PROCESS AND POWER IN
SOVIET FOREIGN POLICY

PROCESS AND POWER IN SOVIET FOREIGN POLICY

Vernon V. Aspaturian

The Pennsylvania State University

LITTLE, BROWN AND COMPANY Boston

To Heidi and Nancy

PREFACE

A long book deserves a short Preface, so this one will be brief. In the following pages I have tried to provide an account of Soviet foreign policy that focuses on the processes, institutions, and inputs into Soviet foreign policy behavior rather than present a descriptive analysis of Soviet foreign policy during the past fifty years. The Introduction defines the Soviet Union as an actor in the international community, which is crucial to an understanding of Soviet behavior, and offers a framework for analysis that seeks to illuminate the linkages between inputs, domestic and external, and outputs in Soviet foreign policy. It is not intended as a model or theory to be empirically tested or verified, nor is it designed to predict future Soviet behavior. Its function is far more modest: to assist in the understanding and explanation of past, current, and future Soviet foreign policy.

The emphasis of the book as a whole is on the processing of Soviet foreign policy: how ideology, interests, wills, and capabilities are converted into policy by institutions, structures, and personalities, operating within various internal and external environmental milieus that constantly shape and influence what goes into the making of Soviet foreign policy, what comes out, what the feedback effects are, and finally what consequences are wrought when Soviet policy intersects with the policies of other countries. Hence the book deals extensively with the linkages and interrelationships between domestic social demands and pressures, internal factional politics, and Soviet foreign policy, a dimension that

I first explored in 1957. Special emphasis is placed upon the decision-making apparatus and the administrative and diplomatic institutions of Soviet policy, particularly the Soviet Foreign Ministry and diplomatic service. An important place is also assigned to the impact of the nationalities on Soviet foreign policy, initially as instruments of policy, and later, increasingly, as sources of input and influence on actual formulation, execution, and behavioral configuration. Soviet relations with Eastern Europe, China, and other Communist parties are related to the overall Soviet role in the interstate system as a Global Power, with an explanation of how this role is influenced by, as well as influences and reshapes, the Soviet role and status as the leader of an international revolutionary movement.

The book represents a complete and integrated statement of my own analyses, perceptions, and interpretations, most of which have appeared elsewhere over the past decade, whose major themes are supplemented or amplified by contributions selected from the writings of other scholars, who approach the subject from other perspectives. None of the contributions have been edited or truncated, with the exception of some of my own, which have been updated and expanded. My judgments, interpretations, and forecasts, however, have not been retrospectively tampered with and remain chronologically, in situ, to impartially and ruthlessly render their own implacable verdict.

I owe thanks to many institutions and individuals for their direct and indirect assistance and support, only a few of whom can be acknowledged here. I wish first to express my deep appreciation to the Pennsylvania State University, its Slavic and Soviet Language and Area Center, political science department, and College of Liberal Arts for their generosity in providing encouragement, time, and material assistance. I am especially indebted to Thomas Magner, Robert S. Friedman, and Stanley Paulson in this connection. I wish also to thank the generations of students, both graduate and undergraduate, in my classes and seminars on Soviet foreign policy, not only at Penn State, but also at Columbia, the Johns Hopkins School of Advanced International Studies, and U.C.L.A., where many of the ideas in this book first germinated and others were reshaped and redefined in the give and take of the classroom. I cannot, of course, fail to convey my appreciation to the many libraries and research institutions that assisted me in various ways at different times: the Hoover Institution, the RAND Corporation, the Lenin Library in Moscow, the Graduate Institute of International Studies in Geneva, Switzerland, the Library of Congress, the Widener Library at Harvard, and of course the Pattee Library at Penn State. It would be very difficult to recount the individual kindnesses and privileges extended by the people connected with these institutions. And, for financial support over the years, I must thank the Rockefeller Foundation, the Inter-University Committee on Travel Grants, and the Central Fund for Research at Penn State. I am also grateful to the publishers of the works reprinted here and the contributors for being particularly generous in granting their permissions.

Special acknowledgments and gratitude are also due those individuals most directly involved with the production of this work. I am particularly indebted to Donald Hammonds of Little, Brown, without whose persistence and tenacity this book might not have appeared for a few more years, and to Al Browne and Janet Bane for shepherding the manuscript to publication. To my current and former graduate students, who assisted me in various ways, I also express my appreciation: Joseph Mastro, Vincent McHale, Merlyn Clarke, Jay Gurmankin, and most of all Peter Vanneman, who carried the main burden of proofing the galleys. And then there are those indispensable magicians, the typists, and, in particular, Linda White, the secretary of the Slavic Language and Area Center, who was responsible for most of the typing and other clerical matters connected with the manuscript. Others who helped with the typing are Amy Howard Schlitt, Linda McCarty, and Jean Fitzgerald.

And finally, I owe greatest thanks to my wife, Suzanne, and my two daughters, to whom this book is dedicated, whose inexhaustible capacity for enduring more than the usual share of pugnacity, cantankerousness, broken promises, missed vacations, absences, and absentmindedness associated with the writing of a manuscript, can never be repaid with mere expressions of gratitude.

Vernon V. Aspaturian

TABLE OF CONTENTS

PROCESS AND POWER IN
SOVIET FOREIGN POLICY

INTRODUCTION

THE NATURE OF SOVIET FOREIGN POLICY BEHAVIOR: ANALYSES AND PROCESSES

I. THE SOVIET UNION AS AN ACTOR IN THE INTERNATIONAL SYSTEM

A definition of the Soviet Union as an actor in the international system is necessary for a proper analysis of Soviet behavior in world affairs. Despite a wide array of attempts to generalize and conceptualize about actors in the international and interstate political system, these broader attempts do not satisfactorily or comprehensively define the Soviet Union. Since the Soviet Union obviously betrays many characteristics in common with other actors, particularly the Great Powers, the usual pattern is to stress these characteristics and subsume it under a conceptual rubric or to include it in a broader category of states or actors within an overall classificatory or theoretical framework. Thus, the Soviet Union is variously defined and classified in terms of its power magnitude (Great Power, Super Power, Global Power, Nuclear Power, Missile Power, etc.), socio-political system (closed, totalitarian, monocratic, monolithic, single-party, authoritarian, ideocratic, etc.), territorial dimensions (large, super large, extensive, intercontinental, etc.), demographic size (large), demographic structure and composition (literate, multinational, skilled), stage of economic development (industrialized, post-industrialized, advanced, developed, pre-mass consumptionists, etc.), or general orientation (revolutionary, utopian, movement-regime, messianic, universalist, etc.).[1]

[1] Various classificatory schemes and typologies of international actors, including the Soviet Union, can be found in the following: R. Barry Farrell, editor, *Approaches to Comparative and International Politics* (Evanston, Illinois, Northwestern University Press, 1966), especially the contributions

Although these classifications are often useful in demonstrating the similarities and differences between the Soviet Union and other actors in the international system, they obscure the fact that in its total complex the Soviet Union is an absolutely unique political and international entity, and that it is the totality of its behavioral definition as an actor that sets it apart from all other states, past or present, in the international order. Subsuming the Soviet Union into a general category allows for only partial or fragmentary analysis of Soviet behavior in international affairs and tends to reenforce the assumption that its behavior is different only in details from that of other states with which it shares some important common characteristics. Thus, although Soviet behavior is comparable to that of other states in many important dimensions — some with this state, some with that — there is no other state — past or present — whose total behavior is comparable to that of the Soviet Union, and some aspects of Soviet behavior have no precedent whatsoever. The unique character of the Soviet Union does not derive from such idiosyncratic factors as culture, geographical location, national traditions, etc., since in this sense each and every state can be defined as a unique entity, but rather its uniqueness is defined in terms of the type of international actor it is, *i.e.*, if the Soviet Union were to be conceptualized as a type of international actor, it would be the only one of its type.

The two existing states with which the Soviet Union is usually compared are the United States and the Chinese People's Republic; historical types with which it is sometimes compared are imperial states such as Russia before World War I and the Hapsburg, Ottoman, and Byzantine empires, among others. And it does share a number of characteristics with all of these. In today's world comparisons and contrasts with the United States and Communist China are most prominent. All three share a richly endowed large territory (extra large in the Soviet case), a large population (extra large in the Chinese case), and possess a nuclear capability. Beyond this point, few significant characteristics are held in common by the three powers, but the Soviet Union shares other important characteristics with the other two that they do not share with each other. Thus, like the United States, the Soviet Union is a developed, industrial, and technological society and

by Rosenau, Friedrich, Long, and Farrell; James N. Rosenau, *The Adaptation of National Societies: A Theory of Political System Behavior and Transformation* (New York, The McCaleb-Seiler Co., 1970); John H. Herz, "The Territorial State Revisited: Reflections on the Future of the Nation-State," *Polity*, January 1968, pp. 12–34; Harold and Margaret Sprout, *Foundations of International Politics* (Princeton, N.J., Van Nostrand, 1962), pp. 73–105; Bruce M. Russett, "Delineating International Regions," in J. David Singer, editor, *Quantitative International Behavior* (New York, The Free Press, 1968); Karl W. Deutsch, *The Analysis of International Relations* (Englewood Cliffs, N.J., Prentice-Hall, Inc., 1968), pp. 21–39, Richard Merritt and Stein Rokkan, editors, *Comparing Nations* (New Haven, Conn., Yale University Press, 1966); and R. J. Rummel, "Some Empirical Findings on Nations and Their Behavior," *World Politics*, January 1969.

a Global Power with a large stockpile of nuclear warheads, intercontinental delivery systems, and a wide array of conventional armaments. The Soviet population, like that of the United States, is highly literate and skilled. And both are leaders of a politico-military coalition of allied states and provide a shelter for sundry client states at the periphery of their protective umbrellas.

On the other hand, the Soviet Union shares with China a common socio-political order (Marxist-Leninist-Socialist) variously described as closed, totalitarian, authoritarian, or single party. Furthermore it shares with China a dualistic identity as both a State and Revolutionary Party, inspired by a systematic ideology and dedicated to facilitating, encouraging, and sometimes fomenting revolution in various parts of the world. With its large territory, immense multinational population, and growing technological and industrial power, China is potentially a carbon copy of the Soviet Union as a Communist Global Power, and whatever uniqueness the Soviet Union enjoys in this dimension is purely transitory.

The duality of the Soviet Union as a revolutionary power center and as a Russian state has long been recognized, as has the singular political and behavioral schizophrenia that has resulted from this fusion and confusion of identities and roles. But, as noted above, although the Soviet state was uniquely endowed with this dualistic nature until the emergence of a powerful Communist China, it now must to a certain degree share this characteristic with Peking. To be sure, the Chinese leaders have never adopted the pretension of China being the nucleus of a future Communist state, as did the Soviet Union for nearly four decades of its existence, but they do offer China as a model for other countries (particularly in the underdeveloped world) to emulate, and they probably do envisage China as the center and leader of a future constellation of Communist states. The current posture of the Soviet Union approximates this and in fact has been adopted in response to the Chinese repudiation of the universalist pretensions of Moscow, although residual aspects of universalism continue to characterize Soviet rhetoric and behavior. As a consequence of this rivalry in the Communist world, the emergence of two constellations of Communist states, centered around Peking and Moscow respectively, is a distinct possibility as China's power and leverage in world affairs continue to wax over the long run.

Confusion about Soviet motives, misperceptions of her intent, and puzzlement in comprehending Soviet behavior have always characterized, and continue to characterize, any attempt to analyze, describe, and explain foreign policy. This results not only from failure to properly relate Soviet conduct to one of these two identities and roles, but even more seriously from perception of the Soviet Union as a dual entity, an oversimplification of a more complicated existence. The Soviet Union is not merely a dualistic entity but a multiple one, whose constituent parts have both contradictory, conflicting — even irreconcilable — motives, intentions, interests, and constituencies, as well as overlapping, intersecting, and harmonious ones. The identity of the Soviet Union as merely a revolutionary center and Russian state is simply insufficient to account for Soviet behavior in international politics, although it does explain a great deal.

Another dimension of the Soviet identity stems from its multinational composition. The Soviet Union is also frequently compared to the United States, China, and other extended societies because of its multinational, multiracial, and multireligious character, although the Soviet ethno-cultural mosaic is far more finely variegated and complicated. Its specific multinational character has been a crucial influence not only in shaping its policies and behavior in world affairs, but also in arousing responses and reactions to its internal and external policies.[2]

One of the most striking characteristics of the Soviet Union is its singular ethnic diversity: a demographic tapestry woven of more than 100 different nationalities, tribes, and linguistic groups, some of them little more visible than slender glistening exotic threads alongside broad and bold stripes, of which the most conspicuous is the Great Russian nation. To be sure, there is a propensity for the Soviet authorities to exaggerate the ethnic heterogeneity of the U.S.S.R. for propaganda purposes by even including "nationalities" with populations of less than 1,000. Nevertheless, the ethnic diversity of the country remains impressive. Twenty-two of the nationalities enumerated in the 1970 census number more than one million each and account for over ninety-five per cent of the total population. The other eighty or more "nationalities" total fewer than ten million, and only twenty-nine number more than 100,000 people each. The nationalities are organized into a unique multinational juridical state complex that simultaneously exhibits characteristics that are unitary, federal, and confederal in both internal and external dimensions. Fifteen (up from eleven in 1936, down from sixteen since 1956) of the major nationalities are invested with quasi-sovereign status as Union Republics.

Under international law the Soviet Union is recognized as a single composite (plural, multiple) state entity in its capacity as a Union State, but at the same time two of its constituent republics, the Ukraine and Byelorussia, enjoy separate, but partial, recognition under international law as members of the United Nations and other international and multilateral bodies and associations.[3] The thirteen remaining Union Republics are equally endowed constitutionally with potential separate recognition under international law and are juridically entitled to engage as individual actors in the international community while remaining a part of the Union and retaining their representation as well. As

---

[2] See Selection 4. *Cf.* also Zbigniew Brzezinski and Samuel P. Huntington, *Political Power: USA/USSR* (New York, Viking, 1964); and Alfred G. Meyer, "Theories of Convergence," in Chalmers Johnson, editor, *Change in Communist Systems* (Stanford, Calif., Stanford University Press, 1970) for a comparative treatment of Soviet and American political behavior and processes.

[3] See Selection 19.

a composite juridically plural state, the Soviet Union consists of fifteen Union Republics and twenty Autonomous Republics, all of which are considered by Soviet jurists to be endowed with some form of state existence or sovereignty, although only the Union Republics are endowed with the legal capacity to secede from the Union, raise armies, contract treaties, and engage in diplomatic relations with the outside world, *i.e.*, are juridically invested with all the trappings of an actor in the interstate system. In addition to the Union and Autonomous Republics, eight Autonomous Oblasts and ten National Okrugs are endowed with lesser juridical powers.

The Soviet federal system is a multinational federalism, *i.e.*, all its federal units are juridical expressions of nationhood or nationality. However, only sixty-three nations and nationalities of the more than 100 in the Soviet Union are endowed with one of the four national units described above. The remaining nationalities, some of which are national minorities (Germans, Poles, etc.) that are not indigenous Soviet nations, are bereft of any formal legal recognition in the structure of the state, although some of them are microscopic in size. Table 1 lists the major nationalities in the Soviet Union as of the 1970 census. The national unit that represents each nationality is shown in parentheses.

Thus, the uniqueness of the Soviet Union as an actor in the world state system stems neither from its character as a Revolutionary Party,

TABLE 1

MAJOR NATIONALITIES OF THE U.S.S.R. 1939–1970

Nationality	1939	1959	(%)	1970	(%)
Russian (UR)	99,019,000	114,114,000	(54.6)	129,015,000	(53.4)
Ukrainian (UR)	28,070,000	37,253,000	(17.8)	40,753,000	(16.9)
Byelorussian (UR)	5,267,431	7,913,000	(3.8)	9,052,000	(3.7)
Uzbek (UR)	4,844,021	6,015,000	(2.9)	9,195,000	(3.8)
Tatar (AR)	4,300,000	4,969,000	(2.4)	5,931,000	(2.5)
Kazakh (UR)	3,098,000	3,622,000	(1.7)	5,299,000	(2.2)
Azerbaidzhan (UR)	2,274,805	2,940,000	(1.4)	4,380,000	(1.8)
Armenian (UR)	2,151,884	2,787,000	(1.3)	3,559,000	(1.5)
Georgian (UR)	2,248,566	2,692,000	(1.3)	3,245,000	(1.3)
Lithuanian (UR)	—	2,326,000	(1.1)	2,665,000	(1.1)
Jewish (AO)	3,020,141	2,268,000	(1.1)	2,151,000	(.9)
Moldavian (UR)	—	2,214,000	(1.1)	2,698,000	(1.1)
German (NONE)	1,423,534	1,619,000	(.8)	1,846,000	(.8)
Chuvash (AR)	1,367,930	1,470,000	(.7)	1,694,000	(.7)
Latvian (UR)	—	1,400,000	(.7)	1,430,000	(.6)
Tadzhik (UR)	1,928,964	1,397,000	(.7)	2,136,000	(.9)
Polish (NONE)	626,905	1,380,000	(.7)	1,167,000	(.5)
Mordvin (AR)	1,451,429	1,285,000	(.6)	1,263,000	(.5)
Turkmen (UR)	811,769	1,002,000	(.5)	1,525,000	(.6)
Bashkir (AR)	842,925	989,000	(.5)	1,240,000	(.5)
Kirgiz (UR)	884,306	969,000	(.5)	1,452,000	(.6)
Estonian (UR)	—	989,000	(.5)	1,007,000	(.4)
Others	—	7,215,000	(3.5)	8,313,000	(3.4)
Total	190,678,000	208,827,000	(100.0)	241,720,000	(100.0)

nor from its character as a closed totalitarian, authoritarian, or single-party socio-political order, nor from its socialist system or multinational population, but rather because the Soviet Union is invested with all these characteristics in addition to others. As a consequence the Soviet Union is endowed with a multiplicity of identities and roles in international affairs, responding to and influenced by a wide spectrum of internal and external constituencies and interests that intersect to fundamentally impinge upon the contours of Soviet behavior.[4] The Soviet Union emerges as the only authentic multiple actor in the international community of states. It reveals itself as five distinct but interrelated, congruent, and concentric institutionalized personalities, each performing one or more distinct roles. These five institutionalized identities can be grouped for analytical convenience as follows: (1) state; (2) party; (3) Russian nation; (4) non-Russian nation (variable); and (5) multinational commonwealth.

Each of these identities has separate and separable roles and operates within several different socio-political environments and socio-historical parameters. The Soviet Union thus endeavors to serve a wide spectrum of domestic and external social, ideological, and national constituencies, whose distinct concerns intersect to form a kaleidoscope of interests, demands, and supports. Sometimes these interests, demands, and supports can be compromised and blended into a larger whole; at other times they may overlap or be in coexistential congruence, yet remain still separate and distinct; sometimes they manifest themselves in serial progression, depending upon circumstances and opportunities, but frequently they are in various stages and degrees of subtle or overt conflict or contradiction, pushing and pulling the Soviet Union in various directions, sometimes tangentially and at other times toward diametrically opposed poles. Thus, Soviet behavior can take place simultaneously, successively, harmoniously, contradictorily, or independently in five different environments: (1) the Soviet socio-political order; (2) the Soviet multinational order; (3) the Communist interstate sub-system; (4) the World Communist movement; and (5) the general interstate system. All these environments involve varying demands and supports and thus condition and influence Soviet behavior.

Multiple identities performing multiple roles in multiple environments constitute a recipe for confusion both for Soviet leaders who must act and observers of Soviet behavior who must analyze and explain. The possible mutations and permutations of inputs and outputs are thus staggering. The problem of analysis is further complicated by the more than usual difficulty in securing reliable and verifiable data concerning even past Soviet foreign policy, to say nothing about acquiring information about recent or current policy.

The long period of Stalinist rule tended to obscure both the multiple personality of the Soviet Union and its diverse roles, since they were all coordinated and orchestrated by one person, who could, more or less arbitrarily, in accordance with his own perceptions, drives, ambi-

[4] See Selection 13.

tions, values, and judgments, process into decisions the tensions, conflicts, strains, demands, contradictions, and priorities inherent in the Soviet system through the totalitarian instrumentalities that he created and adopted for this purpose. Soviet policy under Stalin was essentially, but not exclusively, a process of converting his will into policy and implementing it with the capabilities at his disposal. Over time, and particularly since Stalin's death, as Soviet capabilities grew and operational choices and options proliferated correspondingly, the totalitarian glue that bound these identities together became progressively unstuck and the constituent personalities of the Soviet Union have increasingly become more manifest. And as these various identities exert themselves, the various roles and functions of the Soviet Union have become more distinct, impinging themselves more consciously and forcefully upon Stalin's successors, who have been singularly incapable of sustaining a unified viewpoint in formulating policy. As a consequence, Soviet policy betrays a tendency to become increasingly less synchronized, resulting in contradictory, inconsistent, and ambivalent behavior, due more to the inability of the Soviet leaders to select out the principal referent-identity in dealing with particular situations and events rather than to calculated and premeditated changes in thrust and direction. As a concrete illustration of this dilemma, should the Soviet Union respond to China's territorial demands as the custodian of historic Russia's interests, the protector of the interests of its Central Asian nations, or as a party representing the abstract interests of advancing world Communism? Depending upon the identity in which it chooses to function, the response will vary. Needless to say, the Soviet leaders will continue to avoid such confrontations of roles and identities, but ultimately a new balance among these various identity roles must be established, and some may have to be renounced, modified, altered, adjusted, or even added.

The behavioral configurations of the Soviet Union thus constitute an absolutely unique historical phenomenon. No other state in history has assumed as many masks as the Soviet Union. All its identities and roles are not equally significant and some are essentially composite in nature. Depending upon conditions and circumstances, one or more identities and roles may assume greater importance than the others during different periods in the evolution of the Soviet system. Their relative importance varies not only with the changing values and goals of the leadership but also in response to the demands and pressures of its various constituencies and the opportunities and risks that manifest themselves in the international environment in terms of its own evolving capabilities.[5]

1. *The Soviet Union as a State*

As a state, the Soviet Union possesses all the traditional formal properties of a state in the interstate or international system, which

[5] See Selection 1.

needs no extensive elaboration here. It operates within the parameters of a definite interstate system, which objectively and externally imposes common standards of behavior upon all its actors in accordance with a shifting and flexible equilibrium of power among them. As a state, it must accept certain minimum obligations and responsibilities in return for corresponding rights and privileges on a reciprocal basis. The separate identity of the Soviet Union as a state has impressed itself deeply upon the consciousness of the Soviet leaders, who from time to time choose to stress with particular force the identity of the Soviet Union as a state in contradistinction to its other identities. This is frequently done in order to divest itself of the obligations and responsibilities it has incurred in its other identities and to press certain advantages and opportunities that accrue to it as a state.

This applies with particular force when the Soviet Union wishes to distinguish its state identity from its party identity in relations with both Communist and non-Communist states. Thus, before World War II, the Soviet leaders consistently disclaimed state responsibility for the behavior of the Comintern and its constituent Communist parties in other countries on grounds that they were not to be considered as acts of the Soviet Union as a state, although it was common knowledge that the Soviet leaders controlled both the Soviet state and the Comintern, and through it the activities of various Communist parties operating throughout the world in other countries.[6] Similarly, it has justified interference in the internal and external affairs of other Communist states on grounds that it was not functioning as a state intervening in the affairs of other states, but as a fraternal Party dispensing advice and direction in accordance with the rules and processes of the international Communist movement.

Non-Communist powers have been generally ineffective in dealing with this dualistic posture, except for the Axis Powers, who imaginatively riposted with an anti-Comintern Pact, which was allegedly directed not against the Soviet state, but against the Comintern, for whose activities the Soviet state disclaimed responsibilities. In this way Germany, Italy, and Japan forged an anti-Soviet alliance in the guise of an anti-Comintern organization. Similarly, the United States enunciated various doctrines (such as the Truman and the Eisenhower) that were directed not against the Soviet state but against "international Communism," which, after the dissolution of the Comintern in 1943, was a formless and amorphous movement bereft of organizational identity. Needless to say, the Soviet leaders considered both responses to be directed against the Soviet state and hence indirectly conceded the inseparability of the two identities.

But in dealing with other Communist states, it soon became apparent that they, too, could function in a dualistic capacity in their relations with the Soviet Union. Thus when Stalin attempted to discipline Tito and Yugoslavia through the Cominform and subversion of

---

[6] See Selection 11.

the Yugoslav Communist Party, Marshal Tito responded by condemning this as Soviet state interference in the internal affairs of the
Yugoslav state in violation of the norms of international law. Little
more than a decade later, when the Chinese leaders, emulating the
Soviet pattern, attempted to alter Soviet policies by disseminating propaganda and literature critical of the Soviet leadership and its policies
through its embassy in Moscow, the Soviet Union charged that Peking
was violating international law by grossly intervening in the affairs of
the Soviet state.[7] The Chinese retorted that it was merely an attempt to
engage in a dialogue with the Soviet Communist Party in accordance
with the rules of the international Communist confraternity and was
not to be construed as an act of the Chinese state.

In its capacity as a state, the Soviet Union is charged with defending and advancing the interests of the Soviet Union against the demands and interests of other states in the international community, and
for this purpose maintains both a diplomatic and defense establishment
as do other states. The interests of the Soviet state as a state are
formulated internally in accordance with a set of priorities arrived at
through its own internal processes and in response to the various
domestic constituencies and groups which can influence the process.[8]
The foreign policy of the Soviet state, in its broadest aspects, may assume the patterns of self-perpetuation (security and maintenance), self-
extension (aggrandizement), or self-fulfillment (development and
prestige), separately or in combination.

As a state, the Soviet Union currently functions as a Global Power
in the international community. Its credentials as a Global Power rest
upon possession of advanced technological weapons systems, including
thermonuclear warheads, ICBM delivery systems, as well as a wide array
of conventional armaments.[9] The possession of these capabilities combined with the requisite will and purpose enables the Soviet Union to
unilaterally assert an interest in any part of the globe and to take
corresponding action, including intervention, if necessary or desirable.
Thus, as a Global Power, the Soviet Union has successfully intervened in
both the Caribbean and the Middle East, leading to the creation of allied or client states in both regions. It made an unsuccessful attempt to
intervene in the Congo, and although it has retrenched somewhat in
that area because of overextension, it did establish a precedent and
maintains residual footholds as the basis for a renewed attempt in the
future to establish client states in tropical Africa. Similarly, the Soviet
Union has asserted interests in South Asia and Southeast Asia. As a
general rule, the Soviet Union, as a Global Power, asserts the right to
be consulted and to participate in any international problem in any part
of the globe.

The Soviet Union's role as a Global Power is buttressed by its being
a regional Great Power as well and the leader of an ideological-military

[7] See Selection 18.
[8] See Selections 15 and 16.
[9] See Selections 26 and 28.

coalition, institutionalized as the Warsaw Treaty Organization, and reigns more or less supreme in its own region, Eastern Europe, in which it tolerates no external intrusion by any other power, including the other Global Power, the United States.[10] The simultaneous immunity of the Soviet regional sphere from external intervention by other powers and the reassertion of an exclusive Soviet right to intervene in Eastern Europe has been formalized in the so-called "Brezhnev" or "Socialist Commonwealth Doctrine." Although conceptualized as a collective or multilateral action, this doctrine enables the Soviet Union to militarily intervene in the affairs of any Communist state (Yugoslavia excepted), if in its judgment the internal socialist order of any Communist state is threatened with subversion from within or without. Theoretically any Communist state or group of Communist states enjoys the same right, but in reality only the Soviet Union possesses the power and capability to do so. In some respects, the "Brezhnev Doctrine" resembles very closely the Monroe and Wilson doctrines which have been multilateralized and institutionalized in the Organization of American States.[11] In both instances, a collective or multilateralized right to intervention in the affairs of member states is largely a juridical fig leaf concealing the unilateral right of the regional Great Power to intervene.

The Brezhnev Doctrine constitutes an important theoretical departure in Soviet conceptions of Communist interstate and interparty relations while simultaneously resurrecting a pattern of past Soviet behavior. Before the Soviet occupation of Czechoslovakia in August, 1968, all Soviet interference in the internal affairs of Eastern European countries was defined in terms of interparty relationships. Soviet intervention was accomplished, first by the Soviet Party dictating or directing changes in the leadership structure and ideological orientation of another Communist Party, which would, in turn, then alter the structure and composition of the state and Government, resulting in new policies and directions. Thus, theoretically no Soviet *state* interference in the domestic affairs of another *state* took place. Although Soviet intervention in Eastern European states was frequently blatant and ruthless, particularly during the period 1947–1953, Moscow nevertheless was scrupulous in *disclaiming any right* to intervention on the part of the Soviet state and perennially reaffirmed its devotion to the norms of nonintervention, noninterference, and the absolute sovereignty of states under international law. The Soviet leaders were thus careful in avoiding any precedent that might justify intervention on the part of other powers.

The new doctrine, however, is applicable to relations between *states* and not parties and is thus sometimes called the "Doctrine of Limited Sovereignty," in that individual Communist states are precluded from the right and authority to replace their socialist system with

[10] See Selections 22, 25, and 28.
[11] See Selection 18 for a discussion of the impact of the "Brezhnev" Doctrine" on diplomatic representation between the Soviet Union and other Communist states.

another on the grounds that the subversion or displacement of the socialist system in one country endangers its existence in others. Thus, the socialist commonwealth of states is entitled to intervene as an act of collective and individual self-defense of their internal socio-political orders.[12] Conceived both as a retroactive justification for the occupation of Czechoslovakia and as a threat of future action by the Soviet Union, the doctrine has been roundly condemned by Yugoslavia, Rumania, and China in varying degrees as being in violation not only of international law, but of proper norms of behavior between socialist states.

The Brezhnev Doctrine clearly blurs the distinction between the Soviet Union as a state and Party in theory as well as practice. The distinction between the two in practice has always been imperfect, since the Soviet state from its very conception has been conceived as an instrumentality of the Party and under its direct control and thus has always been an instrument of the Party's will. The distinction has never been as fastidious in internal policy as in foreign policy, since the Party possesses ultimate control over domestic juridical norms, which it does not, of course, have in the realm of international legal and juridical relationships. The Party then has been the first and most important constituency of the state, although since Stalin's death, the Party itself has become an arena of conflict and rivalry among various personalities, factions, and socio-functional and socio-institutional groups. These groups become not only constituencies of the Party but, directly and indirectly, of the state as well.

The Soviet state, *qua* state, functions in four of the five environments to which the Soviet Union must respond. These are the internal socio-political order, where it must articulate the interests of the various social constituencies in the Soviet system in accordance with a given, but shifting, structure of power and priorities among them in the formulation and execution of foreign policy; the Soviet multinational order, where it must do the same for the various nations and nationalities that make up the Soviet Union; in the Communist interstate subsystem, where it functions as the leader and defender of a coalition of allied states; and in the general interstate system, where it currently functions as a Global Power. Only in the environment of the World Communist Movement is the Soviet Union, as a state, supposedly not an actor, although, here again, it functions within this environment indirectly and covertly.

2. *The Soviet Union as a Revolutionary Party*

Before the advent of the Soviet state, there existed, of course, the Communist (Bolshevik) Party. The Soviet state was inspired and created by the Party in response to the goals, values, and norms of its ideology, Marxism-Leninism. One of its important norms was to facilitate and/or encourage the communization of the world, allegedly

[12] *Cf.* V. V. Aspaturian, "Soviet Aims in East Europe," *Current History,* October 1970.

in consonance with the dictates of inexorable historical laws of development.[13]

In its capacity as a revolutionary Party, the Soviet Union performs the following roles and functions: (1) as the ideological guardian of the multinational socio-political order at home and the initiator and architect of its future development; (2) as the ideological and organizational leader of the ruling Communist Parties and the ultimate arbiter of the ideological parameters within which their socio-political existence and development take place; and (3) as the ideological leader and source of inspirational and material support of the World Communist movement, made up of both ruling and nonruling Communist Parties. As a Party, the Soviet Union functions in three distinct environments: the domestic socio-political, the Communist interstate subsystem, and the World Communist Movement. The Soviet Union, as a Party, has no status under international law and does not function as a formal actor in the general interstate system. Its role within the multinational environment inside the Soviet Union is not readily distinguishable from the second role-function listed above.

These roles as a Party identity have metamorphosed over the past five decades, and the definitions given above correspond largely to the current roles of the Soviet Union as a revolutionary Party. Therefore, a brief descriptive summary of the evolving nature of these roles might serve to clarify the current situation. The Communist (Bolshevik) Party antedated the Soviet state. In fact, the Soviet state, the Soviet socialist order, the World Communist Movement, and the Communist interstate subsystem were all initially creations of the Party, which means that the Party fashioned the very environments within which it functions. The feedback effects of these creations, however, have in turn influenced the changing roles and functions of the Party both domestically and abroad.

Originally, the Soviet state was conceived as an instrument of the Party in its mission of communizing the world. The revolution that it inspired and the social system that it spawned were designed as models for other countries and Communist Parties. The Soviet Union was envisaged successively, and often simultaneously, as the inspiration, model, base, arsenal, and center of world revolution. For several decades, the Soviet Union also posed as the nucleus or the embryonic embodiment of a future world Communist state. To this end, the Party inspired the creation of Communist Parties in other countries and established the Comintern (Communist International) in 1919 to coordinate the revolutionary activities of all Communist Parties and to assist the Soviet state to defend itself against external enemies.[14] As the only Communist Party in power for nearly three decades, the Soviet Party supported, nurtured, counselled, directed, and eventually controlled the activities of both the Comintern and its constituent members in other

[13] See Selection 10.
[14] See Selections 20 and 21. *Cf.* also Richard Lowenthal, *World Communism* (New York, Oxford, 1964).

countries. They thereupon became instruments of Soviet foreign policy.

With the advent of new Communist states in Eastern Europe, the Soviet Party through its control of the Eastern European Communist Parties established varying degrees of control over their states. In this way, a system of Party control and dependency was transformed into a system of vassal and client states. This resulted in the simultaneous creation of a subsystem of Communist states within the general inter-state system and a subsystem of ruling Communist Parties within the World Communist Movement. Institutions were created to coordinate both subsystems: the Cominform (1947–1956) for the subsystem of ruling parties, and Comecon (Council of Mutual Economic Assistance) in 1949 and the Warsaw Treaty Organization (1955) to coordinate the economic, military, and political policies of the interstate subsystem. The three Asian Communist states (China, North Korea, and North Vietnam) were never *institutionally* members of these subsystems, although they were informally parts of both. Furthermore, Albania was never a member of the Cominform, although the non-ruling parties of Italy and France were.

Because of various internal and external developments since Stalin's death, most notably de-Stalinization and the Sino-Soviet conflict, the Soviet grip on both subsystems and on the World Communist Movement has been loosened in varying degrees. China has emerged as a rival of the Soviet Union both inside and outside the movement, while the Eastern European Communist states and Parties have achieved varying degrees of autonomy in domestic matters during the years since 1956. Under Khrushchev, the Soviet Union unilaterally and explicitly renounced its position as the leader of the World Communist Movement, but it has in fact simply been retrograded to the *de facto* leader of a rump World Communist Movement, of which China, Albania, and a number of non-ruling parties and splinter groups are not formal members. It would be an exaggeration to describe China as the leader of another rival World Communist Movement, but potentially, Peking is the possible leader of both another World Communist Movement and another Communist interstate subsystem.

Although the distinction between the state and Party identities of the Soviet Union has attenuated over the years, the confusion still persists. Furthermore the history of the relationship between the two identities is an important prerequisite to understanding Soviet behavior in world affairs. There has always been a rivalry between the two identities, not only because their functions and roles were in large measure both overlapping and contradictory, but also because each had a tendency to attract and respond to different, if frequently overlapping, constituencies and clients — both in internal and external policy.[15] Over the years, the state identity has gained over the Party, largely because it is capable of more effectively appealing to and aggregating the interest and demands of a larger constellation of constituencies than

[15] See Selection 16.

can the Party. Thus, although the role and function of the state was originally designed to be instrumental, *i.e.*, essentially a holding operation, ultimately to "wither away" and that of the Party more or less permanent, during the past fifty years their respective positions have been virtually reversed.

Contradiction and tension between the roles of the state and Party in international affairs have been chronic problems during the entire existence of the Soviet system.[16] The Party was assigned the mission of subverting and transforming the international environment in which the state functioned in preparation for the disestablishment of the state as a distinct entity. But as the Soviet state has adapted to the interstate system and, since about 1956, has integrated itself into the system as one of two major Global Powers, its stake in the system has intensified.[17] The mission of World Communism that is vested in the Party tends to undermine not only the interstate system, but to seriously complicate the role and effectiveness of the Soviet Union as a Global Power. With the emergence of Communist China as a rival within the Communist movement, the Soviet stake in world Communism seems further diminished as its role as a Global Power grows in (*relative*) importance.

3. *The Soviet Union as a Russian Nation-State*

As the historical and juridical successor to the Russian state, the Soviet Union also functions as the custodian and heir to the interests of the Russian nation, an imperial and traditionally ruling nation, and in this capacity fulfills the role of preserving and extending the values, goals, and interests of historic Russia. The Soviet Union includes within its territory the entire Great Russian Nation and is territorially and demographically indistinguishable from the Russian Empire that preceded it. As a Russian national state, its constituency is the entire Great Russian Nation, irrespective of class distinctions or social status. As a Russian national state, the Soviet Union manipulates patriotic symbols, commemorates national glories, venerates historic heroes (mostly tsars and generals), worships at the national shrines, and celebrates the lofty goals, purposes, and achievements of Holy Mother Russia. This never fails to stir the Russian people who are more likely, in times of crisis, to rally around the symbols of Holy Russia than those of Communism.

Since the Great Russian Nation constitutes the demographic backbone of the Soviet state, its loyalty and dedication is indispensable for both the survival of Russia and the development of Communism. Frequently, Russian and Communist symbols and institutions are fused into something called "Soviet," in which either form or content is Russian, depending upon time and circumstance, and in this manner, Russian goals and values are imposed upon the non-Russian population in the name of science, progress, and historical inevitability.

One of the primary purposes of a state is to articulate, preserve,

[16] See Selection 17.
[17] See Selection 23.

As a consequence of this pervasive institutionalization, Russian is ⸱ imperial language of the Soviet Union, or as the Soviet authorities ᵗmselves euphemistically characterize it, "the language of interna- ᵗality communication." As a practical matter, Russian is eminently ᵗctional as the *lingua franca* of Soviet society, but this nevertheless ᵗelibly imparts to the Soviet state a definite Russian character. No ᵗrist regime was ever able to successfully achieve this despite its ᵗlculated efforts.

The institutionalization of the Russian identity of the Soviet state ᵗ powerfully reinforced by the progressive acculturation of Soviet ᵗciety as a whole to Russian norms (russianization). As the sole ᵗnguage of "internationality communication," Russian is the vehicle of ᵗmmunication not only between Russians and non-Russians but among ᵗe various nationalities of the Soviet state. A Lithuanian, for example, ᵗnd a Buryat Mongol or Yakut citizen can thus communicate, because ᵗey are not merely citizens of the same territorially-extended state, but ᵗecause they share a common *lingua franca*, which is Russian.

The universalization of the Russian language in the Soviet Union ᵗas been paralleled by the universalization of Russian literature, art, ᵗmusic, dance, and theater, all of which somehow become "Soviet" once ᵗhey are translated into non-Russian idioms. In this way Russian aesthetic norms and forms become Soviet models to be emulated by non-Russians in the development of their own culture. Similarly the Cyrillic alphabet has become virtually a "Soviet" alphabet, or perhaps more appropriately a Communist alphabet, since all nations whose languages employ the Cyrillic alphabet are now under Communist rule. All non-Russian languages except the Lithuanian, Latvian, Estonian, Georgian, and Armenian, now use variations of the Cyrillic alphabet, including many that have historically employed the Arabic (Moslem nationalities) or the Latin (Moldavians and Karelians) alphabets. The Cyrillization of the non-Russian languages serves simultaneously to facilitate the learning of Russian, to erect artificial barriers to com- munication with related peoples outside the Soviet Union who speak the same language but employ different alphabets, and finally to psy- choculturally condition non-Russians to think that similarity of alpha- bets indicates general cultural kinship to the Russians.

Aside from Cyrillization as a vehicle for russianizing the non- Russian languages, all non-Russian languages have been generously infused with a steady stream of Russian vocabulary, again often dis- guised as "Soviet," "scientific," or "modern" terminology. In some cases the Russian impact upon non-Russian languages has distorted both the grammar and syntax of the language to make it conform more closely to Russian.

The most durable effects of russianization, however, are likely to be psychocultural. Thus, even minor aspects of russianization such as the near-universal adoption of the Russian form of the patronymic by non-Russians leaves its indelible imprint. Many non-Russians have also russianized their family names by adopting Russian endings. Thus

and extend the interests, values, and norms of the
a juridical expression. The Soviet state registers
score insofar as its role and function as a Russian
cerned. As a consequence, the Russian identity of
terms of the consequences and effectiveness of its r
and guardian of Russian national interests and its
even more durable and tenacious than that of the
state. Under Soviet rule, Russian imperial national i
"internationalized" and advanced in the name of Cor
values have been internalized as Marxist canons and
non-Russians, as Russian cultural norms, "univers
norms, have been adopted and assimilated by non-Rus
All this has been done in the name of "progress" rat
russification and therefore has been more effective a

The touchstone of national identity is language,
state has clearly done more to preserve, strengthen,
Russian language than any Russian state in history. Th
direct effects of universalizing education, most of which
the Russian language, reenforces the Russian identity
state among both Russians and non-Russians. Russians
intensively conscious of their national identity, as nor
"modernized" via Russian norms and vehicles. The Rus
of the Soviet state is thus manifested institutionally and
ally as a consequence. Some of the principal institutionaliz
tions of the Russian character of the Soviet state are as follo

1. Russian is the official language of the state, dip
international contact.
2. Russian is a mandatory official language in all
areas alongside the local language.
3. Russian is the single language of command in the ar
whose multinational members are dispersed among Russian
Slavs.
4. Russian is the only language inscribed on all offici
decorations, medals, postage stamps, money, and currency,
special or commemorative issues.
5. The legend "Proletarians of all countries unite!" is in
Russian on the coats-of-arms of all non-Russian republics toge
the native language.
6. All public institutions and localities in non-Russian a
identified in Russian along with the local language.

[18] Cf. Vernon V. Aspaturian, "The Non-Russian Nationalities,"
Kassof, editor, Prospects for Soviet Society (New York, Praeger, 1968)
extended analysis of the implications of russianization and russific
Soviet nationality policy. Soviet Russian Nationalism (New York,
1936) by Frederick C. Barghoorn, although focused primarily on the S
era, is a valuable study of the effects of Stalinist nationality policies. C
Richard Pipes, " 'Solving' The Nationality Problem," Problems of Comm
September/October 1967.

virtually every Soviet citizen not only speaks Russian but bears a russianized individual identity in one form or another.[19]

The vaunted "new Soviet man" allegedly emerging in Soviet society appears to be a little more than an intensely more nationally conscious Russian in the Russian areas of the country and a more or less russianized non-Russian in other areas. Originally envisaged as a culturally deracinated and historically disumbilicized citizen, totally disembodied of his national consciousness and identity, the "new Soviet man" was to be "pure" man, the pristine representative of mankind or humanity, unencumbered by class distinctions or national identity. Upon the variegated multinational Soviet population, the Soviet leaders were not to impose parochial Russian norms and values but the universal humanistic values of Marxism. These norms and values however were not introduced by faceless, nationless, floating cosmopolites, but by leaders who were mostly Russians or russianized non-Russians, who were themselves products of the same cultural-demographic environment they wished to fashion into a new humanity. The "new Soviet man" emerged in Russian areas as a modernized Russian, whose outlook is conditioned by a curious mixture of traditional Russian values and Marxist norms, whereas in the non-Russian areas, the "new Soviet man" is conditioned by an even more unstable amalgam of Marxist, Russian, and indigenous norms and values, whose stability and durability varies considerably from one nationality to another. As a consequence, not only the Russians but the non-Russians are "more Russian" than they ever were under the overtly imperial Russian state of the tsars.

Although the Soviet Union remains a multinational state, only half of whose population consists of Russians, the Russian character of the state is unmistakable. Its Russian identity constitutes the irreducible residue of the Soviet Union when all else is trimmed away. Without Russia, the Soviet Union could not exist in any form, whereas Russia is independent of its Soviet identity and character. The Russian identity of the Soviet state thus remains its most durable role and, as the protector and promoter of Russian national interests, its most traditional. It has performed its functions in this regard with consummate effectiveness in the following ways:

1. The Russians have been preserved as the ruling nationality of the state through different devices, although this is cloaked in various euphemisms.[20]

2. Lost territories have been recovered on behalf of historic Russia, other territorial demands have been made, and a sphere of influence has been established in Eastern Europe indistinguishable from

[19] As, for example, Mirzamakhmud Mirzarakhmanovich Musakhamov, an Uzbek male deputy, and Gaziza Kabievna Zhangabulova, a female Kazakh deputy to the Supreme Soviet.

[20] Cf. Yaroslav Bilinsky, "The Rulers and the Ruled," *Problems of Communism*, September/October 1967, and Seweryn Bialer, "How Russians Rule Russia," *Problems of Communism*, September/October 1964.

the fondest hopes of the imperial tsars. Even those territories annexed on behalf of the non-Russian nationalities are simultaneously annexations on behalf of *Rossiya* or imperial Russia and are apt to be so viewed by Russians.

3. Not only have Russian values and culture been preserved, but they have been given wider dissemination among Russians because of expansion of educational institutions, the growth of literacy, the printing of books and magazines in large numbers, and the subsidization and promotion of the traditional Russian and aesthetic forms in the dance, theater, cinema, and music.

4. Russian culture has been actively promoted and advanced among non-Russian nationalities, and cultural imperialism has always been the hallmark of an aggressive self-assured national state. [21]

5. Finally, Soviet leaders consistently single out the Russian nation for special praise, extolling its moral altruism, political *noblesse oblige* and material generosity.[22] This serves to infuse the Russians with feelings of self-esteem, personal satisfaction, and a sense of moral accomplishment. In this way, both territorial annexations and cultural imperialism have been transformed into the highest acts of nobility.[23]

The Russian character of the Soviet state is further reenforced by the following characteristics: (1) the Russian share of membership in the Communist Party has ranged from 75 per cent (1926) to 62 per cent (1967); (2) the leadership of the Party and state have always been overwhelmingly Russian; (3) the upper echelon of the Armed Forces is a virtual monopoly of Russians and russianized Slavs (Marshals Bagramyan and Babadzhanyan and Fleet Admiral Isakov are the only non-Slavs to serve and to have served in the highest echelon of the Armed Forces since World War II, and all three come from one small non-Slavic nation, the Armenian); (4) the Foreign Ministry and the Diplomatic Service are virtual monopolies of the Russians;[24] and (5) Russians serve as high Party, Government, Economic, and Secret Police

[21] *Cf.* the excellent study by Yaroslav Bilinsky, "Education of the Non-Russian Peoples in the USSR, 1917–1967: An Essay," *Slavic Review,* September 1968.

[22] Thus, Stalin at a Kremlin banquet for Red Army commanders after victory in Europe: "I drink first of all to the health of the Russian people because it is the most outstanding nation of all the nations forming a part of the Soviet Union." *Pravda,* May 25, 1945.

[23] See Selection 13. Boris Ponomarev, a high Party functionary, only recently reaffirmed this image as he ostensibly condemned tsarist imperialism. Although not all wars waged by the tsars, he conceded, were "just and progressive," as was virtually the line under Stalin, Ponomarev, nevertheless, managed to assert that the "dialectic of history is such that despite the reactionary aims and methods of Tsarism, the annexation of the peoples to Russia, the uniting of their power with the power of the Russian people . . . in the final analysis led to the liberation of all peoples of the Tsarist Russian Empire, and the creation of a hitherto unknown socialist community of nations, inhabiting our Motherland." *Kommunist,* No. 1, 1963, pp. 21–22.

[24] See Selection 18.

officials in almost all of the non-Russian Republics, the degree of the Russian presence varying considerably from one Republic to another.[25]

For all these reasons, some observers have always maintained that the essential key to understanding the behavior of the Soviet Union lies in perceiving its basic identity as Russia rather than its identity as the agent of an ecumenical cause or as the embodiment of a multinational state.

4. *The Soviet Union as a Variable Nation-State*

The preceding discussion of the Soviet Union's role as a Russian nation-state should not serve to obscure or denigrate its role as a variable nation-state, representing individually and collectively the interests of more than a dozen nations in addition to those of Russia. The Soviet Union is not unique in its capacity as a single state representing the interests of more than one nation. The standard image of an international system made up of nation-states in which each nation is represented by a single state and each state represents a single nation, *i.e.*, the mono-ethnic state, has always been an ideal or incomplete normative type. The international system is more properly an *interstate* system, since the basic actors in the international community are *states*, not nations. States also exist in the international community that represent a single nation, two nations, several nations, a fragment of a nation, or none at all. On the other hand, many nations in the world have little or no recognition or representation under international law, in international organizations, or in the international community generally.[26]

One state has frequently represented more than one nation, and, before 1870, the ideal type of the nation-state was applicable to not more than a handful of states, principally in Europe. The more typical state was the multinational empire, the residual feudal state (monarchy, principality, duchy, etc.), and the colonial empire-state. In Europe, the epicenter of nineteenth century diplomacy, states embracing several nations were not referred to, out of racial deference perhaps, as *colonial* empires, but as *multinational* empires, although in fact they were multinational only insofar as the composition of their population was concerned rather than the political and juridical structure of the state.

[25] *Cf.* Michael Rywkin, *Russia in Central Asia* (New York, Collier Books, 1963), and Bilinsky, "The Rulers and the Ruled," *op. cit.*

[26] For philosophical and theoretical discussions of the relationship between state and nation, see the following: Benjamin Akzin, *States and Nations* (London, Hutchinson and Co., Ltd., 1964); Rupert Emerson, *From Empire to Nation* (Cambridge, Mass., Harvard University Press, 1960); Frederick Hertz, *Nationality in History and Politics* (London, Kegan Paul, 1944); K. R. Minogue, *Nationalism* (New York, Basic Books, 1967); J. V. Stalin, *Marxism and the National Question* (New York, International Publishers). *Cf.* also Ivo Duchacek, *Nations and Men* (New York, Holt, Rinehart, and Winston, 1971, second edition); Grey Hodnett, "What's in a Nation?," *Problems of Communism*, September/October 1967; Elliot Goodman, *The Soviet Design for a World State* (New York, Columbia University Press, 1960); and Karl Deutsch, *Nationalism and Social Communication* (Cambridge, Mass., The M.I.T. Press, 1953).

Before World War II, neither imperial Russia, the Ottoman Empire, the German Empire, nor the Hapsburg Empire was an authentic juridical multinational state. Austria-Hungary was a binational state; Germany was a German national state with a fragment of the Polish nation as part of its population. Imperial Russia and Ottoman Turkey were autocratic, centralized national states with multinational populations.

The Soviet Union today is an authentic juridical multinational state. It claims to be the nation-state of all its major nationalities and is not described as a Russian state, constitutionally or legally. Other contemporary authentic multinational states are Switzerland, Yugoslavia, and the United Kingdom. Belgium, Czechoslovakia, and Canada are authentic binational states. South Africa is a binational state representing only its two European nationalities. The non-European population is not part of the state structure but is a subordinate subject population. Multinational or binational states can assume confederal, federal, or unitary form; special autonomy for the component nations is not a prerequisite for a state to be an authentic multinational state. The indispensable criteria are: (1) equal official status for the languages, cultures, and religions, of the member nations of the state; (2) equal official recognition and commemoration of the national symbols, values, shrines, and institutions of the component nations; (3) equal or proportionate access to all levels of the political and social system; and (4) the official name of the state should clearly identify its component nations (Yugoslavia, Austria-Hungary, Czechoslovakia) or should assume a neutral form reflecting a traditional geographical or regional characteristic (Switzerland, Belgium, Canada, South Africa) or an artificial construct (Union of Soviet Socialist Republics [Soviet Union]).

Authentic multinational states should not be confused with contemporary national states containing national minorities or fragments of other nations. Thus, pre-war Poland was self-identified as a *Polish* national state, although much of its population was non-Polish in character. Communist China, although it initially paid lip-service to the idea of a multinational state, frankly considers itself to be a Chinese, rather than a multinational, state, although it employs the territorial-imperial concept of China (*Chung-hua*) rather than the ethnic-racial concept (*Han*) in its official title as a state (*Chung-hua Jen-min Kung-ho Kuo*). In this manner, Peking can lay claim to territories historically a part of China, whose population is not *Han*, but who are nevertheless called "Chinese," because they inhabit traditionally Chinese territories. The Chinese concept *Chung-hua* is thus similar to the concepts *Rossiya* and Britain.

Alongside the multinational state, whether it be unitary, pluralistic, composite, federal, or confederal, is its inverted mirror-image, the divided nation. Just as one state can represent several nations in international affairs, one nation can be served (or disserved) by two or more states. The German nation is currently represented by three states (the German Federal Republic, the German Democratic Republic, and Austria), a special separate entity, West Berlin, and Switzerland, whose largest component nation is a fragment of the German nation. Vietnam, Korea, and China are also served by more than one state, as in the "Arab nation," which is dispersed among more than a dozen "Arab" states.

Thus, the role of the Soviet Union as a single state (although composite or multiple in form) representing more than one nation in international affairs is by no means unique in recent history or even today. For states of this character the concept national interest is inappropriate, since the state represents not *a* national interest but the interests of more than one nation. For this reason, as well as others, the term *state* interests would be a more appropriate characterization not only for multinational states but for all states, since even so-called *national* states often serve only the interests of élites or restricted constituencies in the state rather than the entire nation. A state such as the Soviet Union thus attempts to sort out and accommodate conflicting national interests at the domestic level before they are articulated as the interests of the state in foreign policy. Not only must various national interests be accommodated, but these must also be accommodated to the interests of social constituencies as well, within individual Soviet nations and across them.[27]

The uniqueness of the Soviet Union as a variable nation-state thus stems neither from its multinational character nor even from its peculiar juridical status under international law, but from its attempt, which no other state in recent history has made, to simultaneously function as the nation-state for an enormous array of disparate nations and nationalities of varying sizes and in uneven stages of national development. The Soviet federal structure attempts to give each nation a juridical semblance of both nationhood and statehood through a hierarchical system of federal national units (National District, Autonomous Oblast, Autonomous Republic, and Union Republic), of which the highest form, the Union Republic, approaches statehood in virtually all ceremonial and institutional norms, including the constitutional right to engage in diplomacy, raise armies, and even secede from the Union. As a consequence, Soviet citizens can be endowed with a bewildering set of juridical and national identities. For example, a Cherkass (Circassian) living in the Abkhazian Autonomous Soviet Socialist Republic is simultaneously: (1) a citizen of Abkhazia; (2) a citizen of The Georgian Republic, of which Abkhazia is a juridically subordinate national unit; (3) a citizen of the Soviet Union; and (4) a member of the Cherkass nation, which also possesses its own Autonomous Oblast. Before the educational reform acts of 1959, such a citizen could be legally obligated to learn Cherkass, Abkhazian, Georgian, and Russian in school.

As a variable nation-state, the Soviet Union serves separately and simultaneously as a Ukrainian, Georgian, Armenian, Uzbek, Lithuanian, etc. nation-state in the international community, since these nations have no other state representation under international law or in the international community save their existence as recognized juridical

---

[27] See Selection 13 and Aspaturian in Kassof, *op. cit.*

national components of the U.S.S.R. This responsibility of the Soviet state to function as a variable nation-state for its member nations is clearly recognized and explicitly and readily accepted by Soviet authorities, who claim that in this way small nations have, in effect, Great Power recognition because of their membership in the Soviet Union.[28]

As a variable nation-state, the Soviet Union has problems articulating the interests of more than a dozen major nations and several score minor ones. It must first deal with the conflicting interests and demands that the Soviet nations have against each other, which results in the establishment of a hierarchy of national priorities, with those of Russia at the top, followed by the Ukraine and the other nations in conformity with their size, strategic importance, resources, skills, or in response to their capacity for political leverage. Except for Russia and the Ukraine, the hierarchy of priorities is not fixed but changes with time and circumstance. In its capacity as a variable nation-state, the Soviet Union has claimed or annexed territories on behalf of Russia, the Ukraine, Byelorussia, Lithuania, Georgia, Armenia, and Azerbaidjan, although most of these territories were annexed from neighboring Communist states (whose interests Moscow is also supposed to guard in her capacity as leader of the World Communist Movement) and were subject to conflicting claims by the different Soviet nations themselves.[29]

In the past, the expansion of the Russian empire was the explicit aggrandizement of a Russian national state, called *Rossiya*, which corresponds to a territorial rather than ethnic concept of Russia and roughly approximates the term "all the Russias." This concept of a territorial *Rossiya* is a tradition that remains preserved in the juridical name of the Russian Soviet Federated Socialist Republic (R.S.F.S.R.) as "*Rossiiskaya . . . Respublika*," not *Russkaya Respublika*, since the R.S.F.S.R. is not a purely Russian republic but a lesser multinational federation within the U.S.S.R. Significantly, the R.S.F.S.R. has neither a separate Russian Communist Party organization (although every other national unit has one), nor a separate "*Russkaya . . . Respublika*," although it has numerous autonomous national Republics and Oblasts. Furthermore, Stalin did not demand separate representation of the R.S.F.S.R. in the United Nations (although it is by far the largest and most important Union Republic), thus reenforcing the view that the Russian character of the Communist Party, the Government, and the socio-cultural system is sufficient to allow a Russian citizen to identify himself with the Soviet Union as a Russian state.

5. The Soviet Union as a Multinational Commonwealth

Over and above the identity of the U.S.S.R as a juridical entity in the international system and its identities as a Russian nation-state and a variable or multiple non-Russian nation-state, it further functions in its total capacity as a unified collection of nations which adds up to

[28] See Selection 19.
[29] See Selections 13 and 14.

more than the simple sum total of its national components. Although russianized, it represents in this capacity the distilled and consensual interests of all its member nations and their commitment to each other as parts of a juridical polyethnic entity, which we will call its multinational commonwealth identity.

The specific ethnic distribution and composition of this commonwealth is a consequence of historical geography, a legacy of the Eurasian multinational and colonial empire assembled by the Russian tsars after several centuries of virtually uninterrupted territorial expansion and conquest. Today, the Soviet Union is the only intercontinental, multijuridical, multiracial, multilingual, and multicultural state in the world, and its Eurasian character has served not only to define its past evolution but continues to control its future destiny as a multinational commonwealth and to condition its behavior in world affairs.

Both Lenin and Stalin were quick to recognize and exploit the special advantages that the Soviet state enjoyed as a Eurasian multinational state. It gave to the Soviet Union the glow of an incipient, genuine universalism. The multinational character of the Soviet state was the principal rationale for its organization: a juridically federal state with residual confederal features, based upon national republics and ethnic units. Marxism as a doctrine was hostile to federalism, but Lenin and Stalin saw in a multinational federation the beginnings of what might eventually expand into a global federation of Communist states. This strategy became dogma under Stalin, with the result that some Communist states, in their zeal to model themselves with precision on the Soviet Union, sought to justify their programs by claiming to be synthetic multinational states on a smaller scale. The most conspicuous illustration was Yugoslavia, which slavishly aped the Soviet Union, though it modeled itself more on the R.S.F.S.R. than on the U.S.S.R. in anticipation of becoming a future subfederation of the U.S.S.R. It was also Mao Tse-tung's original intention to organize a Communist China into a multinational federation, but gradually, between 1934 and 1949, he retreated from one federal position after another until the idea was repudiated entirely in favor of a unitary state with severely limited ethnic autonomy for the non-Han population. Rumania also abandoned all pretense of being a multinational state. Both China and Rumania have either expelled their national minorities, tried to assimilate them, or reduced them to a condition of distinct ethnic subordination. Only Czechoslovakia, aside from Yugoslavia, has instituted, since 1968, a binational federal system in which Czechs and Slovaks enjoy juridical equality as distinctive autonomous units.

The centrality of the Soviet Union's geographical location as a Eurasian state has given it immense opportunities for self-extension—territorially, culturally, and ideologically. No less than 250,000 square miles of territory were annexed between 1939 and 1946, and a dozen new Communist states proliferated outward from the Soviet center in Europe and Asia. Counting the three Baltic states, fifteen nations have been brought under Communist rule in Eurasia due to direct or indirect

Soviet action and support. As Communist states were generated on the Soviet periphery in response to Soviet military, political, and ideological action, the Soviet Union, once simply the center of a revolutionary movement, became the hegemonic center of a new universe of ideologically related states that were simultaneously potential Union Republics of the U.S.S.R.

The proliferation of Communist states adjacent to the Soviet Union thus functioned initially to advance the ideological, political, and military frontiers of the U.S.S.R into Central Europe in the West and toward Southeast Asia in the East. Immediately after the war, Soviet leaders may have expected that some of these states would be incorporated into the U.S.S.R. as Union Republics, thus moving the Soviet border to the frontiers of new potential recruits to the Communist world. Stalin placed great emphasis on the territorial contiguity of Communist states, particularly on the territorial contiguity of these states with the U.S.S.R. Only by the successive incorporation of expanding concentric rings of new Communist party-states, Stalin believed, could the Soviet Union maintain a dynamic frontier in direct contact with future members of the Communist state system.

The defection of Yugoslavia and the emergence of a new Communist giant, China, prevented the implementation of this design, and after Stalin's death it was repudiated in favor of a "commonwealth" of independent socialist nation-states, whose future organizational relationships would be empirically determined. As polycentric tendencies developed and China emerged as a rival of the Soviet Union, what was initially conceived as a vehicle for the further sovietization of Europe and Asia became, in the West, a buffer between the Soviet Union and central-western Europe and, in the East, an impassable barrier to further Soviet expansion. Communism would now proliferate as a secondary emanation; that is, it would radiate outward from the non-Soviet Communist states rather than directly from the Soviet Union—or it would be, as in the case of Cuba, a spontaneous and independent eruption geographically remote from the Communist center.

The multinational character of the Soviet State has, since Stalin's death, outlived its usefulness as an instrument of Soviet expansion or as an embryonic world-state.[30] Actually, the multinational nature of the Soviet Union may become a handicap now that the Chinese have challenged the right of the Soviet Union to pose as an Asian or Eurasian state and have accused it of being a European imperial power masquerading in Asia as a multinational state. On this basis, China vetoed Soviet participation in the second Afro-Asian Conference, although other Asian and African states have continued to recognize the U.S.S.R. as an authentic Asian power. [31]

The replacement of a "capitalist encirclement" of the Soviet Union by a "socialist encirclement" has thus been a mixed blessing. On the

[30] Cf. Elliot Goodman, op. cit., for an examination of the world state idea in Soviet ideology and policy, and Lowenthal, op. cit.

[31] See Selection 10.

one hand, it increases the territorial security of the Soviet state by creating a buffer between it and the capitalist world, but on the other hand, this belt of Communist party-states on the Soviet periphery inhibits further Soviet territorial expansion. The Soviet Union, because of its extremely long border, has been able to annex more territories from neighboring countries than any other Communist state. Seven neighboring states, five of which are Communist, have relinquished territory to the U.S.S.R: Finland, Germany, Poland, Czechoslovakia, Rumania, China, and Japan. The Soviet Union made unsuccessful territorial demands upon two non-Communist states, Iran and Turkey, but was able to incorporate three entire states, Estonia, Latvia, and Lithuania. Of the Communist states sharing borders with the Soviet Union, only Hungary and North Korea have not been victims of Soviet territorial expansion, and if pre-1938 frontiers are used as a base point, Poland is the only Communist country that has annexed territory from another kindred state (East Germany).

These annexations were made by Stalin essentially through the use or threat of force. In the future, the de-Stalinization movement may take up the question of Soviet conquests as instances of Stalinist abuses and excesses against fraternal Communist states. Mao Tse-tung already has questioned the justice of virtually all Soviet territorial annexations and tsarist conquests in Central Asia and the Soviet Far East, which has been interpreted by Moscow as a virtual demand for the territorial dismemberment of the U.S.S.R.

Territorial questions were almost certain to be raised once the Soviet Union acquiesced in accepting and preserving the nation-state as the definitive form of the state in the Communist state system. This retention of the nation-state is an explicit recognition of class solidarity's failure to submerge national distinctions, and proletarian internationalism's inability to prevail over the traditional and historical interests that such states represent. Even in a system in which all nation-states are allegedly proletarian in class content, the specter of mutual territorial demands upon one another and multiple territorial claims against the Soviet Union in the name of national irredenta continues to haunt the Communist state system. It is unlikely that the Communist alliance system will be any more successful than non-Communist alliance systems in its ability to rise above the centrifugal force generated by nationalism. Since it is clear that the "nation-state" is a function both of people and of geography, the ethnographic configuration of the Soviet Union and its impact on the Communist system of states demands close examination, and its feedback effects upon the evolution of the Soviet multinational system itself also bears close examination, since both are crucial factors in conditioning Soviet foreign policy behavior.

Since the non-Russian nationalities of the Soviet Union inhabit the border regions of the country from the White Sea to the Black and from the Baltic to the Pacific (except for the Maritime Province), and frequently spill over into adjacent states, some of them actually constitute the national irredenta of bordering countries. This is true of the Karelian areas adjacent to Finland, of Eastern Galicia bordering on Poland, of the Moldavian Republic next to Rumania, and of the Buryat-Mongol regions north of Mongolia. Although no Chinese ethnic irredenta are within Soviet borders, the Turkic nationalities of Central Asia are culturally and linguistically related to ethnic groups inhabiting Sinkiang.

The strategic location of the non-Russian nationalities and their character as unredeemed national kinsmen of neighboring states pose a potential threat to the integrity of the Soviet state. From a potential instrument of integration, the multinational character of the Soviet Union has become a possible vehicle for its disintegration. Now that the separate existence of national Communist states is to be perpetuated indefinitely and the nation-state becomes the basic state form of the proletariat, the Soviet federation can no longer sustain the pretense of being an embryonic universal federation. The subversion of the ideological rationale justifying the Soviet Union's existence as a single-state complex has compelled Soviet leaders to fall back upon other justifications, mainly traditional and historical ones. Even the propriety of subordinating the non-Russian nationalities as bogus nation-states in the form of Union Republics might be raised inside and outside the Soviet Union, since in the present Communist confraternity of nation-states these nationalities do not enjoy separate participation but exist as juridically inferior nations. As long as the destiny of the other Communist party-states was incorporation into the U.S.S.R., their existence as subordinate Soviet Republics was ideologically defined as a superior and more progressive status, but now that the Bulgarians, Albanians, Mongols, and other Communist nations can enjoy national independence, why must the Ukrainians and other Soviet nations be satisfied with only the external ornaments of statehood that their vicarious national existence as Union Republics affords them?

As a terminal multinational commonwealth, instead of a potential world state, the Soviet Union has been forced to transform some of its original goals and purposes. "World Communism," even as an abstraction, must now be visualized as a world of independent Communist states, rather than as a universalized U.S.S.R. or hegemonic system under Soviet control. The transformation of "World Communism" from a monolithic into a decentralized conception raises profound questions with respect to the ultimate fate and destiny of the nations under Soviet rule. Is the U.S.S.R. to be dissolved into its component national Communist units to become separate and independent members of the Communist community? Are they to continue as autonomous units within the U.S.S.R. as juridically inferior or "second class" Communist states? Or, are they to dissolve into the numerically preponderant Russian nation or fuse into a new Soviet nation?

The future of the nations under Soviet rule is a fundamental question that requires resolution, and one form that the resolution appears to be taking is the preservation of the current dimensions of the Soviet state by transforming it into an integrated, permanent, indivisible multinational commonwealth. The expanding tsarist empire swallowed, but was never able to fully digest, this variegated and mutually antagonistic collection of races and nationalities. The imperial response was to establish the numerically preponderant Great Russians as the ruling nationality, and Russia became a "prison of nations," not a multinational commonwealth in fact or fiction. It is generally acknowledged that one of the principal factors contributing to the revolution of 1917 was the disaffection of the major non-Russian nationalities and especially of their educated classes. All the revolutionary parties of Russia counted among their leaders outstanding individuals of many nationalities. The failure of Imperial Russia to grapple intelligently with the nationality question was instrumental in accelerating its demise in the midst of national agony and crisis.

Although most of the Russian Empire was preserved intact as the U.S.S.R., the federal approach to the nationality problem was undermined by the political policies and ideological goals of the Soviet regime and can be considered only a limited success before World War II. The nationality problem in many ways remains a matter of life and death for the Soviet state because of the strategic location of the border nationalities. The geographical balance and distribution of the nationalities of the Soviet Union give rise, in fact, to a "Russian" problem as well as a "Soviet" problem since the Great Russians, occupying the continental interior of Eurasia, are fringed on all sides by a virtually uninterrupted belt of non-Russian nationalities that forms a buffer on the international borders of the Soviet Union. Along virtually the entire Baltic coast of the U.S.S.R. are the Estonians, Latvians, and Lithuanians; the Byelorussians, Ukrainians, and Moldavians inhabit the territories bordering Poland, Czechoslovakia, and Rumania. In the Caucasus, the Georgians, Armenians, and Azerbaidzhani Turks inhabit the regions bordering on Turkey and Iran, and in Central Asia, the Turkmen, Uzbeks, Kazakhs, Tadzhiks, and Kirgiz occupy the border areas adjacent to Iran, Afghanistan, and the Sinkiang Province of a menacing China, and a multitude of Turkic, Mongol, and Tungusic tribes occupy the border regions with Outer Mongolia. Only in the Soviet Far East do Russians inhabit territories adjacent to international frontiers, and this is a region remote from the heartland of the Russian nation.

Because of the strategic location of the border nationalities, their loyalty to Moscow and their relationship to the Russian people has always been a vital factor in Russian and Soviet security considerations. The federal solution whereby each major nationality was organized into a separate republic with its own language, culture, constitution, and other symbols of nationhood was only a partial success in winning the loyalty and reliability of these nationalities. During World War II, the Germans were welcomed in some of the border regions, and hundreds of thousands of Soviet prisoners of war of many nationalities agreed to enlist in Nazi-organized National Legions to fight against the Soviet Union. The nature and intensity of this defection still remains the subject of considerable speculation and controversy, since it is not exactly clear whether the motivations were basically anti-Soviet, anti-Russian, anti-Stalin, or just simple national self-determination and self preservation, but undoubtedly all of these elements were involved.[32]

Currently, the Soviet leadership, given the altered landscape in the international system, within the Soviet Union, and in the world of Communist states, is confronted with three alternative solutions *to the national problem*, all of which have their advocates and proponents among the various national elites. These three alternatives can be conceptualized as follows:

1. *The Nation-Building Model.* This appears to be the dominant, official position of the Soviet leadership, as judged by Party resolutions, directives, and pronouncements. It is a modified version of the Stalinist vision of a unilingual, unitary nation formed out of the amalgamation, merger, or "coming together" of all the nationalities to form a new nation, which would be heavily "russianized."[33] Whether the common language was to be a new linguistic creation or Russian was subject to periodic controversy, with the Russian option clearly emerging as dominant. This process would be similar to visions of nation-building animating India, Nigeria, and other new polyethnic, multilingual states.

2. *The Assimilation Model.* This solution presupposes the assimilation of the non-Russian nationalities by the Great Russians, in contrast to the nation-building model that assumed a melting down of all nationalities, including the Russian, into a new composite national identity.[34]

[32] *Cf.* the following for an accounting of the behavior of the Soviet nationalities in areas of German occupation during World War II and Stalin's reactions: Alexander Dallin, *German Rule in Russia* (New York, St. Martin's Press, 1957); Robert Conquest, *The Soviet Deportation of Nationalities* (New York, St. Martin's Press, 1960); and George Fischer, *Soviet Opposition to Stalin* (Cambridge, Mass., Harvard University Press, 1952).

[33] The Soviet debate on the future of Soviet nationalities, because of its delicate character, has evolved an esoteric terminology of its own, in which various writers seek to express themselves in the choice of words, and the intensity with which they advocate what appear ôn the surface to be similar or indistinguishable goals. The ambiguity of the Party position itself contributes to both the ambiguity and ambivalence of many commentators. Code words for the assimilationist position appear to be "merging" (*sliyaniye*), "fusion," "amalgamation," and "complete union" or "unity." Code words for commonwealth-building appear to be "flourishing" (*rastvet*) of nations and employment of the term "Soviet people" (*narod*) rather than the more integralist "Soviet Nation" (*natsiya*), which is a code word of the nation-builders, as is "coming together" (*sblizheniye*). The "nation-building" model is not only implausible but both ambiguous and ambivalent and hence becomes essentially an arena of controversy between assimilationists and commonwealth-builders, who pull and stretch the Party position to coincide with their view. The "merging together" formula is thus apparently a stop-gap concept designed to permit debate and discussion, and which can be readily adapted either to the assimilationist or commonwealth-building model once a definitive policy has been established.

[34] Since explicit assimilationist views are officially proscribed, the assimilationist model is essentially a more militant and uncompromising restatement of nation-building. P. G. Semyonov (Russian) is one of the few writers

This alternative is essentially indistinguishable from tsarist policies of "russification," with the exception that it is conceived more rationally and is dominated by an egalitarian ethos rather than the blatant tsarist pattern of discrimination against some nationalities as unfit for transformation into Russians.

3. *The Commonwealth-Building Model.* This alternative presupposes the preservation of the federal system and even its creative development in new directions and assumes the perpetuation of individual national identities, loyalties, sentiments, and consciousness for a considerable period into the future.[35] Emphasis would be on the creation and fashioning of new bonds that would generate immutable ties of mutual interest, incapable of being subverted by separate national identities, no matter how intensively articulated. Switzerland is a microcosmic prototype of this model, and Yugoslavia is faltering in the same direction as it progressively unburdens itself of its original Stalinist conceptions of multinational federalism.

The Soviet leadership has apparently rejected the assimilationist model, although some marginal assimilation (russification) will continue. It has not definitively decided between the nation-building and

---

to employ the term assimilation and thus is a prominent target of the commonwealth-builders. For his assimilationist views, Cf. *Sovetskoye Gosudarstvo i Pravo*, No. 12, 1961. Other assimilationists, masquerading as militant nation-builders are M. A. Sverdlin (Jewish) and P. M. Rogachev (Russian), who have jointly published several articles in *Filosofskiye Nauki*, 1964, No. 2 and 5; *Kommunist*, June 1963, No. 6; and *Voprosy Istorii*, 1966, No. 1.

[35] For a typical commonwealth-building view, disguised as lukewarm advocacy of nation-building, Cf. E. V. Tadevosyan in *Voprosy Istorii*, 1964, No. 5, who stresses the creative potential of Soviet federalism and criticizes Semyonov for underrating the latent possibilities in Soviet federalism. "In the field of national state construction to try to hasten artificially the extinction of the forms of socialist national statehood, as well as refusal further to perfect and develop them, can only bring harm." Other commonwealth-building views are M. S. Dzhunusov (Kirgiz) in *Voprosy Istorii*, 1966, No. 4; M. O. Mnatsakanian (Armenian) in *Voprosi Istorii*, 1966, No. 9; N. A. Tavakalian (Armenian) in *Voprosy Istorii*, 1967, No. 2; I. E. Kravtsev (Russian) *Razvitiye Natsionalnykh Itnishevii v SSSR* (Kiev, 1962); I. P. Tsamerian (Armenian), in *Voprosy Istorii KPSS*, 1968, No. 9. For nation-builders, *i.e.* those who would apear to envisage a "russianized" multinational state rather than a "russified" one, Cf. M. Kh. Khakimov, "Some Problems of the Development of National Soviet Statehood During the Present Period," in *Obshchestvennyye Nauki v Uzbekistane*, 1964, No. 6, where he suggests that the progressive "internationalization" of the Union Republics redistributes the sovereignty of the Republic to the eponymous nation and its population as a whole; B. L. Manelis, another nation-builder, develops this theme even further by asserting that "internationalization" shifts sovereignty from the nation giving the Republic its name to the whole people inhabiting the Republic, "who are homogeneous and monolithic in the social sense and becoming more and more heterogeneous in the national sense." "The Identity of the Sovereignty of the USSR with the Sovereignty of the Union Republics in the Period of Full-Scale Communist Construction," in *Sovetskoye Gosudarstvo i Pravo*, 1964, No. 7.

commonwealth-building models but seems to be in a state of animated suspension between the two. Its official pronouncements appear to endorse the former, which is also strenuously supported by articulate jurists and nationality specialists, whereas its actual policies appear to reflect the latter, which also has a conspicuous coterie of adherents, particularly among the nationalities with ancient and powerful credentials of national consciousness, such as the Georgians, Armenians, and Lithuanians. This ambivalence suggests not only indecision, but also factional cleavages over the issue in the leadership. But since the nation-building model presupposes an extended period of transition, initial steps in the process of nation-building are indistinguishable from commonwealth-building, which can be viewed as a prerequisite to the former as well as a terminal goal.

Proponents of the assimilationist model are also still active, and all three views find expression in Soviet newspapers, books, and articles, and a lively debate and discussion has been in progress for over a decade.[36] Many advocates of the commonwealth-building model prudently pay lip service to the nation-building model by not explicitly endorsing the commonwealth idea as a terminal state and simultaneously extolling the vitality and creative potentialities of Soviet federalism and emphasizing the remoteness of the day when national boundaries, languages, and consciousness are supposed to "wither away."

In the meantime, as the debate continues and history marshals its forces for the future, the Soviet Union exists as a russianized multinational commonwealth, alongside its other identities. As it attempts to press along the road to the amalgamation of nationalities in the face of internal counter-pressures, the Soviet regime must, at the same time, project its personality as a multinational commonwealth in its external behavior, thus contributing confusion and contradiction to Soviet policy. Whatever may have been the intentions of the Soviet leaders in the past, they, for the forseeable future at least, have abandoned the idea of the Soviet Union as the embryonic nucleus of a universal Soviet state and have accommodated themselves to the acceptance of the Soviet Union as a terminal multinational commonwealth within an expanding community of independent Communist states. The Soviet leaders are thus no longer committed to the territorial or juridical expansion of the Soviet state, although they are still committed to the expansion and extension of the Communist world of states. They are, however, implacably determined to preserve the current dimensions of the Soviet state and its multinational character in *some* form for the forseeable future.

Preserving the Soviet Union as a terminal multinational commonwealth in an age of resurgent national consciousness throughout the world, including the appearance of even micro and mini nationalism

[36] For further discussions of the debate between various proponents, *Cf.*, Hodnett, *op. cit.*, and Jurij Borys, "The Concept of the Soviet Nation," a paper presented at the Far Western Slavic Conference, Stanford University, April 25–26, 1969.

among groups whose national consciousness has been hitherto under-developed or unaroused, is bound to create manifold difficulties for the Soviet leaders. After more than a quarter of a century without a major war and with the gradual attenuation of the "Cold War," the overriding imperative of territorial and state integrity has eroded, and various sub-national groups within individual states are being infected with the heady prospect of independent sovereign existence as states and as members of an international organization, the United Nations, whose very name emphasizes the higher priority of national sovereignty and identity over that of state sovereignty. The crumbling of colonial em-pires, the movements of national liberation and secession, and de-mands for national self-determination by national, linguistic, ethnic, tribal, and racial minorities has set into motion a dynamic from which the Soviet Union is not likely to remain immune. The awakening of racial consciousness among American blacks and national awareness among Chicanos and Indians is matched by the revival of French Canadian nationalism in Quebec and Basque nationalism in Spain, which is likely to provoke similar movements in Catalonia. Irish ir-redentism has reappeared in Northern Ireland, while various manifesta-tions of mini-nationalism have appeared among the Welsh and Scotch in the United Kingdom. The Bretons in France have revived demands for some form of official recognition of their national identity, and Provencal speakers in the South of France have raised the issue of official recognition for their *patois* as a distinct language.

Binational states such as Belgium and Czechoslovakia are under severe strain as Flemings and Slovaks demand greater attention to their distinct identity, and in Yugoslavia, the renewal of the Serbo-Croat na-tional conflict has aroused the national consciousness of the Slovenes, Bosnian-Moslems, Albanians, Macedonians, and even Montenegrins. The infectious virus of nationalism is thus no respecter of ideologies or juridi-cal systems and threatens to undermine and dissolve Communist and non-Communist states, whether they be federal or unitary in character.

The national question in the Soviet Union and its future as a functioning multinational state is thus part of a larger process operating throughout the globe, and the manner in which the problem is resolved elsewhere is likely to influence developments inside the U.S.S.R. On the other hand, the way in which the problem of multinationalism is handled inside the Soviet Union may affect developments elsewhere, particularly for nationally inchoate multitribal, polyethnic, and multi-religious states that have proliferated in Asia and Africa since World War II. To the degree that the Soviet Union succeeds in satisfying the demands of individual national self-expression with the broader im-perative of membership in a larger complex, then to that degree can the Soviet multinational system serve as a possible model for countries such as India and Nigeria.

The implications of the internal evolution of the Soviet multi-national system for Soviet security and foreign policy has thus been drawn into the debate between the proponents of various solutions. The nation-builders, and even more emphatically the residual assimilation-ists, strongly suggest that federalism and multinational pluralism are inherently centrifugal, divisive, and disintegrative in character. They maintain that an effective and active foreign policy requires that ideo-logical unity be given priority over national diversity, which would also minimize the vulnerability of the Soviet Union to external irredentist demands and racist appeals, particularly by the Chinese.

The commonwealth-builders, on the other hand, stress the impor-tance of the Soviet multinational system, not as an active factor in Soviet foreign policy, but as a beacon attracting other countries. Ac-cording to commonwealth-builders, only an authentic commonwealth of nations that can meet the imperatives of both socialism and national identity can effectively enhance the Soviet image abroad and serve as a model to beckon other nations toward Soviet values and socialism. Thus, M. O. Mnatsakanian, an articulate advocate of commonwealth-building and creative federalism, argues that failure to respect the deep attachment people have for national identity can damage the Soviet Union both internally and in foreign policy:

> Belittling the role of national statehood in general, and Soviet [state-hood] in particular, cannot serve the goal of further consolidating the friendship of peoples of the U.S.S.R., of strengthening the unity of the socialist system, nor the goal of winning over ideologically and politically the masses of both developed capitalist states and of young countries liberated from colonial oppression.[37]

The multinational character of the Soviet Union thus has a poten-tial of tremendous magnitude as an influence on the evolution and development of the international system. Up to now, the Soviet leaders have energetically supported movements of national liberation, seces-sion, and independence, since they were ideologically committed to the principle of national self-determination as a pragmatic vehicle for the dissolution of multinational capitalist states and colonial empires. But just as Lenin quickly recognized that national self-determination was as effective in eroding the Bolshevik state as the tsarist empire, and called for a pragmatic retreat, so Soviet leaders are increasingly aware that their support of national liberation and independence movements in colonial empires may establish a precedent for similar demands at home.

II. THEORIES, MODELS, AND FRAMEWORKS OF ANALYSIS

1. Predicting Soviet Behavior

One perennial purpose in the systematic study of any country's foreign policy is to understand the reasons and uncover the causes for its past and current behavior in world affairs. This inevitably involves

[37] M. O. Mnatsakanian, in *Voprosy Istorii*, 1966, No. 9, p. 34, as cited in Hodnett, *op. cit.*, p. 13. See also Selection 4.

FIGURE 1
CONSTITUENCIES, IDENTITIES, AND EXTERNAL CONTACTS OF THE SOVIET UNION

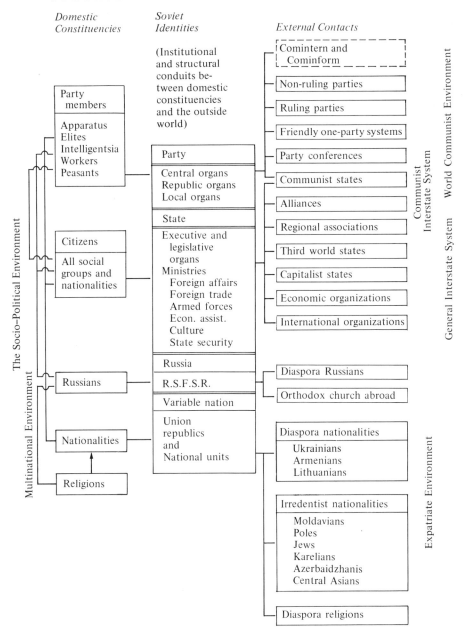

an examination of the motives, purposes, and intentions of the state toward other states in the international community, as well as an examination of how it reacts and responds toward the perceived intentions and demands of the international community upon it. Purpose and analysis are thus inextricably interwoven: The objective of analysis is often to discover the purposes of the state in foreign policy; the analysis of purpose often reduces itself to speculating about intent and attempting to predict future behavior.

Preoccupation with intent and obsession about the prediction of future behavior, however, achieves a level of intensity in the study of Soviet foreign policy rarely reached in the study of the foreign policy of most other states, save perhaps that of Communist China. The systematic study of United States foreign policy, for example, rarely involves speculation about the intent and motives of decision-makers, nor is any special attention devoted to predicting future foreign policy. Awareness of the many fortuitous factors and innumerable voluntaristic and spontaneous variables involved renders the prediction of United States foreign policy a futile exercise. In fact, even the description of past policy invites acrimonious controversy and divergent interpretations among United States scholars. The appearance of an American school of "revisionist" historians, for example, reflects little more than an attempt to retrospectively predict foreign policy since 1939 (sometimes since 1900 or 1914) disguised as a reexamination of the "origins" of the "Cold War" and a retroactive reconstruction of the motives, intent, and purposes of the United States and its decision-makers in the light of not only new data and information but new ideological moods and attitudes among the younger generation of historians as well as older scholars who subscribe to Marxist or quasi-Marxist interpretations.[38] The results have been neither particularly edifying nor conclusive and in some instances have merely repeated earlier Marxist (including Soviet) analyses.

Predicting the future behavior of any country in foreign policy is a hazardous process at best. *Ex post facto* explanations of foreign policy are only slightly less susceptible to the hazards and pitfalls that afflict the prediction of future behavior, since the problem of coping with the underlying purposes and intentions of international actors and their agents is compounded by the problems posed by the intentions, purposes, and integrity of the scholars and historians, to say nothing of the ideological predispositions that animate them or the methodological preferences that may intellectually mesmerize them.

It is the relative openness of American society, the accessibility to data and personalities, the abundance of information, and the profusion of contradictory and divergent opinions and interpretations that impel the student of American foreign policy to realize the futility of developing a theory or framework with which to predict future American behavior and to abjure serious attempts to devise such mechanisms. Yet

[38] See Selections 5, 6, and 7.

the demand for theories, frameworks, models, and systems that can provide the basis for predicting future Soviet behavior continues unabated, based upon the assumption that if enough energy, imagination, and scientific methodology is applied, somehow a predictive system will be contrived. This is an intellectual malady that afflicts virtually all students of Soviet foreign policy, including the author, and its tenacious persistence demands explanation.

Aside from the obvious fact that Soviet area studies developed within the context of the "Cold War" and were infected with the "know your enemy" syndrome that carried over from wartime studies of Nazi Germany and Imperial Japan, the predictive component is persistent in the study of Soviet foreign policy for other reasons. Among the more important are the following two:

1. *The Apparent Simplicity of the Soviet Decision-Making System.* In accordance with the general assumption that decision-making in authoritarian, totalitarian, and dictatorial political systems was a relatively uncomplicated procedure, it was assumed that Soviet decisions in foreign policy were made by a single person or a small group of visible individuals (Politburo). The decision-makers were perceived as intelligent, rational, and calculating men, who were relatively free from internal institutional restraints, domestic pressure groups, public opinion, criticism, or even advice and also unencumbered by moral compunction, international law, or world public opinion. Accordingly, Soviet decisions were arrived at after coolly and rationally examining all alternatives, calculating resources and capabilities, dispassionately awaiting openings and opportunities, unerringly determining timing with precision, and acting quickly, decisively, and with dispatch. The Soviet leaders, under this simple model, were restricted only by their own intelligence, rationality, adeptness, and capabilities.[39]

2. *The Apparent Simplicity in Assessing Soviet Intent, Purposes, and Motives.* Since Soviet decisions were made by a small, identifiable group of individuals, it was conveniently assumed that decipherment of Soviet intent was essentially a matter of divining the intentions of the

[39] This view was given wide dissemination in many elementary and introductory textbooks on international relations, especially when contrasting the relative efficiency of "dictatorships" and "democracies" in making foreign policy decisions. It should be noted that the conclusions drawn were not incompatible with the definition of the "problem," but rather with actual reality. Because of the relative ignorance prevailing about the "totalitarian" decision-making systems, observers were particularly conscious of the pressures, restraints, and impositions upon "democratic" decision-makers, which did not seem to be operative in totalitarian systems. What they were unaware of was that "totalitarian" decision-makers labored under a different set of pressures, restraints, and obstacles, most of which were concealed and hence invisible to the outside observer, but far from nonexistent. Thus, democratic decision-makers were relatively free from constraints and pressures like factional intrigue, conspiracies, *coup d'etats*, assassinations, purges, ideological struggles, and the resultant paranoia that often developed to haunt and persecute the decision-maker and undermine his efficiency in totalitarian systems.

Soviet leaders. This objective was rendered almost ridiculously simple because the Soviet leaders were governed by a systematic ideology, periodically and publicly interpreted, that defined Soviet norms, goals, and purposes, made explicit the strategy and tactics to be employed, and communicated these ends and means in public via the printed and spoken word, although in a special, esoteric jargon. Mastering the Soviet jargon was the key to understanding Soviet ideology that, in turn, was the lock in the door that opened into the hidden, inner recesses of Soviet intent.

As a consequence of these two assumptions, several simple predictive models of Soviet foreign policy behavior were implicitly developed, of which four were initially the most conspicuous:

1. *The ideological model,* which assumed that Soviet behavior was almost automatically a function of the norms and stated purposes of Marxism-Leninism, to which the Soviet leaders subscribed undeviatingly and with fanatic devotion. [40]

2. *The personality model,* which was somewhat more sophisticated than the ideological model, since it was postulated on the view that the interests, drives, ambitions, and psychocultural conditioning of the Soviet leaders would invariably affect the way the ideology was perceived, developed, and applied. Soviet behavior was thus defined as a combination of ideological and personality factors.[41]

3. *The capabilities model,* which reached a slightly higher level of sophistication than the personality model, since it recognized that Soviet behavior would be limited and conditioned by its own resources and capabilities as measured against the resources and capabilities of other powers, irrespective of ideology or personality drives, and thus an external input into Soviet behavior was recognized. In this model, Soviet behavior was defined in terms of ideologically conditioned personalities making decisions in the context of capabilities analysis. A simplistic capabilities model was one in which Soviet decisions were almost automatically restricted or unleashed by the changing balance of capabilities (power).[42]

[40] Cf., for example, W. H. Chamberlain, editor, *Blueprint for World Conquest* (Chicago, Ill., Human Events, Inc., 1963); Fred Schwarz, *You Can Trust the Communists (To Do What They Say)* (Englewood Cliffs, N.J., Prentice-Hall, 1960); and Anthony Bouscaren, *Soviet Foreign Policy* (New York, Fordham University Press, 1962).

[41] Cf. Stefan T. Possony, *Lenin, The Compulsive Revolutionary* (Chicago, Ill., Henry Regnery, 1964); Edward E. Smith, *The Young Stalin* (New York, Farrar, Straus and Giroux, 1967); Paul Sheffer, "Stalin's Power," *Foreign Affairs,* July 1930; Diplomaticus, "Stalinist Theory and Foreign Policy," *Review of Politics,* Vol. 14, 1952.

[42] Simple capabilities models, often based upon geopolitical formulations, were at one time popular in professional military circles during the late forties and fifties, particularly in the Air Force, whose course of instruction in ROTC programs often included a course in "Aeropolitics" as a substitute for international politics.

4. *The Russian imperialism model,* which assumed that the Soviet state was the imperial Russian state in modern dress and that ideology and Communism were merely convenient masquerades for Russian imperialist expansion. Standing alone in this manner, it was the most simplistic model of all, but by being grafted upon the other three, it achieved a relatively high level of sophistication: Soviet behavior was defined as a function of Russian Marxist leaders, whose ambitions and drives were a combination of personality factors, traditional Russian interests, and Marxism, making decisions within the context of the changing balance of capabilities.[43]

In general, intellectuals, whether favorably disposed or in opposition to Soviet policies, subscribed to the ideological model. Statesmen and politicians favored the personality model, and professional military people were partial to the capabilities model, whereas diplomats and professional historians were attracted to the Russian imperialism model. These were only general tendencies and represented essentially the dominant, not exclusive, motif in their thinking about Soviet foreign policy, which was generally multicausal in conception, although usually a single factor was so dominant as to give it the appearance of mono-causal analysis.

The paucity of knowledge concerning Soviet behavior combined with the conspicuous and novel emphasis upon ideology in Soviet pronouncements thus combined to produce the notion that the foreign policy of a Communist dictatorship was particularly susceptible to systematic prediction, if one could only have access to data and information. It was this belief that eventually resulted in the inordinate emphasis placed upon intelligence and espionage in dealing with the Soviet Union. Faith in the miraculous power of espionage where Soviet behavior was concerned became an obsession, although it was obvious in the case of other powers that increased access to data and availability of information seemed to be of only peripheral significance in the development of a framework that could predict future foreign policy behavior.[44] Ignorance concerning the total universe of variables and factors that affected Soviet policy and the matrix within which they operated resulted in the conclusion that the variables and factors were few in number and simple in operation; all that was necessary was complete information about them to develop an effective predicting machine. More information, however, when it materialized, proved disappointing. As the availability of data concerning Soviet behavior enhanced, it became apparent that the Soviet decision-making system was extremely

[43] See Selections 10 and 11. *Cf.* R. S. Tarn, "Continuity in Russian Foreign Policy," in Robert Goldwin, *et al.,* editors, *Readings in Russian Foreign Policy* (Chicago, American Foundation for Political Education, 1959).

[44] *Cf.* Allen Dulles, *The Craft of Intelligence* (New York, Harper and Row, 1963), especially pp. 220–236; Paul W. Blackstock, *The Strategy of Subversion* (Chicago, Ill., Quadrangle, 1964); and Sanche de Gramont, *The Secret War* (New York, Putnam, 1962).

complex and that the number of variables and inputs involved were both extremely numerous and their interrelationships very complicated. The earlier simplistic theories and models crumbled and gave way to a profusion of more intricate and involved frameworks, but instead of enhancing the predictability of Soviet behavior, just the opposite transpired. The earlier simple certainties concerning Soviet behavior, founded on relative ignorance, gave way to confusion, controversy, and uncertainty, not only over Soviet behavior, but whether Soviet behavior was, in fact, predictable. The earlier assurance that more data and access would mean greater reliability of the analysis has proven to be exaggerated. More information and data have resulted in a greater awareness of the numerous variables and factors involved in Soviet policy; more access has meant a greater appreciation of the complicated and complex character of the Soviet system. Furthermore, the availability of more data has undermined our previous certitudes and reveals even more vividly the extent of our continuing ignorance concerning the totality of the Soviet system.

As a consequence, we have more speculation and "informed opinion," not less; more contradictory and divergent interpretations; more theories, models, and frameworks; and more methodologies and techniques of analysis. Surely we are now less confident in our ability to predict Soviet behavior simply on the assumption of more information, but apparently not necessarily less certain that quantitative techniques and computers will succeed where previous methods have failed.[45] As information and data have become more accessible and available, frameworks, models, and theories have become more complex. But just as the simplicity of early frameworks was based upon ignorance, the complexity of new frameworks reflects largely an awareness of the complexity of the problem and not necessarily a more effective predictive tool. The new frameworks are more interesting and exciting, certainly more illuminating, about past and current Soviet behavior, but just as ineffective in predicting future behavior, if the total universe of factors and variables continues to remain beyond reach, and this is certainly the case with respect to Soviet foreign policy.

2. Analyzing Soviet Behavior

The known variables, constants, factors, and inputs that influence and shape Soviet behavior are enormous, and their significance, relatively as well as absolutely, has varied considerably over time and space (and will continue to do so). It has been these variables, plus those that remain unknown or unborn, and their uneven importance over time that has generated so many single-factor analytical frameworks or theories: ideological, geographical, historical, personality, psychocultural, developmental, power, national interest, etc. Many of these single-factor theories were developed when a particular variable loomed

---

[45] Faith in the success of these methods was especially high in the Defense Department and its outside research contracting agencies during Secretary McNamara's tenure. Cf. Alain C. Enthoven and K. Wayne Smith, How Much Is Enough? (New York, Harper and Row, 1971).

larger than others in shaping Soviet behavior; others were generated in response to fads, trends, and fashions in academic research; still others were reflections of the specific identity ascribed to the Soviet Union as an actor in world affairs by scholars and observers, who ignored the multiple roles and identities that characterized the Soviet state. Thus, to a certain extent history explains (not necessarily justifies) the successive appearance of these single-factor analytical theories and approaches. Not only are we still not cognizant of all the variables and inputs into Soviet behavior, but knowledge about those that are visible is often incomplete, distorted, and subject to speculative evaluation and assessment.

During the early years of the Soviet state, ideological explanations of Soviet behavior were dominant, among both proponents and opponents of the Soviet regime. In large measure this was due to the conspicuous emphasis that Lenin and other Soviet leaders assigned to ideology as a guide to action, both before and after the Bolsheviks came to power. Ideology as an explicit guide to foreign policy behavior was a novelty in the twentieth century and was surely the most important factor influencing Soviet behavior during the earlier years of the regime, challenging at times even the pragmatic imperatives of survival.[46] The Soviet state was new; its capabilities were extremely limited, its social system largely in a state of disarray. Ideological explanations (the pursuit of world revolution, as noted earlier) were later supplemented with or displaced by theories emphasizing development (as the Soviet socio-economic order assumed shape), personalities (following Lenin's death and the succession controversy), national interest (as the Soviet Union reentered the main stream of European diplomacy), and imperialist expansion (following Soviet expansion in 1939–1940). All these theories and approaches have left their deposits and residues in the study of Soviet behavior. Since World War II, with the tremendous growth of Soviet power and influence in world affairs, capabilities explanations became the vogue, often combined with geopolitical ruminations.

What have often been overlooked in the examination and manipulation of variables shaping Soviet foreign policy are the changes in one variable or the appearance of new ones that affect the relative importance of others. Multiple changes in several variables give rise to various possible new mixes or mutations and permutations insofar as the total impact on Soviet behavior is concerned. The single most important characteristic of the Soviet state since World War II, for example, has been its immense absolute and relative power, the manner in which it has employed it, and above all, the enormous range in choices and options these capabilities have provided. After five decades of Soviet foreign policy, as another illustration, the role of ideology in Soviet foreign policy, as both a source of ends and as an instrument of

[46] This was especially true during the early years of Bolshevik rule, when, first Nikolai Bukharin and the "Left Communists," and then Leon Trotsky and his doctrine of "Permanent Revolution" assigned a higher priority to ideological fidelity than to survival and self-preservation as a state.

other goals, emerges more clearly. Viewed in historical perspective, ideology has not been a constant in shaping Soviet policy, but a relative factor whose relationship to other variables has shown considerable fluctuation as an input. This protean and variable characteristic of ideology has been and continues to be a prime source of controversy in assessing its significance for Soviet policy. As other variables have altered in their dimensions, the relative role of ideology has been correspondingly transformed.[47]

Finally, these changing variables and the kaleidoscopic matrix within which they operate must be related to the multiple identities of the Soviet Union and the interests of the constituencies that they serve, since the relative importance of individual variables tends to emphasize one Soviet identity over the other, while simultaneously favoring the constituencies associated with that identity. Thus, the priority of ideology in foreign policy (world Communism) reflects the Soviet identity as a party and serves the interest of the party apparatus, professional ideologues, and non-ruling Communist parties abroad. Emphasis on power, prestige, and influence reflects its identity as a state and the state bureaucracy (including the diplomatic service) and to the degree that it involves the enhancement of military capabilities, it serves the interests of the professional military and heavy industrial interests.[48] Territorial expansion is multi-dimensional in its effects, since it can simultaneously reflect several identities and serve the interests of a number of constituencies.[49] Thus territorial expansion can result in the following:

1. The enhancement of the Soviet Union as a Global Power (state).

2. The extension of the Communist socio-political system (party).

3. The expansion of Russia or the Russian empire (Russian nation).

4. The expansion of the territories of non-Russian nationalities (variable nation).

5. The extension of the multinational character of the Soviet Union (multinational commonwealth).

[47] See Selections 1, 10, 11, 12, and 25 for discussions of the ideological factor in various contexts of Soviet behavior. Cf. also Zbigniew K. Brzezinski, "Communist Ideology and International Affairs," in *Ideology and Power in Soviet Politics* (New York, Praeger, 1962); Adam B. Ulam, "Soviet Ideology and Soviet Foreign Policy," *World Politics*, Volume XI, No. 2, 1959.

[48] See Selection 15. For other analyses of the relationship between domestic politics and Soviet foreign policy, Cf. Alexander Dallin, "Soviet Foreign Policy and Domestic Politics: A Framework for Analysis," *Journal of International Affairs*, Volume XXIII, 1969, No. 2; Sidney Ploss, "Studying the Domestic Determinants of Soviet Foreign Policy," *Canadian Slavic Studies*, Volume I, No. 1, Spring 1967; John Armstrong, "The Domestic Roots of Soviet Foreign Policy," *International Affairs* (London), January 1965; and Henry A. Kissinger, "Domestic Structure and Foreign Policy," in Stanley Hoffman, editor, *Conditions of World Order* (Boston, Houghton, Mifflin and Co., 1968).

[49] See Selection 14.

All these explanations and justifications for Soviet territorial expansion have been offered by Soviet leaders at one time or other.

Soviet behavior, of course, is not as tidily compartmentalized as the above oversimplification suggests, since it frequently reflects diverse motives and is often the result of fortuitous opportunities. In critical situations, the multiple identities of the Soviet Union are more visible as contradictory impulses, and imperatives are generated simultaneously by two or more identities. Just as territorial expansion reflects the multidimensional functions of the Soviet Union, territorial claims against the U.S.S.R. can force a confrontation between the various Soviet identities.

Thus, Chinese territorial claims against the Soviet Union force the Soviet leaders to choose between the identity of the Soviet Union as a Party and its other identities. The Chinese demand for a return of territories annexed by tsarist Russia is directed at the Soviet Union in its capacity as a fraternal party, in accordance with the principles of "proletarian" or "socialist internationalism," which require that injustices perpetrated by one nation against another when both were "bourgeois," "imperialist," or "feudal," be rectified once the proletariat is in power in both places. Since the Chinese demand does not conflict with the Soviet Party's commitment to preserve and extend the Communist system (alteration of boundaries and territorial exchanges between Communist states does not diminish the ambit of Communist jurisdiction), the Soviet response should have been favorable, if its Party identity had highest priority in the calculation of its leaders. But since a Soviet acceptance of the demand (which might trigger similar territorial demands upon the U.S.S.R. by other Communist states), would serve to erode and diminish the position of the Soviet Union as a regional and global power (state), reduce the dimensions of the R.S.F.S.R. (Russian nation-state), reduce the territory of some non-Russian republics in Central Asia (variable nation-state), and remove some nationalities out of the Soviet Union entirely (multinational commonwealth), the Soviet leaders have reacted viscerally and negatively.[50]

Theories, approaches, and frameworks for analyzing and predicting Soviet behavior are many and continue to proliferate in response to the continuing inadequacy of all existing theories, singly or in combination. These may be grouped for purposes of expository convenience in the following categories, recognizing that each grouping contains a number of related and inter-related theories, frameworks, and approaches that may vary greatly in sophistication, complexity, and logical consistency.[51]

[50] See Selection 13.

[51] See Selection 9. Cf. also John S. Reshetar, Jr., *Problems of Analyzing and Predicting Soviet Behavior* (New York, Doubleday, 1955), and William A. Glaser, "Theories of Soviet Foreign Policy: A Classification of the Literature," *World Affairs Quarterly,* July 1956, for a discusion of various problems and approaches to the study of Soviet behavior. Cf. also Richard F. Rosser, *An Introduction To Soviet Foreign Policy* (Englewood Cliffs, N.J., Prentice-Hall,

1. *Ideological:* analyzing the basic components of Marxism, Leninism; modes of interpretation and application of the doctrine; its epistemology, teleology, value system, assumptions, expectations, analytical categories, concepts, strategies, and tactics. The basic thrust of these approaches is that Soviet behavior is largely a product of voluntaristic inputs structured into a deterministic ideology, and that the prediction of Soviet behavior is largely a matter of deciphering Soviet ideology.[52]

2. *Personality:* analyzing the personalities and characters of the decision-makers in the Soviet system (dictator and/or Politburo-Secretariat members), their ambitions, values, intelligence, abilities, competence, career patterns, biographies, statements, psychocultural conditioning, modes of behavior, skills, unconscious drives, and mental stability. The principal thrust of these approaches is that Soviet behavior is essentially an extension of the behavioral characteristics of Soviet leaders and that Soviet behavior can best be predicted by analyzing the decision-makers.[53]

3. *Capabilities:* predicting Soviet behavior on the basis of capabilities can assume a number of forms, and framed within a uni-dimensional or multi-dimensional context. Soviet behavior is assumed to be, at the very least, limited by its capabilities (objective or subjective), and in some cases to be determined by the nature and extent of its capabilities

---

1969), pp. 15–38, for a useful survey of different approaches and explanations.

[52] For various ideological explanations of differing degrees of complexity and sophistication, *Cf.* the following: Gerhart Niemeyer and John S. Reshetar, Jr., *An Inquiry Into Soviet Mentality* (London, Atlantic Press, 1956); "Historicus" (George Morgan), "Stalin on Revolution," *Foreign Affairs,* January 1949; R. N. Carew-Hunt, "The Importance of Doctrine," *Problems of Communism,* March–April 1958; and W. W. Kulski, *Peaceful Co-Existence* (Chicago, Ill., Henry Regnery, 1959). Nathan Leites' monumental work, *A Study of Bolshevism* (Glencoe, Ill., The Free Press, 1953), is perhaps the most ambitious attempt to establish causal connections between Soviet ideology and Soviet behavior, but in combination with a historico-psycho-cultural analysis of the impact of the Russian national character on the Bolshevik leaders, particularly Lenin and Stalin, as personality types. Like many studies produced during the same period, the work was essentially a study of the Stalinist era, and mistakenly assumed to be the definitive model of the Soviet system. *Cf.* also Robert Strausz-Hupe, *et al., Protracted Conflict* (New York, Harpers, 1959).

[53] Although based upon his *A Study of Bolshevism,* which it preceded, Nathan Leites' shorter work, *The Operational Code of the Politburo* (New York, McGraw-Hill, 1951), is more explicitly based upon a model of Soviet leaders as distinctive Bolshevik personality types guided in their behavior by an implicit code which Leites attempts to formulate explicitly. For other personality and related psychocultural explanations of Soviet behavior, *Cf.* the following: Margaret Mead, *Soviet Attitudes Toward Authority* (New York, McGraw-Hill, 1951); Dinko Tomasic, *The Impact of Russian Culture on Soviet Communism* (Glencoe, Ill., The Free Press, 1953) and also his *Personality and Culture in Eastern European Politics;* Geoffrey Gorer and John Rickman, *The People of Great Russia* (London, Cresset Press, 1950). Robert C. Tucker, "The Dictator and Totalitarianism," *World Politics,* Vol. XVII, 1965, No. 4.

in a positive sense, in accordance with the principle of "pushing to the limit." Capabilities can be defined in terms of military, economic, political, geographic, demographic, and technological capacity or potential.[54]

4. *Historical:* predicting Soviet behavior on the basis of regularities, uniformities, and persistent configurative patterns of past behavior, whether restricted only to the Soviet period or extending backward into the pre-revolutionary era. Historical explanations of Soviet behavior are among the oldest, most ubiquitous, and multiform. The basic thrust of these theories is that future Soviet behavior can most reliably be projected on the basis of examining previous behavior.[55]

5. *Systemic:* postulating Soviet society as an integrated, rational, and self-contained organic entity or mechanical system in which all of its components are interrelated and interdependent and whose behavior is largely a product of the structure and function of its institutions, processes, and norms. Systemic theories are sometimes expressed in terms of models, simulations, or games. The main thrust of these theories is that Soviet behavior is to be predicted and explained in terms of the *basic character* of the Soviet system as a total entity whose chief goals may be system maintenance, system growth, or system expansion, depending upon the particular theory in question.[56]

[51] *Cf.* Thomas W. Wolfe, *Soviet Power and Europe,* 1945–1970 (Baltimore, The Johns Hopkins Press, 1970); Arnold Horelick and Myron Rush, *Strategic Power and Soviet Foreign Policy* (Chicago, Ill., University of Chicago Press, 1966); Herbert S. Dinerstein, *War and the Soviet Union* (New York, Praeger, 1959); Malcolm M. MacIntosh, *Strategy and Tactics of Soviet Foreign Policy* (New York, Oxford, 1962); Raymond L. Garthoff, *Soviet Military Policy* (New York, Praeger, 1966).

[55] *Cf.* "X" (George Kennan), "The Sources of Soviet Conduct," *Foreign Affairs,* July 1957, and George Kennan, *Russia and the West Under Lenin and Stalin* (Boston, Mass., Atlantic-Little, Brown, 1961) for explanations of Soviet behavior as a combination of historical, personality, and ideological factors. See also Adam B. Ulam, *Expansion and Coexistence* (New York, Praeger, 1968), and Philip E. Mosely, *The Kremlin in World Politics* (New York, Vintage Press, 1960).

[56] The most durable and controversial system explanation of Soviet behavior is that based upon the totalitarianism model in its various forms and adaptations, beginning with Merle Fainsod's impressive and influential work, *How Russia Is Ruled* (Cambridge, Mass., Harvard University Press, 1953). *Cf.* also Raymond Bauer, Alex Inkeles, and Clyde Kluckhohn, *How the Soviet System Works* (Cambridge, Mass., Harvard University Press, 1956); Alex Inkeles and Raymond Bauer, *The Soviet Citizen: Daily Life in a Totalitarian Society* (Cambridge, Mass., Harvard University Press, 1959); Alex Inkeles, *Social Change in Soviet Russia* (Cambridge, Mass., Harvard University Press, 1968); Alfred G. Meyer, *The Soviet Political System* (New York, Random House, 1966); Frederick C. Barghoorn, *Politics in the U.S.S.R.* (Boston, Little, Brown, 1966); John Armstrong, *The Politics of Totalitarianism* (New York, Random House, 1961); Bertram Wolfe, *Communist Totalitarianism* (Boston, Beacon Press, 1961). For a survey of alternative models to the totalitarian model, *Cf.* H. Gordon Skilling and Franklyn Griffiths, editors, *Interest Groups in Soviet Politics* (Princeton, N.J., Princeton University Press, 1970), especially the three contributions by Skilling.

6. *Quantitative:* applying quantitative methods to any of the various theories and approaches outlined above. The principal objective of quantitative methodology is to impart greater rigor and precision to existing theories, reducing them to hypotheses that can be subjected to empirical tests of verification or confirmation. These methods attempt to distinguish between "hard" and "soft" data, where possible; to "harden" soft data where appropriate; to apply statistical methods of analysis; and to reduce qualitative factors to quantifiable terms capable of precise measurement. Content-analysis, multi-factor analysis, cross-tabulation matrices, etc., whether capable of computer-programming or not, are various ways in which quantitative methods are being applied to the study of Soviet behavior.[57]

Finally, the terms *Kremlinology* and *Sovietology* must be explained and related to these various theories. Neither theories nor methods, both are descriptive labels (originally terms of derision) for the study of Soviet behavior. To the extent that one can distinguish between the two, Sovietology (which has achieved a measure of acceptance as a descriptive label by Soviet specialists) is the more inclusive since it applies to the full spectrum of Soviet studies, whereas Kremlinology refers to the more limited exercise of describing and analyzing the behavior of the Soviet decision-makers.[58]

[57] The most ambitious effort to employ quantitative methods in the study of Soviet foreign policy is J. F. Triska and D. D. Finley, *Soviet Foreign Policy* (New York, The Macmillan Co., 1968). Described in the introduction as an "experiment" that hopes to go beyond a mere "synthesis" of diverse interpretations of Soviet foreign policy, it seeks to "explain diversity rather than to reconcile it." The study is also frankly heuristic and quantitatively oriented: "We want to open doors for the student and persuade him that new techniques of political analysis show some prospect for allowing more precise handling of the available data in a field still relegated by many to the occult arts. . . . No modes of analysis have been rejected here per se. History, legal analysis of institutions, functional and content analysis all find some place. We confess, however, that because frustrating differences occur from impressionist interpretation, we were inclined to use quantitative indicators wherever we found them available and the relevant questions amenable to quantitative analysis. In this fashion we sought to break through the formidable distortions that stem from cultural diversity" (pp. xiii–xiv). Although the overall result is actually another interpretation, rather than an exercise in empirical verification or scientific proof, and one that coincides largely with existing interpretations arrived at by less exotic methods, it is nevertheless an impressive study, rich in factual and descriptive data, both illuminating and insightful. For a discussion of the relative merits of the Triska and Finley book and Ulam's more traditional *Expansion and Coexistence,* see the excellent review article by Charles Gati, "History, Social Science, and the Study of Soviet Foreign Policy," *Slavic Review,* December 1970. *Cf.* also Jan F. Triska, editor, *Communist Party States* (New York, The Bobbs-Merrill Co., 1969).
[58] *Cf.* Sidney Ploss, *The Soviet Political Process* (Waltham, Mass., Ginn and Co., 1971), for representative examples of "Kremlinology," together with a sympathetic elucidation. See also Vernon V. Aspaturian, *Who's On Top — New Power Struggle in the Kremlin?* (Santa Monica, California, The RAND Corp., 1965).

None of these theories, individually or collectively, is sufficient to fully explain past or future Soviet action. All are tentative, provisional, and perhaps even premature. The lacunae in our knowledge, due to various reasons, remain enormous, and precision and accuracy in the prediction of Soviet behavior remains, and will remain for quite some time, an elusive goal. Although there is no intention here to become enmeshed in an elaborate analysis of the deficiencies of various methods employed in scrutinizing and analyzing Soviet behavior, some comment is in order concerning not the relative merits of one method or another, but their common purpose and function.

Given the current state of the art and/or science of human behavior, including international politics, all theories, models, methodologies, frameworks, and research techniques are essentially processes whereby available information and data are processed into *judgments about* behavior rather than *proof*, although the former is often passed off as the latter by some scholars. Quantitative methods, including multifactor analysis, statistical analyses, computer programming, etc., no matter how refined the technology or complex the methodology, serve essentially the same function, the making of judgments. The employment of "hard" methods and techniques to process "soft" data cannot perform the miraculous feat of transforming judgment into proof, since much of the data accumulated are subjectively classified and categorized and thus come pre-packaged with judgmental inputs. The use of scaling methods, for example, conceals rather than eliminates the judgmental input, and the more "pretesting" that is done, the more the judgmental increment of the investigator is buried in his methodology. The issue is not which method provides the basis for the soundest judgments about international politics and Soviet foreign policy, since that determination cannot be made by comparing methods, but by comparing results, which is futile at this stage since the analysis and judgments produced by various methods converge and coincide to a remarkable degree. Differences in judgment and analysis about Soviet foreign policy are more likely to be inspired by divergent ideological convictions, philosophical predispositions, political persuasions, and value orientations than by differences in methodology. To put it more bluntly, "hawkish" or "dovish" analyses are more likely to reflect the prior commitments of the scholars than the methodologies they employ.

Behind every methodology is the intellect of a scholar, the quality of whose judgment will depend upon his personal capabilities rather than the method he employs to process his knowledge. At this stage, and for the foreseeable future, dependable knowledge concerning Soviet behavior is more likely to be the product of the intelligence, skill, industry, and imagination of individual or aggregate scholarship rather than particular methodologies or frameworks, and each scholar should employ the method that inspires self-confidence, sharpens his creative powers, heightens his insights, and in general proves more effective for him personally, either as a heuristic device or one that processes his knowledge into judgments about Soviet behavior.

3. *Some Conceptual Problems*

The study of international politics and foreign policy, including Soviet foreign policy, is often unduly complicated by persistent demands that research be conducted in accordance with standards of methodological rigor and precision that cannot be sustained either by the state of the art or available data.[59] And when such rigor is attempted, nevertheless, it often results in premature conceptualization, based upon fragmentary, transient, elusive, and often unreliable data, leaving a trail strewn with obsolete and discarded concepts as both changing political reality and new information outdate concepts.

It is sometimes stated that a rubbish heap of archaic concepts is the price of scientific progress, and that even in the "hardest" of sciences, such as physics and astronomy, concepts are developed and discarded along the road to progress. But most concepts in the social sciences are qualitatively different from concepts in the "hard" sciences. Concepts in the physical sciences most frequently are outdated by progress in *discovering new knowledge,* which renders archaic concepts based upon fragmentary or false knowledge. Concepts in the social sciences are outmoded primarily, not by the discovery of new knowledge, but by changing events and reality brought about by human volition in one form or another. Thus, the concept "ether" was discarded in physics, not because ether changed, but because new knowledge demonstrated that it never existed. On the other hand, the concept *monarchy* will soon become outmoded not because it didn't exist, but because it will disappear. Thus, although all concepts are essentially synthetic and artificial constructs of the human mind in both hard and soft sciences, the concepts in the physical sciences represent perceptions of natural realities independent of human volition, whereas the most important concepts in the social sciences represent perceptions of social realities, which themselves are synthetic and artificial constructions of individual or aggregate human volition, and hence are arbitrary, transient, and ephemeral. Thus when human beings change social reality, the concepts that represent them are rendered outmoded.[60]

[59] According to Webster's Third International Dictionary, *rigor* means "harsh inflexibility in opinion, temper, or judgment . . . the quality of being unyielding or inflexible." *Precise* is defined as "exactly or sharply defined or stated . . . minutely exact . . . strictly conforming to rule or convention." This is what I mean by these terms and I assume this is what is meant by those who demand rigor and precision in social science concept formation. *Cf.* Frederic J. Fleron, Jr., *Communist Studies and the Social Sciences* (Chicago, Rand McNally and Co., 1969), especially Fleron's Introduction, and the two contributions by Erik P. Hoffman, "Methodological Problems of Kremlinology" and "Communication Theory and the Study of Soviet Politics," and those by Fleron, "Toward a Reconceptualization of Political Change in the Soviet Union," Robert S. Sharlet, "Concept Formation in Political Science and Communist Studies," and William A. Welsh, "Toward a Multiple Strategy Approach to Research on Comparative Communist Political Elites: Empirical and Quantitative Problems."

[60] A debate of sorts between "scientists" and "traditionalists" concerning the applicability of scientific techniques and methods to international politics

The fate of "totalitarianism" as a concept emphasizes a second fundamental difference between concepts in "hard" and "soft" sciences, the fact that most concepts in social science, and particularly those that define and ask the most important and fundamental questions, are often normative in character rather than neutral or value-free. Often invested with emotion, passion, overt or structured bias, value preferences, and ideological prejudice, concepts in social sciences thus serve not only to facilitate communication, assist in the discovery, organization, and elucidation of knowledge, but also become active factors in changing, reshaping, condemning, praising, and outmoding the social realities they are designed to reflect. The normative input into the construction of concepts varies considerably, in terms of explicitness, intensity, and in accordance with the intellectual temper of the times. Even the most "scientific" concepts in the social sciences have a structured value-normative-volitional input and are sometimes cleverly calculated devices for promoting normative goals, whether they be substantively reactionary, conservative, liberal, revolutionary, or radical. In this way, normative concepts are draped in the august garments of "neutral," "impartial," and objective science to conceal their normative character in order to enhance the prestige and persuasiveness of the results generated by methods utilizing these concepts.[61]

---

has been taking place for nearly two decades. The debate is somewhat barren intellectually since the controversy reflects not so much conflict over methods as it does diametrically opposite assumptions concerning human nature, human behavior, and social organization in general, which, of course, are not susceptible to verification one way or another. Many of the same issues were raised decades ago by E. H. Carr, *The Twenty Years Crisis, 1919–1939* (New York, 1940); and Hans F. Morgenthau, *Scientific Man vs. Power Politics* (Chicago, Chicago University Press, 1946), but since the issues are essentially postulational rather than propositional in nature, and hence unresolvable, the controversy continues unabated. *Cf.* Hedley Bull, "International Theory: The Case for a Classical Approach," *World Politics*, April 1966, and the rejoinder by Morton A. Kaplan, "The Great Debate: Traditionalism versus Science in International Relations," *World Politics*, October 1966. See also the following: Charles A. McClelland, *Theory and the International System* (New York, 1966); Hans F. Morgenthau, *Politics Among Nations* (New York, Knopf, 4th edition, 1967) and K. J. Holsti, "The Concept of Power in the Study of International Relations," in *Background: Journal of the International Studies Association*, February 1964; Morton A. Kaplan, editor, *New Approaches to International Relations* (New York, St. Martin's Press, 1968) and the contributions by Kenneth W. Thompson, Charles A. McClelland, Raymond Aron, and Hans Morgenthau in Norman D. Palmer, editor, *A Design for International Relations Research: Scope, Theory, Methods, and Relevance* (Philadelphia, The American Academy of Political and Social Science, 1970).

[61] *Cf.* The insightful article by Kenneth W. Thompson, "Normative Theory in International Relations," *Journal of International Affairs*, 1967, Vol. XXI. Just as some behavioralists and empiricists have been attacked by the New Left as covert or inadvertent supporters of the status quo, others have been accused of employing quantitative methods as a convenient screen to conceal their essentially "reformist" or utopian goals and values. Thus psychologist Ralph K. White was moved to concede at a conference convened to debate once again the issue of traditional versus scientific methods in the study of international politics: "They [*i.e.*, the sociologists] haven't reached

The heated controversy swirling around the concept totalitarianism concerning its origins, historical accuracy, utility, and propriety as a concept in political science serves to bring into sharp focus the problems posed both by premature conceptualization and value bias in concept formation in the social sciences. Before World War II the concept was coined primarily to define Nazi Germany as a distinctive type of political system, to which Fascist Italy was soon assigned but not without inconsiderable violence to a concept that was originally conceived to serve both as a conceptual tool of empirical analysis and as a mark of moral reprobation.[62] The Soviet Union was subsequently added to form a totalitarian triad, and although this did further violence to the loosely conceived original concept, Soviet entry into the war against Hitler resulted in its temporary declassification as a totalitarian state and thus made it unnecessary to tidy up a concept that was already becoming obsolescent.

After the war, with the destruction of the Nazi and Fascist states, totalitarianism was in danger of passing into the ash cans of history, but instead it was redefined and reconceptualized now to fit primarily the lone survivor of the unholy totalitarian trinity. Increasingly the concept was restricted to Communist states, since the surviving Fascist state (Spain) failed to meet the new criteria for totalitarian status. Just as the concept was a symbol of anti-Fascism before the war, it now became a symbol of anti-Communism and was employed as a major ideological weapon in the "Cold War." The concept was progressively redefined and refined between 1948 and 1956, when it was offered as a consummate model of rigorous and precise conceptualization that sharply delineated the common properties of a class of political systems, of which only one authentic representative remained (the U.S.S.R.).[63]

the synthesis that, I think, some of us psychologists have reached, which consists of being 'do-gooders' much of the time, but also scientists. These people I have just mentioned are psychologists of this type. [Herbert] Kelman was a conscientious objector; Frank was a pacifist and, I suppose, still is. Charles Osgood, Morton Deutsch, Dean Pruitt, Harold Guetzkow—this is basically a 'do-goodish' crowd, very much so. The very title of the journal that they helped to start, *Conflict Resolution*, is a 'do-goodish' title. There were lots of doubts as to whether this was too boldly 'do-goodish,' to call a journal *Conflict Resolution* rather than something innocuous like *International Tensions*. But they have been contributing. They have done solid, theoretical, and empirical work. I suspect the reason is that they have come to terms with 'do-goodism.' " Comments of Ralph K. White in Norman D. Palmer, editor, *A Design For International Relations Research: Scope, Theory, Methods, and Relevance* (Philadelphia, The American Academy of Political and Social Science, 1970), pp. 50–51. The real question is whether the scholars who came to terms with their "do-goodism" did so by structuring it into their methods in such a way that certain hypothetical solutions were *a priori* excluded, *viz*, resort to war as the most "scientific" way of resolving a problem in international politics, as, for example, a war of independence by an oppressed people.

[62] *Cf.* Carl J. Friedrich, Michael Curtis, and Benjamin R. Barber, *Totalitarianism in Perspective* (New York, Praeger, 1969), for a brief history of the concept and three different views concerning its validity and appropriateness.

[63] Totalitarianism was apparently first formalized as a concept in political science by Sigmund Neumann, in *Permanent Revolution: Totalitarianism*

By 1956, when the definitive conceptual work on totalitarianism was published,[64] the Soviet regime, with almost calculated perversity, began a series of internal changes that shattered the major pillars upon which the concept rested, thus rendering it obsolete once again almost immediately. Methodological purists now assail the concept precisely because of the recurrent necessity to revise it, labeling it an example of false conceptualization of a nonexistent class of political systems.[65] Yet, all concepts in the social sciences, and the theories and models based upon them, have a peculiar habit of being rendered obsolete almost at the moment they achieve their definitive, immutable parameters.[66] The social realities upon which they are based start coming apart, sometimes because of the corrosive normative impact of the concept itself, releasing the painstakingly accumulated reservoirs of factual and empirical data to flood and wash out the carefully contrived concepts that contained them.

Yet totalitarianism as a concept was probably more rigorous and accurate than most concepts in political science. Its adaptability was more a sign of strength than weakness, and its very elasticity enabled it to keep march with changing political realities. If it has outlived its utility as a concept, it is not for the reason that totalitarian systems as a class of political organisms never existed, but rather that they no longer do.[67] Thus, it was Khrushchev who eloquently confirmed the accuracy of the totalitarian model in describing the Stalinist system and

---

in the Age of International Civil War (New York, 1942), although, of course, he did not coin the word which apparently was invented by one of Mussolini's ideologues, Alfredo Rocco. It received further theoretical impetus by Hannah Arendt in *The Origins of Totalitarianism* (New York, Harcourt, Brace and Co., 1950), and was subjected to critical examination in the symposium, *Totalitarianism* (Cambridge, Mass., Harvard University Press, 1954), edited by Carl J. Friedrich. Fainsod's *How Russia Is Ruled* appeared about the same time.

[64] Carl J. Friedrich and Zbigniew Brzezinski, *Totalitarian Dictatorship and Autocracy* (Cambridge, Mass., Harvard University Press, 1956). A revised edition (revised by Friedrich alone) was published in 1965, and Arendt revised her work first in 1958 and then again in 1966.

[65] For sharp critical comments of the concept, Cf. Robert Burrowes, "Totalitarianism: The Revised Standard Version," *World Politics*, January 1969; Benjamin Barber, "Conceptual Foundations of Totalitarianism," in Friedrich, Curtis, and Barber, *op. cit.* Cf. Friedrich's defense of the concept, "The Evolving Theory and Practice of Totalitarian Regimes," in Friedrich, *et al., op. cit.*

[66] Cf. Giovanni Sartori, *Concept Misinformation in Comparative Politics*, for an incisive methodological critique of static formulations and Henry S. Kariel, "Creating Political Reality," for an ideological critique of positivist political science, both in *The American Political Science Review*, December 1970.

[67] Not only Khrushchev's revelations, but additional data made available on conditions during the Stalin era continue to give retrospective empirical verification to the applicability of the concept "totalitarianism" to the Stalinist period. Ironically, at the moment that American scholars are attacking the concept, dissidents inside and defectors from Communist countries are increasingly finding the concept applicable to their own experience.

at the same time sounded the death knell of totalitarianism as a concept, not the methodological purists who attacked its conceptual deficiencies, nor those who assailed it from ideological barricades. Both are essentially demanding that it be permanently buried but for divergent reasons: To the methodologists, totalitarianism is a monumentally embarrassing example of premature conceptualization, whereas for the "New Left" it is an outrage that tends to link radical and revolutionary movements and Third World one-party systems with the evils of Hitler and Stalin.[68]

Those who condemn totalitarianism as a concept for ideological reasons are on firmer ground than the methodologists. Conceptual deficiencies can be remedied and the defenders of the concept have already redefined and reconceptualized it several times to bring it into focus with changing reality,[69] but it is doubtful if the concept can ever be purged of its original normative inspiration and functions. One need not agree with the "New Left" substantively to see merit in its charge that the concept, no matter how empirically precise or objectively accurate it may be in its periodically revised state, is indissolubly linked with Nazism in origins and with Stalinism in its development and thus can never be purged of its morally repugnant connotations and associations.

It was the unfortunate fate of totalitarianism that it was assailed from two directions simultaneously, which exposed both its methodological imperfections and normative impurities at the same time. Were other cherished concepts in political science (democracy, dictatorship,

[68] Cf. Herbert J. Spiro and Benjamin R. Barber, "The Concept of Totalitarianism as the Foundation of an American Counter-Ideology in the Cold War," paper delivered at the 1967 Annual Meeting of the American Political Science Association. Cf. also Barber, op. cit. pp. 40–41. Totalitarianism as a concept was devised by "liberal-democrats" to conveniently lump together under one pejorative label ideological enemies on both the Left and Right. Its ethical reference point is thus "liberal democracy," which simultaneously is the dual antithesis of both Communist and Fascist totalitarianism. Totalitarianism, in a sense, is essentially a liberal-democratic counterpart to the Soviet formulation "capitalist-imperialist" states, which embraces under one rubric both liberal democratic states and Fascist regimes, and to the Nazi notion of the Jewish-Bolshevist plutocracies, which grouped Moscow and the Western Powers under one roof. The fact that totalitarianism was a more elegant and sophisticated construct should not obscure its ideological content and purpose.

[69] In spite of its imperfections, there appears to be a continuing need for the use of the concept or a surrogate for the class of political phenomena it purports to describe. Barber would discard the concept entirely; Burrowes appears to be amenable to a substitute. Some scholars have already offered working substitutes. Robert C. Tucker suggests its replacement with "movement regimes," in "Towards a Comparative Politics of Movement Regimes," American Political Science Review, March 1961; Alfred G. Meyer appears to favor "bureaucratic" systems as a substitute, in The Soviet Political System; Allen Kassof prefers the term "administered society" or "totalitarianism without terror," in "The Administered Society: Totalitarianism Without Terror," World Politics, July 1964. Cf. also John Kautsky, "Communism and the Comparative Study of Development," Slavic Review, March 1967.

law, justice, government, system, freedom, state, nation, etc.) subjected to the identical tests of perfection, even the concept political science itself would fail to survive.

Basic concepts in international politics are constantly subjected to a purifying process in an attempt to purge them of the impurities associated with their original inspiration and conception. This is doomed to be a futile exercise, however, since not only do concepts rarely stay in focus with the realities they are supposed to represent, but also because normative impurities are almost incapable of being cleansed. The entire concept must be repudiated and some scholars are advocating precisely that, and new ones are devised, founded on a narrow hard data base discoverable in even the softest of disciplines. Two traditionally basic concepts in international politics, "power" and "national interests," have already been measured and found wanting by some scholars, who find it easier to eliminate them from the discipline than from their own vocabularies, for without the two words intelligent communication about international politics would be impossible.

Controversies over the precise meaning of terms often leads to the conclusion that since all hard sciences possess a scientific terminology that is both precise in meaning and universally accepted by all scholars in the discipline, the first step in the creation of a science is to establish a technical vocabulary with a common set of definitions, which, together with a common methodology, should be imposed upon all scholars in the field.

What results is not a "science," but an "academy," in the intellectual rather than the institutional sense, whereby a particular school of thought within the discipline may seize the commanding heights of the field and impose a consensus upon the discipline with respect to the definition of terms, concepts, and rules and criteria of evidence and proof. In the absence of demonstrated methods of replicability of results by others, however, verification procedures that are based solely upon disciplinary consensus cannot be a surrogate for the objective replicability of results. Consensus is a form of judgment, informed opinion, but not the same as proof. Agreement on definitions of terms and concepts may facilitate communication and maximize consistency in research methods, but it does not necessarily produce "science."[70] If the

70 The "consensus" character of the social sciences is now being conceded by some scholars, under the hammer blows of the New Left, with whose ideological goals they largely agree, but whose charges they now wish to mitigate through admissions that their preoccupation with methodological problems may have emasculated them politically. Thus, Alvin Gouldner in his influential *The Coming Crisis of Western Sociology* (New York, Basic Books, 1970), calls for an end to "The schism between Marxism and Academic sociology," which will necessitate a repudiation of conservative "Parsonianism" in favor, perhaps, of a "Left-Parsonianism." Thus, what I refer to as "academy consensus," Gouldner calls "domain assumptions," *i.e.*, the ideological parameters of a social science discipline that structurally decides in advance the questions that can be raised and the answers that may be entertained. "Domain assumptions concerning man and society," Gouldner writes, "are built not only into substantive social theory but into methodology

agreed-upon definitions and concepts turn out to be faulty, they may actually hinder the pursuit of knowledge rather than promote it, in the absence of any objective tests of verification independent of institutionalized academy consensus.[71] Under these conditions, "consensus

---

itself." Furthermore: "Stated otherwise, information-gathering systems or research methods always premise the existence and use of some system of social control. It is not only that the information they yield may be used *by* systems of social control, but that they themselves *are* systems of control. . . . When viewed from one standpoint, 'methodology' seems a purely technical concern devoid of ideology; presumably it deals only with methods of extracting reliable information from the world, collecting data, constructing questionnaires, sampling, and analyzing returns. Yet it is always a good deal more than that, for it is commonly infused with ideologically resonant assumptions about what the social world is, who the sociologist is, and what the nature of the relation between them is," pp. 49–50. *Cf.* also Tom Bottomore, "Has Sociology A Future?" *The New York Review of Books,* March 11, 1971. Bottomore suggests that Gouldner's notion of "domain assumptions" seems "to correspond closely with what Kuhn and others have called a 'paradigm'; namely the constellation of values and beliefs shared by the members of a scientific community that determines the choice of problems which are regarded as significant and the approaches to be adopted in attempting to solve them. It is evident that 'domain asumptions' or 'paradigms,' in this sense are necesarily linked with, or include, a 'structure of sentiments,' " p. 37.

[71] Fleron correctly notes that "There are those whose wish to retain 'totalitarianism' in studying Communism because of its negative connotations . . . so that we can continue to pin a 'boo' label on a 'boo' system of government." *Communist Studies and the Social Sciences,* p. 33, note 82. What Fleron ignores is that those who wish to eliminate totalitarianism as a concept and to abolish "Area Studies" in the name of reintegrating Communist studies with the mainstream of social science, may also be motivated more by ideological than scientific considerations. Using his own formulation, "I should guess that if we knew enough of the psychology of research, we would find that there are those who wish" to abandon totalitarianism as a concept and "Area Studies" as a focus in order to eliminate possible obstacles and barriers to a rapprochement or convergence of systems. If totalitarianism and Area Studies constitute part of the academy consensus or "domain assumptions" of the Cold War liberals, then opposition to the two ideas and the advocacy that Communist studies should be integrated into the mainstream of contemporary social science may simply reflect the "domain assumptions" of anti-Cold War liberals. Thus a new "academy science" can reflect not only changes in political reality but more importantly changes in ideological perspective. Changing methodologies, reflecting changing ideological perceptions, can, in turn, hopefully shape the direction of changes in reality itself, and thus the normative circle is closed, all in the name of science. But before there can be rapprochement or convergence in the real world, the Communist systems must be rescued from the methodological Siberia to which they have been consigned by "Area Studies" and concepts like totalitarianism. On the other hand, some partisans of the "New Left" are not simply content to remove the stigma of totalitarianism from leftist regimes, but demand that it now be attached to the United States and its allied and client states. I should emphasize at this point that I do not object to the normative character of "consensus science" or "domain assumptions" but merely suggest that the normative character of disciplinary parameters should be consciously and explicitly recognized—in fact, I believe that normative inputs are unavoidable—rather than fatuously claiming that methodological innovations are being made purely in an endeavor to advance the discipline and make it more scientific.

science" may resemble "Lysenkoism," but with the academy rather than the state (or Church in the Middle Ages) establishing the Procrustean bed, to which all scholars shall be tailored.

The international system at any given instance in history, and the contours and characteristics of its basic actors, is the aggregate product of human volition, not the autonomous, objective materialization of nature, independent of human will, ambitions, drives, values, and action. Although a given system, whether it be interstate or an individual state, may exist within a given set of parameters over a period of time and in different places, thus giving it the appearance of momentary permanence and the illusion of regularity and uniformity, it is still, nevertheless, subject to sudden and unexpected upheavals that may demolish its parameters and redirect its patterns of regularity and in the process shatter the concepts that were based upon it, if they were too precisely and rigorously designed. Elastic concepts, on the other hand, such as "state" and "nation," will survive to assume the shape of the new parameters as they evolve. A similar situation in astronomy would prevail if the planets periodically and unexpectedly crumbled because of their own volitional energy, only to reconstitute themselves as new bodies, following new orbits around new epicenters, without any change in the total mass of the system. Under these conditions, astronomy as a "hard" science would be in deep trouble. Yet, this is what periodically happens to the interstate system and political systems generally.

Past experience in devising frameworks and methodologies in the social sciences with their "soft" data and basic concepts, whose historical, ideological, psychocultural, and polemical origins and characteristics can never be completely eliminated, should be a caveat against premature preoccupation with the methodological problems. Concepts in international politics, even those borrowed from traditional vocabulary and subjected to a "hardening" process, will remain plastic, fluid, and imprecise, since the boundaries or parameters of the international system are inherently unstable and transient. It should be remembered that neither the Soviet Union nor Soviet foreign policy existed six decades ago, that the entire international landscape has been seriously altered several times since the turn of the century, and that changes of this character are likely to continue.

Under these circumstances, a loose framework that assumes incomplete information, inaccessibility to decision-makers, and inability to replicate and objectively verify results, and thus explicitly requiring a judgmental component involving informed speculation about hidden or inaccessible data remains a better vehicle for understanding past, current, and future Soviet foreign policy behavior, than frameworks and models that rely solely upon the manipulation of "hard data" and visible variables.

The following framework, which is largely skeletal and schematic in form, is not designed to *predict* Soviet foreign policy, except in broad outlines, but to provide a basis for explaining past and current Soviet foreign policy and to understand and analyze future behavior as it occurs. The individual variables are not new but are grouped and related to one another differently, not only to account for the multiple identities of the Soviet Union as an international actor, but also to demonstrate the inseparability of voluntaristic and objective factors that are involved in the shaping of Soviet foreign policy and the distortions that would result if quantifiable factors and inputs alone were calculated.

III. A FRAMEWORK FOR ANALYZING SOVIET FOREIGN POLICY

A comprehensive and usable framework for the analysis of Soviet foreign policy, at this point in the state of the art or science, should be sufficiently elastic and plastic not only that it might offer insights into current and future behavior, but also so that it can be quickly and appropriately reshaped to adjust and accommodate to new realities, data, fortuities, and situations, which themselves are unpredictable, such as sudden deaths of key leaders through accident, illness, and assassination. Such a framework would seek to intelligently utilize all avenues of knowledge, all methods of measurements, and all theories, selectively and with imagination and skill. The variables, constants, factors, and inputs that contribute to Soviet behavior are enormous, and their significance, relatively as well as absolutely, has varied so considerably over time and space (and will continue to do so) that it would be more hazardous to rely upon a rigid, closed, and tightly integrated model or theory than one that remains open-ended and subject to continuous modification, as distinct from the necessity of "patching up" or "rectifying errors" in closed models or theories. The variables, defined as inputs or factors, whether domestic or external, that condition, shape, or animate Soviet foreign policy can be classified into five groups of gross variables, as follows:

1. *Motivations/Purposes/Intentions:* These variables are subjective preferences defined in terms of purposes, goals, values, norms, and interests, organized into a dynamically related scheme of priorities and formulated in terms of demands upon the outside world.
2. *Capabilities/Power:* These variables, some of which are subject to precise measurement if access to the data and information is possible, include the means, instruments, institutions, structures, and resources whereby demands upon the outside world are asserted, activated, or realized.
3. *Risks:* The risk variables are defined in terms of three interrelated perceived calculations of chance involved in the initiation of a voluntary action (demand, threat, lack of response), whose outcome is uncertain, but whose consequences can be harmful: (a) chance of success, (b) chance of harm, and (c) chance in the magnitude or level of harm.
4. *Costs/Benefits:* These variables represent perceptions of calculated anticipated or certain costs measured against perceptions of

anticipated or certain benefits under three sets of circumstances: (a) if voluntary action is initiated to press or realize demands, (b) if responses are made to events or conditions taking place in the external environment, and (c) no action or response is taken.

5. *Opportunities:* These variables are perceived situations where optimal intersection of demands, capabilities, risk, and cost variables occur.

These groups of variables are in constant dynamic interaction with each other over space and time, their absolute and relative significance varying accordingly. As will be seen below, when broken down into more discrete categories and individual factors, most of them are qualitative and judgmental in character, rather than quantifiable and measurable. The variables themselves may not be quantifiable, although information about them is susceptible to quantification in various forms. Thus, although ideology as a variable cannot be objectively measured, content analysis can be employed to gain an insight as to its relative weight as an input into policy, depending upon time and circumstance. Similarly, the personality variable cannot be quantified, but aggregate biographical data may be subjected to quantitative analysis as aids in arriving at judgments concerning their relative significance as an input. Applying quantitative methods to information variables should not, however, be confused with the measurement of the variable itself.[72] The only variables subject to objective measurement are those involving material and human resources, economic, technological, and military hardware, etc., provided the data are available.

The individual variables within the five categories of variables can be characterized qualitatively into two types, voluntaristic (*i.e.*, normative, volitional, subjective) and deterministic (*i.e.*, nonvolitional, objective). Voluntaristic variables are those whose weight and effect can be directly varied by the action of human will, whether individual or aggregate, whether conscious, inadvertent, or fortuitous. Deterministic variables are those whose effects and weight are independent of direct human will, but whose relative impact may vary because of conscious changes in the dimensions and value of the voluntaristic variables. For example, geographical location is not subject to significant change through human action (except in cases where territorial expansion significantly alters the geographical character and dimensions of the state), but the relative value of geography in contributing to Soviet behavior in foreign policy has been fundamentally altered by the advent of nuclear-missile capabilities developed by human technology. Similarly, a state's natural resources may be fixed and finite, but its weight as a factor varies with the human ingenuity, effort, and will invested in their development.

Some variables betray both voluntaristic and deterministic charac-

---

[72] On this point, *Cf.* the perceptive and penetrating critique by Giovanni Sartori, "Concept Misinformation in Comparative Politics," *The American Political Science Review,* December 1970.

teristics in mixed proportions. Political culture, including national character, for example, is the aggregate, cumulative product of human volition and changes slowly over time. Nevertheless it is essentially deterministic in its effects, since decision-makers cannot readily alter national character nor easily shed both the conscious and unconscious (especially the latter) conditioning effects it has had upon the shaping of his individual personality. In many instances, the deterministic or voluntaristic quality is a dominant rather than exclusive characteristic, but the transformational direction of change is generally for volun-taristic variables to assume deterministic characteristics. This has been the case, for example, of religion and ideology, whose impact may initially have been almost entirely voluntaristic in their effects, but which tend to take on deterministic attributes as they are progressively assimilated into the political culture.

1. Motivations/Purposes/Intentions

Although this tripartite label for a group of variables suggests the intricate interrelationships among motives, intent, and purposes, they can be distinguished. *Motivations* are those underlying forces that acti-vate a state in its political behavior; they are the driving power that energizes the will to action. Examples in the case of the Soviet Union would be the messianic urge to liberate mankind from capitalism or imperialism that originates in ideology (Party-oriented motivation) or the urge to enhance and advance the greater glory of the Soviet Union and/or Russia (state and Russian nation-oriented motive).

Purposes are the objects or goals toward which the motivational energy is directed, for example, the impulse to liberate mankind from capitalism will find its ultimate fulfillment in achieving the goals of world revolution and world Communism, and the passion to advance the greater glory of Russia could be achieved by the goal of territorial expansion.

Intentions are closely related to purposes and are often used inter-changeably. As used in this framework, intentions (or intent) character-ize a psychological or mental readiness to act as opposed to the urge or impulse to act. It is possible to be both motivated and purposive in orientation, but without the readiness to act in order to realize purposes prompted by motives, a crucial ingredient in the formulation of foreign policy is absent.

As noted earlier in another connection, Soviet motives, purposes, and intentions have often been misrepresented as the total of foreign policy in the past; although they combine to constitute attitudes and desires at the most, one must resist the temptation to readily equate motives, purposes, and intentions with foreign policy.[73] The general predisposition of scholars to be fascinated with the prospect of con-

---

[73] Cf. The excellent study of William Zimmerman, *Soviet Perspective on International Relations* (Princeton, N.J., Princeton University Press), which examines the Soviet outlook on international politics, which is distin-guishable from Soviet foreign policy, *per se.*

structing a framework that can predict Soviet foreign policy stems largely from the fact that basic Soviet motives, purposes, and intentions, *i.e.*, attitudes and desires, are constantly articulated and expressed in speeches, documents, pronouncements, resolutions, books, laws, and articles. By now, everybody knows that the "ultimate aim" of Soviet policy is something called "World Communism," and that it possesses a "blueprint" (strategy and tactics) for action. According to some, even a "timetable" or "schedule" for its realization can be distilled out of Soviet speeches and writings. Although all this may constitute inputs into Soviet foreign policy, it is not policy itself. There is little doubt that, if the Soviet leaders had their way, they would indeed establish something called "World Communism," although this idea has undergone a multiple transmutation in perception and meaning for the Soviet leaders over the past fifty years. Thus, Khrushchev somewhat petulantly noted in 1964:

> If it depended only on our desire to make revolution, I can guarantee you that the Central Committee would have done everything so that there would be no bourgeois world and the Red Flag would wave over the entire world. But comrades, let's not indulge in fantasies, let's be people who think realistically. Just to want something is not enough, even if the Party wants it.[74]

a. *Words and Intent in Soviet Foreign Policy.* Since a principal, but by no means exclusive, source for divining Soviet motives, purposes, and intentions, has been Soviet verbal output, the relationship between Soviet words and intent should be clarified. The assumption that Soviet speeches, resolutions, and other published output are significant sources for clues to current or future intent is, of course, true in a limited sense. But just as Soviet verbal output is not the exclusive repository of Soviet intent, Soviet speeches and writings are not exclusively concerned with intent, since they perform multiple functions and serve many purposes, only one of which is to communicate or reveal (deliberately or inadvertently) Soviet intent in foreign and strategic policy. Aside from the multiform purposes served by Soviet words, the important time dimension should be considered as well: The relationship between *words* and *policy* varies with the nature of the factional balance or conflict within the Soviet leadership itself. Thus the relationship between verbal output and policy during the Stalinist years was substantially different than it has been since his death. Stalin was an all-powerful and unchallenged dictator, the sole fount of ideological wisdom and orthodoxy and the ultimate arbiter of policy. Everything stated or published during the Stalinist era was essentially an elaboration of the dictator's output, and a systematic examination of Soviet publications and speeches could plausibly provide guidelines to Soviet policy.[75] Soviet-published output

[74] *Pravda*, April 6, 1964.
[75] *Cf.* George Morgan ("Historicus"), *op. cit.*, Robert C. Tucker, *The Soviet Political Mind* (New York, Praeger, 1963), and the two works by Nathan Leites, cited earlier. In an effort to do for the Khrushchev period what he did for the Stalin period but with less successful results, *Cf.* Nathan

was relatively limited and hence manageable as well; furthermore, it was predictably uniform in content at any particular time, enabling the observer to detect with relative ease changes and variations in content.

Since Stalin's death, the Soviet leadership has been in a state of chronic factional conflict, with the eruption of acute crises in the leadership making themselves manifest during periodic intervals, resulting in shifts, realignments, dismissals, promotion, and rotation of various personalities in accordance with the given factional balance or consensus. On the basis of nearly twenty years of post-Stalinist behavior, a basic assumption of Soviet politics, in contrast to the Stalinist era, is that factional conflict (and even institutional conflict) is a continuing characteristic of the Soviet leadership. This means that the relationship between words and policy has become considerably more complicated as compared to the Stalinist years, since statements contain not only possible intent, but conflicting possible policies. In other words, Soviet-published output now communicates (deliberately, esoterically, exoterically, or inadvertently) not only intent but controversy about future policy.

All statements, writings, and speeches by Soviet civilian and military leaders can be viewed as possible sources of information concerning current and future intentions. But the question of whose intentions becomes the supreme conundrum in the post-Stalinist period. Under Stalin, policy formulation and decision-making were tightly centralized in his person. Under his successor, however, the inconclusive struggle for power has resulted in the fragmentation of the decision-making structure, distributing power among various individuals and factions, each in command of parallel institutional power structures. Ideological orthodoxy has been divorced from personalities and policy formulation, which in turn has been frequently out of phase with the administration and execution of policy as rival factions assumed control over policy-making bodies. The fragmentation of the decision-making structure meant that factional politics replaced one-man decisions in the Soviet leadership. Personalities, factions, and eventually socio-functional and socio-institutional groupings assumed a more variable role in the shaping of Soviet behavior, and a new fluid relationship was established among Soviet capabilities, ideology, personalities, and institutions in the decision-making process. Although this made it even more difficult to judge Soviet intentions and predict Soviet behavior, it was compensated for by the corresponding inability of the Soviet Union to pursue the single-minded and precisely calibrated type of foreign policy that was characteristic of the Stalin era, since Soviet leaders are apparently as uncertain as western Kremlinologists in charting the course and outcome of internal factional conflict.[76]

Leites, *Kremlin Moods* (Santa Monica, Calif., The RAND Corporation, 1964). No sooner was the study completed than Khrushchev was toppled, just as two decades earlier, Stalin mysteriously died soon after the appearance of *A Study of Bolshevism.*

[76] See Selections 15, 17, 23, 24, and 30. *Cf.* also Herbert Dinerstein, *War and the Soviet Union,* 2nd edition (New York, Praeger, 1959); Carl Linden,

It is thus no simple matter to elicit future intentions from Soviet words, uttered or printed. Three general observations should be stated at the outset: (1) long-range intentions have always been and continue to be more clearly discernible than short-range, although even in this realm, as the Sino-Soviet conflict illustrates, long-range Soviet intentions are by no means clearly charted and, as noted earlier, are constantly subjected to erosive and corrosive internal and external influences; (2) the more distant and remote in time a statement of policy intent, the more unified the outlook of the Soviet leadership is likely to be; and (3) debate, controversy, and differences over long-range strategy and goals are most likely to be explicitly echoed by contrasting statements and pronouncements issued by foreign Communist leaders and parties, most notably those of Communist China.[77]

Thus, although Soviet words are not always statements of intention, they are vehicles of communication, for both external and internal audiences, often serving different and even contradictory purposes. Soviet words may represent: (1) propaganda (for various internal or external audiences); (2) deception; (3) concealment and camouflage of actual intent; and (4) rationalization, legitimization, or justification of various actions and policies.

b. *Intent and Factions.* The appearance of factional groupings and conflict in the Soviet leadership has thus added yet another dimension to the relationship between words and intent, as various individuals and factions articulate their views through newspapers, periodicals, and other media subject to their control or influence, and sometimes even implement their views as policies through Party and state institutions and organs under their direct administrative control, thus conveying the impression of contradictory, inconsistent, and ambivalent behavior in Soviet policy. Although this is the net effect for the Soviet system as a whole, it is not necessarily true of individual groups, factions, or personalities whose own views may be consistent and firm but are unable to prevail over equally consistent and obdurate views held by other groups and individuals. The possibility of factional vacillation and ambivalence is, of course, not ruled out.

Collective leadership, therefore, may not necessarily contribute to more rational or controlled action but may, under certain conditions, be even more unpredictable, dangerous, and difficult to contend with than one-man rule. Under some circumstances collective leadership may turn out to be collective irresponsibility as decisions are made and unmade by shifting conditions or autonomous action is taken by powerful socio-institutional bodies in the face of factional paralysis or bureau-

---

Khrushchev and the Soviet Leadership: 1957–1964 (Baltimore, The Johns Hopkins Press, 1966); Sidney Ploss, editor, *The Soviet Political Process* (Waltham, Mass., Ginn and Co., 1971); Roman Kolkowicz, *The Soviet Military and the Communist Party* (Princeton, N.J., Princeton University Press, 1967); Thomas Wolfe, *Soviet Strategy at the Crossroads* (Cambridge, Mass., Harvard University Press, 1964); and Raymond Garthoff, *Soviet Strategy in the Nuclear Age* (New York, Praeger, 1958).

[77] See Selection 20.

cratic inertia. The deliberations of a divided oligarchy are not only secret but anonymous as well and can yield many surprises. More than ever Soviet decisions in foreign policy may reflect the anxieties, fears, insecurities, and ambitions of individual factions and personalities involved in secret and faceless intrigue and maneuver. In the absence of crisis situations, whether acute or chronic, the assumption of Soviet rationality will continue to be valid. As personalities and as individual factions, the Soviet leaders appear to be a sober and calculatingly rational group and in their separate capacities are determined, forceful, and animated by purpose. But in the absence of a stable majority or durable consensus and with the fluidity of the decision-making process characterized by rapidly dissolving and reconstituted majorities on various issues, the behavior of the Soviet leadership as a collectivity is likely to be fluctuating and inconsistent. The multiplication of divergent rational inputs can thus produce a collective, irrational output. In this restricted sense institutionalized irrationality may come to characterize Soviet behavior. Under these conditions, Soviet verbal output can thus represent debate, controversy, and conflict, making it even more difficult to determine intent, since the Soviet leaders themselves may not know the outcome of the controversy. As a consequence, Soviet verbal output may reflect a bewildering variety of possibilities, as even the correspondence between statements of formal office-holders and those actually wielding power becomes disjointed. Thus, for brief periods of time Malenkov and Bulganin, successively, retained their formal positions as head of the government and hence were official spokesmen, although they articulated views to which they did not presumably subscribe personally. As clues to whose intent Soviet verbal output actually reflects, Soviet words must be examined within the various possible contexts from which they issue, and in particular, the status and role of the leader making them. Thus, for purposes of convenience and clarification, the possible implications of statements issued by the formal spokesmen of the Party (Secretary-General) and state (Chairman, Council of Ministers) will be listed separately from those made by other leaders.

Thus, whenever a statement is made by the Secretary-General of the Party and/or the Chairman of the Council of Ministers, the formal spokesmen of the Party and state, it can reflect one or more of the following:

1. the unanimous view of the leadership;
2. the dominant (majority) view in the leadership, including his own personal view;
3. the view of a plurality faction, including his own view;
4. his personal view;
5. the dominant view in the leadership, but with which he personally may disagree; and
6. the consensus or compromise view of the leadership.

On the other hand, when other Soviet leaders make statements, they can reflect one or more of the following:

1. the unanimous view of the leadership;
2. the dominant (majority) view in the leadership, including his own view;
3. view of a plurality faction, of which he is a member;
4. view of a minority faction, of which he is a member;
5. his personal view;
6. the consensus or compromise view of the leadership; and
7. the view of a socio-functional or socio-institutional group or sub-faction (Armed Forces, Party Apparatus, Heavy Industry, etc.) that may or may not accord with other factional views, dominant, plurality or minority.

The most nettlesome and yet fascinating situations are those reflected by statements made by a formal spokesman who must articulate positions with which he is in disagreement, but which represent those of the dominant faction. This can occur when the formal spokesman is on his way out (Malenkov, late 1954) or when he has temporarily lost his majority and represents perhaps only a plurality or fluctuating majority (Khrushchev between May, 1960, and May, 1963).

c. *Factions and Policy.* Under conditions of factional differences and cleavages in the Soviet leadership, distinctions must be drawn between verbal statements that correspond with actual policy and behavior and those that are in contradiction. Three possible relationships can exist: (1) correspondence or compatibility between actual policy and behavior and all verbal statements of intent and views; (2) correspondence or compatibility between actual policy and behavior and some statements of verbal intent and substantial divergence or incompatibility with other statements and views; and (3) no correspondence or compatibility between actual policy and behavior and any of two or more mutually divergent or incompatible statements of intent and policy (Khrushchev during the period May, 1960–May, 1963). The relationships among verbal output, factions, capabilities, and policies are further discussed below.

Soviet verbal output is thus only one possible source for clues or information concerning intentions. Information concerning Soviet motives and intentions are derived from four principal sources: (1) words, (2) conduct, (3) personal contact with the Soviet leadership, and (4) intelligence and espionage, technological and otherwise. And since Soviet intentions, individually or collectively, ultimately reflect the intentions of individuals, Soviet behavior cannot be analyzed in separation from the character and personality traits of the principal decision-makers in the Kremlin, who constitute a well-defined, if not always united, oligarchy.

Verbal statements that correspond with actual policy and behavior can be defined as "output policy," and statements that diverge or are incompatible with existing policy can be characterized as "factional intent." Policy or actual behavior that continues in the absence of positive correspondence or compatibility with any of two or more mutually divergent statements of intent reflects "continuity policy," that is, "muddling through." The implications of these relationships are as follows:

1. *Output Policy:* Output policy refers to the official intent of the Soviet state as articulated by its designated spokesmen, together with supplemental and support positions by various spokesmen and media representing various socio-institutional and socio-functional entities. Normally, output policy is articulated by the Secretary-General of the Party and/or the Chairman of the Council of Ministers (Premier). Whenever the two positions are occupied by a single individual (Stalin, 1941–1953; Khrushchev, 1958–1964), the authoritative character of the output is maximized. Whenever the two positions are occupied by two different individuals (1953–1955: Malenkov, Premier; Khrushchev, First Secretary; 1955–1958: Bulganin, Premier; Khrushchev, First Secretary; 1964–present; Brezhnev, Secretary-General; Kosygin, Premier), the situation is more complicated and may represent one of the following:
   a. Rivalry between the two leaders as individuals and/or as leaders of two chief factions in uneasy equilibrium or consensus.
   b. Factional instability or acute conflict, involving more than three contending personalities or factions, coexisting in uneasy and unstable accommodation, usually temporary or provisional. Under these conditions, other individuals assume a prominence and explicit influence approximating that of the two official spokesmen, whereupon the situation can be characterized as a triumvirate, quadrumvirate, etc.
   c. A stable coalition between two or more factions operating on a consensus or majority basis.
   d. The existence of a dominant faction with a continuing majority. Under these conditions the Party leader enjoys definite primacy, with the Premier as a definite number two man in the hierarchy. This condition in the past has usually been a prelude to a struggle between the two, with the Party Secretary usually assuming the position of Premier as well in order to eliminate any ambiguity in ultimate authority.
   Note: Sometimes, there is a time lag of varying duration between the time a factional power conflict has been decided and resolved and the time that legal-constitutional adjustments are made. Under these conditions, the Premier is a "Lame Duck" for several months and is no longer the authoritative spokesman for official policy (Malenkov between September, 1954 and February, 1955; Bulganin between July, 1957 and March, 1958; no time-lag was permitted following the decision

to dethrone Khrushchev as Party and government spokesman).

2. *Factional Intent:* Factional intent represents statements, etc. that significantly deviate from output policy. These may vary in number and intensity depending upon the number of factions, the intensity of the conflict, and the relative role and power position of the contending groups. Factional views may constitute alternatives to output policy, in which case they constitute potential output policy. If the faction wins out, its factional views become output policy in total or in part. Under conditions of chronic conflict, a faction may be sufficiently powerful to actually modify, change, or reshape the direction of output policy. It operates, in effect, as a pressure group: powerful enough to influence policy and force a compromise output but not sufficiently powerful to reverse or displace existing policy.

3. *Continuity Policy:* Continuity policy is not an intent, but a condition. It represents continuing policy in the absence of any explicit accompanying statements of intent. Continuity occurs because of the following:

   a. Factional standoff or paralysis, in which case existing policy continues by default or inertia because of inability to make decisions to arrest, modify, or reverse existing policy. It represents essentially a condition of drift.

   b. Bureaucratic or institutional momentum, inertia, or sabotage. Policy continues because administrative or executive agencies are under the control of individuals who are out of sympathy with changes in policy, in which case continuity represents a form of factional policy. (Beria, Molotov, and Marshal Zhukov, among others, have been charged with refusing to execute changes in policy in their respective administrative jurisdictions.) In the absence of agreement at the top, continuity sometimes represents simply the functional and role momentum of lower-level bureaucrats and officials.

   c. Policies carried over from the preceding period because they are noncontroversial, uncontested, or represent the ongoing, spontaneous, and natural output of technical and scientific research and development. In the latter case, continuity is essentially deterministic rather than the product of explicit intent.

   Note: It should be emphasized that in large, complex, and unwieldy bureaucracies, policies are often deterministically influenced by the role, structure, ingrained habits, competence, and normal functioning of the organization. Thus, with specific reference to a possible relationship between strategic arms development and continuity as the result of bureaucratic momentum: Assume that at a given time, the Soviet leadership was united in achieving strategic superiority and that the necessary development, production, and deployment decisions were made. Now assume that, for various reasons, the majority on this issue broke down, but no majority could be formed to reverse or arrest earlier decisions. That is, the Soviet leadership was divided three or more ways. Development, production, and deployment of weapons in accordance with previous decisions continues. Consequence: development and production may result in a de facto policy of seeking strategic superiority, although the policy does not enjoy an explicit endorsement by the leadership. Bureaucratic momentum continues and results in a policy without conscious intent. Needless to say, the Soviet bureaucracy is also not immune from the maddening and bizarre concatenation of phenomena subsumed under the rubrics of "Parkinson's Law" and the "Peter Principle."

Analyzing Soviet intentions purely on the basis of documents, speeches, and ideological statements gives undue weight to "rational" factors since the irrational, non-rational, accidental, and fortuitous factors can hardly be divined from verbal sources. On the other hand, calculating Soviet motives on the basis of capabilities or past responses and patterns of behavior can also result in faulty projections, since significant acts can depart from past behavioral patterns. Two historical illustrations are pertinent in this connection. During the final years of the Eisenhower Administration, extrapolations of future Soviet missile strength were based upon existing productive capabilities, resulting in the famous "missile gap" controversy. The Soviet leaders, however, for various reasons did not produce the missiles they were capable of producing, and the "missile gap" turned out to be an illusion.[78] Similarly, in 1962, it was the general consensus of Soviet specialists (inside and outside the government) that the Soviet Union would not attempt to establish nuclear-tipped missiles in Cuba, a judgment that also turned out to be erroneous. In both cases, judgments were based upon past Soviet behavior. In the past, Soviet leaders usually employed their productive capacities to the limit, and Soviet leaders had scrupulously avoided establishing nuclear-based missiles on non-Soviet territory.

As a general rule, the more dominant the role of a single personality in Soviet foreign policy, the more voluntaristic the behavior of the Soviet Union in the choice of values and purposes, in the latitude for fulfilling personal ambitions, drives, and aspirations of the leader, and the more apparent the idiosyncratic characteristics (neuroses, psychoses, anxieties, suspicions, maturity, emotional balance, volatility, temperament, and style) of the personality in the behavior of the Soviet state.

[78] Cf. Horelick and Rush, op. cit.

On the other hand, if the regime is governed by an oligarchy, Soviet policy is more likely to allow wider latitude for the influence of deterministic factors such as history, force of tradition, pattern maintenance, bureaucratic routine, inertia, or momentum. This is likely to condition Soviet behavior to be more prudent and less innovating. The sober and pedestrian nature of Soviet behavior under Brezhnev and Kosygin thus reflects not only their own personalities but also the absence of a dominating charismatic leader, whereas the cautious character of Soviet behavior under Stalin, as well as the mercurial flamboyance under Khrushchev, were reflections of two dominant personalities.

Estimates of the "human equation" in Soviet behavior, whether derived from personal observation or biographical or psychoanalytical studies of the Soviet leadership are themselves essentially subjective in character. They originate with observers and scholars who are free from neither ignorance, prejudice (cultural or individual), nor gullibility, and their estimates are apt to vary accordingly. Any attempt to distill the essence of Soviet intentions solely from personality considerations is thus also likely to be seriously deficient. A sound analysis of Soviet intentions must take into consideration words, conduct, and personalities, not as separate and independent articles, but as basic variables whose relative and relational significance is in a constant state of flux. Furthermore, they should be examined within the fivefold framework of variables and factors mentioned above and outlined in detail below.

The following table is a simple partial checklist of the variables that should be considered when assessing Soviet motivations, purposes, and intentions:

Group I Checklist

A. *Ideological* (Teleological and normative components only)
   1. Beliefs, assumptions, perceptions (dialectical laws, class struggle, economic determinism, theories of human nature and behavior, scientific inevitability, etc.)
   2. Definitions of normative and purposive goals (world revolution; world Communism; stateless, classless, conflictless society; proletarian internationalism, etc.)
   3. Definitions of strategy and action (revolutions: proletarian, national, colonial, anti-imperialist; just wars: class, popular, anti-imperialist, national liberation, etc.)
B. *Self-Interest*
   1. Self-preservation (maintenance, survival)
      a. Leader, oligarchy
      b. State
      c. Party
      d. Social system
      e. Russian nation
      f. Non-Russian nation (variable)
      g. Multinational Commonwealth

    2. Development (material well-being, growth, wealth)
      a. State
      b. Social system (according to structured hierarchy)
      c. Party
      d. Russian nation
      e. Non-Russian nation (variable)
      f. Multinational Commonwealth
    3. Self-image (self-esteem, pride, prestige)
      a. State
      b. Social system
      c. Leaders
      d. Party
      e. Russian nation
      f. Non-Russian nation (variable)
    4. Self-extension (territorial, ideological, system)
      a. Social system
      b. State
      c. Party
      d. Russian nation
      e. Non-Russian nation (variable)
      f. Multinational Commonwealth
C. *Power* (As a goal or purpose)
    1. Leader, oligarchy
    2. State
    3. Party
    4. Social system (various institutions, Armed Forces, Secret Police, etc.)
    5. Russian nation
D. *Personalities*
    1. Drives
      a. Conscious (ambitions, goals, purposes, values, self-fulfillment)
      b. Unconscious (resentments, frustrations, sublimations, displacements, personal idiosyncrasies)
    2. Character (moral, amoral, deceitful, trustworthy, etc.)
    3. State of mind (sanity, rationality, emotional balance)
    4. Style or mode of behavior
    5. Biographic variables (national origin, social origins, age, education, etc.)
E. *Political Culture/National Character* (The cumulative, aggregate, and generationally transmitted psychocultural patterns of reaction, response, and behavior to various internal and external circumstances, conditions, and events that condition the attitudes and actions of both leaders and various groups and strata of the population, both Russian and non-Russian)
    1. Behavior under conditions of stress (privation, deprivation, war, destruction, occupation, surprise, oppression, suppression, etc.)

       a. Toward leaders, socio-political system, and institutions
       b. Toward outsiders (enemies, allies, neutrals)
       c. Toward each other (social groups; Russians *vis à vis* non-Russians and *vice versa*)
    2. Behavior under conditions of success, victory and/or prosperity (victory in war, occupation of foreign territory and population, economic prosperity, relaxation of tensions, domestic reforms, etc.).
       a. Toward leaders, socio-political system, and institutions
       b. Toward outsiders (the defeated and occupied, allies, neutrals)
       c. Toward each other (social groups, nationalities)
  F. *Historical Traditions and Legacy*
    1. Unconscious
       a. Russian
       b. Non-Russian (variable)
    2. Conscious (*i.e.*, assimilated to "Soviet" values and norms)
       a. Russian
       b. Non-Russian (variable)

2. *Capabilities/Power*

Past experience has shown that predicting Soviet foreign policy on the basis of Soviet capabilities can be as unreliable as predicting Soviet behavior purely on the basis of stated intentions and purposes. Even a marriage between intentions and capabilities, *i.e.*, raising capabilities to match desires, does not always produce policy either. Actually, there can be an intimate dynamic interaction between capabilities and intentions, whereby although the latter originally may inspire the development of capabilities, as these grow, they feed back to influence and reshape intentions and purposes. As Soviet capabilities have expanded, the Soviet leaders have reevaluated original goals and intentions (particularly those inspired by Marxism-Leninism) in the light of the risks involved in relation to possible returns. Factional differences not only result from changing and conflicting perceptions of risks, but they also represent changing configurations of purpose and interests, both domestic and external. Furthermore, growing capabilities in a context of factional differences create new choices and options, giving rise to new perceptions of priorities and the consequent erosion of commitment to earlier purposes and goals.

In recent years, the growth of Soviet capabilities, instead of reenforcing or intensifying commitment to ideological goals like "World Communism," has actually contributed to the erosion of commitment in that direction and its partial redirection toward other purposes and goals, more restrictive and traditional in character. Soviet commitment to ideological goals thus has been attenuated, not only because of factional conflict, but also because the commitment is now more widely diffused among the goals and purposes generated by its five identities. It becomes increasingly more difficult for the Soviet leaders to sacrifice the interests of one Soviet identity for another, and since intense commitment to ideological interests (Party identity) seriously undercuts and even endangers the interests of the other identities and their constituencies, they become increasingly reluctant to pursue it.

As noted earlier, statements of intent are far from sufficient to explain Soviet foreign policy. Statements of intent must therefore be correlated with capabilities and when there is a correspondence between the two, it suggests very strongly that statements of intent should be taken seriously. Thus, another clue to predicting future Soviet behavior is the relationship between statements of intent ("intent observables") and the observed development of capabilities ("capabilities observables"), particularly, but not exclusively so, in the field of weapons development and deployment. Because of the fragmented character of the Soviet decision-making system, among other reasons, the relationship can assume a number of forms, depending upon the given factional balance internally or the balance of power externally. These relationships, together with their possible explanations, are as follows:

1. *Intent observables correlate with compatible capabilities observables, i.e.,* statement of intent is accompanied or followed by compatible capabilities development. *Hypothetical illustration:* Statement that Soviet Union possesses inter-continental ballistic missile (ICBM) correlates with information that ICBMs are being produced: This suggests that the intent observables represent official policy, which in turn can mean the existence of (a) a dominant faction; (b) majority coalition; (c) a consensus, compromise, or accommodation; (d) a unified position.

2. *Intent observables fail to correlate with compatible capabilities observables, i.e.,* statement of intent is not accompanied or followed by any compatible capabilities development. *Hypothetical illustration:* Statement that conventional Armed Forces are to be reduced is not accompanied or followed by any actual reduction in forces: This suggests a wide range of possibilities: (a) inability to form a stable majority or to arrive at a consensus, compromise, or accommodation; (b) sabotage by executing or administering agency controlled by dissident leaders; (c) change of policy due to change in factional balance; (d) change in policy, due to external reactions, responses, or situations; (e) technical, resource, or research difficulties or failures; (f) desire to deceive or conceal.

3. *Intent observables correlate with incompatible or contradictory capabilities observables, i.e.,* statement of intent is accompanied or followed by capabilities development or deployment that contradicts statement of intent. *Hypothetical illustration:* Statement by Soviet leader that Soviet Union will not establish nuclear missile bases on foreign territory is accompanied or followed by establishment of such bases: This also suggests a wide range of possibilities: (a) desire to mislead, misinform, or deceive; (b) change in the factional balance, particularly if the capabilities observable is compatible with an earlier statement of an alternative intent; (c) cleavage between official Party and state

spokesmen and the dominant factional or consensus policy; (d) ongoing fluctuational factional conflict, resulting in modifications and changes of policy; (e) changes in the external situation; (f) perception of new opportunities stimulated by the development of the weapons systems themselves.

The relationships between intent and capabilities observables become even more complicated and fascinating when two or more incompatible or contradictory statements of intent correlate with capabilities developments as outlined above. Aside from the fact that the coexistence of contradictory statements of intent confirm sharp factional or institutional conflict, the possible explanations of these relationships can be extrapolated from the three basic relationships between intent observables and capabilities observables outlined above.

In the instance of situations outlined in number three above, the relationship between intent observables and capabilities observables would be reversed: *The appearance of capabilities observables would probably be followed by the expression of new intent observables* to correspond with the capabilities achieved or being developed—whether or not these intent observables had earlier appeared as the view of the minority or dissident faction.

In the following partial checklist of capabilities/power variables, it will be noted that certain variables reappear from the first checklist. This is because variables such as ideology and personality possess different dimensions and are simultaneously factors of both intent and capabilities. Thus, the analytical, epistemological, communication, and legitimization components of ideology are capabilities, rather than purposive, factors, as are the intelligence, skill, and abilities of Soviet leaders.

Group II Checklist

A. *Military* [Immediate and potential]
   1. Strategic
   2. Tactical
   3. State of readiness
   4. Alliances
B. *Economic* [Immediate and potential]
   1. Industrial
   2. Agricultural (food supply)
   3. Transportation and communication
   4. Trade and aid
   5. Autarchical (self-sufficiency)
   6. Technological and scientific
C. *Ideological*
   1. Cognitive, epistemological, and analytical
   2. Mobilizational and inspirational (internal and external)
   3. Legitimizational (internal and external)
   4. Communicational

D. *Political/Institutional*
1. Decision-making (effectiveness, rapidity of response, etc.)
2. Conflict-resolving and conflict-containing
3. Mobilizational and communicational
4. Crisis management
5. Self-correcting
6. Legitimizational
7. Diplomatic
E. *Personalities* (Leadership)
1. Abilities, skills, competence, intelligence
2. Education
3. Character (imagination, courage, audacity, nerves, etc.)
F. *Systemic* (Socio-political)
1. Legitimizational and socializational
2. Mobilizational and inspirational
3. Integrative
4. Functional and structural
G. *Demographic*
1. Size, diversity, distribution, and density of population
2. Skills, education, industriousness
3. Loyalty, morale, endurance
H. *Geographical*
1. Size, location, and distribution of territory
2. Topographical, physical, and climatic
3. Natural resources
   a. Sufficiency
   b. Availability (immediate and potential)
   c. Location and distribution

3. *Risks*

The risks variables are highly subjective, involving almost pure perception, judgment, and chance, rather than something that can be objectively measured. Judgments about Soviet risk-taking propensities can, of course, be quantified, as can other forms of opinion or attitudes, but the quantification of opinion about Soviet risk-taking is not the same as objectively measuring it. The degree of risk (whether high or low) should not be confused with anticipated or actualized level of gain or loss.[79] The risk variable, as defined here, involves the perception of the Soviet leaders as to the probable chance of: (1) success or failure, (2) harm, and (3) high level of harm. For example, when Khrushchev decided to establish nuclear missile bases in Cuba, he had to assess simultaneously its chances of success, estimate the chances of harm in the process, and finally to chance the level or magnitude of harm that

[79] Cf. Jan F. Triska, *Pattern and Level of Risk-Taking in Soviet Foreign Policy Making: 1945–1963* (Stanford, Stanford Studies of the Communist System, 1964); and Robert Jervis, *The Logic of Images in International Relations* (Princeton, Princeton University Press, 1970), pp. 237 ff.

might be inflicted. Although all three risk components are organic links in a single decision, each chance factor is independent of the other and may be unevenly distributed among the three risk components. Thus, not only is the calculation of the risks on the part of the Soviet leaders essentially subjective in character, varying with individual decision-makers, but the analyst's judgment of the decision-maker's risk judgments is equally subjective and varies with the individual observer. Thus, the analysis of Soviet risk-taking carries within it a built-in futility, because the only concrete reference points are the decision itself and its success or failure. The outcome of a particular action cannot be used to retrospectively validate or invalidate the risk calculation, since, by definition, the consequence of a risk is uncertain and any of various outcomes are possible, although the degree of probability for various outcomes can be calculated differently. A successful outcome cannot serve to validate a low-risk assessment any more than failure can invalidate it, since either result is possible, irrespective of the risk calculated. *Ex post facto* quantitative analyses of Soviet risk-taking, as measured in terms of success or failure, thus cannot yield results of any higher certitude, because the success or failure of an action can total 100 per cent, although the probabilities of success may have been calculated at 99 per cent before the event. Similarly a 1 per cent chance of success may result in a 100 per cent actual success. As an illustration, it has been said by one of the participants in the decision that the Bay of Pigs action was rated as a 95 per cent probability of success, but that it resulted in a 100 per cent failure. A similar relationship between the calculation of risk and the outcome was probably the case eighteen months later when Khrushchev attempted to establish nuclear-missile bases in Cuba. Anticipating gains and losses of the risk operation, although crucial in determining whether a risk action should be taken, is not causally related to the probabilities of success or failure and is a separate and distinct variable, which, however, can be employed retrospectively to judge whether the risk was worthwhile.

Measuring the risk level of a particular action thus involves simultaneous assessment of the perceptions of three risk components, which, however, cannot be "averaged" out. The three risks are not additive in character. How then can we distinguish between a high-risk action and one that is low risk? The simple Risk Matrix Chart below might be helpful in this connection by clarifying the various combinations that are possible among the three risk components in a decision. It should be emphasized that the matrix is extremely simplified; it characterizes risk levels only in terms of high or low, although it is obvious that the chance element can be more precisely calibrated in terms of perception, if not objective measurement. The matrix is for illustrative purposes only and is not meant to be analytical. The suggested historical illustrations reflecting various combinations of risk are based on the author's judgment, as are the expected gain level and the designation of the action as a success or failure. Furthermore, the matrix does not pretend to

SIMPLIFIED RISK MATRIX

			Chance of:			
	Failure	Harm	High level of harm	Gain expecta- tions	Suggested illustrations	Outcome[a]
1	High	High	High	High	Nazi-Soviet Pact — 1939	F
2	High	Low	High	Low	Sino-Soviet Border Conflict — 1969	S
3	High	Low	Low	High	Congo Crisis — 1960	F
4	High	High	Low	High	Berlin Crisis — 1961	F
5	Low	Low	Low	Low	Suez Crisis — 1956	S
6	Low	Low	High	High	Berlin Crisis — 1948	F
7	Low	High	High	High	Cuban Missile Crisis — 1962	F
8	Low	High	Low	High	Czech Occupation — 1968	S

[a] S=success; F=failure.

account for risks whose effects may be protracted or delayed, since this would involve intricate calculations of the impact of interstitial decisions taken between action and effect.

The column labeled "expectations" refers to the decision-maker's anticipation of the level of gain from the risk, again described simply in terms of high or low. Gain is defined not only in positive terms but also as a prevention of loss. The Soviet occupation of Czechoslovakia in 1968, for example, is given as an illustration of a risk in which the gain expectation is rated high, although in actuality the action was taken to prevent possible serious losses that would be risked by inaction.

The confusing and frequently contradictory comparisons and contrasts often made between Stalin's foreign policy behavior and that of Khrushchev results not only from an inability to distinguish between risk and cost estimates as two distinct variables (this is discussed below), but also because the risk among the three components in their decisions were different combinations of high and low. Khrushchev is sometimes characterized as being a higher risk-taker than Stalin, whose foreign policies, in restrospect, appear cautious by comparison. The reasons for the contradictory perceptions are several, a significant one being the accelerated and unprecedented technological revolution in weaponry after Stalin's death. Under these conditions, any high or low risk policy, involving a confrontation between the U.S. and the U.S.S.R., risks a high level of harm.

Khrushchev's political career was that of a man who favored combining high risk of failure with low risk in the level of harm. He was by nature a shrewd and calculating gambler who played long shots but bet small stakes and shied away when the ante was raised. In the domestic political realm, Khrushchev could exercise some control over the stakes involved, but once he appeared on the world stage, his penchant for gambling and bluffing, plus his instinctive survival impulse to quickly retreat if the stakes were raised, made him vulnerable to a counter-strategy of "brinksmanship" or "eyeball to eyeball" confrontation.[80] For this reason, Khrushchev sedulously sought to redefine Soviet-American relations so that he could indulge his penchant for flamboyant and extravagant risk-taking without losing control over the magnitude of the stakes. His détente policy, for example, sought to remove the vital interests of both parties from the arena of confrontation, leaving only peripheral interests to be contended over, which would thus enable him to bluff, bluster, and gamble at high levels of risks, secure in the knowledge that in the event of failure, the costs would be acceptable.[81]

His hope to gain agreement with Eisenhower after the Camp David preliminaries however, was undercut by the U-2 affair and led him to seriously underestimate Kennedy's will and resolution (based upon his perception of the Bay of Pigs fiasco) at their meeting in Vienna, and he carelessly embarked upon a risky venture over Berlin and was forced to retreat when Kennedy unexpectedly raised the ante. The Berlin failure impelled him to embark upon an even more perilous adventure that resulted in the Cuban missile crisis and another Soviet retreat after the president raised the stakes.[82] Finally, the partial Test Ban Treaty provided Khrushchev with the kind of arrangement he was seeking, but events were to overtake both Kennedy and Khrushchev, as the former was assassinated four months after the treaty was signed, and Khrushchev was toppled less than a year later.

In contrast to Khrushchev, Stalin was a more calculating personality, who combined low risk-taking with high stakes.[83] Unlike Khrushchev, he did not find it necessary to virtually disown the goal of "World Communism," since he pursued it pragmatically, cautiously, and without excitement, at a level likely to arouse serious counteraction only from the ideologues of Fascism and the right. Stalin constantly warned against the revolutionary penchant for inadvertently "showing one's true colors" or prematurely "raising the Red Flag," (warnings, incidentally, that were disregarded by both Tito and Mao, who gambled instead and won). Whereas Khrushchev's preferred risk behavior was typically combinations three and four in the chart on p. 74, which allowed him to project a flamboyant and risky image, Stalin preferred risks approximating combination six, i.e., actions that were low risk in terms of failure and harm, but high risk in possible level of harm combined with high-gain expectations. Since scholars as a general class are low-risk-taking personality types, their perceptions of the level of risk may vary widely

[80] Cf. Horelick and Rush, op. cit.

[81] See Selections 23 and 30.

[82] Cf. Arnold Horelick, The Cuban Missile Crisis: An Analysis of Soviet Calculations and Behavior (Santa Monica, Calif., The RAND Corporation, 1965); and Ole R. Holsti, Richard Brady, and Robert C. North, "Measuring Effect and Action in International Reaction Models: Empirical Materials from the 1962 Cuban Missile Crisis," in Louis Kriesburg, editor, Social Processes in International Relations (New York, Wiley, 1968).

[83] Cf. Marshall Shulman, Stalin's Foreign Policy Reappraised (Cambridge, Mass., Harvard University Press, 1963).

from that of the decision-makers whose risk they are examining. What may appear risky to the scholar may not be perceived as risky to the individual statesman. This wide divergence in perceptions of the level of risk between scholars and decision-makers raises a formidable barrier to rendering meaningful conclusions about risk-taking. And when the observers are part of a larger socio-cultural milieu in which risk-taking is frowned upon, it becomes even more difficult to render judgments about perceptions of risks taken by decision-makers who are products of a political system that catapults risk-taking personalities to positions of power.

The risk variable thus involves an intricate and complex judgment about personalities, both on the part of the decision-maker contemplating the risk and the scholar who attempts to make judgments about the risk-taking propensities of the decision-maker. All other factors are essentially peripheral to the personality factor, although the institutional matrix within which he functions serves to create some restraint and conditioning mechanism. But statesmen in both authoritarian and democratic countries appear to be able to evade these restraints if their commitments are sufficiently intense, their self-confidence high, and their temperament appropriate. Not only the Bay of Pigs, but the Franco-British assault on Suez, the two Israeli Blitz attacks on Egypt, and the escalation of the Vietnamese war by President Johnson are all examples of substantial risk-taking by democratic decision-makers.

On the surface it would appear that decision-makers in authoritarian states have greater latitude in taking risks than statesmen in democratic countries, if they are so inclined. This is probably true, but an authoritarian regime does not, *per se*, induce high risk-taking. Politics as a vocation is a risky enterprise, and in authoritarian regimes probably riskier than most, which thus results in a higher proportion of successful risk-taking personalities occupying decision-making positions. Newly formed revolutionary regimes probably contain the highest proportion of risk-taking personalities, since revolution is an extremely risky business to begin with.

Aside from personality considerations, which are dominant in the risk variables, some objective conditions may facilitate high risk-taking. These are:

1. *Flexibility of the decision-making system,* i.e., the relative freedom of decision-makers to act and react quickly without institutional restraints;

2. *Command control,* i.e., the ability of the decision-maker to communicate, execute, and implement high-risk decisions through the chain of command;

3. *Image projection,* i.e., the ability to project a false image of strength, determination, or boldness and to sustain a bluff for a considerable period of time;

4. *Information security,* i.e., the ability to control and manipulate all internal items of information concerning the risk operation; and

5. *Recovery capability*, i.e., the ability to retreat, fall back, or recover with minimum loss in the event the operation is exposed before it is launched.

In the final analysis, risk, like beauty, is in the eye of the beholder, and what may appear risky to one individual may not to another.

4. *Cost/Benefits*

The risk variables are obviously closely related with the costs/ benefits variables and at points the two tend to merge and become blurred. Both are highly subjective and vary widely in accordance with the personalities and capabilities of the decision-makers. Costs and benefits are usually assessed in terms of advanced estimates and calculations, but no matter how carefully calibrated in terms of assessing relative capabilities, or as Soviet leaders themselves say, "calculating the correlation of the world forces," the estimates remain highly subjective and uncertain. What Soviet leaders can do is to carefully estimate the anticipated costs of certain decisions and policies and decide whether the benefits are sufficiently compensating to absorb them if necessary. Analysts of Soviet foreign policy also develop frameworks that attempt to assess the kinds and dimensions of costs that Soviet leaders may find acceptable ("acceptable damage" in the event of nuclear war, for example) in order to arrive at judgments as to when and where the Soviet leaders may risk as acceptable certain precalculated levels of damage and cost in the event of action.[84] The decision to invade Czechoslovakia in 1968, for example, involved intensive debate concerning the relative levels of cost in the event of action as opposed to inaction.[85] Indications are that the Soviet leaders were prepared to accept a higher level of cost than they actually had to endure. Similarly, with respect to the Soviet presence in Egypt, costs of the Soviet decision to arm Egypt and support her diplomatically involved a calculation not only of the risks involved in such a venture, but also the costs.

There is still another intricate relationship between risks and potential costs that requires exploration, particularly where Soviet foreign policy is concerned. Sometimes a high-risk policy is confused with a high-cost policy, and conversely a low-cost policy is confused with a low-risk policy. Although there is obviously some correspondence between the level of potential cost and the level of risk involved, the two can nevertheless be discretely separated for analysis. If risk is defined in terms of the estimated chance of success or failure, it can stand independently of the level of costs that are perceived as acceptable or must be endured, since the cost level can be calculated in advance often more accurately than the risk variables. Thus, it becomes possible to devise a

[84] *Cf.* Herman Kahn, *On Thermonuclear War* (Princeton, Princeton University Press, 1960); J. David Singer, *Deterrence, Arms Control and Disarmament* (Columbus, Ohio State University, 1962).

[85] See Selection 25.

high-risk, potentially high-cost policy, as well as a high-risk policy, whose potential cost level is calculated to be relatively low. Similarly, it is possible to combine a low-risk policy with a potentially high-cost or low-cost factor.

A prudent and cautious foreign policy would be one that combined low-risk with low potential costs; an adventurous one would be a combination of high-risks, and high potential costs. The confusing and frequently contradictory comparisons and contrasts often made between Stalin's foreign policy and that of Khrushchev result from an inability to distinguish between the risk and cost estimates as two distinct variables, as well as the failure to appreciate the uneven combination of risk components.

In summary, it can be said that Stalin ran low risks in pursuit of high stakes, whereas Khrushchev preferred high risks for low stakes but was impelled to run high risks for high stakes instead.

Costs variables (benefits variables are in most cases simply the mirror-image of the costs variables), generally speaking, are of two types: limited and unlimited. Unlimited costs are by their very nature intrinsically unacceptable, but such costs may result through miscalculation of both risks and costs.

Group IV Checklist

A. *Limited Costs*
 1. Material/physical loss
  a. Territorial loss
   (1) Annexation
   (2) Occupation (temporary or permanent)
   (3) Demilitarization, depopulation of territories
  b. Demographic/population loss
   (1) Diminished size
    (a) Deaths
    (b) Loss through annexations
    (c) Loss through deportations, emigration, defections
   (2) Diminished capabilities
    (a) Loss of skilled populations
    (b) Loss of ethnic and national groups
    (c) Casualties (cripples)
    (d) Altered sex ratio and structure
    (e) Altered age structure and ratios
    (f) Altered fertility rates, birthrates, deathrates
    (g) Altered capacity for livelihood because of economic dislocation, etc.
  c. Economic loss
   (1) Physical destruction (partial or total) of cities, economic structures, buildings, transportation and com-

munications facilities, food supply, natural resources, etc.
- (2) Loss of same through annexation of territory
- (3) Reparations and compensations
- (4) Other financial loss
  d. Military loss and diminished security
  - (1) Loss of strategic territory
  - (2) Reduction of forces
  - (3) Destruction or surrender of equipment
  - (4) Loss of trained manpower
2. Intangible loss (psychological and social)
   a. Diminished confidence in political, social, and economic system
   b. Diminished motivation, energy, enthusiasm, and industry on the part of the leadership and/or sectors of the population
   c. Psychological feelings of inferiority and incapacity on the part of the population
   d. Lowered civilian and military morale and self-confidence
   e. Diminished national pride, self-esteem, and prestige
   f. Increased social and ethnic instability
   g. Loss of allies, client states; dissolution of alliances
   h. Increased vulnerability to pressures, threats, and demands
   i. Diminished diplomatic capabilities and influence
B. *Unlimited Costs*
   1. Material/physical
      a. Total physical destruction of structures
      b. Total annihilation of population
   2. Social/political loss
      a. Annihilation of political and social elites
      b. Dissolution and disestablishment of the socio-political system
      c. Dissolution of state (or national) sovereignty and existence
      d. Total territorial dismemberment
      e. Total military occupation or political subjugation

The defeat of Nazi Germany is a recent concrete illustration of a state suffering a type of unlimited costs as a consequence of its policies. The Nazi socio-political order was disestablished, its elites annihilated or imprisoned, and the country dismembered territorially and politically and subjected to total military occupation. Soviet leaders have traditionally viewed the outcome of a war between the U.S. and the U.S.S.R. as one that will involve various forms of unlimited costs for the loser, although the traditional expectation of system annihilation has been conjoined since about 1953 with various versions of physical and demographic annihilation as well. Thus, Stalin, in 1952, before the advent of perceptions of mutual annihilation, provided the orthodox Marxist-Leninist vision of an unlimited type of cost: "War with the U.S.S.R., as a socialist land, is more dangerous to capitalism than war between capitalist countries. . . . War with the U.S.S.R. must certainly put in question the existence of capitalism itself."[86] This apocalyptic consequence of a war between the U.S. and the U.S.S.R. perceived as a war between social systems rather than states, *per se*, is still adhered to in various degrees by Stalin's successors, but unlike Stalin they reject the inevitability of such a war.[87] For a brief period during Khrushchev's incumbency, various notions of perceived mutual physical annihilation in the event of nuclear war were directly and indirectly formulated. This view was vigorously rejected by Mao in 1957 and by some in the Soviet leadership. Currently, the Soviet leadership appears divided over the *inevitability of mutual annihilation* in the event of nuclear war as distinct from the inevitability of war, and some factions appear to believe that one side can emerge relatively victorious under certain conditions and circumstances.[88]

5. *Opportunities*

Opportunity variables are extremely difficult to conceptualize, but they constitute nevertheless an essential ingredient in the calculation of Soviet foreign policy. Opportunities are by definition perceived situations and hence are essentially subjective. Like beauty and risk, opportunity is in the eye of the beholder and outside observers can do little more than catalogue past opportunity situations and how they were apprehended by the Soviet leaders. Somewhat akin to the risk variable, in that it is related to chance, the opportunity variable is different in that it is frequently a perceived stroke of fortune or a fortuitous concatenation of favorable events not directly assembled or brought about by conscious action. The opportunity variable is particularly significant as an input in Soviet behavior, because Leninist strategy and tactics have explicitly conditioned the Soviet leaders to be in a state of constant search for opportunities and readiness to quickly perceive and exploit favorable combinations of events that may materialize and dissipate quickly or that may appear unexpectedly and evaporate just as suddenly.[89]

[86] J. V. Stalin, *Economic Problems of Socialism* (New York, International Publishers, 1952), p. 29.

[87] See Selections 10 and 12.

[88] *Cf.* Roman Kolkowicz, *The Red "Hawks" on the Rationality of War* (Santa Monica, Calif., The RAND Corporation, 1966), and *The Dilemma of Superpower: Soviet Policy and Strategy in Transition* (Washington, D.C., Institute for Defense Analysis, 1967); and Thomas Wolfe, *Soviet Military Policy Trends Under the Brezhnev-Kosygin Regime* (Santa Monica, Calif., The RAND Corporation, 1967).

[89] The image that politicians may have of the Soviet predilection for opportunity situations is sometimes very graphic. "I regard the Soviet Union," Senator Henry Jackson has been quoted as saying, "as an opportunistic hotel burglar who walks down corridors trying all the door handles to see which door is open." *The Washington Post*, March 7, 1971.

The opportunity variable can be defined in terms of both timing and chance and often involves both. Unlike the risk variable, which is a conscious initiative based upon a subjective calculation and voluntary acceptance of blind chance (a gamble), the opportunity variable is the manifestation of an unambiguously favorable combination of circumstances determined externally and objectively by good fortune (a windfall). Thus, the risk variable involves a situation in which, if action is taken, the outcome is doubtful or uncertain, whereas the opportunity variable is a perceived situation where the outcome will be favorable if action is initiated.

The opportunity presents itself when intentions, capabilities, risks, and costs fortuitously intersect to maximize the possibility of realizing goals or objectives. It is thus a kind of dialectical astrology, whereby the Soviet Union is the beneficiary of objectively determined dialectical forces intersecting to provide the occasion for successful behavior. The opportunity situation in foreign policy is the external counterpart to what Lenin described as a "revolutionary situation" in the domestic realm.

Thus an opportunity may differ little from a low-risk situation in terms of consequences, but the genesis of the two situations are different, and the psychological attitudes required for behavior are distinguishable from one another. Risk, even low risk-taking, requires positive action to create situations, whereas opportunity spontaneously develops. Sharp distinctions between the two, however, cannot always be drawn.

6. Summary

In analyzing Soviet foreign policy, the relevant variables from these five sets must be viewed in dynamic interaction with each other, as not always explicitly deliberated upon by the Soviet leaders but nevertheless constantly scanned, screened, and related to each other in their minds. Serious changes in one gross variable can result in fundamentally restructuring the relative relevance of the others, which may then recombine to feedback and again alter the initial variable. Thus, originally, it was envisaged by the Soviet leadership that since the normative goals and purposes of its ideology were constant and absolute truths, their realization would be maximized by the development of Soviet resources and capabilities. In other words, once capabilities developed to the point that they could implement purposes, policy behavior would result. Theoretically, as Soviet capabilities grew, ideological goals would be progressively transformed into policy goals. World Communism would thus exfoliate more or less in accordance with the expansion of Soviet power and capabilities, until they were sufficiently developed to universalize Communism.[90]

But as capabilities developed, other variables were seriously affected. The risks of converting ideological purposes into policy goals, however, appeared to grow even faster than Soviet capabilities, since, as

[90] See Selection 4.

Soviet power grew, while ideological goals remained constant, other powers revised their estimates of Soviet intent, assigned greater seriousness to ideological purposes, and reacted in a defensive or hostile manner to Soviet behavior. The rise of Hitler in Germany was largely attributable to the growing capabilities of the Soviet Union, which served to impart greater credibility to Soviet ideological intentions and to the "Bolshevik danger."

With the advent of nuclear weapons in 1946, the risks of a forward ideological policy were sharply increased and qualitatively assumed a perceptibly different character, since Stalin would now have to calculate the costs/benefit variables not simply in terms of limited material/physical and unlimited social costs, but in terms of unlimited material/population costs. With the development of thermo-nuclear weapons and the advent of missile delivery systems, the risk and costs variables were actually qualitatively transformed as a consequence. The more powerful the Soviet Union became in terms of advanced weaponry, the riskier and potentially more costly became a militant commitment to a policy of advancing World Communism.

As a consequence, the commitment to ideological goals and purposes was seriously eroded and the Soviet leaders searched for new surrogate objectives that could be consummated with their new capabilities without running grave risks or involving potentially suicidal costs. New options and avenues proliferated as a result of enhanced capabilities, and a new equilibrium was established among the five sets of variables in Soviet calculations.

Because of the multiple identities of the Soviet Union, Soviet leaders possess a wide range of constituencies they can serve and cultivate to more than compensate for those that they would lose as a consequence of their attenuating commitment to World Communism. In concrete terms, this meant shifting away from serving the interests of external constituencies (ruling and non-ruling Communist Parties, particularly China), as the Soviet leadership under Khrushchev directed greater attention to serving domestic Soviet constituencies.[91] This also involved a subtle but fundamental redefinition of ideological priorities. "Building Communism" (internal development) replaced "world revolution" (condemned as "export of revolution" by Khrushchev), as the highest ideological priority of Soviet policy.

Technological advances in weapons systems or other factors that might seriously alter the existing strategic balance between the United States and the Soviet Union can also feed back to fundamentally alter the equilibrium among the variables determining Soviet foreign policy. Just as the relative weight of ideology as a motivating factor diminished as risks multiplied and increased, a substantial reduction in the risk variable and/or potential costs could trigger a rise in the relative weight of the ideological factor. For example, the strategic balance could shift radically in favor of the Soviet Union because of one or more of the

[91] See Selection 15.

following developments: (1) failure, through inability or unwillingness, to match Soviet technological and scientific developments in weapons technology; (2) failure, through inability or unwillingness, to match the production and deployment of weapons systems sufficient to preserve the existing strategic balance; (3) paralysis of political will develops in the United States because of domestic racial conflict, student disorders, economic disturbances, war weariness, and mass demoralization because of the Vietnam war, etc.; and (4) failure to freeze the existing strategic balance through mutually agreed upon controls over weapons stockpiles, deployment, and development via the SALT Talks.

If any of the above happens, individually or in combination, the stage would be set, for a rearrangement of the variables mix in the calculation of Soviet foreign policy and alter the relative attractiveness of various options.[92] But as noted earlier, the relationship between intent and capabilities is not a simple one-to-one factor, since the other three gross variables, like intent, are largely functions of leadership perceptions. The character of the leadership and the goals it selects from the array of purposes and objectives will largely determine which options the Soviet Union will exploit, whether it be to enhance the Soviet role as a Global Power, as a revolutionary Party, a Russian state, or as a multinational commonwealth, individually or in combination.

[92] See Selections 27, 29, and 30.

I THE SWEEP OF SOVIET FOREIGN POLICY

1. A HALF CENTURY OF SOVIET FOREIGN POLICY

Vernon V. Aspaturian

The balance-sheet of Soviet foreign policy over the past fifty years shows an impressive range of accomplishments when measured against a comparable period for any other power of similar magnitude. An outlaw state in 1917, governed by a pariah regime, beset on all sides by powerful enemies, racked internally by social convulsions, civil war, fragmentation, and foreign occupation, whose chances for survival were extremely poor, the Soviet Union stands today as a modernised global power, second only to the United States in power, prestige, and influence. This evolution was no orderly unilinear development, preordained by history, but rather the outcome of periodic collisions between utopian hopes generated by ideology and the limitations imposed by the interests and ambitions of other states. For while it is true that "the record of Soviet diplomacy shows an inability to distinguish between the real and the imaginary, a series of miscalculations about the capabilities and intentions of foreign countries, and a record of clumsy co-ordination between diplomacy and propaganda," it is also true that the many spectacular failures of Soviet foreign policy have been more than matched by its spectacular successes.[1]

The incalculable factor of luck has undoubtedly played a crucial role in the successes of both Soviet external and internal policy, beginning with the revolution itself, although Soviet leaders have not been

Originally published under the title of "Moscow's Foreign Policy," in *Survey*, October, 1967, pp. 35–60. Reprinted by permission.
[1] Max Beloff, *Foreign Policy and the Democratic Process* (Baltimore, 1955), p. 98.

loath to capitalise on the follies and misjudgments of other states. If luck was the principal ingredient which explains Lenin's success in seizing power and preserving it against an impressive array of internal and external enemies, whose failure to co-ordinate their actions was decisive for the survival of the Soviet regime, luck was even more emphatically the crucial factor which rescued Stalin's Russia from defeat and annihilation during the second world war. Stalin's misjudgment of the internal social and political forces and trends in Germany in the years before Hitler's assumption of power, his near catastrophic miscalculation of the balance of power between the Axis and the western powers in 1939, and his imprudent rejection of all evidence of an impending German attack, by all logic should have resulted in the destruction of the Soviet state; but fate intervened in the form of Churchill's decision to accept Russia as an ally and Japan's attack upon Pearl Harbor which brought the United States into the war.

It would be absurd, of course, to attribute all Soviet successes in foreign policy to sheer luck, just as it would be unfounded to ascribe them all to an innate shrewdness of Soviet leaders, who perceived every opportunity, exploited every advantage, and capitalised on every blunder with uncanny astuteness. Since success and failure in foreign policy are highly relative and often symbiotically interdependent, it is both captious and self-deceiving to pretend that Soviet "successes" are in reality little more than the "failures" of other states. Yet it would be difficult to quarrel with George Kennan's judgment that "the standard components for a rousing Soviet diplomatic success" are "one part Soviet resourcefulness and singlemindedness of purpose, two parts amateurism, complacency, and disunity on the part of the West," and that it was this which enabled the Soviet Union to advance from "the initial weakness of 1921 to the pinnacle of power and success it occupies in the wake of World War II."[2]

Throughout most of its history, Soviet foreign policy has operated within a self-defined framework of a two-camp or bi-polar world with two basic players, communism (the Soviet Union) and capitalism (everybody else), so that all losses in the capitalist world were automatic gains for the Soviet Union. While such an image of the world was a crude distortion of reality, it is true that the Soviet addiction to this grim view could not but redefine the international situation and superimposed upon international politics the synthetic impression of a zero-sum game whereby a loss for one player was automatically a gain for the other. For nearly two decades the Cold War was pursued within this framework as the bi-polarisation of power around Moscow and Washington increasingly assumed the objective character of a zero-sum game as defined by Moscow and increasingly by western statesmen as well in response. The disintegration of the European colonial empires, the advent of weapons of instantaneous and universal destruction, the progressive dissolution of the Soviet bloc, the erosion of the NATO alliance,

[2] George Kennan, *Russia and the West under Lenin and Stalin* (Boston, 1961), p. 223.

and the eruption of the fratricidal Sino-Soviet conflict, however, have all but destroyed the bi-polarised international community in which gains and losses could be registered with zero-sum gamelike simplicity.

While Soviet foreign policy achievements are impressive, this does not mean that the Soviet Union today has fulfilled the expectations of its founders and leaders, past and present. Actually, its present status and position in the world community represent a blend of objective success and subjective failure, i.e. it has been a resounding success when its achievements are measured against the traditional yardstick of power politics, but a conspicuous failure when measured against its initial ideological inspiration and purpose. Instead of transforming the world, it is the Soviet Union which has been transformed. From a self-anointed centre of world revolution dedicated to the destruction of the existing social and political status quo, it has been objectively transformed into a mature global power whose interest in stabilising the status quo now virtually matches its dedication to revolution. From an embryonic world communist state the Soviet Union has been objectively metamorphosed into an arrested Russianised multinational community, burdened by supplicants and blessed by clients and allies as well as harassed and tormented by enemies and rivals in both the sub-community which it inspired and created as well as in the world which it sought originally to subvert. From a self-perceived instrument of history ordained to save mankind from the evils and injustices of capitalism and mandated to construct a new world communist society of universal justice, liberated from class, national, and racial conflict, the Soviet Union is now content to offer itself as a model for rapid modernisation and industrialisation of underdeveloped societies, with its eschatological and apocalyptic rhetoric largely muted. And finally, its ideology has been transformed from a vehicle legitimising world revolution into one legitimising communist rule in Russia; instead of raising the standard of revolution abroad, Moscow emphasises raising the standard of living at home in the name of ideology; instead of justifying further social changes in the Soviet system, it rationalises the social status quo; instead of inspiring the masses to charge the barricades, Soviet ideology now erects barricades against the heresies of Peking.

If we employ the traditional criteria of success in foreign policy (power, influence, and prestige), it is indisputable that the Soviet Union has been more successful than any other state in the past fifty years, save the United States. The most significant factor in the simultaneous rise of Soviet power and decline in the power of other states was the second world war. Germany was dismembered and occupied; Japan was squeezed back into her main islands and disarmed; Italy was shorn of her colonial empire, while a weakened France, Great Britain, and Netherlands progressively relinquished theirs. During the same period, the Soviet Union annexed 250,000 square miles of territory in Europe and Asia, established vassal and subservient states in east Asia and eastern Europe, displacing Japan and Germany respectively as the dominant powers in those two regions. It supported a successful communist take-over in China, sponsored the growth and proliferation of communist parties abroad, which it manipulated as instruments of its foreign policy, and continued to maintain the largest military establish ment in the world poised to move into new vacuums which might be created by the convulsions and agonies of colonial empires in dissolution and by the internal turmoil and political uncertainties which swept western Europe in the post-war period.

Although the Soviet Union has certainly failed in its original ideological mission of communising the world, its half-century attempt has left a lasting imprint upon the physiognomy of the globe and has fundamentally restructured the social, political, economic, and ideological configurations of one-third of the world and reoriented the direction in which the rest is moving. As a consequence of its endeavours, an international sub-system of fourteen communist states, comprising nearly one-third of the world's population and territory, has been established. These fourteen states not only share a common ideology, of which individual variants have emerged, but a common socio-economic system with a distinctive set of property relationships, giving rise to a shared social structure, governed and regulated by highly similar political institutions and processes.

Furthermore, communist parties, large and small, powerful and insignificant, are to be found in some seventy additional countries on five continents, ranging from minuscule and furtive illegal conspiratorial groups to large mass parties, such as those in France, Italy, and India. All these parties are inspired by variants of a common ideology, Marxism-Leninism, and are thus derivative emanations from the Bolshevik revolution of 1917.

The failure of the Soviet Union to achieve its ideological goal of universal communism is largely attributable to American power, which grew even more rapidly and spectacularly than Soviet power. Unlike the Soviet Union, however, the United States was a status quo power. Ironically, its strength was largely sustained and accelerated by the remarkable expansion of Soviet power and the threat it posed to the world at large. Unlike the growth of Soviet power, which was largely relative, due in large measure to the destruction of the great powers on her periphery, the growth in American power was largely incremental and absolute, although it experienced a relative enhancement of its power as well resulting from the corresponding shrinkage in the number of great powers after the war. While the Soviet Union avidly fell heir to the power spheres left vacant by the collapse of Japan and Germany because of its advantageous geographical position, the United States, reluctantly, erratically, and often inadvertently, progressively assumed the burdens carried by the declining and retreating western European powers. What the United States lacked in geographical advantage it more than made up for by its control of the seas, its inexhaustible economic resources, and its atomic monopoly. From the Soviet perspective, the only obstacle in the way of communist universalism was the American "ruling class" armed with nuclear weapons, and Soviet postwar foreign policy for over a decade was largely designed to nullify, immobilise, neutralise, skirt, surround, or even destroy this impediment, which ultimately proved impassable and insurmountable.

The failure of Soviet foreign policy to find its way around American power signalled the success of the containment policy which had been inaugurated in 1947. It is a silent but eloquent tribute to this policy that when the great colonial empires dissolved, not a single former colonial dependency was sucked into the communist orbit (save North Vietnam), although the Soviet Union had devoted considerable thought, energy, effort, and expense to capitalise upon an event which Soviet leaders had been predicting and expecting for decades.

Both Lenin and Stalin had formulated elaborate theories of colonialism, imperialism, and "bourgeois-nationalist" revolutions; they framed imaginative strategies of multi-staged revolutionary upheavals and multi-phased transition processes designed to adapt the exotic political ferments and forces in the colonies and semi-colonies to the general Marxist historical perspective. If ever a political leadership was psychologically poised and intellectually prepared to take advantage of one of history's most extensive and profound shifts in the global balance of power, it was the Soviet leadership, which had repeatedly predicted and eagerly awaited the revolutionary disintegration of the colonial empires, from which they expected a flood of recruits to the world of communism.

But the colonial empires dissolved in more or less orderly fashion into more than sixty new states, which were then shielded by the power of the United States from being sucked into the Soviet orbit. The American shield, however, not only protected the new states from being absorbed by the communist world but it also had the unfortunate effect in many cases of protecting unsavoury and oppressive native systems and regimes from their own disaffected populations, and this was bound to drive a wedge between the United States and many non-communist revolutionary movements and regimes in the new states. Thus, while the containment policy succeeded in arresting the expansion of Soviet and/or communist power, it also had the distressing tendency to contain and limit the range of non-communist options open to many of the new states in order to organise their social and political life.

Deprived first of its self-asserted character as an embryonic communist world state and then effectively denied its role as the centre of a world revolutionary movement articulating the interests of mankind, the Soviet Union was forced by objective circumstances to revert more and more to its irreducible role as a traditional great power, responding and reacting to its own national interests. And the more it reverted to its character as a great state, the more the other communist countries were likely to act as autonomous states rather than as parts of an organic movement.

The recrudescence of the nation-state as the state form of the communists has thus effectively demolished the pretensions of the Soviet Union as an embryonic universal state and has in effect forced its transformation into a modern version of the Russian Empire, purporting to represent the national interests not only of Russia but of all the major nations of the USSR.

These profound transmutations and revisions in the communist world have shattered the Marxist-Leninist expectation that a common ideology and a common social system would first surmount and then eradicate conflicts of national interests among communist states. After the reams of ideological nonsense written about the character of the new socialist international system, founded on the basis of mutual trust, harmony of interests, and the absence of conflict, it must come as a profound shock to Soviet ideologists to be now charged with the thankless task of justifying the dissolution of the communist bloc and explaining the Sino-Soviet dispute. Thus one Soviet writer, obviously dismayed by the gross inadequacy of Marxist-Leninist propositions, ruefully concedes that relations among socialist states, in spite of a common ideology and similar socio-economic systems, are still determined by factors traditionally associated with national distinctions:

> The formation of the world socialist system — a commonwealth of sovereign socialist states with equal rights — gave rise to a number of great theoretical and political problems which communists had never encountered before. . . . When the international relations among national detachments of the working class turned into relations between states, a new situation arose that required creative application of the general principles of Marxism-Leninism, the development of a number of propositions of the theory and actualisation of political decisions. How are the national and state interests of each socialist country to be brought in line with the interests of the entire system? How are the diverse interests of separate socialist states to be harmonised? How is the turbulent flow of national consciousness and national pride, caused by the success of socialist construction and the acquisition of genuine national independence, to be directed along the course of socialist internationalism?

He then concedes the essential naïveté of the orthodox Marxist-Leninist proposition that a common social system would be sufficient to eradicate conflicts of national interests:

> In our time such a formulation of the question seems natural and even trite. But to arrive at it required more than a year of intense searching that was frequently accompanied by practical errors and theoretical confusion. Let us recall the state of theory before the opening of the sixties. A formula of approximately this sort was set forth: All socialist states are of the same socio-economic nature, they have the same types of political power, and the same ideology prevails in them; consequently, there should not and cannot be any disagreements or contradictions in the relations among the countries of socialism. The very fact of the establishment of socialist production relations in a number of countries was considered to be an adequate guarantee of good relations among them, a guarantee that national and international interests would somehow automatically be harmonised.

Ideology, he points out, foundered on the traditional shoals of national interest, whose diversity and contradictory character have their source in the national peculiarities of history, culture, geography, and socio-economic development, whose significance had been seriously under-rated. Optimistically, but without much conviction, the writer maintains that concerted policy should be able to overcome the baneful effects of national interests:

> Life has proved to be more complicated and contradictory than this formula. The actual practice of contact among the countries of socialism has shown that this homogeneity of socio-economic, political, and ideological structures is a necessary but insufficient prerequisite for the real establishment of the principles of fraternity and cooperation, complete trust and mutual understanding in the relations among social-ist states. Historical experience bears witness to the fact that a complex intertwining of objective and subjective factors connected with the con-siderable disparity in the levels of socio-economic development of the individual countries of socialism, with differences of an historical-cultural and geographical nature, and with varying degrees of cog-nisance by the various parties of the laws of development of socialism, can lead in practice to deviations from the internationalist principles which are supposed to regulate relations in the socialist commonwealth. And an abstract reliance on the fact of a single type of ownership or state power is of no help here. Only the conscious, purposeful policy of the ruling communist parties is able to neutralise the influence of factors that lead to collisions and contradictions. Such a policy presup-poses a determined fight against attempts to present what is desired for what is real and to put actual problems of the socialist system in a simplified, bureaucratically optimistic form. Such a policy is based on the fact that each socialist state may have its own national interests, connected with peculiarities of its history, geographical location, eco-nomic development, etc. This is a fact that, when understood, is of direct significance for correct — both theoretically and politically cor-rect — application of the basic principles of relations among socialist states.[3]

The failure of the Soviet Union as a universal state should not, however, obscure its achievements as a traditional great power. In many respects, the current position of the Soviet Union exceeds the fondest aspirations of its Tsarist predecessor. Russia's historical irredenta have been largely reincorporated into the Soviet Union, and the new Soviet empire has been consolidated into an integrated and stable modern society, with a broad base of social and multinational support; the country is substan-tially self-sufficient militarily and economically; it presides over a retinue of client and allied states in eastern Europe; a dismembered Germany lies impotent in the west, a disarmed Japan has been shoved back into its indigenous islands in the east, and a belt of weak buffer states carved out of colonial empires lies to the south. Only the revival

[3] A. Bovin, "The International Principles of Socialism," *Izvestia,* Sep-tember 21, 1966.

of an expansionist China threatens the Soviet Union as a state and as the abortive leader of a residual revolutionary movement.

When Lenin established Soviet power in the former Russian Empire, he thought not only that he could sever irrevocably the umbilical cord with Russia's past but that he could also rid the new state of traditional Russian goals and purposes in foreign policy. Neither geography, nor history, nor national interests would govern the behaviour of the Soviet state in its relations with the outside world; rather its outlook and conduct would be uniquely and exclusively determined by its self-anointed ideological mission of world revolution as inspired by the doctrines of Marx and Engels. There is little doubt that at first Lenin was genuinely convinced that this was possible and that the new Soviet state could unilaterally unburden itself not only of Tsarist purposes and goals in foreign policy but also of Russia's heritage and culture, could overcome the deterministic influences of its geography, surmount the complex aggregate behaviour patterns of its population (national character), relieve itself of the manifold liabilities and dispel the enmities acquired by its Tsarist predecessor in the pursuit of its aims, and of whatever designs, claims, grievances, and demands Russia's enemies might have against her. All this, however, was more easily asserted than accomplished, for while Lenin could plausibly abjure the goals and purposes of Russia's traditional foreign policy and could selectively retain the fruits of four centuries of Russian expansionism wherever possible, he could not entirely disown the objective consequences of Tsarist diplomacy nor dictate the attitude of other states towards the new regime. Even if the Soviet state refused to remain Russia, Japan remained Japan, Poland remained Poland, Germany remained Germany, the Straits remained the Straits, and Russians remained Russians.

Thus, partly by choice, partly of necessity, and partly against its will, the Soviet state could not but assume many of the contours of its predecessor in foreign policy. This fact served not only to complicate Soviet foreign policy for many decades but also to plunge into seemingly insoluble and futile controversy all discussion and analysis concerning its motivations and nature. Was the Soviet Union motivated by traditional Russian national interests and manipulating revolutionary ideology as an instrument of its national purposes, or was Russia merely the national vehicle for a messianic universalism?

While there is no intention here to rehash the innumerable variations on this theme, ranging from the pathetically simplistic to the inordinately sophisticated, with virtually all possibilities in between, some comment is indispensable. After fifty years, the role of ideology in Soviet foreign policy, as both a source of ends and an instrument of other purposes, emerges more clearly and can now perhaps finally be placed in definitive perspective. Historically, ideology appears as a protean force and influence on Soviet foreign policy behaviour, shaping its eschatological goals operatively rather than operationally, and also as a cognitive and epistemological philosophy, embracing a theory of socio-historical reality, a theory of human nature and behaviour, and a theory of international and interstate behaviour. Instrumentally, ideology has also functioned as a theory or strategy of action, i.e. as a framework for the analysis, mobilisation, and manipulation of social and political power in a variety of conditions and circumstances. It has enabled Soviet leaders to recognise that interstate and intrastate social conflicts, tensions, frustrations, and resentments are potential reservoirs of energy which can be tapped, mobilised, and transmuted into concrete political power subject to the manipulation of Soviet policy. In calculating what the Soviet leaders call the international correlation of forces, internal social forces and the direction of their movement have always assumed an important value in the balance-of-power equation. Furthermore, ideology serves to justify and rationalise Soviet behaviour and the social status quo in the Soviet Union; it serves as the foundation of legitimacy upon which Soviet rule reposes and provides ethical sanction for the extension or intensification of Soviet power.

The relative influence of ideology as a motivating factor in Soviet foreign policy has been indissolubly linked with the utility of the world communist movement as an instrument of Soviet foreign policy. Hypothetically, the Soviet state was merely the creator and advance guard of a wider entity, the international proletariat, but not its directing centre. This was the theory. It simply represented the Russian national section of the international proletariat which had seized power in its own country. Consequently its policies and behaviour were supposed to reflect the interests of the world revolution and the international proletariat, which would be determined by the Comintern and its Executive Committee. Instead of being the master of the Comintern, the Soviet state was supposed to be its instrument. But since the Soviet state was the only communist state in existence and the headquarters of the Comintern could be located only in Moscow, it was inevitable that, as prospects for additional revolutions faded away, the position of the Soviet party would be correspondingly enhanced and its role transformed.

The Soviet state soon assumed an identity and existence of its own, separate yet related to that of the Comintern. As a state, the conditions for survival were sharply different from those of a movement whose existence, independent of state organisation, was still possible. Consequently the Soviet Union gradually assumed the contours of a traditional state operating within a system of states, yet in conflict with it. It assumed a configuration of interests not entirely congruent with those of the revolutionary movement, since the impulse and requirements for survival as a state frequently collided with its obligations as an instrument of the Comintern and the world revolutionary movement.

The entire history of Soviet relationships, first with foreign communist parties, then with communist states, and then with rivals for leadership, has been determined by the two essentially contradictory purposes of either serving the interests of foreign constituencies (world revolution, foreign communist states, China), or responding to the interests of internal constituencies (survival as a state, national interest, Soviet elites). The first purpose necessarily implies self-abnegation since it demands that the interests of the Soviet Union's internal constituencies be subordinated to the interests of external constituencies, while the second is subversive of internationalism, since it gives higher priority to internal needs than to external obligations.

Tension between these two conflicting sets of demands was inevitable and not capable of easy resolution. One purpose was bound to subordinate the other. Either the Soviet state was to become an expendable instrument of the international proletariat, or the Comintern would be reduced to a creature supinely responsive to the demands of the Soviet state. This contradiction was resolved by adjusting the interests and behaviour of the Comintern and foreign communist parties to those of the Soviet state. Comintern interests were thus reshaped and subordinated to Soviet state interests in order to ensure full coordination of action and congruence of interests. This, of course, ran counter to the theory of their relationship, since the interests and behaviour of the Soviet state were supposed to be adjusted to meet the demands and requirements of the Comintern. The orthodox rendition of the Stalinist formula ran as follows:

> The USSR has no interests at variance with the interests of world revolution, and the international proletariat naturally has no interests that are at variance with the Soviet Union.[4]

The basic philosophy justifying this submission to Moscow's control was defined by Stalin as "proletarian internationalism":

> A revolutionary is he who, without evasions, unconditionally, openly, and honestly . . . is ready to uphold and defend the USSR. . . . An internationalist is he who unconditionally, without hesitation and without provisos, is ready to defend the USSR because the USSR is the base of the revolutionary movement, and to defend the advance of this movement is impossible without defending the USSR.[5]

With the installation of communist regimes in the countries of eastern Europe, the Soviet Union was automatically deprived of its unique position as the only communist state, whose ruling proletariat pre-empted the articulation of the class interests of the entire world proletariat languishing in oppression and exploitation in capitalist countries. As long as the Soviet Union was the only communist state, it could be argued that good communists everywhere should display first loyalty to the only fatherland of the proletariat. Loyalty, however, was not founded on the inherent moral superiority or priority of interests of the Soviet proletariat over all others; the international proletariat gave its loyalty to the Soviet Union on the premise that the Soviet Union was the only authentic representative of the class interests of proletarians in all countries. That it was the Russian proletariat which ruled the first

[4] W. K. Knorin, *Fascism, Social Democracy and the Communists* (Moscow, 1933).

[5] J. V. Stalin, *Sochineniya* (Moscow, 1949), X, p. 61.

communist state was historically fortuitous and legitimised neither its moral nor its political superiority.

Stalin, however, extrapolated his meaning of "proletarian internationalism" from the period of "capitalist encirclement" into the period of multiple communist party-states, each with its own ruling proletariat. Proletarian internationalism became, in effect, a device for converting party subservience into state vassalage. Entire countries were subjugated and their interests subordinated to that of the Soviet state. Some satellite leaders, however, demurred and interpreted the Stalinist theory of proletarian internationalism as applicable only to parties in capitalist countries; otherwise it was a philosophical justification for Soviet imperialism and colonialism. The divergence of interests between the Soviet Union and foreign communist parties, particularly those in power, was exemplified by the break with Yugoslavia in 1948, and the potential character of the conflict was discernible when Stalin directed the execution or removal of satellite leaders who betrayed even a faint tendency towards national autonomy — all in the name of proletarian internationalism.

While Stalin's death set the stage for the disintegration of the world communist movement into its constituent state and national parties, ironically enough the underlying cause of the divorce between Soviet interests and those of other communist parties was the rapid growth of Soviet power and capabilities. Hypothetically, this should have brought Soviet ideological goals into closer alignment with policy; but as Soviet power grew, so did the risks and costs of implementing an ideological foreign policy. And as these increased, the general tendency was for Soviet ideological goals to crumble into ritualistic rhetoric, while the growth in Soviet power created greater opportunities and more options for the achievement of traditional great-power goals in foreign policy. Thus as Soviet power has increased to the point where ideological purpose could have been converted into state policy, there has been a corresponding tendency for the costs and risks of converting ideology into policy to escalate as well. As Peking has been quick to point out, the expansion of Soviet capabilities has served to debase some cherished ideological goals into little more than propaganda rhetoric.

In the fourteen years since Stalin's death, the Soviet Union has been forced to adjust itself to changing configurations of interests and power at home, in the communist interstate community, in the world communist movement, and in the international community at large, which has resulted in a fundamental shift of priorities in Soviet foreign policy.

While Stalin subordinated the interests of foreign communist states and parties to the security and foreign policy interests of the Soviet state, he rarely viewed the material prosperity of the Soviet population as a significant factor in coordinating Soviet interests with those of the communist movement. Stalin catered to internal constituencies only to the degree necessary to maximise the effectiveness and power of the state at his command. Once the communist monolith started to disintegrate into its component parts, and external constituencies could articulate their demands upon the Soviet Union to discharge its international ideological obligations in accordance with the theory that the Soviet Union was a servant of the movement and not its master, Stalin's successors, under pressure from their own internal constituencies, altered both the priorities and the theory underlying them, so that in both theory and practice the interests of Soviet social constituencies now assume priority over those of external constituencies.

Not only does the Sino-Soviet dialogue on this point demonstrate how international ideological commitments can be subordinated to internal economic requirements by a developed and an underdeveloped communist state sharing a common ideological commitment; it also illustrates how each perceives its ideological obligations in such a way that their implementation automatically serves the internal interests of the state concerned. Thus, while Moscow asserts that rising Soviet standards of living help to promote world communism, Peking contests this view and argues that the world revolution can best be furthered if the developed communist states postpone their affluence in favour of bolstering up the economies of their deprived communist allies. In either case, it reduces itself to the crude formula "What's good for the Soviet Union (or China) is good for the world revolution." While in the past this formula was applied by Stalin almost entirely in terms of the foreign policy and security needs of the Soviet state as the bastion of the world communist movement, it is only since his death that this formula has been applied to purely domestic economic considerations. To be sure, Moscow insists that raising the standard of living in the Soviet Union strengthens the most powerful state and hence alters the global balance of power in favour of world revolution, psychologically if not militarily; but this proposition is both dubious and transparently self-serving. It also serves to support the Chinese charge that in the face of possible thermonuclear war, the Soviet leaders have lost their revolutionary militancy and may be willing to settle for a status quo which will allow them to divert resources and energies from a counterproductive and dysfunctional policy of revolutionary aggressiveness to improving the standard of living at home and expanding and consolidating the social legitimacy of their power and authority as a great power.

Soviet foreign policy over the past fifty years has thus passed through a succession of distinct phases, each with its characteristic patterns of behaviour shaped in accordance with a changing mix of personalities, perceived interests, ideology, and objective capabilities. A change in one variable has always significantly altered the impact of the others with corresponding reciprocal feedback effects.

When the Bolsheviks seized power and proclaimed eternal war against all capitalist states, the permanent diplomatic isolation of the Soviet state appeared inevitable; yet, during the fifty years of its existence, the Soviet state has achieved diplomatic recognition by a world it was committed to liquidate, has entered into commercial relations with capitalist states, has formed alliances with a variety of bourgeois powers which it earlier condemned as wicked and hostile, joined international organisations which it previously denounced, formed military coalitions with capitalist states against common enemies, divided the spoils of power-politics and conquest, and alienated powers which it previously courted, and wooed states which it had previously condemned or shunned.

While the dictates of Soviet ideology imposed upon the Soviet Union a unique diplomatic unilateralism, the realities of power-politics forced upon it an equally unique dualism: accommodation to an existing system of states which it was dedicated to destroy.

We can demarcate two broad periods in Soviet foreign policy, linked by an overlapping transitional phase, whose basic parameters can be defined in terms of the Soviet Union's relative power position in the world at large and of the balance between capabilities and intentions or demands in foreign policy. The first, which can be described as the period of relative impotence, covers the years 1917–39, during which time Soviet intentions and demands greatly exceeded objective capabilities and Soviet leaders were principally preoccupied with maintaining a balance between their ideological utopianism and the imperatives of survival in a more power hostile environment. This period gradually merged into the second, extending from 1944 to the present, during which time the Soviet Union was transformed from a relatively weak power into a great power, then a super-power, and finally a global power, when its objective capabilities increased to the point where some of its ideological goals were realisable and rhetoric was converted into concrete policy, resulting in the partial transformation of a world communist movement into a communist interstate system. The years 1940–43 (actually the period between the German-Soviet pact and the Red Army's expulsion of the Germans from Soviet territory) were both a transitional phase overlapping the two periods and a watershed dividing them.

Each of these two broad periods passed through a succession of diplomatic stages or phases, dominated by a particular strategy, reflecting the increasingly sophisticated employment of various instruments as Soviet leaders became accustomed to the methods of international politics and diplomacy, in response to changing perceptions of interest, alterations in the balance of power, and shifting opportunities in the international scene.

After 1921, when foreign intervention failed to strangle the new regime and the prospects for communist revolutions elsewhere had faded, Lenin was forced to acknowledge an objectively imposed balance of power between the new Soviet state and the outside world, which Stalin was to conceptualise as the objective strategy of "peaceful coexistence" and to institutionalise as the "dual policy" whereby the Soviet state would accommodate itself to international realities while the Communist Party through the Comintern would simultaneously endeavour to alter them.

The Stalinist image of the world was one of imposed coexistence between a single socialist state and a hostile capitalist environment — a coexistence forced upon both antagonists by objective historical conditions. It was not conceived as a subjective norm of Soviet foreign policy, as many in the West appeared to believe, but rather as a condition which the Soviet Union would have to accept on a temporary basis; since neither side was sufficiently powerful to liquidate the other, they were fated to exist together temporarily on the basis of an unstable and constantly shifting balance of power:

> The fundamental and new, the decisive feature, which has affected all the events in the sphere of foreign relations during this period, is the fact that a certain temporary equilibrium of forces has been established between our country . . . and the countries of the capitalist world; an equilibrium which has determined the present period of "peaceful coexistence."[6]

The temporary equilibrium was not to be upset so long as the Soviet Union was in a weakened condition. War between the two camps was inevitable, but could be temporarily avoided and delayed by astute maneuvering within the conflicts raging in the capitalist world:

> England's attempts to form a united front against the USSR have failed so far. The reasons for this failure are: the antagonisms of interests in the camp of the imperialists. . . . Hence the task of taking into account the antagonisms in the camp of the imperialists, of postponing war by "buying off" the capitalists. . . . We must not forget what Lenin said about very much in our work of construction depending upon whether we succeed in postponing war with the capitalist world, which is inevitable, but which can be postponed either until the moment when the proletarian revolution in Europe matures, or until the moment when the colonial revolutions have fully matured, or lastly, until the moment when the capitalists fight among themselves over the division of the colonies.[7]

During Stalin's lifetime, despite his periodic strictures against "dogmatism," this image of the two-camp world remained remarkably fixed, although the centre of the anti-Soviet conspiracy passed from England to nazi Germany and finally to the United States.

Before the war the Soviet Union sought to maximise its security against the capitalist world while simultaneously seeking to subvert it. Not only did Moscow utilise "contradictions" and conflicts of interest among bourgeois powers in the pursuit of its aims, when it aligned itself with Weimar Germany at Rapallo in 1922, and at Genoa in the same year excited the appetites and competition of capitalist countries with the prospects of a giant Soviet economic market which proved illusory; it also capitalised in its propaganda on the widespread desire for peace and disarmament. Furthermore, it sedulously sought the protection of

    [6] J. V. Stalin, *Political Report of the Central Committee to the 14th Congress of the CPSU* (Moscow, 1950), p. 8.
    [7] J. V. Stalin, *Political Report of the Central Committee to the 15th Congress of the CPSU* (Moscow, 1950), p. 29.

the traditional forms of international law as it pursued diplomatic recognition and negotiated treaties of neutrality, non-intervention, and non-aggression with neighbouring states. Soviet leaders recognised that international law, although bourgeois in inspiration and largely ineffectual, afforded some incremental security value, and they eagerly sought whatever protection it might provide in spite of its obvious marginality. Thus the Soviet Union sought diplomatic recognition, more avid for de jure than de facto, but happy to accept either, and betrayed an unexpected solicitude for the sanctity of international legal norms like "diplomatic immunity," "non-intervention," and "state sovereignty," which she had no real intention of observing at all. After all, these were bourgeois legal norms, and if Bolsheviks had little respect for the legal norms of their ideological and class enemies (which was understandable), this was no reason for bourgeois states to contravene and outrage their own cherished legal and moral precepts; ordinary decency required that their behaviour towards the Soviet Union should be governed accordingly. While under few illusions that capitalist powers would be limited by either moral self-restraint or international law in dealing with Moscow on matters involving vital interests or security, the Soviet leaders recognised that in ordinary conditions international law would probably function as a restraining influence, and the Soviet state would have to be treated as a member of the international community in good standing by those states with whom it had diplomatic relations.

Legal protection was, of course, insufficient as a security shield, and so the Soviet Union searched for limited political arrangements which might enhance her security. Although the Soviet position on international law was the classic status quo posture, in its political attitudes the Soviet regime associated itself with the anti-Versailles or revisionist group of European states, notably Weimar Germany, a fellow international pariah (political rather than ideological), and from 1924 to 1934 Soviet policy was oriented towards Germany. The Rapallo Agreement of 1922 was followed by a neutrality pact in 1926 and supplemented by informal military collaboration. Until 1932, Moscow considered France, Britain, and Poland to be her "immediate" enemies, and thus she automatically associated herself with their potential capitalist adversary, Germany. The Soviet government supported revision of the Versailles Treaty and in general supported the Germans against the victors of the 1914–18 war.

This seemingly idyllic partnership, however, was rudely complicated by Anglo-French diplomacy in the form of the Locarno Treaty (1925), which was designed to prevent German-Soviet collaboration from being converted into a possible anti-Versailles military alliance. By opening up the prospect of satisfying German revisionist demands at the expense of Moscow should the necessity arise, the British and the French provided another possible option to a revitalised Germany. Just as Moscow was utilising Germany's revisionist resentments against the Anglo-French powers (the chief centres of anti-Soviet sentiment), the British and French contrived the Locarno formula, which the Soviet leaders accurately recognised as a potential inducement to Germany to turn East should her appetite for territory become uncontrollable. The western powers would not be predisposed to interfere with the satisfaction of the aspirations in the East, particularly if they served simultaneously to minimise or eradicate the contagion of Bolshevism, if, in return for this demonstration of unconcern for the status quo in the East, the Anglo-French powers received a solemn German renunciation of all territorial claims against the West, thus *politically* reaffirming the legal provisions of the Versailles Treaty in this connection.

Locarno thus impelled the USSR to search for new instruments of security, and once again her resourceful statesmen and diplomats were able to convert bourgeois international law to their own purposes. Since the League of Nations was viewed as an anti-Soviet organisation inspired by the fear of Bolshevism and preserved as the skeletal structure of a future anti-Soviet coalition dominated by the same powers which sought to divert Germany eastward at Locarno, Moscow saw little profit in searching for security in the League. Consequently, Soviet diplomacy entered into a new phase, during which Moscow reinforced whatever protection was afforded by diplomatic recognition by the device of contractual arrangements with neighbouring states which, since they required only passive reciprocal political obligations, would not entangle the Soviet Union in any positive commitments to bourgeois powers. This took the form of concluding a series of neutrality and nonaggression treaties with virtually all her border states and possible sources of aggression. By these treaties the signatories undertook to remain neutral if one of them was involved in war, and to refrain from engaging in or supporting aggression directed at the other party. Since these treaties did not entangle the Soviet Union in positive obligations to capitalist states, the Soviet leaders continued to congratulate themselves on retaining their Bolshevik virtue intact, although it was obvious that this was a further step in the reinvolvement of Russia in the European balance of power. Furthermore, it did serve to counteract Locarno in some degree, since the Soviet Union succeeded, between 1926 and 1932, in negotiating treaties of this character with virtually every neighbouring country, including Germany and Poland, the two potential spearpoints of any future anti-Soviet crusade.

With the advent of the nazi regime in Germany, however, Soviet diplomacy was once again channelled into a new phase.

The revisionism of nazi Germany was as dangerous to France as to Russia, since Hitler openly repudiated the military provisions of the Versailles Treaty, reoccupied the Rhineland, and denounced the Locarno Treaty, signifying his refusal to accept the territorial status quo in the West. Stalin at first refused to take Hitler's anti-Bolshevism seriously, and only reluctantly severed his connections with the principal revisionist power of Europe. But eventually he had to seek a rapprochement with the most powerful bulwark of the status quo on the European continent, France. German revisionism constituted a greater immediate danger to French security than communism, and similarly German expansionist aspirations eastward appeared to be a greater threat to Moscow than the *cordon sanitaire* policy of France. The Franco-Soviet military alliance of 1935 not only signified the resurgence of traditional alignments, based on national interests and not ideology; it also constituted a new and important shift in Soviet strategy. For the first time, the Soviet Union formally allied itself with one bourgeois power against another. Even more fundamentally, this shift in alignment for the first time openly subordinated the interests of world revolution to Soviet security interests as the Comintern was instructed to arrest its revolutionary agitation in bourgeois countries friendly to the Soviet Union and to seek the formation of anti-fascist fronts and popular front governments in alliance with bourgeois parties. In effect, the Soviet Union abandoned a revisionist foreign policy in favour of a temporary support of the status quo.

In 1934 Stalin explained this reversal of policy not only in terms of the German danger; it also reflected outside respect for growing Soviet power:

> Change for the better . . . has taken place recently in the relations between the USSR and Poland and between the USSR and France. As is well known, our relations with Poland in the past were not good. . . . The relations between the USSR and France were no better. . . . What is the cause of this change? . . . Primarily, the growth in the strength and might of the USSR. In our times it is not the custom to give any consideration to the weak — consideration is given only to the strong. Besides, there have been some changes in the policy of Germany which reflect the growth of imperialist and revenge sentiments in Germany.[8]

At the same time, he justified the change almost exclusively in terms of national interest:

> Some German politicians say that the USSR has now taken an orientation towards France and Poland; that from an opponent of the Versailles Treaty it has become a supporter of that treaty, and that this change is to be explained by the establishment of the fascist regime in Germany. That is not true. . . . We never had any orientation towards Germany nor have we any orientation towards Poland and France. Our orientation in the past and our orientation at the present time is towards the USSR, and towards the USSR alone. And if the interests of the USSR demand rapprochement with one country or another . . . we take this step without hesitation.

The underlying significance of the Franco-Soviet alliance, based upon reciprocal opportunism, turned out to be not so much that Moscow had aligned herself with the status quo powers in Europe, but rather that Stalin had decided that Soviet interests could be served no longer by remaining outside the European balance-of-power; but by becoming an active participant in the balance of power. As the Soviet perception and definition of immediate enemies changed, Soviet alignments were correspondingly shifted. This strategy guided Stalin when he was abandoned

[8] J. V. Stalin, *Problems of Leninism* (Moscow, 1947), p. 466.

by France at Munich, and made him ready to ally himself again with the forces of German revisionism in order to divert their energies against his erstwhile status quo partners. In his address to the eighteenth party congress on March 10, 1939, Stalin, in dissecting the motives of Britain and France after Munich, gave a pointed indication of the motives behind the startling reversal of Soviet policy which was to follow five months later with the conclusion of the German-Soviet Pact:

> England and France . . . have taken up . . . the policy of . . . conniving at aggression, giving free reign to . . . an eagerness, a desire . . . not to hinder Japan, say, from embroiling herself in a war . . . with the Soviet Union; not to hinder Germany . . . from embroiling herself in a war with the Soviet Union; to allow all the belligerents to sink deeply into the mire of war, to encourage them surreptitiously in this; to allow them to weaken and exhaust one another; and then, when they have become weak enough, to appear on the scene with fresh strength, to appear, of course, "in the interests of peace," and to dictate conditions to the enfeebled belligerents. Cheap and easy.[9]

When, in the same speech, he accused Britain and France of attempting "to incense the Soviet Union against Germany, to poison the atmosphere, and to provoke a conflict with Germany without any visible grounds," he threw a broad hint to Germany that Moscow was not averse to an arrangement which might prove mutually beneficial. "It can now be seen," Molotov reported after the Pact was signed, "that on the whole Germany correctly understood these statements of Stalin and drew practical conclusions from them." Molotov's justification of the Pact is an almost classic formulation of the motives underlying Soviet foreign policy:

> France and Great Britain . . . had shown that the conclusion of a pact of mutual assistance could not be expected, [and] we could not but explore together possibilities of ensuring peace and eliminating the danger of war between Germany and the USSR. If the British and French governments refused to reckon with this that is their affair. It is our duty to think of the interests of the Soviet people, the interests of the Union of Soviet Socialist Republics. All the more since we are convinced that the interests of the USSR coincide with the fundamental interests of the peoples of all countries. . . . Is it really difficult for these gentlemen to understand the purpose of the Soviet-German Non-Aggression Pact, on the strength of which the USSR is not obligated to involve itself in war either on the side of Great Britain against Germany or on the side of Germany against Britain? Is it really difficult to understand that the USSR is pursuing and will continue to pursue its own independent policy, based on the interests of the peoples of the USSR and only their interests?[10]

The identical principle governed Soviet participation in the Grand Coalition during the second world war, although Stalin at first expected the

---

[9] Ibid., p. 602.
[10] Text of Molotov's speech in *Strategy and Tactics of World Communism* (Washington, D.C., GPO, 1948), p. 160.

Western powers to stand aside to watch the two totalitarian giants engage in a battle of mutual annihilation. It should have come as no surprise then that after the war Moscow's wartime allies were suddenly transformed into "immediate" enemies, and the Stalinist two-camp image of the world was resurrected with renewed conviction. But now the Soviet Union was moving from a position of power and not weakness, and the identical principle yielded not only diplomatic gains but ideological ones as well, as Soviet capabilities were brought into closer alignment with Soviet intentions. A system of vassal communist states was established in eastern Europe, while in the Far East a communist regime was installed in North Korea and opportunities were created for the assumption of power by Mao Tse-tung and the Chinese Communist Party, although the rapidity and extent of Mao's victory may have surprised Stalin and were not entirely in harmony with Soviet interests.

Stalin's post-war policy assumed an inevitable conflict with the West, mobilised by the United States. The organisation of the Cominform and the forced unity of the communist orbit, the expulsion of Tito from the communist fraternity, the extraction of public statements of loyalty from communist leaders in all countries, the urgency with which Stalin sought to eliminate all possible power vacuums between the two blocs along the periphery of the communist world were all preparatory measures based on the false assumption that Washington was preparing the final Armageddon. At the founding convention of the Cominform, Zhdanov gave an authoritative Soviet interpretation of the emerging bipolarisation of power:

> The fundamental changes caused by the war on the international scene and in the position of individual countries have entirely changed the political landscape of the world. A new alignment of political forces has arisen. The more the war recedes into the past, the more distinct become two major trends in post-war international policy, corresponding to the division of the political forces operating on the international arena into two major camps; the imperialist and anti-democratic camp, on the one hand, and the anti-imperialist and democratic camp, on the other. The principal driving force of the imperialist camp is the USA. . . . The cardinal purpose of the imperialist camp is to strengthen imperialism, to hatch a new imperialist war, to combat socialism.[11]

Based on this grim image of imminent conflict, Soviet foreign policy became increasingly bellicose, which naturally provoked the belief in the West that the Soviet Union was itself preparing to overrun western Europe and all of Asia. Friction along the entire periphery dividing the two worlds was frequent and finally erupted in the Korean War, when Stalin sanctioned the move into South Korea on the assumption that it had become a vacuum between the two blocs. This accelerated defensive preparations in the West, and Stalin's policies, by predicting the increasing hostility of the West, actually ensured its materialisation.

During the Korean War and just before the nineteenth party

[11] *Strategy and Tactics*, p. 216.

congress in 1952, a debate had apparently taken place in the Politburo concerning the validity of the expectation of imminent war between the two camps. Two essentially divergent views were discussed by Stalin in his *Economic Problems of Socialism:* (1) That wars between capitalist countries had ceased to be inevitable and hence war between the two camps imminent, the view then current; and (2) that wars between capitalist states remained inevitable, but that war between the two camps was unlikely. Although the first view was the basis of Soviet postwar policy, Stalin ascribed it to "mistaken comrades," and elevated the second to doctrinal significance:

> Some comrades hold that, owing to the development of new international conditions since the second world war, wars between the capitalist countries have ceased to be inevitable. They consider . . . that the USA has brought the other capitalist countries sufficiently under its sway to be able to prevent them going to war among themselves and . . . that the foremost capitalist minds have been sufficiently taught by the two world wars . . . not to involve the capitalist countries in war with one another again. . . . It is said that the contradictions between capitalism and socialism are stronger than the contradictions among the capitalist countries. Theoretically, of course, that is true. It is not only true now, today; it was true before the second world war. . . . Yet the second world war began not as a war with the USSR, but as a war between capitalist countries. Why? . . . because war with the USSR, as a socialist land, is more dangerous to capitalism than war between capitalist countries; for whereas war between capitalist countries puts in question only the supremacy of certain capitalist countries over others, war with the USSR must certainly put in question the existence of capitalism itself. . . . It is said that Lenin's thesis that imperialism inevitably generates war must now be regarded as obsolete. . . . To eliminate the inevitability of war, it is necessary to abolish imperialism.[12]

Stalin's only modification of the two-camp image was thus to concede that imminent war between the two blocs was no longer inevitable, but would first be preceded by a series of inevitable wars among the capitalist powers themselves.

If it was Stalin who transformed the Soviet Union into a great power, it was under Khrushchev that Soviet Russia was transformed into a global power, directly challenging the United States for paramountcy and unilaterally claiming the right to intervene in any part of the world to assert an interest and influence developments. Stalin pursued essentially a cautious continental policy, oriented towards the communisation, first of the Soviet periphery and then of the new geographical periphery of the expanded communist bloc, relying on direct physical contiguity and the concentrically radiating expansion of communism from the Soviet base. The experience of the Hungarian Soviet Republic and other geographically isolated attempts to establish com-

[12] J. V. Stalin, *Economic Problems of Socialism* (New York, 1952), pp. 27–30.

munist regimes after the 1914–18 war convinced Stalin that the capitalist world would never tolerate an isolated communist state in its midst; it would be crushed through internal subversion or direct assault.

Stalin was loath to overcommit the Soviet Union militarily, politically, or ideologically, and was reluctant to burden himself with obligations which he could not or preferred not to fulfil. This may explain his refusal to assume a legal obligation to defend Albania, which after 1948 was separated from the rest of the Communist bloc by Yugoslavia's defection and hence was exposed to attack or subversion. Only with the creation of the Warsaw Pact in 1955 did Albania come under formal Soviet military and political protection. Similarly, Stalin abjured any legal commitments to North Korea and North Vietnam, both of which were parts of divided states and hence susceptible to involvement. It was apparently Stalin's design that as the communist periphery was gradually expanded outward from the centre, all communist states would be territorially adjacent to at least one other communist state. In the meantime, communist parties in non-contiguous countries would be supported and encouraged until the movement of the communist periphery to their borders created the possibility of their transformation into communist states.

Khrushchev, on the other hand, broke out of the shell in which Soviet diplomacy had been encapsulated and embarked upon a bold global strategy of reaching out over oceans and continents in search not only of possible recruits to the communist bloc but of diplomatic client states as well in any part of the world. Whereas Stalin divided the world into two hostile camps and worked largely through local communist parties, Khrushchev carved a generous "zone of peace" out of the capitalist camp as the immediate object of Soviet diplomacy. Consisting largely of underdeveloped, newly emancipated countries, strongly influenced by the Leninist theory of imperialism and predisposed to socialism of various national hues, the countries in the "zone of peace" were perceived by Khrushchev as intrinsically anti-imperialist, anti-capitalist, and hence anti-western, rather than as bogus appendages of the capitalist camp.

Khrushchev's global strategy, pursued in the wake of Soviet space spectaculars which he tried to transform into military power, was designed to breach the non-communist world at its vulnerable points all along the "zone of peace" — in the Middle East, Southeast Asia, Africa, and even Latin America. In the process, Soviet foreign policy was largely, but not entirely, de-ideologised, since the maximisation of possible diplomatic gains in the non-communist world dictated a minimisation and dilution of the ideological content of Soviet foreign policy. Ultimately this was self-defeating, although advantageous momentarily, since it entailed the abandonment of certain foreign policy strategies associated with Moscow for decades. It meant, in some instances, sacrificing the future of local communist parties in return for diplomatic gains in the third world; it also meant the diversion of scarce resources from internal development and allied communist countries to seduce the newly independent countries of Asia and Africa with economic bribes; it meant the assumption of new risks, costs, and burdens in areas far removed from the centres of communist power and vulnerable to American sea and air power. For a time Khrushchev capitalised on the alleged "missile gap" to unfurl a protective nuclear-missile umbrella over the three continents of Asia, Africa, and Latin America, in the mistaken conviction that the United States could be deterred or dissuaded from resisting Soviet policy or local shifts of power promoted or encouraged by the Soviet Union.

While Khrushchev transformed the Soviet Union into a global power, he did it at the expense of weakening Soviet control in its own sphere, alienating Moscow's strongest ally, China, overcommitting the power and resources of the Soviet Union, and increasing the danger of thermonuclear war by his persistent prodding and probing of weak spots in the western world and forcing the United States into a series of confrontations, in the hope that this would result in the settlement of outstanding issues on Soviet terms and force the United States to withdraw from exposed positions. The Suez crisis of 1956, the Middle East crisis of 1958, the spasmodic Berlin crisis of 1958–61, and finally the Cuban missile crisis of 1962 were either manifestations or consequences of Soviet risk-taking in foreign policy in pursuit of substantial diplomatic gains.

It was also Khrushchev's fate to preside over the breakdown of the Sino-Soviet alliance, the disintegration of the Soviet bloc, and the dissolution of the world communist movement into captious states and fractious parties, unable to reconstruct a new consensus.

By denouncing Stalin, Khrushchev simultaneously, but unwittingly, shattered the foundations of Soviet ideological hegemony — the myths of Soviet moral superiority and doctrinal infallibility on which rested the Soviet claim to priority on the political loyalty of all communists and communist parties, and on the resources of communist states. By demolishing the "cult of Stalin," Khrushchev inadvertently unleashed tremendous convulsive reactions in eastern Europe and provoked the wrath of the Chinese leadership; the virtual dissolution of the Soviet bloc and the Sino-Soviet conflict followed within a few years.

While the condemnation of the Stalin cult resulted in profound changes in Soviet relations with communist states and parties, it was Khrushchev's repudiation of certain specific doctrinal formulations associated with Stalin (and Lenin in some instances) which was to have profound consequences for Soviet foreign policy. By renouncing the Leninist-Stalinist thesis on the "fatal inevitability of wars," Khrushchev jettisoned the suicidal implications of a formula whose grotesque self-fulfilling properties inspired terror in friend and foe alike, since the inevitability of war between East and West in the thermonuclear age promised not the inevitable victory of world communism but the inevitability of coextinction. By dismantling the Stalinist two-camp image and interposing a broad "zone of peace" between the capitalist and communist worlds, Khrushchev not only introduced a convenient buffer between two contending giants but also freed Soviet diplomacy from the dogmatic restraints of the Stalinist dictum that all non-communist states were by definition part of the capitalist camp and hence to be treated as enemies rather than potential friends or allies. By renouncing the doctrine of "capitalist encirclement," Khrushchev not only demolished the main ideological prop justifying the preservation of the apparatus of terror at home but also dispelled the psychological atmosphere of a Soviet state besieged on all sides by powerful enemies intent upon its annihilation. The renunciation of this doctrine enabled the Soviet Union to adopt a normal diplomatic posture although it served simultaneously to dilute its ideological content. Khrushchev thus sought to free the Soviet Union from its psychological self-encirclement so that it might, in turn, forge an encirclement of the remaining bastions of world capitalism, whose territorial and demographic dimensions had been substantially diminished by the loss of the "zone of peace."

Khrushchev's repudiation of another Stalinist concept, the doctrine of the progressive "intensification of the class struggle" as the final victory of communism drew nearer, also had important implications for Soviet foreign policy. Extrapolated onto the world scene, this doctrine dictated the progressive aggravation of relations between the two camps and the exacerbation of international tensions generally. Its renunciation enabled Khrushchev to de-dogmatise Soviet diplomacy, redefine "peaceful coexistence," and elevate it to doctrinal significance as something approximating a policy norm of Soviet foreign policy rather than an objective description of an unwanted equilibrium. The substantive meaning of peaceful coexistence, however, remains indeterminate and this absence of precision probably reflects disagreement among the Soviet leaders as to its precise contemporary ideological significance. What is clear is that the Stalinist concept of peaceful coexistence has been disavowed, and while it may not accord in all particulars to the Chinese charge that the new Soviet concept is indistinguishable from a rationalised acceptance of the international status quo, in some respects Soviet behaviour corresponds to the Chinese accusations.

Khrushchev's global strategies were marked by serious contradictions, ambivalent goals, blatant opportunism, inept execution, and frequent adventurist excursions bordering on the irrational. For over a decade he alternated threats and blandishments, militancy and diffidence, responsible behaviour and irresponsibility, decorum and outrageous personal conduct. This ambivalence, while apparent in Khrushchev's personal idiosyncrasies, actually reflected the increasing difficulty of choosing between the Soviet Union's role as a responsible global power, dictated by the objective conditions of its industrial and technological maturation, and its role as an agency of messianic revolution.

Increasingly, Soviet ideological responsibilities to its communist allies and the world communist movement come into conflict with its responsibilities and interests as the second most powerful state in the international community. As a global power with proclaimed rights and responsibilities all over the world based upon its objective capabilities rather than upon the moral force of its ideology, to behave as the centre of a messianic movement would automatically limit the influence of the Soviet Union in areas where Soviet ideology is unwelcome. It should be noted, however, that at many points the role of the Soviet Union in the world communist system merges harmoniously with its self-assumed role in the general international system, particularly in its support of revolutionary movements and regimes in underdeveloped areas; occasionally they also collide, as the relations between the Soviet Union and radical nationalist regimes in Egypt, Indonesia, Guinea, Algeria, and elsewhere have demonstrated.

This dual role calls for both conflict and cooperation with the United States; conflict as the residuary leader of the communist movement ostensibly still seeking to universalise itself, and cooperation as a partner-rival in the general international scene, where it seeks to relax international tensions. This cooperation not only gives greater physical security but also enables greater attention to be given to domestic needs. On the other hand, it involves the possible sacrifice of the interests of some of its allies (China, Cuba, North Vietnam), and the postponement or abandonment of some of its diplomatic and ideological objectives in foreign policy.

To minimise these conflicts, Soviet leaders have devised surrogates for the obligations to the world communist movement which they have deferred or renounced. They are providing greater material assistance to communist countries, are allowing, tolerating, or acquiescing in the assertion of greater autonomy in external and internal affairs on the parts of its east European allies, and in the underdeveloped countries they are supporting a variety of revolutionary-nationalist regimes and movements, frequently to the detriment of local communist parties, who are left to their own devices. This has created a gap, that the Chinese are trying to exploit, between the Soviet-supported nationalist regimes and the more radical guerrilla communists in many underdeveloped countries. As a global power the Soviet Union seeks client states of all political hues; as the residuary centre of a revolutionary movement, it welcomes ideological adherents. In an effort to merge these two objectives, Moscow hopes to attract the radical nationalist regimes into the Soviet diplomatic orbit and then guide their "ethnic" brands of socialism in a Soviet direction through the conversion from above of radical nationalist regimes into communist regimes.

The emergence of the Soviet Union as a thermonuclear-missile power with global interests and responsibilities transcending ideological allegiances and rivalries, the resurgence of national autonomy in the communist system, the appearance of China as a national threat to Russia and ideological rival to the Soviet Union, and the fear of thermonuclear annihilation have combined to give the Soviet Union a greater interest in maintaining the status quo than in attempting to alter it in its favour by pursuing high-risk policies, whether ideologically inspired or not. There is a certain pathos and more than a grain of truth in the

Chinese charge that the fear of thermonuclear annihilation, given the ingrained Bolshevik instinct for survival first implanted by Lenin at Brest-Litovsk in 1918, has become the principal animating force of the Soviet leadership:

> The Soviet leaders seek only to preserve themselves and would let other people sink or swim. They have repeatedly said that so long as they themselves survive and develop, the people of the world will be saved. The fact is they are selling out the fundamental interests of the people of the world in order to seek their own momentary ease.[13]

The avoidance of thermonuclear war, which was established by Khrushchev as the highest priority item in Soviet foreign policy, thus continues to have top priority under his successors, and this almost automatically impels the Soviet Union to minimise its confrontations with the United States. The recent Middle East crisis was a striking illustration of this.

[13] Chinese statement of August 15, 1963, *Peking Review*, August 16, 1963.

2. SOVIET DIPLOMACY: G. V. CHICHERIN, PEOPLES COMMISSAR FOR FOREIGN AFFAIRS, 1918–1930

Theodore H. Von Laue

In 1923, five years after the humiliating treaty of Brest-Litovsk, the government of Soviet Russia, according to its new federal constitution, considered itself the nucleus of a global association of Soviet socialist republics. To an observer unencumbered by ideology and judging international relations by prewar standards, the millennial goal of the new regime might have seemed preposterous. With the resources of imperial Russia, which had been so recently found wanting and which were further reduced by loss of territory and civil war, the Bolsheviks tried to sustain a political ambition far exceeding the boldest aspirations of the Tsars. The discrepancy between a weakness so recently demonstrated and an ambition so boldly proclaimed would have forever discredited the Soviet leaders, had they not developed, at ferocious cost, two novel sources of power: a totalitarian dictatorship to expand Russia's military and industrial potential; and a totalitarian type of foreign relations. This chapter cannot deal with the type of arrangements that mobilized Russia's internal resources as never before. What matters here is that with their new plenitude of controls the Bolshevik leaders were able to manipulate every phase of the relations between Soviet Russia and the outside world; they could fit every point of contact

Reprinted from Gordon A. Craig and Felix Gilbert, editors, *The Diplomats 1919–1939* (Copyright 1953 by Princeton University Press). Reprinted by permission of Princeton University Press.

between Soviet citizens and foreign nationals into their central scheme of foreign relations. The new regime thus evolved an armory of foreign policy instruments exceptionally complete for that time. It had at its disposal the Comintern, Profintern, the secret police and military intelligence, as well as the traditional channels of diplomacy, the foreign trade agencies, the Society for Cultural Relations with Foreign Countries (VOKS), Intourist, and a host of other organs. This multitude and variety of agencies with contacts abroad helped Soviet foreign policy to offset the weakness of Soviet Russia and gave the Soviet impact on other countries an unusual intensity. Through these channels the Bolsheviks made bold to transmit their techniques of class warfare and social disintegration into the struggle between states. And by the example of their intentions, properly interpreted by Bolshevik ideology, they also claimed the leadership of all "progressive" causes. In short, they arrogated to their rule as universal a significance as was implicit in the cultural preeminence of the Great Powers of the West; and, in doing so, they issued a profound challenge to the world order inherited from the nineteenth century.

It was understandable that the role of diplomacy, the traditional tool of international relations, should be changed under an avowedly revolutionary regime, for it found itself in an alien milieu. In the competition for power, in which the Bolsheviks, after their revolution, joined with such seemingly unlimited aims, diplomacy had to accommodate itself to an inferior role. It was the tragedy of Chicherin, who assumed the post of Peoples Commissar for Foreign Affairs after Trotsky's resignation in March 1918 and who carried the burden of office longer than any contemporary Foreign Minister, that he was placed in the center of the turbulent confluence of diplomacy and social revolution. In order to be intelligible, Soviet diplomacy, and Chicherin's role in it, must therefore be viewed not in isolation but as a fragment, and a rather unrepresentative one, of Bolshevik policy in world affairs. This [paper] will deal, above all, with the relationship between the two seemingly discordant instruments of Bolshevik foreign relations, between diplomacy and revolution, leaving out the other less important agencies of policy and treating the main lines of Soviet foreign policy proper in a necessarily summary fashion.

I.

Strictly speaking, Soviet diplomacy did not begin with Chicherin, but with Trotsky; and Trotsky began by abolishing diplomacy. Named Peoples Commissar for Foreign Affairs after the seizure of power, he took an optimistic view of his tasks at the Foreign Office, now renamed Peoples Commissariat for Foreign Affairs (Narkomindel): "I will issue some revolutionary proclamations to the peoples and then close up the joint."[1] Admittedly, he exaggerated, but not without reason.

[1] L. Trotsky, *Mein Leben* (Berlin, 1930), p. 327. See also Lenin's startled comment: "What, are we going to have foreign relations?" Ibid.

Diplomacy — if one may extend Trotsky's unspoken thought — was part of the capitalist superstructure, like the national state. The revolutionaries of all countries would know how to deal more simply and honestly among themselves; and the advanced national states, now locked in ferocious imperialist war, would disappear in the world revolution which had begun in Petrograd. What was needed most at this historic moment in the foreign relations of the new regime were stimulants to set the sluggish masses of Europe and the European dependencies throughout the world into revolutionary motion, primarily to assist in the revolution at home, and perhaps, in a series of chain reactions, to spread and even complete the world revolution.

From the first, Bolshevik foreign policy aimed at world revolution. Asked early in the world war what he would do if he should come to power, Lenin gave the daring answer: "We would propose peace to all the belligerents, the liberation of all colonies and all dependencies, all the oppressed, and those peoples who do not have equal rights. Neither Germany nor England and France would accept these conditions with their present governments. Then we would have to prepare and conduct a revolutionary war: i.e. not only would we carry through our whole minimum program with decisive means, but we would at once systematically start to incite rebellion among all the peoples now oppressed by the Great Russians, all the colonies and dependent countries of Asia (India, China, Persia, and others). And we would also raise in rebellion the socialist proletariat of Europe against their governments. . . . There is no doubt that the victory of the proletariat in Russia would create very favorable conditions for the development of the revolution in Asia and Europe."[2]

Having seized power in Petrograd, Lenin proceeded at once to put that master strategy into effect. The opening act of the new regime was its Proclamation on Peace, the starting-point of Soviet foreign relations, which outlined a revolution in international relations no less drastic than that accomplished in civil society. First of all, by its peace proposal the Bolshevik regime eliminated itself from the traditional European system. As a socialist government, it considered itself outside the pale of "capitalist" nations. Bent upon liquidating the most Westernized elements in its population (and later, by the same token, in the Bolshevik party), and following an ideology which, in strict theory at least, permitted no dealings with "capitalism," Soviet Russia lapsed into profound isolation. A citadel of suspicion and hostility, she lived henceforth as though in a different world, which remained obscure to the outside and, in turn, permitted only a distorted picture of the alien realities of Western democracy. Secondly, in calling for world revolution, Lenin's Proclamation on Peace envisaged a global, rather than a European, system of international politics. Although, in its special appeal to the workers of England, France, and Germany, it obliquely recognized the traditional preponderance of Europe, it counted more on the nationalist

---

[2] Quoted from D. Shub, *Lenin* (New York, 1948), p. 144.

and anti-Western stirrings of the non-European, and particularly the Asiatic, world; for the new regime was dedicated to the overthrow of the global balance of power inherited from the nineteenth century. Finally, in preferring revolutionary agitation to traditional diplomacy, Lenin's Proclamation introduced a new dimension into the field of power politics, the dimension of social revolution. What was the use of armament factories, of imposing armies and navies, and of strategic strongpoints, if the social structure was crumbling underneath them? Thus, cohesion again took its place as a factor of political power, and subversion became a potent weapon of power politics. As for the Bolsheviks, who in the months after November 1917 commanded practically none of the traditional weapons, revolutionary agitation was almost the sole effective instrument at their disposal. Besides, from their own upbringing, it was one especially dear to them; they were superior to all statesmen of the liberal tradition in handling it. Circumstances in due time apprenticed them in the use of the traditional tools as well, even of diplomacy; but to this day revolutionary agitations remain closest to the revolutionary core of the party.

The attempts which Lenin made before the foundation of the Communist International to exploit war-born and war-nurtured unrest in Europe and Asia may be studied in Merle Fainsod's *International Socialism during the War*. With the formation of the Comintern in March 1919, the preliminary, experimental phase of these efforts was ended. Henceforth, revolutionary agitation became institutionalized as a permanent feature of Soviet foreign relations. To be sure, the Comintern, with its related agencies, was not a flawless tool of Soviet policy; it could not be as freely wielded as was sometimes assumed. But, at a time when they possessed few other resources, it brought great advantages to the Soviet leaders. Through it, they could extend the techniques of revolutionary agitation into the realm of international relations. The conditions for admission into the Comintern were such as to mold its members in the Bolshevik pattern. They were ordered to establish an underground organization beside their legal party apparatus and to infiltrate not only into every proletarian organization but also into the armed forces of their country. And above all, they were commanded to observe Bolshevik discipline, which made them subject to the decisions of the Comintern Executive, dominated in turn by the Russian Communists. Lenin himself was the chief Russian delegate; Trotsky, Bukharin, and Zinoviev were his associates on the Executive Committee.[3] This revolutionary organization, which soon had its own information service and intelligence center in Moscow, followed closely Lenin's original aim: the immediate preparation for the dictatorship of the proletariat.

[3] The close ties between the Comintern and the Politburo were inadvertently revealed by Zinoviev at the Twelfth Party Congress, when he spoke of immediate consultation with the Politburo on a matter of Comintern policy. See P. Miliukov, *La Politique Extérieure des Soviets* (2nd ed., Paris, 1935), p. 135.

In the center of that struggle, as the guiding policy of the Comintern stated,[4] stood the Soviet Republic. It was surrounded and protected by the proletarian vanguard of all countries and the liberation movements of the colonial and suppressed peoples — the revolutionary *glacis*. Beyond lay the hostile capitalist world, doomed by the very laws of its existence to be reborn into Soviet socialist society. It was the task of the Comintern to hasten the dialectical development, with the active assistance of the Soviet Republic. How far that active assistance might go was made clear by events. In March 1919 Lenin dispatched troops to help Bela Kun, although he had to recall them almost immediately because of the advance of Denikin's White Armies; and in the following year, during the offensive against Poland, he undertook to "break the crust of the Polish bourgeoisie with the bayonet." Soviet Russia's weakness again interfered, and for the next two decades its revolutionary agitation abroad was carried forward with minimum effort and without the active assistance of the Red army. But, according to the main strand of Bolshevik theory, revolutionary war remained part of the revolutionary outward thrust, as it was part of the domestic attack. As Stalin expressed it in 1924: "The victorious proletariat of one country should stand up against the remaining capitalist world, attracting to itself the oppressed classes of other countries, raising revolts in those countries against the capitalists, in the event of necessity coming out even with armed force against the exploiting class and their governments."[5]

The policies of the Soviet regime or its novel techniques of agitation and organization within the framework of the Comintern may be studied elsewhere. The record is clear: between 1919 and 1930 Soviet domination increased until it amounted to tightest possible control. Through the far-flung activities of international communism, the Politburo manipulated to a considerable extent the revolutionary forces of Europe and Asia in order to suit its own ends according to its interpretation of world affairs. Through the Communist parties it reached into the center of domestic politics in other countries where, at least in the recent history of the sovereign state, no foreign Power had ventured in such strength.

But while the Bolsheviks perfected their revolutionary instruments of foreign relations, they were confronted with new situations in which these instruments were patently inadequate, or even harmful to their interests. Even at the time of the foundation of the Comintern, revolutionary agitation, in which Trotsky had put such hope, had ceased to be the sole tool of Soviet foreign relations. What, in the eyes of the faithful, had been intended to do away permanently with power politics had become merely another dimension of the same old evil. For, contrary to Trotsky's prediction, the Narkomindel had not yet closed shop. Almost

[4] Lenin, "Theses on the Nationality and Colonial Question," submitted at the Second Comintern Congress, July 1920.
[5] In "The October Revolution and the Tactics of the Russian Communists," quoted by Historicus, "Stalin on Revolution," *Foreign Affairs*, January 1949.

from the beginning, its diplomatic activities were expanding, with aims that were eventually to differ radically from those of the Comintern. Diplomacy, indeed, had been implicit in Lenin's Peace Proclamation (which, in regard to the relation between revolution and diplomacy, maintained a revealing ambiguity). And when the Central Powers, who alone among the belligerents had accepted the Soviet proposal for peace negotiations, pressed home their ruthless terms, and when the German revolution did not come to the rescue, the Bolshevik leaders were forced to resort to the traditional forms of international relations. "The given relation of forces in the world arena," read a party resolution of March 1918, left no choice except negotiating with the Central Powers and signing the Treaty of Brest-Litovsk. In its precarious position, both at home and abroad, the Soviet government was thus compelled to recognize the existence of capitalist governments and to adapt itself, for the time being, to the conditions of capitalist encirclement. While the international revolutionary movement gained momentum, with active Soviet assistance but still far too slowly, "we must . . . stick to our tactics of waiting," Lenin reported to the party on May 14, 1918, "taking advantage of the conflict and antagonisms among the imperialists and of slowly accumulating strength. . . ." He promised "everything diplomacy can do," in the execution of that policy. On July 4, 1918, before the Fifth All-Russian Congress of Soviets, Chicherin reported on the new situation in yet greater detail. After the revolutionary offensive which had followed immediately upon the seizure of power, he explained, a radical change had come over Soviet policy. It was now on the defensive, trying to gain time while the international revolution matured and Soviet institutions took hold at home. There were certain assets upon which Soviet foreign policy could draw: the split among the capitalist Powers just then fighting the fiercest battles of the war, and disagreements within each capitalist Power between military and industrial groups, and between those who favored intervention in order to restore the Russian front and those who wanted thereby to overthrow the Bolshevik regime. Bolshevik diplomacy, he claimed, had already been maneuvering among these forces.

The record of Soviet diplomacy in the two years after the seizure of power (which need not be told here) substantiated Chicherin's analysis.[6] But, of course, while there was still a chance for a White victory in the civil war, Soviet diplomacy could make little headway among the "capitalist" Powers. The only direction in which it could move with greater assurance was Asia. But even on that continent, its actions were rather in the nature of gestures; and, despite their enthusiastic recep-

[6] The length to which Soviet diplomacy would go in this period in order to attract attention and aid might be seen in Litvinov's and Vorovskii's letter to the Norwegian lawyer Ludwig Meyer, in which they offered the reinstatement of the political emigrés, reconsideration of the repudiation of the Tsarist debt, and cessation of all propaganda. These promises, needless to say, would never have been honored by Lenin. See Jane Degras, ed., *Soviet Documents on Foreign Policy* (London, Royal Institute of International Affairs, 1951), I, 133.

tion, particularly in China, they brought no immediate relief to the hard-pressed Soviet regime. The full opportunity for Soviet diplomacy inevitably lay in the West.

When at last in 1920 the struggle between the White armies assisted by foreign intervention and the Bolshevik outward thrust for revolutionary penetration had been fought to a stalemate, Soviet diplomacy came into its own. Peaceful coexistence between capitalism and socialism, proclaimed by the Narkomindel long before capitalist stabilization was conceded by the Comintern, demanded machinery for formal relations. The New Economic Policy, a reluctant retreat on the home front, called even for capitalist assistance in the construction of socialism in Soviet Russia. At the Genoa Economic Conference in April 1922 (a time of famine in Russia), the Soviet delegation, headed by Chicherin, officially made its debut in European diplomatic circles. The old-time diplomats noticed with pleasure that the Soviet representatives, in frock coats and striped trousers, behaved exactly as diplomats were expected to behave. Chicherin even went to a royal reception and exchanged toasts with an archbishop. Henceforth, Soviet diplomats became known as sticklers for diplomatic etiquette.

Soviet diplomacy, indeed, had come a long way in the five years since Trotsky's casual repudiation of diplomacy. It now occupied a legitimate place in the Soviet scheme of government, helping the revolutionary regime to adjust itself to its capitalist environment and even to derive a limited benefit from it. On this unrevolutionary plane of its policy, the Soviet republic was merely one state among others. It had to be informed of the plans of other governments so as to know how to cope with their presumably hostile designs, to exploit their separate needs, and to support within each of them the groups most favorable to itself. For that reason it had to maintain normal relations, and to cultivate at least a minimum of goodwill. Thus, by the logic of survival in a capitalist world, diplomacy was foisted upon a revolutionary regime. But it was tainted from the start with defense, retreat, concessions, insincerity, and the weakness of revolutionary Russia in general.[7]

II.

Needless to say, in the process of evolution these two almost antithetical planes of Soviet policy — the revolutionary one close to the Bolshevik core and the more peripheral one of diplomacy — became only gradually differentiated. At the very beginning, of course, diplomacy and revolutionary agitation were almost indistinguishable. Even after Trotsky's resignation, the Narkomindel, barred from formal relations with other governments, continued in his spirit. It was the first Foreign Office to put the "new diplomacy" into effect. All diplomatic

[7] One can detect a defensive note even in Chicherin's formal and informal analyses of Soviet diplomacy. Particularly in the early years he constantly stressed the complexity of international relations, as if to justify his work as a necessary and autonomous field of government activity.

correspondence was conducted in the open with an eye to its publicity value both in revolutionary and nonrevolutionary circles. In July 1918 Chicherin frankly admitted that assistance to non-Russian revolutionary movements was a recognized function of revolutionary diplomacy,[8] and in the following January the invitation to the first Congress of the Comintern went out through his Commissariat; moreover, he attended it in person. In his more strictly diplomatic utterances he tried to mobilize Western labor unions over the heads of their governments on behalf of Soviet interests. In the inner councils of the Narkomindel he, Karakhan (its eastern expert), and Radek functioned as a triumvirate, joined for a time by Kamenev. Radek was in charge of the central European department, whose main function consisted of agitation among German prisoners of war; he founded the Karl Liebknecht brigade from their ranks. But, as a brilliant journalist, Radek was also the commissariat's chief publicist. Only later, when diplomacy and revolution had become divorced, did he drift into work with the Comintern in order to stay nearer the center of revolutionary power. (He remained, however, always closer to diplomacy than Zinoviev.) Among the Soviet plenipotentiaries abroad the identity of revolutionary action and diplomacy was still more prominent. Joffe, who was sent to Germany after the Treaty of Brest-Litovsk, at once formed close relations with the Independent Socialists and worked to the utmost to strengthen the revolutionary movement. A few days before the revolution in Germany he was expelled for his machinations — his baggage had burst open (not entirely by accident) in a Berlin railway station and was found stuffed with revolutionary propaganda. Lenin at the time fully conceded that the Soviet embassy in Berlin was "a carrier of the revolutionary contagion";[9] and Chicherin, in his annual report to the Seventh All-Russian Congress of Soviets in December 1919 commented upon the incident in a telling formulation, saying that "the rising revolutionary wave in Germany [had] gradually forced the technical diplomatic work into the background."[10]

Even the very paraphernalia of diplomacy were affected by the original association with revolution. The first Soviet delegation to the Brest-Litovsk negotiations was distinguished by the presence of a worker, a peasant, and a soldier; the proletarian touch was even preserved, although in a far more dignified manner and for more concrete reasons as well, in the Genoa delegations which contained top repre-

[8] Quoted by Bruce Hopper, "Narkomindel and Comintern," *Foreign Affairs,* July 1941. Chicherin had told Bruce Lockhart already in the spring of 1918 of the coming Third International.

[9] Speech on the anniversary of the October Revolution, November 6, 1918; also the following day before the Extraordinary All-Russian Congress of Soviets.

[10] Quoted by T. A. Taracouzio, *War and Peace in Soviet Diplomacy* (New York, 1940), p. 76, note 40. Later when the Soviet government began to insist upon the fiction of the complete separation of the two spheres, the incident was fiercely denied and the blame cast upon White agents, who were accused of having smuggled the compromising material into Joffe's suitcase.

sentatives of Soviet trade unions. A further revolutionary note was carried into diplomacy in June 1918, when it became clear that diplomacy was here to stay: all diplomatic ranks as established by the Congress of Vienna were declared abolished, and equality was decreed between diplomatic and consular agents. Henceforth the heads of Soviet missions abroad were to be known simply as "plenipotentiary representatives." In this connection the old distinction between small and Great Powers, another hangover from the capitalist system, was also considered dropped. Unfortunately, when formal relations were later established with capitalist countries, it proved rather difficult to determine the exact position of a "plenipotentiary representative" in the diplomatic corps of a foreign capital; and the Soviet government had to recognize the old titles, albeit in an indirect way. In the same year (1924) the government also prescribed for all Soviet diplomats abroad "the simplicity of form and the economy of expenditures fitting the ideals of the Soviet regime."[11]

After the formation of the Comintern and the end of the civil war, the separation of the two spheres of Soviet foreign relations proceeded apace. If the Soviet government wanted to deal with capitalist governments it had to conform to their standards of diplomacy. The issue of revolutionary propaganda cropped up at once as an almost insurmountable obstacle to diplomatic recognition and even to the resumption of trade relations. The result was a strict outward separation of the two spheres.[12] The Soviet government denied any complicity whatever with the activities of the Comintern; it always protested any contrary view as an unfriendly act.

Underneath the fictional separation, however, the relationship between the two spheres was always a troublesome problem. In most areas of the East, where from the Leninist point of view national and

[11] T. A. Taracouzio, *The Soviet Union and International Law* (New York, 1935), app. viii. This regulation, incidentally, did not prevent Rakovsky from wearing silk breeches in his audience with the King of England. How far Soviet diplomats would go in submitting to capitalist or feudal ceremonial practices depended to a large extent upon the current political situation. If the Politburo desired good relations, its diplomats could conveniently drop their Bolshevik simplicity. There seemed to be almost no end to Soviet adaptability: in 1926, at the death of the Mikado, the Soviet representative deposited the official wreath with the Soviet insignia, but without the inscription: "Proletarians of all countries unite," which was part of it. See Bessedovsky, *Den Klauen der Tscheka Entronnen* (Leipzig, 1930), p. 99.

[12] The clearest formulation of this separation was given by Chicherin in 1922: "The Communist party stands at the head of a great government. As a government it enters into relations with all other governments and establishes close friendly relations, guarding the political and economic interests of its republic. . . . Speaking in the name of the government organs we leave [party policy] on the side. The fate of the communist movement, the successes and experiences of communist parties belong in the realm of other organs. Our attention is given to the fate of the Soviet government." "Za piat liet," *Mezhdunarodnaia Zhizn*, 1922, No. 15. There is, of course, much discussion of this point in Soviet literature on international law, which obscures rather than clarifies the relationship.

revolutionary movements tended to coincide, there were far fewer sources of conflict.[13] But where, as in the West or in Japan, there was a sharp distinction between the established government and the revolutionary movement, the two branches of Soviet policy were bound to collide. One strained its utmost to overthrow the governments with which the other tried to maintain friendly relations. Which branch would prevail in the conflict depended upon circumstances. According to Chicherin's felicitous phrase, a rising revolutionary wave would always force "the technical diplomatic work" into the background; in that respect diplomacy was forever inferior to revolution. But in the uncertain setting of the 1920's a twilight zone developed, with revolution and diplomacy holding each other in balance. In the end, the relative success of each branch determined to a large extent its standing in regard to the other. Insofar as the revolutionary ventures of the Comintern and its chief, Zinoviev, collapsed, diplomacy gained;[14] and, insofar as diplomacy failed, revolutionary agitation again advanced. The two branches were in constant adjustment to each other through most of the 1920's for reasons of foreign as well as domestic policy. The period ended, however, with a net gain for diplomacy.

While the prevailing impression is thus one of considerable friction, there is no doubt that the two branches also supplemented each other. The members of the Comintern were always bound, unless otherwise instructed, to support the diplomacy of the Soviet government in their own countries, often much to their chagrin.[15] And without the diplomatic immunity which Comintern agents enjoyed as members of a Soviet foreign mission, they could not have done their work either. Despite their friction, then, a degree of cooperation was indispensable to both.

At the top level of the Politburo, foreign relations, of course, appeared again as one. All disputes between the two main instruments of foreign policy were submitted to it, and it chose the tool, or more commonly the combination of tools, that seemed best to fit the particular occasion. Sometimes diplomacy won an outright victory, as in the case of the Soviet Union's friendly relations with Mussolini in the mid-1920's. Sometimes the Politburo seemed to pursue two seemingly con-

[13] After the Congress of the Peoples of the East in September 1920 no more revolutionary congresses were held. In relations with the Near and Middle East, the Comintern did not seem to have played an active part. Thus, communications with the Indian communists were maintained, according to M. N. Roy, through diplomatic channels.

[14] This may be the point to comment on *Pravda's* famous cartoon, showing Zinoviev haranguing a revolutionary crowd while Chicherin, in the background, held his head in despair. This cartoon appeared before the Fifth Congress of the Comintern in June 1924, when a new equilibrium between diplomacy and revolution was in the making. But the pictorial design of the cartoon still leaves no doubt of Zinoviev's superiority. . . .

[15] At the Fourth Congress of the Comintern in 1923, Bukharin found it necessary to justify the ways of Soviet diplomacy to the members of the Comintern. See B. Moore, *Soviet Politics: The Dilemma of Power* (Cambridge, Mass., 1950), p. 208.

tradictory policies, as in regard to the Kellogg-Briand Pact, which it supported on the diplomatic level while the Comintern denounced it. Sometimes again, as in relations with Germany in the fall of 1923, the revolutionary impulse gained the upper hand without, however, depriving diplomacy of its usefulness. One might say then that each of the two main branches of Soviet policy had an area of maximum effectiveness, with a relatively small area of friction separating them. In the case of the divided attitude towards the Kellogg-Briand Pact, the Soviet leadership tried to make the most of each dimension of its foreign relations, the contradiction not really being as prominent as one might expect (except in the eyes of a few intellectuals) because both dimensions were usually kept apart also in the life of most contemporaries.

The Politburo's analysis of the basic factors of Soviet strength in world affairs likewise counted on the two dimensions. As Stalin put it in the Political Report to the Fifteenth Party Congress, the position of the Soviet Union depended upon three interrelated elements: the inner strength of the Soviet Union; the strength and weakness of the capitalist states; and the strength and weakness of the suppressed classes all over the world and of their revolutionary movements. The first element, the only one entirely under Soviet control, remained, of course, uncomfortably insufficient from the Politburo's point of view, despite all strenuous effort to build up Russia's internal security, her army, and — above all — her industrial potential. All the more significant were the other two, in which the Soviets operated as much as their preoccupation with their internal reconstruction permitted. Their joint significance was also revealed in the chief party documents. In the Political Reports of the Central Committee, particularly in Stalin's methodical rendition from 1925 on, one is apt to find a passage dealing with the world situation in general, analyzed in Marxist terminology, followed by a section on the tasks of the party in the international revolutionary movement and another one on the tasks of diplomacy.[16]

In assessing the scope of Soviet foreign relations, one cannot overstress the fact that from the beginning the Soviet leaders insisted in their dealings with capitalist countries upon the combination of revolutionary activity, with all its illegal components, and traditional diplomacy. The Soviet regime had reverted permanently and wholeheartedly to a more brutal interpretation of the nature of international relations than had become customary in the West. As with diplomats in the age of royal absolutism, Soviet foreign missions were designed to spy, to lie, and to intrigue abroad for the welfare of their masters. But while the Machiavellian diplomat combined the legitimate with the illegitimate business in his own person, the Soviet regime, recognizing that the standards of diplomacy had been raised in a liberal age, relieved its

[16] The fact that the spokesman of the Central Committee gave a Leninist analysis of the world situation, from which Soviet diplomacy in its official reports was barred, showed again the relative inferiority of that branch of government.

diplomats[17] of the more unsavory functions. It created a number of separate agencies for spying and subversion, for which, in the eyes of the gullible, it need not assume responsibility. The advance over the days of cabinet policy lay in the vastly improved technique of socio-political agitation, the chief contribution of Leninism. To be sure, in the period under consideration, much of its revolutionary agitation in Europe and Asia remained an idle boast and an act of self-deception. The revolutionary tide had receded and the bulk of Soviet effort came to be concentrated at home. But, for the conduct of Soviet foreign relations, the combination of diplomacy with revolution remained standard practice. In an age of almost universal social and political crisis the Soviets had opened up, for better or worse, the cohesion of society as a new field of power politics, which demanded new instruments, new organizations, and new concepts of theoretical analysis. The Soviets thus started their career with a more comprehensive grasp and control of the factors of power in the twentieth century than their liberal-democratic opponents were to possess for another generation.

And to ask the Soviet regime in its weakness to refrain from making use of its revolutionary tools was as futile as to ask the British Empire to scrap its fleet.

III.

One can imagine the difficulties of Chicherin as Soviet Russia's chief diplomat in such a setting. The Soviet Foreign Office had lost the monopoly over the conduct of foreign relations. In the Comintern, it always had a jealous rival and one which was closer to the ears of its superiors.[18] Traditionally, the Foreign Minister had always enjoyed a leading position in the government, and the Foreign Office was an honored branch of the government. There had been notable exceptions to the undisputed monopoly of foreign relations in the hands of Foreign Offices, but never had diplomacy fallen to such a humble and suspect position as it now did. In an avowedly revolutionary society, diplomacy was an anomaly, a standing contradiction to the essential spirit of the regime. Its imitation of the formalities practised by other states was — even while patently insincere — disconcerting and unpleasant to the hard-bitten professional revolutionaries who dominated the government. No one, for instance, could have been unhappier than Kalinin, when he was forced, in his capacity as Chairman of the Presidium of the all-Union Congress of Soviets, to receive King Amanullah of Afghanistan.[19] It is not surprising that the Narkomindel was often by-passed. When

[17] Except Joffe, who on all his foreign assignments (in Berlin and Vienna, and on his trip to the Far East) combined the two elements.
[18] For a long time Radek (and never Chicherin) was the Politburo's rapporteur on foreign affairs. See Bessedovsky, *Revelations of a Soviet Diplomat* (London, 1931), p. 62.
[19] A. Barmine, *Memoirs of a Soviet Diplomat* (London, 1938), p. 221.

something really important seemed in the offing, as for instance the revolutionary upsurge in Germany after July 1923, the Politburo took over, acting through the Comintern; and, for the promotion of the Chinese revolution, it appointed a special Chinese Affairs Commission, in which the Narkomindel was represented by a Far Eastern expert only.[20] In short, at the slightest pretext the Politburo was always inclined to deal directly with all matters within the jurisdiction of the Narkomindel, thus reducing its significance. In many ways, an early uncomplimentary characterization of the Narkomindel as "just a diplomatic chancellery attached to the Central Committee"[21] stated the simple truth. And as a true clerk it was not necessarily admitted into the secret purposes of its masters.

Chicherin's low position in the Communist party, the center of Soviet power, also reflected the inferior status of his office. A former Menshevik, admitted into the party in January 1918, Chicherin could not expect to be heard in the inner councils. Even foreigners knew how much he depended upon Lenin in all major decisions.[22] An early tiff with Stalin over the nationality question, in which he lost out, may have also shown him his powerlessness.[23] His timidity towards the chief leaders increased with the years; rarely did he dare to assert himself. Party distrust was also expressed in the appointment of Litvinov, an old Bolshevik, who in April 1919 joined the *collegium* of the Narkomindel as an informal party guardian over his chief. Joffe, Krestinsky, Rakovsky, Krassin, and others who in the 1920's represented the Soviet government abroad, stood higher in the party than their official chief. Until the Fourteenth Party Congress in 1925, the Narkomindel had not even a voice in the Central Committee, while its rival, the Comintern, had from the beginning several spokesmen in the Politburo, not to mention Radek on the Central Committee. At the Party Congress of 1925, because of the changing balance of power in the party and the successes of Soviet diplomacy in the previous year, Chicherin was promoted to the Central Committee, but by that time this body had lost its original significance; and in 1930, at the Sixteenth Congress, he was deprived of this prefer-

[20] Bessedovsky, *Revelations*, p. 122. This commission was headed by Unschlicht, the head of foreign military intelligence.

[21] Ascribed by Bessedovsky to the acting head of the Ukrainian Narkomindel, Yakovlev, in 1920. *Revelations*, p. 20. Important notes were drafted by members of the Politburo themselves; so Trotsky drew up the reply to the Curzon Ultimatum in May 1923. It is significant also that the official *History of the Communist Party* barely mentions Soviet diplomacy in the period under discussion.

[22] Lenin's private opinion of Chicherin may be gathered from his letter to Trotsky after Chicherin had suggested that substantial concessions be made at the Genoa Conference: "Send Chicherin at once to a sanitarium." Trotsky, *Mein Leben*, p. 455.

[23] At the Tenth Congress (March 1921) Stalin attacked Chicherin over a series of articles in *Pravda* written by the latter, entitled: "Against Stalin's Theses." Although nominated to the Committee on the National Question at that Congress, Chicherin was not elected to it. See the stenographic protocols of the Tenth Congress (ed. N. N. Popov, 1933).

ment without his successor Litvinov at once being elected in his place.[24] Obviously, the Narkomindel was left very much on the outer fringes of the party.

Under these circumstances it was not easy to organize and operate an efficient foreign service. Soviet diplomacy, to discuss briefly its internal organization, was handicapped from the outset because, unlike most other branches of the Soviet government and unlike its foreign equivalents, it had to start entirely from scratch. The Narkomindel's historian has described the tense scene when Trotsky took over the Foreign Office.[25] Upon his arrival he ordered the entire staff inherited from the previous regime to assemble and announced to them curtly: "Those for us go to the left, those against us go to the right." The *chinovniks*, after deliberating among themselves, went right to a man. Only the menials remained to shake hands with the new Commissar. Shortly thereafter all Foreign Office personnel abroad was recalled or repudiated. Within two months, however, the personnel of the Narkomindel already numbered about two hundred, including the revolutionary guards from the Siemens-Schuckert works and a nearby pipe-rolling mill. But even after the arrival of Chicherin, the organization and routine of the new Peoples Commissariat reflected for some time the shiftlessness of that hectic phase of Soviet rule. By 1921 it had at last achieved some stability. Its internal organization was sanctioned by a decree of the Council of Commissars; and the treaties with Soviet Russia's neighbors, the trade negotiations with England, and expanding relations with the outside world in general provided its officials with a steadily growing volume of business. But for a long time it had a reputation for amazing inefficiency.[26]

The top personnel, constituting the *collegium*, which ran the Narkomindel in the mid-1920's, was a remarkable body in the annals of diplomacy. Georgii Chicherin himself, his country's chief diplomat, was considered rather an oddity.[27] A shy, timid little man with an intelligent and gentle glance, utterly negligent of dress, an aesthete and hypochondriac, he had little of the outward polish of the diplomat, despite his aristocratic birth. Those who knew him closely called him a visionary who had shut out all reality and who lived with his job twenty-four hours a day — although occasionally he would lock himself up in a room adjoining his study and for hours play Mozart on the piano. They praised him as a man above pettiness and party intrigue, almost too fragile for the rude hurly-burly of Bolshevik politics. The foreign correspondents discussed his unorthodox methods of work, his custom of receiving foreign diplomats and other callers in the small hours of the

[24] Litvinov was elected in 1934, at the Seventeenth Congress.

[25] See the Narkomindel's publication *Desiat Liet Sovietskoi Diplomatiia* [*Ten Years of Soviet Diplomacy*] (Moscow, 1927), p. 4.

[26] See O. Blum, *Russische Köpfe* (Berlin, 1923), p. 406.

[27] Characterizations of Chicherin's personality can be found in Louis Fischer, *Men and Politics;* Bruce Lockhart, *Memoirs;* Lincoln Steffens, *Autobiography;* Louise Bryant, *Mirrors of Moscow;* G. Bessedovsky, *Revelations;* O. Blum, *Russische Köpfe;* E. Cerruti, *Visti da Vicino;* etc.

morning, his dislike of modern office equipment. The gossipers traded stories of how, because he was unable to delegate work, he drafted, wrote, typed, sealed, and posted diplomatic notes himself; or how, in his absentmindedness, he mislaid important documents, for which then the whole department had to search. In such an event, they related, he even routed his colleagues from bed or the ballet. But everyone who knew Chicherin respected his abilities as diplomat: his brilliant mind, his sharp repartee, and that amazing memory which made foreign diplomats wince.

Only revolution could have placed such an unusual man in charge of Russian diplomacy; but even among the revolutionaries he remained a stranger. Among the matter-of-fact life stories of Old Bolsheviks, Chicherin's authorized biography (which only he himself could have written) reads like a chapter from Dostoievsky.[28] There were no revolutionary deeds in the underground to record; there was only the tortuous metamorphosis of a Russian aristocrat into a Menshevik, who during the world war found himself in agreement with Lenin's revolutionary internationalism rather than the "social chauvinism" of the bulk of European socialists.[29] In his case the making of a Menshevik consisted of a series of inner crises: the adjustment problems of an only child reared in an emotionally surcharged and highly religious atmosphere; the sufferings and inhibitions of a poor relation in the fast and superficial northern capital; the tensions which led to his final break with his aristocratic past. His intense spiritual struggles, which he later described with introspective detail, carried him from bourgeois respectability, Nietzschean yearning for the superman, and tortured compulsions towards self-destruction to the optimistic collectivism of Marxism. They left his physique undermined from an early age; he was not fit for active revolutionary duty. But there was also a more stable side to his development: his interest in foreign policy.

Diplomacy had been in the family. His father, before he took up pietism and retired to his estate in the province, had been secretary to the Piedmont legation in 1859 and shortly thereafter, counselor at the Paris embassy. His maternal grandfather, Count Stakelberg, had been the Russian ambassador at Vienna, at the time of the Congress of Vienna; hence the self-avowed Metternich touch in Chicherin's diplomacy.[30] This tradition compelled the young Chicherin to join the Tsarist Foreign Office. He entered, however, not as an active diplomat, but as an archivist and scholar, who was set to work on Russian foreign policy between the Crimean war and the Congress of Berlin, a fact which may account for his special interest in the Near and Middle East and for his anti-British bias in later years.

After 1904 the two strands of his life interests, diplomacy and

[28] Printed in *Entsiklopedicheskii Slovar Russkago Bibliograficheskago Instituta Granat* (hereinafter cited as *Granat*), XLI, part III, 215ff.

[29] See Trotsky, *Mein Leben,* p. 334, for Chicherin's initial leanings towards patriotism.

[30] See his biography, cited in note 28 above.

social justice, separated to be united again only after the revolution. Quietly giving up his position at the Foreign Office, he left Russia and studied the social-democratic movement in Germany, where he became a close friend of Karl Liebknecht. It was indicative of his ability that, within three years, he assumed an important post in the revolutionary movement by becoming secretary of the foreign bureau of the Russian Social-Democratic party, which tried to coordinate the work of the various Marxist emigré centers. At the same time he took a deep interest in the socialist youth movement. After the outbreak of the war, he shifted from Paris to Brussels and London, where he worked for the relief of Russian political refugees and took a hand in the antiwar agitation of the Independent Labor party. After the March Revolution, he headed a committee for the repatriation of political exiles, was arrested after the Bolshevik coup for his propaganda activities, and was finally exchanged in January 1918 for Sir George Buchanan, the British ambassador to Russia. Upon his return he joined the Bolshevik party. As he was the only comrade with Foreign Office experience, an excellent linguist, and otherwise well-qualified except perhaps in party staunchness, Lenin assigned him at once to the Peoples Commissariat for Foreign Affairs, and, even before Trotsky's resignation as Commissar in March 1918, he assumed control. Thus, at the age of 45, "a new page of his life," as he wrote, began for him. It was not to be an altogether happy one, for, as he confessed in his autobiography, the revolutionary and the aesthete did not always blend in him, either before or after the revolution.

Next in importance in the Narkomindel, and eventually to replace his chief, came M. M. Litvinov, Vice-Commissar, whose work will be evaluated in a subsequent chapter of this book. Beside Litvinov stood L. M. Karakhan, also Vice-Commissar, and specialist for Far Eastern affairs.[31] His background was rather undistinguished both from a revolutionary or intellectual point of view. Born in the Transcaucasus (his name indicates Armenian origin) and trained in the law, he joined the Russian Social-Democratic Workers party in 1904, and worked for a while in its Far Eastern organization. Later he went to the capital where he became a permanent member of the international committee. He was said to have proved himself a competent agitator, propagandist, and organizer, who remained outside the factional strife. A "defeatist" during the war, he was banished to Tomsk, where he continued his revolutionary work and extended it into eastern Siberia. He joined the Bolsheviks after the March Revolution and appeared for the first time in the limelight as a member of the Brest-Litovsk delegation, owing his selection to Lenin. His background in Asiatic Russia seemed to fit him particularly for Soviet relations with the East; in 1925 he was Soviet

[31] The following biographies are based on *Granat*, XLI. It should be noted, however, that these official biographical sketches are by no means reliable. All revolutionaries had to censor their *curricula vitae* both before and after the revolution. See also Bessedovsky's characterization of Karakhan as "the ass with the classical profile."

ambassador in Peking. He was generally described as an able, but by no means outstanding person, who impressed some of the younger Bolsheviks like Barmine as the department's diplomatic dandy.[32]

A fourth member of the *collegium,* who joined it in 1923, was V. L. Kopp, who, like Karakhan and Litvinov, stemmed from petty bourgeois background. He had studied engineering but had soon followed the revolutionary call and became a member of the "transport administration" which received and distributed revolutionary materials within Russia. After organization work among St. Petersburg metal workers in 1905, he had gone into foreign exile and newspaper work with Trotsky and the German Social Democratic party. After the outbreak of the war, he served in the Russian army — an unusual turn for a future Bolshevik commissar — but was captured by the Germans in 1915. Joffe obtained his release in the fall of 1918 and made him counselor at the Berlin embassy. He then served as Soviet representative in Berlin until his promotion to the *collegium.* In 1925 he was Soviet ambassador in Japan, where he proved quite susceptible to the geopolitical teachings of Haushofer.

The *collegium* of the Narkomindel, in which the Commissar was *primus inter pares* rather than undisputed chief, was far from a unanimous body. Litvinov, the Old Bolshevik, had been set to watch over Chicherin. In the ensuing jockeying for power, which divided the Commissariat ever more deeply towards the end of the 1920's, Karakhan sided with Chicherin, Kopp with Litvinov. It was said that a fifth member, T. A. Rothstein, was appointed to break the deadlock. Rothstein, however, who had been an editor of the London *Daily News* and had his sons educated at Oxford, proved unequal to the task. More of a scholar than a diplomat, he was put in charge of publicity and press affairs. At times other men also joined the *collegium* — Rakovsky as Ukrainian delegate and Vice-Commissar, and after him the party economist Schlichter. As a body, the *collegium* may be said to have been made up of the least revolutionary type of Bolsheviks, most of whom had fairly extensive knowledge and experience of western European life. They were "halfway men," making their career in the twilight zone between the outside world and the Bolshevik core. But, apart from Chicherin, its chief members would have hardly qualified for Sir Ernest Satow's characterization of a diplomat as an "educated gentleman." The *collegium* was apparently not a congenial environment for profitable common work. Bessedovsky, a minor diplomat, found it shot through with intrigue and scandalmongering.

Under the *collegium* there operated, besides the numerous secretariat, the various geographical and functional departments.[33] The

[32] Barmine, *Memoirs,* p. 155. Maybe Trotsky's quip was directed at him (or was it Litvinov?): "I absolutely cannot understand those revolutionaries who like to become ambassadors and swim in their new role like a fish in water." Trotsky, *Mein Leben,* p. 348.

[33] *Desiat Liet,* p. 19. They were organized under the *Sovnarkom* decree of November 12, 1923. This decree is reprinted in French in the Yearbook of the Narkomindel for 1929.

latter dealt with administrative and personnel affairs, the press, economic and legal matters. As to the geography of its foreign relations, the Narkomindel knew only East and West, the Eastern Department being divided into Near East (including Africa), Middle East, and Far East, and the Western, according to the decree of November 12, 1923, into Central Europe, the Baltic limitrophes and Poland, Scandinavia, Anglo-Roman (Britain, France, Italy, Spain, United States, and Latin America), and the Balkans. In 1927, as an economy measure, the Balkan division was dissolved and its countries assigned either to the Anglo-Roman or Central European divisions.[34] Altogether, between 450 and 550 men and women seem to have been employed at the central offices during the mid-1920's,[35] a number roughly comparable to the personnel of the central offices of the Comintern.[36] Paul Scheffer, the German correspondent, found the department overworked and somewhat neglected.[37] Indeed, a position in the Narkomindel was not considered an easy berth, particularly in the early 1920's, not only because of Chicherin's unusual hours but because of the low pay scale. Other government departments paid their officials three to four times as much[38] — a further indication of the relative unimportance of the Narkomindel in the Soviet scheme. By comparison the experts of the Comintern, mostly pampered foreign comrades, lived like kings.

The Narkomindel as part of the formal government structure was subordinate to the Council of Peoples Commissars and through it responsible to the all-Russian Congress of Soviets and its Central Executive Committee (vtsik).[39] Occasionally Chicherin or Litvinov reported before these bodies on the state of international relations, and their Commissariat submitted its annual report to them. One may assume that the few public discussions on foreign affairs in these bodies,[40] prepared beforehand, were no problem to the Narkomindel; at least Soviet diplomacy was spared the worry over parliamentary pressure groups or public opinion. The relations of the Narkomindel with other executive agencies, however, were more complicated. Within its extensive bureaucracy the Soviet government found it difficult to coordinate all its formal foreign relations. In 1927, for instance, the *Naphtha Trust* was discovered negotiating on its own with the Spanish government[41] (which had not yet recognized the Soviet Union), despite the recent

[34] *Desiat Liet*, p. 23.

[35] Ibid., p. 17. For 1924 the number of "responsible workers" (corresponding roughly to the Tsarist *chinovniki*) was given as 484, 376 of them being party members.

[36] P. Scheffer, *Sieben Jahre Soviet Union* (Leipzig, 1930), p. 286.

[37] Ibid., p. 416.

[38] *Desiat Liet*, p. 12.

[39] For the place of the Narkomindel in the constitutional structure of the ussr, see J. Towster, *Political Power in the USSR, 1917–1947* (New York, 1948).

[40] See, for instance, the debates of the Third All-Union Congress of Soviets in May 1925, and the analysis of them in Towster, *Political Power*, pp. 217ff.

[41] Bessedovsky, *Revelations*, p. 205.

decree of *Sovnarkom* that all business between the branches of the Soviet government and foreign governments be conducted through the Narkomindel.[42] Under that decree only strictly nonpolitical matters could be handled directly; otherwise the Narkomindel was to be informed immediately. Military and naval authorities were to arrange with the Commissariat their modes of communication with their attachés (who were outside the jurisdiction of the Narkomindel). That decree incidentally suggests that, even within the relatively narrow legitimate sphere of foreign relations, the Narkomindel had found it difficult to enforce its monopoly. The very size of government in the twentieth century — the Soviet government took the lead in "big government" — created new problems for the conduct of diplomacy.[43]

The Narkomindel's relations with other government departments, however, were far less of a problem to it than its relations with the Comintern, the OGPU, and the party, i.e. with those interlacing agencies which by their nature were closer to the Bolshevik core. The full extent of the domestic pressures bearing down upon the Narkomindel will probably never be known with certainty; but the few available glimpses into that fluid and carefully hidden realm of internal Soviet politics, although to be interpreted with caution, tell their own story. There is no evidence of any routine liaison between the Narkomindel and the central office of the Comintern (the OMS — International Liaison Section) headed by O. A. Piatnitsky. But there were two indirect ties, one through the Politburo acting as arbiter between the two agencies; the other through the foreign missions. If Bessedovsky's case was at all typical, a Soviet diplomat about to assume a new post abroad was briefed not only by the Narkomindel but also by the Comintern and the Politburo — not to mention the OGPU and military intelligence.[44] In his embassy then he would have to shift back to the position of mere diplomat. There his job was to come to some working relationship with the Comintern agents and other nondiplomatic personnel who were part of his suite and enjoyed full diplomatic privileges no matter how subversive their real concerns.[45]

Inevitably, the relation between revolution and diplomacy within the walls of a Soviet foreign mission were often stormy. Nowhere else was their rivalry so keen and so intimate. Naturally the Narkomindel wished to rid its embassies of their most compromising members, or at

---

[42] Joint decree of *Vtsik* and *Sovnarkom*, August 27, 1926, reaffirming an earlier one of 1921. See Taracouzio, *Soviet Union*, Appendix x.

[43] There is no room here to discuss the federal aspects in the organization of the Narkomindel. There is no reason to assume, however, that they were of any special concern either to Chicherin or Soviet diplomats in general.

[44] Bessedovsky, *Revelations*, pp. 127ff.

[45] As the presence of Comintern agents in Soviet diplomatic missions was public knowledge, it was the desire of all governments to limit the size and number of Soviet missions in their territory; hence the protracted negotiations over the status of Soviet trade delegations in England and other countries.

least curtail their powers.[46] And many times it carried the dispute over the disciplinary rights of its diplomats to the Politburo.[47] Over the years the position and influence of the subversive agents in Soviet embassies and trade delegations were reduced. After the failure of the German revolution in 1923 the Comintern agents were given more subordinate functions as translators or press agents, and their work was organized separately to reduce friction with the diplomatic staff. But individual Comintern agents with strong backing in Moscow occasionally defied these regulations. And while the Narkomindel succeeded in limiting the power of the Comintern in its foreign missions, it never could eliminate it altogether; diplomatic immunity was too essential for its work. Sometimes it would even occur that a diplomat was asked to aid directly in some Comintern transaction, which he was apt to refuse if he was worth his salt.[48] But while individual diplomats might resist such compromising orders at some risk to their careers, diplomatic mail pouches would unfeelingly carry dynamite, weapons, propaganda, or money for revolutionary purposes. And the couriers of the Narkomindel were all said to be OGPU men.[49]

The Narkomindel's relations with the secret police resembled somewhat its relations with the Comintern. As part of the subversive machinery abroad and closely related to the Comintern at the center,[50] the police agents constituted an equally compromising part of foreign missions. In the home office in Moscow, the presence of a Cheka man was reported in the early 1920's.[51] In 1927 Chicherin confessed to Bessedovsky that his office (like most others in the government) was wired with hidden microphones by the OGPU.[52] That agency also interfered in matters of policy. Paul Scheffer, the German correspondent, reported that after 1927 the OGPU, staffed ever since Dzerzhinsky's days with Poles, manufactured anti-German incidents to the embarrassment of Chicherin.[53] It meddled furthermore in the censorship exercised by Rothstein of the Narkomindel's press department over foreign correspondents, often stopping dispatches previously passed by him.[54] Litvinov, who could afford to be bolder than his chief, took a vigorous stand against OGPU penetration, with scant success.[55] Here, still more than in the case of its struggle with the Comintern, Soviet diplomacy had its hands tied. This does not mean that harmony prevailed between the

[46] The second secretary of the mission was usually the Comintern agent, the third secretary the OGPU man (or woman). Miliukov, *Politique extérieure*, p. 136.
[47] Bessedovsky, *Revelations*, pp. 69ff.
[48] Ibid., p. 166.
[49] Krivitsky, *In Stalin's Secret Service* (New York, 1939), p. 38.
[50] Piatnitsky, the head of the OMS, was a close friend of Trillisser, in charge of the foreign section of the OGPU. G. Agabekov, *OGPU* (New York, 1931), p. 269.
[51] Louise Bryant, *Mirrors of Moscow* (New York, 1923), p. 191.
[52] Bessedovsky, *Revelations*, p. 196.
[53] P. Scheffer, *Sieben Jahre*, p. 441.
[54] Ibid., p. 421.
[55] Agabekov, *OGPU*, p. 269.

agencies closer to the core of the party — there was some friction also between the OGPU and the Comintern; but the two were apt to present a common front against diplomacy. And yet, no doubt, Soviet diplomacy also benefited from the code cracking and espionage services of the OGPU.

The link between the Narkomindel and the party was kept fairly well out of sight, for obvious reasons. Of course, all its chief officials were party members and thus under party discipline. Lenin commented proudly on the close penetration of the Narkomindel by the party. Chicherin's speeches, and still more Litvinov's, although adapted to diplomatic non-Marxist parlance, reflected the official line. At party congresses, Chicherin after 1921, and later Litvinov and Karakhan, appeared only as nonvoting delegates for their department; they took no part in the discussion. The report on foreign policy, as part of the Political Report, was entirely in the hands of the leading member of the Politburo, Lenin, Zinoviev, or Stalin.[56] But while Soviet diplomacy was silent at party congresses, the head of the Comintern submitted a lengthy and fully publicized report. As to the attitude of the Politburo towards the Narkomindel, it was what would be expected: tolerance because of a limited usefulness but not respect. In public, Lenin had treated Chicherin and his work with a certain friendly solicitude; even Zinoviev in delivering the Central Committee's report in 1923 found a few good words for him, but Stalin was cool. Only after 1928 was he said to have taken a greater interest in the department, when Chicherin was already on his way out. Bessedovsky reports many instances when Stalin ignored the views of the department; he also tells of Stalin's private correspondence with diplomats over the heads of their chief and of errands on which he sent them contrary to official diplomatic policy.[57] Needless to say, the fact that the Politburo was occasionally divided in itself on foreign policy was another source of complications to Chicherin.[58] Of cordiality between the Narkomindel and the chief figures in the party there was no trace; Chicherin disliked Stalin, and both he and Litvinov disliked Molotov.

[56] Litvinov once spoke, at the Fifteenth Party Congress in December 1927, reporting on the Preparatory Committee on Disarmament of the League of Nations, in whose work he had recently participated. But his speech was an exception prompted by a very special reason. At that congress Stalin played a difficult and ambiguous game. On one hand he had been forced to set a sharp Left course, which implied bitter hostility to the League. On the other hand, he had already determined upon a policy of cautious rapprochement with the Western Powers. It was left to Litvinov, just back from Geneva, to reconcile the two incompatible policies by giving a strongly Left interpretation to Soviet policy at Geneva. Judging by the hilarious reception of his speech, he acquitted himself successfully of his difficult task. See also Towster, *Political Power,* on the discussion of foreign policy at party congresses.

[57] Bessedovsky, *Revelations,* p. 210. The issue here was Bessarabia.

[58] As in the Ghilan affair. See L. Fischer, *The Soviets in World Affairs* (new ed., Princeton, 1951), I, x. (Not to mention the party division over the Chinese revolution.)

While Soviet diplomacy at the center was hampered by internal friction and hostile crosscurrents, Soviet diplomatic missions abroad operated on the whole — if one may trust Bessedovsky or Barmine — no more efficiently or harmoniously. And yet they did not lack able diplomats. During its first ten years the Soviet government drew on the services of Krassin, who in the past had followed an unusual, but successful, career as an electrical engineer, big businessman, and revolutionary, and who was also its Commissar for Foreign Trade;[59] of Joffe, who as a young man of means had given his time to studies and revolutionary underground work until he was exiled to the Siberian *taiga* to rise after his return to the inner circles of the party;[60] of Krestinsky, who had been a lawyer, a Bolshevik candidate for the Fourth Duma, and later chairman of the Ural committee of the Communist party before he was made secretary of the Central Committee; and finally of Rakovsky, the Ukrainian communist who for years had practiced medicine in France before he became chairman of the Ukrainian Council of Peoples Commissars and its Commissar for Foreign Affairs.[61] To be sure, Krestinsky and Rakovsky were sent to their foreign posts as a form of political exile; they had become *personae non gratae* in Moscow. In the years of Stalin's rise, assignment to the diplomatic service became a favorite method of isolating potential opponents, a practice which reflects again the relatively inferior position of diplomacy. During the struggle against the "left deviation," Kamenev thus became ambassador in Rome, and Mme. Kollontai, the Soviets' first woman diplomat (and much advertised as such), minister to Norway and later ambassador to Mexico. Unfortunately, no study of the background of Soviet diplomats in the 1920's is available. It appears, however, that not only Bolsheviks secured diplomatic assignment. Bessedovsky, a career diplomat, had been a Ukrainian Social Revolutionary and forestry expert; Leonid Obolensky, Soviet plenipotentiary in Warsaw until 1925, an aristocrat and Tsarist tax collector in Siberia.[62] In the subordinate positions, at least in the first years after the revolution, all sorts of revolutionary riffraff could be found. In general, the conditions were such that the Narkomindel was forced from an early time to undertake the training of suitable Bolshevik cadres to make the most of the opportunities for distinction which Soviet diplomacy afforded.

The position of Soviet diplomats in foreign capitals, indeed, was a

[59] His biography in Lubov Krassin, *Leonid Krassin, His Life and Work;* and more revealingly in Simon Liberman, *Working for Lenin's Russia,* which contains interesting glimpses of Soviet diplomacy in the early years.

[60] *Granat,* XLI. Also for the following.

[61] One might also mention Vorovsky, who was of Polish noble background and had received a scientific education. He was the Bolshevik representative among the Polish Social Democrats and lived in Stockholm, as a contact man, during the war. After the February revolution he became a member of the foreign bureau of the Bolshevik Central Committee, to be sent back to Scandinavia after the seizure of power.

[62] Bessedovsky, *Revelations,* p. 40. He was appointed, it seems, because he had done a favor to a Bolshevik exile in Siberia.

very challenging one, although not without obvious physical dangers.[63] Their job was twofold: to overcome the often extreme hostility against the Soviet regime — a feeling so intense on occasion that Litvinov, upon his first arrival in Copenhagen for negotiations with the British over the return of prisoners of war, was unable to secure lodging in any respectable hotel — and to make a position for themselves which would enable them to wield at least some political influence. Their situation was not unlike that of the diplomats of an earlier period, when, in the absence of instantaneous communication with their home office, they had to rely upon their own resources. The Soviet diplomat, of course, could always resort to the telegraph. But as his success depended upon adaptation to a very alien scene, the home office could not always assist him. This suggests, incidentally, that it was not only modern communications but also the increased uniformity of conditions and diplomatic practices among the Western governments that deprived diplomats in general of their former independence. Where there was little common ground between governments, as between the Soviet Union and the outside world, the diplomat — at least potentially — had a chance to regain his former stature. That was true, not only of Soviet diplomats with spirit and boldness, such as Rakovsky in Paris, but also of foreign diplomats in Moscow, when political circumstances favored their assignment, as was the case with Brockdorff-Rantzau. The independence enjoyed by these men, however, could not last. Rakovsky's attempts to manipulate French domestic politics (entirely without recourse to revolutionary forces) finally led to a demand for his recall;[64] and the tightening control of the Stalinist regime soon limited whatever opportunity existed for Soviet diplomats abroad or Western diplomats in Moscow. What Stalin expected of his diplomats may be gathered from his admonition to Bessedovsky as he set out for Tokyo: "Talk to the Japanese as little as possible and telegraph us as often as possible. And don't think yourself the cleverest of us all."[65]

Here, in short, was the constant dilemma of Soviet diplomats. They had to attempt to bridge the profound gap between the core of the revolutionary regime, with its Leninist-Stalinist sense of reality, and the "capitalist" governments to which they were accredited. If they played too much the professional revolutionary or kept too much to themselves, they could not hope to make their way abroad and to be of maximum usefulness to their government. If, on the other hand, they made their way too well, they laid themselves open to the charge of submitting to capitalist influences. Few members of the Soviet foreign service knew how to strike a balance acceptable to their masters and true to their

[63] Two Soviet diplomats, Vorovsky and Voisky, and a courier, Nette, were assassinated in the 1920's. Throughout, Soviet embassies lived in fear of attack.

[64] The official reason was that he had signed a manifesto of the Left opposition which encouraged foreign soldiers to desert to the Red Army in case of war with the Soviet Union.

[65] Bessedovsky, *Revelations*, p. 131.

craft. Some, like Krassin, found their influence increasingly limited; others, like Bessedovsky, Solomon, and Dimitrievsky, fled from Soviet service when the disparity between the Soviet Union and the outside world, between the Stalinist regime and their political ideas, became too uncomfortable. These dramatic defections were followed by the adoption of greater security measures. But, as the later examples of Barmine and Kravchenko show, the loyalty problem was never completely solved, despite very strict supervision within Soviet missions abroad.

Apart from the supervision of the diplomats by the agents of the secret police and the Comintern within their mission, there was the scrutiny by the party cell, the secretary of which reported directly to party headquarters. In appointments to foreign posts, loyalty checks played a great part by 1930, with the chief of the foreign section of the OGPU and the members of the Central Committee in charge of party cells abroad conferring with the Narkomindel or the Commissariat for Foreign Trade on every candidate.[66] The activities of the party cells in foreign missions often descended to a rather unpleasant personal level. Relatively idle and almost completely isolated from "capitalist" society, Soviet missions abroad, particularly the lesser ones, often stagnated in their own sordid little messes. A touch of scandal or insurmountable personal animosity often led to the transfer of personnel from one post to another. These circumstances may have contributed in part to the low esteem in which diplomats were held in inner party circles.[67]

Nor could they, on the whole, make a good impression abroad on grounds of their professional integrity or competency. How could a Soviet diplomat fulfill the conditions which Lord Balfour set for the good diplomat?[68] As a party member and representative of the Soviet government, he could not expect to gain the confidence of the government to which he was accredited. Nor could he honestly and clearly convey the policies of the Politburo to that foreign government, for he voiced only the surface segment of Soviet foreign relations. And again, if he reported to his Soviet superiors accurately and understandingly on the intentions and policies of foreign governments, and particularly on general conditions abroad, he always ran the danger of being accused of lacking in revolutionary rectitude. The safest procedure for a Soviet diplomat under the circumstances was to forget professional standards and, as a diplomatic technician, adapt himself to the outlook demanded of him, at whatever cost to Soviet interests or world peace.[69]

[66] Agabekov, *OGPU*, p. 269. The penalties for desertion were further increased in the 1930's.
[67] That is the picture conveyed by Bessedovsky, and to a lesser extent by Barmine. There was, however, also the example of Iureniev, Soviet representative in Rome, who conducted his embassy according to the best Bolshevik ideals. See Barmine, *Memoirs*, p. 206.
[68] Lockhart, *Memoirs*, p. 271.
[69] The effects upon diplomatic negotiations resulting from such close supervision of diplomats may be seen in Philip E. Mosely, "Some Soviet Techniques of Negotiation," in *Negotiating with the Russians,* ed. Raymond Dennett and Joseph E. Johnson (New York, 1952).

The individual diplomat's dilemma, however, only reflected the larger quandary of Soviet diplomacy. In all countries the Diplomatic Service must mediate between foreign reality and domestic pressures; for that reason, it is bound to encounter hostility at home. Particularly in countries where social cohesion is insufficient for the purposes of government, those who urge the need for adjustment to the nature and the needs of foreign peoples are under suspicion, for they introduce an alien element into a society which fears any challenge to its orthodoxy. In Soviet Russia, the Bolshevik norm was increasingly narrowly defined; hence the professional handicaps of diplomacy increased during the 1920's. In order to win successes abroad, Soviet diplomacy was forced to indulge in a degree of adaptation to "capitalist" environment; by its very nature, then, it had a bias towards the "right deviation" — just as, in the case of capitalist countries dealing with socialist governments, the conscientious diplomat is apt to be accused of Leftist sympathy. No wonder, then, that Soviet diplomats were put under very strict observation.

What, then, was the outward appearance of Soviet diplomacy as a halfway station between the revolutionary core and the capitalist world? As the legitimate segment of Soviet policy it had to serve as a shield of the revolutionary core; its task in carrying out its assignments was to explain away, to conceal, to deny, or to ignore the revolution. For all its actions, it had to find nonrevolutionary motives. And here Soviet diplomacy, which was to be "open diplomacy," presumably averse to all secrecy or camouflage, found itself often in another insoluble dilemma, from which it escaped only by employing the most preposterous lies, half-truths, or arguments which, in strict theory, were incompatible with Soviet ideology.

Among the outright falsehoods frequently employed was the contention that the Soviet government had nothing to do with the Comintern. In his speech to the Central Executive Committee of the all-Russian Congress of Soviets on March 4, 1925, to quote but one example, Chicherin rejected a German protest that a member of the presidium of that body had signed a revolutionary appeal to the German Communist party: "We have already been forced once before to advise the German government formally that our government is not responsible for the activities of the Comintern and has nothing in common with it." The German government, bound to Soviet Russia by political necessity, did not pursue the point further. In 1921 and 1922, the British government under Curzon had disputed the same Soviet assertion and had been met with a series of evasions[70] and claims that British information about the connection between the Comintern and the Soviet government was false (it was in form, although not in substance); that it was fabricated by White agents (who, indeed, were active forgers in that period); and that the British, too, were employing

[70] See the documents in Degras, *Soviet Documents*, I, 209, and Krassin, *Leonid Krassin*, pp. 135ff.

subversive agents against Soviet influence (which presumably was also true but beside the point); and that members of the British Cabinet were also members of international organizations (which again was irrelevant). If Soviet diplomacy admitted the existence of the Comintern at all, it argued — and this was another half-truth — that capitalist and colonial conditions inevitably made for revolution, regardless of Soviet propaganda.[71]

When Soviet diplomacy was not rubbed so hard against uncomfortable verities, it resorted to more congenial subterfuges. It took a line which might be called homeopathic revolution; it would be progressive, anti-capitalist, even proletarian, but without the Bolshevik sting. Chicherin's speech at the opening session of the Genoa Conference, carefully prepared with Lenin's help, may serve as an illustration of this mode. He said that the Russian delegation came in the interest of peace and the economic reconstruction of Europe and recognized, without surrendering their Communist principles, the parallel existence of the old and the new order in the present historical period. He even put the economic opportunities for foreign business under the NEP in a rather favorable light. But then he introduced issues not on the agenda: various measures of disarmament; a better League of Nations, in which the distinction between small and Great Powers, between the victorious and the vanquished, was abolished; and even a plea for planned global distribution of industrial resources. In short, he presented a picture of the Soviet government as the leader in progressive reforms of international relations, advocating drastic but not necessarily revolutionary measures for an admittedly bleak postwar world. On other occasions, Soviet diplomacy harped on the foibles of capitalist international relations in general, the brutal character of the Versailles settlement, the shortcomings of the League, the friction between the Great Powers, and the high cost of power politics in general; it delighted in pointing out the injustices of the existing balance of power and the hypocrisy of all capitalist diplomacy (as it was quick, in retaliation, to show up the dirt in the politics of any other government). In the 1920's, the climax of this propaganda policy without the revolutionary corollary was of course Litvinov's famous first performance before the Preparatory Commission on Disarmament in November 1927. While Chicherin did not approve of Litvinov's policy, he himself had many times sung a similar gloating tune on other issues; it was the *basso continuo* of Soviet diplomacy. The closest Soviet diplomacy came to admitting an interest in revolution — and it did this only in the early 1920's — was to claim that it represented the foreign policy of the international proletariat.

Another motif of Soviet revolutionary not-so-revolutionary diplomacy, in which Chicherin, the Metternich pupil, felt particularly at home, was its frank *Realpolitik*. It sought to exploit the "contradictions"

[71] In Chicherin's circular to Soviet representatives abroad (September 10, 1920) concerning a note from the American Secretary of State Bainbridge Colby to the Italian ambassador in Washington. Degras, I, 210. Also Stalin, Political Report to Sixteenth Congress.

among the capitalist powers. These "contradictions" were always listed in any Soviet survey of the foreign situation and often much exaggerated, particularly in the case of Anglo-American relations. Soviet diplomacy tried to aggravate these cleavages and thus sided with the revisionist powers and with the weaker against the stronger, like any practitioner of the traditional balance of power policy. At the same time — and here it reverted somewhat to Marxist analysis — it made much of the divisions among capitalist groups within a given country, attempting particularly to bait certain commercial and industrial interests with concessions in Russia. On this level of its diplomacy, social revolution played no part whatever; any traditional practitioner of power politics might have acted likewise.[72]

Considering Chicherin's background (and also the fact that the Bolshevik revolution represented a strong upwelling of Russian national feeling), the strong trace of nationalism in the rationalizations of Soviet diplomacy should not cause surprise; it again helped to obscure the revolutionary segment of Soviet foreign relations. In many cases, the same policy could be equally interpreted from a revolutionary or from a nationalist point of view, as was true, for instance, of the monopoly of foreign trade. Justified on grounds of socialist theory, this was equally acceptable to non-Bolshevik Russian mercantilists.[73] Similarly, the revolutionary fear of contamination through contact with the West reappeared in diplomatic talk as the nationalist fear of Western economic and political penetration, which had been quite widespread in Russia before and during the war. In the same category, also, belongs Chicherin's championship of the protection of Russian boundaries, shores, and access to its shores, his claim to Bessarabia, his clash with Curzon over the Straits, and his demand for Soviet participation in all diplomatic arrangements involving traditional Russian interests like the Aaland Islands and Spitzbergen. In September 1926, he even pressed for Soviet participation in the current Tangiers negotiations, because Tsarist Russia, he argued, had been a signatory to the Algeciras Treaty,[74] (although the foreign debts of the regime had been repudiated, it will be remembered, precisely because they had been contracted by that government). And who could not hear the voice of traditional Russia in Chicherin's impassioned fulmination against Curzon at the Lausanne Conference in 1923: "The Russian revolution has transformed the Russian people into a nation whose entire energy is concentrated in its government to a degree hitherto unknown in history; and if war is forced upon that nation it will not capitulate. You are uneasy because our horsemen have reappeared on the heights of the Pamirs and because you no longer have to deal with the half-witted Tsar who ceded you the

---

[72] How much Chicherin was at home in the intellectual milieu of *Realpolitik* may be gathered from his articles, signed *postscriptum*, in *Mezhdunarodnaia Zhizn*, the Narkomindel's organ.

[73] Krassin, *Leonid Krassin*, p. 167.

[74] Reported in *Osteuropa*, I (1926), 697.

ridge of the Hindukush in 1895. But it is not war that we offer but peace. . . ."[75]

England, with whom Russia had clashed so often in the past, was also the main enemy of Soviet Russia in Chicherin's eyes. Hoetzsch, the German observer, was right in saying that the second Commissar for Foreign Affairs had always at his heart the *Staatsgedanke* of Russia; it was enshrined by him at the Narkomindel.

No further illustration is needed to show Chicherin's efforts to motivate and conduct Soviet diplomacy as if it were the sole instrument of Soviet foreign policy, and a nonrevolutionary one at that. Those familiar with the discussions of Soviet foreign relations on the Politburo level will be amazed how much Chicherin's conception of foreign policy differed from his masters'. But it must be remembered that, quite apart from the Soviet leadership's ability to accommodate itself to halfway stations, Bolshevik theory permitted any conceivable expedient in the relations with the capitalist world.[76] And no matter how unrepresentative the stated motivations of Soviet diplomacy — to take a view above the quarrels and disabilities from which it suffered at home, and to see it from the perspective of the Politburo — its successes aided the revolution, too, at least indirectly. In the security of its boundaries, its prestige in the world (even a "capitalist" world), in the matter of foreign economic assistance and loans, national and revolutionary interests overlapped or coincided. The only conflict on this higher level arose perhaps from a difference of emphasis. A diplomatic course which represented the *Staatsgedanke* of Russia was apt to consume prematurely the national resources which Bolshevik leadership wanted to husband for the further domestic development of the revolution. There prevailed in this period, from the Treaty of Brest-Litovsk to Stalin's willingness to surrender the Russian claim to Bessarabia and the sale of the Chinese Eastern Railway, a considerable inclination at the revolutionary center (not shared by the Narkomindel) to make territorial concessions for the sake of strengthening the revolution at home. But there was no reason why the territorial and strategic viewpoint should not again come to the fore and be justified in Leninist-Stalinist terms, once "the given relation of forces in the world arena" had changed in favor of the Soviet government.

[75] Degras, *Soviet Documents*, I, 348. Chicherin, indeed, often interpreted the Bolshevik revolution as a source of renewed unity and energy in Russian foreign policy.

[76] The variability of Soviet attitude towards the western world goes probably far deeper than mere expediency. Soviet foreign relations in the first decade show the same "variability in depth" that can be found in the personal attitudes of the revolutionary leaders. They could range from the surface level of polite and seemingly sincere compliance with western standards, the give-and-take with foreign visitors through a whole gamut of intermediary moods to the raw revolutionary inner core of relentless hate. Under Stalin, however, this variability, born of the prerevolutionary contact between Russia and the West, has been greatly reduced.

IV.

In conclusion, the analysis set forth in the previous pages will be illustrated by a brief and necessarily casual survey of Soviet foreign relations in the crucial period between 1921 and 1928. The following sketch will change the observer's vantage point from the Narkomindel to the Politburo and cast into bold relief what appears so flat from a survey of Soviet foreign policy premised on the fiction of the Narkomindel's effective monopoly of foreign affairs. As seen from the Kremlin, foreign relations stretched over a broad and deep front, with the revolutionary detachments of the Comintern and Profintern deployed on the left flank, along with the OGPU and military intelligence, with its various organizations for foreign cultural contact and foreign trade arrayed in the center, and with diplomacy engaged on the right flank. Unfortunately no picture of the fascinating complexity of interaction along this extended phalanx, of its coordinated maneuvers, sallies, feints, and ambushes, can here be given. Only the barest outline of the chief ventures on both flanks, the diplomatic and revolutionary, in their interplay and common relation to domestic conditions, is possible.[77]

As the Soviet government considered itself the spatial nucleus around which other Soviet Socialist republics might eventually gather, its relations with its immediate neighbors assumed special significance. In the West, the postwar settlement, based on Soviet weakness, had surrounded Russia with a *cordon sanitaire* of buffer states. A barrier had thus been established separating the Soviet regime from other countries with a revolutionary potential, such as Germany. While communist parties were forbidden by law in all of these border countries, the Bolsheviks maintained the usual underground organizations with the help of whatever local communist forces they could rally. The establish-

[77] No history of Soviet foreign relations in the Chicherin period has yet been written from the Politburo point of view, covering the entire foreign policy phalanx and coordinating its actions with domestic development. Most existing texts suffer from an overemphasis upon Soviet diplomacy. Louis Fischer's indispensable volumes were conceived largely from the Narkomindel's point of view (in unusually close collaboration with Chicherin himself). P. Miliukov, *La Politique Extérieure des Soviets*, does far greater justice to the complexity of the subject. I. Deutscher's account of "Foreign Policy and Comintern I" in his biography of Stalin gives the best general background to the study of Soviet foreign policy in the Chicherin period, without devoting, however, much space to Chicherin's work. The essays by Boris Nikolaievskii, "Vneshnaia Politika Moskvy"; "Sovietskoie IAponskoie Soglashenie 1925 g"; "Revoliutsia v Kitaie, IAponia i Stalin" (in *Novyi Zhurnal*, 1942–1944); and "Russia, Japan, and the Pan-Asiatic Movement to 1925" in *The Far Eastern Quarterly*, VIII, May 1949, no. 3, show by far the greatest insight into the problems encountered in a detailed study of Soviet policy in this period. Least helpful, of course, from the point of view here taken is the official version of Soviet diplomacy in V. V. Potemkin's volumes: *Istoriia Diplomatii*. On the other hand, the introductory paragraphs of the article on "Soviet Foreign Policy" in the official *Diplomatic Dictionary* (II, 650ff.) confirm, although in general terms, the tenor of Soviet foreign relations as viewed in this chapter.

ment of White Russia as a Union Republic and the creation of an autonomous Moldavian Republic were, at the same time, designed to create pro-Soviet sympathy among the Russian minorities in Poland and Rumania respectively.

In Soviet relations with all the border states, diplomacy necessarily stood in the foreground. In a series of treaties in 1920 and 1921, the Soviet government recognized the existence of these states with stipulations safeguarding Russia from attack through their territories; only relations with Rumania, which had seized Bessarabia in 1918, remained unsettled. Chicherin succeeded also, by playing Lithuania off against Poland, in preventing the creation of a Baltic bloc under Polish leadership. It seems in the last analysis, however, that it was the obvious threat of Russian power which discouraged dangerous adventures on the part of the border states. As things stood, they continued to be unfriendly to the Soviet Union, and they effectively blocked her revolutionary outward thrust; but, at the same time, by their very existence, they afforded the Soviet government a measure of protection against foreign intervention.

In the Near and Middle East, Soviet Russia faced an entirely different situation. Lenin had stressed the revolutionary importance of anti-western nationalism in colonial and semicolonial countries. In accordance with this, Soviet policy towards Turkey and Persia at once repudiated the Tsarist heritage and supported the national aims of the new governments. Thus, Soviet Russia supported Kemalist Turkey in her struggle with the Western Powers, helped the rise of Riza Khan in Persia and granted assistance to King Amanullah in Afghanistan. In their relations with Turkey, the men of the Politburo appear to have played a straightforward game, although the sincere friendship which Chicherin displayed toward Kemal's government was probably no more than mere expediency to Stalin.[78] In the vast territory stretching from Azerbaijan to Manchuria, however, Soviet policy and Tsarist expansion tended to coincide, despite Soviet professions to the contrary. In repudiating imperialism, the Bolshevik leaders were careful to hold on to the many concrete advantages they had inherited, such as the fishery rights in the Southern Caspian, the domination of Outer Mongolia, the operation of the Chinese Eastern Railway, and the disposition of the Russian share in the Boxer indemnity.

In the long run, the Politburo counted on the natural dissemination of its ideals and accomplishments in the Asiatic hinterland. Its agents were not only its diplomats, consuls, trade officials, OGPU and Red Army men, but also its telegraphs, railways, tractors, and the example of Uzbek and Turkmen autonomy. It was as though Soviet Russia had attached a series of suction cups[79] to adjacent territories. How successfully and quickly these cups would work depended on local circumstances and the world balance of power.

[78] Bessedovsky, *Revelations*, p. 187. On Soviet policy with regard to Turkey, see above, Chapter 6, § II.
[79] Scheffer, *Sieben Jahre,* p. 355.

In the last analysis, however, the important question was not that of Soviet Russia's relations with the border states, but rather of her relations with the three great capitalist Powers of the West, Great Britain, France, and the United States. Germany and Japan, which — in Stalin's mind — occupied somewhat analogous positions, were more ambiguous factors; they were capitalist Powers which nonetheless contained strong anti-Western elements. Finally, there was a lesser Power, Italy, and the host of the small ones, which, apart from certain propaganda and nuisance aspects, counted for little. It was towards the centers of world power that the Politburo directed its diversified foreign policy instruments.

In 1920, Lenin had confidently set them all to work in order to break the blockade that had been imposed upon Soviet Russia. He had built up the Comintern to intensify the revolutionary pressure; he appealed to labor organizations and humanitarian groups for political and economic assistance; he held out the promise of concessions to foreign businessmen, trying to draw rival business groups into competition for Soviet favor; through his diplomats, he shouted peace to the victorious Allies and whispered consolation to the wounded nationalism of the defeated; and he tried to stir up the colonial peoples of the East. The question was: on what part of his broad foreign policy front the first breakthrough would occur and which foreign policy instruments would be the most effective in the long run. The first opening — there never was a breakthrough — occurred on the diplomatic flank, in relations with Great Britain. Lloyd George, in an attempt to secure the Russian market for British business, met the Soviet offer for a trade agreement, and thus *de facto* established relations. The Soviet government, through Krassin, proved most accommodating and even curtailed its anti-imperialist propaganda in the East. Yet trade relations nevertheless developed rather slowly. At the same time, Lenin directed his special attention towards Germany. As early as 1919, Radek, from his prison cell in Berlin — (he had been caught while organizing the revolutionary underground in Germany) — had negotiated with German industrialists and militarists; and in the next two years, against a backdrop of retreating revolutionary waves in Germany and Soviet threats of a rapprochement with France, the groundwork for future nonrevolutionary German-Soviet collaboration was laid.[80]

A still more satisfying gain was made, again on the economic-diplomatic wing (but with the support of the revolutionary wing),[81] in 1922 at the Genoa Conference, the first European diplomatic gathering to which the Soviet government was invited. The invitation was made possible by a widespread anxiety among European business groups to overcome the postwar depression by restoring the prewar economic ties between Russia and Europe. The danger for Soviet Russia in this

[80] See Wipert von Blücher, *Deutschlands Weg nach Rapallo* (Wiesbaden, 1951), p. 155.

[81] The Comintern had been instructed to agitate everywhere for economic relations and political recognition.

juncture lay in the creation of a European consortium strong enough to force a breach in the Soviet monopoly of foreign trade. The Politburo, however, succeeded in dealing separately with interested parties, selecting one, the Urquhart interests, as proof that it was possible to do business with Russia (but repudiating the contract the moment the demonstration had outlasted its usefulness). Despite these maneuvers, the Politburo (acting through Chicherin and Krassin) could not create such competition among Western economic interests for the Russian trade as to weaken their demands for a prior settlement of the Tsarist debt and for concessions limiting its monopoly of foreign trade. The Genoa Conference thus failed, as did the subsequent Hague Conference. But at the same time a more important matter than economic relations was decided: a course of German-Soviet collaboration.

The Rapallo Treaty, skillfully brought forward at Genoa by Chicherin at a time when the Germans were feeling their isolation most keenly, signified that with Soviet help Germany would try to pursue an independent national policy; it sanctioned a major split among the capitalist Powers. Through Radek, the Politburo had made a strong bid to enlist on its side the anti-Western elements of German nationalism and had succeeded. This tie not only weakened the force of capitalist encirclement but, through the influx of a variety of German experts, directly assisted the socialist reconstruction of Russia. This guarantee of a Soviet-induced and partly Soviet-controlled division of the capitalist world remained one of the major features of Soviet diplomacy, as well as of Politburo policy, throughout the Chicherin period.

It cannot be claimed, however, that at the time even the combined power of Germany and Soviet Russia altered the political situation appreciably. In the following year the French occupied the Ruhr, and Russian diplomacy, unable to prevent an adverse settlement of the Straits question, had also to back down before the Curzon Ultimatum, by which the British Government, in terms so peremptory as to suggest an imminent rupture of relations, demanded compensation for outrages against British subjects and a cessation of anti-British activities in the Middle East. Obviously, it was more difficult than Lenin had anticipated to raise Soviet Russia's position in the world. And he had to face the fact that the concrete gains (such as they were) had been won by diplomacy rather than revolutionary measures.

In 1923 revolution, however, seemed to be in the ascendancy. In that year the entire front of Soviet foreign policy was on the move, with revolution and diplomacy in close interaction. The Ruhr occupation — to concentrate upon the events in Germany — had set the stage for intensified revolutionary agitation and incited the hopes of Soviet leaders. For half a year after the French had moved, Soviet policy still stuck to the spirit of the Rapallo agreement. Chicherin vigorously protested against the Ruhr occupation, branding it a crime; protest demonstrations were held in Soviet cities; and the Red Army forwarded munitions to the *Reichswehr*. Through the Comintern, Radek preached the Schlageter line: communist cooperation with German nationalism.

In thus supporting the German government's policy of passive resistance, the Soviet leaders hoped, at best, for a national war of the defeated against the victors. In mid August, however, the Politburo abruptly changed its tune from diplomatic alliance to social revolution. What had happened to cause this sudden shift of initiative from the right flank of the Soviet foreign policy front to the left?

For one thing, seven months of French occupation had increased the likelihood of a genuine revolution in Germany. On August 12, a series of bitter strikes broke out throughout the country. Secondly, faced with such turmoil, the German government, now headed by Stresemann, decided to abandon passive resistance. With British mediation it now pursued a more moderate course of fulfilment and worked for pacification at home. At this point of Stresemann's retreat — which seemed also a retreat from Rapallo — the Politburo began to play for revolution through the Cominterin.[82] Its agents had been ready since the beginning of the year; now they set up the necessary organizations. Thousands of Russian party members with a knowledge of German were alerted and the government of the new Soviet Socialist Germany was designated.[83]

But in preparing the German revolution, the Politburo faced two major decisions: how much direct aid could it give to the Germans, and what was it to do if a revolutionary victory should be followed by foreign intervention in Germany? Considering the unprepared state of her army and the conditions of the country in general, Soviet Russia was in no position to face war. Territorially separated from Germany, its leaders — at the time of Lenin's illness divided among themselves — could not send armed force without provoking a major international conflict. They dispatched, therefore, a variety of experts, but kept their material contributions at a minimum. The German communists thus had to fend for themselves, the Politburo staking all on their native strength and determination, although it gave serious thought to what would follow a communist victory.

Unable to prevent French meddling, as the French were already in occupation of the Ruhr, the Bolsheviks at least set out to neutralize hostile intervention from the east. They did this on the diplomatic front by sending Kopp to Poland and the Baltic limitrophes to arrange with them an agreement keeping them neutral and permitting the Soviet government to transship grain and other supplies to Germany. Kopp went so far as to threaten the Poles with an attack from the rear if their army should move against Germany. On the revolutionary side, the Politburo's program called for diversionary sabotage in Poland, not to mention aid to the German workers enjoined upon all communists through the Comintern. The risk taken by the Politburo thus included war only in case of Polish intervention in Germany, and it was assumed that the Russian threat would in itself prevent the emergency creating

[82] See Ruth Fischer, *Stalin and the German Revolution* (Cambridge, Mass., 1951), pp. 300ff.

[83] Bessedovsky, *Revelations,* pp. 46ff.

that risk. During these months diplomatic, economic and military relations with the German government of course continued as before, as though nothing had been changed. And after the failure of the German revolution in November 1923, the Politburo conveniently fell back upon its formal ties and the Rapallo policy, having lost very little ground in its unsuccessful revolutionary offensive.

The setback in Germany (and a simultaneous failure in Bulgaria), however, prepared the regrouping of units in the Soviet foreign policy phalanx resulting in greater freedom of action for the diplomats, particularly as the failure on the revolutionary flank was followed by further gains on their sector of the front. Early in 1924 both Great Britain and Italy granted *de jure* recognition to the Soviet government; later in the year France followed suit. The "objective circumstances" seemed to favor the diplomats. The change of government in England and France and the more relaxed atmosphere of international relations raised the position of the Soviet Union as a state among others in the comity of nations. It was in this new situation, calmer than any Soviet Russia had yet experienced, that Lenin's death occurred and the problem of the succession became acute. For the next four years — highly complex years in Soviet foreign relations — Soviet foreign policy was conditioned not only by the changes in world politics but more than ever by the changing internal scene.

At the time of Lenin's death, Soviet policy was determined by the "troika" of Zinoviev, Kamenev, and Stalin, who still followed the basic directives evolved by Lenin. Zinoviev, as head of the Comintern, naturally wielded a dominant influence over foreign relations, which meant continued strong emphasis upon revolutionary agitation. The failures of 1923 weakened his standing in the party, but during 1924 the Left course represented by him still prevailed. For that reason the Politburo remained cool, even hostile, towards the friendly overtures of the Mac-Donald government. Nor could it share the optimism welling up in Western Europe. The new calm in the international sphere began to reduce communist voting strength abroad; and this made the revolutionary weapons of Soviet foreign relations less effective. Furthermore, under the Dawes Plan, Germany was drawn into economic cooperation with Western countries, which portended a weakening of the Rapallo policy. Finally, there were signs of outright hostility, such as the raid upon the Berlin trade delegation in April, and the reaction of the British public to the Zinoviev letter in the elections of October. In the face of such facts, Soviet leaders were divided. The old policy seemed no longer adequate; the direct incitement of revolution became increasingly ineffectual and even ridiculous. Zinoviev's miserable Reval putsch in December 1924 was the last expression of that policy. What new line should be taken?

Considering the unsettled situation in the party, it is not surprising that the answer came from domestic politics. While Zinoviev's policy still prevailed, a new trend based on internal considerations gained ground in the party. A group called "the economists," eager to rebuild

Russian prosperity, even with foreign assistance, advocated less revolution and more foreign trade, which could be obtained only with the help of diplomacy. Zinoviev himself, in delivering the Central Committee's report at the Thirteenth Party Congress in May 1924, alluded to this trend, saying that now more than ever foreign policy stood in close relation to domestic policy. More than that, he even played up Chicherin's significance. There existed, indeed, an intimate connection between Soviet diplomacy and the Russian peasants. The more plentiful the supply of foreign capital for industrial development and the better Soviet Russia's standing with the capitalist Powers, the less sacrifices were demanded of the peasantry. For that reason, as Zinoviev put it, the Narkomindel should be one of the most popular Peoples Commissariats in the villages. In this manner a right turn in Soviet domestic policy meant also a promotion for Soviet diplomacy.

Such a turn took place in the spring of 1925. The uprising in Georgia, a minor Kronstadt, had demonstrated the necessity for greater concessions to the peasants; and the trend abroad was patently against revolution and for diplomacy. At the Fourteenth Party Conference, the new line in domestic as well as foreign policy was proclaimed; as to the latter, its aims were now to be based on the assumption of capitalist stabilization. The Fourteenth Party Congress confirmed the new orientation and also accepted the implicit corollary that, at a time of capitalist consolidation in the world, Soviet socialism would have to advance first of all within Russia. The new status of diplomacy, however, did not mean surrender of the revolutionary flank of the Soviet foreign policy front. But the previous direct incitement of violent revolution wherever possible was now replaced, under Bukharin's guidance,[84] by a more peaceful policy of gradual transition. Communists everywhere were instructed to cooperate with socialists; a link between Soviet trade unions and the British Trade Union Council was established in the form of the Anglo-Russian Trade Union Committee. Bukharin himself admitted, at the time of the English general strike, that revolution in England might not conform to the Bolshevik prototype. In China, too, Borodin was committed to a policy of cooperation with the Kuomintang rather than to outright sovietization. In the mid-1920's, in short, Soviet foreign policy, somewhat in line with the spirit of the times, had moved towards greater moderation. The original predominance of revolutionary agitation was ended; diplomacy had risen to equal rank. But the extreme hopes of some Soviet diplomats for a return by their government to prerevolutionary power politics and a settlement of spheres of influence with the leading colonial powers, were not fulfilled; although with clipped claws, revolutionary agitation continued. And furthermore, the preferment of diplomacy did not imply greater tractability on the part of the Soviet masters. It only meant a partial shift back to European standards in the choice of foreign policy instruments. The total effect of

[84] See B. Nikolaievskii, *Novyi Zhurnal*, no. IV, 1943, pp. 302ff., for an analysis of Bukharin's views. Zinoviev, incidentally, was dropped from the Presidium of the Comintern Executive Committee in 1926.

the change upon foreign capitals was thus bound to be negligible, as was fully revealed in 1927.

While diplomacy now enjoyed greater prestige with the Politburo, it did not become more conciliatory and cooperative in its relations with Western governments. Its elevation coincided with the conclusion of the Locarno agreements and the preparation for Germany's entry into the League of Nations. In order to offset such capitalist solidarity under League auspices Chicherin undertook in 1925 and 1926 a vigorous diplomatic offensive. He strengthened Soviet ties with Turkey, secured the continued adherence of Germany to the Rapallo policy (with a commercial treaty and a 300 million mark credit added) and then set out to construct an anti-League of Soviet Russia's neighbors through non-aggression pacts, not all of which, however, could be concluded even after protracted negotiation. Only Lithuania, Turkey, Afghanistan, and Persia responded favorably. After a while the diplomatic offensive bogged down amidst signs of mounting British hostility. Chicherin's diplomatic weapons could not provide an effective antidote to determined British counteraction against the revolutionary wing of Soviet foreign policy; and, in May 1927, disaster overtook him in the rupture of diplomatic relations by that country.

The chief activities on the revolutionary wing of Soviet foreign policy under the new course, which had so provoked the British conservatives and caused Chicherin's failure, had been the offer of extensive Soviet financial support to the British strikers (who rejected it) and particularly Borodin's energetic promotion of the Chinese revolution. From the summer of 1926 on, the events in China claimed the intense attention of the men in the Politburo, who again set to work all the foreign policy instruments to attain their end. Only a few features of an extremely complex situation can here be mentioned.

Formal Soviet relations with the Far East were established in the spring of 1923, after the Japanese evacuation of Siberia and the absorption of the Far Eastern Republic by the Soviets. In a short time the Politburo negotiated with the chief authorities in China: to wit, the official government in Peking, Chang Tso Lin, the *tuchun* of Manchuria, and Sun Yat Sen in the south, dealing with each in their own terms. Most promising from the Soviet point of view was the incipient nationalist movement of Sun Yat Sen. The Politburo at once dispatched Borodin, an acquaintance of Sun's, together with military advisors, arms, and money, to help organize the Kuomintang as a militant mass party with a progressive social and strongly anti-imperialist program. It was clear to the Politburo that the success of such a movement in China with its 400 million population would create a valuable ally and have immense repercussions through eastern and southeastern Asia and affect even the balance of power in the Pacific. In support of the Kuomintang, the Politburo also enlisted the help of Soviet diplomacy: for a time Karakhan was stationed in Peking; in Manchuria the Soviet officials of the Chinese-Eastern railroad defended Soviet interests against Chang Tso Lin, an enemy of the Kuomintang. In 1925 a settlement with Tokyo was negotiated, stabilizing Soviet-Japanese relations and creating a new *point d'appui* in the Tokyo embassy. In addition, Comintern agents were busy in all major cities of China, among the Korean nationalists, and in the Japanese Communist party. Finally, there was the Red Army, a far more active and influential agent in the Far East than in Europe, stationed along the Manchurian border.

After June 1926, with the Kuomintang striking north to the Yangtse, a decisive period was reached. Would the left or the right wing of the Kuomintang prevail? If the right wing under Chiang Kai-shek won out, the Kuomintang would be lost to Soviet Russia, as the seaboard cities with their Western orientation would determine its foreign policy. The Politburo, therefore, supported the left wing, without, however, advocating an all-out Bolshevik social policy. There were bitter disputes in and around the Politburo as to how far to the left the course ought to be set, with Stalin taking a relatively moderate view. The diplomats at the Narkomindel, on the other hand, worried about English reaction and, uninitiated into the projects of the Politburo, stood vigorously opposed to any revolutionary venture, even to the extent of Stalin's commitment.[85] They argued that China was not ready for more than a Kemalist revolution and they warned of Japanese hostility to a Soviet China. The clash between diplomacy and revolution assumed here a novel form, that of a conflict between an Eastern and Western orientation. The Politburo, having been repeatedly disappointed in its revolutionary expectations in Europe, had now turned to the East; for the present it braved British hostility and staked all upon success in China. The diplomats, considering the European scene with its global repercussions of greater importance, sought to minimize first of all friction with the British conservatives whom they greatly feared. On this dispute, the position of Japan also had to be considered, not only because of the extensive Japanese interests in northern and eastern China, but because Chinese nationalism was also anti-Japanese. In order not to antagonize Japan it seems that Stalin, through Comintern agents, tried to stifle the anti-Japanese agitation in the Kuomintang, while through his diplomats he cultivated friendly relations with the Japanese government. He valued the anti-Western potentialities of Japanese nationalism as highly as he did those of German nationalism.[86] During the height of the Chinese crisis in the spring of 1927 and the sharply rising British reaction, he even put his diplomatic representative in Tokyo under unusual pressure to wrest, in a sort of Far Eastern Rapallo, from the Japanese government a Soviet-Japanese nonaggression pact, in order to forestall active British intervention in China (which he thought possible only with Japanese help).[87] Yet even Japanese neutrality could not save the revolutionary venture in China.

The final crisis in the relations between the right and left wings of the Kuomintang merged with a general crisis in Soviet foreign relations

[85] Bessedovsky, *Revelations*, pp. 120ff.
[86] Nikolaievskii, *Novyi Zhurnal*, no. III, pp. 205ff.
[87] Bessedovsky, *Revelations*, pp. 156ff.

and domestic politics. While at home the left opposition prepared its final demonstration, the foreign situation went from bad to worse. In April the Soviet embassy in Peking was raided; elsewhere in China consulates were searched. At the end of May the British government, after the Arcos raid, broke off diplomatic relations. British hostility radiated into other quarters. In June the Soviet ambassador in Warsaw was assassinated. In the same month Borodin was ordered home and the Chinese revolution, for all practical purposes, written off. In October the French government demanded Rakovsky's recall, after which Franco-Soviet relations reached a low point. Even in Germany the former enthusiasm for the Rapallo policy had waned. The trend of adversity even extended to Russia's hitherto reliable mid-eastern auxiliaries. In Persia and Afghanistan Great Britain won back lost ground; Turkey grew cooler as her relations with the Western Powers improved. Obviously the anti-imperialist shibboleths of the immediate postwar years no longer carried their old weight. At the end of the year the Soviets had lost all ground in China, and in Japan Count Tanaka, the protagonist of an active Manchurian policy, had been made Prime Minister. The crisis extended throughout the entire length of the Soviet foreign policy front. It was a defeat of diplomacy as much as of revolution; it affected Chicherin as adversely as Bukharin and the Comintern, not to speak of Stalin, who in the eyes of the left opposition was also responsible for the alarming turn of events. And yet, in the end, it helped to thrust the party's General Secretary, whose hand had been noticeable here and there even during the period of Bukharin's greatest influence, to the fore in a field in which he had hitherto held back. With his rise, the confusion and uncertainty in Soviet foreign relations dating from Lenin's last days began to disappear. Soviet foreign relations were reconstituted around a new set of convictions, Stalin's convictions.

The serious setback in the tenth year of the revolution on both the diplomatic and revolutionary flanks of the Soviet foreign policy front brought into sharper focus again the old bleak assumptions about the incompatibility of socialism and capitalism and the isolation of revolutionary Russia. A different leader might have chosen the other alternative and abandoned all revolutionary agitation and reverted to the traditional scope of power politics; and this would have also been the inclination of Chicherin. With Stalin there was no chance of such a course. His ascendancy deepened the distrust of the outside world. The former optimism about the imminence of world revolution or of universal formal recognition by "capitalist" governments — both had been conspicuous earlier, despite their contradictory nature — had gone. The "objective circumstances" of the world situation that had seemed to favor the Soviet regime in earlier years had changed. The instruments of international revolution designed to draw strength from these favorable constellations for the Soviet regime therewith also lost much of their reliability. The failures of 1927 thus put the naked fact of Soviet weakness back into bold relief: Soviet Russia could not play the part of a Great Power without the internal resources of a Great Power. In 1927, therefore, Stalin put the course of domestic politics again to the left: he answered the failure in foreign relations with terror at home and increased antiforeign agitation; he fabricated a war-scare that would justify the drastic measures to come, particularly the policy of rapid industrialization at all costs, out of Russian resources and at the expense of the Russian peasant. Only through the fastest possible development of Russian industries could he provide Soviet Russia with the means for victorious participation in the intensified struggle for world power which he saw ahead. At the Fifteenth Party Congress in December 1927 and the Sixth Congress of the Comintern in 1928, which ended Bukharin's uncertain influence over Soviet foreign policy, the ideological foundation for the new line (for which, of course, there was much cause from purely domestic considerations) was laid down. The brief era of capitalist stabilization was declared ended. Instead Stalin envisaged a new period of capitalist disintegration with attendant wars and crises, which would require that Russia be ready, not only to repel any capitalist attack, but to throw in her weight for the ultimate decision which would decide the fate of the world. In terms of practical politics, Stalin's policy, which he presented as a continuation of the old Left course, meant a drastic break with it. Now, the order of the day was concentration upon the domestic tasks of the First Five Year Plan. Foreign policy, despite the revolutionary flourishes of the Fifteenth Congress, was relegated, for a long time to come, to second place. Its sole task was to work relentlessly for peace and Soviet security in the period of socialist industrialization. No realignment of its forces was needed; the foreign policy phalanx remained roughly in the order in which it had been cast in 1925. But the freedom of the diplomats was sharply curtailed and the units on the revolutionary wing were reorganized. The Comintern was thoroughly "Bolshevized," i.e. transformed into a pliant tool for extensive foreign espionage and underground work. All along the policy front, the aggressive tactics of the earlier years gave way to a new defensive quiescence. The millennial hopes of the early period, although not forgotten, were replaced by ruthlessly realistic aims for the immediate future.

In Soviet diplomacy the change became obvious even before the break with England. Even in the latter part of 1926, foreign observers had noticed increased anxiety and uncertainty in Soviet foreign policy, foreshadowing a change of course.[88] In the following spring the new policy emerged as the crisis of Soviet foreign policy deepened. A renewed but fruitless effort was made to win American recognition. As to Europe, the Narkomindel in a sharp reversal gave up its former unconditional hostility towards the League and dispatched a delegation under Sokolnikov to the World Economic Conference in Geneva, where it stoutly maintained the possibility of peaceful coexistence and coopera-

---

[88] See P. Scheffer, *Sieben Jahre,* p. 304. Also O. Hoetzsch in *Osteuropa*, II, 397.

tion between the two systems.[89] Even more significant was Litvinov's participation, after November 1927, in the work of the preparatory Commission on Disarmament, not to speak of Soviet support of the Kellogg-Briand pact in the following year. Soviet weakness drove the regime to seek closer diplomatic ties with the League of Nations, thus dimly foreshadowing a reaction which, in the 1930's, led to membership in it.

The new turn of Soviet foreign relations also affected Chicherin's position[90] and aggravated the physical ills that had always plagued him. Quite apart from the incompatibility between his temperament and that of Stalin, their political differences made further cooperation difficult. Chicherin, who had much in common with the Right opposition, refused to concede the necessity for the change in Soviet diplomacy dictated by Stalin. He had always opposed the League and did not agree now with the Stalin-Litvinov policy of cautious rapprochement; nor did he accept the necessity for the anti-German agitation that was part of the domestic course. He could not share the dictator's apprehension about the imminence of capitalist attack. And finally he who had always stood for the defense of Soviet state power in critical border areas, as well as in the world in general, could not willingly consent to such a far-reaching subordination of foreign relations to domestic reconstruction. For that reason, he spent much time away from his desk, ill and grumbling, leaving most of his business to Litvinov, who was better adjusted to the totalitarian spirit of the Stalinist regime and found the new policy more congenial to his talents. After an absence of a year and a half, the ailing Commissar was finally released from his position by the Sixteenth Party Congress in July 1930, to die six years later in utter obscurity. As Chicherin disappeared from the scene, Stalin abandoned for the time being any intention to engage in competition for new power abroad and rallied all his energies to the single task of strengthening his home base. He drew the line which he was prepared to hold with his foreign policy phalanx in his report to the Sixteenth Party Congress, insisting that: "We do not seek a single foot of foreign territory, but we will not surrender a single inch of our territory either." By this statement, it is safe to say, he also implied: We will not seek any foreign revolution even during the tempting opportunities of a world depression.

In summary, then, what were the aims of Soviet policy in world affairs as they evolved during the first dozen years of capitalist encirclement? The principal one, which overshadowed all others, was to guarantee the absolute independence and security of the revolutionary development within its world base, Soviet Russia. This, incidentally,

[89] In order to make Soviet attendance possible, the Narkomindel, after having rejected the original invitation, suddenly asked for another invitation. See Nikolaievskii, *Novyi Zhurnal*, no. VIII, p. 376.

[90] On Chicherin's position in the late 1920's, see L. Fischer, *Men and Politics;* and Bessedovsky, P. Scheffer, and O. Hoetzsch in the books previously quoted.

implied a far stricter interpretation of sovereignty (manifested in an extreme reluctance to enter binding political, economic, or even technical arrangements with non-Soviet governments) than prevailed in Western countries. From the first aim followed the second: to make the Soviet government as strong as possible through the planned organization of its human and material resources. Throughout the Chicherin period (and for at least a decade afterwards) Soviet Russia was, despite her often pathetic attempts to exaggerate her significance in world politics, if a Great Power at all, certainly a very weak one. Consequently, her main energies as well as her chief domestic controversies were concerned with the best and quickest ways of overcoming that weakness. The aims and means of her relations with other countries in turn were all conditioned by that weakness. From its narrow base of yet undeveloped strength, the Politburo conducted what might be called "negative" power politics; it counted less on the determining force of its material power than upon the opportunities provided by unrest and disunity among its opponents. The greatest desideratum of Soviet foreign relations was foreign revolution fomented by propaganda and local organization, not alliance or territorial gain. In the absence of such revolution (which, to be sure, in a country like Germany might have made all the difference), the position of Soviet Russia in the world depended to an amazing extent upon the minor ups and downs of parliamentary politics in the West, the turn of the business cycle, local, social, and economic conditions, and still other factors not normally controlled by foreign governments. No wonder then that, given its soring political ambition, the Soviet regime perfected its revolutionary techniques so as to gain at least some measure of control over these hitherto so elusive and hence neglected factors of power politics; no wonder that it strove to intensify its impact abroad by manipulating all phases of its foreign contact and by putting to maximum use every shred of sympathy and loyalty which it could find. Such dependence upon foreign conditions also made the Soviet regime unusually sensitive to regional and national differences; it was forced at the risk of being contradictory to identify itself very closely with local circumstances and the political forces there at play. In other words, it had, in its weakness, to seek for sources of power where the powerful countries had hitherto not yet penetrated, because their traditional resources of strength seemed still adequate.

In the new dimensions of international relations thus opened up by the Bolsheviks, Chicherin and the Narkomindel could play only a limited part. Social agitation was a highly specialized field which called for an experience and a mental outlook far different from those required in the conduct of strait-laced diplomacy. As a result, Soviet diplomacy was excluded from a large share of Soviet foreign relations. And Chicherin faced in acute form many of the difficulties which sooner or later beset diplomats everywhere when their governments are driven to cope with the instability of state and society in vital areas of the world. Within his restricted sphere of activity, he proved a very able craftsman, who justly earned the respect of his critics. His tactical skill in the negotiations at Genoa and Rapallo and his sallies against Curzon at Lausanne raised his prestige even in party circles. But his major successes, like Rapallo, and his failures, like the breach with Britain in 1927, were not of his own making. They were caused by the policies and actions of the Politburo, over which Chicherin had very little control. He was, after all, Foreign Minister in name only. His importance was exaggerated by foreign journalists who were guided in their interpretations by the example of Western governments, where Foreign Ministers enjoyed a large measure of influence in foreign relations, and who failed to realize that this was not true in Russia. Chicherin succeeded, however, in giving credence to their fiction, largely, one suspects, because it was his ambition to make it a reality. Whether unintentionally or by design, he thus effectively camouflaged the real politics of his masters.

Chicherin's main contribution, however, should be sought, not so much in the history of international relations in the 1920's, as in the changing formulations of Soviet foreign policy among the inner circles of the party. He stood for a continued validity of *Realpolitik* in the tradition of Metternich and Bismarck at a time when the professional revolutionaries were all but throwing diplomacy overboard. In his efforts to preserve the *Staatsgedanke* of Russia, he carried over into the new regime the heritage of Tsarist diplomacy. He was responsible for the element of continuity which links Tsarist and Soviet foreign policy and which, despite the great contributions of Leninism, seems to grow stronger as the years go by.

3. MAXIM LITVINOV: SOVIET DIPLOMACY, 1930–1939

Henry L. Roberts

Maxim Litvinov, Peoples Commissar for Foreign Affairs from 1930 to 1939, was undoubtedly the Soviet diplomat most widely and familiarly known in the West during the interwar period. At international conferences and at sessions of the League of Nations his chubby and unproletarian figure radiated an aura of robust and businesslike common sense that was in striking contrast to the enigmatic brutality of the Politburo or the conspiratorial noisiness of the Comintern. Although he was an old revolutionary — he was born Meyer Wallach in 1876 and like Lenin, six years his senior, and Stalin, three years his junior, he assumed a *nom de guerre* while dodging the Tsarist police — to him perhaps more than to any other single person may be traced the impression that revolutionary Russia was returning to the family of nations and could be counted upon as a force of stability and peace. Indeed, the most perplexing problem in Litvinov's career is that of the relation of his role to the totality of aims and intentions of the Soviet regime.

This problem was most sharply posed in the blatant contrast between Litvinov's appeals after 1933 for collective security against Nazi Germany and the provisions of the German-Soviet agreement of August 23, 1939. Was Litvinov really striving for the determined cooperation of the peacefully inclined Powers or was Lord Lothian right in his belief that the ulterior aim of Litvinov's policy was "to maintain

Reprinted from Gordon A. Craig and Felix Gilbert, editors, *The Diplomats 1919–1939* (Copyright 1953 by Princeton University Press). Reprinted by permission of Princeton University Press.

discord in Europe"?[1] Is it correct to assume that there was a distinctive "Litvinov policy"[2] or was his role throughout an essentially subordinate one in the Soviet hierarchy?[3] Were there important differences between Litvinov's outlook and that of the Politburo? If so, how did he survive the great purges which decimated the Foreign Commissariat; if not, why was he so abruptly retired in May 1939? Finally, did his retirement represent a real turning point in Soviet policy or was it only a tactical shift, the importance of which should not be overrated?

In attempting to come to closer grips with these questions — their definitive resolution seems impossible in the absence of evidence from the Soviet archives — this paper will consider in turn three topics: (1) the content of Litvinov's diplomatic policy, so far as it can be ascertained from his public pronouncements and recorded conversations; (2) the connection of this policy with the aims of the Politburo; (3) the relations between Litvinov, the Foreign Commissariat, and the Bolshevist high command.

I.

Although it may be a matter of temperament one can detect a definite and largely consistent flavor of Litvinov's diplomatic attitude and behavior. Never the firebrand or the theoretician, he was always valued for his efficiency and practical abilities. Before the 1905 Revolution, the nickname Papasha (little father) was given to him by party comrades. In 1918, when hopes of general revolution were running high, when Chicherin was suggesting that the League of Nations be based on the expropriation of the capitalists of all countries and was intimating to President Wilson that the latter's government was to be replaced by a Council of Peoples Commissars,[4] Litvinov, writing to Wilson two months later, struck a quite different note. He attempted to explain the Red Terror as a defensive measure, protested against the intervention as leading only to the final devastation of Russia, and concluded: "The dictatorship of toilers and producers is not an aim in itself, but the means of building up a new social system under which useful work and equal rights would be provided for all citizens, irrespective of the class to which they had formerly belonged. One may believe in this ideal or not, but it surely gives no justification for sending

[1] See his speech of April 2, 1936, in *Germany and the Rhineland* (London, Royal Institute of International Affairs, 1936), p. 55.

[2] "Soviet foreign policy between 1929 and May 1939 followed the pattern of Litvinov's mind more than of his chief's." Louis Fischer, *Men and Politics* (New York, 1941), p. 127.

[3] Max Beloff, reflecting on his study of Soviet foreign policy, commented, in 1950: "It is probable, too, that I did not lay enough stress upon the essentially subordinate nature of Litvinov's role." "Soviet Foreign Policy, 1929–1941: Some Notes," *Soviet Studies* (Oxford), II (October 1950), 127.

[4] See his note to Wilson of October 24, 1918, in Jane Degras, ed., *Soviet Documents on Foreign Policy* (London, Royal Institute of International Affairs, 1951), I, 112–120.

foreign troops to fight against it, or for arming and supporting classes interested in the restoration of the old system of exploitation of man by man."[5]

One cannot be sure, of course, whether Litvinov's moderation was merely adroit diplomatic address — it was clearly to the advantage of the struggling regime to persuade the Western Powers to give up their intervention — or whether it actually reflects the absence of revolutionary expectation and belligerence. Louis Fischer reported Litvinov as saying to him some years later, "The prospect of world revolution disappeared on November 11, 1918."[6] In any event, this tone of unrevolutionary reasonableness remained a permanent trade mark of Litvinov's dealings with the outside world.

During the years when Litvinov served as Chicherin's second in the Narkomindel, the principal goals of Soviet diplomacy were, after the flurry of revolution and civil war, to achieve recognition and to increase the security of the Soviet Union by means of treaties of neutrality and nonaggression. The reason for these goals is evident and requires no discussion. Less evident is the Soviet purpose in entering the League discussions concerning disarmament, discussions which first brought Litvinov's name to general prominence.

The initial Soviet attitude on the subject of war and peace is stated in the Narkomindel's Appeal to the Toiling, Oppressed and Exhausted Peoples of Europe, of December 19, 1917: "We do not attempt to conceal the fact that we do not consider the existing capitalist Governments capable of making a democratic peace. The revolutionary struggle of the toiling masses against the existing Governments can alone bring Europe nearer to such a peace. Its full realization can only be guaranteed by the victorious proletarian revolution in all capitalist countries."[7] As a logical consequence the League of Nations was viewed as a "mere mask, designed to deceive the broad masses, for the aggressive aims of the imperialist policy of certain Great Powers or their vassals."[8] Despite this hostile attitude, Litvinov appeared at the Preparatory Commission of the Disarmament Conference to propose "the complete abolition of all land, marine, and air forces."

Litvinov never denied these Soviet views concerning peace under capitalism. In 1922 he granted that the present social-economic structures of the majority of countries made the removal of the possibility of armed international conflict "unthinkable."[9] In 1927 he reiterated the Soviet Union's lack of confidence in the readiness and capability of

[5] Telegram from Litvinov to Wilson, December 24, 1918, ibid., pp. 129–133.

[6] Fischer, *Men and Politics*, p. 127. Litvinov's American biographer, Arthur Upham Pope, states that as early as 1920 Litvinov had declared that the project of world revolution was impossible. (*Maxim Litvinoff*, New York, 1943, p. 334).

[7] Degras, *Soviet Documents*, I, 19.

[8] Ibid., I, 381.

[9] *The Soviet Union and Peace* (New York, n.d.), p. 117.

capitalist countries to destroy the system of war between nations.[10] Nevertheless, this fundamental skepticism did not, in Litvinov's view, preclude the possibility of negotiating for disarmament. On November 6, 1930, he made this point quite clearly: "To us, the representatives of the Soviet Union, and exponents of definite socio-economic theories, the impossibility of removing the politico-economic antagonisms of capitalist society, and hence the ultimate inevitability of war, is perfectly clear. We believe, however, or we should not be here, that the danger of war might be considerably diminished, or made comparatively remote, by some measure of real disarmament."[11] It would appear that something which is ultimately inevitable may, however, be reduced as an imminent likelihood by appropriate action.

But was the Soviet proposal for complete disarmament such an appropriate action? Did it represent an effort, as Litvinov put it, "to find a common language" with the other Powers? It is easy to understand the embarrassed and irritable reaction of the other nations, which were trying — without notable success — to fit disarmament into a more general program encompassing security and arbitration. But to the charge that the Soviet scheme could not guarantee security or destroy international distrust, Litvinov simply answered that he was not offering a universal remedy ("We cannot recommend you any such panacea, for we know you would not entertain it for a moment.").[12]

The other Powers also had suspicions, though they were reluctant to express them, that the real intent of the Soviets was to weaken other states militarily and increase the effectiveness of the Communist weapons of insurrection and subversion. To this charge Litvinov replied with a mixture of frankness and disingenuousness. He stated that the Soviet government had no intention of participating with any other government in working out questions "regarding the class war or the struggle against revolution," and asked caustically if the purpose of armaments was to put down possible revolution. He also gave the customary Soviet denial of any responsibility for the actions of the Comintern.

A more serious doubt about the sincerity of the Soviet disarmament proposal arises from the basic premises of Leninism. The argument has been advanced that the Soviets by their own theory could not be advocates of disarmament: True peace is achievable only in a classless and stateless world. Such a world cannot come about by a process of peaceful evolution, but involves the establishment of the dictatorship of the proletariat. This dictatorship explicitly rests on force, of which the Red Army is, equally explicitly, a vital element. Hence, complete disarmament would be, for the Soviets, a "suicidal act."[13] This

[10] Ibid., p. 134.
[11] The Soviet's Fight for Disarmament (New York, n.d.), p. 34.
[12] The Soviet Union and Peace, pp. 188–189.
[13] See T. A. Taracouzio, War and Peace in Soviet Diplomacy (New York, 1940), pp. 266–276, for an able expression of this argument.

argument, however, is not wholly conclusive since the Communist response would be that their analysis and consequent tactics were based on the real nature of modern imperialist states. If these states were to prove capable of overcoming their own nature by the act of disarmament, then the Soviet Union could likewise disarm the Red army. Such indeed was the implication of Litvinov's report to the Fifteenth Congress of the Russian Communist party: "If the capitalist governments doubt our sincerity, they have a simple means of proving it. This means is their adherence to our programme. Let them decide on this. If they do not do this, if they cannot do this, if they do not wish to do this, then, before the whole world, against their will, they testify to the fact that a proposal for full disarmament and abolition of war can emanate only from the Soviet Government; that it can be accepted and executed only when the Soviet system has been adopted by all the countries of the world, when their policies and principles will, of course, be at one with those by which the USSR is guided."[14]

In retrospect the real criticism to be made of Litvinov's stand on disarmament in the 1920's is not that it was insincere propaganda but that by viewing the world in the black and white of Communism versus Capitalist Imperialism it misrepresented the significance of the relations between the non-Communist Powers, and reduced them to the sinful bickerings of reprobates.[15] By making the sweeping generalization that "economic competition is the true cause of war" it falsely placed the issue of security, which could not be separated from disarmament, on an all-or-nothing basis.

With such an outlook collective security was, of course, impossible. In 1924 Chicherin had said: "The Soviet Government therefore rejects any plan for an international organization which implies the possibility of measures of constraint being exercised by any international authority whatsoever against a particular state. . . . In the present international situation, it is impossible in most cases to say which party is the aggressor. Neither the entry into foreign territory nor the scale of war preparations can be regarded as satisfactory criteria. . . . The Soviet Government considers, therefore, that it is absolutely impossible to adopt the system of deciding which State is the aggressor in the case of each conflict and making definite consequences depend upon such decision."[16] In 1928 Litvinov expressed somewhat the same view: "Owing to the lack of exact criteria as to what constitutes an offensive and what a defensive war, the system of regional guarantee pacts based upon mutual assistance . . . may end in something perilously akin to the prewar system of alliances and other military and political combinations."[17]

[14] The Soviet Union and Peace, p. 162.
[15] In his report to the Fifteenth Congress Litvinov said: "It may be said that on all questions considered by the Commission, a clear sharp line was drawn between us and the other delegates. It was a case of *we* and *they*. And this is as it should be."
[16] Degras, Soviet Documents, I, 432-433.
[17] The Soviet Union and Peace, p. 167.

Even the innocuous Kellogg Pact was regarded with deep suspicion. Chicherin, in August 1928, flatly termed it "an organic part of the preparation for war against the USSR." Litvinov, too, intimated that the proposal to prohibit war as an instrument of national policy implied the possibility of war as an instrument for the defence of "civilization" against "barbarism" — i.e. against the Soviet Union.[18] Nevertheless, after having criticized its origins, its omissions, and its reservations, Litvinov not only announced that the USSR would subscribe to the pact but then turned it to advantage by achieving a regional reaffirmation of its terms through the Litvinov Protocol, signed by the Soviet Union and most of its Western neighbors, in February 1929. The Protocol, however, represented "negative security"; it was not a step toward positive cooperative action. When, in 1929, the United States government attempted to invoke the Kellogg Pact in the Russian-Chinese dispute in Manchuria, Litvinov brusquely rejected all efforts at diplomatic intervention and declared that the Pact did not provide any one of its signatories with the function of being its guardian. Clearly, he was not thinking of collective security at this point.

In July 1930, Chicherin, who had been in ill health for some years, was retired, and Litvinov became chief of the Narkomindel. It is generally agreed that the relations between the two men were far from friendly. Their temperaments clashed, each was suspicious of the other's intentions, and Litvinov, who, despite his amiable appearance, was not an easy person to get on with, appears to have been not overly scrupulous in his ambitions to become Foreign Commissar.[19]

With regard to a new course in foreign policy, Litvinov, on July 25, 1930, informed correspondents that his appointment did not imply any change, not only because he had been for ten years a close associate of Chicherin's but because, under the dictatorship of the proletariat, foreign policy was determined by the will of the working masses and hence not subject to fluctuations.[20] Nevertheless, the German ambassador in Moscow, Dirksen, felt, or so he related twenty years later, that his task had become more difficult because Litvinov was not a really convinced adherent of the Rapallo policy but gave it only lip service.[21] Dirksen

[18] Louis Fischer (*Men and Politics*, pp. 88–89) states that neither Litvinov nor Chicherin really believed that the Soviet Union was threatened with attack in 1927–28. Litvinov is quoted as saying, "That was merely idle gossip here of some people and the press. . . . It is wrong to suppose, as many of us do, that Russia is the center of all international affairs. . . ."

[19] See A. Barmine, *Memoirs of a Soviet Diplomat* (London, 1938), pp. 217–218.

[20] M. Litvinov, *Vneshniaia politika* SSSR (Moscow, 1937), p. 59.

[21] Herbert von Dirksen, *Moskau, Tokio, London: Erinnerungen und Betrachtungen zu 20 Jahre deutscher Aussenpolitik, 1919–1939* (Stuttgart, 1950), pp. 94–95. Dirksen also commented: "Although he [Litvinov] almost passionately denied any deviation from the pure Rapallo doctrine, his sympathies were with Great Britain, where he had passed the years of his exile and met his wife. So he had to be earnestly admonished from time to time when he was disposed to deviate from the correct faith to the Western heresy."

went on to say, however, that Litvinov did not really deviate from the German orientation until the Nazi seizure of power gave him the perhaps not unhoped for opportunity to be one of the first to abandon the Rapallo connection.

In fact, it was not his new post as Foreign Commissar but rather developments abroad between 1931 and 1933 which led Litvinov to a new course. The process was gradual, but several stages may be observed.

The Soviet Union continued its policy of signing neutrality and nonaggression pacts with its neighbors. Treaties were made with Turkey, Lithuania, Iran, and Afghanistan between 1925 and 1927. A new treaty with Afghanistan was signed on June 24, 1931. Then, in September 1931 Japan launched its attack on Manchuria. On January 21, 1932, the Soviet Union and Finland signed a treaty which resembled its predecessors, but included a significant new clause: "Should either High Contracting Party resort to aggression against a third Power, the other High Contracting Party may denounce the present treaty without notice." This clause appeared in all subsequent Soviet nonaggression treaties up to but definitely not including the pact with Germany of August 1939.[22]

If this double negative — denouncing a nonaggression pact — be considered a positive step, it may be concluded that this initial move toward collective security, at least by indirection, was stimulated by the first overt aggression of the 1930's.

Litvinov, however, still challenged the possibility of improving international relations except by the path of disarmament. On February 11, 1932, at the Disarmament Conference he declared: "Security against war must be created. This security can never be achieved by roundabout ways, but only by the direct way of total general disarmament. This is no communist slogan. The Soviet delegation knows that the triumph of socialistic principles, removing the causes giving rise to armed conflicts, is the only absolute guarantee of peace. So long, however, as these principles prevail only in one-sixth of the world, there is only one means of organizing security against war, and that is total and general disarmament."[23]

A year later, on February 6, 1933 — that is, after Hitler had come to power — Litvinov took a different line. He expressed, somewhat reluctantly, his willingness to consider the French security proposals, and in conjunction with a French plan submitted a draft definition of aggression. He was now attempting to supply the criteria which in 1928 he had said were lacking. Litvinov's original draft, which defined as aggressions declarations of war, invasions without a declaration, bombardments and naval attacks, landings and unpermitted occupations, and blockades, did not include a notable phrase, subsequently added by a subcommittee of the Disarmament Conference: "Provision of support

[22] Such pacts were signed with Estonia, Latvia, Poland, and France in 1932, and with Italy in 1933.
[23] The Soviet Fight for Disarmament, p. 23.

to armed bands formed on its territory which have invaded the territory of another state, or refusal, notwithstanding the request of the invaded State, to take on its own territory all the measures in its power to deprive these bands of all assistance or protection."[24] Moreover, Litvinov's original draft in its second clause was far more vigorous than the subsequent convention in spelling out the political, military, economic or other considerations which could *not* serve as an excuse or justification for aggression as defined: in substance, revolutionary regimes were not to be subject to retaliation for their revolutionary acts of expropriation and civil violence, "backward areas" were not to be exploited by force or penalized by gunboat assault for their actions against capitalist exploitation. It is interesting to note, in view of the publicity later given to the definition of aggression, that Litvinov said frankly, "I admit, however, that the Soviet delegation itself attributes infinitely greater importance to the second clause in its declaration."[25] Thus, the Soviet Union was at this time definitely less interested in establishing a criterion for aggression — which could provide the basis for collective measures — than in protecting its position as a revolutionary state in a presumably hostile world.

A modification of the convention was proposed by a subcommittee on May 24, 1933, and was accepted by the Soviets. While it fared no further at the Disarmament Conference, at the London Economic Conference Litvinov proposed that Russia and its neighbors sign this convention. The proposal was accepted, and in July 1933 a series of treaties bound the Soviet Union, Afghanistan, Estonia, Latvia, Persia, Poland, Rumania, Czechoslovakia, Turkey, Yugoslavia, Finland, and Lithuania to accept this definition of aggression.

On December 29, 1933, shortly after his return from the United States, where he had successfully negotiated for American recognition,[26] Litvinov delivered an important speech to the Central Executive Committee of the USSR. In this speech a distinct change in outlook was

[24] It is worth noting that when the USSR in November 1950 presented a definition of aggression to the Political Committee of the U.N. General Assembly, it reverted to the original Litvinov formulation — i.e., without mention of indirect aggression by armed bands — and not to the revised formula accepted by the Soviet Union in 1933 and used in its treaties with neighboring powers.

[25] League of Nations, *Records of the Conference for the Reduction and Limitation of Armaments*, Series B, Minutes of General Commission, II, 238.

[26] For the negotiations leading to the establishment of American-Soviet diplomatic relations and for an account of the mutually disappointing aftermath, see *Foreign Relations: Diplomatic Papers: The Soviet Union, 1933–1939* (Washington, 1952). American-Soviet relations are not discussed here primarily because they were not of great importance to Litvinov's major diplomatic efforts. As George F. Kennan wrote from Moscow in November 1937: "When he can be found in Moscow, Litvinov has frequently shown a reluctance to discuss topics other than those he considers to be major political matters. These seem at present to be the success or failure of efforts to induce other states to take strong measures against Germany, Italy and Japan. The result is that few of the current problems of Soviet-American relations attract his interest." Ibid., p. 447.

apparent. The era of "bourgeois pacifism" had come to an end; new and dangerous ideologies were arising. But whereas Litvinov had previously tended to lump all capitalist states together, he now differentiated between actively belligerent powers, those that were temporarily passive but that would not mind a bit of fighting in the world, especially if it were directed against the USSR, and those powers actively interested in the preservation of peace. With regard to the latter, "I am not entering into an estimation of the motives for such a policy, but am merely stating a fact which is highly valuable to us." Moreover, while stressing that the Soviet Union was perfectly capable of defending itself, "and even the approaches to it," he went on to say that "the maintenance of peace cannot depend upon our efforts alone. It depends upon the cooperation and assistance of other countries as well. By striving, there-fore, toward the establishment and maintenance of friendly relations with all countries we devote particular attention to the strengthening of relations and maximum rapprochement with those countries which, like ourselves, furnish proof of their sincere desire to preserve peace and show that they are prepared to oppose any violators of peace."[27]

The chief trouble makers, of course, were Germany and Japan, to whom Litvinov devoted a considerable amount of attention. He pointed out that for ten years Germany and Russia had enjoyed particularly close political and economic relations, which were advantageous to both Powers. Nevertheless, relations had deteriorated beyond recognition in the course of the last year. The new German regime was showing itself openly hostile to the Soviet Union; its leaders in the past had frequently advocated an anti-Soviet policy, which they had not disavowed since they had come to power. He denied that the Nazi attack on the German Communists was the source of friction: "We have, of course, our own opinion of the German regime. We are, of course, sensitive to the suffer-ings of our German comrades, but we Marxists are the last who can be reproached for permitting our feelings to dictate our policy." He empha-sized that the Soviet Union desired good relations with Germany, but that the responsibility lay with the new regime to desist from its current attitude. In concluding, Litvinov fell back upon the older view that the USSR was, after all, surrounded by capitalist Powers and had ultimately to rely upon the Red army, navy, and air force.

In passing, it is interesting to compare this speech with the one delivered by Stalin to the Seventeenth Congress of the Communist party a few weeks later, on January 26, 1934.[28] While the main lines of foreign policy were quite similar, there was a certain difference in emphasis. Stalin's speech, naturally, was more pontifical and grimmer in tone. He expounded at greater length on the reasons for the changes in the world scene, stressing, as always, the economic crisis of capi-talism (Litvinov had given less weight to this, and suggested such other

[27] *Vneshniaia politika* SSSR (Moscow, 1937), pp. 74–96.
[28] J. Stalin, *Problems of Leninism*, 11th edition (Moscow, 1940), pp. 470–486.

factors as the rise of a new generation which had not experienced war). His talk was more "revolutionary": "The masses of the people have not yet reached the stage when they are ready to storm capitalism; but the idea of storming it is maturing in the minds of the masses." While criticizing the attitude of the new German regime, he was by no means friendly to the "peaceloving" capitalist Powers. He denied any new orientation: "Our orientation in the past and our orientation at the present time is towards the USSR, and towards the USSR alone."

The year 1933 seems definitely to have marked a major turning point in Litvinov's diplomatic orientation. To be sure, in subsequent years Communist spokesmen would say that the Soviet Union had anticipated the mounting crisis of the 1930's and point to a multitude of statements about the precarious state of the capitalist world and the emergence of fascism. But in these earlier statements the jeremiads against the capitalist world were general volleys against all the Western Powers, just as the term fascism was a general epithet for quite indiscriminate use in domestic politics. The specific menace of a National Socialist Germany was something else again, and it took the unpleasant experiences of 1933 to bring Litvinov, and the Soviet Union, to the position he adopted in his speech at the end of the year.

For the next two and a half years, however, Litvinov proceeded in high gear down the road of collective security and cooperation with the peace-loving Powers. These were the years when the USSR joined the League, when mutual assistance pacts were signed with France and Czechoslovakia, and when Litvinov made some of his most constructive pronouncements on the means to preserve peace, which he now declared to be "indivisible."

In the spring of 1934, on May 29, Litvinov was prepared to admit that "international life and particularly political events in some countries during recent years had prevented the [Disarmament] Conference from carrying out its direct task of drawing up a disarmament convention." After all, however, disarmament was only a means to an end: "Could not the Conference feel its way towards other guarantees for peace?" — a possibility he had categorically denied some years earlier. He then went on to say that, "Even if there should be dissident States, that should by no means prevent the remainder from coming still more closely together to take steps which would strengthen their own security."[29]

In line with this approach was a new and amiable view toward the League of Nations. As late as December 1933 Litvinov had denied that Russia was likely to join the League in any foreseeable future, but by the following spring his attitude was quite different, and in September the USSR obtained a permanent seat in the Council. Of course, one specific reason for joining the League was that a mutual assistance pact with France, the negotiations for which began in 1934, could be recon-

---

[29] League of Nations, *Records of the Conference for the Reduction and Limitation of Armaments,* Series B, III, 657–661.

ciled with the Locarno Treaty only if France's partner were a member of the League.[30]

Although Litvinov was unsuccessful in persuading Germany to join in guaranteeing the Eastern European frontiers or in creating an Eastern Locarno pact, France and Russia did achieve a mutual assistance pact, which was signed on May 2, 1935. On May 16 was also signed a Soviet-Czech mutual assistance pact, with provisions similar to those of the French pact, but stipulating that they should come into force only if France gave assistance to the country attacked.

Although the Soviet Union was thus drawing closer to some of the capitalist Powers, at the same time, in 1935 and 1936, the Fascist states struck three decisive blows at the structure of European peace: Germany's repudiation of disarmament, the Italian attack on Abyssinia, and the march into the Rhineland. While each of these events did not directly concern the USSR and while the Soviet government did not actually take any important measures, a good deal of Litvinov's positive reputation rests on the speeches he delivered in response to these actions.

In his speech of April 17, 1935, he stated that while the Soviet Union neither favored the Versailles Treaty nor was bound by it, the German action did violate the Covenant of the League, and "one of the foundations of peace is the observance of international relations directly affecting the security of nations."[31] He agreed in principle to the right of equality of armament, but not "if a country which demands or assumes the right to arm is exclusively led by people who have publicly announced as the programme of their foreign policy a policy which consists, not only in revenge, but in the unrestricted conquest of foreign territory and the destruction of the independence of whole States."

On September 5, 1935, when Italy was threatening Abyssinia, he pointed out that while the USSR had no interests involved, the Italian action could set a dangerous precedent: "The repetition of the precedent would certainly have a cumulative effect and, in its turn, would stimulate new conflicts more directly affecting the whole of Europe."[32]

On September 14, in speaking of the Fascist Powers' technique of advocating bilateral pacts, he stated: "We know of another political conception that is fighting the idea of collective security and advocating bilateral pacts, and this not even between all States but only between States arbitrarily chosen for this purpose. This conception can have nothing in common with peaceful intentions. Not every pact of nonaggression is concluded with a view to strengthening general peace. While nonaggression pacts concluded by the Soviet Union with its neighbors, include a special clause for suspending the pact in cases of aggression committed by one of the parties against any third State, we

[30] Max Beloff, *The Foreign Policy of Soviet Russia* (2 vols., London, 1947, 1949), I, 135.
[31] Maxim Litvinov, *Against Aggression* (New York, 1939), pp. 18–19.
[32] League of Nations, *Official Journal*, 16th Year, No. 11, November 1935, p. 1142.

know of other pacts of nonaggression which have no such clause. This means that a State which has secured by such a pact of nonaggression its rear or its flank, obtains the facility of attacking with impunity third States."[33] Perhaps this statement indicates why Litvinov was not quite the man to negotiate the German-Soviet pact of August 1939.

When Germany marched into the Rhineland in March 1936, Litvinov again urged collective action: "One cannot fight for the collective organization of security without taking collective measures against the violation of international obligations. We, however, do not count among such measures collective capitulation to the aggressor."[34]

His funeral speech, on July 1, 1936, for the demise of Abyssinia was one of his best. "We are gathered here," he began, "to close a page in the history of the League of Nations, the history of international life, which it will be impossible to read without a feeling of bitterness." The League had been unable to maintain the territorial integrity and political independence of one of its members, and it was possible that the League itself would be declared bankrupt. Litvinov undertook to combat this defeatist mood and to strengthen the collective security provisions of the Covenant: "I say we do not want a League that is safe for aggressors. We do not want that kind of League, even if it is universal, because it would become the very opposite of an instrument of peace. . . .

"We must educate and raise people up to its lofty ideas, not degrade the League. We must seek to make the League universal, but we must not by any means make it safe for the aggressor to this end. On the contrary, all new members and all ex-members wishing to return must read on its portals: 'Abandon all hope of aggression and its impunity all ye who enter here.' . . .

"As for myself, I would rather have a League of Nations that tries to render at least some assistance, even if it proves ineffective, to a victim of aggression, than a League of Nations that closes its eyes to aggression and lets it pass unperturbed. . . .

"In an ideal League of Nations military sanctions, too, should be obligatory for all. But if we are yet unable to rise to such heights of international solidarity, we should make it our concern to have all continents, and for a start, at least all Europe, covered with a system of regional pacts, on the strength of which groups of States would undertake to protect particular sectors from aggression."[35]

Finally, on September 28, 1936, he warned against the sense of apathy that was spreading under the impact of the Axis: "The legend of the invincible aggressor is being created even outside his country; it is engendering fatalistic and capitulatory sentiments in some countries, which gradually — sometimes even without their noticing it — are beginning to lose their independence and are becoming vassals of the

[33] League of Nations, *Official Journal, Special Supplement to No. 138*, p. 73.
[34] Litvinov, *Against Aggression*, p. 23.
[35] Ibid., pp. 35–45.

aggressor. Thus begins the process of the formation of a hegemony which is to culminate in the crushing of all refractory countries by force of arms."[36]

Toward the end of 1936, however, there were signs that the Soviet Union's new policy was not proving particularly fruitful. The growing menace of Germany, Italy, and Japan was not being checked. The efforts at collective security did not develop into anything substantial, and indeed the outbreak of the Spanish Civil War introduced new strains in the relations between the Soviets and France and Great Britain. The Popular Front adopted by the Comintern did not diminish the suspicions of the non-Communist states which continued to find that the activities of domestic Communists were a major impediment to collaboration with the Soviet Union. The great purges within Russia were under way and served to weaken Western confidence in the character and stability of the Soviet regime.

In Litvinov's speech before the Extraordinary Eighth Congress of Soviets, on November 28, 1936, a new note, or rather an old one, made its appearance. After commenting on the danger of fascism, not as a form of government but as a source of external aggression, after stressing the specifically anti-Soviet content of the anti-Comintern pact (he clearly had very accurate information on its secret terms), Litvinov waxed bitter over the policy of nonintervention in Spain, and uttered a definite word of warning to the non-Fascist Powers:

"The Soviet Union, however, does not beg to be invited to any unions, any *blocs*, any combinations. She will calmly let other States weigh and evaluate the advantages which can be derived for peace from close cooperation with the Soviet Union, and understand that the Soviet Union can give more than receive. . . .

"Other States, other territories are menaced most. Our security does not depend upon paper documents or upon foreign policy combinations. The Soviet Union is sufficiently strong in herself."[37]

From this time on, in Litvinov's speeches and reported statements two distinct themes are detectable: on the one hand, a continued appeal for collective security; on the other, increasing animus against Great Britain and France and the threat of a Soviet return to isolation. The first theme needs no further development as it is largely the exposition of the principles set forth in the preceding two or three years. The second and ominous theme tends to become more and more dominant.

On February 4, 1937, Litvinov complained to the United States ambassador, Joseph E. Davies, that "he could not understand why Great Britain could not see that once Hitler dominated Europe he would swallow the British Isles also. He seemed to be very much stirred about this and apprehensive lest there should be some composition of differences between France, England and Germany."[38] On February 15 he said that "Germany was concerned solely with conquest and it was a

36 Ibid., p. 49.
37 Ibid., pp. 78–79.
38 Joseph E. Davies, *Mission to Moscow* (New York, 1941), p. 60.

mistake to magnify Hitler's importance by engaging in discussions of the character which France and England were projecting."[39]

In a speech to the electors of Leningrad, on November 27, 1937, Litvinov reiterated the old theme that imperialism was inherent in all bourgeois states, and was heavily sarcastic about the efforts of France and Britain to pretend that the Fascist Powers were not aggressive: "I see it is a puzzle to you how experienced bourgeois diplomats could fail to understand the meaning of the aggressor's tactics. You think they are only pretending to disbelieve the aggressor's statements and, under cover of negotiations for confirmations and explanations, they are groping for a deal with the aggressor. You can think so if you like, but my position does not allow me to express such doubts, and I must leave them to your responsibility."[40]

In December Litvinov had an interview with a foreign correspondent in which he was reported, some years later, to have made the following significant remarks:

"Anti-Comintern Pact? What nonsense! Can you never look at things without your cheap bourgeois prejudice? The Anti-Comintern Pact is no threat to the Soviet Union. It is dust in the eyes of the Western democracies. . . . Ideologies mean little to the Fascist brigands. The Germans have militarized the Reich and are bent on a brutal policy of gangsterism. Those contemptible peoples, the Japanese and Italians, are following at the German heels, hoping to share in the spoils of German conquest. It is the rich capitalist countries which will fall an easy prey. The British and French peoples are soft under leaders who are blind. The Soviet Union is the last foe to be attacked by the Anti-Comintern powers. They will loot your countries, but we have the Red Army and a vast extent of territory. . . .

"Hitler and the generals who control Germany read history. They know that Bismarck warned against war on two fronts. They know that he urged the reinsurance policy with Russia. They believe the Kaiser lost the first world war because he forgot Bismarck's admonitions. When the Germans are prepared at last to embark upon their new adventures, these bandits will come to Moscow to ask us for a pact."[41] According to this report, he predicted the *Anschluss* and the attack on Czechoslovakia, and pointed out that the Soviet Union need not come to Czechoslovakia's aid unless France did: "Well, France won't fight. France is through."

By the spring of 1938 Litvinov had adopted a comparatively passive role, though still affirming that the Soviet Union was ready to join in collective action to arrest further aggression, and was willing to discuss measures within the League or outside it. In March 1938 he told Davies that Czechoslovakia would probably fall because it lacked confidence in France; for that matter "France has no confidence in the Soviet

[39] Ibid., p. 79.
[40] Litvinov, *Against Aggression*, pp. 106–107.
[41] J. T. Whitaker, *We Cannot Escape History* (New York, 1943), pp. 207–208.

Union, and the Soviet Union has no confidence in France. . . . The only thing that would prevent a complete Fascist domination of Europe was a change of government or policy in Great Britain." He appeared to envisage within the near future a Europe dominated by fascism and opposed only by Great Britain on the West and the USSR on the East.[42]

The prolonged Czechoslovakian crisis of 1938 is far too complex for even summary discussion here. In general, it may be said that Litvinov, publicly and apparently privately, stood by the position that the Soviet Union would honor its obligations to Czechoslovakia if France came to the latter's aid. On the other hand, he repeatedly indicated that the responsibility for taking the initiative lay with France, and this included the thorny question of obtaining Polish and/or Rumanian permission for Russian troops to come to Czechoslovakia's assistance.

There does not seem to be much evidence, however, that he was expecting Russia to be required to take forceful action. It is striking that neither the British nor the German diplomatic representatives in Moscow felt that the Soviet government showed any sign of preparing itself or the Russian people for the defense of Czechoslovakia. The German ambassador, Schulenburg, commented that Litvinov's speech of June 23, 1938, showed distinct aloofness and a desire to retain freedom of action. Moreover, "the tone of the speech has remarkably little aggressiveness and strives to leave open all possibilities. The attempt to arrive at an objective attitude toward the policy of the Third Reich is striking."[43] On August 22, 1938, Litvinov, in a conversation with Schulenburg was quite frank in charging Germany with aggression and a desire to destroy Czechoslovakia. He went on to say, however, "If the old democratic Germany still existed, the Czech question would have a quite different aspect for the Soviet Union." While the Soviet Union approved of national self-determination and had had no part in the creation of Czechoslovakia, the threat to its independence affected the balance of power: an increase in Nazi strength would be bad for the Soviet Union.[44] According to a British report the Germans felt that in this conversation Litvinov was opening the door for a possible German-Russian rapprochement.[45] Schulenburg, however, did not thus interpret his conversation, and its content as reported need not lead to such an interpretation.

Was Litvinov considering the possibility of independent Soviet action even if France failed to act? This question remains somewhat obscure. In May 1938 he asked the French ambassador Coulondre what France, the ally of Poland, would do in case the latter, having attacked Czechoslovakia, was itself attacked in turn by the USSR? Coulondre replied that the answer was obvious since France was also allied with Czechoslovakia, and both treaties were defensive. Coulondre also pointed out that France recognized that Russia was not bound to move

[42] Davies, *Mission to Moscow*, p. 291.
[43] *German Documents*, series D, I, 1924.
[44] Ibid., II, 604, 630.
[45] *British Documents,* 3rd series, II, 141, note 3.

unless France intervened. Litvinov replied, "That is right, but there is another hypothesis: the case in which the USSR for one reason or another should intervene without France having moved."[46] The question naturally presents itself, as it did to Coulondre at the time, whether the Soviet Union was envisaging military action against Poland and whether such action was possible without a preliminary understanding with Germany.

As far as the Czechs themselves are concerned, it is still not altogether clear whether, and if so how, they were led to believe that Russia would aid them even if France did not. Apparently Litvinov, through the Soviet minister in Prague, Alexandrovsky, did inform the Czech government that if the case were submitted to the League of Nations and Germany were found an aggressor, the Soviet Union would give assistance regardless of France.[47] This was clearly not a very rash promise under the circumstances. It has also been stated, though the evidence seems less satisfactory, that Alexandrovsky later informed the Czech government that the Soviet government would come to the support of Czechoslovakia as soon as Moscow was informed that the League had been seized of the case and would not wait for a decision to be reached at Geneva.[48] Some years later Benes referred to "the fact that, in spite of the insistence of Moscow, I did not provoke war with Germany in 1938."[49] Some light on this remark may be cast by a statement in a recent Soviet work: "More than that, J. V. Stalin, in conversation with K. Gottwald, said that the Soviet Union was ready to give military aid to Czechoslovakia, even if France did not do this, but on the condition that Czechoslovakia defend itself and ask for Soviet assistance. Gottwald told Benes to that effect."[50] Although this statement requires a good·deal of elucidation, it would indicate that such approaches, if made, may not have been through diplomatic channels but through the Communist party. In any event there appears to be no direct evidence connecting Litvinov with any measures more extensive than those to which the USSR was publicly committed: the Czech Treaty and the League of Nations. Furthermore, although Litvinov told the Germans that he thought France and England would assist Czechoslovakia, he seems to have been thoroughly skeptical. On September 16, in discussing with a foreign journalist ways and means of Soviet assistance, he remarked, "This is also unrealistic. . . . They have already sold Czechoslovakia down the river."[51]

In his last major speech in the League, on September 21, 1938, Litvinov bitterly criticized the record of the last few years: "A fire brigade was set up in the innocent hope that, by some lucky chance,

[46] Robert Coulondre, *De Staline à Hitler* (Paris, 1950), p. 153.
[47] Cf. Beloff, *Foreign Policy*, II, 151.
[48] John W. Wheeler-Bennett, *Munich — Prologue to Tragedy* (New York, 1948), p. 127.
[49] Letter from Eduard Benes to L. B. Namier, in Namier, *Europe in Decay*, p. 284.
[50] *Diplomaticheskii Slovar'* (1950), II, 198.
[51] Fischer, *Men and Politics*, p. 561.

there would be no fires. Things turned out differently, however. Fires have broken out in defiance of our hopes, but luckily not in our immediate vicinity: so let us dissolve the fire brigade — of course not forever, but merely temporarily. Directly the danger of any fire disappears, we shall reassemble the fire brigade without a moment's delay." He also carefully relieved the Soviet Union of any responsibility in the debacle: "At a moment when the mines are being laid to blow up the organization on which were fixed the great hopes of our generation, and which stamped a definite character on the international relations of our epoch; at a moment when, by no accidental coincidence, decisions are being taken outside the League which recall to us the international transactions of prewar days, and which are bound to overturn all present conceptions of international morality and treaty obligations; at a moment when there is being drawn up a further list of sacrifices to the god of aggression, and a line is being drawn under the annals of all postwar international history, with the sole conclusion that nothing succeeds like aggression — at such a moment, every State must define its role and its responsibility before its contemporaries and before history. That is why I must plainly declare here that the Soviet Government bears no responsibility whatsoever for the events now taking place, and for the fatal consequences which may inexorably ensue."[52] He concluded: "The Soviet Government takes pride in the fact that it has no part in such a policy, and has invariably pursued the principle of the two pacts I have mentioned, which were approved by nearly every nation in the world [the League Covenant and the Briand-Kellogg Pact]. Nor has it any intention of abandoning them for the future, being convinced that in present conditions it is impossible otherwise to safeguard a genuine peace and genuine international justice. It calls upon other Governments likewise to return to this path."

Despite these concluding remarks it was generally felt among European diplomats that the Munich agreement did mark the bankruptcy of the Litvinov policy and that the USSR would inevitably examine other possibilities. The German reaction is particularly interesting. Counselor of embassy in Moscow, von Tippleskirch, on October 3 and 10, 1938, wrote: "That the policy of Litvinov has suffered a complete fiasco, that the war, from which chaos and weakening of Germany were expected, has not broken out, that the policy of pacts and alliances has failed, that the collective idea has collapsed, and that the League of Nations has disappointed the hopes reposed in it, can in my opinion not remain without consequences for Soviet policy. . . .

"In the light of our experiences it seems to me probable that Stalin will draw conclusions about personalities from the failure of Soviet policy. In that connection I naturally think in the first place of Litvinov, who has made fruitless efforts in Geneva throughout the crisis. . . .[53]

"Litvinov will certainly try to convince the Soviet Government that the policy hitherto pursued by him was the only right one and that it must

[52] Litvinov, *Against Aggression*, p. 127.
[53] *German Documents*, series D, IV, 602–605.

be continued in the future as well. . . . If I judge Litvinov correctly, he will continue to defend his policy of collective action in the conviction that Germany's growth of power . . . will lead to a change in the European balance of power in which sooner or later a definite role must quite automatically fall to the Soviet Union. . . . In other words he will continue to recommend measures against the aggressors in the hope of having more success next time."[54]

This German observer was, perhaps, unduly persuaded that Litvinov still had the opportunity to pursue his policy, or that he really felt capable of pressing it vigorously any longer. Shortly after Munich, Potemkin, Litvinov's assistant, after coldly receiving Coulondre, burst out: "My poor friend, what have you done? As for us I do not see any other outcome than a fourth partition of Poland."[55] And on October 16, Litvinov himself said: "Henceforth the USSR has only to watch, from the shelter of its frontiers, the establishment of German hegemony over the center and southeast of Europe. And if by chance the Western Powers finally decided to wish to stop it, they must address themselves to us, for," he added throwing me a sharp look, "we shall have our word to say."[56] He then went on to remark that he had made the following declaration to Lord Halifax: "Once its hegemony is solidly established in Europe, and France neutralized, Hitler will be able to attack either Great Britain or the USSR. He will choose the first solution because it will offer him much greater advantages with the possibility of substituting the German Empire for the British Empire, and, to succeed in this undertaking, he will prefer to reach an understanding with the USSR."

In his discussions with the British after Munich Litvinov was distinctly cool; he saw no evidence that the Western Powers would cease their policy of capitulation, and said that the Soviet Union would probably remain "aloof" henceforth, since its interests were not directly threatened.[57] In late March 1939, in a conversation with R. S. Hudson, Litvinov was reported as saying that "he foresaw in the not far-distant future a Europe entirely German from the Bay of Biscay to the Soviet frontier and bounded, as it were, simply by Great Britain and the Soviet Union. Even that would not satisfy German ambitions, but the attack, he said smiling happily, would not be directed to the East."[58]

It is true that Litvinov was willing to embark on the final round of fruitless negotiations after the German march into Prague, but it was

[54] Ibid., p. 605.

[55] Coulondre, *De Staline à Hitler*, p. 165. On September 29, 1938, Potemkin said to Schulenburg: "The Powers now taking part in the destruction of Czechoslovakia would bitterly regret their submission to militant nationalism. In the first place, Poland, for there were a 'great many' Germans in Poland; in particular it must not be forgotten that several million Ukrainians were living in Poland, who were already beginning to 'move'." *German Documents*, series D, II, 998.

[56] Coulondre, *De Staline à Hitler*, p. 171.

[57] E.g., his conversation with Sir William Seeds, February 19, 1939. *British Documents*, 3rd series, IV, 124.

[58] Ibid., p. 585.

clear that he displayed no confidence in the Western Powers. On May 3, 1939, he was relieved of his post.

From this review of Litvinov's diplomatic career several general observations may be made. In the first place, his advocacy of collective security was limited in time: before the rise of the Fascist Powers, he denied the possibility of such methods of providing international security. Moreover, from 1936 on there is an increasing note of isolationism: if the other Powers would not cooperate the Soviet Union could follow its own interests independently. In the second place, the idea of collective security was restricted conceptually. Basically the world was still divided into two camps and the Fascist Powers belonged to the capitalist camp. "Peaceful coexistence" was not in the permanent order of things, nor were the motives inducing certain capitalist Powers to be peaceloving necessarily fundamental or enduring. Litvinov's collective security is not to be identified with the idealism of some of his Western admirers.

On the other hand, it is difficult to find evidence that Litvinov had any revolutionary expectations in these years or that by his diplomacy he was bent on fomenting strife. To be sure, the Soviet Union's total impact abroad, its unofficial as well as its official activities, remained troublesome and disturbing. It is also true that Litvinov's speeches to Soviet audiences displayed a truculent and scornful attitude toward the capitalist world which was moderated though not entirely eliminated in his diplomatic addresses to the League. Even so, his speeches on collective security in the League and elsewhere do have a most convincing ring of sincerity and urgency. By 1938 most foreign diplomatic observers in Moscow — Germans as well as French and English — seem to have felt that Litvinov was an ardent supporter of the course he had advocated since 1933.

If, with the above-mentioned qualifications, Litvinov's campaign for collective security was something real and not merely misleading oratory on his part, then the question arises whether his views and those of the Politburo coincided.

II.

From all that is known of the structure of the Soviet state and the Communist party it would be absurd to assume that Litvinov could have pursued a diplomatic course at odds with that desired by Stalin and the inner circle of the Politburo. Clearly the general lines of his foreign policy had the official blessing. Nevertheless, an examination of the available record does reveal a number of instances during his career in which Litvinov was reportedly not in agreement with his superiors. Some of the more illuminating examples may be given, in chronological sequence:

In 1919 a British naval officer, who had an interview with Litvinov in Reval, reported that "M. Litvinoff stated that from the first he had opposed his Government's repudiation of their external debt, as he felt certain that such a course would tend to unify the resistance of other nations against them."[59]

In 1924, according to Christian Rakovsky, Litvinov wished to recognize Rumanian sovereignty over Bessarabia in order to settle the matter. Opposed to his view were Rakovsky, Chicherin, and Stalin, who felt it desirable to maintain Bessarabia as a "Soviet irredenta."[60]

Litvinov seems not to have been convinced of the value of Soviet and Comintern maneuvers in the colonial and Asiatic world at the expense of relations with the Western Powers. He is reported as having said, in March 1929, "I think an agreement with England about Afghanistan and the East generally is possible, but the government takes a different view."[61]

In 1938 it was the opinion of the German ambassador that the new evidence of Soviet antiforeign feeling shown in the closing of numerous consulates was not Litvinov's doing: "Litvinov has to accommodate himself to this predominance of domestic policy."[62]

In January 1938 both Zhdanov and Molotov publicly criticized the Foreign Commissariat, though not Litvinov in person, for its presumed lenience with France, which was accused of harboring anti-Soviet elements, terrorists, and diversionists.[63]

In the summer of 1938 Coulondre told Schulenburg that Litvinov was willing to agree to Soviet participation in defraying expenses occasioned by the withdrawal of volunteer troops from Spain, but had encountered opposition in the Politburo. Litvinov seemed willing to cut losses in the Spanish affair, but the Politburo had prestige considerations.[64]

On March 1, 1939, Schulenburg, referring to Soviet economic negotiations with Germany and Japan, remarked that "M. Litvinov does not regard M. Mikoyan's negotiations with a friendly eye at all. If by obstinacy toward Japan he can sabotage the zealous activities of the Commissar for Foreign Trade, he will intensify rather than moderate this line of action.[65]

Louis Fischer has remarked that Litvinov "has never by word or hint approved of Stalin's pact policy with Hitler."[66] It is obvious, of course, that the German-Soviet rapprochement of 1939 was hardly in the spirit of collective security, that the nonaggression pact of August 23 did not contain the escape clause in the event one of the signatories attacked a third Power. On the other hand, as should be apparent from the above, it is not difficult to find a number of hints of a possible German-Soviet agreement in Litvinov's private remarks from 1937 on.

[59] *British Documents*, 1st series, III, 659.
[60] Fischer, *Men and Politics*, p. 135.
[61] Ibid., p. 128. See also David Dallin, *The Rise of Russia in Asia* (New York, 1949), p. 240.
[62] *German Documents*, series D, I, 905.
[63] Beloff, *Foreign Policy*, II, 113–114.
[64] *German Documents*, series D, III, 714.
[65] Ibid., IV, 628.
[66] Louis Fischer, *The Great Challenge* (New York, 1946), p. 46.

Still, it is worth noting that after the German attack on the USSR in June 1941, and after Stalin in his speech of July 3 had defended the wisdom of the nonaggression pact, Litvinov, in a broadcast in English on July 8, indicated that agreements of any sort with Hitler were worthless because the Nazi gang considered themselves above all conceptions of international obligations. While commenting on the failure to organize collective resistance, he stressed Hitler's technique of dividing his prospective victims: "His strategy is to knock down his victims and strike them one by one in an order prompted by circumstances. He intended first to deal with the Western countries so that he would be free to fall on the Soviet Union." Not only was this no defense of the German-Soviet pact — which would hardly have been a tactful approach to the British and American audience at whom the broadcast was directed — but the whole line of argument was that Hitler's treachery was inevitable and predictable.[67]

Finally, evidence of Litvinov's disapproval of Soviet policy following World War II has been provided by two American reporters writing shortly after his death. C. L. Sulzberger stated that on April 5, 1945, Litvinov, then an isolated figure in Moscow, expressed his pessimism about East-West relations: "The situation is developing badly: First, the Western Powers make a mistake and rub us the wrong way. Then we make a mistake and rub you the wrong way."[68] Richard C. Hottelet wrote that in June 1946 Litvinov indicated to him that the Soviets would continue pressing demands on the West. "As far as I am concerned the root cause is the ideological conception prevailing here that conflict between the Communist and capitalist worlds is inevitable." He declared that the Soviet rulers would not call on him for advice and had reverted to the outmoded concept of security in terms of territory.[69]

While it is difficult to weigh the importance of these scattered examples, they do seem to have a certain consistency: in each case Litvinov appears to have favored practical accommodation with the Western Powers as against moves to create or abet revolution, disturbance, or international disorder. To be sure, such an attitude would be part of his diplomatic function: his job as Foreign Commissar was not made easier by the Communist temptation to kick things around.

Less tangible than these evidences of disagreements on policy but perhaps as important are the subtler indications of a difference in emphasis and interpretation. In a political system where all action and policy are dependent upon a "party line" enunciated by the supreme authority, emphasis and interpretation are all-important, especially since the "line" is often not wholly unambiguous. For example, the theme which underlies Soviet diplomacy throughout most of the interwar period — "the temporary coexistence of the two systems" — can in practice be given two entirely different meanings depending upon the emphasis accorded "temporary" or "coexistence." Although it is perilous

[67] *New York Times*, July 9, 1941.
[68] *New York Times*, January 3, 1952.
[69] *New York World-Telegram*, January 28–February 1, 1952.

to draw conclusions from purely external evidence, there appear to be a number of respects in which Litvinov's interpretation differed from that of the Politburo — Stalin and the rather murky figures of his inner circle.

While Litvinov always acknowledged that the possibilities of co-operation with the capitalist Powers were temporary, that ultimately the capitalist system was doomed to destruction, in the period after Hitler came to power he recognized the Nazi menace as something requiring the cooperative resistance of the peace-loving Powers, not as the turbulent prologue to the victory of Communism. This mood is quite apparent in his speech of December 29, 1933. Yet at the same time, on December 31, 1933, the official journal *Bolshevik* could still give the following interpretation of the German situation: "In Germany the proletarian revolution is nearer to realization than in any other country; and victory of the proletariat in Germany means victory of proletarian revolution throughout Europe, since capitalist Europe cannot exist if it loses its heart. . . . He who does not understand the German question does not understand the path of the development of proletarian revolution in Europe."[70] Stalin's speech of January 26, 1934, while less far out on the limb, is much more revolution-conscious than Litvinov's.[71] One receives the impression that the Politburo was reluctant and regretful in accepting the new course.

Indeed, Litvinov as a diplomat seems always to have found the irrepressible revolutionary yearnings of the Bolsheviks an uncomfortable problem. In a letter to an English negotiator in December 1919, he said: "From the point of view of the vital interests of both countries there should be no obstacle to the establishment of real peace, excepting the bogey of revolutionary propaganda. If formal guarantees from the Soviet Government on this point be considered insufficient, could not means of preventing this propaganda be devised without barring the way to mutual representation?"[72]

The change in the Comintern line at the Seventh Congress in 1935 did not really eradicate this difference. Although Litvinov's diplomatic policy of "collective security" and the Popular Front are often identified, it is doubtful whether this identification should be pressed too far, even though both had Stalin's approval in some fashion. A reasonably attentive reading of Dimitrov's speeches at the Seventh Congress can dispel the popular notion that the Comintern had now really concealed its hard revolutionary core. Certainly, the energetic behavior of the comrades under the new line caused Litvinov perpetual embarrassment. In 1936, for example, Coulondre pointed out to him that the interference of the Comintern in French internal affairs was imperiling the Franco-Soviet pact. In response, Litvinov, after assuring him that the Soviet Union had no intention of interfering and that the Soviet ambassador in Paris had

[70] Quoted in David Dallin, *Russia and Post-War Europe* (New Haven, 1943), p. 62.
[71] Ibid., p. 62, ¶1.
[72] *British Documents*, 1st series, III, 740.

received instructions to that effect — which he would make even more precise — was obliged to fall back on the old claim that the Comintern had nothing to do with the foreign policy of the Soviet government. Coulondre felt, however, that Litvinov was fully aware that this customary disclaimer of responsibility for the Comintern carried no conviction. "But the question went beyond him. It concerned the other side of the double ladder on the top of which sat Stalin alone."[73]

Although Litvinov frequently expressed disapproval and suspicion of the capitalist nations and, in the years after 1936, was extremely critical of the policies of France and Great Britain, he does not seem to have been so deeply imbued with that xenophobia which has increasingly blighted the perception of Soviet leaders. It should not be forgotten that he lived a decade in England, from 1908 to 1918, during which time he settled rather thoroughly into a middle-class existence and married an English wife.

With regard to Germany, while Litvinov certainly subscribed to the general line that the Soviet Union did not desire bad relations with Germany and would welcome a resumption of cordial relations should the German government drop its menacing attitude, he does not seem to have shared the enthusiasm which a number of Russians and Germans had for the Russo-German connection. Dirksen, as mentioned earlier, felt that Litvinov was not a true believer in the Rapallo policy and was pro-English at heart. In March 1936, following the march into the Rhineland, the Soviet statements concerning Germany seemed to display some confusion. On the one hand, Litvinov in the League castigated Germany's recent actions in very sharp terms; on the other, Molotov said to a French editor: "The main trend among our people, the trend which determines the policy of the Soviet Government, considers an improvement in relations between Germany and the Soviet Union possible. . . . The participation of Germany in the League of Nations would be in the interest of peace and would be favorably regarded by us." "Even of Hitler Germany?", asked the French journalist. "Yes, even of Hitler Germany."[74] While there may be no logical contradiction between the two Soviet statements, they have a quite different flavor.

The German-Soviet pact of 1939 inevitably created the suspicion that some Soviet leaders, including Stalin, were always eager for a rapprochement with Germany and had made secret contacts with Hitler even during the period of so-called collective security. Coulondre, who said that he was convinced that Litvinov was, like himself, "a sincere worker for the Franco-Soviet entente within the framework of the League of Nations,"[75] also commented, "I am not even sure that during all that period of my mission in the USSR, certain clandestine contacts had ever ceased between Moscow and Berlin."[76] He was of the opinion that something was definitely in preparation in the spring of 1937, only

---

[73] Coulondre, *De Staline à Hitler*, pp. 32–33.
[74] See Beloff, *Foreign Policy*, II, 51–54.
[75] Coulondre, *De Staline à Hitler*, p. 32.
[76] Ibid., p. 45.

to be dropped in April.[77] The former Soviet intelligence officer, Krivitsky, professed to know that in the spring of 1937 an agreement had been drafted by Stalin and Hitler, with one David Kandelaki as the intermediary, but had broken down.[78] This source also stated, however, that the Commissariat for Foreign Affairs had no part whatever in this undertaking.

In general, even after one has made deductions for the fact that Litvinov, as a diplomat dealing with the outside, capitalist world, was likely to adopt a less revolutionary stance than Communists dealing with Communists or, perhaps, dictators with dictators, there still seems to remain a not unimportant difference between the diplomatic policy advocated or desired by him and the temper of the Politburo, a difference occasionally showing up in specific disagreements but more persistently if less tangibly in shadings of interpretation and emphasis. These, however, form a sufficiently coherent pattern to warrant the conclusion that there was a tension of ideas within the monolithic framework of the Soviet government. If so, is it possible to form any notion of the political or bureaucratic relations behind this tension?

III.

A preceding chapter has shown that diplomacy as such did not stand very high in the hierarchy of instruments developed or revamped by the new Soviet order. Foreign considerations tended to rank below domestic considerations during most of the interwar period, and even in the field of foreign relations the diplomatic arm lacked the prestige of the revolutionary and the military arms. At the same time, because of the peculiar sensitiveness attaching to foreign policy decisions there came to be "a particularly close, direct, and continual relationship . . . between the Politburo and the Narkomindel in the conduct and control of foreign affairs."[79] Consequently the post as Peoples Commissar for Foreign Affairs did not, in itself, carry a great deal of weight in the Soviet system.

[77] Ibid., p. 125.
[78] W. G. Krivitsky, *In Stalin's Secret Service* (New York, 1939), pp. 225–226. The thesis that Stalin was, all along, seeking for a deal with Hitler encounters difficulties in having to explain all the anti-German steps taken by the Soviet Union between 1933 and 1938. Krivitsky contended that the entry into the League, collective security, the pact with France, the intervention in Spain were all undertaken with a view to making Hitler find it "advantageous to meet his [Stalin's] advances." This seems a singularly round-about way to achieve a rapprochement. Still, this tactic of trying to win an ally by making things uncomfortable for him is not unknown in the history of diplomacy. William II and Holstein tried to woo Britain by the threat of a continental bloc against it.
[79] Julian Towster, *Political Power in the USSR., 1917–1947* (New York, 1948), p. 162. Towster points out that in the late 1920's while nearly all the governmental organs were scheduled to report before the Politburo, the Narkomindel apparently was not, presumably because decisions concerning foreign issues were continuously on the agenda of the Politburo itself.

Nor did Litvinov, despite the fact that he was an "old Bolshevik,"[80] rank high in the Party. He was never in the all-important Politburo, though he was a member of the Party's Central Committee for a number of years. Two reasons may help to explain why he was never admitted to the inner circle despite his obvious ability and long record as a party member. He had not returned to Russia from England to participate in the Bolshevik revolution. From the very first he was concerned not with the establishment of the revolutionary state but with its relations abroad. Moreover, even before the revolution he seems to have been valued primarily as a competent technician. In Lenin's references to him during the war as "our legal representative in the International Socialist Bureau," the term "legal" is charged with the characteristic double meaning of being official and public but not really part of the illegal or extralegal revolutionary core. While part of his function as Chicherin's second in the 1920's may have been as Bolshevik guardian over a former Menshevik,[81] it is doubtful whether in the long run his party status was any higher than that of his predecessor; in the opinion of the German ambassador who worked with both men, it was lower.[82]

Consequently, neither as Peoples Commissar nor as a party member was Litvinov in a position to follow his own policy or even to initiate policy. Indeed, late in his career he is reported as remarking rather sourly: "You know what I am. I merely hand on diplomatic documents."[83]

It is, therefore, difficult to see just how Litvinov was in any position to differ significantly with the Politburo. Moreover, Litvinov's term in office overlapped the years of the Great Purges, in which, so it seems, even half-formed or possibly-to-be-formed disagreements were sufficient to destroy a man. Yet Litvinov retained not only his health but his post.

His success in surviving the purges was something of a surprise and miracle to contemporary observers. He was an old Bolshevik; old Bolsheviks were dropping like flies. He headed the Foreign Commissariat; the Foreign Commissariat and the embassies abroad were swept clean. The former Soviet diplomat, Alexander Barmine, comments on Litvinov's "inexplicably surviving all his friends and collaborators": "Two of Litvinov's four assistants were executed, the third was put in prison and the fourth disappeared. His old friends and personal protégés, Ambassadors Yurenev and Rosenberg, disappeared also. Almost all the heads of departments of his ministry and the leading diplomatic personnel abroad, gathered and trained by him over fifteen years, were shot. But Litvinov continued to smile enigmatically. 'They were traitors; all is well!' Was he so confident because he deemed himself indispensable, or

---

[80] He joined the Russian Social Democratic Labor party in 1898 and was on Lenin's side when the latter formed the Bolshevik faction against the Mensheviks in 1903.

[81] See, for example, Simon Liberman, *Building Lenin's Russia* (Chicago, 1945), p. III.

[82] Dirksen, *Moskau, Tokio, London*, p. 94.

[83] Fischer, *Men and Politics*, p. 497.

did he have to keep a good face because his family were held as hostages?"[84] Litvinov does seem to have been jolted by the arrest of his assistant Krestinsky,[85] but in general his recorded remarks indicate approval of the purges as a necessity to rid the Soviet Union of treasonous elements.

Inasmuch as the underlying intent of the purges remains one of the major riddles of Soviet history,[86] it is impossible here to unravel their meaning in the Foreign Commissariat. While some observers have been inclined to regard the diplomatic housecleaning as a preparation for the agreement with Hitler, the part played by foreign policy considerations is by no means clear beyond the fairly obvious fact that people with foreign contacts and foreign experiences were frequent victims, but this may have been for reasons other than the direction of foreign policy itself. The effect of the purge was to reduce even further any independence of action or decision on the part of foreign service officials, an increasing number of whom apparently were attached to the NKVD, and to leave Litvinov a general without an army.

As to Litvinov's own survival, a few comments may be made. In the first place, he may have been fortunate in the fact that while an old Bolshevik he had *not* been one of the inner circle which made the revolution, and consequently had not become enmeshed in the struggle for power within the party, a struggle which produced a very high death rate among the contestants. Moreover, so long as the policy of "collective security" was officially upheld by the Soviet Union, Litvinov's removal or disappearance would have had unfavorable foreign repercussions. By the time he was dropped the purges had subsided. Finally, it is clear that Litvinov must have possessed in some sense or another Stalin's confidence. It is difficult to believe that for all his international political value he could have survived those years of unimaginable suspicion had Stalin not had confidence in his personal as well as his political loyalty. The thesis, however, that Litvinov really believed that Stalin was purging the Foreign Commissariat to rid it of a Fascist fifth column seems quite unlikely, especially since the course of the purges generally started with a suspected chief and spread out through the ranks of his associates and subordinates. Nor does the contrary thesis that Litvinov and Stalin were clandestinely retooling the Narkomindel for a German rapprochement carry conviction; besides making utter nonsense of Litvinov's public policy it increases the difficulty of accounting for his dismissal.

The conclusion that seems able to deal with these confused and contradictory problems most satisfactorily is the one which sees Stalin as always having several strings to his bow. If one assumes that he was capable of considering simultaneously two separate and even conflicting

[84] Alexander Barmine, *One Who Survived* (New York, 1945), p. 121.
[85] Davies, *Mission to Moscow*, p. 262.
[86] Two authors, with firsthand experience in the purges, have recently enumerated seventeen theories which have been advanced to explain the purges: F. Beck and W. Godin, *Russian Purge and the Extraction of Confession* (New York, 1951). With unusual reserve they do not pretend to know the answer.

lines of policy, not making up his mind in advance but waiting to see how events developed, then it is possible, perhaps, to reconcile the elements of difference discussed above and the fact that Litvinov was not a victim of the purge.

According to this interpretation, which is the most this paper can attempt to offer, there were at least two contending lines of foreign policy within the Politburo, and perhaps within Stalin's own mind, in the 1930's: one, the "Litvinov policy," of which Litvinov himself was not only the agent but probably also the advocate and possibly even the formulator (even in a monolithic state ideas cannot all originate at the apex of the pyramid); the other, the policy which emerged with the pact of August 23, 1939, and acquired explicit characteristics in the two years following. Stalin, while perhaps inclined toward the second, was willing to give the first a trial, especially since no other alternative appeared profitable after 1933: the revolutionary line had brought few results and did not fit well with domestic developments, the Rapallo connection seemed impossible with Hitler's Germany behaving in an exceedingly unfriendly fashion. On the other hand the "Litvinov policy" depended upon achieving results. When these failed to come about the balance — whether between persons in the Politburo or between ideas in Stalin's own mind — would swing away from it. Thus, Litvinov's warnings after 1936 that "collective security" could be wrecked if the Western Powers did not change their ways may be regarded as a reflection of a decision still in suspension in the Politburo, a forewarning of a course which he himself may not have favored but which was in the cards if collective security failed.[87]

This interpretation also seems able to meet the question of Litvinov's resignation on May 3, 1939. The terse Soviet announcement merely stated that his resignation had been at his request because of ill health. Since the war, however, the official Soviet explanation has been that in the spring of 1939, when the international situation was deteriorating, when the Soviet Union was threatened with a hostile combination of capitalist Powers, "it was necessary to have in such a responsible post as that of Peoples Commissar for Foreign Affairs, a political leader of greater experience and greater popularity in the country than M. M. Litvinov."[88]

While this statement is true in the sense that the authority of the Politburo was now concerned with the immediate direction of foreign

---

[87] When discussing the possible failure of collective security, Litvinov often indicated that the USSR might do well to return to isolation. Now the Molotov-Ribbentrop Pact was scarcely a return to isolation but, as it proved, a decision to collaborate in aggression (the purely defensive interpretation of Russia's advances during the period of the pact seems inadequate in light of the documents published in *Nazi-Soviet Relations*, esp. pp. 258–259). Hence in his occasional predictions that the Germans would seek a pact with the Soviet Union, Litvinov may have been predicting a development which he himself did not approve.

[88] *Falsifiers of History*, Supplement to "New Times" (Moscow), No. 8, February 18, 1848, p. 9. See also *Diplomaticheskii Slovar'*, II, 162 and 675.

relations, it does not suggest the possibility of a change in policy. At the time, quite naturally, the Soviet government and its representatives abroad assured the other Powers that the switch in Foreign Commissars meant no alteration in the direction of Soviet policy. These assurances were received with justified skepticism, however, and one of the most interested parties, Hitler, later said, "Litvinov's dismissal was decisive."[89] To be sure, Stalin's speech of March 10 at the Eighteenth Congress of the Communist Party had served to pave the way, as had the remarks on April 17 by the Soviet ambassador in Berlin.[90] Nevertheless, it can be concluded that Litvinov's retirement was a very important step in the German-Soviet rapprochement, if only because he was a Jew and had come to symbolize the effort at collective security against German aggression.

While Litvinov's retirement certainly facilitated the German-Soviet negotiations which led to the pact, was it a mark of "no confidence" in him or his diplomacy? His American biographer, whose account of the event was obtained directly from Litvinov during the latter's ambassadorship in the United States during the war, denies that he was discharged or abruptly dismissed. According to this account, Litvinov, after Munich, decided that a rapprochment with Germany was necessary, that he was an obstacle, and suggested his own retirement. The resignation took place untheatrically after a series of conferences with Stalin, and Litvinov himself proposed his friend Molotov as a successor.[91]

This interpretation has Litvinov's authority for its authenticity. And while it is true that he was, in 1942–1943, an official representative of the Soviet government and therefore not likely to stress conflicts in the conduct of Soviet diplomacy, it is also true that he was often surprisingly frank in such matters and not inclined to allow personal concerns to flavor his thinking. Nevertheless, there are certain difficulties with this interpretation. The postwar Soviet explanation seems to imply, quite ungraciously if the change had been marked by full harmony, that Litvinov was not a big enough man for the job. The picture of Litvinov, not a member of the Politburo, nominating the powerful Molotov to be his successor, appears incongruous. Moreover, there is some evidence that Litvinov was in disgrace with fortune and Stalin's eyes. Early in May 1939 the unusually communicative, and perhaps unreliable, Soviet chargé in Berlin, Astakhov, told Coulondre that for six months Litvinov's fall had been foreseeable, since he and Molotov were no longer in accord, and Stalin, while esteeming him, did not like him.[92] After his retirement he seems to have received a cold shoulder at Soviet public functions.[93] In a speech on August 31, 1939, Molotov criticized those

[89] "Notes on Hitler's Conference with his Commanders-in-Chief, August 22, 1939," *Documents on International Affairs 1939–46*, I, 446.

[90] *Nazi-Soviet Relations*, pp. 1–2.

[91] Pope, *Litvinoff*, pp. 441–442. The author is grateful to Mr. Pope for his letter explaining that Litinov had personally confirmed this account of his resignation.

[92] Quoted in Georges Bonnet, *Fin d'une Europe* (Paris, 1946), p. 184.

[93] It may be worth mentioning that the daughter of a former NKVD official attached to the Foreign Commissariat has recently written that

"short-sighted people even in our own country who, carried away by oversimplified anti-Fascist propaganda, forgot about this provocative work of our enemies [the machinating Western European politicians],"[94] a remark that may be interpreted as a slap at Litvinov. On February 20, 1941, Litvinov was dropped from the Central Committee of the Communist party for "inability to discharge obligations."[95]

It is possible, then, that Litvinov was under a cloud; that Stalin had weighed his policy and found it wanting. At the same time he was not officially damned, partly because the policy connected with his name had been Stalin's also, at least nominally; partly, it would seem, because he might still be useful should circumstances change, as they did in June 1941. Still, the remainder of his career is an anticlimax. During his brief ambassadorship in the United States from 1941 to 1943 he was not the leading figure he had been in the 1930's. After the war he sank again into obscurity. At his death on December 31, 1951, he was a minor Soviet hero — with members of the Foreign Ministry as pall-bearers, but no one from the Politburo. In the second volume of the Soviet Diplomatic Dictionary, published in 1950, the favorable but brief biography of Litvinov occupies 92 lines, compared with 54 for Chicherin and 292 for Molotov. Stalin's accomplishments as a diplomat were, of course, too vast for inclusion or comparison.

IV.

In retrospect Litvinov's "collective security" can be seen to have been largely a phrase, never a reality. Neither the Soviet Union nor the Western Powers were ever really guided by the principle of common action against the rising danger from Germany; both ardently hoped that the hurricane, if it developed, would not come in their direction. The "appeasement" policies of France and Great Britain have been thoroughly criticized by disapproving citizens of those states. There was also, however, a corresponding tendency in Russia which sought a reconciliation with Nazi Germany. This tendency was naturally less apparent so long as the major force of Hitler's propaganda was directed against Soviet Communism.

Even Litvinov's position appears reasonably clear and unambiguous only during the short span from 1933 to 1936 — before Germany was equipped to fight a war. After it was clear that the Third Reich was,

---

immediately after Litvinov's resignation and replacement by Molotov her father was purged as a part of a general, though unexplained, house cleaning in that ministry. Nora Murray (née Korzhenko), *I Spied for Stalin* (New York, 1951), pp. 116–129.

[94] V. M. Molotov, *The Meaning of the Soviet-German Non-Aggression Pact* (New York, 1939), p. 8.

[95] According to Pope, *Litvinoff*, p. 460, this step was taken because "Stalin was determined to give no offense to the Germans." In that case it is difficult to see why Maisky, Soviet ambassador to Great Britain, should have been elevated to alternate membership on the Central Committee at the same time.

willy-nilly, going to become a powerful military state, his pleas for collective measures were interspersed with warnings of a Soviet return to isolation. By the time of the Munich crisis his support of collective security was form without content: he was sure that France and England would not move; the French, the British — and the Germans — were equally convinced the Russians would not move.

Nor, in the long run, did Litvinov's efforts to "find a common language" between the Soviet Union and the rest of the world succeed. This failure needs no emphasis today. Indeed Litvinov may have been a cause for deepening the rift. The atmosphere of practical cooperativeness which he created partly concealed but in no way softened the hard core of the Stalinist regime. As a result, collisions with that hard core were not only bruising but carried the additional sting of disillusion.

Still, after this has been said and after one recognizes that future documentary revelations may further darken the picture of Soviet policy between the wars and present Litvinov in a more doubtful light, the late Foreign Commissar does have claim to two things of lasting significance: his ideas and his acumen as a diplomat. Regardless of the aims of Soviet foreign policy or of Litvinov's connection with those aims, the ideas he expressed in his major League speeches are important in themselves. Indeed, whole paragraphs describe, in mood as in content, the tasks facing the world today in its effort to check the new danger of Soviet expansion. His ability to detect the major trends in the 1930's and to anticipate the course of events indicates an extraordinary understanding of that decade. The most recent historian of the League of Nations has remarked on Litvinov's role in that organization: "No future historian will lightly disagree with any views expressed by Litvinov on international questions. Whatever may be thought of the policy and purposes of his government, the long series of his statements and speeches in the Assembly, the Council, the Conferences, and Committees of which he was a member between 1927 and 1939 can hardly be read today without an astonished admiration. Nothing in the annals of the League can compare with them in frankness, in debating power, in the acute diagnosis of each situation. No contemporary statesman could point to such a record of criticisms justified and prophecies fulfilled."[96]

While one might quarrel with the inclusion of the years 1927–1933, it is difficult to disagree with this conclusion for the six years between Hitler's coming to power and Litvinov's retirement from the diplomatic scene.

[96] F. P. Walters, *A History of the League of Nations* (2 vols., London, 1952), II, 712.

II THE SOVIET UNION AS A SUPER-POWER
The Soviet Challenge at Mid-Century

4. THE CHALLENGE OF SOVIET FOREIGN POLICY: REVOLUTION OR EXPANSION

Vernon V. Aspaturian

It is customary, to the point of triteness, to speak of the multiple revolutions of our age — the Communist, the colonial, and the technological. At the same time, obscured by a fog of platitudes, is the fact that the Soviet Union has maneuvered itself into becoming the main reservoir of power in each case, threatening to channel all the revolutions into a single overpowering torrential surge which will wash out the old social order in favor of a new social system, allegedly ordained by the mandate of history.[1]

The most imposing challenge of Soviet foreign policy in the mid-twentieth century is that it has established a virtual monopoly on revolutionary change, establishing its tempo, guiding its direction, and determined to shape its ultimate configuration. The Bolshevik Revolution of 1917, seen from a perspective of more than four decades, emerges as one of the great watersheds in the drama of human history. The multiple revolutions and transformations of the last four decades have been powerfully shaped and influenced by its ideas and by the power of the Soviet State it brought into being.

Reprinted from M. A. Kaplan, editor, *The Revolution in World Politics* (Copyright 1962 by John Wiley and Sons, Inc.). Reprinted by permission.
[1] The new Program of the Communist Party adopted by the Twenty-Second Party Congress reads: "Socialist revolutions, national liberation and anti-imperialist revolutions, people's democratic revolutions, broad peasants' movements, the struggle of the masses for the overthrow of fascism and other despotic regimes, and general democratic movements against national oppression are all being merged into a single world revolutionary process undermining and destroying capitalism," *Pravda*, July 30, 1961.

In the 1960's, little more than one hundred years after the appearance of the *Communist Manifesto,* Communism is no longer a simple idea — it is a way of life embracing thirteen states, with a population of nearly one billion people, occupying approximately one-third of the earth's total land surface. Within this world are to be found over two hundred different nationalities and ethnic and linguistic groups, most of the races of mankind, numerous cultures, and religions representing every major system in the world, except Hinduism. Furthermore, Communist Parties, large and small, powerful and impotent, are to be found in sixty-eight additional countries on five continents, ranging from minuscule and furtive illegal conspiratorial groups to large mass parties such as those of France, Italy, and Indonesia. All of these parties are inspired by the common ideology of Marxism-Leninism and are dedicated to bringing Communism to their own countries by force, revolution, subversion, conquest, or election, under the protective umbrella of Soviet nuclear and missile capability.

The most significant elements in the progression of Communism from an idea to a potential world civilization are the almost uninterrupted and relentless movement upward and outward and the continuing dynamism it demonstrates in its zeal to supplant all existing ways of life. Only the great universal messianic religions of history, such as Islam and Christianity, have had comparable success in the transmutation of an idea into a social system.

Communism, in forty years, has transformed Russia irrevocably. In the process, the ideas of Communism have also undergone substantial revision and reshaping. The Communism which challenges the world in the mid-twentieth century is not the hypothetical, untried, utopian dream of Marx and Engels but the concrete realities of a new social order, forged in the Soviet Union during the past four decades.

Communism as an ideology of internal change is transformed into an ideology of universal revolution when its norms become effective foreign-policy objectives of the Soviet State. From the very inception of the Soviet State, the ultimate objectives of Soviet foreign policy have been universal and ecumenical in character; even the transformation of the Russian social order was calculatedly designed to provide a concrete model which was to be universalized by the very power capabilities with which it equipped the Soviet State. The concrete social system of the Soviet Union thus becomes transcendentalized as a universalized configurative goal of Soviet foreign policy. Since the growing power of the Soviet state stands prepared to translate this goal into reality, world Communism cannot be dismissed simply as an abstract philosophical goal to be fervently aspired. It is instead a utopian norm, reflecting a concrete social system, elevated to the level of state policy.

THE REVOLUTIONARY CHARACTER OF SOVIET FOREIGN POLICY

Soviet foreign policy is authentically revolutionary because its objectives transcend simple territorial expansion, self-defense, or a redistribution of power in its favor; neither is it the simple propagation of an ideology or religious faith. It seeks nothing less than the total annihilation of what it calls the "capitalist-imperialist" system and the residual pre-capitalist social orders which are dependent on it. In their place it seeks to install a new universal ideo-social system, modeled on itself and the Soviet orbit as a whole. Wherever Soviet or Communist power or both have been established, profound and fundamental socio-economic changes have been instituted. They result in the transfer of power from one class to another and the destruction of the economic foundations of power enjoyed by the former paramount or governing classes, through the expropriation and nationalization of land, natural resources, industrial establishments, financial institutions, all media of transportation, communication, and information — all of which become the property of the state; the state, in turn, is reduced to the instrumentality of a new revolutionary power elite. These fundamental changes are considered basic, and they constitute the minimum transformations that must be executed in order to eradicate the old social system and create the foundations for the new.

No matter what internecine heresies may flourish within the Communist orbit, or what schisms may develop, all Communist parties accept these transformations as fundamental and indispensable. How they should be executed and what pattern of reconstruction should be adopted in each case may be a matter of fierce controversy, but the area of ideological consensus remains extraordinarily broad and intense.

With the expansion of the Communist world, the possibilities of schisms and heresies are correspondingly maximized, particularly if separate centers of power crystallize around disputed ideological issues. This will inevitably fragment the Communist movement into a polycentric system — as indeed it has already been so fractured — and to that degree will result in the dilution and corruption of the ideology itself; but it will not necessarily interfere with its continuous advance. The ideological corruption of Communist doctrine and the erosion of the monolithic character of its power are not unmixed blessings for the West. If history is any guide, it surely demonstrates that the universalization of the great religions — Christianity, Islam, and Buddhism — has been accelerated by the corruption and erosion of their doctrinal purity because it enabled them to absorb marginal adherents, who are always more numerous than the true believers.

The proceedings of the Twenty-Second Party Congress have brought to the surface the simmering ideological, personality, and power disputes between the Soviet Union and China — opening interesting opportunities for the West — but for the foreseeable future, the Soviet Union remains the *de facto* power center of the Communist world. Without the Soviet Union, the entire Communist movement could be easily crushed by the overwhelming superiority of the Western world. Just as the United States is the main prop of the Western world, the Soviet Union is the mainstay of the Communist world. Even China recognizes that this condition will persist until she becomes an autonomous nuclear power, in which case both the Soviet Union and the West will be confronted with one of those rare moments in history (which, however, have been all too frequent in the post Second World War era) when a fundamental shift will take place in the power structure of international relations.

Nevertheless, for the present, as the power of the Soviet Union grows relative to that of the non-Communist world, the less utopian becomes its universal ideological mission, even though its absolute control over its direction and tempo becomes less firm. The development of polycentrism in the Communist orbit, and the evolution of quasi-autonomous Communist movements in non-Communist countries, should not obscure the fact that the Soviet Union remains the central inspiration of all these forces, although it is becoming increasingly less dictatorial in its coordination and direction of the world Communist movement.

Although the Soviet will to transform the world may erode in response to external cohesion and internal fragmentation, it would be a mistake to assume that this erosion is inevitable or will take place automatically. Such an expectation, on the contrary, will virtually ensure the continuing vitality of the Soviet ideological mission rather than encourage its diminution. Only when Soviet power is confronted with a permanent situation in which its security and existence are jeopardized more by keeping its ideological norms wedded to state policy than by permitting their separation will world Communism in Soviet calculations lose its political significance and be disarmed as another unfulfilled universal mission, content to remain a regional civilization.

Since the Soviet leaders recognize power as the magic which converts utopia into reality, the day-to-day diplomacy of the Soviet Union appears to be framed within the traditional canon of power politics: the maximization of its power to realize the fulfillment of state interests. This has led many observers, particularly those versed in traditional diplomacy, to mistakenly assume that Soviet foreign policy was fundamentally indistinguishable from that of any other great imperialistic and aggressively minded power, and that the Soviet state was, in fact, motivated by traditional Russian "national interests," which were somehow timeless in their persistence. According to this view, the extraordinary emphasis which the Soviet Union has placed upon the use of subversion, espionage, mass propaganda, and the direction of manipulation of partisans and organizations in other countries is not really unique, except that these techniques and practices are employed in a cruder, more ruthless and primitive manner by Moscow than by other contemporary Great Powers.

It is neither the character nor the style of its diplomatic instruments that makes Soviet foreign policy unique but the nature and conception of the Soviet "State." "State" interests of the Soviet Union — the Soviet Union is a multinational not a national state — are defined in ideological terms which not only transcend the Western ideological consensus but the idea of the territorial state as well. Whereas in the mid-twentieth century the national interests of most powers, although sometimes framed in inordinately ambitious and extravagantly platitudinous terms, are limited in space, subject to the ravages of time and events, and more or less ideologically vapid, the "State interests" of the Soviet Union continue to be universalist in conception, seemingly immune from the effects of time. Although subject to ideological metamorphoses, they remain stubbornly messianic in their implacability. The Soviet conception of "security" is not territorial or geographical in conception, but ideological, since Soviet leaders persist in the belief that the permanent security of the Soviet social order can be ensured only by the destruction of all competing social systems and by transforming the world into a modified image of itself — that is, they seek to forge a new universal consensus.

Although Khrushchev has declared the Stalinist conception of "capitalist encirclement" obsolete and now boasts that the Soviet Union is immune from capitalist intervention and that capitalist restoration in the Soviet Union is an impossibility, the ideological content of Soviet "State interests" remains unaffected: The security of the Soviet State is inextricably linked with the fate of the ideology of Communism itself, not with the existence of the Soviet State as a distinct and separate entity. As long as rival ideological and power centers are in possession of modern weapons of instantaneous mass destruction, the possibility of seriously damaging the Soviet Union and delaying the Communist millennium is the real fear, not the destruction of the Soviet State or Communism as an ideology, since they are currently considered to be immune from destruction. Soviet leaders consider it possible that the capitalist "ruling classes," in a final desperate effort to stave off the inevitable, may irrationally unleash terrible nuclear destruction and leave only the ruins of civilization to a "victorious" Communism.[2] The "dilemma" which confronts the Kremlin is how to bring about the realization of the Communist millennium without triggering widespread devastation at a time when the class enemy possesses precisely such a capability.[3]

[2] "The imperialists' intrigues must never be forgotten. Our tremendous successes in building a new life should not lead to complacency, to relaxation of vigilance. . . . As the solidarity of the peoples of the socialist countries grows, the imperialists' hopes for the restoration of capitalist ways and for the degeneration of the socialist countries fade. World reaction therefore becomes more and more oriented toward striking a blow at the socialist states from outside in order through war to achieve the rule of capitalism throughout the world, or at least, to check the development of the countries of socialism. The most rabid imperialists, acting on the principle of 'after us the deluge,' openly voice their desire to undertake a new war venture. The ideologists of imperialism, intimidating the peoples, try to instill a kind of philosophy of hopelessness and desperation. Hysterically they cry: 'Better death under capitalism than life under communism.' . . . Blinded by class hatred, our enemies are ready to doom all mankind to the catastrophe of war. . . . They behave like a feeble and greedy old man whose powers have been exhausted, whose physical capacity has weakened, but whose avid desires remain." Khrushchev's Report to the Twenty-Second Party Congress, *Pravda*, October 18, 1961.

[3] Soviet leaders continue to toy with the notion of "buying off" the capitalists when the jig is up as an alternative to blowing up the world on an

As long as the Western Powers maintain and sustain a retaliatory capacity sufficient to lay waste the Soviet landscape and can convey a credible determination to employ it, Soviet striking power is effectively nullified as a rational instrument for the universalization of its system. But that power becomes transformed into a protective umbrella under which spontaneous and inspired revolutionary changes can take place in various parts of the world without external interference from the Western world. Whether a prolonged period of nuclear stalemate or effective mutual deterrence reacts to the advantage of the West or the Soviet East thus depends upon the direction in which the social equilibrium in various parts of the world happens to be moving. In countries gripped by revolutionary ferment, the nuclear stalemate tends to assure the free development of that revolutionary process; where the status quo is firmly established and accepted, the possibilities of external intervention to impose revolutions by bayonets are considerably reduced. In either instance, direct *armed intervention* on behalf of maintaining the status quo by force or overthrowing it by violence will risk self-destruction for either side.

SOVIET DETERRENT STRATEGY AND REVOLUTION

Deterring Soviet military action, it soon becomes clear — whether nuclear or conventional, limited or unlimited — can only provide the West with a new foundation for policy; it cannot constitute an end in itself as a surrogate for policy, even if permanently sustained. The establishment of mutual deterrence merely shifts the rivalry from the military arena to the social, political, and sub-belligerent levels. Even the achievement of a permanent symmetrical deterrence at every level of external interference from sub-belligerent instruments of subversion, infiltration, and guerrilla warfare to massive nuclear attack cannot frustrate the natural development of social forces and movements operating in individual countries.

A condition of mutual symmetrical deterrence means that the issue of revolution or status quo in individual countries will be determined by the given internal equilibrium of power. In those areas, where the internal forces of the status quo are stronger than the forces of change, external forces cannot be employed to alter the balance of internal power. But it also means that in those countries where the internal forces of revolution are greater than those in support of the existing order, external forces will be precluded from intervening to arrest the developing revolution.

---

irrational impulse. Thus, the new Party Program advises: "It may well be that under conditions of the ever-growing strength of socialism, the consolidation of the working movement and weakening of the position of capitalism in some countries may lead to a situation in which, as foreseen by Marx and Lenin [and also by Stalin, it might be added], it will be profitable for the bourgeoisie to agree to the sale of the basic means of production and for the proletariat to buy them." *Pravda*, July 30, 1931.

Whether a condition of absolute mutual deterrence between East and West at all levels serves to benefit Soviet foreign policy or that of the West will be determined by the internal social and economic conditions prevailing in the major areas of the world. Thus, while the West seeks deterrence to prevent the Soviet Union from intervening to assist revolution, the Soviet Union pursues it to prevent the United States from intervening to arrest change or support counterrevolution. It should be pointed out, however, that the Soviet union will persist in its endeavor to assert a position of military supremacy even in the nuclear age, through technological break-throughs of a fundamental character. Whether or not a condition of deterrence exists depends upon the West's willingness and capacity to match or exceed Soviet military technological achievements. A self-executing deterrence does not exist and the permanent, absolute, and symmetrical character of deterrence must be sedulously pursued and sustained.[4]

In Soviet calculations, the forces for revolutionary change are spontaneous and inevitable on a universal scale and are likely to develop more intensely in the immediate future; hence, the immediate objective of Khrushchev's foreign policy is to deter the United States as the "gendarme of reaction" from intervening to arrest revolution.[5]

[4] The possibility of achieving a permanent, absolute, and symmetrical mutual deterrence is very remote. Military technology, economic shifts, unexpected or fortuitous occurrences, social movements, etc., are much too fluid, dynamic, and uneven in their development to permit this. Deterrence will always be less than permanent, absolute, and symmetrical. Both sides, and this is absolutely certain in the case of the Soviet Union, will continue to seek a "margin of preponderance" through technological breakthroughs which may provide momentary advantages; the possibility that one side (more likely the United States) may be victimized by a "maginot line" psychology and, through ineptness or unwillingness to sustain financial costs, mistakenly assume that mutual deterrence is a static condition and once achieved, will remain permanent, should not be discounted. Furthermore, it is even more likely that one side may fail to recognize a technological achievement or capacity as altering a hitherto balanced situation. Indications are that the United States does not fully appreciate the strategic, military, diplomatic, and psychological implications of a Soviet Union unilaterally armed with 50 and 100 megaton nuclear warheads; nor does it seem to appreciate what would happen if the Soviet Union unilaterally acquired a reliable anti-missile system. As long as perfect symmetry and deterrence are not likely, external forces will continue to affect internal social forces in individual countries, and vice versa. This makes it all the more imperative that internal social forces within individual countries and the world at large, for and against the status quo, be precisely calculated in any estimate of the general balance of power.

[5] "Of course, warring classes have always sought to rely on the support of kindred forces from outside. For a long time the bourgeois class had an advantage in this respect. The world bourgeoisie, acting in concert, stamped out centers of revolution everywhere and by every means, including armed intervention. Obviously, even at that time the international proletariat was not indifferent to the struggle of its class brothers, but more often than not it could express its solidarity with them in the form of moral support. Now the situation has changed. The people of this or that country who rise in the struggle will not find themselves engaged in single combat with world imperialism. On their side are powerful international forces, possessing everything necessary to give effective moral and material support. The imperial-

American official calculations seem to be based on the assumption that revolutionary currents are Communist inspired and stimulated externally by Soviet action and that their success depends upon some form of outside intervention at various levels.

Under conditions of mutual deterrence, the issue will be decided largely in accordance with that perception and expectation which most closely approximates international social reality. If, indeed, revolutionary movements are externally stimulated by the Soviet Union (or "International Communism") and their ultimate success depends upon some form of outside help, then the exclusion of that help will favor the status quo; if, on the other hand, these forces are indigenous and spontaneous, and Soviet assistance is only catalytic and supplementary, then military deterrence will not be sufficient to meet the challenge of Soviet foreign policy. Consequently, it is of the utmost importance that Western perceptions of international reality more closely approximate actuality than Soviet perceptions. For, if Soviet perceptions of the fundamental forces affecting international politics and the direction of their movement are more accurate reflections of reality than the perceptions of the West, then correspondingly, its foreign-policy objectives are likely to be achieved more often than those of the West.

SOVIET PERCEPTIONS OF INTERNATIONAL POLITICS IN A REVOLUTIONARY WORLD

In analyzing Soviet intentions and behavior in international politics, it is first necessary to understand the multiple and discrete functions which ideology performs for Soviet foreign policy, for it is quickly apparent that a major component of the Soviet challenge is ideological in character. Six discrete functions are performed by Soviet ideology in Soviet policy behavior. It functions as a: (1) Theory of social norms; (2) Theory of knowledge and analysis; (3) Theory or strategy of action;

---

ists, alarmed at the scale of the revolutionary struggle, are not ceasing their attempts to interfere in the internal affairs of peoples and states. This is why they have reserved, in military pacts and agreements, the 'right' to armed intervention in the event of so-called internal unrest, that is, to suppress revolutions, to put down actions by the masses of the people against reactionary regimes. The imperialists charge at every crossroads that the communists export revolution. The imperialist gentlemen need this slander to camouflage in at least some way their claim to the right to export counterrevolution. . . . The communists are against the export of revolution, and this is well known in the West [sic]. But we do not recognize anybody's right to export counterrevolution, to perform the functions of an international gendarme. This too should be well known. The attempts of the imperialists to interfere in the affairs of peoples rising in revolution would constitute nothing less than acts of aggression — a threat to world peace. We must state outright that in the event of imperialist export of counterrevolution the communists will call on the peoples of all countries to rally, to mobilize their forces and, relying on the might of the world socialist system, firmly to repel the enemies of freedom, the enemies of peace." Khrushchev's Report to the Twenty-Second Party Congress, *Pravda*, October 18, 1961.

(4) System of social rationalization; (5) Symbol of continuity, authority, and legitimacy; (6) System of communication. Only the first three functions will be discussed at any great length.

The normative goals of Soviet foreign policy have already been amply outlined, and so it is necessary to devote attention at this point to Soviet ideology as a theory of analysis and of action. It should be apparent that to meet the Soviet challenge it is not sufficient merely to dissect, catalogue, and scrutinize Soviet ideological goals and the various strategies and tactics which have been devised to implement Soviet policies.

Typically, Western reaction has been an overwhelming preoccupation with the "strategy and tactics of world Communism," which invariably resolves itself into an unambiguous condemnation of world Communism as a wicked and evil goal to be fervently frustrated, together with exhortations that the West develop "strategies and tactics" — frequently based upon images of Communist strategy and tactics — to prevent the victory of world Communism. This manifests itself in programs designed to improve our propaganda, intelligence, and espionage services; to develop techniques of subversion, infiltration, and guerrilla warfare — all based on the mistaken notion that if we can develop these techniques and instruments more effectively than the Soviet Union, the West will be more likely to achieve its objectives than Moscow. The goal of Western policy thus becomes the obverse of the Soviet's goals — anti-world Communism. Unfortunately, this resolves itself into a "strategy and tactics" for preserving the status quo, whatever and wherever it might be, as long as it is anti-Communist.

If the assumption that Communism is not a universally desired social goal is valid, it can have only limited spontaneous and autonomous appeal throughout the world. Consequently, it must be extended by the power of an external force. A parallel assumption is that an effective response would require the establishment of a permanent and absolute symmetrical deterrence from the lowest levels of sub-belligerence like subversion, infiltration, and guerrilla warfare, through conventional instruments of conflict, on up to the highest levels of nuclear and rocket technology.

The first assumption is valid, but the second emphatically is not. Consequently, a policy based upon it will fail to respond effectively to the revolutionary thrust of Soviet foreign policy. It is at this point that we must turn our attention to comparative systems or theories of analysis of the social and political forces operating in international politics. Soviet strategy and tactics do not rest upon the assumption that Communism is a universally desired goal and that the success of world Communism rests upon its immediate attractiveness as a social order; neither does Soviet strategy rest upon the notion that world Communism can be imposed willy nilly by external Soviet power. Rather, Soviet policy rests upon the assumption that in most of the non-Communist world, particularly in Asia, Africa, and Latin America, the existing social orders, that is the status quo, are universally disliked, and that the major spontaneous revolutionary social forces in these regions are directed against the status quo — that is, the same status quo which the West supports against Soviet Communism. Thus, Western policy emerges not only as anti-Soviet or anti-Communist, but also, unwittingly, as opposed to indigenous social revolutionary movements. Since the status quo has a single defender — the West — and two opponents — the Communists and native revolutionary movements — the latter two are forced into a marriage of tactical convenience which manifests itself in many obvious ways. All too frequently, this results in their being lumped together in American foreign-policy calculations.

The strategy of harnessing the energies of native revolutionary movements in underdeveloped areas to the Communist dialectic was established in its broad outlines by Lenin more than four decades ago. In 1920 the founder of the Bolshevik state laid down the principal lines of analysis for exploiting revolutionary movements in underdeveloped countries, even before they had actually appeared, but which, on the basis of Lenin's analysis of imperialism, were inevitable. These ideas have since then been modified, renovated, refined, and adapted to various areas under a variety of circumstances. What is important is that Soviet leaders have had at their disposal a systematically articulated theoretical framework for analyzing and exploiting movements against the status quo for more than forty years. Thus, four decades ago, Lenin observed:

> The characteristic feature of imperialism is that the whole world, as we see it, is at present divided into a large number of oppressed nations and an insignificant number of oppressing nations possessing colossal wealth and powerful military forces. The overwhelming majority of the population of the world . . . about 70 per cent of the population of the world belongs to the oppressed nations, which are either in a state of direct colonial dependence or belong to the outlying colonial states such as Persia, Turkey and China, or else, after being conquered by the armies of a big imperialist power, have been forced into dependence upon it by treaties. . . . We argued about whether it would be correct, in principle and in theory, to declare that the Communist International and the Communist Parties should support the bourgeois-democratic movement in backward countries. As a result . . . we unanimously decided to speak of the national revolutionary movement instead of the "bourgeois-democratic" movement. . . . The meaning of this change is that we Communists should, and will, support bourgeois liberation movements in the colonial countries only when these movements are really revolutionary, when the representatives of these movements do not hinder us in training and organizing the peasants and broad masses of the exploited in a revolutionary spirit. Even if these conditions do not exist, the Communists in these countries must fight against the reformist bourgeoisie, among whom we include the heroes of the Second International. Reformist parties already exist in colonial countries, and sometimes their representatives call themselves Social-Democrats and Socialists. . . . There can be no argument about the fact that the proletariat of the advanced countries can and must assist the backward toiling masses, and that the development of the backward countries can

emerge from its present stage when the victorious proletariat of the Soviet republics stretches out a helping hand to these masses.[6]

The Soviet objective, thus, is to use non-Communist revolutionary movements against the West and, in the process, establish control over their direction and merge them into the general stream of Communist expansion. Thus, in 1927 Stalin outlined as an accomplishment what was in fact an expectation:

> The October Revolution has shaken imperialism not only in the centers of its domination, not only in the "mother countries." It has also struck blows at the rear of imperialism, its periphery, having undermined the rule of imperialism in the colonial and dependent countries. . . . The proletariat cannot emancipate itself without emancipating the oppressed nations. . . . The October Revolution has *ushered* in a new era, the era of *colonial* revolutions which are being conducted *in the oppressed countries* of the world in *alliance* with the proletariat and under the *leadership* of the proletariat. . . . The era of undisturbed exploitation and oppression of colonies and dependent countries *has passed away.* . . . The era of revolutions for emancipation in the colonies and dependent countries, the era of its *hegemony* in the revolution, *has begun.*[7]

The more implacable and unyielding the forces of the status quo against these non-Communist revolutionary forces, the more they are impelled in the direction of the Soviet Union, and the more easily they fall under its control. In this way, the Soviet Union emerges as the champion not only of Communism, but also of revolution in general. According to Khrushchev's Report to the Twenty-Second Congress:

> Attempts are made to blame us Communists for any action by the masses against their oppressors. When the working people of any capitalist or colonial country rise in struggle, the imperialists begin to cry: "This is the handiwork of the Communists" or "the hand of Moscow." Of course we are glad to have the imperialists ascribe to communists all the good actions of the peoples. By so doing, the imperialists are involuntarily helping the masses to gain a better understanding of communist ideas.[8]

In a world seething with revolutionary ferment and convulsion, the Soviet Union, with its own revolutionary ideology, is thus in a position to exploit most of the opportunities created by the maintenance of a nuclear stalemate. Although the main direction of the revolutionary tide is neither Communist in character nor Communist-inspired, it soon becomes Soviet encouraged and supported, since it is directed against the residual bastions of Western paramountcy in the underdeveloped regions of Africa, Latin America, and Asia. The supreme tragedy for the

[6] V. I. Lenin, *Selected Works* (International Publishers, 1943), Vol. 10, pp. 239–41.
[7] J. V. Stalin, *Problems of Leninism* (Moscow, 1940), pp. 199–201.
[8] Khrushchev's Report to the Twenty-Second Party Congress, *Pravda,* October 18, 1961.

Western world and the United States is not so much that they have been boxed into becoming the most formidable bulwark against the revolutionary tide, but that neither Western statesmen, nor the vast Western public, are consciously aware of this fact. This is particularly true of the United States, where revolutionary verbalism and conservative action have coexisted for so long that a supreme and heroic gesture will be required to leap out of an ever-deepening quagmire of self-deception concerning the social and economic forces which impel revolutionary movements.

The United States is not always aware of its role as the gendarme of the status quo, although the character of the regimes which the United States has supported in the past and at the present time — together with its well-known aversion to socioeconomic reforms which transgress the sanctity of private property relationships (no matter where it exists, how it was acquired in the first place, or how venal and corruptive its impact on a given country) — ineluctably stamps the United States as the main bulwark of the status quo in a revolutionary world. Although the image of the United States in most of the world, whether it be Moscow or Peking, New Delhi or Cairo, Accra or Havana, becomes increasingly etched as the mainstay of an old order, there has been a corresponding self-image in the United States of a revitalized and resurgent America leading the forces of freedom and reform against the Communist legions of slavery and reaction. This wide and seemingly incompatible discrepancy between the self-image of the United States as a revolutionary force and that in the revolutionary world as a conservative, sometimes reactionary, force requires critical examination.

During great revolutionary moments in history, when not simply the fate of this or that state, but the destiny of entire ideo-social or civilization systems, is involved, failure to include the various internal social equilibriums between the forces of the status quo and revolution into the calculations of the balance of power can result only in a distorted perception of developing reality. The entire structure of the Soviet image of reality and international politics, the Soviet understanding of power, its manipulation and deterrence, rests upon an awareness of this fundamental truth. The Soviet dialectical method of analysis furnishes Soviet decision-makers not only with dynamic analytical categories, but also with a unique ordering of events, relating them to one another, no matter how widely dispersed in time and space, and coordinating the effects of the various and sundry conflicting forces within individual countries as well as the world as a whole. Thus, according to a recent Soviet scholarly view:

> The foreign policy of socialism is based on science and founded on the only correct science of society, the theory of Marxism-Leninism. . . . Marxism is a reliable compass for understanding reality and reconstructing society in a revolutionary manner in accordance with socialist principles. The strength of Marxism-Leninism lies in the fact that it gives the Communist Party and the Soviet State the possibility of

discovering the objective laws of the historical process, of steering the correct course in accordance with the internal and external situation, of understanding the inner connection between events and of ascertaining not only how and in what direction events are developing in the present, but also how and in what direction they will develop in the future. . . . However, the mere understanding of the objective laws of social development, and in particular of international relations, is not in itself sufficient to determine the correct course in foreign politics by which major victories can be won. The decisive source of the strength or weakness of foreign policy, of its historical prospects or lack of prospects is the correlation of that policy and social progress; its conformity or non-conformity to the laws of development.[9]

Soviet leaders recognize that social conflicts, tensions, frustrations, and resentments, particularly between classes, conceal tremendous reserves of pent-up social power, which can be detected by dialectical analysis, and then tapped, mobilized, and transmuted into concrete political power subject to the manipulation of Soviet policy. These stored up social energies of a world in ferment and convulsion are released with tremendous force during periods, which Lenin described as "revolutionary situations":

> For a Marxist there is no doubt that a revolution is impossible without a revolutionary situation. . . . What are, generally speaking, the characteristics of a revolutionary situation? We can hardly be mistaken when we indicate the following three outstanding signs: (1) it is impossible for the ruling classes to maintain their power unchanged; there is a crisis of the "upper classes" taking one form or another; there is a crisis in the policy of the ruling class; as a result, there appears a crack through which the dissatisfaction and the indignation of the oppressed masses burst forth. If a revolution is to take place, it is usually insufficient that "the lower classes do not wish," but it is necessary that "the upper classes be unable," to continue the old way; (2) the wants and sufferings of the oppressed classes must become more acute than usual; (3) in consequence of the above causes, there is considerable increase in the activity of the masses who in "peacetime" allow themselves to be robbed without protest, but in stormy times are drawn both by the conditions of the crisis and by *"the upper classes" themselves* into independent historic action.[10]

In calculating what the Soviets call the international "correlation of forces," or "the relation of forces in the world arena," these internal social factors, and the direction of their movement — for or against the status quo — constitute important elements in the power equation. As a systematic framework for the analysis, mobilization, and manipulation of social and political power under a variety of conditions and circumstances, individually and collectively, separately or simultaneously,

[9] M. Airapetyan and G. Deborin, "Foreign Policy and Social Progress," *International Affairs* (Moscow, 1959), No. 2, pp. 21–22.
[10] V. I. Lenin, *Collected Works* (International Publishers, 1930), Vol. 18, p. 279.

Soviet ideology performs an invaluable service for Soviet policy-makers, which is far too often underrated by Western observers.

Soviet ideology is responsible for neither the invention nor discovery of the social "contradictions," nor for the conflicts in international or internal politics upon which Soviet policy thrives. And we can, of course, dispense with the spurious and largely irrelevant claim to "scientific" pretensions made on behalf of Marxism-Leninism which has diverted virtually an army of scholars and publicists into expending inordinate energy and time in refutations and exposés, in the naive belief that if the "scientific" pretensions of Soviet ideology can be disproven, the entire Soviet ideological edifice will crumble and perhaps the regime and system with it.

What cannot be disproven, however, is that Marxism-Leninism is *a* theory of social reality and, hence, a theory of power, its origins, manifestations, forms, calculations, deterrence, and manipulation; and it is a very powerful and effective theory. Its effectiveness as a guide to action and policy does not rest upon its being "scientific," for it can only be relative in this regard, not absolute, and the only valid measurement of its effectiveness as a theory of analysis and action is to compare it with the effectiveness of corresponding analytic systems employed by Western decision-makers. A true measure of its validity, thus, does not rest upon whether it is indeed "scientific" or not. Its validity is contingent upon its comparison, not with the profusion of theories, models, systems, processes, and games devised by Western scholars, but with comparable theories of analysis employed by Western statesmen as a basis for policy and action, whether they be implicit or explicit, eclectic or synthetic, *ad hoc* or systematic, pragmatic or dogmatic, empirical or *a priori* in character.

Although "contradictions" or conflicts were not discovered by Marxism, the Soviet method of exploiting conflicts to advantage is unique. What distinguishes the Soviet method is that conflicts are viewed in qualitatively different perspective. They are viewed as being in constant flux, as inevitably moving to a foreordained climax and resolution, rather than as being chance or fortuitous occurrences. The Soviet approach to international politics slices deeper than simply the exploitation of state and national interests in conflict (which it recognizes as conflicts between "ruling class" interests). It searches for the more profound, passionate, and explosive animosities and resentments of conflicting social classes and submerged races and nationalities within individual countries, continents, or the world as a whole. The Soviet analytical system provides a scheme for ordering these contradictions and conflicts, establishing priorities, differentiating them into discrete social and power equations, and for manipulating them as the occasion may demand or the opportunity presents itself.

The application of the dialectic to international relations turns up five contradictory equations, each with dynamic formulae, whose values fluctuate in response to changing conditions and opportunities. Each has its decisive moment in history, and each is endowed with its distinctive instruments and forms which can be exploited with maximum effect, singly or in combination. These five general contradictions are:

1. Contradictions between the "bourgeoisie" and the "proletariat" within individual countries, in which the local Communist Party is the chief instrument of exploitation.

2. Contradictions between the "ruling classes" of capitalist states in general for markets, territory, colonies, prestige, and general advantage over the other, which are exploited by economic and political maneuvering by the Soviet Union.

3. Contradictions between the victorious group of capitalist states and the defeated group after the most recent general war, in which the former group seeks to preserve and perpetuate its advantages (status quoism), while the latter group seeks to recoup its former position and plots revenge (revisionism).

4. Contradictions between the capitalist states and the colonial dependencies and former colonial territories which currently receive their greatest exploitation and which promise fruitful results in Latin America, Africa, and Southeast Asia. The chief instrument of exploitation here is "anti-imperialism" or "anti-colonialism," and the "struggle for peace."

5. Finally, the supreme contradiction is that between the capitalist camp and the Communist camp, whose resolution must be delayed until the exploitation of the other contradictions has sapped capitalism of its moral vigor and physical power, rendering it impotent and encircled.

It would be a mistake, therefore, to conclude that Soviet ideology is little more than a manipulative instrument designed to obscure what is in fact an opportunistic exploitation of essentially fortuitous situations and events. This applies only to its theory of action, which is essentially a systematic opportunism, executed within a calculated framework of analysis and devoted to the fulfillment of fixed ideological ends, in accordance with Lenin's admonition "to master the tactics of maneuver, while remaining loyal to the end to principles in the struggle for socialism."

In responding to the Soviet challenge, one of the obvious questions requiring attention is the relative validity and effectiveness of the Western systems of analysis, of which its policy must inevitably be an expression. Does the West have as accurate an image of social and political realities in a revolutionary world as the Soviet leaders, or is this image distorted by factors which have not received sufficient attention from scholars? Is the Soviet system of the class analysis of forces and events in the underdeveloped world more or less accurate than the Western basis of analysis, which sedulously avoids referring to classes or class conflict? Are the social and political realities in the underdeveloped world better understood when analyzed in class categories than within the context of impersonal forces like "poverty," "disease," "hunger," "misery"? Is the "class struggle" in underdeveloped countries a more accurate representation of the tensions and conflicts than "democracy versus dictatorship" or "law and order versus violence and chaos"? Do approximations, in varying degrees, of the Marxist conception of a "ruling class" exist in Middle Eastern countries and many Latin American states or is this simply a figment of the Soviet imagination?

A successful response to the challenges posed by Soviet foreign policy will require a courageous and unevasive answer to these vital questions. For, if a class analysis provides better insights as to real events and forces in a revolutionary world, Western policy-makers must devise a strategy that will work with these forces and not rely upon an analysis and strategy that fails to take them into account. A desirable strategy for the West must seek and uncover a common denominator of interests and action between the social status quo in the Western world and the revolutionary forces in the underdeveloped world. Only in this way can the tremendous social and political energies released by revolution in much of the world be tapped to stabilize and preserve the status quo elsewhere against the universalist pretensions of Soviet Communism.

IMAGES OF THE SOVIET CHALLENGE

Although Communism, as a social order, has little attraction for revolutionary elites in the underdeveloped world, they are nevertheless impressed with the tremendous advances made by the Soviet Union in the name of achieving a Communist society. What Communism has done for Russia, in a material way, constitutes a concrete challenge which repels the advanced Western countries and strikes fear into the ruling classes of feudal and quasi-feudal societies but which excites revolutionary elites who are interested in quick social transformations.

The Soviet achievement merits careful analysis, for, despite the present success of Soviet efforts, there is still a fundamental hiatus between the ideological goals of Soviet foreign policy and the aims of revolutionary elites. The Soviet system is, first of all, a historical *process* of industrialization and modernization. It rivals that of Western capitalism, whether free and spontaneous or state-directed, as in the cases of Imperial Germany and Japan. Before the advent of the Soviet system, capitalism was the only historical method by means of which states modernized. In its second dimension, it is a *way of life* or *civilization* rival to that of the West.

The original purpose of Marxism was to displace a bourgeois-oriented civilization with one centered on the interests and aspirations of the proletariat. Socialism and Communism were envisaged as systems designed not to compete with Western capitalism as processes of industrialization and change, but to supersede capitalism as a superior and more progressive form of social and economic organization of society — as simultaneously more efficient and equitable. But, because Marxism was adapted to a society for which it was never intended — an underdeveloped rather than an advanced one — it was first converted into a process of industrialization and modernization.

Whenever the Soviet Union has tried to impress its ideological norms upon revolutionary elites, as in Egypt and Iraq, this has resulted in forcing underlying incompatibilities to the surface. From the vantage point of Western policy, the distinction between the Soviet system as a *process of change* and as a *civilization* must always be borne in mind. For just as Moscow and the revolutionary elites are united against the status quo, with respect to the process of change, the West and the same revolutionary elites may find common ground in a determination that the status quo, with respect to some civilized values, will not be supplanted by Communism. This unique triangular relationship not only bears the seeds which may destroy the alliance between the revolutionary nationalist elites and Soviet foreign policy, but it also represents the submerged foundation upon which a durable alliance can be erected between these nationalist movements and the West against Communism as a world system.

The underdeveloped countries are more interested in the process of modernization than in the civilization developed by the Soviet Union, while the Western world is interested in neither (except for substantial sections of the populations in France and Italy, who apparently would welcome some variation of the Communist system). These different perspectives of the Soviet system result in the projection of contradictory images of the Soviet Union and, hence, in varying responses to its foreign policy goals at any given instance. In order to fully appreciate the total charter of the Soviet challenge, it is necessary to reconstruct, as accurately as possible, these different images of the Soviet system and determine what they have in common as well as what separates them.

Nothing could be more subversive than to project unwittingly a single image of the Soviet challenge and to act upon the assumption that it is universally recognized and accepted. The Western view that Soviet Communism represents a despotic regime, born in conspiracy, preserved by violence and terror, extended by military conquest, subversion, espionage, and deception, animated by a wicked doctrine, and governed by venal or misguided rulers, is only one image of the Soviet system and is far from being the most universally accepted. No matter how valid this image may be from the perspective of the West, it is not the image seen by large parts of the world, for it represents, primarily, the image of those societies and social groups who benefit from the status quo the Soviet system is dedicated to annihilating. Thus, it is the image held by a mortal enemy and is ideologically biased, since it is a reflection of the interest perspective of the West. Correspondingly, it is rejected by increasingly larger segments of the underdeveloped world and by those classes and social groups in the West who bear no great enthusiasm for preserving the status quo which Soviet foreign policy seeks to subvert and destroy.

Aside from the Communist image (whether it be the self-image of the Soviet leaders, the image of rivalry held by the Chinese, or the image of patron held by other Communist leaders) of the Soviet Union as the engine of progress, three general images of the Soviet system coexist simultaneously and these images in turn determine the reception accorded to Soviet foreign-policy goals. Each image is shaped largely by the distinctive historical or social experience of a particular community or social group together with the perceived implications and contemplated consequences for a given country or social group if Soviet foreign policy objectives are either partly or wholly fulfilled. These discretely different images of the Soviet system thus represent ideological perceptions of self-interest and the degree to which these self-interests are promoted or retarded by the advance of Soviet power.

The Image in the West

The images of the Soviet Union with which the West is most familiar are two variations of the Soviet Union as an aggressive imperialistic power bent upon world domination. These two variants reflect the views of those already subjugated by Soviet power on the one hand and on the other of those who are its contemplated victims. In Eastern Europe, the image of foreign imperialist domination is endemic among the population, and this image is strongly reinforced by historical memories. Russia has traditionally sought to dominate this region and, thus, Soviet Communism appears simply as a more brutish, if technologically more efficient, continuation of Russian imperialism in new garb. With the exception of Yugoslavia and Albania, Communism in Eastern Europe was imposed upon these countries by Soviet conquest and military occupation.[11] The Soviet system never registered any great internal appeal among the population of these countries before their occupation, and the alien regimes imposed from the outside remain highly unpopular in spite of the amelioration of Soviet control since 1956.

The image of the Soviet Union projected to the West is not only of an imperialistic behemoth bent upon world conquest, but also that of a rival world civilization determined to eradicate the spiritual values and social institutions of Western civilization. The West thus represents, in a sense, a former world system in decline, a system whose power and influence have catastrophically shrunk to metropolitan power centers as a consequence of its own internecine and fratricidal conflicts (understandably enough, the two World Wars are viewed by many articulate Asians as essentially European civil wars), the revolutionary pressures released in their colonial empires as a result of these intramural wars, and finally because of the relentless push of the growing might of the

[11] This undoubtedly serves to explain why it is precisely Yugoslavia and Albania that have dared to defy the authority of the Soviet Party. Both Yugoslavia and Albania do not have frontiers with the Soviet and are relatively inaccessible, but geography alone does not explain the defiance. Like the Chinese Party, they are primarily indigenous in their evolution. Since most of the large Parties outside the Communist Orbit also are basically indigenous, if they come to power, the Communist World is likely to become decentralized even more than it is today. As Yugoslavia, Albania, and China demonstrate, the decentralization need not follow a single ideological heresy but may produce many.

Soviet Union. The true meaning of the term "world domination" thus emerges as the dominance of a given set of ideological values and social institutions and relationships in the world at large. In this sense, the struggle between the Soviet world and the West is truly a contest for "world supremacy."

The Image in the Underdeveloped World

In the underdeveloped countries of the world two images of Soviet power are also to be found. The image among the beneficiaries of the status quo — the ruling classes and landowning groups in Asia and Latin America — is similar to that found in the West, but Soviet power represents a more direct challenge to their ruling position because the image of the Soviet Union among the other sectors of population may be a favorable one. Soviet power, even its very existence, constitutes an important element in the internal equilibriums of feudal and quasi-feudal social orders, because both the ideas of Communism and the example of the Soviet Union serve to mobilize internal opposition to the existing order. The saving virtue here is not so much an overwhelming attitude of revulsion towards Communist ideas, as the ignorance of the masses who are insufficiently educated to understand them; on the other hand, there is the fear on the part of ruling groups that once the masses do understand Communist ideas they may revolt.

The second image of the Soviet Union is to be found among the revolutionary middle-class nationalist elites, whether they have come to power or are seeking it. These emerging elites neither fear nor reject the idea of radical social transformation but, in fact, pursue it; neither do they share in the recognition of the Soviet Union as a neo-colonial empire bent on world conquest. On the contrary, they view the Soviet Union as at least a temporary ally against the status quo and, further-more, see in the Soviet Union a former underdeveloped country which has made rapid industrial, military, and cultural progress outside the pattern of Western capitalism — in the face of relentless and implacable hostility from the Western world in fact. In the Soviet *process* of modernization and industrialization, revolutionary nationalist elites see an alternative to the capitalist pattern which can be adapted to their own needs and purposes. A brief comparison between the Russia of 1914 and the Soviet Union of the 1960's can perhaps provide us with an insight as to what excites the revolutionary elites about the Soviet system. [See tables 1 and 2.]

In 1914 Russia was militarily weak, having suffered defeat after defeat since 1850, culminating in the humiliating victory of an upstart Japan in 1905. Her rapidly declining military strength was further confirmed by defeat, occupation, and revolution during the First World War. Today, Russia rivals the United States for military paramountcy and in some respects appears to be in the lead.

In 1914 Russia ranked last among the industrial states of the world, but by 1960, the Soviet Union had already outstripped all the great industrial powers of Western Europe (and Japan) in the basic

TABLE 1

FROM UNDERDEVELOPMENT TO WORLD POWER

Basic Indices of Industrialization and Modernization in the USSR

Industry	1913	(Est.) 1961	(Projected) 1965	1980
Steel (mill. tons)	4.2	71	86–91	250
Pig iron "	4.2	51	65–70	
Rolled metal "	3.5	55	65–70	
Coal "	29.1	513	600–612	1118–1200
Oil "	9.2	166	230–240	670–710
Electricity[a]	1.9	327	500–520	2.7–3 trillion
Cement (mill. tons)	1.3	51	75–81	233–235
Machine tools (thousands)	1.5	175.8	226–236	
Gross indust. prod. (bill. rubles)		155		970–1 trillion

Education, Culture, Health	1913	1959
Literacy	24%	98.5%
Higher education, total	290,000	13,400,000
Students, higher ed., current	127,000	2,200,000
All students	10,000,000	55,000,000
Doctors and dentists	28,000	375,000
Hosp. beds	207,300	1,500,000
Life expectancy	32 yr	68 yr
Urbanization	15%	49%
Total population	159,000,000	215,000,000

[a] Billion kilowatt hours (KWH).

Sources: Narodnoye Khozyaistvo SSSR v 1959 Godu (Moscow, 1960), Pravda (October 19, 1961).

indices of industrial production and is second only to the United States, which it avowedly aims to surpass.

In 1914 Russia had a vast unskilled, uneducated, superstitious, agricultural, and largely demoralized population, 76 per cent illiterate, which had been released from serfdom less than seventy-five years earlier. She produced a few outstanding individual scientists, writers, and composers, but in general Russia lagged far behind the rest of Europe in educational, technological, and scientific achievement. By 1960 the Soviet Union had achieved 98.5 per cent literacy (up from as low as 1 per cent in parts of Central Asia) in a country in which there are nearly twenty-five major languages and linguistic groups, to say nothing of three dozen additional minor ones, all with their own schools, newspapers, and books. Today, the Soviet Union has four times as many students enrolled in institutions of higher education as Great Britain, France, Italy, and West Germany combined. Nearly 2,500,000 students are to be found in 766 institutions of higher learning, 3346 technicums,

TABLE 2
INDUSTRIALIZATION AND MODERNIZATION IN
SOVIET CENTRAL ASIA, 1913–1960

Republic	Steel (tons)	Electricity (thousand KWH)	Coal (tons)	Oil (tons)	Tractors
Uzbek					
1913	0	3,300	0	13,000	0
1959	273,000	5,143,100	2,933,000	1,465,000	69,000
Kazakh					
1913	0	1,300	90	118,000	0
1959	287,900	9,583,400	31,674,000	1,544,000	291,000
Kirgiz					
1913	0	0	103	0	0
1959	0	800,000	3,463,000	424,000	16,000
Tadzhik					
1913	0	0	28	0	0
1959	0	1,151,300	817,000	17,000	14,100
Turkmen					
1913	0	2,590	27	129,000	0
1959	680	662,500	0	4,577,000	14,700

Education, Culture, Health

Republic	H. Ed. Insts.	Libraries	Books	Doctors	Hosp. Beds	School Enr.
Uzbek						
1913	0	0	118,000	128	1,000	17,300
1959	34	3,099	19,398,000	10,618	42,400	1,431,000
Kazakh						
1913	0	139	4,000	196	1,800	10,500
1959	26	6,126	15,701,000	12,490	60,900	1,631,000
Kirgiz						
1913	0	0	0	15	100	700
1959	9	1,095	3,165,000	2,842	10,100	360,000
Tadzhik						
1913	0	0	0	13	40	400
1959	8	922	3,487,000	2,279	9,800	366,000
Turkmen						
1913	0	0	400	56	300	700
1959	9	1,173	3,301,000	2,631	10,400	260,000

Note: The *non-Asian* proportion of the population in the Central Asian Republics is as follows: Uzbek, 15 per cent; Kazakh, 55 per cent; Kirgiz, 36.8 per cent; Tadzhik, 14.7 per cent; Turkmen, 20 per cent.
Source: *Narodnoye Khozyaistvo SSSR v 1959 Godu* (Moscow, 1960).

and other specialized secondary schools, as compared with less than 128,000 students enrolled in 1914. The Soviet Union graduates every year nearly four times the number of engineers as the United States and the total number of Soviet citizens with some higher education now totals more than 13,000,000. In many respects, the Soviet Union has established, virtually from scratch, an educational system second to none in the space of a single generation. Furthermore, this was all accomplished during a period when the Soviet population was subjected to unprecedented and unspeakable natural and political calamities, whether it was war, famine, economic dislocation, civil war, terror, purges, foreign occupation, or depredation.

The story is virtually identical in the field of social services, particularly medicine. In 1914 Russian medical science was woefully retarded, and medical care was available only to the very wealthy. The number of physicians and dentists before the Revolution was 28,000 for a population of 159,000,000. By 1960 it was nearly 375,000 for a population of 214,000,000, which gives the Soviet Union today the largest number of doctors in proportion to the population of any country in the world, including the United States and except Israel. Today, every citizen is entitled to free medical care. Life expectancy in Russia has gone up from an average age of 32 before the Revolution to 68 in 1959, which is now among the highest in the world. The number of hospital beds during the same period has increased from 207,300 to nearly 1,500,000.

As in many pre-industrial societies, pre-revolutionary Russia did not provide many opportunities for women. Today in the Soviet Union, 53 per cent of all Soviet citizens with some secondary education are women. Before the Revolution, 10 per cent of all physicians were women; today, they constitute 75 per cent of the total. In the Soviet Union women are to be found in increasingly impressive numbers at all levels of cultural, scientific, and social life — 70 per cent of the teachers, 57 per cent of the economists and statisticians, 32 per cent of the lawyers and judges, 30 per cent of the engineers, 39 per cent of the technicians, 36 per cent of Soviet scientific workers, and 20 per cent of the Communist Party are women. Before the Revolution 88 per cent of the women of Russia were illiterate.

These are substantial achievements, and they transcend the issues of ideologies or social systems, for industrial power, military strength, scientific and technological progress, medical care, and emancipation of women are universally desired goals among the new elites. These are the undeniable marks of a modernized, industrialized, and Westernized society. They symbolize power and prestige — dignity and pride for the communities which bear them, whether large or small. The underdeveloped countries are interested in results, for they have no vested interests in dogmas and doctrines, and they are inexorably attracted to that process and system which appear most easily adaptable to their needs and which promise to accelerate their entry into the modern industrial and technological age. In the Soviet experience, they see the concrete fulfillment of the dreams and aspirations of a previously underdeveloped country. This is a fascinating and powerful attraction and its magnetic pull should not be underestimated. What is of singular significance is that the Soviet achievement was not only spectacularly quick, but was virtually a do-it-yourself operation which triumphed over overwhelming odds and in the face of almost universal predictions of failure in the Western world.

In this connection, the fate and progress of the non-Russian nationalities, particularly those in Soviet Central Asia, should be treated separately to see whether the Soviet achievements of the past four decades were reserved only for a ruling European nationality. Progress has been made across the entire spectrum of nationalities, of which there are more than two dozen, having a total population of at least one million, in the Soviet Union. This is an important point, for if it can be demonstrated that Soviet progress largely left the populations and territories of the non-Russian nationalities untouched, and that they are exploited for the benefit of the ruling nationality, then a charge of Soviet colonialism would be both valid and effective, and the Soviet anti-colonial posture can be exposed as a brazen exercise in hypocrisy. Progress in Soviet Central Asia, however, under the Soviet regime, has been even more dramatic and sweeping than in most parts of the Soviet Union. In the two Caucasian Republics of Georgia and Armenia, the quality of progress has been positively embarrassing, for per capita achievement outstrips even that of the Slavic Republics of the Union.

The Uzbek Republic is the home of the largest and most advanced of the Central Asian Turks, and its progress under Soviet rule provides a good example of Soviet "colonialism." Before the Revolution, only 2 per cent of the population was literate; institutions of higher learning were non-existent; 160 schools were attended by 17,300 children of the privileged land-owning classes. Native engineers or doctors did not exist, nor were there any teachers with higher educational training. In 1960 the Republic had an Academy of Sciences, an Academy of Agricultural Sciences, 34 institutions of higher learning, 100 technicums, 50 special technical schools, 5800 general ten-year schools, 12 pedagogical institutes, and 1400 kindergartens. Altogether 1,431,000 children are in school, with more than 50 per cent of 80,000 teachers possessing some higher education. The literacy rate in 1959 was over 95 per cent. Before the Revolution, the Republic possessed no libraries; today there are over 3000. The number of books printed in 1913 was 118,000; in 1960 it exceeded 22 million. Of more than 8,000,000 specialists in the national economy of the entire Union who possess a higher or specialized secondary education, Uzbeks accounted for 86,100, while the total number of native Central Asians in this category exceeds 211,000.

Today, the Uzbek Republic follows Japan, China, and India as the fourth most highly industrialized and mechanized state in Asia. In 1913, the region produced only 3.3 kilowatt hours of electricity; in 1959, it was 5,143,100 million kilowatt hours, which means that the Republic produces today five times as much electricity in one day as it did during an entire year in 1913. The Republic alone possesses two and a half times as many electric power stations as all of Russia before the Revolution. In 1960, the Uzbek Republic produced two-thirds of all cotton products in the Soviet Union, three-quarters of the entire Soviet output of spinning machinery, and was the main producer of agricultural machinery for cotton growing and harvesting in the Union. More than 69,000 tractors are to be found on its farms. The Republic has its own chemical industry and a steel industry which produced 275,000 tons of steel and 177,000 tons of rolled metal in 1959, as compared with none in 1913.

Although Central Asia has by no means been converted into a biblical paradise, and its achievements are not likely to look impressive to Western Europeans, it is clear that Soviet Central Asia has clearly outstripped its adjacent neighbors in the Middle East and Southeast Asia, whether independent or formerly under colonial rule. It is, therefore, hardly surprising that the Uzbek Republic has been transformed into a showcase for visiting dignitaries from Africa and Asia. Instead of being an example of Soviet colonialism in the eyes of Afro-Asians, the Soviet achievement stands as a monumental tribute to Western hypocrisy, since the standard colonial rationalization has been that generations were required to achieve even modest levels of education and technical training in underdeveloped countries. After nearly 500 years of Portuguese rule, only 1 per cent of the native population in Angola is barely literate, to cite an extreme example. Although the record for low-level literacy has been better in the Belgian Congo, it is notorious that after a century of Belgian rule, hardly a dozen university graduates existed in a country of 13,500,000 in the year of independence, 1960. Although the performance of the British and the French has been much better, and the American record in the Philippines is really extraordinary in comparison, neither can really compare with the Soviet achievement of providing nearly 250,000 native Central Asians (Uzbeks, Kazakhs, Tadzhiks, Turkmen, and Kirgiz) out of a total population of about 13,000,000 with higher or specialized secondary education [see table 3] and of raising the general literacy rate from 1 to 2 to 95 per cent within the span of four decades. These are the comparisons and images which revolutionary elites in underdeveloped countries see. An idea of what might further impress them can be gleaned from information tabulated on tables 1 and 2.

TABLE 3
HIGHER EDUCATION IN SOVIET CENTRAL ASIA BY NATIONALITIES, 1959

Nationality	Size	Students, Higher Education	Specialists[a]	Scientists
Uzbeks	6,004,000	30,500	86,100	3,121
Kazakhs	3,581,000	22,000	68,800	2,057
Kirgiz	974,000	6,500	17,000	528
Tadzhiks	1,397,000	6,800	22,000	749
Turkmen	1,004,000	5,700	17,900	622

[a] With higher education and specialized secondary education, working in the national economy.

Source: *Narodnoye Khozyaistvo SSSR v 1959 Godu* (Moscow, 1960).

Conclusion

The Soviet achievement is by no means terminal in character, for during the next two decades, Soviet leaders project even greater accomplishments, with the main objective being no less than to outstrip the United States in major areas of material production and technological attainment. The sustained rapid annual growth of the Soviet economy conveys an impression of tremendous vitality and determination. Even a cursory examination of Soviet target goals for 1980 (an annual production of 250 million tons of steel for example) indicates that Soviet production goals are designed to meet both internal and external-ideological policy of the Soviet Union. The foreign-policy implications of these production goals are quite clear, for the tremendous productive capacity of the Soviet Union in 1980 can be used not only to supply economic and technical assistance to underdeveloped countries, but also to disrupt and shatter the commercial and trade structure of the West.

Aside from the ideological and essentially semantic goals of Communist society, the target goals of 1980 set by the new Program of the Communist Party adopted by the Twenty-Second Party Congress literally stagger the imagination, when measured not only against 1913, but against 1962 as well. Although these are only targets and one can question their feasibility, it must be noted that the Soviet Union has demonstrated a remarkable record in achieving her planned goals. Even if the Soviet targets fall short of fulfillment by 25 per cent, the achievement will remain extraordinary. Furthermore, the steady progression toward these goals during the next decade may itself generate an irreversible psychological shift in the world balance of power, unless the Western world responds with a comparable demonstration. One can hardly quarrel with the anxious warning of the Shah of Iran that "even if this plan [the new Soviet twenty-year plan] is only 50 per cent fulfilled, the world will be faced with a new Communist society," adding that "if we waste our time in countries like mine, time is not going to be on our side."[12]

Soviet Communism thus emerges as a process for the rapid transformation of backward agrarian and semi-feudal states into advanced industrial communities, and although this may be a far cry from the original norms of Marxism (as has been repeatedly demonstrated by various critics), this does not diminish its appeal to the underdeveloped. The Soviet process promises quick transformation of illiterate populations into educated communities, rapid conversion of raw, unskilled peasant hands into skilled technicians and workmen, quick elimination of disease and pestilence, the early emancipation of women, and the promise of a quick improvement in the standard of living. But, above all, it promises the quick acquisition and mobilization of power, influence, and dignity for emerging national communities, whose aspirations currently exceed their capacities.

[12] *The New York Times,* November 5, 1961.

In short, Soviet Communism offers a seductive and effective way to meet the demands of the "revolution of rising expectations" which is sweeping the underdeveloped lands. After languishing under the long shadow of Western colonialism for many decades, Soviet Communism promises to give the new and the underdeveloped nations a place in the sun. An effective response to this challenge does not lie in denigrating the Soviet achievement or its promise but in providing a more glittering alternative.

The challenge of Soviet foreign policy lies not only in its military might and in its aggressively anti-colonial posture, but also in its formulas for overcoming the poverty, illiteracy, and economic retardation of the underdeveloped countries. These formulas show more promise than anything offered by the West. As protagonists of the status quo, the West is not particularly adept at revolutionary solutions for pressing social and economic problems, frequently forgetting to recall that its own progress was released only after a revolutionary rupture with obsolete and stagnant social systems. These episodes remain only a dim memory, and the mistaken notion has taken root that Western civilization has developed along a gradual, evolutionary, and non-convulsive arc of progress. The Soviet Union, on the other hand, as did revolutionary France more than a century earlier, represents the forces of revolutionary change and, thus, is more likely to manifest greater sympathy for the aspirations and expectations of retarded societies where discontent and dissatisfaction with the existing social order are widespread and endemic.

During the next four decades, the population of the world is expected to rise from 3 to nearly 6.3 billion. According to current scientific opinion, the total resources of the world are sufficiently ample to meet the demands of this explosive population increase, provided they are efficiently exploited, processed, and distributed. The supreme conundrum of the twentieth century is likely to be whether the Soviet system or that of the West can most effectively mobilize the human and natural resources of the world in the interests of social justice. Soviet leaders boast that in the twentieth century all roads lead to Communism, because it has already demonstrated its superiority in this connection. Unless the Western world, led by the United States, is both willing and able to renovate and universalize the values, institutions, and material abundance which it cherishes, and unless it can demonstrate an alternative promising both the material results of Soviet Communism and the freedoms of Western civilization, then Communism or some variant of it is likely to become the universal ideology of revolutionary salvation as the only doctrine that adequately articulates dissatisfaction and protest against the injustices and insufficiencies of the status quo.

5. ORIGINS OF THE COLD WAR

Arthur Schlesinger, Jr.

The Cold War in its original form was a presumably mortal antagonism, arising in the wake of the Second World War, between two rigidly hostile blocs, one led by the Soviet Union, the other by the United States. For nearly two somber and dangerous decades this antagonism dominated the fears of mankind; it may even, on occasion, have come close to blowing up the planet. In recent years, however, the once implacable struggle has lost its familiar clarity of outline. With the passing of old issues and the emergence of new conflicts and contestants, there is a natural tendency, especially on the part of the generation which grew up during the Cold War, to take a fresh look at the causes of the great contention between Russia and America.

Some exercises in reappraisal have merely elaborated the orthodoxies promulgated in Washington or Moscow during the boom years of the Cold War. But others, especially in the United States (there are no signs, alas, of this in the Soviet Union), represent what American historians call "revisionism" — that is, a readiness to challenge official explanations. No one should be surprised by this phenomenon. Every war in American history has been followed in due course by skeptical reassessments of supposedly sacred assumptions. So the War of 1812, fought at the time for the freedom of the seas, was in later years ascribed to the expansionist ambitions of Congressional war hawks; so the Mexican War became a slaveholders' conspiracy. So the Civil War has been pronounced a "needless war," and Lincoln has even been accused of manœuvring the rebel attack on Fort Sumter. So too the

Reprinted by special permission from *Foreign Affairs*, October, 1967. Copyright, 1967, the Council on Foreign Relations, Inc., New York.

Spanish-American War and the First and Second World Wars have, each in its turn, undergone revisionist critiques. It is not to be supposed that the Cold War would remain exempt.

In the case of the Cold War, special factors reinforce the predictable historiographical rhythm. The outburst of polycentrism in the communist empire has made people wonder whether communism was ever so monolithic as official theories of the Cold War supposed. A generation with no vivid memories of Stalinism may see the Russia of the forties in the image of the relatively mild, seedy and irresolute Russia of the sixties. And for this same generation the American course of widening the war in Viet Nam — which even non-revisionists can easily regard as folly — has unquestionably stirred doubts about the wisdom of American foreign policy in the sixties which younger historians may have begun to read back into the forties.

It is useful to remember that, on the whole, past exercises in revisionism have failed to stick. Few historians today believe that the war hawks caused the War of 1812 or the slaveholders the Mexican War, or that the Civil War was needless, or that the House of Morgan brought America into the First World War or that Franklin Roosevelt schemed to produce the attack on Pearl Harbor. But this does not mean that one should deplore the rise of Cold War revisionism.[1] For revisionism is an essential part of the process by which history, through the posing of new problems and the investigation of new possibilities, enlarges its perspectives and enriches its insights.

More than this, in the present context, revisionism expresses a deep, legitimate and tragic apprehension. As the Cold War has begun to lose its purity of definition, as the moral absolutes of the fifties become the moralistic clichés of the sixties, some have begun to ask whether the appalling risks which humanity ran during the Cold War were, after all, necessary and inevitable; whether more restrained and rational policies might not have guided the energies of man from the perils of conflict into the potentialities of collaboration. The fact that such questions are in their nature unanswerable does not mean that it is not right and useful to raise them. Nor does it mean that our sons and daughters are not entitled to an accounting from the generation of Russians and Americans who produced the Cold War.

II.

The orthodox American view, as originally set forth by the American government and as reaffirmed until recently by most American scholars, has been that the Cold War was the brave and essential response of free men to communist aggression. Some have gone back well before the Second World War to lay open the sources of Russian expansionism. Geopoliticians traced the Cold War to imperial Russian

[1] As this writer somewhat intemperately did in a letter to *The New York Review of Books*, October 20, 1966.

strategic ambitions which in the nineteenth century led to the Crimean War, to Russian penetration of the Balkans and the Middle East and to Russian pressure on Britain's "lifeline" to India. Ideologists traced it to the Communist Manifesto of 1848 ("the violent overthrow of the bourgeoisie lays the foundation for the sway of the proletariat"). Thoughtful observers (a phrase meant to exclude those who speak in Dullese about the unlimited evil of godless, atheistic, militant communism) concluded that classical Russian imperialism and Pan-Slavism, compounded after 1917 by Leninist messianism, confronted the West at the end of the Second World War with an inexorable drive for domination.[2]

The revisionist thesis is very different.[3] In its extreme form, it is

[2] Every student of the Cold War must acknowledge his debt to W. H. McNeill's remarkable account, *America, Britain and Russia: Their Cooperation and Conflict, 1941–1946* (New York, 1953) and to the brilliant and indispensable series by Herbert Feis: *Churchill, Roosevelt, Stalin: The War They Waged and the Peace They Sought* (Princeton, 1957); *Between War and Peace: The Potsdam Conference* (Princeton, 1960); and *The Atomic Bomb and the End of World War II* (Princeton, 1966). Useful recent analyses include André Fontaine, *Histoire de la Guerre Froide* (2 v., Paris, 1965, 1967); N. A. Graebner, *Cold War Diplomacy, 1945–1960* (Princeton, 1962); L. J. Halle, *The Cold War as History* (London, 1967); M. F. Herz, *Beginnings of the Cold War* (Bloomington, 1966) and W. L. Neumann, *After Victory: Churchill, Roosevelt, Stalin and the Making of the Peace* (New York, 1967).

[3] The fullest statement of this case is to be found in D. F. Fleming's voluminous *The Cold War and Its Origins* (New York, 1961). For a shorter version of this argument, see David Horowitz, *The Free World Colossus* (New York, 1965); the most subtle and ingenious statements come in W. A. Williams' *The Tragedy of American Diplomacy* (rev. ed., New York, 1962) and in Gar Alperowitz's *Atomic Diplomacy: Hiroshima and Potsdam* (New York, 1965) and in subsequent articles and reviews by Mr. Alperowitz in *The New York Review of Books*. The fact that in some aspects the revisionist thesis parallels the official Soviet argument must not, of course, prevent consideration of the case on its merits, nor raise questions about the motives of the writers, all of whom, so far as I know, are independent-minded scholars.

I might further add that all these books, in spite of their ostentatious display of scholarly apparatus, must be used with caution. Professor Fleming, for example, relies heavily on newspaper articles and even columnists. While Mr. Alperowitz bases his case on official documents or authoritative reminiscences, he sometimes twists his material in a most unscholarly way. For example, in describing Ambassador Harriman's talk with President Truman on April 20, 1945, Mr. Alperowitz writes, "He argued that a reconsideration of Roosevelt's policy was necessary" (p. 22, repeated on p. 24). The citation is to pp. 70–72 in President Truman's *Years of Decision*. What President Truman reported Harriman as saying was the exact opposite: "Before leaving, Harriman took me aside and said, 'Frankly, one of the reasons that made me rush back to Washington was the fear that you did not understand, as I had seen Roosevelt understand, that Stalin is breaking his agreements.'" Similarly, in an appendix (p. 271) Mr. Alperowitz writes that the Hopkins and Davies missions of May 1945 "were opposed by the 'firm' advisers." Actually the Hopkins mission was proposed by Harriman and Charles E. Bohlen, who Mr. Alperowitz elsewhere suggests were the firmest of the firm — and was proposed by them precisely to impress on Stalin the continuity of American policy from Roosevelt to Truman. While the idea that Truman reversed Roosevelt's policy is tempting dramatically, it is a myth. See, for example, the that, after the death of Franklin Roosevelt and the end of the Second World War, the United States deliberately abandoned the wartime policy of collaboration and, exhilarated by the possession of the atomic bomb, undertook a course of aggression of its own designed to expel all Russian influence from Eastern Europe and to establish democratic-capitalist states on the very border of the Soviet Union. As the revisionists see it, this radically new American policy — or rather this resumption by Truman of the pre-Roosevelt policy of insensate anti-communism — left Moscow no alternative but to take measures in defense of its own borders. The result was the Cold War.

These two views, of course, could not be more starkly contrasting. It is therefore not unreasonable to look again at the half-dozen critical years between June 22, 1941, when Hitler attacked Russia, and July 2, 1947, when the Russians walked out of the Marshall Plan meeting in Paris. Several things should be borne in mind as this reëxamination is made. For one thing, we have thought a great deal more in recent years, in part because of writers like Roberta Wohlstetter and T. C. Schelling, about the problems of communication in diplomacy — the signals which one nation, by word or by deed, gives, inadvertently or intentionally, to another. Any honest reappraisal of the origins of the Cold War requires the imaginative leap — which should in any case be as instinctive for the historian as it is prudent for the statesman — into the adversary's viewpoint. We must strive to see how, given Soviet perspectives, the Russians might conceivably have misread our signals, as we must reconsider how intelligently we read theirs.

For another, the historian must not overindulge the man of power in the illusion cherished by those in office that high position carries with it the easy ability to shape history. Violating the statesman's creed, Lincoln once blurted out the truth in his letter of 1864 to A. G. Hodges: "I claim not to have controlled events, but confess plainly that events have controlled me." He was not asserting Tolstoyan fatalism but rather suggesting how greatly events limit the capacity of the statesman to bend history to his will. The physical course of the Second World War — the military operations undertaken, the position of the respective armies at the war's end, the momentum generated by victory and the vacuums created by defeat — all these determined the future as much as the character of individual leaders and the substance of national ideology and purpose.

Nor can the historian forget the conditions under which decisions are made, especially in a time like the Second World War. These were tired, overworked, aging men: in 1945, Churchill was 71 years old,

---

testimony of Anna Rosenberg Hoffman, who lunched with Roosevelt on March 24, 1945, the last day he spent in Washington. After luncheon, Roosevelt was handed a cable. "He read it and became quite angry. He banged his fists on the arms of his wheelchair and said, 'Averell is right; we can't do business with Stalin. He has broken every one of the promises he made at Yalta.' He was very upset and continued in the same vein on the subject."

Stalin had governed his country for 17 exacting years, Roosevelt his for 12 years nearly as exacting. During the war, moreover, the importunities of military operations had shoved postwar questions to the margins of their minds. All — even Stalin, behind his screen of ideology — had become addicts of improvisation, relying on authority and virtuosity to conceal the fact that they were constantly surprised by developments. Like Eliza, they leaped from one cake of ice to the next in the effort to reach the other side of the river. None showed great tactical consistency, or cared much about it; all employed a certain ambiguity to preserve their power to decide big issues; and it is hard to know how to interpret anything any one of them said on any specific occasion. This was partly because, like all princes, they designed their expressions to have particular effects on particular audiences; partly because the entirely genuine intellectual difficulty of the questions they faced made a degree of vacillation and mind-changing eminently reasonable. If historians cannot solve their problems in retrospect, who are they to blame Roosevelt, Stalin and Churchill for not having solved them at the time?

III.

Peacemaking after the Second World War was not so much a tapestry as it was a hopelessly raveled and knotted mess of yarn. Yet, for purposes of clarity, it is essential to follow certain threads. One theme indispensable to an understanding of the Cold War is the contrast between two clashing views of world order: the "universalist" view, by which all nations shared a common interest in all the affairs of the world, and the "sphere-of-influence" view, by which each great power would be assured by the other great powers of an acknowledged predominance in its own area of special interest. The universalist view assumed that national security would be guaranteed by an international organization. The sphere-of-interest view assumed that national security would be guaranteed by the balance of power. While in practice these views have by no means been incompatible (indeed, our shaky peace has been based on a combination of the two), in the abstract they involved sharp contradictions.

The tradition of American thought in these matters was universalist — i.e. Wilsonian. Roosevelt had been a member of Wilson's subcabinet; in 1920, as candidate for Vice President, he had campaigned for the League of Nations. It is true that, within Roosevelt's infinitely complex mind, Wilsonianism warred with the perception of vital strategic interests he had imbibed from Mahan. Moreover, his temperamental inclination to settle things with fellow princes around the conference table led him to regard the Big Three — or Four — as trustees for the rest of the world. On occasion, as this narrative will show, he was beguiled into flirtation with the sphere-of-influence heresy. But in principle he believed in joint action and remained a Wilsonian. His hope for Yalta, as he told the Congress on his return, was that it would "spell the end of the system of unilateral action, the exclusive alliances, the spheres of influence, the balances of power, and all the other expedients that have been tried for centuries — and have always failed."

Whenever Roosevelt backslid, he had at his side that Wilsonian fundamentalist, Secretary of State Cordell Hull, to recall him to the pure faith. After his visit to Moscow in 1943, Hull characteristically said that, with the Declaration of Four Nations on General Security (in which America, Russia, Britain and China pledged "united action . . . for the organization and maintenance of peace and security"), "there will no longer be need for spheres of influence, for alliances, for balance of power, or any other of the special arrangements through which, in the unhappy past, the nations strove to safeguard their security or to promote their interests."

Remembering the corruption of the Wilsonian vision by the secret treaties of the First World War, Hull was determined to prevent any sphere-of-influence nonsense after the Second World War. He therefore fought all proposals to settle border questions while the war was still on and, excluded as he largely was from wartime diplomacy, poured his not inconsiderable moral energy and frustration into the promulgation of virtuous and spacious general principles.

In adopting the universalist view, Roosevelt and Hull were not indulging personal hobbies. Sumner Welles, Adolf Berle, Averell Harriman, Charles Bohlen — all, if with a variety of nuances, opposed the sphere-of-influence approach. And here the State Department was expressing what seems clearly to have been the predominant mood of the American people, so long mistrustful of European power politics. The Republicans shared the true faith. John Foster Dulles argued that the great threat to peace after the war would lie in the revival of sphere-of-influence thinking. The United States, he said, must not permit Britain and Russia to revert to these bad old ways; it must therefore insist on American participation in all policy decisions for all territories in the world. Dulles wrote pessimistically in January 1945, "The three great powers which at Moscow agreed upon the 'closest coöperation' about European questions have shifted to a practice of separate, regional responsibility."

It is true that critics, and even friends, of the United States sometimes noted a discrepancy between the American passion for universalism when it applied to territory far from American shores and the preëminence the United States accorded its own interests nearer home. Churchill, seeking Washington's blessing for a sphere-of-influence initiative in Eastern Europe, could not forbear reminding the Americans, "We follow the lead of the United States in South America"; nor did any universalist of record propose the abolition of the Monroe Doctrine. But a convenient myopia prevented such inconsistencies from qualifying the ardency of the universalist faith.

There seem only to have been three officials in the United States Government who dissented. One was the Secretary of War, Henry L. Stimson, a classical balance-of-power man, who in 1944 opposed the creation of a vacuum in Central Europe by the pastoralization of Germany and in 1945 urged "the settlement of all territorial acquisitions in the shape of defense posts which each of these four powers may deem to be necessary for their own safety" in advance of any effort to establish a peacetime United Nations. Stimson considered the claim of Russia to a preferred position in Eastern Europe as not unreasonable: as he told President Truman, "he thought the Russians perhaps were being more realistic than we were in regard to their own security." Such a position for Russia seemed to him comparable to the preferred American position in Latin America; he even spoke of "our respective orbits." Stimson was therefore skeptical of what he regarded as the prevailing tendency "to hang on to exaggerated views of the Monroe Doctrine and at the same time butt into every question that comes up in Central Europe." Acceptance of spheres of influence seemed to him the way to avoid "a head-on collision."

A second official opponent of universalism was George Kennan, an eloquent advocate from the American Embassy in Moscow of "a prompt and clear recognition of the division of Europe into spheres of influence and of a policy based on the fact of such division." Kennan argued that nothing we could do would possibly alter the course of events in Eastern Europe; that we were deceiving ourselves by supposing that these countries had any future but Russian domination; that we should therefore relinquish Eastern Europe to the Soviet Union and avoid anything which would make things easier for the Russians by giving them economic assistance or by sharing moral responsibility for their actions.

A third voice within the government against universalism was (at least after the war) Henry A. Wallace. As Secretary of Commerce, he stated the sphere-of-influence case with trenchancy in the famous Madison Square Garden speech of September 1946 which led to his dismissal by President Truman:

> On our part, we should recognize that we have no more business in the *political* affairs of Eastern Europe than Russia has in the *political* affairs of Latin America, Western Europe, and the United States. . . . Whether we like it or not, the Russians will try to socialize their sphere of influence just as we try to democratize our sphere of influence. . . . The Russians have no more business stirring up native Communists to political activity in Western Europe, Latin America, and the United States than we have in interfering with the politics of Eastern Europe and Russia.

Stimson, Kennan and Wallace seem to have been alone in the government, however, in taking these views. They were very much minority voices. Meanwhile universalism, rooted in the American legal and moral tradition, overwhelmingly backed by contemporary opinion, received successive enshrinements in the Atlantic Charter of 1941, in the Declaration of the United Nations in 1942 and in the Moscow Declaration of 1943.

IV.

The Kremlin, on the other hand, thought *only* of spheres of interest; above all, the Russians were determined to protect their frontiers, and especially their border to the west, crossed so often and so bloodily in the dark course of their history. These western frontiers lacked natural means of defense — no great oceans, rugged mountains, steaming swamps or impenetrable jungles. The history of Russia had been the history of invasion, the last of which was by now horribly killing up to twenty million of its people. The protocol of Russia therefore meant the enlargement of the area of Russian influence. Kennan himself wrote (in May 1944), "Behind Russia's stubborn expansion lies only the age-old sense of insecurity of a sedentary people reared on an exposed plain in the neighborhood of fierce nomadic peoples," and he called this "urge" a "permanent feature of Russian psychology."

In earlier times the "urge" had produced the tsarist search for buffer states and maritime outlets. In 1939 the Soviet-Nazi pact and its secret protocol had enabled Russia to begin to satisfy in the Baltic states, Karelian Finland and Poland, part of what it conceived as its security requirements in Eastern Europe. But the "urge" persisted, causing the friction between Russia and Germany in 1940 as each jostled for position in the area which separated them. Later it led to Molotov's new demands on Hitler in November 1940 — a free hand in Finland, Soviet predominance in Rumania and Bulgaria, bases in the Dardanelles — the demands which convinced Hitler that he had no choice but to attack Russia. Now Stalin hoped to gain from the West what Hitler, a closer neighbor, had not dared yield him.

It is true that, so long as Russian survival appeared to require a second front to relieve the Nazi pressure, Moscow's demand for Eastern Europe was a little muffled. Thus the Soviet government adhered to the Atlantic Charter (though with a significant if obscure reservation about adapting its principles to "the circumstances, needs, and historic peculiarities of particular countries"). Thus it also adhered to the Moscow Declaration of 1943, and Molotov then, with his easy mendacity, even denied that Russia had any desire to divide Europe into spheres of influence. But this was guff, which the Russians were perfectly willing to ladle out if it would keep the Americans, and especially Secretary Hull (who made a strong personal impression at the Moscow conference) happy. "A declaration," as Stalin once observed to Eden, "I regard as algebra, but an agreement as practical arithmetic. I do not wish to decry algebra, but I prefer practical arithmetic."

The more consistent Russian purpose was revealed when Stalin offered the British a straight sphere-of-influence deal at the end of 1941. Britain, he suggested, should recognize the Russian absorption of the Baltic states, part of Finland, eastern Poland and Bessarabia; in return, Russia would support any special British need for bases or security arrangements in Western Europe. There was nothing specifically communist about these ambitions. If Stalin achieved them, he would be fulfilling an age-old dream of the tsars. The British reaction was mixed. "Soviet policy is amoral," as Anthony Eden noted at the time; "United States policy is exaggeratedly moral, at least where non-American interests are concerned." If Roosevelt was a universalist with occasional leanings toward spheres of influence and Stalin was a sphere-of-influence man with occasional gestures toward universalism, Churchill seemed evenly poised between the familiar realism of the balance of power, which he had so long recorded as an historian and manipulated as a statesman, and the hope that there must be some better way of doing things. His 1943 proposal of a world organization divided into regional councils represented an effort to blend universalist and sphere-of-interest conceptions. His initial rejection of Stalin's proposal in December 1941 as "directly contrary to the first, second and third articles of the Atlantic Charter" thus did not spring entirely from a desire to propitiate the United States. On the other hand, he had himself already reinterpreted the Atlantic Charter as applying only to Europe (and thus not to the British Empire), and he was, above all, an empiricist who never believed in sacrificing reality on the altar of doctrine.

So in April 1942 he wrote Roosevelt that "the increasing gravity of the war" had led him to feel that the Charter "ought not to be construed so as to deny Russia the frontiers she occupied when Germany attacked her." Hull, however, remained fiercely hostile to the inclusion of territorial provisions in the Anglo-Russian treaty; the American position, Eden noted, "chilled me with Wilsonian memories." Though Stalin complained that it looked "as if the Atlantic Charter was directed against the U.S.S.R.," it was the Russian season of military adversity in the spring of 1942, and he dropped his demands.

He did not, however, change his intentions. A year later Ambassador Standley could cable Washington from Moscow: "In 1918 Western Europe attempted to set up a *cordon sanitaire* to protect it from the influence of bolshevism. Might not now the Kremlin envisage the formation of a belt of pro-Soviet states to protect it from the influences of the West?" It well might; and that purpose became increasingly clear as the war approached its end. Indeed, it derived sustenance from Western policy in the first area of liberation.

The unconditional surrender of Italy in July 1943 created the first major test of the Western devotion to universalism. America and Britain, having won the Italian war, handled the capitulation, keeping Moscow informed at a distance. Stalin complained:

> The United States and Great Britain made agreements but the Soviet Union received information about the results . . . just as a passive third observer. I have to tell you that it is impossible to tolerate the situation any longer. I propose that the [tripartite military-political commission] be established and that Sicily be assigned . . . as its place of residence.

Roosevelt, who had no intention of sharing the control of Italy with the Russians, suavely replied with the suggestion that Stalin send an officer "to General Eisenhower's headquarters in connection with the commission." Unimpressed, Stalin continued to press for a tripartite body; but his Western allies were adamant in keeping the Soviet Union off the Control Commission for Italy, and the Russians in the end had to be satisfied with a seat, along with minor Allied states, on a meaningless Inter-Allied Advisory Council. Their acquiescence in this was doubtless not unconnected with a desire to establish precedents for Eastern Europe.

Teheran in December 1943 marked the high point of three-power collaboration. Still, when Churchill asked about Russian territorial interests, Stalin replied a little ominously, "There is no need to speak at the present time about any Soviet desires, but when the time comes we will speak." In the next weeks, there were increasing indications of a Soviet determination to deal unilaterally with Eastern Europe — so much so that in early February 1944 Hull cabled Harriman in Moscow:

> Matters are rapidly approaching the point where the Soviet Government will have to choose between the development and extension of the foundation of international cooperation as the guiding principle of the postwar world as against the continuance of a unilateral and arbitrary method of dealing with its special problems even though these problems are admittedly of more direct interest to the Soviet Union than to other great powers.

As against this approach, however, Churchill, more tolerant of sphere-of-influence deviations, soon proposed that, with the impending liberation of the Balkans, Russia should run things in Rumania and Britain in Greece. Hull strongly opposed this suggestion but made the mistake of leaving Washington for a few days; and Roosevelt, momentarily free from his Wilsonian conscience, yielded to Churchill's plea for a three-months' trial. Hull resumed the fight on his return, and Churchill postponed the matter.

The Red Army continued its advance into Eastern Europe. In August the Polish Home Army, urged on by Polish-language broadcasts from Moscow, rose up against the Nazis in Warsaw. For 63 terrible days, the Poles fought valiantly on, while the Red Army halted on the banks of the Vistula a few miles away, and in Moscow Stalin for more than half this time declined to coöperate with the Western effort to drop supplies to the Warsaw Resistance. It appeared a calculated Soviet decision to let the Nazis slaughter the anti-Soviet Polish underground; and, indeed, the result was to destroy any substantial alternative to a Soviet solution in Poland. The agony of Warsaw caused the most deep and genuine moral shock in Britain and America and provoked dark forebodings about Soviet postwar purposes.

Again history enjoins the imaginative leap in order to see things for a moment from Moscow's viewpoint. The Polish question, Churchill would say at Yalta, was for Britain a question of honor. "It is not only a question of honor for Russia," Stalin replied, "but one of life and death. . . . Throughout history Poland had been the corridor for attack on

Russia." A top postwar priority for any Russian régime must be to close
that corridor. The Home Army was led by anti-communists. It clearly
hoped by its action to forestall the Soviet occupation of Warsaw and, in
Russian eyes, to prepare the way for an anti-Russian Poland. In addition, the uprising from a strictly operational viewpoint was premature.
The Russians, it is evident in retrospect, had real military problems at
the Vistula. The Soviet attempt in September to send Polish units from
the Red Army across the river to join forces with the Home Army was a
disaster. Heavy German shelling thereafter prevented the ferrying of
tanks necessary for an assault on the German position. The Red Army
itself did not take Warsaw for another three months. None the less,
Stalin's indifference to the human tragedy, his effort to blackmail the
London Poles during the ordeal, his sanctimonious opposition during
five precious weeks to aerial resupply, the invariable coldness of his
explanations ("the Soviet command has come to the conclusion that it
must dissociate itself from the Warsaw adventure") and the obvious
political benefit to the Soviet Union from the destruction of the Home
Army — all these had the effect of suddenly dropping the mask of
wartime comradeship and displaying to the West the hard face of Soviet
policy. In now pursuing what he grimly regarded as the minimal requirements for the postwar security of his country, Stalin was inadvertently showing the irreconcilability of both his means and his ends
with the Anglo-American conception of the peace.

Meanwhile Eastern Europe presented the Alliance with still another crisis that same September. Bulgaria, which was not at war with
Russia, decided to surrender to the Western Allies while it still could;
and the English and Americans at Cairo began to discuss armistice
terms with Bulgarian envoys. Moscow, challenged by what it plainly saw
as a Western intrusion into its own zone of vital interest, promptly
declared war on Bulgaria, took over the surrender negotiations and,
invoking the Italian precedent, denied its Western Allies any role in the
Bulgarian Control Commission. In a long and thoughtful cable, Ambassador Harriman meditated on the problems of communication with
the Soviet Union. "Words," he reflected, "have a different connotation to
the Soviets than they have to us. When they speak of insisting on
'friendly governments' in their neighboring countries, they have in mind
something quite different from what we would mean." The Russians, he
surmised, really believed that Washington accepted "their position that
although they would keep us informed they had the right to settle their
problems with their western neighbors unilaterally." But the Soviet
position was still in flux: "the Soviet Government is not one mind." The
problem, as Harriman had earlier told Harry Hopkins, was "to
strengthen the hands of those around Stalin who want to play the game
along our lines." The way to do this, he now told Hull, was to

be understanding of their sensitivity, meet them much more than half
way, encourage them and support them wherever we can, and yet
oppose them promptly with the greatest of firmness where we see them

going wrong. . . . The only way we can eventually come to an understanding with the Soviet Union on the question of non-interference in the internal affairs of other countries is for us to take a definite interest in the solution of the problems of each individual country as they arise.

As against Harriman's sophisticated universalist strategy, however, Churchill, increasingly fearful of the consequences of unrestrained competition in Eastern Europe, decided in early October to carry his sphere-of-influence proposal directly to Moscow. Roosevelt was at first content to have Churchill speak for him too and even prepared a cable to that effect. But Hopkins, a more rigorous universalist, took it upon himself to stop the cable and warn Roosevelt of its possible implications. Eventually Roosevelt sent a message to Harriman in Moscow emphasizing that he expected to "retain complete freedom of action after this conference is over." It was now that Churchill quickly proposed — and Stalin as quickly accepted — the celebrated division of southeastern Europe: ending (after further haggling between Eden and Molotov) with 90 percent Soviet predominance in Rumania, 80 percent in Bulgaria and Hungary, fifty-fifty in Jugoslavia, 90 percent British predominance in Greece.

Churchill in discussing this with Harriman used the phrase "spheres of influence." But he insisted that these were only "immediate wartime arrangements" and received a highly general blessing from Roosevelt. Yet, whatever Churchill intended, there is reason to believe that Stalin construed the percentages as an agreement, not a declaration; as practical arithmetic, not algebra. For Stalin, it should be understood, the sphere-of-influence idea did not mean that he would abandon all efforts to spread communism in some other nation's sphere; it did mean that, if he tried this and the other side cracked down, he could not feel he had serious cause for complaint. As Kennan wrote to Harriman at the end of 1944:

> As far as border states are concerned the Soviet government has never ceased to think in terms of spheres of interest. They expect us to support them in whatever action they wish to take in those regions, regardless of whether that action seems to us or to the rest of the world to be right or wrong. . . . I have no doubt that this position is honestly maintained on their part, and that they would be equally prepared to reserve moral judgment on any action which we might wish to carry out, i.e., in the Caribbean area.

In any case, the matter was already under test a good deal closer to Moscow than the Caribbean. The communist-dominated resistance movement in Greece was in open revolt against the effort of the Papandreou government to disarm and disband the guerrillas (the same Papandreou whom the Greek colonels have recently arrested on the claim that he is a tool of the communists). Churchill now called in British Army units to crush the insurrection. This action produced a storm of criticism in his own country and in the United States; the American Government even publicly dissociated itself from the intervention, thereby emphasizing its detachment from the sphere-of-influence deal. But Stalin, Churchill later claimed, "adhered strictly and faithfully to our agreement of October, and during all the long weeks of fighting the Communists in the streets of Athens not one word of reproach came from *Pravda* or *Izvestia*," though there is no evidence that he tried to call off the Greek communists. Still, when the communist rebellion later broke out again in Greece, Stalin told Kardelj and Djilas of Jugoslavia in 1948, "The uprising in Greece must be stopped, and as quickly as possible."

No one, of course, can know what really was in the minds of the Russian leaders. The Kremlin archives are locked; of the primary actors, only Molotov survives, and he has not yet indicated any desire to collaborate with the Columbia Oral History Project. We do know that Stalin did not wholly surrender to sentimental illusion about his new friends. In June 1944, on the night before the landings in Normandy, he told Djilas that the English "find nothing sweeter than to trick their allies. . . . And Churchill? Churchill is the kind who, if you don't watch him, will slip a kopeck out of your pocket. Yes, a kopeck out of your pocket! . . . Roosevelt is not like that. He dips in his hand only for bigger coins." But whatever his views of his colleagues it is not unreasonable to suppose that Stalin would have been satisfied at the end of the war to secure what Kennan has called "a protective glacis along Russia's western border," and that, in exchange for a free hand in Eastern Europe, he was prepared to give the British and Americans equally free hands in their zones of vital interest, including in nations as close to Russia as Greece (for the British) and, very probably — or at least so the Jugoslavs believe — China (for the United States). In other words, his initial objectives were very probably not world conquest but Russian security.

V.

It is now pertinent to inquire why the United States rejected the idea of stabilizing the world by division into spheres of influence and insisted on an East European strategy. One should warn against rushing to the conclusion that it was all a row between hard-nosed, balance-of-power realists and starry-eyed Wilsonians. Roosevelt, Hopkins, Welles, Harriman, Bohlen, Berle, Dulles and other universalists were tough and serious men. Why then did they rebuff the sphere-of-influence solution?

The first reason is that they regarded this solution as containing within itself the seeds of a third world war. The balance-of-power idea seemed inherently unstable. It had always broken down in the past. It held out to each power the permanent temptation to try to alter the balance in its own favor, and it built this temptation into the international order. It would turn the great powers of 1945 away from the objective of concerting common policies toward competition for postwar advantage. As Hopkins told Molotov at Teheran, "The President feels it essential to world peace that Russia, Great Britain and the United States work out this control question in a manner which will not start each of the three powers arming against the others." "The greatest likelihood of eventual conflict," said the Joint Chiefs of Staff in 1944 (the only conflict which the J.C.S., in its wisdom, could then glimpse "in the foreseeable future" was between Britain and Russia), ". . . would seem to grow out of either nation initiating attempts to build up its strength, by seeking to attach to herself parts of Europe to the disadvantage and possible danger of her potential adversary." The Americans were perfectly ready to acknowledge that Russia was entitled to convincing assurance of her national security — but not this way. "I could sympathize fully with Stalin's desire to protect his western borders from future attack," as Hull put it. "But I felt that this security could best be obtained through a strong postwar peace organization."

Hull's remark suggests the second objection: that the sphere-of-influence approach would, in the words of the State Department in 1945, "militate against the establishment and effective functioning of a broader system of general security in which all countries will have their part." The United Nations, in short, was seen as the alternative to the balance of power. Nor did the universalists see any necessary incompatibility between the Russian desire for "friendly governments" on its frontier and the American desire for self-determination in Eastern Europe. Before Yalta the State Department judged the general mood of Europe as "to the left and strongly in favor of far-reaching economic and social reforms, but not, however, in favor of a left-wing totalitarian regime to achieve these reforms." Governments in Eastern Europe could be sufficiently to the left "to allay Soviet suspicions" but sufficiently representative "of the center and *petit bourgeois* elements" not to seem a prelude to communist dictatorship. The American criteria were therefore that the government "should be dedicated to the preservation of civil liberties" and "should favor social and economic reforms." A string of New Deal states — of Finlands and Czechoslovakias — seemed a reasonable compromise solution.

Third, the universalists feared that the sphere-of-interest approach would be what Hull termed "a haven for the isolationists," who would advocate America's participation in Western Hemisphere affairs on condition that it did not participate in European or Asian affairs. Hull also feared that spheres of interest would lead to "closed trade areas or discriminatory systems" and thus defeat his cherished dream of a low-tariff, freely trading world.

Fourth, the sphere-of-interest solution meant the betrayal of the principles for which the Second World War was being fought — the Atlantic Charter, the Four Freedoms, the Declaration of the United Nations. Poland summed up the problem. Britain, having gone to war to defend the independence of Poland from the Germans, could not easily conclude the war by surrendering the independence of Poland to the Russians. Thus, as Hopkins told Stalin after Roosevelt's death in 1945, Poland had "become the symbol of our ability to work out problems with the Soviet Union." Nor could American liberals in general watch with equanimity while the police state spread into countries which, if they had mostly not been real democracies, had mostly not been tyrannies either. The execution in 1943 of Ehrlich and Alter, the Polish socialist trade union leaders, excited deep concern. "I have particularly in mind," Harriman cabled in 1944, "objection to the institution of secret police who may become involved in the persecution of persons of truly democratic convictions who may not be willing to conform to Soviet methods."

Fifth, the sphere-of-influence solution would create difficult domestic problems in American politics. Roosevelt was aware of the six million or more Polish votes in the 1944 election; even more acutely, he was aware of the broader and deeper attack which would follow if, after going to war to stop the Nazi conquest of Europe, he permitted the war to end with the communist conquest of Eastern Europe. As Archibald MacLeish, then Assistant Secretary of State for Public Affairs, warned in January 1945, "The wave of disillusionment which has distressed us in the last several weeks will be increased if the impression is permitted to get abroad that potentially totalitarian provisional governments are to be set up without adequate safeguards as to the holding of free elections and the realization of the principles of the Atlantic Charter." Roosevelt believed that no administration could survive which did not try everything short of war to save Eastern Europe, and he was the supreme American politician of the century.

Sixth, if the Russians were allowed to overrun Eastern Europe without argument, would that satisfy them? Even Kennan, in a dispatch of May 1944, admitted that the "urge" had dreadful potentialities: "If initially successful, will it know where to stop? Will it not be inexorably carried forward, by its very nature, in a struggle to reach the whole — to attain complete mastery of the shores of the Atlantic and the Pacific?" His own answer was that there were inherent limits to the Russian capacity to expand — "that Russia will not have an easy time in maintaining the power which it has seized over other people in Eastern and Central Europe unless it receives both moral and material assistance from the West." Subsequent developments have vindicated Kennan's argument. By the late forties, Yugoslavia and Albania, the two East European states farthest from the Soviet Union and the two in which communism was imposed from within rather than from without, had declared their independence of Moscow. But, given Russia's success in maintaining centralized control over the international communist movement for a quarter of a century, who in 1944 could have had much confidence in the idea of communist revolts against Moscow?

Most of those involved therefore rejected Kennan's answer and stayed with his question. If the West turned its back on Eastern Europe, the higher probability, in their view, was that the Russians would use their security zone, not just for defensive purposes, but as a springboard from which to mount an attack on Western Europe, now shattered by war, a vacuum of power awaiting its master. "If the policy is accepted that the Soviet Union has a right to penetrate her immediate neighbors for security," Harriman said in 1944, "penetration of the next immediate neighbors becomes at a certain time equally logical." If a row with Russia were inevitable, every consideration of prudence dictated that it should take place in Eastern rather than Western Europe.

Thus idealism and realism joined in opposition to the sphere-of-influence solution. The consequence was a determination to assert an American interest in the postwar destiny of all nations, including those of Eastern Europe. In the message which Roosevelt and Hopkins drafted after Hopkins had stopped Roosevelt's initial cable authorizing Churchill to speak for the United States at the Moscow meeting of October 1944, Roosevelt now said, "There is in this global war literally no question, either military or political, in which the United States is not interested." After Roosevelt's death Hopkins repeated the point to Stalin: "The cardinal basis of President Roosevelt's policy which the American people had fully supported had been the concept that the interests of the U.S. were worldwide and not confined to North and South America and the Pacific Ocean."

VI.

For better or worse, this was the American position. It is now necessary to attempt the imaginative leap and consider the impact of this position on the leaders of the Soviet Union who, also for better or for worse, had reached the bitter conclusion that the survival of their country depended on their unchallenged control of the corridors through which enemies had so often invaded their homeland. They could claim to have been keeping their own side of the sphere-of-influence bargain. Of course, they were working to capture the resistance movements of Western Europe; indeed, with the appointment of Oumansky as Ambassador to Mexico they were even beginning to enlarge underground operations in the Western Hemisphere. But, from their viewpoint, if the West permitted this, the more fools they; and, if the West stopped it, it was within their right to do so. In overt political matters the Russians were scrupulously playing the game. They had watched in silence while the British shot down communists in Greece. In Jugoslavia Stalin was urging Tito (as Djilas later revealed) to keep King Peter. They had not only acknowledged Western preëminence in Italy but had recognized the Badoglio régime; the Italian Communists had even voted (against the Socialists and the Liberals) for the renewal of the Lateran Pacts.

They would not regard anti-communist action in a Western zone as a *casus belli;* and they expected reciprocal license to assert their own authority in the East. But the principle of self-determination was carrying the United States into a deeper entanglement in Eastern Europe than the Soviet Union claimed as a right (whatever it was doing underground) in the affairs of Italy, Greece or China. When the Russians now exercised in Eastern Europe the same brutal control they were prepared to have Washington exercise in the American sphere of influence, the American protests, given the paranoia produced alike by Russian history and Leninist ideology, no doubt seemed not only an act of hypocrisy but a threat to security. To the Russians, a stroll into the neighborhood easily became a plot to burn down the house: when, for example, damaged American planes made emergency landings in Poland and Hungary, Moscow took this as attempts to organize the local resistance. It is not unusual to suspect one's adversary of doing what one is already doing oneself. At the same time, the cruelty with which the Russians executed their idea of spheres-of-influence — in a sense, perhaps, an unwitting cruelty, since Stalin treated the East Europeans no worse than he had treated the Russians in the thirties — discouraged the West from accepting the equation (for example, Italy = Rumania) which seemed so self-evident to the Kremlin.

So Moscow very probably, and not unnaturally, perceived the emphasis on self-determination as a systematic and deliberate pressure on Russia's western frontiers. Moreover, the restoration of capitalism to countries freed at frightful cost by the Red Army no doubt struck the Russians as the betrayal of the principles for which *they* were fighting. "That they, the victors," Isaac Deutscher has suggested, "should now preserve an order from which they had experienced nothing but hostility, and could expect nothing but hostility . . . would have been the most miserable anti-climax to their great 'war of liberation.'" By 1944 Poland was the critical issue; Harriman later said that "under instructions from President Roosevelt, I talked about Poland with Stalin more frequently than any other subject." While the West saw the point of Stalin's demand for a "friendly government" in Warsaw, the American insistence on the sovereign virtues of free elections (ironically in the spirit of the 1917 Bolshevik decree of peace, which affirmed "the right" of a nation "to decide the forms of its state existence by a free vote, taken after the complete evacuation of the incorporating or, generally, of the stronger nation") created an insoluble problem in those countries, like Poland (and Rumania) where free elections would almost certainly produce anti-Soviet governments.

The Russians thus may well have estimated the Western pressures as calculated to encourage their enemies in Eastern Europe and to defeat their own minimum objective of a protective glacis. Everything still hung, however, on the course of military operations. The wartime collaboration had been created by one thing, and one thing alone: the threat of Nazi victory. So long as this threat was real, so was the collaboration. In late December 1944, von Rundstedt launched his counter-offensive in the Ardennes. A few weeks later, when Roosevelt, Churchill and Stalin gathered in the Crimea, it was in the shadow of this last considerable explosion of German power. The meeting at Yalta was still dominated by the mood of war.

Yalta remains something of an historical perplexity — less, from the perspective of 1967, because of a mythical American deference to the sphere-of-influence thesis than because of the documentable Russian deference to the universalist thesis. Why should Stalin in 1945 have accepted the Declaration on Liberated Europe and an agreement on Poland pledging that "the three governments will jointly" act to assure "free elections of governments responsive to the will of the people"? There are several probable answers: that the war was not over and the Russians still wanted the Americans to intensify their military effort in the West; that one clause in the Declaration premised action on "the opinion of the three governments" and thus implied a Soviet veto, though the Polish agreement was more definite; most of all that the universalist algebra of the Declaration was plainly in Stalin's mind to be construed in terms of the practical arithmetic of his sphere-of-influence agreement with Churchill the previous October. Stalin's assurance to Churchill at Yalta that a proposed Russian amendment to the Declaration would not apply to Greece makes it clear that Roosevelt's pieties did not, in Stalin's mind, nullify Churchill's percentages. He could well have been strengthened in this supposition by the fact that *after* Yalta, Churchill himself repeatedly reasserted the terms of the October agreement as if he regarded it, despite Yalta, as controlling.

Harriman still had the feeling before Yalta that the Kremlin had "two approaches to their postwar policies" and that Stalin himself was "of two minds." One approach emphasized the internal reconstruction and development of Russia; the other its external expansion. But in the meantime the fact which dominated all political decisions — that is, the war against Germany — was moving into its final phase. In the weeks after Yalta, the military situation changed with great rapidity. As the Nazi threat declined, so too did the need for coöperation. The Soviet Union, feeling itself menaced by the American idea of self-determination and the borderlands diplomacy to which it was leading, skeptical whether the United Nations would protect its frontiers as reliably as its own domination in Eastern Europe, began to fulfill its security requirements unilaterally.

In March Stalin expressed his evaluation of the United Nations by rejecting Roosevelt's plea that Molotov come to the San Francisco conference, if only for the opening sessions. In the next weeks the Russians emphatically and crudely worked their will in Eastern Europe, above all in the test country of Poland. They were ignoring the Declaration on Liberated Europe, ignoring the Atlantic Charter, self-determination, human freedom and everything else the Americans considered essential for a stable peace. "We must clearly recognize," Harriman wired Washington a few days before Roosevelt's death, "that the Soviet program is the establishment of totalitarianism, ending personal liberty and democracy as we know and respect it."

At the same time, the Russians also began to mobilize communist resources in the United States itself to block American universalism. In April 1945 Jacques Duclos, who had been the Comintern official responsible for the Western communist parties, launched in *Cahiers du Communisme* an uncompromising attack on the policy of the American Communist Party. Duclos sharply condemned the revisionism of Earl Browder, the American Communist leader, as "expressed in the concept of a long-term class peace in the United States, of the possibility of the suppression of the class struggle in the postwar period and of establishment of harmony between labor and capital." Browder was specifically rebuked for favoring the "self-determination" of Europe "west of the Soviet Union" on a bourgeois-democratic basis. The excommunication of Browderism was plainly the Politburo's considered reaction to the impending defeat of Germany; it was a signal to the communist parties of the West that they should recover their identity; it was Moscow's alert to communists everywhere that they should prepare for new policies in the postwar world.

The Duclos piece obviously could not have been planned and written much later than the Yalta conference — that is, well before a number of events which revisionists now cite in order to demonstrate American responsibility for the Cold War: before Allen Dulles, for example, began to negotiate the surrender of the German armies in Italy (the episode which provoked Stalin to charge Roosevelt with seeking a separate peace and provoked Roosevelt to denounce the "vile misrepresentations" of Stalin's informants); well before Roosevelt died; many months before the testing of the atomic bomb; even more months before Truman ordered that the bomb be dropped on Japan. William Z. Foster, who soon replaced Browder as the leader of the American Communist Party and embodied the new Moscow line, later boasted of having said in January 1944, "A post-war Roosevelt administration would continue to be, as it is now, an imperialist government." With ancient suspicions revived by the American insistence on universalism, this was no doubt the conclusion which the Russians were reaching at the same time. The Soviet canonization of Roosevelt (like their present-day canonization of Kennedy) took place after the American President's death.

The atmosphere of mutual suspicion was beginning to rise. In January 1945 Molotov formally proposed that the United States grant Russia a $6 billion credit for postwar reconstruction. With characteristic tact he explained that he was doing this as a favor to save America from a postwar depression. The proposal seems to have been diffidently made and diffidently received. Roosevelt requested that the matter "not be pressed further" on the American side until he had a chance to talk with Stalin; but the Russians did not follow it up either at Yalta in February (save for a single glancing reference) or during the Stalin-Hopkins talks in May or at Potsdam. Finally the proposal was renewed in the very different political atmosphere of August. This time Washington inexplicably mislaid the request during the transfer of the records of the Foreign Economic Administration to the State Department. It did not turn up again until March 1946. Of course this was impossible for the Russians to believe; it is hard enough even for those acquainted with the capacity of the American government for incompetence to believe; and it only strengthened Soviet suspicions of American purposes.

The American credit was one conceivable form of Western contribution to Russian reconstruction. Another was lend-lease, and the possibility of reconstruction aid under the lend-lease protocol had already been discussed in 1944. But in May 1945 Russia, like Britain, suffered from Truman's abrupt termination of lend-lease shipments — "unfortunate and even brutal," Stalin told Hopkins, adding that, if it was "designed as pressure on the Russians in order to soften them up, then it was a fundamental mistake." A third form was German reparations. Here Stalin in demanding $10 billion in reparations for the Soviet Union made his strongest fight at Yalta. Roosevelt, while agreeing essentially with Churchill's opposition, tried to postpone the matter by accepting the Soviet figure as a "basis for discussion" — a formula which led to future misunderstanding. In short, the Russian hope for major Western assistance in postwar reconstruction foundered on three events which the Kremlin could well have interpreted respectively as deliberate sabotage (the loan request), blackmail (lend-lease cancellation) and pro-Germanism (reparations).

Actually the American attempt to settle the fourth lend-lease protocol was generous and the Russians for their own reasons declined to come to an agreement. It is not clear, though, that satisfying Moscow on any of these financial scores would have made much essential difference. It might have persuaded some doves in the Kremlin that the U.S. government was genuinely friendly; it might have persuaded some hawks that the American anxiety for Soviet friendship was such that Moscow could do as it wished without inviting challenge from the United States. It would, in short, merely have reinforced both sides of the Kremlin debate; it would hardly have reversed deeper tendencies toward the deterioration of political relationships. Economic deals were surely subordinate to the quality of mutual political confidence; and here, in the months after Yalta, the decay was steady.

The Cold War had now begun. It was the product not of a decision but of a dilemma. Each side felt compelled to adopt policies which the other could not but regard as a threat to the principles of the peace. Each then felt compelled to undertake defensive measures. Thus the Russians saw no choice but to consolidate their security in Eastern Europe. The Americans, regarding Eastern Europe as the first step toward Western Europe, responded by asserting their interest in the zone the Russians deemed vital to their security. The Russians concluded that the West was resuming its old course of capitalist encirclement; that it was purposefully laying the foundation for anti-Soviet régimes in the area defined by the blood of centuries as crucial to Russian survival. Each side believed with passion that future international stability depended on the success of its own conception of world order. Each side, in pursuing its own clearly indicated and deeply cherished principles, was only confirming the fear of the other that it was bent on aggression.

Very soon the process began to acquire a cumulative momentum. The impending collapse of Germany thus provoked new troubles: the Russians, for example, sincerely feared that the West was planning a separate surrender of the German armies in Italy in a way which would release troops for Hitler's eastern front, as they subsequently feared that the Nazis might succeed in surrendering Berlin to the West. This was the context in which the atomic bomb now appeared. Though the revisionist argument that Truman dropped the bomb less to defeat Japan than to intimidate Russia is not convincing, this thought unquestionably appealed to some in Washington as at least an advantageous side-effect of Hiroshima.

So the machinery of suspicion and counter-suspicion, action and counter-action, was set in motion. But, given relations among traditional national states, there was still no reason, even with all the postwar jostling, why this should not have remained a manageable situation. What made it unmanageable, what caused the rapid escalation of the Cold War and in another two years completed the division of Europe, was a set of considerations which this account has thus far excluded.

VII.

Up to this point, the discussion has considered the schism within the wartime coalition as if it were entirely the result of disagreements among national states. Assuming this framework, there was unquestionably a failure of communication between America and Russia, a misperception of signals and, as time went on, a mounting tendency to ascribe ominous motives to the other side. It seems hard, for example, to deny that American postwar policy created genuine difficulties for the Russians and even assumed a threatening aspect for them. All this the revisionists have rightly and usefully emphasized.

But the great omission of the revisionists — and also the fundamental explanation of the speed with which the Cold War escalated — lies precisely in the fact that the Soviet Union was *not* a traditional national state.[4] This is where the "mirror image," invoked by some psychologists, falls down. For the Soviet Union was a phenomenon very different from America or Britain: it was a totalitarian state, endowed with an all-explanatory, all-consuming ideology, committed to the infallibility of government and party, still in a somewhat messianic mood, equating dissent with treason, and ruled by a dictator who, for all his quite extraordinary abilities, had his paranoid moments.

Marxism-Leninism gave the Russian leaders a view of the world according to which all societies were inexorably destined to proceed along appointed roads by appointed stages until they achieved the classless nirvana. Moreover, given the resistance of the capitalists to this development, the existence of any non-communist state was *by definition* a threat to the Soviet Union. "As long as capitalism and

[4] This is the classical revisionist fallacy — the assumption of the rationality, or at least of the traditionalism, of states where ideology and social organization have created a different range of motives. So the Second World War revisionists omit the totalitarian dynamism of Nazism and the fanaticism of Hitler, as the Civil War revisionists omit the fact that the slavery system was producing a doctrinaire closed society in the American South. For a consideration of some of these issues, see "The Causes of the Civil War: A Note on Historical Sentimentalism" in my *The Politics of Hope* (Boston, 1963).

socialism exist," Lenin wrote, "we cannot live in peace: in the end, one or the other will triumph — a funeral dirge will be sung either over the Soviet Republic or over world capitalism."

Stalin and his associates, whatever Roosevelt or Truman did or failed to do, were bound to regard the United States as the enemy, not because of this deed or that, but because of the primordial fact that America was the leading capitalist power and thus, by Leninist syllogism, unappeasably hostile, driven by the logic of its system to oppose, encircle and destroy Soviet Russia. Nothing the United States could have done in 1944–45 would have abolished this mistrust, required and sanctified as it was by Marxist gospel — nothing short of the conversion of the United States into a Stalinist despotism; and even this would not have sufficed, as the experience of Jugoslavia and China soon showed, unless it were accompanied by total subservience to Moscow. So long as the United States remained a capitalist democracy, no American policy, given Moscow's theology, could hope to win basic Soviet confidence, and every American action was poisoned from the source. So long as the Soviet Union remained a messianic state, ideology compelled a steady expansion of communist power.

It is easy, of course, to exaggerate the capacity of ideology to control events. The tension of acting according to revolutionary abstractions is too much for most nations to sustain over a long period: that is why Mao Tse-tung has launched his Cultural Revolution, hoping thereby to create a permanent revolutionary mood and save Chinese communism from the degeneration which, in his view, has overtaken Russian communism. Still, as any revolution grows older, normal human and social motives will increasingly reassert themselves. In due course, we can be sure, Leninism will be about as effective in governing the daily lives of Russians as Christianity is in governing the daily lives of Americans. Like the Ten Commandments and the Sermon on the Mount, the Leninist verities will increasingly become platitudes for ritual observance, not guides to secular decision. There can be no worse fallacy (even if respectable people practiced it diligently for a season in the United States) than that of drawing from a nation's ideology permanent conclusions about its behavior.

A temporary recession of ideology was already taking place during the Second World War when Stalin, to rally his people against the invader, had to replace the appeal of Marxism by that of nationalism. ("We are under no illusions that they are fighting for us," Stalin once said to Harriman. "They are fighting for Mother Russia.") But this was still taking place within the strictest limitations. The Soviet Union remained as much a police state as ever; the régime was as infallible as ever; foreigners and their ideas were as suspect as ever. "Never, except possibly during my later experience as ambassador in Moscow," Kennan has written, "did the insistence of the Soviet authorities on isolation of the diplomatic corps weigh more heavily on me . . . than in these first weeks following my return to Russia in the final months of the war. . . . [We were] treated as though we were the bearers of some species of the plague" — which, of course, from the Soviet viewpoint, they were: the plague of skepticism.

Paradoxically, of the forces capable of bringing about a modification of ideology, the most practical and effective was the Soviet dictatorship itself. If Stalin was an ideologist, he was also a pragmatist. If he saw everything through the lenses of Marxism-Leninism, he also, as the infallible expositor of the faith, could reinterpret Marxism-Leninism to justify anything he wanted to do at any given moment. No doubt Roosevelt's ignorance of Marxism-Leninism was inexcusable and led to grievous miscalculations. But Roosevelt's efforts to work on and through Stalin were not so hopelessly naïve as it used to be fashionable to think. With the extraordinary instinct of a great political leader, Roosevelt intuitively understood that Stalin was the *only* lever available to the West against the Leninist ideology and the Soviet system. If Stalin could be reached, then alone was there a chance of getting the Russians to act contrary to the prescriptions of their faith. The best evidence is that Roosevelt retained a certain capacity to influence Stalin to the end; the nominal Soviet acquiescence in American universalism as late as Yalta was perhaps an indication of that. It is in this way that the death of Roosevelt was crucial — not in the vulgar sense that his policy was then reversed by his successor, which did not happen, but in the sense that no other American could hope to have the restraining impact on Stalin which Roosevelt might for a while have had.

Stalin alone could have made any difference. Yet Stalin, in spite of the impression of sobriety and realism he made on Westerners who saw him during the Second World War, was plainly a man of deep and morbid obsessions and compulsions. When he was still a young man, Lenin had criticized his rude and arbitrary ways. A reasonably authoritative observer (N. S. Khrushchev) later commented, "These negative characteristics of his developed steadily and during the last years acquired an absolutely insufferable character." His paranoia, probably set off by the suicide of his wife in 1932, led to the terrible purges of the mid-thirties and the wanton murder of thousands of his Bolshevik comrades. "Everywhere and in everything," Khrushchev says of this period, "he saw 'enemies,' 'double-dealers' and 'spies.'" The crisis of war evidently steadied him in some way, though Khrushchev speaks of his "nervousness and hysteria . . . even after the war began." The madness, so rigidly controlled for a time, burst out with new and shocking intensity in the postwar years. "After the war," Khrushchev testifies,

> the situation became even more complicated. Stalin became even more capricious, irritable and brutal; in particular, his suspicion grew. His persecution mania reached unbelievable dimensions. . . . He decided everything, without any consideration for anyone or anything.
> Stalin's wilfulness showed itself . . . also in the international relations of the Soviet Union. . . . He had completely lost a sense of reality; he demonstrated his suspicion and haughtiness not only in relation to individuals in the USSR, but in relation to whole parties and nations.

A revisionist fallacy has been to treat Stalin as just another Realpolitik statesman, as Second World War revisionists see Hitler as just another Stresemann or Bismarck. But the record makes it clear that in the end nothing could satisfy Stalin's paranoia. His own associates failed. Why does anyone suppose that any conceivable American policy would have succeeded?

An analysis of the origins of the Cold War which leaves out these factors — the intransigence of Leninist ideology, the sinister dynamics of a totalitarian society and the madness of Stalin — is obviously incomplete. It was these factors which made it hard for the West to accept the thesis that Russia was moved only by a desire to protect its security and would be satisfied by the control of Eastern Europe; it was these factors which charged the debate between universalism and spheres of influence with apocalyptic potentiality.

Leninism and totalitarianism created a structure of thought and behavior which made postwar collaboration between Russia and America — in any normal sense of civilized intercourse between national states — inherently impossible. The Soviet dictatorship of 1945 simply could not have survived such a collaboration. Indeed, nearly a quarter-century later, the Soviet régime, though it has meanwhile moved a good distance, could still hardly survive it without risking the release inside Russia of energies profoundly opposed to communist despotism. As for Stalin, he may have represented the only force in 1945 capable of overcoming Stalinism, but the very traits which enabled him to win absolute power expressed terrifying instabilities of mind and temperament and hardly offered a solid foundation for a peaceful world.

VIII.

The difference between America and Russia in 1945 was that some Americans fundamentally believed that, over a long run, a modus vivendi with Russia was possible; while the Russians, so far as one can tell, believed in no more than a short-run modus vivendi with the United States.

Harriman and Kennan, this narrative has made clear, took the lead in warning Washington about the difficulties of short-run dealings with the Soviet Union. But both argued that, if the United States developed a rational policy and stuck to it, there would be, after long and rough passages, the prospect of eventual clearing. "I am, as you know," Harriman cabled Washington in early April, "a most earnest advocate of the closest possible understanding with the Soviet Union so that what I am saying relates only to how best to attain such understanding." Kennan has similarly made it clear that the function of his containment policy was "to tide us over a difficult time and bring us to the point where we could discuss effectively with the Russians the dangers and drawbacks this status quo involved, and to arrange with them for its peaceful replacement by a better and sounder one." The subsequent careers of both men attest to the honesty of these statements.

There is no corresponding evidence on the Russian side that anyone seriously sought a modus vivendi in these terms. Stalin's choice was whether his long-term ideological and national interests would be better served by a short-run truce with the West or by an immediate resumption of pressure. In October 1945 Stalin indicated to Harriman at Sochi that he planned to adopt the second course — that the Soviet Union was going isolationist. No doubt the succession of problems with the United States contributed to this decision, but the basic causes most probably lay elsewhere: in the developing situations in Eastern Europe, in Western Europe and in the United States.

In Eastern Europe, Stalin was still for a moment experimenting with techniques of control. But he must by now have begun to conclude that he had underestimated the hostility of the people to Russian dominion. The Hungarian elections in November would finally convince him that the Yalta formula was a road to anti-Soviet governments. At the same time, he was feeling more strongly than ever a sense of his opportunities in Western Europe. The other half of the Continent lay unexpectedly before him, politically demoralized, economically prostrate, militarily defenseless. The hunting would be better and safer than he had anticipated. As for the United States, the alacrity of postwar demobilization must have recalled Roosevelt's offhand remark at Yalta that "two years would be the limit" for keeping American troops in Europe. And, despite Dr. Eugene Varga's doubts about the imminence of American economic breakdown, Marxist theology assured Stalin that the United States was heading into a bitter postwar depression and would be consumed with its own problems. If the condition of Eastern Europe made unilateral action seem essential in the interests of Russian security, the condition of Western Europe and the United States offered new temptations for communist expansion. The Cold War was now in full swing.

It still had its year of modulations and accommodations. Secretary Byrnes conducted his long and fruitless campaign to persuade the Russians that America only sought governments in Eastern Europe "both friendly to the Soviet Union and representative of all the democratic elements of the country." Crises were surmounted in Trieste and Iran. Secretary Marshall evidently did not give up hope of a modus vivendi until the Moscow conference of foreign secretaries of March 1947. Even then, the Soviet Union was invited to participate in the Marshall Plan.

The point of no return came on July 2, 1947, when Molotov, after bringing 89 technical specialists with him to Paris and evincing initial interest in the project for European reconstruction, received the hot flash from the Kremlin, denounced the whole idea and walked out of the conference. For the next fifteen years the Cold War raged unabated, passing out of historical ambiguity into the realm of good versus evil and breeding on both sides simplifications, stereotypes and self-serving absolutes, often couched in interchangeable phrases. Under the pressure even America, for a deplorable decade, forsook its pragmatic and pluralist traditions, posed as God's appointed messenger to ignorant and sinful man and followed the Soviet example in looking to a world remade in its own image.

In retrospect, if it is impossible to see the Cold War as a case of American aggression and Russian response, it is also hard to see it as a pure case of Russian aggression and American response. "In what is truly tragic," wrote Hegel, "there must be valid moral powers on both the sides which come into collision. . . . Both suffer loss and yet both are mutually justified." In this sense, the Cold War had its tragic elements. The question remains whether it was an instance of Greek tragedy — as Auden has called it, "the tragedy of necessity," where the feeling aroused in the spectator is "What a pity it had to be this way" — or of Christian tragedy, "the tragedy of possibility," where the feeling aroused is "What a pity it was this way when it might have been otherwise."

Once something has happened, the historian is tempted to assume that it had to happen; but this may often be a highly unphilosophical assumption. The Cold War could have been avoided only if the Soviet Union had not been possessed by convictions both of the infallibility of the communist word and of the inevitability of a communist world. These convictions transformed an impasse between national states into a religious war, a tragedy of possibility into one of necessity. One might wish that America had preserved the poise and proportion of the first years of the Cold War and had not in time succumbed to its own forms of self-righteousness. But the most rational of American policies could hardly have averted the Cold War. Only today, as Russia begins to recede from its messianic mission and to accept, in practice if not yet in principle, the permanence of the world of diversity, only now can the hope flicker that this long, dreary, costly contest may at last be taking on forms less dramatic, less obsessive and less dangerous to the future of mankind.

6. THE COLD WAR, REVISITED
AND RE-VISIONED

Christopher Lasch

More than a year has passed since Arthur Schlesinger, Jr. announced that the time had come "to blow the whistle before the current outburst of revisionism regarding the origins of the cold war goes much further." Yet the outburst of revisionism shows no signs of subsiding. On the contrary, a growing number of historians and political critics, judging from such recent books as Ronald Steel's *Pax Americana* and Carl Oglesby's and Richard Shaull's *Containment and Change,* are challenging the view, once so widely accepted, that the cold war was an American response to Soviet expansionism, a distasteful burden reluctantly shouldered in the face of a ruthless enemy bent on our destruction, and that Russia, not the United States, must therefore bear the blame for shattering the world's hope that two world wars in the twentieth century would finally give way to an era of peace.

"Revisionist" historians are arguing instead that the United States did as much as the Soviet Union to bring about the collapse of the wartime coalition. Without attempting to shift the blame exclusively to the United States, they are trying to show, as Gar Alperovitz puts it, that "the cold war cannot be understood simply as an American response to a Soviet challenge, but rather as the insidious interaction of mutual suspicions, blame for which must be shared by all."

Not only have historians continued to re-examine the immediate origins of the cold war — in spite of attempts to "blow the whistle" on their efforts — but the scope of revisionism has been steadily widening.

Reprinted from *The New York Times Magazine,* January 14, 1968. © 1968 by The New York Times Company. Reprinted by permission.

Some scholars are beginning to argue that the whole course of American diplomacy since 1898 shows that the United States has become a counterrevolutionary power committed to the defense of a global status quo. Arno Mayer's monumental study of the Conference of Versailles, *Politics and Diplomacy of Peacemaking*, which has recently been published by Knopf and which promises to become the definitive work on the subject, announces in its subtitle what a growing number of historians have come to see as the main theme of American diplomacy: "Containment and Counterrevolution."

Even Schlesinger has now admitted, in a recent article in *Foreign Affairs*, that he was "somewhat intemperate," a year ago, in deploring the rise of cold war revisionism. Even though revisionist interpretations of earlier wars "have failed to stick," he says, "revisionism is an essential part of the process by which history . . . enlarges its perspectives and enriches its insights." Since he goes on to argue that "postwar collaboration between Russia and America [was] . . . inherently impossible" and that "the most rational of American policies could hardly have averted the cold war," it is not clear what Schlesinger thinks revisionism has done to enlarge our perspective and enrich our insights; but it is good to know, nevertheless, that revisionists may now presumably continue their work (inconsequential as it may eventually prove to be) without fear of being whistled to a stop by the referee.

The orthodox interpretation of the cold war, as it has come to be regarded, grew up in the late forties and early fifties — years of acute international tension, during which the rivalry between the United States and the Soviet Union repeatedly threatened to erupt in a renewal of global war. Soviet-American relations had deteriorated with alarming speed following the defeat of Hitler. At Yalta, in February, 1945, Winston Churchill had expressed the hope that world peace was nearer the grasp of the assembled statesmen of the great powers "than at any time in history." It would be "a great tragedy," he said, "if they, through inertia or carelessness, let it slip from their grasp. History would never forgive them if they did."

Yet the Yalta agreements themselves, which seemed at the time to lay the basis of postwar cooperation, shortly provided the focus of bitter dissension, in which each side accused the other of having broken its solemn promises. In Western eyes, Yalta meant free elections and parliamentary democracies in Eastern Europe, while the Russians construed the agreements as recognition of their demand for governments friendly to the Soviet Union.

The resulting dispute led to mutual mistrust and to a hardening of positions on both sides. By the spring of 1946 Churchill himself, declaring that "an iron curtain has descended" across Europe, admitted, in effect, that the "tragedy" he had feared had come to pass. Europe split into hostile fragments, the eastern half dominated by the Soviet Union, the western part sheltering nervously under the protection of American arms. NATO, founded in 1949 and countered by the Russian-sponsored Warsaw Pact, merely ratified the existing division of Europe.

From 1946 on, every threat to the stability of this uneasy balance produced an immediate political crisis — Greece in 1947, Czechoslovakia and the Berlin blockade in 1948 — each of which, added to existing tensions, deepened hostility on both sides and increased the chance of war. When Bernard Baruch announced in April, 1947, that "we are in the midst of a cold war," no one felt inclined to contradict him. The phrase stuck, as an accurate description of post-war political realities.

Many Americans concluded, moreover, that the United States was losing the cold war. Two events in particular contributed to this sense of alarm — the collapse of Nationalist China in 1949, followed by Chiang Kai-shek's flight to Taiwan, and the explosion of an atomic bomb by the Russians in the same year. These events led to the charge that American leaders had deliberately or unwittingly betrayed the country's interests. The Alger Hiss case was taken by some people as proof that the Roosevelt Administration had been riddled by subversion.

Looking back to the wartime alliance with the Soviet Union, the American Right began to argue that Roosevelt, by trusting the Russians, had sold out the cause of freedom. Thus Nixon and McCarthy, aided by historians like Stefan J. Possony, C. C. Tansill and others, accused Roosevelt of handing Eastern Europe to the Russians and of giving them a preponderant interest in China which later enabled the Communists to absorb the entire country.

The liberal interpretation of the cold war — what I have called the orthodox interpretation — developed partly as a response to these charges. In liberal eyes, the right-wingers made the crucial mistake of assuming that American actions had been decisive in shaping the postwar world. Attempting to rebut this devil theory of postwar politics, liberals relied heavily on the argument that the shape of postwar politics had already been dictated by the war itself, in which the Western democracies had been obliged to call on Soviet help in defeating Hitler. These events, they maintained, had left the Soviet Union militarily dominant in Eastern Europe and generally occupying a position of much greater power, relative to the West, than the position she had enjoyed before the war.

In the face of these facts, the United States had very little leeway to influence events in what were destined to become Soviet spheres of influence, particularly since Stalin was apparently determined to expand even if it meant ruthlessly breaking his agreements — and after all it was Stalin, the liberals emphasized, and not Roosevelt or Truman, who broke the Yalta agreement on Poland, thereby precipitating the cold war.

These were the arguments presented with enormous charm, wit, logic and power in George F. Kennan's *American Diplomacy* (1951), which more than any other book set the tone of cold-war historiography. For innumerable historians, but especially for those who were beginning their studies in the fifties, Kennan served as the model of what a scholar should be — committed yet detached — and it was through the perspective of his works that a whole generation of scholars came to see not only the origins of the cold war, but the entire history of twentieth-century diplomacy.

It is important to recognize that Kennan's was by no means an uncritical perspective — indeed, for those unacquainted with Marxism it seemed the only critical perspective that was available in the fifties. While Kennan insisted that the Russians were primarily to blame for the cold war, he seldom missed an opportunity to criticize the excessive moralism, the messianic vision of a world made safe for democracy, which he argued ran "like a red skein" through American diplomacy.

As late as 1960, a radical like Staughton Lynd could still accept the general framework of Kennan's critique of American idealism while noting merely that Kennan had failed to apply it to the specific events of the cold war and to the policy of containment which he had helped to articulate. "Whereas in general he counseled America to 'admit the validity and legitimacy of power realities and aspirations . . . and to seek their point of maximum equilibrium rather than their reform or their repression' — 'reform or repression' of the Soviet system were the very goals which Kennan's influential writings of those years urged."

Even in 1960, however, a few writers had begun to attack not the specific applications of the principles of *Realpolitik* but the principles themselves, on the grounds that on many occasions they served simply as rationalizations for American (not Soviet) expansionism. And whereas Lynd in 1960 could still write that the American demand for freedom in Eastern Europe, however misguided "expressed a sincere and idealistic concern," some historians had already begun to take a decidedly more sinister view of the matter — asking, for instance, whether a country which demanded concessions in Eastern Europe that it was not prepared to grant to the Russians in Western Europe could really be accused, as the "realist" writers had maintained, of an excess of good-natured but occasionally incompetent altruism.

Meanwhile the "realist" interpretation of the cold war inspired a whole series of books — most notably, Herbert Feis's series (*Churchill-Roosevelt-Stalin; Between War and Peace; The Atomic Bomb and the End of World War II*); William McNeill's *America, Britain and Russia: Their Cooperation and Conflict;* Norman Graebner's *Cold War Diplomacy;* Louis J. Halle's *Dream and Reality* and *The Cold War as History;* and M. F. Herz's *Beginnings of the Cold War.*

Like Kennan, all of these writers saw containment as a necessary response to Soviet expansionism and to the deterioration of Western power in Eastern Europe. At the same time, they were critical, in varying degrees, of the legalistic-moralistic tradition which kept American statesmen from looking at foreign relations in the light of balance-of-power considerations.

Some of them tended to play off Churchillian realism against the idealism of Roosevelt and Cordell Hull, arguing, for instance, that the Americans should have accepted the bargain made between Churchill and Stalin in 1944, whereby Greece was assigned to the Western sphere of influence and Rumania, Bulgaria and Hungary to the Soviet sphere, with both liberal and Communist parties sharing in the control of Yugoslavia.

These criticisms of American policy, however, did not challenge the basic premise of American policy, that the Soviet Union was a ruthlessly aggressive power bent on world domination. They assumed, moreover, that the Russians were in a position to realize large parts of this program, and that only counterpressure exerted by the West, in the form of containment and the Marshall Plan, prevented the Communists from absorbing all of Europe and much of the rest of the world as well.

It is their criticism of these assumptions that defines the revisionist historians and distinguishes them from the "realists." What impresses revisionists is not Russia's strength but her military weakness following the devastating war with Hitler, in which the Russians suffered much heavier losses than any other member of the alliance.

Beginning with Carl Marzani's *We Can Be Friends: Origins of the Cold War* (1952), revisionists have argued that Russia's weakness dictated, for the moment at least, a policy of postwar cooperation with the West. Western leaders' implacable hostility to Communism, they contend, prevented them from seeing this fact, a proper understanding of which might have prevented the cold war.

This argument is spelled out in D. F. Fleming's two-volume study, *The Cold War and Its Origins* (1961); in David Horowitz's *The Free World Colossus* (1965), which summarizes and synthesizes a great deal of revisionist writing; in Gar Alperovitz's *Atomic Diplomacy: Hiroshima and Potsdam* (1965); and in the previously mentioned *Containment and Change.*

But the historian who has done most to promote a revisionist interpretation of the cold war, and of American diplomacy in general, is William Appleman Williams of the University of Wisconsin, to whom most of the writers just mentioned owe a considerable debt. Williams's works, particularly *The Tragedy of American Diplomacy* (1959), not only challenge the orthodox interpretation of the cold war, they set against it an elaborate counterinterpretation which, if valid, forces one to see American policy in the early years of the cold war as part of a larger pattern of American globalism reaching as far back as 1898.

According to Williams, American diplomacy has consistently adhered to the policy of the "open door" — that is, to a policy of commercial, political and cultural expansion which seeks to extend American influence into every corner of the earth. This policy was consciously and deliberately embarked upon, Williams argues, because American statesmen believed that American capitalism needed ever-expanding foreign markets in order to survive, the closing of the frontier having put an end to its expansion on the continent of North America. Throughout the twentieth century, the makers of American foreign policy, he says, have interpreted the national interest in this light.

The cold war, in Williams's view, therefore has to be seen as the latest phase of a continuing effort to make the world safe for democracy — read liberal capitalism, American-style — in which the United

States finds itself increasingly cast as the leader of a world-wide counterrevolution.

After World War II, Williams maintains, the United States had "a vast proportion of actual as well as potential power vis-a-vis the Soviet Union." The United States "cannot with any real warrant or meaning claim that it has been *forced* to follow a certain approach or policy." (Compare this with a statement by Arthur Schlesinger: "The cold war could have been avoided only if the Soviet Union had not been possessed by convictions both of the infallibility of the Communist word and of the inevitability of a Communist world.")

The Russians, by contrast, Williams writes, "viewed their position in the nineteen-forties as one of weakness, not offensive strength." One measure of Stalin's sense of weakness, as he faced the enormous task of rebuilding the shattered Soviet economy was his eagerness to get a large loan from the United States. Failing to get such a loan — instead, the United States drastically cut back lend-lease payments to Russia in May, 1945 — Stalin was faced with three choices, according to Williams:

1. He could give way and accept the American peace program at every point — which meant, among other things, accepting governments in Eastern Europe hostile to the Soviet Union.
2. He could follow the advice of the doctrinaire revolutionaries in his own country who argued that Russia's best hope lay in fomenting world-wide revolution.
3. Or he could exact large-scale economic reparations from Germany while attempting to reach an understanding with Churchill and Roosevelt on the need for governments in Eastern Europe not necessarily Communist but friendly to the Soviet Union.

His negotiations with Churchill in 1944, according to Williams, showed that Stalin had already committed himself, by the end of the war, to the third of these policies — a policy, incidentally, which required him to withdraw support from communist revolutions in Greece and in other countries which under the terms of the Churchill-Stalin agreement had been conceded to the Western sphere of influence.

But American statesmen, the argument continues, unlike the British, were in no mood to compromise. They were confident of America's strength and Russia's weakness (although later they and their apologists found it convenient to argue that the contrary had been the case). Furthermore, they believed that "we cannot have full employment and prosperity in the United States without the foreign markets," as Dean Acheson told a special Congressional committee on post-war economic policy and planning in November, 1944. These considerations led to the conclusion, as President Truman put it in April, 1945, that the United States should "take the lead in running the world in the way that the world ought to be run"; or more specifically, in the words of Foreign Economic Administrator Leo Crowley, that "if you create good governments in foreign countries, automatically you will have better markets for ourselves." Accordingly, the United States pressed for the "open door" in Eastern Europe and elsewhere.

In addition to these considerations, there was the further matter of the atomic bomb, which first became a calculation in American diplomacy in July, 1945. The successful explosion of an atomic bomb in the New Mexican desert, Williams argues, added to the American sense of omnipotence and led the United States "to overplay its hand" — for in spite of American efforts to keep the Russians out of Eastern Europe, the Russians refused to back down.

Nor did American pressure have the effect, as George Kennan hoped, of promoting tendencies in the Soviet Union "which must eventually find their outlet in either the break-up or the gradual mellowing of Soviet power." Far from causing Soviet policy to mellow, American actions, according to Williams, stiffened the Russians in their resistance to Western pressure and strengthened the hand of those groups in the Soviet Union which had been arguing all along that capitalist powers could not be trusted.

Not only did the Russians successfully resist American demands in Eastern Europe, they launched a vigorous counterattack in the form of the Czechoslovakian coup of 1948 and the Berlin blockade. Both East and West thus found themselves committed to the policy of cold war, and for the next 15 years, until the Cuban missile crisis led to a partial détente, Soviet-American hostility was the determining fact of international politics.

Quite apart from his obvious influence on other revisionist historians of the cold war and on his own students in other areas of diplomatic history, Williams has had a measurable influence on the political radicals of the sixties, most of whom now consider it axiomatic that American diplomacy has been counterrevolutionary and that this fact reflects, not a series of blunders and mistakes as some critics have argued, but the basically reactionary character of American capitalism.

Some radicals now construe these facts to mean that American foreign policy therefore cannot be changed unless American society itself undergoes a revolutionary change. Carl Oglesby, for instance, argues along these lines in *Containment and Change*. From Oglesby's point of view, appeals to conscience or even to enlightened self-interest are useless; the cold war cannot end until the "system" is destroyed.

Williams thought otherwise. At the end of the 1962 edition of *The Tragedy of American Diplomacy,* he noted that "there is at the present time no radicalism in the United States strong enough to win power, or even a very significant influence, through the processes of representative government" — and he took it for granted that genuinely democratic change could come about only through representative processes. This meant, he thought, that "the well-being of the United States depends — *in the short-run but only in the short-run* — upon the extent to which calm and confident and enlightened conservatives can see and bring themselves to act upon the validity of a radical analysis."

In an essay in *Ramparts* (March, 1967) he makes substantially the same point in commenting on the new radicals' impatience with conservative critics of American diplomacy like Senator Fulbright. Fulbright, Williams says, attracted more support for the position of more radical critics than these critics had attracted through their own efforts. "He hangs tough over the long haul, and that is precisely what American radicalism has never done in the twentieth century."

As the New Left becomes more and more beguiled by the illusion of its own revolutionary potential, and more and more intolerant of radicals who refuse to postulate a revolution as the only feasible means of social change, men like Williams will probably become increasingly uncomfortable in the presence of a movement they helped to create. At the same time, Williams's radicalism, articulated in the fifties before radicalism came back into fashion, has alienated the academic establishment and prevented his works from winning the widespread recognition and respect they deserve. In scholarly journals, many reviews of Williams's work — notably a review by Oscar Handlin of *The Contours of American History* in the *Mississippi Valley Historical Review* a few years ago — have been contemptuous and abusive in the extreme. The result is that Williams's books on diplomatic history are only beginning to pass into the mainstream of scholarly discourse, years after their initial publication.

Next to Williams's *Tragedy of American Diplomacy*, the most important attack on the orthodox interpretation of the cold war is Alperovitz's *Atomic Diplomacy*. A young historian trained at Wisconsin, Berkeley, and King's College, Cambridge, and currently a research fellow at Harvard, Alperovitz adds very little to the interpretation formulated by Williams, but he provides Williams's insights with a mass of additional documentation. By doing so, he has made it difficult for conscientious scholars any longer to avoid the challenge of revisionist interpretations. Unconventional in its conclusions, *Atomic Diplomacy* is thoroughly conventional in its methods. That adds to the book's persuasiveness. Using the traditional sources of diplomatic history — official records, memoirs of participants, and all the unpublished material to which scholars have access — Alperovitz painstakingly reconstructs the evolution of American policy during the six-month period March to August, 1945. He proceeds with a thoroughness and caution which, in the case of a less controversial work, would command the unanimous respect of the scholarly profession. His book is no polemic. It is a work in the best — and most conservative — traditions of historical scholarship. Yet the evidence which Alperovitz has gathered together challenges the official explanation of the beginnings of the cold war at every point.

What the evidence seems to show is that as early as April, 1945, American officials from President Truman on down had decided to force a "symbolic showdown" with the Soviet Union over the future of Eastern Europe. Truman believed that a unified Europe was the key to European recovery and economic stability, since the agricultural southeast and the industrial northwest depended on each other. Soviet designs on Eastern Europe, Truman reasoned, threatened to disrupt the economic unity of Europe and therefore had to be resisted. The only question was whether the showdown should take place immediately or whether it should be delayed until the bargaining position of the United States had improved.

At first it appeared to practically everybody that delay would only weaken the position of the United States. Both of its major bargaining counters, its armies in Europe and its lend-lease credits to Russia, could be more effectively employed at once, it seemed, than at any future time. Accordingly, Truman tried to "lay it on the line" with the Russians. He demanded that they "carry out their [Yalta] agreements" by giving the pro-Western elements in Poland an equal voice in the Polish Government (although Roosevelt, who made the Yalta agreements, believed that "we placed, as clearly shown in the agreement, somewhat more emphasis" on the Warsaw [pro-Communist] Government than on the pro-Western leaders). When Stalin objected that Poland was "a country in which the U.S.S.R. is interested first of all and most of all," the United States tried to force him to give in by cutting back lend-lease payments to Russia.

At this point, however — in April, 1945 — Secretary of War Henry L. Stimson convinced Truman that "we shall probably hold more cards in our hands later than now." He referred to the atomic bomb, and if Truman decided to postpone the showdown with Russia, it was because Stimson and other advisers persuaded him that the new weapon would "put us in a position," as Secretary of State James F. Byrnes argued, "to dictate our own terms at the end of the war."

To the amazement of those not privy to the secret, Truman proceeded to take a more conciliatory attitude toward Russia, an attitude symbolized by Harry Hopkins's mission to Moscow in June, 1945. Meanwhile, Truman twice postponed the meeting with Churchill and Stalin at Potsdam. Churchill complained, "Anyone can see that in a very short space of time our armed power on the Continent will have vanished."

But when Truman told Churchill that an atomic bomb had been successfully exploded at Alamogordo, exceeding all expectations, Churchill immediately understood and endorsed the strategy of delay. "We were in the presence of a new factor in human affairs," he said, "and possessed of powers which were irresistible." Not only Germany but even the Balkans, which Churchill and Roosevelt had formerly conceded to the Russian sphere, now seemed amenable to Western influence. That assumption, of course, had guided American policy (though not British policy) since April, but it could not be acted upon until the bombing of Japan provided the world with an unmistakable demonstration of American military supremacy.

Early in September, the foreign ministers of the Big Three met in London. Byrnes — armed, as Stimson noted, with "the presence of the bomb in his pocket, so to speak, as a great weapon to get through" the conference — tried to press the American advantage. He demanded that the Governments of Bulgaria and Rumania reorganize themselves along lines favorable to the West. In Bulgaria, firmness won a few concessions; in Rumania, the Russians stood firm. The American strategy had achieved no noteworthy success. Instead — as Stimson, one of the architects of that strategy, rather belatedly observed — it had "irretrievably embittered" Soviet-American relations.

The revisionist view of the origins of the cold war, as it emerges from the works of Williams, Alperovitz, Marzani, Fleming, Horowitz, and others, can be summarized as follows. The object of American policy at the end of World War II was not to defend Western or even Central Europe but to force the Soviet Union out of Eastern Europe. The Soviet menace to the "free world," so often cited as the justification of the containment policy, simply did not exist in the minds of American planners. They believed themselves to be negotiating not from weakness but from almost unassailable superiority.

Nor can it be said that the cold war began because the Russians "broke their agreements." The general sense of the Yalta agreements — which were in any case very vague — was to assign to the Soviet Union a controlling influence in Eastern Europe. Armed with the atomic bomb, American diplomats tried to take back what they had implicitly conceded at Yalta.

The assumption of American moral superiority, in short, does not stand up under analysis.

The opponents of this view have yet to make a very convincing reply. Schlesinger's recent article in *Foreign Affairs*, referred to at the outset of this article, can serve as an example of the kind of arguments which historians are likely to develop in opposition to the revisionist interpretation. Schlesinger argues that the cold war came about through a combination of Soviet intransigence and misunderstanding. There were certain "problems of communication" with the Soviet Union, as a result of which "the Russians might conceivably have misread our signals." Thus the American demand for self-determination in Poland and other East European countries "very probably" appeared to the Russians "as a systematic and deliberate pressure on Russia's western frontiers."

Similarly, the Russians "could well have interpreted" the American refusal of a loan to the Soviet Union, combined with the cancellation of lend-lease, "as deliberate sabotage" of Russia's postwar reconstruction or as "blackmail." In both cases, of course, there would have been no basis for these suspicions; but "we have thought a great deal more in recent years," Schlesinger says, ". . . about the problems of communication in diplomacy," and we know how easy it is for one side to misinterpret what the other is saying.

This argument about difficulties of "communications" at no point engages the evidence uncovered by Alperovitz and others — evidence which seems to show that Soviet officials had good reason to interpret American actions exactly as they did: as attempts to dictate American terms.

In reply to the assertion that the refusal of a reconstruction loan was part of such an attempt, Schlesinger can only argue weakly that the Soviet request for a loan was "inexplicably mislaid" by Washington during the transfer of records from the Foreign Economic Administration to the State Department! "Of course," he adds, "this was impossible for the Russians to believe." It is impossible for some Americans to believe. As William Appleman Williams notes, Schlesinger's explanation of the "inexplicable" loss of the Soviet request "does not speak to the point of how the leaders could forget the request even if they lost the document."

When pressed on the matter of "communications," Schlesinger retreats to a second line of argument, namely that none of these misunderstandings "made much essential difference," because Stalin suffered from "paranoia" and was "possessed by convictions both of the infallibility of the Communist word and of the inevitability of a Communist world."

The trouble is that there is very little evidence which connects either Stalin's paranoia or Marxist-Leninist ideology or what Schlesinger calls "the sinister dynamics of a totalitarian society" with the actual course of Soviet diplomacy during the formative months of the cold war. The only piece of evidence that Schlesinger has been able to find is an article by the Communist theoretician Jacques Duclos in the April, 1945, issue of *Cahiers du communisme*, the journal of the French Communist party, which proves, he argues, that Stalin had already abandoned the wartime policy of collaboration with the West and returned to the traditional Communist policy of world revolution.

Even this evidence, however, can be turned to the advantage of the revisionists. Alperovitz points out that Duclos did not attack electoral politics or even collaboration with bourgeois governments. What he denounced was precisely the American Communists' decision, in 1944, to withdraw from electoral politics. Thus the article, far from being a call to world revolution, "was one of many confirmations that European Communists had decided to abandon violent revolutionary struggle in favor of the more modest aim of electoral success." And while this decision did not guarantee world peace, neither did it guarantee 20 years of cold war.

Schlesinger first used the Duclos article as a trump card in a letter to *The New York Review of Books*, October 20, 1966, which called forth Alperovitz's rejoinder. It is symptomatic of the general failure of orthodox historiography to engage the revisionist argument that Duclos's article crops up again in Schlesinger's more recent essay in *Foreign Affairs*, where it is once again cited as evidence of a "new Moscow line," without any reference to the intervening objections raised by Alperovitz.

Sooner or later, however, historians will have to come to grips with the revisionist interpretation of the cold war. They cannot ignore it indefinitely. When serious debate begins, many historians, hitherto disposed to accept without much question the conventional account of the cold war, will find themselves compelled to admit its many inadequacies. On the other hand, some of the ambiguities of the revisionist view, presently submerged in the revisionists' common quarrel with official explanations, will begin to force themselves to the surface. Is the revisionist history of the cold war essentially an attack on "the doctrine of historical inevitability," as Alperovitz contends? Or does it contain an implicit determinism of its own?

Two quite different conclusions can be drawn from the body of the revisionist scholarship. One is that American policy-makers had it in their power to choose different policies from the ones they chose. That is, they could have adopted a more conciliatory attitude toward the Soviet Union, just as they now have the choice of adopting a more conciliatory attitude toward Communist China and toward nationalist revolutions elsewhere in the Third World.

The other is that they have no such choice, because the inner requirements of American capitalism *force* them to pursue a consistent policy of economic and political expansion. "For matters to stand otherwise," writes Carl Oglesby, "the Yankee free-enterpriser would . . . have to . . . take sides against himself. . . . He would have to change entirely his style of thought and action. In a word, he would have to become a revolutionary Socialist whose aim was the destruction of the present American hegemony."

Pushed to what some writers clearly regard as its logical conclusion, the revisionist critique of American foreign policy thus becomes the obverse of the cold-war liberals' defense of that policy, which assumes that nothing could have modified the character of Soviet policy short of the transformation of the Soviet Union into a liberal democracy — which is exactly the goal the containment policy sought to promote. According to a certain type of revisionism, American policy has all the rigidity the orthodox historians attribute to the U.S.S.R., and this inflexibility made the cold war inevitable.

Moreover, Communism really did threaten American interests, in this view, Oglesby argues that, in spite of its obvious excesses, the "theory of the International Communist Conspiracy is not the hysterical old maid that many leftists seem to think it is." If there is no conspiracy, there is a world revolution and it "does aim itself at America" — the America of expansive corporate capitalism.

Revisionism, carried to these conclusions, curiously restores cold war anti-Communism to a kind of intellectual respectability, even while insisting on its immorality. After all, it concludes, the cold warriors were following the American national interest. The national interest may have been itself corrupt, but the policy-makers were more rational than their critics may have supposed.

In my view, this concedes far too much good sense to Truman, Dulles, and the rest. Even Oglesby concedes that the war in Vietnam has now become irrational in its own terms. I submit that much of the cold war has been irrational in its own terms — as witness the failure, the enormously costly failure, of American efforts to dominate Eastern Europe at the end of World War II. This is not to deny the fact of

American imperialism, only to suggest that imperialism itself, as J. A. Hobson and Joseph Schumpeter argued in another context long ago, is irrational — that even in its liberal form it may represent an archaic social phenomenon having little relation to the realities of the modern world.

At the present stage of historical scholarship, it is of course impossible to speak with certainty about such matters. That very lack of certainty serves to indicate the direction which future study of American foreign policy might profitably take.

The question to which historians must now address themselves is whether American capitalism really depends, for its continuing growth and survival, on the foreign policy its leaders have been following throughout most of the twentieth century. To what extent are its interests really threatened by Communist revolutions in the Third World? To what extent can it accommodate itself to those revolutions reconciling itself to a greatly diminished role in the rest of the world, without undergoing a fundamental reformation — that is, without giving way (after a tremendous upheaval) to some form of Socialism?

Needless to say, these are not questions for scholars alone. The political positions one takes depend on the way one answers them. It is terribly important, therefore, that we begin to answer them with greater care and precision than we can answer them today.

7. RE-READING THE COLD WAR

Adam B. Ulam

There is no better way of summarizing the main preoccupation of American writing and thinking on international affairs since World War II than by recalling the titles of two celebrated Russian novels of the 19th century: *Who Is Guilty?* and *What Is To Be Done?* To be sure, the books' authors, Herzen and Chernyshevsky, both belonged to the radical camp, while in the United States the preoccupations epitomized by the two titles have been shared by writers of different ideological coloration and political aims. But the fact remains that, confronted by the puzzling and depressing phenomenon of the Cold War, historians, men of affairs, and finally, to a smaller or larger extent, all of us have sought to assess the responsibility for and the means of getting out of the dangerous predicament in which the republic and the world have found themselves for the past quarter century.

But the universality of this concern and the understandable emotions it arouses does not excuse the historian from his special responsibility, which is, to use the current jargon, "telling it like it is" — or rather, was. Before he becomes a philosopher of history or a judge, he must tell us what actually happened. His primary duty is not to be attuned to the currently fashionable trends in public thinking or to be a counselor to statesmen. It is to ascertain what, in terms of our knowledge, is a fact, what could be a reasonable hypothesis, and what must remain a conjecture. If he does not meet that test, he is a moralist or a publicist but not an historian.

Now, all this might appear a platitude, and a pedantic one at that.

Reprinted from *Interplay*, March, 1969, pp. 51–53. Reprinted by permission.

But it must be said before we proceed to consider the by now considerable literature concerning the origins of the Cold War. Much of this literature reflects what has come to be known as the revisionist point of view. This view challenges the main thesis underlying American policies since World War II: that the responsibility for the drastic deterioration in US-Soviet relations since 1945 must be attributed wholly or mainly to the actions and designs of the rulers of the Soviet Union. On the contrary, some, almost all of the blame, say the revisionists, depending on the given author, can be traced to actions and intentions of American policy-makers.

REVISING THE REVISIONISTS

Let us for the moment leave apart the wider question of whether the whole inquiry is meaningful or profitable. But do the arguments adduced by the revisionists make sense in their own terms? Mr. Schlesinger, who once impatiently brushed off the whole school, has since[1] come to believe that historical revisionism in general "is an essential part of the process by which history . . . enlarges its perspectives and enriches its insights." Hence one should not deplore the rise of Cold War revisionism. Well, let us see. Dr. Alperovitz's *Atomic Diplomacy, Hiroshima and Potsdam* (New York, 1965) is the most concentrated dose of the revisionist argument. Its thesis is simple: the first atomic bomb was dropped not because of any military necessity but in order to *impress the Russians.* Subsequently, US policy-makers used their monopoly of the atom bomb as a bargaining weapon in order to wrest from the Russians their sphere of influence in Eastern Europe. Since that sphere had been conceded by Roosevelt, Truman's policy represented a significant reversal of American foreign policy. Confronted with this breach by the United States of the solemn pledges he had secured, Stalin naturally withdrew into a policy of isolation, suspicion and hostility toward the West. Hence the Cold War.

Now some reviewers have criticized Alperovitz's book by questioning his assertion that Truman reversed Roosevelt's policy vis-à-vis Russia, by expostulating that it is impossible to talk about the Cold War without taking into account Stalin's personality, etc. Justified as these complaints are, they miss the central point. The book stands or falls with the thesis that there was in fact "atomic diplomacy," *i.e.*, that in bargaining with the USSR over Eastern Europe or any other area, the United States used its possession of the bomb as a threat or a bargaining counter. Hence one would expect Alperovitz to adduce at least a single instance of an American negotiator saying in effect to a Russian during the period in question (1945–46), "You ought to remember we have the bomb," or "If you go easy on the Poles we might share our nuclear know-how with you." Or he might offer a *public* statement by an American official that "the Russians ought to keep in mind before they go too far

[1] *Foreign Affairs*, October 1967.

in Rumania that we have this weapon." Dr. Alperovitz does not cite any such instances because there weren't any.

To put this in perspective, one must recall an official Soviet note to the British government following the Suez crisis of 1956 in which the British were informed that the USSR had nuclear weapons, and long-range missiles; or a similar communication in 1958, this time to Macmillan and Eisenhower during another Near East crisis, in which the Western statesmen were reminded rather needlessly that the Soviet Union "possessed atom and hydrogen bombs . . . ballistic missiles of all kinds including intercontinental ones"; or Khrushchev's warning in July 1960 that Castro was being protected by Soviet missiles. Or we should recall Mr. Dulles' incantation in the 1950s about "massive retaliation." But in 1945? Dr. Alperovitz quotes what various US officials committed to their diaries or what they said to each other concerning the US diplomatic position being strengthened by its possession of the atomic bomb. But what does that prove? If one Soviet official said to another in 1945, "We have larger land forces in Europe than the West has," is this a *prima facie* case for maintaining that the Soviets were blackmailing the British and Americans?

But if no case at all can be made for the existence of "atomic diplomacy" in 1945 or for many years afterwards, can one rescue something from the revisionist argument by adopting Dr. Alperovitz's secondary complaint, *i.e.*, that no *positive* policy was being pursued to dissipate Soviet fears and suspicions? Why did the US quibble over the character of governments the USSR was establishing in its sphere of interests in Eastern Europe? Why, especially, did not the US offer to share its nuclear technology with the USSR, as indeed was suggested at one time by Secretary Stimson? Here the argument must hinge on circumstantial evidence concerning the Russians' (*i.e.*, Stalin's) probable reaction to the US possession of the bomb, and to the United States' quibbling over the extent of Russian influence in Eastern Europe. And as such, it fares no better than the one about the US having practiced atomic diplomacy in 1945.

Dr. Alperovitz believes that Stalin's "post-Hiroshima reversals in Manchuria, Hungary and Bulgaria testify to a new conviction that the power realities required him to yield considerably more than he may have originally thought necessary" [page 233]. What were those reversals? In Hungary the Communists suffered electoral setbacks, but they had been guaranteed leading posts in the government before, whatever the outcome of the elections. In Bulgaria it is arguable that the American delay in recognizing the Soviet-sponsored regime postponed for some time the execution and imprisonment of some anti-Communist politicians. In Manchuria the Soviets were to have very much their own way: they looted the country of its industrial equipment and were soon to distribute seized Japanese stockpiles of arms to the Chinese Communists. What Dr. Alperovitz means by Russian reversals in Manchuria remains a mystery.

Would an American offer of sharing the alleged atomic secrets have made the Russians less suspicious, more tractable, more humane in their policies in Eastern Europe and elsewhere? This is implicit in all the revisionists' writings, since it is not a part of their argument that Soviet policies in Eastern Europe were *entirely* blameless, or that the governments there represented *exactly* the popular will. Soviet repressions and exactions are held as an understandable over-reaction to American atomic blackmail. But as we have seen, Dr. Alperovitz has just argued that had Stalin not been afraid of the atom bomb he would have asked for more rather than less.

A more extended version of revisionism can be found in D. Horowitz's *The Free World Colossus* (London, 1965). With him we come closer to the theory of a *plot* by the US policy-makers to destroy the USSR. The minimum US objectives, he writes, were ". . . to deny Russia the influence she had won in Europe . . . to *compel* Russia to relinquish her positions in Eastern Europe." The maximum US objectives looked "to the breakup of Soviet power itself and beyond that, to the collapse of the Russian Revolution" [page 278]. Those are far-reaching charges, but where is the evidence? Mr. Horowitz relies heavily on the work of Professor Fleming, *The Cold War and Its Origins* (New York, 1961). The professor's work is, in turn, a collection of clippings from newspapers, of excerpts from speeches by Congressmen, from various works suspicious of Western policy, etc., all strung together by his soliloquizing about America's over-commitment and about the sinfulness and futility of stockpiling nuclear arms. But what could one not prove by this method? And indeed Mr. Horowitz's discovery that the American leadership had as its maximum goal in 1945 the "breakup of Soviet power" and "the collapse of the Russian Revolution" belongs in the same class as some of the more extravagant assertions of the late Senator McCarthy.

THE IMPERSONAL VILLAIN

Unlike the preceding, Professor William Appleman Williams' *The Tragedy of American Diplomacy* (New York, 1962) is the work of an historian (*i.e.*, of a man who has respect for the facts). By the same token, it displays most glaringly the defects of the "who is guilty?" and "what is to be done?" approaches to history. Here the guilty party is impersonal: it is the Open Door Policy bias written into American foreign policy, its well-meaning, impractical and dangerous impulse to recast the whole world in the American image. And what is to be done is "a radical but noncommunist reconstruction of American society in domestic affairs" [page 308]. These are legitimate reflections, and one may grant them, depending on one's point of view, a varying degree of validity. But do they help us a great deal in understanding what happened in 1945? And what is one to do about nuclear proliferation, the Near East, China, etc., while a "radical reconstruction . . . of American society," obviously a long and laborious process, is taking place?

What then is the answer? And following Gertrude Stein, what is the question, or rather questions? Here an historian of the Cold War will do well to begin by asking small and unpretentious questions. What accounts for the exceptional case of Finland, the country defeated in the war and which found itself in the Soviet sphere of interests, but which, unlike other countries in that sphere, was allowed to retain its internal freedom? Why did the Soviets pull out of northern Iran in 1946, while the West's previous expostulations about the USSR breaking its wartime pledges in the case of Eastern Europe had been ineffective? There are no hard and fast answers in either case, but a study of both these "exceptions" will yield some interesting tentative conclusions about USSR policy, and the degree to which it would have been influenced by a different American posture.

Then, too, we must not see international affairs merely as a clash of grim historical forces and ideologies, and of sordid or otherwise material interests. Much depends on personal characteristics of the actors involved, on their intelligence and alertness as to the meaning of the given situation. This is such a commonplace that one blushes to put it in writing, yet this factor is strenuously dismissed or minimized both by academic defenders and assailants of American policy. Thus one cannot escape the conclusion, much as it was vulgarized by hack politicians and tendentious journalists, that American diplomacy in 1944–45 was inept, and American policy-makers were strangely naïve and insensitive as to the nature of the Soviet system and its rulers. Professor Williams strenuously defends Roosevelt from the charge of being naïve in his attitude toward Stalin. Yet Professor Williams' credentials on judging what was or was not naïve concerning Russia are not convincing. Writing in 1962, he still believes that Stalin in 1945 had difficulties "in controlling doctrinaire revolutionaries within his own camp" [page 233]. If one believes that, one will believe anything.

Evidence abounds as to the low esteem in which the Soviets held the political acumen of the American policy-makers: Stalin telling Roosevelt at Yalta that he would have difficulties with his Ukrainian and Byelo-russian constituents unless those two republics were seated in the United Nations; Stalin answering Harry Hopkins's plea on behalf of the Soviet-imprisoned Polish underground leaders with the observation that, under the Soviet constitution, he, Stalin, could not interfere with the judicial process; Stalin again in December 1945 telling Secretary Byrnes that the Soviet troops had to stay in northern Iran beyond the agreed date because there was danger of the Iranian army attacking oil fields in Baku. And one could go on.

Granting the psychology of a totalitarian system, the very gullibility of Americans in their initial negotiations with the Russians was to become a factor in increasing tensions and discords of the Cold War. Any stiffening of the American position, any attempt at hard bargaining was to arouse disproportionate Soviet suspicions. While the atom bomb does not seem to have disturbed Stalin's equanimity, there is much circumstantial evidence that fantastically sinister implications were read by Soviet leaders into the Marshall Plan.

Was the Cold War, then, the result of vast impersonal forces or of human errors and passions? Here it is useful to make some distinctions. Few things in history appear as inevitable as that there should have been tension and competition between the US and the USSR following the conclusion of the war. The nature of both systems made it inevitable. How could Stalin's suspicion have been allayed even by a vast American loan and dispatch of sample atomic bombs? Here was a man who imprisoned hundreds of thousands of his countrymen merely for having been prisoners of war, who had executed his closest collaborators, exiled the families of those who continued being his faithful servants, like Molotov and Mikoyan, and was to turn against the leaders of Yugoslavia, until 1948 his most fanatical followers.

Could Stalin's fears have been appeased by a firm agreement on spheres of influence throughout the world between the two superpowers? As I tried to point out in my recent book, if carefully qualified, this argument possesses some validity. But in its extreme form it has its own unreality. With the war over, it was simply impossible for public opinion in the West to remain indifferent to tales of repression, violence and destruction which were pouring in from the East. Had democratic countries been able to practice such cold-blooded realism in foreign policy, it can be argued that there would have been no reason for World War II. What was Hitler doing in Poland and the Japanese in China but carving out their spheres of influence? In the vastly different world of 1968 the Soviet effort to discipline Czechoslovakia — and that by means infinitely more humane than those employed by Stalin in Eastern Europe between 1945–48 — still sent a shock through the world.

Could "tougher" policies have worked? Surely — had America been ruled by a dictator or an oligarchy, there was little that this country could not have gotten by threats and pressure. "American omnipotence" was for the period 1945–1950 not a myth but very close to being a reality. The main factor here was not the wretched bomb, but the fantastic record of American industry and production during the war; and secondly, the vast American manpower — in comparison with every other belligerent barely tapped. As against it, Russia's economy was in ruins and Stalin faced his own people with their expectations, which were to be cruelly disappointed, that their sacrifices had won them the right for a better and freer life than they had had before the war. But the real America of 1945 could no more embark upon a pushful foreign policy than Stalin could have instituted a two-party democracy. In fact, for anybody with even a superficial knowledge of the period, it is evident that the main concern of the American policy-makers was not to deny Russia the fruits of victory nor to destroy the Russian Revolution, as the revisionists tell us in their tirades, but to prevent the American people from lapsing back into isolationism when confronted with the sinful and complex postwar world.

SOVIET REALPOLITIK

Within the limits circumscribed by the character of both societies, there was still a great deal that skillful, well-informed and alert diplomacy could have accomplished. On the Polish issue, a key one in inter-allied diplomacy between 1943–45, the Western leaders and their diplomatic advisers were abysmally ignorant. They simply could not keep up with Stalin, who was excellently informed and who could take the most outrageous liberties with facts without any of his interlocutors catching on. Thus a careful study of the Teheran Conference will bear out the conclusion that on Poland the Soviets were offered more than they had expected. Soviet diplomacy was alert and tenacious. It perceived and exploited the West's fears and foibles. At Teheran Stalin played masterfully on Churchill's embarrassment over the delay on the second front, and his obvious apprehension that the invasion of the Continent might bring casualties on the scale of those of World War I. At Yalta the Russians diagnosed carefully the exaggerated importance attached by the Americans to the framework of the United Nations. The Russians would raise objections concerning membership, procedures, etc., and then drop them in a manner that would earn American gratitude and the feeling that it would be too embarrassing now to quibble over Poland or the German reparations.

Soviet diplomacy was not superhuman nor were the Russians rigid in their thinking, with a blueprint worked out for every contingency. On the German issue, it is obvious, the Soviets in 1945 were not clear in their own mind what they wanted, what kind of Germany would eventually serve their interests best. But American diplomacy was operating by fits and starts. People were already asking questions unanswerable because of their vastness and impracticality. Was Soviet Russia out to conquer the world or was Stalin going to abide faithfully by the charter and spirit of the United Nations? That there were a great number of possibilities and opportunities between those majestic and fatuous alternatives was but dimly perceived.

An American philosophy of international relations was thus launched on that course of grandiose rhetoric that in due time was to produce the would-be magic solutions and incantations: "massive retaliation," preparation for "brushfire wars" and eventually the "we were guilty" chant of the revisionists. While looking for a sign in heaven indicating who was right or for a magic formula to solve *all* problems, we have overlooked those occasions where tenacious, well-informed diplomacy could have made a difference, and where hard bargaining rather than posturing might have brought partial solutions and lowered the international tension. It is in illuminating those occasions — such as the German question in 1947 and 1952, or the opportunities presented for American diplomacy by the already irrefutable evidence of the Sino-Soviet conflict in the late '50s — that the historian can be of help to the men of affairs and to public opinion, rather than by pondering the unanswerable and futile question: who started it all?

Thus one cannot endorse a tolerant view of "cold war revisionism" which sees in it but a necessary part of a dialogue that will lead to a deeper historical truth. As history this revisionism is fallacious. As polemic it is an attempt to exploit the currently fashionable mood of guilt, which is as harmful as a guide to reflection and action as is national arrogance and moral self-righteousness.

8. THE COLD WAR: CONTAINMENT OF SOVIET POWER OR COUNTERREVOLUTION?

Vernon V. Aspaturian

One of the great ideological battlegrounds between the Western world and the Sino-Soviet nations is the universe of underdeveloped countries scattered across Africa, Asia, and North and South America. Whether the ideological allegiances of these countries will be attracted toward the West or toward the Communist world may determine the fate of Western civilization and the social and political systems that it has developed. As the world becomes trifurcated into distinct, if somewhat nebulously organized, ideosocial consensus systems, a triangular pattern of tension and conflict takes shape and demands release and resolution. These tensions and conflicts originated first in the Bolshevik Revolution of 1917 and the challenges that it represented, and later, in the disintegration of the Western colonial systems and the resultant clash between the aspirations of the emerging states and the vestigial bastions of Western rule and domination.

In short, the underdeveloped world is convulsed by social upheaval and seething with revolutionary passion for a place in the sun, long denied them by the dark shadow of colonialism. The Western world, on the other hand, seeks to arrest the social revolution that is sweeping the underdeveloped world, whether in colonial territories, newly emancipated states, or countries with ancient credentials of independence and sovereignty. This revolutionary assault is directed against two distinct

Originally published under the title, "Revolutionary Change and the Strategy of the *Status Quo*," in Laurence Martin, editor, *Neutralism and Nonalignment* (Copyright 1962 by Frederick A. Praeger, Inc.). Reprinted by permission.

targets: (1) the indigenous feudal or quasi-feudal social relics of medievalism; and (2) colonial or foreign domination, be it political or economic in character — that is, opposed to Western imperialism. Thus, the revolutions in underdeveloped countries are directed against the status quo, both in their internal social orders and their external relationships with the Western powers. Since the underdeveloped countries are against what is supported by the Western world and the United States, the latter emerge as the main bulwarks of the status quo, which is under attack.

Since this status quo has been under siege from the Soviet Union since the Bolshevik Revolution of 1917, the underdeveloped world and the Soviet Union find themselves tactically united, while American policy, in its zeal to preserve the status quo everywhere, emerges as both anti-Soviet and antirevolutionary in general. Moreover, since the status quo has a single defender — the West — and two challengers — Soviet Communism and native revolutionary movements — the two challengers are forced into a marriage of tactical convenience. This, all too frequently, results in their being lumped together as a single force in American foreign-policy calculations.

However, it should be made clear from the outset that this tactical alliance between Soviet Communism and the nationalist revolutionary movements in underdeveloped countries is essentially ephemeral and transitory in character because its common goals are limited to the destruction of feudalism (internally) and imperialism (externally). Soviet Communists consider support for the achievement of these objectives to be a necessary preliminary to subsequent Communist revolutions, but the underdeveloped world does not reciprocate with absolute support for Soviet foreign policy or ideological goals. Although the underdeveloped world is opposed to the status quo, it does not wish to replace that status quo with a Communist social system. Instead, it seeks to achieve the social order of the Western world. In this lie both irony and tragedy for the West, for a submerged common denominator of interests and action exists between the preservation of the status quo in the Western world and revolutionary change in the underdeveloped countries. The tremendous social and political energies released by one part of the world in revolution against its status quo could be tapped by the West to stabilize, expand, and strengthen the status quo in the West against the transcendental pretensions of Soviet Communism. Instead, skillful Soviet exploitation of the conflicts between the West and the underdeveloped countries may tap these energies to both subvert the status quo in the West and abort the social order that the underdeveloped countries seek to establish.

Although the main revolutionary tide in the underdeveloped world is neither Communist nor Communist-inspired, it soon becomes Soviet-encouraged and supported. The more implacable and unyielding the forces of the status quo against these non-Communist forces, the more they are impelled toward Moscow, and the greater the danger that they may fall under its control. In this way, the Soviet Union hopes to emerge

262 THE COLD WAR

as the champion not only of Communism, but of revolutionary change and progress in general. Indeed, the new program of the Communist Party of the Soviet Union arrogantly boasts that all revolutionary roads lead to Communism. The multiple revolutions of the mid-twentieth century are merged into a single force dedicated to annihilating the bastions of the status quo:

> Socialist revolutions, national liberation and anti-imperialist revolutions, people's democratic revolutions, broad peasants' movements, the struggle of the masses for the overthrow of fascism and other despotic regimes, and general democratic movements against national oppression are all being merged into a single world revolutionary process undermining and destroying capitalism.[1]

Thus, in a world charged with revolutionary passion, the Western world and the United States are being trapped into becoming the gendarmes of a reactionary status quo, since American policy increasingly assumes the pattern of desperately preserving the status quo, wherever and whatever it might be, whether under attack from Communists or from nationalist revolutionary movements. Simultaneously, American statesmen, and much of the American public, frequently imagine the United States to be in the vanguard of the very revolutionary surge that its policies and instruments appear to thwart. While the image of the United States in most of the world is increasingly that of the mainstay of the status quo, America has recalled its colonial past in an orgy of revolutionary verbalism, although its actions remain implacably conservative. In a desperate attempt to preserve its revolutionary image while simultaneously opposing revolutions, American policy often identifies purely indigenous non-Communist revolutionary movements as Communist-inspired, directed, or infiltrated. This identification is enthusiastically welcomed by Moscow, since, instead of discrediting non-Communist revolutionary movements, it has the unfortunate effect of identifying Communism with popular causes. Thus, at the Twenty-second Party Congress, Khrushchev almost exultantly observed:

> Attempts are made to blame us Communists for any action by the masses against their oppressors. When the working people of any capitalist or colonial country rise in struggle, the imperialists begin to cry: "This is the handiwork of the Communists" or the "hand of Moscow." Of course, we are glad to have the imperialists ascribe to Communists all the good actions of peoples. By so doing, the imperialists are involuntarily helping the masses to gain a better understanding of Communist ideas.[2]

This dangerous discrepancy between the self-image of the United States as revolutionary, and its image in the revolutionary world as conservative, even reactionary, requires critical investigation. The usual American response is to call for "a better selling job" or "propaganda

[1] *Pravda*, July 30, 1961.
[2] *Pravda*, October 18, 1961.

effort," or to contrast the weekly hours the Communists spend on radio broadcasts with the puny response of the Voice of America. Characteristically, there is never any investigation of the content of American propaganda efforts, as if it were self-evident that what is said is unimportant when compared with how it is said and how often. Americans are rightly bewildered that the "land of the free," with the highest standard of living in the world, and a material culture second to none, should be represented as opposing progress. Yet, the reason is simple. Most Americans are satisfied with their status quo and resent the pretensions of Soviet Communism to liberate them from an imaginary oppressor; they fail to realize, however, the intensity with which any movement opposed to the status quo is greeted, whether or not it is Communist. There is no passion against Communism in the underdeveloped countries, because Communism is not a threat, to them, but to conditions that they detest and refuse to defend. In defending a popularly accepted status quo against the Soviet threat, the United States has been trapped into defending it everywhere against all revolutionary forces.

The so-called great debates on American foreign policy have never clearly presented the issues in terms of revolution versus status quo; the American public has never been asked whether the national interest, as distinguished from the special vested interest of some American corporations, requires that the status quo be preserved on four continents against popular revolutionary movements. Indeed, the American public has not even been told that a status quo is being defended, or what the ideological and geographical definition of the status quo that is being defended is. Yet there is a status quo that must be defended, and defended against the Soviet threat. What is required is a general theoretical definition of the status quo and a strategy for the most effective way of preserving it. Such strategy would reveal that, historically and logically, defending a given status quo is not incompatible with supporting revolutions against status quos elsewhere, for often one can best defend a given status quo in one part of the world by supporting revolutions against another elsewhere. Correspondingly a status quo may actually be weakened and subverted if status quos are indiscriminately supported everywhere.

In answering the challenges of a revolutionary world, and the Soviet threat to exploit it, one of the obvious points requiring attention is the degree of validity and effectiveness of the Western system of social analysis, for an effective strategy of action must rest upon a sound foundation of analysis. Does the West have an accurate idea of the social and political realities in a revolutionary world, or has it been distorted by factors that have not received sufficient attention from scholars? To what extent have Western analyses of social and political forces been subverted by propaganda clichés and sanctimonious proclamations? Even more important, is it possible that the Soviet system of analyzing forces and events in the underdeveloped world in terms of social classes and class conflict gives a more accurate appraisal than the

Western system — which sedulously avoids resorting to a class analysis? To what extent are Western distortions of social and international realities due to faulty perception and self-deception, resulting from the employment of imperfect analytical categories; and to what degree are they a result of calculated deception on the part of powerful pressure groups and influential cliques that have a stake in distorting and concealing realities? As concrete illustrations of tensions that might exist between vested interests and social realities: (1) How "real" are the "free" institutions of Laos, Jordan, and South Vietnam, which the United States has committed itself to defend against revolutionary insurrections, as compared with the realities of outside vested interests and the interests of local feudal landowning classes? (2) How "real" is the claim that the commitment to destroy "Castroism" in Cuba reflects the American passion to preserve the "democratic" institutions of Guatemala, Honduras, Nicaragua, Haiti, El Salvador, Panama, Peru, and Paraguay, as compared with the realities of the huge financial investments that American companies and corporations have in Latin America?

To ask these questions is not always to answer them, but it is indisputable that wrong answers, whether by calculation or through ignorance, will provide a poor foundation for a successful policy of defending the status quo in the Western world. An effective framework for analysis and strategy of action demands: (1) a realistic appraisal of forces and events in the underdeveloped world; (2) a knowledge of how the Soviet Union analyzes these forces and events, and how it arrives at assumptions concerning Western response and behavior; (3) a bold, unevasive, and realistic definition of the status quo that is to be preserved and extended, as well as of the status quo that must be abandoned, not to the mercies of Soviet Communism, but to the innovating and invigorating shock of bourgeois-nationalist revolutions; (4) a precise appraisal of the social forces that can be relied upon to defend a given status quo, and a plan as to how these forces can be broadened and strengthened; and (5) an equally precise appraisal of those social forces that are irrevocably committed to the destruction of the status quo that the West wishes to maintain, and a plan for preventing these forces from recruiting additional adherents among dissatisfied and frustrated populations.

What, then, is the status quo that the United States should be committed to preserve and strengthen? It is an ideosocial system that the Communists call "capitalist-imperialist," and which Americans variously refer to as "Western," "the free world," "the democratic world," or "capitalism," not always being certain which has priority, since they are not always compatible with one another. Clearly, there is a "free world," a "democratic world," and a "capitalist world," but they bear little relation to the "free world" of the propaganda clichés, which includes some of the most despotic, venal, and feudalistic systems on the globe. The United States finds itself supporting regimes whose vices often exceed those ascribed to Soviet totalitarianism. The vices against which the

United States is committed are similarly distorted; they include "dictatorship," "the slave-world," and "totalitarianism."

The current status quo policy is anti-Communism, which has become an increasingly elastic and arbitrary concept, since it constitutes the ideological standard against which American objectives are measured. Reduced to their operational level, the shop-worn clichés of "freedom" and "free world" refer to freedom from Soviet (or Sino-Soviet) Communism, irrespective of any other conception of freedom that might be violated. Similarly, the vices to be resisted, "tyranny," "despotism," and "slavery," have operational relevance only with respect to Communist "slavery," "despotism," and "tyranny." Otherwise, how can one explain the zeal with which the United States defends despotism and tyranny in Iran, Saudi Arabia, Yemen, South Vietnam, and elsewhere, as opposed to the totalitarian systems in the Soviet circle, which, at least, are mitigated by accelerated cultural, economic, and technological progress? Can one maintain that life in the despotic and socially retrograde regimes of the feudal Middle East is really more free and more bountiful than in the Communist countries? If so, one must ask, "More free and bountiful *for whom?*" And when this question is answered, one begins to understand the concrete meaning of freedom.

It is indisputable that there exists a free world to defend, but it has little resemblance to the "free world" of the propaganda cliché. It is also incontestable that this free world must be defended against Soviet Communism. But there is a larger world that is neither free nor Communist, and in order that it might be defended more effectively, it should be made "free" rather than be preserved in its current state. Thus, one key to an effective status quo policy is not simply to defend it, but also to extend it.

The revolutionary ferment in the underdeveloped world is also motivated by a pursuit of "freedom" — freedom from colonial domination, foreign economic exploitation, and indigenous feudal ruling classes. The beneficiaries of the status quo in the underdeveloped countries coalesce to preserve a reactionary system from which they benefit while keeping in social bondage millions who ache for the very freedoms that the West vows to preserve, but often helps to deny.

Revolutions are not impersonal forces, but movements designed to serve the interests of distinct social groups and classes, just as a given status quo does. Movements aiming for the destruction of social systems that benefit some classes, in order to build other systems that reflect the interests of other classes, are authentic revolutionary movements. The wider the spectrum of classes that benefit from a given social order, the more "progressive" the system and the wider the ambit of "freedom" that characterizes the social system. Although a certain social system may have been established in the interests of a definite class, its class *origin* is not necessarily identical with the social interests it serves, for a social order originally designed to serve the interests of a given class may be gradually transformed into a social system from which all classes benefit.

The social status quo that should be defended, and extended, is an outgrowth of the great bourgeois revolutions that swept across Western Europe and the Thirteen Colonies in the seventeenth, eighteenth, and nineteenth centuries. These revolutions unleashed invigorating and innovating forces that fashioned a distinct civilization or ideosocial system whose benefits were diffused among all classes in society, transcending those of the bourgeoisie, or middle class, whose values and aspirations have become not merely the values of a particular nation, but those of an entire community of states we call the Western world. The middle-class social orders of the West are a system with a certain fluid, dynamic equilibrium of social, economic, and political power. The more the class interests of the social class that brought the order into being is transcended, the more "classless" the society becomes, in the sense that all classes of society become gradually "bourgeosified" as they adopt the middle-class values. In some countries, notably France and Italy, where the diffusion of interests has been fragmentary, class distinctions prevail, as the working class is denied the opportunity to become "bourgeois." Hence the substantial support that the Communist Party of each of these countries enjoys.

The revolutions that are imminent or temporarily arrested in Latin America, the Middle East, and Africa, as well as those already consummated or in the process of stabilization, are essentially a resumption of the great revolutionary flood unleashed by the French and American revolutions. Such revolutions were aborted in Eastern Europe by Soviet Communism, and arrested in Asia, Africa, and Latin America by the intrusion of Western colonialism and the unholy alliance between Western capitalism and local feudal classes in Latin America and Asia. In the African regions south of the Sahara, most of which were tribal, preliterate and even prefeudal in character, feudalism was arrested, and a landowning aristocracy did not take shape at all. The colonial authority moved in and, where European settlement was possible, white colonists became surrogates for a landowning aristocracy. This situation led to the development of a caste system rather than a class social order, a development that reached its consummate evolution in South Africa, and, to a lesser degree, in Kenya, the Congo, Southern Rhodesia, and the Portuguese colonies. In Central America and in the Caribbean area, large foreign-owned latifundian enterprises further complicated the socioeconomic system. In general, a symbiotic relationship, which still persists, was established between foreign investors and the local landowning classes. Both groups had a common interest in frustrating the emergence of an indigenous capitalist class; the landowners were afraid that a powerful capitalist class would threaten their dominant power position, and foreign economic interests feared local competition.

Consequently, the development of the middle class was first arrested and then reshaped within the socioeconomic mold created by the alliance between the local landowners and the foreign economic interests. There emerged a new type of middle class — a class whose social locus of power was not material wealth or ownership of factories, but the possession of special skills and the ability to perform certain functions — a group that might be called the bureaucratic intelligentsia. Thus, the European middle class, which created a new civilization in Europe and the United States from which all classes now benefit, aided in the preservation of feudal despotism and barbarism in the underdeveloped world and, indeed, intensified the exploitation of the population.

The distinguishing characteristic of an ideosocial system is to be found in the equilibrium of power that has been established among the social classes. The distribution of power among these classes can vary considerably, from the extreme of the Marxist-Leninist image of a "ruling class," which remains a valid approximation of social reality in many of the underdeveloped countries, to an informal graduated structure of power in which different classes share in the distribution of power, not necessarily in equal proportions, but usually in a structural hierarchy that is, to a greater or lesser degree, mobile and dynamic.

A given ideosocial system might also be defined in terms of the social class that constitutes the center of gravity in the system, whether it is the "ruling class," the most powerful class, the most numerous class, or the social class that acts as a bond between the social groups above and below it. Within this context, the ideological status quo the West is committed to defend is the middle-class social order, which is the dominant, but not universal, social system outside the Soviet orbit. A middle-class social system is not necessarily conterminous with a capitalist economic order, but includes "socialist" states like the Nordic countries, Great Britain, and others as well. In these countries, public ownership of economic enterprises is carried out by the middle classes, who continue to provide the social and political leadership in their countries. These countries are usually described as "democratic-socialist" systems, but they could more properly be called "middle-class socialist" systems, as opposed to the proletarian-socialist systems within the Soviet orbit. While it is true that the former are democratic and the latter authoritarian, the "socialist" systems emerging in the underdeveloped countries are also "middle class" in character, but nondemocratic. The fundamental factor is the character of the system rather than the political or economic forms by which the pivotal class exercises its power and radiates its influence.

Any ideosocial system allows considerable latitude for variation in institutions, processes, and social equilibrium. As a general rule, the more mature the system, the more variegated the internal mutations and permutations become; the newer the system, the more rigid and uniform it tends to be. In mature ideosocial systems, whose dominance has long been unchallenged, internal variations and differences are exaggerated and appear to be fundamentally incompatible until confronted with the challenge of a totally new ideosocial system.

Concepts like "democracy," "freedom," and "authoritarianism" have relevance only when they relate to a given ideosocial system, which inevitably provides their substantive definition and operational character. Therefore, authoritarian and democratic systems within a common ideosocial order are more congenial to each other than to their counterparts in another ideosocial framework, and dichotomies between "dictatorships" and "democracies," or "free systems" and "slave orders" are superficial and deceptive. The current struggle between East and West is neither a struggle between "democracy" and "despotism," nor between "freedom" and "slavery." It is a more profound struggle between ideosocial systems whose substantive definitions of common platitudes like "justice," "freedom," "democracy," "peace," and "justice," are intrinsically incompatible because their reference points are two conflicting social equilibriums.

In the revolutionary transfer of power from one class to another, the new ruling class may perpetuate itself, or it may create conditions in which class rule is transformed into a distinct culture and way of life whose social and ethical values are diffused and imparted to all classes in society. This enables a class civilization to assume political forms ranging from democracy to despotism, and economic orders ranging from "rugged individualism" to a wide measure of public ownership. It is neither the political nor the economic system that imparts to a system its distinctive flavor, but rather the class origin of its way of life. Soviet society represents a proletarian culture, not because the proletariat rules, but because the values and goals of the proletariat have become the values and goals of society as a whole.

An effective status quo policy consequently depends upon a clear definition of the status quo, of which an ideological, rather than geographical, definition appears to be least ambiguous and most defensible morally, militarily, and psychologically. Furthermore, such a definition imparts both consistency and uniformity over a wide range of possibilities. A status quo policy defined in this manner would be dynamic rather than static and would aim to preserve middle-class rule wherever it exists and to support its rise to power in the residual feudal communities wherever it does not exist; each middle class, however, must select the political and economic systems that it considers most appropriate for the stabilization of its authority.

Since, in most of the residual feudal countries of the world, the indigenous middle class has already come to power, or is spontaneously being catapulted in that direction, the question of outside imposition is not involved. The West is not foisting middle-class rule upon the emerging countries; this is taking place spontaneously. Indeed, the greatest danger is that the West will intervene to thwart middle-class revolutions and support the privileged position of the landowning classes. This policy, instead of supporting the ideological status quo, in fact subverts it. The most reliable instrument for supporting a middle-class ideosocial order is the middle class itself. Instead of relying upon a rising revolutionary middle class, which is bound to come to power and which would contribute to the stabilization of an expanding middle-class international system, American policy undermines the status quo by thwarting the aspirations of the middle classes. This forces their orientation toward the main reservoir of social revolution, the Soviet Union.

In analyzing the complex revolutionary patterns in the underdeveloped world, a modified class analysis is likely to be more accurate and, therefore, to offer a sounder foundation for policy than would an analysis within the context of categories like "poverty," "ignorance," "misery," and "hunger," or irrelevant platitudes like "freedom versus slavery" and "democracy versus dictatorship." Since the fundamental ideological issues have been more or less resolved in the United States and Western Europe (except in France, Italy, Spain, and Portugal) into a broad ideological consensus, Americans lose sight of the fact that, in the underdeveloped world, the most immediate and pressing issues to be resolved are concerned with the fundamental nature of the social order itself.

Thus, in the underdeveloped world, leaders and intellectuals analyze social and political issues in terms of class categories, not because they are Marxists, but because the social and political realities of a world searching for an ideological consensus can be better understood and analyzed in these terms. In many Middle Eastern and Latin American countries, approximations of the Marxist conception of a "ruling class" are realities, not figments of the Soviet imagination. For millions, class conflict and the exploitation of classes in the underdeveloped world are a real experience.

American society has gradually "bourgeosified" into a quasi-classless society. Class categories as tools of social and political analysis have become suspect and, as they have become increasingly irrelevant to the American social scene, have fallen into disrepute. A vast vacuum in the sphere of social analysis has been partially filled in recent years by intellectual euphemisms like "interest groups" and "elites." These words are valuable analytical instruments, but they are even more valuable when developed within the broader framework of social classes of which they are subgroups.

One of the great advantages of the Soviet analytical system is that it has been allowed to establish a virtual monopoly on class analysis. Yet, classes, class conflict, and class analysis were not invented, discovered, or contrived by Lenin or Marx. In our own constitutional and political history, references to classes — ruling and otherwise — to class conflict, and so on, are profuse and varied in the writings of Alexander Hamilton, John Adams, James Madison, John C. Calhoun, and others. What happened is that Marxists effectively united a valid and reputable system of social analysis with a disreputable and feared prognosis, and as a result of guilt by association, the respectability of class analysis was ideologically tarnished.

Yet, it should be obvious that a class analysis can be used to stabilize and preserve the status quo just as it is used to disrupt and upset it, a point that was recognized but rejected by both Marx and Lenin. Instead, the Marxist view that a class analysis inevitably supported a revolutionary upheaval was accepted in the West. What has happened, in effect, is that we have become the unwitting victims of a disease often ascribed to the Soviet leaders, whereby we automatically deny the existence of the realities that revolt us, accepting myths as reality simply because it would be most congenial if they were true. However, if the West is effectively to rebut the Soviet challenge, it can no longer enjoy the luxury of denying what exists in many underdeveloped countries: a fierce class conflict and the existence of systems like those of Iran, Saudi Arabia, Yemen, and some Latin American countries, which have living counterparts of the Marxist caricature of the "ruling class."

The social structure of the underdeveloped countries and the role of the revolutionary bourgeoisie vary from area to area. These variations, although important to the understanding of a local situation, do not undermine the essential common bonds between these social structures. Even more striking is the almost uniform character of the emergent revolutionary middle class, irrespective of its geographical location or the cultural environment from which it emerged.

The revolutionary bourgeoisie in underdeveloped countries is distinguished from its European prototype in a number of particulars that obscure its essentially middle-class character. In general, the revolutionary bourgeoisie in some Latin American countries is closest to the European prototype, while that of the African territories is farthest removed. The bourgeoisie in the Middle East adheres more closely to the European pattern than does the bourgeoisie in Southeast Asia.

The primary reason for variations of the revolutionary bourgeoisie from its European prototype is historical and chronological. The West European bourgeoisie was an original social formation; that is, it developed spontaneously within the womb of feudal society and, hence, was the original middle class and the prototype of all others. It was, in the first place, an entrepreneurial and property-holding class. The revolutionary bourgeoisie in underdeveloped countries, on the other hand, is an imitative class and is predominantly a nonentrepreneurial and non-property-owning class. It is, in effect, a secondary proliferation from the bourgeoisie, but its proliferation was not a response to the existence of a native property-owning bourgeoisie, but a response to a foreign capital-owning class.

The main component of the middle class, its revolutionary core, is the bureaucratic intelligentsia. In Western Europe, this was a secondary emanation from the property-owning bourgeoisie, but in underdeveloped countries it was the primary component of the middle class, which assumed prominence in the absence of a strong indigenous capitalist class. As a social group, the bureaucratic intelligentsia includes the various service and professional categories that developed to service the local aristocracy, the property-owning bourgeoisie, and the civil servants, teachers, lawyers, professors, engineers, doctors, professional military officers (in the middle grades), writers, artists, and other white-collar and professional vocations. The status of the bureaucratic intelligentsia was determined not by ownership of land or other property, but by the role it played in society.

In the underdeveloped countries, the bureaucratic intelligentsia serves much the same function and enjoys a comparable social status, but it grew up primarily to service foreign and alien enterprises rather than local higher classes. Consequently, it is even more alienated from its society than was the East European bureaucratic intelligentsia. Because of the closer social proximity of the revolutionary bourgeoisie in underdeveloped countries to the bureaucratic intelligentsia in Eastern Europe, its behavior and aspirations coincide more with that historical group than with the Western European bourgeoisie. It should also be mentioned that the Bolshevik Revolution was forged in the crucibles of this component of the middle class and hence Soviet leaders are probably more aware of the ambiguous and alienated character of this group and more prepared to exploit it.

Since the revolutionary elites in underdeveloped countries fail to meet all the criteria of what constitutes a "middle class" or "bourgeoisie" in the West European historical sense, their middle-class character is rejected in some quarters. Given the unique character of their emergence, the revolutionary elites in underdeveloped countries nevertheless qualify as authentic, if unstabilized and historically distorted, middle classes for the following reasons:

1. The functions that these elites perform in society are traditional middle-class functions.

2. The primary ideological motivation of the revolutionary elites is *nationalism* as an end in itself. Socialist norms, whether Marxist-inspired or not, are acceptable not as ends in themselves, but as more efficient means for consolidating and strengthening the emerging national state. Nationalism is both European and bourgeois in origin and conception. As an ideological norm, it is compatible with Communism. The fact that the Soviet Union has used both nationalism and transnationalist regionalism as instruments for the achievement of its own ends should not obscure the fact that, whereas for Moscow, nationalism is a means and socialism an end, for the revolutionary elites, nationalism is the end, and socialism the means. In the economic sector, the socialism of the underdeveloped countries is, in reality, state capitalism rather than socialism.

3. The revolutionary elite in underdeveloped countries takes its aspirations and values from the European middle classes whom it imitates and by whom it has been educated. As an imitative middle class, it seeks the social approval of European middle classes, and much of its resentment may stem from its feeling of rejection. It does not imitate the classes in the Soviet satellites, nor does it elevate the values of the proletarian class as objectives of national or social policy, as is done in the Communist world.

4. Revolutionary elites do not reject religious norms and principles as guidelines for the organization of society, although they do reject some of the more reactionary and stultifying institutions and attitudes

of religion that sprang up to preserve the sanctity of the old order. On the contrary, in the same way that its role became transformed by the bourgeoisie in Western Europe, religion may become an instrument for stabilizing and sanctifying the new social order.

The most imposing psychological barrier to Western acceptance of the revolutionary elite as a middle class is the fact that it is not a property-owning class — the traditional form of the Western bourgeoisie. Yet, it should be recognized that the peculiar conditions under which the underdeveloped countries emerged made the development of an indigenous property-owning bourgeois class largely impossible. However, wherever the possibilities presented themselves, as in Syria, India, parts of Latin America, and scattered locations elsewhere, an entrepreneurial middle class did emerge alongside the bureaucratic-intelligentsia component. Now that the class structure of the underdeveloped countries has assumed shape, it cannot be expected that they will introduce artificial measures solely to create a property-owning middle class to conform to an abstract ideological norm.

Although centered in the social structure, the bureaucratic intelligentsia is alienated from both the foreign capitalists and its own land-owning aristocracy. Poorly paid, without property, and with little access to power or opportunity for upward mobility, the bureaucratic intelligentsia thrives in a suffocating atmosphere of frustration and resentment. As the native class in a society that possesses a virtual monopoly of the technical, professional, and organizational skills, it is denied political power, social status, and material rewards. Its frustrations intensify as its own estimate of its importance in society becomes aggrandized; its expectations and aspirations consequently accelerate and spiral upward in revolutionary passion. As the most articulate social concentration of resentment and frustration, it sees that the only barriers between it and the pinnacle of power and prestige are a small foreign capitalist class and an enervated and degenerate landowning class. Since members of the bureaucratic intelligentsia have the nearest access to the instruments of violence, it is not surprising that, in a number of cases — Egypt, Iraq, Sudan, South Korea — the leadership of this class has come from the middle ranks of the professional military.

Not sufficiently large to carry through and sustain a revolutionary transformation by itself, the revolutionary bourgeoisie unfurls the banner of nationalism and mobilizes the working class and the landless peasantry against the universally hated foreign capitalists and landowning classes. Where it has not yet come to power, it seeks power; where it has come to power, it seeks to solidify its control against the former ruling groups and to expand its power through modernization and industrialization. In pursuit of the first objective, it expropriates the landowners and nationalizes foreign enterprises. In pursuit of the second objective, it enhances the national power of the state through modernization and industrialization, based mainly on public ownership and centrally directed planning, and this, in turn, enhances its own power and prestige. Since the middle class controls the state, the expansion of state-owned enterprises automatically extends its power as a class. Thus, the immediate objective of the revolutionary middle class in power is to entrench itself permanently by adjusting to socio-economic order to its advantage. It also endeavors to demonstrate to the working class and peasantry that it merits the right to rule as the most progressive and socially responsible class; that its goals, values, and aspirations are as worthy of emulation and universalization as those of the nation or society as a whole. This was perceptively recognized by the aging Stalin during one of his shrewdest and most enigmatic moments when, at the Nineteenth Party Congress, he anticipated that the middle class would fail in this endeavor and called upon the Communists to take possession of the political symbols of the bourgeoisie:

> Formerly, the bourgeoisie permitted itself to be "liberal" and defended democratic freedoms, thus creating popularity for itself among the people. Now no trace remains of liberalism. There is no so-called "personal freedom." . . . The principle of equality among peoples and nations has been crushed and has been replaced by the principle of full rights for the exploiting minority and no rights at all for the exploited majority of citizens. The banner of bourgeois democratic rights has been thrown overboard. I think that this banner must be raised by you, the representatives of the Communist and democratic parties, and must be carried forward by you if you want to rally around you the majority of the people. There is no one else to raise it. . . . Formerly the bourgeoisie was considered the head of a nation. It defended the rights and independence of a nation for dollars. The banner of national independence and of national sovereignty has been thrown overboard. There is no doubt that this banner will have to be raised by you, representatives of Communist and democratic parties, and carried forward if you want to become the leading force of the nation. There is no one else to raise it.[3]

When the revolutionary middle class comes to power in under-developed countries it is extremely shaky because it possesses no material economic foundation to give it permanence. This results in its social instability and ideological ambivalence. This new class is capable of either establishing a new social status quo or, in the interests of preserving itself as a ruling group, abdicating its middle-class outlook, undergoing unilateral communization, and continuing the revolution in more radical directions. In the last instance, it automatically subverts its own character as a middle class and transforms itself into a bureaucratic ruling class, willing to serve any ideosocial system that will ensure its permanence as a collection of ruling individuals rather than a social class. This is precisely what current Soviet thinking about the future of the "national bourgeoisie" contemplates. It is a departure from the orthodox Leninist-Stalinist position on the inherent treachery of the "national bourgeoisie" still subscribed to by Mao Tse-tung.

[3] *Pravda*, October 15, 1952.

The alliance forged between foreign economic interests and the landowning classes of the Middle East and Latin America, and the support of this alliance by the West, threaten to divert the middle-class revolutions into the arms of the Soviet Union. Soviet leaders are prepared to exploit this alliance in accordance with theoretical formulations that have been renovated and refined for more than four decades, ever since Lenin laid down the principal lines of analysis for exploiting revolutionary movements in underdeveloped countries. His dicta have since been modified, renovated, refined, and adapted to various areas under a variety of circumstances, but the important point is that the Soviet leaders, for more than forty years, have had at their disposal a systematically articulated theoretical framework for analyzing and exploiting underdevelopment.

The characteristic feature of imperialism [Lenin observed in 1920] is that the whole world, as we see, is at present divided into a large number of oppressed nations and an insignificant number of oppressing nations possessing colossal wealth and powerful military forces. The overwhelming majority of the population of the world . . . about 70 per cent of the population of the world belongs to the oppressed nations, which are either in a state of direct colonial dependence or belong to the outlying colonial states such as Persia, Turkey, and China, or else, after being conquered by the armies of a big imperialist power, have been forced into dependence upon it by treaties. . . . We argued about whether it would be correct, in principle and in theory, to declare that the Communist International and the Communist Parties should support the bourgeois-democratic movement in backward countries. As a result . . . we unanimously decided to speak of the national revolutionary movement instead of the "bourgeois-democratic" movement. There is not the slightest doubt that every nationalist movement can only be a bourgeois-democratic movement. . . . It would be utopian to think that proletarian parties, if indeed they can arise in such countries, could pursue Communist tactics and a Communist policy in these countries without having definite relations with the peasant movement and without effectively supporting it. But it was argued that if we speak about the bourgeois-democratic movement all distinction between reformist and revolutionary movements will be obliterated; whereas in recent times this distinction has been fully and clearly revealed in the backward and colonial countries, for the imperialist bourgeoisie is trying with all its might to implant the reformist movement also among the oppressed nations. A certain rapprochement has been brought about between the bourgeoisie of the exploiting countries and those of the colonial countries, so that very often, in the majority of cases, perhaps, where the bourgeoisie of the oppressed countries does support the national movement, it simultaneously works in harmony with the nationalist bourgeoisie, i.e., it joins the latter in fighting against all revolutionary movements and revolutionary classes. . . . We came to the conclusion that the only correct thing to do was to take this distinction into consideration and nearly everywhere to substitute the term "bourgeois-democratic." The meaning of this change is that we Communists should, and will, support bourgeois liberation movements in the colonial countries only when these movements are really revolutionary, when the representatives of these movements do not hinder us in training and organizing the peasants and broad masses of the exploited in a revolutionary spirit, even if these countries must fight against the reformist bourgeoisie, among whom we include the heroes of the Second International. Reformist parties already exist in colonial countries, and sometimes their representatives call themselves Social-Democrats and Socialists. . . . There can be no argument about the fact that the proletariat of the advanced countries can and must assist the backward toiling masses, and that the development of the backward countries can emerge from its present stage when the victorious proletariat of the Soviet republics stretches out a helping hand to these masses.[4]

The Cuban revolution offers entirely new possibilities because it illustrates an unforeseen metamorphosis of a "bourgeois-democratic" revolution being transformed from the top into a proletarian revolution by a national bourgeoisie, not as an elite acting as the historical agents of the proletariat, but as a group carrying out an act of volition in response to external threats and attractions. Although Castro has declared himself a Marxist-Leninist, called his regime a "socialist" system, and defined his ultimate purpose as the fulfillment of Marxist-Leninist ideological and social norms, these brazen and unilateral proclamations have yet to be recognized as acceptable in Moscow, since they contradict all previously explored paths to the Communist revolution. Just as Mao Tse-tung claims to have executed a "bourgeois-democratic" revolution without a bourgeoisie, so Castro claims to have executed a proletarian revolution with the help of neither the proletariat nor the Cuban Communist Party.

In his zeal for orthodoxy and acceptance into the Communist confraternity, Castro has implicitly condemned Fidelismo as a manifestation of the "cult of personality," and claims to have shifted to "collective leadership." The leaders of the old-line Communist Party, who played no role in the revolutionary process itself, have been assigned the mission of reorganizing various Cuban revolutionary organizations into a Marxist-Leninist party. To what extent Castro still remains master of the situation and the ultimate fount for delegation of authority to orthodox Communist leaders remains unclear, but it is certain that until such time as Castro no longer possesses the power unilaterally to renounce his latter-day conversion to Marxism-Leninism, he will continue to remain an eccentric leader of an enigmatic and curious bourgeois revolution. The character of this revolution continues to baffle Soviet ideologists, who had to invent a completely new stage to accommodate it — the "national democracy," as distinguished from either "bourgeois democracy" or "peoples' democracy."

The curious evolution of the Cuban revolution has already provoked ideological anguish in the Sino-Soviet bloc, for if the Cuban revolution does metamorphose completely into a Marxist-Leninist society, it will represent the first successful completion of an experiment

[4] V. I. Lenin, *Selected Works* (New York: International Publishers, 1943), X, 239–41.

begun in the early twenties with the Kuomintang revolution in China — the take-over from above of a middle-class revolution by the Communist Party. Mao Tse-tung, stung by the Chiang Kai-shek affair, adheres to the view that the two-phase revolution in underdeveloped countries can safely be executed only if the entire dual-phase operation is conducted under the leadership of the Communist Party, and that it is utopian to expect a bourgeois class to carry out a Communist revolution. He remains convinced that the revolutionary bourgeoisie will arrest the revolutionary movement once the anti-imperialist and antifeudal phase of the revolution has been consummated, and that it will seek to anchor itself as the ruling class in a bourgeois social order. This view, which is in accordance with the orthodox Leninist-Stalinist strategy of revolution in colonial and semicolonial countries, maintains that once the bourgeois revolution has been completed, the Communist Party should prepare a proletarian upheaval against the bourgeoisie. The Soviet view seems to be that it is now possible that the revolutionary bourgeoisie in underdeveloped countries, seeing the balance of power shifting toward the Soviet orbit, may, in its own *national,* if not *class,* interests, carry the revolution forward into its second phase, thus obviating the necessity for organizing a Communist Party and a Communist revolution from scratch.

Soviet leaders clearly perceive the ambivalent character of the revolutionary middle class. These elites simultaneously pose a threat to the middle-class status quo and create an opportunity to help preserve it. These revolutionary middle classes have the capability and the determination to come to power. In some countries, they will come to power with the West or without the West. The direction they take and the ideological alliances they forge will depend upon how skillfully the situation is analyzed and acted upon by Soviet and Western leaders, and how effectively the social forces working for or against the ideological status quo are calculated and manipulated.

At this critical juncture in history, the unparalleled success of Soviet foreign policy during the past four decades challenges the Western world to identify the forces agitating the underdeveloped world, to chart their direction, and to work with them, so that the emerging world will conform to an expanded middle-class ideosocial system rather than to a Communist universalism. Western policy must align itself with the popular aspirations of the middle-class nationalist forces in the underdeveloped countries, not out of sheer sentimentality, but out of absolute necessity. Either the Western world as a civilization — not as a hegemonic empire or series of empires — must universalize itself, its values, and its institutions, or it will inevitably shrink, shrivel up, and pass into the ashbins of history as another great civilization unable to accommodate itself to the demands and expectations of its aroused, disaffected, and discontented populations. Certainly there is no compulsion for the Western world to sow the seeds of its own destruction, as if in response to Communist expectations, by supporting decrepit and doomed feudal ruling classes all over the world.

Since the very existence of a great civilization or ideosocial system is at stake, the pressures of powerful interest groups must be resisted, since the issues transcend the narrow interests of those attempting to preserve the status quo. Increasingly, the national interests of the states of the Western community are colliding with the specific interests that powerful international corporations, consortiums, and cartels have in underdeveloped countries. These groups sometimes convey the impression that they "own" Western civilization and that, unless their position is preserved intact, Western civilization will be undermined. Until the necessary distinctions can be made, and until these groups recognize the necessity of diffusing part of their power and wealth to retain the remainder, the United States and the West will continue to back reactionary feudal regimes — which invariably turn out to be exceptionally congenial to those who have lucrative investments and enterprises in their countries — against revolutionary middle classes under the increasingly untenable and transparent device of supporting "anti-Communists." This point is supported in the following excerpt from an article by Peter F. Drucker in *Harper's:*

> The traditional tools of "foreign aid" — money and trained men — will never do the job until *Latin Americans* face up to the tough things which *they* alone can do: collect taxes from the rich and clean out the sinecure jobs in swollen government services; push through land reform and cheap mass housing; stop subsidizing the wrong crops; get rid of the pettifogging regulations . . . and say "no" to the blackmail of the generals who habitually threaten to overthrow a regime unless they get a few more unneeded jet planes, tanks, or destroyers. [Italics added.]

One must inevitably ask *which* Latin Americans must face up to the tough problems enumerated? Who must "collect taxes from the rich . . . push through land reform . . . say 'no' to the . . . generals"? Obviously, the advice cannot be directed to those Latin Americans who have neither power nor property, unless they are being asked to conduct a revolution. It is this form of stereotyped and ritualized impersonal exhortation that serves to hide and distort social realities. Unless one deals in terms of social classes and elites, it is a mystery why taxes are not collected from the rich, why land reform is not being pushed through, why the wrong crops are being subsidized, why no one will say "no" to the generals; but once it is recognized that "they" refers to a concrete ruling class being asked to execute measures against its own interests, it becomes quite clear why these obviously reasonable objectives (in American context) are not being carried out.

In dealing with underdeveloped countries, it must be recognized that "the people" are subdivided into concrete social groups, classes, and elites, each with its own interests and aspirations. There are people with power and property and those without; people who are satisfied with the status quo and those who are not; people who have "freedom" and enjoy "justice," and those who labor under "tyranny" and "injustice." Impersonal exhortations to "the people," as if social classes did not exist or flourish, are disingenuous self-deceptions that obscure the real situation and result in incorrect analyses. If the "people" refuse to respond to the voice of reason, the attitude of most Americans is to shrug their shoulders and say that if "they" refuse to do anything to help themselves, nothing can be done for them. To say that social problems are insoluble, however, means making the Communists the only agents that can change an intolerable status quo. The Communists, too, appeal to the "people," not in the abstract but to certain social classes. They do not exhort them to reform their governments, which they are not in a position to do, but call upon them to revolt, which they can do. If ruling classes in underdeveloped countries refuse to carry out reforms from above, the social momentum does not simply grind to a halt. It assumes a new dimension — the dimension of a revolutionary upheaval from below.

An effective policy for defending and extending the Western status quo must, therefore, include strategies that can be executed where ruling classes prove obstinate. Otherwise, the West will be confronted with the prospect of supporting ruling classes that are doomed, thus inescapably earning the animosity of the rising revolutionary middle classes determined to assume power. The development of a concerted strategy for defending and extending the middle-class status quo necessitates a realistic appraisal of class relationships and forces in each country, as well as an appreciation of the aspirations, powers, and future of given classes. The United States is not interested in manufacturing revolutions where they do not exist, nor in supporting those that are manipulated and directed by Communists, but it must be interested in why revolutions are taking place, and the directions of their movements.

Assessing revolutions and their characters is a tricky business and requires considerable caution as well as boldness, as the occasion may demand. In any given underdeveloped country and, indeed, in any social system, the population can generally be divided into three great divisions according to the attitude each bears to the social order of which they are all a part: One sector of the population is committed to the status quo and benefits so greatly from it that it is willing to fight and die in its defense. (The issue of patriotism is irrelevant to the status quo in underdeveloped countries and thus cannot be manipulated as a symbol by a regime under attack.) The second group is determined to overthrow the status quo and is willing to risk any sacrifice to bring about its destruction. And the third group comprises those who are indifferent and unwilling to risk their lives either to preserve or overturn the status quo. As long as the forces of the status quo can mobilize more power and support than the forces of revolution, the social order remains stabilized. But social systems are not static, and in the underdeveloped world the great reservoir of humanity that falls into the indifferent category can be stimulated into revolutionary action if its level of dissatisfaction is raised or its expectations for a better life are aroused by political agitation. Once this reservoir of indifference furnishes recruits for the forces arrayed against the status quo, a revolutionary situation is created and its momentum rapidly accelerates.

Communist agitation and propaganda are designed to arouse such expectations among indifferent populations. The successes of Communist propaganda are due not so much to superior techniques and methods as to their ability to create expectations that excite indifferent populations to risk their lives for a better future. These expectations need to be generated only among a relatively small number of people to tilt the internal balance of power against the status quo in favor of the forces of revolution. The great mass of the population can continue to languish in indifference. That is why 180,000 well-trained South Vietnamese troops are no match for 20,000 Viet Cong guerrillas, and why 8,000 ragged Pathet Lao troops can repeatedly make a Royal Laotian Army nearly three times its size turn tail and run, although this Army is trained, equipped, and directed by American military-assistance units. The Pathet Lao and the Viet Cong are imbued with a dedication to overturn the status quo more intense than the dedication of the armies of the Laotian and South Vietnamese governments to defend it, since the latter are drawn mainly from the indifferent segments unwilling to risk their lives for a status quo from which they derive little or no benefit.

In defending the status quo, the United States can pursue three basic strategies as a consequence of a class analysis. It can (1) continue the symbiotic relationship with existing feudal regimes and support them against external attack and internal upheaval to the bitter end, with full knowledge of the limitations of such a strategy; (2) support "revolutions from above" carried out by existing ruling classes or elements from within them; or (3) abandon feudal classes to their historical fate and support the rising middle-class nationalist movements against internal feudalism while mitigating their assaults on Western economic interests.

The first strategy has been the preferred policy of the United States. It does not support an ideological status quo, but rather upholds any anti-Communist social order anywhere, no matter what its ideology, political form, or economic system. This usually takes the form of safeguarding these regimes against external attack and providing assistance against internal revolutions by supplying a margin of power that the forces of the local status quo cannot furnish internally to quash a revolutionary threat. This means supporting existing regimes and landowning classes in their symbiotic relation with foreign economic interests and making a purely military response to a social situation. This is the strategy that failed in Iraq, and is still being executed in Iran, South Vietnam, and Laos. It is a strategy being readied for use in Latin America, particularly in the Caribbean littoral. The most conservative of all possible status quo policies and likely to be the most ineffective, it receives its greatest impetus from powerful economic interests in the United States who are reluctant to permit any changes in the local status quo lest their interests be adversely affected. In areas of substantial European settlement, similar pressures are exerted by the colonists of other Western countries. In some countries still slumbering in the Middle Ages, like Yemen and Saudi Arabia, where revolutionary ferment has not yet developed to any great extent, the existing symbiotic relation can be left virtually intact, without any immediate danger, although it must be recognized that, sooner or later, a revolutionary middle class will assume shape.

A few caveats should be issued in connection with this strategy. The first is that a disintegrating feudal regime being shored up by foreign assistance against indigenous and spontaneous revolutionary upheaval must be distinguished from a status quo regime being unseated by revolutionary forces supplied by outside intervention. The latter is not a true revolutionary situation and there a policy of military intervention on behalf of the existing regime can be successful. One must not, however, naïvely mistake a genuine internal upheaval, no matter how initially stimulated, with one supported externally, since the same response will not succeed in both cases. There is real danger that intervention will give an insurrection the character of war against foreign domination and imperialism, and thus broaden the social base of the revolution, rather than narrow it. Indifferent segments of the population are likely to be provoked into joining the insurrection, and the intervening forces are then sucked into a never-ending spiral of intensified revolutionary activity. Consequently, it is of the utmost importance not to indulge in frivolous fabrication and self-deception solely to justify intervention. If the intervention fails, it becomes necessary to give false reasons for its failure, and self-deception builds upon self-deception until rational and realistic analysis becomes impossible. Although the population of the intervening country may be easily and successfully fooled into believing that intervention is justified because the revolution is being supported from the outside, it is certain that neither the population of the country in revolutionary ferment nor the population of the country accused of outside intervention will be deceived.[5] In any event, an interventionist status quo policy is likely to fail as a long-range policy, since it does not contribute to the expansion of a middle-class ideosocial system, but merely preserves feudal social systems.

The strategy of "revolution from above," however, appears to be emerging as a possible American policy, although in a somewhat pragmatic, nebulous, and not completely coherent manner. Historically, the "revolution from above" is the most effective and reliable method for bringing about an alteration in the social structure resulting in a more

---

[5] A further danger involved in intervention is the real possibility that intervention against a purely internal revolutionary insurrection may in fact provoke foreign intervention on behalf of revolution. While this may serve to document the charge of outside intervention, it may also be a cure worse than the disease. Khrushchev, at the Twenty-second Party Congress, threatened precisely this type of counteraction.

or less peaceful, but nonetheless fundamental, transformation of the social order. This strategy requires that existing ruling classes, or the most perceptive and intelligent elements within them, initiate necessary alterations in the internal balance of forces so that the forces of the status quo may be enhanced by giving hitherto indifferent elements in the population a stake in the reconstructed social order. Thus, while a revolution from below seeks to arouse expectations of a better life among indifferent elements of the population, "revolution from above" provides them with a material stake in preserving the revised status quo. In a mathematical sense, the only changes that need be introduced are those that will continuously maintain a social balance favorable to the status quo and opposed to those dedicated to destroying it. When skillfully executed, a "revolution from above" can even recruit supporters of the status quo from the revolutionary elements by providing them with a stake in the system meaningful enough to persuade them to desert the insurrectionary forces.

A "revolution from above" should be distinguished from a *coup d'état* or a palace revolution, in which personalities and cliques from within the existing governing class displace one another in a game of musical chairs, leaving the basic economic and social substructure of power intact. True "revolutions from above" result in a redistribution of social and economic power; the existing ruling class shares and diffuses its power and rewards with the emergent classes, eventually consummating their social fusion. The most successful continuous "revolution from above" has been that of the British, where successive ruling classes have been the most effective renovating and progressive social groups in British society, always introducing the changes necessary to divert revolutionary upheaval. As a consequence, over an extended period of time, there has been a continuous co-option and fusion between ruling classes and emerging classes. Thus, today some ruling families in a British middle-class socialist society can boast of ancestors who belonged to a ruling feudal nobility.

Not all attempts at "revolution from above" have been successful. Successful "revolutions from above" are delicate operations and can be safely carried out only if several prior conditions exist or can be created. The first requirement is that at least a part of the ruling class must be sufficiently perceptive to realize that the status quo cannot be maintained unaltered. Second, it must be prepared psychologically to share power and rewards with the rising and challenging social class from below, and to accept the risks and consequences of this redistribution of power. Third, it must be able to appraise unerringly the social forces, internal and external, in favor of both revolution and the status quo, and to introduce changes at any given moment just sufficient constantly to shift the balance in favor of a changing status quo. Miscalculation on the side of too little change merely weakens the status quo, whereas changes that are excessive are likely to stimulate expectations that cannot be fulfilled rapidly enough. In either instance, a revolutionary upheaval from below is apt to be provoked.

282 THE COLD WAR

In countries where foreign investments are substantial, these external interests must also agree to share in the distribution of whatever economic and social power they command. Sharing may include the partial nationalization of their enterprises, a reduction of profits, an increase in royalties, better working conditions and opportunities for employees, and a greater sensitivity to local needs. In some instances, the foreign investors may have to accept eventual total nationalization or be prepared to undertake new enterprises that may be nationalized after an agreed-upon profit has been made.

"Revolutions from above" are likely to be dynamic and protracted affairs, but under existing conditions in underdeveloped countries, they would result in the gradual transformation of a neofeudal social order into a middle-class social system and would thus extend and strengthen the middle-class ideosocial system. Instead of a revolution that threatens the violent displacement in power of one class by another, a "revolution from above" would bring about a gradual fusion of the old aristocracy with the rising middle class and stabilize society as a whole.

The Alliance for Progress program announced by the Kennedy Administration is an approach to "revolution from above," but its success will depend upon the willingness of the Latin-American landowning classes to introduce the necessary changes,[6] and upon the ability of the Administration to persuade American corporations to make necessary accommodations. Unfortunately, both the landowning classes and the American business interests are likely to prefer reliance upon military intervention to prevent revolutions or to restore an overturned status quo. Yet, "revolutions from above," executed through the Alliance for Progress program, would have good chances for success in countries like Argentina, Uruguay, Brazil, Venezuela, Mexico, and Costa Rica, whose ruling classes include elements who perceive the threat and are prepared to cope with it. The strategy of "revolution from above" is not likely to succeed in Middle Eastern countries, where two middle-class revolutions have already taken place, one relatively bloodless (Egypt), and the other accompanied by savagery (Iraq). Unfortunately, the same fate awaits Iran, whose feudal landowning classes are among the most venal, corrupt, and shortsighted in the world. It is not likely, once a revolution in Iran develops its momentum, that either outside military intervention or a countercoup by the CIA will save the ruling classes of that ancient country.

[6] The narrow feudal character of Latin-American agricultural economies is demonstrated by the extreme concentration of land ownership in some countries. Whereas in Latin America as a whole, 90 per cent of the agricultural lands belong to 10 per cent of the landowners, some concentrations are even more extreme. In Guatemala, 516 farms (0.15 per cent) include 41 per cent of the farm lands; in Ecuador, 705 farms (0.17 per cent) account for 37 per cent; in Venezuela, 6,800 farms (1.69 per cent) comprise 74 per cent of the farm acreage; in Brazil, 1.6 per cent of the landowners hold 50 per cent of the agricultural lands; in Nicaragua, 362 landlords own one-third of the farm lands; in Bolivia, before land reform, 6.4 per cent of the farms constituted 92 per cent of the farm areas.

The third strategy in defense and extension of the middle-class status quo is the most radical of all, but actually it requires less positive action by the United States than either of the previous two. What it does require is an appreciative and sympathetic attitude to encourage or permit the revolutionary middle class to come to power, and aid in its stabilization. It is not required that the United States stimulate these revolutions; they are developing spontaneously in response to existing conditions. It is not necessary to intervene and give material support to such revolutions; nor need diplomatic relations be ruptured with the government in power while moral support is being expressed for the aspirations of revolutionary middle classes. But extending such moral support to revolutionary middle classes is particularly important in countries where the ruling classes are irrevocably opposed to change.

Although this strategy is the only effective strategy of defending and extending the middle-class status quo that can be pursued in many underdeveloped countries, it is likely to be the most difficult psychologically. Because of the necessity of revolutionary violence to alter the social order, a victorious revolutionary bourgeoisie will almost inevitably expropriate the landowners and destroy them as a social class, although it will not necessarily harm them physically. In some cases, depending upon the individual situation in each country, there is likely to be substantial nationalization of foreign-owned enterprises (American, in many instances), but with compensation. In countries where capitalism is not in complete disrepute or where a local capitalist class exists, localization may take place instead, whereby native capitalists are aided in buying foreign enterprises. Substantial public ownership in all countries where the revolutionary middle class comes to power is a foregone conclusion. But the "socialist" or "welfare states" that will emerge will be middle-class in character, not Soviet, and will be nationalist-socialist states, not international-socialist societies. This means that neither collectivization of agriculture nor nationalization of small business will take place. Depending upon local factors, some countries will emerge as parliamentary and democratic states, which is to be preferred; others will be authoritarian in varying degrees.

As we have seen, a policy in defense of the middle-class status quo can be based upon either encouraging and assisting *real* revolutions from above or supporting the rise of the revolutionary middle class. Both policies are defensible morally and historically, but deciding upon which method to choose in individual cases requires experienced and audacious statecraft operating within a systematic framework of social analysis. Current Soviet policy rests upon the expectation that the United States will continue to support feudal regimes and will assume a negative attitude toward middle-class revolutionary movements and bourgeois-nationalist regimes. If this expectation proves correct, the revolutionary middle classes may have no alternative but to alter the character of their revolution and shift it in a Soviet direction, transforming themselves into a bureaucratic ruling elite on the Soviet model, rather than stabilizing a middle-class revolution that will be under attack from both East and West. In the new Draft Program of the Communist Party, Khrushchev reveals both his expectations and apprehensions concerning the revolutionary role of the middle class in underdeveloped countries:

> The world is experiencing a period of stormy national-liberation revolutions. . . . Young sovereign states have arisen, or are arising, in onetime colonies or semicolonies. Their peoples have entered a new period of development. . . . But the struggle is not yet over. . . . Many of them, having established national states, are striving for economic sovereignty and durable political independence. The peoples of these formally independent countries that in reality depend on foreign monopolies politically and economically are arising to fight against imperialism and reactionary pro-imperialist regimes. . . . The extent to which the national bourgeoisie [roughly, the revolutionary middle class] will take part in the anti-imperialist and antifeudal struggle will depend in considerable measure on the solidity of the working class and peasantry. . . . The national bourgeoisie is dual in character. In modern conditions, the national bourgeoisie in those colonial, onetime colonial, and dependent countries, where it is not connected with the imperialist circles is objectively interested in accomplishing the basic tasks of an anti-imperialist and antifeudal revolution. Its progressive role and its ability to participate in the solution of pressing national problems are, therefore, not yet spent. But as the contradictions between the working people and propertied classes grow and the class struggle inside the country becomes more aggravated, the national bourgeoisie shows an increasing inclination to compromise with imperialism and domestic reaction.[7]

In areas where the revolutionary middle class meets resistance to its objectives from the West, it can utilize the implicit protection of Soviet power to transform itself into a bureaucratic ruling class ready to execute a Communist-type revolution from above — as in Cuba — which, in the Draft Program, is called National Democracy:

> In view of the present balance of world forces and the actual feasibility of powerful support on the part of the world Socialist system, the peoples of the former colonies can decide to take . . . the non-capitalist road of development. . . . This road will require concessions from the bourgeoisie, but those will be concessions on behalf of the nation. . . . Establishing and developing national democracies opens vast prospects for the peoples of the underdeveloped countries. The political basis of national democracy is a bloc of all the progressive, patriotic forces fighting to win complete national independence and broad democracy, and to consummate the anti-imperialist, antifeudal, democratic revolution.[8]

Whether the middle-class revolutions in the underdeveloped countries will establish "national democracies" as temporary way stations on the road to Communism, or whether they will establish authentic middle-class regimes that will "compromise with imperialism and domestic

[7] *Pravda,* July 30, 1961.
[8] Ibid.

reaction," to use the quaint phraseology of the Draft Program, will depend in large measure upon the reception they receive from the United States. And American reaction will, in turn, largely depend upon how we perceive the situation and identify the interests of the West with the aspirations of these revolutionary middle-class movements.

The Cuban episode demonstrates one possibility, but it should be recalled that only a few years ago both Nasser and Kassem had been given up as crypto-Communists. Similar misconceptions have been expressed about the regimes in Indonesia, Guinea, and Ghana. There is no question that repeating the prophecy that certain regimes are "going Communist" may indeed result in its fulfillment.

III THE ANALYSIS OF SOVIET BEHAVIOR
Problems and Theories

9. TEN THEORIES IN SEARCH OF REALITY: THE PREDICTION OF SOVIET BEHAVIOR

Daniel Bell

Surely, more has been written about the Russian Revolution and the ensuing forty years of Soviet rule than about any comparable episode in human history! The bibliography of items on the French Revolution occupies, it is said, one wall of the Bibliothèque Nationale. A complete bibliography on the Soviet Union — which is yet to be compiled and may never be because of the geometric rate at which it multiplies — would probably make that earlier cenotaph to scholarship shrink the way in which the earlier tombs diminished before the great complex at Karnak.

And yet, how little of this awesome output has stood the test of so short a span of time! If hell, as Thomas Hobbes once said, is truth seen too late, the road to hell must now be paved twice over with the thousands of books claiming to discover the "truth" about Russia — while the tortures of the damned are reserved for those, diplomats especially, who committed the fates of millions in the confident belief that they could predict correctly the way in which the Soviet rulers would respond.[1]

In the last ten years there has been, presumably, a new sophistica-

Reprinted from *World Politics*, April 1958, pp. 315–353. Reprinted by permission.
[1] *Pace* President Roosevelt, who wrote on the flyleaf of his personal copy of Joseph E. Davies' *Mission to Moscow*, a book which defended the authenticity of the Moscow Trials: "This book will last." Richard H. Ullman, "The Davies Mission and United States-Soviet Relations, 1937–1941," *World Politics*, IX, No. 2, January 1957, 220.

tion, and an extraordinary amount of research and writing on Soviet society, particularly in the United States. Some of this research has come from Russian defectors; most of it has been done in special institutes set up by universities under government or foundation research grants in an effort to obtain reliable knowledge about Soviet behavior. We have seen, too, the entry of new disciplines — anthropology, sociology, and psychiatry — into the study of political phenomena. In some instances these newer approaches have claimed to provide a total understanding of Soviet behavior; in others, to supplement existing explanation. So thick and heavy is this research that an outside observer, seeking to push his way through the marshes, often finds himself mired (as that wonderful Russian onomatopoeic evocation has it) in *splosh.* And one is bogged down further by the fact that much of this newer research is couched in a special jargon which owes allegiance to other modes of discourse than the common tongue. (As R. P. Blackmur has said of the literary "New Criticism," the terminology rigidifies in the course of time and the "normal pathology of a skill becomes a method, and the method a methodology.")

In this chapter, the writer has attempted a description and, in representative cases, a detailed assessment of these methodologies. This is not a "national estimate" of Russian capabilities and weaknesses, social, military, or economic, such as is made by the government's National Security Council. Nor is it a "survey" of empirical research. The writer has sought to distinguish ten approaches in social theory, each of which, despite some shading or overlap, represents a coherent judgment of Soviet behavior. It is hoped that by "reading" each against the other, some sense of the crucial differences, analytical or methodological, may emerge. Beyond that, such a reading may aid in the formulation of the two judgments which are essential in any stocktaking — namely: (1) Which theories or approaches have "stood up" in explaining events, and which have not? (2) If one were a policymaker, which research would one underwrite in the future, and why?

ENTER PIRANDELLO

Hegel once said that what was reasonable was real. Each of the theories to be discussed seems reasonable, yet not wholly real. Something may be wrong with Hegel, the theories, or both. The reader will have to be the judge.

Characterological Theories

(1) *Anthropological.* Beginning with the work of Ruth Benedict, and taken up by Linton and Kardiner, Margaret Mead, and Clyde Kluckhohn, contemporary anthropologists have developed the concept of "culture and personality." The argument is that members of a given culture share certain common, sufficiently distinct ways of handling emotional drives and regulating social conduct which form a unique life style that differs, often markedly, from the life style of other cultural

groups. The "norms" of the group specify how an individual must manage the key tensions generated in social living (i.e., attitudes to authority, frustration of impulses, aggression, etc.) and how the social controls against violation of those norms (i.e., mechanisms of guilt and shame, disposal of repressed hate, etc.) operate.

Margaret Mead,[2] Geoffrey Gorer and John Rickman,[3] and Henry V. Dicks[4] have sought to apply these "culture and personality" concepts to Russian behavior. Gorer, particularly, has gained a certain notoriety for what skeptics have dubbed "diaperology." Together with the late John Rickman, a respected British psychiatrist who lived in Russia during World War I, Gorer argued that the maternal practice of tightly swaddling the Russian infant produces a privation-gratification cycle. This predisposes the "Great Russian" national character to pendulum swings of submissiveness and violent eruption, of apathy and diffuse persecutory anxiety, or "oral" greed and abstinence.[5] This accounts, too, for the willingness of the Russian adult to submit to brutal authority.

Dicks's work is more specific. A British psychiatrist at the Tavistock Institute (which set up the War Office Selection Boards), Dicks's generalizations are based, principally, on long interviews with Russian defectors.[6] The outstanding trait of Russian personality, says Dicks, is its ambivalence. On one side is the omnivorousness, the tendency to rush at things and to "swallow them whole," the need for quick and full gratification, the spells of manic omnipotence, the anarchic demand for abolition of all bounds and limitations; on the other, the melancholy closeness and suspicion, the anxious and sullen submissiveness, the "moral masochism and grudging idealization of a strong and arbitrary authority which is thought of as the only safeguard against the excesses of Russian nature." Authority, thus, if it is to be *authority*, must be hard, deprivational, arbitrary, and capricious; if the *vlast* were weak, nobody would obey it.

Against the traditional untidiness, lack of system, and formlessness of the Russian masses is the contrasting behavior of the elite. It has to be puritanical, in full control of all sentimentality and self-indulgence, and strong enough to renounce the gratifications which

[2] Margaret Mead, *Soviet Attitudes to Authority* (New York, 1951).

[3] Geoffrey Gorer and John Rickman, *The People of Great Russia* (London, 1949).

[4] Henry V. Dicks, "Observations on Contemporary Russian Behavior," *Human Relations*, V, No. 2, 1952, 111–75.

[5] A dichotomy, like an atom once split, can seemingly be multiplied indefinitely. Thus Dinko Tomasic, in his study of *The Impact of Russian Culture on Soviet Communism* (Glencoe, Ill., 1953), finds the Russian national character is a bisect of two contrasting influences, that of the "power-seeking and self-oriented nomadic horsemen of the Eurasian steppes" and of the "anarchic and group-oriented [Slavic] tillers of the land." One can also point to antinomies, such as Gordon Wasson's discovery that Russians are mycophiles and Anglo-Saxons are mycophobes.

[6] Dicks's original research was done in conjunction with Edward A. Shils. Unfortunately Shils's larger work was never declassified by the RAND Corporation, its sponsor, and therefore was unavailable for discussion.

"traditional" Russian character seeks. At important points there are congruities. The people expect and the elite satisfies the image of authority as severe, arbitrary, and fickle. The system, further, permits the most authoritarian fraction of the population "to act out their intro-jected bad-object relations" — i.e., to step into the shoes of a hated, yet, deep down, secretly identified-with father figure (Tsar, landlord, etc.). "By this hypothesis," says Dicks, "I would explain the rise in Soviet Russia of a rigid, gold-braided, intensely status-conscious and anxious bureaucracy, which is winning in the struggle against the very tendency originally successfully attacked by the new system and its founders during the Revolution.[7]

But this very transformation of goals, on a conscious or an uncon-scious level, provides the "salient" divergence between the Soviet system and the traditional Russian culture-pattern. For the elite, faced with the need of quickly producing a new type of technological and managerial personality, "is using the impetus of its own imperfectly assimilated and conflict-laden goal-drives to force and mould the people into a new cultural norm." Since the greater the pressure, the more intensive the inner conflicts, the elite "projects its own compulsive and sadistic authoritarian dominance needs on to foreign outgroups." Thus it creates a psychological situation of "encirclement" and attributes all failures to the work of the external enemy. "It is difficult to estimate," says Dicks, "how much of this paranoid behavior is the result of conscious design and how much is the effect of an inner compulsion due to cultural-psychological forces into which the top leaders have little insight. In this respect, I can only refer to the amazing discovery of the psychiatric pictures presented by a comparable power clique whom we were able to study: Hitler's entourage. We had assumed a cynical and cold-blooded exploitation of this paranoid dynamic by people like Goebbels and Himmler — and we found they were its victims."[8]

The acceleration of industrialization, says Dicks, will increase the tensions between the elite and the people. The coercions are "resented and stored up against the regime"; the deprivations in the name of some ultimate and impersonal good are interpreted as "withdrawal of love and nurturance." But such unconscious rage also leads to a sense of guilt for having defied authority, and this becomes projected onto the elite (i.e., it creates a feeling, at all levels, that the elite is angry at the masses and wants to punish them), leading to an increase in the atmosphere of "persecutory anxiety and diffuse fear (strakh)." The guilt thus also reduces a tendency to strike out at, or oppose, the regime.

(2) *Psychoanalytic.* An attempt to analyze not Russian but Bolshe-vik character structure, particularly as exemplified in the Politburo, has been made by Nathan Leites in his RAND study, underwritten by the U.S. Air Force.[9] But Leites' work goes beyond the mere codification of behavior in operational terms. In guarded, almost esoteric fashion,

---

[7] Dicks, "Observations," p. 171.
[8] Ibid.
[9] Nathan Leites, *A Study of Bolshevism* (Glencoe, Ill., 1954).

Leites undertakes a psychoanalytic explanation which is fairly breath-taking in its attempt. Bolshevik elite behavior is seen in contrast to that of the nineteenth-century intelligentsia. The latter were moody, nervous, soul-searching, brooding, introspective. "The Bolshevik" is rigid, suspicious, unyielding, ever-aggressive. This character is stamped in the primal image of Lenin, and is derived, psychoanalytically speaking, as a "reaction-formation" to fears of death and latent homosexual impulses. (Since Leites' massive work — 639 pages — is the most ambitious attempt yet to read an "operational code" of Bolshevik behavior, particularly in international strategy, a more detailed exposition of the theory is undertaken in Section II below.)

Sociological Theories

(3) *The Social System.* This socio-psychological theory, developed at Harvard in the Russian Research Center, and expressed most concisely in the recent book by Raymond Bauer, Alex Inkeles, and Clyde Kluckhohn,[10] seeks to identify the functionally relevant "operating characteristics" of the Soviet system — e.g., the overcommitment of resources to particular objectives; "storming"; the refusal to allow independent concentration of power — and the effect of these behavior patterns on the various social groups. In this fashion, the authors seek to locate the points of strain in the Soviet system. (Because it is the summary volume of the largest single research project on Soviet behavior, it is discussed in greater detail in Section III below.)

(4) *Ideal Types.* This approach, exemplified largely in the writings of Barrington Moore, Jr., at Harvard[11] (though it has influenced the thinking of W. W. Rostow at M.I.T. and Henry Dicks at Tavistock), sets up a number of models for the organization of power in a society and seeks to establish how far any society, and the Russian in particular, can go in its commitment to one or another of these forms.

According to Moore, power and position in a society are held in one of a combination of three ways: (a) *traditional:* power and position are transmitted through the family or kinship system, from father to son; (b) *rational-technical:* power and position are attained by an individual on the basis of skill and technical ability, regardless of the status of one's parent; (c) *political:* power and position are awarded on the basis of loyalty to a political leader, party or clique.

The use of any one criterion limits the range of workable alternatives for the solution of other problems. Rationality (b) emphasizes that technical competence should be the criterion for employment. But the nature of power struggles (c) demands that jobs should go to the faithful, to the commissar rather than to the manager, while purges, the most drastic expression of politics, remind individuals that obedience is the first law of the Soviet system. Meanwhile, traditionalism (a) is still

[10] Raymond A. Bauer, Alex Inkeles, and Clyde Kluckhohn, *How the Soviet System Works* (Cambridge, Mass., 1956).

[11] Barrington Moore, Jr., *Terror and Progress — USSR* (Cambridge, Mass., 1954), and *Soviet Politics: The Dilemma of Power* (Cambridge, Mass., 1950).

the "natural" mode of the peasantry, and *sub rosa*, within large sections of Soviet industry, and informal ties have become a necessary means of protection against arbitrary orders.

The political criterion of power in Russia (e.g., the commissars in the army, the control functions of the party in relation to industry) has been employed too ruthlessly, says Moore, at the expense, even, of sacrificing large classes of technicians and experienced army officers (e.g., the *Yezhovschina*, the dreaded 1937–38 purges which bear the name of Yezhov, the head of the secret police at the time). The power of the dictator to intervene arbitrarily at any point in the administrative hierarchy creates a level of insecurity which an ongoing system may find difficult to maintain. The choice now, Moore feels, lies between "creeping rationality" or traditionalism, or some combination of both.

Since the Soviet Union is intent on industrialization, the rationalizing elements are likely to become more deeply embedded in the society: this would mean that technical criteria would replace political decisions, jobs would be allocated according to skill, career expectations would have a higher degree of stability, family privileges could be passed on to the children. In turn, the power and prestige of the industrial manager, the engineer, and the technician would rise, and the share in power and prestige held by the "control" apparatus — the party and the secret police — would decline.

An alternative evolution in a traditionalist direction, which Moore finds politically "somewhat more plausible," would mean that the party and military elements would retain control, but arbitrary intervention would diminish as personal cliques and machines within the bureaucracy become the focal point of such loyalties. Such a development would also imply a rise in local autonomy and a resistance to innovation and change.

Plausible as these alternatives seem, if there is any sense to Khrushchev's vast "decentralization" scheme, it would seem to mean the reassertion of a political criterion, rather than economic rationality, in the handling of economic affairs. Genuine economic decentralization, as Richard Lowenthal points out,[12] would leave the party as a parasitic appendix to the economy. Despite the absorption of managers into the party, the division of function between managers and party whips has been a source of conflict; and this was utilized by Malenkov, speaking for the managerial group. What Khrushchev, whose strength has been in the party secretariats, has now done is to create a union of function, whereby the party secretaries, at the Republic and regional levels, will be responsible for the economic performance of the plan. As Lowenthal concludes: "It is the 'irrational' Khrushchev with his party bosses, and not the 'rational' Malenkov with his managers and economic administration, who has won the latest round; and the reason is to be found precisely in the logic of self-preservation of the party regime."[13]

[12] "The Permanent Revolution Is on Again," *Commentary*, XXIV, No. 2, August 1957, 105–12.
[13] Ibid., p. 109.

If Moore is correct, such logic may yet lead to economic crises; but that remains to be seen. What Moore has done is to focus attention on Soviet development primarily as a function of "forced industrialization," rather than of Marxist or even Bolshevik ideology, and to see Stalinist repression as much the necessary outcome of the speed of industrialization as of internal power struggles or the desire of Stalin to consolidate his rule. This is a theme which has commanded increasing attention from writers with such diverse views as Raymond Aron and Isaac Deutscher, and forms the core of E. H. Carr's interpretative analysis of Soviet history.[14] It has the merit, which few of the writings on Russia have had, of speculating on the possibly different "profiles" of Soviet society once industrialization has been achieved.

Political Theories

(5) *Marxist.* Expressed most directly by Isaac Deutscher, this approach sketches a theory of Soviet development based on the proposition that the level of productive power always acts as a constraint on the possibility of action. It argues that the Stalinist dictatorship was a historically "necessary" stage, therefore, in overcoming the resistance of the masses to industrialization, but that once this social stage has been achieved the dictatorial apparatus will "come into social conflict" with the requirements of the new, higher stages of economic development.[15]

As developed by Deutscher — agreement can be found in the writings of E. H. Carr — the year 1920 represented the crossroads of the revolution:[16] the working class was exhausted, demoralized, shrunken to half its size, anxious for relaxation; in a free election, the Bolsheviks would have been ousted; only the iron will of the Bolshevik leadership saved the revolution, at the expense of putting down democracy in the party (i.e., suppressing the workers' opposition faction, the "levelers or Utopian dreamers"). The result was an anomaly, a workers' revolution without working-class support. The rationale for this paradox was "historical necessity": nationalized property represented a higher stage of social development and therefore had to be defended, even against the workers.

The theory, *sans* Stalinist apologetics, had its origin in Trotsky's *The New Course* (1923) and later *The Revolution Betrayed* (1937). There Trotsky argued that in the growth of bureaucracy Russia faced a crisis: either the release of productive forces from the heavy hand of bureaucracy, or a "Thermidor," a return to some capitalist form, state or otherwise. Deutscher, at this point, feels otherwise. The backwardness of the peasant masses and their reluctance to make the sacrifice for industrialization, he says, required the harsh measures and iron discipline of Stalinism. But with the progress that was achieved in the

[14] See particularly E. H. Carr's *Socialism in One Country,* the fifth installment of his *History of Soviet Russia* (London, 1958).

[15] Isaac Deutscher, *Russia: What Next?* (London, 1953).

[16] Isaac Deutscher, *The Prophet Armed: Trotsky, 1879–1921* (New York, 1954).

1930's, says Deutscher, the Stalinist terrorism and "primitive magic" had outlived their usefulness and were coming into conflict with the "new needs of Soviet society." Industrialization, he believes, "tends to awaken the democratic aspirations of the masses," while the "phenomenal growth of Soviet wealth . . . tends to soften class privileges, and the orthodoxy, the iron curtain and the elaborate mythology of Stalinism tend to become socially useless. . . . Stalinism is untenable in this expanding society at its present level of productive forces."[17]

This theme, with a greater emphasis on the working class as a "political power of a magnitude hitherto unknown in Russian history," has been expanded by Deutscher in a recent publication.[18] The post-Stalin reforms, he notes, are reforms from "above," intended largely to provide some security for the bureaucracy. But the working class, particularly the skilled elements in engineering (which employs about one-third of Russia's industrial manpower), is now displaying long-suppressed egalitarian aspirations. This is evident in the revision of the old "progressive" piece-rate system, the narrowing of wage differentials, the introduction of a new pension scheme, and the abolition of all tuition fees in education.

This egalitarian drive — which is reinforced by the formal ideology that the workers are the ruling power in the country — says Deutscher, must come into conflict with the bureaucracy, which will seek to maintain its privileges and to preserve the status quo. And such an impending conflict must create a problem for a regime. With the power of the secret police diminished, there is only the army as the guardian of the order. But the army, rather than keeping order for the benefit of the party, sooner or later will do so on its own account. "In other words," concludes Deutscher, "the strains and stresses caused by a stormy revival of mass movements lacking leadership and clear political purpose, may lead to the establishment of a dictatorship of the Bonapartist type. All the more so as the military could hardly view with indifference a situation in which they must see a threat to Russia's positions of power and to all the strategic gains she won in the last war."[19]

It is highly debatable whether industrialization leads to a striving for *freedom* (even though it may lead to a demand by workers for a greater distributive share of wealth), or whether the expansion of wealth tends to diminish class privileges. Relative scarcities in the Soviet Union are bound to exist for a long period, however "phenomenal" the growth of Russian productivity. And the congealing of class privileges may become the real brake on any relaxation of the dictatorship, although key social groups at the top may win a measure of security. Certainly, in the downfall of Zhukov, the military has, for the time being at least, once again come under the control of the party. Deutscher clearly underestimated the role of the party, and in *Russia:*

[17] Deutscher, *Russia: What Next?* pp. 123, 125.
[18] Isaac Deutscher, "Russia in Transition," *Universities and Left Review*, I, No. 1, Spring 1957, 4–12.
[19] Ibid., p. 12.

What Next? (published in 1953) failed even once to mention Khrushchev — so remote was he from the inner-elite struggles. What is relevant, however, for this presentation is that in Deutscher's scheme of analysis there is a clearly determinable sense (whether substantively right or wrong) of a mainspring of change; and thus it focuses attention on the question which all social theory must confront: the sources of change in social systems.

(6) *Neo-Marxist.* Leading out of Trotsky's discussion of the nature of Soviet policy, a group of theorists argued that Russia, despite nationalized property, was no longer a workers' state but a new social form, namely, "bureaucratic collectivism."[20] The distinction has been important for the *political* orientations of the Marxist parties and sects. The orthodox Trotskyites, for example, claimed that Russia, although a "degenerated" workers' state, was, because of nationalized property, "historically progressive" and therefore worth defending in the event of a conflict with capitalist powers. The dissident Trotskyites, claiming that a new exploitative class society had been established, took a "neither-nor," "third-camp" position. Analytically — i.e., in terms of its predictive utility — the view that Russian society is bureaucratic collectivist leads its proponents either to adopt a scheme similar to that of Moore, or to analyze the regime in political terms not very different than those who see the USSR as a totalitarian society.

(7) *Totalitarian.* Expressed most forcefully in the categories of political philosophy by Hannah Arendt,[21] this theory argues that a radically new social form, different from tyranny, dictatorship, or authoritarianism, was created in Germany and exists now in Russia. The

[20] The first book to insist that Russia was a new class state — calling it "bureaucratic collectivism" — was that of Bruno R., *La Bureaucraticisation du Monde* (Paris, 1939). The theme was debated in the Menshevik press in the early 1940's, with the late Theodor Dan arguing in *Novy Put* that Russia was still a workers' state, and Rudolf Hilferding and Solomon Schwarz arguing the contrary in *Vestnik.* (Dan, following the invasion of Russia, gave qualified support to the Russian regime.) Hilferding's argument, a classic statement of the neo-Marxist position, was printed in the *Modern Review,* I, No. 4, June 1947, 266–71, under the title, "State Capitalism or Totalitarian State Economy," while Schwarz's data appeared later in his article, "Heads of Russian Factories," in *Social Research,* IX, No. 3, September 1942, 315–33, and in his collaborative effort with Gregory Bienstock and Aaron Yugow, *Management in Russian Industry and Agriculture* (New York, 1944). The debate was carried over into the Trotskyite press in the 1940's, principally in the *New International* and the *Fourth International* in New York. Trotsky's last argument is contained in the collection entitled *In Defense of Marxism* (*Against the Petty-Bourgeois Opposition*) (New York, 1942). The revisionist position can be found in James Burnham's *The Managerial Revolution* (New York, 1941) and in Max Schactman's introduction to the revised edition of Trotsky's *The New Course* (New York, 1943). A long discussion in the French periodical *Le Contract Social,* March 1959, sheds interesting light on the career of Bruno R., an Italian named Bruno Rizzi, and on the origins of the theory of bureaucratic collectivism. For a further discussion see my essay "The Strange Tale of Bruno R.," in *The New Leader,* September 28, 1959.

[21] Hannah Arendt, *The Origins of Totalitarianism* (New York, 1951; published in England as *The Burden of Our Times*).

essentially new fact of totalitarianism is that all intermediate or secondary institutions between the leader and the "masses" have been eliminated, and that the ruler, unrestrained by legal or political checks, rules by terror. The theory, as applied to the Soviet Union by Bertram D. Wolfe, holds that no essential change in the nature of the regime is possible and that totalitarianism, through an inner "ideo-logic" of its own, can never relinquish its combative posture vis-à-vis democratic societies. As a "working tool" to explain specific political situations, the theory of totalitarianism, which Mr. Wolfe draws also from Karl Wittfogel's *Oriental Despotism*, is too sweeping. From such heights the terrain of politics, its ridges and gullies, becomes flattened, and the weary foot-traveler finds few guides to concrete problems. Even on a simpler, intuitive basis, one can question the basic assumption of the theory — namely, that society becomes completely atomized and rule is anomic and direct. In a *crisis* situation, a state can fragment all social life, and through terror, perhaps, mold a people to its will. But can a society live in permanent crisis? Can it hold such a rigid posture without either exploding into war or relaxing? The basis of all social life requires not only a minimum of personal security but the reasonable expectation by parents that their children will be educated, develop careers, and so forth. To that extent, a tendency toward "normalization" is at work in any crisis state.

(8) *Kremlinological.* These speculations, identified principally with the writings of the late Franz Borkenau and of Boris Nicolaevsky, focus primarily on the power struggle within the core elite and seek to identify the shifting coalitions ("who is doing-in whom") within the Kremlin, as a basis for predicting political events. While open to easy satire, it is the supercilious who mock it at their peril, as the New York *Post* once learned when it scoffed at the speculations arising from the fact that all the Bolshevik leaders *but* Beria had appeared en masse at the Bolshoi Ballet. "Perhaps Beria doesn't like ballet," said the *Post* archly. Perhaps he didn't, but we never had the opportunity to find out, for two days later came the announcement that Beria had been arrested as a traitor.

In one form or another, Kremlinology is practiced today by every foreign office and by most journalists. Its emphasis is largely on personality and power groups, and less on the social systems and the way such systems can or cannot constrain these leaders. (See Section IV for an enlargement of this discussion.)

Historical Theories

(9) *Slavic Institutions.* Represented in an earlier generation by Nicholas Berdyaev, Sir Bernard Pares, and Sir John Maynard, and today to some degree by Edward Crankshaw, Ernest Simmons, and Werner Philipp (of the Free University of Berlin), this school states that much of contemporary Russian behavior can be accounted for by traditional Slavic character and institutions. "Too often we forget," said Professor Ernest Barker, in introducing Maynard's *The Russian Peasant: And Other Studies* (London, 1942), "that Russia, with all her changes, still

largely remains the same." The theme is elaborated in Sir John's book: "All Russian regimes have been sudden and arbitrary. . . . Old Russia was always rough, with its Siberian exile. . . . Planning . . . a characteristic feature of the new regime, is not as new at first glimpse as it looks to be. . . . Even the 'Party' — that misnomer of the vocation of leadership — is not really new: but rather a new application of an ancient institution: the priesthood . . . ," etc., etc.

One finds a similar argument in the November, 1951, lecture by Professor Werner Philipp on the "Historical Presuppositions of Political Thought in Russia," inaugurating the Osteuropa Institute of Berlin.[22] As a reviewer summarizes Professor Philipp's argument: "Conditions and traditions have produced a definite political mentality in Russia which goes back for several centuries. . . . The Russian distrust of the West, the cult and consciousness of the precedence of the community over the individual, the recognition of the unlimited power of governmental authority over society, and the discrepancy between political reality and the professed ideal aim, all these phenomena of Soviet thought and life have their roots in conditions which developed in Russia between the beginning of the thirteenth and the end of the sixteenth century."[23] The theme of an "eternal Russia" is propounded, too, by Crankshaw in his *Cracks in the Kremlin Wall* (New York, 1951).

To argue that the roots of Soviet life go down deep in the Russian past is not, of course, to justify those practices (although the argument lends itself sometimes to apologetics, and in the 1930's and 1940's apologists like Bernard Pares or Maurice Hindus did justify Russian behavior in such terms). But like the characterological theories ("parallel travelers," one might call them), the Slavophile theory argues in effect that since Soviet institutions were shaped by historical social forms, and since they are deeply rooted in the traditions of the people, they will change only slowly.

(10) *Geo-political.* This school, which had some vogue during World War II (e.g., Nicholas Spykman at Yale, and William T. R. Fox's *The Super-Powers,* New York, 1944) and still has some supporters, holds that Russian foreign policy is dictated primarily by long-range strategic interests deriving from its position as a great land-mass power, and that its contemporary political aspirations (e.g., in the Middle East) reflect the historic drives of Great Russian policy. The school generally tends to minimize ideology (viz., Walter Bedell Smith's introduction to the Marquis de Custine *Diaries,* New York, 1951) and to see Russian policy primarily as a function of strategic power position. To some extent the early policy views of George Kennan (see his Princeton University lectures, *Realities of American Foreign Policy,* Princeton, N.J., 1954) and those of Henry Kissinger are shaped by these considerations.

[22] Horst Jablonowski and Werner Philipp (eds.), *Forschungen zur osteuropäischen Geschichte,* Vol. I (Berlin, 1954).
[23] Hans Kohn in the *Russian Review,* XIV, No. 4, October 1955, 373.

KTO-KOVO — THE ID AND EGO OF BOLSHEVISM

During the truce negotiations in Korea, a slim book, *The Operational Code of the Politburo*, by Nathan Leites, was used by the American negotiators as a tactical manual. Leites' research, embodied in the larger *Study of Bolshevism*, was sponsored by the U.S. Air Force's Project RAND. The fact that RAND has given strong support to the pioneering method of Leites (which is now being applied to the study of French politics) makes a more detailed examination of his work worthwhile.

Leites begins by attempting to define "Bolshevik character" as a type distinct in social history. The attempt to define historic character is not new. (We have the image, somewhat overworked these days, of the "inner-directed Protestant.") What makes Leites' work unique are the novel categories he chooses and, above all, his method. There is no observation of behavior. Like Max Weber, who drew his "Protestant ethic" from the writings of Luther, Calvin, Baxter, and others, Leites scans the writings of Lenin and Stalin to infer similar norms which guide the Bolshevik party. He reads the Bolshevik character as a "reaction" to the Oblomovs, who slept away their lives; to the Rudins, the high-flown talkers but never-doers; to the indecisive, soul-sick, moody students. The Bolshevik, as Boris Pilnyak put it, is "against the old peasant roots of our old Russian history, against its aimlessness, its non-teleological character . . . against the philosophy of Tolstoy's Karataev." The moral training of the Russian intelligentsia stressed the prohibition against egotism and the prohibition against "dirtying oneself." Chekhov once said, "If all Socialists are going to exploit the cholera for their own ends. I shall despise them." But, for the Bolshevik, refusal to use bad means is merely an expression of sentimentality and stupidity; in Bolshevik doctrine, the worst egotist is precisely he who refuses to soil his hands. The party strives for humanity, and "purity" lies not in a personal refusal to act immorally but in dedication to the party. In such dedication the individual finds his defense against both egotism and personal impurity.

In contrast to the Russian intelligentsia, who spoke of ultimate things and sacred values, the Bolsheviks maintain silence about the sacred. Against the vice of outpouring emotion, the Bolsheviks uphold the virtue of reserve. Against the old Russian tendency to depressed passivity, introspection, nervous impressionability, and excited babbling, against the protracted searching for metaphysical truths and the posing of unanswerable questions — against all these, there is the determinism of history, the certainty of purpose, the commitment to action, the ability to avoid taking personal offense, the "masculinity" of action. Against the fear of a life with nothing to strive for, a life filled with uncontrollable, impulsive gratifications which arouse anxiety and guilt and thus lead to the famous Russian flirtation with death — Gorky tells how in his youth boys would lie immobile on a railroad track while trains passed over them — against this there are the constant goals of work and the party. Death is merely the point at which one had outlived one's *usefulness*. Of the suicide of Marx's son-in-law, Paul Lafargue, Lenin wrote: ". . . if one cannot work for the party any longer, one must be able to look truth in the face and die like the Lafargues."

Out of such elements of ethics and moral temper emerges, in Leites' view, the "operational code" in politics. For Bolshevism, all politics is summed up in the formula, *kto-kovo* — literally, "who-whom," but in its most radical sense, "who kills whom." Political relations are between dominators and dominated, between users and used. There can be no neutrals. If politics is *kto-kovo*, then all political strategies are guided by this fundamental rule: one pushes to the limit, one refuses to be provoked, one acts when one is ready, etc.

Stated in these gross terms, the precepts become political commonplaces, akin to the generalized precepts of military strategists or the maxims of Machiavelli. What gives Leites' analysis its special point and quality are the nuances of detail: the Bolshevik use of procedural points for trading; the expectations that personal insults will be taken politically and not personally (Vishinsky contemptuously calls Romulo "an empty barrel" in the UN General Assembly and then sends roses to a reception at Romulo's home); the role of provocations, and the like.

The same rigidity and calculatedness of behavior the Bolsheviks ascribe to their adversaries. The "big bourgeoisie" are seen as the Bolsheviks see themselves, i.e., as *serious*, calculating men who, wielding power, obey the "laws" of power. Political acts are not accidental; any act of the opposing ruling class can only be a hostile move in the constant war whose final outcome must be the annihilation of one side or the other. For the petty bourgeoisie, on the other hand, particularly the liberals, the Bolsheviks have only deep contempt; they are sentimental, given to illusions, deceived by the content of ideologies, moralistic — in short, fundamentally *unserious*.

Is "Bolshevik" character the same as it was fifty years ago? In important respects, yes; Leites believes that there are certain invariant patterns. Before 1917, Bolshevism as a small party faced a hostile state; now, in its view, it faces a hostile world: its basic posture remains the same. Pre-revolutionary behavior toward rival political organizations once displayed itself in small cafés and drafty meeting halls; now its scene is the great assembly halls of world politics: the same behavior repeats itself. The preoccupation with procedural issues — arising from the belief that a small point will "inevitably" grow into a big one and must not be conceded — which was manifested by Lenin in regard to the constitution of the editorial board of *Iskra* in 1900 (when he was "coexisting" with rival Social Democrats), was duplicated in intraparty disputes in 1921 and, again, at international negotiations at Yalta, San Francisco, and the Conference of Foreign Ministers in 1945.

The political consequence of this analysis is inescapable: if politics is *kto-kovo*, then "coexistence" as a sustained modus vivendi is impossible. Leites sums it up flatly: ". . . a 'settlement' in Western terms, with outside groups — an agreement sharply and indefinitely reducing the threat of mutual annihilation — is inconceivable [although] agreements with them, codifying the momentary relationship of forces, must always be considered and often concluded."[24] But the party "maintains a full awareness of the basic conflict," and at the strategic moment presses forward again. Promises, as Lenin said, are like pie crusts, "made to be broken."

But let us now look more closely at Leites' use of psychoanalytic insight, for the novelty of his book lies there. To say, as Leites does, that the sources of Bolshevik character lie in a reaction to the extreme temper of the Russian intelligentsia in the nineteenth century is still to write history without the help of Freud; Lenin and his co-workers were perfectly *conscious* of their attempt to reverse traditional patterns of Russian character, to overcome Karataev and Oblomov. But when Leites speaks of the Bolshevik character as a "reaction-formation" to *unconscious*, overwhelmingly powerful wishes, he is approaching politics in a way that was impossible before psychoanalysis.

Two principal drives, according to Leites, explain Russian intellectual character: preoccupation with death, and latent passive homosexual impulses. The Russian intellectual displayed a fascination with death that is terrifying to the Bolshevik. (Tolstoy, for example, could not endure the idea of death or sex.) Against the fascination, the Bolshevik defense is to minimize death by work, and, more important, to express a kind of personal omnipotence through the dissolution of the self into the all-embracing, undying party. Thus, Leites writes, "The earlier Russian feeling that life is empty because of death has been replaced by the Bolshevik feeling that death is empty and small and unable to interfere with life."[25]

The code of work becomes all-important. It is a basic defense against threatening feelings. Krupskaya, Lenin's wife, tells of the time in exile when Lenin was absorbed for hours in playing chess. "On his return to Russia Vladimir Ilyich abandoned chess-playing. 'Chess gets hold of you too much, and hinders work . . .'," he said. "From his early youth," she continues, "Vladimir Ilyich was capable of giving up whatever activity hindered his main work." In exile, many political refugees went often to the cinema, while others, scorning this mode of enjoyment, preferred to take physical exercise in walking. The group divided, said Krupskaya, into cinemists and anti-cinemists, who were jokingly called "anti-Semites." "Volodya," wrote Krupskaya to Lenin's mother, "is a decided anti-cinemist and a fierce walker."[26]

The theme of latent homosexuality, lying deep in the arcanum of psychoanalysis, is seen as a pervasive yet repressed element of Russian intellectual desire. In Dostoevsky, the utmost demonstration of emotion by the usually overwrought and emotionally charged characters is to embrace and clasp one another. To Bolshevism, the fantasy of men embracing each other is repulsive and frightening. When Lenin de-

[24] Leites, *A Study of Bolshevism*, p. 527.
[25] Ibid., p. 137.
[26] Ibid., pp. 135, 261.

scribed those once close to him who had now made common cause with his enemies, he would say that they "kissed" and "embraced" one another. ("The Scheidemannites kiss and embrace Kautsky"; "The followers of Bernstein are impudently blowing kisses to [Plekhanov].")

To Leites, a further significant clue lies in the number of Lenin's intimate friendships which ended in violent ruptures. These included Struve, a close collaborator in the 1890's; Potresev, an early *Iskra* associate; Plekhanov, Lenin's "ambivalently loved master" who "capitulated" to the Mensheviks; Alekinsky, perhaps Lenin's most intimate associate in the years after 1905, who later denounced him as a German agent; and Malinovsky, the Bolshevik whip in the Duma, of whom Lenin said, "He will not be another Alekinsky," and who turned out to be a police agent.

"One might speculate —" says Leites, "the data discussed here allow no more than that — whether the Bolshevik insistence on, in effect, killing enemies and being killed by them is not in part an effort to ward off fear-laden and guilty wishes to embrace men and be embraced by them. This hypothesis is consistent with the existence of certain pervasive Bolshevik trends described in this study; the fear of being passive, the fear of being controlled and used, the fear of wanting to submit to an attack. Once one denies one's wish to kiss by affirming one's wish to kill, this is apt to reinforce one's belief in the enemy's wish to kill by virtue of the mechanism of projection, probably heavily used by the Bolsheviks."[27]

On the basis of what documentation can one make such sweeping inferences? Even if we fully accept the psychoanalytic theories, how does one validate these judgments without putting the Bolshevik leaders on the couch, so to speak? Leites' method is to examine the imagery fantasy, the characteristic literary metaphors employed by Bolshevik leaders, and the fictional models in Russian literature with which the Bolsheviks identify, or those they assail. Russian literature and the Russians' attitude toward it seem to make this possible. In few cultures have fictional characters become such sharply defined national types: Dostoevsky's gallery — the Karamazovs, Raskolnikov, Myshkin, Verkhovensky; Turgeniev's Rudin, Gogol's Chichikov, Goncharov's Oblomov, Chekhov's multifarious characters.[28] These are all models which are accepted or rejected by Russians as psychological masks. The Bolsheviks, as Leites points out, cite these types in their own speech and homiletics with great frequency and emphasis (e.g., "Oblomovism" as a disease of slothfulness which the party must avoid).

Taking off from these literary sources, Leites draws on Freudian theory to highlight the latent meanings of specific imagery. For example, fear of impotence, fear of being beaten (in Stalin's famous

[27] Ibid., pp. 403–4.
[28] Less easily and much less intensely and completely, we accept or reject Hemingway's character, Fitzgerald's youths, Horatio Alger's theories, Huck Finn, the cowboy and the gangster as American types, embodying aspects of our national character.

speech to the managers of Soviet industry in 1931, the image of beating or being beaten occurs eleven times in a single paragraph), jokes about "cleaning out" the party, fear of being used as a "tail," etc. As chief evidence for his theories Leites relies on the marshaling of images, in a vast profusion. The result is a strange and fascinating medley of quotations — roughly three thousand cited for various points.

This method of analysis immediately provokes a charge of "reductionism," namely, that all ideas are seen as being *au fond* something more primitive. Thus, Lenin's fierce attack on solipsism is seen as expressing panic about annihilation, while his attack on the "spontaneity of the masses" is seen as a defense against desires for impulsive, orgiastic gratification. In what sense, one may ask, is the primitive impulse behind an idea more "real" than the idea itself? This is a difficulty one often encounters in connection with psychoanalytic thinking. It is obvious that the psychological impulse *behind* an idea is no test of its truth; the test of truth comes *after* the idea has originated. Yet we have learned not to scoff at these hidden mainsprings, *for we are dealing less with the ideas than with the way in which they are held and used.* What Leites is arguing is that any view held with stubbornness, exaggeration, and intensity — as all Communist views are held — and which violently rejects all rational tests, raises the presumption that it may constitute a defense against strong unconscious wishes or fears which stand in contradiction to the idea. To follow a pronouncedly masculine profession like soldiering does not label a man as a "latent homosexual," but if we find him compulsively, violently, and beyond reason insisting on his military posture, "common sense" permits us to suspect that he may be afraid of being less a man than he would like to appear.

Granting even the validity of the psychoanalytic method in the study of personality, we must still ask whether it can legitimately be extended to the analysis of politics.

Erich Fromm has argued in *Escape from Freedom* (New York, 1941), that the sado-masochistic character, typical of the German middle class, found an outlet in the Nazi party. T. W. Adorno and his associate authors of *The Authoritarian Personality* (New York, 1950) have pointed to the rigid, compulsive individuals who seek authoritarian values. Harold Lasswell, in the early *Psychopathology and Politics* (Chicago, 1930), sought to show how the political arena acts as a displacement of personal needs. (For example, adolescents, feeling guilty about sex strivings, find sublimation in the generalized "love" appeal of political movements that emphasize brotherhood.) In these studies, characteristic of modern social science, the social structure is taken as fundamental and the personality components are seen as the responses.[29]

[29] The effort to construct "social character" out of unconscious strivings is not limited to psychoanalysis. It is central, for example, to Pareto's sociology. For Pareto, the springs of social action were "interests" (or rational assessments), "derivations" (or rationalizations), and "residues" (or fundamental drives). As George Homans, a quondam follower of Pareto, once wrote: "American historians are given to discussing at length the 'Pioneer

Leites' view, however, goes beyond this. He says, in effect, that *character determines politics*. Since the mainspring of Bolshevism is action, the movement, by impressing its character on others, transforms all politics and, in the end, the social structure itself. (Compare the purposeful Bolshevik-type organization with interest-group parties, or tepid ideological parties, to see the difference.) Bolshevism, in this sense, can be considered as one of the few successful movements of pure will in history; its only competitors in this respect are certain religious orders. Because, in modern life, ideas (abstract, philosophical conceptions of truth) have become transformed into ideologies (active strivings to implement a creed as truth), Leites' type of analysis is possible, reflecting as it does a social reality. For ideologies are, in effect, attempts to unite ideas, behavior, and character; they demand a hardening of commitment. The Communist (or the Fascist, or the kibbutznik, or the 100 per cent American) is not only supposed to believe certain things; he is supposed to act, to *be* something, and, in acting, to fix his character. If one is "serious," one "lives" one's ideology. Thus ideology may be said to presuppose character.

But again, what basically determines character? The liberal and utopian answer, as given, say, by Robert Owen in his *New View of Society* or by Edward Bellamy in *Looking Backward*, was that environment bred character: e.g., the rapacious nature of capitalism shaped the competitive character ("Withdraw these circumstances in order to create crime in the human character and crime will not be created," said Owen in a classic phrasing of the liberal belief; in the utopian society where abundance prevailed, a different character would emerge).

What determined Bolshevik character? Leites stops short of an answer to this question, possibly because the purpose of his book lies elsewhere: he is interested in describing the pattern of Bolshevik action in order to develop a practical way of counteracting communism. Whether or not his picture of this operational code is a true one is, he argues, independent of the origins of Bolshevik impulses. Formally he is correct, for the code's validity depends upon its internal consistency, upon its confirmation by other analysts using the same data, and finally upon its usefulness in making predictions. Yet, intellectually, the sources of that code are important, for only by tracing them can we have a complete model of social analysis.

The conventional answer regarding Bolshevik character is that the conspiratorial nature of the conditions of underground work in the days before the Revolution — the environment — shaped the peculiar structure of the Bolshevik elite and its unique code and discipline. But there were other parties, Marxist and Social Revolutionary, which operated in the same environment. And the ideological debates between Lenin and Martov in 1903 on the nature of the party membership antedated the

---

character,' the 'Pioneer spirit.' What they are talking about when they are not simply romancing is the prominence in the 'pioneers' of certain residues, notably those of the integrity of the individual."

development of "party work": Martov argued that a Social Democrat was one who sympathized generally with the party's program, while Lenin argued that only a professional revolutionary, only a conspirator, could be a party member. Thus the pattern was prefigured in the thinking of Lenin.

Leites, it seems to me, would be forced to argue that the Bolshevik pattern was a product of pure will shaped by the intense unconscious drives. Further, if he is to be consistent with the psychoanalytic approach, he would have to argue that *it was the character of Lenin, the "primal father," which shaped the party* (his followers did call themselves Leninists) *rather than the party organization and the environment which shaped Lenin* and the other Bolsheviks. And it was the will of Lenin alone which altered the party's politics, as in the crucial decisions in April and July, 1917. The Bolshevik party, more than any other party in history, has demonstrated the nature of will. It was, and is, one of the most highly self-conscious movements in history. Its patristic writings are not only canonical; they are also "training documents" in the tempering of a "hard core" party membership. Individuals may join from a variety of motives, but all must be stamped in the mold or driven out. "The Narodniks," Lenin jibed, "are more united . . . and with them the abundance of grouplets is not accompanied by sharp splits . . . [yet] the Narodniks are politically impotent . . . incapable of carrying through any political mass action . . . [while] the dogmatic 'Marxists' who have an endless number of splits . . . are successfully active."

The splits and expulsions (becoming blood purges after power is achieved) which characterize Communist parties may thus be seen in a different, sociological light, as a process of personnel, and personality, selection: the true Bolshevik is the man who has thus been tempered, and remains.

If we can sum up the argument schematically: Bolshevik character is a reaction, consciously and unconsciously, to elements in the character structure of the old Russian intelligentsia.[30] This is seen most characteristically in the person of Lenin and his emotional and intellectual temper. In Lenin's mold the party became stamped.

With the Leites study we come full circle in the theories of history and politics. It was the fashion a hundred years ago to ascribe historical change to "great men" and the force of their personalities. Subsequently we interpreted history in terms of abstract "social forces" — population pressure, search for markets, etc. — which somehow, but never fully understandably, translated themselves through individual actors into tangible events. The glaring inadequacies of these deterministic theories have led to the reintroduction of psychological and, through Freudian

---

[30] Leites has elaborated his view in a subsequent volume, *Ritual of Liquidation* (Glencoe, Ill., 1954), to explain the Moscow Trials of the late thirties. His view, briefly, is that the old Bolsheviks were caught, psychologically, in the wheel of their own logic and, having lost, fatalistically submitted and confessed.

influence, of characterological explanations. Even ex-Marxists have not been immune. Is not the current fashionable theory of the "primacy of politics" over economic forces simply a smuggled-in psychological theory of "power"? Most attempts to explain the situation in Russia today find expression in the "power" formula. But actually the formula of "power" explains little. It tells nothing about different tactics, different social groups, the different purposes for which power will be used. If a psychological theory of politics is to be employed, then the Leites view — with its emphasis on character as blending a power drive with ideology — is, in spite of all its limitations and uncertainties, far more subtle and imaginative than the contraband psychology of the political scientist.

However, two questions remain to be asked of the method: How are continuities of character established, and how, and with what difficulties, does an elite group impress its character upon a country?

In the Leites model, as we have seen, there is the implication that the initial change in the character of the intelligentsia — the emergence of Bolshevism — was a reaction-formation, and that the character of the "primal father" determined its political course. If that was true of Lenin, how does it apply to Stalin and to his heirs? In his study of *Hamlet,* Ernest Jones remarks that there are two kinds of sons: those who reject their fathers, and those who take over and internalize the essential characteristics of the father, often caricaturing his features in the process.[31] From this point of view, Stalin was the son who took over the lineaments of the father. The touches, however, were grosser. Where in Lenin's time it was the party that had the monopoly on foresight, under Stalin it became a group within the party, and eventually the Leader alone, in whom all wisdom resided. Devices once reserved for the enemy, particularly deception and terror, were exercised on the masses which the party claimed to represent, and later against rivals within the party itself. Lenin had opposed personal touchiness and insisted on the irrelevance of personal prestige; Stalinism reacted intensely to minor slights, but only after giving them a political interpretation. Lenin opposed bragging; the Stalinist regime went in for the greatest self-glorification in history. Lenin opposed the creation of "scandals" in the party; Stalin liquidated the party cadres under the most fantastic charges.

These changes in Bolshevik behavior *do not necessarily reflect changes in the unconscious wishes and fears* which Leites posits as the ultimate sources of the Bolshevik character. Psychological *defense* patterns may change; indeed, they often *must* change as older defenses become inadequate. But when such changes take place on a broad political scale, they become extremely important, and we are bound to ask why the changes in defense mechanisms have occurred, why *these* particular changes, and what further changes are likely to occur. Here

31 *Hamlet . . . With a Psycho-Analytic Study by Ernest Jones,* M.D. (London, 1947), p. 22. The argument is elaborated in Jones's *Hamlet and Oedipus* (New York, 1951), pp. 83–90.

Leites offers little assistance. His theory deals with the dynamics of Bolshevism in the process of its formation, but once Bolshevism has come to birth, the model, as he presents it, is static. Take, for example, the initial turning on Stalin by Khrushchev and company. One could say that this, in turn, represents a reaction to the overbearing, almost paranoid Stalin; or there may be more "rational" explanations: the need to win mass support, etc. Further, how are we to explain the seeming "openness" and marked vulgarity of Khrushchev's character? We have no guide in the model itself to the possibility or the nature of the change.

The static quality of the model comes in part from its methodology. The basic outlines of Bolshevik character are drawn not from the empirical world of action, but from the abstract canons of Bolshevik doctrine. In itself this is not too great a fault, since the doctrine itself is evident. The greater fault of the theory — and, paradoxically, its strength — lies in the fact that, starting from static doctrine, it posits a static force called "character" and then gathers all human action into that one hedgehog force.[32] But how often in social action does character or will actually impose itself on events? People live largely in social systems, and they are "chained" to one another in complex ways. All of us, no doubt, would like to impose our "character" on the world, but in practice we find ourselves forced to modify our demands to conform with *possibilities*. Leites may thus be claimed to have given his concept of "character" a false autonomy, and in applying this concept to politics, which is par excellence a phenomenon of change within possibilities, to have falsified the nature of the subject.

How the Harvard System Works

Turning now to the sociological approach, the study by three Harvard social scientists, Raymond A. Bauer, Alex Inkeles, and Clyde Kluckhohn, *How the Soviet System Works*, is the best that contemporary sociology offers, and on this score alone merits attention. Their book is a revised presentation of a report, *Strategic Psychological Strengths and Vulnerabilities of the Soviet Social System*, that was prepared for the U.S. Air Force, the agency which commissioned and paid for the five years' research that went into the study. In one respect, the study illustrates the hazards of such sponsored research, since the authors found themselves under pressure to produce a "popular" book which the Air Force sponsors could show to their own controllers. The result is not a happy combination: "theses" are condensed and presented with only partial documentation; the book is written in an attempted vernacular style which just does not come off. The project, based on systematic interviewing of defectors, drew data from 329 extended life-history

---

[32] As George Ivask has said, if all men may be divided into foxes and hedgehogs, they may also be divided, following the satire of Saltykov-Schedrin, into boys with pants and boys without pants. If Lenin wore pants, is Khrushchev without them?

interviews, including detailed personality tests; 435 supplementary interviews; almost 10,000 questionnaires on special topics; 2,700 general questionnaires, and 100 interviews and psychological tests, administered for control purposes, to a matched group of Americans. In all, 33,000 pages of data were accumulated. These, together with the list of over fifty specialized unpublished studies and thirty-five published articles on which the authors drew in preparing the book, indicate how rich their source materials were.

Economic and political matters were not considered to be within the scope of the project. The key concept was that of the "social system," and this is the heart of the Harvard contribution. A "social system" is simply the characteristic ways in which societies, or sub-groups, organize their activities to achieve specific goals. Since the resultant institutions or behavior patterns are linked, presumably in meaningful fashion, variations in one area should be accompanied by regular — and determinate — variations in others. (Thus a change in the rate of capital accumulation, one of the fundamental determinants of an economic system, must precipitate changes in the rate of consumption, etc.) In the social system, reorganization of the structure of authority in the factory would presumably entail corresponding changes in the organization of the school system, the family, etc. For example, when Stalin introduced one-man rule and tight labor discipline in the factories in 1931, one could imagine a manager, confronted with a disrespectful student from a "progressive" school, asking, "What kind of a hooligan is this?" and insisting that school methods be changed so that students would learn obedience. The educational commissars, however, confronted with "wild" children from broken homes, would be forced to demand that the family be strengthened and divorce be made more difficult. And so, in linked fashion, we find the reintroduction of older, traditional forms of authority.[33] Yet such social change may become self-defeating, for as repression in the factory becomes pervasive, individuals need to find protection and do so in close family ties. And thus, after a while, the regime begins to complain about undue familialism. This example oversimplifies a social process, but it is not unjust.

The Harvard group has concentrated, however, not on locating change in the conventional institutions of society — family, political system, education, industry — but on the typical adaptive patterns of behavior which regulate the life of the ruled. These "central patterns" are: the need to conform to an explicit ideology; the refusal to allow independent sources of power; the centralization of all planning and control; the overcommitment of resources to particular objectives; the use of terror and forced labor; "storming" as a method of reaching objectives; the tolerance of evasions which fulfil the plan (e.g., *blat*, the network of informal deals), etc. On the basis of these "operating characteristics," the Harvard group seeks to identify the general strengths and

[33] The example has been adapted from Alex Inkeles, "Understanding a Foreign Society: A Sociologist's View," *World Politics*, III, No. 2, January 1951, 269–80.

weaknesses of the *system*. To wit: Weaknesses: there are no orderly processes of succession in office; economic growth in heavy industry is disproportionate to that in consumer industries; there are constant purges and insecurities. Strengths: the atomization of resistance; the Russians' ignorance of the realities of the outside world; the deep loyalties to the system on the part of the managerial groups.

One trouble with this approach is that one does not know, actually, which of these "operating characteristics" are central and which are not, for the Harvard group seems to lack an organizing principle which determines the selections. Is "forced labor," for example, an "inherent" aspect of the system, or a fortuitous element which got out of hand and may be discarded? And, if the latter, how is the judgment made? — on the basis of the fact that the terror has become self-defeating or that it is uneconomic, or because of moral disapprobation from the outside, or what? Moreover, if one seeks to forecast the "likely responses . . . of various segments of the Soviet leadership" in order to gauge the degree of loyalty and disaffection among the major social groups, the "central patterns" may be of less importance than an accurate definition of the different interests of such segments and of their power vis-à-vis other interest groups. The question is, What do we look for in a mode of analysis?

A mode of analysis is a function of the particular categories one uses to group together related characteristics. In political theory, one can classify regimes, as Aristotle did, as monarchies, oligarchies, or democracies; or, as Max Weber did, as traditional, rational, and charismatic. One's purpose dictates one's perspectives. The danger is that one tends to think of categories as realities rather than as theoretical constructs. This error has been appallingly true of Marxist thought, which in rudimentary fashion first employed the concept of a social system. Since in a simple Marxist model of capitalism, classes are formed in relation to the means of production, to the simple-minded Communist there could be no exploitation in Russia since the "people" owned the factories and there were, therefore, no exploiting classes. Hence, too, the fierce doctrinal debates as to whether Russia was a "workers' state," a "degenerated workers' state," or what.

But, once that is admitted, a large element of indeterminacy has to *tial* nature of a system is that one can locate the causal factors (in modern jargon, the independent variables), the changes in which affect all other parts of the system. (To Marx, for example, the essential nature of capitalism is the compulsion to accumulate and reinvest. Crises are deemed inevitable because of ensuing gaps between consumption and production, because of overproduction, and because of the falling rate of profit, which is a function, presumably, of high capital and low labor inputs.)

The Harvard group, however, shrinks from seeking to specify the motor forces in the social system as they have conceived it. "It is difficult, if not impossible," they say, "to assign a rank order of importance to those operating characteristics since they constitute an interlocking system in which each has implication for the other."[34] Apart from the fact that one may question the "tightness" of such "interlocks" (what, for example, is the link between "storming" and "forced labor" as characteristics of the system?) or even the congruence of the different "operating characteristics," *is it so difficult to single out the factor of prime importance?* Is it not quite clear, really, that the Soviet system is characterized, essentially, by the centralized control of political power, that it is a *command* system, with few institutional checks, and that all other aspects of the system — the refusal to allow independent power, the overcommitment of resources, etc. — derive from that fact?

But, once that is admitted, a large element of indeterminacy has to be admitted as well. For, in such a command system, the decisions of a few men — and, in the case of Stalin, of one — become decisive in changing the nature of the system. If Bukharin, rather than Stalin, had won, would not Russia be a different society? Or if Molotov, rather than Khrushchev, had kept power, would not the profile of Russia be somewhat different today? The development of Soviet society depends thus on the nature of Soviet political developments.

If this be true, then, in seeking to understand the Soviet Union, we are back to Kremlinology, the endlessly fascinating and often exasperating occult game of charting the petty protocol at the dinner table or seeing who is called on to speak at the Supreme Soviet, and in what sequence, in order to guess who is "on first."

The essential fact is that the Harvard system, lacking a sense of motor, cannot locate the sources of change in the system. While it is important to know the "limits" of social action (e.g., how far one can push recalcitrant peasants before offering new incentives, or which groups have the greatest potential for independent action), in *politics* one has to know who composes a ruling group, how the group arrives at a decision, how the claims of subordinate groups are adjudicated, and so on. For in a society like Russia, where institutional and behavior patterns are not autonomous, a "social system" has no meaning unless it can be defined within the context of politics.

Who Eats before Whom

The basic assumption of Kremlinology is that every move at the Russian *verkhuska* is shot through with the struggle for protocol, prestige, and power. Thus the manifest need to decentralize the Russian economy, because of the increasing inability of a single center to direct the operation of 300,000 enterprises, becomes a problem as well of whose power is increased and whose power is reduced by such a shift. Thus, not in the final analysis, but in the immediate one, all rational technical criteria bow to the political. And thus, in analyzing any move of Russian policy, we are forced to thread our way through the Byzantine intrigues which are spun in such power fights.

[34] Bauer, Inkeles, and Kluckhohn, *How the Soviet System Works,* p. 20.

The real problem arises, first, in the definition of the contending power groups, and, second, in the way we identify the alignments of individuals, particularly subordinates. One approach has been to define power groups in "functional" terms — e.g., party, army, secret police, state bureaucracy, etc. — and to locate spokesmen for those groups from the positions they hold. Thus the late Franz Borkenau, a leading practitioner of Kremlinology, wrote in the *New Leader* of May 6, 1957: "Since Stalin's death, an undisguised struggle has raged between Khrushchev, as representative of the Party dictatorship, and onetime Premier Georgi Malenkov as spokesman of the managers' demand for independence. Over the last four years, the managers have been making more and more effective demands for greater decentralization in the economy. Hence, Khrushchev and his ally Lazar Kaganovich have devised this scheme as a circuitous plan for undermining the managerial class." In a later article (June 3) Kaganovich was seen as standing on the sidelines, rather than at Khrushchev's side.

There are several difficulties with this sweeping type of statement. A word like "managers" contains a basic ambiguity. Are the managers the men who head the factories in the field, the heads of economic ministries in Moscow, or the planners in the Gosplan? If the "managers" include all three categories, is there an identity of interests among them? (Surely one would expect considerable friction between a factory seeking greater control over its own activities and a ministry in Moscow.) And, if not, which of the three are the real "managers"?

A second difficulty arises from mechanically countering bloc with bloc. While it is true that there are often interest conflicts between functional groups, the very nature of a political power struggle carried on by small cliques and coteries requires the power figure to have his allies within *all* groups. Thus the fight may not be simply "managers" vs. "party," or "army" vs. "party," but may cut across these groupings. Is the army, for example, a unitary interest group (united on what interests?), or does Zhukov line up with X and Koniev with Y and Vasilievsky with Z? From what we know of armies elsewhere, certainly such internal conflicts and differing outside alliances take place — e.g., in the U.S. Army the Marshall-Eisenhower group vs. MacArthur. The problem, then, is to locate those issues on which the army would stand united and those on which its top officers would divide. And, in so doing, one faces the problem of determining what it is that ties cliques and coteries together: school affiliation, loyalties to one who has made promotion possible, differences in generation, common wartime or service experiences, etc., etc.

Nor can one say that ideology determines alignments, for on key policy issues — consumer goods vs. heavy industry, tough or soft line toward the West, tough or soft line toward the satellites — there may be no unitary ideology which dictates a consistent attitude toward such issues. Malenkov may have wanted relaxation at home so as to be more tough with the West. Moreover, a top figure will often switch ideological sides opportunistically in a bid for support. Certainly Stalin's history is instructive in this regard. (The question is often put: does Khrushchev represent the "Stalinist" faction or does Malenkov? The difficulty with these formulations is that what we are observing is the breakup of a faction and, in such a highly personal situation, few of the formal sociological criteria for charting allegiances seem to hold.)

Even greater difficulties are faced in the task of locating the links of support down the line. Every foreign office and propaganda organization maintains extensive biographical dossiers on members of the Soviet elite in an effort to keep track of the shifting personnel as a means of measuring the relative strength of the contenders at the top. And often, as the example cited below shows, the method is highly tenuous.[35] How

[35] The *Radio Liberation Daily Information Bulletin* of May 14, 1957, carried the following news item, headed "Andropov — Head of the Satellite Countries Department of the CC":

"*Pravda* for May 12, 1957 twice mentions the former ambassador of the USSR in Hungary, Yu. V. Andropov, as 'head of a department of the Central Committee of the CPSU.' According to *Pravda*, Andropov was present at Khrushchev's reception for the government delegation from the Mongolian People's Republic and also at a lunch given by Bulganin in honor of the same delegation.

"Although the Tass reports do not state precisely which department Andropov controls, it may be assumed that it is the fairly secret satellite countries department (even its official name is not known).

"In the past, B. N. Ponomarev, who was invariably called 'a member of the Central Committee of the CPSU' usually took part in such receptions and banquets in honor of party and government delegations from the satellite countries. The position occupied by Ponomarev has never been mentioned anywhere. In this connection it is interesting to note that at the lunch given by Bulganin and Khrushchev in honor of the Albanian party and government delegation on April 12th this year (*Pravda*, April 13, 1957) the order of those who attended was as follows:

". . . Serov — Ponomarev — Palgunov — Nikitin . . .

"At the lunch which was recently given by Bulganin for the Mongolian delegation, the order of protocol was as follows:

". . . Serov — Andropov — Nikitin — Palgunov. . . .* [Footnote: *The protocol order at the reception given by Khrushchev was as follows: Gromyko — Pisarev (ambassador in Mongolia) — Andropov; however, it should be remembered that according to protocol, at a reception for a foreign delegation, the Soviet ambassador of the country concerned is always given the place of honor, whether or not he actually merits it 'on the protocol ladder.']

"Despite all these facts, it would be premature to conclude that Ponomarev has been replaced by Andropov, because Ponomarev is also to some extent connected with the international communist movement. (For example, he was a member of the delegation of the CPSU to the Fourteenth Congress of the French Communist Party in July 1956.) A more probable explanation is that an 'international division of labor' has been carried out in the Central Committee; Ponomarev will henceforth maintain contact only with those Communist parties outside the orbit, while Andropov deals with the satellites.

"*Bearing in mind the fact that Andropov was released ('in connection with a transfer to other work' — Pravda, March 7, 1957) in the course of a reshuffle of senior officials of the Ministry of Foreign Affairs which was begun by Shepilov immediately before his withdrawal from the post of Minister of Foreign Affairs, there can be no doubt to whom Andropov owes his promotion* (on the 'protocol ladder' he is now several stages above his former chief — V. V. Kuznetzov, first deputy Minister of Foreign Affairs — see *Pravda*, May 12, 1957)."

far one can go with this detailed, yet mechanical, scoring is open to question. One observer, in reviewing Boris Meissner's *Das Ende des Stalin-Mythos*, complains: ". . . he believes that he can say of any party functionary, from the top on down through lower ranks, whether he is a Khrushchev or a Malenkov man, a supporter of this or that tactical nuance of party policy. Very often these assertions are based on extraneous biographical information. Whoever served under Malenkov at some time in the past must, in Meissner's opinion, be considered a Malenkov adherent in all present-day situations. Whoever worked with Khrushchev twenty years ago in the Ukraine still must be his confidant today."[36]

And sometimes the same event — in this instance, the appointment of Frol R. Kozlov to the key post of candidate member of the party Presidium — is interpreted in diametrically opposite fashion. Harrison Salisbury, in the New York *Times* of February 16, 1957, reported that Kozlov was a member of a group to which Mr. Pervukhin belonged, and was "probably an adherent of Mr. Malenkov." Kozlov, said Salisbury, was one of the authors of the key propaganda documents of the "doctors' plot" of 1953; and one can surmise, therefore, in line with the logic of Kremlinology, that Malenkov was one of the directors of the plot. But Richard Lowenthal commented a day later in the London *Observer*: "Mr. Khrushchev's inner-party position has been reinforced not only by Mr. Shepilov's return to the party Secretariat, but by the promotion of Frol Romanovich Kozlov, the first secretary of the Leningrad region, to candidate membership of the party Presidium. . . . Having returned to obscurity during the early Malenkov era, he was at the end of 1953 promoted by Khrushchev's personal intervention to take the place of Malenkov's protege, Andrianov, as head of the Leningrad party organization." And, by equal logic, since Kozlov had signaled the campaign of vigilance at the start of the "doctors' plot," Khrushchev was thus tied to the execution of the plot.

This is not to say that the method is wrong, but that someone's information is inadequate. (For the record, Mr. Lowenthal was right about Kozlov, and Salisbury wrong.) How excruciatingly difficult the problems of Kremlinology can be is seen from a report in the New York *Times* of August 10, 1957, which stated that the U.S. State Department simply did not know who was running the Soviet foreign office and writing its *démarches*. Said the report:

> The State Department has been trying for some time without success to solve a new Kremlin riddle.
> The question: Who is the man who really operates Soviet foreign policy? who is the Soviet opposite number to Secretary of State Dulles? . . .
> It is argued that Mr. Khrushchev and Marshal Bulganin have been away from Moscow so much, unaccompanied by foreign policy experts,

---

[36] Immanuel Birnbaum, "Destalinization: Motives and Consequences," *Problems of Communism*, VI, No. 1, January–February 1957, 41.

that they cannot possibly have had time to "mind the store" during recent months.

Yet the State Department feels that the quality of Soviet diplomacy has improved noticeably during this period and now shows an unusual degree of sophistication in its understanding of the West. . . .

The Secretary has asked the United States intelligence agencies to examine the evidence, but so far the investigators have drawn a complete blank. . . .

The effect in Washington is to make it extremely difficult for the State Department to appraise either the Soviet Union's present intentions or the probable future of its foreign policy.

Consider, too, the dilemma of the Kremlinologist in having to make spot interpretations of a major change in the status of leading personnel when the announcement of the change itself offers no clue to its meaning. Thus, the day after a terse announcement appeared that Marshal Zhukov had been relieved of his post, Harry Schwartz, the New York *Times* specialist, began his story in this fashion: "Two principal possibilities have emerged from Marshal Georgi K. Zhukov's removal yesterday as Soviet Defense Minister: a substantial decline in his real power or a step toward his promotion in the Soviet hierarchy" (October 27, 1957).

One can sympathize with these occupational hazards. Henry Adams, in his *Autobiography*, remarks that when he was in London during the American Civil War, serving as secretary to his father, the United States Minister, he was making reports on the splits in British Cabinet opinion, reports which became the basis of American policy (e.g., the Mason-Sliddel affair) and which, he felt, were based on first-hand information. Twenty years later, when the Cabinet papers were opened, he found to his dismay that his reports had been completely wrong. Shortly after the revolt in Budapest, Hugh Gaitskell raised the question in the House of Commons whether the Russians had been emboldened to intervene because of the news of Eden's action at Suez. The question, even if Gaitskell intended it only to press a political advantage, was not an unfair one. It would be important to know if this were so. Is there an answer? We have no access to sources.

But one *can* raise a question regarding method, at least regarding the way in which Kremlinology has been applied. Put most simply, Kremlinology often becomes the obverse side of the Bolshevik mentality — that is, it becomes over-deterministic. The characteristic fact about Bolshevik mentality is its refusal to admit of accident and contingency. Everything has a reason, a preordained motive. Hence the sinister refrain in Bolshevik rhetoric: "It is no accident, comrade, no *mere* accident, that . . ." or, "Why at this time, why at *this particular moment*, does the enemy choose . . . ?" And so all such questions lead, with insidious intent, to the ultimate question: *kto-kovo*, who is using whom? One is reminded of the episode some years back when two Ukrainian delegates to the UN wandered into a small New York delicatessen during a holdup, and failing to understand the command of the robbers, one of them was shot in the thigh. Vishinsky, either to embarrass the United States, or because he was truly suspicious, rejected the explanation of the New York police department that, since it was a holdup, the shooting could not have been political. "How could it have been a holdup?" he asked. "It was a *small* delicatessen." In wealthy, capitalist America, who would bother to hold up a *small* store?

One sometimes finds a similar logic among the Kremlinologists.[37] Every move — both of personnel in the power conflicts within, and of policy in the international arena without — is seen as a carefully plotted, conspiratorially conceived, predetermined plan whose every consequence is anticipated; every move has a secret meaning which detailed charting of protocol and word counting can uncover. (Imagine what the Kremlinologist and/or the psychoanalyst could do with the statement of Indian Ambassor K. P. S. Menon, the last foreigner to see Stalin alive, that at the interview Stalin occupied himself throughout the entire session with making doodles — of wolves.) But from what we know of every chancellery in the world, few campaigns in political (or even military) affairs are ever calculated with such precision. And the analyst who fails to consider contingency runs the same risk as the Bolshevik in over-determining the political game.

And with one more step we come full circle. Whatever the importance of power at the top, no group of power figures, however absolute their rule, can wield infinite power. The problem with the Kremlinological approach is the same as with that of Leites. Every attempt to impose one's will has to take into account the finite limits of natural resources and the recalcitrance of human institutions[38] — but how?

[37] Perhaps the most extraordinary attempt to trace Soviet elite maneuverings by means of "Kreminological" methods is the RAND study of Myron Rush, *The Rise of Khrushchev* (Washington, D.C., 1958). In 1955, Rush observed that Khrushchev's title as first secretary of the party (*pervi sekretar*), which normally appeared in Russian press in lower case, suddenly was given in *Pravda,* of May 25, 1955, as *Pervi Sekretar.* (The next day the capital S was diminished, but the capital P retained, and the title appeared thereafter as *Pervi sekretar.*) From a clue as slim as this, and from others which at first glance might seem to be equally tendentious (e.g., Khrushchev's emulation of Stalin's use of the word *otriskoi*, or "belching forth," to characterize Malenkov as a right deviationist), Rush argued, in a paper prepared for RAND at that time, that Khrushchev was beginning to make his bid for power, and that he would use Stalin's ladder, the party secretariat apparatus, in his ascent. For some detailed questioning of Mr. Rush's reasoning, see my review of his book in *Problems of Communism,* Vol. VII, No. 2, March–April 1958.

[38] Insufficient attention has been paid, for example, to the techniques of evasion practiced by Soviet scientists in carrying out their work in accordance with the common fund of scientific knowledge. Alexander Weissberg-Cybulski, who was an editor of the physics journal in the Soviet Union and later a director of an institute in Kharkov before being jailed in the 1937–38 purges, tells the highly amusing story of how, in the journal articles, research advances in Russia were attributed, out of political necessity, to the wisdom derived from dialectical materialism, and of the problem that confronted the editors when the German Academy of Science asked for the secret of the new method. (See *Science and Freedom,* Proceedings of the Hamburg Conference [London, 1955].)

More recently, Ivan D. London has noticed wholesale evasions of *partinost* in science: "For example, it is not difficult to show, on the basis of

THE ONE ROAD AND THE MANY — EXIT PIRANDELLO

Now that we have investigated many roads, are there some which can lead us to reality better than others? (Says a passage in the Talmud: "If you don't know where you are going, any road will take you there.") Perhaps a few distinctions — and questions — are in order.

The Different Moments

There should be a clear distinction between the types of change which take place: between changes in Soviet society (the social system) and in Soviet politics, although in crucial moments one is dependent on the other. The difference is one of distinguishing between a process and an event; or, to revive an old distinction of the crusty sociologist William Graham Sumner, between *crescive* and *enacted* change.

Crescive changes are those which surge, swell, go on willy-nilly, and develop with some measure of autonomy. They variously derive from organic growth of tradition, or from changes in values (e.g., the decision of people to have fewer children or more), or from technical imperatives, once a key decision has been taken (e.g., the need for training more engineers, once a country industrializes).

Enacted changes are the conscious decisions or intents of legislators or rulers (e.g., the declaration of war, the collectivization of agriculture, the location of new industry, etc.). Those who enact change have to take into account the mores of the people and the resources at their disposal, but these serve only as limiting, not determining, factors.

Sociological analysis is most sure when it deals with crescive changes. These can be identified, their drift charted, and, like iceberg floes, their course and even their breakup specified more readily than others. But sociological analysis often fails in predicting political decisions. There are in history what Hegel called the "unique moments," and, in calling the turn, not pure reason but practical judgment (that unstable compound of information, intuition, and empathy) has to take hold. Bolshevism has been par excellence a movement minutely conscious of the past and supremely aware of the tactical and strategic

---

items abstracted from speeches, prefaces, introductory paragraphs, etc., that in the Soviet Union the whole development of physiology of the sense organs was prescribed by the Communist Party in order to provide a 'concrete basis for Lenin's theory of reflection' and to meet the 'demands of practice': industrial, medical, and military, the latter two in particular. Yet a detailed scrutiny of the technical literature, the published minutes of various meetings, conferences, etc., over the years reveals little to suggest that the serious programs of research in the field of sensory physiology in the Soviet Union have been really influenced in any respect, by either practical considerations or Party dicta. Of course, superficially there may seem to be a planned compliance with practical programmatic aims — after all, 'Soviet language' fulfills, besides communicative, also prophylactic functions — but any sensory physiologist who is alert to his subject will recognize the dust-in-the-eyes purpose of certain parts of research programs. . . ." ("Toward a Realistic Appraisal of Soviet Science," *Bulletin of the Atomic Scientists*, XIII, No. 5, May 1957, p. 170.)

nuances of events. It has been this constant awareness of "unique moments" (the "revolutionary situation," as Lenin first conceived it) and its ability to adapt its timing to the changing situation that have given Bolshevism its unique political advantage in the past.

The Problem of Prediction

The nature of the changes which one describes conditions the kind of prediction one can make. One can define, and predict, the limits of broad crescive changes (e.g., if one knows the resource pattern of the Soviet Union — amount of arable land, minerals, manpower — one can make a guess about the slowdown in the rate of economic growth), but in predicting the short-run policy turns one comes up against the variabilities of accident, folly, and simple human cantankerousness. The situation is reminiscent of two radicals in the 1920's debating the future course of Soviet politics. "The objective situation," said one, "requires that Trotsky do so and so and so and so." "Look," replied the other, "you know what Trotsky has to do, and I know what Trotsky has to do, but does Trotsky know?"

One of the key problems in the analysis of power is the mode of succession. In the Soviet system, as opposed to a constitutional regime, there seems to be no formal definition of legitimacy, and no system of investiture of power. In seeking to duplicate Stalin's rise, Khrushchev used the party secretariat as a power lever. But in doing so he was taking a big gamble. In the war years and after, Stalin had emphasized his governmental and military titles rather than his party position. At the time of his death in 1953, Stalin was only one of nine party secretaries, but was, uniquely, the Chairman of the Council of Ministers of the USSR. Malenkov relinquished his post as party secretary, when forced to make a choice, and sought to legitimize his authority through the post of Premier and the Council of Ministers. It is the measure of Khrushchev's shrewdness that he assumed correctly that, despite the rise of the technical and military classes, the mechanics of political power had not changed essentially since the 1930's. Yet can we assume that these "laws of mechanics" will hold in the naming of Khrushchev's successor? How do we define the balances of forces and predict the direction in which they will tip?

(Given all these problems and pitfalls, it would be a forward step in the social sciences if a group of Soviet experts were, at regular intervals, to make predictions, at different levels, of probable Soviet developments and state the reasons for their inference. Bauer, Inkeles, and Kluckhohn, for example, stated that the collegial system of power in Russia *could stabilize itself;* Myron Rush said that it would not, and predicted Khrushchev's bid for power.[39] By systematic review of the predictions, the successes and failures, one could probably obtain a more viable operational model of Soviet behavior.)

---

[39] Bauer, Inkeles, and Kluckhohn, *How the Soviet System Works*, p. 239; Rush, *The Rise of Khrushchev*, p. 21.

The Role of the Irrational

In social theory, the weight of analysis has always been thrown on the side of the rational explanation. The presumption (cf. Moore, Rostow, Deutscher, Aron, etc.) is that a society ultimately makes its choices on the basis of the rational alternatives which confront it. But how much meaning can one make of the role of pique (e.g., Tito's anger, as reported in the Dedijer biography,[40] at the fact that "we were treated like Komsomols," or Khrushchev's resentment at being forced by Stalin to dance the *Gopak*) in explaining the precipitateness or intensity of political acts? And, taking into account the researches of Leites, what weight can be given to the role of emotional components, conscious or unconscious, as a clue to political stance? Is it simply that rationality dictates the political course, and emotions the choler, or what?

Myth and Monolith

One difficulty with analysis in social science is that it deals with categories, not people. In recent analyses of the Communist movement, particularly in the United States, the movement has been seen as a monolith, with each adherent a disciplined soldier or a "true believer" ready always to follow orders of "the party."

To some extent, the West itself has been seduced by the very image of "The Bolshevik" with which the Communist rulers have sought to mold the "new" Soviet man. For, like any human group, the Communists have not been immune to personal rivalries and, more important, they have not been immune to the inherent factionalism which besets all radical movements. In fact, one might argue that factionalism, if only the need at times to chop off a "left" wing or a "right" wing, has been necessary in order for the party to maintain a myth of inviolate correctness. Certainly, however, the strains and factions of earlier years (the defections of Levi, Ruth Fischer, Brandler, Thalheimer, Souvarine, Rappaport, Rosmer, Bordiga, Silone, Cannon, Lovestone, Wolfe) have had their counterparts — although the struggles were more hidden and suppressed — in the defections and expulsions and murders of Marty, Tillon, Lecoeur, Hervé, Cucchi, Magnani, Reale, Tito, Petkov, Gomulka, Rajk, Nagy, and thousands of others. In fact, not monolithism but factionalism has been a basic law of the Communist movement. And we have failed to see this and exploit it. For from general political experience — whether it be in the trade-union movement or political parties — we know that ruling groups rarely collapse, but fall through the defection of key power figures who control substantial followings. This was the experience of the CIO with the "Communist problem" in the United States, and the meaning of Tito, Nagy, and (perhaps) Gomulka in the international Communist movement.

But more than a tactical inability to exploit the fissures and cracks is involved. In the character approach, and in Kremlinology, too, there has often been a "false concreteness." One saw all Communists as "the

[40] Vladimir Dedijer, *Tito* (New York, 1953), p. 327.

enemy," as "The Bolshevik," and any unrest, particularly in the satellites, purely as power conflicts between rival leaders. But there was more than this. There was also the simple recalcitrance and the simple decency of the human being which lay underneath. Who becomes the *apparatchik*, seduced by sadism and power, and who does not? Who the bureaucrat and who the lurking idealist? Who the Rakosi and who the Gyulya Hay? These questions are not, as we saw in Poland and Hungary in 1956, a closed book.

We can now see, in retrospect, the real meaning of the first Nagy regime in 1954–1955, how the momentum gathered when people were able to communicate with each other, exchange experiences, and realize that some hope of change was possible.[41] But why did almost all the specialists in Soviet affairs fail to catch the significance of those clues in 1954–1955? Was it because they were so mesmerized by the thought of "power" alone as the singular clue to the meaning of social conflict as to forget its impact on people?

Having said this, we must also recognize that political events do not return in the same trajectory. Having failed to catch the "unique moment," we are apt to forget that the moment may not return. The lesson of the last few years, from East Berlin to Budapest, is that a "thaw" breaks up glaciers and log jams, creates rifts and fissures, and sends massive floes down the sea of history. But have not the Russians — who are more sensitive than most to the lessons of history — seen this as well and, learning from these events, may they not have decided that, if they can help it, to control any new "thaws."

The Word and the Deed

Every society, every social organization, lives for certain goals which in considerable measure are dictated by its ideology. We know — to use an example from modern trade-union experience — that many individuals act quite pragmatically when their doctrinaire ideological goals conflict with the ongoing reality, and they compromise accordingly. Yet, when called upon to take a stand on issues far removed from their immediate experience, the only vocabulary, the only rhetoric, the only categories of analysis or even simple formulae available to them, are the old ideological banners. They use them and become trapped; for ideology is a hardening of commitment, a freezing of opinion.

Since the Bolshevik ideology is the only formal canon of Soviet intentions that we have, an answer to this question is of prime impor-

[41] We realize, too, the profound wisdom of de Tocqueville: ". . . it is not always when things are going from bad to worse that revolutions break out. On the contrary, it oftener happens that when a people which has just put up with an oppressive rule over a long period of time without protest suddenly finds the government relaxing its pressure, it takes up arms against it. . . . Patiently endured so long as it seemed beyond redress, a grievance comes to appear intolerable once the possibility of removing it crosses men's minds. For the mere fact that certain abuses have been remedied draws attention to the others and they now appear more galling. . . ." Alexis de Tocqueville, *The Old Regime and the French Revolution* (Anchor ed.; New York, 1955), pp. 176–177.

tance: To what extent are the Soviet leaders committed to the formal Bolshevik ideology (e.g., the incompatibility of compromise, the attribution to capitalism of inherent imperialist aims, etc.), and to what extent are they prepared to modify it on the basis of experience and reality?

The answers are contradictory: (1) If one accepts the "characterological evidence" (e.g., Dicks, Leites), compromise is precluded. The rigid psychological postures and even paranoid suspicions of the Soviet rulers make it difficult for them to appraise realistically the changes in the Western world. (2) An extreme Kremlinologist might say that the Soviet rulers are cynical and regard the ideology simply as a necessary myth for the masses. (3) A geopolitical theorist, taking a completely rationalist view, would argue that strategic interests rather than ideology determine the behavior of Soviet rulers. (4) The weight of some evidence (see pp. 29–35 of the Bauer, Inkeles, and Kluckhohn book) is that ideology, even though cynically used by the Soviet rulers, is a real factor in the way they think and in the formulation of their goals.

But all this was before Khrushchev. While in the fields of literature and the arts the party has moved to reassert *partinost* (ideological control), in other fields practical considerations rather than ideology seem to determine policy. Soviet economists, for example, in conformity with the Marxist theory of value, could not admit of the productivity of capital or utilize the interest rate to measure the rational allocation of capital. But even under socialism, capital scarcities exist, and if cost economies were to be achieved, some disguised techniques had to be created in order to carry out the functions of the interest rate. After the war, these evasions of dogma were attacked by the ideologists. "In the hot debate which followed," writes Robert Campbell, "the conflict between the very real problem of the planners and the demand of purity in doctrine was made quite clear. The Soviet leaders faced an impasse; one of the central assumptions of Marxist economic theory had been proved wrong by their own experience, and they were faced with a painful choice between ideology and rational expediency. . . . So long as Stalin was alive, no official line emerged to break the deadlock. About a year after his death, however, the Gordian knot was cut, and cut in such a way as to constitute a surrender of orthodoxy to reality."[42]

In the field of agriculture, Khrushchev has taken the dramatic, drastic step of abolishing the machine and tractor stations, which, in the Stalinist scheme, represented a giant step forward in the elimination of the peasantry, and is turning their equipment over to the *kolkhozes*. And, we can surmise; in the fields of nuclear physics, the pressure to squeeze all theories into the ritualistic formulae of dialectical materialism has diminished. Certainly no one today talks, as they did twenty-five years ago, of the "bourgeois" physics of Einstein.

And yet, at some point — but where? — some essential aspects of the regnant ideology — but which? — must be maintained, for without

[42] Robert W. Campbell, "Some Recent Changes in Soviet Economic Policy," *World Politics*, IX, No. 1, October 1956, p. 8.

a central belief system with some continuity, disintegrative opinions begin to spread (e.g., Poland). Nothing demonstrates better the incalculable effects of such opinions, and of the role of single events in politics, than the corrosive effects of the Khrushchev speech denigrating Stalin. Once the charade is exposed, how can the large masses of people, particularly the youth, retain any belief, when the leadership itself has destroyed the moral and psychological basis of believing? Paradoxically, this may lead the rulers to an even more intensive effort to assert the validity of the central features of the ideology. A movement is never more fanatical than "when prophecy fails," or when hypocrisy is exposed, for in an effort to still the panicking doubts of the believers, it redoubles its efforts to assert the fundamentals of the faith.[43] And however cynical a ruling group may become about the "myths" that are necessary for the masses, in such situations they may find themselves psychologically trapped by the verbal formulae they employ, and act as if the ideology were real.

Foreign and Domestic

In the past, a determining factor in the behavior of foreign Communist parties, and in the policy of the Soviet government, has been the internal power struggles in the Soviet party. But one can argue now that the primary motives of internal Soviet development (e.g., the continued emphasis on heavy industry) are in reflex to the tense world situation. (And today how much of Russian foreign policy is determined with an eye to the rise of Red China as an autonomous power?) In any assessment, how do the Soviet rulers weigh these considerations?

Both the characterological and the geopolitical approach state, in effect, that whatever the internal developments in the Soviet Union, Soviet policy will be combative and expansionist, and that internal and external calculations affect only the timing of aggressive moves. But this leads, with deliberate intent, to the question which is the purpose of this discussion: To what extent is the Soviet system a qualitatively new phenomenon, subject to its own laws and indestructible from within; to what extent can the Soviet Union evolve gradually from within into a more stable, normal society?

The approaches broadly labeled characterological, Kremlinological, and totalitarian would argue the former, while the sociological and the Neo-Marxist, plus some of the historical school, would argue the latter proposition.

Derivative questions immediately arise: Was Stalin an aberration, or does communism, by its very nature (e.g., vanguard party, dictatorship of the proletariat, Bolshevik ideology), take one through a period of the Stalinist type even without a Stalin? Can Communist regimes in Europe, and especially in Asia, "leap directly" to a mellowed phase without going through the type of upheaval which Russia experienced?

[43] In this connection, see the interesting study, *When Prophecy Fails* (Minneapolis, 1956), by Leon Festinger, Henry W. Riecken, and Stanley Schacter.

Are the repressive phases merely a function of forced industrialization? At this stage the author, like Pirandello pursuing the illusion of reality, is tempted, almost, to repeat the ten theories which first set him off in search of reality. But, except for a coda, the play is done.

There is one large variable which these theories, in the nature of things, cannot adequately take into account: the behavior of the free world, which is the most important "reality factor" limiting the freedom of action of the Communist leaders. Here the role of social science becomes characteristically ambiguous. For the theories we have been discussing are designed to shape the behavior of the free world in its opposition to communism, but in doing so they set up the risk of a self-confirming hypothesis whereby we, because of our judgment of how the Communist may be expected to act, adopt policies forcing them to confirm or negate that judgment (just as the Russians force us into similarly prefigured molds). This is always a danger, but we can minimize it if we remember that no matter how far our social science sophistication has come, it cannot take the place of that practical flexibility which is demanded by two necessary humilities: an awareness of the limitations of our knowledge, and of the openness of history.

IV IDEOLOGY AND SOVIET FOREIGN POLICY

10. IDEOLOGY AND NATIONAL INTEREST IN SOVIET FOREIGN POLICY

Vernon V. Aspaturian

CONTINUITY AND CHANGE IN RUSSIAN FOREIGN POLICY

One of the most baffling aspects of Soviet foreign policy is its remarkable capacity for evoking the most variegated and contradictory responses to its diplomacy. "In its distant objectives," writes Edward Crankshaw, "the foreign policy of the Soviet Union is less obscure and more coherent than that of any other country," yet its immediate intentions and the motivations behind its day-to-day diplomacy often appear incoherent, capricious, and almost always enigmatic.[1]

The foreign policy of any country, the Soviet Union included, is not, however, simply the sum total of its avowed intentions, no matter how sincerely and devotedly they are adhered to, but must depend upon the capacity, in the present or in the future, to carry out its intentions. "In order to transform the world," Stalin told H. G. Wells in 1934, "it is necessary to have political power . . . as a lever of change."[2] Marxist ideology, reinforced by the early experiences of the Soviet regime, thus has persuaded the Kremlin that the capacity to transform intentions into reality is indistinguishable from power, a power which is objectively determined by the economic and social foundations of society, but

From Vernon V. Aspaturian, "Soviet Foreign Policy," in Roy C. Macridis, editor, *Foreign Policy in World Politics*, © 1957, 1962, and 1968. By permission of Prentice-Hall, Inc., Englewood Cliffs, New Jersey.

[1] *New York Times Book Review*, July 3, 1949, p. 4.
[2] J. V. Stalin and H. G. Wells, *Marxism vs. Liberalism* (New York, 1934), p. 14.

which, in turn, can dictate the evolution of society towards particular ethical and political goals.

In order to draw a proper appraisal of Soviet diplomacy at any given time, the voluntaristic aspects of Soviet foreign policy must always be measured against its power to overcome the deterministic impediments of international reality. Thus, although the Soviet Union can plan the calculated growth of the economic and military foundations of its power, it cannot "plan" foreign policy. This fact was eloquently stated by Maxim Litvinov to the Central Executive Committee in 1929:

> Unlike other Commissariats, the Commissariat for Foreign Affairs cannot, unfortunately, put forward a five-year plan of work, a plan for the development of foreign policy. . . . In . . . drawing up the plan of economic development, we start from our own aspirations and wishes, from a calculation of our own potentialities, and from the firm principles of our entire policy, but in examining the development of foreign policy we have to deal with a number of factors that are scarcely subject to calculation, with a number of elements outside our control and the scope of our action. International affairs are composed not only of our own aspirations and actions, but of those of a large number of countries . . . pursuing other aims than ours, and using other means to achieve those aims than we allow.[3]

The balance between the voluntaristic and deterministic components of Soviet foreign policy is neither fixed nor stable, but is in a state of continual and deliberate flux. In the initial stages of the Bolshevik Republic, its foreign policy was virtually at the mercy of external forces over which it could exercise little control, and Soviet diplomacy assumed the characteristic contours of a weak power struggling for survival under onerous conditions. As its economic and military position improved, it gradually assumed the characteristics of a great power and, given its geographical and cultural context, it took on the distinctive features of its Tsarist predecessors and the impulse to subjugate its immediate neighbors.

The Geographic and Historical Inheritance

"Marxism," writes a contemporary Soviet specialist on diplomacy, "teaches that economic factors determine the foreign policy and diplomacy of a state only in the long run, and that politics and diplomacy are, in a certain sense, conditioned by the concrete historical period and by many other elements (not excluding even, for instance, the geographical situation of a given country)."[4] Although Soviet writers may still tend to agree with the observation of the hapless Karl Radek, that "it is silly to say that geography plays the part of fate, that it determines

---

[3] *Protokoly Zasedani Tsentralnovo Ispolnitelnovo Komiteta Sovetov,* Bulletin 14 (Moscow, 1930), p. 1.

[4] F. I. Kozhevnikov, "Engels on 19th Century Russian Diplomacy," *Sovetskoye Gosudarstvo i Pravo* (No. 12), December 1950, pp. 18–34.

the foreign policy of a state,"[5] geography is nonetheless the most permanent conditioning factor in a country's foreign policy; for location, topography, and natural resources are significant — and often decisive — determinants of a country's economic and military power. Geography's effects, however, are relative, rarely absolute, always dependent upon the more variable factors in a country's character, such as its cultural traditions, political institutions, the size and diversity of its population, the exploitation of its natural resources, and the skill of its statesmen. A country's geography, with rare exceptions, cannot be remade; it can only be utilized more effectively. Thus, although Radek's contention that "the questions raised by geography are dealt with by each social formation in its own way . . . determined by its peculiar economic and political aims," remains incontestable, it was the blessing of Providence that this vast empire secreted all the basic ingredients for the erection of a powerful industrial and military state, given the necessary will and determination of its leadership. Had Russia been a wasteland with limited raw materials, she would have been doomed to be permanently a pre-industrial society. The character of her foreign policy — her very existence — would have been vastly different, and her vaunted ideology would have long been relegated to the ash cans of history.

The Soviet Union, like Tsarist Russia before it, is the largest single continuous intercontinental empire in the world. Embracing fully half of two continents, the Soviet Union has the world's longest and most exposed frontier, which is at once both its greatest potential hazard and one of its prime assets in international politics. As a part of both Europe and Asia, and embracing more than 150 ethnic and linguistic groups ranging from the most sophisticated nations to the most primitive, the U.S.S.R. achieves a unique microcosmic character denied any other country, including the United States with its ethnically variegated but linguistically assimilated population. Russia's serpentine frontier is both a consequence of the indefensibility of the central Russian plain and, at the same time, an important conditioning factor in the further evolution and execution of its foreign policy. For a weak Russia, such a frontier affords maximum exposure to attack, but for a powerful Russian state, this extended frontier, bordering on nearly a dozen states, offers an enviable and limitless choice for the exertion of diplomatic pressure. Since 1939, the Soviet Union has annexed four of its former neighbors, seized territory from seven more, and has made territorial demands upon two others; most of this territory was previously lost by a weakened Russia. Of all her bordering states, only Afghanistan has not been imposed on to cede territory to the Soviet Union.

In the past, Russia's geographical position has exposed her to continuous depredations and subjugation from all directions — an inevitable consequence of political disunity in a geographically indefen-

[5] Karl Radek, "The Bases of Soviet Foreign Policy," in H. F. Armstrong, ed., *The Foreign Affairs Reader* (New York, Harper & Row, Publishers, Inc., 1947) p. 173.

sible community. But if geography simplified the conquest of a divided Russia, it also facilitated the expansion of a united and powerful Russian state, which pushed out in all directions until it was arrested by superior force.

In the absence of more obvious geographical obstacles to her enemies, Russia's physical security became irrevocably attached to land space, while her psychological security became inseparable from political centralization. This conviction was confirmed by Stalin, himself, on the occasion of Moscow's 800th anniversary in 1947.

> Moscow's service consists first and foremost in the fact that it became the foundation for the unification of a disunited Russia into a single state with a single government, a single leadership. No country in the world that has not been able to free itself of feudal disunity and wrangling among princes can hope to preserve its independence or score substantial economic and cultural progress. Only a country united in a single centralized state can count on being able to make substantial cultural-economic progress and assert its independence.[6]

It is a persisting fact of Russian history that this dual quest for physical and psychological security has produced, in Russian foreign policy, a unique pattern. A divided Russia invites attack, but a united Russia stimulates expansion in all directions. The Revolutions in 1917, and the terrible purges of the Thirties which Stalin undertook to enforce unity at home exposed Russia's internal schisms to the world and stimulated foreign intervention. In each crisis, after surviving the initial assault from without, she embarked on a campaign designed to carry her beyond her self-declared national frontiers. The campaign failed in 1921, but she succeeded, after World War II, in bringing all of Eastern Europe under her hegemony.

The Bolsheviks fell heir not only to Russia's geography and natural resources, but also to the bulk of her population, her language, and the Russian historical and cultural legacy. Marxism gave Russia new goals and aspirations, but once the decision was taken to survive as a national state, even on a temporary and instrumental basis, the Soviet Union could not evade assuming the contours of a Russian state, and falling heir to the assets and liabilities of its predecessors. Although Lenin thought that he had irrevocably severed the umbilical cord with Russia's past, it was not entirely within his power to unburden the new Soviet Republic of the disadvantages of Tsarist diplomacy. Foreign attitudes remained remarkably constant; fears and suspicions, sympathies and attachments, were reinforced more than erased. Designs on Soviet territory still came from the same quarter, exposure to attack remained in the same places, and the economic and commercial lifelines of the Tsars became no less indispensable to the new regime. In short, even if the Soviet Union refused to remain Russia, Japan remained Japan, Poland remained Poland, and the Straits remained the Straits.

Moreover, the Russian language, permanently encrusted in its

---

[6] *Pravda*, September 11, 1947.

Cyrillic shell, became the official speech of Soviet diplomacy, and, as the vehicle of the Marxist dogma, it was pompously proclaimed the "language of the future." Russian cultural and scientific achievement became the basis for Soviet claims to cultural supremacy, of which Soviet science and culture were pronounced a continuation; the symbolism of Holy Russia was revived. Moscow eagerly laid claim to all the advantages of historic Russia, and the outside world just as assiduously refused to permit her to evade the liabilities and vulnerabilities of the Russian past. Thus, partly by choice and partly by necessity, the foreign policy of the Soviet Union could not but assume some of the contours of its predecessors.

The impact of a voluntaristic doctrine like Marxism on the geographical facts of Russia and her messianic traditions not only reinforced the psychological obsession for security, but provided an ideological rationale for assuming the implacable hostility of the outside world and sanctified Russian expansion with the ethical mission of liberating the downtrodden masses of the world from their oppressors. The hostile West of the Slavophils became the hostility of capitalism and imperialism; instead of the parochial messianism of the pan-Slav enthusiasts, Marxism provided Russia with a mission of universal transcendence — transforming the outside world into her own image, in fulfillment of her historic destiny and as the only permanent guarantee of absolute security. Up until the Twentieth Party Congress, in 1956, the Leninist-Stalinist thesis that "the destruction of capitalist encirclement and the destruction of the danger of capitalist intervention are possible only as a result of the victory of the proletarian revolution, at least in several large countries,"[7] continued to be in force. Although "capitalist encirclement" was declared ended by Stalin's successors, the recent events in Poland and Hungary may have convinced the Kremlin that this proclamation was premature.

To assume, however, that Soviet foreign policy is merely Russian imperialism in new garb would be a catastrophic mistake on both sides. Soviet foreign policy was bound to assume "Russian" characteristics during one phase of its metamorphosis, but now that the maximum, but still limited, aims of Tsarist imperialism have been virtually consummated, the aggressive (no longer necessarily expansionist) aspects of its foreign policy will assume a purely Marxist character, while only the defensive aspects (i.e., the preservation of its present power position) of its diplomacy will retain distinctively "Russian" features. That these two aspects of current Soviet foreign policy are in flagrant contradiction is self-evident, even to the Kremlin and other communist leaders. Chinese accusations of "Great Power chauvinism," the de-Stalinization campaign, and the uprisings in Poland and Hungary are all manifestations of this fundamental schism in Soviet foreign policy. Whereas in the past, when the Soviet Union was weak, indiscriminate emphasis on the revolutionary aspects of its foreign policy tended to undermine its basic instinct to survive, now, its defensive reflexes tend to subvert not

[7] *Kommunist* (No. 2), January 1953, p. 15.

only its continuing leadership of world communism, but the eventual success of the movement itself.

World Revolution and National Interest in Soviet Diplomacy

Deciphering Soviet motives is an elusive and hazardous undertaking, yet it must be done systematically and with calculation, otherwise *ad hoc* and unconscious assumptions acquire priority by default. Miscalculation of motives can often be catastrophic since foreign policy expectations are built upon assumptions concerning the motives and capabilities of other powers, and diplomatic success or failure often depend on the degree of accuracy with which these assumptions approach actuality. Much of the agony of postwar Western diplomacy can be traced directly to illusory expectations resulting from false calculations of Soviet motives by Western leaders. Diplomacy, however, is not an intellectual exercise, and motives are not always susceptible to rational and logical analysis. Assessment of motives, in any event, is rarely certain and in most cases calls not only for acute analytical intelligence, but espionage, and, above all, for the intuitive wisdom of long experience in statecraft.

Information concerning Soviet motives is derived from three principal sources: (1) word; (2) conduct; and (3) personal contact with the Soviet leadership. In general, whenever there exists a discrepancy between publicly stated intention and conduct, the latter is a more reliable indicator of motives on a short-run basis. Actually there are three possible relations between speech and practice in Soviet diplomacy: (1) *identity;* (2) *approximation,* usually implying a temporary accommodation or modification of a preconceived intention; unless the latter itself receives explicit reformation; and (3) *divergence.* Cleavages between word and conduct may, in turn, result from faulty execution, misinformation, miscalculation, or deliberate confusion.

Analyzing Soviet diplomacy purely from documents, speeches, and ideological statements, give undue weight to "rational" factors, since the irrational and accidental aspects of diplomacy can hardly be culled from documentary sources, and, although such a study may give a fairly lucid picture of the long-range outlines of Soviet policy, it is of limited validity as an investigation of Soviet diplomacy. On the other hand, calculating Soviet motives purely on the basis of day-to-day conduct and responses to particular situations can easily produce a distorted conception of Soviet foreign policy and lead to the erroneous conclusion that it is only slightly distinguishable from traditional Great Power diplomacy.

Diplomacy is neither impersonal nor automatic in its execution — although its working executors may often be both — but it is a human enterprise. Soviet motives cannot be separated from the character and personality traits of the principal decision makers in the Kremlin. Any evaluation of the foreign policy of the Soviet Union, whose principal decision makers are a well-defined oligarchy, without a prudent and careful examination and consideration of the various estimates and observations of the "human equations" in Soviet diplomacy is bound to be defective. The personal factor, particularly in the last fifteen years of Stalin's life, and during Khrushchev's incumbency, was of crucial significance in any evaluation of Soviet foreign policy. Personal observations of the Soviet leadership, however, are essentially subjective; they originate with observers who are free from neither ignorance, prejudice, nor gullibility, and the observations are apt to vary accordingly. Any attempt to distill the essence of Soviet diplomacy solely from personality considerations is in fact doomed to hopeless confusion and sterility. A sound analysis of Soviet motives must take into consideration ideology, conduct, and personalities, not as separate and independent entities, but as basic variables whose relative and relational significance is in a constant state of flux.

One question that inevitably arises is whether Soviet policy is actually motivated by ideological ends, such as world revolution, or by some other more mundane consideration, such as "power" or "national interest." Soviet ideology itself defines "national interest," "power," and "world revolution" in such a way as to make them virtually as indistinguishable and inseparable as the three sides of an equilateral triangle. The transcendental goal of Soviet foreign policy, world revolution, was defined by Lenin even before the existence of the Soviet state, when he declared in 1915 that "the victorious proletariat of [one country] . . . would stand up against . . . the capitalist world . . . raising revolts in those countries against the capitalists, and in the event of necessity coming out even with armed force against the exploiting classes and their states."[8] " 'The fundamental question of revolution is the question of power,' " wrote Stalin, quoting Lenin, and he went on to say that, as the effectiveness of the Soviet Union as an instrument of world revolution is measured in terms of power, "the whole point is to retain power to consolidate it, to make it invincible."[9] As a contrived and temporary nation-state, the Soviet Union assumed particular interests, but "the U.S.S.R. has no interests at variance with the interests of the world revolution, and the international proletariat naturally has no interests that are at variance with the Soviet Union."[10] Stalin's final fusion was to identify the consolidation and extension of his own power with the interests of the world revolution.

The abstraction of a Soviet national interest outside the context of Soviet ideology, no matter how superficially attractive it may appear to be as a useful analytical tool, ruptures the image of Soviet reality and results in the calculation of Soviet foreign policy on the basis of false assumptions. Soviet foreign policy is based on the image of reality provided by the Marxist-Leninist ideological prism, and whether this image be faulty or not is totally irrelevant in the calculation of Soviet motives, although such a foreign policy will eventually reap its toll in

[8] V. I. Lenin, *Selected Words* (New York, International Publishers Company, Inc., n.d.), V, p. 141.
[9] J. V. Stalin, *Problems of Leninism* (Moscow, Universal Distributors, 1947), p. 39.
[10] W. K. Knorin, *Fascism, Social-Democracy and the Communists* (Moscow, 1933).

diplomatic failure. The Soviet conception of "interest" cannot be separated from class categories, and its determination is essentially horizontal rather than vertical. Although the legal expression of class interests is temporarily articulated through the nation-state, and assumes the character of a "national interest," nonetheless in the Soviet view there exist within each state not one but several parallel "national interests," corresponding to its socio-economic development. The "national interest" reflected by the state in its diplomacy, however, can only represent the interests of the "ruling class," and no other, regardless of its pretensions.

Soviet ideology recognizes the coexistence of three qualitatively distinct national interests in the modern world, owing to the uneven development of society: (1) the national interest of the feudal aristocracy, surviving only in extremely backward societies; (2) the national interest of the bourgeoisie, which allegedly is the dominant expression of most non-communist states; and (3) the national interest of the proletariat, receiving diplomatic expression only in communist states, which is presumed by the dialectic to be coterminous with that of society as a whole.

Marxism tenaciously holds to the view that the community of interests that binds identical classes of different nations is more fundamental and decisive than that which binds different classes within the same nation-state. Although division and disunity are inherently characteristic of the bourgeois classes of different states, whose conflicts of interest are periodically expressed in war, the interests of all proletarians (together with their peasant and colonial allies) are considered to be in total harmony, their basic identity being temporarily obscured by artificially stimulated national distinctions.

Given the premise of the total identity of interests on a class basis, the Soviet Union, as the only avowed proletarian state in existence and the self-proclaimed embryo of a universal proletarian state, pronounced its interests to be identical with those of the world proletariat:

> The Communist Party of the Soviet Union has always proceeded from the fact that "national" and international problems of the proletariat of the U.S.S.R. amalgamate into one general problem of liberating the proletarians of all countries from capitalism, and the interests . . . in our country wholly and fully amalgamate with the interests of the revolutionary movement of all countries into one general interest of the victory of socialist revolution in all countries.[11]

Although this view is vigorously contested, is far from universally recognized, and does not correspond to actual facts, it is not thereby invalidated as a basis for diplomatic action or analysis.

The presence of one of two factors, both capable of objective verification, is sufficient to impart to the national interests of a particular state an authentic international quality. These factors are: (1) the creation of appropriate forms of political organization designed to

[11] *Kommunist* (No. 2), January 1953, p. 15.

articulate the national interests of one state as those of the world at large; and (2) mass recognition in other countries that the national interests of a foreign state are identical with a higher transcendental interest. Not one, but both of these desiderata characterize Soviet foreign policy. It was a cardinal aim to replace the nation-state system with a world communist state, by shifting allegiance and loyalty from the nation-state to class. This not only invited the nationals of other countries to recognize a higher, class, loyalty to the Soviet Union, but meant active engagement in fostering the appropriate political institutions, such as the Comintern, foreign communist parties, front organizations, and the like, to implement this fusion.

The Soviet invitation to commit mass disloyalty has elicited wide response, and the formula identifying Soviet interests with the interests of the world proletariat has been accepted by millions of communists throughout the world as a basis for political action. This gives to Soviet national interests an undeniable transcendental quality denied to the national interests of any other state except China. No matter how persistently a state may claim to be motivated by the interests of all mankind, if such a claim is accompanied neither by a serious effort at implementation nor evokes a response in other countries, it remains an empty and pious pretension. Transcendental ethical ends in foreign policy, irrespective of their substantive nature, have relevance only if they function as effective instruments or stimulants for the limitation, preservation, or further accumulation of power, or as instruments for its focalization. Otherwise, they are meaningless slogans and utopias, devoid of anything but peripheral significance in the calculation of a country's foreign policy.

Expansionism is thus inherent in the Leninist-Stalinist ideology, since the Soviet state was conceived as an ideological state without fixed geographical frontiers. Not only did this idea of the Soviet Union as the nucleus of a universal communist state receive expression in the basic documents of the Comintern,[12] but the Soviet Constitution of 1924 proclaimed the new Union to be open to all future Soviet republics and a "decisive step towards the union of workers of all countries into one World Socialist Soviet Republic."[13] And at Lenin's bier, Stalin vowed "to consolidate and extend the Union of Republics."[14] Since it was the indispensable instrument and base of the world revolution, the extension of Soviet power and territory, by any means, was equated with the exfoliation of the revolution.

Stalin's attempt to preserve the dominant and privileged status of the Soviet proletariat in the postwar communist fraternity of nations resulted in a specific form of Soviet imperialism that brought about

[12] *Cf.* W. C. Chamberlin, ed., *Blueprint for World Conquest* (Chicago, Human Events, Inc., 1946).
[13] Full text in M. W. Graham, *New Governments of Eastern Europe* (New York, Holt, Rinehart & Winston, Inc., 1927), p. 608.
[14] *History of the Communist Party of the Soviet Union* (New York, International Publishers Company, Inc., 1939), p. 269.

Tito's defection and unleashed corrosive forces within the orbit as a whole. The subsequent failure of Khrushchev and Mao Tse-tung to reconcile their divergent national interests may have produced an irreparable schism in the movement as a whole. The failure of Stalin and his successors to calculate accurately the persistence and vitality of the community of interests based on national peculiarities is actually a reflection of the inadequacy of Marxist categories to deal with the conflicting interests of national communities, whether they be communist or bourgeois.

Paradoxically, as long as the Soviet Union was the only communist state, its universalistic pretensions were unchallenged by foreign communist parties. But with the eclipse of the Soviet monopoly of the interests of the world proletariat, occasioned by the emergence of a Communist China and national communism in Eastern Europe, the universalistic pretensions of the Leninist doctrine have been blunted, while, at the same time, stimulating a more limited "regional interest" aimed at synthetizing the various national interests of the communist orbit. The transmutation of several national interests into a single supranational interest remains an insuperable difficulty in the communist world, so long as the incompatibility of individual communist national interests, which the Marxist dogma fails to perceive accurately, prevails:

> Marxism-Leninism has always strongly advocated that proletarian internationalism be combined with patriotism. . . . The Communist Parties of all countries must . . . become the spokesmen of the legitimate national interests and sentiments of their people [and] . . . effectively educate the masses in the spirit of internationalism and harmonize the national sentiments and interests of these countries.[15]

Less than seven years later, however, it had become quite clear that "the spirit of internationalism" could not prevail over the conflicting and incompatible national interests of the two great communist powers, each with its own national goals, aspirations, and image of the outside world. Since both the Soviet Union and China function within an identical ideological matrix, each has attempted to reshape and subordinate the interests of the communist movement to its own national interests, and each has provided an ideological rationalization for the transmutation of its national interests into the universal interests of all mankind. In 1963, Moscow denounced with eloquence the very vice which she had hitherto practiced with such consummate skill:

> The statements of the Chinese leaders reveal a growing tendency to speak on behalf of the peoples of practically the whole world, including the Soviet people, the peoples of other socialist countries, and also the young national states of Asia, Africa, and Latin America. "Yet, who has given the Chinese leaders the right," the Soviet people inquire with

[15] Statement by the Chinese Communist Party, "Once More on the Historical Experience of the Dictatorship of the Proletariat." Full text in *Pravda*, December 31, 1956.

indignation, "to decide for us, for the Soviet government, for the communist party, what is in keeping, and what is not in keeping with our interests? We have not given you the right and we do not intend to give it to you."[16]

SOVIET IDEOLOGY AND FOREIGN POLICY

The exact relationship between Soviet ideology and foreign policy has been subject to great controversy, ranging from the view that it is substantially irrelevant to the conviction that foreign policy is rigidly dictated by ideology. Actually, aside from providing the transcendental objectives of Soviet diplomacy, Soviet ideology performs five additional and distinct functions in foreign policy: (1) As a system of knowledge and as an analytical prism, it reflects an image of the existing social order and the distinctive analytical instruments (dialectical laws, and categories like the "class struggle," "historical stages," and so on) for its diagnosis and prognosis. (2) It provides an action strategy whereby to accelerate the transformation of the existing social order into the communist millennium. (3) It serves as a system of communication, unifying and coordinating the activities of its adherents. (4) It functions as a system of higher rationalization to justify, obscure, or conceal the chasms that may develop between theory and practice. (5) It stands as a symbol of continuity and legitimacy.

This compartmentalization of Soviet ideology is frankly arbitrary, and actually ruptures its basic unity, which is not necessarily to be found in its logic or reason, but in the intuitive faith and active experience of its partisans — factors which often elude rational analysis. Elements of Soviet ideology that appear logically incompatible, in fact, are, but these rational contradictions can be unified only in the crucibles of revolutionary action, not in the intellectual processes of the mind. The true meaning of the Marxist-Leninist insistence on the "unity of theory and practice" is that contradictions cannot be resolved by logic, but by action, which is the final judge of "truth." Communist "truth" cannot be perceived without intuitive involvement, i.e., revolutionary action and experience, and to the outsider it remains as enigmatic as the mysteries of Zen.

The Soviet Image of the World

The Soviet ideological prism reflects an image of the world that is virtually unrecognizable to a non-communist, yet it is on this image that Soviet foreign policy is based. It reflects a world of incessant conflict and change, in which institutions, loyalties, and philosophies arise and decay in accordance with the convulsive rhythm of the dialectic which implacably propels it on a predetermined arc to a foreordained future — world communism. This image is accepted as the real world by Soviet

[16] Soviet government Statement of August 21, 1963, *Pravda*, August 21, 1963.

leaders. Their foreign policy rests upon the conviction that Marxism-Leninism is a scientific system that has uncovered and revealed the fundamental and implacable laws of social evolution and, hence, affords its adherents the unique advantage of prediction and partial control of events. This conviction has imparted to Soviet diplomacy an air of supreme confidence and dogmatic self-righteousness:

> Soviet diplomacy . . . wields a weapon possessed by none of its rivals or opponents. Soviet diplomacy is fortified by a scientific theory of Marxism-Leninism. This doctrine lays down the unshakeable laws of social development. By revealing these norms, it gives the possibility not only of understanding the current tendencies of international life, but also of permitting the desirable collaboration with the march of events. Such are the special advantages held by Soviet diplomacy. They give it a special position in international life and explain its outstanding successes.[17]

The history of Soviet diplomacy, however, is by no means a uniform record of success, though "errors" in foreign policy are ascribed not to the doctrine, but to the improper apprehension and application of these infallible laws. Failure to apply these laws properly, according to the Soviet view, divorces foreign policy from international realities, and although it is true that "the record of Soviet diplomacy shows an inability to distinguish between the real and the imaginary, a series of false calculations about the capabilities and intentions of foreign countries, and a record of clumsy coordination between diplomacy and propaganda,"[18] still, it is fatuous to deny that Marxism-Leninism, on the whole, has furnished a system of analysis that gives a sufficiently accurate comprehension of power, its calculation and distribution in the world, and the opportunities and limitations such calculations afford for Soviet foreign policy. The dogmatic reliance on techniques and methods that have proven successful under other conditions, the frequent refusal to jettison concepts that either have outlived their usefulness or consistently produce dismal results in terms of foreign policy aims, and the concentration of all decision-making authority in one man or in a tight oligarchy — these practices at times tend to convert Marxism-Leninism from a unique asset for Soviet diplomacy into a strait jacket.

The Dialectical Image of History. Soviet ideology exposes the forces and tendencies operating in international politics, but it is up to the leadership to calculate these forces properly, seek out the most decisive trends, and coordinate Soviet diplomacy with the inexorable march of history. The success of Soviet diplomacy, according to the Soviet view, is maximized as it is attuned to the rhythm of the historical dialectic, and its failures are multiplied as it falls out of harmony. Conversely, the

[17] V. P. Potemkin, ed., *Istoriya Diplomatii* (Moscow, 1945), III, pp. 763–64.

[18] Max Beloff, *Foreign Policy and the Democratic Process* (Baltimore, The Johns Hopkins Press, 1955), p. 98. Cf., also V. V. Aspaturian, "Diplomacy in the Mirror of Soviet Scholarship," in *Contemporary History in the Soviet Mirror*, ed. J. Keep (New York, Frederick A. Praeger, Inc., 1964), pp. 243–74.

occasional successes of bourgeois diplomacy are due to fortuitous and haphazard coordination with historical development, or to the equally accidental deviation of Soviet foreign policy from the implacable dictates of history. These accidental deviations are attributed to faulty application of historical laws by individual leaders.

Without attempting any extended discussion of Soviet dialectics, it can be said that, in the communist view, history progressively exfoliates as a series of qualitative stages, each with its own peculiar economic organization of society, which gives rise to corresponding social, political, and religious institutions. This inexorable movement, from lower to higher forms of economic and social organization is propelled by means of a dialectical duel between perpetually developing economic forces of society and the social and political institutions that attempt to preserve the economic order in the interests of a particular ruling class, whose servants they are. As long as the institution of private property survives, class distinctions between property holders and the propertyless, whose interests are irreconcilable, are perpetuated, and will eventuate in conflict, war, and revolution, only to be replaced by a new economic system that perpetuates class divisions and conflicts in new form. The class struggle, which is the principal motivating force of historical revolution, comes to an end only with the overthrow of the capitalist system by the proletariat, after which class distinctions, conflict, and war are finally eliminated. Once communism achieves victory on a world scale, the state itself and its coercive institutions are supposed to "wither away."[19]

The communists recognize five qualitative historical stages: primitive communism, slave-system, feudalism, capitalism, and socialism-communism, all of which, except for the first and last, are characterized by the institution of private property, two main contending classes (owners of the means of production and workers), and a state that represents the interests of the ruling class. Although the movement of history is from lower to higher stages, this movement is neither uniform nor without complications, and it does not pursue a uniform and rigid chronological evolution. This has been particularly true of the twentieth century. At the present time, communists acknowledge the coexistence of all historical stages; and this recognition has had a profound influence on Soviet foreign policy.

The recognition of new or unforeseen historical stages or transitional forms in the dialectical movement of history is the most delicate and crucial problem of "creative Marxism," since Soviet policy must be based on a constantly changing historical reality and its strategy is subordinated to the dictates of each stage and varies geographically in accordance with different co-existing stages. Major doctrinal schisms arise whenever serious differences about the existence or nature of

---

[19] For a more elaborate statement of the author's views on the nature of Soviet ideology, see Vernon V. Aspaturian, "The Contemporary Doctrine of the Soviet State and Its Philosophical Foundations," *American Political Science Review*, XLVIII, December, 1954.

historical stages and their transitional forms cannot be reconciled. According to Stalin, Marxism is not

> . . . a collection of dogmas that "never" change despite changes in the conditions of the development of society. . . . Marxism as a science cannot stand still, it develops and improves. In its development Marxism cannot but be enriched by new experience, new knowledge — consequently some of its formulae and conclusions cannot but change with the passage of time, cannot but be replaced by new formulae and conclusions, corresponding to new historical tasks. Marxism does not recognize invariable conclusions and formulae obligatory for all epochs and periods.[20]

Even seemingly unambiguous concepts like "inevitability" are neither absolute nor fatally deterministic, but must be understood within the context of a particular historical stage and under given conditions. Thus what may appear inevitable, *viz.*, war, in one stage and under one set of conditions may no longer be inevitable if the conditions change or a new historical stage manifests itself. The single absolute is the abstraction of the dialectical movement itself; its content varies and hence is relativistic. Consequently, interpretation of Soviet dogma often assumes the character of tortured scholastic wrangling and frequently leads to tautological absurdities like "fatal inevitability," which presumably means inevitability in the absolute sense as differentiated from inevitability in the relative sense.

Soviet ideology is not self-executing; that is, it does not interpret itself automatically and does not reflect images of reality that can be unambiguously perceived, but rather it is based upon an authoritative interpretation of changing events by the Soviet leaders, who must choose from among a variety of possible interpretations, only one of which can be tested at a time for truth in the crucible of action. As long as Stalin was alive, interpretation of doctrine was a monopoly reserved for him alone, and it was his interpretation, whether it was concerned with the materialistic basis of the thought processes of the deaf and dumb or with the nature of the state, that became the basis for official policy. All other possible interpretations were consigned to heretical oblivion, to be resurrected later by him or by his successors who silently disputed his conception of reality.

The Two-Camp Image. Stalin's image of the world after the Russian Revolution was one of forced "co-existence" between a single socialist state and a hostile capitalist world surrounding it — a co-existence imposed upon both antagonists by objective historical conditions. Neither side being sufficiently powerful to end the existence of the other, they were fated to exist together temporarily on the basis of an unstable and constantly shifting balance of power:

> The fundamental and new, the decisive feature, which has affected all the events in the sphere of foreign relations during this period, is the

[20] J. V. Stalin, *Political Report of the Central Committee to the Fourteenth Congress of the C.P.S.U. (B)* (Moscow, 1950), p. 8.

fact that a certain temporary equilibrium of forces has been established between our country . . . and the countries of the capitalist world: an equilibrium which has determined the present period of "peaceful co-existence."[21]

The establishment, in a capitalistic world, of a socialist bridgehead which was inevitably destined to envelop the entire globe was, for Stalin, the supreme and ineluctable contradiction in the international scene. Although the capitalist world was infinitely stronger and could overwhelm the Soviet Republic if it could embark on a common enterprise, it was viewed as torn by internal divisions and conflicts that prevented the organization of an anti-Soviet crusade. Beside the overriding contradiction between the socialist camp and the capitalist camp, the bourgeois world was plagued with four additional inescapable contradictions: (1) the contradiction between the proletariat and the bourgeoisie in each country; (2) the contradiction between the *status quo* and the revisionist powers (Stalin referred to them as "victor" and "vanquished" capitalist states); (3) the contradiction between the victorious powers over the spoils of war; (4) the contradiction between the imperialist states and their colonial subjects.

The contradiction between the socialist and capitalist camps was considered by Stalin the most fundamental and decisive, but it was not to be aggravated so long as the Soviet Union was in a weakened condition. War between the two camps was viewed as inevitable; however, it could be temporarily avoided and delayed by astute maneuvering within the conflicts raging in the capitalist world.

> England's attempts to form a united front against the U.S.S.R. have failed so far. The reasons for this failure are: the antagonisms of interests in the camp of the imperialists. . . . Hence the task of taking into account the antagonisms in the camp of the imperialists, of postponing war by "buying off" the capitalists. . . . We must not forget what Lenin said about very much in our work of construction depending upon whether we succeed in postponing war with the capitalist world, which is inevitable, but which can be postponed either until the moment when the proletarian revolution in Europe matures, or until the moment when the colonial revolutions have fully matured, or, lastly, until the moment when the capitalists fight among themselves over the division of the colonies.[22]

During Stalin's lifetime, despite his periodic strictures against "dogmatism," his image of the two-camp world remained remarkably fixed although the center of the developing anti-Soviet crusade passed first from England to Nazi Germany and finally to the United States, which he had predicted as early as 1925 would become the final bastion

---

[21] J. V. Stalin, *Political Report of the Central Committee to the Fourteenth Congress of the C.P.S.U.* (B) (Moscow, 1950), p. 8.
1950), p. 8.
[22] J. V. Stalin, *Political Report of the Central Committee to the Fifteenth Congress of the Communist Party of the Soviet Union* (Moscow, 1950), pp. 29–30.

of world capitalism. Although this image of reality failed to apprise correctly the nature and motivations of Nazi Germany and incorrectly assumed the impossibility of a Soviet alliance with the Western Powers, Stalin's fixed vision of "two camps" poised in uneasy co-existence dominated Soviet diplomacy in the postwar period, becoming even more indelibly etched in Soviet ideology.

Stalin's postwar policy was predicated on an inevitable conflict with the West, organized by the United States. The organization of the Cominform and the forced unity of the communist orbit, the expulsion of Tito from the communist fraternity, the extraction of public statements of loyalty from communist leaders in all countries, the urgency with which Stalin sought to eliminate all possible power vacuums between the two blocs along the periphery of the communist world, all were preparatory measures based on the false assumption that the American ruling class was betraying anxiety at the growth of Soviet power and was preparing the final Armageddon. At the founding convention of the Cominform the late Andrei Zhdanov revealed the authoritative Soviet interpretation of the emerging bipolarization of power:

> The fundamental changes caused by the war on the international scene and in the position of individual countries have entirely changed the political landscape of the world. A new alignment of political forces has arisen. The more the war recedes into the past, the more distinct become two major trends in postwar international policy, corresponding to the division of the political forces operating on the international arena into two major camps; the imperialist and antidemocratic camp, on the one hand, and the anti-imperialist and democratic camp, on the other. The principal driving force of the imperialist camp is the U.S.A. . . . The cardinal purpose of the imperialist camp is to strengthen imperialism, to hatch a new imperialist war, to combat Socialism.[23]

Based on this grim image of the imminent expectation of violence, Soviet foreign policy assumed increasingly bellicose tendencies, which, in turn, evoked the natural response in the West that the Soviet Union, itself, was preparing to overrun Western Europe and all of Asia. Friction all along the periphery dividing the two worlds was frequent and finally erupted in the Korean war, when Stalin sanctioned the move into South Korea on the assumption that it had become a vacuum between the two blocs. This action accelerated defensive preparations in the West, and Stalin's policies, by predicting the increasing hostility of the West, actually forced its materialization.

During the Korean war and just prior to the Nineteenth Party Congress in 1952, a "great debate" had apparently taken place in the Politburo concerning the validity of the expectation of imminent war between the two camps. Two essentially divergent views were discussed by Stalin in his *Economic Problems of Socialism:* (1) that wars between capitalist countries had ceased to be inevitable and hence war between

[23] Full text reprinted in *Strategy and Tactics of World Communism* (Washington, D.C., G.P.O., 1948), pp. 216–217.

the two camps was imminent, the view that was then current; and (2) that wars between capitalist states remained inevitable, but that war between the two camps was unlikely. Although the first view was the basis of Soviet postwar policy, Stalin ascribed it to "mistaken comrades," and elevated the second to doctrinal significance:

> Some comrades hold that, owing to the development of new international conditions since the Second World War, wars between the capitalist countries have ceased to be inevitable. They consider . . . that the U.S.A. has brought the other capitalist countries sufficiently under its sway to be able to prevent them going to war among themselves and . . . that the foremost capitalist minds have been sufficiently taught by the two world wars . . . not to involve the capitalist countries in war with one another again. . . . It is said that the contradictions between capitalism and socialism are stronger than the contradictions among the capitalist countries. Theoretically, of course that is true. It is not only true now, today; it was true before the Second World War. . . . Yet the Second World War began not as a war with the U.S.S.R., but as a war between capitalist countries. Why? . . . because war with the U.S.S.R., as a socialist land, is more dangerous to capitalism than war between capitalist countries; for whereas war between capitalist countries puts in question only the supremacy of certain capitalist countries over others, war with the U.S.S.R. must certainly put in question the existence of capitalism itself. . . . It is said that Lenin's thesis that imperialism inevitably generates war must now be regarded as obsolete. . . . That is not true. . . . To eliminate the inevitability of war, it is necessary to abolish imperialism.[24]

Stalin's only modification of his two-camp image was thus to concede that war between the two blocs was no longer imminent, but would be preceded by a series of wars among the capitalist powers themselves — between the United States and its satellite allies, France and Britain, on the one hand, and its temporary vassals, Germany and Japan, on the other. The resentment of the ruling classes of these vassal countries over American domination would provoke national revolutions and a renewed war over the ever-shrinking capitalist market, occasioned by the emergence of a parallel communist market, which would remain outside the arena of capitalist exploitation. The Soviet Union would remain outside the conflict, which would automatically seal the doom of world capitalism. However, Stalin's policies actually accentuated the very conflict — that between the two camps — he wished to temporarily deemphasize, while submerging those — among the capitalist states — which he wished to exacerbate. Soviet policy, by predicting war, was threatening to make inevitable a nuclear holocaust which would destroy both worlds.

The Post-Stalin Image. Stalin's image of reality was first challenged by Tito in 1948 and apparently later by his own colleagues on the Politburo. Khrushchev admitted that these differences were so serious that Stalin was plotting to liquidate all of his old associates for daring to

24 J. V. Stalin, *Economic Problems of Socialism* (New York, International Publishers, 1952), pp. 27–30.

question his ideological infallibility. Stalin's obstinate refusal to keep in step with changing conditions resulted in converting Soviet ideology from a prism that reflected reality into a prison that concealed it, resulting not only in a series of diplomatic blunders, but also in blinding Moscow to new diplomatic opportunities. As the man, next to Stalin, most closely associated with Soviet foreign policy, Molotov confessed on behalf of his departed chief:

> We do not infrequently still remain prisoners of habits and patterns formed in the past, before World War II, and which now hinder the deployment of new, wider, and more active forms of struggle. . . . We not infrequently still suffer from underestimation of the new possibilities which have opened before us in the postwar period. . . . We must stop underestimating the immense possibilities which we have. . . . In the field of foreign policy our Party proceeds from the need for the most serious consideration of concrete conditions and from the need for understanding the given situation and the prospects of historic development. The Leninist combination of adherence to principle and elasticity in pursuance of the foreign policy line is the factor which insures success for our Party in the solution of internal tasks.[25]

At the Twentieth Party Congress, Stalin's image of the world was considerably modified, in an attempt to bring it into closer focus with the realities of international politics. These modifications were made to eliminate the threatening schisms in the communist camp, to break up the unity of the non-Soviet world and dismantle anti-Soviet instruments like NATO, to head off the impending nuclear war that Stalin's doctrines and policies were unwittingly encouraging, and to enhance the flexibility of Soviet diplomacy in exploiting the contradictions of the capitalist world.

In place of Stalin's fatalistic image of a polarized world, the Twentieth Party Congress drew a more optimistic, and, in many respects, a mellower picture:

1. "Capitalist encirclement" was officially declared terminated, as major speakers like Molotov echoed the Titoist doctrine that "the period when the Soviet Union was . . . encircled by hostile capitalism now belongs to the past." The permanent insecurity of the Soviet Union, pending the worldwide victory of communism, as visualized by Stalin, was replaced with the image of a permanently secured Soviet Union, surrounded by friendly communist states in Europe and Asia, embracing nearly one-third of the world, with imperialism in an irrevocable state of advanced decay.

2. In place of Stalin's fixed vision of coexistence between two irreconcilable camps poised in temporary balance, which was declared obsolete and inapplicable to the postwar world, his successors recognized a third, "anti-imperialist" but nonsocialist, group of powers, carved out of decaying colonial empires, which had separated from the capitalist camp but had not yet joined the communist. Stalin's inflexible two-camp image needlessly alienated these new states and tended to force them into the

---

[25] Full text as broadcast by the Moscow Radio, February 20, 1956; cf. also *The New York Times*, February 21, 1956.

capitalist orbit. This belt of neutralist states — a concept which Stalin refused to recognize — insulated the entire communist orbit from the capitalist world and, together with the socialist states, was viewed as constituting "an extensive 'zone of peace,' including both socialist and nonsocialist peace-loving states of Europe and Asia inhabited by nearly 1,500,000,000 people, or the majority of the population of our planet."[26]

3. Stalin's doctrine of the "fatal inevitability" of wars was pronounced antiquated, since its emphasis on coercive and violent instruments of diplomacy tended to render the Soviet peace campaign hypocritical, accelerated the formation of anti-Soviet coalitions, and, in an era of nuclear weapons, appeared to doom both worlds to a war of mutual annihilation.

4. Stalin's five main contradictions were retained as valid and persistent, but the radical shift in the equilibrium of class forces in the world dictated a change of emphasis and the reordering of priorities. Stalin stressed the conflicts among the major capitalist countries as the main object of Soviet diplomacy, relegating other contradictions to minor roles, but his successors saw the main contradiction of the current historical stage to be that between the anticolonial and the imperialist forces. In short, the world has moved out of the stage of the "capitalist encirclement" of the Soviet Union and, during the current phase of coexistence, is moving into the stage of the "socialist encirclement" of the United States, as a prelude to the final victory of communism.[27]

The new image of the world drawn by Khrushchev at the Twentieth Party Congress was by no means the consequence of a unanimous decision. It was opposed by at least four, and possibly five, full members of the eleven-man Presidium. Aside from his vigorous opposition to Khrushchev's adventurist innovations in industry and agriculture, Foreign Minister Molotov and the so-called Stalinist faction bitterly resisted the demolition of the Stalin myth and the entire de-Stalinization program; and they systematically sabotaged the foreign policy decisions of the Twentieth Party Congress, which they publicly accepted.

Molotov's disagreement with the Khrushchev faction was not merely over the execution of foreign policy but over fundamental doctrinal propositions as well. Thus he disputed the thesis on the "fatal inevitability of wars" that was one of the key decisions of the Party Congress. "Comrade Molotov," according to the resolution of the Central Committee which expelled him from the Presidium on June 29, 1957, "opposed the fundamental proposition worked out by the party on the possibility of preventing wars in the present condition." Furthermore, he controverted the Titoist doctrine "on the possibility of different ways of transition to socialism in different countries," and resisted the decision "on the necessity of strengthening contacts between the CPSU and the progressive parties abroad [i.e. non-Communist socialist parties]."[28]

[26] Full text as broadcast by Moscow Radio, February 18, 1956; cf. also *The New York Times,* February 19, 1956 (Mikoyan Report).

[27] Ibid.

[28] Full text of the resolution reprinted in *The New York Times,* July 4, 1957. These and all subsequent references to this resolution are taken from this version.

Molotov's doctrinal differences had practical consequences in the actual formulation and execution of foreign policy. His constant carping criticism of existing policies, together with the precarious nature of Khrushchev's majority in the Presidium, introduced an uncharacteristic hesitancy into Soviet diplomacy. The vacillations, abrupt reversals, hesitations, discrepancies between policy and administration, and other eccentricities of Soviet diplomacy after Stalin's death were due not only to the incapacitating incompatibilities in the Presidium but also to Molotov's use of the foreign ministry and Soviet missions abroad as instruments to subvert the Government's policy in favor of his own.

Molotov objected to the decisions to seek a reconciliation with Marshal Tito and to meet President Eisenhower at Geneva. When Khrushchev and Bulganin returned from Geneva, Molotov was waiting with sarcastic and biting comments on their personal diplomacy. As a result of his persistent criticism and obstructionism, he was disciplined by the Central Committee in July, 1955, and his "erroneous stand on the Yugoslav issue was unanimously condemned." This was followed shortly by his forced and pained confession of doctrinal error, which superficially appeared to have no connection with foreign policy but appeared designed to tarnish his ideological orthodoxy and was an unmistakable sign that he was on his way out. His unrelenting sabotage through the foreign ministry, in particular his determination to poison relations with Tito, finally led to his ouster as foreign minister in favor of Shepilov on the eve of Tito's visit to Moscow in June, 1956. Apparently Shepilov also fell out of sympathy with the foreign policy he was supposed to execute and for opportunistic reasons (Khrushchev scathingly characterized him as "the careerist Shepilov who . . . showed himself to be a most shameless double-dealer") cast his lot with the Stalinist faction. The Molotov group suddenly contrived a majority in the December, 1956, Plenum of the Central Committee, but when Khrushchev regained control at the February, 1957, Plenum, Shepilov was summarily dismissed as foreign minister in favor of Andrei Gromyko, who was a professional diplomat and thus could be counted upon not to pursue a personal foreign policy.

In the bill of particulars against Molotov, who was supported most consistently by Kaganovich and sometimes by Malenkov, there was revealed an almost complete alternative foreign policy to the one currently adopted by the Soviet Government, one that in effect unwittingly constitutes the platform of a "disloyal opposition." In the sphere of foreign policy," according to the indictment, "the group, in particular Comrade Molotov, showed narrow-mindedness and hampered in every way the implementation of the new pressing measures intended to ease international tension and promote universal peace." It was charged:

> 1. For a long time, Comrade Molotov in his capacity as Foreign Minister, far from taking through the Ministry of Foreign Affairs measures to improve relations between the U.S.S.R. and Yugoslavia, repeatedly came out against the measures that the Presidium . . . was carrying out to improve relations with Yugoslavia.

2. Comrade Molotov raised obstacles to the conclusion of the state Treaty with Austria and the improvement of relations with that country, which lies in the center of Europe. The conclusion of the Austrian Treaty was largely instrumental in lessening international tension in general.

3. He was also against normalization of relations with Japan, while that normalization has played an important part in relaxing international tension in the Far East.

4. Comrade Molotov repeatedly opposed the Soviet Government's indispensable new steps in defence of peace and security of nations. In particular he denied the advisability of establishing personal contacts between the Soviet leaders and the statesmen of other countries, which is essential for the achievement of mutual understanding and better international relations.[29]

Besides these publicly stated charges against Molotov, it was reported from Warsaw that Khrushchev admitted in the Central Committee that Dulles was "practically right" when he accused Moscow of "trying for months to torpedo the disarmament talks," but he qualified this by saying that "it was not the Soviet Union that tried to torpedo the talks but Molotov, Kaganovich, and Shepilov."[30] He also accused Molotov of enflaming relations with other communist parties, probably those of China, Poland, Japan, Italy, and the United States.

"Molotov," Khrushchev bluntly stated in a later speech, "found more convenient a policy of tightening all screws, which contradicts the wise Leninist policy of peaceful co-existence." Thus, it can be assumed that Molotov advocated a continuation of the basic foreign policies of the Stalinist era, as modified during the Malenkov regime, based on a perpetuation of the two-camp image. It was Molotov's contention that Soviet policy could reap its greatest dividends by maintaining international tensions at a high pitch and running the risks of nuclear war, on the assumption that an uncompromising, cold-blooded policy would force Western statesmen, through lack of nerve and under pressure of public opinion to continually retreat in the face of Soviet provocation, for fear of triggering a war of mutual extinction. It appears that he considered as un-Marxist the idea that the ex-colonial countries could be regarded as having deserted the capitalist camp and as constituting an "extensive zone of peace" together with the Soviet bloc, but rather he considered their behavior in international politics to be motivated purely by considerations of opportunism and expediency. The main arena of rivalry for Molotov remained in Western Europe and the Atlantic area — the bastions of capitalism — and not in Asia or Africa, and he continued to view the new countries of Asia and Africa with hostility and suspicion as appendages to the capitalist camp.

Molotov's policy of "tightening all screws" was opposed by the Soviet army, and also by Peking, which had its own reasons, although it

[29] The last point is probably a reference not only to the Geneva Conference but also to the various junkets of Bulganin and Khrushchev throughout Asia and Europe, none of which included Foreign Minister Molotov.

[30] *The New York Times,* July 7, 1957.

was later revealed that the Chinese and Molotov seemed to agree on a wide range of issues. Speaking in Peking, Anastas Mikoyan, reputedly the principal Kremlin architect of the new diplomatic strategy, invoked Lenin in support of the current policy. Quoting Lenin's famous formula that "in the last analysis, the outcome of the struggle will be determined by the fact that Russia, India, China, etc. constitute the overwhelming majority of the world's population," he roundly condemned the Stalinist two-camp image to which Molotov still subscribed:

> We must consider it harmful that all countries not belonging to the socialist system are sometimes put in the same category and then are mechanically included in the capitalist camp. . . . The paths which are now being followed and blazed by India, Burma, Indonesia, Egypt and other countries which have won their independence have a general international significance. . . . The development of these countries and their policies weaken imperialism, deepen the crises in the capitalist system, destroy colonialism as one of the mainstays of this system and hasten the end of capitalism.[31]

Soviet diplomatic strategy in the underdeveloped countries of Asia, Africa and Latin-America appears to contradict the basic revolutionary strategy of communism. Although Moscow's support of the so-called "bourgeois-nationalist" (roughly, "neutralist" under existing conditions) independence or revolutionary movements in the underdeveloped regions (colonies and "semi-colonies") against Western colonialism, economic dependence upon the West and internal feudalism, is fully compatible with Leninist-Stalinist doctrine on revolution in the under-developed world, the Soviet pattern of political and economic assistance to regimes like those in India, Egypt, Iraq, Ghana and, to a lesser extent, Cuba, does not fully conform to communist doctrine. Red China has stepped into this breach and has challenged Moscow's refusal to encourage and support indigenous communist parties in their efforts to overthrow native "bourgeois-nationalist" governments and establish authentic communist-controlled regimes. Instead, according to Peking, Moscow supports governments which persecute and imprison local communists.

The Soviet position on this point is extraordinarily non-doctrinaire and pragmatic, for whereas China stresses the view that the Communist Party is the only reliable instrument of revolution, Khrushchev and his successors appear to be toying with the idea that under favorable circumstances, particularly when the balance of power has shifted decisively in favor of the communist world, native bourgeois-nationalist leaders may be won over to communism and the revolution could be consummated from above rather than below. The transformation of the Castro regime in Cuba, from an anti-imperialist, nationalist regime into a communist regime, was apparently viewed by Khrushchev as a prototype of this process. As a practical diplomatic position, Moscow feels that any move to encourage communist insurrection in these areas

---

[31] *Pravda*, September 18, 1956.

would simply stampede them all into the capitalist and anti-communist camp, a development which Peking considers — along with Molotov — as inevitable in any event. Peking's present strategy seems to stem from the conviction that the bourgeois nationalists will betray the Soviet Union (as Chiang Kai-shek did in 1928) and that, by supporting the local Communist parties now, China will have earned their gratitude and support.

11. SOVIET CONCEPTIONS OF DIPLOMACY

Vernon V. Aspaturian

I. INTRODUCTION

"Honesty in politics," Lenin shrewdly observed, "is the result of strength; hypocrisy is the result of weakness."[1] Duplicity, perfidy, deceit, chicanery, and cruder forms of dishonesty have been the indelible stigmata of Soviet diplomacy in the past, as tortured falsehood, palpable distortion, and disingenuous fabrication have characterized Soviet scholarship in this area. The death of Stalin introduced a fresh breeze, at first a barely distinguishable zephyr in the storm of destalinization, which has done much to cleanse the halls of Soviet scholarship. The more powerful and confident the Soviet Union has become in the post-Stalin era, the more its diplomatic behavior tends to abjure the hypocrisies and deceits of the past in favor of more forthright postures in both internal and external policy, and the less urgent becomes the need to distort history. One of the distinguishing features of post-Stalinist diplomacy is its greater reliance upon the innate power position of the Soviet Union in a world in which the equilibrium of military, psychological, and political forces are shifting perceptibly in favor of the Communist orbit. Less reliance upon the hypocritical gestures and debased contrivances of the past, and more on the momentum of history to accomplish purposes and objectives seems to be the emerging trend.

Soviet diplomatic behavior now corresponds more faithfully to the

Originally published in a shorter form under the title, "Diplomacy in the Mirror of Soviet Scholarship," in J. Keep and L. Brisby, editors, *Contemporary History in the Soviet Mirror* (Copyright 1965). Reprinted by permission of Frederick A. Praeger, Inc. and George Allen and Unwin Ltd.

[1] V. I. Lenin, *Sochineniya*, vol. XVII, p. 138.

norms of Soviet ideology, although residual elements of Stalinist diplomacy continue to be secured in reserve to be resurrected in moments of stress and unexpected lapses into weakness, as demonstrated by the Soviet army intervention during the Hungarian uprising in 1956. It should come as no surprise that the Hungarian Revolution and its repression is the "dead rat," to use the quaint phraseology of Khrushchev, in the throats of contemporary Soviet scholars, for none of the routine falsifications and unsophisticated propaganda devices of the Stalinist era that were so conspicuous here, could create "legions" of Horthy and American fascists where none existed, or conceal the dismay and chagrin of Soviet scholars, who were forced to revert to the unlamented but unburied devices of the past.

As the Soviet system becomes more entrenched, and if the balance of power continues to shift in its favor, there may be a corresponding but distressing tendency on the part of the western powers, particularly the United States, to desperately resort to gimmicks and devices of deception and hypocrisy in achieving their objectives. The Suez conspiracy, the revelations of the U–2 affair, and the ignoble and awkward fabrications and confessions made by the highest responsible authorities of the American Government, together with the ill-concealed and equally fumbling adventure into subversion demonstrated by the Cuban fiasco, correspond increasingly to Soviet expectations of "bourgeois" diplomatic behavior. If current post-mortems and reappraisals of American foreign policy are indications of future diplomatic action, the increasingly weakened position of the West is likely to result in not less, but more resort to tricks and gimmicks, such as more "effective" propaganda, guerrilla warfare, and subversion, rather than upon power, prestige, and policy to achieve or preserve foreign policy objectives. Diplomacy conducted from positions of impotence is an art in itself, which frequently becomes a diplomacy of wits or duplicity.

There is no intention to imply that the Soviet Union and the West have in fact exchanged diplomatic postures, for the gap between the residues left by forty years of systematically nurtured diplomatic deceit and this disturbing trend in western diplomacy is still substantial, but it would be a foolish self-deception to ignore these increasingly perceptible changes in diplomatic behavior.

II. GRAPPLING WITH THE STALINIST LEGACY
IN THE ACADEMIES

During the Stalinist era international politics and diplomacy were matters reserved exclusively for the Politburo. A regime of fabrication and stultification descended upon Soviet scholarship and all journals and books dealing with foreign policy. Works on diplomacy implicitly bore the imprimatur, not merely of official tolerance, but of quasi-official inspiration. For each subject, an official textbook was the rule, which was invariably superseded by another work, usually a symposium, in accordance with changes in policy. General texts on international relations, Soviet foreign policy, and international organization were virtually non-existent. Specialized monographs on international legal subjects and official textbooks on international law pre empted the ficld.

The two general reference works on diplomacy, the *Diplomatic Dictionary* in two volumes, and the three-volume *History of Diplomacy*, edited in both cases by active or retired officials of the Soviet Foreign Ministry, constituted the *summa theologica* of Stalinist scholarship on diplomacy.[2] By way of documentation, there was a collection of treaties published annually and a handy series of compilations of Soviet foreign policy documents, which ceased publication around 1950. Since the writing of a textbook on Soviet foreign policy was only slightly less hazardous than writing a history of the party, not a single scholar could be found to undertake the task, and no comprehensive account of Soviet foreign policy was in fact published. The only book on the United Nations was an innocuously descriptive volume by S. B. Krylov, published in 1946.[3] As surrogates for scholarship there was a profusion of tendentious propaganda booklets paying tribute to Stalin's genius as a statesman.

The special risks involved were dramatized by the fate of one of the chief editors of Volume I of the *Diplomatic Dictionary* (published in 1948), S. A. Lozovsky, an old Comintern functionary and a former Deputy Commissar of Foreign Affairs, who vanished just before the appearance of the second volume in 1950, in which he was not even given an entry. His dismal end was officially recorded in the second edition of the *Large Soviet Encyclopedia* (Vol. 51, p. 180).

Things started to change soon after Stalin's death. In 1954 the Soviet journal *Mezhdunarodnaya Zhizn* was revived, and while its contents did not materially deviate from the Stalinist tradition, its appearance alone was a welcome innovation. (A journal with the same title was published in the twenties as an organ of Narkomindel.) It was the Twentieth Party Congress, however, which relieved Soviet scholarship of the Stalinist incubus. Characteristically, the party leaders blamed the intellectuals for the deficiencies and stagnation of Soviet scholarship and rebuked them for not taking a more imaginative and active role in discussing international relations and contemporary history, and for failing to demonstrate more courage in resisting the fabrications of the Stalinist era.[4] The depressing state of affairs was revealed in a series of letters to the editors of *Mezhdunarodnaya Zhizn* in 1956–7,[5] which read like a carefully rehearsed five-year plan in which scholars, publishers, and propagandists exchanged mutual recriminations and confessions of negligence in a mood of inspired self-criticism.

[2] *Diplomaticheskii slovar*, I, edited by A. Y. Vyshinsky and S. A. Lozovsky (Moscow, 1948); II, edited by A. Y. Vyshinsky (Moscow, 1950). *Istoriya diplomatii*, 3 vols., edited by V. P. Potemkin (Moscow, 1945).
[3] S. B. Krylov, *Materialy k istorii Organizatsii Obedinennykh Natsii* (Moscow, 1946).
[4] Cf. the speeches by A. I. Mikoyan and Madame A. Pankratova.
[5] *International Affairs*, 1956, No. 12, 98–9; 1957, No. 1, 159–68; No. 2, 133–6.

The first letter was submitted by four distinguished scholars, headed by the veteran jurist Yevgeny Korovin, in which the publishing house Gospolitizdat was censured for publishing only propaganda to the exclusion of serious works of scholarship on foreign policy, and the journal itself reprimanded for not demanding higher standards from its contributors:

> We are of the opinion that the necessary stimulation of research work on the study of current world affairs is proceeding too slowly. Evidence of this is to be found above all in the fact that new and original scholarly works of research into the most important current international problems are not being published . . . We find that popular booklets on general themes occupy the dominant position . . . Actually no monographs on the basic problems in world affairs are available . . . Furthermore, books on general political subjects, history, economics, and law are reviewed very irregularly in our periodicals. So far there has not been a single work of any importance . . . generalizing and offering a scientific evaluation of the activities of the UN and its agencies. The present paucity of reference works on international economic and political problems is impermissible. Why, for example, have we no works of biographical reference containing information on the political figures of various countries, no scientifically edited and systematically published editions of documents of foreign powers, no reference books dealing with political parties and government bodies, no year-books of world events, such as are very widespread abroad, etc.?[6]

The four scholars went on to urge that "the teaching of the history of international relations and international law in higher educational institutions . . . be radically improved." Existing courses, they noted, "devote too little attention to questions of the history of diplomacy."

The letter elicited two responses in the next issue, one from S. Mayorov, the head of the Department of Literature on International Problems of Gospolitizdat, and another from I. Ivashin, head of the faculty of International Relations of the Higher Party School, whose sacred cows had been attacked by Korovin and company. Mayorov, recognizing true inspiration, responded with reluctant but equally inspired agreement. The charge was accurate but the target was a case of mistaken identity. The real culprits were the scholars themselves, who refused to produce suitable manuscripts.

> We applied to all the appropriate research institutes . . . and the higher educational establishments with departments of international relations and general history, requesting that they inform us of their plans for research . . . The result was a great disappointment, for very little of the material offered could be included in our publication plan.

The scholars, it seemed, under the spell of some strange malady or subject to equally strange idiosyncrasies, were eminently uninterested in current problems of international relations and organizations, but

[6] *International Affairs*, 1956, No. 12, 98–9. The letter was also signed by Academician A. Guber and Professors N. Lyubimov and A. Manfred.

were enamored of "topics dealing with the past." The deficiencies in the area of Soviet foreign policy were truly monumental and just short of scandalous. "The most serious shortcoming," Mayorov asserted, "in the work of research institutes and university departments studying international affairs . . . is the absolutely unsatisfactory state of the study of Soviet foreign policy, its history, and relations between the USSR and other countries." Not a single scholar in the Institute of History of the Academy of Sciences — the *sanctum sanctorum* of Soviet scholarship — was engaged in the study of Soviet foreign policy, and its "research programmes for 1955 and 1956 did not contain a single Soviet foreign policy topic and not a single such topic was studied." Even more reprehensible, "the institute does not train any experts in this field. Not a single post-graduate submitted or even prepared a thesis on Soviet foreign policy."

Comrade Ivashin's reply was less humble and in some respects positively aggressive. Whereas Korovin and company were disturbed by the rate at which scholars and scholarship were being displaced by hacks and propaganda tracts "on peaceful co-existence," Ivashin castigated the scholars for producing works that were worthless for the propagandist. "They indiscriminately censure all booklets on the peaceful co-existence of the two systems," he complained, and in turn exacted his vengeance by gratuitously noting that a recent article by Korovin "is an example of a careless attitude to the reader . . . evidently composed in a hurry and . . . nothing but a compilation of sentences and facts covering a period of forty years." He went on:

> At the present time there are almost no educational establishments to train qualified propagandists in the field of international affairs. Humanity departments of higher schools either offer no courses on international affairs whatsoever or make these courses purely optional. Unfortunately, in 1956 the course on international relations and Soviet foreign policy was dropped from the curriculum of republican, territorial, and inter-regional party schools where many propagandists receive their training . . . Great anxiety is caused by the fact that current history (the most important and vital part of general history) is not taught at all in secondary schools and is only touched upon in the part of the syllabus covering the post-October period of the history of the USSR. Thus, knowledge of the most important contemporary events abroad is kept from millions of young people. Our historians should be ashamed of the fact that we have no textbooks on current history. A number of works on general history are carried only as far as 1917.

Sarcastically, he noted that "work on a world history has been going on for about twenty years but so far only Volume I has been completed."

It was now time for the historians and the provincial constituencies to be heard from. Professor Galkin, head of the Modern History Department of Moscow University, in turn accused the publishing houses "of converting scholarly papers into popular, or at best popular science, booklets, a practice which does not attract serious authors."[7] Further-

---

[7] Letters from Professors Galkin and M. Yanovsky (Assistant Professor, Tashkent State University) are in *International Affairs*, 1957, No. 2.

more, "repeated abridgements of history books have transformed them into a compendium of titles and brief sociological generalizations [in which] . . . history has been deprived of its pulse." Conceding that "training of post-graduates in the field of international relations has been stopped," he announced proudly that his department at least had one post-graduate in this subject.

This was the state of Soviet scholarship and teaching in the field of international relations and diplomacy some years ago. Since then, however, a veritable avalanche of books, monographs, symposia, reference works, and documentary collections has poured forth from Soviet universities, research institutes, and publishing houses, on all types of international and diplomatic subjects. In 1957 there appeared the first history of Soviet foreign policy, produced by Ivashin's Higher Party School, which was almost immediately attacked and criticized by other scholars for its superficiality.[8] A lively discussion on Soviet foreign policy ensued in the pages of *Mezhdunarodnaya Zhizn* in 1958-9,[9] and dozens of works on Soviet foreign policy alone have been published since 1957.[10] The number of books and monographs on other aspects of diplomacy run into hundreds, including numerous translations of western books.

The recent output is distinguished by its relatively high level of scholarship, sophisticated approach to ideological questions, and its varied use of foreign publications, though these are selected from among those western works which either present the Soviet position in a sympathetic light or represent extremely hostile positions which seem to confirm Soviet preconceptions and expectations of "bourgeois" behavior. Tendentious and stereotyped propaganda tracts, shorn of the more vulgar excrescences of the Stalinist era, continue to appear, but with diminishing frequency, and they must now compete for attention with the output of genuine scholars.

The publication of documents was inaugurated with the annual series of *Documents on Soviet Foreign Policy*, the first volume of which appeared in 1957.[11] In contrast to Stalinist practice, documents signed by former Soviet luminaries later consigned to oblivion appear with their original signatures. Soviet scholars and the Soviet public can now see for themselves the important parts played by personalities such as Trotsky, Krylenko, Joffe, Kamenev, Shlyapnikov, Karakhan, Rakovsky, Sokolnikov, and others during the early days of Soviet diplomacy, with-

[8] *Istoriya mezhdunarodnykh otnoshenil i vneshnei politiki SSSR 1870–1957 gg.* (Moscow, 1957). An earlier outline, *Mezhdunarodnye otnosheniya i vneshnyaya politika SSSR 1917–1941 gg.*, had been published in 1955 for use in military academies.

[9] *International Affairs*, 1958, No. 2, 63–70; No. 5, 71–5; No. 7, 59–64; No. 8, 65–71.

[10] For a list of recent Soviet works on international relations, cf. the 400-page bibliographical handbook compiled by V. Yegorov, *Mezhdunarodnye otnosheniya: bibliograficheskii spravochnik: 1945–1960* (Moscow, 1961). Not a single work by Stalin is listed, although speeches and articles by Lenin and Khrushchev appear in profusion.

[11] *Dokumenty vneshnei politiki SSSR* (Moscow, 1957–in progress).

out benefit of gratuitous annotations explaining their subsequent "treason."

The change creates problems of adjustment for non-Soviet observers of the scene. Under Stalin, there was nothing to study but speeches by Stalin, Molotov, and their minions, the pages of *Pravda*, *Izvestia*, and *Bolshevik*, and the few quasi-official texts and reference works on international law and diplomacy. Virtually anything in print could be safely assumed to be an expression of official attitudes. Things are different now. Books, periodicals, and even newspapers can no longer be accepted as automatic expressions of official thinking; increasingly they represent the views of individual authors writing within the bounds of official latitude, which are relatively broad and allow for considerable variation on a single ideological theme.

While the official textbook seems to be a relic of the past, the conceptual framework which is common to all Soviet scholars remains fixed in its essentials. It is the identical ideology which governed during the Stalinist period, but shorn of its excesses, rigidities, and dogmatic sterility. Even the new editions of the *Diplomatic Dictionary* and the *History of Diplomacy*, whose first volumes have appeared, will not enjoy the official standing of their predecessors, although they, too, are being compiled by a group of active and retired diplomats and distinguished scholars.[12] The announcement on the *History of Diplomacy* promised that "great care will be taken to preserve the first edition's popular presentation, laconic style, and profoundly scholarly exposition."[13] It is still too early to say whether this is a promise or a threat.

Soviet scholarship on international relations and diplomacy has been further enhanced by the resurrection of old research institutes and the creation of new ones. Within the Soviet Academy of Sciences, not only the Institute of History, but the new Institute of World Economics and International Relations,[14] and the Soviet International Law Association conduct research on international and diplomatic matters, while under the central committee both the Academy of Social Sciences and the Higher Party School sponsor quasi-scholarly works on diplomatic history and contemporary international relations. *Mezhdunarodnaya Zhizn* is published by the All-Union Society for the Dissemination of Political and Scientific Knowledge, but seems actually to be a quasi-official organ of the Soviet Foreign Ministry.

The teaching of international relations and modern history in universities, pedagogical institutes, and other establishments of higher learning has also experienced a renaissance since the twentieth CPSU

---

[12] *Diplomaticheskii slovar*, edited by A. A. Gromyko, S. A. Golunsky and V. M. Khvostov, I (Moscow, 1960); II (1961). *Istoriya diplomatii*, edited by V. A. Zorin, V. S. Semenov, S. D. Skazkin and V. M. Khvostov, I (Moscow, 1959).

[13] *International Affairs*, 1958, No. 7, 115.

[14] Its monthly publication is *Mirovaya Ekonomika i Mezhdunarodynye Otnosheniya*. The institute continues the work of Varga's Institute of World Politics and World Economics, which was dissolved in 1949, as was its publication, *Mirovoe Khozyaistvo i Mirovaya Politika*.

congress, and in recent years many conferences on international relations, law and organization, and diplomatic historiography in general, have been held.

III. DIALECTICS AND DIPLOMACY

Soviet diplomatic scholarship operates within ideological limits set by Marxist-Leninist theoretical conceptions of diplomacy. For Marx and Engels, as for Lenin, diplomacy was essentially a bourgeois institution, either inappropriate or superfluous for a proletarian state. According to Trotsky, when the Bolsheviks met to organize their first government and the question of foreign relations was raised, Lenin exclaimed: "What, are we going to have foreign relations?" And upon his own appointment as the first Foreign Commissar, Trotsky announced: "I will issue a few revolutionary proclamations and then close up shop."[15]

The failure of the world revolution to exfoliate according to expectations and the *de facto* survival of the Soviet state in a hostile world forced the Bolsheviks to re-appraise diplomacy as a means of conducting foreign relations with capitalist powers during the period of co-existence. Initially, Soviet diplomacy was overtly connected with the espionage, subversion, and propaganda carried on by the regime, but after 1924 the bulk of these operations was shifted to the Comintern and other agencies.

Soviet writers, like their western counterparts, draw a distinction between foreign policy and diplomacy, but also concede that frequently the two are confused and, indeed, at times barely distinguishable. Like the state itself, foreign policy and diplomacy are pre-determined and shaped by the structure of society, the nature of its inner conflicts, and the interests of its ruling classes.

I. D. Levin, in his book *Diplomatic Immunity,* defines foreign policy as:

> a combination of the aims and interests pursued and defended by the given state and its ruling class in its relations with other states, and the methods and means it uses to achieve and defend these purposes and interests. The aims and interests of a state in international relations are realized by various methods and means: first of all, by peaceful official relations, maintained by a government, through its special agencies, with the corresponding agencies of other states, by economic, cultural, and other contacts, maintained by state agencies, as well as by public and private institutions (economic, political, scientific, religious, etc.), which provide a state with wide opportunities for exercising economic, political and ideological influence on other states; finally by using armed force, i.e. by war or other methods of armed coercion.[16]

[15] Leon Trotsky, *Moya zhizn* (Berlin, 1930), II, p. 64. Cf. L. Trotsky, *My Life* (New York, 1930), p. 341.

[16] I. D. Levin, *Diplomaticheskii immunitet* (Moscow, 1949), pp. iv–v. Cf. also I. D. Levin, "On the Question of the Concept of Diplomacy," *Sovetskoe Gosudarstvo i Pravo,* 1948, No. 9.

This definition is unusually broad and frank, and would include, among other Soviet devices, the activities of foreign communist parties, the Comintern, Cominform, and cultural exchanges as instruments of Soviet foreign policy; although the *Diplomatic Dictionary*, Volume I of which appeared in the same year as Levin's monograph, carefully eschews any references to the activities of foreign communist parties or the Comintern in the long entry on "Soviet Foreign Policy." Diplomacy, however, Levin views more narrowly:

> Diplomacy, on the other hand, is precisely the kind of state activity which consists in realizing the foreign policy aims and interests of a state by means of official relations maintained by a government, its special agencies, both within its own state and abroad, in the form of negotiations, correspondence, agreements, etc. Thus, the concept of diplomacy does not cover the concept of foreign policy, but is a part of it. Diplomacy is a method or means of foreign policy of states, and alongside it there exist other methods and means . . . Diplomacy is not merely one of the methods of foreign policy. Among all the methods of foreign policy, it is of primary importance in times of peace, and usually dominates over other methods, or their successful application depends upon it. The history of the diplomacy of slave-owning, feudal, and capitalist states reveals that diplomacy prepares for wars, trying to create an advantageous correlation of forces, to secure allies and to isolate the future enemy by the time war begins. Diplomacy completes wars by striving to secure the fruits of victory with the greatest possible advantage, or to mitigate the consequences of defeat . . . The correlation between foreign policy and diplomacy may to a certain extent be compared with the correlation between strategy and tactics.[17]

The Soviet view that diplomacy is inseparable from, and incapable of, rising above the class character of the state and society which it represents, provides a deeper insight into its inner workings and functions than the views held in the West by the traditional practitioners of diplomacy. The Soviet concept is inextricably linked to the general socio-historical categories of Marxism, and differs from western notions in being overtly rooted in a systematic philosophy of social norms and objectives which not only inspire and guide the policies and diplomacy of the Soviet state, but in fact transcend them. What Soviet writers and statesmen consider to be the chief source of Soviet diplomatic successes is precisely what continues to baffle veteran western diplomats. Confronted with the arrogant assertion by Professor Tarle in Volume III of the *History of Diplomacy*, that "Soviet diplomacy . . . wields a weapon possessed by none of its rivals or opponents . . . the scientific theory of Marxism-Leninism,"[18] Sir Harold Nicolson wrote:

[17] Ibid., pp. v–vi. For virtually identical conceptions, cf. "Diplomacy," in *Diplomaticheskii slovar*, I, 1948, 569–91. On the relationship between foreign policy and diplomacy and their theoretical constructs in general, no significant difference exists between the Stalinist period and the post-Stalinist. Cf. "Diplomacy," in *Diplomaticheskii slovar*, I, 1960, 457–68.
[18] *Istoriya diplomatii*, III, p. 764.

You will have observed that in these lectures I have made but slight reference to the diplomacy of the Soviet Union. Mr. W. P. Potjomkin [V. P. Potemkin], in his *History of Diplomacy,* assured us that the Russians possess one powerful weapon denied to their opponents — namely "the scientific dialectic of the Marx-Lenin formula." I have not observed as yet this dialectic has improved international relationships, or that the Soviet diplomatists and commissars have evolved any system of negotiation that might be called a diplomatic system. Their activity in foreign countries or at international conferences is formidable, disturbing, compulsive. I do not for one moment underestimate either its potency or its danger. But it is not diplomacy: it is something else.[19]

Nicolson's contempt for Soviet diplomacy derives from the misplaced notion that the function of diplomacy is to improve international relationships, and since the dialectic has not contributed to this objective, it must perforce be worthless. The value of the dialectic to Soviet diplomats is indeed formidable, for it provides them with an integrated scheme of analysis and prognostication which, while frequently out of focus with reality and far from being as scientific as they claim, is at any rate an effective system of analysis and strategy in terms of Soviet objectives.

The frequent assertion by western diplomats and scholars alike that the so-called laws of the dialectic have little or no application to foreign policy and constitute a sort of ritualistic mumbo-jumbo, is a dangerous self-deception. In fact, the entire structure of the Soviet image of reality and international politics rests upon a dialectical analysis which furnishes Soviet decision-makers and diplomats with analytical categories, creates for them an integrated ordering of events, relating them to each other, no matter how widely dispersed in time and space, and co-ordinates the effects of the various and sundry conflicts within individual countries as well as the world as a whole. Through dialectical analysis, Soviet statesmen and diplomats see events and forces in motion and interrelation, not statically and in isolation; measure their direction and tempo; and above all are able to mobilize the energies of a world in ferment and movement, transmuting them into political power, subjecting them to the manipulation of Soviet policy. In short, Marxism-Leninism is a framework for the analysis, mobilization, and manipulation of social and political power under a variety of conditions and circumstances. Thus, according to a recent Soviet appraisal:

> The foreign policy of socialism is based on science and founded on the only correct science of society, the theory of Marxism-Leninism . . . Marxism is a reliable compass for understanding reality and reconstructing society in a revolutionary manner in accordance with socialist principles. The strength of Marxism-Leninism lies in the fact that it gives the communist party and the Soviet state the possibility of dis-

[19] Sir Harold Nicolson, *The Evolution of Diplomatic Method* (London and New York, 1954), p. 90.

covering the objective laws of the historical process, of steering the correct course in accordance with the internal and external situation, of understanding the inner connection between events and of ascertaining not only how and in what direction events are developing in the present, but also how and in what direction they will develop in the future . . . However, the mere understanding of the objective laws of social development, and in particular of international relations, is not in itself sufficient to determine the correct course in foreign policy by which major victories can be won. The decisive source of the strength or weakness of foreign policy, of its historical prospects or lack of prospects, is the correlation of that policy and social progress, its conformity or non-conformity to the laws of development.[20]

On the other hand, in the Soviet view, western diplomacy relies upon chance, personalities, opportunism, adventurism, sentimentalism, and other subjective factors for its successes, and correspondingly attributes diplomatic failures to similar factors, over which western diplomats claim to have little control or understanding:

> The bourgeois press attempts to explain the failure of imperialist foreign policy by psychological factors, individual features and miscalculations of certain bourgeois statesmen and diplomats, by the greed and envy of some of them, by "communist propaganda" and the like. Thus Adlai Stevenson . . . maintains that the crisis of American foreign policy "has its seat in the minds and hearts of Americans." Some American bourgeois historians put themselves out to prove, for instance, that it was Truman's "stinginess" in subsidizing the Chiang Kai-shek clique, Marshall's "inflexibility," etc., that resulted in the defeat of American policy in China. But such arguments are untenable, for their authors, basing themselves on idealist conceptions, consider individual defeats and also the crisis of imperialist foreign policy in isolation from the acute and profound crisis of the whole capitalist system.[21]

Now, it may be argued, and frequently is, that the "scientific" discovery of "contradictions" in international politics is a spurious claim, since contradictions are neither more nor less than conflicting state or national interests, such as have existed for ages, and that the Soviet exploitation of rivalries among their adversaries is a technique as hoary as politics itself. Even if this is true, the Soviets would not claim to have either discovered these conflicts or invented the device of exploiting them for diplomatic advantage. What distinguishes the Soviet view is that these conflicts are seen in qualitatively different dimensions, and in a condition of dynamic flux, moving to a foreordained conclusion, rather than being chance or fortuitous occurrences. Thus, whereas the traditional function of diplomacy is to seek adjustment, accommodation, and even the resolution of these conflicts to the maximum advantage of the state concerned, these conflicts are viewed by the Soviets as irreconcilable; the function of diplomacy is to facilitate a resolution by bringing about the annihilation, liquidation, absorption, or submission of one

[20] M. Airapetyan and G. Deborin, "Foreign Policy and Social Progress," *International Affairs*, 1959, No. 2.
[21] Ibid.

pole of the contradiction. The dialectical approach to international politics, furthermore, goes deeper than an examination of state or national interests in conflict; it seeks to uncover the more profound, passionate, and explosive animosities and resentments of social classes and submerged populations, which Soviet diplomacy then attempts to manipulate to its own advantage. It provides a scheme for relating conflicts in foreign policy to internal social conflicts, and for ordering these contradictions into a coherent frame, establishing priorities, differentiating and arranging them into social and power equations which can be added, subtracted, multiplied, or divided as the occasion demands or the opportunity arises.

We can brush aside the claim that the Marxist-Leninist dialectic constitutes the only valid scheme of analysis, but it is not so easy to ignore its effectiveness as a basis for action. Historical inevitability and scientifically derived laws of social change may indeed be intellectual residues of the nineteenth century, little more than sophisticated and sophistic nonsense, but this misses the main point. Reality, in whatever dimension, is plastic, and while its transformations may not be pre-determined, the implacable voluntarism of fanatics determined to real-ize what they say is inevitable, may render the difference between "objective inevitability" and the "self-fulfilling prophecy" irrelevant; for no matter how successfully they may be distinguished in the intellectual processes of the mind, the distinctions in terms of consequences in the world of reality are essentially nil. A purely intellectual critique of Marxism inevitably wins the theoretical battle and loses the war on the plains of reality.

All theories of reality are approximations and can to a certain degree influence the development of reality in the direction desired by their sponsors; and a serious examination of Marxism-Leninism, not as a "science," but simply as a mundane theory of reality, particularly as it applies to international politics, is long overdue. Its effectiveness as a guide to policy is necessarily relative, since it must be measured against the effectiveness of corresponding analytical systems employed by others. A true measure of its validity requires it to be compared, not with the great profusion of theories, models, systems, processes, and games devised by western scholars, but with comparable theories of reality and analysis employed by western statesmen and diplomats, whether implicit or explicit, eclectic or synthetic, *ad hoc* or systematic, pragmatic or dogmatic, empirical or *a priori*.

Soviet ideology is not simply a conglomeration of abstract norms, but an ideology cemented to state power, providing a framework for the execution of Soviet foreign policy. Consequently, whether it is, in fact, superior or inferior to the array of analytical devices contrived by western professors is almost totally irrelevant, unless, of course, they eventually enjoy the same relationship to state power as does Marxism-Leninism. The pertinent question is not: "is Marxism-Leninism a sci-ence?", which has diverted attention from the real issue, but: "how effective is it in providing Soviet leaders with a map of international reality, enabling them to see their way through the complicated and bewildering maze of events to their objectives, as compared with the effectiveness of the maps of reality implicitly or explicitly employed by their western counterparts?" Furthermore, in assessing the past forty years, have the expectations of the Soviet Union in world affairs, based upon the insights gained from their ideological prism, been more or less accurately fulfilled than those of their enemies?

Really, the Soviet leaders had little more than this map of reality called dialectics as a surrogate for experience, but it served their purpose and yielded immense returns, against heavy odds, within the span of a single generation. Like the hedgehog of the Greek poet, Archilochus, Soviet diplomacy "knows one big thing," while the western foxes "know many things," none of which, so far at any rate, has been able to cope with the one big thing that Soviet diplomacy knows. Since the Soviet dialectic has been so effective during moments of weakness in Soviet history, is it any wonder that Soviet leaders remain even more convinced of its "scientific" character, now that their country is so strong?

A fundamental redistribution of power has taken place more or less in accordance with Soviet expectations. While Soviet predictions have not been borne out in all particulars and the record has been marked by reverses, defeats, and retreats, the overall pattern of expectations has been depressingly favorable. Thus, the following general expectations have been substantially realized: (1) The western world has shrunk in power, influence, and territory; (2) The United States has emerged as the leader of the western world; (3) The colonial empires have disintegrated in response to movements for independence supported by the Soviet Union; and (4) The communist world has expanded in territory and in power at the expense of the western world.

Thus, when we compare the balance-sheet to date of the "successes" and "defeats" of Soviet foreign policy, it is indisputable that the net balance is heavily weighted in favor of the Soviet Union and/or Soviet communism. In less than fifty years, Soviet communism has grown from an obscure Russian conspiratorial sect into a distinctive world civilization embracing more than a dozen states with a combined population of nearly one billion people, occupying about one-third of the earth's land surface. Communist parties, large and small, growing and diminishing, conspiratorial and legal, exist in seventy-five countries and command substantial electorates in France, Italy, Indonesia, and India. Soviet power and influence have intruded into South-east Asia, Africa, and Latin America, where only two decades ago the western powers were in complete control.

Soviet ideology has apparently provided the Soviet leadership with a system of analysis more effective than that at the disposal of the western powers. Otherwise, we must fall back upon the explanation that the forty-year record of the rise of Soviet power can only be explained by good luck, cunning, cupidity, accident, personalities, Providence, treachery, perfidy, etc., all of which, to be sure, played their part, but within the given framework of Marxism-Leninism.

Soviet scholars do not exclude these factors, but deny their contrality or decisive character, and subsume them under what they call the "art" of diplomacy, as distinguished from its scientific foundations, in which personalities play their role. But "without an understanding of the objective laws manifested in international relations," writes one Soviet scholar, "even very talented diplomats may prove unable to attain the main foreign-political aims of their country." He then proceeds to taunt:

> It is true that during recent decades, bourgeois diplomacy has not brought to the fore any single figure rising above mediocrity. But the chief source of its repeated major miscalculations and failures, however, is that it lacks an understanding of the new historical trends.[22]

On the other hand, Soviet diplomacy does not become victimized by confusing the fundamental with the transitory, because:

> Marxism regards politics as both a science and an art; as a social science, whose laws are applied to change reality, this application constituting an art, as an art based on the scientific perception of reality, the rules of which are based on the laws of social science. . . . The view of politics as an art is applicable both to diplomacy. . . . Diplomatic activity, however, cannot take the form of a mere application of definite scientific rules. . . . Naturally, they require constant adjustments, necessitated by the changes in the situation and the corresponding emergence of new tasks subordinated to the overall aims, and these adjustments are creatively made by persons applying the rules. . . . The operation of these rules is inseparable from the subjective capabilities of the persons applying them. They are rules not of science, but of art. . . . Not without reason is diplomacy compared with warfare in precisely this sense. . . . Lenin compares politics, in general, to warfare. . . . It would be naive, of course, to confine the entire diplomatic art to certain subjective qualities of a diplomat, as is often done by bourgeois authors. Yet, it can hardly be denied that mastery of the rules of the diplomatic art . . . occupies not the last place among the conditions indispensable for the successful achievement of foreign policy aims.[23]

The absence of a valid system of social analysis in the West, however, is neither accidental nor the result of inactivity on the part of western scholars, but rather due to the fact that the capitalist "ruling classes are acutely aware that their interests are fundamentally incompatible with developing reality, which threatens to erode and subvert their privileged positions. Hence, according to the Soviet point of view, western scholarship and diplomacy are not devoted to revealing social reality, but to concealing it:

> An unscientific interpretation of foreign relations and the development of international relationships is intended to serve the class interests of the imperialist bourgeoisie. Being an ideological weapon of reaction, it is designed to confuse public opinion. By representing the dynamics of international relations and politics as a mere game of chance, the apologists of capitalism try to prove that it is impossible to understand this domain of social life, and prove their claim that absolute chance reigns here. In so doing they wish to impress upon the

[22] I. D. Levin, *Diplomaticheskii immunitet,* pp. IX–X.
[23] Ibid.

working masses that it is futile and senseless to fight for their basic and vital interests . . . that is to condemn them to be passive onlookers of events. All these and similar arguments put forward by the modern bourgeois ideologists are intended not to disclose, but, on the contrary, to hide the objective causes of crises and failures of imperialist foreign policy, to create the illusion that, given different, more "flexible methods," that policy could "succeed."[24]

It is this incompatibility between the interests of the "ruling classes" in the capitalist world with the implacable dictates of dialectical truth that ineluctably imparts to "bourgeois" diplomacy and to the diplomacies of all preceding socio-historical systems, their characteristic qualities. The nature of diplomacy varies historically with the social system, for whereas during the period of feudal absolutism, when diplomacy was the monopoly of a small aristocratic elite, it was not surprising "that deceit, perfidy, bribery, intrigues, and court conspiracies were widely employed in diplomatic activity," whereas,

> During the epoch of capitalism . . . the social foundations and political forms of the state have changed, and the art of diplomacy, though preserving its inner essence, underwent considerable modernization. The tasks and methods of diplomacy became much more intricate and varied. Diplomacy had to resort now to deceiving not only individuals from among a narrow governing circle, but also wider groups of the governing class and even wider sections of the population, both abroad and in its own country, and to make skillful use of the services of political propaganda and of various methods of influencing public opinion and the press both in the foreign state and at home. . . . Yet the old methods of the diplomacy of absolutism remain: bribery, various political diversions, conspiracies, etc.[25]

In the Soviet view, individuals, nations, and classes can be fooled, cheated, and diverted, but history is immune from ordinary human vices, and the inexorable dialectic of development is destined to overwhelm the "bourgeoisie," no matter how clever and cunning it may be in fabricating contrivances, artifices, and diversions to delay, derail, or deter the "locomotive of history."

IV. DIALECTICS AND DUPLICITY: STALINIST
CONCEPTIONS OF DIPLOMACY

The psycho-semantic identification of diplomacy with duplicity in Soviet thinking is not only rooted in Marxist ideology, but above all in Stalin's character and personality, which in large measure shaped the definitive contours, not only of Soviet diplomacy, but of Soviet politics in general. In the hands of Stalin, Marxism-Leninism became a powerful tool of analysis, upon which he superimposed his own social norms under the rubric of "creative Marxism." The nature of Stalin's person-

[24] Airapetyan and Deborin, "Foreign Policy and Social Progress," p. 21.
[25] I. D. Levin, *Diplomaticheskii immunitet*, pp. XIV–XV.

ality is bound to preoccupy scholars for some time: Was it due to innate causes, or perhaps to the cultural and environmental influences of his childhood, his work in the Bolshevik underground? Or was it shaped later in life by sudden flashes of insight after the seizure of power, as to the inner motivations, hypocrisies, and pretenses of human behavior; and discovering, in the words of Gracian, "each man's thumbscrew"? Whatever the reason, the institutionalized deception which Marx ascribed to the bourgeois "ruling class," and which Lenin converted into an instrument to be used only against the "class enemy," was personalized by Stalin and used against capitalist and communist alike, against friend or foe.

The Marxist view of diplomacy was summed up by Engels in 1890 in his essay on "The Foreign Policy of Russia's Tsars," which was specifically restricted to the diplomacy of Imperial Russia and not to "bourgeois" diplomacy in general.[26] The fate of this essay in Stalin's Russia is itself a commentary on the state of diplomatic history there. Although the essay was included in the Russian edition of the collected works of Marx and Engels, it did not have wide circulation. In 1934, the editors of *Bolshevik* naïvely planned to reprint the essay in a special issue, but were overruled by Stalin. In a letter dated July 19, 1934, but not made public until May 1941, Stalin criticized Engels for exaggerating the role of Tsarist Russia as the "bulwark of European reaction," assigning it a monopoly in the "policy of conquest" and imparting to its diplomacy a unique venality, which seemed to transcend history, classes, and ideology as the inseparable characteristic of an "eternal" Russia.[27]

If Engels was correct, Stalin noted, then "it must be clear that war, let us say, between bourgeois Germany and Tsarist Russia is not an imperialist war, not a war of plunder, but a war of liberation or almost of liberation." As for the implication that a policy of conquest was "a monopoly of the Tsars," Stalin said:

> Everyone knows that a policy of conquest was also characteristic . . . of the kings and diplomats of all the countries of Europe, including an emperor of such a bourgeois cast as Napoleon, who . . . successfully practised intrigue, deceit, perfidy, flattery, atrocities, bribery, murder and arson in foreign policy. Obviously it could not be otherwise.

What apparently infuriated Stalin was Engels' grudging admiration for the unparalleled mendacity and effectiveness of Tsarist diplomacy, which, to give the devil his due, justified Stalin's observation that it was "un-Marxist" in its analysis. Engels had written:

> The Russian diplomatic corps forms, so to speak a modern Jesuit order . . . [a] secret society, recruited originally from foreign adven-

[26] Cf. K. Marx and F. Engels, *The Russian Menace to Europe*, edited by Bert Hoselitz and Paul W. Blackstock (Glencoe, 1952) for an English translation of Engels' essay.
[27] J. V. Stalin, "On Engels' Article, 'The Foreign Policy of Russian Tsarism,' " *Bolshevik*, No. 9, 1941.

turers, which has raised the Russian Empire to its present plenitude of power. With iron perseverance, eyes fixed on the goal, not shrinking from any breach of faith, any treason, any assassination, any servility, distributing bribes lavishly . . . It is this gang, rather than all the Russian armies put together . . . which made Russia great, powerful and feared, and has opened up the way to world domination.[28]

"One might get the impression,'" Stalin wrote caustically, "that in Russian history and foreign policy diplomacy was everything, while Tsars, feudal lords, merchants and other social groups counted for nothing or almost nothing," and added that, far from being peculiarly Tsarist, "perfidy, treachery, bribery . . . and similar 'qualities' of diplomacy . . . are the characteristic sores of any . . . capitalist diplomacy."

Apart from any anxiety that Engels' description of Tsarist diplomacy might appear too close an approximation to his own, prompting one of his legal experts, Kozhevnikov, to warn that "Russia cannot be identified with Tsarism and autocracy,"[29] the republication of the essay would have needlessly compromised Stalin's planned resurrection of Russian nationalism and the retrospectively re-interpreted "progressive" character of Imperial Russian expansion, which came to dominate Soviet historiography. "Russian rule," Kozhevnikov later observed, apprehensively citing Marx, "plays a civilizing role for the [people of the] Black and Caspian Seas [area] and Central Asia, for the Bashkirs and Tatars."[30]

Just as the Soviet state was conceived initially as an inverted version of the Leninist model of the bourgeois state, of which the concrete historical manifestation was the Russian autocracy, Soviet diplomacy has inexorably evolved within the context of the Stalinist image of "bourgeois" diplomacy. Engels' version of Tsarist diplomacy was universalized as the authentic expression of bourgeois diplomacy in its pristine form, and served as the inverted model for Soviet diplomatic behavior. Soviet diplomacy was further embellished with the devices and methods that Stalin imagined were characteristics of British diplomacy and espionage, for which he betrayed a grudging, but silent, respect, similar to that exhibited by Engels for the intrigues and machinations of Imperial Russia.[31]

[28] Hoselitz and Blackstock, *The Russian Menace to Europe*, p. 26.
[29] F. I. Kozhevnikov, "Engles on 19th Century Russian Diplomacy," *Sovetskoye Gosudarstvo i Pravo*, No. 12, December 1950, 18–34. For another commentary on Stalin's letter, cf. A. L. Narochnitsky, "On Engels' Article 'The Foreign Policy of Russian Tsarism' " (Moscow, 1950). For a post-Stalin view on Marx and Engels' views on diplomacy, cf. E. Bogush, "Karl Marx on the Foreign Policy of the Working Class," *International Affairs*, No. 5, 1948, 19–25. Stalin is not cited once in this article, whereas all pre-1953 items on diplomacy profusely cited Stalin's "Letter."
[30] Cited in Kozhevnikov, "Engels on 19th Century Russian Diplomacy."
[31] This can be inferred from Stalin's weird accusations that General Velebit was a British spy in the Tito regime, that Marshal Voroshilov had become a British spy, as well as other allusions to British diplomacy and espionage. The British ruling class, for Stalin, was the most cunning and

Even before the Revolution, Stalin's image of diplomacy had crystallized into its characteristic form. In a 1913 speech, Stalin ominously intoned:

> A diplomat's words must have no relation to action — otherwise what kind of diplomacy is it? Words are one thing, actions another. . . . Sincere diplomacy is no more possible than dry water or iron wood.[32]

As a synonym for deceit, diplomacy was not restricted to foreign policy but was frequently employed by Stalin to characterize the speeches and actions of his critics and opponents, who were charged with being "diplomatic and insincere." On one occasion, he accused Trotsky of plotting "diplomatically to support the opposition . . . while pretending to support the Central Committee," a maneuver that Stalin said "bore the stamp of duplicity."[33] At a conference of the party, held in 1923, he said:

> One report diverged very widely from reality . . . It was not even a report, it was sheer diplomacy, for everything that is bad . . . was obscured, glossed over, whereas everything that glitters on the surface and strikes the eye was pushed into the foreground, for display . . . I think that we have gathered at this conference not for the purpose of playing at diplomacy with one another, of making eyes at one another, while surreptitiously trying to lead one another by the nose, but for the purpose of telling the whole truth.[34]

In Stalin's mind, this identification of diplomacy with deceit persisted until his death in 1953. At Yalta, for example, Stalin expansively ruminated with Churchill:

> I am talking as an old man; that is why I am talking so much. But I want to drink to our alliance that it should not lose its character of intimacy, of its true expression of views. . . . In an alliance the allies should not deceive each other. Perhaps that is naïve? Experienced diplomatists may say: "Why should I not deceive my ally?" But I as a naïve man may think it is best not to deceive my ally even if he is a fool. Possibly our alliance is so firm just because we do not deceive each other; or is it because it is not so easy to deceive each other?[35]

Theoretically, of course, in identifying diplomacy with deceit, Stalin was characterizing "bourgeois" diplomacy and "bourgeois" behavior, but since Soviet diplomacy before the war was necessarily restricted to diplomatic contact with the capitalist world, it was forced into the same mold, for, in the words of the late dictator, it would be "naïve to preach

---

experienced in all Europe. Cf., *The Soviet-Yugoslav Dispute* (RIIA, 1948), pp. 16–17, 33–34.

[32] Stalin, *Sochineniya* (Moscow, 1946), II, p. 277.

[33] Stalin, *Works,* p. 397.

[34] Ibid., p. 338; cf. also pp. 331, 312.

[35] Winston Churchill, *Triumph and Tragedy* (Cambridge, 1953), pp. 362–363.

morality to people who do not recognize morality. Politics is politics, say the old, hardbitten bourgeois diplomats."[36] Whereas deceit and deception were appropriate in dealing with the "class enemy," they were not suitable forms of behavior for communists, whose relations, according to Stalin, would be governed by absolute respect for sincerity, truth, trust, and confidence. According to this peerless master of simulation and dissimulation:

> *Either* we are Leninists, and our relations one with one another as well as relations with the sections and with the Comintern, and vice versa, must be built on mutual confidence, must be as clean and pure as crystal — in which case there should be no room in our ranks for rotten diplomatic intrigue; *or* we are not Leninists.[37]

Implicitly, of course, relations based upon mutual trust and confidence would continue to prevail once other communist parties came to power in their own countries creating a new socialist type of diplomacy which would challenge and eventually supplant that of the bourgeoisie. Stalin, however, in his relations with his own colleagues, with satellite and other communist leaders, victimized them even more than his implacable "bourgeois" enemies, yet he continued to subscribe verbally to a theoretical double standard of diplomatic behavior. In 1948, Stalin, in effect, accused Tito of failing to observe this double standard in his dealing with the Soviet ambassador:

> Tito and Kardelj . . . identify the Soviet ambassador . . . with an ordinary bourgeois ambassador; a simple official of a bourgeois state, who is called upon to undermine the foundations of the Yugoslav state. . . . They, therefore, put the foreign policy of the USSR on a par with the foreign policy of the English and Americans and feel that they should follow the same policy towards the Soviet Union as towards the imperialist states.[38]

Thus, the institutionalized deception which Marx and Engels ascribed to the bourgeois "ruling class," and which Lenin converted into an instrument to be used only against the "class enemy," was personalized by Stalin and used against capitalist and communist alike, against friend and foe. Soviet diplomacy has inexorably evolved within the context of the Stalinist image of "bourgeois" diplomacy; Engels' image of Tsarist diplomacy was universalized as "bourgeois" diplomacy in general and served as the inverted model for Soviet diplomatic behavior.

This view of diplomacy was carried over intact into the body of Soviet historiography. In Volume III of the *History of Diplomacy*, for example, there is a chapter entitled "The Tactics of Bourgeois Diplomacy," written by Academician E. V. Tarle, whose unifying theme he claims he owes to "one of the great masters of the diplomatic art," the

---

[36] J. Stalin, "Report to the 18th Communist Party Congress," March 10, 1939.
[37] J. Stalin, *Stalin's Speeches on the American Communist Party*, p. 15.
[38] *The Soviet-Yugoslav Dispute*, p. 42.

seventeenth-century Swedish statesman, Axel Oxenstierna, who allegedly said:

> Diplomacy always has at its disposal two obedient slaves: *simulation* and *dissimulation*. Simulate what is *not*, but that *which is* dissimulate . . . The diplomats of the seventeenth century, as well as their colleagues of the eighteenth, nineteenth, and twentieth centuries made profitable use of these two "slaves": they affirmed what did not exist, but concealed what did, practising with skill both simulation and dissimulation.[39]

Professor Tarle proceeds to enumerate eleven discrete techniques of this dual tactic, embellished with historical illustrations from the diplomatic history of Europe, liberally interpreting "bourgeois" diplomacy to include the writings of Machiavelli — to whom is attributed the device of inciting internal differences for diplomatic advantage — and the policies of Louis XIV. A caveat is issued that neither the list nor the historical examples exhaust the rich and varied artifices of bourgeois diplomacy. Illustrations are selected almost indiscriminately, irrespective of century, form of government, or ideology, since in the Soviet view the bourgeois state can assume many forms, but remains the instrument of the ruling class. Thus, whether the states are autocracies, absolute monarchies, petty principalities, representative republics, parliamentary democracies, or fascist dictatorships, they are all classed as bourgeois. In the words of another Soviet authority:

> The methods of the diplomacy of the fascist states, in their perfidy, cynicism and corruption, went beyond the worst examples of the diplomacy of absolutism. . . . The diplomacy of the other bourgeois states did not differ radically in political substance and moral characteristics from that of fascist states.[40]

Although the eleven tactics of bourgeois diplomacy are illustrated by examples from the diplomatic behavior of Nazi Germany and Mussolini's Italy, Professor Tarle distinguishes the "systematic employment of lies and extortion" as specific techniques of fascist diplomacy. Nevertheless, the eleven general tactics of bourgeois diplomacy are sordid enough, and are in fact easily recognized as the tactics of Stalinist diplomacy inverted to simulate those of the western powers and to dissimulate its own.

As reconstructed by Professor Tarle, they are:

1. Aggression masquerading as self-defence.
2. Aggression camouflaged by "disinterested" motives.
3. Peace propaganda employed to deceive the adversary.
4. Concluding "friendship" treaties for the purpose of subverting the vigilance of the adversary.
5. Aggressive plans disguised as a struggle against Bolshevism and the USSR.

---

[39] *Istoriya Diplomatii*, III, p. 702. Tarle also notes the Latin original: "Simulantur quae non sunt, quae sunt vero dissimulantur."

[40] I. D. Levin, *Diplomaticheskii immunitet*, p. XV.

6. "Localized conflicts" disguised to facilitate the successive elimination of victims.
7. Diplomatic exploitation of internal antagonisms in the camp of the adversary.
8. The exploitation of national differences and conflicts of interest in the camp of the enemy.
9. Demogogic appeal to struggle against the hegemony of the victorious group of imperialist powers.
10. Systematic employment of threats to terrorize the adversary.
11. The "protection" of weak states as a pretext for aggression.

The first edition of the *Diplomatic Dictionary* pursued these themes with even greater vigor and pungency, embellishing the biographical entries of "bourgeois" statesmen and diplomats with a varied array of vices and unflattering observations. In contrast, many of the Tsars of Russia are treated as virtual members of the communist confraternity, thus deviating considerably from the unflattering description of Tsarist diplomacy provided by Engels.

Thus, whereas Napoleon's basic principle of diplomacy, "to divide his opponents and strike at them separately," is condemned, the same vice is extolled in Peter the Great, who successfully and extensively exploited "the internal contradictions in the countries hostile to Russia" in the interests of Russia. Sir Edward Grey is denounced as the author of the greatest number of secret treaties concluded by a British Foreign Secretary, and Wilhelm II's diplomatic talents are shown as emphasizing "the art of lying, hypocrisy and the denunciation of one 'imperial' friend to another," as Ivan the Terrible's diplomacy was based on "definite principles" and "concern for the 'honor' of his state," and Peter the Great's most important principle "was to be faithful in word and to fulfill all obligations entered into."

Clemenceau is the embodiment of "the militant policy of French Imperialism," President Wilson is a self-proclaimed "messiah," obviously false, as Lloyd George, who was portrayed favorably in the *History* only five years earlier, is described in Volume II as one who "eagerly resorted to sensational methods designed to deceive public opinion . . . embalming his words with democratic-pacifist unction, or alternately threatening to use the English pound or fleet," although his opposition to the Chamberlain government is also mentioned.

Of the more recent "bourgeois" diplomats, Ribbentrop is described as "mad," Anthony Eden is portrayed as the son-in-law of a banker, and Georges Bonnet is cited as a feverish agent of French, British, German, and American financial circles and bankers, who scandalously bribed journalists, officials, and legislators with both public and private funds at the behest of his masters. Neville Chamberlain is contemptuously etched as "a narrow-minded, obstinate, arrogant bourgeois, with the mentality of a provincial entrepreneur, a poor orator and a crude politician. . . . The embodiment of mediocrity." His ability to become Prime Minister during the most serious period in British history demonstrated

not only the power and influence of social origins and family connections, but also reflected "the profound decomposition of the British
ruling class."

The most picturesque and un-chivalrous language, however, was
reserved for Stalin's wartime comrade-in-arms, Winston Churchill, whose
Fulton, Missouri "Iron Curtain" speech had never been forgiven by
Stalin nor his successors:

> Churchill's political personality is characterized by a singular com-
> bination of the specific features of a military-political adventurer of the
> feudal era with those of a consummate imperialist of the 20th century.
> . . . From early childhood, Churchill had an extraordinary fascination
> for everything military . . . drawing particular inspiration from his
> ancestor, the Duke of Marlborough. . . . During the First World War,
> Churchill as Naval Minister, organized the unsuccessful Dardenelles
> Campaign, which turned out to be the purest form of military adven-
> turism. During the Second World War, Churchill continuously interfered
> with the direction of military operations, imagining himself to be a
> British Napoleon, called upon to remake the map of Europe to his own
> taste. . . . As a typical imperialist of the 20th century, for Churchill,
> the British Empire is the beginning and end of everything. . . . Feign-
> ing verbal devotion to the principles of democracy, Churchill demon-
> strates at every step his extreme hostility to democracy, especially in
> connection with the colonial peoples. . . . Both sides of his political
> physiognomy — the nobiliary-feudal and the bourgeois-imperialist — are
> "harmoniously" blended in his attitude towards the U.S.S.R.

Ambassador Davies (who was awarded the Order of Lenin),
Cordell Hull, and President Roosevelt emerge unscathed because of
their friendly and cooperative attitude to Soviet Russia. Among the
Soviet diplomats, Chicherin is described as a "gifted diplomat" (in 1956,
Izvestia promoted him to "an outstanding Soviet diplomat whose memory is cherished by the Soviet people"), Litvinov is called an "eminent
Soviet diplomat and one of the oldest workers of the Bolshevik Party,"
whereas Vyshinsky, as befitting one of the co-editors, is simply described
as a "Soviet statesman, diplomat, and scholar." Molotov's entry is dignified and flattering, but not nearly as effusive as the encomiums he received from his rivals, Dulles, Byrnes, and Churchill:

> As a diplomat, Molotov is well-known for his consistent energy and
> profound adherence to principle. Molotov combines pungency in pre-
> senting a problem with extraordinary firmness and frequently disarms
> his opponents with his composure.

One Soviet scholar, in reviewing the *Diplomatic Dictionary*, gloats
that:

> In the age of the general crisis of capitalism, the imperialist bour-
> geoisie has not been able to produce one figure that might be marked as
> an outstanding talented diplomat.[41]

[41] A. Yerusalimsky, "Concerning the 'Diplomatic Dictionary,'" *Literaturnaya Gazeta*, February 6, 1950. The preceding characterizations can be
found under the appropriate biographical entries in both volumes.

V. POST-STALIN IMAGES OF THE DIPLOMACY OF THE PRE-WAR PERIODS: THE LIMITS OF DE-STALINIZATION

The death of Stalin in 1953 had little impact on the foundations of Soviet ideology, but it did much to change the Stalinist emendations and extrapolations. The repudiation of the inevitability-of-war thesis, capitalist encirclement, the two-camp image, of the doctrine of the accelerated intensification of the class struggle as final victory approaches, the *de facto* abandonment of a communist orbit tightly controlled and directed from Moscow, and the recognition of a favorable shift in the world equilibrium of power, were bound to modify seriously Soviet conceptions of international relations and diplomacy and the historiography which they shape and support. Although doctrinal continuity persists, considerable variation, deviation, transformation, and even repudiation of Stalinist content, style, form, and methodology have taken place. Soviet conceptions of both diplomacy and historiography have benefited from Khrushchev's recognition of altered international conditions which Stalin was either unable or unwilling to acknowledge.

The first noticeable change in post-Stalinist literature on diplomacy and foreign affairs is the relative absence of abusive language, and the greater effort to bolster interpretations of the past with at least some outward display of scholarship and documentation. It has been largely shorn of its Stalinist distortions, arrant fabrications, and piercing invective. Some distortion persists, but omission of damaging facts and events is becoming more usual than the overt invention of falsehoods.

Post-Stalinist treatment of Munich and the Nazi-Soviet Pact provides revealing glimpses of both contrasts and similarities to the Stalinist era. The unrelenting theme of Soviet historiography on pre-war diplomacy remains one of continuous conspiracy on the part of the Anglo-French imperialist camp to maneuver Germany into a war with the Soviet Union, and with a single stroke to weaken its imperialist adversaries and destroy the Bolshevik state. Thus, a commentary on a new Soviet history of the war being compiled by the Institute of Marxism-Leninism maintains:

> It would be an over-simplification to say that the present policy of British ruling circles towards German militarism is an exact replica of the policy pursued with such tragic consequences in the 1930s . . . Nevertheless, those who rule Britain are largely following the pre-war pattern in their policy. Throughout the post-war years the British monopolies . . . have been guided by the desire to build up German militarism and imperialism as both a bulwark and an assault force against the forces of socialism.[42]

The major difference between pre-war and post-war western machinations against the Soviet Union stems, not from any change in the intentions of the western powers, but from the change in the world

---

[42] M. Andreyeva and K. Dmitrieva, "From the Pre-history of the Second World War." *International Affairs*, 1961, No. 5, 73.

balance of power which imparts to western post-war policy an air of unreality. Whereas before the war it was possible to aim at the destruction of the Soviet Union, since the war this is so no longer.

How the Soviet Union managed to foil these conspiracies and strategems is tediously recounted in terms of a simple morality play. Intervention, blockade, Leagues of Nations, *cordons sanitaires*, Young and Dawes plans, Locarnos, Kellogg-Briand pacts, Anti-Comintern pacts, and Munichs were fended off in a series of intrepid Soviet diplomatic strokes, such as Rapallo, non-aggression and neutrality pacts, the Litvinov protocols, disarmament conferences, collective security appeals, and, the most stunning coup of all, the Nazi-Soviet Pact, which, in the words of the old *Dictionary*, frustrated "the double game of British-French diplomacy" and "upset all the designs of the ruling circles of Britain and France."[43] This remains the *leitmotiv* of post-war Soviet diplomatic historiography, increasingly buttressed by the publication of documents, old and new, the memoirs and diaries of western statesmen and diplomats, and accounts by "bourgeois" historians, all cited to support the Soviet position. Recent Soviet literature has also quoted unpublished material from the archives of the Soviet Foreign Ministry, which means that Soviet scholars have at last been given at least limited access to unpublished sources.

The theme of Volume III of the old *History of Diplomacy* was revealed in its title, "Diplomacy in the Period of the Preparation of the Second World War"; Volume I of the new projected six-volume *History of the Great Patriotic War of the Soviet Union 1941–1945*, is called "Preparation and Unleashing of the War by the Imperialist States." Virtually all Soviet general accounts of the diplomacy of the inter-war period carry a similar title.

A comparison of two pre-war episodes, the Czech crisis and the Nazi-Soviet Pact, in Stalinist and post-Stalinist literature, reveals interesting divergences. It should be noted that there was a sharp difference in tone, language, and degree of distortion between the *History of Diplomacy* and the *Diplomatic Dictionary*, particularly Volume II of the latter, which appeared in 1950. The former, which was compiled while the Grand Alliance was still intact, distinguished between the "reactionary bourgeoisie" (Chamberlain, Halifax, the "Cliveden set," etc.) and far-sighted members of the British ruling class (Churchill, Eden, Lloyd George, Duff Cooper), but no such distinctions are apparent in the *Dictionary*. In post-Stalin accounts the distinction is once again resurrected, although Churchill cannot be forgiven for his Fulton speech.

While historians do their best to present Soviet diplomatic behavior at the time of Munich in the most favorable light, the "dead rat" caught in the throats of Soviet historians, to use Khrushchev's phrase, remains the Nazi-Soviet Pact. Since the Soviet Union has not yet publicly acknowledged the existence of the secret protocols to the pact, while their existence is universally known outside the Soviet Union, Soviet

[43] *Diplomaticheskii slovar*, II, p. 176.

374 SOVIET CONCEPTIONS OF DIPLOMACY

historians are left with the impossible task of justifying something whose existence is not admitted. They are reduced to pleading that the Soviet Union signed a treaty of non-aggression in self-defence, as a result of the acknowledged equivocation of Britain and France; but their arguments cannot support the entire structure of Nazi-Soviet negotiations, agreements, and discussions during the period April 1939–June 1941.

In Soviet historiography Munich and the Nazi-Soviet Pact are linked, Anglo-French behavior at Munich being the moral justification for the Pact. Every effort is made to show that the Soviet Union was the only country sincerely willing and ready to act against fascist aggression. The joint publication of Czech-Soviet documents on Munich,[44] and the Soviet transcript of the ill-fated Anglo-French-Soviet military negotiations, were both designed to supply documentary ballast to an old position.[45] The first does throw new light on the Munich crisis, but the latter adds little more than trivia to the record.

Although the point was not mentioned in Volume II of the *History*, Volume II of the *Dictionary* asserts that Stalin asked Gottwald to assure Beneš that the Soviet Union was ready to aid Czechoslovakia, even if France failed to fulfil her treaty obligations, but "the ruling clique of the Czechoslovak bourgeoisie, afraid for its class interests, preferred capitulation," and Beneš spurned the offer (p. 198). No further details are offered. The documents published in 1960, however, prove, according to the Soviet commentator, that:

> In the middle of May 1938 Klement Gottwald, who was in Moscow at that time in connection with the activities of the Comintern, had a long talk on the Czechoslovak question with J. V. Stalin, who stated that the Soviet Union was ready to help Czechoslovakia even if this was not done by France, but only on condition that Czechoslovakia defended herself and asked for assistance. J. V. Stalin authorized Gottwald to communicate this to President Beneš.[46]

The most interesting thing about this revelation is the uninhibited manner in which the Comintern (not mentioned in the *Dictionary*) is implicated in Soviet foreign policy. Why this so-called assurance was never given through official diplomatic channels is not explained. At the time, Stalin held no official position in the Soviet Government, and since the assurance did not constitute an official act, verbal or written, it could hardly commit the Soviet Government.

The documents do not shower much credit on the British or French; but neither do they prove that the Soviet Union was ready or able to go beyond its commitments if Beneš would only give the signal.

---

[44] *Novye dokumenty iz istorii Myunkhena* (Moscow, 1958).

[45] Cf. *International Affairs*, 1959, No. 2, 107–23 and No. 3, 106–22 for a transcript of the military negotiations, and a commentary on their significance.

[46] I. Zemskov, "New Documents on the History of Munich," *International Affairs*, 1958, No. 10, 70. Cf. also V. G. Polyakov, *Angliya i Myunkhenskii sgovor* (Moscow, 1960).

In its official and public diplomatic activity, amply supported by the record, the Soviet Union made much of the fact that neither Poland nor Rumania was ready to facilitate Soviet assistance to Prague (after all, Poland was also making territorial demands on the Czechs), but no explanation is offered as to how Stalin's assurance to Gottwald could possibly negotiate the geographical barrier.

The first public Soviet admission of the secret Nazi-Soviet negotiations preceding the Hitler-Stalin Pact, and a hint at the possible existence of the secret protocols, seems to have been made in Volume I of the new *History of the Great Patriotic War*. Only the most tantalizing of outlines is provided, combined with the deliberate omission of embarrassing material and a perceptible, but not scandalous, bending of the truth. Up to this time, all Soviet accounts had conveyed the impression that the Pact suddenly materialized out of thin air.

The Soviet version, as given by this source, deviates sharply from that in the German documents. According to this sketchy chronology, negotiations started on May 30, 1939, with a meeting between Astakhov and Weizsäcker; the non-aggression pact was a German idea, and Moscow twice spurned German offers to sign a secret protocol (thus leaving the impression that no secret agreements were in fact signed). The German documents show, on the other hand, that the story actually began on April 17th, with a meeting between the Soviet ambassador, Merekalov, and Weizsäcker, and that Soviet attaché, Astakhov, had two meetings with a German official, Schnurre, and another with Weizsäcker, prior to May 30th. Furthermore, a meeting between Molotov and Schulenberg on May 20th is not mentioned. The German documents also show that, whereas the Germans took the initiative in proposing a deal, the specific form and execution of the arrangements were all suggested from the Soviet side: The non-aggression treaty and the special protocol, as well as a preparatory trade and credit agreement, were all first advanced by Moscow.

The Soviet account leaps from May 30th to August 3rd when, according to this version, Ribbentrop told Astakhov that no "insoluble" question between the two countries existed, and "suggested a secret German-Soviet protocol to delimit the interests of the two powers 'all along the line from the Black to the Baltic Sea'," but the Soviet Union was "unwilling to enter into such an agreement" (p. 174); neither contention is supported by the German documents. The next date mentioned is August 14th, when Schulenberg makes a second "verbal offer" of a non-aggression treaty and a secret protocol to Molotov but "the Soviet Government again declined the German proposal" (p. 175), which again is not supported by the German evidence. The German documentation shows that both the non-aggression treaty and a special protocol as well as a trade and credit agreement were all suggested for the first time on August 17th by Molotov, who furnished the German ambassador with a Soviet draft treaty two days later — all of which elated the Germans, because they themselves were not yet ready to formulate such a daring proposal.

The Soviet account then records Hitler's anxiety to make an agreement immediately, on the ground that a crisis was likely to break out any day, possibly involving the Russians, expressed in the telegram he dispatched on August 20th insisting that Ribbentrop be received in Moscow on the 22nd or 23rd (all of which is supported by the German documents); but Stalin's personal reply to Hitler the next day accepting Ribbentrop is not mentioned. "The Soviet Union was left with no choice," the book relates, "because an attack by Germany upon the Soviet Union could well have developed into a 'crusade' of the capitalist world against our state . . . The only thing that could still be done was to deliver the western Ukraine, western Byelorussia, and the Baltic countries from German invasion. With this in mind, the Soviet Government succeeded in obtaining a German commitment not to cross the rivers Pissa, Narew, Bug and San" (p. 176).[47]

The reader is thus left with the impression that secret treaties were offered and spurned twice, but finally some sort of agreement (which was never made public) establishing a territorial delimitation between the two countries was reached, the main purpose of which was to deliver the peoples of eastern Poland and the Baltic States from Nazi tyranny. This also makes it just a little bit easier for Soviet historians to persist in their tedious assault on the pernicious "secret" diplomacy of the "bourgeoisie," for they can now concede the existence of an unpublicized agreement, and continue to deny that it was "secret."

VI. Discovering Soviet Foreign Policy:
The Agonies of Diplomatic Periodization

One new development is the discovery by Soviet historians of Soviet foreign policy as a distinct field of diplomatic study. The first general history of Soviet foreign policy, *History of International Relations and Foreign Policy of the USSR (1870–1957)*, appeared in 1957, edited by F. G. Zueva and bearing the imprimatur of the Higher Party School of the central committee.[48] The work was almost immediately criticized for faulty "periodization." One of the main obstacles in the past to a work on Soviet foreign policy was the completely justified fear on the part of Soviet historians that they might unwittingly devise heretical "periodizations," to say nothing of the perplexities and embar-

[47] Molotov's meeting with Hitler and Ribbentrop in November 1940 in Berlin is not mentioned.

[48] Actually an outline had appeared two years earlier with a terminal date set at 1941. The 1957 work was followed in 1958 by I. F. Ivashin's *Ocherki istorii vneshnei politiki SSSR* (Moscow, 1958), which was equally unsatisfactory. A new work on the same subject, *Mezhdunarodnye otnosheniya i vneshnyaya politika Sovetskovo Soyuza, 1950–1959*, 2 vols., edited by V. P. Nikhamin, appeared in 1960, but it was restricted to one decade. In 1961, the three authors joined forces to edit a new general work on Soviet foreign policy, *Mezhdunarodnye otnosheniya i vneshnyaya politika SSSR 1917–1960* (Moscow, 1961). This work was also issued by the Higher Party School of the central committee.

rassments of having to deal with a subject in which most of the principals and personalities had been purged and liquidated. As it is, even
post-Stalinist literature avoids mentioning Soviet personalities, apart
from Lenin and occasional references to Stalin, although bourgeois
statesmen and diplomats flit through its pages with relative abandon.
General MacArthur comes into the picture several times, but Litvinov is
not mentioned once, either in connection with the famous Litvinov
protocols following the Kellogg-Briand Pact, or during the period
1930–9, when he was People's Commissar for Foreign Affairs. All his
statements and activities are ascribed to anonymous Soviet representatives or to the Narkomindel. Neither is Molotov's replacement of Litvinov in 1939 mentioned, although the *Dictionary* called this a significant
move.

Although the "periodization" fear has evaporated and Soviet historians are now free, within limits, to discuss the "periodization" of
Soviet foreign policy, the role and influence of personalities still create
complications.[49] This is never stated explicitly, however; no hard party

[49] Although only the first two volumes of the new edition of the *Diplomatic Dictionary* (A-I and K-P) had been published when this essay was
written, the general contours of the new retrospective historical treatment of
Soviet diplomatic personalities have been set. The criteria established for
those to be resurrected, those to remain in oblivion, and those to be consigned
to the ranks of obscurity never fail to arouse the curiosity of both Soviet and
non-Soviet historians. Comparing biographical entries in the new edition with
those in the old is not necessarily conclusive in its implication, since the new
edition is much less ambitious in scope than the old. All biographical entries
have been shortened and the colorful language (whether invective or
panegyric) has been substantially excised. The entries for active Soviet
diplomats are extraordinarily meagre, particularly the new diplomats drawn
from the party apparatus, who often have no more than three or four lines.
Foreign Minister Gromyko is given barely a half-column. "Bourgeois" diplomats, however obscure, fare much better: Joseph Beck, for example, is
awarded nearly three times as much space as Gromyko; Imperial Russian
diplomats are generously treated; and the late John Foster Dulles is awarded
three full columns. In contrast, V. M. Molotov, who was head of the Soviet
Foreign Office for longer than any other individual, is not even entered, while
Vyshinsky is given a curt half-column and Litvinov a skimpy fourteen lines.
Of the pre-purge diplomats, S. S. Aleksandrovsky (Soviet ambassador to
Czechoslovakia at the time of Munich), Antonov-Ovseyenko and L. M.
Karakhan (twenty-three lines), are among those rehabilitated, whereas veteran pre-purge diplomats like Jan Berzin, I. Joffe, D. V. Bogomolov, Davtian,
Arosev, Aralov, Krestinsky, and Bekzadian remain in limbo, although documents bearing the names of both Joffe and Berzin appear in *Dokumenty
vneshnei politiki SSSR*. Manuilsky has also been excluded from the new
edition, although he was in the old. Since most of the first volume of the new
history of the war is simply a survey of the diplomacy of the inter-war period,
and its format indicates that it is destined to be the definitive history produced by the current regime, it is interesting to make a quantitative check of
the number of entries various personalities, Soviet and non-Soviet, have been
given in the index. Of the Soviet personalities, Lenin leads with 50, followed
by Khrushchev with 24, Stalin with 22, and Voroshilov with 12. Khrushchev
is the first to be mentioned, on the first page of the introduction, with a
quotation on the significance of the war, whereas Stalin appears only five
pages later and then only as a name in another quotation from a Khrushchev

line has been established on periodization and none seems likely. The job is visualized as essentially the responsibility of historians, who still betray the caution and prudence of their craft.

A general discussion of the problem was initiated in the pages of *Mezhdunarodnaya Zhizn* in February 1958 by M. Airapetyan, in an article entitled "The Periodization of the History of Soviet Foreign Policy." Fundamental importance is assigned to periodization, because:

> To define the historical periods of Soviet foreign policy correctly and scientifically is of paramount importance in understanding its basis and the place in history of each stage in the struggle for peace and the creation of favorable international conditions for the building of socialism and communism in the USSR, and in clarifying the ever-growing influence of our foreign policy on the whole course of international development and its transformation into a decisive factor of contemporary world history. It enables us to understand the social laws governing the transition from one stage of foreign policy to another and permits a better understanding of the nature of historical turns in Soviet foreign policy, reveals their causes and consequences, and demonstrates the many-sided role played by the communist party of the Soviet Union as the leader and guiding force of Soviet foreign policy.

The basic principles of Soviet foreign policy, "proletarian internationalism" and "peaceful co-existence," he writes, do not vary, but "the specific forms and methods of their application change as the international situation and the world balance of forces change," and "the transition from one stage of Soviet foreign policy to another is determined not by chance combinations of circumstances or diplomatic tactics, but by objective economic and political factors both at home and abroad."

Airapetyan divides the entire history of Soviet foreign policy into "two basic strategic stages," the first stretching from the revolution to the end of the Second World War, when socialism was transformed into a world system. The second period covers the years from 1945 to the present. Each is then divided into periods, the two most interesting of

---

speech; this is his only appearance in the introduction. Altogether Khrushchev is quoted five times in the introduction and has four other entries in the introductory section. Stalin is not quoted at all, while Lenin merits four entries, of which two are quotations. Bulganin, Kaganovich, and Malenkov do not appear in the index at all, whereas Engels has 8 entries, Marx 7, and Mao Tse-tung 6. Kalinin has 5 entries, Kollontai, Marshals Blyukher and Timoshenko, 3 each. Gomulka and Gottwald also merit 6 apiece, while Vyshinsky and Chicherin go unmentioned. Ordzhonikidze, Potemkin, and, strangely enough, L. P. Beria have 2 entries each, while a sprinkling of military figures have 1 apiece. A. A. Kuznetsov and Antonov-Ovseyenko have 1 entry each, while Voznesensky is given 2. Molotov, Mikoyan, Zhdanov, and Litvinov have 1 entry each. Of the non-Soviet personalities, who on the whole get much more coverage than Soviet figures, Hitler leads all entries with 117, followed by Chamberlain with 33, Mussolini with 24, Ribbentrop with 23, Goering with 22, Churchill with 22, Hull with 17, Halifax and Roosevelt with 11 each, and de Gaulle and Bullitt with 10.

which are those called "The Early Stages of the Second World War (September 1939–July 1941)," i.e. the years of the Nazi-Soviet honeymoon, and "The Period of the Emergence and Consolidation of the World Socialist System (1945–1953)," whose terminal point is, of course, the year in which Stalin died. Whether coincidental or not, every year in which an important personality shift occurred appears as the terminal point of a period, although not all of his periods are defined by this criterion. What is interesting is that the year in which Stalin died, 1953, has been proposed as a dividing line rather than 1956 (the Twentieth Party Congress). The major event of the former year is obvious to everyone even though its significance cannot be explicitly recognized. "The tremendous impact of Soviet peace policy after 1953," wrote Academician Khvostov, "and the extension of the Soviet peace effort, justify its choice as an important milestone on the straight road of development of the Leninist peace policy."[50] Yet the major shifts in foreign policy actually took place after 1955.

Airapetyan's article was offered as "a basis for discussion" and reactions were solicited. Aside from quibbling about periods, and the implied question of the relationship between personalities and periods, two other issues emerged as continuing problems for Soviet historians of Soviet foreign policy. The first is the Nazi-Soviet Pact. Khvostov, in his outline published in 1957, frankly suggested that the period September 1939–July 1941 be called the "Period of the Soviet-German Pact," but Ivashin of the Higher Party School thought this "an unhappy and narrow definition."[51] Virtually all Soviet scholars now subsume it under some variation of "The Early Stages of the Second World War," which is appropriately innocuous.

More serious methodologically is the co-ordination of Soviet foreign policy with internal developments, in accordance with the doctrine that foreign policy is an extension of internal policy. The chief problem here is that, whereas 1936 constitutes, in the official mythology, the most fundamental dividing-point in Soviet internal development, it does not correspond with any comparable development in Soviet foreign policy. Some of Airapetyan's critics pointed out that the year in which socialism was established in the USSR failed even to produce a ripple in his periodization. The underlying difficulty is, of course, that whereas Stalin could unilaterally declare the existence of a "fundamental" internal transformation by ideological fiat, he could hardly decree a corresponding change in foreign policy.

In a "summing-up" article Khvostov justified departures between the periodization of internal and external development on the common sense ground that, although internal development was determined exclusively by the Soviet Government, its influence on external policy had

[50] *International Affairs*, 1958, No. 8, 71.
[51] *International Affairs*, 1958, No. 7, 62. Cf. also *Novaya i Noveishaya Istoriya*, 1957, No. 4. Khvostov's outline covered only the first forty years of Soviet foreign policy and constituted the framework for his short book, *40 let borby za mir* (Moscow, 1958).

to be shared with the outside world. Thus, although the basic divisions of Soviet foreign policy should coincide with internal developments, the "periods" themselves need not precisely coincide. In an interesting review of the discussion, completely devoid of abusive language, threats, or admonitions, so characteristic of discussions during the Stalin era, Khvostov writes:

> In defining periods in any aspect of the historical process . . . the historians must necessarily proceed from the general historical periods that embrace the development of a people as a whole. The history of a country's foreign relations is just one aspect of its over-all process of historical development . . . the developments and requirements in its economy, the progress of the class struggle and other domestic factors. . . . All this implies that a periodization of foreign policy hinges largely upon the general periods of a country's history. This does not by any means imply that the more fragmentary periods in the development of a country's foreign relations should always be identified with phases in the development of industry, agriculture or, say, literature and art. The attempt to define periods separately in the history of Soviet foreign policy is, therefore, perfectly justified. It must be based on the general periods in the history of the U.S.S.R., but must not necessarily coincide with them. One of the difficulties confronting students of Soviet foreign policy when they try to define its periods is that the general periods of Soviet history are as yet far from comprehensively defined and that Soviet historians are not as yet of one opinion regarding them. . . . Airapetyan's periods diverge greatly from the research of a large group of historians who prepared the textbook, *History of the U.S.S.R. — The Socialist Epoch* . . . (which) draws the line between these two periods in 1937. In other words, Airapetyan's "two basic strategic stages" in the history of Soviet foreign relations diverge sharply from the "two general phases" of the textbook. What does this disparity imply? First of all, that the periods in the history of foreign policy may easily differ from the periods in a country's general history. Yet this is not as it should be (since) . . . all policy is determined in the final analysis by the development of the social basis. . . . It appears to me, however, that in defining the periods of Soviet foreign policy, we must not ignore so important a fact as the completion, in the main, of the building of a Socialist society in the Soviet Union. . . . If there are to be any "strategic stages," this connection is absolutely essential in defining such major divisions.[52]

VII. THE IDEOLOGICAL PARAMETERS OF DIPLOMACY: A RUPTURED INTERNATIONAL CONSENSUS

It is not always recognized that, while certain externals of diplomacy seem to transcend both ideologies and centuries, they are in fact given new content and often serve other purposes than those for which they were originally conceived. Each historical era has its own specific diplomacy, the features of which are determined not only by the given state of technology and geographical communication but also by the

[52] Khvostov, *International Affairs*, No. 8, 1958, 67–69.

socio-economic and political order which prevails within a given civilization, and the ideological consensus which binds it together. Diplomacy, as a part of the prevailing customary inter-state legal system, no matter how nebulously conceived and ambiguously executed, can function effectively only when fundamental ideological and social questions are no longer a matter of dispute. It functions to preserve the given ideo-social system by seeking to accommodate and adjust conflicts which are bound to arise within it. Diplomacy is thus most effective when it serves to lubricate frictions and resolve conflicts between states in such a way that the system itself is never brought into question. Even when force is employed to resolve issues, the unwritten premise guarantees that it will simply result in the re-arrangement of a new political mosaic within the existing order, which itself is never at stake.

Immanuel Kant, in his essay on *Eternal Peace*, expressed much the same idea when he wrote that "no state shall, during war, permit such acts of hostility which would make mutual confidence in the subsequent peace impossible," for "it follows that a war of extermination, in which the destruction of both parties and of all justice can result, would permit perpetual peace only in the vast burial-ground of the human race."[53] These maxims apply only if there exists a consensus to preserve the given order, but if that order itself is challenged they are invalidated. The distinctive feature of a world without an international ideological consensus is precisely that conflict can be resolved only within the framework of "extermination" and "annihilation," not necessarily in the physical sense, but certainly in the ideological and spiritual. This international consensus is absent from the world today; the old order has been challenged now for over four decades and the challenger repeatedly and without reservation asserts that its ultimate objective is to replace the existing consensus by a new one.

It is an intrinsic tendency of a diplomatic system to universalize its premises in order the better to perform its function of preserving the basic elements of the civilization it serves. By nature it cannot and does not tolerate or endure for any length of time a rival diplomacy representing another system or civilization, which it always seeks to subordinate to its own forms and rules. This happened when the European diplomatic system collided with those of the Ottoman Empire and China; both systems were eventually subjugated and subordinated to the European system by means of the peculiar diplomatic institutions known as capitulations and extra-territoriality.

In the absence of basic challenges to its supremacy, the diplomacy of a given order tends to assume that it is eternally valid and universally applicable, as the unwritten presuppositions of its existence recede into invisibility. Since nothing fundamental is at stake, variations in form, technique, style, and tempo are exaggerated out of all proportion to their intrinsic importance; ritual and ceremony assume greater superficial prominence. The art of diplomacy becomes the manipulation of exter-

53 Immanuel Kant, *Critique of Practical Reason and Other Writings in Moral Philosophy*, edited by L. W. Beck (Chicago, 1949), p. 309.

nals to maximum advantage and the avoidance of fundamental controversy. At its best, such a diplomacy functions in an atmosphere of good
faith and tact, but it is frequently forgotten that these qualities in large
measure apply to relations between social equals. Characteristically,
only those who are excluded from the consensus are conscious of their
non-universal character. These values are exposed as ephemeral in their
operative sense only when different social orders or ideologies come into
collision, for each devises its own framework within which these identical qualities and virtues are defined. In a world where the conception of
"truth" is in dispute, where the existence of "facts" is subject to contradictory epistemological doctrines, and a common definition of "lying"
does not exist, the values resting upon differing social perspectives may
lose all relevance in judging diplomatic behavior between rival civilizations. While the Bolsheviks made it explicit that they would endeavor
to deceive and cheat the "bourgeoisie," it is not often recalled that, in its
reaction to the Bolshevik revolution, the West confirmed Lenin's contention that the existing international order was "bourgeois" by casting the
Soviet republic outside the framework of the western pattern of law and
ethics for its refusal to be bound by prevailing norms of property law;
the Bolshevik regime was declared more than once an outcast government and hence outside the protection of international law. In short, no
holds were barred in dealing with the Bolsheviks, since they were
"outlaws" and the normal restrictions of international law governing
intervention and retaliation were suspended in dealing with the Bolshevik state. The refusal to recognize the Soviet Government during the
early years of its existence — and the refusal of the United States to
recognize communist China since 1949 — reflect the belief that rules of
international law and diplomacy are essentially based upon an international ideological consensus. Many aspects of current American
policy with respect to countries in the Soviet orbit and to Cuba operate
upon the unstated assumption that these countries are really outside the
framework of the law, and hence the normal restraints do not apply. No
attempt is being made here to justify or condemn these attitudes, but
merely to show that they confirm the ideological basis of a given diplomatic and international order — a point that is only too rarely recognized.

Thus, while a diplomacy which governs relations between members
of a common ideo-social order must rely upon a fund of good will and a
reservoir of trust which transcends their conflicts, the diplomacy which
governs relations between different ideo-social systems often ignores
these factors, since the ultimate issue at stake is the existence of this or
that civilization itself. A triumphant ideological bloc will write its own
history and pass ethical judgement on its own conduct independently of
the standards or values of the vanquished order.

The Bolshevik revolution not only rejected the prevailing ideo-
social system and repudiated its fundamental values and ethical principles, but declared eternal war against it, undertook to overturn it, and
to supplant it with a radically new order. Since the prevailing diplomatic

system functions to preserve the order it was rejecting, the Soviet regime refused to re-establish relations on the basis of existing diplomacy but demanded and received certain modifications and adjustments of existing diplomatic institutions and processes to accommodate its entry into the diplomatic community. In the initial phase of collision between the old and the embryonic new, it was the old system which made adjustments to accommodate the Soviet Union. Thus, from the very beginning, the Soviet Union was able to impose its radical diplomatic norms upon traditional diplomacy; and this pressure has steadily increased until today the full complement of western diplomatic norms applies to an ever-shrinking geographical area.

In the western world, it is generally accepted that what passes under the rubric of the "new" diplomacy was inspired by Woodrow Wilson, but a close examination of the Wilsonian influence reveals that each and every innovation that Wilson purportedly introduced into the practice of international relations had already been put forward by Lenin. What is called Wilsonian diplomacy in the West is called Leninist in Soviet literature. The five ideological principles which have shaped the diplomacy of the past four decades and which have been attributed to Wilson, but of which Lenin was in fact the author are: 1) national self-determination; 2) equality of all nations and states, large and small; 3) open diplomacy; 4) popular participation (elections, plebiscites, etc.) and/or popular involvement (propaganda, manipulation of opinion, etc.); and 5) internationalism. These principles were first enunciated by the Bolshevik Regime in 1917, although their ideological foundations were developed much earlier, and President Wilson appropriated them a year later precisely because they had caught the popular imagination and evoked widespread approval beyond the confines of the Bolshevik State itself.[54] The Wilsonian principles and norms were identical in form, but not in substance or in universality of application. In each case they were designed to perform diametrically opposed functions. Through these new principles Wilson sought to renovate, reform, and preserve the existing international order by accommodating diplomacy to the increasing involvement of populations and developing technology; for Lenin the identical principles were devised to destroy the same order.

During the inter-War period, the liberal-democratic application of these norms was to dominate international relations, much to the chagrin of the professional diplomat who was either unable or unwilling to adjust to new conditions and continued to sigh for the "good old days," which he still often does, whereas the Soviet version remained essentially programmatic. The Soviet conception, however, was bound to increase in influence in proportion to its increase in power, until today,

[54] Cf. "The Decree on Peace," issued on November 8, 1917 and the "Declaration on the Rights of the Nations of Russia" in *Dokumenty Vneshnei Politiki SSSR*, I, 11–15; and V. Khvostov, "*Leninskiye Printsipy Vneshnei Politiki*," in *Voprosy Vneshnei Politiki SSSR i Sovremennykh Mezhdunarodnykh Otnoshenii*, 89–102.

the Soviet version of these principles has wider application than the western. Increasingly, western diplomats complain that international diplomacy and negotiation must proceed on Soviet terms and at the Soviet level. Western spokesmen continually vow not to engage in Summit or public diplomacy, but to operate through normal diplomatic channels rather than through propaganda media. However, it all becomes a futile endeavor unless the Soviet Union "cooperates," and as long as the methods that the West finds an anathema remain congenial and advantageous to the Soviet Union, the Russians will continue to call the diplomatic tune. Their influence is now so pervasive that the West finds itself at a disadvantage whether it refuses to deal on Soviet terms or conducts business at the Soviet pace.

VIII. Soviet Conceptions of Diplomacy in a Fractured International Community

(1) Post-Stalin Images of "Bourgeois Diplomacy"

The ideo-social consensus which prevailed before 1917 and the diplomacy which it reflected have since 1917 been shattered, but only after the Second World War has this been generally recognized in the West. Two competing social and ideological systems have arisen where before there was one, and each has its diplomatic projection, but instead of only two diplomatic systems, there are in fact three: (1) Western diplomacy ("bourgeois" in the Soviet version), which is now restricted by and large to the NATO powers and those countries associated with them. (2) "Socialist" diplomacy, which governs relations among the states of the Soviet orbit and which is still in the development stage and not yet a fully integrated system. (3) The diplomacy of "co-existence," which governs relations between states of the Soviet and western worlds and the "neutralist" universe of states, which accept neither the communist nor western norms in their totality and deal with those of each system. These states do not constitute an ideo-social system nor do they have their own distinctive diplomatic projection. In the Soviet view, these three diplomacies are closely inter-related and in dynamic flux, in accordance with their dialectical framework, whereby the new (communist diplomacy) is in a continuous state of expansion at the expense of the old (western diplomacy) through the medium of a transitional phase (co-existence diplomacy).

Interestingly enough, the post-Stalinist image of "bourgeois" diplomacy has mellowed considerably and the old vulgar invective and clichés have noticeably diminished. But the basic ideology has not changed; neither has the view taken of "bourgeois" diplomacy. It is in fact now bolstered by sociological analyses of the "bourgeois" states and their external functions, as they relate to internal purposes. Bourgeois diplomacy persists in the Soviet version as the instrument of capitalist "ruling circles" in the representation of their class interests abroad, but clearly as a diplomacy in an advanced state of degeneration corresponding to the decline of the system which it represents. Hence it is no longer viewed as a serious threat, although its capacity for mischief is continually emphasized. The entry on "Diplomacy" in the first volume of the second edition of the *Diplomatic Dictionary* has been completely re-written and shorn of much of its crudity in favor of a more "objective" Marxist description. Bourgeois diplomacy is no longer linked with fascist diplomacy; the Stalinist image of bourgeois diplomacy is now ascribed to the diplomacy of feudal absolutism, but with the observation that some of its features were inevitably carried over into the bourgeois era. Diplomacy is defined as

> the official activity of heads of states, governments and special agencies engaged in foreign relations . . . designed to accomplish the aims and purposes of the foreign policy of a state as determined by the interests of the ruling class, and also to uphold the rights and interests of the state concerned.[55]

Soviet writers now view bourgeois diplomacy as a once great institution in decline. There is even a certain patronizing nostalgia which reflects the smug conviction that history is moving in Moscow's direction and that therefore a more generous and charitable tone can be used in describing bourgeois diplomacy in the final phases of its agony. Whereas its objective before the war was to isolate, encircle, and destroy the USSR, it can now do no more than put up futile rearguard actions and fight desperately for survival against the relentless advance of communism. Instead of denunciations, Soviet writers offer more "critiques" and "analyses" of bourgeois diplomacy, exposing its frailties and errors and taunting its practitioners for not being able to rise to the brilliant heights of their "illustrious" predecessors, Metternich and Talleyrand, Bismarck and Canning, Disraeli and Gorchakov, and the writer-practitioners Satow, Nicolson, and Cambon, all of whom are presented in a favorable light in contrast to their inept and fumbling contemporary counterparts. Instead of following the sage counsel of the illustrious diplomats of the past to use intelligence, tact, compromise, common sense, and decency in diplomacy, and to avoid involvement with general staffs, espionage establishments, and the use of deceit and trickery, modern bourgeois diplomacy increasingly subordinates itself to military strategy, espionage, and sabotage to achieve its purposes. Soviet writers and historians are now indulging in the luxury of dispensing gratuitous advice to the "bourgeoisie" on how to view their own interests — that is, to join up with history instead of futilely resisting its implacable mandate — much in the same way that western scholars define the interests of the Soviet Union for the benefit of the Kremlin, imploring it to renounce its

---

[55] *Diplomaticheskii slovar*, I, 1960, p. 457. The new *Dictionary* continues to emphasize deception as an important "objective" characteristic of "bourgeois" diplomacy, but its effectiveness is said to have been blunted because of its exposure by the Soviet Union. The might of the socialist camp, it is held, has forced bourgeois diplomacy to employ new devices, which are becoming increasingly difficult to contrive, forcing it to become less dishonest contrary to its own will.

childish notion that an outmoded social doctrine like Marxism can have any real relevance for the present or the future, and to accept the permanence of a non-Soviet world. The wheel of history has made a complete revolution, in the view of Soviet writers, for only a generation ago the bourgeoisie was refusing to acknowledge that the Soviet system had any claim to permanent existence, but now the bourgeoisie is itself pleading for survival.

Instead of subscribing to Bismarck's wise observation that politics is the "art of the possible," modern bourgeois diplomats are accused of following the idiotic notion of Alfred Rosenberg that politics is "the art of making the impossible possible."[56] Consequently:

> Western diplomats, who are by no means lacking in knowledge, intelligence and professional skill . . . stubbornly pursued impracticable aims. However, there is essentially nothing surprising in this. Indeed, only that is realizable which corresponds to the historical demands of the period, that is, the objective laws of development. Those who set themselves goals which are at variance with these objective processes, sooner or later — but unfailingly — suffer failure. . . . Phenomena which arise objectively and develop tempestuously as a result of historical laws which operate in reality and are not a product of armchair deductions, are explained as "accidental"; facts are denied if they do not suit the tastes of the capitalist ruling classes. . . . The cold war compelled bourgeois diplomacy to operate in an imaginary world. A long string of "doctrines" and "theories" was evolved — some dealing with "global" policy and others designed for "local" use, some being discarded and others replacing them. Their common feature, however, was that they were artificially contrived. It followed logically from this that diplomacy became "inert" and "negative," as the Western Press complained, and that it became doctrinaire and scholastic—and degenerated. . . . Routine, the absence of initiative and unwillingness to make any move, have become salient features of bourgeois diplomacy. . . . Western diplomacy has sunk to the wide use of slander and incitement, espionage, subversion and sabotage against the socialist countries. . . . It has become an adjunct not only to General Staffs, but also to organizations dealing in espionage, sabotage, and terror. "Cloak and dagger diplomacy" is an inevitable fellow traveller of "atomic diplomacy." . . . In its best days, the old bourgeois diplomacy was able to grasp that the essence of its art was the ability to adapt to new situations.[57]

(2) From "Proletarian Internationalism" to "Socialist Diplomacy"

With respect to the international relations and diplomacy of the communist orbit, three main innovations have been introduced, corresponding to the transformation of socialism from a system restricted to one country into an international system: (1) The restoration of the so-called Leninist norms of behavior between communist parties and states, which were consistently violated by Stalin, although repeatedly reaffirmed doctrinally, as the basis of inter-communist relationships. (2)

[56] P. Tolmachov, "Bourgeois Diplomacy Today," *International Affairs*, No. 1, 1960, 23–29.
[57] Ibid.

The transformation of the principles of "proletarian internationalism" from a norm of inter-party relations into a diplomatic norm of inter-state relations. (3) The transformation and expansion of Soviet diplomacy into "socialist" diplomacy and the appearance of a new parallel and self-contained diplomatic and international order, bound by a common ideology, in which inter-state and inter-party relations have been virtually merged.

One of the most striking innovations is the retrospective assimilation of pre-war inter-party relations and institutions in diplomatic history. Since the communist states are now governed by parties which were out of power before the war, pre-war inter-party activities have been, *mutatis mutandis*, retroactively extrapolated into the past as part of the diplomatic history of the communist orbit. The old pretence of a dichotomy between party and official relations has been abandoned. Corresponding institutional changes have also been made in the diplomacy of the communist universe. The Soviet ambassador, for example, now functions overtly as both a party and state representative and in the first capacity attends communist functions in the state to which he is accredited. All Soviet diplomatic emissaries to communist capitals are now career party functionaries rather than professional diplomats such as those who serve outside the communist orbit.

The idea of a communist system of international relations was not ideologically orthodox under Stalin, who tried to maintain the artificial distinction between state and party relations because of certain advantages that accrued to his rigid control over the satellite states. "Proletarian internationalism" remained a party principle. Its essence was that all communists, whether in or out of power, owed first loyalty to the Soviet party and state just as if no change had taken place since before the war. Consequently, during the Stalin era a "communist" diplomatic system did not exist, but only Soviet diplomacy. In contrast to the mendacity of bourgeois diplomacy, Soviet diplomacy, according to a 1948 account:

> cannot use the amoral and anti-popular methods practised by the diplomacy of absolutist and bourgeois states; it cannot have recourse to deceiving its own and other peoples . . . since its aims meet with the sympathy of all progressive mankind . . . The art of Soviet diplomacy . . . differs fundamentally from the diplomatic art of the bourgeois states . . . in the realization of its declared principles, clearness and straightforwardness in the formulation of its demands . . . It is alien to "combinations" . . . to unscrupulous transactions, intrigues, intimidation, or disguising real tendencies by false formulas and "doctrines" . . . Not resorting to the traditional . . . methods of the "diplomatic game" — threats, perfidy, and lies — the Soviet diplomatic art invariably insures the realization of all the foreign policy aims of the Soviet state, and at the same time wins deep moral support.[58]

The absurdity of this description merits neither elaboration nor extensive documentation, but it remains substantially unaltered as the con-

---

[58] I. D. Levin, *Diplomaticheskii immunitet.*

temporary Soviet description of communist diplomacy which is simply the internationalization of the Soviet version of Soviet diplomacy. These principles apply only among socialist states and are not extended to the "bourgeois" world; and then only to parties and states which accept the ideological consensus of the Soviet orbit; they cease to apply in the event of heresy (the Nagy regime) or non-acceptance (Tito).

The Sino-Soviet conflict, however, added, by implication, a new element to the Soviet perception of the problem of international relations. Stalin could avoid recognizing "contradictions" between the socialist states by declaring Tito's Yugoslavia a non-socialist state. Since Moscow still considers Albania and China to be socialist states, Soviet leaders are hoisted upon their own ideological petard. They are faced with a problem which is not explicable either in terms of the principle of "proletarian internationalism," nor that of "peaceful co-existence."

Just as "bourgeois" diplomacy is conceived as dedicated to the preservation of the ideo-social order of which it is a part, socialist diplomacy is devised to preserve the communist consensus, not to facilitate its disruption. Thus if "bourgeois" diplomacy was governed by the implicit principle of "capitalist internationalism" and an "aristocratic international" dominated the era of feudal diplomacy, the principle of "proletarian internationalism" governs socialist diplomacy. That is, it applies only to the members of the diplomatic club, all of whose members have "ruling classes" that are proletarian in character. Proletarian internationalism, which was simply an idea before 1917, has undergone two qualitative transformations in the past four decades, that have had relevance for diplomacy:

> After . . . the establishment of the Soviet socialist state, the principles of proletarian internationalism remained basically unchanged (unity, solidarity, mutual support) and acquired a new significance in world relations. . . . The principles of proletarian internationalism found expression in the Soviet Government's approach to every world problem. . . . At this stage of history, class-conscious workers in all countries for the first time found a socialist fatherland in the Soviet socialist state. . . . Therefore, as a result of the socialist revolution in Russia, proletarian internationalism for the first time became a state policy, in the policy of the Soviet Union, the socialist fatherland for the working people of the world.[59]

After World War II, the second transformation of "proletarian internationalism" took place, its conversion from the state policy of a single state into that of several:

> The inception of a number of socialist states and the establishment of the world socialist system opened up a new stage in the revolutionary struggle of the working class. The feature of it is that the principles of proletarian internationalism, formerly the principles of the international working class movement and of the policy of one state only (the Soviet state), have become the basis for the international relations of all the

[59] E. A. Korovin, *Osnovnye Problemy Sovremennykh Mezhdunarodnykh Otnoshenii* (Moscow, 1959), pp. 58–60.

socialist countries and the entire world socialist system. These principles determine the relations between the socialist states and their attitude towards countries liberated from or in the process of liberation from the colonial yoke, and also their policy in regard to capitalist countries.[60]

The third transformation will take place when "proletarian internationalism" and socialist diplomacy become the universal norms of the international order. "The future," writes one Soviet authority, "belongs to relations of a new socialist type in the sphere of international relations. The capitalist system is doomed . . . and the same is equally true of the corresponding type of international relations."[61]

The revolutionary changes in Soviet conceptions of diplomacy are not only manifested in the assimilation of inter-party relations and institutions into socialist diplomacy, but the old artificial dichotomies between state and party relations, elsewhere are also no longer maintained with any great conviction or urgency to deceive. In a sense, this is indeed a franker and more straightforward approach to foreign policy, which the Soviets maintain is a prime characteristic of their diplomacy. Proletarian internationalism as a principle not only fuses party and state relations in the Soviet orbit, but it also constitutes an organic link with future communist states through ideological communion with their future ruling communist parties, which are not yet in power. A curious predisposition remains that maintains a penumbra of international legality by drawing a tenuous distinction between "ruling" and "non-ruling" communist parties, the former invested with official status, but the latter constituting only a potential officiality. Nevertheless, the old pretences and shams of keeping official and party activities in air-tight legal compartments are no longer asserted with the same legal precision and meticulous attention to protocol. Thus, Korovin, who in the past has been next to none in preserving the sanctity of international law from the extraneous intrusions of party activities, now writes:

> The concept of proletarian internationalism was extended to become a concept of socialist internationalism in so far as the realization of its principles, which remain those of the world working-class movement, is at the same time one of the most important functions of each socialist state. . . . The most prominent manifestation of proletarian (socialist) internationalism in inter-state relations is the new type of relations between countries of the world socialist system. These are characterized in the statements of socialist statesmen, in joint declarations by Governments of socialist countries *and the documents of Communist and Workers' parties.*[62]

[60] Ibid., p. 60. Cf. Ronin, S. L., *Printsip Proletarskovo Internatsional-izma v Sovetskom Sotsialisticheskom Prave* (Moscow, 1956).

[61] S. Sanakoyev, "The Basis of the Relations Between the Socialist Countries," *International Affairs*, No. 7, 1958, 23. Cf. the article by the same author Novy Tip Mezhdunarodnykh Otnoshenii," in *Voprosy Vneshnei Politiki*, 18–150.

[62] Korovin, *Osnovnye Problemy Sovremennykh Mezhdunarodnykh Otnoshenii*, pp. 60–61.

(3) *The Diplomacy of Co-existence: The Soviet Image of Non-Consensus Diplomacy*

At present, the Soviet theory asserts that while the principles of "proletarian internationalism" govern relations in the Soviet orbit, the principle which governs relations with the non-Soviet world is "peaceful co-existence," which in the Soviet view is no longer a tactical expedient but a distinct historical phase of transition from one ideo-social system to another, and hence is characterized by the simultaneous existence of contradictory systems which must establish some form of relationship with one another. It is, in effect, a period in which a single ideo-social system does not prevail, and the diplomacy it reflects is correspondingly provisional in character and a diplomacy of non-consensus. It is a diplomacy which does not seek to resolve disputes within the given order or orders — as is the case with both "bourgeois" and "socialist" diplomacies — but rather seeks to resolve them within the framework of annihilating, liquidating, or assimilating one pole (capitalism) to the other (communism), not necessarily physically or through the use of external force (which has been rendered impractical by technological developments), but its elimination nevertheless. Soviet spokesmen, from Khrushchev down, are vociferous in their condemnation of the view that peaceful co-existence is based upon the *permanent* as opposed to the *temporary* co-existence of different ideo-social systems:

> The principle of peaceful co-existence is a most important principle governing the relations between the socialist and capitalist countries. Peaceful co-existence does not presuppose any similarity between the social systems of co-operating countries; on the contrary, as emerges from the phrase itself, it means that on our planet there simultaneously exist countries with differing social and economic systems. The principles of proletarian internationalism are much wider and deeper than the principles of peaceful co-existence. They express the interests of the working class, the class interests of the workers of the socialist countries.[63]

The temporary character of "peaceful co-existence" is pre-ordained by the inexorable laws of history, which preclude any resolution on the basis of a permanent existence of differing ideo-social systems. Co-existence is simply another way of defining the class struggle on the international level. Referring to the words of the Italian communist leader, Togliatti, one Soviet writer characterized "as absurd the attitude of those who regard peaceful co-existence as a 'division into two parts: on the one side socialism, on the other capitalism. The struggle of classes . . . and above all the struggle of the working class for its vital interests, for an end to exploitation . . . will continue as long as a single capitalist

[63] Sanakoyev, "The Basis of the Relations Between the Socialist Countries," p. 30. Cf. also Korovin, "Mirnoe sosushchestvovanie kak osnova sovremennykh nezhdunarodnykh otnoshenii i mezhdunarodnogo prava," in *Osnovnye Problemy;* and V. Vasileyev, "Peaceful Co-existence — the Basis of International Relations," *International Affairs,* 1958, No. 3.

country exists, so long as capitalism survives.' "[64] Peaceful co-existence, under no conditions, must permit any relaxation of the ideological struggle to extirpate capitalism:

> The class struggle, including one of its concrete manifestations — the struggle between socialist and bourgeois ideologies — is determined by the objective laws of social development. The operation of these laws can be abolished neither by individuals, nor parties, nor Governments. The only thing that depends on the latter is the means (peaceful or non-peaceful) by which this struggle is waged. . . . Communists proceed from the premise that in the sphere of *inter-state relations* the positions of the socialist and the capitalist countries can and must be brought closer together, specifically through mutually acceptable concessions and compromises, and that ideological differences and disputes must not hinder the further relaxation of international tension. But as for *class relations*, including the struggle between opposing ideologies, in this sphere there can be no easing of the struggle, no depolarization. So long as antagonistic classes exist in the world, the class struggle will inevitably continue to grow in one form or another.[65]

As Khrushchev himself has put it in an unusually frank manner, co-existence would otherwise be superfluous:

> If there were only one ideology in the world and the same social order held sway in all countries, there would be no antagonistic systems and there would be no emergence at all of the problem of co-existence in the sense in which we refer to it now. In that case, it would simply be existence and no co-existence.[66]

The co-existence of two diplomatic systems representing two ideo-social consensus orders also implies a double-standard of diplomatic behavior, for identically expressed international legal and diplomatic norms and forms may have diametrically opposite effects, depending upon whether they are applied to the communist orbit or to the capitalist states. This flows from Lenin's dictum that "one and the same idea in different, concrete, historical circumstances may be, according to the case, reactionary or progressive."[67] Or, as Korovin has reformulated it more recently:

> A legal norm that has positive (progressive) value in relations between capitalist states may, in a number of cases, acquire the opposite (reactionary) character when transferred to the relations between socialist states.[68]

Thus norms and forms like "non-intervention," "sovereignty," "diplomatic immunity," "neutrality," "national self-determination," "aggres-

---

[64] T. Timofeyev, "Inter-State Relations and Social Contradictions," *International Affairs*, No. 3, 1958.

[65] Ibid., p. 17.

[66] Speech to Supreme Soviet, January 14, 1960. Moscow Radio Broadcast of January 14, 1960.

[67] A. Zhdanov in *Voprosy Filosofii*, No. 1, 1947, p. 263.

[68] Korovin, *Osnovnye Problemy Sovremennykh Mezhdunarodnykh Otnoshenii*, p. 77.

sion" (indirect or otherwise), and even "annexation," when invoked against capitalist states are "progressive" and correspondingly reactionary if employed against the interests of socialist countries.[69] They will have different concrete applications, depending upon whether they operate in the universe of "bourgeois," "co-existence," or "socialist" diplomacy. It was this bewildering world to which President Kennedy was introduced when he met with Premier Khrushchev in Vienna:

> The facts of the matter are that the Soviets and ourselves give wholly different meanings to the same words: war, peace, democracy, and popular will. We have wholly different views of right and wrong, of what is an internal affair and what is aggression. And above all, we have wholly different concepts of where the world is and where it is going.[70]

Thus, the Soviet Union has managed to transform diplomatic and legal norms that were designed to preserve the *status quo* into instruments for digging its grave, by first changing their ideological content and then universalizing their application. The main Soviet reliance is that non-communist states will continue to be absolutely bound by the norms of international law that they consider to be sacred; should the "bourgeois" states in desperation violate their own ethical and legal norms, they can then be exposed as hypocritical or their norms to be no more universal than those of the Soviet orbit. On the other hand, the Soviet Union can freely violate "bourgeois" norms of international law and diplomacy because the Soviet Union has renounced them and thus is not committed to their sanctity. Thus the Soviet Union can simultaneously observe and violate norms of international law and diplomacy, since it will be observing them in the "socialist" sense and violating them in the "bourgeois." This naturally creates certain advantages for the Soviet Union. Even if the Soviet Government violates its own norms, it is relatively immune from "exposure" since its system is not as articulated as the western, and it still remains the final judge of the content of its own norms.

The diplomacy of co-existence, in the Soviet view, is supposed to constitute a meeting ground in which both "bourgeois" and "socialist" norms mix and overlap, and are acceptable to both sides, although the

[69] For the Soviet position on the relativity of norms and forms of international law and diplomacy, cf. F. I. Kozhevnikov, *Sovetskoye Gosudarstvo i Mezhdunarodnoye Pravo* (Moscow, 1948), especially Chapters I, II, III, and V; and *Mezhdunarodnoye Pravo* (Moscow, 1957), Chapters III and V. For Soviet metamorphoses of the concept of "aggression" and "non-aggression" cf. K. A. Baginyan, *Aggressiya-Tyuagchaisheye Mezhdunarodnoye Prestupleniye* (Moscow, 1955); Y. Yudin and I. Vanich, "Indirect Aggression — A Weapon of Imperialist Powers," *International Affairs*, No. 11, 1958; K. A. Baginyan, *Narysheniye Imperialistichekimi Gosudarstvami Printsipa Nevmyeshatelstva* (Moscow, 1954); on changing conceptions of "neutrality," cf. Korovin, "Neitralitet v Proshlom i Nastoyashchem," in *Osnovnye Problemy*, pp. 135–150; on the relativity of the sanctity of treaties (Pacta Sunt Servanda), cf. V. M. Shurshalov, *Osnovaniya Deistvitonosti Mezhdunarodnykh Dogovorov* (Moscow, 1957).

[70] *Time*, June 16, 1961, p. 14.

elements of the mixture are explosive and constantly changing in proportion to one another. Co-existence diplomacy thus functions as an instrument of both conflict and cooperation between two irreconcilable ideo-social systems, one of which is doomed to inevitable non-existence. As Isaiah Berlin has so perceptively demonstrated, ideologies of determinism develop attitudes of moral irresponsibility in that they assign the burden of responsibility to the impersonal forces of history.[71] Dealing and negotiating with the Soviet Union is frustrating because its representatives deny all personal responsibility for their inflexibility, assigning it to the inexorable laws of history, forcing western statesmen to negotiate not with Moscow but with the dialectic, to which the West is advised to lodge all of its complaints concerning the "class struggle" and the inevitable doom of capitalism. Clearly, western diplomacy in its traditional garb is no match for maneuvers of this character.

IX. Postscript

Khrushchev's attempt to install missile bases in Cuba in 1962 once again suggests that no matter how far the process of de-Stalinization may have progressed in Soviet domestic policy and intra-Bloc relations, the basic rules that governed Soviet diplomatic behavior toward the western world remained depressingly Stalinist in their essentials, and the Soviet invasion of Czechoslovakia in 1968 suggests a partial relapse into Stalinist practices where Eastern Europe is concerned. The so-called "Brezhnev doctrine" is, in effect, the latest operational manifestation of both "proletarian internationalism" and "socialist diplomacy." Duplicity, perfidy, deceit, chicanery, and cruder forms of dishonesty have characterized Soviet diplomacy in the past, and both the Cuban and Czechoslovak episodes betray a distressing continuity in behavior. The Cuban case, in particular, illustrates the manner in which Soviet leaders employed both deceit and lesser forms of deception in their dealings with the United States in order to gain an improvement in their strategic position.

Khrushchev's Cuban escapade was totally in character with his political physiognomy as an audacious and clever operator — an experienced and successful political adventurer skilled in the arcane arts of intrigue and machination, simulation and dissimulation, simple deception as well as refined duplicity. His entire political career has been marked by successive and successful political maneuver and calculated gambles as he has pursued and preserved his power at home: the arrest and execution of Beria, the dethronement of Malenkov, the reconciliation with Tito, the denunciation of Stalin, the intervention in Hungary, the Virgin Lands program, the expulsion of the anti-party group, the shelving of Marshal Zhukov, the drastic reorganization of the Soviet economy, and finally his current ideological shadow-boxing with Peking all attest to both his personal intrepidity and artful double-dealing.

Khrushchev's duplicity, however, was more than a simple reflection

---

[71] Isaiah Berlin, *Historical Inevitability* (London, 1954).

of his moral personality, for as we have seen, duplicity in dealing with the class enemy is deeply rooted in Soviet doctrine and practice. It is a noxious weed whose seeds were sown by Marx and Engels, watered by Lenin, cultivated and nurtured by Stalin, and whose poisonous fruit continues to be harvested by his successors. It is significant that in his condemnation of Stalin and his methods, it was not the late dictator's double-dealing with the class enemy which Khrushchev subjected to excoriation, but rather Stalin's employment of methods in dealing with communists which were properly reserved for use only against the bourgeoisie. On the contrary, Khrushchev praised Stalin for his "struggle against the enemies of Marxism-Leninism," and in this connection, he once asked that "may God grant that every Communist will be able to fight as Stalin fought."

It has been widely heralded that Khrushchev's withdrawal of his missiles from Cuba at least verified the assumption that the Soviet leaders are rational (even if the Chinese and Albanians are not) in that they preferred to retreat — even ignominiously — rather than risk self-destruction. This is certainly in accordance with orthodox Leninist principles and by itself should not be a great occasion for rejoicing, for Khrushchev also simultaneously demonstrated that his conception of rationality is not incompatible with entertaining the grave risk of thermonuclear war if the possible dividends are correspondingly high. Although Khrushchev's Cuban enterprise failed, it was nevertheless a rational gamble which only narrowly missed being successfully executed. In return for running the risk of nuclear war, the Soviet leader hoped to convert Cuba into an advanced missile outpost which might have eroded the entire American position in the New World. Cuba would have been provided with a local nuclear deterrent and Latin American revolutionary forces would have found protection behind a Soviet nuclear shield against possible American intervention. The credibility of American commitments around the globe would have been undermined and wars of liberation and popular uprisings might have erupted in many parts of the world. The United States would have been exposed as a toothless tiger and the entire world balance of psychological, military, and social power might have shifted irrevocably in favor of the communist world.

It is sometimes forgotten that the calculation of risks is also rational behavior, while, frequently, rationality is mistakenly identified with other virtues, such as prudence, wisdom, and even honesty. It is possible to act rationally, yet to be misinformed, imprudent, adventurous, and dishonest, for rational behavior does not guarantee against the effects of accident, miscalculation, ignorance, and bad luck. In retrospect, to be sure, a calculated gamble which fails frequently appears more reckless than audacious, and hence irrational.

While it may be true that Khrushchev mistakenly expected President Kennedy to procrastinate rather than risk the use of force in the event his movement of missiles into Cuba was prematurely discovered, there is considerable evidence that Khrushchev was relying as much, if not more, on his ability to deceive the President as on an expectation that the President was "too liberal to fight" and would protest and fulminate but in the end do nothing. He was aided in his gamble by the prevailing conviction in official Washington that Khrushchev would never install missiles in Cuba because (1) he had never established missiles on non-Soviet territory; (2) he was too rational to install missiles ten thousand miles away from home, where they might be exposed to capture; (3) he was too shrewd to allow an erratic and unstable Castro to share in the control of Soviet missiles and nuclear warheads; (4) he did not need missile bases in Cuba for military purposes; (5) a combination of the above.

Ever since von Clausewitz warned that a shrewd general would always expect the enemy to do the unexpected, it has been bad business to tell your rivals in advance what you expect them not to do. Above and beyond this unwitting assistance to Khrushchev's design, the crucial role of duplicity in the entire operation is also betrayed by the following:

1. Khrushchev disarmingly, if somewhat insultingly, promised not to press the Berlin issue until after the November elections, at which time he would expect a summit conference. In retrospect, we can assume that he expected to confront Kennedy with the *fait accompli* of nuclear-tipped missiles aimed at the United States.

2. He publicly and repeatedly asserted that Soviet assistance to Cuba was "purely defensive." In this he was further encouraged by Kennedy's public statements that the Soviet build-up was indeed defensive in character, which meant either that the United States was unable to detect the true nature of the Soviet action or was afraid to acknowledge it publicly for fear that it would have to back down openly before Soviet might.

3. The President was assured through informal channels by a lower ranking Soviet diplomat carrying a message to Kennedy from Khrushchev and Mikoyan that the Soviet Union would not emplace weapons in Cuba capable of reaching the United States. This was a deliberate, premeditated, and unambiguous act of perfidy.

4. Both Foreign Minister Gromyko and Soviet Ambassador Dobrynin personally reassured the President about the "defensive nature" of Soviet installations being erected in Cuba. These reassurances were given in spite of the crisis atmosphere which had since developed, and in spite of Republican charges that Soviet missiles were indeed being placed in position.

5. After the President's quarantine speech and the official accusation that missiles were detected in Cuba, Soviet spokesmen and the Soviet press continued to deny the charge, hoping apparently that vigorous denial might gain them sufficient time to render the missiles operational, in which case the exposure would have been rendered irrelevant.

While François de Callières' observation that "deceit is indeed the measure of the smallness of the mind of him who uses it and proves that he does not possess sufficient intelligence to achieve results by just and reasonable means" is undoubtedly true, the conscious and brazen participation of the highest political and diplomatic officials of the Soviet state in an overt act of diplomatic duplicity transcends ordinary vices conventional to diplomacy. Their minds are neither small nor unintelligent. This forces us to re-examine critically the roots of duplicity in Soviet thought and action so that we may know whether it is institutionalized in Soviet dialectics — and hence likely to recur automatically — or whether it reflects simply a conscious act of policy, subjective and personal in character. For if it is institutional or ideological in character, only a change in ideology will eliminate it, whereas if it is personal, a change of heart or leaders is sufficient.

It may be argued validly that ideological controversies over the substantive meaning of ideas cannot be identified with double-talk or duplicity, except in the institutionalized sense. This would be true if Soviet leaders and spokesmen would make the substantive nature of their views clear, but when they rely upon the ambiguity of their words for success in their diplomacy, then they engage in deception at best, and perfidy at worst. Furthermore, the substantive meanings which Soviet leaders assign to various ideas are themselves subject to change and alteration without advance notice in accordance with Lenin's dictum that "one and the same idea in different, concrete, historical circumstances may be, according to the case, reactionary or progressive."

There is the view in the West that because the term "peaceful co-existence" has acquired a favorable image and is thus endowed with a certain positive psychological value, it can be given a new non-Soviet content and should therefore be retained as a useful symbol. Of course, it may be possible to do this, but as noted above, Soviet spokesmen are alert to attempts by the bourgeois ideologists to appropriate and distort the meaning of "peaceful co-existence"; consequently, this is apt to be a rather formidable operation. As past masters in converting devices and slogans invented by others to their own purposes, Soviet leaders are always on guard against possibilities in reverse. Furthermore, appropriation of communist slogans may create the false impression that the West has exhausted its own fund of ideas and solutions.

Even President Kennedy has been accused of trying to distort the meaning of "peaceful co-existence." Thus one Soviet writer charges that,

> During his Vienna meeting with N. S. Khrushchev, President Kennedy outlined his conception of peaceful coexistence. This, in effect, meant halting the movement of the peoples for national and social liberation. In the name of "peaceful coexistence," he demanded that the Socialist nations refrain from supporting national revolutions and liberation movements. Thus, American understanding of peaceful coexistence is seen as "unconditional surrender" of socialism to capitalism, not as equal cooperation of free peoples and independent nations.[72]

The deceptive character of the Soviet view of peaceful co-existence is easily revealed by allowing one Soviet authority to define what it is not.

[72] Ye. Korovin, "Semantic Camouflage of Imperialist Politics," *International Affairs* (Moscow), No. 11 (1961), 44.

Condemning what Soviet writers call western "misconceptions" and "distortions" of co-existence, including views expressed by George Kennan, Raymond Aron, and others, Timofeyev pointed out that:

> The idea of peaceful coexistence is wrongly interpreted at times. Specifically, attempts are being made artificially to tie up the task of improving international relations with problems of an ideological nature; expectations of "concessions" by Communists in the Marxist-Leninist ideology are associated with peaceful coexistence . . . that there will be an "inevitable smoothing over" of differences between the socialist and capitalist states . . . as a result of some kind of fundamental "changes" in the social and economic system, political structure and ideology in the socialist countries . . . [or] that a slackening of the class struggle within capitalist countries is possible. . . . The idea of the gradual "elimination" of the basic differences between states with contrary social and economic systems is being preached more vigorously now that world tensions are easing. . . . Another no less important aspect is . . . the reactionary Utopian thesis that an "approximation" of the social purposes of communism and capitalism is possible, and to support the false idea that the Soviet system is "drawing closer" to the "Western pattern." It goes without saying that there is not much logic to such a twist. Why, in fact, should the . . . socialist countries strive for the notorious "Western pattern?" After all, if, as is generally recognized, socialism is scoring ever new successes, including victories in the "battle for the minds of the people," in the international arena . . . is it not natural to assume that an opposite process is inevitable?[73]

It is important to understand fully the Soviet meaning of "peaceful co-existence," the ideological foundations upon which it rests, and the expectations it envisages since the term itself is ambiguous and deceptive. Relying on the deceptive and platitudinous character of the formula, the Soviet regime has been fairly successful in its attempt to have the principles of peaceful co-existence accepted as a universal basis for diplomacy, so that the idea is widely heralded on both sides of the Iron Curtain as the only alternative to a thermonuclear war of mutual

[73] Timofeyev, "Inter-State Relations and Social Contradictions," pp. 12–15. According to the author, the expansion of contacts between East and West in the interests of relaxing inter-state tensions may actually result in the exacerbation of ideological tensions. With peerless dialectical logic, he observes: "It is necessary, furthermore, to take into account some specific features of modern diplomacy, the forms of contacts between states. . . . High-level visits, which are becoming more and more frequent . . . enable statesmen to address the population of other countries directly. . . . This results in a *considerable extension of the battleground where socialist and bourgeois ideologies clash*." Ibid., p. 12. The various advocates of "ideological co-existence," according to this article, range from the "frankly bourgeois theories" (Rostow, Berle, Kennan, Aron), the "Right-Wing Socialists" (Strachey, Reuther, Meany, C. Crosland), to the "Revisionists" (Browder, Starobin, Gates, Lefebvre, and the "Titoists"). Whereas the first group argues that technological and industrial progress leads to similar results in socialist and capitalist countries, the second emphasizes the "gradual transformation of capitalism into democratic socialism," whereas the third group maintains that the class struggle is diminishing.

annihilation. But as the Sino-Indian conflict demonstrates, even a documentary enumeration of the principles of co-existence does not guarantee a common agreement as to the substantive meaning of the idea. The impact which Soviet conceptions of international relations and diplomacy have had upon the western world and its diplomacy raises three fundamental questions: (1) To what extent do western states-men and diplomats recognize that a single diplomatic order no longer exists, that it is incapable of imminent restoration, and that the traditional diplomacy for which many of them nostalgically yearn is beyond resurrection? (2) In the absence of a single ideological consensus, how can a non-consensus diplomacy as a medium of communications and negotiation with the Soviet orbit be organized as long as Soviet leaders remain seriously dedicated to their ideological objective of universalizing their own ideo-social order? (3) Is the formula of peaceful co-existence a sufficiently common basis for the creation of a non-consensus diplomacy?

There is no question but that a non-consensus diplomacy would be both possible and desirable in today's divided world, but such a diplomacy must not rest upon the Soviet conception of peaceful co-existence by default. Instead of relying upon clichés and platitudes and the risky endeavor to appropriate communist slogans and convert them to our own use, it would be better to define in concrete terms what the Soviet meaning of "peaceful co-existence" presupposes, and enumerate the principles of a non-consensus diplomacy which the West will accept as an indispensable minimum condition.

We can summarize the current Soviet meaning of "peaceful co-existence" (the Chinese meaning would permit even graver risks of war, for it visualizes the initiation of war to promote communist ends in the thermonuclear age) as follows:

1. Two irreconcilable social systems are forced to co-exist with one another because of the given balance of forces between them, but the co-existence is purely transitory.

2. History has ordained the inevitable doom of capitalism which has been in a state of continuous decomposition since 1917, and the inevitable victory of communism as the universal social system of the future.

3. The communist world is invested with the historical right to accelerate the eradication of capitalism and the expansion of communism by non-violent means and through the support of wars of liberation and popular uprisings, which are just wars.[74]

4. The western world must implicitly accept the inevitability of its own demise and accommodate to it gracefully. It must refrain from using local wars to arrest wars of liberation or popular uprisings, because

[74] This is not to imply that all wars of liberation and popular uprisings are Communist inspired or assisted. One of the vexing problems of American foreign policy is to distinguish between authentic wars of liberation and popular uprisings from Communist insurrections stimulated, manipulated, and supported externally.

such measures are unjust wars and would provoke Soviet retaliation, while it must also refrain from using non-violent or violent means to roll back communism, since this would be contrary to the will of history and would result in general war.

5. The existence of thermonuclear weapons of mass destruction rules out the use of *general war* as an instrument of policy by either system, because it threatens mutual annihilation. Thermonuclear war is not inevitable but it is possible if madmen in the western world resort to force to prevent the collapse of capitalism. Thus, any nuclear war which may materialize is automatically and in advance the fault of the West.

As President Kennedy has so aptly stated, such a diplomacy means for the Soviet leaders, "What's mine is mine; what's yours is negotiable." Since diplomacy on this basis requires that the West acquiesce and cooperate in bringing about its own non-existence, it is clearly an unacceptable framework for diplomacy.

A non-consensus diplomacy acceptable to the West, on the other hand, must be based upon the following indispensable, objective conditions:

1. Both social systems are equally permanent or transitory and there is always the possibility that other social systems may emerge. All are subject to expansion, contraction, or dissolution.

2. History (and God) is neutral where social systems are concerned and none has received any special blessing or mandate as the duly sanctified universal order of the future.

3. Each system will strive to preserve its existence and this always involves the risk of war. Each side may endeavor to expand at the expense of the other as long as this does not involve the risk of self-destruction.

4. Each system will adopt whatever social and ideological principles it chooses for organizing its own life.

5. Various possible relations between systems may evolve: (1) permanent co-existence of various systems based upon *de facto* mutual acceptance (as in the case of irreconcilable religions); (2) the triumph and universalization of a single system; (3) the mutual accommodation, convergence, or assimilation of various systems. In all cases, both cooperation and conflict, mutations and permutations within individual systems will take place.

These conditions for a non-consensus diplomacy are objective in character and require only *de facto* acceptance by the Soviet Union. They cannot be arrived at through negotiation, since no Soviet leader would accept them. They must be imposed upon Soviet leaders so that they will recognize that their own survival depends upon the recognition of these conditions. In the final analysis, this means that Soviet leaders must be confronted at all times with only two options: (1) the risk of certain destruction in the event they attempt to impose their system upon the rest of the world by force; *or* (2) survival on the basis of the *de facto* observance of the conditions enumerated above. This does not mean that either side will have to give up its ideology but only that it confine its ideology to matters of domestic concern, or, to be realistic, attempt to extend its application only when there is no risk of general war.

How are these conditions to be established without a negotiated agreement? They can be initially established only by unilateral action by the West. The Cuban crisis confirms that Moscow exhibits a healthy regard for its own survival and that its respect for our survival is maximized as its survival is made contingent upon our own. Neither sweet words, nor blandishments, nor sympathetic understanding will serve as a reliable foundation for a diplomacy of non-consensus in the immediate future. Soviet diplomacy will continue to rely upon duplicity — personal and dialectical — to achieve its objectives, and since this impulse is deeply imbedded in Soviet doctrine and behavior, the hope that a change of heart on the part of Soviet leaders will miraculously establish a condition of mutual trust and confidence is a frangible reed to rely upon.

The security and survival of the West cannot be left to the capricious moral sense of Soviet leaders, but must continue to rest upon the maintenance of an overwhelming deterrent and retaliatory capability and a credible determination to use it in order to re-enforce Soviet respect for its own survival, so that it either "lives and lets live" or risks certain destruction. Only when Soviet ideology is explicitly reformulated to rule out the moral double standard in dealing with the "class enemy" can Soviet behavior be expected to limit itself only to ordinary vices and exclude the venal; only when the Soviet regime explicitly separates its ideological goals from foreign policy can the West begin to feel that the Soviet Union has finally made peace with the rest of the world. The de-ideologization of Soviet foreign policy and diplomacy may be a long and protracted process, and the West must be alert at all times for any signs of the further erosion of ideological commitment, although it may initially be manifested in behavior rather than rhetoric. The process will not be linear, but erratic, and thus the possibilities of slippage or reversion in varying degrees must be expected as Soviet behavior in foreign policy is disentangled from its ideological rhetoric. The de-ideologization of Soviet diplomacy is by no means either automatic or inevitable, but will materialize in response to changing patterns of interest, power, and factional groupings at home and adaptation to the shifts in the equilibrium of power and the balance of risks in the international community. This also includes, of course, changing patterns of interest, ideological commitment, and political goals within the world of communist state and parties.

12. COMMUNIST OUTLOOK ON WAR

Thomas W. Wolfe

Communist thinking on war has been shaped by many factors —
Marxist-Leninist theory, the historical experience and policies of the
Soviet state, the personalities of various leaders, interaction with the
West, the impact of modern technology, the rise of a rival center of
Communist power and ideological authority in Peking, to mention a few.
Before taking up the evolution of the Communist outlook on war in light
of such formative influences, it may be useful at the outset of this essay
to comment briefly on the matter of differences which have tended to set
the Communist interpretation of war apart from that generally to be
found in the West.

In the fullness of time, the differences may one day come to appear
less notable than the similarities between Communist and Western
thought on the age-old phenomenon of war. Indeed, as Professor Norman Gibbs has observed in a companion piece to this essay, despite
certain fundamental cleavages between the Soviet system and the
societies of the Western world, there always has been some common

Reprinted by permission from paper P-3640. Copyright © 1967 by the
Rand Corporation.

Any views expressed in this paper are those of the author. They should
not be interpreted as reflecting the views of The RAND Corporation or the
official opinion or policy of any of its governmental or private research
sponsors. Papers are reproduced by The RAND Corporation as a courtesy to
members of its staff.

The present paper is an expansion of a lecture intended for presentation
at a Seminar on the History of War, taught by Dr. John S. Patton at Catholic
University, Washington, D.C. In its present form, the paper is to appear in
The Soviet System and Democratic Society: A Comparative Encyclopedia,
edited by C. D. Kernig.

ground in their understanding of war, deriving if nothing else from a shared European politico-cultural heritage. One need only recall, for example, that Marxism itself grew out of Western thought, and that its conceptions of war took their original point of departure, at least, from Marx's general theory of capitalist development. Or again, it may be noted that the early nineteenth-century views of Clausewitz on war owed much to his study of warfare in Russia, a debt later returned with interest by such Soviet figures as Lenin and Stalin, who drew heavily on Clausewitz's philosophy of war in forming their own doctrines a century later.

More recently, tendencies toward what some people regard as convergence between Soviet and Western societies in the industrialized world of the mid-twentieth century may also be having the effect of narrowing to some extent the gap between Communist and Western views on the many-sided question of war. The technology of the nuclear-missile age, itself an accompaniment of the modern industrialization process, is another factor often credited with imposing its dictates alike upon both Communist and non-Communist states, and with thus wiping out ideological distinctions that seemed more valid before the nuclear genie was let out of the bottle. As neatly summed up in the cryptic comment of the Soviet Communist Party in its quarrel with Peking in 1963: "The atomic bomb does not adhere to the class principle; it destroys everybody within range of its devastating force." Nevertheless, despite various similarities and overlapping conceptions, from our present perspective at least, one must say that the Communist outlook on war and its place in human affairs still differs in important respects from Western thought on the subject.

SALIENT DIFFERENCES BETWEEN WESTERN AND COMMUNIST THOUGHT ON WAR

Perhaps the most salient difference lies in the diversity of Western views on the causes, functions, and potential eradicability of war in human society, as contrasted with the relatively narrow but more cohesive Communist interpretation. In the West, for example, one finds a wide and historically variable range of explanations for the causes of war. Some of these explanations are cast in essentially economic terms: Wars arise from tension between haves and have-nots; from quarrels over territory, resources, markets and the like. Other explanations emphasize the political roots of war, viewing it as a vehicle of national or imperial aggrandizement; as a projection of domestic policies or an expression of dynastic disputes; or as the ultimate recourse in international politics for settling differences between states. Ideological and religious causes are sometimes stressed, as when war is attributed to conflict between belief systems or religious convictions; or to defense of a way of life or a civilization. Still other explanations of the causes of war draw upon anthropology, psychology or various popular theories of human behavior; man is by nature a fighting animal and war the expression of his aggressive instincts; war is merely a more highly organized form of the struggle and competition which are integral elements of human society; war is the outlet for man's deep-seated "death urge"; it is the product of Malthusian pressures or of racial antagonism or of arms races; or it is simply a misfortune visited upon naturally good and peace-loving peoples from time to time by evil or power-seeking rulers — Kings, Munitions Makers, Militarists, Fascist or Communist Dictators and so on.

Western thought offers an equally broad menu of theories on the functions of war: to maintain or alter a particular balance of power; to expand the influence of advanced countries over more backward areas; to preserve or upset the dominant role of ruling classes and elites; to build up national unity; to defend "right" and "freedom" against "aggression"; to promote processes of stability or change in the relationships among human groupings — tribes, states, societies, civilizations.

Similarly, the West is of varied mind on the prospect of eradicating war from human affairs. It offers an array of views from the essentially pessimistic one that war is as old as history and is not likely to disappear even though the destructiveness of modern war dictates that men should learn to settle their differences without it, to the more optimistic belief that war is not necessarily an immutable aspect of the human condition, and that men may in fact learn through some combination of political, social and moral invention to control and eventually eliminate it from their affairs. However, Western thought makes no pretense of having hit upon a single formula for the future which may serve better than such conceptions of the past as the *Pax romana* or the Christian *Pax gentium* to eliminate war and bring about lasting peace.

By contrast with this open-ended approach of Western thought, which in effect eschews a single-track explanation for a phenomenon so complex and many-sided as war, Communist thought characteristically has sought to explain war in terms of a single body of theory, insisting, indeed, that *only* Marxism-Leninism offers a key to its understanding, as well as to its abolition. In the words of a contemporary Soviet treatise dealing with the nature of war and strategy, for example, war is said to be a social phenomenon "whose essential meaning can be revealed solely by using the only scientific method: Marxist-Leninist dialectics."[1]

While the analysis of war served up over the past century or so by Marx, Engels, Lenin and their various disciples has by no means been immune to change, as we shall see later, its essential points for the most part have remained relatively intact. For the moment, let us consider briefly what this analysis has to say about the "essential meaning" of

---

[1] V. D. Sokolovskii *et al.*, *Voennaia strategiia*, 1st ed., 1962, English version *Soviet Military Strategy*, translated and annotated by H. S. Dinerstein, L. Gouré, and T. W. Wolfe of The RAND Corporation, (Englewood Cliffs, N.J.: Prentice-Hall, 1963), p. 270. See also *Bol'shaia sovetskaia entsiklopediia* (Large Soviet Encyclopedia), 2nd ed. (Moscow, 1949–1958), Vol. 8, p. 571. (Hereafter referred to as *BSE*.)

404 COMMUNIST OUTLOOK ON WAR

war, in terms of its causes, functions and the conditions for its abolition, recalling meanwhile that despite the claims for Marxist-Leninist
theory to a unique insight into the meaning of war, some of the concepts
embodied in it actually had their genesis in Western thinking.

Just as Marxist-Leninist teaching holds that the class struggle is
the principal motivating force in history,[2] so it maintains that "the real
explanation for all social phenomena and events, including wars, must
be found in the relationship between classes."[3] Since, according to the
Marxist-Leninist schema, this relationship in a class society is inevitably
antagonistic because of private ownership of the means of production
and the attempt of the ownership class to serve its economic interests by
exploitation of the working class, the underlying cause of both the class
struggle and of wars to which it gives rise is therefore economic. In
short, from the viewpoint of Marxism-Leninism, "war is a continuation
of the politics of particular classes in their pursuit of class goals,"[4]
which in turn are determined by the existing system of production.

This explanation of the cause of war, which insists that war is a
phenomenon of class society, innate in the capitalist system, carries
over to the classical Marxist-Leninist position on both the functions of
war and its eradicability. So long as capitalism still exists, and especially in its present and allegedly final stage of "imperialism," the
capitalist order, as Marxism-Leninism sees it, will seek to serve essentially three purposes through war: to extend capitalist domination over
colonial peoples; to achieve the redivision of the world among rival
capitalist countries; and to arrest the process of history by desperate but
unavailing last-ditch resistance to the new Communist order.[5] From the
Marxist-Leninist standpoint, wars in this same final stage of imperialism serve an essentially revolutionary function which "capitalist imperialism" fears but can do little about: namely, they help to disrupt
and break down the old order and to facilitate the takeover of the
new — serving, in other words, as the "midwife" of progress and
revolution.[6]

[2] *Fundamentals of Marxism-Leninism*, O. W. Kuusinen, ed. (Moscow:
Foreign Languages Publishing House, 1961), p. 202. Or, as Marx put it in the
Communist Manifesto: "The history of all hitherto existing societies is the
history of the class struggle." See also Fredrich Engels, "Karl Marx," in *Karl
Marx and Frederick Engels: Selected Works*, Vol. II (Moscow: Foreign Lan-
guages Publishing House, 1949), pp. 149–151.

[3] P. Fedoseev, "Marxism and Mao Tse-tungism," *Kommunist*, No. 5,
March 1967, 110–111; N. P. Prokop'ev, *O voine i armii* (On War and the
Army) (Moscow: Voenizdat, 1965), pp. 4–5.

[4] *Kommunist*, March 1967, 111; I. Sidel'nikov, "V. I. Lenin on the Class
Approach to Defining the Nature of Wars," *Krasnaia zvezda*, September 22,
1965. See also *Sochineniia V. I. Lenina* (Works of V. I. Lenin), 4th edition,
Izdatel'stvo politicheskoi literatury, Moscow, 1941–1966, Vol. 24, pp. 363–
364. (Hereafter cited as Lenin, *Sochineniia*.)

[5] Kuusinen, *Fundamentals of Marxism-Leninism*, pp. 317–322, 626–
629; Lenin, *Sochineniia*, Vol. 22, pp. 233–285; Vol. 23, p. 67.

[6] Marx supplied the image of "midwife" and Lenin later the theory of
imperialism which produced this Marxist-Leninist view of the revolutionary
function of war. Although Lenin condemned the misery and suffering which
past wars in history had caused, he also took pains to point out that even the

THOMAS W. WOLFE   405

As for the eradicability of war, it follows from the Marxist-Leninist contention that war is a product of class society, inseparable from capitalism, that war "will cease to exist only with the destruction of capitalism and the victory of the socialist order in the whole world."[7] All other theories and proposals for the "abolition" of war, according to Marxist-Leninist teaching, "are nothing but deceptions calculated to perpetuate the system of exploitation and war."[8] Until the dawn of that Utopian day when a classless and stateless Communist order is universally established and political revolution has run its historical course, the danger of war will continue to exist, as Marxist-Leninist theory sees it. For most of the lifetime of the Communist movement, at least until after the advent of the nuclear age, it was held that wars of various kinds, including a final cataclysmic clash between the capitalist and Communist systems, were in fact "inevitable" during the historical passage from the old order to the new. Khrushchev's amendment in 1956 of the thesis of "the inevitability of war while imperialism still exists" was among the more significant changes imposed upon the classical Communist doctrine of war by nuclear-age conditions, and one which marked the beginning of divergencies between Moscow and Peking over Marxist-Leninist teaching on war and peace.

Before we take up specifically the influence of modern technology and today's international power balance upon Communist theories of war, however, it may be useful to review in somewhat more detail than above three centrally important and closely related aspects of pre-nuclear age Communist thinking on war. These are: the development of Communist views on the relationship of war to revolution and politics; the Marxist-Leninist classification or typology of wars; and the question of prescribed Communist attitudes toward wars of various types.

RELATIONSHIP OF WAR TO REVOLUTION AND POLITICS

That portion of Communist theory and doctrine dealing with war was most fully elaborated by Lenin, who transformed what had been Marx's general body of critical theory of the capitalist system into a specific "Marxist-Leninist" ideology and operational code for the seizure

---

most predatory and unjust wars had often served "progressive purposes" by "helping to break up harmful and reactionary institutions." V. I. Lenin o voine, armii i voennoi nauke (V. I. Lenin on War, the Army and Military Science) (Moscow: Voenizdat, 1957), Vol. 1, p. 416. See also E. I. Rybkin, Voina i politika (War and Politics) (Moscow: Voenizdat, 1959), p. 25.

[7] BSE, Vol. 8, p. 572; Lenin, Sochineniia, Vol. 21, p. 271; Vol. 24, pp. 46, 363. For a current restatement of the view that abolition of war must await "the victory of socialism and communism on a universal scale," see: A. Migolatev, "On the 50th Anniversary of V. I. Lenin's Work 'War and Revolution,'" Krasnaia zvezda, May 27, 1967.

[8] "Measures for the Struggle Against the Danger of Imperialist War and the Tasks of the Communists," Theses adopted at the Sixth Congress of the Comintern, July–September 1928, in Xenia J. Eudin and Robert M. Slusser, Soviet Foreign Policy 1928–1934: Documents and Materials, Vol. I (Pennsylvania State University Press, 1966), p. 129.

of political power. However, while it may be said that Communist thinking on war and its relationship to revolution and politics owes more to Lenin than to Marx, Engels and others who preceded him, the matrix of ideas which Lenin bent to his purposes was nevertheless largely laid down by his precursors. Let us therefore begin by reviewing briefly the legacy of contributions by Marx and Engels to what subsequently emerged as "Marxist-Leninist" theory on war and revolution.

The revolutionary creed of Karl Marx, epitomized by the declaration in his *Theses on Feuerbach* that "All philosophies have sought to explain the world; our business is to change it," provided ambiguous guidance at best to successive generations of his followers as to just how they should go about the business of replacing one historic order of society by another. Marx's own thinking pointed in at least two possible directions: that of peaceful evolutionary transformation of society and that of violent revolutionary change. For example, his concept of the economic origins of social development, in which transition from an old to a new order was held to occur after contradictions between productive forces and the prevailing property system had ripened to a certain stage, lent itself equally to the notion of either peaceful or violent overthrow of the existing socio-political superstructure. On the other hand, his concept of the class struggle as the prime motivating force behind the dialectic of history was weighted rather heavily in the direction of violent revolutionary change. With its assumption that the ruling or exploiting class would always resist being dislodged, this concept naturally lent itself to the idea, expressed by Marx himself in an addendum in 1872 to the *Communist Manifesto*, that the exploited class must smash the "existing state machine" and take power by force. Or as Marx put it elsewhere: "The last word of social science on the eve of each general reconstruction of society will always remain: 'struggle or death, bloody war or nothingness.' "[9]

Like Engels, whose views we shall come to in a moment, Marx looked expectantly to each of the wars of his time to speed up the revolutionary process. As it turned out, he was left disappointed by events, and in fact toward the end of his life was obliged upon occasion to concede that the route to socialism might lie in a lengthy and relatively peaceful transition rather than in immediate revolutionary action. Nevertheless, although the revolutionary failures of his day served to temper his expectations, Marx did not abandon the notion that war and violence would help to deliver the child of revolution, an idea which at least some of his epigones were to find more persuasive than the prospect of peaceful evolutionary transition to socialism.

Partly as a consequence of the ambiguities in Marx's own teachings, when his followers subsequently split into schools — one composed of moderates tending to follow the intellectual leadership of men like Bernstein and Kautsky, and believing in the possibility of peaceful evolution and reform; the other of extremists led by Lenin and

[9] Karl Marx, *The Poverty of Philosophy*, (London: Martin Lawrence, Ltd., 1936), p. 147.

convinced that violence would be necessary to overthrow the existing order — each school could appeal with some justification to Marxian authority.[10]

Similarly, the views of Marx's close associate, Friedrich Engels, also were sufficiently contradictory on the question of evolutionary versus revolutionary socialism to enable adherents of both to claim him as their master.[11] However, Engels, a lifelong student of military affairs, doubtless contributed more than Marx to laying down the basis for a revolutionary strategy that would recognize the role of armed forces as an agent of social change. In keeping with his times, when no socialist state yet existed to give the revolutionary movement an organized power base, Engels' interest lay in developing a realistic revolutionary strategy that would enable the proletariat ultimately to take over for its own purposes the existing military organization of capitalist society. As the weight of the lower classes increased within the "nation in arms" through such devices as universal conscription, the army would, Engels argued, serve increasingly as the channel for transition to socialism. It was this notion that led Engels in 1891 to observe that "contrary to appearance, compulsory military service surpasses general franchise as a democratic agency."[12]

Apart from emphasizing the importance of arming the proletariat as a long-term preparatory measure for the same when the world revolutionary situation would ripen, Engels also gave attention to the more immediate possibility that one or another of Europe's wars in the latter half of the nineteenth century might trigger off a major revolutionary upheaval. Although his hopes in this regard went unrewarded, the searching analyses he made of these wars in terms of their revolutionary potential not only set a precedent which other Communist theoreticians were to follow, but also provided a store of lessons upon which they drew. One of these, later quoted approvingly by Trotsky, was that "a disorganized army and a complete breakdown of discipline has been the condition as well as the result of every victorious revolution."[13] Another was that "the day of the barricades, of street corner revolutions" was gone, and that henceforth a successful revolutionary strategy would have to rest, among other things, on proletarian understanding of modern technology and fighting methods.

It was, of course, Lenin, the revolutionary leader to whom fell the historic opportunity to put Marxist theory into practice amidst the chaotic conditions created in Russia by World War I, who brought together the main conceptions of pre-nuclear age Communist thought on

[10] See R. N. Carew Hunt, *The Theory and Practice of Communism*, rev. ed. (New York: The Macmillan Company, 1951), p. 70.

[11] See Sigmund Neumann, "Engels and Marx: Military Concepts of the Social Revolutionaries," in *Makers of Modern Strategy: Military Thought from Machiavelli to Hitler*, Edward Mead Earle, ed. (Princeton University Press, 1948), p. 169.

[12] Ibid., p. 169.

[13] See Edward Mead Earle, "Lenin, Trotsky, Stalin: Soviet Concepts of War," in *Makers of Modern Strategy*, p. 337.

the links between war, revolution and politics. Although Lenin's genius may have lain more in adapting the theories of others to fit the practical pursuit of power than in breaking original theoretical ground on his own, nevertheless his very success as a maker of revolution tended to confer the sanction of dogma upon his ideas, which became the foundation for all subsequent Marxist-Leninist teaching on problems of war and revolution.

Thus, Lenin's rejection of the evolutionary path to socialism and his conviction that the overthrow of capitalism could not be accomplished without violence became articles of dogma for the Communist movement, leaving scant trace of the ambiguity originally to be found in Marx. Consider, for example, the blunt and unambiguous declaration set forth in the *Theses of the Sixth Congress of the Communist International* in 1928: ". . . the overthrow of capitalism is impossible without violence, without armed uprising and wars of the proletariat against the bourgeoisie."[14] However, let us review here the formulation of some of Lenin's ideas prior to their subsequent hardening into the clichés of "Leninism."

Among the conceptions central to Lenin's teaching that war is the progenitor of world revolution was his theory of imperialism, which served in effect as the bridge between Marx's general theory of capitalist contradictions and economic crises and Lenin's specific contention that imperialist war was the "final contradiction" which would bring about collapse of the capitalist order.[15] Borrowed largely from ideas of Marxist theorists like Kautsky, Otto Bauer, Rudolf Hilferding and even non-Marxists like J. A. Hobson, Lenin's theory of imperialism — spelled out most fully in his 1916 pamphlet, *Imperialism, The Highest Stage of Capitalism* — held that as capitalist economies matured the declining opportunities for profit and investment at home would drive the capitalist states into increasing global competition for raw materials, labor and markets in the backward areas of the world.[16] Once these areas had been divided up, the pressures of imperialist competition would mount, leading to wars among the imperialist powers over "redistribution" of the colonies. Such wars, which Lenin described as symptomatic of the "internal contradictions" of the world capitalist system in its final imperialist stage and as "absolutely inevitable,"[17] would, he argued, provide the necessary "objective" historical conditions for world revolu-

---

[14] In Eudin and Slusser, *Soviet Foreign Policy*, p. 129. Or as Lenin himself once put it, there was never "in history an important revolution not linked with war." *Sochineniia*, Vol. 29, p. 133. Although the present paper does not deal with Communist attitudes toward disarmament, it is pertinent to note that Lenin's views on the necessity of violent revolution colored his outlook on disarmament. Thus, he warned against the "pacifist" longing for disarmament, and asserted that the proletariat would not throw away its arms until the world bourgeoisie was overthrown and disarmed. *Sochineniia*, Vol. 23, pp. 71, 84.

[15] See Frederick S. Burin, "The Communist Doctrine of the Inevitability of War," *The American Political Science Review*, June 1963, 335–336.

[16] Lenin, *Sochineniia*, Vol. 22, pp. 233–262 *passim;* Vol. 26, p. 139.

[17] Ibid., Vol. 21, p. 23; Vol. 24, pp. 64, 372–373, 431; Vol. 26, pp. 134, 140.

tion. Parenthetically, one may note here that Lenin pushed his theory of imperialism to conclusions not shared by all Marxist theorists of imperialism, some of whom suggested that the capitalist powers might come to agreement among themselves to divide up the world for their mutual benefit without going to war.[18]

Two propositions important to subsequent Marxist-Leninist concepts of the revolutionary role of war were thus tied to Lenin's theory of imperialism: Wars among the imperialist countries were inevitable, and they possessed the makings of world revolution. From this theoretical basis, and in the context of the "imperialist" war that was actually being waged in 1916, Lenin advanced the essentially activist argument that the time was ripe to transform the imperialist world war into civil war and social revolution. It was merely up to the proletariat, or more precisely its vanguard party, to take advantage of the revolutionary situation spawned by wartime misery and discontent.

Needless to say, the revolutionary success of the Bolshevik Party in Russia in the wake of World War I served in the eyes of Marxist-Leninists to validate the theoretical connection which Lenin had drawn between "inevitable imperialist war" and revolutionary opportunity. At the same time, however, this very success underlined the need to formulate a revised doctrinal approach to the question of war and world revolution, for with the emergence of the first proletarian state upon the world scene, the problem of war was no longer one to be viewed in the context of struggle among imperialist powers alone. The hitherto dormant issue of a potential war between a proletarian state and the capitalist powers now came to the fore, along with the need to adjust Communist doctrine on war to the foreign policy objectives of the Soviet state.

Historically, it fell largely to Stalin to deal with the questions posed by the entry of the Soviet Union into world politics; however, Lenin himself added several new dimensions to Communist thinking on war before his life came to an end in 1924. Among Lenin's more important post-revolution contributions was his conversion of the doctrine of inevitable imperialist wars into the new thesis of the inevitability of war between the rival systems. Although lacking the theoretical foundation upon which his doctrine of inter-imperialist wars had rested,[19] the new formulation was to become firmly embedded in Marxist-Leninist theory until the advent of the nuclear age counseled its partial revision. As expressed by Lenin in 1919, in what is probably one of the most widely quoted bits of Leninist writing, the formulation was as follows:

> We are living not merely in a state but in a system of states and the existence of the Soviet Republic side by side with the imperialist states for a long time is unthinkable. One or the other must triumph in the

---

[18] Kautsky, for example, in "Zwei Schriften zum Umlernen," *Die Neue Zeit*, Vol. 33 (1915), p. 144, cited by Burin, "The Communist Doctrine," p. 335. Lenin, it may be noted, fulminated at great length against what he called Kautsky's "harmful" theory of peaceful redivision of the world by "ultra-imperialism." See *Sochineniia*, Vol. 22, pp. 240, 260.

[19] See Burin, "The Communist Doctrine," p. 337.

end. And before that end supervenes, a series of frightful collisions between the Soviet Republic and the bourgeois states will be inevitable. That means that if the ruling class, the proletariat, wants to hold sway, it must prove its capacity to do so by its military organization.[20]

Although this Leninist formulation itself left somewhat ambiguous the question of who would attack whom, the idea that capitalism would strike out in a desperate effort to avert its historical doom — the "dying beast" theory — was already a part of Marxist-Leninist dogma. Stalin later removed any ambiguity from the formulation by linking his theory of "capitalist encirclement" with the specific threat of capitalist war against the Soviet Union;[21] Stalin's further contribution to the doctrine of inevitable war to the finish between the opposing systems was to propound the policy of avoiding such a clash as long as possible while the Soviet Union built up its industrial-military might.

To return to Lenin's time, a second doctrinal development which followed the Bolshevik seizure of power in Russia was Lenin's renewed advocacy of the doctrine of revolutionary war,[22] based on the idea that the new Soviet state had a revolutionary obligation to come to the aid of the proletariat abroad in the course of what was expected to be a world-wide revolt to throw off the yoke of capitalism. When this expectation proved premature after abortive revolutionary movements in Germany and Hungary, as well as failure of the Red Army's campaign against Poland in the first years of Soviet rule, Lenin himself tended to drop the idea of sending the Red Army to the aid of the proletariat in bourgeois countries — about the closest he ever came to espousing "revolution by Red bayonets."

Throughout the early twenties, however, even for some months after Lenin's death in early 1924, the question of developing a dual mission for the Red Army — defense of the Soviet homeland and support of proletarian revolution abroad — remained a matter of keen debate among Soviet theorists and military strategists.[23] Only after the

[20] Lenin, *Sochineniia*, Vol. 29, p. 133.

[21] See, for example, Stalin's report to the 18th Congress of the CPSU, March 10, 1939, in I. V. Stalin, *Problems of Leninism* (Moscow: Foreign Languages Publishing House, 1940), pp. 623–630, 656–662. See also I. V. Stalin, *Sochineniia* (Works), Vol. X, Moscow, 1952, pp. 288–289.

[22] Strictly speaking, the doctrine of revolutionary war by a proletarian state was formulated even before the Bolsheviks came to power in Russia, Lenin having offered in 1915, for example, a program of revolutionary war for the hypothetical day when, after the victory of socialism in at least one country, the proletariat of that country would go to the support of "revolt against the capitalists" in other countries, "appearing if necessary with armed force against the exploiting classes and their states." It was only after the revolution in Russia produced the "first proletarian state," however, that Lenin's advocacy of this doctrine took on practical significance. Lenin, *Sochineniia*, Vol. 21, p. 311. See also E. H. Carr, *A History of Soviet Russia*, Vol. III, *The Bolshevik Revolution 1917–1923* (New York: The Macmillan Company, 1953), pp. 562–563.

[23] Marshal M. N. Tukhachevskii was among the more articulate proponents of the idea that the Soviet Union should adopt a strategy of the military-political offensive under which its armed forces, together with an

assumption of power by Stalin did this debate die out. Thereafter, as Stalin's doctrine of "socialism in one country" gained ascendancy, the Comintern took over as the chief instrument of Soviet revolutionary aims abroad. Curiously enough, it was Stalin himself who later revived the notion of the Red Army's revolutionary mission, when, after World War II, the "liberating" presence of Soviet armies in Eastern Europe made possible the takeover of power there by Communist regimes. As Stalin put it in a conversation with a Yugoslav visitor in 1945:

> This war is not in the past; whoever occupies a territory imposes on it his own social system. Everyone imposes his own system, as far as his army can reach. It cannot be otherwise.[24]

A third effect of Bolshevik acquisition of state power upon Lenin's latter-day doctrinal approach to war was that it gave new significance to his borrowing of the Clausewitzian conception of war as the continuation of politics by other means.[25] This formula found a congenial place in Lenin's thinking, as well as Stalin's, because it permitted war to be pictured as an extension of class conflict to the international arena.[26] The Clausewitzian coupling of war and politics also served another important theoretical function in the Marxist-Leninist schema. Without it, Marxist-Leninist theory — which insisted that war was a phenomenon of capitalist society — lacked a logical device for demonstrating that war might serve as an instrument of policy for Communist as well as capitalist states. Under the new conditions of Soviet statehood, when wars between the Soviet Union and the capitalist countries had to be taken into account, it was just as important to assert that the war aims and policies of the Soviet state should be regarded as the continuation of its progressive peace-loving policies as to argue that warmongering capitalist powers intended to use war as an instrument for continuation of their predatory policies. Moreover, as Lenin, no less than Trotsky, was aware, it was necessary after the Bolsheviks came to power to undo the anti-war propaganda they had so vigorously fostered during the

---

international proletarian army organized under a Comintern general staff, would launch an attack on "world armed capital." Curiously enough, Trotsky, though an advocate of "permanent revolution," argued against this concept of a world revolutionary mission for the Red Army, partly on the grounds that it should not usurp the revolutionary role of the indigenous proletariat in other countries. For discussion of this debate of the early twenties, see: Earle, "Lenin, Trotsky, Stalin," pp. 342–347; John Erickson, *The Soviet High Command: A Military-Political History 1918–1941* (London: Macmillan and Company, 1962), pp. 107–143; D. Fedotoff-White, *The Growth of the Red Army* (Princeton University Press, 1943), pp. 158–182.

[24] Milovan Djilas, *Conversations with Stalin*, (New York: Harcourt, Brace & World, Inc., 1962), p. 114.

[25] Lenin, of course, had discovered Clausewitz well before he found himself the head of a proletarian state, and had often applied the concept of war as a continuation of politics in his analyses of World War I. See Lenin, *Sochineniia*, Vol. 21, p. 293; Vol. 24, p. 364; Vol. 30, p. 131.

[26] Cf. T. A. Taracouzio, *War and Peace in Soviet Diplomacy* (New York: The Macmillan Company, 1940), p. 27.

"imperialist" war just ended, and which could prove embarrassing to the military strengthening of the new proletarian state.[27] This purpose too was served by a concept permitting wars in which the Soviet Union might become involved to be depicted as a continuation of "progressive" policies advancing the Communist cause.

It was, of course, necessary to purge the Clausewitzian formula for Marxist-Leninist purposes; its link between war and politics was accepted, but for Clausewitz's "idealistic" definition of politics was substituted the Marxist-Leninist idea of the class origin of politics — a distinction still stressed today by Soviet theorists.[28] This amendment of Clausewitz's original statement on the relationship between war and politics had provided Marxist-Leninists with a convenient means for classifying wars according to their "regressive" or "progressive" effect in serving Communist policies, and consequently with a yardstick for determining appropriate attitudes toward a given war.[29] Let us next examine these aspects of the Communist approach to war.

TYPOLOGY OF WARS AND PRESCRIBED ATTITUDES TOWARD THEM

The Communist classification of wars has been revised and amended from time to time since Lenin defined the types of wars he considered possible in his day, but the convenient yardstick of "progressive" and "regressive" wars — more frequently labeled "just" and "unjust" wars — has remained in constant use. Within these two broad categories, the varieties of war recognized by Marxist-Leninist theory have been juggled around to fit political and ideological expediency to the point that even Communist theoreticians have sometimes lost their way among the maze of overlapping definitions.

The purposes of this discussion may best be served by describing the classifications in vogue at certain representative periods: first, the intricate typology of wars set out by Lenin in his day; the amended version promulgated under Stalin by the Sixth Congress of the Comintern in 1928; Khrushchev's simplified classification popularized in 1961; and the more complicated typology to which currently authoritative Soviet literature on the subject has returned today.

Lenin's standard typology distinguished three main types of wars: imperialist, national and proletarian-revolutionary wars.[30] What he meant by each is summarized briefly below.

[27] See Earle, "Lenin, Trotsky, Stalin," p. 339.

[28] See, for example: *BSE*, Vol. 8, p. 571; N. Ia. Sushko and S. A. Tiushkevich, editors, *Marksizm-Leninizm o voine i armii* (Marxism-Leninism on War and the Army), 4th ed. (Moscow: Voenizdat, 1965), pp. 12–15; T. Kondratkov, "Advocates of Aggression," *Krasnaia zvezda*, August 24, 1966.

[29] As frequently pointed out in Soviet writing: "The Leninist-Stalinist formulation on just and unjust wars . . . makes it possible to define the tactics of the working class and its Marxist party toward this or that specific war." *BSE*, Vol. 8, p. 573.

[30] *BSE*, Vol. 8, p. 571; Lenin, *Sochineniia*, Vol. 21, pp. 271–276, 315. See also Vols. 22, pp. 294–298; 23, p. 68; 26, p. 362; 27, p. 106; 30, p. 131.

Imperialist Wars

Wars of this type, "unjust" by definition, Lenin further subdivided into three varieties, depending upon the parties involved. If adversaries on both sides were imperialist powers, the conflict was a pure inter-imperialist war. Toward such wars, the prescribed Communist attitude was to conduct anti-war and defeatist propaganda aimed at transforming the inter-imperialist war into civil war for overthrow of the bourgeoisie. In the second instance, if the war pitted an imperialist power against an "oppressed" nation, it was an "imperialist war of counterrevolution," while in the third instance, if an imperialist state waged war against a country with a proletarian regime, this was a counterrevolutionary war of the purest degree. In principle, since all three brands of imperialist war were assumed to occur at imperialist initiative, the Communist position was to oppose them with appropriate tactics designed to convert them into revolution against the bourgeoisie, with the added injunction that in war against a state already under a proletarian regime, the proletariat must defend its "own socialist fatherland."

National Wars

In this category, Lenin placed wars waged by colonial or semi-colonial peoples against their imperialist masters. Although the immediate initiative for such wars might not appear to come from the imperialist side, they were seen as the "just" outgrowth of colonial resistance to imperialist policies. From this Leninist category of wars stems the type better known nowadays as "national-liberation" war, which Communists then as now were obligated to support.

Proletarian-Revolutionary Wars

Wars of this kind were in Lenin's typology those conducted by the proletariat to realize the overthrow of the capitalist order. If fought by the proletariat of a capitalist state against its own bourgeoisie, such a conflict might take the form of civil war. If an established proletarian state were involved against a capitalist state, the war would assume an international character. As Lenin and others made clear, such wars fought to advance the Communist cause were innately "just," whether waged offensively or defensively by the Communist side.[31] Indeed, Lenin argued that by its very nature, a proletarian state could conduct only a just war.[32] Under this doctrine, resort to arms by the proletariat in a "preventive" war was even justified, since such a war would, by definition, be "a progressive and revolutionary type."[33]

[31] See Taracouzio, War and Peace, p. 30.
[32] BSE, Vol. 8, p. 573; Lenin, Sochineniia, Vol. 22, p. 295; Vol. 23, p. 187.
[33] So argued by Boris M. Shaposhnikov, Mosg armii (Brain of the Army) (Moscow, 1928), Vol. III, p. 251. The doctrine of "just" wars in the Communist cause also had important implications for the Soviet stand on disarmament. As Lenin observed, advocacy of disarmament could not be

The somewhat abbreviated version of the foregoing Leninist classification of wars which was advanced in 1928 at the Sixth Congress of the Comintern was as follows:

> In the present epoch, the following three types of wars can be distinguished: first, wars between the imperialist states; second, wars of imperialist counterrevolution against the proletarian revolution, or against countries in which socialism is being built; third, national revolutionary wars, especially of colonial countries against imperialism, which are connected with wars of imperialist suppression against these countries.[34]

It may be noted that this classification formally omitted the Leninist category of proletarian-revolutionary wars, partly in deference perhaps to Stalin's general line of "building socialism in one country" and of avoiding revolutionary adventurism abroad while the process of developing Soviet industrial-military might was being carried out. However, the text amplifying the 1928 theses of the Sixth Congress still specified that the proletariat "supports and conducts . . . socialist wars against imperialism," which in effect served to recognize the missing Leninist category.

In between the period of these earlier classifications of war under Lenin and Stalin, and Khrushchev's appearance upon the doctrinal scene, lay the great watershed of the nuclear age. Although we shall take up the broader doctrinal implications of this nuclear watershed subsequently, it should be observed that Khrushchev's contribution to the classification of wars was itself greatly influenced by the advent of the nuclear era, so that in a sense we shall be anticipating here part of our later discussion. In general, Khrushchev was a simplifier who, though usually maintaining the Communist distinction between "just" and "unjust" wars, seldom sought to lay out a methodical typology of wars. His best-known characterization of the various categories of wars was given in his January 1961 report on the Moscow Conference of Representatives of Communist and Workers' Parties.[35] According to Khrushchev:

> In modern conditions, the following categories of wars should be distinguished: world wars, local wars, liberation wars, and popular uprisings. This is necessary to work out the correct tactics with regard to these wars.

This typology, with its borrowing from Western usage of the term "local war," was considered a bit too casual, for it was soon amended to give — in more characteristic Marxist-Leninist style — a breakdown into three "fundamental types of war in the present epoch." These were:

---

carried to the point of opposing even "just" wars. "A socialist, without ceasing to be a socialist, cannot be opposed to any war." Lenin, *Sochineniia*, Vol. 23, p. 65.

[34] In Eudin and Slusser, *Soviet Foreign Policy*, pp. 129–130.

[35] N. S. Khrushchev, "For New Victories of the World Communist Movement," *Kommunist*, No. 1, January 1961, 17–19.

world war; small imperialist wars of local, limited scale; and national-liberation wars, a category also including civil war.[36] The main features associated with each of these types of war, as described either by Khrushchev himself or by various Soviet theorists in his day, were as follows.[37]

World War

War of this category would be global and nuclear in character, with missiles as the main means of nuclear delivery. It would be a war of coalitions, with the capitalist states opposing a group of socialist states for the first time in history, and it would be fought for unlimited ends, namely, the existence of one system or the other. Although tracing its lineage to Lenin in the sense of envisaging "a decisive armed clash between the two opposing world social systems," this nuclear-age Soviet image of world war no longer included the notion of inevitability. As Khrushchev argued, "the emergence of the mighty socialist camp" makes it possible to "forestall the outbreak of a world war." Should such a war occur, however — and in the Soviet literature of Khrushchev's day the initiation of any future world war invariably was ascribed to the imperialist camp, most likely through launching of a surprise attack — there would be no question of the political essence of the war for the opposing sides: "Such a war would be aggressive, predatory, and unjust for the imperialists, but liberating, just, and revolutionary for the socialist commonwealth."[38]

Small Imperialist Wars

This category of wars, to which Khrushchev himself simply pinned the label of "local wars," was a scaled-down version of the original Leninist category of imperialist war. It applied mainly in Khrushchev's definition to small wars of local, limited scope, undertaken by the imperialists to suppress national-liberation movements or to hold on to colonies. Small local wars between imperialist states were not excluded, but in general Khrushchev held that the imperialists had become "afraid of starting wars among themselves" because they must keep an eye on the Soviet Union. This marked a departure from the position taken by Stalin in 1952 in his last theoretical treatise, *Economic Problems of Socialism in the USSR*, in which the possibility of a major new clash among the capitalist powers was given renewed emphasis.[39] Another doctrinal novelty introduced into Khrushchev's treatment of local war was the assertion that while opportunities for the imperialists to unleash

[36] See, for example, *Soviet Military Strategy*, pp. 282–283.

[37] Among Soviet descriptions, see: Marshal P. Rotmistrov, "The Causes of Modern Wars and Their Characteristics," *Kommunist Vooruzhennykh Sil* (Communist of the Armed Forces), No. 2, January 1963, 29–32; Colonel P. Derevianko, "Some Features of the Contemporary Revolution in Military Affairs," ibid., No. 1, January 1964, 17–25; Colonel General N. A. Lomov, "New Weapons and the Nature of War," *Krasnaia zvezda*, January 7, 1964.

[38] *Soviet Military Strategy*, p. 282.

[39] Joseph Stalin, *Economic Problems of Socialism in the USSR* (New York: International Publishers, 1952), pp. 28–29.

such wars were diminishing, there was great danger that once started, a local war might draw in the nuclear powers and escalate to global nuclear war. The constraint upon support of revolutionary conflicts implicit in this doctrine of escalation, especially in its occasional form of "inevitable escalation," was caustically noted by the Chinese Communists, whose criticism may have been a factor in removal of the "inevitable" label even before Khrushchev left the scene.[40]

National-Liberation Wars

This category, into which were fitted also civil wars and popular uprisings, received particular emphasis in Khrushchev's classification; indeed, the stress placed on Communist support of national-liberation struggles in his 1961 report led to a rather widespread belief in the West that the Soviet Union was about to embark on a major campaign of fostering such conflicts in the underdeveloped world. Wars in this category, as in earlier periods, were defined as just and revolutionary, stemming from the uprising of colonial peoples against their oppressors. In discussing national-liberation wars, Khrushchev's 1961 report made the point that they should not be identified with local wars between states. Presumably, Khrushchev intended by this distinction to exempt national-liberation wars, to which strong Communist support was pledged, from the doctrine of nuclear escalation applying to local wars.[41]

Dissatisfaction among Soviet theorists with Khrushchev's classification of wars became evident even before Khrushchev left the political scene. In 1963, for example, the author of a brochure on military doctrine indicated that confusion arose from the concept of local wars which would be waged "within local territorial limits." "If one takes this position," he wrote, "then one must also place in this category wars of national liberation and civil wars — that is, just wars which also are waged within territorial limits. The only correct criterion for defining the character of wars is their sociopolitical content."[42] After Khrushchev's downfall, his simplified classification of wars was attacked directly by other Soviet writers on similar grounds,[43] and more elaborate constructions replaced it in official texts.

[40] For a discussion of this question, see the author's *Soviet Strategy at the Crossroads* (Cambridge, Mass.: Harvard University Press, 1964), pp. 123–128.

[41] *Kommunist*, January 1961, p. 20. An example of the Soviet effort to disassociate the idea of nuclear escalation from national-liberation wars may be found in a 1964 article which stated that such wars were "not only permissible, but inevitable," and which then dismissed the escalation problem by asserting that in national-liberation wars "the question of using nuclear weapons will not arise." Major General N. Sushko and Major T. Kondratkov, "War and Politics in the Nuclear Age," *Kommunist Vooruzhennykh Sil*, No. 2, January 1964, 23.

[42] N. A. Lomov, *Sovetskaia voennaia doktrina* (Soviet Military Doctrine), Izdatel'stvo "Znanie" (Moscow, 1963), p. 21.

[43] See, for example, Colonel I. Sidel'nikov's previously cited article in *Krasnaia zvezda*, September 22, 1965. It should be noted that Soviet criticism of Khrushchev's classification of wars tended to distort his position. Even though he employed the shorthand Western term of "local war," he also used the "just-unjust" criterion which he was accused of overlooking.

Representative of these revised classifications of the post-Khrushchev period was one spelled out with lengthy accompanying commentary in the 1965 edition of *Marxism-Leninism on War and the Army*. Although the format differed somewhat, the doctrinal content of this new description of wars remained essentially what it had been in the Khrushchev period. In addition to reiterating in detail the doctrine of "just and unjust wars," the 1965 treatment identified five categories of wars, two of which overlapped to a considerable degree. The categories were: [44]

World War Between Opposing Social Systems

The global, nuclear and unlimited character of this category of war was treated as before, with the injunction that the Soviet armed forces must be prepared for such a war, even though its destructiveness would create great difficulties for the world revolutionary process, hence making it highly important to prevent nuclear war if possible. Western proposals for "city-sparing" and restrained targeting in event of nuclear war were rejected as attempts to deceive the people and to "mask plans for preventive war through a first strike against the socialist countries." Should the imperialists unleash a world war, many factors, in addition to Soviet military might, would work to their disadvantage, such as the vulnerability of Western lines of communication, loss of capitalism's former "reserves" in the colonial world, and the anti-war activities of the "forces of peace" in the capitalist countries, including the United States.

War in Defense of the Socialist Fatherland

Essentially a variant version of war between opposing social systems, since an attack by one socialist state upon another was not posited, this category of war was described as "unconditionally just," fulfilling the "historical duty" of the working class to defend the achievements of socialism. The "constant threat of military attack by the imperialists" was stressed, with the United States pictured as taking up the role of aggressor where Hitler left off. War of this kind would have a revolutionary character as a "continuation of class struggle against the imperialist bourgeoisie," and it would be international in the sense of not only defending the "socialist fatherland" but of fulfilling the latter's "liberation mission and its international duty" toward the world proletariat. The historical obligation of other socialist states to join in defense of the "socialist fatherland" was cited as the basis for mutual defense arrangements within the "commonwealth of socialist states." Only Communist parties, it was asserted, could guarantee the "international unity of socialist peoples and their armies" which would lead to victory in such a war. World War II, after the Soviet Union became a belligerent, was cited as the prime past example of this type of war.

[44] *Marksizm-Leninizm o voine i armii*, 4th edition (Moscow: Voenizdat, 1965), pp. 69–160. For other slightly varying classifications, see: Prokop'ev, *o voine i armii*, pp. 50–65; E. Khomenko, "Wars: Their Character and Type," *Soviet Military Review*, No. 9, September 1965.

Civil Wars

This category of war was described as "armed struggle between antagonistic classes within a country," with Communist countries excepted, of course, by definition. While not necessarily leading to socialist revolution, civil wars, depending on their political content, could "serve the cause of historical progress" by eliminating the old ruling regime and "preparing the soil" for socialist development. Intervention by imperialists in such wars on the side of reactionary regimes, although less promising to the imperialists than formerly because of the changed "correlation of forces in the international arena in favor of socialism," was still being practiced and should be resisted by the world proletariat. Imperialist intervention against the revolutionary forces in a civil war would convert the war into a national-liberation struggle against the imperialists. The Korean War of 1950–1953 was cited as a pertinent example, as well as the war in Vietnam.

National-Liberation Wars

In this category of wars were placed "armed struggles against colonialists by oppressed peoples for their national independence" and "wars by newly-independent states against imperialist aggressors seeking to restore the colonial regime." Communist support was pledged for both types of war. Such wars, it was asserted, were always "in the nature of a response" to violence by the colonialists. A large role could be played in such wars by the "national bourgeoisie," especially in the less developed countries of Africa and Asia where conditions were not yet suitable for proletarian leadership of the anti-colonial struggle. While the national-liberation movement was ascribed great importance, issue was taken with the position of those "leftist" Communists like the Chinese who argued that "the leading role in the world revolutionary process is no longer played by the international workers movement, but by the national-liberation struggle." This was a reassertion of the long-standing Soviet position under both Stalin and Khrushchev that the main front in the world revolutionary movement lay in the advanced countries. Among examples given of national-liberation wars were the Indonesian war against the Dutch, the Algerian war against France, and the wars in Vietnam against the French and Americans in turn.

Wars Between Bourgeois States

This category of war, described as the constant companion of the capitalist order, completed the 1965 classification of wars. Although the "main contradiction" of the times is that between the Communist and capitalist systems, deep contradictions remain within the capitalist world, it was asserted, and therefore the possibility of war between the imperialist countries "cannot be excluded." However, the warning was given that it would be "premature" to reach the conclusion that "differences between the bourgeois states are stronger than the forces which unite them." On the other hand, it was observed, America's hope of "uniting the entire bourgeois world under its aegis has proved unrealizable." While the prospect of a major inter-imperialist war was rated no higher than by Khrushchev, Communists were reminded of Lenin's injunction that in the event of a war between imperialists their task would be not only to bring about "peace in place of war," but to "replace capitalism with socialism . . . to utilize the crisis bred by war to speed the overthrow of the bourgeoisie." Among examples given of past imperialist wars were World War I and the first part of World War II, until the entry of the Soviet Union "completed the conversion of the war into a just war of liberation on the part of the anti-Hitler coalition."

Impact of Modern Technology upon Communist Thinking on War

The advent of the nuclear age brought substantial changes in Soviet thinking on war, some of which have been noted in the foregoing discussion of Communist typologies of war. Many of these changes, such as those felt in Soviet military doctrine, strategy and defense policy, lie outside the immediate scope of this essay, and hence will only be touched upon tangentially, if at all.[45] Here we shall be concerned primarily with the impact of the military-technical revolution of the nuclear age upon certain basic and long-standing Marxist-Leninist doctrinal tenets.

Although strictly speaking, the Soviet Union was introduced to the nuclear age under Stalin, historically it devolved upon Khrushchev to preside over the process of adapting both Communist doctrine and Soviet policy to what has sometimes been called the "imposed rationality" of the new technological environment. Perhaps none of Khrushchev's tasks presented more fundamental perplexities at both the doctrinal and operative levels of Soviet policy than that of finding ways to translate Soviet military power into effective political power in a nuclear world where the machinery of power itself had taken on awesome new dimensions of destructiveness. Khrushchev (and for that matter, his successors also) faced the paradox that even as technology invested military power with an ever-increasing coercive potential, the constraints upon its use also grew apace, tending to multiply the risks and narrow the opportunities for turning military power to political advantage. This was, of course, a universal paradox confronting not the Soviet leadership alone; however, it proved to have particularly damaging effects upon the doctrines of a Marxist-Leninist leadership elite schooled to take a tough-minded view of force and violence as agents of revolutionary sociopolitical change.

While pre-nuclear-age Communist doctrine neither embraced the notion of violence for its own sake nor stressed, except for brief intervals, the spread of revolution by red bayonets, it did regard war, as we have seen, as the legitimate "midwife" of revolution. The experience of

[45] For treatment of these questions by the author elsewhere, see *Soviet Strategy at the Crossroads.*

two world wars seemed to confirm this diagnosis, for it was after each of these wars that Communism enjoyed its greatest expansion in the world.[46] In a nuclear environment, however, another world war began to look much too dangerous to perform the function of enhancing the conditions for a third wave of Communist advance. Moreover, a new constraint fell upon lesser forms of revolutionary conflict also, for small wars might escalate into a large nuclear conflagration which could jeopardize the Soviet system itself. All of this helped to account for a shift of Soviet doctrinal emphasis, after the advent of the nuclear age, to the idea that revolution is no longer "obligatorily linked with war."[47]

Symptoms of a doctrinal crisis growing out of the Soviet leadership's appreciation of the destructiveness of nuclear-age war first came to the surface with Malenkov's short-lived thesis in 1954 that a nuclear war could result in the "mutual destruction" of both capitalist and Communist society.[48] If this were so, then long-held Leninist dogma on the inevitability of war to the finish between the capitalist and Communist systems was patently the counsel of despair. Khrushchev himself initially opposed Malenkov's unorthodox and unsettling assertion, but later, after establishing his own leadership credentials, he swung progressively around to views essentially similar to those of his discredited colleague.

Khrushchev's first step in this direction was his revision at the Twentieth Party Congress in 1956 of the Leninist tenet on the inevitability of war,[49] on the grounds that the growing strength of the Communist camp made it possible to avert war even though "imperialism" retained its aggressive character. This doctrinal revision provided the theoretical underpinning for Khrushchev's advocacy of the policy of peaceful coexistence as the safest and most reliable form of class struggle in the international arena, and it also reflected a leaning toward the concept of deterrence around which Khrushchev's military policy was to be largely fashioned. In terms of Marxist-Leninist theory, Khrushchev's new position,[50] although removing one doctrinal liability,

[46] An authoritative Soviet doctrinal manual, published in 1959, put the point as follows: "Up to now historical development adds up to the fact that the revolutionary overthrow of capitalism has been linked each time with world wars. Both the first and second world wars served as powerful accelerators of revolutionary explosions." *Osnovy Marksizma-Leninizma* (Foundations of Marxism-Leninism) (Moscow: Gospolitizdat, 1959), p. 519.

[47] Ibid., pp. 519–520. See also: Migolatev, in *Krasnaia zvezda*, May 27, 1967; *Marksizm-Leninizm o voine i armii*, 4th ed., p. 91.

[48] Election speech of G. M. Malenkov, *Pravda*, March 13, 1954.

[49] Khrushchev's speech to 20th Party Congress, *Pravda*, February 15, 1956. The passage in which Khrushchev revised Lenin's notion of inevitable war began with the words "There is, of course, a Marxist-Leninist precept that wars are inevitable as long as imperialism exists" and ended with the statement: "But war is not fatalistically inevitable. Today there are mighty social and political forces possessing formidable means to prevent the imperialists from unleashing war."

[50] It should be noted that Khrushchev's "new position" of 1956 on the non-inevitability of war was not in fact altogether unprecedented in Communist argumentation Twenty years earlier, at the 7th Congress of the

created another. If war was henceforth to be regarded as avoidable, what would happen to the old Leninist link between war and revolution? Would not the absence of war, which was supposed to represent the "final contradiction" of the capitalist system in its old-age, also mean a slowing down of the world revolutionary process? Khrushchev dealt with this doctrinal inconsistency essentially by arguing, in connection with his advocacy of the strategy of "peaceful coexistence," that the latter form of struggle would in fact provide a reliable road to revolution — a view which, as we shall see, was contested by Peking.

Another revisionist tendency which manifested itself under Khrushchev was the gradual erosion of the dogma of inevitable Communist victory, should a new world war somehow occur. Although Khrushchev neither fully nor consistently embraced the "no victory" notion promulgated by some Soviet publicists during his tenure, the logic of his occasional admissions that nuclear war might mean mutual annihilation seemed to argue that he placed little stock in the doctrinaire formula of inevitable Communist victory in any new world war.[51]

A related symptom of doctrinal crisis over the political implications of modern weaponry arose during the Khrushchev period around the question whether the Leninist thesis on war as an instrument of politics — which, as we have seen, originally found its way into Lenin's thinking via Clausewitz — still retained its validity under nuclear-age conditions. Debate on this question tended to find Soviet military writers persistently defending the validity of Lenin's dictum that war is a continuation of politics and an instrument of policy, while some political writers openly argued that in the nuclear age the formula should be changed to: "War can be a continuation only of folly."[52] Again, Khrushchev himself stopped short of outright repudiation of Lenin's formula. His public remarks on the implausibility of erecting Commu-

---

Comintern, when the general foreign policy line of the Soviet Union was stressing the Popular Front as a device against the war danger posed by the rise of Nazi Germany, Georgii Dimitrov, then general secretary of the Comintern, had criticized "Left phrasemongers" who "propagate fatalistic views to the effect that war is *inevitable* and the maintenance of peace *impossible.*" See G. Dimitroff, *The United Front: The Struggle Against War and Fascism* (New York: International Publishers, 1938), p. 174. World War II, of course, took the wind out of Dimitrov's argument that war was avoidable. After the war the doctrine of inevitable war, buttressed by the Stalin-Zhdanov concept of "two hostile camps," came back into vogue until nuclear-age conditions began to erode it. Prior to Khrushchev's formal amendment of the doctrine in 1956, an obscure Soviet writer, M. Gus, had partially anticipated him by arguing in *Zvezda,* November 1953, that the Marxist doctrine of the inevitability of war was merely an expression of "regularities," rather than of "fatal inevitability."

[51] See, for example, Khrushchev's speech to the USSR Supreme Soviet, *Pravda,* December 13, 1962.

[52] Boris Dimitriev, "Brass Hats: Peking and Clausewitz," *Izvestia,* September 24, 1963. See also N. Talenskii, "Disarmament and Its Opponents," *Mezhdunarodnaia zhizn'* (International Affairs), No. 12, December 1961, 19; N. Nikolskii, *Osnovnoi vopros sovremennosti* (Basic Question of the Times) (Moscow: Izdatel'stvo MDO, 1964), p. 381.

nism on the radioactive rubble of a nuclear war, however, seemed to reflect a personal belief that the Leninist link between war and politics was no longer tenable, at least with respect to nuclear war.[53]

Interestingly enough, in 1965 about a year after Khrushchev's political demise, the debate over the obsolescence of war in the nuclear age was reopened, with various military theorists challenging the "fatalistic notion" promulgated under Khrushchev that victory is impossible in nuclear war. As one writer put it, to accept this view, "would not only be false on theoretical grounds, but dangerous also from a political point of view."[54] A dissenting note, however, was heard from other Soviet sources. As an editorial article in early 1967 observed,[55] proponents of the view that victory was feasible provided a country conducted a nuclear war so as to minimize damage to itself, had unfortunately skirted some of the problems arising under nuclear-age conditions. Although the article reiterated doctrinaire claims of Communist victory if war should come, its main emphasis lay upon the need for "anti-imperialist forces" to oppose nuclear war "as a means for resolving international disputes," thus seeming to imply that theorizing on the prospects of nuclear victory should not be carried too far.

Divergencies in Soviet and Chinese Thinking on War

While we cannot, of course, explore here either the range of causes or the full implications of the schism which has developed during the past decade between the two leading Communist powers, it is pertinent to our subject that differences relating to the question of war in the nuclear age have been among the issues at the center of the quarrel between Moscow and Peking. Perhaps the fact that the Soviet Union exploded its first atomic device in 1949 while China was obliged to wait until 1964 for the same experience has had something to do with the differences in outlook between the Soviets and the Chinese on the question of war and its relation to political struggle in a nuclear world. In any case, the airing of these differences has contributed in a large way to the contrasting public images of a Soviet Union sobered by the potential consequences of a nuclear war and desperately anxious to avoid its risk as opposed to an intransigent China prepared to court the huge losses of a nuclear war in order to bring about the worldwide

[53] For a fuller discussion of this question, see *Soviet Strategy at the Crossroads*, pp. 70–78.

[54] Lt. Colonel E. Rybkin, "On the Essence of World Missile-Nuclear War," *Kommunist Vooruzhennykh Sil*, No. 17, September 1965, p. 55. Among others advancing similar arguments were: Lt. Colonel V. Bondarenko, "Military-Technical Superiority — The Most Important Factor in Defense of the Country," ibid., No. 17, September 1966, pp. 7–14; Colonel I. Grudinin, "The Question of the Essence of War," *Krasnaia zvezda*, July 21, 1966; N. Ia. Sushko and T. R. Kondratkov, eds., *Metodologicheskie problemy voennoi teorii i praktiki* (Methodological Problems of Military Theory and Practice) (Moscow: Voenizdat, 1966), pp. 33–34.

[55] "On the Essence of War," *Krasnaia zvezda*, January 24, 1967.

triumph of Communism. While allowing for a good deal of polemical exaggeration, one may take it that there is a genuine residue of disagreement between the disputants around the central question of how best to extend Communist power and influence in the world without risking nuclear war and extinction.

From the start, the Chinese leadership seems to have challenged the Soviet departures from orthodoxy which began with Khrushchev's revision of the thesis of inevitable war in 1956. Peking disputed Khrushchev's view that nuclear technology had fundamentally altered the link between war and politics and outmoded the thesis of inevitable war, although Chinese appraisal of nuclear war was by no means as primitive as Soviet denunciations subsequently pictured it.[56] The Chinese conceded that the growing military power of the Communist camp might restrain the imperialists; indeed, the Chinese tended to place a higher estimate on the deterrent value of modern Soviet weaponry than Moscow itself, for the essence of the Chinese position was that the capitalist powers would not respond to revolutionary provocation with the kind of nuclear escalation that Moscow feared.[57] At the same time, however, the Chinese argued that it is "sheer illusion" to expect permanent avoidance of war "before imperialism has been eliminated," and they took the persistent stand that if a general nuclear war should come the net result would be the destruction of capitalism and the triumph of world Communism.[58]

Without following the dispute over issues of war and peace in detail, one may note a few of the other principal themes around which it developed. From the Soviet side, a recurrent theme was the alleged tendency of the Chinese leaders to regard war as "an acceptable and, in fact, the only means of settling contradictions between capitalism and socialism."[59] Eventually Mao Tse-tung was accused of substituting for Marxism-Leninism a "theory of violence" which, "under the cover of revolutionary phraseology," assumed that "war is the principal means of solving all social conflicts."[60] The Chinese, in turn, while denying that they were deliberately courting war, argued that to dwell on its horrors would merely discourage the revolutionary ardor and will-to-fight of the masses. They countercharged that the Soviet position meant "to beg

[56] See Morton H. Halperin, "Chinese Nuclear Strategy," *The China Quarterly*, January–March 1965, 85.

[57] See Donald S. Zagoria, *The Sino-Soviet Conflict 1956–1961*, (Princeton, N.J.: Princeton University Press, 1962), pp. 154–172; Alice Langley Hsieh, *Communist China's Strategy in the Nuclear Era* (Englewood Cliffs, N.J.: Prentice-Hall, 1962), pp. 83–99, 169.

[58] *Long Live Leninism* (Peking: Foreign Languages Press, 1960), pp. 20–22. See also *Peking Review*, No. 24, June 14, 1960, and No. 25, June 21, 1963.

[59] Speech by M. A. Suslov at the Central Committee Plenum, February 14, 1964, published in *Pravda*, April 3, 1964.

[60] Fedoseev, in *Kommunist*, March 1967, p. 111. Fedoseev and other Soviet theorists linked the contemporary Soviet attack on Mao's "theory of violence" and his "ideology of militarism" with the earlier opposition of Marx, Engels, and Lenin to Dühring's "voluntaristic conception of history."

imperialism for peace" and to rely on the false hope of averting war by seeking "mutual accommodation" with imperialism.[61]

Another series of arguments from the Chinese side centered on charges that the Russians were too preoccupied with the problems of nuclear war, including the danger of small wars escalating into global nuclear war, and that this "nuclear fetishism" with its lopsided emphasis on "technology over man" helped to account for the failure of Soviet policy to serve the needs of the national-liberation movement.[62] The Soviet side in turn reminded Peking that the countries of the Communist camp as well as the national-liberation movement lived under the protection of Soviet nuclear power, and that the real turning point in modern history came when the Soviet Union back in 1949 broke the atomic monopoly of the West.[63] The Chinese were accused of inviting war on the basis of military theories that would pit manpower against nuclear weapons, and the alleged Maoist fallacy of thinking that war can be won through "weakness" when "modern techniques of war are ignored" was branded as "naive, to say the least, if not criminal."[64]

While the Chinese often accused the Soviets of making a fetish of nuclear weapons during the polemics of the early sixties, they never made a secret of their own ambition to become a nuclear power. Their achievement of nuclear status in 1964 enabled them to claim that they had nullified a plot between the Soviet Union and the United States to preserve a superpower nuclear duopoly in order to "contain" China. On the other hand, China's entry into the nuclear club had no appreciable effect in tempering her advocacy of a militant and aggressive revolutionary struggle.

Underlying much of the polemics on war and peace was an apparent concern on the part of the Chinese leaders about where the policy of peaceful coexistence, as espoused by Khrushchev and his successors, might lead. Even though the Soviets never conceded that peaceful

[61] "The Differences Between Comrade Togliatti and Us," in *Peking Review*, No. 1, January 3, 1963. See also "Two Different Lines on the Question of War and Peace. . . ." in *Peking Review*, No. 47, November 22, 1963.

[62] Among relevant Chinese statements, see: "Two Different Lines on the Question of War and Peace. . . ." in *Peking Review*, No. 47, November 22, 1963; "The Proletarian Revolution and Khrushchev's Revisionism," *People's Daily-Red Flag* article of March 31, 1964, in *Peking Review*, No. 14, April 1964; Kao Ko, "Road to Victory in the National Liberation War," *People's Daily*, July 31, 1963; Lu Chih-chao, "Examination of the Question of War Must Not Run Counter to the Marxist-Leninist Viewpoint on Class Struggle," *Red Flag*, August 15, 1963; General Lo Jui-ching, "Commemorate the Victory over German Fascism," *Red Flag*, May 10, 1965.

[63] See Soviet Government Statement, *Pravda*, September 21, 1963; D. Vol'skii and V. Kudriavtsev, "Practical Reality and the Fantasies of the Splitters," *Red Star*, October 10, 1963; Colonel P. Trifonenkov, "The Most Pressing Problem of the Present Day and the Adventurism of the Chinese Dogmatists," *Kommunist Vooruzhennykh Sil*, No. 21, November 1963, pp. 23–28.

[64] Major General S. Koslov, "Against Dogmatism and the Distortion of Marxist-Leninist Teaching About War," *Narodna Armiya* (People's Army) broadcast on Sofia radio, October 8, 1963.

coexistence means giving up the class struggle, their admission that nuclear weapons do not "subscribe" to the "class principle" became a dangerous heresy in Peking's view. It raised a very disturbing question: How does one save a basic dogmatic principle after exception has been made to it? Perhaps Peking's uneasiness rested on a suspicion that the policy of peaceful coexistence, originally conceived as a means by which pressure on the West was to be carefully regulated so as not to provoke a nuclear disaster, might become in time a way of life — a mellowing of earlier militant Communism, with subsequent divergence between the aims of the world Communist movement and the national interests of the Soviet Union. At the end of this road might lie a durable rapprochement between the Soviet Union and the United States, a development which the leaders in Peking were likely to look upon as a threat to China's own long-term interests.

How the Sino-Soviet dispute will end, no one can predict. Conceivably, it might lead to an outright military collision between the two countries, voiding one of the most long-standing dogmas of Marxist-Leninist theory: that war is a product of the capitalist order, unthinkable between two Communist states. Even well short of such a dénouement, however, the Sino-Soviet dispute already seems to have demonstrated that the world is a much more complicated place than Marxism-Leninism once pictured it. Damaged beyond repair is the simplistic image of a unitary Communist movement in which the binding force of a common ideology was expected to prove more potent than the world's great diversity of peoples, nationalisms and cultures. Along with the splitting of Communism into local variants — the Soviet brand, Maoism, Titoism, Castroism and other approaches — it seems likely that the Communist outlook on war also will lose whatever unitary character it once may have had.

V DOMESTIC INPUTS AND INSTRUMENTS OF SOVIET FOREIGN POLICY

13. NATIONALITY INPUTS IN SOVIET FOREIGN POLICY: THE U.S.S.R. AS AN ARRESTED UNIVERSAL STATE

Vernon V. Aspaturian

The Soviet Union did not emerge full-blown from the dialectic of history. Before it was the Soviet Union, it was Soviet Russia, and before that it was the Russian Empire. The Bolsheviks inherited the ruins of the Russian state — its geography, its population, its culture and traditions, its history of glory and failure, its friends and enemies, and above all, its complex of behavioral patterns called "national character." As a territorially truncated version of the Russian Empire, the Soviet state ruled the same people, a multinational, multiracial population, most of whom were Russians, who with their religions, cultures, skills, knowledge, ignorance, prejudices, superstitions, and fears and anxieties now became peoples of the Soviet Union. This was the raw material upon which were imposed the ideological norms of Marxism, but these norms were imposed by leaders whose lives and attitudes were conditioned by the very raw material which they wished to fashion into a qualitatively new world order.

Reprinted from Vernon V. Aspaturian, *The Soviet Union in the World Communist System*, with the permission of The Hoover Institution on War, Revolution and Peace, Stanford University. © 1966 by the Board of Trustees of the Leland Stanford Junior University.

BELIEF SYSTEM AND NATIONALISM:
THE "RUSSIAN" FACTOR IN SOVIET BEHAVIOR

The Russian inheritance inevitably left its imprint on the social transformations which were to serve as a model for the future world. This society, as it emerged, was both "Russian" and "Marxist," that is, Bolshevik and Soviet. It was simultaneously ethnocentric and ecumenical. As the most numerous and influential element in the population, the Russians became the national vehicle for "internationalization" of the Soviet system. Marxism was poured into Russian containers. Russian culture, language, alphabet, and messianic fervor became the carriers of the universal redemptionist doctrine of Marxism, now called Marxism-Leninism. The Russian language became the lingua franca of the Union, while the Cyrillic alphabet became a multinational alphabet applied to all languages in the Union except those of the tiny minority of Estonian-, Lithuanian-, Latvian-, Georgian-, and Armenian-speaking peoples (only 11 million out of the more than 225 million persons in the Soviet Union).[1]

Both psychological momentum and practical necessity dictated the Russianization of the non-Russian nationalities. Under Soviet rule, Russian culture was converted from a purely national phenomenon into a multinational civilization, while Russian took its place as a "world language" alongside English, French, and Spanish. The superimposition of Russian culture on the non-Russian nationalities is reminiscent of the Hellenization and later Arabicization of the Middle East, the Latinization of Western Europe and the Hispanicization of the New World. The diffusion of English and French in the colonial empires, insofar as they became the lingua franca of the local elites, is also a comparable process.

Under Stalin Marxism was completely fused with the Russian legacy, and it was Stalin's conviction that his ethnocentric model of a socialist society would be systematically extended to new Communist party-states. They were to be simultaneously Russianized and communized. Stalin's successors have recognized the limitations of this process, and it has been arrested and reversed outside the Soviet Union. But

---

[1] Until the Soviet government adapted the Cyrillic alphabet to the numerous non-Slavic languages in the Soviet Union, the Cyrillic alphabet was restricted only to Slavonic languages, the other modern languages employing it being the Serbo-Croatian and Bulgarian. It is now being used by more than fifty non-Slavic languages in the Union, including languages like Moldavian and Karelo-Finnish, whose kinsmen in Finland and Rumania employ the Latin alphabet. Although Mongols in both the U.S.S.R. and the Mongolian People's Republic, as well as the Turkic and Tungusic peoples of Soviet Central Asia and the Soviet Far East, have been using Cyrillic now for nearly three decades, Peking has imposed the Latin alphabet on Mongols, Kazakhs, Kirgizes, Tadzihks, Uzbeks and other Turkic and Tungusic peoples living in China. Just as Stalin wanted to erect a barrier between the Moldavians and the Rumanians, and the Karelo-Finns and the Finns, Mao wants to minimize the cultural and ideological infection of his minorities from the Soviet side of the border.

there is no apparent intention of undoing it within the U.S.S.R., although in the non-Russian areas the purely Russian norms in Soviet communism no longer enjoy equal legitimacy with Marxist norms.

THE U.S.S.R. AS A SELF-FULFILLING UNIT: NATIONAL INTERESTS AND WORLD COMMUNISM

The establishment of the nation-state as the form of the Communist party-state signalled not only the victory of nationalism in its confrontation with class universalism, but also effectively demolished the pretensions of the Soviet Union as an embryo universal state. Arrested in its development as a universal state, the Soviet Union has in effect been transformed once again into a modern *Rossiya* — a Soviet commonwealth of nations (U.S.S.R.) with an ideological military sphere of influence in Eastern Europe. In many respects, the current position of the Soviet Union represents the fondest aspirations of its Tsarist predecessor: the Russian Empire has been consolidated into a unified and stable society, broadly based and militarily and economically self-sufficient. It has a retinue of client states in Eastern Europe, a dismembered Germany on the west, a disarmed Japan on the east, and a belt of weak buffer states in the Middle East. Only the revival of an expansionist China threatens the Soviet Union as a state and as the leader of a revolutionary movement.

Nationalism has been relegitimized not only in the smaller party-states, but in the Soviet Union as well. The more the other party-states behave and respond as nation-states, the more the Soviet Union is impelled to behave in similar fashion. Because of the multinational character of the Soviet state, this imposes new imperatives of internal adjustment and accommodation. The Soviet Union cannot, as under Stalin, respond simply as a Russian national state. A change has occurred in the internal distribution of influence and power among the various Soviet nations, with the result that the "national" interests of the major non-Russian nationalities must be calculated in formulating the state interests of the U.S.S.R. Under Stalin, the "national" interests of the Great Russian nationality were the dominant and virtually pre-emptive national inputs in Soviet external policy, just as the interests of the Soviet state enjoyed primacy in the Communist party-state system and movement.

Under the pressures generated in the past several years, both within and outside the Communist system, the role of the Soviet Union in its relationship to the various external environments in which it has functioned has been gradually revealed as a tight compound of many roles synchronized to respond to various internal and external constituencies in several different environments. Tightly cemented together by a compelling ideology, these multiple roles had been rendered indistinct, except for the obvious dichotomy between the Soviet Union as a state and as the institutionalized party center of a world revolutionary movement. With the re-emergence of nationalism in the movement, the

Soviet Union's various roles are becoming increasingly more distinct, responding almost independently to the demands of various political and social environments. The duality of the Soviet Union as a state and as a party has long been recognized, and its behavior has always betrayed a certain amount of political schizophrenia. But the Soviet Union operates not in just two, but actually in several different political and social environments, serving a wide spectrum of social, ideological, and national constituencies, whose distinct concerns intersect to form a kaleidoscope of interests. Sometimes these interests blend into a larger whole; at other times they overlap or are congruent; sometimes they simply coexist or appear successively; and frequently, they are in various degrees of subtle or overt contradiction.

As these various roles become more distinct, Soviet responses are likely to become less synchronized, resulting in contradictory and inconsistent behavior. For example, the response of the Soviet Union as a nation-state to Communist China's implied territorial demands on the Soviet Far East and Central Asia is totally divorced from its character and role as the center of a world revolutionary movement. Ultimately, a new balance among these various roles must be established, and some of them may be renounced (the role of center of world communism, for example), and others modified, altered, adjusted, or even added.

These roles, shaped and conditioned by the separate yet concentrically related environments in which the Soviet Union is called upon to act, represent a wide spectrum of responses. Some roles are unilaterally assumed, others have been deterministically imposed by history, geography, or the nature of the social and political situation. These roles are dynamic rather than static, ambivalent and ambiguous rather than precise and measurable, fluctuating and relational rather than fixed and absolute. Instead of a stabilized pattern of behavior, Soviet responses are subject to periodic reconfiguration. Alterations or diminutions in the demands of one role may force unforeseen changes in the imperatives of another. Also, the feedback effect of these changing roles frequently affects conscious motivation as well as Soviet thought and action.

For analytical convenience these roles can be grouped in a number of ways, but perhaps the most fruitful is to define them as institutionalized entities acting in specific environments. The Soviet Union reveals itself as four distinct but often interrelated, congruent, and concentric institutionalized personalities, each performing one or more distinct roles. These four institutionalized identities of the Soviet Union are: (1) state; (2) party; (3) nation (Russia); (4) multiple nation. As a total complex, it functions as a Russianized socialist multinational party-state, but it can also operate as a narrower entity, such as a party-state, a Russian state, or as a multinational state.

The prevailing current tendency in the behavior of the Soviet Union and other party-states is for the role functions performed by the state to assume priority over role functions performed by the party. The various constituencies to which the state responds are more numerous, broader, more concrete and more sustaining than those represented by the party, particularly in the smaller states where the party's interests and constituencies have been particularly narrow.

The external constituencies represented by the party are largely alien, that is, they consist of the abstraction "proletarian internationalism" and the interests of "fraternal" parties. In the past, the *de facto* external constituency of foreign Communist parties was the Soviet Union, and their role in reducing their countries to vassalage is likely to remain an ugly legacy which the parties in the smaller states may find difficult to overcome. The state, on the other hand, represents a longer historical continuity. Compared to the party, the state is perceived as more responsive to indigenous constituencies and less prone to have a commitment to the residual vestiges of the Stalinist era.

The behavioral configurations of the Soviet Union are an absolutely unique historical phenomenon. No other state or similar institution in history has assumed as many masks as the Soviet state. One of the few environments in which it refuses to assume a role is the supernatural, although Soviet dialectical disquisitions are frequently as metaphysical and scholastic as those of any theologian.

The most flagrant Soviet masquerade has been its attempt to separate its identity as a state from its status as a party and thus disclaim responsibility for its manipulation of foreign Communist parties. Now that the fiction of separateness has become a hindrance in the Soviet dispute with China and in relations with other Communist states and parties, the Soviet Union tries to minimize the distinction. Conversely the Chinese now find it useful to characterize their attack as one upon the Soviet party, not upon the Soviet state.

But the ambiguity of the Soviet political personality has reflected itself in other ways as well, even in its capacity as a state. The precise "national" character of the Soviet state, for example, remains elusive. Like a chameleon, it has masqueraded as Russia, as a multinational complex, and as a denationalized entity. Juridically, the state is called the Union of Soviet Socialist Republics, an artificial and abstract entity. Almost everywhere, inside and outside the Soviet Union, it is also identified as Russia, and not only by political and legal illiterates. "Russia" and "the Soviet Union" are used interchangeably everywhere, except in official documents. Both Soviet leaders and rank-and-file citizens of all nationalities continue to refer to their country as *Rossiya*. For, in fact, the Soviet Union is in many ways a continuation of *Rossiya*, as distinct from *Rus* (the Great Russian nation), which means "all the Russias" or "all-Russian" and conveys the concept of a multinational state with the Russian nation as the guardian and protector of the other nations joined together in an historically evolved commonwealth. Lenin and Stalin often referred to the "peoples of Russia" or the "nations of Russia (*Rossiya*)." Even today, the concept of *Rossiya* is juridically preserved in the constitutional identity of the Russian Republic — Rossiiskaya Sovetskaya Federativnaya Sotsialistichestkaya Respublika (R.S.F.S.R.) — which is also a multinational federation within an even larger multi-national Union state.[2]

But the Soviet Union frequently behaves as historic *Rus* as well, separately or in combination with its identity as *Rossiya*. Sometimes, these identities cause confusion, even among Soviet leaders. At Yalta, according to James Byrnes and Churchill, Stalin (a Geogian) com-plained:

> Some people wanted Russia [*Rossiya*] to take less than Curzon and Clemenceau had conceded. That would be shameful. When the Ukrain-ians came to Moscow [*Rus*], they would say that Stalin and Molotov were less trustworthy defenders of Russia than Curzon or Clemenceau.[3]

Perhaps those who, out of ignorance, think that the U.S.S.R. stands for the "United States of Soviet Russia," may in their naïve juridical illiteracy express more aptly the national substance of the Soviet state: a Russianized multinational party-state.

These four identities, state, party, nation, and multiple nation, act in five political environments, again as distinct personalities or in vari-ous combinations. These environments may also be congruent, concen-tric, overlapping, or simply coexistent or concurrent. Behavior in these various environments has taken place simultaneously, successively, harmoniously, contradictorily, or independently. These five political environments are: (1) the Soviet social order; (2) the Soviet multi-national order; (3) the Communist inter-state system; (4) the general inter-state system; and (5) the world Communist movement.

Each of these political environments represents a definite spectrum of internal and external social, political, and ideological constituencies, whose interests impinge upon and influence the behavior of the Soviet Union in its multiple political roles. The impact of these interests and Soviet response to them have been highly uneven and have fluctuated through time. Not only must the Soviet Union periodically establish a balance between its "state interests" and its party "ideological interests," but it must now increasingly adjust to the internal social changes result-ing from the divergent demands that arise among various internal social elites and social classes. Furthermore, greater attention must be paid to the different demands and pressures arising from the changing distribu-tion of influence and power among the various non-Russian nations.

This changing balance is affected not only by the internal evolution of the non-Russian nations of the U.S.S.R., but also by their relative significance in the foreign-policy aspirations of the Soviet Union. The Soviet bid for status as an Asian state, for example, derives from its claim to be the juridical representative of the Central Asian and other Asian nations of the U.S.S.R. Thus, Khrushchev, in addressing a joint

[2] See Frederick C. Barghoorn, *Soviet Russian Nationalism* (New York: Oxford University Press, 1956).

[3] James Byrnes, *Speaking Frankly* (New York: Harper and Brothers, 1947), p. 30. See also Winston Churchill, *Triumph and Tragedy* (Boston: Houghton Mifflin Company, 1953), p. 370.

meeting of the Kirghiz Central Committee and Supreme Soviet, on August 16, 1964, rebutted the Chinese:

> You live in the very center of Asia. The Soviet Republics of Central Asia are a beacon summoning all the peoples of the East. . . . True, some persons [i.e., the Chinese leaders] doubt that you, as well as other Soviet Republics of the East, belong to the Asian countries. They doubt that the Soviet Union is both a European and an Asian country, although a considerable part of its territory consists of republics and land of the Asian continent, and many peoples are among the most indigenous peoples of Asia, having an ancient history and a thousand-year culture. The Soviet Union is not only a European country, it is an Asian one, too. And this is so whether some adults who disregard geography and history want it so or not.[4]

In its capacity as a state, the Soviet Union functions first of all within a distinctive social environment called "socialist society," organized and developed originally in response to ideological norms, but which has now achieved its own internal dynamic and social equilibrium. The Soviet Union acts in this environment in response to the demands and interests of various social elites and social groups, in accordance with the socio-political balance of power among them. The Soviet Union thus represents the internal interests of its dominant and articulate social groups in the various other environments in which it is called upon to act; and its first order of business, since its leaders and decision makers are recruited from these same social forces, is to preserve the social order from which they benefit.

[4] Khrushchev speech in Frunze (*Pravda,* August 17, 1964). When *Pravda* complained on May 5, 1964, that the Chinese blackballed Soviet participation in the second Afro-Asian Conference on grounds that the Soviet Union was a European and not an Asian power, Peking retorted as follows: "*Pravda* argued that the Soviet Union, 'two-thirds of whose territory lies in Asia, is naturally not only a European but also an Asian country,' and therefore it is qualified to participate in the Asian African Conference. This assertion is untenable. True, Soviet territory spreads over Europe and Asia. But each state is a single entity, and it cannot be said that the Soviet Union is qualified as an Asian as well as a European state simply because its territory extends over both continents. . . . The political center of the Soviet Union as a single entity has already been in Europe, and it is internationally acknowledged that the Soviet Union, in history and tradition, has always been a European country. . . . It must be pointed out further that the Asian union republics of the Soviet Union cannot take part in the Asian-African Conference either. A state can have only one, and not more than one, unified central government. The Asian union republics of the Soviet Union are component parts of the Soviet Union and not states independent of it." ("What Right Have Soviet Leaders to Issue Orders to Asian and African Countries?," *Peking Review,* No. 23, June 5, 1964, 9.) See also "Statement of the Government of the People's Republic of China," ibid., 608. The Chinese reference to the Soviet Asian republics was designed to controvert the separate complaints issued by the Uzbek (*Pravda Vostoka,* May 10, 1964), Turkmen (*Turkmenskaya Pravda,* May 9), Tadzhik (*Kommunist Tadzhikstana,* May 13), and Kazakh (*Kazakhstanskaya Pravda,* May 10) Republics against Chinese arguments that the Soviet Union was not an Asian state. See also *Pravda,* April 25, May 5 and 9, 1964.

Degree of Integration within
the Union: The Primacy of Russia

In addition to the social order, the Soviet state acts within another significant internal environment, the environment of nationalities.

If the first role which we defined for the Soviet Union acting as a state within the context of a specific social system can be identified as its "socialist" identity, then in its second capacity as a state it functions as a "multinational" state. It functions not as just any kind of multi-national state, but specifically as a socialist multinational state. This means that the demands and interests of the various national entities of the Soviet Union must be expressed within the predetermined ideological parameters of the Soviet social order. This immediately rules out the articulation of any "national" interests which conflict with the prior imperatives of the Soviet social order, contribute to the dismemberment of the Soviet Union, or emphasize religious norms or racial exclusiveness.

The interests of the various nations of the Soviet Union must thus be expressed within the official formula, "national in form, socialist in content." Even within the confines of this formula, the national interests of the various nations can be expressed in both form and substance, as long as the substance is "socialist." This means that the various nations of the Soviet Union can register demands upon the system and one another that are not inconsistent with their socialist character as nations within a family of Soviet socialist nations. These demands might be, for example, greater national representation in the local and national organs of the state and party, greater investment and resource allocations for services and enterprises in their national locality, and territorial adjustments and claims against other national republics or foreign states. As long as these demands threaten neither the social imperatives of the system nor the external security and territorial integrity of the Soviet Union, they are considered legitimate expressions of national interest. Their satisfaction depends, however, upon the balance of power among the various nations of the Union and the degree to which they impinge upon the interests of purely social constituencies.

In recent years, the Soviet government has tried to eliminate the friction between the interests of social and national constituencies. The major illustration of this sensitivity to national interests has been the national quota system. The Soviet regime has formally and informally been using quotas, in which each nationality is represented according to its proportion of the total population (Table 1), in staffing state and party institutions and in enrolling students in institutions of higher learning. National sensitivities are also reflected in the periodic adjustments of territorial claims between various national units. These measures are designed to harmonize the national interests of the various nationalities with those of the state as a whole, the party, the social system, and the other nations in the U.S.S.R. The tendency is to establish proportional national representation in all political and social institutions. The tempo

TABLE 1
INTERSECTION OF NATIONAL, SOCIAL, AND POLITICAL CONSTITUENCIES

	Nationalities[a]		Political Constituencies & Institutions										Social Constituencies			
Nationality 1970	Population 1970		Supreme Soviet 1970[b]		Council of Ministers 1966		Communist Party 1965[c]		Central Committee 1966[d]		Politburo and Secretariat 1966[d]		Intelligentsia 1965[e]		Scientists 1968[f]	
	N	%	N	%	N	%	N	%	N	%	N	%	N	%	N	%
Russians	129,015,000	53.3	647	42.65	50	72.5	7,335,200	62.38	198	55.00	14	58.33	7,040,800	62.58	544,035	66.11
Ukrainians	40,753,000	16.9	203	13.38	14	20.3	1,813,400	15.42	57	15.83	4	16.67	1,734,300	15.41	87,578	10.64
Byelorussians	9,052,000	3.7	59	3.89	1	1.5	386,000	3.28	12	3.33	2	8.33	342,600	3.04	16,358	1.98
Uzbeks	9,195,000	3.8	51	3.36	0	0	193,600	1.66	5	1.38	1	4.17	143,500	1.27	10,312	1.25
Kazakhs	5,299,000	2.2	37	2.44	0	0	181,300	1.54	5	1.38	1	4.17	106,800	.94	6,475	.78
Georgians	3,245,000	1.3	50	3.30	0	0	194,300	1.65	3	.83	1	4.17	187,600	1.66	15,697	1.90
Azerbaidzhanis	4,380,000	1.8	47	3.10	0	0	141,900	1.21	2	.55	0	0	129,700	1.15	11,564	1.40
Lithuanians	2,665,000	1.1	32	2.11	0	0	61,500	0.53	3	.83	0	0	99,600	.88	6,932	.84
Moldavians	2,698,000	1.1	21	1.38	0	0	40,300	0.34	3	.55	0	0	44,300	.39	2,003	.24
Latvians	1,430,000	.6	28	1.85	0	0	44,300	0.38	4	1.11	1	4.17	78,900	.70	5,442	.66
Kirgiz	1,452,000	.6	23	1.52	0	0	35,000	0.30	2	.55	0	0	26,900	.23	1,474	.17
Tadzhiks	2,136,000	.9	33	2.18	0	0	41,900	0.36	2	.55	0	0	32,100	.28	1,949	.23
Armenians	3,559,000	1.5	45	2.97	1	1.5	187,900	1.60	5	1.38	0	0	163,700	1.45	17,182	2.08
Turkmens	1,525,000	.6	26	1.72	0	0	32,400	0.28	2	.55	0	0	27,700	.24	1,595	.19
Estonians	1,007,000	.5	28	1.85	0	0	33,900	0.29	3	.83	0	0	60,000	.53	4,174	.50
Jews	2,151,000	.9	6	.39	1	1.5			1	.27	0	0	482,400	4.28	60,995	7.41
Tatars	5,931,000	2.45	18	1.19	1	1.5			1	.27	0	0	173,000	1.53	9,905	1.20
Chuvash	1,694,000	.7	8	.53	0	0			0	.00	0	0	44,400	.39	1,543	.19
Others	8,313,000	3.4	156	10.28	1	1.5	1,035,000	8.80	53	14.72	0	0	331,400	2.94	17,697	2.15
Totals	241,720,000	100.0	1517	100.0	69	100.3	11,738,200	100.02	360	100.18	24	100.01	11,249,700	99.89	822,910	99.92

[a] Total population, as of January 15, 1970 was 241,748,000. Nationality data from the 1970 from *Pravda*, April 17, 1971.
[b] Nationality identification taken from *Deputaty Verkhovno Soveta SSSR: Sedmoi Sozyu* (Moscow: 1970).
[c] As of January 1, 1965. "*KPSS v Tsifrakh* (1961-1964 Gody)," *Partinaya Zhizn*, May 1965, p.12.
[d] *Pravda*, April 9, 1966. Nationality identification taken from source cited under (b) above, 1966 and 1970.
[e] As of November 15, 1964. *Narodnoye Khozyaistvo SSSR v 1965 Godu* (Moscow: 1966), p. 582.
[f] As of the end of 1968. *Narodnoye Khozyaistvo SSSR v 1968 Godu* (Moscow: 1969), p. 697.

with which this is accomplished varies with the significance, size, and development of the individual nationalities, and with the degree to which their interests serve those of the social system and the state as a whole.

However, certain priorities still remain. The interests of various social elites continue to enjoy the highest priority in the decisions and policies of the Soviet Union, and within the context of nationalities, the national interest of the great Russian nation still enjoys the highest priority, outweighing the interests of all other nations, individually or combined. This is evidenced not only by the preponderance of Great Russians in the Communist party and in the ranks of the various elite groups, by their greater urbanization, and by the distribution of investments, but also by the presence of Russians at strategic points in the political and social institutions of individual non-Russian republics. Russian is the official language of state, diplomacy, and military command. It is the official language in the major institutions of higher learning, and it is virtually a compulsory second language for all non-Russians. Whether all of this is a response to calculated chauvinistic impulses or the automatic response to a situation in which the Russian nation is numerically preponderant, it serves to infuse the policies and decisions of the state with a heavy dose of Russian national interests.

In recent years, however, a substantial retreat has been made from the advanced points of Stalinist Great Russian chauvinism, which ruthlessly and needlessly overrode the national interests, pride, and sensitivity of other nations and was threatening to undermine the multinational foundations of the Soviet state. Reconciling the national interests of the various nations of the Union to the national interests of Russia was an important dimension of the Soviet "national problem" over and above that involved in the coordination of the national interests of all nations in the Union with the normative social imperatives of the Communist party itself. Stalin's gross insensitivity, especially in his later years, to the national interests of other nations was such that Beria apparently thought he could utilize national dissatisfactions and latent resentments as a power base from which to move against his rivals. Thus among the charges leveled against the deposed police chief was that he endeavored to mobilize the non-Russians against the Russians. Although it was claimed that he was "deprived of any social support within the U.S.S.R.," he nevertheless did in fact attempt to organize a sociopolitical base among the non-Russian nationalities:

> Beria and his accomplices undertook criminal measures in order to stir up the remains of bourgeois-nationalist elements in the Union Republics, to sow enmity and discord among the peoples of the U.S.S.R. and, in the first place, to undermine the friendship of the peoples of the U.S.S.R. with the Great Russian people.[5]

The interests of the Great Russians continue to predominate as the chief national input into the Soviet system. The national interests of

[5] *Pravda*, December 17, 1953.

other nations also serve as inputs into the calculation of Soviet state interests, but in accordance with an informal hierarchy of national priorities. This structure of priorities reflects the degree to which the various nations have national demands upon one another; it reflects the degree of compatibility of these interests with those of the Russian nation and the Soviet state, and also the degree to which their interests can be articulated in the policies of the Soviet Union abroad. This informal hierarchy of national priorities should not be confused with the purely formal hierarchy of national autonomy: (1) Union Republics; (2) Autonomous Republics; (3) Autonomous Oblasts; and (4) National Okrugs.

The primacy of the Russian nation is so pronounced that its position in the hierarchy of nations is qualitatively distinct from that of the others. Consequently, in its *national* behavior, the Soviet state acts as two different national entities: (1) The Great Russian nation-state (historic *Rus*), and (2) a multinational state representing the national interests of various nations (a modification of the concept *Rossiya*). In an era when each nation is demanding its own state, and the nation-state has emerged as the definitive form of the Communist party-state, these two aspects of the national substance of Soviet behavior will tend to become increasingly differentiated both in the Communist party-state system and in the general international system.

In the realm of foreign policy, the spectrum of national interests from which inputs are selected is restricted almost entirely to the nations organized as Union Republics. The informal order of national priorities also should not be confused with the rank order of Union Republics listed in the constitution of the U.S.S.R., since the latter order is based, with a single exception, on size of population. Currently, the informal ranking of the non-Russian nations in terms of the priority given their demands against one another and against the Russian nation, and their demands upon the Soviet state is as follows: (1) the Ukraine, the second-largest nation and, since 1953, formalized as the second-ranking nation, or *secundus inter pares;* (2) the two Christian nations of the Caucasus, Georgia and Armenia, which received preferential treatment during the Stalinist era, and the third of the "other Russias," Byelorussia, which, like the Ukraine, is a closely related but smaller and less nationally conscious Slav relative of Great Russia; (3) the two historic Turkic nations, predominantly Moslem in background, Azerbaidzhan and Uzbekistan; (4) the three Baltic nations (Estonia, Latvia, and Lithuania) and Moldavia, whose national priorities will advance as they become more integrated into the Soviet system; (5) the Kazakh, Kirghiz, Turkmen, and Tadzhik nations, in that order.

This informal hierarchy of officially "equal" nations in the U.S.S.R. is reflected in various ways: in the distribution of national representatives in various party and state institutions; in the proportion of indigenous citizens in the national party and state organizations; in the level of cultural, educational, and technological development, which in turn reflects the investment ratio of resources and funds; in the urban-rural ratio; in the rate and level of economic development; and in the representation of their "national interests" in Soviet foreign policy.

Except for the institutionalized second place held by the Ukraine, this informal hierarchy is subject to change and will continue to be determined by a variety of factors, such as the ethnic, historical, and cultural (including religious) ones; by the political relationship with the Great Russian nation; and by the degree to which the traditional interests and attitudes of the nations have coincided with or deviated from those of the Great Russian nation. Thus the reference point in articulating the interests of the non-Russian nations remains the national interests of the Russian nation, but this interest is no longer understood as chauvinistically as it was during the Stalinist era.

The functioning of the Soviet state within its own borders as a multiple nation-state is relatively uncomplicated when compared with its behavior in the international arena. The formal constitutional structure of the Union gives the impression that it can simultaneously act in international affairs as sixteen separate states — the Union as a whole, and fifteen individual national states — but in reality the Soviet state functions as a collectivized entity, representing the combined interests of all Soviet social and national constituencies in accordance with the given structure of social and national priorities.

The role of the Soviet Union as the guardian of the national interests of all its major nations is both crippled and enhanced by the peculiarly ambivalent legal character with which Soviet jurists encumber the Soviet state. The U.S.S.R. claims to be not only the successor state of the Russian Empire, and thus the legal heir to all its rights, privileges, and property, but it simultaneously claims to be an entirely new state, unencumbered with the legal and political delinquencies or "negative" characteristics of its predecessor. Thus one Soviet jurist writes:

> The U.S.S.R., as before, remains a Union State. Above all and principally, it functions externally in the capacity of a subject of international law. Its international obligations and rights pertain to the entire territory of the Union. It functions as the successor to the rights of Russia as a whole in the international arena.[6]

Pravda, however, in a long editorial in 1964, rejecting implied Chinese territorial claims upon Soviet lands in the Far East and Central Asia, disassociated the Soviet Union from the Russian Empire, whose predatory annexations and "unequal" treaties were the basis of Chinese complaints:

> The Soviet Union is an absolutely new state formation which emerged as a result of a voluntary unification of soviet republics created on the ruins of the Tsarist empire. Whereas the borders of Tsarist Russia were determined by the policy of imperialist predators, the borders of the Soviet Union were formed as a result of a voluntary statement of the

[6] F. I. Kozhevnikov, *Sovetskoye Gosudarstvo i Mezhdunarodnoye Pravo* (Moscow, 1948), p. 64. See also I. P. Blishchenko and V. N. Durdenevskii, *Diplomaticheskoye i Konsulskoye Pravo* (Moscow, 1962), pp. 38–41.

will of the peoples on the basis of the principle of free self-determination of nations. The peoples which joined the Soviet Union will never
allow anyone to encroach upon the right to settle their destiny themselves.[7]

The Soviet Union thus continues to function simultaneously as the
Russian national state, the national state of individual non-Russian
nations, and finally as one single state entity for all of the nations
combined. In an international system and subsystem of states, the
interests of nations can be served effectively only if they have the
organized power of a state to articulate their demands. In the present
era, this assumes the standard pattern of each nation organizing itself
into a nation-state, so that the interests of the nation and state are
completely congruent and coterminous. While this may not solve the
problem of conflicting social and political interests *within* the nation, it
does serve to eliminate conflicts between nations, which continue to
characterize states made up of two or more nations. Binational and
multinational states represent deviations from the standard norm; and
in almost all such states, national conflicts are chronic, since the equal
representation of the national interests of more than one nation by a
single state is extremely difficult. This problem exists in more or less
aggravated form in Canada, Belgium, South Africa, Yugoslavia, Czechoslovakia, the U.S.S.R., China, and even Switzerland.

As the largest multinational state, representing the widest spectrum of nations in the world, the Soviet Union has tried to solve this
problem through the flexible juridical device of a multiple state. Each of
the fifteen Union Republics is organized as a nation-state, with all of the
external ornamentation and symbols of such status, though with little of
the substance.

Thus, in accordance with Soviet conceptions of sovereignty and
international law, the fifteen Union Republics are endowed with the
rights and obligations of statehood and have been invested with all the
external ornaments of statehood in their separate capacities. Each
Republic is constitutionally equipped to establish separate diplomatic
representation with other countries and international organizations, to
contract treaties, and to establish its own national troop formations. But
the ability of the Soviet state to function as a multiple nation-state in
international affairs does not depend upon its own will alone, but must
also involve the recognition and acceptance by other states as well.
Consequently, the ability of the Soviet Union to represent the national
interests of its member nations in their separate capacities is severely
handicapped and limited. Only the Ukraine and Byelorussia, however,
enjoy partial and limited recognition as separate state entities in the
international system, and even they have virtually none in the Communist sub-system.

According to Soviet jurists, the multiple juridical character of the

[7] Issue of September 2, 1964.

U.S.S.R. also invests the smaller national republics with the full panoply of Great Power status in the international system:

> Membership in the U.S.S.R. guarantees each Republic full protection of its rights and interests on the international level. If each Republic acted in international affairs as a separate state . . . it would have little participation and influence in the consideration of major international questions. It is only as part of the Union structure that each Republic, irrespective of its size, has equal opportunity with others to assume the position of a Great Power — the U.S.S.R. — in international affairs.[8]

In foreign policy, the Soviet Union has been most conspicuous in representing the national interests of its member nations on territorial questions. Since the Union Republics as separate states might not have been in a position to reclaim their irredenta or to maintain their territorial integrity, there is a degree of truth to the Soviet claim that as parts of the U.S.S.R. they derive certain advantages which they might not otherwise enjoy. Almost all of the territorial adjustments made in favor of its national republics have been at the expense of other members of the world Communist party-state system. For this reason alone, the multinational character of the Soviet state is a crucial factor in its relationship to other Communist states. The most important territorial changes favoring the Soviet Union have been made on the pretext that these territories constituted unredeemed national lands of various national republics in the Soviet Union.

The Soviet Union has detached territories from Poland on behalf of the Lithuanian, Byelorussian, and Ukrainian nations, and from Czechoslovakia and Rumania on behalf of the Ukraine. Southern Sakhalin and the Kuriles were "reunited" with Russia, and territories were seized from Finland on behalf of the Karelian nation. Unsuccessful territorial demands were made upon Turkey for the redemption of Georgian and Armenian national irredenta.

While these territorial acquisitions and demands may have been prompted by considerations other than the national interests of various Soviet nations, and while Stalin's exploitation of their irredentist character may have been little more than cynicism, it is true nevertheless that these territorial settlements and demands coincided with the national interests of the individual nations involved. The boast that the Soviet Union is the national redeemer and unifier of the Ukraine, Byelorussia, and Lithuania is not entirely unfounded, and neither is Thesis 19 of the "Theses on the 300th Anniversary of the Reunion of the Ukraine with Russia (1654–1954)," which reads as follows:

> The growing might and strength of the Union of Soviet Socialist Republics made it possible to realize the yearning for national reunion which the Ukrainian people had carried through the centuries. The reunion of all the Ukrainian territories was completed thanks to the

---

[8] V. Vadimov, *Verkhovny Sovet SSR i Mezhdunarodnye Otnosheniya* (Moscow, 1958), pp. 1, 16.

wise policy of the Communist party and the Soviet Government. In 1939, the Western Ukraine was reunited with the Soviet Ukraine, Bukovina and the Ismail region were reunited with the Ukrainian S.S.R. in 1940, and Transcarpathian Ukraine in 1945. With the reunion of all the Ukrainian territories, the Soviet Ukraine became one of the biggest states in Europe.[9]

The intensity with which the Soviet Union will defend the national interests of its border nations may soon be put to the test again. In the interview which Mao Tse-tung gave to a group of Japanese visitors in August 1964, the Chinese leader not only made implicit demands upon Soviet territory on behalf of China, but in effect also encouraged Poland, East Germany, Czechoslovakia, Rumania, Finland, and Japan to resurrect their own territorial grievances against the Soviet Union. These territorial issues involve not only "Russia," but the Kazakh, Kirghiz, Tadzhik, Ukrainian, and Byelorussian nations as well. Five of the states having territorial grievances, latent or otherwise, with the Soviet Union and party-states: China, Poland, Czechoslovakia, East Germany, and Rumania. Stalin, cynically or not, gave higher priority to the interests of the border nations of the U.S.S.R. than to those of the fraternal party-states. In the cases of Poland and Rumania, the Soviet Union also annexed territories that can with equal justification be considered national territories of those two countries, rather than of the Ukraine. This is certainly true of Lwow and the Polish-inhabited regions of Eastern Galicia and the Moldavian- (Rumanian-) inhabited territories of the Moldavian and Ukrainian Republics.

National Irredentism and the Communist System

Much has been made of the Soviet claim that only under their membership in the Soviet Union has the historic territory of the Lithuanian, Byelorussian, and Ukrainian nations been assembled under a single national roof. In consequence the Soviet regime may soon be confronted with an embarrassing opportunity to preserve the national territorial integrity of these nations whose lands it has so recently gathered together. Both China and Rumania have made implied territorial demands upon the Soviet Union, and while Soviet leaders have not mentioned Rumania's renewed interest, they have made vociferous attacks upon the Chinese demands.

From the tenor of *Pravda's* remarks concerning Mao Tse-tung's discussion of Soviet territorial acquisitions with a group of visiting Japanese socialists, Moscow apparently expects multiple territorial demands to be made in the near future. According to Japanese sources, Mao was supposed to have said:

> There are too many places occupied by the Soviet Union. In correspondence with the Yalta agreement, the Soviet Union, under the

[9] *Pravda*, January 12, 1954. In connection with the celebration of the unification of Russia and the Ukraine, the R.S.F.S.R. also magnanimously ceded the Crimean Peninsula to the Ukrainian Republic on February 19, 1954.

pretext of guaranteeing the independence of Mongolia, actually put that country under its rule. . . . In 1954, when Khrushchev and Bulganin arrived in China, we raised this question, but they refused to talk with us. They have appropriated part of Rumania. Detaching part of East Germany, they drove out the local inhabitants to the Western area. Detaching part of Poland, they included it in Russia and as compensation gave Poland part of East Germany. The same thing happened to Finland. They detached everything that could be detached. Some people have said that Sinkiang Province and the territory to the north of the Amur River must be included in the Soviet Union. The U.S.S.R. is concentrating troops on its borders.[10]

There is a further profound significance in Mao's remarks if the Japanese version correctly noted his use of "Russia" and "the Soviet Union" interchangeably in the course of the discussion. Charging Peking with a desire to detach the Soviet Far East and parts of Kirghizia, Tadzhikstan, Kazakhstan (up to Lake Balkash) and Sakhalin, *Pravda* apprehensively noted:

> Mao Tse-tung pretends to attack the interests of only our country, but is it not clear to everybody that such a provocative appeal to revise borders, if it is taken seriously, would invariably generate a whole series of mutual claims and insoluble conflicts between countries of Europe and Asia? The self-evident nature of all this cannot be doubted and is cause for stating that only those who find it profitable for some reasons to sow mistrust and animosity between people of socialist countries can act in such a manner. It is precisely with this aim that Mao Tse-tung is trying to fabricate so-called territorial issues between a number of socialist countries. However, these attempts are doomed to failure in advance. No one will ever succeed in undermining the friendship and cooperation of the people of the socialist countries.[11]

The most cherished treasure of a nation is its territory, and, historically, territorial disputes have evoked the deepest emotional reactions. As the custodian of the "national" interests of their own people, Polish, Chinese, and Rumanian Communist leaders must be prepared to defend

[10] "Concerning Mao Tse-tung's Talk with a Group of Japanese Socialists," *Pravda*, September 2, 1964. Since no official Chinese version of the interview has been published, all information concerning the content of the interview is derived from Japanese sources. On September 2, *Pravda* reprinted a version of the interview carried by *Sekai Shuho* on August 11. This is the version from which Mao's alleged statements are cited, and *Pravda*'s rebuttal is based on it. Moscow accepted the version as authentic because "it was thought that Peking would refute this report, but no denial was forthcoming." Soviet attempts to elicit confirmation or denial were rebuffed, while other Chinese statements seemed to confirm the substance of the interview. "After this," *Pravda* explained, "no doubt remained that the Japanese press had indeed reproduced a statement of the Chairman of the Communist Party of China."

[11] Ibid. Mao also reportedly said: "About a hundred years ago the area east of Lake Baikal became Russian territory, and since then Vladivostok, Khabarovski, Kamchatka, and other points have been territories of the Soviet Union." And then he ominously warned: "We have not yet presented the bill on this list." Ibid.

their national territories with a zeal equal to that of Soviet leaders. Since most of the foreign claims on Soviet territory are claims to territories of non-Russian republics, Soviet leaders, in defending the territorial sanctity of the U.S.S.R., will be simultaneously acting in their capacity as representatives of their border nations.

Since the border nations are deprived of their ability to function as independent state entities, they must rely upon the Soviet government to act on their behalf. Unless the Soviet Union is willing to forfeit its claim to be the legitimate defender of the national interests of its member nations, it must live up to this claim. Soviet leaders can hardly expect their member nations to accept possible future dismemberment simply because this would satisfy the national impulses of other Communist states. It must in the event of conflict continue to assign higher priority to the "national" interests of its member nations than to the interests of neighboring party-states. The degree to which the interests of various Soviet nations coincide with the higher interests of the Soviet state and party will determine the intensity with which these interests will be pursued.

The territorial issues being raised by Peking are thus of crucial importance for the Communist system. In the words of *Pravda*, "Mao Tse-tung . . . is not only claiming this or that part of Soviet territory, but is portraying his claims as a part of some general territorial question."[12] The newspaper further warned: "we are faced with an openly expansionist program with far-reaching pretensions."

Six weeks after Mao's interview with a group of Japanese visitors, Khrushchev addressed another Japanese group in Moscow and devoted almost the entire interview to a diatribe against Mao's territorial pretensions. Pointedly reminding Peking that China, too, is a multinational state, Khrushchev warned Mao that territorial demands against the U.S.S.R. might easily backfire. While not stating the point explicitly, Khrushchev intimated that China was in possession of territories that

---

[12] Ibid. Khrushchev publicly explored the explosive irredentist claims of Poland, Rumania, the Ukraine, and Byelorussia in an unusually frank speech in Leipzig on March 7, 1959:

"The matter of boundaries . . . exists in socialist countries as well. Take the Soviet Union and Poland. If one were to ask the Ukrainians or Byelorussians, they would say that even at present Poland holds a number of areas that were formerly a part of the Ukraine and Byelorussia. . . . I speak of this not because there are any territorial disputes between the Soviet Union and Poland. There are no such disputes, though I feel sure that there is a section of the Polish population which . . . would probably like them [the boundaries] to pass farther to the East. . . . We also know that part of the present Moldavian Soviet Republic had been seized by the King of Rumania and subsequently reunited with the Soviet Union. Yet there is no dispute between the Soviet Union and the Rumanian People's Republic over boundaries, because both are socialist countries guided by common interests. . . . But that does not mean that there are no people in Rumania who believe that Moldavia is a part of Rumania. We are not blind to the possibility that such sentiments may arise." N. S. Khrushchev, *World without Arms, World without Wars* (2 vols.; Moscow, 1960), I, 194–195.

might more accurately be described as the national irredenta of Soviet Central Asian nations:

> Let us take Sinkiang, for example. Have the Chinese been living there from time immemorial? The Sinkiang indigenous population differs sharply from the Chinese ethnically, linguistically, and in other respects. They are Uighurs, Kazakhs, Kirghizes, and other peoples. Chinese emperors conquered them in the past and deprived them of their independence. . . . The Chinese state is also a multinational state. It also took shape as a result of historical processes. Chinese emperors were in no lesser degree robbers than the Russian tsars and accumulated big wealth by robbery. The independent Mongolian People's Republic was formed and is developing as a result of the national liberation struggle, while another part of the territory populated by Mongols forms part of the Chinese state. The territory on which the Kazakh people live forms part of the Soviet Union. On this territory, the Kazakh people set up the Kazakh Soviet Socialist Republic. This is the sovereign state of the Kazakh people, and according to the constitution, the Kazakh people have the right, if they wish so, to secede from the Soviet Union. Some of the Kazakhs and the territory they occupy form part of the Chinese state.[13]

Describing the situation of the Kirghizes, in terms identical to that of the Kazakhs, Khrushchev warned that "territorial and national questions in the land of the Soviets have been settled in conformity with the expression of the will of the peoples," and cautioned the Chinese that they should "not engage in incitement."[14]

As a state more or less satisfied with its existing frontiers, the Soviet Union has become, territorially speaking, a *status quo* power, and this more than anything else accounts for Moscow's sudden interest in a general convention outlawing the use of force in the alteration of borders between states. In his statement to the Japanese, Khrushchev recalled his earlier suggestion:

> In the Soviet government's message of December 31, 1963, we proposed that the states should not violate existing frontiers, not resort to

[13] Khrushchev's interview took place on September 15, 1964, and was published in *Pravda* on September 19. The issue of Sinkiang and its Soviet-related populations became very acute in April 1962, when an anti-Chinese uprising erupted in the Ili Valley and lasted for several months. According to Soviet sources, tens of thousands of Kazakhs and other Turkic nomads sought and were given asylum in the Soviet Union. (*Kazakhstanskaya Pravda*, September 29, 1963.) According to the Chinese: "In April and May 1962, the leaders of the CPSU used their organs and personnel in Sinkiang, China to carry out large-scale subversive activities in the Ili region and enticed and coerced several tens of thousands of Chinese citizens into going into the Soviet Union. The Chinese government lodged repeated protests and made repeated presentations, but the Soviet government refused to repatriate these Chinese citizens on the pretext of 'the sense of legality' and 'humanitarianism.' To this day this incident remains unsettled." ("The Origin and Development of the Differences between the Leadership of the CPSU and Ourselves," *Peking Review*, No. 37, September 13, 1963, 6–23.) For the Soviet rejoinder see *Pravda*, September 21 and 22, 1963.

[14] *Pravda*, September 19, 1964.

forcible methods of solving territorial problems. War must not be a means of changing frontiers. Only in this condition can peace be safeguarded. The only acceptable way of revising frontiers is talks. Any other way, as a rule, leads to war.[15]

"Frontier problems are complex," he said, admitting that "some states are dissatisfied with the existing frontiers for one reason or another." He made it quite clear that Soviet borders, except for minor adjustments, are sacrosanct and not subject to negotiation: "The frontiers of the Soviet Union are sacred and he who dares violate them will meet with a resolute rebuff from the peoples of the Soviet Union."[16]

The Soviet position on the territorial question conforms precisely with Clausewitz's observation that "a conqueror is always a lover of peace," which Lenin noted in the margin of his personal copy as being very witty. A recurrent claim of Soviet spokesmen is that the Soviet border "has developed historically and was fixed by life itself, and treaties concerning the border have a basis which cannot be disregarded."[17] Since the territorial annexations of the tsars are a matter of

[15] Khrushchev's reference to "talks" as a method for settling boundary questions seems to contradict an observation he made to the Germans in March 1959: "The lessons of history show that boundaries are not changed by conferences. What a conference can do is merely formalize in its decisions the existing relation of forces. And that relation is the result of victory or surrender in war, or of other factors." (*World without Arms*, I, 194.) For a text of Khrushchev's message on the peaceful solution boundary questions see *Pravda*, January 4, 1964. On September 21, 1964, Moscow asked that the proposal be placed on the Agenda of the Nineteenth Session of the General Assembly. (*New Times*, October 7, 1964, pp. 39–40.) Nevertheless, Soviet spokesmen have repeatedly stated that they are willing to discuss "a more precise definition of the border line," but "the Chinese side has avoided such consultations, at the same time continuing to violate the border." (*Pravda*, September 21 and 22, 1964.) Consultations on the border did start in February 1964, but nothing concrete has materialized. During the same month, Khrushchev said: "we got this border as our inheritance, and we must maintain it," while Suslov said: "only certain more accurate definitions of the frontier can be discussed," thus making it clear that Moscow had no intention of surrendering territory as such. See *Manchester Guardian*, February 29, 1964, and *Pravda*, April 3, 1964. After Suslov's speech was published in April, Chou En-lai claimed that "countries whose territories have been invaded and occupied by imperialism naturally have every right to recover the lost territory by every means." *Reuters*, April 26, 1964.

[16] *Pravda*, September 19, 1964. According to Moscow: "Starting in 1960, Chinese military and civilian personnel have been systematically violating the Soviet border. More than 5,000 violations of the Soviet border by the Chinese were recorded in 1962 alone. They are even making secret attempts to 'assimilate' individual sections of Soviet territory." (*Pravda*, September 21 and 22, 1963.) Increasingly, the military factor seems to be entering into the Sino-Soviet border issue. In his statement to the Japanese, Mao is reported to have said: "the U.S.S.R. is concentrating troops on its borders." Adzhubei told *Der Spiegel* soon after: "the entire military might of the U.S.S.R. stands guard over Soviet frontiers in the west as well as in the east." (*Der Spiegel*, August 3, 1964.)

[17] *Pravda*, September 19, 1964. The Soviet leaders are not totally oblivious of the *status quo* quality of their stand on territorial issues. "I realize that you Germans," Khrushchev admitted in 1959, "might say: 'It's all very well

indisputable historical record, Moscow does not deny them; but it views the whole history of Tsarist expansion as irrelevant, since the transformation of Russia into the U.S.S.R. cleansed the Soviet Union of all the sins of its predecessor. Thus, Khrushchev explained,

> The territory of the Soviet Union took shape as a result of historical processes. The October Revolution granted all peoples of Russia the right to self-determination, up to and including secession, and they used this right. Some peoples seceded from Russia, others voluntarily united to form the Union of Soviet Socialist Republics. The peoples of the Soviet Union do not want foreign lands, but they will allow nobody to encroach on their lands.[18]

Not only do territorial claims against the Soviet Union create agonizing internal and external problems for Moscow, but they also

---

for Khrushchev to talk that way, for it was Germany, and not the Soviet Union, that lost territories as a result of the Second World War.' " (*World without Arms*, I, 194.) And on September 21, 1963, the Soviet government told the Chinese: "The Soviet Union has no border conflicts with a single state. And we take pride in this, because such a situation accords not only with the interests of the Soviet Union but with the interests of all the socialist countries, the interests of the cause of peace throughout the world." (*Pravda*, September 21 and 22, 1964.) As far as the Soviet Union is concerned, until the advent of utopia, the Second World War legitimized existing boundaries and another war would result if Peking made an attempt to change them. According to *Pravda* (September 2): "Mao Tse-tung crossed out with amazing ease the entire system of international agreements concluded after the Second World War which meets the interests of strengthening peace and the security of people. He declared: 'The places occupied by the Soviet Union are too numerous,' and even named some territories with the obvious aim of adding inflammatory material to fan nationalistic passions. It is hard to believe that the Chinese leader does not understand the causes and historic circumstances of the present borders between states in Europe and Asia. Also it is difficult to assume another thing—that he is not aware of the most dangerous consequences to which any attempt to recarve the map of the world could lead under present conditions."

[18] *Pravda*, September 19, 1964. See also Khrushchev's speech to the Kirghizians on August 16, in which he implied that Tsarist expansionism coincided with the basic yearnings of inarticulate Central Asians to be united with Russia: "The centenary of Kirghizia's voluntary incorporation in Russia is a great and important event in the history of the peoples of our country. . . . Kirghizia's voluntary incorporation in Russia was . . . a progressive phenomenon. To touch upon history, it is well known that at the beginning of the nineteenth century the Kirghiz lands became the object of aspirations of conquest on the part of foreign predators. The historical setting of that time, the complicated foreign-policy situation, confronted the Kirghiz people with an important problem—to join with Russia. . . . Kirghizia's incorporation in Russia made it possible for Kirghizia to rid herself of enslavement to the Kokand Khans and constant persecution by the Chinese feudal lords and to avert the menace of disappearance of the Kirghizes as an independent people. . . . The voluntary incorporation in Russia took place in contradictory historical circumstances. The colonialist policy of Russian tsarism hindered the development of the Kirghiz economy and culture. But progressive representatives of Russian culture did everything to help the development of the Kirghiz people. . . . In joining Russia, Kirghizia became part of the country that turned into the center of the world revolutionary movement in the twentieth century." (*Pravda*, August 17, 1964.)

threaten to revive territorial disputes between other members of the Communist world. As the state which has been the main consumer of neighboring party-state territory, the Soviet Union is the one most threatened by the revival of territorial demands. If the Soviet Union could justify territorial annexations against smaller party-states on the grounds of national self-determination, why cannot these states justify their demands upon the Soviet Union on the same grounds. Since Stalin, in adding to the Soviet empire, invoked virtually every possible justification, including historical conquest, why is it so outrageous when Mao invokes the same arguments against the Soviet Union?

Under Stalin, Soviet retention of territory which was properly the irredenta of neighboring states was justified on the specious grounds that the territorial expansion of a socialist state was progressive if it was at the expense of a bourgeois state, regardless of the national character of the territory in question. The interests of socialism took precedence over those of nationalism. But this argument can no longer be invoked, since the countries demanding their irredenta are also socialist states seeking to reunite their national proletariat. If it were proper for Moscow to reunite the Ukraine, Byelorussia, and Lithuania, is it not just as appropriate for Rumanian, Hungarian, Polish, and other nationalities to seek the national reunification of their territories, even at the expense of the U.S.S.R.?

The Soviet Union is not likely to relinquish voluntarily any of its territories, no matter what justifications are advanced, and the other party-states are not likely to be in a position to seize lands from the Soviet Union by force. But this is hardly the issue. The point is that relations among party-states are likely to be poisoned by territorial disputes, and the position and role of the Soviet Union in the Communist world is bound to suffer as a consequence. This is more than a hypothetical possibility, as even *Pravda* concedes:

> As already noted above, the Chinese leaders are trying to elevate territorial claims to the level of some general principle. However, this involves the mainstays of international relations. What would happen if all states would follow the Peking recipe and begin presenting mutual claims to each other for a revision of historically formed borders? There is no difficulty in answering this question. This road would mean an inevitable aggravation of international tension and be fraught with military conflicts and all the consequences ensuing from them.[19]

It would be ironic indeed if the Communist party-state system should founder on such a patently bourgeois issue as territorial conflict, especially since such a conflict between Communist states was one of those "non-problems" of Marxism-Leninism. Whether it be the root cause or not, this conflict certainly threatens the stability of the system, since no alliance system can long survive mutual territorial claims of one state upon another or multiple territorial demands upon the most powerful member of the alliance.

Once the nation-state was established as the standard state form in

[19] *Pravda*, September 2, 1964.

the Communist system, problems of national irredenta were bound to re-emerge. There is also a definite danger of feedback into the Soviet Union from this revival of nationalism. As long as the avowed destiny of all Communist states was incorporation into the U.S.S.R. as Union Republics, Soviet leaders could rationalize the status of the Union Republic as representing a higher form of statehood than formal independence. But now that Albania, Bulgaria, Mongolia, and the rest are to become permanent national states, the Union Republic is automatically degraded to second-class, or even dependent, statehood. While this may not be an immediate issue in the Soviet Union, and while the Union Republics cannot realistically envision violent secession, they may become increasingly restive as more and more obscure tribal and ethnic groups are awarded statehood and become independent actors in international diplomacy. Nations like the Ukraine, with nearly 40 million people, are likely to demand either more significant attributes of statehood or a greater share in managing the affairs of the Union.

Instead of being the nucleus of a world Communist state, the Soviet Union, by 1965, was little more than a Russianized socialist multinational state, controlling an East European empire of dependent states. Essentially, the "Russian" character of the Soviet Union ultimately undermined its bid for universalism, since few independent nation-states were willing to recognize the inferiority of their own national traditions or to renounce them in favor of a Russianized civilization masquerading as an international proletarian civilization. Marxist dogma legitimized the rule of the Communist party in the Soviet Union, but nothing comparable existed that could justify system-primacy for the Russian proletariat and its national legacy. Once the party-states had achieved the "dictatorship of the [national] proletariat" and Marxist social and economic objectives, submerged national distinctions began to reappear in the Communist world.

The ouster of Khrushchev in October 1964 seems to have temporarily muted the territorial aspects of the Sino-Soviet conflict. Khrushchev's removal may have been closely connected with his intemperate and shrill overreaction to Mao's interview with the Japanese socialists. Khrushchev significantly was the only Presidium leader who seized upon the territorial issue, and in the eyes of his colleagues he may have deliberately exaggerated the nature and urgency of Mao's territorial claims against the U.S.S.R. in order to inflame public passions against Peking preparatory to a formal break with the Chinese, which the other Soviet leaders may have considered premature. The chronological sequence of events preceding Khrushchev's downfall strongly suggests that his treatment of the territorial issue was a crucial factor in the decision to remove him from authority. The Mao interview took place on July 10, 1964; it was published in the Japanese press on August 11; *Pravda* reprinted the Japanese version on September 2, together with a long and impassioned denunciation. The issue reached a crescendo in mid-September with Khrushchev's interview in Moscow with another group of Japanese visitors when he implicitly disputed the legitimacy of

Peking's rule over Sinkiang and other border areas, hinting that these might more properly be the property of Soviet Asian republics. Less than a month later, he was relieved of power and office.

The territorial issue burned out as quickly as it was ignited. Neither Moscow nor Peking has paid serious attention to it since, although Peking has rebuffed all attempts by the Brezhnev-Kosygin regime to patch over the differences and denounces their policies as representing "Khrushchevism without Khrushchev." The Sino-Soviet territorial issue has thus once again been submerged, but it is likely to surface again and perhaps in more violent form. Yet one must question Mao's precise motives in generating the issue and the choice of forum, although Khrushchev's explosive reaction is fully explicable. It should be emphasized that the Mao interview was not publicized in the Chinese press, nor is there an official Chinese version of his statement. Chinese claims to Soviet territory have not yet been formalized or even given wide currency in China. They have always been expressed esoterically and indirectly. This suggests that Mao's statement prematurely and imprudently reflected a future intention rather than an imminent demand and that Khrushchev sought to bring the issue to the surface and force it to a head, in the hope that the Chinese would take a formal position which could be effectively exploited for his own political ends. His colleagues, sensing that perhaps the Sino-Soviet conflict was assuming the proportions of a personal feud between Khrushchev and Mao, apparently opposed this strategy and sought instead to head off a possible open break between the two Communist giants by de-emphasizing Sino-Soviet differences and purging the polemics of abuse and invective.

14. THE UNION REPUBLICS AND SOVIET NATIONALITIES AS INSTRUMENTS OF SOVIET TERRITORIAL EXPANSION

Vernon V. Aspaturian

INTRODUCTION

More than twenty-five years have elapsed since the Soviet Government dramatically amended its Constitution on February 1, 1944, in the midst of war, to permit its sixteen constituent Republics to establish separate foreign offices, diplomatic services, defense commissariats and national troop formations. By empowering each Republic with the constitutional authority to engage in diplomatic relations, conclude international agreements and organize national armies, the Amendments intended to confer upon the Republics the missing legal essentials of statehood and sovereignty.

Although these changes provided Soviet legal hair-splitters with an unparalleled opportunity to write reams of scholastic and tedious nonsense about the juridical character of the renovated Union, and the diplomatic consequences of these constitutional innovations may have been less than world-shaking, they have also been far from trivial.

These Amendments of February 1, 1944 introduced a new phase in the role of the Union Republics and the Soviet nationalities both as subjects and as pawns of Soviet diplomacy. Any valid assessment of why the Amendments were introduced in 1944 must begin with the somewhat ambiguous and Aesopian justification made by Foreign

Reprinted from Vernon V. Aspaturian, *The Union Republics in Soviet Diplomacy* (Geneva, 1960). Reprinted by permission of the Institut Universitaire de Hautes Études Internationales.

Commissar Molotov to the Supreme Soviet, and the curious comments made by Supreme Soviet deputies from various Union Republics in the brief "debate" which followed, The decision, however, to adopt the Amendments was made not by the Supreme Soviet or in its presence, but in a meeting of the Central Committee of the CPSU, held a few days earlier. Beyond the bare announcement in an information communiqué of January 27, 1944, that the question of decentralizing Soviet foreign affairs was discussed, no other details of the proceedings of this meeting have been made public.[1] Although a more candid exposition than that in Molotov's speech of the reasons why the Amendments were adopted exists in the records of the Central Committee, it is still possible to reconstruct partially the motives which prompted the Amendments, the conditions which made them necessary or desirable, and the range of diplomatic benefits envisaged by the Soviet leaders. This may be accomplished by super-imposing the content of Molotov's report upon the contours of Soviet diplomacy in the years which followed, and by examining the laborious output of Soviet legal exegetes and publicists on international affairs. Furthermore, by means of such a scrutiny, not only the past diplomatic and military successes, near misses and failures of the Amendments can be evaluated, but their potential for future diplomatic mischief can be projected as well.

The general purpose of the Amendments, as pointed out by *Izvestia* two days after their adoption, was to enable the Soviet Union "to acquire . . . a flexible organization which will provide for the further growth of the power of the motherland." Molotov had observed in his report that centralization of foreign affairs "was necessary at a certain stage in the development of our state and yielded its positive results," but that under existing international conditions formal centralization was a drawback. "Changes in the international situation and national development," he said, "call forth organizational changes in the machine of the Soviet state."[2] These changes, he warned, were not designed merely to meet the needs of the individual Republics, but were "dictated by the interests of the Union as a whole:"

> Lastly, it should be acknowledged that this is in the interests not only of this or that individual Republic, but also in the entire cause of the expansion of international connections . . . of the U.S.S.R. with other states, which is of such importance in time of war and which will yield fruit also in the postwar world.[3]

It would be erroneous, of course, to assume that the Soviet leaders foresaw all possibilities and opportunities, carefully plotted all moves in accordance with a time-table, or catalogued all missions of the Amendments with the assiduity of a lexicographer. The changes did, however,

[1] KPSS y Rezolyutsiyakh i Resheniyakh Sezdov, Konferentsii i Plenumov Tsk 1898–1954, three volumes (Moscow, 1954), III, p. 475. *Cf.* also Zlatopolsky, *Obrazovaniye i Razvitiye,* p. 200.

[2] *Molotov Report,* pp. 239–240.

[3] Ibid., p. 241.

immeasurably enhance the flexibility of Soviet diplomacy. The Amendments appear to have been inspired by a peculiar and even fortuitous concatenation of internal problems and external opportunities which required immediate attention. These were: (1) To facilitate the legal incorporation of Western Byelorussia and the Western Ukraine into the Soviet Union by converting an ethically dubious claim based essentially on conquest into the more palatable context of Ukrainian, Byelorussian and Lithuanian national self-determination. (2) To provide a fresh basis for legalizing the accession of the Baltic States to the U.S.S.R. and to make it easier for the United States to retreat from its position of non-recognition. (3) To prepare a juridical foundation for multiple representation in the projected international organization. (4) To provide a legal basis for demanding multiple representation at the Peace Conference. (5) To counter the noxious effects of the renegade national troop formations organized by the Nazis with those formed in the Republics.

These were the urgent and precise objectives of the Amendments, but their enactment, of course, opened up other opportunities as well, such as: (1) To facilitate the accession of new Republics to the Union without disturbing their juridical status under international law. (2) To employ the irredentism (real or contrived) of the border nationalities as a basis for territorial expansion. (3) To permit individual Republics to support their independent diplomatic and territorial adventures with localized military operations without legally implicating the Union as a whole. (4) To create the impression at home and abroad that the Soviet system was on the verge of decentralization and democratization. (5) To create the basis for multiple representation in future international and multilateral diplomatic assemblies and organizations.

The architectonic design of the two Amendments was to transmute serious separatist forces released by the German occupation into useful levers of centripetalization and to simultaneously enable the multinational character of the Soviet state to be employed as an effective instrument of Soviet diplomacy. The Union Republics could be manipulated not only as objects of Soviet diplomacy, but as subjects as well. The constitutional changes would enable the Union Republics to be employed as instruments of territorial expansion by exploiting the manifold ambiguities of the principle of national self-determination and to be manipulated as subjects of plural representation for the Union in multilateral diplomatic bodies and assemblies by taking advantage of the generous elasticity of certain legal norms of international law like multiple sovereignty.

I. MULTINATIONAL SELF-DETERMINATION IN SOVIET DIPLOMACY

The multinational character of the Soviet Union and the fortuitous existence of numerous nationalities inhabiting the entire periphery of the Union from the Barents Sea to the Sea of Japan, which are related to kindred populations living in a dozen border states, afford Soviet diplomacy unique opportunities for exploiting the irredentist claims and national aspirations not of one nation, but of more than a dozen, in the pursuit of its objectives. National self-determination, however, for a multinational state, can be a double-edged sword. If Stalin shrewdly recognized that the Soviet Union as a weak polyglot empire was endangered by the principle of national self-determination, he also realized that the identical principle in the service of a powerful Soviet state could be transformed from a menace into an instrument of Soviet expansion. Accordingly, the Soviet attitude toward national self-determination has been shaped by Lenin's dictum that "one and the same idea in different, concrete, historical circumstances may be, according to the case, reactionary or progressive."[4]

The Bolsheviks, of course, have a long history of independent support for the principle of national self-determination and, together with President Woodrow Wilson, Lenin and Stalin bear the principal responsibility for its introduction into international politics, first as an ethical norm and subsequently as a quasi-legal norm. Whereas for Wilson self-determination had an absolute character and was the ethical justification for the dismemberment of the polyglot German, Hapsburg and Ottoman Empires, for the Bolsheviks it was essentially a utilitarian device of only transitory and relative moral relevance, designed to bring about the decomposition of all multinational states and colonial empires, including the Russian, insofar as such dissolutions promoted the advance of the Communist Revolution. When the convulsive and unpredictable forces thus unleashed by its application after the Revolution threatened to destroy the Soviet regime itself, Lenin and Stalin quickly retreated from their exposed position and resurrected the discarded idea of multinational federalism as a surrogate, not only to arrest the utter disintegration of the former Russian Empire, but also to justify its reconstitution in new guise.[5] By 1921, Stalin could warn that "we have long ago abandoned the nebulous slogans of national self-determina-

---

[4] Andrei Zhdanov in *Voprosy Filosofi*, 1947 (No. 1), p. 263.

[5] Vernon V. Aspaturian, "The Theory and Practice of Soviet Federalism," *Journal of Politics*, and Julian Towster, *Political Power in the U.S.S.R. 1917–1947* (New York, Oxford University Press, 1948), pp. 50–65. Stalin revealed the opportunistic character of his conception of national self-determination even before the Revolution. In 1917, he said: "We are at liberty to agitate for or against secession, according to the interests of the proletariat, the proletarian revolution. Hence, the question of secession must be determined in each particular case independently, in accordance with existing circumstances, and for this reason the question of the recognition of the right to secession must not be confused with the expediency of secession in any given circumstances." J. V. Stalin, *Marxism and the National and Colonial Question* (London, Lawrence and Wishart, 1936), p. 64. The Soviet principle of national self-determination (which is Leninist-Stalinist and not Marxist in origin) was incorporated into the program of the Second Party Congress, held in 1903, a decade and a half before it came to President Wilson's attention. By the time the Bolsheviks seized power, a considerable body of Communist literature on national self-determination was already in existence. *Cf.* V. I. Lenin, *The Right of Nations to Self-Determination* (New York, International Publishers, 1951).

tion," because the principle "has in effect become an empty slogan easily adaptable to the use of the imperialists."[6]

The Soviet regime, however, has never repudiated the idea of national self-determination for all time and even reluctantly accepted it as a legitimate basis for the assertion of independence by the seceding border states which successfully thwarted Soviet domination, but the idea was carefully reformulated within the context of class expressions of national self-determination and unambiguously subordinated to the "higher interest" of the dictatorship of the proletariat to consolidate and extend its power. In accordance with Soviet doctrine, *proletarian* national self-determination has supreme ethical priority over all other forms. It is superior to *bourgeois* national self-determination, which, in turn, is more progressive than imperialist domination or feudal rule.[7]

As a weak multinational state easily subject to national fragmentation, the Soviet Union did not press the application of the principle with either much energy or conspicuous enthusiasm between the two World Wars except for giving it indiscriminate support in the colonial empires. Although the principle in the Wilsonian sense had exhausted its major potentialities in Europe by giving each major nationality its own state, the post-Versailles frontiers were not drawn to coincide faithfully with ethnic or linguistic contours, but had been distorted by the overriding imperatives of geography, economics, power-politics and retribution. Under these conditions, national self-determination was gradually

---

[6] Stalin, *Marxism and the National and Colonial Question*, p. 106. *Cf.* also *Works*, V, pp. 42–43, 48.

[7] "As regards the question, who is the bearer of the nation's will for secession, the RCP stands on the historical class point of view, taking into consideration the stage of historical development of the given nation: is it on the road from medievalism to bourgeois democracy or from bourgeois democracy to Soviet or proletarian democracy, etc.?" *Vsesoyuznaya Kommunisticheskaya Partiya (b) v Rezolyutsiakh Sezdov, Konferentsii i Plenumov Ts.K., 1898–1935*, two volumes (Moscow, 5th edition, 1936), pp. 295–296. "It should be borne in mind," Stalin reported to the 12th Congress in 1923, "that in addition to the right of nations to self-determination, there is also the right of the working class to consolidate its power, and the right of self-determination is subordinate to this latter right. There are cases when the right of self-determination conflicts with another, a higher right — the right of the working class that has come to power to consolidate its power. In such cases — this must be said bluntly — the right of self-determination cannot and must not serve as an obstacle to the working class in exercising its right to dictatorship. The former must yield to the latter." Stalin, *Works*, V, p. 270. After the rise of Hitler in Germany, the Soviet conception of national self-determination acquired another tactical phase: the subordination of the right of self-determination to the struggle against fascism. Thus, on March 11, 1939, D. Z. Manuilsky told the 18th Party Congress that "while upholding the right of the colonial peoples to self-determination, including even secession, Communists follow the teachings of Lenin and Stalin in subordinating the actual realization of this right of secession . . . to the interests of defeating fascism." *The Land of Socialism Today and Tomorrow* (Moscow, 1939), p. 82. After the German attack on Russia, the Comintern ordered a halt to all agitation for independence and self-determination in the British Empire, particularly India, since this was incompatible with the successful prosecution of the war against Germany by Moscow's ally.

transformed from an instrument of national independence into a device for raking in unredeemed territories, that is, into irredentism. In the hands of the revisionist powers, national self-determination became a vehicle not only for the dismemberment of the very states which it had spawned, but also for the territorial aggrandizement of those against which it had been first employed.

After 1933, when Hitler virtually established a monopoly over the principle and converted it into a moral justification for the territorial dismemberment or liquidation of Germany's neighbors, the Kremlin appeared to abandon all interest in the concept because of its dangerous implications for the Soviet Union itself. From the Soviet viewpoint, the troubled waters stirred up by national self-determination in these circumstances provided meager promise for Bolshevik fishing lines, since it would result only in transfering territory from one enemy to another. As *Pravda* prophetically warned when Hitler demanded the Sudetenland on the basis of German national self-determination:

> The Soviet Union views with equanimity the question as to which imperialist robber gives orders in one or another colony, in one or another vassal state, for it sees no difference between German and English robbers. . . . But these questions cannot be a matter of indifference to the "democratic countries" of Western Europe. In agreeing to robbery at Czechoslovakia's expense, and in giving their blessing, Great Britain and France are *playing with fire;* for tomorrow the same questions may be put before them with reference to some territories in Asia or Africa under the domination of the "democratic powers."[8]

Stalinist diplomacy, however, manifested a remarkable capacity for accommodating its style and tempo to the ideological precepts and

[8] *Pravda*, September 21, 1938. Until 1933, the Soviet Union generally supported Germany's claims to her "unredeemed" ethnic territories in Poland, Czechoslovakia and elsewhere. Even the Czech Communist Party supported "self-determination to the point of separation" for the German minority in the Sudetenland. In a speech of June 23, 1938, Litvinov suggested that Moscow's position on the Sudeten question was due to Berlin's hostile attitude and on August 22, 1938, he candidly told Count von der Schulenburg that "if the old democratic Germany still existed, the Czechoslovak question would have quite a different aspect for the Soviet Union. We have always espoused the cause of self-determination of peoples." *Documents on German Foreign Policy*, Series D, II, p. 604; *cf.* also pp. 629–631. In his speech to the 18th Congress, Manuilsky recognized the Nazi appropriation of the principle of national self-determination: "The fascist war-mongers are . . . trying to turn the democratic slogan of 'national self-determination' into a counter-revolutionary weapon for the furtherance of their own aggressive plans. Hypocritically adopting the guise of supporters of national self-determination, they are trying to desintegrate the multinational capitalist states which lie in the path of fascist expansion. . . . The Communists concentrate their main fire in the present historical situation on the fraudulent fascist "self-determination" of nations. Communists lay prime emphasis on the struggle for the achievement of self-determination by the nations enslaved by the fascist states. They demand free self-determination for Austria, which was forcibly annexed by fascist Germany on the eve of the plebiscite, and for the Sudeten region, which Germany seized from Czechoslovakia." Manuilsky, *Land of Socialism*, p. 82.

psychological conditioning of Moscow's diplomatic partners, whether they were fascist or democratic states. During the brief period of flirtation with Hitler, Stalin sedulously tailored his diplomatic strategy to suit the German dictator's political prejudices and psychological preconceptions, without, at the same time, repudiating a single Soviet ideological objective. In particular was this true of the way Stalin skillfully re-chiseled the principle of national self-determination to fit the Nazi irredentist pattern of "race and community" when advancing Soviet territorial claims. Just as Hitler morally disarmed the West by turning the principle against the authors of Versailles, Stalin ideologically disarmed Hitler by couching his claims to territory within the irredentist formula, buttressed by plebiscites, a formula which the Nazi dictator had himself so successfully exploited.[9]

Although opportunities for invoking the principle of multinational self-determination existed on the Western frontiers of the Soviet Union, in the Caucasus, in Central Asia and in the Far East, Stalin advanced Soviet territorial claims only in the West and in the Caucasus, since it was neither opportune nor immediately practicable to advance them in Asia. The collapse of colonialism in the Middle East and Southeast Asia and the triumph of Communism in China, however, not only once again rendered national self-determination obsolete for Soviet purposes, but actually created possibilities for invoking the principle against the Soviet Union itself in Asia.

1. *Ukrainian, Byelorussian and Lithuanian Irredentism*

Before World War II, the Soviet Government did not directly advance territorial claims against neighboring states on grounds of national self-determination. Its only official claim to territory was against Rumania because the Soviet regime had never recognized the annexation of Bessarabia. This claim, however, was juridical rather than ethnic. Unofficially, of course, Moscow retained a deep interest in the Ukrainian and Byelorussian minorities across the border. The Fifth Congress of the Comintern in 1924, for example, stated that it "considers it necessary for the Communist Parties of Poland, Czechoslovakia and Rumania to launch the general slogan of the separation of the Ukrainian lands from Poland, Czechoslovakia and Russia, and their union with the Soviet Ukraine and through it, with the U.S.S.R."[10] This resolution was adopted after D. Z. Manuilsky, the Soviet delegate, invoked the principle of "revolutionary irredentism":

> The question of irredentism . . . has a two-fold form: the question of irredenta between a workers' and peasants' state, and the question of irredenta between two bourgeois states. This group of questions is all the more important as the imperialist re-distribution of the world which followed the European war, has dismembered nations and peoples. The

[9] *Cf.* Hans J. Morgenthau, "The Paradoxes of Nationalism," *The Yale Review,* Summer 1957.

[10] *Communist International,* December 1924–January 1925 (No. 7), 96.

problem of revolutionary irredentism assumed a very concrete form in the relations between the U.S.S.R. and the states adjoining it. Thus, at the Second Congress of the Polish Communist Party, the Polish Party decided to support the movement of the Ukrainians and White Russians forming part of the Polish State for their inclusion into the Workers' and Peasants' Republics of the U.S.S.R. Similar declarations were made by Estonian Communists, Communists of Carpathian Russia, etc.[11]

Although the Communist Parties of Poland and Rumania were commended by the Congress for their support of Ukrainian self-determination, all efforts to stimulate pro-Soviet sentiment among the Ukrainians outside the Soviet Union registered increasingly diminishing returns. By 1938, even the Communist Party of the Western Ukraine abandoned the demand for self-determination and union with the U.S.S.R. in favor of autonomy within Poland.[12] Just as the enthusiasm of the Ukrainians and Byelorussians to unite with their kinsmen in the Soviet Union reached its nadir, the Soviet Government suddenly renewed its active interest in Poland's minorities, by ominously questioning the legitimacy of Polish rule over its eastern provinces when Poland demanded Teschen from Czechoslovakia on grounds of national self-determination in 1938:

> If one were to reckon how many Poles live in the Ukrainian and Byelorussian territories of the Polish State, it is doubtful whether the result of this calculation would serve as an argument in favor of these provinces belonging to Poland. Further, if one is interested in ticklish questions, the answer to the question by what right of national self-determination, and in general by what right, Poland rules the Ukrainian and Byelorussian population, would be no less revealing.[13]

The Nazi-Soviet Period, 1939–1941. In the Secret Protocols to the Nazi-Soviet Pact signed on August 23, 1939, not a word was printed about Soviet claims to Polish territories on the basis of Ukrainian and Byelorussian national aspirations. Actually, in the original delimitation of the territorial partition of Poland, a considerable area of solid Polish-inhabited territory was included in the Soviet share. Apparently the Soviet Government decided to invoke the principle of self-determination as justification for its intervention and occupation of eastern Poland at the last minute. As early as September 3, Ribbentrop invited Moscow to occupy its share of Polish territories, but Molotov pleaded for time and, on September 10, revealed to the German Ambassador that the Soviet

[11] Speech delivered on June 30, 1924 at the Fifth Congress of the Comintern. *Fifth Congress of the Communist International* (London, The Communist Party of Great Britain, 1924), p. 190.

[12] Cf. *Communist International*, Vol. 12, June 20, 1935 (No. 12), pp. 563–564; Vol. 13, April 1936 (No. 4), p. 225; *The Communist International Between the Fifth and Six Congresses — 1924–1928* (London, 1928), p. 228; pp. 299–302. The Western Ukrainian Communist Party was constantly infected with "national deviation." Cf. Walter Kolarz, *Russia and Her Colonies* (New York; Praeger, 1952), pp. 135–140.

[13] *Pravda,* September 21, 1938.

Government "intended to take the occasion of the further advance of German troops to declare . . . that it was necessary for the Soviet Union . . . to come to the aid of the Ukrainians and the White Russians 'threatened' by Germany."[14] The purpose of this argument "was to make the intervention of the Soviet Union plausible to the masses and at the same time avoid giving the Soviet Union the appearance of an aggressor."

Four days later, Molotov told the German Ambassador that the Red Army would move into Poland after the fall of Warsaw and he called attention to an article in *Pravda* attacking the condition of minorities in eastern Poland as preparation for the official Soviet public justification for intervention. Ribbentrop, however, objected to the Soviet plan to justify its action on grounds of a German threat to the Ukrainian and Byelorussian populations, but on the day before the Red Army crossed the Polish frontier, Molotov informed the German Ambassador that:

> The Soviet Government intended to motivate its procedure as follows: The Polish state had collapsed . . . the Soviet Union considered itself obligated to intervene to protect its Ukrainian and White Russian brothers.[15]

Conceding that this course might be "jarring to German sensibilities," Molotov further admitted:

> The Soviet Government unfortunately saw no possibility of any other motivation, since the Soviet Union had thus far not concerned itself about the plight of its minorities in Poland and had to justify abroad in some way or other its present intervention.[16]

This was substantially the justification which was presented to the Polish Ambassador and made public following Soviet intervention. Only after the occupation of the sphere allotted to the Soviet Union, did the multinational self-determination formula begin to assume its subsequent form. Stalin voluntarily, and on his own initiative, surrendered the indisputably Polish-inhabited territories between the Vistula and the Bug rivers to Germany, and, on November 1 and 2, the Supreme Soviet formally incorporated the remaining lands into the Ukrainian and Byelorussian Republics after the organization of sham plebiscites and petitions.[17] On October 27, 1939, the Vilna region was transferred by the Russians to Lithuania, which was in its entirety incorporated into the Soviet Union less than a year later. In explaining this move, Molotov said:

[14] *Nazi-Soviet Relations 1939–1941* (Washington D.C., U.S. State Department, 1948), pp. 86, 91.

[15] Ibid., pp. 92–93 and *Pravda*, September 14, 1939. *Nazi-Soviet Relations*, p. 95.

[16] Ibid., p. 96. *Cf.* also John A. Armstrong, *The Soviet Bureaucratic Elite* (New York, Praeger, 1959), pp. 105–108.

[17] *Cf.* Zlatopolsky, *Obrazovaniye i Razvitiye*, pp. 169–177. For texts of the acts of incorporation, *cf. Sbornik Zakonov SSSR . . . 1936–1956*, p. 21.

> The Soviet Union agreed to the transfer of the city of Vilna to the Lithuanian Republic not because it has a predominantly Lithuanian population. No the majority of the inhabitants of Vilna are not Lithuanian. But the Soviet Government took into consideration the fact that the city of Vilna . . . ought to belong to Lithuania as a city with which are associated both the historical past of the Lithuanian State and the national aspirations of the Lithuanian people.[18]

Byelorussian irredentism had exhausted its diplomatic possibilities with the annexation of Western Byelorussia, although the cession of Vilna to Lithuania hinted at a clash between the irredentism of the two nations. The national aspirations of the Ukraine, however, which was the most territorially dispersed of the nations under Soviet rule, were further utilized to annex Bessarabia and Northern Bukovina from Rumania less than a year later. Although the Soviet claim to Bessarabia for more than two decades had been juridical and its acquisition was rendered possible because of the secret arrangement with Germany, as in the case of the Polish territories, the ethnic principle was nevertheless invoked publicly, not only to ensure a sympathetic response from Berlin, but from the world at large. In its note to Bucharest demanding immediate restoration of Bessarabia, Moscow said:

> In 1918 Rumania . . . robbed the Soviet Union (Russia) by force of . . . Bessarabia, and thus broke the century-old unity of Bessarabia inhabited by Ukrainians, with the Ukrainian Soviet Republic.[19]

The opportunistic character of the ethnic claim was, however, immediately betrayed by the Soviet Government itself, which, instead of uniting Bessarabia with the Ukraine, united most of the province with the miniscule Moldavian Autonomous Republic which was then elevated to the more august status of a Union Republic. In her demands upon Rumania, Moscow said not a word about the Moldavians, but on August 1, 1940, Molotov told the Supreme Soviet that "the Ukrainians and Moldavians who form the main part of the population of Bessarabia obtained the opportunity of joining the united family of Soviet nations."[20]

Together with Bessarabia, the Soviet Union annexed Northern Bukovina. Originally the Soviet Government intended to annex the entire province on Molotov's pretext that "Bukovina is the last missing part of a unified Ukraine."[21] In the face of German objections that a large German minority lived in the southern part of the province, and that the Soviet demand was new and outside previous agreements, Moscow limited her demand only to "that part of Bukovina where the predominant majority of the population is connected with the Soviet Ukraine by common historical destinies, as well as by community of

[18] *Pravda*, November 1, 1939. *Cf.* also Zlatopolsky, *Obrazovaniye*, pp. 181–182.
[19] Text in Jane Degras, ed., *Soviet Documents on Foreign Policy* (London, Royal Institute of International Affairs, 1951), III, pp. 458–459.
[20] Ibid., p. 464.
[21] *Nazi-Soviet Relations*, p. 159.

language and national composition."[22] In spite of the naked character of the Soviet military occupation of the two areas, plebiscites were organized in the territories in order to re-enforce ethnic self-determination with political self-determination, similar to the pattern followed in the Western Ukraine and Western Byelorussia.

After the German Attack, 1941–1946. The German attack on the Soviet Union brought into question the legitimacy of all Soviet annexations of territories, including those from Poland and Rumania. Since Rumania was an enemy state, the annexation of Bessarabia and Northern Bukovina could not excite much interest among Moscow's new allies. But the question of the annexations from Poland aroused fierce passions and stimulated Soviet political and legal ingenuity. Whereas in the Soviet Union's diplomatic dealings with Nazi Germany, national irredentism, strategic necessity and historical association were acceptable rationalizations for naked conquest, in its dealings with the Western Powers, particularly the United States, these justifications alone were insufficient to earn respectability and legitimacy. Since the principle of national self-determination was also a liberal-democratic dogma and Soviet justifications for its annexations had even evoked a sympathetic response among the Western democracies, Stalin adjusted his claim to the same territories to accord more closely with Wilsonian moral prescriptions and the Anglo-American propensity for formal legality. National self-determination in its unique Soviet multinational dimension thus remained a versatile weapon in the Soviet diplomatic arsenal. The Soviet Union not only retained virtually intact all of its annexations made during the Nazi period, but incorporated additional territories as well on the basis of the national aspirations of its Republics.

In September 1939, the Soviet Government had publicly advanced a number of justifications for its military intervention in addition to "its sacred duty to extend the hand of assistance to its brother Ukrainians and Byelorussians inhabiting Poland." These were that "the Polish State and its Government have virtually ceased to exist," that all treaties between Poland and the U.S.S.R. had been rendered inoperative, that Poland was "a fertile field for any accidental and unexpected, contingency, which may create a menace to the U.S.S.R.," and that "its blood-brothers, the Ukrainians and Byelorussians inhabiting Poland, who even formerly were nations without rights . . . now have been utterly abandoned to their fate."[23] While these arguments could legitimately be used to justify *intervention* and *temporary occupation,* after the German attack on Russia and the restoration of relations between Moscow and an Allied Polish Government-in-Exile, only the argument invoking national self-determination could plausibly be invoked to justify *retention* of the territories.

[22] Degras, *Soviet Documents,* III, p. 459.
[23] These justifications were advanced in Molotov's statement to the Polish Ambassador on September 17, 1939, his radio broadcast of the same day, and in his speech to the Supreme Soviet on October 31, 1939.

Although the Soviet Government formally renounced the validity of the territorial agreements with Germany concerning Poland, Stalin refused to disgorge the provinces annexed. In place of the Ribbentrop-Molotov Line, the Soviet Government resurrected the Curzon Line, which differed slightly in Poland's favor, as a political basis for negotiating a final demarcation. The refusal of the Soviet Government, however, to nullify a series of citizenship and nationality laws which blanketed all of the inhabitants of the territories with Soviet citizenship or to alter the juridical *status quo* of the provinces as integral parts of the Ukrainian, Byelorussian and Lithuanian Republics, rendered the repudiation of the Nazi-Soviet agreements little more than an empty formality. Both Molotov and Stalin acted as if the Soviet laws and the constitutional acts of incorporation (the Constitution also stipulates that the boundaries of the Republics cannot be altered without their consent) had suddenly acquired an immutably sacred character and could not be altered, although their existence was made possible only by the Nazi-Soviet protocols, which Moscow had renounced.

After a long period of inconclusive and bitter wrangling, Moscow, on April 23, 1943, severed diplomatic relations with the London Polish Government-in-Exile, after the latter had tactlessly accepted a Nazi invitation to investigate the Katyn Forest Massacre, on grounds that the London Poles were "making use of the slanderous Hitlerite fake for the purpose of wresting from it territorial concessions at the expense of the Soviet Ukraine, Soviet Byelorussia and Soviet Lithuania."[24] It was indispensable that the Soviet Government contrive a new legal basis upon which to justify the retention of these territories.

If the principle of national self-determination provided the moral basis for Soviet territorial claims, Moscow found in the 1944 Amendments the missing legal forms for justifying them under international law. As formal diplomatic entities, the Republics would be empowered to give legal expression to their claims for unredeemed ethnic and historical territories and to exercise all legal rights of self-determination:

> The Soviet Union as a whole and every Union Republic in particular are autonomous subjects of international law with all the rights and obligations toward other states which derive from this status. . . . State sovereignty embodies the right of self-determination, the latter being the right to freely decide all questions relating to the national fate, without, however, infringing in any way upon the rights of other nations. A nation has the right to choose autonomy as a form of its statehood or to enter with other nations into a federation or finally to secede completely, because each nation is sovereign and all nations are equal.[25]

[24] Text in *Polish-Soviet Relations 1918–1943* (Washington D.C., Polish Embassy, 1943), p. 245.
[25] Yevgenyev, *op. cit.*, pp. 76–77. This conception is based upon Stalin's work, *Marxism and the National Question*, first published in 1913: "The right of self-determination means that a nation can arrange its life on the basis of autonomy. It has the right to enter into federal relations with other nations. It has the right to complete secession. Nations are sovereign and all nations are equal." Stalin, *Marxism and the National and Colonial Question*, p. 19.

"It is indisputable," Molotov told the Supreme Soviet in his report on the Amendments, "that the problem of emerging into the arena of external activities has already acquired vital importance for a number of Republics."[26] The most urgent order of business to be dispatched with the aid of the new diplomatic powers of the Republics was the aggravated territorial dispute with Poland. Consequently, it was not pure accident that the Ukraine was the first Republic to organize its Foreign Affairs Commissariat. On February 7, 1944, barely a week after the changes had been adopted, A. E. Korneichuk, Molotov's Deputy Foreign Commissar in charge of Polish affairs, was relieved of his duties in Moscow and appointed with almost unseemly haste as the first Foreign Commissar of the Ukraine.[27] Since the Republics needed a Polish Government to deal with, one was pieced together from a mélange of Kremlin-inspired Polish Communist front organizations to rival the authority of the Polish Government-in-Exile. Almost simultaneously with the establishment of the Ukrainian Foreign Commissariat, the Polish National Council materialized in Moscow, and it was ominously announced that conditions were ripe for "the friendly rapprochement of these two states and . . . the conclusion of special agreements for the strengthening of these friendly connections between them."[28] On March 1st, it was reported from Moscow that the officials of the Polish National Council were already deeply engaged in negotiations with Ukrainian officials, and since one of the most prominent personalities of the Polish group was Wanda Wasilevska, wife of the Ukrainian Foreign Commissar, the intimate character of these relations was beyond dispute.[29]

With breathtaking rapidity, the R.S.F.S.R. organized its Foreign Commissariat on March 4th, and the Byelorussian and Lithuanian Republics followed suit within a month.[30] By fabricating juridical

[26] *Molotov Report*, p. 241.
[27] *The New York Times*, February 7, 1944. Korneichuk, who had been appointed a Deputy Foreign Commissar exactly a year earlier, was dropped as Molotov's deputy on February 3, 1944, the same day that the Ukrainian Constitution was modified. Nikita Khrushchev was simultaneously appointed Chairman of the Ukrainian Council of People's Commissars. *Izvestia*, February 4, 1944.
[28] *The New York Times*, February 7, 1944.
[29] Korneichuk was succeeded as Ukrainian Foreign Commissar by the veteran Comintern functionary and "Old Bolshevik," D. Z. Manuilsky, on July 13, 1944, at least partly because "Ukrainian-Polish" relations were assuming the comic aspects of a private family affair. Ironically, it was Manuilsky who supported Stalin in 1923 against Rakovsky and Skrypnik over the question of separate foreign affairs commissariats for the Republics. *Cf.* Stalin, *Works*, V, p. 344.
[30] The first "Russian" Foreign Commissar, career diplomatic official A. I. Lavrentiev (a specialist on Balkan and Near Eastern affairs) was appointed on March 8, 1944. The Byelorussian Supreme Soviet revised the Byelorussian Constitution on March 26 and K. V. Kiselev was appointed Foreign Commissar on March 30, 1944. P. K. Ponomarenko was simultaneously appointed Chairman of the Byelorussian Council of People's Commissars.

fictions, the Kremlin intended to transform a clear-cut territorial dispute between Poland and the Soviet Union into a bewildering "international" controversy, implicating no less than half-a-dozen legal entities all dancing from strings pulled in Moscow.

As the Red Army crossed the Curzon Line, the Soviet-sponsored Polish National Committee was given *de facto* recognition by the Soviet Government as the administering authority in Polish territory occupied by the Soviet armed forces. This move paved the way for the first bi-lateral diplomatic acts to be conducted by the Union Republics with "foreign states" in their separate capacities. The Ukraine and Byelo-russia on September 9, 1944, and the Lithuanian Republic on September 22, signed agreements with the Polish National Committee governing exchanges of population in the disputed provinces even before the territorial controversy had been definitively settled. The conclusion of these agreements was designed to afford concrete evidence of the diplomatic vitality of the Union Republics and they rarely fail to be hailed as such by Soviet jurists and writers.[31] By embellishing the Soviet Republics with the external ornaments of sovereignty and state-hood, legally affirmed by their international contractual agreements with the Polish National Committee, a serious juridical *lacunae* existing in the Soviet claim could be rectified. As one Soviet jurist was to explain this legal anomaly much later:

> A nation, which has not yet created its own independent state or seceded into such a state, may not be recognized as a subject of inter-national law, because the lack of any public authority deprives this nationality of the capacity for contracting international obligations and guaranteeing their fulfillment.[32]

But as another Soviet jurist points out:

> The struggle of nationalities for the realization of their national sovereignty does not need to take the form of a struggle for an indepen-dent state, i.e., for state sovereignty. . . . A nationality may just as well express the wish to be included in a multi-national state as a member of a federation or as an autonomous unit.[33]

Consequently, in accordance with these juridical gymnastics, Stalin could legally exercise in behalf of the Byelorussian, Ukrainian and Lithuanian nations their rights of national self-determination and pose at Yalta as the defender of the national interests of "All the Russias":

> Some people want that we should be less Russian than Curzon was and Clemenceau was. You would drive us to shame. What will be said by the White Russians and the Ukrainians. They will say that Stalin and

[31] *Cf.* Vernon Aspaturian, *The Union Republics in Soviet Diplomacy* (Geneva, 1960), pp. 174–175.

[32] V. Yevgenyev, *op. cit.*, p. 77.

[33] L. A. Modzhoryan, "The Notion of Sovereignty Under International Law," *Sovetskoye Gosudarstvo i Pravo*, February 1955 (No. 1), 70.

Molotov are far less reliable defenders of Russia than are Curzon and Clemenceau.[34]

Even Churchill was moved to concede that Stalin's "claim was founded not on force but on right."[35]

When Molotov told Count von der Schulenburg in 1940 that Bukovina was the last missing part of a unified Ukraine, he did so only because he was aware that the most sensationally publicized piece of Ukrainian-inhabited territory, the Carpatho-Ukraine, could not be negotiated away from the Germans. During the entire period of Nazi-Soviet collaboration, the Soviet Government not once raised the question of this province which a grateful Hitler had given to Admiral Horthy because of Hungary's exemplary behavior when Hitler occupied Prague and dismembered Czechoslovakia in March, 1939.

The province, however, was not forgotten in Moscow, if only because of its psychological significance as a symbol of Hitler's designs on the Soviet Ukraine. Before the war, rumors were rampant that Hitler intended to use the Carpatho-Ukraine as a lever for dismembering the Soviet State. Although Stalin ridiculed in public the possibility that "there are madmen in Germany who dream of annexing the elephant, that is, the Soviet Ukraine, to the gnat, namely, the so-called Carpathian Ukraine," the Kremlin was genuinely worried in private that the province might be employed by Hitler as a tool for encouraging Ukrainian separatism.[36] When Hitler permitted the native fascist regime to be overthrown by Hungary and the region annexed, the action was recognized in Moscow as a possible sign of impending change in Germany's policy toward the U.S.S.R., which it was.

When and how the question of Soviet annexation of the Carpatho-Ukraine first arose remains obscure.[37] Although the Soviet Union and the Western Powers had solemnly promised to restore the pre-Munich frontiers of the Czechoslovak Republic, curious broadcasts from Radio Kiev early in 1944 demanded that the region be included in the Soviet Ukraine. These broadcasts reached their climax just about the time the province was occupied by Soviet troops. Contrary to previously arranged agreements, Czech administering authorities from the Beneš exile government were prevented from entering the area on one pretext or another, and when "spontaneously" formed local "National Councils" demanded unification with the Ukraine, Molotov informed Beneš that Moscow could no longer remain deaf to the clamor of a Slav brother nation for the completion of its national unity. The province was trans-

[34] James Byrnes, *Speaking Frankly* (New York, Harper and Brothers, 1947), p. 30. *Cf.* also Winston Churchill, *Triumph and Tragedy* (Boston, Houghton-Mifflin, 1953), p. 370.

[35] Churchill, *Triumph and Tragedy*, p. 367.

[36] *Cf.* Stalin's Report to the 18th Party Congress on March 10, 1939 in J. Stalin, *Problems of Leninism* (Moscow, 1947), pp. 603–604.

[37] *Cf.* P. E. Mosely, "Soviet Policy and Nationality Conflicts in East Central Europe," in W. E. Gurian, editor, *The Soviet Union: Background, Ideology, Reality* (Notre Dame, The University of Notre Dame Press, 1951), p. 51, and Armstrong, *The Soviet Bureaucratic Elite*, pp. 108–110.

ferred to the Soviet Union while it was still under military occupation by a treaty signed on June 29, 1945. Although the provisions read that the province "is re-united . . . with its ancient motherland, the Ukraine, and is included in the Ukrainian Soviet Socialist Republic," Ukrainian functionaries neither participated in the negotiations nor signed the treaty in spite of the existence of an independent Ukrainian foreign office.[38] The Treaty, however, was drawn up in the Russian, Ukrainian and Slovak (but not Czech) languages.

At the time the Amendments were discussed in the Supreme Soviet, Ukrainian deputies had predicted a bright future for Polish-Ukrainian and Czech-Ukrainian diplomatic relations, but once Poland and Czechoslovakia surrendered territories to the Ukraine, these visions vanished as abruptly as they had appeared.

Ukrainian Nationalism and Stalin's Diplomacy. The role of Ukrainian nationalism as an active factor in Soviet diplomacy has never been precisely determined and remains shrouded in mystery. The extent to which Ukrainian nationalism and irredentism represented genuine pressures upon Stalin and other Soviet decision-makers has mystified and intrigued both German and Allied statesmen, who watched Stalin with hypnotic fascination as he invoked his "difficulties" with the Ukrainians as justification for his territorial demands. Even the experienced Count von der Schulenburg, in spite of the contrived nature of Molotov's justification for annexing Polish territory, was hoodwinked less than a year later into believing that the territorial demands made in the name of Ukrainian irredentism were due to a formless Ukrainian pressure group exerting its force upon the deliberations and calculations of the Kremlin:

> Regarding the action taken against Rumania, it has aroused general surprise here that the Soviet Union has also demanded the northern part of Bukovina. There has never been any statement of Soviet claims to this region. As is known, the Soviet Government has justified its claim

[38] *Sbornik Deistvuyushchikh Dogovorov, Soglashenii i Konventsii Zaklyuchennykh SSSR s Inostrannymi Gosudarstvami*, XI (Moscow, 1955), pp. 31–32. Cf. *infra*, pp. 194–195. With the annexation of the Carpatho-Ukraine, the unification of the Ukraine was completed, and the Soviet Government could pose as the national redeemer and unifier of the Ukraine (as well as Byelorussia and Lithuania). Cf. Zlatopolsky, *Obrazovaniye i Razvitiye*, p. 212. Thesis 19 of the "Theses on the 300th Anniversary of the Reunion of the Ukraine with Russia (1654–1954)" reads as follows: "The growing might and strength of the Union of Soviet Socialist Republics made it possible to realize the yearning for national reunion which the Ukrainian people had carried through the centuries. The reunion of all the Ukrainian territories was completed thanks to the wise policy of the Communist Party and the Soviet Government. In 1939, the Western Ukraine was reunited with the Soviet Ukraine. Bukovina and the Izmail region were reunited with the Ukrainian S.S.R. in 1940, and Transcarpathian Ukraine in 1945. With the reunion of all the Ukrainian territories, the Soviet Ukraine became one of the biggest states in Europe." *Pravda*, January 12, 1954. In connection with the celebration of the reunion of Russia and the Ukraine, the R.S.F.S.R. ceded the Crimean Peninsula to the Ukrainian Republic on February 19, 1954 *Sbornik Zakonov SSSR . . . 1938–1956*, p. 35.

by the fact that Bukovina has a Ukrainian population. . . . I cannot get rid of the impression that it was Ukrainian circles in the Kremlin who have advocated and put through the claim for cession of Northern Bukovina. On several occasions, for instance during the negotiations regarding the German-Soviet border in Poland, a very strong Ukrainian influence in the Kremlin was evident. Herr Stalin told me personally at that time that he was prepared to make concessions north of the boundary line where it runs through White Russia, but this was impossible in the south where Ukrainians live.[39]

Schulenburg acknowledged, however, that "it has not yet been possible to determine where this strong Ukrainian influence originates," and correctly noted, in one of his dispatches, that "there is no especially influential Ukrainian known to be among the immediate entourage of the leaders of the Kremlin."[40] The two Ukrainian "experts" in the Politburo, Kaganovich and Khrushchev, however, were non-Ukrainians, and Stalin, only a few years earlier, had thoroughly purged all Ukrainian Party and Government leaders who exhibited even a trace of Ukrainian nationalist sentiment.

Playing on the vanity of Western statesmen, Stalin also confided his Ukrainian problems to President Roosevelt at Yalta, provoking a comparable reaction compounded of mystification and ambiguous expectancy. "No one," Stettinius wrote, "has been able to determine the extent of the Ukrainian difficulty, but we, in Washington, of course, had heard talk during the German advance that the Ukraine might leave the Soviet Union."[41] While Stalin's problems with the Ukrainians were real enough, he was putting them to use in the service of Soviet diplomacy.[42] In negotiations, a statesman finds it useful to have a source of internal pressure allegedly beyond his control to use as a bargaining lever. If Hitler had his "Volkdeutsche" and Roosevelt his "Polish voters" to satisfy, then Stalin had his Ukrainians. Stalin deliberately exaggerated the independent role of the Ukraine to enhance his diplomatic leverage and he was successful because the image of his Ukrainian difficulties was cleverly shaped to simulate comparable difficulties which Stalin believed were contrived by his diplomatic counterparts for diplomatic advantage. The mysterious "Ukrainian influence" in the Kremlin was none other than Stalin himself.

2. *Armenian and Georgian Irredentism*

Whereas the Soviet Government justified its territorial demands upon Poland and Rumania in the name of *Ukrainia Irredenta* both before and after the German attack, its demands upon Turkey were framed within irredentist terms only as an afterthought. The postwar

[39] *Nazi-Soviet Relations*, p. 164.
[40] Ibid.
[41] Edward R. Stettinius, Jr., *Roosevelt and the Russians* (New York, Doubleday, 1949), p. 187. Cf. also Aspaturian, *The Union Republics*, p. 102.
[42] Cf. Michael Pap, "Soviet Difficulties in the Ukraine," *Review of Politics*, April 1952; John Armstrong, *Ukrainian Nationalism 1939–1945* (New York, Columbia University Press, 1953).

Soviet Georgian and Armenian claims to territory in eastern Anatolia were little more than an echo of Stalin's unsuccessful effort to extort the same provinces from Hitler in 1940 as part of his price for joining the Axis. No specific provinces were named, and no pretense was made that the Soviet demands were in fulfillment of the national aspirations of the Caucasian Republics. Moscow simply asked Hitler that "the area south of Batum and Baku in the general direction of the Persian Gulf [be] recognized as the center of the aspirations of the Soviet Union."[43] Although Hitler was willing to surrender this part of the world to Stalin, he balked at other demands and no agreements were signed.

The Soviet Union, however, continued its interest in the area. After the War, the Soviet Government revived its claims to virtually the identical territory in the garb of Armenian and Georgian irredentism, encouraged probably by the successful exploitation of Ukrainian nationalism. Soviet designs on Iranian territory assumed a slightly different form in that the Red Army encouraged and supported a Soviet sponsored Autonomous Government in the Azerbaidzhan province of Iran, adjacent to the Soviet Azerbaidzhan Republic. Although Soviet Azerbaidzhan was assigned the preparatory role of fomenting separatism among the kindred population inhabiting the neighboring provinces of Iran, developments did not progress to the irredentist phase. Unlike the Georgian and Armenian Republics, which are the only juridical expression of Georgian and Armenian nationhood, the Azerbaidzhanis are closely related to other Turks and Tatars in the Soviet Union and in Turkey and hence did not constitute the only expression of Turko-Tatar nationhood. Under these circumstances, the Soviet Government could not pose with the same credibility as the legitimate redeemer of Turko-Tatar lands beyond the Soviet frontier. Furthermore, unlike the Georgians and the Armenians, the Moslem Azerbaidzhanis have traditionally looked toward Turkey and Iran for protection, rather than to Russia, who has been viewed traditionally as an oppressor. However, had the Soviet-sponsored Autonomous Republic of Azerbaidzhan survived the withdrawal of Soviet troops, the stage would have been set for its annexation not as *irredenta* but probably as voluntary accession.

Characteristically, the first indications of renewed Soviet interest in revising its frontiers with Turkey assumed the form of a denial by Molotov on October 31, 1939:

> Now a few words about our negotiations with Turkey. All kinds of tales are being spread abroad about the substance of these negotiations. Some allege that the USSR demanded the cession of the districts of Ardahan and Kars. Let us say for our part that this is a sheer fabrication and lie.[44]

[43] *Nazi-Soviet Relations*, p. 259.
[44] *Pravda*, November 1, 1939. This speech by Molotov established some kind of record in the annals of diplomacy for the public display of perfidy. In his report, Molotov denied that the Soviet Union (1) coveted Kars and Ardahan, (2) intended to annex Viipuri and the Finnish territories north of Lake Ladoga, (3) planned the sovietization of the Baltic States (which he dismissed as nonsense), and (4) sought a privileged position in the Straits.

A formalized demand for the two provinces of Kars and Ardahan was initially made secretly on June 7, 1945, when Molotov informed the Turkish Ambassador in Moscow that future treaty relations between the two countries presupposed, *inter alia,* the cession of Kars and Ardahan to the Armenian Republic.[45] When Stalin raised the issue at Potsdam, both Truman and Churchill, who had been alerted by the Turks, immediately threw cold water on the entire prospect.[46]

The Armenian claim to Kars and Ardahan was the most modest and tenable of the Caucasian irredentist demands and it received the most serious attention from the Soviet Government, although the Armenian Republic carried the burden of the propaganda effort. The Soviet claim was remarkably strong by any irredentist standard. Not only were the two provinces historically Armenian, but they also formed a part of the Russian Empire from 1878 to 1918 and were initially seized by the Turks under terms of the Treaty of Brest-Litovsk, imposed upon the Soviet regime by the Central Powers, and confirmed in 1921 by Treaty with the Soviet Government. The Soviet claim aroused widespread and passionate support from expatriate Armenian communities dispersed throughout Europe and the Near East as a result of Turkish policies during the First World War. Virtually all Armenian political groups, including implacably anti-Soviet nationalists, recognized the propriety of Moscow's actions on behalf of the Armenian nation. Notwithstanding the opportunistic exploitation of the Armenian Question by the Tsarist regimes, Stalin was acting in accordance with good historical precedent when he told one reporter that "Russia wants Kars and Ardahan given back to Armenia, because Russia felt they rightfully belong to Armenia."[47]

The Soviet claim was seriously complicated, however, because of the fact that an Armenian population no longer inhabited the two provinces and hence irredentism could not be blessed with the principle of national self-determination as in the case of the Ukraine. Before 1917, the Armenians constituted the numerically preponderant nationality in the two regions, but they were evacuated virtually in their entirety to Russian territory as the Russian Army was forced to retreat.[48] To

---

These notions, he said, were malicious fabrications and slanders invented by the foreign press. Within a year, Molotov proved himself to be a liar on all four counts. The moral is, apparently, that what the Soviet Union covets, it will first deny.

[45] These demands were not made public until June 24, 1945. *Cf.* Necmeddin Sadak, "Turkey Faces the Soviets," *Foreign Affairs,* April 1949, for details.

[46] Churchill, *Triumph and Tragedy,* p. 635.

[47] *The New York Herald Tribune,* October 10, 1945.

[48] Before the First World War, according to one authority, when the provinces were under Russian rule, Kars and Ardahan were populated with 600,000 Armenians, 525,000 of whom retreated into Russian Armenia in the face of the Turkish advance. Of these, an estimated 400,000 remained on Soviet territory and the others emigrated elsewhere. J. H. Simpson, *The Refugee Problem* (London, 1939), p. 71.

further bolster the Soviet position and at the same time to demolish the argument of the Turkish Premier that "there is not a single Armenian living there,"[49] the Soviet Government took the unusual step, first in November 1945, and then in October 1946, of inviting all ethnic Armenians, irrespective of place of origin, former residence, or both, to assume automatic Soviet citizenship by emigrating to the Armenian Republic.[50] Nearly 100,000 Armenians responded, and since the vast bulk of them were survivors of the Turkish massacres and deportations, or their descendants, Stalin not only hoped to impart a moral and humanitarian tone to the Soviet claim, but also to compensate for the absence of an Armenian population in the two provinces.

No sooner had the Armenians made their claim to Kars and Ardahan, than the Georgians unexpectedly made even more extensive territorial demands upon Turkey, laying claim to no less than 180 miles of Black Sea coastal lands embracing the region known in classical times as Lazica. Since the Georgian claims conflicted in part with those of the Armenians, a superficial facade of autonomy was imparted to the actions of the two Republics. These claims were first made by two Georgian professors on the Tiflis Radio and in the Georgian newspaper *Kommunisti* on December 14, 1945, and would have passed unnoted had the article not been reprinted in full in *Pravda, Izvestia* and *Krasnaya Zvezda* on December 20, 1945:

> We appeal [the two professors said] to world public opinion concerning our ancient lands wrested from us by Turkey. This is not a matter of an insignificant territorial infringement, but of the seizure from us of the cradle of our individuality as a nation, of a crime which cut in two the living national body. . . . The Georgian people must get back their lands which they never gave up and cannot give up.

Although Georgian aspirations were vividly expressed in prose, song, poetry and even drama, the effective Western opposition to the modest and more plausible claim to Kars and Ardahan made it highly unlikely that Georgia *irredenta* could be pried loose from Turkey, and the Soviet Government (although Stalin himself was a Georgian) never made a formal diplomatic demand upon Turkey to relinquish Georgia's ancient provinces.

Multiple irredentism in the case of the Caucasian Republics failed principally because the Soviet Union overplayed its hand. Had it restricted its demands only to Kars and Ardahan, the prospects for their recovery might have been better. By coupling them with a demand for "joint control" of the Straits, frivolously exciting the national passions of the Georgians, and sponsoring Communist separatist movements among

---

[49] Cf. Khvostov, "The Facts of the Case," *New Times*, February 1, 1946, for a Soviet rejoinder to Premier Saracoglu's infelicitous observation that there were no Armenians in the region. Cf. also George Ginsburgs "The Soviet Union and the Problem of Refugees and Displaced Persons 1917–1956," *American Journal of International Law*, April 1957.

[50] For the text of the decree of October 19, 1946, cf. *Sbornik Zakonov . . . 1938–1956*, p. 70.

the Azerbaidzhanis and Kurds in Northern Iran as well, the Soviet Union succeeded only in exacerbating the already strained relations with the Western Powers. Since the postwar territorial interests of the Caucasian Republics coincided with "the area south of Batum and Baku" which Stalin unsuccessfully sought to have recognized as a Soviet sphere of influence by Hitler, Moscow's desire for additional territory was undoubtedly genuine, but a strong case can also be made for the view that the manipulation of the irredentism of the Caucasian Republics was chiefly designed as leverage to achieve Soviet objectives in the Straits and to gain generous oil concessions in Northern Iran.

Four months after Stalin's death, the Soviet claims against Turkey were formally renounced with proper diplomatic apologies in an obvious bid for Turkish goodwill.[51] Of all the territories which belonged to the Russian Empire in 1914 (with the exception of Poland and Finland), only Kars and Ardahan were not retrieved by Soviet diplomacy.

II. THE ACCESSION OF NEW REPUBLICS

When the "Molotov Cocktail" was first dropped upon an unsuspecting world, immediate private reaction in Washington was remarkably similar to Berlin's public charge that it was "another attempt to hoodwink the world," and that it was a scheme for the creation of a "Soviet World State." Western journalists freely speculated that the changes might be an invidious device for the communization of Europe and Asia by facilitating the incorporation of new states into the Soviet Union. Although the Comintern had been dissolved in the previous year, the basic presuppositions of Soviet ideology and Stalin's unrenounced doctrine that the U.S.S.R. was a World Soviet State in embryo were still in force, and the fear that the Soviet Union had boldly taken over the functions of the discarded Comintern was by no means unwarranted. Molotov's inscrutable remarks that the constitutional changes "reveal still more fully the historic meaning of the existence of the Soviet Union to the peoples of East and West," and that "the solution of the national problem in the U.S.S.R. is of great importance from the viewpoint of all progressive humanity," was not exactly calculated to dispel these deep anxieties in Western capitals.[52] After all, five additional Republics had been re-shaped out of territories annexed in 1940 — three of them formerly independent states.

Although the new changes would make it possible for states to

[51] In its statement to the Turks, Moscow said that "in the interests of preserving good-neighborly relations and strengthening peace and security, the governments of Armenia and Georgia take the opportunity of renouncing their claims against Turkey. . . . Thus the Soviet Government declares that the Soviet Union has no territorial claims whatsoever against Turkey." *Pravda*, July 19, 1953. *Cf.* also P. Moiseyev and Yu. Rozaliev, *K Istorii Sovetsko-Turyetskikh Otnoshenii* (Moscow, 1958), p. 73. To the last the Soviet Government maintained the fiction that it was acting in behalf of the Republics of Georgia and Armenia.

[52] *Molotov Report,* pp. 238, 244.

accede — voluntarily or forcibly — to the Soviet Union without sacrificing their international identity or forfeiting their separate membership in international organizations, five Soviet Republics already had been added without benefit of these Amendments. Consequently, the Amendments had among their purposes not only to facilitate the accession of new Republics but also to make past annexations politically and juridically more palatable and to facilitate the annexation of neighboring states to existing Soviet Republics of the same nationality.

1. *Legalizing the Accession of the Baltic States*

A problem no less pressing in 1944 than the territorial controversy with Poland was legalizing the annexation of the Baltic States which were subject to imminent re-occupation by the Red Army. The Soviet claim to the three small states was extremely weak morally and legally. They had been under actual Soviet rule for barely a year, in contrast to their existence as independent states for nearly two decades. Even the protean and elastic principle of national self-determination could not be plausibly invoked to justify their retention, because the normal application of this principle would have eventuated in the restoration of their independence. Soviet rule was based on naked conquest thinly veiled by transparently contrived acts of voluntary accession to provide the flimsiest basis for their incorporation. Furthermore, even this flimsy basis would be deprived of what little validity it might possess once the real story of how the small states were bartered away in a series of secret protocols and diplomatic intrigues with Nazi Germany became public knowledge. Stalin was anxious to settle all juridical issues before the secret dealings with Germany became public, since the United States continued to refuse recognition of their incorporation in accordance with the Stimson Doctrine and had even prevailed upon the British to abandon their intention to accord such recognition in 1942.[53]

Stalin's only credible justifications for their retention were historical, economic and strategic, but he was implacably determined to keep possession of the three small countries. Official Washington circles expected that Stalin could somehow be persuaded to restore their independence, and Roosevelt confided to Secretary Hull that when he met the Soviet leader face to face at Teheran "he intended to appeal to him on grounds of high morality . . . that in Russia's own interest, from the viewpoint of her position in the world, it would be a good thing for her to say that she would be willing, two years or so after the war, to hold a second plebiscite in the Baltic countries."[54]

Although *Krasnaya Zvezda* in July, 1943, once again reiterated the authoritative Soviet view that "the Baltic States were and shall remain Soviet states," and an irritated Stalin told Roosevelt at Teheran that the question was absolutely closed to discussion, the view that they could be peacefully pried away persisted with unusual tenacity. The drift of

[53] Cordell Hull, *The Memoirs of Cordell Hull*, two volumes (New York, Macmillan, 1948), II, pp. 1171–1174.
[54] Ibid., p. 1266.

President Roosevelt's discussion with Stalin at Teheran on the question of the Baltic States apparently convinced the Soviet leaders that the Amendments could make the incorporation of the Baltic States more palatable to the legalistic-moralistic psychology of American official and popular opinion. Furthermore, Roosevelt had unnecessarily and imprudently interjected a note of personal political opportunism in the discussion with Stalin, when he pleaded that the Baltic issue was important to him politically because of the views of a large bloc of American voters of Baltic ancestry who had a paramount interest in the independence of the three Baltic states. Stalin's reaction was a grim suggestion that "some propaganda work should be done among these people."[55]

The curious comments made by deputies from the Baltic Republics in the "debate" on Molotov's report to the Supreme Soviet two months after the Teheran Conference revealed that the Amendments were expected not only to mollify the legal and moral objections of Washington, but also to ease Roosevelt's internal political burdens. A Latvian deputy, V. T. Latsis, observed that the changes would be useful in "countering the anti-national counter-revolutionary activities conducted in the United States by representatives of the fascist government which had been overthrown by the Latvian people,"[56] while Yu. I. Paletskis, a Lithuanian deputy said that the three million Lithuanians living abroad (chiefly in the United States) had to be taken into account when judging the necessity of the Amendments.[57]

The small circle of émigré Baltic diplomats and officials in the United States immediately recognized that the Amendments were designed to make a salutary impact on American opinion by eliminating formal barriers to American recognition of their annexation. They wasted little time in denouncing the constitutional changes as a legal ruse to render legitimate the illicit annexations of 1940.[58] The traditional American preoccupation with legal formalities may have persuaded the Kremlin into surmising that clever legal legerdemain would be sufficient to dispel American objections to the annexations since the Amendments gave them the color of independent statehood. Still, had the Amendments been in effect before the war, the irritating problem of recognition might never have arisen. Former Secretary of State Cordell Hull conceded almost as much in his *Memoirs*, where he wrote that the United States was powerless to object to the extortionist pre-annexation treaties of alliance imposed by Moscow upon the three states in 1939, because, since "nominally Estonia, Latvia, and Lithuania retained their governments and independence, there was no diplomatic step we felt

[55] Robert E. Sherwood, *Roosevelt and Hopkins* (New York, Harper and Brothers, 1948), p. 796; *cf.* also p. 861. The question of the Baltic States was unexpectedly raised by Stalin at Teheran due to a misconstruction of Roosevelt's remarks. The President was discussing freedom of navigation for Russia through the Baltic Sea, when Stalin indignantly retorted that the issue of the Baltic States was not open to discussion. Ibid., p. 782.

[56] Zlatopolsky, *Obrazovaniye*, p. 203.

[57] Ibid.

[58] *Cf. The New York Times*, February 7, 1944.

called upon to take."[59] By giving the three Republics their own foreign and defense departments, Moscow, in effect, was re-endowing them with "nominal independence."

Although the adoption of the Amendments made no appreciable impact on the official American determination not to give explicit recognition to the annexations, Moscow made several attempts to inveigle the United States into extending tacit recognition. At Yalta, Molotov and Stalin made a futile attempt to gain the separate admission of Lithuania to the United Nations alongside the Ukraine and Byelorussia, and later made a more serious and persistent effort to gain membership for all three Baltic states to the Paris Peace Conference, in what can be described as backdoor maneuvers to secure at least implied recognition. Other stratagems, like the annexation of northern East Prussia (whose only physical connection with the U.S.S.R. is through Lithuania), the inclusion of the three Baltic Foreign Ministers as members of the Soviet delegation to the Peace Conference, and assorted attempts by the three Republics to join international, technical and functional organizations also failed to induce the United States to retreat from its position. To this day, the United States continues to refuse recognition of the annexations on the basis of the Stimson Doctrine, and in this purpose the Amendments were a distinct failure.

2. Irredentism in Reverse — Karelia and Moldavia

The Karelo-Finnish Republic and the Moldavian Republic were designed to play yet another role in Soviet diplomacy — that of a reverse *irredenta*. Both Republics were organized in 1940; both were fashioned out of territories annexed from neighboring states joined together with lands already a part of the U.S.S.R. Most significantly, the eponymic populations of both Republics, in contrast to the Slavic and Caucasian, were and are the unredeemed kinsmen of neighboring Finland and Rumania. As Soviet Socialist Republics, they were the self-proclaimed custodians of the national sovereignty of the Finnish and Rumanian proletariats and thus their existence constituted a grim threat to the independent existence of both states.

This was particularly true of the Karelo-Finnish Republic which was organized after the war with Finland in 1940 in patent violation of two out of the three indispensable criteria laid down by Stalin himself only four years earlier as pre-conditions for Union Republican status. Not only was its population far less than the required minimum of one million, but only one-third (instead of the required majority) of its people were made up of the eponymous Karelians, Finns and Veps. The only criterion which it met was its location on the border (so, according to Stalin, "The right to secede . . . does not become a meaningless scrap of paper").[60] The capricious existence of the Republic served one purpose only — to facilitate the accession of Finland to the Karelo-Finnish Republic. This mission of the Karelo-Finnish Republic was not

---

[59] Hull, *The Memoirs of Cordell Hull*, I, p. 701.
[60] Stalin, *Problems of Leninism*, p. 563.

simply a national mission, but a higher class mission — a manifestation of *proletarian* national self-determination.

This "higher mission" was implicitly conceded by the Soviet Government soon after the Soviet invasion of Finland in 1939, when a spurious "Democratic Republic of Finland" was created in Moscow with the veteran Comintern functionary and Stalinist crony, Otto Kuusinen, as its President. On December 2, 1939, Moscow signed a "Treaty of Mutual Assistance" with this bogus government. "The time has come," the preamble of this document reads, "to give effect to the age-old aspirations of the Finnish people for re-union of the Karelian people with their Finnish kindred in a single Finnish State." Accordingly, Article I of the Treaty provided:

> In token of friendship and of the profound confidence of the Soviet Union in the Democratic Republic of Finland, and to meet the national aspirations of the Finnish people for reunion of the Karelian people with the Finnish people in a single State of Finland, the Soviet Union agrees to transfer to the Democratic Republic of Finland the districts of Soviet Karelia with a predominant Karelian population, amounting altogether to 70,000 kilometers.[61]

Since the Kremlin does not have the reputation of parting with sacred Soviet soil unless it expects its imminent return with compounded interest (as in the case of the transfer of Vilna to Lithuania in 1939), Moscow's generosity was predicated upon the expectation that Kuusinen would shortly be installed in Helsinki by the Red Army. When the Kuusinen Government failed to advance beyond Moscow and the war with Finland was brought to a close in March, 1940, instead of meeting "the age-old aspirations of the Finnish people for re-union with the Karelian people" by ceding Soviet Karelia to Finland, the Soviet Union united some of the territories ceded by Finland with its Karelian provinces and established the Karelo-Finnish Soviet Republic.[62] Since the new unit contained less than 10,000 Finns and Kuusinen was installed

[61] *Pravda*, December 3, 1939. This generous offer, however, was never made to the "bourgeois" government in Helsinki. In his statement of November 29, 1939 — on the day the war broke out — Molotov fatuously intoned that "had Finland herself pursued a friendly policy towards the USSR, the Soviet Government would have been prepared to discuss favorably even such questions as that of the reunion of the Karelians inhabiting . . . Soviet Karelia with their Finnish kinsmen in a single independent Finnish State." *Pravda*, November 30, 1939.

[62] The draft law on the creation of the Karelo-Finnish Republic was introduced and supported by Andrei Zhdanov on March 31, 1940, and was adopted on the same day by the Supreme Soviet. In his supporting speech, Zhdanov stressed the national and racial kinship between the Finns and Karelians and argued that "the conversion of the Karelian ASSR into the Karelo-Finnish SSR will further the future economic and cultural development of these two related peoples and strengthen their fraternal relationship." *Shestaya Sessiya Verkhovnovo Soveta SSSR (stenograficheskii otchet)* (Moscow, 1940), p. 49. Cf. also Zlatopolsky, *op. cit.*, pp. 178–179. The new Republic included Viipuri and other territories annexed from Finland, but after the end of World War II, when all of the Finnish population fled to Finland, Viipuri and the Karelian Isthmus were unceremoniously detached and incorporated into the R.S.F.S.R.

as its head, the name of the Republic obviously implied that Stalin was contemplating the reunion of the Finns and Karelians within a new framework. When Molotov was in Berlin in 1940, he indirectly sought Hitler's approval for a second opportunity to annex Finland by suggesting that the Finnish issue be resolved "on the same scale as in Bessarabia and in the adjacent countries [the Baltic States]," but was rebuffed by the Fuehrer.[63]

In July 1956, the Karelo-Finnish Republic suddenly — and without prior discussion in the local press or the formal participation of its own electorate — exercised its unconstitutional right to self-liquidation. Kuusinen complained that three-quarters of its population of 600,000 was made up of Great Russians and asked that the Republic revert to its pre-1940 status as an Autonomous Republic within the R.S.F.S.R. and that the "Finnish" part of its name be dropped.[64] No mention was made of the possible impact on Finland by the change, but it was obvious that Stalin's successors had repudiated the "higher mission" of the Republic as a gesture of friendship to the Finns. As compensation for his loss of "prestige," Kuusinen was elevated to membership in the Party Presidium after the expulsion of the Molotov group in July, 1957.

The existence of the Moldavian Republic does not rest upon foundations as fragile as those which supported its sister Republic to the north. But since the Moldavians are Rumanians linguistically and ethnically, except that Moscow has compelled them to use a modified Cyrillic alphabet rather than the Latin alphabet used by their kinsmen in Rumania, its mission during the Stalin era was similar to that of the Karelo-Finnish Republic — to facilitate the union of Rumania with the Moldavian Republic within the Soviet family of nations. Unlike the former Karelo-Finnish Republic, the Moldavian Republic meets all the formal criteria of Union Republican status, but since the communization of Rumania, the class nature of its mission has been clouded. The position of this Republic is unique because it is the only Union Republic which is the unredeemed territory of another communist state, which means that even within the peculiar class context of the Soviet doctrine of self-determination, Rumania is morally and ideologically justified in demanding the reunification of the Moldavians with their national proletariat in Rumania — thus bringing into complete focus class, national and state sovereignty. Because of its sensitive relationship to Rumania, the future of this Republic also appears dim.

While it is true that not a single state (with the exception of the

---

[63] *Nazi-Soviet Relations*, p. 240.

[64] *Pravda*, July 17, 1956. It was claimed that the question of self-liquidation was discussed in an April 24, 1956, session of the Karelo-Finnish Supreme Soviet, although no public announcement was ever made prior to its alleged convocation. Strangely enough, Kuusinen's arguments in favor of dissolution in 1956 were remarkably similar to Zhdanov's arguments in favor of creation in 1940, with one significant exception: whereas Zhdanov stressed the kinship between the Finns and Karelians, Kuusinen emphasized the cultural and historical association of the Karelians and Russians. Cf. A. V. Yurchenko, "The Liquidation of the Karelo-Finnish SSSR," *Bulletin, Institute for the Study of the USSR*, October 1956.

bogus Tuvinian People's Republic) has been taken into the Soviet Union since the adoption of the Amendments, there is ample reason to believe that future accessions were at one time seriously contemplated. Immediately after the war, the leaders of at least one satellite country, Yugoslavia, expected eventual incorporation into the U.S.S.R. According to I. V. Sadchikov, the Soviet Ambassador to Belgrade in 1945, the Yugoslav Foreign Minister, Edvard Kardelj, told him on June 1, 1945, that:

> He would like the Soviet Union to regard them, not as representatives of another country, capable of solving questions independently, but as representatives of one of the future Soviet Republics . . . that is, that our relations should be based on the prospect of Yugoslavia becoming in the future a constituent part of the USSR.[65]

Although Kardelj was told that "it was necessary to recognize the facts as they are at present, namely to treat Yugoslavia as an independent State," and Stalin later dismissed Kardelj's statement as "primitive and fallacious reasoning," it appears certain that the Yugoslav leaders were not thinking in an ideological vacuum.[66] Since Yugoslavia did not share a frontier with the Soviet Union, the contemplated incorporation of Yugoslavia presupposed the prior accession of the continuous countries between the two states. In view of Molotov's earlier rejection as "nonsense" of all speculation "about the Sovietization of the Baltic countries" in his speech of October 31, 1939, less than a year before their forcible annexation, no necessary contradiction existed between Kardelj and Stalin.[67]

Although the Soviet Union is still juridically capable of incorporating additional states, since Stalin's death, and particularly after the events in Poland and Hungary in 1956, the Soviet leaders have apparently abandoned the Stalinist formula of spreading the Communist revolution through the forcible multiplication of Union Republics. The dissolution of the Karelo-Finnish Republic is further evidence that this policy has been renounced as either out of tune with existing political and national realities or is considered to be generally undesirable.

III. The Union Republics and Soviet Diplomacy in Asia

The Union Republics as instruments of Soviet diplomacy have generally outlived their usefulness insofar as Europe is concerned. The incorporation of the Carpatho-Ukraine into the U.S.S.R. not only eliminated the last potential center of Ukrainian separatism outside the Soviet Union, but also signalled the superfluity of the Republics as agents of Soviet territorial expansion in Europe. The last tenable Soviet irredentist demand west of the Urals — that against Turkey — was effectively blocked by the Truman Doctrine in 1947 and renounced by Moscow herself in May, 1953. Furthermore, the system of vassal states

[65] *The Soviet-Yugoslav Dispute* (London, Royal Institute of International Affairs, 1948), p. 38.
[66] Ibid.
[67] *Pravda,* November 1, 1939.

organized in Eastern Europe, rendered the missions of the Republics superfluous in this area and infinitely unappealing to Western Europe.

1. The Central Asian Republics and Soviet Diplomacy

Although the Soviet Government has never formally posed as the national redeemer of the "lost lands" of its Central Asian Republics, the most conspicuous opportunities for exciting the local irredentism of the Soviet Republics are to be found along the southern periphery of Soviet Central Asia. Stalin had limited his irredentist strategy to advancing the claims of Soviet nationalities traditionally associated with Holy Russia or for which Russia in the past has posed as guardian, although he had by no means ignored the explosive potentialities of the national aspirations which might be cultivated in his Central Asian subjects. Essentially, it was a question of proper timing, for Stalin was aware that while it was historically and traditionally appropriate for him to pose as the Little Father of "All the Russias" and the Lord-Protector of the Christian Georgians and Armenians, in view of the fact that the overwhelming bulk of the population in Central Asia (and in Azerbaidzhan) are Moslem Turks, it would have been fatuous of him to masquerade as the Grand Turk.

All along the serpentine southern periphery of the Soviet Union, from the Caspian Sea to Korea, the native nationalities spill over into the adjacent countries of Iran, Afghanistan, Sinkiang and Outer Mongolia. In some cases, the minority segment of these nationalities is found on the Soviet side of the frontier and in other cases on the other side. This naturally complicates the picture for the Soviet Union insofar as conventional national self-determination and irredentism are concerned.

The most important of the Soviet Asian nationalities are segregated into five Union Republics — the Uzbek, Kazakh, Kirgiz, Turkmen and Tadzhik — while lesser nationalities are organized into Autonomous Republics or Regions, mostly within the R.S.F.S.R. The indigenous populations of Central Asia are Moslem in faith, Islamic in cultural traditions and preponderantly Turkic linguistically. These people have been traditionally anti-Russian, non-Christian and oriented toward their Moslem co-religionists in the Middle East. National consciousness in this region was developed only in the Uzbek nationality which, as the successor to the residual authority of the Mongol and Tatar Khans, constituted the native ruling element through whom the Tsars exercised their control. While separatism has always been widespread in this region, it was manifested primarily by the Uzbeks, who flirted not only with independence but with various movements like Pan-Turkism, Pan-Turanism and Pan-Islamism.[68] While the Turkmen, Kirgiz and Kazakhs, like the Uzbeks, are Turkic, the Tadzhiks are Iranic and are linguistically and culturally related to the Persians, Afghans and Pakistanis.

---

[68] For a somewhat romanticized account of Pan-Turkism and its future, cf. Charles W. Hostler, *Turkism and the Soviets* (New York, Praeger, 1957).

In order to isolate and weaken the hold of the separatist-minded Uzbeks, the Bolsheviks organized the five nationalities into five Republics. While this policy served to cultivate and exaggerate the cultural and linguistic differences among the four Turkic nationalities and succeeded in creating four nations where before there was but one, it is also undeniable that this policy of *divida-et-impera* served politically and psychologically to emancipate the four other nationalities from Uzbek domination.[69] All of the Central Asian languages have been provided with modified Cyrillic alphabets which serve not only to further separate them from their Moslem and linguistic brethren outside the Soviet Union, but also to reorient them toward Russian culture and language.[70] The organization of these five nationalities into Union Republics imparts to them a juridical expression of nationhood which could allow them to register irredentist claims against neighboring countries in which are located their national kinsmen.

Originally, the Central Asian Republics were designed to play a pivotal role not in Soviet diplomacy but in world Communism — to generate discontent in European colonial dependencies as a prelude to their communization. Because of the circumstances of internal policies and the absence of external opportunities, their missions were postponed and they actually played little part in Soviet diplomacy or world communism. Their potentialities in this connection were prematurely overrated. The original idea was to create a model eastern Republic which would act as a magnetic attraction to the populations on the other side of the Soviet frontier. This was the mission originally conceived for the Turkestan Autonomous Republic, which embraced much of the area subsequently divided into five Republics. As Stalin observed in 1923:

> Turkestan is the most important Soviet Republic from the point of view of revolutionizing the East. . . . The task is to transform Turkestan into a model Republic, into an advanced post for revolutionizing the East.[71]

Subsequently, for the less noble purpose of facilitating Soviet rule, instead of one "model republic," in Central Asia, there appeared several, but the mission of Central Asia remained unchanged. Thus, when the Kirgiz and Kazakh Republics were established a decade later, one Soviet

---

[69] For the basic documentation on the political and ethnic reconstruction of Central Asia, cf. *Istoriya Sovetskoi Konstitutsii*, pp. 482–498.

[70] The adoption of the Cyrillic Alphabet facilitates both sovietization and russianization. "Of great significance in the enrichment of the vocabularies of the peoples of the Soviet Union is the language of the Russian people. . . . Large numbers of Russian political, economic, agricultural and industrial words are now commonplace in the Turkmen vocabulary." *Turkmenskaya Iskra*, October 16, 1954. The most comprehensive and perceptive work on the russianization of the non-Russian nationalities is Frederick C. Barghoorn, *Soviet Russian Nationalism* (New York, Oxford University Press, 1956). *Cf.* also G. A. von Stackelberg, "The Second Turkmen Linguistic Congress and Its Political Significance," *Bulletin, Institute for the Study of the USSR*, January 1955.

[71] Stalin, *Sochineniya*, V, p. 329; *cf.* also Stalin, *Works*, V, p. 336.

writer vicariously rejoiced in their transcendental revolutionary mission:

> One cannot overlook the fact that Kazakhstan and Kirgizstan are situated on the borders of the Soviet land. They are objects of tremendous interest for their foreign neighbors — China, Persia, and for the comparatively near Afghanistan; every forward step carried out by the Soviet Republics meets with a longing echo in the hearts of those peoples suffering under the yoke of imperialistic States. . . . They see from the example of the national republics located near them and belonging to the U.S.S.R. how national and social liberation can be achieved. . . . We can be bold enough to declare that the transformation of Kirgizstan and Kazakhstan will have a great echo beyond our frontiers.[72]

The usefulness of the Central Asian Republics as handmaidens of Soviet foreign policy presupposed the establishment of three specific conditions: (1) Nationalism in the Republics would have to be domesticated and subordinated to Soviet ideology and reliable native cadres trained who could be counted on not to be corrupted by separatist nationalist sentiment. (2) Soviet power would have to be enhanced to the point where it could challenge British supremacy in the area. (3) The neighboring states would have to remain under foreign colonial control and their populations kept languishing in social and economic poverty visibly lower than that of the adjacent Soviet Republics.

The problem of transforming the Central Asian Republics into model Republics proved to be a formidable operation, and their assigned mission of revolutionizing the East encountered serious obstacles, not the least conspicuous of which was Soviet policy in the area itself. It was not easy to find or train reliable native Communists who could carry out the sovietization of the region because they were invariably drawn from the literate elite of the old social order, and they were attracted more to nationalism than to Communism. As Stalin complained in 1921:

> Communists from the local native population who experienced the harsh period of national oppression . . . often exaggerate the importance of specific national features in the Party work, leave the class interests of the working people in the shade, or simply confuse the interests of the working peoples of the nation concerned with "national" interests of that nation. . . . That, in turn, leads to a deviation from communism towards bourgeois-democratic nationalism, which sometimes assumes the form of Pan-Islamism, Pan-Turkism.[73]

When Stalin was criticized in 1923 for supporting Sultan-Galiyev, who betrayed communism in favor of Pan-Turkism, he answered:

> As far back as the beginning of 1919, the "Left" Comrades reproached me with supporting Sultan-Galiyev, with trying to save him for the

---

[72] S. M. Dimanshtein, in *Revolyutsiya i Natsionalnosti*, July 1936, as cited in Kolarz, *Russia and Her Colonies*, p. 258.
[73] Stalin, *Works*, V, pp. 28–29; see also p. 300.

Party, with wanting to spare him, in the hope that he would cease to be a nationalist and become a Marxist. . . . There are so few intellectuals, so few thinking people, even so few literate people, generally in the Eastern republics and regions, that one can count them on one's fingers. How can one help cherishing them? It would be criminal not to take all measures to save from corruption people of the East whom we need and to preserve them for the Party.[74]

Strenuous efforts to develop reliable native Communist leaders were periodically frustrated not only by the persistent attraction of nationalism, but also by the schisms which developed within the Party, with the Central Asian Communist Parties producing their individual quotas of Trotskyites, "Leftists" and "Rightists," who had to be purged. These purges reached their climax in 1938, when the two outstanding Communist leaders of Central Asia, Faizulla Khodzhayev, Chairman of the Uzbek Council of People's Commissars, and Akmal Ikramov, the First Secretary of the Uzbek Communist Party, were tried with Bukharin and the "Rightists" and executed for alleged nationalist and separatist activities.[75]

Consequently, sovietization in Central Asia was carried out principally by Russians and other non-Turks. Since the Moslem faith was persecuted by nominal Christians, the Islamic culture assaulted by the Russians, and local nationalism stifled by alien bureaucrats assigned by Moscow, sovietization of the Central Asian Republics, as far as the natives were concerned, was indistinguishable from colonialism, a fact which Stalin frequently noted with distress and chagrin. The industrialization of the Republics brought in hordes of Russians to infest the metropolitan centers, while the collectivization and mechanization of agriculture decimated the local population, especially the nomadic Kazakhs, and resulted in the deportation of hundreds of thousands of Ukrainian peasants to take over lands expropriated from the native landholders by Russian Commissars.

The general unreliability of the Central Asian Turks as well as of other Moslem groups was amply demonstrated during World War II, when thousands deserted to the Germans and were recruited into various national legions to fight against the Soviet regime.[76]

Since the war, a new generation of Central Asians has grown up under Soviet rule, from which a corps of comparatively young and reliable native leaders have been recruited and educated. For the most part, they are russianized and bi-lingual, and while not completely immune from the infection of local nationalism, they probably have a greater vested stake in the Soviet system than in separatism. Although the influx of Russians into Central Asia has been enormous, most of the high Republican offices are staffed with fairly reliable, if not always

---

[74] Ibid., p. 310.

[75] Cf. In the Case of the Anti-Soviet "Bloc of Rights and Trotskyites" (Moscow, 1938).

[76] Cf. Aspaturian, The Union Republics, Chapter VII, note 14.

competent, indigenous Communists. Russians are still conspicuously evident in strategic posts in the Party apparatuses, while many key executive and administrative posts in the Republican Governments are also still occupied by Russians. Virtually all military, police and economic posts are staffed by Russians and the post of Second Secretary of the Party is normally held by a non-native Communist.[77]

Russian domination of the Central Asian Republics varies from one Republic to another and depends not only upon the size of the Russian population, but also upon the competence, size and reliability of the native Communist elite. The Kazakh Republic is now virtually governed as a second Russian Republic, since the native Kazakhs, who are the most primitive of the Central Asian Turks, have been reduced to less than a majority in their own Republic. The Republic least infested with Russians is the Tadzhik, and since they are not Turks, they probably are the most reliable of the Central Asian peoples.[78]

The relationship between Party and State in Soviet Central Asia faithfully mirrors that of the Soviet system as a whole, but since the Party is controlled by Russians and Republican governmental officials are natives for the most part, the power relationship is not dissimilar from traditional forms of indirect colonial rule. Instead of a Governor-General issuing orders to a native Emir, a Russian Party Secretary (who gets his orders from Moscow) issues instructions to a native Presidium Chairman or Premier. The rules and the ruled are still separated by race, religion, language and culture. It would be a mistake to exaggerate the colonial features of Soviet rule, since they are not designed to be permanent but are imposed by the objective consequences of trying to achieve and secure preconceived ideological and social objectives. Furthermore, in recent years, Moscow has been scrupulous in its concern to establish a proportional quantitative distribution (not necessarily qualitative) of posts in both Party and State corresponding to the population ratios between Russians and natives.[79] Moreover, native Communists are also to be found in increasing numbers in Party and State posts of the Central Government, although not proportional to their population.

What is most important, however, is that a numerically impressive native intelligentsia, made up of government and Party officials, scien-

[77] Cf. the excellent analysis by H. Carrère D'Encausse and A. Benningsen, "Pouvoir Apparent et Pouvoir Réel dans les Républiques Musulmanes de l'U.R.S.S." in *Problèmes Sovietiques*. April 1958, pp. 57–73.

[78] The Kazakhs, who were reduced in number by nearly a million inhabitants between the time of the Soviet censuses of 1926 and 1939, by that time were already less than a majority in their own Republic. Since then the population of the Republic has grown from 6,094,000 to 9,301,000 in 1959, as a result of great population movements eastward, mass deportations of unreliable nationalities and individuals, the rapid industrialization program and the "virgin lands" projects. The Turkmen and Kirgiz Republics are also threatened with the loss of their slender majorities.

[79] Cf. D'Encausse and Benningsen, "Pouvoir Apparent et Pouvoir Réel dans les Républiques Musulmanes de l'U.R.S.S."

tists, technicians and intellectuals, loyal to the Soviet regime have been trained, especially in the Uzbek Republic.

Just as Moscow had weeded its Central Asian garden of most of the poisonous nationalist and separatist growth and had enhanced its power to the point where it could challenge the supremacy of Britain, the entire colonial structure collapsed in the Middle East and Southeast Asia. Instead of colonial dependencies, the Central Asian Republics were now competing with a number of highly nationalistic independent states, threatening the mission of the Central Asian Republics with immediate oblivion. While genuinely native Soviet Asian Republics might conceivably have a magnetic attraction for nations under colonial rule, it has yet to be demonstrated that "national self-determination" within the Soviet framework is a more powerful attraction than what Soviet ideologists call "bourgeois-nationalist" independent states. Countries like Iran and Afghanistan (and recently Iraq), however, which continue to be governed by feudal and semi-feudal social orders may still be susceptible to such attractions. Consequently, a radical reformulation of the missions of the Central Asian states was necessary.

Since Stalin's death, Soviet policy in Central Asia has undergone a substantial alteration, both in the direction of more intense russification and de-russification. While the Kazakh Republic is being increasingly russified by the "Virgin Lands" program and the accelerated industrialization of the Republic, the Uzbek Republic is being simultaneously de-russified. Stalin's crude and currently inopportune multidimensional irredentist formula has been jettisoned as an instrument of Soviet diplomacy, and the original notion of a "model republic" has been resurrected, not as an instrument of revolution, but of diplomacy. Instead of being used to expand the territory of the U.S.S.R., the Central Asian Republics are to be used as diplomatic spearheads to establish Soviet influence among the new independent states of Asia and Africa, to swing them into the Soviet diplomatic orbit as a prelude to their eventual and inexorable gravitation to communism.

Khrushchev has taken great pains to emphasize that the Soviet Union "is simultaneously a European and Asian power,"[80] but for this claim to have a non-colonial validity and a legitimate basis for asserting a role in Afro-Asian affairs, Soviet Asian States must be under the control of Asians and the benefits of Soviet policy channeled to the native Central Asian populations. To implement the Soviet bid for a role in Asian affairs, Khrushchev has employed a device almost elemental in its simplicity — that of a chosen instrument to promote Soviet objectives in all Asia and Africa, not simply as a means for the accretion of marginal border territories.

Moscow's chosen instrument in Asian-African affairs is the Uzbek Republic, the closest approximation to a model republic in Central Asia. The Uzbeks, who are the most populous, virile, culturally advanced and politically articulate nationality in Central Asia, are the traditional ruling nationality and were the chief instruments of indirect Tsarist rule

[80] Khrushchev speech in Rangoon, December 6, 1955. Full text in *International Affairs* (Moscow), January 1956 (No. 1), p. 236.

before the Revolution. Thus, in more respects than one, current Soviet policy is a refinement of the methods of its predecessor. The Uzbek Republic contains the ancient Islamic centers of Central Asia, is sufficiently populated with Russians to establish a balance between the security interests of Moscow and Uzbek ethnic supremacy, and is one of the most highly industrialized and mechanized states of Asia, ranking only behind Japan, China and India. Soviet policy in Central Asia currently appears to assume the pattern of russifying the Kazakh and Kirgiz Republics by flooding them with Russians, possibly as a bulwark against China, while sharing real authority in this area with the powerful Uzbek nation, in a shrewd effort to convert it from a center of separatism into an instrument of centralization. This is an apparent reversal of the Stalinist policy of isolating the Turkic nationalities from their old ruling group. The concrete application of this new policy is taking place at three levels: (1) The acceleration of the "Uzbekization" of the local Party and Government apparatus; (2) the admission of native Uzbeks to the inner sanctum of Soviet power, such as the appointment of N. A. Mukhitdinov as a full member of the Party Presidium and Secretariat in Moscow; (3) the employment of Uzbek state officials as formal and informal representatives of Soviet diplomacy in Asian and African affairs.[81] A further elaboration of this policy may develop into the recruitment of selected Uzbek officials into the Soviet diplomatic service for appointment in Moslem and Asian countries.

Alongside the Uzbek Republic, the small Tadzhik Republic appears destined to play a subsidiary role in relations with the Iranic-Moslem countries of Iran, Afghanistan and Pakistan, with which it shares cultural, historical, religious and linguistic traditions and treasures.

This unique and clever shift in the manipulation of the Central Asian Republics can have far reaching diplomatic results and should not be underestimated. Under any standards, the industrial and cultural progress of the Uzbeks and Tadzhiks has been impressive, and if it can be demonstrated that a substantial proportion of the material benefits of Soviet rule is enjoyed by the native populations, then model republics have indeed been established. Although from the standpoint of European standards the economic and cultural progress of the Uzbek Republic may be uninviting, the harsh truth is that its social, cultural and economic development has clearly outstripped that of its adjacent independent neighbors, and for this reason it may turn out to be a powerful magnet for Soviet diplomacy. Aside from political rights, which the vast majority of the populations of Asia and Africa have never enjoyed or exercised, and religious freedom, which often has been a brake on progress in the Moslem countries, the Uzbek Republic tends to approach the notion of a model republic in Eastern eyes.

2. *Soviet and Chinese Communist Multinationalism in Rivalry*

The Kazakh and Kirgiz Republics were designed to play a role with respect to Sinkiang corresponding to that contrived for the other three Central Asian Republics in relation to Iran and Afghanistan. Sinkiang is

81 *Cf.* Aspaturian, *The Union Republics,* Chapter VIII.

united by geography, religion, culture and language more with the people of Soviet Central Asia than with China, but more with China than with Russia — facts which are appreciated by both Chinese and Russians. Important Kazakh and Kirgiz minorities live in Sinkiang, but the most numerous Turkic nationality is the related Moslem Uighur, which number approximately three million.[82] Both China and the Soviet Union have sizeable Mongol minorities living respectively south and north of the Mongol People's Republic, which is a Soviet satellite only recently detached from China.

Chinese cultural influences among Soviet minorities radiate as far westward as the North Caucasus to the steppe country of the Buddhist Kalmyks. In 1923, Stalin — ironically, in retrospect, since he liquidated their Republic for collaboration with the Nazis — singled out the Kalmyks for special concern as even more important than the Ukrainians in Communist revolutionary strategy:

> The Eastern peoples, which are organically connected with China
> . . . are of primary importance for the revolution. The relative impor-
> tance of these small nationalities is much higher than that of the
> Ukraine. If we make a slight mistake in the Ukraine, the effect upon the
> East will not be great. . . . We have only to commit a slight mistake in
> the small Kalmyk Region, the inhabitants of which are connected with
> Tibet and China, for the effect to be far worse.[83]

As one moves eastward across Siberia, Chinese influences — cultural and religious — are more in evidence, particularly east of Tuva. Most of these territories, whose indigenous Tungusic, Mongol and Turkic tribes (except for the orthodox Yakuts) have cultural and historical ties with China (which may not impel them toward Peking but nevertheless makes them objects of Chinese attention) were at one time nominally parts of the Celestial Empire and were considered by Kuomintang authorities to be unredeemed Chinese territories.[84] Some provinces, like Outer Mongolia and Tuva, were juridically parts of China as recently as fifteen years ago, and it is not likely that the Chinese, who have long memories, have forgotten these border provinces or have irrevocably renounced their claims. Both regions, the latter incorporated

[82] Cf. Owen Lattimore, *Pivot of Asia* (Boston, Little Brown, 1950), pp. 103–151 for an ethnographic analysis of Sinkiang.
[83] Stalin *Works*, V, p. 283. The Kalmyks, like the Buryat-Mongols, are adherents of the Lamaistic Buddhist sect and acknowledge the spiritual authority of the Dalai Lama in Tibet. In December 1943, the Kalmyk Republic was dissolved and its entire population deported to Siberia. This action was denounced by Khrushchev in 1956 and the Republic was restored first as an Autonomous Oblast and then reconstituted as an Autonomous Republic in its former location. Cf. *Izvestia*, February 12, 1957 and *Zakony SSSR*, 22–25 *Dekabrya 1958*, p. 122. In view of Peking's bigger mistake in Tibet, Moscow's "slight mistake" with respect to the Kalmyks need have no serious repercussions in China or Tibet.
[84] Cf. Allen Whiting, "Foreign Policy of Communist China," in Macridis, *op. cit.*, p. 268, for a tabulation of China's "Lost Territories" as compiled by Chinese Nationalist sources.

into the R.S.F.S.R. in 1944, and the former proclaimed independent in 1946, have long been under Russian and Soviet influence, but they were detached from a Kuomintang China recently enough to warrant their return to a "People's China."

Chinese Communist leaders still retain an interest in all of the territories which were historically part of the Chinese Empire. In 1936, Mao Tse-tung stated to Edgar Snow:

> It is the immediate task of China to regain all our lost territories. . . . We do not, however, include Korea, formerly a Chinese colony. . . . The Outer Mongolian republic will automatically become a part of the Chinese federation, at their own will. The Mohammedan [Sinkiang] and Tibetan peoples, likewise, will form autonomous republics attached to the Chinese federation.[85]

This point was re-emphasized five years later in a Chinese Communist statement of April 21, 1941, that "the sacred task of the whole Chinese people" is "to win back all the lost lands of China."[86]

China's unredeemed territories, however, are not populated by Chinese, but by peoples related to her border minorities, with the exception of the Russians and Ukrainians who form the bulk of the population of the Soviet Far East. But China, like the Soviet Union, claims to be a multinational state, although not with the same degree of legitimacy. Of the more than 600,000,000 people of China, Peking recognizes only 6% to be national minorities, but these minorities inhabit roughly 60% of the country's total territory.[87]

The attitude of the Chinese Communists toward the juridical organization of the Chinese multinational state betrays a curious and revealing evolution. Orginally, in patent imitation of the Soviet Union, the Chinese leaders approached the principle of national self-determination for China's minorities within the same juridical formula upon which the Soviet federation was based. In 1930, according to a resolution of the First All-China Congress of Soviets:

> In such regions as Mongolia, Tibet, Sinkiang . . . in which a majority of the population belongs to another, non-Chinese nationality, the

[85] Edgar Snow, *Red Star Over China* (Modern Library, 1944), p. 96.

[86] Anna Louise Strong, *China's New Crisis* (London, n.d.), p. 50. At the time the statement was made, in view of the fact that it was accompanied by a declaration of support for Soviet policies in Outer Mongolia, it was widely interpreted that Outer Mongolia was beyond the scope of this "sacred task". One Chinese Communist writer rationalized in 1950 that reunification of Outer Mongolia was undesirable because Outer Mongolia was well on the road to socialism whereas China was entering into the phase of New Democracy. Cf. John De Francis, "National and Minority Policies," in H. A. Steiner, editor, *Report on China* (Philadelphia; The Annals for September, 1951), p. 149. It is well known that in the Communist view changing conditions can reshape national missions, and when China overtakes Mongolia on the highroad to Communism, it is not unlikely that the question of reunification may be reopened.

[87] Liu Shao-chi, *The Political Report of the Central Committee of the Communist Party of China to the Eighth National Congress of the Party* (Peking, 1956), p. 71.

toiling masses of these nationalities have the right to determine by themselves whether they want to secede from the Chinese Soviet Republic and form their own independent state, *or to join the Union of Soviet Socialist Republics*, or to form an autonomous region of the Chinese Soviet Republic.[88]

By November 1931, the formula was modified to exclude the right of secession to join the U.S.S.R.:

> The Soviet Government of China recognizes the right of self-determination of the national minorities in China, their right to complete separation from China, and to the formation of an independent state for each national minority. All Mongolians, Tibetans . . . and others living on the territory of China shall enjoy the full right to self-determination, i.e., they may either join the Union of Chinese Soviets or secede from it and form their own state as they prefer.[89]

Within a few years national self-determination within the secessionist formula was apparently renounced in favor of limiting it to autonomy for the non-Chinese nationalities within a federal union, as evidenced, for example, by Mao's statement to Edgar Snow in 1936 that Outer Mongolia would automatically become a part of the Chinese federation. In 1945, Mao Tse-tung was still expounding the idea of the New China granting the non-Chinese minorities "the right of self-determination and of forming a Union with the Hans [the Chinese] on a voluntary basis" within the context of a "Union of Democratic Republics."[90] First the right of the border regions to secede and join the Soviet Union, then the right to secede itself, and finally, after victory, the right to be organized into a federal unit were successively jettisoned in favor of what the Chinese Constitution now unambiguously defines as a "unified, multi-national state."[91] This idea was emphatically reaffirmed in January, 1958, when Peking ominously reminded the non-Chinese nationalities that China is "not a federation of Republics." In a long article condemning the "dangerous nature and seriousness of separationist activities" among the minorities, the Peking *People's Daily* accused the nationalities of exhibiting hostility toward Han bureaucrats sent out to the border regions by Peking and warned them, particularly the Uighurs in Sinkiang, that the Chinese authorities would not tolerate any move to establish national republics either within the framework of a federal union or as independent states.[92]

Just as the collapse of colonialism in the Middle East and in Southeast Asia forced a redefinition of the mission of the Turkmen, Uzbek and

---

[88] *Sovety v Kitaye* (Moscow, 1933), p. 440. (Italics added.)

[89] Constitution of the Soviet [Chinese] Republic (November 7, 1931), in Conrad Brandt, et al., *A Documentary History of Chinese Communism* (Cambridge, Harvard University Press, 1952), p. 223.

[90] Mao Tse-tung, *The Fight for a New China* (New York, 1945), pp. 35, 44.

[91] *Constitution of the People's Republic of China, 1954* (New York, Far Eastern Reporter, New York, n.d.), Article 3.

[92] *The New York Times,* January 18, 1958.

Tadzhik Republics, so the victory of Communism in China has not only rendered obsolete whatever missions were originally envisaged for the Kazakh and Kirgiz Republics, but threatens to turn the multinational irredentist formula against the Soviet Union itself. In Sinkiang province and in Inner Mongolia, Peking has forged a chain of autonomous regions for its non-Chinese nationalities, adjacent either to the mosaic of ethno-autonomous units in the Soviet Union or to the southern border of Moscow's Mongolian satellite. Most of Sinkiang has been organized into the Sinkiang Uighur Autonomous Region, but along the borders of Soviet Central Asia, China has established Tadzhik, Kirgiz, Kazakh and Mongol autonomous regions.[93] Who will attract whom is destined to be an intriguing question.

Not without reason did Peking, in April 1954, with much ceremony, move the bones of Genghis Khan to Inner Mongolia and erect an impressive mausoleum in 1955. As one writer observes, "it is a gesture which cannot be dismissed lightly," for "it suggests that the Chinese Communist leaders in Peking are aware of the long range political implications of the fact that they now have in their possession historic relics of great significance to all Mongols."[94] On June 7, 1958, for reasons best known to itself, the Presidium of the Supreme Soviet of the U.S.S.R. decreed an obscure amendment to the Constitution, altering the name of the Buryat-Mongol ASSR to simply the Buryat ASSR.[95]

Not only has the triumph of Communism in China virtually erected a barrier to Soviet direction of the Communist movement in the Far East, but along the Sino-Soviet frontier, the principle of national self-determination once more has the grim potentialities of becoming an instrument for the dismemberment of the U.S.S.R. rather than for its aggrandizement, although this appears to be remote for the present. Khrushchev is not unaware of the potential friction and rivalry between China and the Soviet Union, as Chinese population pressures mount and China's industrial and military power progressively increases. Publicly at least, Soviet leaders continue to dismiss the possibilities of Sino-Soviet friction. In his characteristically quaint but revealing manner, Khrushchev told the Burmese:

> I often have to talk with foreigners [he said, in a speech at Rangoon University]. Not so long ago I had a talk with a bourgeois leader who offered me 'good advice.' He said: 'The Soviet Union is helping China a great deal. Is it right for you to do that? After all, you have a population of 200 million, whereas China has 600 million. Isn't that dangerous to your state? When China has set up an industry of her own and consolidated her independent state she will threaten the Soviet Union. . . . A strong China will threaten both the Soviet Union and other European

[93] The juridical basis for national autonomy is covered by Articles 67–72 of the 1954 Constitution. All autonomous regions are governed from the center and there is, of course, no right to secede. Cf. Peter S. H. Tang, *Communist China Today* (New York, Praeger, 1957), pp. 205–212.

[94] Howard L. Boorman, "The Borderlands and the Sino-Soviet Alliance," in *Moscow-Peking Axis* (New York, Harper and Brothers, 1957), p. 157.

[95] *Zakony SSSR . . . 22–28 Dekabrya 1958*, p. 122.

countries — she will bring pressure to bear upon them.' . . . Under the law prevailing in the capitalist world, unless you oppress someone you will be oppressed yourself. . . . We follow a different doctrine. . . . We say that if there is an equitable distribution of the wealth created by man and if there is no exploitation of man by man . . . all men will be brothers regardless of the color of their skin.[96]

Irrespective of the Soviet leaders' blind ideological faith, they are quite aware that the paradise on earth about which they wax so eloquently is far from fulfillment and that before the conditions about which Khrushchev spoke materialize, national rivalries, even among Communist states, will be resolved not by the fabric of good intentions, but by the configurations of power. In an earlier speech to the Indians, Khrushchev shrewdly noted:

> We must view things soberly and assess the situation correctly. Every beast has its own food. The tiger, for example, lives on meat, and the buffalo on grass. You cannot force the buffalo to feed on meat, nor the tiger to feed on grass.[97]

The Soviet Premier may be expert in taming Uzbeks, but it is doubtful whether he really believes that he can train the voracious Chinese tiger to feed on grass.

[96] *International Affairs*, No. 1 (Moscow, January 1956), p. 236.
[97] Speech of November 26, 1955, *International Affairs*, No. 1 (Moscow, January 1956), p. 199.

15. INTERNAL POLITICS AND FOREIGN POLICY IN THE SOVIET SYSTEM[1]

Vernon V. Aspaturian

SOCIAL STRUCTURE AND FOREIGN POLICY IN THE SOVIET SYSTEM

Marxist thinkers were among the earliest to analyze systematically the interconnection between internal politics and foreign policy. Marx and Lenin both characterized foreign policy as the continuation of

Reprinted from R. Barry Farrell, editor, *Approaches to Comparative and International Politics* (Copyright 1966 by Northwestern University Press). Reprinted by permission.

[1] The intentions and political objectives attributed to Khrushchev in this chapter are applicable with equal force to his successors, Brezhnev, Kosygin, and Mikoyan, who were members of the Khrushchev faction. They have been pursuing essentially the same policies but with less bombast, irascibility, and personal identification, and with more sophistication, rationality, and open-mindedness to innovation and criticism. Khrushchev's colleagues apparently viewed him as the chief barrier to the successful execution of the very policies with which he had come to be identified in the public eye. In the realm of foreign policy, the decision to remove Khrushchev may have been prompted by the conviction that he had become a personal impediment in the way of a reconciliation with Peking. His sudden removal, however, also plunged the Communist world into temporary confusion and provoked widespread criticism in Eastern Europe and in Western European Communist parties, whose leaders had also identified themselves with Khrushchev's policies. His removal may have also served to mollify temporarily the factional opposition to his policies in the Soviet leadership itself, although the main factional and socio-functional and socio-institutional cleavages described in this chapter have remained substantially intact. Khrushchev's successors have actually accelerated the implementation of his tension-lessening policies, and relations with China have deteriorated even more,

domestic politics. According to Marxist and Soviet observers, the state as the instrument of the dominant ruling class articulates the interests of the ruling class outside the boundaries of the state under its control. What passes as the interest of the state, the "national" interest, is in effect the interest of the ruling class in society. In foreign policy as in domestic policy, the state is viewed as the chief instrument for defending the existing social order from external threats and for promoting the interests of its ruling class abroad.

Soviet definitions of "foreign policy," "diplomacy," and "international law" have betrayed remarkable uniformity over the years in terms of their class-oriented character. A leading Soviet authority on diplomacy defined foreign policy in 1949 as follows:

> Foreign policy is a combination of the aims and interests pursued and defended by the given state and its ruling class in its relations with other states, and the methods and means used by it for the achievement and defense of these purposes and interests. The aims and interests of a state in international relations are realized by various methods and means: first of all, by peaceful official relations, maintained by a government, through its special agencies, with the corresponding agencies of their states; by economic, cultural and other contacts, maintained by state agencies, as well as by public and private institutions (economic, political, scientific, religious, etc.), which provides a state with wide opportunities for exercising economic, political and ideological influence on other states; finally by using armed forces, i.e., by war or other methods of armed coercion.[2]

Elsewhere in the same book he writes that foreign policy is "closely bound up with the character of the social and state system of the states in question, since foreign policy is a direct continuation of domestic policy, and the diplomatic machinery constitutes a part of the entire machinery of state."[3] The Stalinist edition of the *Diplomatic Dictionary* observes that

> Foreign policy is determined in slaveowning, feudal and capitalist society by the interests of the ruling classes, but in socialist society by the interests of the entire toiling people. Diplomacy, on the other hand, whilst by no means free from the influence of the social structure . . .

---

although the new regime unilaterally suspended its public attacks upon the Chinese for over a year. Peking's characterization of the Brezhnev-Kosygin regime as "Khrushchevism without Khrushchev" appears to be substantially accurate.

[2] I. D. Levin, *Diplomaticheskii Immunitet* (Moscow, 1949), pp. 4–5. In 1962 Levin expanded the introduction to his work on *Diplomatic Immunity* into a monograph entitled *Diplomatiya, Yeye Sushchnost, Metody i Formy* (Moscow, 1962) and repeated this passage, word for word, without change on p. 17.

[3] Ibid. For a more detailed account of Soviet conceptions of foreign policy and their relationship to the social system, cf. V. V. Aspaturian, "Diplomacy in the Mirror of Soviet Scholarship," in J. Keep, ed., *Contemporary History in the Soviet Mirror* (London, Allen and Unwin, 1964), pp. 243–85.

is all the same merely the technical means for the realization of foreign policy.[4]

Diplomacy is usually defined by Soviet authorities as subordinate to foreign policy and its chief instrument during times of peace. Just as foreign policy reflects the social interests of the ruling class in society, diplomacy represents the formal expression of the interests of the state. Thus diplomacy represents the transformation of internal social class interests into official and legal state interests in foreign policy, just as domestic law represents a similar transformation of domestic class interests secured by power into legal rights. While diplomatic relations represent, in effect, the indirect collision of interests and resolution of conflicts between internal interest groups or social classes of various states masquerading as the national interests of the country as a whole, "international law can be defined as the aggregate of rules governing relations between states in the process of their conflict and cooperation . . . expressing the will of the ruling classes of these states and defended in case of need by coercion applied by the states individually or collectively."[5]

The foreign policy of the Soviet Union, like that of other states, is shaped by the interests of the dominant social groups in society, ideologically rationalized as the will of all social classes in the country and legalized as the official interests of the state. The Soviet regime in its foreign policy also purports to articulate the interests of deprived classes, particularly the proletariat, in non-Communist countries as well, although this aspect of its foreign policy is now challenged by that of Communist China.[6] "In the Soviet Union," according to a recent

[4] A. Y. Vishinsky and S. A. Lozovsky, eds., *Diplomaticheskii Slovar* (Moscow, 1948 and 1950), Vol. I, p. 570.

[5] F. I. Kozhevnikov, ed., *Mezhudnarodnoye Pravo* (Moscow, 1957), pp. 3–4.

[6] Both Peking and Moscow have challenged each other's unilateral attempts to articulate the interests of the deprived social classes in other countries. In its letter of June 14, 1963, to the C.P.S.U. Central Committee, Peking charged: "Certain persons [i.e., Khrushchev] now go so far as to deny the great international significance of the anti-imperialist revolutionary struggles of the Asian, African, and Latin-American peoples and, on the pretext of breaking down the barriers of nationality, color, and geographical location, are trying their best to efface the line of demarcation between oppressed and oppressor nations and between oppressed and oppressor countries and to hold down the revolutionary struggles of the peoples in these areas. In fact, they cater to the needs of imperialism and create a new 'theory' to justify the rule of imperialism in these areas and the promotion of its policies of old and new colonialism. Actually, this 'theory' seeks . . . to maintain the rule of the 'superior nations' over the oppressed nations." *Peking Review*, June 21, 1963. Khrushchev, for his part, has publicly complained: "The Chinese splitters would like to become the leaders and mentors of the revolutionary movement in Asia, Africa, and Latin America. They are maliciously counterposing the national-liberation struggle of the peoples of these continents to the workers' movements and the countries of socialism. Even here they are striving to introduce a split, distrust and estrangement. Their reactionary idea that whites will allegedly never understand blacks and yellows, that their interests are allegedly different, serves this purpose."

Soviet textbook on international law, "diplomacy for the first time in the history of mankind wholly serves the interests of the working people, not only of the U.S.S.R. but also of all other countries."[7]

While the foreign policy of the state is traditionally defined as being shaped by the interests of the state, more frequently called the "national interest," this becomes an empty, sterile concept unless it is related to the ideological or social substance of what constitutes the "national interest." Ultimately the concept of state interests must have as its reference point the concrete interests of people, either as individuals, as groups, or as aggregates of groups in some ordered structure of a concentrically radiating consensus. The policies of the state, external and internal, register unevenly upon the interests of various individuals and groups on society, and represent in effect a societal distribution of power reflecting either an informal or a formal consensus pattern or a nonconsensual structure of active and passive coercion. The lowest common denominator of consensus is willingness to defend the integrity of the state and its independent existence. Sometimes it is assumed that all states qualify for this distinction, but this is manifestly not the case. States have existed, and still do, whose very existence is opposed by substantial sectors of their population. This is particularly true in cases where a single nation is divided into several states and where the basic loyalty of the population is to the "nation" divided rather than the state of which it is a part. This may even assume the pattern of giving higher loyalty to another state because it represents the interests of the nation as a whole, in which case the interests of this state assume a transcendental significance. Historical and current illustrations of this phenomenon are so abundant that concrete recitation is unnecessary.

What is more often overlooked, however, is that even within a state consisting of a single nation in its entirety, hostility may still be directed at the separate existence of the state by sectors of the population whose primary loyalty has been transferred to another state, ideology, or class. The efforts of the Communist movement to effect a transfer of primary loyalty from state or nation to the proletarian class are well known. This indicates that a level of consensus higher than that of the state and nation may exist at the level of the social system. Social groups and classes in a particular state may experience such deprivation that they seek to rupture and disestablish the existing social order to the advantage of another state, even if the cost to their own state or nation is a heavy one. Such was the case with the Bolsheviks after the Russian Revolution, the French émigrés and the French Revolution, and the American colonists with respect to their separation from Great Britain. In such instances the interests of a social group or class assume higher priority than those of the state and nation.[8]

Pravda, April 16, 1964. For a discussion of a related issue, cf. pp. 509–510, this text.

[7] Kozhevnikov, *Mezhudnarodnoye Pravo*, pp. 281–82.

[8] The classic illustrations of states disappearing because of a higher loyalty to "nation" than to state are, of course, the processes whereby Italy

The priority of ideological or social interests (ideo-social interests) over the interests of the state and nation is by no means an exclusive monopoly of deprived or revolutionary groups. It is not unknown for privileged or ruling groups to have also been ready to sacrifice the interests of other social groups in society, and even of the state and nation, in order to preserve or recover their former privileged status in society. This has been accomplished in the past by either merging their state into another or inviting outside powers to intervene on their behalf, in return for a guarantee that their privileged status will be preserved in one form or another.[9]

Civil wars and revolutions are thus more often the consequence of a shattered or challenged social consensus than of a disintegrating consensus at the abstract level of the state or nation.

---

and Germany were unified in the nineteenth century. The phenomenon of "Nasserism" in the Arab world represents, in effect, a higher loyalty on the part of many Arabs to Nasser and his dream of a single Arab state than to their own independent Arab states. Bi-national and multi-national states, like Belgium, Canada, South Africa, the U.S.S.R., etc., are chronically subject to internal stresses and strains because of the higher pull of "nation" on the loyalty of many citizens than of the "state." Theoretically, the nation-state was designed to eradicate tensions originating in conflicting loyalties to nation and state by making the two congruent. But the nation-state did not solve the latent tensions generated by social class differences, and a nation-state may be swallowed up into a larger state unit, such as a federation, because substantial sectors of the population see their interests served better within such a state than as an independent "nation-state." Cf., F. Hertz, *Nationality in History and Politics* (London, Kegan Paul, 1944); R. Schlesinger, *Federalism in Central and Eastern Europe* (London, Oxford University Press, 1944); A. Cobban, *National Self-Determination* (Chicago, University of Chicago Press, 1944); R. Emerson, *From Empire to Nation* (Cambridge, Harvard University Press, 1960); Karl Deutsch, *Nationalism and Social Communication* (New York, Wiley, 1953); Joel B. Montague, Jr., *Class and Nationality* (New Haven, College and University Press, 1963); and V. V. Aspaturian, *The Union Republics in Soviet Diplomacy* (Geneva, Librairie Droz, 1960).

[9] Historical illustrations of privileged classes or groups sacrificing the interests and even the very existence of their state in order to preserve their privileged position as either subordinate local rulers or as co-opted members of the conquering ruling group can be found as far back as classical antiquity. The Alexandrine, Persian, Roman, Islamic, Ottoman, and Habsburg empires were all expanded and consolidated in this manner. The acceptance of indirect rule by local aristocracies subordinate to external authority was a key factor in the establishment and preservation of the European colonial empires. Whenever a ruling group invites outside intervention to quash an internal uprising, it is often sacrificing national or state interests to its own class interests; conversely, the Bolsheviks were willing to sacrifice Russian territory at Brest-Litovsk in order to stay in power as a ruling group. According to Hertz, "in the centuries after the Middle Ages the word 'nation' was used in Germany and France for designating the higher ruling classes in opposition to *Volk* or *peuple*, which corresponded to the English word 'populace' or 'common people.'" Hertz, *Nationality in History and Politics*, p. 6, note 1. Cf. also, J. B. Montague, Jr., *Class and Nationality* (New Haven, College and University Press, 1963), pp. 44–53. Social class and nation, like state and nation are not always congruent, and under various circumstances the discrete interests of each may come into violent conflict.

Thus when we speak of state or national interests in foreign policy, it is necessary to examine the social structure, the interrelation of interest groups and social classes, the degree of ideo-social consensus, and the process whereby conflicts among various groups are resolved without rupturing the social consensus — and how foreign policy decisions are a product of these processes while at the same time reacting upon them. Just as foreign policy decisions may register different consequences for various groups in society, so is the influence which various groups bring to bear upon foreign policy highly uneven.

The substantive character of the social and power structure of state and society varies considerably and so accordingly does the substantive content of the national interest. Basic alterations in the social or power structure of the state frequently generate different perceptions of national interest, although the territory, resources, and population of the state may remain largely intact. The foreign policy of Castro differs substantially from that of Batista because the nature of the social order and the threats which its dominant groups perceive are correspondingly different, not because Cuba has been transplanted geographically or because its population has been replaced or its history altered.

Generally speaking, all social groups which have a common interest in preserving a given social and political system will develop a process for resolving their conflicts into decisions in such a way as not to injure seriously the social system from which they benefit, even though deprivations in individual cases might be severe. When severe deprivations result systematically and with great frequency for certain groups or social classes, however, one can expect an alienation of these groups and classes from the system and the state which protects it and articulates its interests.

In foreign policy, as in domestic, the interests of the state reflect the socio-power structure of the community, although the precise manner in which divergent internal interests are resolved in foreign policy decisions may vary considerably. The interests of the state in foreign policy thus inevitably reflect the spectrum of domestic interest groups which are affected by foreign policy decisions and are capable of making their demands known and their influence felt in the shaping of these decisions.

Those individuals and groups whose tangible interests are either unaffected by foreign policy decisions or are incapable of making their requirements known or their influence felt remain outside the ambit of participation and are objects rather than subjects of policy. In an absolute sense, perhaps, it would be difficult to imagine a situation whereby substantial groups would be either unaffected by foreign policy decisions or incapable of even passive influence; yet it is nevertheless true that such has been the case not only in the Soviet Union but the United States as well. Under Stalin the active participation of Soviet elites and the passive influence of the non-elites were virtually nonexistent where foreign policy decisions were concerned. In the United States, relations with Latin America were largely shaped and executed to meet the requirements of the business community with investments in that area, since the great mass of Americans were largely unaffected by our relations with Latin America and hence correspondingly indifferent to policy in that region. Before World War II the American Negro community was effectively deprived of any means of exerting influence on American foreign policy decisions. With the rise of a militant Negro elite and the emergence of Africa from under colonial rule, the situation has been altered considerably and the Negro community not only can but does register an increasing impact upon American foreign policy calculations.

It is obviously impossible to quantify precisely the proportion of power which various groups and individuals can command in a given state — since this varies in time and space from one country to another and in individual countries from one time to another, and can even vary considerably in accordance with specific policies. The range is both wide and diverse, stretching from societies in which power is the exclusive monopoly of a small elite, oligarchy, or ruling class to pluralistic societies exhibiting a structural distribution of power in which virtually every group and individual has a basic minimal share in the power structure.

Even the most widely representative society, however, is graduated in its power structure in a sort of inverse relationship between the size of the group and what might be called effective power density. Thus whereas 70 per cent of a society's power may be distributed among a thousand groups, while 30 per cent is concentrated in a small number, the effective power of the latter is substantially greater than 30 per cent. A good analogy for this mode of power distribution is the modern corporation, where 10 per cent of the stock in a few hands may effectively control an organization, 90 per cent of whose stock may be widely diffused and hence relatively ineffective. Since it is impossible to be as precise in calculating the social distribution of power, inevitably some equation about the distribution of power in society is wittingly or unwittingly made on the basis of less reliable and complete data.

The foreign policy of the Soviet Union is largely formulated by decision-makers who are recruited from, and largely represent, the interests of social elites who possess a tangible share of effective political power based upon their functional skills. To the degree that these elites have interests which fortuitously correspond with those of non-elite groups in Soviet society, they also indirectly articulate the interests of the latter groups as well. But the non-elites in Soviet society exert their demands largely by indirection rather than by active participation. As in other modern totalitarian societies they may be actively involved and manipulated in the political process, but they neither directly participate in it nor exercise positive power. This is not necessarily a permanent condition, and the relationship between the non-elites and political power may change abruptly or gradually, depending upon a variety of conditions. Continued conflict among the elites may provoke certain elites to contend for the passive allegiance of the non-

498 INTERNAL POLITICS AND FOREIGN POLICY

elites by deliberately fostering policies which coincide with the basic interests and aspirations of the non-elites. If competition becomes keen among elites for the passive support of the non-elites, dialectical quantification may take place as manipulation from above leads to *passive involvement,* which in turn may be metamorphosed into *active participation,* at first limited and indirect and then more substantial. Under such conditions, power becomes inevitably diffused and an elite power configuration may give way to an evolving system of graduated pluralistic power. Thus political conflicts originally restricted to factional groups may spread first to larger social elites representing social constituencies based upon functions, skills, and talents and finally may be extended in the process, wittingly or unwittingly, to the non-elite masses, as the elites compete with one another in searching for new increments of social power which might give them an advantage in the struggle for power. Khrushchev's consumer-oriented and tension-reducing policies, whether designed consciously or not for this purpose, provided him with a latent reserve of social constituencies which might have proved invaluable and even decisive in intraparty conflicts. Just as Khrushchev successfully mobilized a constellation of elites represented in the Central Committee against the "antiparty group," which constituted a majority in the Presidium, it is not at all implausible that some day another leader may attempt to mobilize these numerically larger social groups (inside and outside the party) against a formal majority in the Central Committee. It is more likely, however, that skillful association or identification with the interests of these larger social constituencies may actually enable certain leaders and factions to avoid confrontations of such a nature in higher bodies.

The Interplay of Domestic Interests and Foreign Policy in the Soviet Political Process

The state or national interests of the Soviet Union, which are reflected in its foreign policy, can be divided into four distinct components, which are wholly traditional and not unconventional in their formal abstract conception:

1. Assuring the security and safety of the state, its territory, its property, and its population, as a distinct entity.
2. Preserving or enhancing the power, prestige, and influence of the Soviet state in the international scene.
3. Preserving the social order at home and securing and promoting the social and economic well-being and prosperity of its people within the structure of priorities established by the existing order.
4. Extending the ideological values and social system of the Soviet Union to other parts of the world.

What is basically innovating and unconventional about the state interests of the Soviet Union is the substantive character of the third and fourth components, since the first two are intrinsically universal for large states in a multiple international state system. The third and fourth components are also characteristic of large states, but lack the definition and systematic explicitness that characterize Soviet behavior in international relations. This stems from the fact that the character of social groups in Soviet society, and their economic and social interests which function as inputs into the Soviet political system, represent substantially unique characteristics, as does the substantive nature of the ideological values of the system. These four components are clearly interrelated and interdependent, and frequently reinforce one another, but they are also inherently contradictory and likely to collide significantly at various points, depending upon certain internal and external variables. The contradiction between the first and fourth components has always been apparent, but it has been only in recent years that the fourth component has come into periodic collision with the second and third. Soviet leaders now perceive not only that an aggressive ideological orientation in foreign policy tends to mobilize the capitalist world against them but also that it serves to drain scarce resources required to enhance the material prosperity of the Soviet population, ideologically described as "building Communism."

While the contradiction between Soviet security interests and ideological goals in foreign policy has long been recognized by observers of the Soviet scene, a new variable in Soviet policy is the contradiction between enhancing economic prosperity at home and fulfilling international ideological obligations. In Soviet jargon, this emerges as a contradiction between the requirements of "building Communism" and the cost and risks of remaining faithful to the principle of "proletarian internationalism."

This new factor has not gone unnoticed by the Chinese. They accused Khrushchev of abandoning Soviet ideological and material obligations to international Communism and the national-liberation movement in favor of avoiding the risks of nuclear war and building an affluent society to satisfy the appetites of the new Soviet "ruling stratum" — in the guise of pursuing peaceful coexistence and "building Communism." Thus in a long editorial entitled "On Khrushchev's Phoney Communism and Its Historical Lessons for the World," the authoritative Chinese organ, *Jen Min Jih Pao*, charged on July 14, 1964:

> The revisionist Khrushchev clique has usurped the leadership of the Soviet party and state and . . . a privileged bourgeois stratum has emerged in Soviet society. . . . The privileged stratum in contemporary Soviet society is composed of degenerate elements from among the leading cadres of party and government organizations, enterprises, and farms as well as bourgeois intellectuals. . . . Since Khrushchev usurped the leadership of the Soviet party and state, there has been a fundamental change in the state of the class struggle in the Soviet Union. Khrushchev has carried out a series of revisionist policies serving the interests of the bourgeoisie and rapidly swelling the forces of capitalism in the Soviet Union. . . . Under the signboard of "peaceful coexistence," Khrushchev has been colluding with U.S. imperialism, wrecking the socialist camp and the international Communist move-

ment, opposing the revolutionary struggles of the oppressed peoples and nations, practicing great-power chauvinism and national egoism, and betraying proletarian internationalism. All this is being done for the protection of the vested interest of a handful of people, which he places above the fundamental interests of the peoples of the Soviet Union, the socialist camp, and the whole world. . . . The members of this privileged stratum have become utterly degenerate ideologically, have completely departed from the revolutionary traditions of the Bolshevik party, and discarded the lofty ideals of the Soviet working class. They are opposed to Marxism-Leninism and socialism. They betray the revolution and forbid others to make revolution. Their sole concern is to consolidate their economic position and political rule. All their activities revolve around the private interests of their own privileged stratum.[10]

While initially the basic purpose of external security and state survival was to develop into a power center for the purpose of implementing ideological goals in foreign policy (world Communism), increasingly the primary purpose becomes in fact to protect and preserve the existing social order in the interests of the new social groups who dominate it and benefit from it.[11] To the extent that the implementation of Soviet foreign policy goals, whether ideologically motivated or otherwise, is compatible with the preservation and enhancement of the social order and serves to reward rather than deprive its beneficiaries, no incompatibility between internal and external goals is experienced. If, however, the pursuit of ideological goals in foreign policy undermines or threatens the security of the Soviet state and the social groups who dominate it (or even arrests the progress of their material pros-

[10] *Jen Min Jih Pao,* July 14, 1964. The Chinese statement continues with its catalogue of Khrushchev's sins: "In putting up the signboard of 'building Communism,' Khrushchev's true aim is to conceal the true face of his revisionism. . . . Khrushchev has ulterior motives when he puts up the signboard of Communism. He is using it to fool the Soviet people and cover up his effort to restore capitalism. He is using it to deceive the international proletariat and the revolutionary people the world over and betray proletarian internationalism. Under this signboard, the Khrushchev clique has itself abandoned proletarian internationalism and is seeking a partnership with U.S. imperialism for the partition of the world; moreover, it wants the fraternal socialist countries to serve its own private interests and not to oppose imperialism or to support the revolutions of oppressed peoples and nations, and it wants them to accept its political, economic, and military control and be its virtual dependencies and colonies. . . . He does not regard the struggle of the working class for Communism as a struggle for the thorough emancipation of mankind as well as itself, but describes it as a struggle for 'a good dish of goulash. . . .' Khrushchev's 'Communism' takes the United States for its model. Imitation of the methods of management of U.S. capitalism and the bourgeois way of life have been raised by Khrushchev to the level of state policy. . . . Thus it can be seen that Khrushchev's 'Communism' is indeed 'goulash Communism' — the 'Communism of the American way of life.' " Ibid.

[11] Cf. V. V. Aspaturian, "Social Structure and Political Power in the Soviet System," a paper presented to the 1963 Annual Meeting of the American Political Science Association; and R. C. Macridis and R. Ward, eds., *Modern Political Systems: Europe* (Englewood Cliffs, New Jersey, Prentice-Hall, 1963), pp. 453–72 and 492–502.

perity), the primacy of internal interests is ideologically rationalized, and the energies and efforts devoted to external ideological goals are correspondingly diminished.

It must be realized that the relationship between internal interests and external ideological goals is a dynamic one which fluctuates in accordance with opportunities and capabilities but that in the long run the ideological goals which threaten internal interests tend to erode and to be deprived of their motivating character. The persistence of ideological goals in Soviet foreign policy, which tend to raise international tensions, reflects socio-functional interests which have been traditionally associated with the Party Apparatus and professional ideologues. The fact that the concrete policies which have resulted from the pursuit of ideological goals in foreign policy have created special vested interests for other socio-political or socio-institutional groups, like the secret police, the armed forces, and the heavy-industrial managers, should not obscure the fact that the definition, identification, and implementation of ideological goals, whether in foreign or domestic policy, has been the special function of the Party Apparatus and its attendant ideologues. The area of common interest which remains among some members of the Party Apparatus and the armed forces and heavy-industrial managers in pursuing policies which are tension producing will be discussed later in another connection. Tension-producing policies in an era of increasing technological complexity, however, not only tend automatically to enhance the power of professionalized and technologically oriented groups in the Soviet Union — to the relative detriment of the status and power of the Party Apparatus — but also tend to alienate from the Apparatus other more numerous social groups whose interests are more in consonance with tension-lessening policies. Among these groups are the consumer-goods producers and light-industrial managers, the intellectuals, artists, professionals, agricultural managers, and finally the great mass of Soviet citizenry, comprising the lower intelligentsia, workers, peasants, and others, whose priorities are always low during periods of high international tensions. Since these latter social forces are more numerous than those whose interests are served by tension-producing policies, the social function of the Party Apparatus was in danger of being rendered superfluous as it lost relatively in power and influence to the professional military and the heavy-industrial managers. At the same time its own ideological interests were being increasingly alienated from those social groups that would benefit from a relaxation of tensions.

In an endeavor to avoid this impending collision between the interests of numerically large and potentially powerful social groups in Soviet society and the international ideological commitments of the Party Apparatus, and thus simultaneously to preserve its primacy in the Soviet socio-power structure by finding larger and more numerous social constituencies to rely upon, Khrushchev's policies appeared to have been designed to provide the Apparatus with a more durable internal ideological function — the building of Communism, i.e., raising the standard of living of the Soviet people. This was reflected periodically in Khrushchev's preferences for cutting down on defense expenditures, bringing about a relaxation of tensions in the international scene, and shifting more money and resources to the production of consumer goods and services. Even more cogently, Khrushchev in August 1964 introduced pensions for collective farmers and hiked the salaries of teachers, doctors, medical personnel, service workers in communal housing and in the trade and public catering enterprises, and local government officials. Some 30 million people were the beneficiaries of these social welfare policies and wage increases, and Khrushchev specifically mentioned that one purpose of the wage increases was to enhance the social status of these groups. He also clearly revealed the relationship between tension-lessening policies and a higher standard of living for the Soviet population:

> Comrade deputies: The projected wage increase is one of the most important measures envisaged by the Party to further raise the well-being of the Soviet people. It had been intended to implement the measures under discussion at the present session earlier in 1962. But then, for certain reasons of external and internal order, we were obliged to postpone their implementation temporarily. The international situation obtaining at that time forced us to take certain measures to strengthen the country's defense. In this connection it was necessary to increase the allocation of funds for these purposes, and this found full approval from the Soviet people. Our efforts aimed at achieving agreement on disarmament have not yet been crowned with success. So we must keep our powder dry so that the enemy knows that it is impossible to attack us unpunished, and that if an attack is made he will receive an answering crushing blow.[12]

He cryptically noted that "not all our people in leading positions have really understood how important it is to increase constantly the output of consumer goods," and after citing an innocuous illustration, he

---

[12] *Izvestia*, July 14, 1964. The fact that Peking issued its statement on "Khrushchev's Phoney Communism" on the day after Khrushchev's address to the Supreme Soviet is not entirely accidental. Peking has also apparently perceived Khrushchev's alteration of the class character of the C.P.S.U. as part of his design to provide the Party Apparatus with a new internal social function. "Besides making a great fuss about a 'party of the entire people,' Khrushchev has also divided the party into an 'industrial party' and an 'agricultural party' on the pretext of 'building the party organs on the production principle.' The revisionist Khrushchev clique says that they have done so because of 'the primacy of economics over politics under socialism' and because they want to place 'the economic and production problems, which have been pushed to the forefront by the entire course of the Communist construction, at the center of the activities of the party organizations' and make them 'the cornerstone of all their work.' Khrushchev said: 'We say bluntly that the main thing in the work of the party organs is production.' . . . The real purpose of the revisionist Khrushchev clique in proposing a 'party of the entire people' was completely to alter the proletarian character of the C.P.S.U. and transform the Marxist-Leninist party into a revisionist party." *Jen Min Jih Pao*, July 14, 1964.

chastised the Gosplan, the U.S.S.R. Sovnarkhoz, and party organizations for deficiencies in this connection.[13]

Indications of such resistance to these goals can be surmised from the periodic attacks upon members of the "anti-party group," particularly Molotov, who supposedly represented constituencies external to Soviet society; cryptic references to resistance or opposition from various social groups to particular policies; and charges against the Chinese that they were either utilizing or seeking to create factional differences within the Soviet hierarchy for their own purposes.

At the Twenty-second Party Congress, for example, F. R. Kozlov's justification for the retention of the ban on factionalism in the new party statutes was an oblique admission of a continuing and chronic condition in the Soviet political process:

> Under present circumstances, need the statutes contain any formal guarantees against factionalism and clique activity? Yes, . . . such guarantees are needed. To be sure, there is no social base left in Soviet society that could feed opportunistic currents in the party. But the sources of ideological waverings on the part of particular individuals or groups have not yet been entirely eliminated. Some persons may fall under the influence of bourgeois propaganda from the outside. Others, having failed to comprehend the dialectics of society's development and having turned . . . into dying embers, will have nothing to do with anything new and go on clinging to old dogmas that have been toppled by life.[14]

Although factionalism is usually associated with the antiparty group as a transitory problem and Soviet leaders had been coupling denunciations of factionalism and Molotov with charges of Chinese attempts to undermine Khrushchev's position in the Soviet party, it was hardly likely that Peking was directing its appeal to defunct members of the antiparty group. Rather it had reason to believe that the Soviet professional military and individuals in the Party Presidium and Secretariat might have shared a common interest with Peking in ousting Khrushchev from power, if for different reasons.[15] It was also plausible that the periodic denunciation of Molotov and the association of his views with those of Peking were in fact veiled warnings against those within the Soviet hierarchy who might have seen an opportunity in Peking's invitation to upset the Khrushchev faction. That these internal dissensions existed was more than implied by Suslov — who may have been a specific target of Peking's appeal — in his report to the February 1964 Plenum of the Central Committee. He confirmed the Chinese bid for factional support in the Soviet leadership and simultaneously protested much too much that Khrushchev and the Central Committee were solidly united. Suslov's statement may actually have been an esoteric

13 *Izvestia*, July 14, 1964.
14 *Pravda*, October 29, 1961.
15 For an interesting exposition of this point, cf. Sidney I. Ploss, "Mao's Appeal to the Soviet 'Conservatives'" (Princeton University, Center of International Studies, 1963).

signal to the Chinese that for one reason or another Peking should not
rely upon him for its intrigues:

> In their struggle against the C.P.S.U. and its Leninist course, the
> Chinese leaders are concentrating their fire primarily against Nikita
> Sergeyevich Khrushchev. Of course, they cannot fail to see that it is
> Nikita Sergeyevich himself who stands at the head of those remarkable
> processes that arose in our party and country after the 20th Party
> Congress that are ensuring the Soviet people's successful progress
> toward Communism. This is why, for their subversive purposes, they
> would like to isolate Comrade Khrushchev from the Central Committee
> and place our Central Committee in opposition to the Party and the
> Soviet people. But this filthy scheme is adventurist and hopeless; it is
> doomed to complete and shameful failure. Our Central Committee,
> headed by that true Leninist, Nikita Sergeyevich Khrushchev, is united
> and monolithic as never before, and the Chinese leaders — and not they
> alone — should make up their minds to that. Comrade N. S. Khru-
> shchev . . . is the recognized leader of our party and people. He ex-
> presses the most cherished thoughts and aspirations of the Soviet people.
> The Leninist line pursued by our party cannot be divorced from the
> Central Committee, from Nikita Sergeyevich Khrushchev.[16]

While Stalin subordinated the interests of the world Communist
movement to the security and foreign policy interests of the Soviet state,
the material prosperity of the Soviet population was rarely viewed by
him as a significant factor in coordinating Soviet interests and those of
the Communist movement. When Soviet security and foreign policy
interests were not threatened, Stalin apparently — like Molotov and
Mao — welcomed heightened international tensions, even at the expense of material prosperity at home, since they functioned to rationalize totalitarian controls. Hence Soviet ideological commitments abroad
were rarely subordinated to the interests of raising the Soviet standard
of living under Stalin.

Since Stalin's death, and particularly during the rule of Khrushchev, the balance between Soviet internal economic and cultural needs
and the ideological imperatives of foreign policy had been increasingly
altered in favor of the former, so that it now seems to enjoy priority in
the formulation of foreign policy. Under attack from Peking for allegedly betraying the world Communist movement, Khrushchev did not
directly deny the Chinese charge but in effect rationalized that the most
effective way in which the Soviet Union could meet its ideological
commitments to the revolutionary movement was constantly to raise the
standard of living of the Soviet people, which would have presumably
stimulated revolution in other countries because of the attractiveness of
Soviet society. Thus, M. A. Suslov, in his report to the C.P.S.U. Central

---

[16] *Pravda*, April 3, 1964. Suslov's report was delivered on February 4,
but publication was delayed until April for obvious internal political reasons.
Cf., also *Pravda*, September 22, 1963. After Khrushchev's removal it was
widely rumored in Communist circles that Suslov delivered the main indictment of Khrushchev at the Central Committee Plenum which demanded
Khrushchev's resignation.

Committee in February 1964, reiterated this position in asserting that "Communist construction is the greatest contribution to the fulfillment of the internationalist duty of the Soviet people." He then amplified as follows:

> The prime role in the world revolutionary process belongs to the socialist countries. This is demonstrated first in the fact that the working class, the working people of these countries are . . . creating a new society . . . for the sake of which the peoples are working toward revolution. In creating the material and technical base of socialism and Communism, the socialist countries are delivering imperialism blow after blow in the decisive sphere of social activity — the sphere of material production. . . . All this revolutionizes the masses, helps accustom them to the active struggle against the capitalist system and for social and national liberation. . . . It is the internationalist duty of the Communists of the socialist countries to build the new society well and successfully, to develop the economy, to strengthen defense·capability, to consolidate the socialist camp, and to strive to ensure that through practical implementation of the ideas of socialism they become increasingly attractive to all working people. . . . Distorting the essence of the matter, the C.P.C. leadership is attempting to prove that economic competition allegedly means that "the oppressed peoples and nations have in general no need to wage a struggle, to rise up in revolution" . . . and that "it remains for them only to wait quietly, to wait until the Soviet Union overtakes the most developed capitalist country in the level of production and material well-being. . . ." Such myths are being circulated from Peking expressly to discredit the idea of economic competition between the two systems. In fact, Marxist-Leninists see the revolutionary importance of the victories of socialism in economic competition precisely in that they stimulate the class struggle of the working people and make them conscious fighters for socialism.[17]

Thus, in summary, we can isolate six characteristics of Soviet foreign policy which can be termed generalizable and applicable to the foreign policy behavior of all states:

1. Foreign policy is a continuation of domestic policy.
2. The interests of the state in foreign policy are a function of the interests of internal social groups.
3. Internal policy requirements generally have primacy over external policy requirements in the event of incompatibility.
4. Foreign policy, including external defense, is more a function of preserving the social order and the interests of its dominant groups than of the state or the national interests in the abstract.
5. Foreign policy, including external defense, functions more to serve tangible internal interests than intangible or abstract ideological interests abroad.
6. Thus we can also conclude that if the pursuit or achievement of ideological goals in foreign policy threatens or undermines the interests and security of dominant social groups, these will not be pursued even if the necessary capability is available.

[17] Ibid.

In the realm of motivating factors, two unique factors in Soviet foreign policy can be isolated:

1. In the past when there has been no incompatibility between the security and/or internal power interests of social groups and the promotion or implementation of purely ideological goals in foreign policy, the latter has functioned as a significant motivating force in shaping foreign policy, and the Soviet regime has diverted relatively substantial resources and devoted considerable energies in the pursuit of ideologically determined goals in foreign policy. The fact that at some stage in the process, ideological goals were converted into instruments serving Soviet national interests should not obscure the fact that this was not always the case during the early years of the Soviet regime. Whether Soviet foreign policy will continue to be shaped by ideological considerations and whether ideological goals can still be converted to Soviet national purposes are becoming moot questions. Not only are the psychological and material drains on the Soviet system becoming increasingly burdensome and costly, but the emergence of Red China as an ideological rival threatens to render ideological goals in foreign policy dysfunctional and counterproductive for the Soviet system. This is particularly the case if the Soviet charge is true that the Chinese advocate a policy which would artificially reduce the economies of developed Communist countries to a common level. In October 1963 *Kommunist* claimed that the Chinese "asserted that the obligation of socialist countries that had moved forward in their economic development allegedly consisted in 'waiting for' the lagging ones and giving them everything that had been created by the forward-moving countries, as distinct from the lagging ones."[18] This charge was to be repeated by *Kommunist* in the following year in even blunter terms:

> The Chinese interpret the question of internationalism in relations between the socialist countries in a spirit of national egoism. It was not too long ago when they were saying that the most economically developed countries must turn over to the backward countries the entire portion of their national income that exceeded the level of the backward ones.[19]

Not only does the Sino-Soviet dialogue on this point demonstrate how international ideological commitments can be subordinated to internal economic requirements by a developed and underdeveloped Communist state sharing a common ideological commitment, but it also illustrates how each can perceive its ideological obligations in such a way that their implementation automatically serves the internal interests of the state concerned. Thus while Moscow asserts that the enhancement of the Soviet standard of living furthers the promotion of

[18] "Marxism-Leninism Is the Base for the Unity of the Communist Movement," *Kommunist,* No. 15, October 1963, 15.
[19] "Proletarian Internationalism Is the Banner of the Working People of All Countries and Continents," *Kommunist,* No. 7, April 1964. Citation is from the version published in *Pravda,* May 6, 1964.

world Communism, Peking controverts this view and argues that the world revolution can best be furthered if the developed Communist states postpone their affluence in favor of bolstering the economies of their deprived Communist allies. In either case it reduces itself to the crude formula: "What's good for the Soviet Union (or China) is good for the world revolution." In the past this formula was applied by Stalin almost entirely in terms of the foreign policy and security needs of the Soviet state as the bastion of the world Communist movement; only since the death of Stalin has this formula been applied to purely domestic economic considerations. To be sure, Moscow insists that raising the standard of living in the Soviet Union strengthens the most powerful Communist state and hence alters the global balance of power in favor of world revolution, psychologically if not militarily, but this proposition is both dubious and transparently self-serving. It also serves to support the Chinese charge that in the face of possible thermonuclear war, the Soviet leaders have lost their revolutionary militancy and may be willing to settle for a status quo which will allow them to divert resources and energies from a counterproductive and dysfunctional policy of revolutionary aggressiveness to bolstering the standard of living at home and expanding and solidifying the social legitimacy of their power and authority.

The history of Soviet foreign policy thus demonstrates that the Soviet elite has been and may still be willing to divert considerable resources and energies to the pursuit of ideological objectives in foreign policy, although their achievement may result in little more than psychological satisfaction, as long as its security and vital interests are not undermined. Enthusiasm for ideological causes wanes, however, if their implementation subjects the dominant social groups in Soviet society to chronic and continuous exposure to destruction or deprivation for an indefinite period. It should be noted that Soviet behavior in this regard is not a simple counterpart to the altruistic and humanitarian efforts exercised in foreign policy by other countries, since the Soviet state has exerted itself in behalf of international ideological goals to a degree which other states would normally regard as seriously self-denying or self-depriving.

2. The second unique characteristic in the content of Soviet ideological goals in foreign policy is that the Soviet Union desires the ultimate restructuring of the social order of the outside world in its own image. This process started with the Stalinization of the Comintern and foreign Communist parties before World War II and was implemented in areas that fell under Soviet control after the war. Soviet policy was not content with the simple establishment of economic, political, or military control of client states, but rather dictated their total social transformation and restructuring of the internal social foundations of authority and power. This aspect of Soviet policy is not *historically* unique, but it cannot be generalized either. It is generally a characteristic of revolutionary great powers and thus is currently applicable to the foreign policy configurations of Communist China.

Five factors, however, have developed outside the Soviet Union that have tended to blunt the cutting edge of Soviet ideology in foreign policy and to deny the Soviet system a universalist character.

1. The growth of polycentrism and diversity within the Soviet orbit, which allowed local Communist leaders to reshape their policies so that they were more responsive to the internal needs of their own countries than to the interests of Moscow.

2. The real possibility of new adherents to the Communist world emerging spontaneously out of initially non-Communist revolutionary movements and regimes, of which Cuba is a prototype. This allows for an even more diluted and impure type of Communism and greater deviation from the Soviet norm.

3. The implied diversity in even more radical dimensions of future Communist social orders in Western Europe and other areas, as reflected in the changing programs and strategies of the Italian and French Communist parties, to say nothing of the bizarre nature of emergent Communism in tropical Africa.

4. The appearance of intermediate-type noncapitalist, non-Communist social systems in Africa and Asia, like those in Algeria, Egypt, Ghana, Guinea, Indonesia, etc., which subscribe to a local "national" or "ethnic" socialism that Moscow wishes to attract to its ideological and political orbit.

5. Finally the most crucial factor, the emergence of Red China as a revolutionary rival to the Soviet Union within the Communist world and its objective of universalizing what Moscow calls "sinified" Communism.[20]

All these factors have impelled the Soviet leaders to adjust and accommodate to the proliferation of revolutionary movements and regimes — Communist and non-Communist — and settle for a strategy which will disestablish capitalism and imperialism without necessarily replacing them with variants of the Soviet social order.

[20] According to *Pravda*, "Our party . . . has buried the very idea of the 'hegemony' of one party to another in this movement. The Chinese leaders, however, clearly wish to revive this idea, assuming the right to decide by themselves theoretical and political questions that concern the entire movement. What else can explain the hullabaloo raised in China about the 'ideas of Mao Tse-tung' as the summit of Marxist thought for all peoples, for the entire movement? In Peking they have gone so far as to declare that the theoretical generalization of the historical tasks of the present day has become incumbent upon Mao Tse-tung alone, that our epoch itself is the 'epoch of Mao Tse-tung'. . . . Such statements not only are permeated with an adulation and glorification of the leader that is unworthy of Communists. Behind them are obvious feeble attempts to assert a 'monopoly' in Marxism-Leninism on the part of Chinese theoreticians. To counterpoise the great doctrine of Marx, Engels, and Lenin, the Chinese leadership is attempting to foist the so-called 'sinified Marxism' upon the Communist movement as its ideological banner." "Marxism-Leninism Is the International Doctrine of the Communists of All Countries," *Pravda*, May 10, 1964. Cf. also, *Pravda* for May 11 and 12, 1964, and "Against Splitters, for Unity of the Communist Movement," *Partiinaya Zhizn*, No. 11, June 1964, 8–20.

The challenge of China and its implied threat to mobilize the underdeveloped, non-white areas of the world against the European and developed areas, including the Communist countries, in a mind of global war between the Northern and Southern hemispheres, has, however, caused Soviet and European Communist leaders even to doubt the wisdom and productivity of prematurely encouraging the proliferation of Communist regimes in the underdeveloped regions of the world. Such a proliferation might result not only in contributing incrementally to China's power in the Communist world, but also in radically upsetting the balance between developed and underdeveloped Communist countries and imposing serious burdens on the economies of the Soviet and Eastern European Communist states in the name of "proletarian internationalism" and "fraternal assistance." The European Communists are equipped neither temperamentally nor in terms of resources to divert their energies from internal construction in order to protect militarily or bolster economically a profusion of underdeveloped Communist states. The Sino-Soviet dispute thus reflects microcosmically the global confrontation between the European "haves" and the non-European "have-nots." This has been explicitly confirmed by Moscow and implicitly by Peking, although both have conspired to subsume such an East-West or North-South conflict in a smoke screen of jargon about whether the main feature of the current epoch is the contradiction between the working class (mainly European) and capitalism or the national liberation movement (mainly non-European) and imperialism. Thus the Soviet leaders perceive Chinese motives as follows:

> The Chinese leaders represent matters as though the interests of the peoples of Asia, Africa, and Latin America were especially close and understandable to them, as though they were concerned most of all for the further development of the national-liberation struggle in order to turn them into a tool for the realization of their hegemonic plans. . . .
> The C.P.C. leaders have circulated their infamous myth that the C.P.S.U. "underestimates" the historical role of the national-liberation movement, that the Soviet Union, under the pretext of the struggle for peaceful coexistence, is "refusing to help" the national-liberation movement. . . .
> The Chinese delegates at this conference [Afro-Asian Conference in Moshi] . . . suggested to the representatives of the African and Asian countries that inasmuch as the Russians, Czechs, and Poles are white, "you can't rely on them," that they will allegedly "always be in collusion with the Americans — with whites," that the peoples of Asia and Africa have their own special interests. . . . In the light of the Chinese leaders' practical activities in recent years, the true political meaning of the slogan they have advanced — "The wind from the East is prevailing over the wind from the West" — has become especially clear. . . . This slogan . . . substitutes for the class approach a geographical and even racist one. It plainly bespeaks a belittling on their part of the role of the world socialist system, the working class and popular masses of Western Europe and America. . . . The long years of enslavement and exploitation by the imperialists . . . are nurturing among part of the population of the former colonies and semicolonies a mistrust of people

of the white race. The Chinese leaders are trying to fan these feelings, in the hopes of setting the peoples of the former colonies and semicolonies against the socialist countries, against the working people in the developed capitalist countries. . . . For if one is to expose the secret scheme that stands behind the Chinese slogan, if one is to reveal the long-range goal of the C.P.C. leaders, it consists of the following: China, they reason, is the largest country of the East and embodies its interests; here are born the "winds of history" that are to prevail over the "winds of the West." Thus this slogan is nothing but an ideological and political expression of the hegemonic aspirations of the Chinese leadership.[21]

INTERNAL AND EXTERNAL FORCES SHAPING SOVIET FOREIGN POLICY

Soviet foreign policy decisions, like those of any state, are products of internal responses to both external factors and domestic political considerations operating in dynamic interrelation or as discrete variables. Increasingly, however, the distinctions between foreign policy and internal policy decisions have become blurred, and nearly all policy decisions have both internal and external effects which are continuously feeding back and forth in a reciprocal, if uneven, manner. Bearing this *basic interconnection* in mind and recognizing that foreign policy decisions may result from external or internal factors separately or in fortuitous or calculated combination, and correspondingly have internal and external effects separately or in combination, fortuitously or otherwise, expected or unexpected — we can nevertheless enumerate some of the more significant external and internal influences upon Soviet external behavior.

External Factors

It has been frequently and mistakenly assumed in the past that foreign policy is largely a patterned response to the behavior or condition of the outside world and that internal factors and effects are largely fortuitous, incidental, or supplemental. External factors which influence Soviet foreign policy can be either defensive or nondefensive in character or a combination of the two. Although nondefensive factors cannot always be discretely distinguished from defensive and security considerations, defensive factors, generally speaking, have priority in the event of conflict. Under Stalin the security interests of Soviet client or ideologically allied states generally had priority over the non-security interests of the Soviet Union. This may no longer be the case, although Soviet leaders continue to vow that all socialist states (with the possible exception of China and Albania) will be defended with the same alacrity and effort as the Soviet Union itself. Since the Cuban missile crisis, however, the credibility of this commitment has been rendered dubious and has been openly doubted by China. This in turn has elicited Soviet reactions which can be interpreted as withdrawing the protective

[21] Suslov's report to the February 1964 Plenum of the Central Committee, *Pravda*, April 3, 1964.

umbrella of Soviet strategic power from China, although the Sino-Soviet military alliance has not yet been formally or publicly denounced.[22] The external factors (defensive and non-defensive) that shape Soviet foreign policy are listed below in the order of priority most probably perceived by the Soviet leadership today:

1. Threats or objective conditions that have a direct, adverse effect on the security safety, and well-being of the Soviet state, its territory, property, and population.

2. The fulfillment of international legal obligations to other states or international organizations which are interrelated with the first factor, i.e., treaties of alliance with Communist states, whose security is intimately connected with the security of the Soviet state.

3. The fulfillment of international legal obligations to other states

[22] In the Soviet government statement of August 21, 1963, Moscow charged the Chinese with having the audacity to criticize the Soviet Union only because Peking enjoyed the protection of Soviet nuclear power: "Can the C.P.R. leaders place their hands over their hearts and say that without the nuclear might of the U.S.S.R. . . . China could today peacefully engage in solving its internal problems of economic and state construction? No, the C.P.R. leaders would have to admit that they can permit themselves even the luxuries of their . . . rude attacks against the Soviet Union and the C.P.S.U. only because the external security of China is protected by the might of the Soviet Union and the whole socialist commonwealth." *Pravda*, August 21, 1963. *Krasnaya zvezda*, four days later, carried the implied threat of withdrawing Soviet nuclear support one step further: "China today is indebted to the power of Soviet nuclear weapons for the fact that it can calmly engage in solving its internal tasks of economic and state construction. The leaders of the Chinese People's Republic ought to recognize that they can permit themselves such luxuries . . . as their gross attacks on the Soviet Union and the C.P.S.U. only because the external security of China is guarded by the might of the Soviet Union and of the whole socialist commonwealth. . . . The great Chinese people have an ancient proverb: 'When you drink water, remember who dug the well.' It seems the Chinese leaders, judging by their statements, assume this wisdom can be disregarded." Colonel A. Leontyèv, "Dogmatists at the Well," *Krasnaya zvezda*, August 25, 1963.

And in June 1964, *Izvestia* hinted that perhaps Peking may have taken itself out of the socialist camp and out from Soviet military protection: "Casting doubts on the efficacy of the Soviet-Chinese treaty of friendship, alliance, and mutual aid, C.P.R. Minister of Foreign Affairs Chen Yi alleged in December 1963 that Soviet assurances are of no value. 'Such promises are easy to make,' he said cynically, 'but they aren't worth anything. Soviet protection is worth nothing to us.' Trying to justify the C.P.R. government's flirting with reactionary regimes, Marshal Chen Yi today declares that China is a 'nonaligned' country. In political language, this means in fact that Chen Yi does not consider China a part of the world socialist camp. . . . True, the Chinese leaders assert occasionally that in a 'complex situation' the U.S.S.R. and the C.P.R. would line up together against imperialism. A legitimate question arises: When are the Chinese leaders to be believed?" "Combine National and International Interests," *Izvestia*, June 4, 1964.

For further details on the Sino-Soviet dialogue concerning nuclear weapons and the Sino-Soviet alliance, cf. Alice L. Hsieh, "The Sino-Soviet Dialogue: 1963" (Santa Monica, RAND Corporation, 1964); and "Communist China and Nuclear Force" by the same author in R. N. Rosecrance, ed., *The Dispersion of Nuclear Weapons: Strategy and Politics* (New York, Columbia University Press, 1964).

or international organizations, which serves to reduce the danger to Soviet security, i.e., treaties of alliance with non-Communist states, of nonaggression, neutrality, and international cooperation, such as the test ban treaty.

4. Opportunities which enhance the power and prestige of the Soviet state, not directly connected with security *per se*.

5. Opportunities in international relations which enhance the material well-being of the Soviet state and its people (defined in terms of the Soviet structure of social priorities).

6. Threats or objective conditions adversely affecting the security interests of Communist allies, but not necessarily of the Soviet Union, which require the fulfillment of international ideological and/or legal obligations, i.e., a treaty of alliance or informal commitment to defend a small client state only remotely connected with Soviet security interests, like Cuba or North Vietnam.[23]

7. The fulfillment of unilaterally assumed international ideological obligations to Communist parties, revolutionary movements, and "oppressed peoples" everywhere, i.e., the obligations subsumed under the rubric of "proletarian internationalism" not covered by formal legal commitments.

8. The fulfillment of international legal obligations to non-Communist states or international organizations, which have little or no connection with the direct interests of the Soviet Union or its ideological allies.

The Sino-Soviet conflict, or what we know of it to date, has raised significant questions concerning the interrelationship of Soviet interests with those of other Communist states, particularly Red China. According to the Chinese view, which is not entirely unmerited, the Soviet Union now gives higher priority to the nondefensive external and internal interests of the Soviet Union than to Chinese security interests, to say nothing of Soviet international ideological obligations to the "world revolution" in general. The test ban treaty is held up as a scandalous example of the sacrifice of Chinese security interests at the altar of the Soviet passion for affluence — since from the Chinese point of view the primary purpose of the test ban treaty was to deny nuclear weapons to China in return for a lessening of international tensions. It is difficult to assess the Chinese accusation precisely, since it is not yet sufficiently clear whether Soviet leaders have actually subordinated Chinese security interests to their passion for affluence or whether they really perceive Chinese demands for the satisfaction of Chinese national interests as jeopardizing their own security.

The issue, of course, is not this clear-cut. What the Soviet leaders may believe is that China in reality is trying to maneuver the Soviet regime into giving higher priority to Chinese non-security interests than to its own by masquerading them under the rubric of security considera-

---

[23] The mild Soviet reaction to the systematic U.S. bombing of North Vietnam for over a year would seem to confirm the relatively low priority of these obligations in Soviet policy, just as Peking has charged.

tions. This interpretation is plausible because of the emphasis the Chinese leaders place on the obligations that the developed Communist countries allegedly have to their underdeveloped Communist brethren and because of the indignant manner in which they condemn the new Soviet party program designed to usher the Soviet Union into the epoch of Communist abundance.

In any event, the Soviet leaders have openly questioned the legitimacy of Chinese motives in foreign policy, as being unrelated to Chinese security interests and hence unworthy of being defended by the Soviet Union and the Communist camp as a whole:

> If the leaders of China are actually following the principles of proletarian internationalism, why are they striving so hard to obtain their own atom bomb? People who stop at nothing in their desire to provide themselves with new types of destructive weapons must have some motive. What is behind this desire? From our point of view, the very idea of the need to provide themselves with nuclear weapons could occur to the leaders of a country whose security is guaranteed by the entire might of the socialist camp only if they have developed some kind of special aims or interests that the socialist camp cannot support with its military force. But such aims and interests can manifest themselves only among those who reject proletarian internationalism . . . and . . . peaceful coexistence. After all, it is impossible to combine with the peace-loving foreign policy course of the countries of the socialist system plans for nuclear weapons of one's own in order, for example, to increase one's influence in the countries of Asia, Africa, and Latin America or to create for oneself a "position of strength" in disputed international questions, or, finally, to exacerbate international tension. We say directly: We would not like to think that the C.P.R. government is guided by such motives.[24]

The Chinese, in turn, have charged that Soviet power serves exclusively the interests of the Soviet Union and that "in fighting imperialist aggression and defending its security, each socialist country has to rely in the first place on its own defense capability."[25] And even more emphatically, the Chinese Foreign Minister, Chen Yi, has declared:

> Atomic bombs, missiles, and supersonic aircraft are reflections of the technical level of a nation's industry. China will have to resolve this issue within the next several years; otherwise, it will degenerate into a second-class or third-class nation.[26]

While the Soviet leaders may feel that a powerful China armed with nuclear weapons might embark on independent adventures in foreign policy which might inflame the international situation and thus force unwanted and difficult choices upon Moscow, Peking perceives in the Soviet position a desire to control the foreign policy of China and subordinate it to the interests of Russia. "Soviet protection is worth

[24] *Pravda*, September 21 and 22, 1963.
[25] *Jen Min Jih Pao*, August 15, 1963.
[26] As reported by KYODO, Tokyo, October 28, 1963, and cited in A. L. Hsieh, "The Sino-Soviet Nuclear Dialogue: 1963," p. 29.

nothing to us," Chen Yi has asserted. "No outsiders can give us protection, in fact, because they always attach conditions and want to control us."[27]

Internal Factors

All decisions, whether internal or external, frequently bring about unexpected or unanticipated consequences bearing on both internal and external affairs, which in return may modify the original action in one way or another. It is not always clear whether the effects of foreign policy decisions upon the internal situation in the Soviet Union were intended or unintended. Thus a whole series of fundamental decisions in Soviet foreign policy since Stalin's death have left their impact upon the Soviet domestic scene. This is the case with respect to foreign policy decisions concerning the rapprochement with Tito, the de-Stalinization of the satellite system, the regularization and then fracturing of relations with China, the repudiation of the doctrinal propositions concerning the "inevitability of war," "capitalist encirclement," and "peaceful coexistence," frequent resort to summit meetings and personal diplomacy, the Austrian peace treaty, the test ban treaty, etc. It is extremely difficult to determine whether these decisions were deliberately designed to bring about the internal consequences which eventuated or whether the internal changes were the incidental or unanticipated consequences of external policy decisions made for other purposes. Cause and effect are intertwined and cannot always be disentangled in any meaningful way. Undoubtedly some of the effects were intended and anticipated, and others were not; some constituted a welcome fall-out, and some did not. Events and forces were often set in motion which could not be easily reversed and thus were either arrested, domesticated, permitted to run their course, or adjusted to.

There is little question but that the relaxations of Soviet society which have progressively taken place since Stalin's death are closely related to foreign policy decisions and that these relaxations in turn have influenced subsequent foreign policy decisions. But to what degree foreign policy decisions were made for the purpose of justifying these domestic relaxations and to what degree these internal changes came about as consequences remains a methodological enigma.

Internal pressures shaping Soviet foreign policy decisions, not involving security considerations, have in the past been assigned a subordinate role. Yet even during the early years of factional strife in the Soviet Union — like that between Stalin and Trotsky — Soviet leaders and personalities saw opportunities to shape their foreign policy views in a manner calculated to bolster their internal political position in the struggle for power, and these opportunities thus played a significant role in the formulation of Soviet foreign policy. Stalin's doctrines of "socialism in one country," temporary "peaceful coexistence" with capitalism, and his support of Chiang Kai-shek in China were all calculated, at least in part, on one assumption: that a foreign policy of

[27] As reported in the *Washington Post,* December 8, 1963.

relative retrenchment, with its promise of physical and psychological respite, and concentration on internal construction would probably find a wider response within the party and the population at large than a militantly aggressive revolutionary external policy. Hence such a policy would result in associating Stalin's political fortunes and interests with larger and more powerful social constituencies than his opposition could muster in support of its views.

Once Stalin consolidated his power, however, a political process *per se* ceased to have any existence in the Soviet system, and foreign policy calculations were subordinated almost entirely to the bolstering and reinforcing of Stalin's power at home and his grip on the Comintern and foreign Communist parties abroad. Soviet "state" interests were systematically defined in terms of Stalin's political interests, although various social and institutional groups emerged which also developed a vested interest in preserving and maintaining the Stalinist totalitarian order. After World War II a political process re-emerged in which these quasi-autonomous factional, social, and institutional groups developed discretely divergent interests and imposed these on Soviet foreign policy to the degree that they were either able to influence Stalin or resort to administrative distortion in the implementation of policies with which they were charged.

After Stalin's death these differences were to erupt through the surface of totalitarian secrecy and reveal themselves in various ways, as individual Soviet leaders assumed different positions on a large number of foreign policy issues, all of which not only were to have a pronounced impact on the struggle for power among Stalin's heirs but probably were articulated in the first place to bolster the political posture of various personalities and factions. Malenkov's early bid for a relaxation of international tensions, combined with a policy of greater production of consumer goods and services and a loosening of the reins on the satellite states, was designed to widen the social basis of his political support through an appeal to those sectors of Soviet society that suffered deprivations under the Stalinist system.[28] At the same time, however, the same gesture was perceived as a threat by other groups, like the Armed Forces, the heavy-industrial managers, and members of the Party Apparatus, who saw in a policy based on the relaxation of international tensions, and greater priority to consumer goods and services, a restructuring of priorities for resources and money which would leave them relatively deprived and diminish their role, status, and power in the Soviet system. The interests of these groups during the years 1953–1955 were most vocally articulated by Khrushchev, who emerged as the personal rival of Malenkov.

[28] Malenkov's policies were spelled out in his speech to the Supreme Soviet on August 8, 1953: "The government and the Central Committee of the Party consider it necessary to increase significantly the investments in the development of the light, food, and fishing industries and in agriculture, and to improve greatly the production of articles of popular consumption." On Malenkov's hope to reduce international tensions, cf. H. S. Dinerstein, *War and the Soviet Union* (New York: Praeger, 1959), pp. 65–90.

Malenkov's bid for support from a wider and more numerous constellation of social constituencies appears, in retrospect, to have been premature. The light-industrial managers, the rank and file state officials, the intellectuals and professionals, the ordinary Soviet citizens — all of whom would be the beneficiaries of Malenkov's policies — had not yet developed either the political leverage or awareness to mobilize their latent power so as to prevail against the powerful combination of party bureaucrats, industrial managers, and the professional military, who exercised a near monopoly control over the instruments of coercion and means of production.

This powerful coalition, however, was not entirely monolithic in its outlook, and discrete but sharp divergencies of views existed among them which were temporarily submerged in the opposition to Malenkov only to reappear once Malenkov was dethroned. First, those members of the coalition with the narrowest internal constituency, like Molotov, were almost immediately isolated on questions of foreign policy, particularly as it related to relations within the Communist bloc, which at this stage was restricted essentially to bringing Yugoslavia back within the Communist confraternity and eradicating the conditions that were causing a rapid deterioration of relations with China. Thus even before Malenkov was formally removed from authority, the spokesmen for the victorious coalition journeyed to Peking and Belgrade to mend Soviet relations with those two Communist states.

After Malenkov's resignation as Premier, the anti-Malenkov coalition started coming apart and new combinations were reorganized. Khrushchev's coalition continued the policy of isolating Molotov by coming out in favor of a relaxation of tensions, but without a substantial reduction in defense expenditures or abandonment of the priority for heavy industry in economic development until after 1956. The innovations introduced by Khrushchev at the Twentieth Party Congress introduced the next stage in the political struggle and the manipulation of foreign policy for internal factional political advantage. Not only was the isolation of Molotov completed with the doctrinal emendations relating to the "inevitability of war," "capitalist encirclement," "peaceful coexistence," "peaceful transition," and negation of the Stalinist "two-camp" image, but some of the heavy-industrial managers were also threatened with isolation by the new regime's proposals to deconcentrate and decentralize the Soviet economic establishment. The denunciation of Stalin reinforced the isolation of Molotov and also was designed to tarnish Malenkov, Kaganovich, and other Soviet leaders and officials closely identified with the late dictator. Khrushchev, however, was careful not to alienate the military, for while he called for a relaxation of international tensions, he did not diminish the overall military budget too drastically nor did he decentralize the economic ministries connected with armaments production. Marshal Zhukov was elected an alternate member of the Party Presidium, while the denunciation of Stalin, the rehabilitation of military victims of Stalin's purges, and the relaxation of party controls in the military widened the area of common interest between the Khrushchev faction and the military.

The consequences of Khrushchev's innovations at the Twentieth Party Congress were extremely complicated and mixed, for they did not have the intended effect of simply polarizing Soviet politics into sharp and unambiguous cleavages. Khrushchev's emendations, however, not only served to drive his new rivals into the arms of his old, but the wide sweep of his formulations also either threatened members and groups within his own coalition, or created situations which some of his allies perceived as opportunities to preserve or advance their own political fortunes and interests against his. Furthermore, consternation was provoked within the Communist bloc itself, as factional cleavages developed within satellite parties, leading to the Hungarian uprising and the emergence of a defiant Poland under Gomulka's leadership. The denunciation of Stalin, in particular, threatened not only Khrushchev's political rivals at home, but some of his own allies, and various Communist leaders in Eastern Europe and in China, all of which served to feed inputs back into the Soviet political system which threatened Khrushchev and his faction.

The events of the Twentieth Party Congress and its aftermath were welcomed in general by those forces which were deprived under Stalin, such as the light-industrial managers, who saw in the decentralization scheme a relative diminution of power and status for the heavy-industrial managers; by the intellectuals, artists, scientists, and other professionals, who expected de-Stalinization at home and relaxation of international tensions abroad to result in further liberalization of controls; and by the rank and file Soviet citizenry, who saw in the Khrushchev policies an implied promise for production of goods and services. But above all, the professional military under Marshal Zhukov's direction, felt that its interests were being amply protected by Khrushchev, and it saw in the coalition with the Khrushchev faction perhaps an opportunistic maneuver which would render it dependent upon the military, once the other groups were politically disarmed.

The net internal political effect of the Twentieth Party Congress and its aftermath was the polarization of the Soviet elites into two fragile coalitions: (1) The so-called "anti-party group" was made up of the various personalities and groups threatened by Khrushchev's policies, or who saw an opportunity for more rapid enhancement of power by deserting Khrushchev. This included the so-called "Stalinist" faction, made up of those who were threatened by the denunciation of Stalin, like Molotov, Malenkov, Kaganovich, and Voroshilov; the heavy-industrial managers, Pervukhin and Saburov, who viewed with distaste the economic decentralization and reorganization program, which would reduce their power and status; and the "opportunists," Bulganin and Shepilov, who deserted Khrushchev in anticipation of improving their position. (2) Within the Presidium, Khrushchev could rely on the undivided loyalty of only two full members, Mikoyan and Kirichenko, and the ambiguous support of Suslov, but among the alternate members, he was to find wider support, in particular that of Marshal Zhukov, who at a critical moment announced that the military was solidly behind Khrushchev. This caused the "anti-party group" to fracture into its separate components at various stages in the crisis, and this accounts in part for the different forms of punishment which were meted out.

The party leadership was reorganized after June 1957 with Khrushchev's supporters generously rewarded and Marshal Zhukov elevated to full membership in the Party Presidium. In the meantime, the open factional strife at the highest level of the Soviet political system unleashed political forces inside the Soviet Union and within the Soviet bloc which have since proved to be irreversible. Factionalism became rampant within Communist parties everywhere, while social groups within the Soviet Union, particularly the intellectuals, which were hitherto silent and only latent in their power, were stimulated into political awareness and assumed greater assertiveness. As the Soviet leadership divided into factions, social groups within the Soviet system were increasingly drawn within the vortex of the struggle as various factions issued direct or indirect appeals for support. As a consequence, the Communist party has been considerably expanded in numbers, and increasingly larger numbers of people, especially within the intelligentsia, are being drawn directly or indirectly into the Soviet political process. Whether by design or default, the Khrushchev faction of the Party Apparatus was increasingly shifting to broader social foundations of support, and its internal and external policies increasingly registered this tendency.

The Soviet military in the person of Marshal Zhukov, however, emerged as a potential threat, since if Zhukov's support could enable Khrushchev to prevail over a majority in the Presidium, could it not also support a minority against Khrushchev? Acting swiftly and skillfully, and relying upon personal animosities and factional cleavages within the military, Khrushchev sent Zhukov to Albania on a junket and effectively removed and separated him both from the party hierarchy and the military upon his return. No professional military man has since occupied a seat on the Presidium.

The neutralization of the Soviet military as an immediate political threat allowed for pressures to develop from within Khrushchev's new constellation of social constituencies to couple his policy of relaxing international tensions with a radical shift in emphasis from heavy industry to consumer goods and services. Such a policy would entail a reduction in investment for both heavy industry and the military, and consequently residual, but effective opposition has come from both sectors — enough to slow down the shift but not sufficient to arrest it completely, except when international developments render it unavoidable, as was the case during the period between the U-2 crisis and the test ban treaty.

As a result, a new sociopolitical balance has emerged in the Soviet political process, whereby the previous gross disparity in power among various groups has been sharply diminished, so that the Soviet system has assumed the characteristics of a limited quasi-pluralistic polity. This has brought about a greater relaxation of controls at home, a higher level of tolerance for diversity and dissent, and less fear of severe deprivation or punishment. Policies and views which have been advanced and defeated survive to be advanced once again, to be repeatedly rebuffed, or to emerge as finally victorious. Discussion and debate of an internal character (in public or in camera), preceding decisions, are becoming increasingly significant characteristics of Soviet domestic policy, although discussion and debate concerning foreign policy still remain largely behind closed doors. But even in this connection, significant differences in opinion concerning both military and foreign policy are increasingly apparent in journals, periodicals, and books. Furthermore the open polemics with Red China have been a useful surrogate for a public debate on foreign policy, particularly for outside observers.

Thus while foreign policy has always been subordinate to internal political needs, this was not always apparent during the Stalinist era. During the past decade, however, it has become increasingly obvious not only that foreign policy decisions reflect internal political processes, but that the consequences of these decisions feed back and affect the fortunes of various individuals and groups differently. Whereas under Stalin the interplay between foreign policy and internal politics was extremely narrow — the interests of Stalin and a handful of other personalities and groups being the only social inputs into the process and all other Soviet citizens being subject to the consequences — now the spectrum of individuals and groups whose interests constitute inputs into the Soviet political system is incomparably larger. In some respects Soviet foreign policy now reflects a social spectrum of interests — numerically, not substantively — similar to the initial phases of the de-aristocraticization and gradual democratization of foreign policy in Western Europe and the United States.

Increasingly many Soviet foreign policy decisions are designed principally for the impact they will have on various internal forces. Without any attempt to organize these internal purposes served by foreign policy into a structured pattern of priorities or to distinguish among them too discretely or precisely, it can be said that the following internal purposes have influenced and will continue to influence Soviet foreign policy decisions, separately or in combination with one another or with external purposes discussed earlier:

1. To provide a faction or coalition of factions in the Soviet hierarchy with an advantage in the struggle for power.

2. To justify the continuation, modification, or repudiation of existing policies, practices, institutions, and decisions.

3. To justify the perpetuation of the existing distribution of resources, rewards, and deprivations.

4. To justify the redistribution of resources, rewards, and deprivations.

5. To pacify or satisfy the demands of particular social groups.

6. To use foreign policy decisions as a diversionary maneuver to conceal, obscure, or falsify the real reasons for certain internal policies, actions, and failures.

7. To encourage the creation or alteration of a particular internal mood.

8. To justify the retention, modification, or repudiation of certain ideological propositions whose effects are substantially internal in character.

INTERNAL SOCIAL AND POLITICAL POLARIZATION ON FOREIGN POLICY ISSUES

Soviet foreign policy decisions are nearly always marked by controversy and conflict. The allegedly monolithic will and policy of the Soviet regime have been repeatedly exposed as little more than a veneer beneath which conflict rages more or less continuously. This was true even during Stalin's rule, although conflict was largely muted. Six months before Stalin's death on the eve of the Nineteenth Party Congress Stalin ominously reported that serious controversy had taken place within the Politburo over basic questions of both internal and external policy. The "doctors' plot," which unfolded in January 1953, was apparently designed to resolve these conflicts in a way characteristic of Stalin's rule — the blood purge. Khrushchev's secret speech at the Twentieth Party Congress provided the outside world with further information and insight as to how foreign policy decisions were made under Stalin. Since these matters have already been treated in greater detail, they need not detain us here.[29]

What is significant, however, is that in spite of these fierce inner conflicts the Soviet elite at the very top has demonstrated an unusual degree of ideo-social consensus, which has been sustained over a long period of time. It is some sort of tribute to the Soviet system that after nearly half a century of cataclysmic existence, no significant coterie of prominent exiled Soviet politicians exists anywhere. The indisputable truth is that not a single Soviet official with the former status of government minister, Central Committee member, or high Union Republican or party official has defected since the forced exile of Trotsky in 1928. This is all the more remarkable since many Soviet officials stationed abroad, including heads of diplomatic missions, returned home to Stalin's abattoir and concentration camps rather than defect. Many high Soviet state and party officials have had and continue to have opportunities to flee abroad or to remain outside the country. Even during the war, no prominent Soviet official defected or went over to the opposition. The same has not been true, of course, of lower ranking officials from the secret police, armed forces, diplomatic service, and elsewhere.[30]

This indicates that members of the Soviet elite at the very top

[29] Cf. pp. 514–515, this text.

[30] Cf., for example, Alexander Barmine, *One Who Survived* (New York, Putnam's, 1945); W. G. Krivitsky, *In Stalin's Secret Service* (New York, Harper, 1939); Alexander Orlov, *The Secret History of Stalin's Crimes* (New York, Random House, 1953); Peter Deriabin and Frank Gibney, *The Secret World* (Garden City, Doubleday, 1959); Aleksandr Kaznacheev, *Inside a Soviet Embassy* (Philadelphia, Lippincott, 1962).

assign highest priority to the preservation of the Soviet social order, even if it results in their individual self-destruction. Even the Soviet secret police, formerly one of the principal institutional actors in the Soviet political system, was dismantled and its elite decapitated without producing more than an insignificant ripple of defection.

The Soviet elite, we can therefore assume, assigns highest priority to the security and survival of the Soviet state and its social order. Whether the Soviet elite would sacrifice the social order to assure the survival of the physical components of the Soviet state — its territory, material property, and population — is difficult to say, but the author's guess would be that it would not; that is, it would risk thermonuclear destruction rather than allow the Soviet social order to be disestablished. This high degree of ideo-social consensus is not characteristic of other Communist countries, with the possible exception of China.

Soviet foreign policy decisions are formulated within the party and executed through state organs.[31] Differences and conflicts over foreign policy in the party may result from several factors, individually or in combination:

1. Personality differences at the very highest levels, involving personal ambitions for power, prestige, and status.

2. Group differences at a lower level of the hierarchy, a factor which may reflect itself in factional conflicts — resulting from divergent perceptions of the impact of foreign policy decisions upon the status, role, and power of the various social elites, institutional groupings, regional combinations, national groups, and cliques and factions within these major groupings — for ascendancy within their particular grouping or institution. This factionalism may reflect itself in conflict between state and party institutions, between various state institutions, between various party organizations, between young, ambitious individuals and their older superiors, between various sectors of the economy, between local and national priorities, and between various geographical and nationality areas.

3. Differences over doctrinal interpretations, stemming largely, under existing conditions, from differing perceptions of how doctrinal positions may affect the role and status of the individual and collective actors in the system as each attempts to define and shape ideology to accord with its own interests. While doctrinal interpretations are frequently shaped to meet social interests, very often, because of the peculiar role ideology plays in the Soviet system, ideological differences may assume a separate significance which transcends conflicts of social interests.

4. Differences over strategy and tactics; that is, differences over the most effective way to achieve agreed-upon common objectives, defined in terms of the social priorities established in the process of implementing common goals. Frequently several strategies or tactical

[31] Cf. V. V. Aspaturian, "Soviet Foreign Policy," in R. C. Macridis, ed., *Foreign Policy in World Politics* (Englewood Cliffs, New Jersey, Prentice-Hall, 1962), pp. 152–76.

approaches may have equal chance of success, but a different set of social priorities may be involved in the process in each case. This type of conflict has become very explicit with respect to the Sino-Soviet dispute as was discussed earlier in another connection. Just as individuals, groups, institutions, etc., seek to shape ideology to satisfy or accord with their particular interests, so are strategies and tactics subject to similar distortion.

Soviet doctrine considers personality factors to be of little consequence in policy decisions, but ever since the denunciations of Stalin and the "cult of personality," it has become virtually impossible to sustain this view in word or deed. Indeed, since Stalin's death, Soviet sources have repeatedly conceded that personal ambitions and personal animosities have played an important role in Soviet political behavior. Stalin is characterized as having abused his position in order to enhance his personal power, while Beria, Malenkov, Molotov and the antiparty group, and Zhukov have been successively accused of seeking personal power or making decisions which would settle "personal scores."[32]

Even more important, Soviet sources seem to emphasize that these individuals were acting as representatives of groups and using institutional structures as vehicles of power against the Party Apparatus (always identified as "The Party"). Thus Beria was charged with using the secret police as a vehicle of power,[33] Malenkov with the state bureaucracy, Molotov with the Foreign Ministry and the Ministry of State Control, Pervukhin and Saburov with various economic agencies, Kaganovich with the Ministry of Supply, and Marshal Zhukov with the armed forces.[34]

[32] Kosygin, for example, charged that the "basic motive" of the antiparty group was "personal resentment and ambition"; that they "felt they had little power." *Pravda*, July 4, 1957. S. D. Ignatiev revealed Bulganin's craving for more power and prestige by asserting: "Nikita Sergeyevich [Khrushchev] was right when he said: 'Bulganin ran after a piece of gingerbread which the antiparty group offered him. Although the gingerbread was poisonous, Bulganin, being dissatisfied with his position in the Party, nevertheless ran after it when it was promised to him.'" *Plenum Tsentralnovo Komiteta Kommunisticheskoi Partii Sovietskovo Soyuza, 15–19 Dekabria 1958 Goda, Stenograficheskii Otchet* (Moscow, 1958), p. 350.

[33] The statement announcing the arrest of Beria made the following charges: "It has been established by the inquiry that Beria, using his position, forged a treacherous group of conspirators, hostile to the Soviet State, with the criminal goal of using the organs of the Ministry of Internal Affairs, both central and local, against the Communist Party and the Government of the U.S.S.R. in the interests of foreign capital, striving in its perfidious schemes to set the Ministry of Internal Affairs above the Party and Government in order to seize power and liquidate the Soviet worker-peasant system for the purpose of restoring capitalism and the domination of the bourgeoisie." *Pravda*, December 17, 1953.

[34] For details concerning this aspect of the factional struggles in the Soviet hierarchy, cf., H. S. Dinerstein, *War and the Soviet Union* (New York, Praeger, 1959); Robert Conquest, *Power and Policy in the U.S.S.R.* (New York, St. Martin's Press. 1961), esp. pp. 292–328; Roger Pethybridge, *A Key to Soviet Politics* (New York, Praeger, 1962); and Aspaturian in Macridis, *Modern Political Systems*, pp. 152–68; cf. pp. 535–536, this text.

It might be pointed out that in all cases mentioned above the personal passion for power, and the attempt to use institutional structures successfully as power bases, failed because Khrushchev, the chief beneficiary of all these failures, was able to use the Party Apparatus skillfully, in alliance first with one group and then another, to establish the supremacy of the Party Apparatus in the system and the dominance of his faction within it.

Without going into a detailed accounting of the intricate maneuvers and intrigues involved, it can be assumed that these factional conflicts arise because a symbiotic relationship becomes established between the interests of certain individual leaders and the interests of certain elites. While these functional elites are fairly well defined, considerable lateral mobility exists at various levels among them, and personal attachments to certain institutions are likely to be transitory and opportunistic rather than permanent, insofar as the leaders are concerned.

Furthermore, the institutional and functional-interest groupings are themselves divided by personality and factional conflicts over the relative importance of various branches and sectors of the government and the economy, the allocation of budgets, and the assignments of role and mission. To the degree that foreign policy decisions affect these relationships, they give rise to internal factional strife.

The foreign policy and defense posture of the Soviet state establish a certain configuration of priorities in the allocation of budgetary expenses and scarce resources. Various individuals and groups develop a vested interest in a particular foreign policy or defense posture because of the role and status it confers upon them. Correspondingly, other individuals and groups in Soviet society perceive themselves as deprived in status and rewards because of existing allocation of expenditures and resources; hence they might initiate proposals that could alter existing foreign policy and defense postures or support proposals submitted by other groups or individuals.

Herbert S. Dinerstein has demonstrated rather impressively how Khrushchev cleverly manipulated the fear of war to his advantage in his struggle first with Malenkov and then with the antiparty group in 1957. "Alarms of war," he writes,

> may offer political advantage to the alarmist in a factional fight. To the factionary, of course, his attaining office, or continuing in it, is a matter of major ideological import. The opponent's faction, he believes, will take the country to the dogs by perverting true Bolshevism or by failing to adjust it to the changing situation. When, in the early months of 1957, Khrushchev raised a wholly contrived danger of war, he himself and those who supported him probably believed that his displacement would be accompanied by dangerous political changes. The alarm of war was raised to keep one faction in office and this suggests that a lower probability was assigned in fact to the likelihood of war.[35]

[35] Dinerstein, *War and the Soviet Union*, p. 93.

The Soviet Union, like the United States, is involved in a continuous great debate over foreign policy and national security matters centering around the issue of whether the heightening of international tensions or the relaxation of international tensions best serves the "national interests." In both countries there are important spokesmen on both sides, although in the Soviet Union those who may be interested in maintaining international tensions make their views known only behind closed doors or in the esoteric type of communication which has inspired the profession of "Kremlinology." The polemics with Peking, however, provide the outside world with some idea of how the debate behind closed doors may be taking place. Thus on June 19, 1964, *Izvestia* published the substance of an alleged interview between a Latin-American Communist and Mao Tse-tung, in which the Chinese leader purportedly said:

> Who benefits from international tension? The United States? Great Britain? The world proletariat? In this lies the problem. Personally, I like international tension. The United States will realize that the tension they themselves have created is not advantageous to them, since it can force the supporters of peace and all working people of the entire world to think, and will bring a greater number of people into the Communist Parties. . . . There is a Chinese proverb: "People dare to touch the tiger's whiskers." This is why I think that we should not fear international tension.[36]

And a year earlier, Moscow, in an "open letter" to Soviet party members, bluntly asserted:

> One gets the impression that the leaders of the C.P.C. think it to their advantage to maintain and intensify international tension, especially in relations between the U.S.S.R. and the U.S.A. They obviously think that the Soviet Union should answer provocations with provocations, should fall into the traps set by the "madmen" from the imperialist camp, should accept the challenge of the imperialists to enter a competition in adventurism and aggressiveness — i.e., a competition not to ensure peace but to unleash war.[37]

On the other hand, the official Soviet position is that a relaxation of tensions is beneficial to the Soviet Union, the Communist world as a whole, and the revolutionary movement:

> In a situation of rising international tension war hysteria strengthens the influence of militarist and reactionary forces; with the successes of the policy of peaceful coexistence, on the other hand, more favorable conditions arise for the masses' gains on the side of socialism, for development of the revolutionary movement.[38]

[36] *Izvestia*, June 19, 1964. Cf. also *Pravda*, September 21 and 22, 1963.
[37] *Pravda*, July 14, 1963.
[38] "For the Triumph of Creative Marxism-Leninism, Against Revising Course of the World Communist Movement," *Kommunist*, No. 11, July 1963, pp. 19–20. Yury Zhukov, in an article entitled "Who Is For, Who Is Against?" linked the Chinese position with the "madmen" in the United States on the

Only Molotov and the antiparty group have been specifically identified by the Soviet leadership with a policy of favoring international tensions. Nevertheless the factional conflicts in the Soviet Union — over budgets, military strategy, the likelihood of war and violence, the nature of imperialism, perceptions of American "ruling class" behavior, and the proper balance between the production of consumer goods and services and heavy industry in the Soviet economy — clearly indicate that tension-producing policies tend to favor certain groups within Soviet society and tension-lessening policies tend to favor others. Although a residual fervor of an ideological commitment to specific goals and policies remains operative in the thought and behavior of Soviet leaders, there has also been an inexorable tendency for individual leaders and factional interest groups to perceive the interests of society as a whole through their own prism and to distort and adjust the national interest accordingly. Ideological distortion takes shape in similar fashion in order to impart the necessary symbolic legitimacy to policies and interests demanded by the Soviet system as part of its political ritual.

A particular interest group or social formation may often have a role or function imposed upon it by events, circumstances, policies, and the mechanism of a given social system in response to certain situations not of its own making or, in some instances, situations that objectively provided the basis for its very creation and existence. Particular interest groups may not have sought such a role, or have taken any initiative in acquiring it; they may not even have existed before the function was demanded. Yet once this role or function has been thrust upon them, they adjust to it and develop a vested interest in it as the source of their existence and status. As individual members adjust to their role, develop it, and invest their energies and careers in it, they almost automatically resist the deprivation or diminution of this function in their self-interest.

The same is true of groups which have been assigned limited or

basis of the formula embodied in the title of his article. *Pravda,* July 29, 1963. Another *Pravda* writer, F. Burlatsky, in an article entitled "Concrete Analysis Is a Major Requirement of Leninism," rejects the Chinese view "that the revolutionary struggle of the working class in capitalist countries and the national liberation movement can develop successfully only if there is constant international tension — 'cold war,'" and rhetorically asks: "What effect does an increase in international tension and a heightening of war psychosis have on internal conditions, on the political struggle of the masses? There can be only one answer to this question: a highly negative effect. . . . By using the bugbear of the 'threat of war' and inflaming nationalist prejudices and chauvinism the ruling classes in the capitalist countries have striven and are still striving to undermine the international solidarity of the proletariat and to isolate its advanced forces. An atmosphere of war hysteria makes it easier for the forces of reaction to carry out repressions against the Communists. . . . On the other hand, a slackening of tension and successes of the policy of peaceful coexistence are accompanied by an intensification of the workers' movement and a new upsurge of class struggle in the capitalist world." *Pravda,* July 25, 1963. Cf. also N. Inozemtsev, "Peaceful Coexistence and the World Revolutionary Process," *Pravda,* July 28, 1963.

arrested roles or functions in society — except that they develop a vested interest in expanding the role, dignifying it with greater status and prestige, and demanding greater rewards. Consequently it is extremely difficult to distill out of Soviet factional positions those aspects of thought and behavior which express conflicting perceptions of self-interest on the part of various individuals, factions, and groups as opposed to authentic "objective" considerations of a broader interest, whether national or ideological — since they are so inextricably intertwined and interdependent.

All that we can assume at this point is that certain individuals, factions, and socio-institutional functional groups seem to thrive and flourish and others to be relatively deprived and arrested in their development under conditions of exacerbated international tensions, while the situation is reversed when a relaxation of international tensions takes place.

Without attempting to speculate on the motives for a particular foreign and security policy, let us examine the possible impact upon the interests of various social groups in Soviet society of a foreign policy based upon expectations of high international tensions (whether generated from without or within) as opposed to one which would be based upon the expectation of a relaxation of international tensions and *détente* (irrespective of whether generated from without or within). It should be made clear that a one-to-one relationship between cause and effect is much too simple an explanation even for hypothetical purposes, but the reconstructions below are based on actual reactions of individual Soviet spokesmen representing various groups in Soviet society, as reported in the Soviet press or attributed to them by other Communist sources, including the Chinese.

"WHO BENEFITS" IN SOVIET SOCIETY FROM INTERNATIONAL TENSIONS?

Soviet writers are fond of citing Lenin's injunction that the rewards of a particular social system should not be defined in terms of "who favors" a particular policy but rather of "who benefits" from a given policy. Thus one Soviet writer, in applying Lenin's maxim to an examination of the role of the "military-industrial complex" in American society, made the following observation:

> Lenin taught us that behind every proposal and every measure are the real interests of quite definite political and social groups and that in each specific case it is necessary to elucidate whom these proposals and measures benefit. "The important thing is not *who* directly upholds a certain policy, for to defend any of his views in the conditions of the noble modern capitalist system a rich man can always 'hire' or buy or enlist any number of lawyers, writers, even members of parliament, professors, priests, and so on. We live in the business times when the bourgeoisie is not ashamed of trading in both honor and conscience. . . . No, in politics it is not so important who directly upholds certain

views. The important thing is *who benefits* by these views, these proposals, these measures."[39]

A great deal has been said and written about the military-industrial complex in the United States and its alleged vested stake in maintaining and even fanning the Cold War. While individuals and groups undoubtedly exist in the United States whose interests might be adversely affected by a relaxation of international tensions and a *détente*, it is not generally recognized that a counterpart to the American military-industrial complex exists in the Soviet Union, whose interests are also favored under conditions of international tension and Cold War. We already have it on the highest Soviet authority that the social foundations exist in Communist-governed societies for individuals and groups to develop a vested interest in maintaining international tensions, since the current Soviet leadership has explicitly charged that both the anti-party group in the C.P.S.U. (which almost seized power in 1957) and the Chinese Communist leaders at the present time have a vested interest in keeping international tensions at a high pitch.

It would be absurd to maintain, as Lenin does implicitly, that because certain individuals and groups are favored by policies flowing from an exacerbation of the international environment these groups necessarily favor or deliberately promote policies designed to sustain or create international tensions, any more than it can be asserted that individuals and groups favored by a peacetime economy would deliberately favor or promote policies which would expose the country to external danger simply to avoid a rise in defense expenditures which might adversely affect their interests. It cannot be excluded, however, that motivations of this character also exist. The problem is much more complicated than conscious motivation. Aside from the phenomena of "false consciousness," false perceptions, mistaken judgment, false or incomplete information, misinterpretation, etc., which are always involved in attempting to relate social motivation to policy behavior, there is the more serious problem of genuine and unconscious distortion of the objective situation through the prism of individual or group self-interest. Perception itself is frequently a reflection of self-interest rather than objective reality, and even more frequently it is simply a distortion of objective reality to a greater or lesser degree.

What can be assumed, because of these complicated psychological dialogues between perceptions of self-interest and perception of objective reality, is that groups that are favored by a particular policy or situation have a greater inclination to perceive objective reality in terms of their self-interest. Hence groups that are objectively favored by heightened international tensions might have a greater propensity to perceive external threats and a corresponding disinclination to recognize that the nature of a threat has been altered, reduced, or eliminated, thus requiring new policies which might adversely affect them. On the

[39] I. Yermashov, "The Warfare State," *International Affairs* (Moscow), No. 7, July 1962, 19.

other hand, groups that are objectively favored by relaxation of international tensions or a peacetime economy might be more prone to perceive a premature alteration, diminution, or elimination of an external threat and a corresponding tendency to be skeptical about external threats which arise if they would result in a radical upsurge in defense expenditures and a reallocation of resources and social rewards.

Even sophisticated Soviet writers now find it difficult to apply consistently the Leninist maxim of "who benefits" to the American political and social scene in a simplistic manner, since it would result in contravening other cherished dogmas of Soviet ideology. Thus one influential Soviet specialist on U.S. affairs, after a trip to the United States, revealed an increasing sophistication in observing and reporting on American society and politics:

> The picture of political and intellectual life in the U.S.A. is extremely complex and varied and is in many ways contradictory; we saw this more than once during our trip. It is perfectly natural to find completely different ways of thinking among people occupying diametrically opposite positions in the social structure — representatives of "big business" and of the working class, say. But there are considerable differences even within the basic classes. For instance, there are great differences in position and views between the 4,000,000 unemployed and the best-paid strata of the working class. We also encountered the following situation: In conditions where the overwhelming majority of the American working class favors a disarmament program, the segment of workers who are directly connected with arms production favors the preservation of this production in full. . . . It is common knowledge that in the conditions of capitalist reality, monopoly capital is the center of political reaction. However, the monopolistic bourgeoisie of the U.S.A. is by no means unified or homogeneous; by no means all of its representatives support the "madmen" or the "war party." . . . There are deep contradictions between the group of influential monopoly associations directly engaged in war production and all the other industrial and banking corporations, some of them very large but still deprived of access to the "pie" of government military orders. These contradictions find acute expression in the approach to many practical questions: tax cuts, the military budget, foreign economic policy and others.[40]

Factional differences over foreign policy and budgetary questions are not directly expressed in Soviet media of information and communications, since neither political factions nor the social foundations for divergent interests on such questions are supposed to exist. Only after a serious debate, which leads to an open struggle for power, has been definitively resolved are retrospective factional activities admitted, but the standard Soviet ritual is that they have been eliminated and that no social basis exists for their perpetuation or revival.[41] Some Soviet

[40] N. Inozemtsev, "The Hopes and Anxieties of Americans," *Pravda*, December 25, 1963.

[41] Cf. Kozlov's explanation at the 22nd Party Congress cited above, p. 227. The statement announcing Beria's arrest, for example, asserted: "Deprived of any social support within the U.S.S.R., Beria and his accomplices

sociologists, with empirical and behavioral orientations — which is a distinctive intellectual innovation in itself — are beginning to concede that social and other differences in Soviet society influence and shape social and political attitudes. "The opinion of each person polled," according to a Soviet experimenter with public-polling techniques, "is influenced by the nature of his attitude toward life, by his moral evaluation of his personal goal and means of attaining it," which, in turn, is dependent on "how the respondent's social situation, age, and so on influenced his opinion." Thus he explained:

> The poll permitted determining the degree of dependence of the judgment of different groups of youth on the nature of their activity (factory workers, collective farmers, officeworkers, engineers, professional people, servicemen, students, and school children, as well as the nonworking); education (incomplete secondary, secondary, higher); age (under 17, 18–22, 23–30); place of residence (Moscow, large cities, other cities, countryside); and sex.[42]

The tyranny exercised by the international situation on Soviet budgetary allocations and the fortuitous and objective impact they have on the fortunes, status, rewards, and deprivations of various groups in Soviet society was more than implicit in Khrushchev's frequent complaints about the allocation of money and resources.

> It is necessary to state frankly: When the government reviews questions of the distribution of means by branches — where to direct how much of the available resources — difficult puzzles often have to be solved. On the one hand, it would be desirable to build more enterprises that make products for satisfying man's requirements, that produce clothing, footwear, and other goods for improving people's lives. It would be desirable to invest more means in agriculture and to expand housing construction. We know that the people need this. The leaders of our party and government themselves come from the people; they know their needs and share their life. To give more good things to the people — this is the basic goal of the Communist Party of the Soviet Union. . . . On the other hand, life dictates the necessity for spending enormous funds on maintaining our military power at the required level. This reduces and cannot help but reduce the people's possibilities of obtaining direct benefits. But this must be done in order to defend the victories of the October Revolution, the victories of socialism, and to keep the imperialists from attacking our homeland, from unleashing a general war. That is why when calculating available resources we must

---

based their criminal calculations on support of the conspiracy by reactionary imperialist forces from abroad." Yet, he was also accused of undertaking "criminal measures in order to stir up the remains of bourgeois-nationalist elements in the Union Republics, to sow enmity and discord among the peoples of the U.S.S.R., and, in the first place, to undermine the friendship of the peoples of the U.S.S.R. with the great Russian people," which indicates that he was looking for internal social support among the border nationalities. *Pravda*, December 17, 1953.

[42] M. Kh. Igitkhanyan, "The Spiritual Image of Soviet Youth," *Voprosy Filosofii*, No. 6, June 1963, 75–84.

soberly consider the needs of the peaceful economy and the requirements of defense and must so combine the one with the other that there will be no overemphasis on either.[43]

The social and institutional groups in Soviet society which appear to benefit from an aggressive foreign policy and the maintenance of international tensions are (1) the armed forces, (2) the heavy-industrial managers, (3) professional party *apparatchiki* and ideologues. By no means do all individuals or sub-elites and cliques within these groups see eye to eye on foreign policy issues. Some individuals and sub-elites, for opportunistic or careerist reasons or functional adaptability, are able to adjust to a relaxation of tensions by preserving or even improving their role and status. The significant point is that the main impetus for an aggressive policy and the chief opposition to a relaxation of tensions find their social and functional foundations within these three socio-functional or socio-institutional groups, whose common perception of

---

[43] *Pravda*, February 28, 1963. A year later, at the February 1964 Plenum of the Central Committee, Khrushchev, in discussing the plan to expand chemical production, once again revealed in graphic, if only schematic form, how various groups protected their interests against attempts to reallocate resources to their detriment. "How is it possible to explain such an attitude toward chemistry in a country that has given the world such great figures of chemical science? . . . Only by the fact that a section of the workers of the Gosplan, by force of their departmental attachment to specific branches of production, did not appreciate the importance of chemistry in time. . . . It would seem beyond question that chemistry should be given priority, . . . that more capital investments should be devoted to the development of the chemical industry. . . . In 1958 we adopted a decision and outlined a program for the development of chemistry, but it is not being fully carried out. Why? Is it that funds have been insufficient? Nothing of the kind. We are overfulfilling the plan for metallurgy, oil extraction, and in other branches. But in chemistry . . . the tasks envisaged by the May Plenum of the Central Committee have not been accomplished. How is this to be explained? How is the process of the distribution of funds among different branches proceeding in our country? Let us take as an example the metallurgy committee. The heads of this committee are little interested in chemistry. They concern themselves primarily with the way metal production is going to develop. . . . Huge quantities of various materials are necessary to build Communism. Hence, workers responsible for the production of steel must understand what is new and draw the necessary practical conclusions. It is this kind of understanding of which there is a shortage in some leading workers. The Gosplan is called upon to correct the narrow-mindedness of branch workers. It is duty bound to redistribute in good time material and financial resources for the benefit of new, progressive branches and to maintain reserves for this purpose. . . . By contrast, we have at times taken the position that a definite place is assigned to every sector of every branch and it is very difficult to change existing proportions. . . . Everyone then guards his own sector within the limits assigned to him. . . . And what shall we do with what is new in the economy, since it is emerging every day and demanding attention and material safeguards? The resources are already distributed among the old branches and trends. This approach impedes the development of new branches, and technical progress. . . ." *Pravda*, February 15, 1964. Cf. also Carl Linden, "Khrushchev and the Party Battle," *Problems of Communism*, September–October 1963, pp. 27–35; S. I. Ploss, *Recent Alignments in the Soviet Elite* (Princeton, Center of International Studies, 1964).

interests results in an informal "military-industrial-apparatus complex." Their attitudes stem almost entirely from the function and role they play in Soviet society and the rewards in terms of prestige, status, and power which are derived from these functions in time of high international tensions as opposed to a *détente*.

The professional military, on the whole, has a natural interest in a large and modern military establishment and a high priority on budget and resources; the heavy-industrial managerial groups have a vested stake in preserving the primacy of their sector of the economy; and the Party Apparatus traditionally has had a vested interest in ideological conformity and the social controls which they rationalized, thus ensuring the primacy of the Apparatus over all other social forces in the Soviet system. All these functional roles are served best under conditions of international tension. Consequently, these groups wittingly or unwittingly have developed a vested interest in either maintaining international tensions or creating the illusion of insecurity and external danger, which would produce the same effect.

To the degree that individuals or sub-elites within these groups are able socially to retool their functions and adapt them to peacetime or purely internal functions, then do they correspondingly lose interest in an aggressive or tension-preserving policy.

The Party Apparatus

The major enigma in relating socio-functional and institutional groups in Soviet society to various internal and external policy positions is the precise nature of the factional pattern within the Party Apparatus. It is relatively easier to decipher internal factional cleavages within the armed forces and heavy industry because of the greater spectrum of technical and functional divisions which characterizes their activities. The Party Apparatus, on the other hand, is the only major socio-institutional group in the Soviet system which performs neither a productive nor a clear service function. While it guides and audits both the economy and the government, and members of the Apparatus have assumed formal administrative responsibility in both the economic and governmental establishments from time to time, it is neither an executive nor an administrative elite. Its sole function in Soviet society stems from its unilaterally preempted role of manipulating and articulating the will of the party. It sets the ideological norms of the Soviet social order, formulates both internal and external policy, and finally audits or checks on their fulfillment by other socio-functional and institutional elites.

Traditionally the Apparatus has been associated with the internal missions of ideological conformity and political direction and the external mission of promoting world revolution. As pointed out earlier, these missions of the Party Apparatus were increasingly alienating it from the numerically large and potentially significant social constituencies, whose will it was allegedly expressing. On the other hand, the dismantling of the special instrument of coercion erected by Stalin as a counter-poise to the armed forces, the secret police, left the Apparatus increasingly dependent upon the armed forces and their allies, the heavy-industrial managers.

Khrushchev's response to the social dilemma of the Apparatus was to provide it with a more durable social function by associating its ideological mission more directly with the will of the Soviet people in the concrete rather than in the historical abstraction of a predetermined proletarian mission. This has assumed the goal of "building Communism" — that is, raising the Soviet standard of living within the ideological norms of a Communist society, which, in turn, required a relaxation of international tensions so that a radical reduction of defense expenditures could be realized.

This social retooling process has been viewed with skepticism by many old-time Apparatus careerists and has given rise to new patterns of factional conflict within the Apparatus, whose outlines are still extremely fluid and hazy. Since the expulsion of the antiparty group in 1957, there are no Stalinists, per se, remaining in the Apparatus. Differences, however, have arisen over the degree and extent of the de-Stalinization process and the treatment of the antiparty group. What can more properly be described as a "conservative" faction — also anonymously called "dogmatists" by their detractors — whose leaders appear to have been the late Kozlov and Suslov, seems to have played a significant role in opposing, slowing down, or arresting Khrushchev's policies and actually may have been in a position to oust him in the spring of 1963, after the Cuban missile crisis. After Kozlov suffered a heart attack in April 1963, Khrushchev's fortunes seemed to take a turn for the better.

This conservative faction represents two subfactional groups within the Party Apparatus, the professional ideologues, whose major spokesman is Suslov, and those who are more directly involved in control and audit functions, whose spokesman seemed to be Kozlov before his heart attack and subsequent death. To the degree that the interests of this faction require greater investment in military and heavy-industrial expenditures, it also serves to articulate the interests of the professional military and of heavy industry, since neither of these groups is directly represented in either the Party Presidium or the Secretariat.

The conservative faction of the Apparatus saw in Khrushchev's policies a threat to the very existence of the Apparatus itself, for if the external ideological function of the Apparatus erodes and its internal functions can be more efficiently performed by technical and administrative specialists, what is the Apparatus to do? The fact that Yugoslavia is still considered to be a "socialist state," although its Communist party has withered into a "league," must be a source of grim anxiety for this group, since it establishes the precedent of a socialist state without a separate party machine.[44]

[44] On April 8, 1963, the May Day slogan for Yugoslavia published by *Pravda* failed to enumerate it among the countries "building socialism," although a Soviet letter to Peking on March 30, 1963, repudiated the Chinese

Other differences between various factions in the Apparatus reflect themselves in divergent perceptions of the American "ruling class" and the likelihood of an American surprise attack, the level of military expenditures, the balance between heavy and light industry, on methods for increasing agricultural production, the degree of ideological conformity imposed upon the arts, sciences, and professions, and finally the degree to which Moscow can afford to alienate Peking.

The periodic and frequent rotation of personnel in the Apparatus as a whole and the constant expansion and contraction of membership in the Party Presidium and Secretariat, particularly after serious changes in the direction of policy, all attest to the factional ferment taking place within the Apparatus. Since the Chinese position on many matters seems to coincide with the views of the conservative faction of the Soviet Party Apparatus, it is likely that Peking was directing its appeal to this group to overthrow Khrushchev, while Suslov's extravagant defense of Khrushchev in response could have been interpreted as a forced profession of loyalty.[45] Peking apparently made a similar esoteric overture to the Soviet military by publicly espousing a position on the validity of Clausewitz's maxim on war and politics much like that of the Soviet professional military and opposed to that adhered to by the Khrushchev faction.[46]

---

view that Yugoslavia had "betrayed Marxism-Leninism" and emphatically affirmed that "we consider that it is a socialist country." On April 11, 1963, *Pravda* published a revised slogan for Yugoslavia, which described it as "building socialism." Cf. Carl Linden, *op. cit.*, and S. I. Ploss, *Some Political Aspects of the June 1963 CPSU Central Committee Session* (Princeton, Center of International Studies, 1963).

[45] The Chinese are apparently making covert appeals to other segments of Soviet society. The noted Soviet writer Konstantin Simonov, in an article entitled, "A Writer's Notes: MAKE NO MISTAKE!" published in *Pravda* on May 24, 1964, broadly hinted that the Chinese apparently thought that they could make some headway among Soviet intellectuals: "The Chinese splitters . . . have no dispute, you understand, with the Soviet people, with the Soviet intelligentsia, with rank-and-file Soviet Communists, with the peoples of the socialist countries or the Communists of the world! They are arguing, you understand, only with the leadership of our party; they have nothing to argue about with us. They are possessed by a hope that, though it reeks of provocation, is still naive in its absurdity — the hope that perhaps some one of us will fall for the bait, will believe that the dispute is not between them and us, not between the Chinese leaders and the world Communist movement, but above our heads, so to speak, only with our leaders. It seems that it is this hope that has called forth the attempts to dose us with ponderous and tedious, clumsily contrived propaganda on the radio and the attempts to distribute to private addresses various documents containing ridiculous attacks on our party and its leadership. . . . I want to say: No, it won't work! It won't work in general, it won't work in particular, it won't work anywhere or with anyone. The bait with which you are trying to catch at least something in our country is rotten, and our people are not the kind who can be caught with this rotten stuff."

[46] The Chinese leaders are apparently making an even more subtle appeal to elements of the Soviet military who did not see eye to eye with Khrushchev on the relationship between politics and war, military strategy and foreign policy, and on the question of whether Clausewitz's maxim that

The Soviet Armed Forces

Unlike the Party Apparatus, the Soviet military has an important and highly valued function to perform in Soviet society, which since World War II has carried the armed forces to a new pinnacle of prestige, esteem, and power. It is axiomatic in any society which is subject to civilian control and ideologically dedicated to the values and goals of peace that in time of war or external danger, the value and esteem of the military are maximized and its role and influence in society magnified, while in time of peace or reduced danger, the opposite effect is likely to take place. Soviet society is conventional in this regard since, unlike fascist or chauvinistic ideologies, war is not glorified in the Soviet Union as a value-end in itself and neither is the martial spirit. Ideologically the Soviet system is committed to the abolition of war and of all military establishments. Yet unlike the Apparatus, which has alienated many groups in Soviet society, the armed forces are a genuinely cherished and popular institution and are considered more or less indispensable. Differences do arise, however, as to the size, composition, and cost of the military establishment, and it is at this point that interest configurations assume shape, and influence the political process and the role of the military in it.

War and international tensions maximize the threat to the state and hence almost spontaneously enhance the role, status, prestige, and power of the armed forces as an institution and its individual members. It guarantees a very high priority in the allocation of money, resources, and personnel. High military officials assume greater influence in the

---

"war is a continuation of politics by violent means" is still a valid proposition during the nuclear age. Although the first edition of Sokolovskii's *Military Strategy* was attacked by various political writers on these points, the second edition reflected little change from the view expressed in the first. Cf. Leon Gouré, *Notes on the Second Edition of Marshal V. D. Sokolovskii's "Military Strategy"* (Santa Monica, RAND Corporation, 1964), and Thomas W. Wolfe, *Soviet Strategy at the Crossroads* (Santa Monica, RAND Corporation, 1964), esp. pp. 71–82. The Chinese in their polemics with Moscow have charged that Khrushchev had abandoned the Leninist twist to the Clausewitz maxim, and the Khrushchev faction confirmed this by asserting that the Clausewitz formula was now outmoded in its traditional application. One Soviet commentator, Viktor Glazunov, has gone so far as to say that the formula no longer even applies to imperialist countries and that war can no longer be considered as a rational instrument of foreign policy: "In general, the views of the Chinese leaders on nuclear arms and the nature of modern warfare can only cause extreme bewilderment. It is said that nuclear rocket arms are merely a 'current type' of weapon introducing nothing new to the nature of war. Consequently, Clausewitz's old narrow formula that war is a continuation of policy still holds true in another form. And Clausewitz is at the moment very popular in Peking. . . . Hitherto there have been victors and vanquished whereas now entire countries and peoples would disappear. For them thermonuclear war would no longer be a continuation of policy, good or bad, just or unjust. For them it would be the end of everything on earth. How, then, can one say that nothing has changed in the nature of war since the appearance of nuclear weapons?" *Moscow International Service* (radio), July 22, 1964.

formulation and execution of policy because of their indispensable expertise; this results in a significant spill-over into nonmilitary areas and retains a high residual political force even as war and external danger recede.

As specialists in manipulating the instruments of violence and coercion and with a high value placed upon its services, during periods of insecurity the military threatens to become a powerful entity in its own right while it dwarfs the immediate power of other elites in Soviet society. Since the Soviet military has rarely been employed as an internal repressive force, its standing and popularity with the public are enviable in the Soviet system, whereas other elites have been tarnished in one degree or another with the stigma of Stalinist repression. This makes a large military establishment even more menacing to the political authorities, who remain haunted by the possibilities of a Bonapartist coup. The recurring fear of a military coup has been dealt with by the party in a number of ways. Stalin not only subjected the military to party and secret police controls, but he also ensured compliance through periodic purges and decapitation. Since Stalin's time, the incubus of police repression has been lifted and techniques of terror no longer employed. The question of party controls and indoctrination remains a source of continuous friction with the professional military, which seeks to limit the role of the party while the Apparatus endeavors to maximize it. Khrushchev also skillfully used personal and clique rivalries and animosities within the military, whether based on professional divisions of military labor, cronyism, or simple opportunism, in order to fracture it into internal factions and keep it disunited. The professional military probably reached its maximum point of development as an autonomous political actor under Marshal Zhukov in 1956 and 1957, when Zhukov not only had administrative direction and control of the military as Minister of Defense but sat on the Party Presidium as well, where his presence was first a comfort and then a threat to Khrushchev and his faction. The fact that Zhukov had also reduced party controls in the military to the vanishing point was also a source of anxiety to the civilian authorities.

The charges leveled against Zhukov after his removal in October 1957 were essentially four in number: (1) he tried to separate the armed forces from the party; (2) he encouraged and promoted a "cult of Zhukov" in the military; (3) he tried to organize the armed forces into a personal political machine; and (4) he was planning to seize power in a Bonapartist coup. Thus the statement issued by the Central Committee contained the following charges:

> The Plenary Session of the C.P.S.U. Central Committee notes that of late the former Defense Minister Comrade Zhukov has . . . pursued a policy of curtailing the work of Party organizations, political organs and military councils, of abolishing the leadership and control of the Party, its Central Committee and Government over the Army and Navy. The Plenary Session of the Central Committee has established that the cult of Comrade Zhukov's personality was cultivated in the Soviet Army with

his personal participation. . . . Comrade Zhukov . . . proved to be a politically unstable leader disposed to adventurism.[47]

All Zhukov's personal enemies and professional rivals, including his successor as Minister of Defense, Marshal Malinovsky, were mobilized to heap criticism and abuse upon the fallen warrior. Marshal Konev repeated the charge that Zhukov sought "a separation between the Army and the Navy on the one hand and the Party on the other" and further specified that he betrayed "a definite tendency to regard the Soviet Armed Forces as his own domain."[48] And two years later Malinovsky intimated that Zhukov was planning to seize power and establish a military regime:

> The C.C. of the C.P.S.U. discerned in an extremely timely manner the aspiration of the former Minister of Defense, Marshal Zhukov, to sever the Army from the Party, and gave this new Bonaparte a sharp rap over the knuckles.[49]

Since the removal of Marshal Zhukov, the armed forces have not been directly represented on the Party Presidium or Secretariat, and Malinovsky's position as defense minister does not entitle him to sit on the Presidium of the Council of Ministers, the chief policy-making organ of the government. He as well as other military professionals, however, are frequently invited in for consultation and discussion.

While the professional military does not currently loom as a direct threat to the party regime as it did under Zhukov, it nevertheless still functions as a powerful political force with its own perception of its interests in Soviet society. On the whole, the professional military assumes a harder position than Khrushchev on foreign policy issues and its outlook was more in tune with the views of the conservative faction in the Apparatus. In general, the professional military has resisted troop cuts and reduced military expenditures; is skeptical of disarmament and arms control measures; is more prone to view U.S. intentions as implacably aggressive; is more concerned with the possibilities of preventive war by the United States; has consistently supported a large military establishment, demanded greater defense expenditures, and more advanced military weapons; and has with equal constancy called for vigilance, preparedness, and readiness to fight any type of war from a local conflict to an all-out thermonuclear war.

The military is by no means united in its outlook. Aside from traditional service rivalries among branches and services, the military is also plagued within each service with internal divisions between "radicals" and "traditionalists"; between technically oriented officers and the conventionally trained professionals; between rocket and nuclear forces and conventional forces; between those who emphasize reliance on missiles and nuclear weapons and those who call for "balanced forces"; between those who think the initial phases of a future war will be

[47] *Pravda*, November 3, 1957.
[48] Ibid.
[49] *Pravda*, February 4, 1959 (speech at the 21st Party Congress).

decisive and those who anticipate a long war of attrition; between those who favor preemption and those who do not; between those who think that the military should be prepared for all kinds of wars and those who think that all wars involving the United States and the U.S.S.R. will inevitably escalate to total thermonuclear war.[50]

Superimposed upon these divisions, which are essentially professional in origin, are, of course, personal rivalries, clique and factional activities which may be independent of professional or technical considerations. Various factions, groups, services, and individuals in the military seek support from various factions and personalities in the Apparatus, so that some groups within the military were closely associated with Khrushchev, while others appear to have been in a state of continuous resistance to his foreign policy and the military policy which was derived from it.[51]

While, generally speaking, the professional military benefits from international tensions, this is not true of some forces, particularly the technically oriented and the rocket specialists, who are viewed with a mixture of awe and contempt by the traditional ground-force officer. Khrushchev's periodic calls for troop cuts and reductions for military spending were invariably accompanied by proposals to increase spending for missile and technical development in the military. Since a *détente* and relaxation of tensions would require in any event the maintenance of a deterrent capability, these forces are not threatened, but in fact may be favored, by a relaxation of international tensions. Furthermore, of all the officers in the military, these are most likely to adjust to peacetime careers without difficulty.[52]

Since 1955, when the first major troop cuts were made in the Soviet military, the size of the military establishment and budget has varied in almost barometric fashion with the state of international tensions. As the prospects for a *détente* and relaxation of tensions went up, as after the Camp David talks, Khrushchev would call for sharp troop reductions and smaller budgetary allocations for the traditional military; as the prospects for a *détente* diminished, as illustrated by the U-2 incident, troop cuts were arrested, military expenditures were increased, and the role of the military enhanced. Thus during the period

[50] For a discussion and elaboration of divergent views between the party and the military and within the military on issues of strategy and foreign policy, see the following: V. D. Sokolovskii, ed., *Soviet Military Strategy*, analyzed and annotated by H. S. Dinerstein, L. Gouré, and T. W. Wolfe (Englewood Cliffs, New Jersey, Prentice-Hall, 1963); Leon Gouré, *Notes on the Second Edition of Marshal V. D. Sokolovskii's "Military Strategy"* (Santa Monica, RAND Corporation, 1964); Roman Kolkowicz, *Conflicts in Soviet Party-Military Relations: 1962–1963* (Santa Monica, RAND Corporation, 1963); Thomas W. Wolfe, *Soviet Strategy at the Crossroads* (Santa Monica, RAND Corporation, 1964).

[51] Cf. Roman Kolkowicz, *Conflicts in Soviet Party-Military Relations: 1962–1963* (Santa Monica, RAND Corporation, 1963).

[52] Cf. Roman Kolkowicz, *The Impact of Technology on the Soviet Military: A Challenge to Traditional Military Professionalism* (Santa Monica, RAND Corporation, 1964).

between the U-2 incident and the Cuban missile crisis, the size of the Soviet military budget and establishment was maintained at a high level; once Khrushchev successfully overcame the opposition of his conservative critics in league with the professional military in the spring of 1963, he signed the test ban treaty; and as the prospects for a *détente* became even brighter, he called for reduced defense expenditures.

Whenever international tensions are reduced and the military's budget correspondingly cut, the professional officers among the traditional services are faced with agonizing choices confronting few other comparable groups in Soviet society: the termination or suspension of a professional career in which half a lifetime or more may have been invested. Factional conflicts between arms and services and various branches of the armed forces are unleashed over the redistribution of a diminished budget. Personal conflicts ensue as difficult decisions concerning the retirement of professional military officers must be made.[53]

Since the Soviet military's chief function is external defense and it plays little role in maintaining internal order, it is threatened with the deprivation of its function as the security of the state is maximized and international tensions are reduced. This means not only the demobilization of thousands of career personnel but also a diminished role and status in society for those who remain on active service. It creates serious morale and recruiting problems, since the military function suffers a depreciation of social value and esteem and suffers a corresponding reduction in social rewards. While these effects are universally applicable to military establishments everywhere, the problem is particularly acute in the Soviet system. Contrary to a widespread misapprehension, the demobilized Soviet officer is likely to suffer more than his counterpart in other countries. Unlike the retired military officer without a peacetime skill in the United States, who might, among other options, go into business for himself, this option and the entire spectrum of possibilities and opportunities offered by a free enterprise economy are closed to his Soviet counterpart.

When Khrushchev's new military policy, enunciated in January 1960, called for a troop reduction of 1,250,000 men, including 250,000 officers, Marshal Malinovsky specifically emphasized that "the demobilization of 250,000 officers will be accompanied by various difficulties."[54] Of the 70,000 officers previously demobilized, he noted that only 35 per cent were able to find civilian occupations commensurate with their previous military positions, while nearly two thirds had to assume lower skilled jobs as ordinary workers. Letters to the Soviet press and interviews with demobilized officers confirmed Malinovsky's account. One demobilized major bitterly complained:

[53] Under budgetary pressures it is usually the officer least equipped to adjust to civilian life by training and education who is the first to be demobilized. Thus Marshal Malinovsky noted in 1960 that "Not even regimental commanders are assured of remaining in their position. If they do not have an academic education, then the cadres personnel don't even want to talk to them." As cited in R. Kolkowicz, ibid., p. 20.

[54] *Krasnaya zvezda*, January 20, 1960.

> I am 46 — that's the trouble. . . . What pleasures are ahead of me? Am I to eat up my pension and wait until I die? Too soon for that. And work does not come easily for me. I need a place in life, do you understand? I need active service. . . . I am an old platoon officer; where does a company officer belong in a civilian job?[55]

Serious morale problems among officers remaining on active duty also develop as they face the prospects of demobilization — and *déclassement*. The social degradation of the demobilized officer also has the effect of insidiously undermining the status and deference shown to officers remaining on active duty by both civilians and conscriptees under their command. *Krasnaya zvezda* reports the case of an impertinent young conscriptee who scorned the advice of his commanding officer by contemptuously noting: "I don't need any teachers. I was in Grade 6 in the factory and had a former major as a metal worker apprentice working under me."[56] Reports of mistreatment, abuse, and unsympathetic consideration of demobilized military officers by local party and government officials also appeared periodically in the Soviet press.

The clever Chinese leaders apparently perceived political capital in the dissatisfactions of the Soviet traditional military and actually made a bold public appeal to the discontented elements of the Soviet military, seeking to associate the interests of Peking with theirs against Khrushchev. The Chinese charged, no less, that Khrushchev intended to destroy the traditional branches of the military in favor of the rocket forces:

> We wish to point out that the great Soviet people and Red Army have been and remain a great force safeguarding world peace. But Khrushchev's military ideas based on nuclear fetishism and nuclear blackmail are entirely wrong. Khrushchev sees only nuclear weapons. According to him, "The present level of military technique being what it is, the air force and the navy have lost their former importance. These arms are being replaced and not reduced." Of course, those units and men having combat duties on the ground are even less significant. According to him, "In our time, a country's defensive capacity is not determined by the number of men under arms, of men in uniform. . . . A country's defense potential depends in decisive measure on the firepower and means of delivery that country commands." . . . Khrushchev's whole set of military theories runs completely counter to Marxist-Leninist teachings on war and the army. To follow his wrong theories will necessarily involve disintegrating the army and disarming oneself morally.[57]

Even more seriously, from the standpoint of the military as an institution, the general relaxation of international tensions and the increasing prospects for a *détente* have engendered a quasi-pacifist and

[55] *Literaturnaya Gazeta*, May 24, 1960.
[56] *Krasnaya zvezda*, February 3, 1961.
[57] "Two Different Lines on the Question of War and Peace," *Jen Min Jih Pao*, November 18, 1963, as translated in *Peking Review*, November 27, 1963, pp. 6–16.

antimilitarist spirit and attitude among the population in general and among artists, writers, and intellectuals in particular. The impact of these tendencies on the status and image of the military was having such an effect upon the morale of the officer corps that in February 1964 the Ministry of Defense and the Chief Political Administration of the Soviet Army and Navy held a conference with writers and artists to arrest these tendencies. General Yephishev, head of the Chief Political Administration, noted that:

> Certain mistaken tendencies that have appeared in recent years in individual artistic works devoted to the military-patriotic theme have been subject to serious and merited criticism. The note of pacifism that was beginning to resound in certain books, films and paintings concerned with the Great Patriotic War has been justly condemned; the mistaken and basically harmful striving by certain masters of the arts to belittle the heroic spirit of military events has been dethroned.[58]

Marshal Malinovsky chastised the writers and artists in the same vein:

> In recent times mistaken tendencies in representing the last war have appeared. Motifs of pacifism and the abstract rejection of war have made themselves felt in certain works of literature and painting and in the movies. Is it correct to represent the war our people waged as merely an accumulation of horrors and deprivations, to trot out onto the stage in naturalistic detail little, confused people? We reject this one-sided approach to an important theme. . . . Of course, this does not mean that we are in favor of depicting war as one long triumphal march. . . . Neither can we ignore certain views that have appeared . . . calling for a rejection of enthusiastic words, of the heroic aspect in works about the war, and claiming, if you please, that all this used to be a feature of the period of the cult of the individual.[59]

Other speakers at the conference bemoaned the negative image of the Soviet officer which was increasingly creeping into Soviet literature and the visual arts; some speakers criticized the artists for belittling the military profession, taking a cynical attitude toward military-patriotic themes, for promoting the "so-called 'theory' of deheroization" and for writing "books that cast doubt on the commander's orders."[60] All this, according to Marshal Malinovsky, was having a baneful effect on the morale of the Soviet officer and the duty and pride of soldiering:

> Through the efforts of our party and the entire people both in the fire of war and in the painstaking work during peacetime, we have reared splendid command cadres. They are leading people in the country. The

[58] *Krasnaya zvezda*, February 9, 1964.
[59] Ibid.
[60] Ibid. In a letter to the editor of *Krasnaya zvezda*, published on January 29, 1961, twenty-five officers, including several Heroes of the Soviet Union, complained about an article which appeared in *Komsomolskaya Pravda* because the typical officer "in the sketch appears as a veritable horror, an aberration, a spiritual Quasimodo. . . . The incriminating sketch concentrates all sorts of imaginable nastiness exclusively in the person of the officer and presents this monstrosity, without concern, to the public."

soldier's unquestioning obedience to his commanders acquires special importance in the army under present-day conditions. In the orders of their commander, Soviet fighting men justifiedly see the orders of the homeland, and they execute them not only because of the law but because of their internal convictions. . . . It is important to us now as never before to preserve the commander's authority, to strengthen it, and to reveal the essence of one-man command as an expression of the collective will. Therefore, for example, certain works that discredit Soviet officers and soldiers evoke a feeling of dismay.[61]

As the relaxation of tensions progresses and the expectations of war recede and pacifist trends grow, the status and prestige of the professional military in Soviet society will continue to diminish. Already the Soviet military is being confronted with the serious problem of attracting and recruiting new officers. Several students in military academies, for example, sent a letter to Marshal Budenny in which they questioned the social values of military service as a profession:

> There can be no beauty where, they say, people are training to kill others. . . . They say that there have been and are bourgeois philosophers and generals who talk of the beauty of war. . . . They say that though the officer profession is necessary at present, it is uninteresting and unromantic and that any civilian profession is better than a military one.[62]

There is little question but that the Soviet professional military as a socio-institutional group views unenthusiastically its diminished stature in Soviet society and the real possibility of a mass *déclassement* of the officer elite in the event of an extended *détente* leading to extensive disarmament measures. Yet it would be incorrect to maintain that the Soviet military is unusually aggressive or warlike or glorifies war. The Soviet military is not particularly interested in actual war, since it is aware that in a thermonuclear conflict it risks not only the lives of its members but its very existence as an institution as well. What the Soviet military seeks is social and institutional security guaranteed by the appearance of insecurity for the state. To ensure its existence as a socio-functional institution, the Soviet military seeks to couple durable security and peace with a large military establishment as the principal guarantor that the aggressors would not dare unleash war for fear of destructive retaliation. Soviet military leaders apparently place little reliance upon a possible political settlement which would lead to a *détente* based upon mutual reduction of military arms and expenditures.

The Soviet armed forces, apparently like armies everywhere, would like to be the final judge of their own requirements, and this can best be accomplished under conditions of heightened military tensions. The peculiar characteristic of the Soviet military is that it is both a social and an institutional entity, whose members are threatened with a mass *déclassement* in the event of an extended *détente*. Until the Soviet

[61] *Krasnaya zvezda*, February 9, 1964.
[62] *Krasnaya zvezda*, January 13, 1963.

system can devise a formula which will enable the Soviet officer to transfer his relative social status to the civilian sector of society, the Soviet military will continue to view an extended relaxation of tensions with grave apprehension and perceive a *détente* as incompatible with its interests.

Heavy Industry

Unlike the Party Apparatus and the Soviet military, the managers of the heavy-industrial sector of the economy do not constitute a socio-institutional group, but rather are a socio-functional interest group whose organizational or institutional existence is amorphous and inchoate. Since 1956–57, when the economic ministries were decentralized and deconcentrated, the heavy-industrial managerial elite has been badly crippled politically and dispersed throughout the country — and has lost what centralized control it had over the levers of industrial production. Consequently it is unable to articulate its interests or to make its influence and pressures felt as pointedly and effectively as the Apparatus and the military.

Traditionally, heavy industry has been associated with defense and international tensions, because of its obvious necessity for the production of armaments. While the primacy of heavy industry assumed virtually the status of sacred writ under Stalin and ritual obeisance continues to be paid to this theme, increasingly it has become apparent that a radical upsurge in the development of the other sectors of the economy cannot be accomplished without subverting this principle. Although Khrushchev was the chief proponent of expanded consumer goods production, he was always careful to pay continued lip service to the primacy of heavy industry. Thus when he proposed his chemicalization of industry and agriculture programs in December 1963, he emphasized the benefits for agriculture and the consumer goods industry, but in February 1964, in order to answer his critics, he emphasized that 61 per cent of chemical production was still for heavy industry.[63]

Although a productionist-consumptionist debate of sorts has been

[63] "The ill-wishers of the Soviet state are also racking their brains as to how to understand the decisions of the December Plenum: Is it a retreat or is it not a retreat from the general line for the preferential development of heavy industry to which the Soviet Union had adhered unwaveringly until now? Voices can be heard now saying that under the blows of reality, because of crop failures, the Soviet Union and the Communist Party are renouncing industrialization and setting a course for the development of light industry and agriculture. We have never renounced the development of the means of production industry. . . . The chemical industry has always been a part of heavy industry. . . . Chemistry, figuratively speaking, synthesizes well the interests of the state and the people in the development of heavy industry, and the interests of Soviet people in the rapid increase of the manufacture of consumer goods. . . . The Party will continue to insure the development of heavy industry. It has never regarded it as an end in itself, however. The Communist Party forced the development of heavy industry in order to create a . . . foundation to achieve a high standard of living for the people." Khrushchev's report to the February 1964 Plenum of the Central Committee, *Pravda*, February 15, 1964.

carried on in the Soviet press since 1959, the ideological rationalizations for Khrushchev's policies were provided for by Academician A. Arzumanyan in a two-part article in *Pravda* on February 24 and 25, 1964, entitled "Current Problems of the Development of Our Economy," in which he suggested not only an equal balance between light and heavy industry but an even higher rate for light industry.[64] Arzumanyan, like Khrushchev earlier, used the experience of the United States to demonstrate that under certain conditions economic growth is consistent and possible with a higher rate of production for light industry.

While the managers of heavy industry were no longer sufficiently powerful to arrest or resist Khrushchev's policies by themselves, the traditional association between heavy industry and a large military establishment, and the traditional association between the latter and national security, is so habitual that the interests of the managers were in fact being defended and promoted by the military and the conservative faction in the Apparatus. The article by Arzumanyan and the program of welfare and wage benefits introduced by Khrushchev in July 1964, however, seem to indicate that the social role and prestige of the heavy-industrial manager will suffer at the expense of his light-industry rivals as the *détente* with the West progresses. Undoubtedly many of the heavy-industrial managerial specialists can convert to light industry, and to the degree that this is possible, resistance by this group will diminish. Its future is by no means as bleak as that of the demobilized military officer or the unhorsed party *apparatchik*.

"Who Benefits" from a Relaxation of International Tensions in Soviet Society?

While the socio-institutional and functional groups in Soviet society who benefit from international tensions are few in number as groups, and in absolute numbers constitute but a small fraction of the total

[64] Cf. A. Arzumanyan, "Urgent Problems of Developing Our Economy," *Pravda*, February 24 and 25, 1964. According to Arzumanyan: "First of all, the question arises of the dynamics of groups 'A' and 'B' in industry. To this day, the establishment of the proportions between them has been hindered by certain theoretical survivals that have their roots in Stalin's erroneous dogmas. . . . Stalin thought it possible to combine a rapid expansion of industrial production with a systematic lag in consumer-goods output. . . . Nevertheless, some of our economists adhere to this day to erroneous views on the question of the relations between production and consumption. Intentionally or unintentionally, they divorce the law of preferential growth of the production of the means of production from personal consumption in a socialist society and . . . the law of preferential growth of the production of the means of production is transformed into an end in itself. . . . During the past decade the Party, while comprehensively developing heavy industry, has at the same time taken an enormous stride forward in expanding group 'B,' in increasing the personal consumption of the Soviet people. . . . Life today insistently advances the task of bringing the rates of growth of groups 'A' and 'B' closer together. N. S. Khrushchev was profoundly right when he asserted at the February plenary session of the C.P.S.U. Central Committee that '*there can be no counterposing of group 'A' and group 'B.'*'"

population, they represent highly concentrated power constituencies in terms of levers of power to which they have access. The military constitutes the only organized structure of violence in the system. The Party Apparatus controls the symbols of legitimacy and functions as an organized power structure to manipulate them. The heavy-industrial managers have access to, if not control of, the basic means of production in Soviet society.

On the other hand, those social groups which tend to benefit from a relaxation of international tensions are more numerous as group entities, more diverse in terms of function and social status, and make up the overwhelming proportion of the population. While the three groups who benefit most from international tensions are relatively small in total membership, they represent power structures as well as social constituencies. The groups who would benefit from a relaxation of tensions represent the whole motley spectrum of social forces in Soviet society, from relatively powerful subgroups within the Apparatus, military and heavy industry, through the politically awakening cultural, professional, and scientific elites, to the passive and politically impotent and largely inarticulate members of the lower intelligentsia (white collar groups), the working class, and the peasantry. Thus whereas the three groups in the first category are social elites which represent a high proportion of members in the party, the second group consists of both social elites and social non-elites, whose overall distribution of party membership is very low — ranging from 100 per cent for the sub-elite in the Apparatus to only 5.5 per cent for the peasantry.[65]

For purposes of analytical convenience, those social groups which would seem to benefit from a relaxation of international tensions can be classified into four general categories.

The State Bureaucracy

The state officialdom in the Soviet Union, though not always precisely distinguishable from members of the Party Apparatus, the economic bureaucracy, or even the military, nevertheless appears to constitute a distinct socio-institutional grouping. While there has been considerable overlap and mutual interpenetration of the party and state bureaucracies, the two institutions are separate, and often rival, entities. The state represents in effect the structure of legality which is supposed to mirror the structure of legitimacy embodied in the party and to translate the social will of the latter into official acts of state. The party, strictly speaking, has no legal or coercive authority except through the state.

The state represents an older institution in Soviet society than does the party (strictly speaking, its Apparatus), since it constitutes a continuation of the historic Russian state and in some degree is the sym-

[65] For an analysis of the social composition of the C.P.S.U. and its higher organs, cf. Aspaturian, in Macridis and Ward, eds., *Modern Political Systems*, pp. 492–502, and Aspaturian, "Social Structure and Political Power in the Soviet System."

bolic heir to its legacy and the deep emotional and passionate sentiments it arouses. Loyalty to the state is patriotism, while loyalty to the
party is ideological rectitude. Furthermore, the state is more inclusive in
its membership, while the party is selective and exclusionist: citizenship is universal, party membership restrictive. Thus although the state
is identified with legality in the official dogma, it is also endowed with a
residual element of the prerevolutionary repository of historic legitimacy
which the Russian state embodied, and hence remains a competitor to
the Apparatus *cum* party.

It was this residual symbolism of patriotism and legitimacy which
Stalin relied upon during World War II to inspire the Soviet population
to resist the Germans. Stalin's assumption of the position as head of the
Soviet government and his appointment as generalissimo of the armed
forces tended to blur the distinction between state and party, to the
disadvantage of the Party Apparatus. If Khrushchev can be believed,
during the war and down to Stalin's death, the party as a distinctive
ruling elite was virtually on the verge of withering away, since its
highest organs were no longer being used by Stalin to govern the
country.

After Stalin's death, Malenkov misjudged the situation and apparently assumed that the state had eclipsed the party in power and
prestige and decided to use it rather than the Party Apparatus as his
socio-institutional base of power. Seeking to expand his social base of
support, Malenkov decided to adopt a policy based upon increased consumer goods production at home and a relaxation of tensions abroad.
This seemed to accord more with the interests of his new social
constituency, the state bureaucracy, than the policies pursued by Stalin
or now advocated by his rival, Khrushchev, who assumed the mantle of
First Secretary of the party. The rank and file employees of the State
Apparatus would be among the first to benefit from a relaxation of
international tensions and a higher standard of living. Thus it was more
than coincidence that among those given substantial salary increases by
Khrushchev in July–August 1964 were rank and file employees of the
State Apparatus. Traditionally, high administrative officials of the state
have been associated with a policy of less tension abroad and a higher
standard of living at home. The first three post-Stalinist chairmen of the
Council of Ministers — Malenkov, Bulganin, and Khrushchev — reversed themselves and became advocates of peace and plenty once they
assumed the office of premier.

As the power and prestige of the state are enhanced, the power of
other institutions diminishes, most notably that of the Party Apparatus
(whose functions become increasingly superfluous), but also that of the
military, since the latter is legally subordinated to the state as its legalized coercive arm. Furthermore, Khrushchev, like Stalin and Malenkov
before him, appeared to have shifted his main institutional base of
power to the State Apparatus as well, not only because of the ineluctable
advantages already mentioned but also because increasingly the glow
and aura which he derived as the chief personal symbol of the Soviet

Union in international affairs radiated back into the Soviet Union. Because diplomacy and foreign policy are official activities of states and not parties, a Soviet leader who chose to govern only through the Party Apparatus would be denied this new powerful increment to his internal authority.

Light-Industrial, Consumer Goods and Services, and Agricultural Managers

These social constituencies represent a numerically impressive, geographically diffused, and politically weak constellation of interest groups. Generally speaking, their status, prestige, and material rewards have had low priority in the Soviet system, especially during periods of war and international tension. This stems from three principal causes: (1) During periods of external danger, their services and products are not as highly valued or needed. (2) Their geographically dispersed character diffuses their power and limits their possibilities for organized and focused articulation of their point of view. (3) Their functions give them little or no access to important institutional levers of power.

These groups become important and rise in the socio-power hierarchy to the degree that they become useful to one or more of the principal socio-power groups. But as their usefulness as social allies grows, so does their relative power position become enhanced, to the degree that they too might become more significant as political actors in their own right.

One of the oldest components of Soviet mythology from Lenin to Khrushchev has been the promise to raise the Soviet standard of living to a level second to none once the problem of external security was solved. A policy of peace and plenty obviously places a higher demand and value upon the services of these groups, resulting in commensurate increases in budgetary allocations and hence status, prestige, and power. This was concretely reflected by Khrushchev's policies. Whenever Khrushchev thought that relations with the United States had improved, he called for greater budgetary allocations for these sectors of the economy; when the international situation turned sour, they were arrested or deferred. The latest acts in this cycle were increased budgetary allocations for agriculture in late 1962 and early 1963 and a steady shift of budgetary allocations to light industry and consumer goods and services, which has been in progress since the Cuban missile debacle.

The Cultural-Professional-Scientific Groups

Except for the professional ideologists, propagandists, and hacks whose positions depend upon their servility before the Party Apparatus, these groups as a whole seem to benefit most during periods when international tensions are relaxed. International tensions are associated with ideological controls and conformity, strict rules of censorship, reduced international contacts, and greater restrictions and restraints on artistic, scientific, and professional expression and development. Relaxation of international tensions is associated with the "thaw" and the "new freedom" for Soviet intellectuals, a freedom which has been progressively expanded since Stalin's death.[66]

The Soviet artistic and intellectual community is one of the most potent forces arguing in favor of a continued relaxation of international tensions. This has found expression in quasi-pacifist and antiwar sentiments expressed in an increasing number of works, much to the dismay of the military, as noted earlier. The artistic and intellectual groups are unique in that they not only have access to media of communication and information whereby to make their views known, but they are among the few social groups in Soviet society who are legally permitted to exist as separate organized societies and associations. While these associations in the past were strictly under Party Apparatus control, increasingly they are becoming vehicles whereby the interests of their members are given voice. The Party Apparatus periodically attempts to reimpose ideological controls, but this has by no means been fully successful. Although Soviet intellectuals are likely to exercise self-restraint during periods of real danger to the state, they are unlikely to accept as supinely as before the ideological controls which the party ideologues would like to impose.

The Soviet "Consumer": The White Collar Groups, the Working Class, and the Peasantry

These three groups, taken together, account for some 90 million of the 100 million adults in the Soviet population. The organized political power of these large social groups is virtually nil. Yet they will be among the principal beneficiaries of the policy of peace and plenty, and this has already been reflected in wage increases for white collar and service groups like doctors, medical personnel, teachers, and restaurant and catering personnel; higher prices for agricultural commodities; relaxation of controls on collective farms; pensions for collective farmers; and higher wages for factory workers.

Since these groups are among the first to be deprived and to suffer during war or periods of international tension, they constitute a numerically impressive group whose political power, though latent and passive, might be of single importance if allied to one of the major socio-power elites in the Soviet system.

SOME CONCLUDING OBSERVATIONS

One of the most conspicuously unique characteristics of the Soviet system is the virtual absence of any meaningful distinction between a

[66] A pertinent illustration of the barometric relationship between the relaxation of international tensions and relaxations of ideological controls over the arts took place in the spring of 1963. When Khrushchev appeared to be in difficulty and was in danger of being ousted by his factional opposition because of the Cuban missile debacle, the Party Apparatus called for an ideological conference which was designed to establish more stringent ideological controls, but after Kozlov suffered a heart attack and Khrushchev's fortunes took a turn for the better, the ideological conference was delayed for a month and, when it met, turned out to be a rather tepid affair. The test ban treaty followed soon thereafter.

public and private sector in Soviet society. Private organizations, associations, and pressure groups, as such, are nonexistent in the forms known to the non-Communist world. In the sense that the public and private sectors are virtually coterminous, the Soviet system is totalitarian, although no longer encumbered with the institutions of terror and arbitrariness which characterized the Stalinist era. This means that its political system is closed; that is, the pluralistic interplay of autonomous and spontaneously organized political organizations and associations is legally prohibited. As a consequence, several aspects of Soviet decision-making in foreign policy appear unique.

1. No internal Soviet interest groups have a vested private interest in countries abroad which might result in the distortion of foreign policy. There is, in general, none of the economic "conflict of interests" on the individual or corporate level which often complicates foreign policy-making in other countries. Private economic interests of a domestic character which might exert pressure upon decision-making also do not exist. What Soviet property exists abroad is owned by the state, and foreign trade is an absolute state monopoly. Thus the Soviet abdication of joint stock companies and other state-owned enterprises in foreign countries could be executed purely on the basis of state policy with no private interests complicating the situation.

In foreign aid and trade policies no internal pressures or lobbyists representing private economic interests can materialize to distort and shape policy. This is also true of geographical and regional pressures. There are no demands for the inclusion of certain commodities, tariff reductions or increases, etc., stemming from interest groups, private or public — although as the Soviet economy increasingly shifts to a consumer-oriented one, foreign trade and aid might become increasingly important to interest and regional groups whose internal markets have been exhausted or eliminated.

2. Soviet officials devote full time to public interests and public policy, and hence they do not divide their time and energies between public and private domains. There are no private fortunes or estates, no private businesses or professions which can drain away energies from their public responsibilities. Their status, prestige, and power in Soviet society stem solely from their public functions.[67]

3. Foreign policy debates are largely secret. While foreign policy is discussed much more widely in the Soviet Union than heretofore, there is still no criticism of a systematic character about Soviet foreign policy.[68] Soviet decision-makers still act without prior public discussion

[67] Cf. Zbigniew Brzezinski and Samuel P. Huntington, *Political Power: U.S.A./U.S.S.R.* (New York, Viking, 1964), for a pioneering and penetrating comparative analysis of the social background and behavior of Soviet and American political elites.

[68] For a discussion of the upsurge in monographic and scholarly discussion of international and foreign policy issues and problems, cf. V. V. Aspaturian, "Diplomacy in the Mirror of Soviet Scholarship," in J. Keep, ed., *Contemporary History in the Soviet Mirror* (London, Allen and Unwin, 1964).

and need not render an accounting in public, although increasingly reports on foreign policy are made to the Supreme Soviet.[69] Foreign policy is too crucial a matter to debate in public, since it would alert the outside world to Soviet intentions. Thus there is no political opposition which can publicly offer an alternative program or policy. Opposition does exist, but behind the closed doors of higher party and state organs. These criticisms and alternative policies are sometimes revealed indirectly through denunciation, rejection, allusions to "bourgeois thinkers," "metal eaters," "certain comrades," "some people," "anti-Marxists," etc. In the condemnation of the antiparty group in July 1957, the foreign policy criticisms of Molotov were revealed to be, in effect, an alternative policy.[70] This revelation constituted the closest approximation to a debate on foreign policy until the initiation of open polemics with the Chinese.

4. The professional military in the Soviet Union is not subordinated in the ordinary sense to civilian control but rather is integrated into the political and administrative apparatus of the Soviet system. The military has direct, active, regular, systematic, and predictable participation and membership in party and state organs which are nominally civilian in character. They are co-opted at all levels and in all branches. In the party, professional military representatives have sat on the Presidium (Zhukov) and are regularly represented in the Central Committee, the Party Congress, and the party organs of the Union Republics and other administrative-territorial regions.[71]

In state institutions they are found in the Presidium of the Supreme Soviet, are regularly elected as members of both chambers of the Supreme Soviet, serve on its committees, and also serve on the Council of Ministers. The defense ministry is administered almost entirely by professional soldiers, who are at all times on active military duty as professional officers. They also serve in Union Republican state institutions.

5. Defeated political leaders have no political base to return to, no private business or law practice, no free opportunity to offer services commensurate with their formerly exalted positions, no status of loyal oppositionists. Under Stalin, defeated political leaders inevitably suffered political and physical oblivion, but now only the former. The net effect is to deprive the country completely of the services of experienced statesmen and politicians.

This more than nullifies the unique advantage of political leaders fully committed to public responsibilities. It should be noted, however,

[69] Cf. V. Vadimov, *Verkhovny Sovet SSSR i Mezhdunarodnye Otnosheniya* (Moscow, 1958); and *Sbornik Osnovnykh Aktov i Dokumentov Verkhovnovo Soveta SSSR po Vneshnepoliticheskim Voprosam 1956–1962* (Moscow, 1962).

[70] For a discussion and description of the Molotov foreign policy "program," cf. Aspaturian in Macridis, *Modern Political Systems*, pp. 150–52.

[71] Cf. T. W. Wolfe, "Role of the Soviet Military in Decision-Making and Soviet Politics" (Santa Monica, RAND Corporation, 1964), and his *Soviet Strategy at the Crossroads.*

that this situation is not necessarily permanent and that the retiring of defeated opponents or the assigning of menial positions to them may result in toleration of their dissident views, particularly if factional stalemates become a permanent feature of the Soviet political system. It is not even inconceivable that factionalism may eventually lead to the organization of competing slates and programs within the Communist party, just as they exist in other one-party systems.[72]

6. One final unique characteristic, which still requires greater exploration, is that Soviet internal politics are closely intertwined with the domestic politics of other Communist states. Factional conflicts assume an intrabloc character, with factions in the Soviet hierarchy reflected in the hierarchies of allied states and parties; the result is the formation of interparty factional alliances designed to aid kindred factions in other states in their struggle against rival factional groupings. In this way the leaders of one state may actively cultivate the allegiance and support of an opposition faction in another state and vice versa. To a certain degree the course of factional conflicts in other Communist states affects the fortunes of factions within the Soviet hierarchy.[73]

The relationship of internal politics to foreign policy in the Soviet system remains in a state of flux and has yet to find its characteristic equilibrium. The tendency, at present, appears to be that foreign policy objectives will increasingly be accommodated to internal interests rather than abstract ideological commitment, although for the moment they remain an inextricable combination of both elements in undecipherable proportions at any given time. As the social consensus within the Soviet system expands and becomes more pluralistic, the tendency will be for ideological norms to have less influence in the shaping of foreign policy.

[72] That a multi-party Communist system is not inconceivable is attested to by the fact that the Chinese have actually called for the toleration of dissident Communist parties in other countries, including presumably the countries of the socialist camp in Europe. This has infuriated the Soviet Party, which has naturally reaffirmed its incompatibility with Marxism-Leninism: "One cannot agree with the concepts now current in the Communist movement that justify fragmentation of the ranks of the Communist movement and the creation of 'several Communist parties' in one country. The supporters of these concepts say that the international Communist movement is now allegedly undergoing a process of 'selection, crystallization, and condensation' and that there are at present in the world Communist movement four types of Communist and Workers' Parties, namely: '(1) the Marxist-Leninist party; (2) the party whose leadership is under the control of revisionists but that has a Marxist-Leninist opposition within it; (3) the party that is completely under the control of revisionists, while the Marxist-Leninists who have been expelled from the party have formed Marxist-Leninist groups; (4) the party whose leadership is under control of the revisionists and alongside which a new Communist Party has formed.' Meanwhile, certain comrades consider it possible for themselves — and call on others — to support to an equal degree liaisons with all the above groups and parties. They thereby support a kind of 'Communist multi-party system.' " "Against Splitters, for Unity of the Communist Movement," *Partiinaya Zhizn,* No. 11, June 1964, pp. 8–20.

[73] Cf. article cited immediately above.

The Chinese ambition to displace the Soviet Union as the center of the world revolutionary movement and usurp the ideological initiative will have an ambivalent impact on the relationship between ideology and Soviet foreign policy. On the one hand, it may drive the conservative faction of the Apparatus to more desperate measures in reasserting the ideological preeminence of the Soviet party in the Communist movement; on the other it may serve to reinforce the conviction of the Khrushchevite faction that the internal burdens of an ideologically oriented foreign policy are too heavy to carry, and hence counterproductive in character.

VI THE DOMESTIC FOREIGN POLICY PROCESS
Formulation, Execution, and Administration

16. THE FORMULATION OF SOVIET FOREIGN POLICY

Vernon V. Aspaturian

INTRODUCTION

Any attempt to describe the formulation of Soviet foreign policy in the crucibles of its decision-making organs is bound to be a hazardous and frustrating enterprise. The absence of periodic or systematic publication of documents, the inaccessibility of archives and officials, the virtual nonexistence of memoirs or diaries of retiring statesmen, the puzzling duplication of state and Party institutions, the perplexing fluctuations in their relationships, the ambiguity of Soviet ideology and the wide discrepancy between theory and practice, the bewildering profusion of constitutional and institutional changes, the arbitrary tendency to ignore or short-circuit elaborately detailed institutional channels, and, finally, the capricious and convulsive turnover of personalities, are the more familiar impediments that must be contended with.

The decision-making process itself is a dynamic interaction between institutions and personalities, whose character varies with the effectiveness of institutions to impose limits on the acts of individuals. In constitutional states, characterized by relatively permanent institutions, the restraints on officials are carefully defined, imposing ineluctable limits not only on the range of policy formulation but upon the choice of means as well. In a totalitarian system like the Soviet Union, where impermanently rooted institutions have been subordinated to relatively permanent personalities, the institutional aspects of the deci-

From Vernon V. Aspaturian, "Soviet Foreign Policy," in Roy C. Macridis, editor, *Foreign Policy in World Politics*, © 1957, 1962, and 1968. By permission of Prentice-Hall, Inc., Englewood Cliffs, New Jersey.

sion-making process are little more than ceremonial. Decision making is essentially personal, and bound to vary with the evolving ideological convictions, character, and judgment of those in control, the nature of the rivalries between them, and, finally, their reaction to the political and social pressures that bear upon them.

The Soviet political superstructure prior to 1953, was a complicated mosaic of shifting and interlocking institutions resting on an entrenched foundation of one-man dictatorship, in which all powers were delegated from above. The institutions of both Party and State, as well as their relationship to one another, were essentially creatures of the late Joseph Stalin and were designed, not to limit his own power, but to limit that of his subordinates and rivals, and to facilitate the solidification of his own authority. As the instruments of his creation and manipulation, they could not, and did not, function as restraints on his latitude of decision. Both institutions and subordinates were liquidated with remarkable dispatch when the occasion demanded.

The system of duplicating and overlapping political organs between the Party and State allegedly reflects a division of functions between the formulation and execution of policy, with policy formulation a monopoly reserved exclusively for the Party, while the function of the government was to be restricted to formalizing and legalizing the decisions of the Party into official acts of state. This dichotomy was never either rigid or absolute, but constantly varied in accordance with the degree of interlocking of personnel at the summits of the Party and State hierarchies.

The Party Congress

In theory the most exalted, but in practice the most degraded of the central Party institutions in the formulation of policy is the Party Congress. Traditionally the most important fundamental pronouncements on foreign policy have been made before the Party Congress, which is empowered to set the basic line of the Party and State, but in actual fact merely hears and rubber-stamps the decisions made elsewhere. All higher organs of the Party, including the Presidium and Secretariat, are responsible and accountable to the Party Congress, which theoretically can remove and replace their membership.

The actual role of the Congress in foreign policy has varied throughout its existence. Under Lenin, and, in fact, as late as the Sixteenth Party Congress (in 1930), serious debate on foreign policy and international revolutionary strategy frequently ensued, although never with the same intensity or wide range of diversity as on domestic policy. Because of its massive size (nearly 2,000 delegates), the Congress became increasingly unwieldy as an organ of debate and discussion, and it gradually was converted into a forum which heard various sides and finally into a subdued sounding board for Stalin's deadly rhetoric. Discussion and debate first slipped behind the doors of the Central Committee and eventually vanished into the Politburo. All decisions were made in the Politburo, then reported to the Central Committee and, with increasing infrequency, to the Party Congress. The principal function of the Party Congress was reduced to the hearing of reports by the prominent figures of the Party.

The two most important reports to Party Congresses relating to foreign policy are the Main Political Report of the Central Committee, delivered in the past by Stalin (except at the Nineteenth Congress), and a report on the activities of the World Communist Movement. At the Nineteenth Congress, Malenkov delivered the Main Report. However, Stalin had ordered published his *Economic Problems of Socialism* on the eve of the Congress, and this set the tone and dominated the entire proceedings. At the Twentieth Congress, Khrushchev delivered the Main Report, incorporating radical doctrinal innovations affecting foreign policy, while Molotov confined himself to praising reluctantly the new policy and resentfully subjecting his own past conduct of foreign policy to self-criticism. The activities of foreign communist parties were reported by their own representatives.

A close examination of the Main Political Reports betrays an almost rigid uniformity in organization. The entire first section is devoted to international affairs; an authoritative interpretation of the world situation; an appraisal of the Soviet position; trends, developments, and opportunities to watch for; warnings, threats, boasts, and invitations to bourgeois powers; congratulations and words of praise for friendly countries; and, finally, a summary of the immediate and long-range objectives of Soviet foreign policy. This report, before the emergence of polycentric tendencies in the World Communist Movement and the onset of the Sino-Soviet dispute, set the line to guide communists everywhere in their activities, and, thus, the Congress became not a forum for debate, but a unique medium of communication.

Debate and discussion vanished after 1930, and meetings of the Congress became so infrequent that they threatened to vanish altogether. In his secret speech to the Twentieth Congress, Khrushchev gave this vivid description of the deterioration of the Party Congress:

> During Lenin's life, party congresses were convened regularly; always when a radical turn in the development of the party and country took place, Lenin considered it absolutely necessary that the party discuss at length all basic matters pertaining to . . . foreign policy. . . . Whereas during the first years after Lenin's death, party congresses . . . took place more or less regularly, later . . . these principles were brutally violated. . . . Was it a normal situation when over 13 years [1939–1952] elapsed between the Eighteenth and Nineteenth Congresses? . . . Of 1,966 delegates [to the Seventeenth Congress in 1934] with either voting or advisory rights, 1,108 persons were arrested on charges of revolutionary crimes.[1]

The Central Committee

As the body that "guides the entire work of the Party in the interval between Congresses . . . and . . . directs the work of the Central and

[1] This extract and all subsequent references to Khrushchev's secret report to the Twentieth Congress are taken from the full text, *New York Times,* June 5, 1956. The speech has been widely reprinted elsewhere.

Soviet public organizations [i.e., the government],"[2] the Central Committee became the principal arena of debate and discussion of foreign policy during the period preceding 1934. According to the Party rules at that time, the Politburo was obliged to report to this body at least three times a year, so that its decisions might be examined, criticized, and judged. The Ceneral Committee elected the members of the Politburo, the Orgburo, and the Secretariat, and theoretically was empowered to appoint, remove, or replace its members. The Central Committee, itself elected by the Party Congress, was empowered to replace its own members by a two-thirds vote, but Stalin removed and appointed members of the Central Committee virtually at will.

On some occasions, the Foreign Commissar (who invariably is at least a full member of the Central Committee), as well as high Soviet functionaries of the Comintern, reported to the Central Committee on foreign policy and international communist activities. More often, the Secretary-General (Stalin) would deliver a report on the nature and scope of the Politburo's work and explain the precise application of the "line" under changing international conditions. A fairly large body, composed of full and alternate members (about equally divided), the Central Committee was empowered to alter the policies of the Politburo and support the views of the minority. Only full members exercised the right to vote, but candidates had the right to participate in debate. Some of these reports, but not all, were made public, particularly if important modifications of the policies announced at the previous Party Congress were made. The records of the Committee's proceedings during the Stalin era remain generally unpublished and inaccessible for examination.

The Central Committee too, in time, was reduced to little more than a sounding board; its meetings became increasingly infrequent, and there is reason to believe that, after 1934, its decisions were unanimous. In Khrushchev's secret speech, he said:

> Even after the end of the war . . . Central Committee plenums were hardly ever called. It should be sufficient to mention that during the years of the Patriotic War [World War II] not a single Central Committee plenum took place. . . . Stalin did not even want to meet and talk with Central Committee members. . . . Of the 139 members and candidates of the Party's Central Committee who were elected at the Seventeenth Party Congress [1934], 98 persons, i.e., 70 per cent, were arrested and shot.

The Party Politburo[3]

There is no question but that the most important organ of decision making in the Soviet Union has been, and continues to be, the Politburo

[2] *The Land of Socialism Today and Tomorrow* (Moscow, International Publishers Company, Inc., 1939), p. 473.

[3] The Party's highest organ was called the Politburo, from 1917 to 1952, and the Presidium, from 1952 to 1966. In 1966, the name Politburo was restored.

of the Party. In accordance with the principle of "democratic central-ism," the ultimate power of the Party is entrusted to this organ. Its internal organization and recruiting procedures, the composition and convictions of its factions, and its voting practices remain essentially a mystery. No proceedings of its deliberations have been made public in decades, and, in the absence of any recent defections from this body, information concerning its procedures and activities can be derived only from the following sources: (1) fragmentary records of very early meet-ings; (2) public exposure of its deliberations by Leon Trotsky and other rivals of Stalin during the period before 1930; (3) accounts by high-ranking diplomats or government and Party officials, whose activities brought them into close range of the Politburo, and who have defected from the Soviet Union; (4) personal accounts and memoirs of foreign statesmen who negotiated with members of the Politburo or with Stalin; (5) accounts of renegade officials of the Comintern and foreign com-munist parties; (6) secrets spilled as a result of the Stalin-Tito feud; (7) Khrushchev's secret speech at the Twentieth Party Congress and its aftermath; (8) calculated leaks by the Polish Party and government since the rise of Gomulka; (9) examination of the decisions already taken; (10) rare public disputes between leading press organs of the Party and government; (11) shifts in Party and government officials; and (12) rare Central Committee Resolutions like that of June 29, 1957.

Under Stalin, all decisions of the Politburo on questions of foreign policy were, in one form or another, his. All rival and dissident views were quashed and their adherents liquidated. The membership of the body was hand-picked by him. In his relations with the Politburo, Stalin could either announce his decisions and expect unanimous approval; submit them for examination and ask for discussion, with or without a vote; simply act without consulting his colleagues; or consult with various members on certain questions, to the exclusion of others. Ac-cording to a former Soviet diplomat, who was an eye-witness to some Politburo meetings in 1933:

> A thin appearance of collective work is still kept up at Politburo meetings. Stalin does not "command." He merely "suggests" or "pro-poses." The fiction of voting is retained. But the vote never fails to uphold his "suggestions." The decision is signed by all ten members of the Politburo, with Stalin's signature among the rest. . . . The other members of the Politburo mumble their approval of Stalin's "proposal." . . . Stalin not only is generally called "the Boss" by the whole bureauc-racy, but *is* the one and only boss.[4]

This general description of Stalin's style of work has been con-firmed many times by diplomats and statesmen of many countries who

[4] Alexander Barmine, *One Who Survived* (New York, G. P. Putnam's Sons, 1946), p. 213. Barmine writes that ". . . thousands of relatively unim-portant, as well as all-important, problems, must pass through Stalin's hand for final decision. . . . Weeks are spent in waiting; Commissars wait in Stalin's office."

observed that Stalin often made important decisions without consulting anyone, while Molotov and others would request time to consult with their "government." The role of the other members of the Politburo could best be described as consultative, although within the area of their own administrative responsibility they exercised the power of decision. Testimony concerning Stalin's intolerance of dissent is uniformly consistent. "Whoever opposed . . . his viewpoint," complained Khrushchev, "was doomed to be removed."

The relationship between the Foreign Ministry and the Presidium has always been unique. Since relations with other states are viewed in terms of a struggle for power among various "ruling classes," and thus directly involve the security and the very existence of the Soviet state, the Party center has always retained a tight supervision over the Foreign Ministry. This supervision assumes different forms, depending upon the Party rank of the individuals who hold the posts of Foreign Minister and of Premier. The Premier has always been a Party figure of the highest rank, while the Foreign Minister may or may not be a member of the Party Presidium.

During the period when Maxim Litvinov was Foreign Commissar, his work was supervised by Molotov, the Premier of the government and his formal superior. Matters of routine interest, not involving questions of policy or fundamental maneuver, were decided by Litvinov himself in consultation with his collegium. More substantial questions were taken to Molotov, who, depending upon the nature of the question, would make a decision, or take it to the Politburo.[5]

The Politburo itself was broken down into various Commissions dealing with different aspects of policy. Questions of foreign policy were first considered by the Politburo Commission on Foreign Affairs, which included the Politburo specialists on the Comintern, Foreign Trade, and Defense. In matters involving exceptional or immediate importance, Molotov would deal directly with Stalin and get a decision.

The procedures of the Politburo were neither systematic nor rigid. Often Stalin would personally consult with the Foreign Commissar and his chief advisers; and Litvinov, on a few occasions, would be asked to make a report to the Politburo. The principal function of the Commission on Foreign Affairs was to act as a coordinating agency of all the departments concerned with foreign relations, to assemble and evaluate intelligence information flowing from different channels, to devise strategy and policy, examine analyses, projects, and reports drawn up by specialists in the Foreign Commissariat, study reports of diplomats abroad, and then make a comprehensive report either to Stalin or to the Politburo as a whole.

Once the decisions were made, they would be transmitted in writing or verbally by Molotov to Litvinov for execution. These bureaucratic channels were often ignored and Stalin would act directly with Molotov, his principal agent, and they would personally give in-

[5] *Cf.* Merle Fainsod, *How Russia Is Ruled* (Cambridge, Mass., Harvard University Press, 1953), p. 282.

structions to Litvinov. Deviation or improvisation from instructions by the Foreign Commissar or his subordinates in the Commissariat was neither permitted nor tolerated. According to Khrushchev, the system of Politburo Commissions was not primarily for organizational efficiency, but was a sinister device whereby Stalin weakened the authority of the collective body:

> The importance of the . . . Political Bureau was reduced and its work disorganized by the creation within the Political Bureau of various commissions — the so-called "quintets," "sextets," "septets" and "novenaries."

When Molotov replaced Litvinov in May, 1939, this cumbersome procedure was simplified. The Nazi-Soviet Pact was worked out principally by Stalin and Molotov, with Zhdanov and Mikoyan the only other members of the Politburo apparently appraised of the crucial decisions contemplated. The Politburo Commission on Foreign Affairs gradually increased in size until, by 1945, it was large enough to be converted by Stalin from a "sextet" into a "septet." As it grew in size, so its importance diminished. During the war, Stalin appeared to consult only Molotov on questions of foreign policy and frequently made decisions on the spot at the Big Three conferences.

Khrushchev's description of how decisions were made by Stalin and the Politburo is probably exaggerated and self-serving, but accurate in its general outline:

> After the war, Stalin became even more capricious, irritable, and brutal; in particular his suspicion grew. His persecution mania reached unbelievable dimensions. Everything was decided by him alone without any consideration for anyone or anything. . . . Sessions of the Political Bureau occurred only occasionally . . . many decisions were taken by one person or in a roundabout way, without collective discussion. . . . The importance of the Political Bureau was reduced and its work disorganized by the creation within the Political Bureau of various commissions. . . . The result of this was that some members of the Political Bureau were in this way kept away from participation in the decisions of the most important state matters.

Decision Making in the Post-Stalin Period: The Agonies
of Collective Leadership and Factional Conflict

The death of Stalin stimulated the expression of various opinions, and unleashed a struggle for power among his successors. Six months before his death, at the Nineteenth Party Congress, Stalin radically reorganized the Party summit, abolishing the Orgburo and replacing the eleven-man Politburo with a Presidium of twenty-five members and eleven candidate members as the key decision-making organ of the Soviet system. Since many of the new members of the Presidium were burdened with permanent administrative responsibilities far from Moscow, and since it was much too large to function as a decision-making body, there was secretly organized, in violation of the new Party charter, a smaller Bureau of the Presidium, whose membership has never been revealed. Whether expansion of the Presidium was designed by Stalin to widen the area of decision making and prevent a struggle for power after his death — thus preparing the conditions for orderly transition from personal to institutional dictatorship — or whether it was a sinister device for liquidating his old associates in favor of a generation ignorant of his crimes, remains an intriguing enigma. According to Khrushchev:

> Stalin evidently had plans to finish off the old members of the Political Bureau. . . . His proposal after the Nineteenth Congress, concerning the selection of 25 persons to the Central Committee's Presidium, was aimed at the removal of the old Political Bureau members and the bringing in of less experienced persons so that they would extol him. . . . We can assume that this was a design for the future annihilation of the old Political Bureau members, and in this way, a cover for all the shameful acts of Stalin.

Immediately after Stalin's death, the old members of Stalin's entourage reduced the Presidium to its former size. The removal of Beria and the dismantling of his secret police apparatus introduced an uneasy equilibrium among the various factions in the Presidium, none of which was powerful enough to overwhelm the others.

In the post-Stalin Presidium, decisions often were taken only after stormy controversies and agile maneuvering among the various factions. As a consequence, necessity was converted into ideology, and conflicting opinions, within carefully circumscribed limits, were given official sanction. The authoritative theoretical journal *Kommunist*, however, warned that "views that are objectively directed toward dethroning the leadership elected by the Party masses," would not be tolerated.[6] This danger is adumbrated in the Party Statutes, Article 28 of which reads:

> A broad discussion, in particular on an all Union scale concerning the Party policy, should be so organized that it would not result in the attempts of an insignificant minority to impose its will on the majority of the Party or in attempts to organize fractional groupings which would break down Party unity, or in attempts to create a schism that would undermine the strength and the firmness of the socialist regime.[7]

The Party Statutes, however, were revised in 1961, at the Twenty-second Party Congress, in order to reflect more realistically the more fluid situation which had developed since Stalin's death and, while factionalism was still proscribed, greater emphasis was placed on ensuring the expression of divergent views within the Party. Thus, Article 27 of the 1961 Party Statues stipulates that:

> Wide discussion, especially discussion on a countrywide scale of questions of Party policy must be held so as to ensure for Party members the free expression of their views and preclude attempts to form fractional groupings destroying Party unity, attempts to split the Party.

[6] *Kommunist*, No. 10 (August, 1956), 3–13.
[7] *Pravda*, October 14, 1952.

The Proliferation of Factional Politics. Diversity and clash of opinion was allowed, initially, to filter down only to the level of the Central Committee. Eventually however, differences of opinion which reflected various factional views erupted — at first gingerly, and then more bodily, in Party Congresses, lower-level Party bodies, the Supreme Soviet, various professional conferences, newspapers and periodicals, and in professional organizations. The disagreements within the Presidium which were unleashed after Stalin's death threatened to crack the Party pyramid down to its very base. It was even possible to envisage the development of a multiparty system, and authoritative voices were openly advocating the nomination of more than one candidate for elective offices.

Decisions in the Politburo are reached by simple majority, with only full members entitled to vote, although alternate members participate in the debate and discussion. Meetings of the Politburo are held at least once a week and, according to both Khrushchev and Mikoyan, most decisions are unanimous. Mikoyan has further elaborated by stating that if a consensus were unobtainable, the Presidium would adjourn, sleep on the matter, and return for further discussion until unanimity was achieved. Since five full members out of eleven were expelled, on June 29, 1957, for persistent opposition and obstruction to the Party line, the unanimity of the Presidium's deliberations appear to have been exaggerated.

In view of Khrushchev's bitter attack on the organization of Politburo Commissions under Stalin, the Politburo's internal compartmentalization may not be as rigidly demarcated as before; foreign policy decisions, instead of being merely the concern of the Commission on Foreign Affairs, are discussed and made by the body as a whole. "Never in the past," said Molotov at the Twentieth Party Congress, "has our Party Central Committee and its Presidium been engaged as actively with questions of foreign policy as during the present period." The vitiating effects of Stalin's commission system, however, have been more than matched by the crystallization of factional groupings and cliques within the Party's highest body.

Under the Soviet one-party system, which does not permit the organization of an opposition with an alternative slate of leaders and policies, factional rivalry within the Party summit becomes a crude and primitive substitute for a two-party contest, while the relationship between the Central Committee and its Presidium constitutes the nearest approximation to a system of institutional responsibility and accountability.

The sharp and close factional divisions in the Politburo have revived the prominence and activity of the moribund Central Committee. Factional differences have been displayed before Plenums of the Central Committee (which are held at least twice a year) where the actions of the Politburo have been appealed. In this relatively large body of 195 full members and 165 alternates, discussion of the various views current in the Politburo is still more ritualized than free, with each faction in the Politburo supported by its own retainers in the Central Committee. Voting is conditioned not only by divisions in the Politburo, but also by considerations of political survival and opportunism, with members being extremely sensitive to the course that the struggle assumes in the higher body. "At Plenums of the Central Committee," according to the revealing statement of one low-ranking member, "Comrade Khrushchev and other members of the Presidium . . . corrected errors in a fatherly way . . . regardless of post occupied or of record."[8]

It was in the Central Committee that Malenkov reputedly indicted Beria and where, in turn, he and Molotov were disciplined and attacked by the Khrushchev faction. Shifts in the balance of factions in the Politburo are almost always immediately registered in the Central Committee, whose proceedings inevitably sway with those of the higher body. The Central Committee, whose decisions are invariably reported as unanimous, is empowered to alter its own membership and that of its higher bodies by a two-thirds vote; and in the June, 1957, Plenum it expelled three full members and one alternate from the Presidium and the Central Committee, demoted one to alternate status, and cut off still another at full membership in the Central Committee. Correspondingly, the Presidium was expanded to fifteen full members and nine alternates.

The Central Committee assumed increasing importance during the Khrushchev era, and it is likely that, after the "anti-Party group" episode, of June, 1957, he considered this body as a counterweight to the opposition which might congeal against him in the Presidium. Khrushchev was almost fastidious in his zeal to enshrine the Central Committee as the ultimate institutional repository of legitimacy in the Soviet system. The body was enlarged and convened regularly by Khrushchev, and all changes in personnel and major pronouncements of policy were either confirmed by or announced at Central Committee Plenums. Thus, the Central Committee was convened to expel Marshal Zhukov, former Premier Bulganin, Kirichenko, and Belyayev, as well as others, and met more often than the two annual meetings specified in the Party statutes. New appointments to the Presidium and the Secretariat were also announced after Central Committee meetings.

Immediately after the expulsion of the "anti-Party group," in mid-1957, and the removal of Marshal Zhukov, the Khrushchev faction appeared to be in full control of both the Presidium and the Central Committee and Khrushchev appeared to be in full command of the ruling faction. Proceedings of the Central Committee were also published more or less regularly under Khrushchev although selective censorship and suppression persisted. Khrushchev's behavior at Central Committee proceedings was often crude, rude, and earthy; commanding, but not domineering. He would deliver a report on the main item on the agenda, which was then discussed in speeches delivered by the other members. These were freely interrupted by the First Secretary, who might affirm, criticise, chastise, admonish, correct, and even warn the speakers, and

[8] Moscow Radio broadcast, February 21, 1956. Speech of Z. I. Muratov, first secretary of the Tatar Oblast Committee.

they would respond with varying degrees of deference, familiarity, meekness, fear, or audacity. At the December, 1958, Plenum, for example, seventy-five speakers discussed Khrushchev's report, and Bulganin, Pervukhin, and Saburov used the occasion to denounce themselves for complicity in the "anti-Party group" conspiracy to oust Khrushchev from power.

Factional Conflict in the Politburo. Differences in the Politburo arise as a result of both personal ambitions for power and fundamental conflict over doctrine and policy. Both factors are so intricately interwoven that attempts to draw fine distinctions between personal and policy conflicts are apt to be an idle exercise. Although Soviet ideology neither recognizes the legitimacy of factional groupings in the Party nor tolerates the doctrinal schisms that are their ideological expression, the Party, throughout its history, has been constantly threatened with the eruption of both. After Stalin's death, the rival cliques he permitted — and may even have encouraged — to form among his subordinates developed into factions, each with its own aspirations and opinions. Since no single faction was sufficiently powerful to annihilate the others, necessity was converted into virtue and the balance of terror in the Presidium was ideologically sanctified as "collective leadership."

Even before the revelations of the resolution that hurled Molotov and his associates from their places of eminence, it was unmistakable that serious factional quarrels kept the Presidium in a continual state of turmoil. At least three factions appear to have existed in the Presidium before June, 1957, although the members of each faction were not permanently committed to issues; and personality and tactical shifts, though not frivolous, were also not unusual. The Presidium was divided on four major issues that had important foreign policy repercussions: the Stalinist issue; the relations between the Soviet Union and other communist states and parties; economic policy and reorganization; and relations with the ex-colonial states.

The so-called Stalinist faction had at its core the veteran Politburo members, Molotov and Kaganovich, and was frequently supported by Malenkov. The nucleus of the anti-Stalinist faction was made up of Khrushchev, Mikoyan, Voroshilov, Bulganin, Kirichenko, and the alternate members of the Presidium. This faction was in decisive control of the Party apparatus and the Central Committee, and it found crucial support in the army, in Peking, Warsaw, and Belgrade, Pervukhin and Saburov made up the so-called "managerial-technical" faction, which appeared to have close connections with Malenkov in the past but generally cast its vote with the Khrushchev group on questions of Stalinism. The group deserted Malenkov for Khrushchev when Malenkov appeared to be the apostle for increased emphasis on the production of consumer goods and Khrushchev continued to rely on heavy industry. These factions were bound together by bonds of common ideological and policy considerations, but personal ambitions and opportunism played a considerable role, allowing wide room for maneuver and realignment of positions as the main chance presented itself.

The events in Poland and Hungary, together with the uncompromising attitude of Marshal Tito, encouraged the Stalinists to believe that the Khrushchev group had fumbled, while Khrushchev's sudden interest in decentralizing the economic structure of the state stampeded Pervukhin and Saburov foolishly to join the Stalinist faction in an anti-Khrushchev coalition that made a desperate effort to thwart the proposed dismantling of their economic empires. At the December, 1956, Plenum of the Central Committee, this combination was sufficiently powerful to arrest the de-Stalinization program temporarily and to guarantee the preservation of the centralized economic structure by installing Pervukhin as the virtual dictator of the economic system. Relations with Tito were once again inflamed, and Satellite policies appeared to harden. During this period, Malenkov — as representative of the new majority — accompanied Khrushchev to the communist gathering held in Budapest, from which both Warsaw and Belgrade were deliberately excluded.

The inconclusive factional strife in the Kremlin, and the ideological ferment in Eastern Europe, provided an opportunity for Peking to intervene, and Chou En-lai embarked upon an emergency trip to Moscow and Eastern Europe to shore up the Khrushchev faction. Because of the unnatural and unstable amalgamation organized against him, Khrushchev's ouster was deferred; but once the crisis had subsided, and it was clear that the armed forces and China preferred Khrushchev's policies in preference to those of his opposition, a realignment of forces in the Presidium enabled Khrushchev once again to reconstitute a majority at the February, 1957, Plenum, and Pervukhin was toppled from his brief perch on the economic throne. The economic levers of power were wrenched from his hands, while Shepilov was ousted from the Foreign Ministry in favor of Gromyko.

With the Presidium so sharply and evenly divided, "collective leadership" threatened to abandon Soviet foreign policy to the mercies of an inconclusive see-saw struggle plunging the Kremlin into a condition of perpetual indecision. While key Khrushchev supporters were out of town, Stalinist forces, by engineering a rump meeting of the Presidium — ostensibly to discuss minor matters — regrouped and resolved to unseat Khrushchev through a parliamentary ruse. When the meeting took place on June 17–18, 1957, the First Secretary found himself momentarily outmaneuvered and apparently irrevocably outvoted. Saburov and Pervukhin once again voted with the Stalinist faction, as did Khrushchev's erstwhile protégé, Shepilov. But the key figure in the new realignment was Bulganin, who miscalculated the power of the anti-Khrushchev forces and underrated the First Secretary's political agility (leading Khrushchev to confide later that some of his colleagues knew more about arithmetic than politics), and in an opportunistic maneuver voted to oust Khrushchev from power in the meeting over which he presided. Refusing to resign, Khrushchev conducted a filibuster while his supporters quickly assembled a special meeting of the Central Committee and its auditing commission (a total of 319 members), which sat from June 22–29, 1957.

After a bitter ventilation of all the contentious issues of doctrines and policy, during which 60 members reportedly took part in the debate and 115 filed statements, the Molotov-managerial coalition was overwhelmed by a unanimous vote tarnished only by a single obstinate abstention by Molotov — the first such publicly admitted dissonance in a Central Committee vote in almost thirty years. The Stalinist wing of the coalition was charged in the resolution which expelled them with engaging in illegal factional activity and cabalistic intrigue:

> Entering into collusion on an anti-Party basis, they set out to change the policy of the Party, to drag the Party back to the erroneous methods of leadership condemned by the Twentieth Party Congress [i.e., Stalinism]. They resorted to methods of intrigue and formed a collusion against the Central Committee.

The others were not specifically condemned, but Saburov lost his seat on the Presidium and Pervukhin was demoted to alternate status. In their humiliating appearances before the Twenty-first Party Congress, held in February, 1959, both confessed their complicity in the plot against Khrushchev, although they maintained that they later switched to Khrushchev on the vote to actually oust him as First Secretary. Saburov was eventually exiled to the obscurity of a factory manager in Syzran, while Pervukhin wound up with the less than exalted post of ambassador to East Germany. Apparently for purposes of concealing the fact that a majority of the Presidium actually voted against him, Bulganin lingered on as Premier until March, 1958, and as a member of the Presidium until the following September, although it was clear that his position had been compromised. He was formally charged with being part of the anti-Khrushchev conspiracy on November 14, 1958, and at the December, 1958, Plenum, Bulganin made a grovelling confession in which he denounced himself as the "nominal leader" of the plot because of his position as chairman of the Council of Ministers. He made an abject plea for forgiveness, unleashed a vicious attack on Molotov and Kaganovich, and was consigned to the demeaning post of chairman of the Stavropol Economic Council.

The victorious group soon betrayed signs of splitting on a wide range of domestic and foreign policies. The leadership tended to polarize around two main factions, a "moderate" group, led by Khrushchev, and a "conservative" group, whose leaders appeared to be M. A. Suslov and F. R. Kozlov, later apparently supported by traditional elements of the professional military and representatives of heavy industry. Generally speaking, the moderate faction sought a relaxation of international tensions and a *détente* with the United States, even at the expense of alienating China; the conservative faction saw little value in a *détente* with the United States, especially at the expense of alienating the Soviet Union's most important ally. Domestically, Khrushchev and the "moderates" were willing to tolerate greater relaxation of controls at home and advocated a change in the economic equilibrium in the direction of producing more consumer goods at the expense of heavy industry. The "conservatives" were opposed to further relaxation at home and may have even demanded some retrenchment, and they were virtually dogmatic in their insistence that priority continue to be given to heavy industry over light industry and agriculture. Under these conditions, formalized debate in the Central Committee gave way to a genuine if largely esoteric, articulation of divergent factional viewpoints, which was also evident from the content of the speeches delivered at the Twenty-first and Twenty-second Party Congresses, in January, 1959, and October, 1961, respectively.

As long as Khrushchev's policy of seeking a relaxation of international tension and a *détente* with the United States seemed to be bearing fruit, he was able to isolate and silence his critics in the leadership, particularly after his meeting with President Eisenhower at Camp David, in mid-1959. Relations with China simultaneously deteriorated catastrophically when Khrushchev unilaterally nullified a secret, 1957, Sino-Soviet agreement on nuclear technology, just prior to his meeting with President Eisenhower. Since an improvement in relations with the United States inevitably meant a further deterioration of relations with China, this became an important and crucial issue which agitated the Soviet leadership. The factional opposition to Khrushchev was strengthened in January, 1960, when the Soviet leader alienated the traditional military by calling for a reduction of the ground forces by one-third and shifting the main reliance for Soviet security to its nuclear deterrent capability. This new strategic policy was based upon the expectation of an imminent settlement of all outstanding issues between Washington and Moscow on the basis of the "Camp David Spirit."

After the U-2 incident, Khrushchev's grip on the Central Committee and its Presidium was weakened and came under increasing attack at home, while criticism in Peking mounted simultaneously. Khrushchev's foreign policy was based upon a fundamental restructuring of the image and character of the American "ruling class," which, according to the "moderates" had split into a "sober" group, on the one hand, and an intractable group, made up of "belligerent," "aggressive," "irrational," and even "mad" elements, on the other. The sober group, whose leader, according to Khrushchev, was President Eisenhower, was dominant, and it appeared ready to negotiate a settlement with the Soviet Union, on a realistic basis, which to Khrushchev meant a *détente* based on supposed Soviet strategic superiority. Neither the "conservative" faction, nor the traditional military, nor the Chinese leaders subscribed to this image. The Soviet Union's leader was, in effect, relying upon the self-restraint of the sober forces in the American ruling class, and his opposition viewed his call for troop reductions and cutbacks in heavy industry with considerable alarm. From the Chinese viewpoint, Khrushchev's search for a *détente* with Eisenhower indicated an erosion in Moscow's commitment to revolutionary goals and a tacit alliance with Peking's principal national enemy.

Although Khrushchev's logic was undermined by the U-2 incident, he managed to remain in power. He pleaded that a new American administration would resume the earlier pacific course of Soviet-American relations, viewed the U-2 crisis as an unfortunate incident, and insisted that the sober American group was still dominant and would be so demonstrated by the forthcoming elections.

Kennedy was unknown to the Russians, but Nixon was a well-known and heartily disliked personality, and so Moscow placed its reliance on a Kennedy victory and a reversal of post–U-2 policy. But the Soviet leader was to be disappointed once again, as the new President embarked on a course of strengthening U.S. military capabilities, supported an attempt to overthrow the Castro regime in Cuba, and refused to be bullied into negotiating a settlement on Soviet terms. The Soviet failure to win a Berlin victory and the steadily growing power of the United States, increased the pressures upon Khrushchev both at home and from Peking and at the Twenty-second Party Congress, he adopted a harsher line towards the United States.

From the time of the Twenty-second Party Congress until Khrushchev's ouster, in October, 1964, the Soviet leadership was plagued by constant factional squabbles and these often found expression in the Central Committee Plenums. Khrushchev stayed in power only because the factional balance was extremely delicate, with some leaders supporting him on some issues and opposing him on others. Thus, Soviet factional politics was not only institutionally and functionally oriented but issue oriented as well, and it was the existence of issue-oriented factionalism which provided Khrushchev with the margins necessary to stay in power.

Khrushchev once again narrowly missed being ousted as a consequence of the Cuban missile crisis of October, 1962, when his opposition at home and his critics in Peking seemed perilously close to having a common point of view. His problems were aggravated, also, by President Kennedy's initial rejection of a Soviet proposal for a limited test-ban treaty based on three annual inspections. The Soviet Premier gained a temporary extension of power, however, when the leader of the "conservative" faction, F. R. Kozlov, suffered an incapacitating stroke in April, 1963. Although Khrushchev mused in public about his possible retirement, the incapacitation of Kozlov gave him a new lease on political power and he quickly took advantage of President Kennedy's offer, in a speech at American University, to reach an agreement on a limited test-ban treaty, which was signed the following month.

Khrushchev thus appeared to have vindicated himself for the "sober" forces were indeed in control in Washington and while the détente was based not upon the assumption of Soviet strategic superiority, but upon the implied assumption of U.S. strategic superiority, it enabled Khrushchev to turn his attention to pressing economic problems at home and to the dispute with Peking. The Chinese called the limited test-ban treaty an act of Soviet betrayal, and there was strong evidence that the treaty was not enthusiastically accepted by the "conservative" faction or the traditional military.

Khrushchev's inept handling of the dispute with China, his generally crude and unsophisticated behavior as a politician, and his constant boasting in public apparently finally alienated some of his supporters, who saw in his person an impediment to a reconciliation with China and an obstacle to a rational approach to domestic problems. In October, 1964, he was ousted, in a coup engineered largely by his own trusted subordinates, Brezhnev, Kosygin, and Mikoyan. He was indirectly accused of concocting "hare-brained schemes," "boasting," and general ineptness. Khrushchev's ouster allegedly took place at a Central Committee Plenum, but the proceedings were not made public. The manner and abruptness of his dismissal caused considerable commotion and disturbance in other communist countries and parties, whose leaders demanded and received an explanation in a series of bilateral conferences.

The Chinese, the conservatives, the traditionalistic military, and the moderates all seemed to have a common interest in removing Khrushchev, if for widely differing and even contradictory reasons, and there seems to be little question that the factional situation at home and the criticisms from Peking combined to bring about the Soviet Premier's political ouster.

The Central Committee is thus emerging as the most important political organ of power and authority in the Soviet system, although it has not yet eclipsed the Politburo, which, however, must be increasingly responsive to its deliberations. The growing power of the Central Committee reflects the increasingly pluralistic character of the Soviet social order. This body is composed of representatives from the most powerful and influential elite groups in Soviet society. It includes the entire membership of the Politburo and the Secretariat, the most important ministers of the government, the first secretaries of republican party organizations and important regional party organizations, the most important officials of the Union Republics, the marshals, generals, and admirals of the armed forces and the police, the important ambassadors, the trade union officials, the cultural and scientific celebrities and leaders, the leading Party ideologists, and the top Komsomol officials. Increasingly, these representatives perceive attitudes reflecting their institutional or functional roles and status in Soviet society and this provides the social basis for the political factions which now characterize the Soviet system.

The transition from Stalinist, one-man rule to quasi-pluralistic political behavior is now all but complete. The Khrushchev decade emerges as a sort of transition period between these two types of political behavior. Under Stalin, conflicts were rendered into decisions after a blood purge in which potential opponents were physically destroyed; under Khrushchev, conflicts were resolved into decisions by the clearcut victory of one faction and the expulsion of the others from important positions of power. The blood purge was replaced with public condemnation and disgrace, demotion, or retirement but, since the execution of Beria in 1954, no fallen leader has been executed or even brought to trial. With the element of terror removed from the political process, however, the risks of opposition and dissent were considerably reduced. Victorious factions divided into new factions, and so the factional conflict resumed on a new level, and around new issues. By late 1959, no single group could establish dominance, and control gradually came to be exercised by a kind of consensus, based on compromise, bargaining, and accommodation. This has introduced an element of instability and uncertainty with respect to any given government or administration, but it has simultaneously stabilized and regularized the Soviet political process and has removed much of the uncertainty which hitherto prevailed.

No formal charges of factionalism have been made against any group or individual in the Soviet Union's hierarchy since 1959. Such a charge can only be levelled if a particular faction is soundly defeated and expelled from the leadership, and this was characteristic of the rule by a single faction which flourished between 1953 and 1959. Factionalism is still prohibited by the Party rules, but its existence was tacitly admitted by Kozlov at the Twenty-second Party Congress:

> Under present circumstances, need the statutes contain any formal guarantee against factionalism and clique activity? Yes . . . such guarantees as needed. To be sure there is no social base left in Soviet society that could feed opportunistic currents in the Party. But the sources of ideological waverings on the part of particular individuals or groups have not yet been entirely eliminated. Some persons may fall under the influence of bourgeois propaganda from the outside. Others having failed to comprehend the dialectics of society's development and having turned . . . into dying embers, will have nothing to do with anything new and go on clinging to old dogmas that have been toppled by life.[9]

Interest Groups and Factional Politics. It is at once obvious that factions could neither arise nor flourish unless they received constant sustenance from powerful social forces in Soviet society. Just as Party factions do not organize into separate political organizations competing with the Party for political power, so interest groups in Soviet society do not constitute separate organizations, but rather seek to make their influence felt as formless clusters of vested interests. Within the context of Marxist ideology, an interest group can only be a social class with economic interests that conflict with the interests of other classes. After the Revolution only the interests of the working class, as distorted by the Marxist prism, were given legitimate recognition — although the concrete political articulation of these interests was usurped by the Communist Party — and all other interests and parties were condemned to oblivion. In 1936 Stalin declared the eradication of class conflict in Soviet society, but he continued to recognize the existence of separate social classes, whose interests had merged into a single identity. The Communist Party was transformed from a party representing only the interests of the working class into one representing the transcendental interests of all Soviet social classes. Consequently, Soviet ideology

[9] *Pravda*, October 29, 1961.

neither recognizes the legitimacy of competing interest groups nor tolerates their autonomous existence. In Soviet jargon, an interest group that develops interests that deviate from the Party line is a hostile class; the faction that represents it in the Party is an attempt to form a party within a party; and its articulated views on policy and doctrine constitute an ideological deviation.

Separate interest groups, however, continue to flourish in Soviet society, but not in conformity with the doctrinaire and contrived premises of nineteenth-century Marxism, nor within the synthetic social divisions given official sanction. The collective-farm peasantry and the working class constitute the numerically preponderant classes in Soviet society, but the major interest groups with sufficient power and influence to apply political pressure do not follow the artificial constructions of Soviet ideology; in accordance with the unique dynamic of Soviet society the privileged elites find their social differentiation within a single recognized group, the intelligentsia, which is not recognized as a social class, but is euphemistically called a *stratum*.

Although the Soviet intelligentsia (roughly identical with what Milovan Djilas labels the "New Class") is a variegated congeries of differentiated elites, they all have in common a desire to perpetuate the Soviet system from which they have sprung and from which they benefit as privileged groups. But each group is immediately concerned with its own vested stake in Soviet society and seeks to force doctrine and policy to assume the contours of its own special interests. Since these groups do not enjoy official recognition, they all seek to exert their influence through the Communist Party, not outside it, and political rivalry assumes the form of competing for control of the Party's decision-making organs and its symbols of legitimacy. Because Soviet ideology rigidly and inaccurately insists on the existence of a single monolithic interest, representing that of society in its collective entity, conflicts between major groups are resolved not by political accommodation, but by mutual elimination and by the attempt of one interest group to establish its supremacy and to impose its views as those of society as a whole. Thus the Communist Party, under the pressures of diverse groups seeking political articulation and accommodation, has become a conglomeration of interests whose basic incompatibilities are only partially obscured by a veneer of monolithic unity. (See Table 1.)

Not all interest groups in the Soviet Union are sufficiently powerful to exact representation for their views by factions in the Party hierarchy. There are six principal groups within Soviet society that have accumulated sufficient leverage, either through the acquisition of indispensable skills and talents or through the control of instruments of persuasion, terror, or destruction, to exert pressure upon the Party. These are: (1) the Party apparatus, consisting of those who have made a career in the Party bureaucracy; (2) the government bureaucracy; (3) the economic managers and technicians; (4) the cultural, professional, and scientific intelligentsia; (5) the police; (6) the armed forces. (See Table 2.)

TABLE 1
THE DISTRIBUTION OF THE INTELLIGENTSIA IN THE COMMUNIST PARTY, 1966

Social category	Total size of social category (employed)	Percentage of social category in party	Party membership[b]	Percentage of party
Mental Workers	26,000,000[a]	20.9%	5,432,196	46.2%
Intelligentsia	11,249,700[c]	36.2	4,450,530	37.8
(women)	(6,940,700)	(13.0)	(900,000)	(7.7)
Executives	1,200,000	76.0	423,700	8.6
Administrators			586,656	
Engineer, technical[d]	4,400,000	40.0	1,765,400	15.0
Cultural, professional, and scientific	5,200,000	24.3	1,265,700	10.8
Trade, services, etc.	470,000 }			
Other office workers	14,000,000[e] }	4.2	510,592	4.3
Armed forces (est.)	3,000,000	29.3	880,000[f]	7.5
Workers (urban and rural)[g]	51,000,000	8.6	4,385,700	37.4
Collective farmers	30,000,000	6.5	1,940,160	16.5
Total	110,000,000		11,758,169	

a As of January, 1966.
b As of January, 1965.
c As of November 15, 1964 (12,065,900 as of November, 1965). Includes all "specialists" working in the national economy.
d Includes agricultural personnel.
e Mainly women.
f Primarily officers and senior noncoms; calculated on the basis of military representation at the Twenty-Third Party Congress (April, 1966).
g Includes all foremen and 8 million rural workers on state farms.

TABLE 2
SOCIAL COMPOSITION OF PARTY CONGRESS, 1952–1966 (VOTING DELEGATES ONLY)

	1952		1956		1959		1961		1966	
	Number	Per cent	Number	Per cent	Number	Per cent	Number	Per cent	Number	Per cent
Total	1,192		1,355		1,269		4,408		4,943[h]	
Workers		7.8[a]		12.2%		32.0%	984	22.3%	1,141	23.0%
Peasants		7.8[b]		4.9	399		469	10.6[c]	554	11.2
Intelligentsia		84.4			870	68.0	2,955	67.1	3,248	65.7
Party apparatus			526	82.9	456	36.0	1,262	28.7[e]	1,330[i]	27.0
State officials			177	37.3[d]	147	11.5	465	10.5	539	10.9
Managerial-tech.				13.1	126	10.0	667	15.0[f]	756[j]	15.3
Cultural-profess.					50	4.0	235	5.3	271[k]	5.5
Military			116	8.5	91	7.0	305	7.0[g]	352	7.1
Other							21	0.5		
Women		12.3	193	14.2	222	17.5	1,073	22.3	1,154	23.3

[a] Includes foremen.
[b] Includes farm directors and rural intelligentsia.
[c] Includes farm directors.
[d] Includes 20 trade-union and Komsomol officials.
[e] Includes 104 trade-union and Komsomol officials.
[f] Includes 260 agricultural specialists.
[g] Includes police officials with military rank.
[h] Includes alternates also.
[i] Includes 82 trade-union and 44 Komsomol officials.
[j] Includes 320 agricultural executives and technical personnel.
[k] Includes "other."

These major groups are by no means organized as cohesively united bodies, speaking with a single authoritative voice, but rather themselves are made up of rival personal and policy cliques, gripped by internal jealousies, and often in constant collision and friction with one another in combination or alliance with similarly oriented cliques in other social groups.

The Party apparatus itself was thus divided into rival cliques, the two main contending groups being those led by Khrushchev and Malenkov. Since the denouncement of Malenkov, his supporters in the Party apparatus were replaced with followers of Khrushchev. Although the function of the Party bureaucracy is essentially administrative rather than policy-making, it has a tendency to feel that it "owns" the Party, and thus seeks first to subordinate the Party to its control and then to force the other major groups to submit to the domination of the Party. After Stalin's death, the serious and imminent threat posed to the Party by Beria and his secret police caused Khrushchev and Malenkov to temporarily bury their rivalry in the apparatus of the Party in order to crush the secret police, which had developed into an independent center of power and threatened to subjugate the Party to its will. The secret police was dismembered with the aid of the army.

There appears to be no systematic attempt to select members of the Central Committee and its Politburo from among the major forces in Soviet society; the composition of these bodies appears to depend upon the balance of forces at any given time (see tables 3 and 4). Ample evidence exists, however, that their composition reflects deliberate recognition of these major interest groups. Traditionally, the Party apparatus accounts for slightly less than half the total membership of the Central Committee, with the government bureaucracy (including the economic administrators) following close behind. The representation of the other groups is substantially less, although, because virtually all members of the Party's two highest bodies who are not career Party bureaucrats are employed by the state, it is often difficult to distinguish the main line of work pursued by a particular member of the Central Committee. This is especially true of individuals who move from one group to another. Consequently, all distinctions are provisional and, in some cases, arbitrary. The composition of the Politburo is more accurately differentiated, although even there, because of the interlocking of the top organs of state and Party, some ambiguity prevails.

Since the membership of the Central Committee is normally determined by the Party Congress, which meets every four years, its composition is not normally affected by day-to-day changes in the factional equilibrium. The Politburo, whose membership can be altered by the Central Committee, is peculiarly sensitive to the fluctuations in the balance of power and is a fairly accurate barometer of changing political fortunes.

Formerly, it could be said that the composition of the Central Committee was determined from the top, by the Politburo, but the relationship between the two bodies is becoming increasingly reciprocal.

TABLE 3
SOCIAL COMPOSITION OF THE CENTRAL COMMITTEE, 1952–1966 (FULL AND CANDIDATE MEMBERS)

Social category	1952	1956	1961	February, 1966	April, 1966
Party apparatus	103	117	158 (48.0%)ᵃ	107 (34.2%)	155 (43.0%)ᵈ
State and economic officials	79	98	112 (34.0)	115 (36.8)	136 (37.9)
Military officers	26	18	31 (9.3)	31 (9.8)	33 (9.7)
Cultural and scientific			18 (5.4)		15 (4.2)
Police	9	3	2		2 (0.5)
Workers and peasants					10 (2.8)
Others	19ᵇ	19ᵇ	9ᶜ (3.3)	61 (19.1)	9 (2.5)
Totals	236	255	330	314	360
Women					15 (4.2)
Over age 40					327 (90.8)
New members					121 (33.6)

ᵃ Includes 9 trade-union and Komsomol officials.
ᵇ Includes cultural and scientific personnel.
ᶜ Includes a few "workers" and "peasants."
ᵈ Includes 10 trade-union and Komsomol officials.

Changes in the composition of the Politburo now reflect, to some degree, changes in the factional balance in the Central Committee as groups and individuals maneuver for position and advantage — bargaining, negotiating, and accommodating. The Central Committee's authority becomes crucial, and perhaps even decisive, when the factional balance is delicate. Then, rival groups seek to gain wider support and alter their policies to meet the demands of wider constituencies. Thus, while the Politburo is the more accurate gauge of day-to-day politics, the composition of the Central Committee is apt to reflect more durable, long-range trends. Table 4 shows only institutional representation on the Politburo, and it should be noted that interest groups tend, increasingly, to cut across institutional entities.

The Party apparatus continues to be the dominant institutional actor in both the Central Committee and its Presidium, but its absolute and relative strength in both bodies, after reaching a post-Stalin high point in 1957, seems now to be diminishing as other groups demand greater representation. As factional cleavages develop within the apparatus, opportunities are created for other groups as they become targets of appeal for support by rival apparatus factions and in turn make demands upon the apparatus. The year 1957, after the expulsion of the "anti-Party group" represented the zenith of single faction rule which was sustained substantially unimpaired until Khrushchev's assumption of the premiership in the following year. Factionalism, however, infected the victorious Khrushchev group itself and the overall representation of the apparatus in the Presidium started to decline and by the time of the Twenty-second Party Congress in October, 1961, two main factions had once again materialized, a "moderate" faction led by Khrushchev and a "conservative" faction, supported by the traditional military, led by F. R. Kozlov, an erstwhile Khrushchev satrap. No less than four full members and four candidate members of the Presidium associated with the "moderate" position were dropped, and the over-all size of the Presidium was substantially reduced. In the Secretariat, the "moderate" faction's dominance was eliminated by the appointment of new members associated with the "conservative" group and the size of this body was raised from five to nine. Thus the "moderate" faction suffered losses in the Presidium by a trimming of its membership while in the Secretariat, its presence was diminished through the addition of new members associated with the other faction. Khrushchev managed to hang on as both Premier and First Secretary, first in order to present a united front to both the United States and China and second, because he adjusted and accommodated his publicly stated views and policies to accord more with the demands of the "conservative" faction, without at the same time abandoning his leadership of the "moderate" faction. From the Twenty-second Party Congress until his ouster in October, 1964, he presided over a regime which was characterized not by single faction rule but by factional consensus and accommodation.

During the Khrushchev era, the government bureaucracy suffered a drastic decrease in its representation on the Presidium, both in the

TABLE 4
DISTRIBUTION OF ELITES IN THE PRESIDIUM/POLITBURO 1952–1970

Category	October 1952	March 1953	February 1956	July 1957	July 1961	October 1961	January 1963	April 1966	1970
Party apparatus[a]	13 (5)[b]	2 (2)	4 (3)	10 (6)	10 (3)	7 (3)	8 (4)	6 (7)	6 (7)
State bureaucracy									
Economic	5 (4)	4	4	1 (2)	2 (1)	2	2	5 (1)	5 (1)
Non-economic	4 (2)	3 (1)	3 (1)	3	2 (2)	2 (2)	2 (2)		
Professional									
Military	0	0	0 (1)	1	0	0	0	0	0
Police	2	1 (1)	0	0	0	0	0	0	0 (1)
Cultural									
Intelligentsia (ideologists)	1 (1)	0	0 (1)	0 (1)	0 (1)	0	0	0	0
Totals	25 (11)	10 (4)	11 (6)	15 (6)	14 (7)	11 (5)	12 (6)	11 (8)	11 (9)
Women	0	0	0	1	1	0	0	0	0

[a] State and police officials, ideologists, and others who were appointed to government positions from the party apparatus are included in this category rather than in their official position. Main career experience determines classification. Thus, M. A. Suslov is classified with the party apparatus rather than with the cultural intelligentsia.
[b] Figures in parentheses are candidate members.

economic and non-economic realms. Since 1958, there has been no active representation of either the professional military or heavy industry, while light industry was amply represented by Kosygin and Mikoyan, both of whom were in high favor with Khrushvhev. The appointment of D. F. Ustinov as a candidate member of the Politburo and as a member of the Secretariat at the Twenty-third Party Congress (1966) marked the first direct representation of heavy industry in the Party's highest body in nearly a decade. A specialist in defense industry, Ustinov represents in his person the symbolic relationship between heavy industry and the traditional military in the Soviet social system. The police were also excluded, although the admission of Shelepin to the Presidium, after he stepped down from his position as chairman of the Committee on State Security, may have given the police some marginal representation. The cultural intelligentsia was represented by professional ideologists like Suslov, who were closely identified with the Party apparatus.

The fall of Khrushchev, in 1964, did not produce any immediate major dislocations or dismissals in the Soviet hierarchy, except for the demotion of a few individuals who were personally close or related to the Soviet leader. The most conspicuous was his son-in-law, Alexei Adzhubei, who was unceremoniously booted out of the Central Committee and relieved of his job as chief editor of *Izvestia*. Shelepin and Shelest, neither of whom were candidate members, were admitted as full members of the Presidium, and Demichev was appointed a candidate member. Shelepin and Demichev were also members of the Secretariat, and their appointment broadened the overlapping membership in the two bodies. It is possible that their elevation was, in part, a reward for their support in ousting their erstwhile patron. There were other dismissals and appointments at lower levels, but they were accomplished with little fanfare. It was quite clear that Khrushchev's ouster had created a series of minor power vacuums which had to be filled, and this resulted in some maneuvering. Three Khrushchev supporters, Ilyichev, Polyakov, and Titov, were dropped from the Secretariat, reducing its size to eight.

In March, 1965, after a Central Committee Plenum, further changes were made. Mazurov was elevated from candidate membership to full membership in the Presidium, and D. F. Ustinov was added as a candidate member. Ustinov's star had appeared to rise, after the Cuban missile crisis, when Khrushchev seemed to be in deep trouble, but it dimmed after Kozlov's stroke and Khrushchev made a temporary political recovery.

Further changes were made in the Party summit in December, 1965, when Ustinov, Kapitonov, and Kulakov were appointed to the Secretariat to replace the three members who had been dropped after Khrushchev's political demise, raising its number once again to eleven. Six members of the Secretariat were also full or candidate members of the Presidium, which suggested a resurgence of the Party apparatus's representation at the Party summit. Podgorny, at this time, also replaced

Mikoyan as Chairman of the Presidium of the Supreme Soviet, and subsequently relinquished his membership in the Secretariat.

The definitive post-Khrushchev composition of the Party summit was made at the Twenty-third Party Congress in April, 1966, when Mikoyan and Shvernik were retired from the Politburo and, Pelshe, a Latvian Party secretary, was appointed a full member over the heads of all the candidate members. Two new candidate members were appointed — Kunayev, a Kazakh Party leader, and Masherov, a Byelorussian Party secretary who had become a full member of the Central Committee only in November, 1964, immediately after Khrushchev's ouster, which suggests that he played a key role in the post-Khrushchev factional maneuvering. The composition of the Secretariat remained unchanged, except that Kirilenko, also a full member of the Politburo, replaced Podgorny in the Secretariat, since the latter's new post as Chairman of the Presidium of the Supreme Soviet is traditionally disassociated from the Secretariat.

The restructuring of the Party summit at the Twenty-third Party Congress strongly suggested that Brezhnev, the General Secretary of the Party, had strengthened his position and that he enjoyed a factional majority or consensus, but by no means had assumed the power of a Khrushchev or a Stalin, irrespective of the symbolic manipulation of nomenclature at the Congress. Of the eleven full members of the Politburo, four were members of the Secretariat, while of the eight candidate members, two were members of the Secretariat. This meant that six members of the eleven-man Secretariat also sat on the Politburo. The clear dominance of the Party apparatus in the Politburo was further indicated by the presence of six Party secretaries of republics (Ukrainian, Latvian, Georgian, Uzbek, Byelorussian and Kazakh) as full or candidate members, thus broadening its ethnic base to include representation from six of the fourteen major non-Russian nationalities, including two Central Asian Moslem nationalities, the Uzbek and Kazakh, and giving the apparatus a total of six full members and six candidate members of the Politburo, or twelve votes out of nineteen, a clear majority. In addition to this, career Party bureaucrats like Podgorny and Mazurov moved into key state offices. The interlocking of institutions and personnel between the Party and the state after the Twenty-third Party Congress is shown in table 5.

It is normal practice to divorce membership in the Secretariat from membership in the Council of Ministers, since the Secretariat is supposed to exercise an independent audit of the government's work and check on the execution and implementation of Party directives and resolutions. The only consistent deviation from this practice occurs when the same personality functions as General Secretary (First Secretary) of the Party and Chairman of the Council of Ministers, as was the case during the later years of the Stalin and Khrushchev eras. Similarly, the Chairmanship of the Presidium of the Supreme Soviet is considered to be incompatible with membership in the Secretariat. Both Brezhnev and Podgorny relinquished their membership in the Secretariat upon their appointment as Chairman of the Presidium of the Supreme Soviet. It is traditional, however, for the General Secretary to be an ordinary member of the Presidium of the Supreme Soviet if he holds no other state post, and it is usual for the Presidium to include several other members of the Party Secretariat, thus ensuring Party audit and control over its activities. It is also customary for membership in the Presidium of the Supreme Soviet to be incompatible with membership in the Council of Ministers, since the latter is juridically responsible to the former. Since the death of Stalin, it has been normal practice to include high state and Party officials of the R.S.F.S.R. and the Ukraine in the Politburo.

Internal Politics and Soviet Foreign Policy: Interest Groups and Factional Polarization on Foreign Policy Issues[10]

The informal recognition of groups with distinctive special interests of their own and the admission of their representatives to the decision-making bodies of the Party cannot but influence the country's foreign policy, although how this influence is exerted, and in what direction, is difficult to determine. Although it is true that none of the major groups has publicly thwarted the decisions of the Party in foreign policy, it has been officially admitted that Party decisions have been administratively distorted by both a Minister of Internal Affairs and two Foreign Ministers. The removal of the managerial bureaucrats from both the Presidium and high government posts was motivated, at least in part, by the fear that their control of the key economic levers of society could be used to frustrate the decisions of the Party.

Marshal Zhukov's leadership of the army posed an even grimmer threat to the supremacy of the Party apparatus, had he been permitted to remain in the Presidium and the Defense Ministry where he could seriously question the basic decisions of the Party concerning military and foreign policy and frustrate their implementation. His removal, in October, 1957, from both strategic positions was essentially preventive, designed to remove a popular and commanding personality who might at some future date challenge even more crucial decisions of the Party and thus produce an internal crisis of incalculable magnitude. Zhukov's denouement was painlessly engineered by skillful exploitation of his own vanity and the intense personal jealousies and factional cleavages within the army leadership itself as well as by adroit manipulation of the Middle-Eastern crisis. His replacement on the Presidium was not another representative from the military, but yet another worker in the Party Apparatus, promoted up from alternate membership.

By 1958, the Party apparatus, under Khrushchev's direction, had dismembered the police, domesticated the managerial bureaucrats and decentralized their empire, exiled the leaders of factional groupings in the Party to Siberia, and subordinated the military to its will. As table 2

[10] This section is adapted from the author's "Internal Politics and Foreign Policy in the Soviet System," in *Approaches to Comparative and International Politics*, ed. B. Farrell (Evanston, Ill., Northwestern University Press, 1966).

TABLE 5
INTERLOCKING OF GOVERNMENT AND PARTY INSTITUTIONS AND PERSONNEL IN THE SOVIET UNION: 1970

First Secretaries of Republics	Presidium of the Supreme Soviet	Secretariat	Politburo	Presidium of the Council of Ministers	Premiers of Republics	Other
	Brezhnev	Brezhnev (General Secretary)	Brezhnev			
			Kosygin	Kosygin (Chairman)		
		Suslov	Suslov			Suslov[b]
	Podgorny (Chairman)		Podgorny			
		Kirilenko	Kirilenko			
			Polyansky	Polyansky (First Deputy)		
			Voronov		Voronov (R.S.F.S.R.)[a]	
			Shelepin			Shelepin (Trade Union Chairman)
Shelest (Ukraine)	Shelest		Shelest			
Pelshe (Latvia)			Pelshe			
			Mazurov	Mazurov (First Deputy)		
	Grishin		Grishin			Grishin (Moscow Party Committee)
Mzhavanadze (Georgia)			Mzhavanadze			
Rashidov (Uzbek)	Rashidov		Rashidov			
			Shcherbitsky		Shcherbitsky (Ukraine)[a]	
		Demichev	Demichev			
		Ustinov	Ustinov			
Masherov (Byelorussia)	Masherov		Masherov			
Kunayev (Kazakh)	Kunayev		Kunayev			
			Andropov	Andropov (State Security)		
		Ponomarev				Ponomarev[c]
		Kulakov				
		Kapitonov				
		Solomentsev				Solomentsev[d]
		Katushev				

[a] Ex officio members, Council of Ministers.
[b] Chairman, Foreign Affairs Commission, Council of Union.
[c] Chairman, Foreign Affairs Commission, Council of Nationalities.
[d] Chairman, Legislative Proposals Commission, Council of Union.

indicates, neither major instrument of coercion in the Soviet system now has a representative in the Party Presidium, which is now overwhelmingly dominated by career Party *apparatchiki.*

Although ideologically the basic purpose of external security and state survival is to develop into a power center for the purpose of implementing ideological goals in foreign policy (world communism), increasingly the purpose becomes in fact to protect and preserve the existing social order in the interests of the social groups who dominate and benefit from it. To the extent that the implementation of foreign policy goals, whether ideologically motivated or otherwise, are compatible with the preservation and enhancement of the social order and serve to reward rather than deprive its beneficiaries, no incompatibility between internal and external goals is experienced. If, however, the pursuit of ideological goals in foreign policy undermines or threatens the security of the state and the social groups who dominate it (or even arrests the progress of their material prosperity), the primacy of internal interests are ideologically rationalized and the energies and efforts devoted to external ideological goals are correspondingly diminished.

It must be realized that the relationship between internal interests and external ideological goals is a dynamic one and fluctuates in accordance with opportunities and capabilities, but in the long run the tendency is that ideological goals which threaten internal interests erode and are deprived of their motivating character. The persistence of ideological goals in Soviet foreign policy reflects socio-functional interests which have been traditionally associated with the Party apparatus and professional ideologues. The fact that the concrete policies which have resulted from the pursuit of ideological goals in foreign policy have created special vested interests for other socio-political or socio-institutional groups, like the Secret Police, the Armed Forces, and the heavy industrial managers, should not obscure the fact that the definition, identification, and implementation of ideological goals, whether in foreign or domestic policy, has been the special function of the Party apparatus and its attendant ideologues. An area of common interest among some members of the Party apparatus and the Armed Forces and heavy industrial managers in pursuing policies which are tension-producing has thus come into being. Tension-producing policies, however, in an era of increasing technological complexity, not only tend to automatically enhance the power of professionalized and technologically oriented groups in the Soviet Union, to the relative detriment of the status and power of the Party apparatus, but also tend to alienate from the apparatus other more numerous social groups in society whose interests are more in consonance with tension-lessening policies, such as the consumer goods producers and light industrial managers, the intellectuals, artists, professionals, agricultural managers, and finally, the great mass of Soviet citizenry, comprising the lower intelligentsia, workers, peasants, and others, whose priorities are always low during periods of high international tensions. Since these latter social forces are more numerous than those whose interests are served by tension-producing policies, the Party apparatus was in danger of alienating itself further from the great masses of the Soviet citizenry and becoming increasingly dependent upon the traditional military and heavy industry.

The Soviet Union like the United States is thus involved in a great debate over foreign policy and national security matters centering around the issue of whether heightening international tensions or relaxation of international tensions best serves the "national interests."

While only Molotov and the "anti-Party group" have been specifically identified by the Soviet leadership with a policy of favoring international tensions, the nature of the factional conflicts in the Soviet Union over budgets, military strategy, the likelihood of war and violence, the nature of imperialism, images of American "ruling class" behavior, and the proper balance between the production of consumer goods and services and heavy industry in the Soviet economy, clearly indicate that tension-producing policies tend to favor certain groups within Soviet society while tension-lessening policies tend to favor others. While the residual fervor of a purely ideological commitment to specific goals and policies remains operative in the thought and behavior of Soviet leaders, there has also been an inexorable tendency for individual leaders and functional interest groups to perceive the interests of society as a whole through their own prism and to distort and adjust the national interest to accord with their own. Ideological distortion takes shape in similar fashion in order to impart the necessary symbolic legitimacy to policies and interests which the Soviet system demands as part of its political ritual.

The foreign policy and defense posture of the Soviet state establishes a certain configuration of priorities in the allocation of money and scarce resources. Various individuals and groups develop a vested interest in a particular foreign policy or defense posture because of the role and status it confers upon them. Correspondingly, other individuals and groups in Soviet society perceive themselves as deprived in status and rewards because of existing allocation of expenditures and resources, and hence they might initiate proposals which might alter existing foreign policy and defense postures or support proposals submitted by other groups or individuals.

A particular interest group or social formation may often have a role or function imposed upon it by events, circumstances, policies, and the mechanism of a given social system in response to certain situations not of its own making, or, in some instances, which provided the basis for its very creation and existence. While particular interest groups may not have sought such a role, nor taken the initiative in acquiring it, or even did not exist before the function was demanded, once this role is thrust upon them, they adjust to it and develop a vested interest in the role and function imposed upon them, since it constitutes the source of their existence and status. As individual members adjust to their role, develop it, and invest their energies and careers in it, they almost automatically resist the deprivation or diminution of this role or function in their self-interest.

585 VERNON V. ASPATURIAN

The same is true of groups which have assigned to them limited or arrested roles or functions in society, except that they develop a vested interest in expanding their role, dignifying it with greater status and prestige, and demanding greater rewards. Consequently, it is extremely difficult to distill out of Soviet factional positions those aspects of thought and behavior which express conflicting perceptions of self-interest on the part of various individuals, factions, and groups as opposed to authentic "objective" considerations of a broader interest, whether national or ideological, since they are so inextricably intertwined and interdependent.

All that we can assert at this point is that certain individuals, factions, and socio-institutional functional groups seem to thrive and flourish and others to be relatively deprived and arrested in their development under conditions of exacerbated international tensions, while the situation is reversed when a relaxation of international tensions takes place. What might be assumed, therefore, because of these complicated psychological dialogues between perceptions of self-interest and perception of objective reality, is that groups that are favored by a particular policy or situation have a greater inclination to perceive objective reality in terms of their self-interest. Thus, groups that are objectively favored by heightened international tensions might have a greater propensity to perceive external threats and a corresponding disinclination to recognize that the nature of a threat has been altered, reduced, or eliminated, thus requiring new policies which might adversely affect them. On the other hand, groups that are objectively favored by relaxation of international tensions or a peacetime economy might be more prone to perceive a premature alteration, diminution or elimination of an external threat and a corresponding tendency to be skeptical about external threats which arise if they would result in a radical rise in defense expenditures and a reallocation of resources and social rewards.

The social and institutional groups in Soviet society which appear to benefit from an aggressive foreign policy and the maintenance of international tensions are (1) the traditional sectors of the Armed Forces; (2) the heavy industrial managers; (3) professional Party *apparatchiki* and ideologues. By no means do all individuals or sub-elites and cliques within these groups see eye-to-eye on foreign policy issues. Some individuals and sub-elites, for opportunistic or careerist reasons or functional adaptability, are able to adjust to a relaxation of tensions by preserving or even improving their role and status. The significant point is that the main impetus for an aggressive policy and the chief opposition to a relaxation of tensions find their social and functional foundations within these three socio-functional or socio-institutional groups, whose common perception of interests results in an informal "military-industrial-apparatus complex." Their attitudes stem almost entirely from the function and role they play in Soviet society and the rewards in terms of prestige, status, and power which are derived from these functions in time of high international tensions as opposed to a *détente*.

The professional military, on the whole, has a natural interest in a large and modern military establishment and a high priority on budget and resources; the heavy industrial managerial groups have a vested stake in preserving the primacy of their sector of the economy; and the Party apparatus traditionally has had a vested interest in ideological conformity and the social controls which they rationalized, thus ensuring the primacy of the apparatus over all other social forces in the Soviet system. All of these functional roles are served best under conditions of international tension. Consequently, this group wittingly or unwittingly has developed a vested interest in either maintaining international tensions or creating the illusion of insecurity and external danger, which would produce the same effect.

To the degree that individuals or sub-elites within these groups are able to socially re-tool their functions and adapt them to peacetime or purely internal functions, then do they correspondingly lose interest in an aggressive or tension-preserving policy.

For purposes of analytical convenience, those social groups which would seem to benefit from a relaxation of international tensions can be classified into four general categories: (1) The state bureaucracy, in the central governmental institutions as well as in the Republics and localities; (2) Light industrial interests, consumer goods and services interests, and agricultural interests; (3) The cultural, professional, and scientific groups, whose role and influence seem to flourish and thrive under conditions of relaxation both at home and abroad; and (4) The Soviet "consumer," the rank and file white collar employees, the working class, and the peasantry, who will ultimately benefit most from a policy which concentrates on raising the standard of living. The technical-scientific branches of the professional military, including the nuclear-missile specialists, also appear to benefit during periods of relaxed international tensions because during periods of *détente* they become the main reliance for national security while the traditional forces are subject to severe budget reductions.

While the contradiction between Soviet security interests and ideological goals in foreign policy has long been recognized by observers of the Soviet scene, a new variable in Soviet policy is the contradiction between enhancing economic prosperity at home and fulfilling international ideological obligations. In Soviet jargon, this emerges as a contradiction between the requirements of "building Communism" and the costs and risks of remaining faithful to the principle of "proletarian internationalism."

This new factor has not gone unnoticed by the Chinese who accuse Khrushchev of abandoning Soviet ideological and material obligations to international Communism and the national-liberation movement in favor of avoiding the risks of nuclear war and building an affluent society to satisfy the appetites of the new Soviet "ruling stratum," in the guise of pursuing peaceful coexistence and "building Communism." Thus, in a long editorial entitled, "On Khrushchev's Phoney Communism and Its Historical Lessons for the World," the authoritative Chinese organ, *Jen Min Jih Pao,* charged on July 14, 1964:

> The revisionist Khrushchev clique has usurped the leadership of the
> Soviet party and state and . . . a privileged bourgeois stratum has
> emerged in Soviet society. . . . The privileged stratum in contemporary
> Soviet society is composed of degenerate elements from among the
> leading cadres of party and government organizations, enterprises, and
> farms as well as bourgeois intellectuals. . . . Under the signboard of
> "peaceful coexistence," Khrushchev has been colluding with U.S. im-
> perialism, wrecking the socialist camp and the international communist
> movement, opposing the revolutionary struggles of the oppressed
> peoples and nations, practicing great-power chauvinism and national
> egoism, and betraying proletarian internationalism. All this is being
> done for the protection of the vested interest of a handful of people,
> which he places above the fundamental interests of the peoples of the
> Soviet Union, the socialist camp and the whole world.[11]

The same charge has also been leveled at Khrushchev's successors, who,
Peking maintains, are simply practicing "Khrushchevism without
Khrushchev."

As the Soviet system matures and becomes inextricably identified
with the interests of its various privileged elites, the decision makers
must give greater consideration in the calculation of foreign policy to
factors affecting the internal stability of the regime; and they will show
greater sensitivity to the effects of decisions on the vested interests of
the various elites in Soviet society. The rise of powerful social and
economic elites in the Soviet Union, and their insistent pressure for
participation in the exercise of political power, could only introduce
stresses, strains, conflicts, and hence new restraints into Soviet diplomacy.

Within the context of an ideology that imposes a single interest
representing society as a whole, each interest group will tend to distort
ideology and policy in an endeavor to give it the contours of its own
interests; the next step is to elevate these to transcendental significance.
Under these conditions, Soviet ideology may be constantly threatened
with a series of fundamental convulsions if one interest group displaces
another in the struggle for the control of the Party machinery. Hence, a
rational system of accommodating conflicting interests appears to be
evolving. As the vested stake of each major group becomes rooted in the
Soviet system, the contours of Soviet diplomacy and national interest
will inexorably tend to be shaped more by the rapidly moving equilibrium or accommodation of interests that develop internally than by
abstract ideological imperatives, which may conflict with the concrete
interests of specific major elites in Soviet society.

Only as long as a major Soviet elite whose vested stake is the
function of maintaining the purity of ideological objectives (the Party
Apparatus) remains in undisputed control of the Party machinery and
can subordinate the other elites to its direction can the transcendental
revolutionary objectives of the Marxist doctrine remain fully compatible
with Soviet national interests. On the other hand, any foreign policy that
threatens to upset the equilibrium of interests in Soviet society or that

[11] *Jen Min Jih Pao*, July 14, 1964.

strikes at the vested position of any powerful social group may encounter resistance, and the group may take desperate measures to
preserve its status, regardless of ideological considerations. In a real
sense, Soviet ideology and national interests will be increasingly shaped
by the internal interests of the Soviet elite — or combination of elites —
that succeeds in establishing control over the machinery of the Party;
thus ideology and interests are bound to undergo periodic transmutations.

17. THE ADMINISTRATION AND EXECUTION OF SOVIET FOREIGN POLICY

Vernon V. Aspaturian

PARTY POLICY AND STATE ADMINISTRATION: CONFLICT AND HARMONY

Responsibility for the actual *execution* of foreign policy as distinct from its *formulation* rests with the Council of Ministers and its Presidium, which is nominally accountable to the Supreme Soviet and its Presidium but in fact is subordinate to the Party Politburo, with which it normally shares key personnel. The relationship between the Party's highest body and the Council of Ministers and its Presidium in the decision-making process, which is often ambiguous and is currently in a state of transition, depends more upon the degree of interlocking membership between the two organs than upon constitutional forms. Under Stalin, particularly after he became Premier in 1941, interlocking membership was virtually complete and was designed to ensure maximum harmony between Party policy and State administration. Distinctions between formulation and execution of policy were ambiguous to the point of complete irrelevance under these conditions. Before Stalin held any formal executive position in the government, the institutions of the Party were the chief decision-making bodies of the regime, but with Stalin's assumption of the premiership, Stalin, the Secretary-General of the Party, made policy, and in his capacity as Premier he was

From Vernon V. Aspaturian, "Soviet Foreign Policy," in Roy C. Macridis, editor, *Foreign Policy in World Politics*, © 1957, 1962, 1968. By permission of Prentice-Hall, Inc., Englewood Cliffs, New Jersey.

also in charge of its execution and administration. As head of both Party and government he did not need to employ all the institutions of decision making; and those of the Party virtually withered away. Since all diplomatic relations with the outside world are carried on through State institutions, the organs of the State had to retain sufficient vitality to legalize Stalin's decisions into formal acts of government.

The apparent rise of the State to a position superior to that of the Party was undoubtedly a major factor in Malenkov's decision to succeed Stalin as Premier rather than as First Secretary of the Party. Legally, as Premier, he had under his control the two principal instruments of violence, the Police and the Armed Forces; and thus he chose the State in preference to the Party Secretariat as his instrument with which to subdue his rivals in the Presidium. The Police and the Army, however, turned out to be virtually separate entities with their own informal lines of organization and loyalty which radically departed from constitutional and legal patterns. By relinquishing control of the Party Secretariat to Khrushchev in favor of the premiership, Malenkov abdicated the symbols of legitimacy in favor of the shell of power, since within the context of the Party rules and institutional controls bequeathed by Stalin, the Premier and the government were mere creatures of the Party's will. As long as the secretariat and the premiership are united in a single personality, relationships of control and subordination are irrelevant, but once they are separated, custom and precedent, as well as ideology, favor the secretariat in any rivalry for supremacy.

With the eruption of factional rivalry in the Presidium and the separation of the Party Secretariat from the government, interlocking membership between the Council of Ministers and the Party's highest body, instead of ensuring harmony between policy and administration, in fact guaranteed conflict and friction, as the Party Presidium came under the control of one faction while key administrative organs of State were in the hands of members of rival factions.

The first overt instance of conflict between Party policy and State administration was Beria's attempt to thwart the decisions of the Party through his control of the Ministry and Internal Affairs. Since then, both major and minor discrepancies between policy administration have taken place. Thus, while Khrushchev could muster narrow majorities in the Presidium, members of the opposition were in strategic administrative positions where they could subvert the implementation of Party decisions. One of the major accusations against Foreign Minister Molotov, and also against Shepilov, was that he was using the Foreign Ministry and Soviet missions abroad to subvert and sabotage, rather than to carry out, the policies formulated by the Party. Similarly, Khrushchev's plan for breaking up the concentration of economic power in Moscow was probably opposed by the managerial bureaucrats like Kaganovich, Pervukhin, and Saburov, who controlled key economic levers in the nation's industrial system and could effectively frustrate the dismantling of their own source of power and influence. Thus, before the reorganization of the Presidium in June 1957, five of the nine members of the Presidium of the Council of Ministers were members of the opposition minority in the Party Presidium. It was untenable that the minority faction in the Party Presidium should enjoy a majority in the Presidium of the Council of Ministers, whose function it was to implement the very policies rejected, in the Party Presidium by a majority of its members.

The power of the Council of Ministers as a policy-making and executive institution was severely curtailed during the brief period of Bulganin's continued incumbency after the 1957 reorganization. Before June 29, 1957, the nine-man Presidium of the Council of Ministers included seven full members of the Party Presidium, but after the reorganization only Bulganin and Mikoyan remained members of both bodies. The displacement of Bulganin by Khrushchev in March 1958 marked a revival in overlapping membership in the two organs, whereby career Party workers moved into top government positions. By 1961, four of the seven-man Presidium of the Council of Ministers were also members of the Party Presidium. The situation became highly fluid as Khrushchev's grip on the leadership started to erode after the Twenty-second Party Congress and in particular after the Cuban missile crisis, when only four full members of the Party's Presidium of 12 full members were also members of the government Presidium of 12 members.

[The primacy of the Party Central Committee and its Politburo continues to be the rule despite occasional lapses in favor of State organs. According to Valerian A. Zorin, veteran career diplomat and member of the Central Committee since 1956:

> An essential condition for the correct and successful implementation of the objectives of this foreign policy by Soviet diplomacy was and is its direction by the Communist Party of the Soviet Union and by its Central Committee, which deals with the most pressing problems of foreign policy from day to day.
>
> V. I. Lenin attributed exceptional importance to the everyday direction of Soviet foreign policy and diplomacy by the Party's Central Committee. In 1923, he emphasized: "Does not the Politburo discuss from a Party point of view many insignificant and important matters related to 'moves' by our side in response to the 'moves' of foreign powers in order to thwart their — let us say — stratagems, so not to have to resort to less decorous language? Is not this flexible combination of state and Party a source of exceptional strength in our policy?"
>
> The leadership of the Communist Party determines and has always determined the proper direction and content and the best methods of Soviet diplomacy. Following Leninist tradition, the CPSU always establishes the objectives of the foreign policy and diplomacy of the Soviet Union at its congresses and at the plenary meetings of the Central Committee. The Central Committee of the CPSU provides day to day direction of the foreign policy measures and of the diplomatic moves implemented by the Ministry of Foreign Affairs of the USSR, insuring successful attainment of the foreign policy objectives of the Soviet state which have been established by the Party.*]

[* Valerian A. Zorin, *Osnova Diplomaticheskoi Sluzhby* (Moscow, 1964), p. 116. The citation for Lenin is taken from "Letters on Tactics," *Polnoye Sobraniye Sochinenii*, vol. 31, p. 132.]

THE CONSTITUTIONAL BASIS OF SOVIET FOREIGN RELATIONS

Under the Soviet Constitution of 1936, as amended, foreign policy is administered and executed at four different institutional levels: (1) the Presidium of the Supreme Soviet; (2) the Supreme Soviet; (3) the Council of Ministers; and (4) the Union Republics, of which there are now fifteen. Although the Soviet constitutional setup is based on the principle of complete fusion of executive, legislative, and administrative power, each institutional level is invested with certain foreign policy functions, which may be permissive, exclusive, or concurrent. These legal relationships, however, do not function in any way as limitations on Soviet diplomacy.

The Presidium of the Supreme Soviet. The Presidium of the Supreme Soviet is vested under the Constitution with a wide range of ceremonial, executive, and legislative functions. Juridically a creature of the Supreme Soviet, for which it acts as legal agent, it is, in fact, its institutional superior and surrogate, since it is empowered with virtually the entire spectrum of authority granted to the Supreme Soviet during the long and frequent intervals between sessions of the Soviet legislature. Technically, all of its actions are subject to later confirmation by the Supreme Soviet, but, in practice, this is an empty ritual.

In the area of foreign affairs, the Presidium, in the person of its Chairman, functions as the ceremonial chief of state, much like the American president and the British monarch:

> In accordance with the universally recognized doctrine of international law, the supreme representation of the modern state is vested in the chief of state, whether he be an actual person (monarch, president of the republic) or a collective body (Presidium of the Supreme Soviet of the U.S.S.R., Federal Council of Switzerland). . . . As a general rule, the competence of the chief of state includes the declaration of war and conclusion of peace, nomination and reception of diplomatic agents, granting powers for the conclusion of international treaties and agreements of special significance, and the ratification and denunciation of these treaties and accords.[1]

In its ceremonial capacity, the Presidium confers all diplomatic ranks and titles of a plenipotentiary character, formally appoints and recalls diplomatic representatives of the U.S.S.R., and receives the letters of credence and recall from foreign envoys. Although foreign representatives almost always present their credentials to the Chairman of the Presidium, they are, in fact, accredited to the Presidium as a collective entity.

The Presidium's substantive powers are considerable. Article 49 of the Constitution authorizes it to interpret all Soviet laws, convene and dissolve the Supreme Soviet, annul decisions and orders of the Council of Ministers, appoint and remove the higher commands of the Armed Forces, and issue decrees in its own right, virtually without limits.

[1] *Istoriya Diplomatii,* III, 765.

Furthermore, the Presidium, during intervals between sessions of the Supreme Soviet, "proclaims a state of war in the event of armed attack . . . or whenever necessary to fulfill international treaty obligations concerning mutual defense against aggression," can order general or partial mobilization, and can proclaim martial law in separate localities or throughout the country. The exercise of many of these powers is not subject to later confirmation by the Supreme Soviet, although the Presidium remains technically accountable for all its activities to the Soviet legislature, which theoretically can replace its personnel.

Certain important powers vested in the Presidium are provisional and delegated. Thus, the Presidium, during periods when the Supreme Soviet is not in session, can appoint and dismiss ministers upon the recommendation of the Chairman of the Council of Ministers, but this is subject to later confirmation. Similarly, if the Presidium promulgates decrees of a fundamental nature, outside its formal constitutional competence, they also are subject to confirmation, although this may be several years later.

Although the Constitution appears to give the Presidium a monopoly on the ratification and denunciation of treaties, a law of the Supreme Soviet, "On the Procedure for Ratification and Denunciation of International Treaties," passed on August 19, 1938, defines as treaties requiring its ratification: (1) treaties of peace; (2) mutual defense treaties; (3) treaties of nonaggression; and (4) treaties requiring mutual ratification for their implementation.[2] By implication, and in accordance with past practice, all treaties not specifically enumerated as requiring ratification by the Presidium are left to the discretion of the Council of Ministers. On the other hand, on rare occasions the Supreme Soviet has been asked to ratify or give preliminary approval to particularly important treaties, although there exists no constitutional imperative.

The Supreme Soviet. As the "highest organ of state authority in the U.S.S.R.," the power of the Supreme Soviet under the Constitution is coterminous with that of the Union.

Composed of two coordinate chambers — the Council of the Union and the Council of Nationalities — of approximately equal size, the constitutional competence of the Soviet legislature in foreign affairs surpasses that of any other organ. In practice, it has abdicated most of its powers to the Presidium and has been left only with the empty shell of ceremony, which may sometimes border on consultation. Both chambers are equally potent or impotent, singly or together, and neither has specific functions or powers denied the other.

The formal authority of the Supreme Soviet in foreign policy falls into seven categories: (1) the enactment of basic legislation and constitutional amendments; (2) the confirmation of the decisions and decrees of the Presidium and the Council of Ministers; (3) ratification of selected treaties; (4) declaration of war and peace; (5) confirmation

[2] *Second Session of the Supreme Soviet of the U.S.S.R.* (New York, International Publishers Company, Inc., 1938), p. 678 verbatim report.

and authorization of territorial changes and of the creation, admission, promotion, demotion, and abolition of new republics; (6) hearing and approving of foreign policy reports delivered by the Premier or the Foreign Minister; and (7) the preliminary examination of treaties prior to ratification by the Presidium. Since Stalin's death, all these activities have been accorded greater publicity.

All proposed laws, treaties, significant statements of policy, results of important conferences, or simply reviews of the international situation — with one or two alleged exceptions, however — were taken on the initiative of the government, under instructions from the Party.

The sessions of the Supreme Soviet are short. Between 1946 and 1954, the Supreme Soviet sat for a total of only forty-five days, the longest session lasting seven days (June, 1950) and the shortest, sixty-seven minutes (March, 1953); its performance before and during World War II was even less auspicious. By far the most significant function of the Supreme Soviet is to hear reports on the foreign policy of the government. It is customary, but by no means the invariable rule, that the Foreign Minister review the government's foreign policy before this body, usually before joint sessions. It listens attentively and enacts the desired legislation. There is "discussion," but a close examination of the official records discloses not a single note of criticism, to say nothing of a negative vote, in all the deliberations of the Supreme Soviet.

In the words of *Kommunist*, "until recently its [the Supreme Soviet's] sessions concerned for the most part consideration of budget questions and approval of the decrees of the Presidium,"[3] but after the replacement of Malenkov by Bulganin, in 1955, it was given a more conspicuous role in foreign affairs. At that time, the Supreme Soviet issued an appeal to other parliaments for a program of parliamentary exchanges in the form of visiting delegations addressing each other's legislatures; more than a dozen such exchanges have taken place. In July, 1955, the Supreme Soviet adhered to the Inter-Parliamentary Union (ITU) and sent a delegation to its forty-fourth annual conference in Helsinki.

Although the two Foreign Affairs Commissions of the two chambers of the Supreme Soviet are supposed to make "a preliminary examination of all matters connected with foreign affairs to be considered by the Supreme Soviet (and its Presidium)," this function had all but withered away and the existence of these bodies was virtually rendered superfluous. They were suddenly brought back to life when the Soviet-Iranian Agreement of 1954, the denunciation of the Anglo-Soviet and Anglo-French Treaties of Alliance, the Warsaw Pact, and the agreement to establish diplomatic relations with West Germany were all submitted to joint sessions of the two Commissions (the Supreme Soviet was not in session) for consideration. After hearing reports by Molotov and his deputies, they recommended approval to the Soviet Presidium. At about the same time, the two Chairmen of the chambers, together with allegedly prominent members of the two Commissions, appeared at

3 *Kommunist,* No. 10, August, 1956, 3–15.

diplomatic receptions, received foreign dignitaries, and pompously pontificated on foreign policy in patent, but bogus, imitation of their counterparts in the American Congress.

It was the Supreme Soviet which proclaimed an end to the state of war with Germany, on January 25, 1955. On August 4, 1955, it was called into special session to hear Bulganin's report on the Summit Conference at Geneva, a procedure not used since Molotov had addressed a special session on the Nazi-Soviet Pact of 1939. On this same occasion, the Supreme Soviet, after "debating" the policy of the government and "interpellating" the Foreign Minister, issued an appeal to the parliaments and governments of the world to "put an end to the arms race." The regular session of the Supreme Soviet coincided with the return of Bulganin and Khrushchev from their tour of Southeast Asia, and both addressed the Supreme Soviet on the results of their trip.

Although the activities of the Supreme Soviet have been stepped up, there is little reason to believe that there has been a corresponding enhancement of its influence and power. It hears more reports on foreign policy, but it has also retained its absolute unanimity. The invocation of the formal prerogatives of the Supreme Soviet, however, is no idle exercise, since it creates certain advantages for Soviet diplomacy: (1) It serves to infuse the citizenry with the notion that their representatives participate in the formulation of foreign policy decisions. (2) As a propagandistic maneuver it strives to create the illusion of evolving constitutionalism in the Soviet system. (3) As a purely diplomatic device, it permits the Kremlin to invoke constitutional procedures as a stumbling or delaying mechanism in negotiations and affords a basis for demanding reciprocal action in the ratification of treaties and other diplomatic instruments.

The possibility, no matter how slight, that ceremony may some day be replaced with substance cannot be ignored, but this expectation must yield to the realization that the flurry of activity we have noted can be arrested as abruptly as it began. Yet it must be stated that periodic suggestions are made in the Soviet press that the Supreme Soviet be given more legislative authority.

The Council of Ministers.[4] As the "highest executive and administrative organ" of the government, the Council of Ministers "exercises general supervision" over the execution and administration of the country's foreign policy, and also directs the state's foreign trade monopoly. Constitutionally, since 1944 the central government no longer exercises a monopoly over foreign affairs, but merely represents the Federal Union as a whole and establishes the "general procedure in mutual relations between the Union Republics and foreign states," and thus shares the conduct of diplomacy with its fifteen constituent republics. In practice, however, foreign policy in the Soviet Union is the most tightly centralized activity of the Soviet government.

The Council of Ministers has the following powers: (1) grant or withdraw recognition of new states or governments; (2) sever and

[4] Formerly the Council of People's Commissars, or *Sovnarkom.*

restore diplomatic relations; (3) order acts of reprisal against other states; (4) appoint negotiators and supervise the negotiation of international treaties and agreements; (5) declare the adherence of the Soviet Union to international conventions not requiring formal ratification; (6) conclude agreements not requiring ratification with other heads of governments (similar to American executive and administrative agreements); (7) ratify all treaties and agreements not requiring ratification of the Presidium; (8) give preliminary examination of all treaties submitted to the Presidium for its ratification; (9) oversee "the current work of the diplomatic organs, effectually direct that work and take the necessary measures in that field"; and (10) appoint and accredit all diplomats below plenipotentiary rank and foreign trade representatives.[5]

Actually, there appears to be a great area of overlapping activity between the Presidium and the Council of Ministers in the conduct of diplomacy, and were it not that the one-party system makes all basic decisions, rivalries and jealousies would almost certainly develop between these two organs, rendering coordination of diplomatic activity virtually impossible.

a) The Chairman and His Cabinet. The most influential member of the Council of Ministers is its Chairman, referred to in the West as the Premier, who is always an important figure of the highest rank in the Party hierarchy. This office, including its predecessors under previous Constitutions, has been filled by only eight men since the establishment of the Soviet state: Lenin (1917–1924); Rykov (1924–1930); Molotov (1930–1941); Stalin (1941–1953); Malenkov (1953–1955); Bulganin (1955–1958); Khrushchev (1958–1964); and Kosygin (1964–   ). After Lenin's death, when Stalin refused to hold formal office, this post was reduced to a mere shadow of the Secretary-General of the Party, but after Stalin assumed formal responsibility for the policies of the government in 1941, the post retrieved its former prestige and power. The rivalries that were unleashed after Stalin's death, in 1953, temporarily revived the division of power between the Premier and First Secretary of the Party, and the two positions were again separated, then reunited and later reseparated. Khrushchev's assumption of the office after Bulganin's resignation reflected the internal and external symbolic significance which it acquired during Stalin's long tenure as well as the fact that it was too risky to permit it to be separately occupied.

The sundering of the two positions, in October, 1964, reflected once again a division of power in the Soviet leadership. The post of Premier serves to legitimize and legalize the power of the First Secretary, just as the latter imparts to the premiership the necessary ideological sanctity. The position has suffered another setback with Khrushchev's ouster and the restoration of the title of General Secretary, but the premiership will continue to exert an attraction to any General Secretary.

[5] *Cf.* A. Y. Vyshinsky, *The Law of the Soviet State* (New York, The Macmillan Company, 1948), p. 376; *Istoriya Diplomatii*, III, 767–68, 806–7; Julian Towster, *Political Power in the U.S.S.R.* (New York, Oxford University Press, 1948), p. 279.

The Chairman, or Premier, has primary responsibility for the conduct of foreign policy and, presumably, the authority to appoint and remove the ministers concerned with its day-to-day execution. Immediately below the Chairman are his First Deputy Chairmen and Deputy Chairmen, who normally are in charge of a specific ministry, or may be without portfolio. The Chairman, his First Deputies, and his Deputies constitute the Presidium (Cabinet) of the Council of Ministers.

The size and composition of the Presidium have undergone serious transformations in recent years and has varied in size up to more than a dozen members. Under Stalin, the Presidium became so large that a Bureau — or inner cabinet — of the Presidium was secretly organized, whose composition and membership have never been made public. After his death, the Bureau of the Presidium was technically abolished, but in fact, the Presidium was reduced to the smaller size of the Bureau.

The Council of Ministers and its Presidium are actually subordinate to the Party Politburo and, in theory, to the Supreme Soviet and its Presidium. If the Premier of the government loses a vote of confidence in the Politburo, the decision is reviewed by the Central Committee; if it is upheld there, he submits his resignation to the Presidium of the Supreme Soviet. The Central Committee, through its First Secretary, nominates the next Premier to the appropriate State organs and a new government is thus formed.

Since the formation of the Bulganin government, the Premier and other key members of the Presidium of the Council of Ministers have played an increasingly personal and active role in the country's diplomacy. This pattern was further accelerated after Khrushchev became Premier. Not only the Premier, but important ministers and the Chairman of the Presidium of the Supreme Soviet, have made state visits to many countries as a part of the Kremlin's new diplomatic offensive. Kosygin and Brezhnev introduced a division of labor in international affairs, each assuming individual personal roles in Soviet diplomacy. While he was Foreign Minister, Molotov played an active personal role in the country's diplomacy, but he apparently objected to the interference of the other members of the government in Soviet diplomatic activity. In particular, he objected to the travels of Bulganin and Khrushchev and their meetings with the heads of various governments.

b) The Foreign Minister. In forty years of Soviet diplomacy, there have been only seven Foreign Ministers: Leon Trotsky (November, 1917–April, 1918); Georgi Chicherin (1918–1929); Maxim Litvinov (1929–1939); Vyacheslav Molotov (1939–1949 and 1953–1956); Andrei Vyshinsky (1949–1953); Dimitri Shepilov (during 1956); Andrei Gromyko (1957–   ). The typical tenure of a Soviet Foreign Minister is ten years, and nearly forty-five years of Soviet diplomacy have been directed by only four individuals, thus giving Soviet diplomacy an enviable continuity except for a few years after Stalin's death, when the changes reflected the bitter conflicts that have raged over foreign policy in the past few years.

The Foreign Minister's influence depends almost entirely upon his Party rank. When the Minister is of relatively low rank in the Party, he is little more than a caretaker of the department. If he is of top Party rank, as Trotsky and Molotov were, he participates in the decisions he is asked to execute and, in at least two cases (Molotov and Shepilov), he has actually flouted the will of the decision makers. Chicherin and Litvinov, like Gromyko, were relatively low-ranking members in the Party hierarchy, but this by no means indicates that they were less effective as diplomats. There is ample evidence to suggest that the Party leaders would prefer a low-ranking Party member as Foreign Minister rather than one of first rank, except under critical circumstances, since it enhances the flexibility of Soviet diplomacy while hampering that of other countries, who are forced to accommodate their diplomacy to the bureaucratic channels of the Soviet Foreign Office. Normally, the Foreign Minister is at least a full member of the Central Committee, although both Chicherin and Litvinov achieved that status some time after they had become Foreign Commissars. Gromyko was elevated to full membership only at the Twentieth Party Congress. Trotsky and Molotov were the only Foreign Ministers who were full members of the Party's highest body; Vyshinsky and Shepilov were alternate members of the Presidium during their incumbency.

The Ministry of Foreign Affairs[6]

Evolution of the Ministry. The government department directly charged with the day-to-day administration of Soviet diplomacy does not materially differ in its structure and organization from its counterparts in the other Great Powers, although its evolution is unique. Since its establishment, it has undergone a triple metamorphosis.

In the beginning, its primary purpose was to trigger a world revolution and thus create the conditions for its own extinction. It was thought that if the world revolution failed, a Soviet diplomacy would be impossible, and, if it succeeded, unnecessary. It was Leon Trotsky's boast, "I will issue a few revolutionary proclamations to the people of the world, and then close up shop."[7] On November 26, 1917, a decree from Trotsky's Foreign Affairs Commissariat virtually disestablished the diplomatic apparatus of the Russian state: all members of the Russian foreign service abroad were summarily dismissed unless they expressed loyalty to the Bolshevik regime. In their places, Bolshevik émigrés abroad were appointed as "unofficial" agents of the new government (Litvinov was such an appointee to Great Britain). Trotsky even neglected to establish a permanent home office; he appeared at his office only once — to dismiss all employees reluctant to pledge loyalty to the new regime and to set up a committee to publish the secret treaties in the archives of the Russian Foreign Office.

The Treaty of Brest-Litovsk imposed upon the new regime diplo-

[6] Formerly the People's Commissariat for Foreign Affairs, or *Narkomindel.*

[7] Cited in E. H. Carr, *The Bolshevik Revolution, 1917–1923* (London, Macmillan, 1953), III, 16.

matic relations with Germany and its allies, so the Council of People's Commissars was forced to re-create a provisional diplomatic service. With obvious petulance, in a decree of June 4, 1918, they attempted to rewrite unilaterally the principle of diplomatic ranks adopted by the Congress of Vienna in 1815, by abolishing all Soviet diplomatic titles in favor of a single designation, "plenipotentiary representative" (*Polpred*). In a naive attempt to impose Soviet egalitarian principles upon foreign envoys, the decree peremptorily announced that "all diplomatic agents of foreign states . . . shall be considered equal plenipotentiary representatives regardless of their rank."[8]

Pending the eventual liquidation of the Foreign Affairs Commissariat, the functions of Soviet diplomacy during this initial period fell into three principal categories: (1) the publication of "secret treaties" in order to expose the duplicity and hypocrisy of the Allies and compromise them in the eyes of their own people; (2) the conduct of necessary negotiations and diplomatic relations, on a temporary basis, with capitalist states in a position to impose them; and (3) the utilization of Soviet embassies and legations abroad as centers of revolutionary propaganda, conspiracy, and activity, in clear violation of treaty obligations. In this connection, the Soviet government announced that "The Council of People's Commissars considers it necessary to offer assistance by all possible means . . . to the left internationalist wing of the labor movement of all countries [and] . . . for this purpose . . . decides to allocate two million rubles for the needs of the revolutionary international movement and to put this sum at the disposal of the foreign representatives of the Commissariat for Foreign Affairs."[9]

The failure of the revolution to spread beyond Russia, the success of the seceding border states in maintaining their independence, and the failure of foreign intervention to subdue the Bolshevik regime forced the expansion of diplomatic contact with the bourgeois world. By 1921 the Soviet foreign office was prepared to pass out of its initial phase into its second, as a quasi-permanent agency for "normalizing" relations with the capitalist powers on the basis of "mutual interests" during the prolonged period of "co-existence" which Lenin now recognized as the inevitable interval between the first and final stages of the world revolution. From an instrument of world revolution the foreign office was converted into an instrument for furthering the interests of the Soviet state.

Since the revolutionary and conspiratorial activities of Soviet diplomats complicated the establishment of desirable trade and political connections with the bourgeois world, the new Commissar of Foreign Affairs, Georgi Chicherin (who succeeded Trotsky in April 1918), was instrumental in shifting the function of revolutionary agitation from the Foreign Office to the Party. A new diplomatic service was organized

[8] Full text in T. A. Taracouzio, *The Soviet Union and International Law* (New York, The Macmillan Company, 1935), p. 383.
[9] Jane Degras, ed., *Soviet Documents on Foreign Policy* (London, Royal Institute of International Affairs, 1951), I, 22.

from scratch by Chicherin, and shortly after he assumed office, the Foreign Commissariat was organized into more than a dozen departments. The first Statute on the Commissariat for Foreign Affairs was issued by the Council of Ministers on July 6, 1921; it defined the sphere of competence of each of the departments. After the formation of the Union and the centralization of diplomacy in Moscow, the Commissariat on November 12, 1923, received its definite statute which still constitutes the juridical basis for the organization and structure of the Foreign Ministry. However, it was not until 1924 that Soviet diplomacy was juridically relieved of its revolutionary mission and it entered into its current phase. According to a decree issued November 21, 1924 and still effective:

> It goes without saying that diplomatic missions abroad are appointed by each of the parties establishing diplomatic relations for purposes which exclude propaganda in the country to which they are accredited. The Soviet diplomatic missions follow and are to follow this principle with absolute strictness.[10]

Although technically the Soviet Foreign Office is supervised by the Council of Ministers, it has always enjoyed a unique, direct relationship with the Party Presidium. Unlike the other departments of government in the new Bolshevik regime, the Foreign Commissariat was unencumbered with holdovers from the old bureaucracy, Chicherin being the only prominent figure who had previous diplomatic experience. Consequently, from the very beginning, it was cherished by Lenin:

> The diplomatic apparatus . . . is quite exceptional in the governmental apparatus. We excluded everyone from the old Tsarist apparatus who formerly had even the slightest influence. Here, the whole apparatus, insofar as it possesses the slightest influence, has been made up of Communists. For this reason this apparatus has acquired for itself . . . the reputation of a Communist apparatus which has been tested and cleansed of the old Tsarist bourgeois and petty bourgeois apparatus to a degree incomparably higher than that attained in the apparatus with which we have to be satisfied in the other people's commissariats.[11]

This quality, in the words of a Soviet diplomat, "helped make it a peculiarly well-fitted apparatus for the expression of new policies."[12]

The Statute governing the Foreign Affairs Commissariat, decreed on November 12, 1923, which has been frequently amended, but never superseded, defined its principal duties as:

> (a) The defence of the political and economic interests of the U.S.S.R. . . . (b) The conclusion of treaties and agreements with foreign countries in accordance with the decisions of the government.

[10] Full text in Taracouzio, *The Soviet Union and International Law*, 389–390.

[11] *The New York Times*, July 1, 1956. Extract is from suppressed Lenin documents distributed at the 20th Party Congress and later made public.

[12] Alexi F. Neymann in S. N. Harper, ed., *The Soviet Union and World Problems* (Chicago, Chicago University Press, 1935), p. 279.

(c) Supervision over the proper execution of treaties and agreements concluded with foreign states, and enabling the corresponding organs of the U.S.S.R. and the Union Republics to exercise rights conferred by these treaties. (d) Supervision over the execution by the competent organs of treaties, agreements, and accords concluded with foreign states.[13]

The Foreign Minister and his Collegium. The administration of the Foreign Commissariat was initially entrusted to a collegium in accordance with the Bolshevik principle of collective responsibility. The Foreign Commissar was forced to share authority and responsibility with a board of three or four other senior officials of the Commissariat.

With the promulgation of the first Constitution in March 1918, the germ of one-man management was implanted, when the Commissar was invested with the personal power of decision relating to matters within the competence of his department, but if this decision conflicted with the views of the collegium, the latter, without the power of stopping execution of the decision, could appeal its differences to the Council or to the Presidium. As a consequence, collective responsibility became a convenient evasion of concrete responsibility and the collegium frequently abused its powers by issuing orders in its own name, thus lowering the prestige and personal responsibility of the Foreign Commissar.

By 1934, defects of collective responsibility became so serious that Stalin condemned the collective principle as obsolete and subversive of efficient administration; the collegium was abolished and the Foreign Minister installed in complete charge of his department and, in turn, he assumed full personal responsibility for its work.

Four years later, in March 1938, the collegium was restored in modified form, but was clearly divested of its former tyrannical power over the Commissar. The Council, which was too large and unwieldy as a decision making or even advisory body, was retained as a convenient institution for the diffusion of policy and administrative decision, and the collegium retained its character as the executive committee of the Commissariat. The Commissar retained his plenary authority and responsibility, but the formal prerogatives of the collegium remained considerable.[14]

The institutional relationship established in 1938 between the Foreign Minister and his collegium has survived, substantially unaltered, till now. Its size and composition appear to vary, depending upon the discretion of the Foreign Minister, except in unusual circumstances, although appointments to the collegium continue to be made by the Council of Ministers. The collegium is presided over by the Minister or one of his First Deputies. It includes not only the First Deputy and

---

[13] The full text of this statute, with amendments through 1927, is reprinted in *Yezhegodnik Narodnovo Komissariata Po Inostrannym Delam Na 1928 God* (Moscow, 1928), pp. 182–193. All subsequent references and extracts refer to this text. Cf. also *Istoriya Diplomatii*, III, 770–71.

[14] Cf. *Vyshinsky*, pp. 387–89.

Deputy Ministers, but also about four to six senior officials in the department, one of whom frequently is the Chief of the Press and Information Division. The number of First Deputies has varied from one to three; their rank roughly corresponds to that of the undersecretary in the American State Department. Immediately below the First Deputies are the Deputies, whose rank corresponds to that of Assistant Secretaries in the American hierarchy; there may be up to six Deputies (in 1966 there was one First Deputy and six Deputies). The other members of the collegium are normally department heads. Thus the size of the collegium may vary up to more than a dozen members.

The institutional prerogatives of the collegium fall just short of the power of actual decision, but without weakening in any way the full responsibility of the Minister. It cannot overrule the Minister's decisions, nor issue orders in its own name, but it is mandatory for the Minister to report any disagreement with his collegium to the Council for disposition. The collegium retains the right, individually or collecticely, to appeal to the Council and the Central Committee of the Party.[15]

The Organization and Structure of the Foreign Ministry. The basic organization and structure of the Soviet Foreign Ministry remain governed by the Statute of 1923, which established a flexible system of administration, permitting a wide latitude for internal reorganization at the discretion of the Minister. The Ministry is organized into "divisions according to the main geographical divisions of the world and the main functions of the department and . . . this apparatus both in its offices in Moscow and its missions in foreign countries does not present any striking differences in structure compared with similar departments in other countries."[16] [See Figure 1.]

At the apex of the Ministry stands the Minister with his collegium, which is provided with a central secretariat — headed by a Secretary-General — performing routine secretarial and staff administrative work for the Minister, his Deputies, and members of the collegium. The functional divisions, which have become increasingly differentiated with the expansion of Soviet diplomatic activity, have been conventional: Protocol, Political Archives, Courier and Liaison, Passport and Visa, Treaty and Legal, Economic, Consular Affairs, Administration, Personnel, Finance, Supplies, and Press Information. Several related functional divisions are grouped together and supervised by Deputy Ministers, and perhaps also by collegium members. As Soviet power and influence in international affairs has increased, the functional divisions have undergone substantial expansion in recent years. There are now seven functional divisions: Protocol, Press, Treaty and Legal, Consular Administration, Archives Administration, Personnel Administration and Administration for Servicing the Diplomatic Corps. In addition, the Foreign Ministry has attached to it two training institutions, The Institute of International Relations and The Higher Diplomatic School. The

---

15 Ibid.
16 Neymann, *The Soviet Union and World Problems,* pp. 226–27.

STRUCTURE AND ORGANIZATION OF THE SOVIET FOREIGN MINISTRY

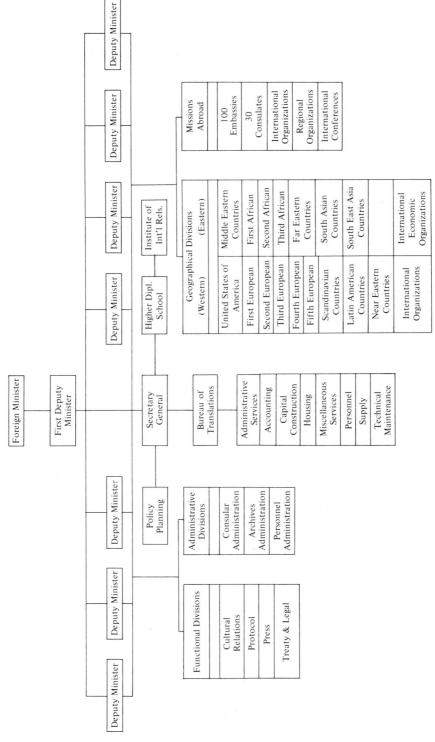

old Economic Division has since proliferated into a separate Ministry called The State Committee for Foreign Economic Relations, which is in charge of the extensive Soviet foreign aid program. Two other Ministries closely related to the Foreign Ministry are the old Ministry of Foreign Trade and The State Committee for Cultural Relations with Foreign Countries.

Since the 1923 Statute does not stipulate the precise number of geographical divisions, the number and composition of these departments vary considerably, and currently are in a phase of expansive reorganization. The Statute merely states that "the divisions of Western Affairs . . . are charged with securing diplomatic relations with the states of Europe and America, the observation and study of the political and economic and other relations between these states and other institutions of the U.S.S.R. which may also have relations with missions in the U.S.S.R." The divisions for "Eastern Affairs" assume identical responsibilities for the states of Asia and Africa.

The political changes of the past twenty years, the massive expansion of Soviet diplomatic relations, and the creation of many new states in Asia and Africa, have profoundly affected the internal organization of the Foreign Office. In the past few years, the number of geographical divisions has been increased, while the number of functional divisions has remained fairly constant. As compiled from press accounts, there are now eight "Western" divisions and eight "Eastern" divisions, plus two separate departments for international organizations, and for international economic organizations. The geographical divisions, which closely resemble those of 1925, are as follows:

Western Divisions

1. United States of America Division
2. Latin-American Countries Division
3. First European Division (France, Benelux, Italy)
4. Second European Division (United Kingdom and white Commonwealth countries)
5. Third European Division (the two Germanies, Austria, Switzerland)
6. Fourth European Division (Poland and Czechoslovakia)
7. Fifth European Division (Balkan countries)
8. Sixth European Division (Scandinavian countries and Finland)

Eastern Divisions

1. First African Division (North African states with the exception of Egypt and Sudan)
2. Second African Division (Black African states)
3. Third African Division (Black African states)
4. Near-Eastern Countries Division
5. Middle-Eastern Countries Division
6. South-Asian Countries Division
7. Southeast-Asian Countries Division

8. Far-Eastern Countries Division (China, Mongolia, North Korea, and Japan)

Normally, a Deputy Minister exercises general administrative supervision over the work of several contiguous geographical divisions, and usually he is a former ambassador with diplomatic experience in the geographical area in question.

The appearance of kindred communist states in Eastern Europe and in the Far East has not modified the geographical divisions of the Ministry. Relations with communist countries through the Foreign Ministry, however, have been reduced to the bare minimum required by international law and protocol, since substantive and policy questions are handled through corresponding Party organizations. Soviet envoys to important communist countries are considered primarily as functionaries and emissaries from the Party, and secondarily as government agents. Thus, when Tito complained that the Soviet Ambassador was meddling in the affairs of the Yugoslav Party, Stalin replied:

> Tito and Kardelj . . . identify the Soviet Ambassador, a responsible Communist . . . with an ordinary bourgeois ambassador, a simple official of a bourgeois state. . . . The Soviet Ambassador, a responsible Communist . . . not only has the right but is obliged, from time to time, to discuss with Communists in Yugoslavia all questions which interest them.[17]

This relationship has been confirmed and emphasized since Stalin's death with the adoption of the practice of dispatching high Party functionaries as ambassadors to important communist states.

In view of the deterioration of relations with China, however, Party relations between the two countries have virtually ceased, and contact has been limited almost exclusively to formal State relations. Already in 1959, Moscow had replaced a highly placed Party official (Yudin) functioning as the Soviet ambassador, with a lower-level Party functionary. And in April, 1965, this lower ranking Party official (Chervonenko) was replaced by a career diplomat, S. G. Lapin, who is not even a candidate member of the Central Committee. There is little question but that the Party standing of Soviet ambassadors to communist countries is indicative of the state of Party relations existing between them.

The Soviet Diplomatic Service. The decree of 1918, reducing all diplomatic ranks to the single and equal rank of plenipotentiary representative, remained technically in force until 1941, although it was neither possible nor desirable to honor it in practice. The principle of diplomatic equality was based on the discarded theory that "the representatives of . . . the U.S.S.R. do not personify a quasi-mythical Leviathan state, but only . . . the plenipotentiary of the ruling class," and that diplomats from bourgeois countries were likewise emissaries of their

---

[17] *The Soviet-Yugoslav Dispute* (London, Royal Institute of International Affairs, 1948), pp. 34–35.

ruling classes.[18] This view was condemned as doctrinaire and subversive of Soviet prestige and diplomacy since, in practice, it amounted to unilateral renunciation of all the privileges and prerogatives of seniority and rank under traditional norms of diplomatic intercourse.

Soviet diplomacy gradually accommodated itself to existing international practice through the extralegal exchange of supplementary protocols granting informal recognition of rank so that Soviet diplomats might avoid forfeiting recognized privileges accorded to those of rank and seniority. On May 9, 1941, the Presidium issued a decree establishing three diplomatic categories: (1) ambassador extraordinary and plenipotentiary; (2) minister extraordinary and plenipotentiary; and (3) *chargé d'affaires*. This decree gave legal sanction to *de facto* distinctions. Two years later, on May 28, 1943, the Presidium decreed the establishment of eleven grades in the diplomatic service and thus brought Soviet diplomatic ranking into complete focus with general diplomatic practice: (1) ambassador extraordinary, and plenipotentiary; (2) minister extraordinary and plenipotentiary of the first class; (3) minister extraordinary and plenipotentiary of the second class; (4) counselor, first class; (5) counselor, second class; (6) first secretary, first class; (7) first secretary, second class; (8) second secretary, first class; (9) second secretary, second class; (10) third secretary; and (11) attaché.[19]

Until Stalin's death, one of the chief peculiarities of the Soviet diplomatic service was the relative permanence of the Foreign Minister as contrasted with the turnover of all ranks below. This is almost precisely the reverse of the situation found in other countries where kaleidoscopic changes occur at the ministerial level in contrast to the relative permanence of the diplomatic bureaucracy as a whole. This frequent turnover of personnel has arrested more than once the orderly development of a career diplomatic service, if that is desirable, or even possible, in a one-Party State. While scores of ambassadors and high Foreign Ministry officials have been arrested or executed on charges of treason, not a single Foreign Minister (Trotsky excepted) has ever been liquidated or charged with high treason. Ministers appointed to other departments have not been so lucky. The disgrace suffered by Molotov and Shepilov recently while the career service survived virtually unscathed indicates the possible existence of a career service that scrupulously avoids involvement in power intrigues and thus may gain immunity from the effects of factional rivalry.

Although it appears that a professional diplomatic service has been assuming shape during the past decade and a half, it is still fundamentally distinguishable from what is generally understood to be a career service. In Western countries, career officials are insulated from political partisanship (except under unusual circumstances) and man-

[18] E. Korovin, *Mezhdunarodnoye Pravo Perekhodnovo Vremeni* (Moscow, 1924), p. 63.
[19] *Cf. Istoriya Diplomatii*, III, 778–80. Date of the decree is mistakenly given as June 14, 1943, in this work.

age to survive the changing fortunes of political parties or movements, serving as impersonal instruments of the party that happens to exercise political power. This was true even of Fascist totalitarian states. In contrast, since the Communist Party has a permanent monopoly on political power, all Soviet diplomats must be members of the Communist Party, and senior officials of the Ministry frequently are members of Party organs corresponding to their diplomatic importance.

As a rule, career Soviet diplomats do not rank very high in the Party hierarchy. The Foreign Minister is at least a full member of the Central Committee and frequently a member or alternate member of the Presidium. First Deputies are normally full members of the Central Committee, while career diplomats rarely achieve higher status than candidate membership in the Central Committee.

Since Stalin's death, the Soviet diplomatic service has been subjected to a unique infusion of new personnel. Alongside members of the career service, who serve as diplomatic technicians, there now exist numerous high-ranking Ministry officials and diplomats who are primarily State administrators and Party functionaries who appear to correspond to the political appointee in the American diplomatic hierarchy. The transfer of high Party officials and State administrators into the diplomatic service has gone through four distinct phases since Stalin's death, corresponding to the principal milestones in the struggle for power after 1953. Each time a major change in the power equilibrium took place in the Presidium, Party officials were shifted to diplomatic work. Consequently, the most obvious trend is that the Foreign Ministry is once again being used as a convenient post of exile from the centers of political power for Party bureaucrats wounded in the power struggles. A second trend is the assignment of career Party bureaucrats — not all of them in disgrace — to Communist capitals, which has resulted in the formation of a distinct parallel diplomatic pattern which serves to combine both Party and State relations in the Communist orbit. A third trend is that a Ministry long under the control of Molotov and exposed to the temptations of the outside world is being placed under quasi-surveillance and provided with Party ballast.

Since 1953, not counting Molotov and the late A. Y. Vyshinsky, no less than six full members and five alternate members of the Party Presidium elected in 1952 have been shifted to the diplomatic service, most of whom are still there. Many of these new Party diplomats enjoy higher Party rank than their technical superior, Foreign Minister Gromyko, and they constitute a distinct cluster of Party luminaries who outshine any combination of career diplomats. The year 1958 represented the high-water mark of Party infusion into the Foreign Ministry, when Gromyko's two First Deputy Ministers and at least six of his ambassadors appeared to outrank him in the Party galaxy, although in most cases their stars were in decline. Five of these new diplomats were admitted to the Party Central Committee in 1939, the same year in which Gromyko entered the diplomatic service as a junior official.

Since 1958 some of the Party officials have worked themselves back into the Party apparatus, others have died, and some have been appointed to quasi-diplomatic ministerial positions. None have fully recovered their former Party eminence, while additional Party and government officials have been shifted to diplomatic careers.

The Channels of Soviet Diplomacy. It is general practice for Soviet envoys to report to the Ministry through routine bureaucratic channels, that is, through the appropriate geographical divisions in the Ministry, but ambassadors in important posts frequently report directly to the Foreign Minister. Reports of an exceptionally important character are also sent directly to the Foreign Minister or his First Deputies, rather than through normal channels. The close supervision of the diplomatic service by the Party center cannot be overemphasized; and diplomatic channels remain deliberately flexible.

Not all Soviet representatives abroad report to the Foreign Ministry. Envoys to communist states, particularly those holding high Party rank, probably report to the Central Committee or the Presidium, except for reports of essentially protocol or legalistic significance, which are funnelled through normal channels. The jurisdiction of the Foreign Ministry over envoys to communist countries appears marginal at best.

Although the Ambassador, as the chief legal representative of the Soviet Union in foreign countries, is charged with general supervision over the activities of Soviet representatives and missions abroad to ensure that they are in accord with the general policy of the government, this responsibility is often of little more than formal or legal significance. According to defectors like Igor Gouzenko and Vladimir Petrov, Soviet missions abroad are organized into five separate divisions, each with separate and independent channels of communication: (1) the Ambassador and his staff, reporting directly to the Ministry of Foreign Affairs; (2) the Commercial Counselor, reporting to the Ministry of Foreign Trade; (3) the Secret Police representative, disguised as a minor diplomat, reporting directly to the foreign section of the Security Ministry (now Committee); (4) the Attachés, reporting directly to the Director of Military Intelligence in Moscow; (5) the Party representative, also disguised as a minor diplomatic functionary, communicating directly with the foreign section of the Central Committee of the Party.

All of these representatives, with the exception of the Ambassador and the embassy staff proper, may be actively engaged in the overt or clandestine collection of intelligence information. In order to comply with the letter of their agreements with foreign countries, the Ambassador is scrupulously insulated from all knowledge of illegal espionage activities organized by the other sections, and although the Foreign Ministry Statute gives him the power to determine whether their activities are in accordance with government policy, in practice the Ambassador rarely sees the reports dispatched by the other sections through their respective channels.

In addition to espionage and intelligence activities, the Secret Police and Party sections maintain general surveillance over the other members of the mission and over each other. If the accounts of high-ranking defectors from the diplomatic and police service are accurate, Soviet missions abroad are often centers of intrigue, personal vendettas, and institutional rivalries and jealousies.

Information coming through various channels is screened, coordinated, and evaluated by a special agency of the Central Committee, which then submits its reports to the Presidium to be used as a factor in the formulation of foreign policy and in the making of decisions.

As instruments, rather than makers of policy, professional Soviet diplomats play a minor role in the formulation of foreign policy. Their work is essentially technical and legalistic; their reports are concerned primarily, if not exclusively, with observations and suggestions for more effective implementation of existing policy. Their area of initiative is carefully circumscribed, and often they are ignorant about the exact intentions of their superiors in the Kremlin. Their reports constitute but a minute fraction of the information on which the Presidium acts, and final disposition of all information from routine diplomatic channels and intelligence sources is made by the Presidium as it sees fit. As Merle Fainsod points out, accurate evaluation of information in the Soviet Union is often subjected to special hazards:

> But the mountains of material have to be reduced to manageable proportions before they are brought to the attention of the leadership. What the rulers read reflects the selection and emphasis of an editorial staff which may be guided by its own preconditioning as well as its sensitivity to the anticipated reactions of its readers. The tendency to embrace data that confirm established predilections while rejecting the unpalatable facts that offend one's preconceptions is a weakness . . . [to] which . . . totalitarian societies appear to be particularly susceptible. . . . Every dictatorship has a tendency to breed sycophancy and discourage independence in its bureaucratic hierarchy. When the pronouncements of the dictator are sacred and unchallengeable, the words which subordinates must throw back at him tend to flatter his whims rather than challenge his analyses. . . . The ideological screen through which facts are recieved, filtered, and appraised constitutes an additional possibility of misrepresentation. . . . Not even the most pragmatically oriented member of the ruling group can wholly liberate himself from the frame of responses that represent the residue of a lifetime in Communist thought patterns.[20]

Khrushchev's explanation of why Stalin ignored repeated warnings, from Churchill and from his own efficient espionage networks, that the Nazis were planning to attack the Soviet Union appears to confirm Fainsod's perceptive appraisal when he revealed that "information of this sort concerning the threat of German armed invasion of Soviet territory was coming in also from our own military and diplomatic sources . . . [but] because the leadership was conditioned against such information, such data were dispatched with fear and assessed with reservation."

[20] Merle Fainsod, *How Russia Is Ruled* (Cambridge, Mass., Harvard University Press, 1953), p. 283.

18. THE EVOLUTION AND ORGANIZATION OF THE SOVIET DIPLOMATIC SERVICE

Vernon V. Aspaturian

Of all the diplomatic services of the major powers perhaps the least is known about the Soviet diplomatic service. Hard information pertaining to the composition, organization, procedures, and personnel of the Soviet diplomatic service and Foreign Ministry is frustratingly elusive and fragmentary. The conventional sources of information are virtually nonexistent. Retired Soviet diplomatists do not keep diaries or write memoirs; nor do they write articles for the press or give vocal expression of their views on current policies in press interviews or before public investigating bodies.[1] The diplomatic correspondence of the Soviet Foreign Office remains, for the most part, locked in its archives. The Soviet Foreign Ministry issues neither a public telephone directory

This chapter was originally written in December, 1959, for the Harvard Russian Research Center Seminar, without footnotes. It has been slightly edited, with grammatical tenses changed, supplied with documentation, and updated through footnoting and the addition of a brief postscript.

[1] This is no longer the case. Some retired Soviet diplomats have written their memoirs. Cf., for example, Ivan Maisky, *Memoirs of a Soviet Diplomat* (New York, Charles Scribner's Sons, 1968), originally published in Russian in 1965 as *Vospominania Sovetskovo Posla: Voina 1939–1943* (Moscow, Izdatelstvo "Nauka"). Many Soviet marshals, generals, and admirals have also produced memoirs touching on Soviet diplomacy and foreign policy, but no top Soviet political figures have yet done so. There are indications, however, that both V. M. Molotov and A. I. Mikoyan are currently preparing their memoirs for possible publication cf. also, Ilya Ehrenburg, *Memoirs: 1921–41* (New York, World Publishing Co., 1964), and *Post-War Years: 1945–54* (New York, World Publishing Co., 1967).

nor a simple manual on its organization and functions. Since about 1929 even Ministerial orders and instructions concerning internal organization, procedures, and functions are no longer accessible for public scrutiny. The number of laws, decrees, orders, etc., dealing with the Soviet Foreign Ministry and the Soviet diplomatic service that have been published barely count two score. The Narkomindel Statute of November 12, 1923, which is the basic law governing the organization, structure, and powers of the Foreign Ministry has not been published in its up-to-date form for more than three decades.[2] The recent collection of documents on international law edited by Modzhoryan and Sobakin, for example, include only extracts from the basic Statute of the Foreign Ministry and then only from the version as it originally appeared in 1923.[3]

I. INTRODUCTION

The Soviet diplomatic service is distinguished from the diplomatic establishments of the other major powers by its historical traditions and links, its continuity, its basic missions, the source and character of its appointments, and its relationship to internal ideological and political forces and conflicts.

The most fascinating distinction is that the Soviet diplomatic service was totally devoid of any direct links with the Tsarist past, either in traditions or in personnel. Aside from Chicherin's brief experience as a *chinovnik* in the Tsarist Foreign Ministry, the diplomatic service established after the Revolution was completely unburdened with professional experience. Because of its pristine revolutionary character, the new diplomatic service was particularly cherished by Lenin, who singled it out as a model for other government departments.[4] Although the Soviet diplomatic service was not tainted by any connection with the ancien régime, even within the span of the post-revolutionary era, the Soviet service has failed to display even the most rudimentary characteristics of continuity in personnel. With perhaps one or two exceptions, all Soviet diplomats today date their entry into the service after 1937.[5] The first Soviet diplomatic service was virtually wiped out during the great purges of the late thirties and its connection with the present service is only marginal.

[2] The full text of this important document, together with amendments through 1927, is reprinted in *Yezhegodnik Narodnovo Kommissariata Po Inostrannym Delam Na 1928 God* (Moscow, 1928), pp. 182–193. The term Narkomindel was the official acronym for the People's Commissariat for Foreign Affairs.

[3] *Mezhdunarodnoye Pravo v Izbrannykh Dokumentakh* (Moscow, 1957), Vol. II, pp. 6–9.

[4] Cf. Chapter 17, p. 589, for the pertinent citation.

[5] This comment refers to the period down to 1960. In the past decade, the Soviet diplomatic service has demonstrated extraordinary continuity in personnel, based upon the personnel recruited between 1937 and 1944, who constitute the elite corps and administrative leadership of the Soviet Foreign Ministry and diplomatic service. Cf. "Postscript," at the end of this chapter.

The fundamental missions of the Soviet diplomatic service have undergone periodic transmutations and still remain highly nebulous in scope, ambiguous in definition, and unorthodox in techniques. Originally, the Bolsheviks did not even envisage the necessity or desirability of diplomacy, which they considered to be a purely bourgeois pastime and eminently unsuited to a revolutionary regime. When diplomacy was forced upon the new regime by the Central Powers, the early Soviet diplomatic service was conceived to be merely another instrument of the forthcoming world revolution. Only later were its missions defined in more conventional terms, although it has still been unable to shed completely the vestiges of its original functions.

Unlike the diplomatic services of other countries, notably the American, appointments to high diplomatic positions have been frequently signs of disgrace and imminent political oblivion rather than rewards for services rendered, political or meritorious. Recruits to the higher echelons of the diplomatic service have frequently been drawn from those wounded in the inner political battles, and in the past the diplomatic service was full of political oppositionists and constituted a nest of political intrigue.

Lastly, the relationship of the Soviet diplomatic service to internal ideological and political forces is unlike that of any other. It is a service whose personnel must be ideologically committed and frequently politically committed as well to one or another of the factions or cliques contending for political power. Consequently, the diplomatic service is inexorably drawn within the inner vortex of the struggle for power of which it bears unmistakable scars. In conformity with its political character it is a service whose high-ranking personnel are co-opted into the outer ring of the decision-making councils of the system, although this characteristic is subject to considerable variation.

In its evolution between 1917 and 1960, the Soviet diplomatic service fell into five rather distinct phases. The first phase corresponded roughly to the period of War Communism, that is to the years 1917–1921. A period of transition and improvisation, it was marked initially by an attempt to repudiate diplomacy, then to use it for revolutionary purposes, and finally to enhance the security position of the Soviet State. It was a period during which the diplomatic service had no firm future and most of its leading personnel were Bolshevik émigrés, whose legal status in the country to which they were accredited was extremely dubious.

The second phase in the evolution of the Soviet diplomatic establishment spanned the years 1921 to 1939, which is the longest and most convulsive of the phases of its development. The fundamental element that served to unify the disparate events of this long period was the essential continuity of diplomatic personnel. This is the period during which the first Soviet diplomatic service was formed and then destroyed.

The third phase was a transitional one embracing the war years and shortly thereafter, 1940–1947. It constituted the flimsiest thread of continuity between the prewar diplomatic service and that which exists today. During these years, diplomatic posts were temporarily filled by personnel drawn from other departments, particularly the Secret Police. Litvinov had been removed and Molotov had taken over the responsibilities of the Narkomindel in addition to his duties as Chairman of the Council of People's Commissars. These were also the years when the shattered service was being reconstituted by Molotov with the help of a small handful of career diplomats who survived the purges and the Secret Police.

The fourth phase started with the elimination of the last veterans of the pre-war diplomatic service and the Secret Police representatives. It signaled the maturation of the new diplomats recruited by Molotov and represented the emerging dominance of the second career service. This period lasted from 1947 until Stalin's death in 1953.

The fifth phase in the evolution of the Soviet diplomatic service was marked chiefly by the mass influx of high-ranking party *apparatchiki* into the diplomatic service alongside the corps of professionals trained by Molotov.[6] Each phase is marked by its own characteristics, determined not so much by the changes decreed in foreign policy as by the consequences of the internal struggles for power, although, of course, changes in external policy and reshaping the missions of Soviet diplomacy have also left their imprint. The chief feature that distinguishes one phase from another, however, is essentially that of personnel.

In its brief four decades of existence, the Soviet diplomatic service had seven chiefs: Leon Trotsky (November 1917–April 1918); Georgi Chicherin (1918–1929); Maxim Litvinov (1929–1939); V. M. Molotov (1939–1949; 1953–56); A. Y. Vyshinsky (1949–1953); Dmitri Shepilov (June 1956–February 1957); Andrei Gromyko (1957–   ). Nearly 35 years of Soviet diplomacy, however, had been directed by only three Ministers: Chicherin, Litvinov, and Molotov. Until 1949, the average tenure of a Foreign Minister was about ten years. Soviet diplomacy at the top represents a remarkable measure of continuity and stability unmatched by that of any power, and in the Soviet regime itself its record is exceeded only by that of the Ministry of Foreign Trade. The foundation of this stability at the top was, of course, the Stalinist dictatorship, but it should be pointed out that Ministers of other departments in the Soviet Government have not been able to demonstrate a corresponding durability.[7]

6 Since this was written in 1960, I would characterize the fifth and latest phase somewhat differently. The infusion of high-ranking Party personnel into the diplomatic service, for various reasons, has not seriously eroded the professional character of the Soviet diplomatic service, but has resulted in a bifurcation of function between those diplomats assigned to Communist states and those assigned elsewhere. See postscript at the end of this chapter for further details.

7 The tradition of continuity and durability at the Ministerial level continues. Gromyko has now been Foreign Minister for 13 years, the longest continuing incumbency of any Soviet Foreign Minister. He has survived a major succession crisis and his position seems secure. Thus, 48 years (out of 52) of Soviet diplomacy has now been directed by only four Ministers.

In contrast to the relative permanence of the Foreign Minister, however, the diplomatic service itself has been unable to establish a similar record of continuity, stability, and durability. Although Foreign Ministers have remained relatively secure (and not one has ever been executed), the same could not be said of their ranking and lesser subordinates, who were arrested, imprisoned, and executed by the score under Stalin. The equilibrium established between the Foreign Minister and the diplomatic service was diametrically opposed to that found in other states, where Foreign Ministers were replaced with kaleidoscopic rapidity as the diplomatic establishment remained unscathed. Foreign Ministers may come and go, but the diplomatic servants remain fixed.

Within six years after Stalin's death, however, the Foreign Ministry changed hands almost as many times as in the previous thirty-five, but the career professionals remained for the most part unmolested, thus indicating the development of a new equilibrium between the professionals and the politicians in the Soviet diplomatic service similar to that found elsewhere. However, other significant transformations took place in the diplomatic service that threatened to alter the basic quality and composition of the service once again.

By 1953, the Soviet diplomatic service appeared to have achieved an inner equilibrium marked by the high professional caliber of its leading personnel, a remarkable breadth of diplomatic experience at home and abroad, the establishment of high standards, the institution of a predictable system of recruitment, rotation, and promotion of personnel, and above all an apparent immunity from the effects of Kremlin intrigues and power struggles. To what extent Molotov shielded and nurtured the foreign service by not forging it into a personal instrument of political manipulation is not clear, but it is known that the Soviet diplomatic apparatus fashioned under Molotov's direction was virtually immune from criticism and its members were rarely targets of abuse by the various contending cliques and factions that surrounded Stalin. With the exception of Beriya's ubiquitous secret police, the Soviet Foreign Office was remarkably free of penetration by Party hacks and status-seeking members of the Party apparatus. Above all, it was not used as a graveyard for Party bureaucrats wounded in the power struggles and on their way to oblivion, as it was so employed before the war and after Stalin's death.

The Foreign Ministry was Molotov's private preserve, although in retrospect it appears that one of the chief purposes of Vyshinsky's appointment as Molotov's Deputy in 1940 was to act as Stalin's "eyes and ears," and the ostensible reason for his displacement of Molotov in 1949 was to de-Molotovize the diplomatic establishment in view of Molotov's bleak future during the final years of Stalin's life. Vyshinsky was the most conspicuous interloper in Molotov's domain, but there were others, particularly during the war period, when Beriya's minions, as V. K. Dekanozov, and Party specialists, as S. A. Lozovsky, were placed in high positions in the Foreign Ministry to ensure reliability and to substitute for those who were slaughtered in the preceding years or those who had not yet matured sufficiently. Although Vyshinsky remained in the Foreign Ministry to become his chief assistant, Molotov was successful in sweeping out Beriya's cronies. By 1947, the new professionals were ready to assume full administrative responsibilities under Molotov's direction.

One further significant characteristic of the diplomatic service under Molotov was that, aside from Molotov and Vyshinsky, who were politicians, none of the professionals had been co-opted into the decision-making organs of the Party until 1952, when Gromyko, Zarubin, and Malik were elected as alternate members of the Central Committee.

II. The Diplomatic Service as a Post of Political Exile

Stalin's death, however, opened up new avenues into the Foreign Ministry from the Party apparatus and the diplomatic service was soon top-heavy with former high-ranking Party officials and State functionaries. Each internal political crisis in the Kremlin appeared to send out a wave of Party bureaucrats to hit the diplomatic service. Between 1953 and 1960, not counting Molotov and Vyshinsky, no less than five full members and five alternate members of the Party Presidium elected in 1952 by the 19th Party Congress were shifted to diplomatic work.[8]

The initial intrusions into the diplomatic service were made immediately after Stalin died, when the game of musical chairs in the Kremlin assumed the pattern of contracting the size of both Party and government summits. Thus when Voroshilov displaced Shvernik as Chairman of the Presidium of the Supreme Soviet, Shvernik, in turn, bumped V. V. Kuznetsov from his post as Chairman of the All-Union Central Council of Trade Unions into the Foreign Ministry as a Deputy Minister of Foreign Affairs (ranking below Vyshinsky and Malik, who were appointed First Deputies) and ambassador to China. He lost his seat in the Presidium but retained his full membership in the Central Committee. Recalled in December 1953 and promoted to First Deputy Foreign Minister, Kuznetsov was replaced in Peking by another Party careerist who was elected an alternate member of the Presidium in 1952 — P. F. Yudin.[9] Yudin was a prominent ideologist and a former

[8] The influx of Party officials into the diplomatic service did not disturb this new emerging trend. Although a substantial number of Party officials exiled into the foreign service after Stalin's death were shunted out again, the professional diplomats survived largely unscathed and many senior diplomats, recruited during the years 1937–1944, match or exceed Gromyko's longevity in the service. Even some of the Party bureaucrats taken into the service have remained to develop new careers. The five full members of the Party Presidium who were exiled into the diplomatic service were Mikhailov, Ponomarenko, Melnikov, Pervukhin, and Kuznetsov, and the five alternate or candidate members were Pegov, Patolichev, Puzanov, Tevosyan, and Yudin.

[9] V. V. Kuznetsov is still with the Soviet Foreign Ministry, having served as First Deputy Foreign Minister since 1955. He functions as one of the Kremlin's top diplomatic trouble-shooters and can now be considered a professional diplomat. He has remained continuously as a full member of the Party Central Committee. P. E. Yudin left the diplomatic service with his departure as ambassador to Peking and died in 1961.

editor of the Cominform journal, *For a Lasting Peace, For a People's Democracy.*

Two other former Presidium members also found themselves shunted off into diplomacy shortly after Stalin's death. L. G. Melnikov, First Secretary of the Ukrainian Party apparatus and an alternate member of the first post-Stalin Presidium, was dethroned from his positions in a power play by Beriya and packed off as ambassador to Rumania for a brief excursion in diplomacy.[10] N. A. Mikhailov, also elected a full member of the Presidium in 1952 and a veteran Party functionary, was dispatched to Warsaw in March 1954 as ambassador.[11] Kuznetsov, Yudin, and Mikhailov retained their positions as full members of the Central Committee, but Melnikov was deprived of his, although he is now an alternate member. Neither Mikhailov nor Melnikov are currently in the diplomatic service.

Within the space of a single year after Stalin's death, no less than four former members of the Party's highest body, the Presidium, were shunted into the diplomatic service for reasons that had little to do with diplomacy. This curious attraction of the diplomatic service for former high Party luminaries was one of the most conspicuous features of the post-Stalin diplomatic service.

The second wave of Party bureaucrats to wash over the Foreign Ministry took place after Malenkov's removal as Premier in February 1955. The most prominent of these was P. K. Ponomarenko, a veteran *apparatchiki* elected to full membership in the Central Committee in 1939, to the Party Secretariat in 1950, and to the Presidium in 1952. Ponomarenko was Stalin's viceroy in Byelorussia for more than a decade, and he was one of the few newcomers to the Party summit in 1952 who was retained as an alternate member after the post-Stalin reorganization. Apparently a key Malenkov lieutenant, he started skidding as soon as Khrushchev displaced Malenkov in the Secretariat. He was appointed in rapid succession as Minister of Culture and First Secretary of the Kazakh Party organization. He was dropped from the Presidium in late 1954 and was sent to Warsaw as ambassador to replace Mikhailov, who returned to Moscow to become Minister of Culture.[12] Aside from Ponomarenko, several Party functionaries were reassigned to the Foreign Ministry during the same period: I. F. Ilyichev, a former editor of *Pravda, Izvestia,* and *Kommunist,* and M. V. Zimyanin, a former Second Secretary of the Byelorussian Party organiza-

[10] Melnikov left the diplomatic service in 1954 to occupy a series of low-ranking government positions.
[11] N. A. Mikhailov, as Kuznetsov, has remained close to diplomacy. He has served as ambassador to Indonesia, Minister of Culture, and Chairman of the State Committee on Publishing. Again like Kuznetsov, he remains a full member of the Central Committee.
[12] P. K. Ponomarenko, after a succession of diplomatic appointments, including India and the Netherlands (where he was involved in a scandal), ended his diplomatic career after a two-year stint (1963–1965) as Moscow's permanent representative with the International Atomic Energy Agency in Vienna. As Melnikov, Ponomarenko was unable to make a successful career in diplomacy.

tion, both of whom suffered a decline in Party rank after their entry into the diplomatic service. Ilyichev became the Chief of the Press and Information Division, as Zimyanin headed up a European Department in the Foreign Ministry.[13]

The third wave of Party officials to hit the Foreign Ministry took place after the 20th Party Congress and Molotov's resignation as Foreign Minister. Between the time of Molotov's resignation as Foreign Minister in June 1956 and his expulsion from the Presidium and government in July 1957, four high Party and government officials, who were elected alternate members of the Party Presidium in 1952 and were still full members of the Central Committee, were reassigned to the Foreign Ministry: I. F. Tevosyan, N. M. Pegov, N. M. Pusanov, and N. S. Patolichev. Three, as Malenkov and Ponomarenko, belonged to the class of 1939; that is, they were elected to the Party Central Committee by the 18th Party Congress. Patolichev was admitted to the Central Committee in that year as an alternate, as Tevosyan and Pegov entered as full members. All four personalities had impressive records of Party and administrative service as Deputy Premiers, Ministers, or Party Secretaries in the central apparatus or of Republican Party organizations. Patolichev was appointed a Deputy Foreign Minister, Tevosyan was sent to Japan, Pegov to Iran, and Puzanav to North Korea.[14]

The fourth wave of highly placed Party officials to deposit its jetsam of the power struggle in the diplomatic service came after the expulsion of the "anti-Party group" in July 1957. Molotov himself was exiled to Ulan Bator Khoto, as M. G. Pervukhin served for a brief period as Chairman of the State Committee for Foreign Economic Relations and then was reassigned as ambassador to East Germany in 1958. Unlike Molotov, he lingered on as a full member of the Central Committee and as a nominal alternate member of the Party Presidium.[15]

[13] L. F. Ilyichev's career has been rather chequered. One of the few "politicals" who made a partial comeback into the hierarchy under Khrushchev, who rescued him from the foreign service and had him appointed a Secretary of the Central Committee, he was mildly purged again after Khrushchev's demise in 1964 and returned to the Foreign Ministry as a Deputy Foreign Minister. In some ways Zimyanin's career has been the obverse of Ilyichev's. As Ilyichev was dropped from full membership in the Central Committee, Zimyanin was advanced from membership in the Central Auditing Commission to full membership in the Central Committee upon his appointment as editor of *Pravda* after Khrushchev's ouster, a job also held in the past by Ilyichev. He vacated his post as Deputy Foreign Minister, the job filled by Ilyichev.

[14] I. F. Tevosyan died of natural causes in 1958, Patolichev has functioned as Minister of Foreign Trade continuously since 1958, as Pegov and Puzanov have made a career of the diplomatic service. After his Iranian assignment, Pegov served as ambassador to Algeria (1964–1967) and was appointed ambassador to India in 1967. Puzanov, after serving as ambassador to North Korea, was assigned to Yugoslavia (1962–1967), and moved on as envoy to Bulgaria in 1967. Both remain as full members of the Central Committee.

[15] After a three year exile in Mongolia, Molotov was rejected by the Dutch Government as the envoy to the Netherlands, and was thereupon appointed permanent representative to the International Atomic Energy

Lateral entry at the apex of the Soviet diplomatic service was by no means reserved only for former members of the Presidium. Lesser Party bureaucrats and state administrators also found their way into diplomacy, some by choice and others involuntarily. At least three current ambassadors, aside from those already mentioned, have held ministerial rank: I. A. Benediktov, who was elected a full member of the Central Committee in 1939, has been a former Minister of Agriculture and State Farms. He served briefly in 1953 as ambassador to India and is once again envoy to New Delhi, having replaced Ponomarenko in late 1959.[16] M. A. Menshikov, another former ambassador to India and later ambassador to the United States, is an ex-Minister of Foreign Trade.[17] N. S. Ryzhov, a former Minister of Light Industry, was appointed ambassador to Turkey.[18]

Five additional Party bureaucrats in the diplomatic service in 1960 were full or alternate members of the Central Committee; two others, who had been demoted from the Central Committee in 1956, were members of the Central Auditing Commission. A number of Party workers from the central apparatus or regional Party organizations who had not achieved sufficient importance to win elections to central Party organs were also reassigned to diplomatic work.

Virtually all of the former Party bureaucrats and high State officials in the diplomatic service carried their Party rank into the Foreign Ministry with them. This introduced a chasm in the Ministry between the professionals, who as a general rule do not rank very high in the Party hierarchy, and their new colleagues. The year 1958 was the high-water mark of Party infusion into the Foreign Ministry. Gromyko's two First Deputy Foreign Ministers, V. V. Kuznetsov and N. A. Patolichev, and at least six of his ambassadors appeared to outrank him in the Party galaxy on the basis of seniority, although in most cases their stars were clearly in decline. First Deputy Foreign Minister Patolichev and four ambassadors had been members of the Central Committee since 1939, the same year in which an outraged official in the American Embassy in Moscow reported back to Washington that an obscure and inexperienced

Agency in Vienna in 1960, from which post he was recalled and retired in late 1961 because he persisted in factional intrigues against Khrushchev. M. G. Pervukhin was finally dropped from his inactive alternate membership in the Party Presidium by the 22nd Party Congress in 1961 and was subsequently recalled from his post in East Germany in 1962 and reassigned to a succession of minor positions in the economic bureaucracy.

[16] I. A. Benediktov resumed his position as Minister of Agriculture for a period after his ambassadorship to India, which he resumed from 1959 to 1967, and then was reassigned as ambassador to Yugoslavia in 1967. He, too, remains a full member of the Party Central Committee.

[17] After a three-year tour as ambassador to the United States, Menshikov was recalled and reassigned to the dubious position of Foreign Minister to the R.S.F.S.R. (1962–1968), whereupon his diplomatic career came to an end.

[18] N. S. Ryzhov served as ambassador to Turkey until his reassignment as ambassador to Italy in 1967, and thus has made the diplomatic service his career.

youngster — "one Gramyko (sic)" — had been placed in charge of the American Desk in the Narkomindel.[19] Thus, in the same year that Gromyko entered into the diplomatic service as a junior official, nearly a half-dozen of his present subordinates were already on the threshold of the inner sanctum of Soviet power. In 1958, Gromyko's non-career subordinates included, aside from Molotov, not only eight former Presidium members, but two former First Secretaries of Republican Party organizations. Altogether, the non-career diplomats accounted for nine full members of the Central Committee, five alternates, and two members of the Central Auditing Commission who had been demoted from membership in the Central Committee.

In dramatic contrast to the Party rank of the non-career diplomats, of the professionals, only Foreign Minister Gromyko was a full member of the Central Committee, to which he was elected an alternate in 1952 and a full member in 1956. Malik, the late Georgi Zarubin, and V. A. Zorin were the only career diplomats to have achieved alternate status, as three or four others were elected to membership in the Central Auditing Commission.[20] Absolutely nothing even remotely resembling this assemblage of diversified administrative and political talent existed in any other Ministry. In the past, the existence of such an anomaly was a portent of tragedy, although this was not necessarily a precedent governing the future. The controlling factor was the unpredictable course of the struggle for power and policy. Nevertheless, the presence of more than a dozen high-ranking Party personalities in a Ministry whose chief and principal professional subordinates had relatively low-ranking status in the Party must have been a source of deep anxiety for the professionals and Party diplomats alike. Although no drastic purge took place in the career service, the lateral entry of the Party bureaucrats into the service has blunted the ambitions of not a few professionals who had to be content with posts of lesser prestige.

III. Major Trends in the Post-Stalin Diplomatic Service

The influx of Party and State officials into the diplomatic service reflected several distinct trends. The most obvious was that the Foreign Ministry was once again being employed as a convenient post of exile — to serve some as a vestibule for meditation, penance, and partial rehabilitation and for others as a temporary way station on the way to political oblivion. Because of the inherently diffused nature of their functions and the dispersed character of their organization, the Foreign Ministry and the diplomatic service constitute a poor power base and correspondingly are effective places to scatter and isolate the opposition.

Ample evidence exists that the diplomatic service was once again converted into a post of political exile. First, there was the reassignment

---

[19] *Foreign Relations of The United States: The Soviet Union 1937–1939* (Washington, D.C., The Department of State, 1952), p. 772. Hereinafter cited as *The Soviet Union, 1933–1939*.

[20] V. S. Semyonov, G. M. Puskin, and S. A. Vinogradov.

of Melnikov after his unambiguous fall from grace, and second, there was the presence of Molotov and Pervukhin, two former giants of the regime who have been publicly and overtly disgraced and humiliated. Further confirmation was less direct but no less eloquent. Of the more than one-fourth of the members of the Party's highest body elected in 1952 who were reassigned to diplomatic work, not a single one managed to climb back up to the Party summit.[21] In contrast to this abysmal record, eight others who were elected to the Party summit in 1952, and were dropped after Stalin's death, managed to be restored to either full or alternate membership in the Presidium by 1960. Furthermore, eleven members of the Presidium in 1960 were not elected to this body in 1952, including several who were not even elected to alternate membership in the Central Committee in that year.[22]

Another trend revealed by the new appointments runs directly counter to the first, but is by no means incompatible with it. In some instances, reassignment to the diplomatic service has been accompanied by a rise in Party rank rather than a decline. This was particularly true of N. P. Firyubin, husband of Presidium member Ekaterina Furtseva, who entered the diplomatic service early in 1954 and was appointed a Deputy Foreign Minister after ambassadorial tours in Prague and Belgrade.[23] Two other clear cases of upward Party mobility were those of Ye. I. Gromov, appointed ambassador to Hungary, and I. K. Zamchevsky, Firyubin's successor in Yugoslavia.[24] The mobility of two other former Party careerists, I. T. Grishin, full member of the Central Committee since 1952, and A. A. Yepishev, an alternate member of the Central Committee since 1952, was not clear, since their Party ranks were unaffected one way or the other by their reassignment to the diplomatic service. Grishin was assigned as ambassador to Czechoslovakia and Yepishev was appointed the Soviet envoy to Bucharest.[25]

A third major trend indicated by the new diplomatic appointments was the closer Party surveillance of a Ministry that was dominated by Molotov for more than a decade and in whose image the career service

[21] With the limited exception of L. F. Ilyichev, who made it partly back up with his appointment as a Party Secretary for a brief period under Khrushchev.

[22] The restored group included L. I. Brezhnev, O. V. Kuusinen, A. V. Aristov, N. M. Shvernik, A. N. Kosygin, D. S. Korotchenko, M. A. Suslov, and N. P. Ignatov. The 10 new members were N. I. Belyayev, Ye. A. Furtseva, A. I. Kirichenko, F. R. Kozlov, P. N. Pospelov, A. P. Kirilenko, K. T. Mazurov, V. P. Mzhavanadze, N. V. Podgorny, and N. A. Mukhitdinov.

[23] N. F. Firyubin has served as a Deputy Foreign Minister since 1957. His wife, Furtseva, has served as Minister of Culture since 1960.

[24] I. K. Zamchevsky is a minor official in the Foreign Ministry; Gromov has become a diplomatic functionary assigned to relations with Communist states.

[25] A. A. Yepishev was reassigned as ambassador to Yugoslavia in 1960, a post he vacated in 1962 to become Chief of the Main Political Administration (Directorate) of the Armed Forces, a position that he still holds. He was advanced to full membership in the Party Central Committee in 1964. Grishin, on the other hand, left the Foreign Ministry in 1960 to become Deputy Minister of Foreign Trade and was dropped from membership in all the Central Party organs.

was largely shaped. This function could be simultaneously served by the very individuals who had been shunted out of the inner sanctum of Soviet power. Essentially *apparatchiki* in their outlook, they could be counted on to keep a jaundiced eye upon the career diplomats whose long exposure to the temptations of the capitalist world may have tainted them with a cosmopolitanism incompatible with the best traditions of proletarian internationalism. In any event, it served to "politicalize" the career service, if that was necessary in the diplomatic establishment of a Communist state.

A fourth major trend betrayed by the infusion of Party bureaucrats in the service was suggested by the geographical distribution of appointments. Virtually all Soviet envoys to Communist countries are former Party bureaucrats, whether in disgrace or not. In the post-Stalinist period Soviet ambassadors to Poland, Czechoslovakia, Yugoslavia, Hungary, Rumania, China, North Korea, North Vietnam, and East Germany were invariably at least alternate members of the Central Committee. This was no longer true of Soviet envoys to China, Poland, and North Vietnam for a brief period when lesser former Party functionaries were now installed. The obvious meaning of the replacement of career diplomats in Communist capitals with Party diplomats was that diplomatic channels to kindred states were being employed as Party lines of communication as well. Although a separate department dealing with Communist states has not been established in the Foreign Ministry (as is the case in the Ministry of Foreign Trade), I confirmed in Moscow that one of the First Deputy Foreign Ministers (Patolichev until his reassignment as Minister of Foreign Trade) supervised relations with Communist countries as one of his principal responsibilities. Once again Soviet envoys perform a dual function, but this time only in ideologically related states, where they double as Party representatives and in this capacity attend local Party congresses and conventions. Whether this is to be a permanent feature of Soviet diplomacy remains unclear, but this procedure was clearly made necessary by the dissolution of the Cominform and the failure to establish a new supranational Party organization.[26]

Finally, one cannot rule out that in individual cases assignments to the foreign service were freely chosen by Party workers who wished to switch careers in mid-stream. As the power and influence of the Soviet Union in world affairs has enhanced, so have the prestige and status of the diplomatic service. For bureaucrats who have spent their lives climbing up the treacherous rungs of the Party apparatus, diplomatic service abroad could have many attractions. Some of the former officials of the Party and other ministries, such as V. V. Kuznetsov and Menshikov, have now been in the diplomatic service so long that they may even be classified as professionals. Others may have preferred reassignment to the diplomatic service rather than elsewhere as a result of the economic reorganization acts that reduced the number of central ministries.

[26] *Cf.* "Postscript," *infra.*

One curiosity revealed by the transfusion of Party into the Foreign Ministry is that service in the Byelorussian Party organization appears to uniquely equip one to be a Soviet diplomat. No less than four former Secretaries of the Byelorussian Party had been transferred to diplomatic work: Ponomarenko, Patolichev, Zimyanin, and P. A. Abrasimov, who was Minister-Counselor to Peking before his later assignment as ambassador to Warsaw.[27]

Paradoxically, reassignment to the diplomatic service of highly placed Party and State officials may be a sign of personal disgrace, but their presence in the Foreign Ministry serves to heighten its status in the Soviet institutional hierarchy. No other Ministry in the Soviet Government could boast of such an accumulation of former Party Presidium members, Deputy Premiers, Party Secretaries, and Ministers as the Foreign Ministry and none could muster as high a number of officials with full or alternate status in the Central Committee.

IV. FOUNDING THE INSTITUTIONS OF SOVIET DIPLOMACY: THE CHICHERIN ERA

This was not the first time that the Soviet diplomatic service had been subjected to a major face-lifting operation and its significance can be placed in appropriate perspective only by examining past precedents in the erratic evolution of the Soviet foreign service during its brief but convulsive four decades of existence. It was the original intention of Lenin and the Bolsheviks to do away with diplomacy and diplomats, since they expected the imminent world revolution to render diplomatic intercourse superfluous, or in the event of its failure, make it equally impossible between the Soviet Republic and the hostile capitalist states it was dedicated to destroying.[28]

Unlike the other branches of the Soviet Government, the Soviet diplomatic service was born without an umbilical connection with the old Tsarist diplomatic establishment. Not a single major or minor diplomat from the ancien régime was carried over, and in this respect it was unique among the government departments of the new Soviet regime. The reason was not, as is sometimes supposed, that the imperial diplomats still serving the Provisional Government could not be trusted; that is true, but the former officials used in other departments and the Tsarist generals and officers taken into the Red Army were equally suspect. The primary reason was that Soviet diplomacy was envisaged to be a purely interim operation with no firm future, but equally important was the fact that not a single diplomat offered to work for the new regime.

[27] Abrasimov, who remains a full member of the Party Central Committee, has been ambassador to East Germany since 1962 and is essentially a Party official filling diplomatic posts to Communist countries.

[28] "What foreign affairs will we have now?" Lenin asked Trotsky, when a Commissariat of Foreign Affairs was proposed after the Bolshevik takeover. Leon Trotsky, *My Life* (New York, Scribners, 1930), p. 341.

When Leon Trotsky reluctantly accepted the post of Foreign Commissar he considered it to be a strictly part-time and transitory appointment whose main function would be to liquidate the diplomatic service. "I will issue a few revolutionary proclamations," he announced, "and then shut up shop."[29] Trotsky paid a visit to the Foreign Ministry, assembled all the workers in the Ministry into a central hall and simply asked that those supporting the new regime divide to the left and those not to the right. None chose the left, whereupon Trotsky demanded the keys and fired them all on the spot. He turned the administration of the new Commissariat over to one of his cronies, I. A. Zalkind.[30] On November 26, 1917, a decree by Trotsky virtually disestablished the diplomatic apparatus of the Russian state. All members of the Russian foreign service abroad were summarily dismissed unless they expressed loyalty to the Bolshevik regime. A committee was set up to publish the secret treaties and Zalkind organized a rudimentary central administration of seven departments, to which were added seven additional departments about six months later.[31] As diplomats abroad, Bolshevik émigrés were charged with what formal or informal representation could be established: Litvinov in London, V. V. Vorovsky in Stockholm, and Jacob Suritz in Copenhagen. Other *ad hoc* appointments followed wherever possible.

The new Soviet leaders soon discovered that jettisoning diplomacy was not an easy matter and they were forced to revive it when negotiations were forced upon them at Brest-Litovsk. Trotsky's fiery declamations over the radio had a spectacular but only ephemeral effect and they proved to be a poor substitute for diplomacy. The Treaty of Brest-Litovsk imposed formal diplomacy upon the regime with Germany and its allies, so a provisional diplomatic service was recreated by the *Sovnarkom*.[32] A. A. Joffe was sent to Berlin, where his attempt to establish a revolutionary center in his embassy became an international diplomatic scandal. Pending the eventual liquidation of the Foreign Affairs Commissariat, the functions of Soviet diplomacy during this initial period fell into three principal categories: (1) the publication of "secret treaties"; (2) the conduct of necessary negotiations and diplomatic relations with capitalist states as a holding operation; and (3) the use of Soviet embassies and legations abroad as centers of revolutionary conspiracy, propaganda, and activity in clear violation of treaty obligations.

Moscow also saw the advantages of establishing informal and formal diplomatic contact with the bourgeois powers. The failure of the

[29] Leon Trotsky, *My Life* (New York, Scribners, 1930), p. 341. "The Commissariat of Foreign Affairs," he wrote, "actually meant freedom from departmental work. . . . The diplomatic department, with the exception of the Brest-Litovsk peace negotiations, took very little of my time." *Ibid.* pp. 341–344.
[30] *Desyat Let Sovetskoi Diplomatii* (Moscow, 1927), p. 5.
[31] *Ibid.* pp. 5 and 8.
[32] Official Soviet Acronym for the Council of People's Commissars, renamed Council of Ministers in 1946.

world revolution to take fire and the successful secession of the border states rendered diplomatic contact even more necessary. Diplomatic relations were even established with the quasi-independent regimes in Byelorussia, the Ukraine, and the Transcaucasian Republics, and within three years the Soviet regime was in active search for diplomatic recognition by the capitalist powers since it provided a measure of security of which they were not immediately aware.

Trotsky's behavior at Brest-Litovsk and his obvious distaste for a bourgeois avocation soon led him to relinquish the Foreign Commissariat to his assistant Georgi Chicherin, the only individual in the Soviet diplomatic service who had even the remotest connection with the previous Russian Foreign Ministry. Trotsky left little imprint on the future contours of the Soviet diplomatic service during his brief tenure as Foreign Commissar and Chicherin can rightly be called the Father of Soviet Diplomacy, although the extraordinary diplomatic establishment which he molded was all but destroyed.[33] Soviet foreign affairs chief longer than anyone, except Molotov (and now, Gromyko), he served during the crucial formative years from 1918–1929, when the Soviet Government was weak, rent with internal political convulsions and struggles, still aggressively revolutionary, and surrounded by hostile states on all sides. In many respects Chicherin's brilliant diplomacy was the shield that protected the Soviet Republic from outside intervention and permitted the internal political quarrels and struggles to rage unimpeded by external interference. Although a valued and close friend of Lenin, the aristocratic-mannered Chicherin had little influence in the formulation of the foreign policy which it was his function to execute. He did not rank very high on the Party totem-pole and was elected a member of the Central Committee six years after his appointment as Foreign Commissar, a seat that he lost immediately upon his removal from office in 1929.

With the formation of the Union in 1923 and the formal unification of the diplomatic agencies of the lesser Soviet Republics, the Foreign Commissariat was provided with its definitive stature decreed by the *Sovnarkom* on November 12, 1923. The Narkomindel was completely reorganized along the lines that still persist today. In conformity

[33] Chicherin had served for a brief period as a minor official in the central office of the Tsarist foreign ministry. *Cf.* A. S. Bakhov, *Na Zare Sovetskoii Diplomatii* (Moscow, 1966) for a recent, relatively objective Soviet account of the origins, development, organs, institutions, personnel, and practices of Soviet diplomacy during the first five years of the Soviet regime. Many of the pre-war diplomats purged or disgraced by Stalin have been progressively rehabilitated since 1956, and this work deals favorably with many, praising their contributions. Even Trotsky is mentioned in passing as providing "untrustworthy ideological leadership" for the *Narkomindel* (p. 28), which is described as "actually led by G. V. Chicherin" (p. 24), who emerges as the founding father of Soviet diplomacy in this work. Litvinov* also comes in for considerable praise, and the following are also given credit for earlier Soviet diplomatic achievements: I. Zalkind, N. G. Markin*, L. M. Karakhan*, Ya. S. Ganetsky*, Ya. A. Suritz, M. A. Stakhovich, L. K. Martens*, Ya. A. Berzin*, Ya. A. Bekzadyan* and others. (Starred names are accompanied with photographs.) *Cf.* also F. I. Kozhevnikov, *Gosudarstvo i Mezhdunarodnoye Pravo* (Moscow, 1967), pp. 136–158.

with early Soviet administrative practice the affairs of the Narkomindel were directed by Chicherin and the Collegium of the Commissariat, on which sat Lev Karakhan, Maxim Litvinov, and Khristian Rakovsky as his Deputy Commissars. In June 1918, the Narkomindel had a personnel roster of 200 employees, but as the international connections of the Soviet Republic expanded, the size of diplomatic establishment increased correspondingly.[34] By the end of 1921, the Soviet Government had a total of 38 representatives abroad, including consular representatives and foreign trade emissaries.[35] The number of workers in the Foreign Commissariat rose to more than 1300 by the time of the formation of the Union. These figures were trimmed somewhat by 1927, when the Narkomindel reported 278 diplomats accredited to Western countries, 375 to Eastern and 93 officials at home, for a total of 746, and a total of 519 employed within the central apparatus itself.[36] The Narkomindel Statute of 1923 defined the principal missions of the Narkomindel, which are still cited by Soviet authorities as the objectives of the Soviet Foreign Ministry today.[37] It was not until 1924, however, that the Narkomindel was juridically relieved of its extra-legal revolutionary missions when a decree of November 21, 1924 stated:

> It goes without saying that diplomatic missions abroad are appointed by each of the parties establishing diplomatic relations for purposes which exclude propaganda in the country to which they are accredited. The Soviet diplomatic missions follow and are to follow this principle with absolute strictness.[38]

Although the decree abolishing diplomatic ranks was not superseded and Soviet diplomatic representatives all carried the same title of *Polpred*,[39] extra-legal arrangements were soon made, the first with China in 1924, which gave informal ranking to Soviet representatives abroad so that they might not forfeit the elementary and obvious advantages of seniority and status among the diplomatic corps.[40] The Soviet egalitarian principle became increasingly intolerable as Moscow's relations were expanded until by 1941–1943, it was finally abolished in favor of a revival of traditional titles.

The prewar diplomatic service was essentially the creation of Chicherin and largely reflected his own predispositions and personality, especially among the younger functionaries. During the entire Chicherin-

[34] *Desyat Let*, p. 6.
[35] *Ibid.*, p. 12.
[36] *Ibid.* p. 13.
[37] *Cf.* Chapter 21 for pertinent extract from the statute.
[38] Full text in T. A. Taracouzio, *The Soviet Union and International Law* (New York, Macmillan, 1935), pp. 389–390. Yet, when Chicherin addressed a Congress in Tblisi in 1925, his earnest protest that the Soviet "government is not responsible for the activities of the Comintern and has nothing at all to do with it," was greeted with loud and derisive laughter by the knowing delegates, much to his embarrassment. Cited in Gustav Hilger and Alfred G. Meyer, *The Incompatible Allies* (New York, The Macmillan Co., 1953), p. 109.
[39] For text of the decree abolishing diplomatic ranks and establishing the title of *Polpred*, cf. Taracouzio, *op. cit.*, p. 383.
[40] For the arrangement with China, *Ibid.* p. 181.

Litvinov era (1918–1939), the diplomatic service was generally looked upon as a slightly disreputable profession for simon-pure revolutionaries, who preferred to work in the Comintern. Like Chicherin himself, the service was slightly suspect and tainted with the brush of bourgeois cosmopolitanism. Again, like Chicherin, a large proportion of his diplomats were pre-revolutionary Marxist intellectuals with non-proletarian backgrounds and bourgeois tastes, former Mensheviks and late-comers to the Party. Many had spent years of exile in Western Europe. An extraordinary proportion of the diplomatic service consisted of Jews, and many cosmopolites of various nationalities who had cast their lot with the Russian Revolution were also to be found in the Narkomindel. The identical talents — knowledge of the outside world and of foreign languages — that formed the foundation of their diplomatic competence also turned out to be their greatest political handicap.[41]

The Foreign Commissariat was treated with contempt by Stalin, who detested Chicherin and apparently never forgave him for daring to challenge his theses on the national question in 1921.[42] Before his rise

[41] These diplomats, naturally, would resent the rubric of "cosmopolitan." Thus, although Ehrenburg refers to his friend Yakov Suritz, as "an old revolutionary, and internationalist and a typical intellectual, Suritz rejected both the labels of 'obsequiousness to everything foreign' and 'cosmopolitanism.'" Ehrenburg, op. cit., p. 282. Furthermore, Ehrenburg confirms Stalin's suspicions that the pre-war professionals were basically hostile toward him and shared common backgrounds and experiences that reinforced their animosity: "Towards the end of his life [Suritz] . . . at times lost control and blurted out whatever was on his mind. He would drop in unannounced . . . and then break out; he could talk for two hours at a stretch, inwardly seething. It nearly always began with the words: 'yesterday I was talking to Litvinov . . .' followed by furious language. Sometimes he attributed Stalin's actions to 'a pathologically split personality'. . . . I shall not repeat his stories about Stalin; they might read like 'exposures'. . . . Suritz tried to find an explanation for certain aspects of Stalin's nature in an inner divergence between theory and practice. . . . He once said in a low voice: 'the trouble isn't only that he doesn't know how the people live, but that he doesn't *want* to know: the people are an *idea* to him and nothing more.' He would leave and then turn up again a month or two later, unable to keep silent any longer, and would start: 'yesterday Litvinov and I were talking about Lozovsky. . . .' There was only one way to soothe him and that was to take him into the room where the Matisse drawings, Falk landscapes and the Chagall paintings hung." *Ibid.* pp. 282–283. Suritz died on the day of Litvinov's funeral. And, in reference to Litvinov, Ehrenburg reports that though he appreciated Stalin's intelligence, Litvinov had a low opinion of Stalin's knowledge of Western ways: "He said with a sigh: 'He [Stalin] doesn't know the West. If our opponents were a bunch of shahs or sheikhs he would outwit them.'" *Ibid.* p. 278. As many other "cosmopolitans" among the "Old Bolsheviks," Litvinov underrated Stalin's abilities as a statesman and patronizingly viewed him as a kind of Caucasian tribal chief, adept at minor intrigue and manipulation, but devoid of real sophistication and subtlety. Stalin, however, in spite of his ignorance of the West, eventually outwitted and outmaneuvered all of his contemporary Western counterparts.

[42] Chicherin had written articles entitled "Against the Theses of Comrade Stalin," which Stalin condemned as not containing "a single practical proposal . . . worthy of attention." J. V. Stalin, *Marxism and The National Question* (New York, International Publishers, 1942), pp. 104–106.

to preeminence, Stalin frequently criticized the Narkomindel for its ineffectiveness in exploiting differences among the capitalist states. The diplomatic service soon became a dumping ground for Stalin's political rivals and their camp followers. Important Party figures as Madame Alexandra Kollontai, Gregory Sokolnikov, Kristian Rakovsky, Nicolai Krestinsky, and others were exiled to or isolated in the Foreign Commissariat. Kamenev was shunted off to Rome, Rakovsky to Paris and London, as Kollontai was kept virtually in permanent exile in Stockholm from 1931–1945. The prewar diplomatic service was a natural haven for intellectuals, Jews, ex-Mensheviks, cosmopolites of various nationalities, tired and disillusioned "Old Bolsheviks," reformed and unregenerate Trotskyites, and a motley assortment of other oppositionists to Stalin. As Gromyko does today, Chicherin found himself uncomfortably surrounded with Party personalities far more exalted and influential than he, even though they were on the downgrade and he was fixed in a permanent state of political stagnation. In this way Stalin employed the Soviet foreign service as a genteel exile for his defeated rivals and their lesser supporters. The parallel could not have been unnoticed by Gromyko's formerly higher-ranking subordinates during the immediate post-Stalin period.

The ailing and abused Chicherin was removed in 1929 and succeeded by his ambitious and equally competent First Deputy, Maxim Litvinov, who, although an "Old Bolshevik" and former crony of Stalin's, was not rewarded immediately with his predecessor's seat in the Central Committee, but had to wait until 1934 for his election to this body — a position that he also forfeited when he was replaced by Molotov in 1939. Chicherin was removed in disgrace, to die a few years later, forgotten and ignored by the regime which he served so well. Both Litvinov and Chicherin, however, were given biographical entries in the *Diplomatic Dictionary* and their diplomatic services recognized. Litvinov even merited a lesser state funeral upon his death in 1951. On July 7, 1956, on the twentieth anniversary of Chicherin's death, *Izvestia* stated that "the Soviet public cherishes the memory of G. V. Chicherin, an outstanding Soviet diplomat," in a belated tribute to his services.[43]

[43] Chicherin's death in 1936 went virtually unnoticed. His ashes were placed in The Kremlin Wall, however, and the first edition of the Soviet *Diplomatic Dictionary* described him as a "gifted diplomat" during the period of the Civil War and foreign intervention. *Diplomaticheskii Slovar*, Vol. II, edited by A. Y. Vyshinsky (Moscow, 1948), p. 663. After the 20th Party Congress in 1956, Chicherin was rehabilitated, beginning with an *Izvestia* observance of the 20th anniversary of his death, in which it was said that "The Soviet public cherishes the memory of G. V. Chicherin, an outstanding Soviet diplomat." *Izvestia*, July 7, 1956. *Cf*. Chicherin's entry in the second edition of the *Diplomatic Dictionary* for a long, highly favorable account of his tenure as Foreign Commissar. *Diplomaticheskii Slovar*, three volumes, edited by A. A. Gromyko, S. A. Golunskii and V. M. Khvostov (Moscow, 1960–64), III, pp. 472–473. On the other hand, Vyshinsky receives a brief entry, curt and dry (Vol. I, p. 328), and Molotov does not even merit an entry!

V. The Destruction of the First Soviet Diplomatic Service: The Litvinov Era

Litvinov inherited the superb diplomatic instrument fashioned by Chicherin virtually intact, but it was his unenviable misfortune to preside over the liquidation of his magnificent band of non-conformists. Kamenev left the diplomatic service but Krestinsky, Karakhan, Kollontai, Troyanovsky, Sokolnikov, and others decided to make a career of diplomacy and together with other lesser figures they developed from a group of amateurs into a remarkably competent corps of diplomats. Furthermore, by 1936, the diplomatic service had already developed traditions, an esprit de corps, and a notable record of continuity.

The diplomatic service, however, was a veritable nest of anti-Stalinist sentiment, if not intrigue, and many indiscreetly voiced their sentiments to their younger subordinates and to foreigners. Stalin had his network of spies in the Foreign Commissariat and he kept abreast of all rumors, real and fabricated, that circulated among Soviet diplomats. It was inevitable that the diplomatic service would be caught in the mechanisms of the great purge, since it was vulnerable on a number of counts.

Disaster, however, came to the Foreign Ministry somewhat later than to the Party and other departments of government, but when it struck, it wiped out the service virtually overnight. There were three main reasons for the delay: (1) many of the diplomats were stationed abroad and it required considerable ingenuity and expenditure of time, to say nothing of trickery and cajolery, to lure them back home; (2) the diplomatic service was isolated and remote from the center of power and constituted little immediate danger to Stalin's authority unlike his rivals in the Party and other government officers; and (3) Soviet diplomacy was in a condition of extreme delicacy since Soviet Foreign Policy was undergoing a radical reorientation and it was imperative that any surgery be carried out without unduly complicating or disrupting relations with countries upon which the new security interests of the Soviet Union depended.

In 1933 Litvinov's Collegium in the Commissariat was made up of three Deputy Foreign Commissars who were prominent members of the opposition and one Bulgarian who had found a home in the Narkomindel. By 1938 all four had vanished. Sokolnikov was the first of Litvinov's deputies to be removed. In 1934 he was shifted to the Commissariat of Finance and arrested in 1936 on charges of treason. He appeared as one of the principal defendants in the second public trial in January 1937.[44] Simultaneously with Sokolnikov's trial, Litvinov's second deputy, Krestinsky, was transferred to the Commissariat of Justice. His third deputy Karakhan had been appointed ambassador to Turkey in 1936, but was recalled in June 1937, and was tried, and executed in camera in December. Almost at the same time Krestinsky was arrested

[44] Cf. *In The Case of The Anti-Soviet Trotskyite Centre* (Moscow, 1937), pp. 146–167, 551–555.

and appeared as a spectacular performer in the third public trial held in March 1938 along with another former Deputy Foreign Commissar, Rakovsky.[45] The fourth member of Litvinov's Collegium, Stomonyakov (the Bulgarian), simply vanished in the same year.

With the removal of Krestinsky in 1937, a veteran Secret Police official, Vasily Korzhenko was installed in Krestinsky's former villa and placed in charge of personnel. According to his daughter's testimony, Korzhenko "was not concerned with diplomacy but had absolute power over Foreign Office employees from cipher clerks to ambassadors . . . not only in Moscow but throughout the world. . . . Father's job was to see that everyone kept the party line. If they made one slip, he put through an order for their immediate recall and banishment."[46]

To maintain the orderly flow of diplomatic routine, V. P. Potemkin, a former professor who had joined the Foreign Service and an ex-Menshevik, was appointed Litvinov's new First Deputy Commissar on April 28, 1937. Potemkin's main functions were to deal with foreign envoys in Moscow when Litvinov was abroad, which was nearly always, and, when Litvinov was in Moscow, to tour Europe's major capitals to keep Stalin's diplomatic fences in a reasonable state of repair. Both appeared unconcerned with the slaughter of their subordinates and between the two of them they virtually carried the burdens of the Soviet Foreign Commissariat until 1939. When Litvinov was queried by foreigners about the convulsions in his Commissariat, he would shrug his shoulders and nervously sputter that even he could not always understand the behavior of his government.[47]

Under Korzhenko's efficient direction, the Narkomindel was converted to an abattoir as virtually the entire diplomatic establishment was wiped out between 1937 and 1939. Most of Russia's major diplomats were systematically recalled in 1937 in carefully prepared stages, on the pretext of routine business, reassignment, or the promise of higher positions, even at the ministerial level. They were, as a rule, housed in a luxurious hotel situated on the outskirts of Moscow, ostensibly awaiting reassignment, but in reality being unsuspectingly readied for the execution chambers. Almost all of Litvinov's ambassadors and ministers were either executed or imprisoned. Litvinov himself became a barrier to Soviet foreign policy objectives and was swept out in May

[45] Cf. In The Case of The Anti-Soviet "Bloc of Rights and Trotskyites" (Moscow, 1938), pp. 152–157 and 730–735 (Krestinsky); and pp. 287–313 and 758 ff. (Rakovsky).

[46] Nora Murry, I Spied for Stalin (London), p. 83; and also Alexander Barmine, One Who Survived (New York, Putnam, 1948), p. 8.

[47] Cf. Hilger and Meyer, op. cit., p. 113. Litvinov's reasons for survival remain obscure. Even his friend Ilya Ehrenburg was bewildered: "Why, having put to death almost all of Litvinov's assistants, did he [Stalin] not have the obstreperous Maxim himself shot? It is extremely puzzling, certainly Litvinov expected a different ending. From 1937 till his last illness he kept a revolver on his bedside table because, if there were to be a ring at the door in the night, he was not going to wait for what came after." Ehrenburg, op. cit., p. 277.

1939.[48] Korzhenko, the purger, beholden to a disgraced Secret Police chief, was himself purged and thrown into Lubyanka Prison by Molotov after he assumed control of the Commissariat.[49]

Molotov carried the purge to its logical conclusions. Within two months what had been left of the residual staff inherited from Litvinov had been replaced. "With only few exceptions," reported the American Embassy in Moscow, "almost the entire staff of the Commissariat has changed since Molotov assumed the functions of the Commissariat for Foreign Affairs. . . . Among the minor officials of the Foreign Office at least 90% have been replaced since the appointment of Molotov."[50]

A few survivors remained to preserve a semblance of continuity and to aid Molotov in reconstituting the shattered diplomatic service. The survivors were a faithful microcosm of the prewar diplomatic service itself. Aside from Litvinov and Potemkin, there were Ivan Maisky, Yakov Suritz, S. I. Kavtaradze, the durable aristocrat Madame Kollontai, Boris Stein, and Konstantin Umansky. Most of them were both ex-Mensheviks and Jews. Others, such as Troyanovsky, also survived but were employed as inconspicuous consultants to the Foreign Ministry. Boris Stein, a veteran diplomat, who had served as chief of various departments and ambassador to a number of important countries, was also relegated to relatively insignificant posts, although he was to become a permanent ornament appended to numerous postwar Soviet diplomatic delegations. All except Maisky, Troyanovsky, and Stein were dead by 1960 — of natural causes. Some, such as Maisky, were to suffer again after 1948, but all were given biographical entries in the *Diplomatic Dictionary* issued in 1948 and 1950.[51]

With the liquidation of Chicherin's extraordinary aggregation of brilliant but ideologically errant talent, it was necessary to erect a new diplomatic establishment upon the ruins of the old. Meanwhile Soviet diplomacy had to continue without faltering. Many important posts in the central office and in missions abroad remained unfilled for a long time. Interim appointments were pressed into service as the diplomatic establishment was being reconstituted. The surviving veterans were dispatched to important embassies abroad as experienced adminis-

---

[48] Murry, *op. cit.*, p. 83. According to Ehrenburg: "At the meeting where Litvinov was attacked and expelled from the Central Committee he indignantly asked Stalin: 'Does this mean that you regard me as an enemy of the people?' As he was leaving the hall Stalin took his pipe out of his mouth and said: 'No we don't.'" Litvinov was not arrested after his removal as Foreign Commissar, but according to Ehrenburg's account: "Stalin removed him from all functions in order to destroy him by enforced inaction. However, this did not quite work out at the time. When Hitler attacked the Soviet Union, Stalin sent for Litvinov, shook hands with him in a friendly manner and appointed him to Washington." Ehrenburg, *op. cit.*, pp. 278–279.

[49] *Ibid.* p. 129.

[50] *The Soviet Union, 1933–1939*, p. 772.

[51] Maisky has published his memoirs, cf. note 1, *supra*. In 1966, Maisky signed a petition with twenty-six other well-known Soviet intellectuals protesting the possible rehabilitation of Stalin by the 23rd Party Congress, Cf. *The New York Times*, March 21, 1966.

trators were borrowed from other departments of government to take up key positions at home and abroad. Many new diplomats were borrowed from Beriya's Secret Police. Potemkin, a veteran diplomatic historian, was retained for window dressing since he was the only top official with any direct knowledge or experience with diplomacy. In May 1939, Molotov appointed S. A. Lozovsky, a veteran Comintern functionary and a leading figure in the defunct Profintern, to be a Deputy Commissar. Lozovsky was also a member of the Foreign Relations Committee of the Council of Nationalities in the Supreme Soviet. V. K. Dekanozov, one of Beriya's fellow Georgian Chekists, was also appointed a Deputy Commissar at the same time. He was sent briefly to Germany as ambassador but returned to resume his duties in the central office shortly thereafter. Molotov's third new deputy was Stalin's prosecutor at the purge trials, Andrei Vyshinsky, appointed in 1940, who became the chief administrator of the Commissariat since Molotov was still chairman of the Council of People's Commissars. Dekanozov was given authority over personnel and security matters as Lozovsky, who became the chief spokesman for the Commissariat, was charged with coordinating the work of the Narkomindel with that of the Comintern.[52]

VI. The Creation of the Second Soviet Diplomatic Service: The Molotov Era

Stalin's purges created a tremendous shortage of experienced administrative talent in the Soviet Union and the priorities of the Foreign Commissariat were relatively low. Consequently the Narkomindel recruited its new personnel from among the young and inexperienced. In the language of an American Embassy official, the vacancies left in the diplomatic service by the purge "without exception have been taken by unknown individuals who have no experience in matters dealing with foreign affairs, no knowledge of foreign languages nor any contacts in general with foreigners or foreign countries."[53] The same contemptuous language was used by foreign diplomats to disparage the diplomatic talents of the new Foreign Commissar as well. According to a report of the British Ambassador, Sir William Seeds, Molotov "knows, or rather speaks, no foreign language, has so far as I am aware, never been outside Russia, and has no practical experience in the conduct of foreign affairs or knowledge of the psychology of foreign countries."[54] The apparent ineptitude and ignorance of the new Foreign Commissar and his subordinates became the scandal of the foreign diplomatic colony in Moscow. Of course, these "unknown individuals" are now well known to the outside world — they are the Gromykos, Maliks, Zorins, Zarubins, and Sobolevs who now form the top echelon of the Soviet

---

[52] *The Soviet Union, 1933–1939*, p. 773.

[53] *Ibid.* p. 772.

[54] *Documents on British Foreign Policy 1919–1939*, Third Series, Volume V. (London, 1952), pp. 544–545. Seeds further lamented that "It is my fate to deal with a man totally ignorant of foreign affairs." *Ibid.*, p. 772.

career service. The Soviet diplomatic service today is second to none in its professional competence, and Molotov subsequently proved to be one of the outstanding diplomatists of all time, according to the testimony of his most implacable antagonists.[55] This is not the first time, nor will it be the last, that foreign observers have underrated the abilities of Soviet personalities by confusing anonymity with ignorance and technical inexperience with incompetence. Similar appraisals were made of Stalin in the twenties and of Khrushchev only a few years ago.

Among the recruits of this period, about a dozen had achieved sufficient prominence to merit biographical entries in the first edition of the *Diplomatic Dictionary*, edited by A. Y. Vyshinsky and S. A. Lozovsky. From these official biographies and those found elsewhere, there emerges a clear prototype of the topflight Soviet career diplomat, who differs from his unfortunate predecessor almost as much as his new colleagues from the Party apparatus differ from him.[56] Born around 1905 (the oldest in 1900 and the youngest in 1912) of working class or peasant parents and of Great Russian ethnic origin, his early childhood was spent under the Tsars and is shrouded in obscurity. He became active in Communist youth organizations after the Revolution and because he demonstrated ideological reliability and genuine native ability he was given an education in a provincial university, industrial institute for workers, or in a military academy. Before entering the Foreign Service, he prepared himself for a career in economics, journalism, teaching, law, engineering, industrial management, or the military. He had never been abroad and had little knowledge of the outside world and foreign languages as was accurately reported by the foreign embassies.

[55] Apparently Molotov's abilities were seriously underrated, if subsequent evaluations by his diplomatic antagonists are any guide. Winston Churchill's appraisal of Molotov, in whom he perceived a "remarkable skill in duplicity," is at once the most trenchant and discerning tribute: "A man of outstanding ability and cold-blooded ruthlessness . . . his cannon-ball head, black mustache, and comprehending eyes, his slab face, his verbal adroitness and imperturbable demeanor were appropriate manifestations of his qualities and skill. He was above all men fitted to be the agent and instrument of . . . an incalculable machine." *Cf.* C. L. Sulzberger's characterizations in *The New York Times*, January 11, 1956. Former Secretary of State James Byrnes, a nimble operator in American domestic politics, grudgingly conceded that he was hopelessly outmatched by Molotov's superior maneuverability in international politics, and complained with bitter admiration of Molotov's deadly virtues — maddening patience, tireless energy, annoying precision, unctuous innocence. James Byrnes, *Speaking Frankly* (New York, Harper, 1947) pp. 277–279. And even before he became Secretary of State, the late John Foster Dulles conceded with obvious but reluctant admiration: "I have seen in action all of the great international statesmen of this century and I have never seen such personal diplomatic skill at so high a degree of perfection as Mr. Molotov's." John Foster Dulles, *War Or Peace* (New York, Macmillan, 1950). *Cf.* V. V. Aspaturian, "Mr. Molotov Nears The End of The Road," *Reporter*, April 5, 1956.

[56] The "prototype" is a composite characterization based upon the biographies and careers of the following Soviet professional diplomats: A. A. Gromyko, Ya. A. Malik, V. A. Zorin, G. N. Zarubin, F. T. Gusev, G. M. Pushkin, A. Y. Bogomolov, V. Z. Lebedev, A. I. Lavrentev, A. A. Lavrishchev, K. V. Novikov, A. A. Sobolev, V. Y. Semyonov, B. F. Podtserob, S. A. Vinogradov, among others, all of whom belong to the same vintage period.

His social and political profile did not materially deviate from that of his contemporaries who were taking their chances in the Party apparatus, the State bureaucracy, and industrial management. But from the time he entered into the diplomatic establishment, he was shaped by a mold like no other in the Soviet system, and the end-product was substantially different a decade later than that fashioned by other institutions in the Soviet order.

During the same period when his new colleagues from the Party apparatus were entering into the charmed circle of Soviet power, our typical diplomat joined the Communist Party and was recruited almost immediately into the foreign service. The Secret Police played an important role in his selection, since veteran N.K.V.D. officials were in charge of personnel during this phase of his career. His opportunities in the diplomatic service were unusually varied and bright, with rapid promotion virtually predetermined with almost indecent haste. After a short indoctrination and orientation at the Institute of Diplomatic and Consular Workers, he was placed in charge of a desk or made an assistant to a geographical or functional department chief, whom he was predestined to supplant in less than a year. He assiduously studied a foreign language and quickly made up for this deficiency in his technical qualifications. After a brief sojourn as a *chinovnik* in the central office, he was dispatched to an important mission abroad to serve his apprenticeship under the man he was slated to displace. Soon after his entry into the service, as if to symbolize the passing of the old diplomatic service and the birth of the new, the revolutionary doctrine of diplomatic equality was jettisoned and the ranks of ambassador, Minister, and *Charge d'Affaires* were reestablished by decree of the Presidium on May 9, 1941.[57]

Within four or five years after his entry into the services, our young diplomat was elevated to the rank of ambassador or Minister to an important capital in place of the aging survivors of the Chicherin-Litvinov era or the strictly interim appointments made after the purge. The year 1943 was a key year in the career of the typical Soviet career diplomat: Gromyko at age 33 replaced Litvinov in Washington, Gusev at 38 replaced Maisky in London, and Malik at 37 was appointed ambassador to Japan.[58] As if to dramatically symbolize the completed

[57] Full text of the decree of May 9, 1941 has been reprinted in Modzhoryan and Sobakin, II, *op. cit.*, pp. 5–6.

[58] Bogomolov, age 43, was appointed ambassador to France in 1943; Zarubin at age 44 was appointed to Ottawa in 1944; Lavrentev, age 37, was appointed envoy to Rumania in 1941; Lebedev, at age 43, was assigned as envoy to the Governments-in-Exile in London, in 1943; and Zorin was appointed to Prague at age 43, in 1945. Apparently, the Soviet victory at Stalingrad was a turning point not only in the War but also in Soviet relations with its allies. Stalin recalled the remaining Western-oriented cosmopolitan diplomats, whom he may have suspected of being insufficiently ruthless. Litvinov and Maisky were unexpectedly and simultaneously recalled from Washington and London against their wishes. According to Ehrenberg: "In 1943, after the Stalingrad victory, Litvinov was recalled to Moscow [and replaced with Gromyko]. He still held the post of Deputy Minister of Foreign Affairs, but was given work of little importance. In 1947 he was pensioned off,

metamorphosis of the diplomatic service, 1943 was also the year in which the full complement of diplomatic ranks was restored by a Decree (*Ukaz*) of the Presidium on May 28th, and Molotov's new diplomats were draped in gilt-edge uniforms, frankly patterned along military lines, strangely reminiscent of the diplomacy of the aristocratic epoch.[59] With jewelled dirks at the ready, Soviet diplomats in full dress uniform carried star-studded shoulder boards that conspicuously displayed their rank: Molotov sported the single large gold star equivalent to that of a Marshal of the Soviet Union, as his deputies and ambassadors were invested with the slightly smaller one ("35 millimeters," according to the fastidious provisions of another official decree) of the lesser Marshals. Ministers carried the four small stars of an army general and so on down the line for a total of eleven distinct grades.[60] It

---

not at his own request." Ehrenburg, *op. cit.*, pp. 278–279. And according to Maisky's *Memoirs*, he, Maisky, was unexpectedly recalled after Stalingrad because he thought Stalin wanted to express his displeasure with the British over the Second Front problem: "The Soviet Government clearly wanted to indicate its dissatisfaction to the British Government by recalling me from London 'for consultations' — the most customary form in diplomatic practice on such occasions" (p. 365). But upon his arrival in Moscow, where he brought bad news to the Soviet leadership concerning the Second Front, he asked Stalin to receive him, "but he did not find it necessary to talk to me." (p. 378). He had a reunion with Litvinov, an old friend with whom he shared exile in Britain before 1917, and took part in minor planning conferences at the Foreign Commissariat as he awaited further instructions. On August 1, 1943, he was called in by Molotov to be curtly informed of his new assignment: " 'You have been appointed Deputy People's Commissar of Foreign Affairs. . . . You will be in charge of the problem of reparations. . . . Are you satisfied with your new appointment?' " (p. 381). It is clear from Maisky's account that he was stunned and he requested to be allowed to return to London to gather his wife, make farewells, collect his belongings, and reassure friends concerning his fate: "I should like to return now for a short time to London, collect my wife for whom in wartime conditions it will not be an easy journey to Moscow, and above all prevent the appearance around my name of gossip which may be quite undesirable and unprofitable for us' " (p. 381). Maisky then reveals the tremendous anxiety and uncertainty that haunted the surviving diplomats of the period: "In the years of the great-man cult there were many cases when Soviet Ambassadors were unexpectedly recalled to Moscow and then vanished without a trace — either into the grave or some camp. Therefore in the West there had been created the impression that, once a Soviet Ambassador was recalled to Moscow, some unpleasantness or other was awaiting him at home. I wanted to protect myself against this kind of interpretation and suspicion." (p. 381). Apparently after consultation with Stalin, Molotov informed Maisky on the next day that he would be granted not more than five days to wind up his affairs in London.

[59] Full text of The Decree of May 28, 1943, can be found in Modzhoryan and Sobakin, II, p. 6. For technical details concerning ranks, Cf. Chapter 17.

[60] The uniforms were apparently authorized by a Decree (*Postanovleniya*) of the Sovnarkom on June 14, 1943, since this date is erroneously given as the date of the Decree (*Ukaz*) establishing the seven diplomatic ranks by V. P. Potemkin, editor *Istoriya Diplomatii*, Vol. III. (Moscow, 1945), p. 779. The same source gives May 28, 1943 as the date for the decision on the uniforms, which is the correct date for the *Ukaz* on ranks. I assume that the dates were erroneously transposed.

was thus only appropriate that Stalin, who measured politics in military terms, proposed a toast to Molotov at a banquet for Marshals and Generals reminding them not to "forget that a good foreign policy sometimes counts far more than two or three armies at the front. To our Vyacheslav!"[61]

The war years afforded the new Soviet diplomats extraordinary opportunities for gaining concentrated diplomatic experience; for comparatively young men, they were assigned unusually important diplomatic responsibilities. At the end of the war, when they had been sufficiently trained to assume full control of the diplomatic apparatus under Molotov's guiding hand, another purge, more genteel and restricted, of the Foreign Ministry was conducted. Nearly 400 workers in the Foreign Commissariat were awarded medals by the Presidium of the Supreme Soviet after the war in 1945. Molotov, Vyshinsky, and eight new professionals, including Gromyko, Malik, Zorin, Gusev, and Vinogradov, received the Order of Lenin, as the survivors of the prewar service, of which there were barely a half-dozen, received lesser awards (a conspicuous gesture of humiliation).[62] Most of the interim appointments had been dropped from the diplomatic service during the war; now it was the turn of the central apparatus to be purged. When Litvinov, Maisky, and Kavtaradze were displaced in foreign capitals by their apprentices, they had been appointed Deputy Foreign Commissars in Moscow. The new career diplomats, after the war, were now ready to supplant them in the home office as well. Maisky was dropped as a Deputy Minister in March 1946, Lozovsky followed on July 26th, and Litvinov was removed on August 22. Their places were assumed by Gusev and Malik on the day of Litvinov's removal; Gromyko joined as a Deputy Minister in December. Dekanozov was sent back into the obscurity of the Secret Police early in 1947 and his place was taken by Bogomolov. Zorin joined as a Deputy Minister in December of the same year. The final threads of continuity with the prewar service were thus irrevocably severed. Only Vyshinsky was retained of the post-purge appointees; Stalin's old crony Kavtaradze lingered on for a few additional years before his retirement. The year 1947 thus marks the completed transition from the old service to the new. From 1947 until Stalin's death all top appointments in the diplomatic establishment at home and abroad were reserved exclusively for the career professionals, as Molotov and Vyshinsky remained the only "politicals," although by then they, too, could legitimately be classified as professional diplomats.

The fate of those relieved after the war was almost uniformly tragic. Lozovsky was reassigned to editorial and diplomatic work, but

[61] *Pravda,* May 25, 1945.
[62] Presidium Decree (*Ukaz*) of November 5, 1945, *Vedomosti Verkhovnovo Soveta SSSR,* No. 78, 1945. Maxim Litvinov, Ivan Maisky, Yakov Suritz, and Boris Stein, for example, received the much less coveted "Order of The Red Banner," which is three orders down from the Order of Lenin, as many of the new young diplomats received the more prestigious "Order of the Patriotic War," Classes I and II. It may have been only coincidental, but the four veteran prewar diplomats cited above were all Jews.

mysteriously vanished after 1948 at the height of the vicious anti-cosmopolitan campaign. Soon after Volume One of the *Diplomatic Dictionary* appeared, listing him along with Vyskinsky as a chief editor. Although he was a co-editor of the first volume, by the time of the appearance of the second volume in 1950 he did not merit a biographical entry. Volume 51 of the *Bolshaya Sovetskaya Entsiklopediya,* which in some respects is a Soviet "Who's Who" of the purged and rehabilitated, gives him a short sketch and dates his death at 1948 without explanation.

Dekanozov once again emerged from obscurity after Stalin's death as one of Beriya's chief henchmen and paid for his life in 1954 for his part in Beriya's abortive bid for power. Kollontai, Suritz, Litvinov, and Potemkim are now dead — presumably of natural causes. Volume 51 of the *Bolshaya* reported Maisky as still alive and, as Troyanovsky, whose son Oleg was one of the principal English interpreters for the Ministry, was listed as a consultant to the Ministry in a professional capacity. Boris Stein functioned as a consultant with the rank of ambassador and was an invariable and invaluable adornment to many Soviet diplomatic delegations before his retirement from the service.

VII. The Soviet Career Diplomat

One of the interesting questions raised by the history of the Soviet diplomatic service is whether a career diplomatic service was at all possible in a totalitarian state. In non-totalitarian societies, career officials are generally insulated and kept out of internal political rivalries and manage to survive the changing fortunes of political parties, revolutionary movements, cliques, and factions. They generally place themselves at the disposal of those who exercise political power as impersonal instruments of their will. They conceive their function to be the implementation of policy, not its formulation. All professional diplomats, in democratic and non-democratic countries, are painfully aware that a certain quota of plush or important diplomatic assignments are reserved for political appointees. It is traditional for the Foreign Minister and his top assistants to be "political" rather than professional, and this is again generally true regardless of ideologies or forms of government. In both Fascist Italy and Nazi Germany, the professional diplomatic service was carried over virtually intact, although it was eyed with wholesome suspicion — and for good reason.

The political environment of the Soviet career services, however, is unique. It stems from the Marxist-Leninist conviction that the permanent bureaucracy of the state machine is the most implacable and ideologically committed institution of the given political order. The political neutrality of the bureaucracy is considered to be a sham; hence in the Soviet scheme, the Soviet bureaucracy must meet the canons of the Marxist-Leninist dogma. By definition, Soviet diplomats are ideologically and politically committed; they cannot and do not stand above the political battle, but are invariably and inexorably drawn into its vortex. For this reason, even the career diplomats of the Soviet service are to some extent assimilated into the decision-making structure of the regime at the political level rather than being confined to the administrative level alone, which is the usual procedure in other systems.

Each given social and political order defines the relationship between the State bureaucracy and the political process in its own way, and it would be a mistake to deny that a career service is possible in such a system as the Soviet. A fundamental distinction exists between the diplomats in the Soviet service who have devoted most of their mature years to diplomacy and those who have entered laterally from the Party apparatus and the State bureaucracy. The first category constitutes the "professionals"; the second, for want of a better term, is made up of "politicals," and their status approximates that of the political appointees in other countries. Just as some of the most important diplomatic posts in the United States foreign service — London, Paris, Bonn, Rome, etc. — are often reserved for political appointees, so are some of the key diplomatic assignments in the Soviet service now given over to politicals rather than professionals.

The professional and career status of the Soviet diplomatic service is beyond dispute. The higher echelons of the Soviet diplomatic establishment no longer fit the patronizing characterization of the American Embassy in 1939 that "the new incumbents without exception appear to be persons with no experience in matters relating to foreign affairs . . . who have had no contact with foreigners or foreign countries and who consequently in their dealings with foreign representatives here, will, knowing no other, reflect only the orthodox Soviet point of view unencumbered by any knowledge or experience of life abroad."[63] In less than two decades of service as a diplomat, the Soviet top-flight professional has accumulated more high level diplomatic experience and has assumed greater responsibilities for longer periods of time than most of his counterparts in other countries, primarily because he was catapulted to ambassadorial and ministerial status as a comparatively young man. Career officials in other countries who have patiently waited to become ambassadors and ministers in their fifties and sixties find that their Soviet counterparts in the diplomatic arena have functioned at that level for an average of more than a decade and a half and still have many years of service before retirement. As a group, the top level of the Soviet diplomatic service exhibits more concentrated diplomatic experience at consistently high levels of responsibility and sustained over a longer period of years than any other corresponding assemblage in the world — an extremely significant factor that is too often ignored.

Since 1943, the typical Soviet high-ranking diplomat has served in several important world capitals, has participated in many important international conferences, has put in a tour at the United Nations, and has served at least once or twice in Moscow as a Deputy Minister of Foreign Affairs. In some cases, he has gained entry into the country's central decision-making organs — an opportunity systematically and

[63] *The Soviet Union, 1933–1939*, p. 772.

deliberately denied to the career diplomats of other countries. The Soviet Foreign Minister himself, since 1957, has been a career diplomat.

The very factors that mark the high professional competence of the Soviet diplomat — wide experience and residence in the outside world — tend to make him suspect in the eyes of his political superiors in Moscow. Of course, this suspicion of the diplomatic service is by no means restricted only to the Soviet system, and diplomats of all countries, for similar reasons, are generally viewed with varying degrees of suspicion by politicians. Although the Soviet diplomat can hardly be accused of cosmopolitanism, his long exposure to the material temptations and intellectual atmosphere of the outside world would tend to make his political superiors slightly dubious of his ideological stability. In this lies the principal dilemma of the career diplomat.

The formative years of a Soviet career diplomat were spent in the atmosphere of suffocating conformity characteristic of the late Stalinist era, and to some degree he still carries the birthmarks of that period. Although he may be the Soviet version of the "organization man" and is ready and willing to express "the orthodox Soviet point of view," since Stalin's death he has found this excruciatingly elusive. If his ideological outlook was shaped by Stalinism, his personality reflects that of Molotov. The career diplomat of this vintage is generally a conformist who frowns upon frivolity, is inclined to be conservative and cautious in manner, somber in outlook, often both sour and dour in expression; he rarely smiles when working and virtually never relaxes. He expresses no personal opinions, keeps his political convictions to himself, and unlike the diplomats of the Chicherin-Litvonov era, who were often unable to resist the temptations of political intrigue and frequently failed to keep their irrepressible revolutionary enthusiasm in check when abroad as diplomats, he has managed to keep his political skirts clean and displays a fastidious passion for the requirements of protocol. He scrupulously avoids compromising his diplomatic status by engaging in "impermissible activities," such as cavorting with indigenous Communists or directing espionage and propaganda operations, although he may "innocently" look the other way as his subordinates use his embassy as a cover for both subversive and spying activities. He cultivates few personal friendships with foreigners, official or private, keeps no diary, and has no intention of writing his memoirs, and although not effusively sociable, and rarely loquacious, he can easily turn on the charm upon signal from Moscow.[64]

In short, the diplomatic house that Molotov built was largely shaped in his own image, and although a new purge in the Stalinist sense did not take place, the career diplomats could have hardly viewed with equanimity the influx of Party bureaucrats into the service, who ousted them from Communist capitals and threatened to pluck the choicest plums in other diplomatic appointments. To what extent the new appointments constituted a suspicious reflection on the career

[64] This also is no longer true, particularly of the younger crop of diplomats, recruited after the war and especially after Stalin's death.

servants raised and nurtured by Molotov and to what degree they simply represented temporary way stations for Party bureaucrats bruised in the Kremlin battles on their way to political obscurity was not clear, but it does appear that both purposes were served simultaneously — an intricate technique employed more than once in the past.

The Soviet diplomatic service is unquestionably a career service. It is difficult to determine at this time, however, whether its career status is predicated upon an undeviating orthodoxy to which the diplomats can accommodate. The real question is whether the ideological orthodoxy demanded of them is to the general Marxist-Leninist doctrine or whether they must choose from amongst the factional interpretations and applications of the doctrine. If, for example, the diplomats have an ideological commitment to a particular orthodoxy that they find as difficult to shed, as did their unfortunate predecessors, or if they are unable to reject the foreign policy objectives that they were charged with executing during the Stalinist period, then they can look forward to a grim future. If, on the other hand, they can avoid involvement in the factional schisms that might arise in the Kremlin and assume an attitude of neutrality, not toward the general Marxist-Leninist doctrine, but simply to the factional and doctrinal disputes, and willingly prostrate themselves before any faction that assumes power and carries out its directives with neither hesitation nor reservation, then the Soviet diplomatic service would be assured of the stability and continuity that characterize the diplomatic establishments found in other countries.

It was not entirely certain that the diplomats would be permitted to remain uninvolved in the internal struggle for power. Their fate hinged upon the degree of personal loyalty and obligation that Molotov demanded or inspired in his subordinates and the tenacity with which they held it, or the Soviet leaders thought they held it. In view of the fact that one of the most serious charges leveled against Molotov when he was ousted from the Presidium was that he used the Foreign Ministry and its missions abroad as instruments to subvert and sabotage the policies of the Party in favor of his own, the future looked ominous for the career people, since it was not clear whether they were willing tools, as Beriya's subordinates in the Ministry of Internal Affairs, or whether they were simply carrying out, without question, the instructions of their superior. In any event, these particular accusations leveled against Molotov illustrate the particular hazards of the Soviet career diplomats who may be charged with serious deliquencies for failing to distinguish between the orthodoxy of the Party line and the personal policies of their constitutional superior. Under these circumstances they are confronted with the awful choice of controvening the directives of the Party or willfully disobeying the instructions of the Foreign Minister. With the appointment of a career servant as Foreign Minister this dilemma, however, is not likely to occur. As Khrushchev bluntly told Averell Harriman in the presence of Gromyko, "Gromyko will do exactly what he is instructed to do or will be removed from office."

The safest refuge of the career professional remains the expressionless shell within which are sealed his innermost thoughts, not only from the outside world but from his superiors as well. On more than one occasion, the depressing composure of the Soviet diplomat, impervious alike to provocation, ridicule, or blandishment, has exasperated and unnerved even his superiors. Former Secretary of State Edward R. Stettinius has written that "Stalin teased Gusev for always being glum and for never cracking a smile,"[65] as more than ten years later Premier Bulganin ridiculed Gromyko as "quite a nice chap, but one of those fellows who will sit around all evening at a party saying only two words and the next day will say 'What a wonderful time we all had last night.' "[66] And in 1959, Nikita Khrushchev told Averell Harriman in Gromyko's presence that he planned to send Gromyko to the Foreign Minister's Conference in Geneva and that if he were told to pull down his pants and sit on a block of ice he would do so until he was told to rise — otherwise he would lose his job. Gromyko's expressionless face failed to betray any emotion.

It is ironic, but what appears to be one of the most effective and irritating assets of the Soviet career servant — his legendary imperturbability in the face of provocation — may be the very thing that will save him from the fate of his pre-war predecessor. Khrushchev, it should be noted, lost his job in 1964, but Gromyko survived to retain his.

POSTSCRIPT: THE SOVIET DIPLOMATIC SERVICE SINCE 1960

The main trends discerned in the development of the Soviet diplomatic service during the first decade after Stalin's death have not only continued into the second decade but have evolved along more sophisticated lines and appear to have been institutionalized into a distinctive division of diplomatic labor that has shaped the recruitment, assignment, and rotational pattern of diplomatic personnel. At the highest level of the diplomatic service, three distinct groups of Soviet diplomats have emerged, distinguished from one another by training, career backgrounds, diplomatic assignments, and membership in central Party organs. These three groups are designated as follows: career diplomats (Group 1); political diplomats (Group 2); and Party diplomats (Group 3).

Tables 1, 2, and 3, respectively, name the principal individuals within each group and show their diplomatic as well as non-diplomatic assignments during the three decades from 1940 to 1970. As can be

---

[65] Edward R. Stettinius, Jr., *Roosevelt and The Russians* (New York, Doubleday, 1949), p. 221.

[66] *Time*, June 17, 1957. Political figures, irrespective of ideologies or political systems, seem to share common attitudes toward their professional diplomatic servants. Roosevelt and Churchill, and Hitler and Stalin periodically suspected the political perspectives and inner thoughts of their ambassadors, frequently betrayed annoyance and irritation at their demeanor, and were often put off by their personalities. The image of the professional diplomat as a cosmopolitan cookie pusher in striped pants is apparently widely held and pervasive among politicians of all varieties.

seen from the charts, virtually all of the top level diplomats in the service were born before 1915 and hence generational cleavages do not distinguish the three groups. Generational cleavages, however, are marked within the career service as a whole, with most of the dynamic and able young diplomats functioning as heads of missions to small countries, particularly in the Third World, and as second level diplomats in major capitals served by the career service. Some, as Dobrynin, Smirnovsky, and Troyanovsky, however, have invaded the domain of the aging career diplomats and this trend is likely to accelerate as attrition takes its toll.

These basic trends, however, have been seriously affected and in some instances even redirected by the tremendous expansion of the Soviet diplomatic service and the proliferation of new departments, agencies, and desks in the bureaucracy of the Soviet Foreign Ministry. This has been brought about as a result of four developments:

1. The diplomatic explosion occasioned by the decolonialization of the Colonial Empires and consequent proliferation of a host of new states. Thus, whereas the Soviet Union maintained diplomatic relations with only 55 states in 1955, which had risen to only 66 in 1959, by January 1965, diplomatic relations had been established with 95 countries. In 1968, the Soviet diplomatic list included 101 countries represented in Moscow, and the Soviet Union itself was represented abroad by 88 embassies, 3 non-resident ambassadors, and 1 legation.[67]

2. The continuing expansion of Soviet participation in the organs, agencies, and activities of International Organizations.

3. The emergence of the Soviet State as a Global Power in the sixties and its assumption of international obligations and commitments in various parts of the world. Summit conferences, disarmament conferences, and other types of conferences as well as expanded military and economic assistance to various countries all contributed to the expansion of the Soviet diplomatic service, which was also accompanied by the expansion of para-diplomatic structures in the military, cultural, Foreign Trade, and Economic Assistance areas.

4. The revival of the Soviet consular service, which by 1968 included consular relations with 19 countries in 30 locations.

Thus, by 1970, Foreign Minister Andrei Gromyko presided over a massive Ministry consisting of many thousands of bureaucrats, foreign service and supporting personnel, distributed throughout more than 90 countries and among dozens of bureaus, departments, and agencies of a perpetually proliferating and expanding bureaucratic empire. The central apparatus of the Foreign Ministry alone consisted of nearly 500 professional and technical personnel.

[67] Cf. *International Affairs*, No. 2, 1965, p. 107. For a description of the training received by fledgling Soviet diplomats before their assignments abroad, and for an inside view of the workings of a Soviet Embassy in underdeveloped countries, cf. Aleksander Kaznacheev, *Inside a Soviet Embassy* (New York, J. B. Lippincott Co., 1962).

Needless to say, this unprecedented growth and expansion of the Soviet diplomatic service has resulted in a greater degree of functional differentiation and geographic specialization commensurate with the widening ambit of Soviet commitments and obligations as a Global Power. In many respects, the Soviet diplomatic service more nearly resembles the diplomatic establishments of the West, most notably that of the United States, whereas in other respects it has retained some residual features of its former uniqueness and has also introduced some innovations peculiar to the diplomatic practices of Communist states.

An examination of the career lines of Soviet diplomatic personnel and the pattern of functional and geographic rotation and assignment of personnel reveals a singular division of labor involving five distinct areas of functional and geographic specialization and several self-contained patterns of rotation among them. The five functional and geographic areas of specialization and assignment are as follows:

1. Western countries;
2. Communist states;
3. Third World countries;
4. International organizations, conferences, and agencies; and
5. The central apparatus in the Foreign Ministry.

In addition, there are two other areas of specialization and assignment outside the diplomatic service that are also involved in the rotation of personnel involved in the diplomatic service: (1) other governmental departments; and (2) the Party apparatus.

These patterns of assignment and specialization have congealed with particular force since Stalin's death (1953), which remains as a major watershed in the postwar evolution of the Soviet diplomatic service. In order to place this evolution within the broadest possible perspective, however, this analysis of assignment and specialization begins in 1937 with the year in which the major Soviet senior career diplomats entered into the diplomatic service (the Gromyko generation). It excludes the hold-overs from the old diplomatic service, transitional "politicals" like Dekanosov, and two Foreign Ministers, V. M. Molotov and A. Y. Vyshinsky. At the other end, it omits the new emerging post-Gromyko generation of senior diplomats, such as Dobrynin.

The analysis is based upon the career patterns of 53 important Soviet diplomatic officials, including some who have since died, retired, or reassigned out of the diplomatic service. These 53 individuals can, in turn, be grouped into three distinct groups, each of which will be discussed separately before relating them to each other. These three groups are:

1. the career professional diplomats;
2. the "political" diplomats; and
3. the "Party functionary" diplomats or "Party diplomats."

1. *The Career Professional Diplomats* (Table 1)

This group consists of 21 diplomats, ranging in age from 58 to 70. All entered the diplomatic service between the years 1937 and 1941.

Two of this group (Zarubin and Pushkin) are dead, and about half-a-dozen are retired or no longer in the diplomatic service.[68] The most distinctive characteristic of this group is that it has exercised a virtual monopoly on ambassadorial assignments to major Western capitals and the United Nations. The typical rotational-assignment pattern has been from a major Western capital, to assignment in the Central Ministry, usually as a Deputy Foreign Minister, and assignment back to a major Western capital or to the United Nations as chief Soviet representative.

Before Stalin's death, however, a discernible degree of geographic specialization also characterized this group. Some diplomats, as Gromyko, Malik, and Zarubin, served only in Western and U.N. assignments, as assignments to Communist countries were virtually pre-empted by diplomats such as Pushkin, Sadchikov, Lavrentiev, and Lavrishchev, who also served in Middle Eastern and Central Ministry assignments, also as Deputy Foreign Ministers. Thus, before Stalin's death a second typical rotational-assignment pattern evolved. These were the two basic rotational patterns, although a few deviations from this routine did take place.

A closer examination of the foreign assignments of the twenty-one career diplomats yields a more precise breakdown of rotational patterns, which, however, does not vitiate the basic tripartite division of specialization: Western, Afro-Asian or Middle Eastern, and Communist countries (see Table 1a below). Of the twenty-one career diplomats included in Table 1, seven have served only in Western capitals, six have served in Western and Communist countries, although four of these are primarily Western specialists. Four of the twenty-one have served in Western and Afro-Asian states, and three have been posted to both Middle Eastern and Communist countries. Only Pushkin has served exclusively in Communist countries from this group.

After Stalin's death, a fundamental change was introduced into the structure of assignments. The professional diplomats specializing in the Eastern Europe-Middle Eastern pattern were either reassigned to minor posts in the bureaucracy or retired from the service, thus suggesting that they may have constituted a special corps of ideological diplomats reporting directly to Party organs rather than to the Foreign Ministry, or perhaps they were under the *de facto* administrative control of Beria and the Ministry of Internal Affairs. In any event, the sudden denouement of their diplomatic careers coincided with the death of Stalin and the elimination of Beriya.

Since Stalin's death, diplomatic assignments to Communist countries have been closed to senior professional diplomats, or rather, they have been virtually monopolized by the Political and Party Functionary diplomats, which assumed shape as distinct entities after 1953.

A second conspicuous characteristic of the Career Professional diplomats is the continuing paucity of their representation in the central organs of the Communist Party. Of the twenty-one diplomats in this

---

[68] Other career diplomats who fall into this category are K. V. Novikov, M. A. Kostyliev, N. V. Novikov, D. A. Zhukov, and N. V. Roshchin. They were omitted from the chart simply for convenience.

TABLE 1
CAREER PATTERNS OF SENIOR PROFESSIONAL DIPLOMATS

644

Career Category	Gromyko, A.A. (1909-) 1937*	Malik, Ya. (1906-) 1937	Zarubin, G.A. (1900-1958) 1940	Gusev, F.T. (1905-) 1937	Fedorenko, N.T. (1912-) 1939	Tsarapkin, S.K. (1906-) 1937	Semenov, V.S. (1911-) 1939	Zorin, V.A. (1902-) 1941	Bogomolov, A.Y. (1900-) 1939	Sobolev, A.A. (1903-) 1939	Soldatov, A.A. (1915-) 1941	Parnyushkin, A.Y. (1905-) 1939	Lebedev, V.V. (1900-) 1940	Vinogradov, S.A. (1907-1970) 1940	Kozyrev, S.P. (1907-) 1939	Podtserob, B.F. (1910-) 1937	Smirnov, A.A. (1905-) 1936	Lavrentev, A.I. (1904-) 1939	Lavrishchev, A.A. (1912-) 1939	Sadchikov, I.V. (1906-) 1939	Pushkin, G.M. (1909-1963) 1937
Party rank																					
Presidium-Politburo Mbr.																					
CC Member	56-																				
Cand. Member	52-56	52-61	52-58		66-71		66-	61-71			56-71	52-61		56-61		52-56					61-63
CAC Member		68-					56-66	56-61				41-52 61-71									56-61
Western countries																					
United Nations	46-48 48-52 68-				62-67			52-53 53-54 60-62		55-60											
U.S.A.	43-46		52-57									47-52									
United Kingdom	52-53	53-60	46-52	43-46							60-66										
France								65-	41-50					53-65							
Germany						66-	53-54	55-56									56-66				
Italy									54-57						57-66						
Japan		42-45			58-62																
Other Western			44-46	42-43 56-62		47-49 42-53							43-44 51-58			65-					
Other I.O.						49-54				46-50 54-55											
Afro-Asian																					
India																					
Iran																	41-43	53-56		46-53	
Turkey														40-48		54-57			48-54		

Algeria												67-70	50-53
Egypt													
Indonesia													
Other A-A													45-46
Communist countries													
Yugoslavia											49-50		
China					39-44 52-53	51-53				45-51			
Poland									52-53 40-41				
Czechoslovakia				45-47	52-54				53-				
Rumania													45-49
Hungary													
Bulgaria									39-40	40-44			
East Germany													49-52 53-58
Other Comm.					Cuba 68-				54-56				
Foreign Ministry													
Foreign Minister	57-												
First Dep. or Dep. FM.	49-52 53-57	46-53 60-68	58-	46-53	55-58	55-	47-55 56-65	51-52	60-64	66-68	66-	52-55 68-	46-49 51-53	52-53 59-63
Dept. Head or Dep. D.H.	42-43				48-49 53-55	38-47 54-65	41-42 54-55	42-43	49-51 53-54	48-60	45-49 53-57	42-52 57-65	43-44 53-57	45-48 53-55
Other		38-42	68-				41-42 57-	39-41	65-	41-48	58-	50-53 39-43	49-55 56-	56-
Non-diplomatic work													
Government													
Bureaucracy												54-	
Party									44-47 54-				
Apparatus													
Unknown													

*The first date refers to life span; second date refers to year of entrance into diplomatic service.

645

TABLE 1a
FOREIGN ASSIGNMENTS OF CAREER DIPLOMATS

1. Western[a]	2. Western-Communist[b]	3. Western-Afro-Asian[c]	4. Communist-Middle Eastern	5. Communist
G.omyko	Zorin[d]	Vinogradov	Lavrentev	Pushkin
Malik	Bogomolov[d]	Smirnov	Lavrishchev	
Zarubin	Sobolev[d]	Kozryev	Sadchikov	
Gusev	Soldatov[d]	Podtserob		
Fedorenko	Panyushkin			
Tsarapkin	Lebedev			
Semenev				

[a] Includes Japan.
[b] Includes Cuba and pre-Communist states in Eastern Europe.
[c] Includes Turkey.
[d] Primarily Western Specialists.

group, *only two* have been full members of the Party's Central Committee (Gromyko since 1956 and Zorin since 1961) and none have been admitted to the Party Presidium/Politburo or Party Secretariat.[69] Although Gromyko has now served continuously as Foreign Minister longer than any previous Soviet Foreign Minister, he is the only Foreign Minister since 1939 never to have served even at the alternate level in the Party Presidium/Politburo. It is even more strange that Gromyko has never been formally admitted to membership in the Presidium or inner Cabinet of the Council of Ministers, nor has he functioned as a Deputy Premier. This not only confirms the relatively low Party status of the professional diplomats, but also corresponds with practice in reference to the Defense Ministry. Since Marshal Zhukov's ouster, no Defense Minister (also a career professional) has been admitted to the Party's Politburo/Presidium or the Presidium of the Council of Ministers. Both positions, curiously enough, are considered to be essentially professional rather than political in status.

Six other career diplomats in this group have served at various intervals as candidate members of the Party's Central Committee, as four others have served on the Central Auditing (Inspection) Commission. But at the 23rd Communist Party Congress in 1966, only Gromyko and Zorin were elected full members of the Central Committee, only V. S. Semenov was appointed a candidate member, and Podtserob and Soldatov were the sole representatives in the Central Auditing Commission from the career diplomatic service. Malik, for some reason, was dropped as a candidate member in 1961, whereas Panyushkin (no longer in the service) retained his tenuous membership in the CAC to

[69] Gromyko emerges as the senior Party man in the career service, having been elected a candidate member in 1952 and promoted to full member in 1956. Thus, during the past decade, only one career diplomat (Zorin) has been elevated to full membership.

which he had been demoted from candidate membership in the Central Committee in 1961.

Membership or candidate membership in the Central Committee for a career diplomat appears to reflect his diplomatic assignment rather than his personal status in the Party. Thus, the Foreign Minister is almost automatically a full member, as all ambassadors to the United States since 1947 (Panyushkin, Zarubin, Menshikov, Dobrynin) have been at least candidate members and have relinquished their membership after reassignment. Judging by the nature of his appointments and his Party rank (Central Committee candidate or full membership since 1956), Zorin clearly emerges as the second most important career diplomat in the service.[70]

Brief mention should be made at this point of the emerging post-Gromyko generation of senior career diplomats, the most important of whom appears to be A. F. Dobrynin, born in 1919, who entered the diplomatic service in 1946 and was appointed ambassador to the United States in 1961 at age 40. One can place in the same category M. N. Smirnovsky, born in 1921, who entered the diplomatic service in 1948, and was appointed ambassador to London in 1966 (at age 45); and Oleg Troyanovsky (son of the first Soviet ambassador to the United States), born in 1919, who entered the diplomatic service in 1944, and was appointed ambassador to Japan in 1967 (at age 48).

2. *The Political Diplomats* (Table 2)

Until Stalin's death, all diplomatic appointments, after the war, whether major or minor, were reserved almost exclusively for the professional diplomatic service, although a special corps within it concentrated on Eastern European countries and strategic Middle Eastern states. The political diplomats as well as the Party functionary group are thus entirely a product of the post-Stalin period and although these two groups share some characteristics in common, they are nevertheless sharply distinguishable from each other. Briefly, the political diplomats as a group constitute former high Party and government officials exiled more or less permanantly from the Party apparatus, whereas the Party functionary group remains largely a corps of Party functionaries who

[70] Only Gromyko and Zorin have retained their Party rank continuously since their election as candidate members. Soldatov has served continuously on the CAC since 1956. The relationship between the Foreign Ministry, the diplomatic service, and the Party Central Committee has been clarified somewhat by Zorin in his book *Osnova Diplomaticheskoi Sluzhby* (Moscow, 1964). As both a veteran career diplomat and a full member of the Central Committee since 1961, Zorin is well qualified to comment on this matter. He writes that although the Central Committee daily guides the multivarious activities of Soviet diplomacy, at the same time it allows wide opportunities for the display of initiative by members of the diplomatic service. Presumably this applies primarily to the diplomats who serve as full and candidate members in the Central Committee. "The Party and Government," he writes, "have always been very exacting in the selection of personnel for the Foreign Ministry," because "political purposiveness, sense of responsibility and political maturity in all activities determine the level of work of the Foreign Ministry staff" (p. 116).

TABLE 2
DIPLOMATIC CAREER PATTERNS OF FORMER HIGH PARTY AND GOVERNMENT OFFICIALS

Career Category	Andropov, Yu. (1914-) 1954 *	Aristov, A.B. (1903-) 1961	Kuznetsov, V.V. (1901-) 1953	Mel'nikov, L.G. (1906-) 1953	Mikhailov, N.A. (1906-) 1954	Mukhitdinov, N.A. (1917-) 1968	Patolichev, N.S. (1908-) 1956	Pegov, N.M. (1905-) 1956	Pervukhin, M.G. (1904-) 1958	Pomarenko, P.K. (1902-) 1955	Puzanov, A.M. (1906-) 1957	Tevosyan, I.F. (1902-1958) 1956	Yudin, P.F. (1899-1968) 1953	Benediktov, I.A. (1902-) 1953	Menshikov, M.A. (1902-) 1953	Ryzhov, N.S. (1907-) 1957
Party rank																
Presidium-Politburo Mbr.	67-	52-53 57-61	52-53	52-53	52-53	56-61	52-53	52-53	52-61	52-55	52-53	52-53	52-53			
CC Member	61-	52-71	52-	52-56	39-71	52-66	39-	39-	39-61	39-61	52-	39-58	52-61	39-71		
Cand. Member				56-61												
CAC Member																66-
Western countries																
United Nations																
U.S.A.															58-62	
United Kingdom																
France																
Germany																
Italy																
Japan												56-58				66-
Other Western										59-61 61-64						
Other I.O.																
Afro-Asian																
India								67-		57-59				53-		
Iran								56-63						59-67	53-57	

648

Category	Entries
Turkey	
Algeria	64-67, 57-66
Egypt	60-65
Indonesia	
Other A-A	68-
Communist countries	
Yugoslavia	53-, 62-67, 67-
China	61-, 54-55, 55-57, 53-59
Poland	
Czechoslovakia	53-54
Rumania	
Hungary	54-57
Bulgaria	58-62, 67-
East Germany	57-62
Other Comm.	
Foreign Ministry	
Foreign Minister	
First Dep. or Dep. FM.	53-, 56-58, 62-68
Dept. Head or Dep. D.H.	
Other	
Non-diplomatic work	
Government	67-, 55-, 55-60, 65-, 58-, 62-, 54-59
Bureaucracy	
Party	58-67, 53-54, 60-
Apparatus	
Unknown	65-, 68-

*The first date refers to life span; second date refers to year of entrance into diplomatic service.

serve as diplomats to Communist countries and may be reassigned back to Party or government work outside the diplomatic service. In both cases, service in the diplomatic corps may constitute political exile or demotion, although this is most markedly apparent in the case of the political diplomats.

Of the 16 individuals classified as political diplomats, all but three have been at some time or other alternate or full members of the Party's highest body, the Politburo/Presidium. Some have also been members of the Party Secretariat as well, or held governmental positions at the Deputy Premier level simultaneously with their membership in the Party's highest decision-making organ. Former Foreign Minister and long-time Politburo member, V. M. Molotov also falls within this grouping, since he was the most conspicuous high political personality exiled to the diplomatic service.

Three members of this group are more properly former high governmental officials rather than Party luminaries: I. A. Benediktov, M. A. Menshikov, and N. S. Ryzhov. All were former Ministers and only Ryzhov was never a candidate or full member of the Central Committee. Ryzhov has apparently made a career of the diplomatic service, but Menshikov suffered further disgrace after his ambassadorship to Washington and was shuffled off as Foreign Minister of the R.S.F.S.R. Benediktov has oscillated between diplomatic assignments to India and Yugoslavia and ministerial status in Moscow (Agriculture).

The political diplomats are sharply differentiated from the career diplomats in terms of former and current Party status and in terms of their diplomatic assignments. Furthermore, some in this group are in various stages of political demotion, exile, and disgrace, whereas in other instances some have established themselves permanently as high-ranking career-political diplomats. In the cases of Molotov, Pervukhin, Melnikov, and Ponomarenko, the diplomatic service was clearly employed as an instrument of political isolation and disgrace, whereas in the instances of Aristov, Mukhitdinov, Pegov, Tevosyan, and Yudin, the diplomatic service was employed as a way of demoting without humiliating and disgracing former high Party officials who merited a more genteel form of exile. Still others such as Kuznetsov, Mikhailov, and Patolichev have managed to stabilize themselves at a sub-Politburo level of Party ranking and cannot be properly described as being either in exile or disgrace. Mikhailov and Patolichev have functioned as Ministers in para-diplomatic structures (Ministries of Culture and Foreign Trade respectively), as Kuznetsov has functioned continuously and without interruption as a Deputy or First Deputy Foreign Minister since 1953, after a brief tour as ambassador to China. Kuznetsov apparently supervises not only important negotiations with the major powers but also may be the official through whom the political and Party functionary diplomats report.

One of the most conspicuous features that differentiates this group of diplomats from the career professionals is their high Party status. Only two career professionals were elected or re-elected full members of the Central Committee in 1966, whereas no less than four members of this group still (as of 1970) in the diplomatic service were re-elected full members in the same year (Aristov, Kuznetsov, Pegov, and Puzanov).* At any given time since 1953, the political diplomats alone have outnumbered the career diplomats in the Central Committee, and when combined with the Party functionary diplomats (seven full members in 1966), the low Party status of the career diplomats becomes particularly evident. As noted previously, all this suggests that various parallel channels of *de facto* administrative authority must exist in a Ministry whose Minister is clearly outranked in Party councils by ostensible subordinates who have greater access to the inner sanctum of political power in Moscow.

The pattern of diplomatic and non-diplomatic assignments reveals not only a sharp geographical division of labor between the political and professional diplomats, but a distinctive functional division as well. These distinctions are so sharp that they appear to be not only calculated but perhaps even institutionalized in the form of hard agreements between the career service and the power elite. Thus:

1. No political diplomat has ever been appointed as chief Soviet representative at the United Nations.
2. With the single exception of Tevosyan (Japan, 1956–1958), no former high Party luminary, has ever been assigned to a major Western capital.
3. With the exception of Kuznetsov and Patolichev (whose positions were discussed earlier), no political diplomat has ever served in a high capacity in the Central Apparatus of the Foreign Ministry.
4. On the other hand, although no career diplomat (except Foreign Minister Gromyko) has ever been elevated to ministerial status, several political diplomats have served at the ministerial level since their entry into the diplomatic service (Melnikov, Mikhailov, Patolichev, Pervukhin, and Benediktov).

Political diplomats are assigned almost exclusively to Communist capitals or to strategically important Arab and Asian states. It appears evident that this group has preempted the former domain of the Lavrentievs and Sadchikovs during the Stalin period. As a general rule, none of this group has ever been reassigned to work in the Party apparatus, with the single exception of Andropov, who became a higher Party luminary and government official *after* his entry into the diplomatic service. In some respects Andropov belongs in the Party functionary class, from which he graduated to Party luminary status. In other respects his career is similar to that of I. F. Ilyichev. Since Andropov's brief tour in the diplomatic service (1954–1957), he moved into the Central Party apparatus as Head of Section for Eastern European Countries (1957–1967), was appointed a Party Secretary (1962–

* All four are former members or candidate members of the Politburo/Presidium. Pegov has served continuously in the Central Committee since 1939, whereas the other three date their membership since at least 1952.

1967), and was elevated to alternate membership in the Party Politburo in 1967 as he assumed the post of Chairman of the Committee on State Security (Secret Police). But as Andropov's career waxed, Ilyichev's waned, as will be described below, and some connection apparently exists between their respective political fortunes, as well as that of Zimyanin.

Of the sixteen individuals in this group, only eight were still in the diplomatic service in 1970 (Aristov, Kuznetsov, Mukhitdinov, Pegov, Puzanov, Benediktov, Menshikov, and Ryzhov). And of the eight, five were still full members of the Central Committee, five had served at one time or other as full or alternate members of the Party Presidium, and two had also served in the Party Secretariat. Four had also served at one time or other as Ministers in the Council of Ministers.[71]

Of the eight who are no longer in the diplomatic service, two are dead (Tevosyan and P. F. Yudin), three are in various stages of oblivion and disgrace (Melnikov, Pervukhin, and Ponomarenko), and three are Government Ministers (Andropov [State Security]; Mikhailov [Press]; and Patolichev [Foreign Trade]). The last three are also full members of the Central Committee.

Employment of the diplomatic service as a vehicle of political exile or disgrace for former Politburo/Presidium and Secretariat members has diminished considerably since 1960. Only Aristov (1961) and Mukhitdinov (1968) have chosen or been reassigned to the diplomatic service after their demotion from the centers of power since 1960. Others bruised in the inner Party battles have been reassigned elsewhere in the Party and State bureaucracy. The diplomatic service remains, however, a post of exile (by choice of reassignment) for sub-Politburo level Party officials, as will be discussed below.

The precise relationship between the political and professional diplomats remains obscure in many respects. Some such as Aristov (1961), Pegov (1956), Puzanov (1957), and Ryzhov (1957) have served continuously in ambassadorial posts abroad since their entry into the diplomatic service. Thus, Pegov, Puzanov, and Ryzhov have served continuously *abroad* as diplomats longer than any other diplomats (professional or otherwise) in the service except for Vinogradov, who died in 1970. For them, the diplomatic service has truly been a post of exile, but not necessarily disgrace.

Because of their continuous membership in the Central Committee as full members, four of the five former members of the Politburo/Presidium (Kuznetsov, Puzanov, Pegov, and Aristov) can be characterized as career "political" diplomats, particularly the first three, and thus have made a successful transition to a diplomatic career.

3. The Party Functionary Diplomats (Table 3)

These diplomats share many characteristics in common with the political diplomats, particularly in their pre-diplomatic career back-

[71] Menshikov's status, as of 1970, was somewhat obscure. After a tour as Foreign Minister of the R.S.F.S.R. (1962–68), he has apparently been retired as a consultant.

grounds, and in some respects are simply lower-level prototypes of the former Presidium/Politburo members in the diplomatic service. Generationally, they are not much different from the other two groups, the overwhelming majority being in their late fifties and sixties. Their aggregate ranking in the Party is relatively lower than that of the political diplomats but substantially higher than that of the career professionals. Thus, of the sixteen individuals in this group, all have been at one time or other at least candidate members of the Central Committee, while no less than thirteen have served as full members, and seven were re-elected full members of the Central Committee by the 23rd Party Congress in 1966.

The presence of these Party functionary types in the diplomatic service represents several distinct and often contradictory trends. As in the case of many of the political diplomats, diplomatic assignments were covert demotions and hence a form of political exile and isolation. Whereas the typical pre-diplomatic career of the political diplomat was that of a high State (ministerial level) or Party official (Presidium/ Politburo and Secretariat), the typical pre-diplomatic career of the Party functionary diplomat was that of a Provincial or Union Republican Party Secretary.

The movement of Party officials in and out of the diplomatic service, as well as their assignments and responsibilities, correlate to a large extent with factional struggles at the political center. Unlike the political diplomats, many of whom found themselves reassigned to diplomatic work soon after Stalin's death, beginning in 1953, the movement of Party functionaries into the diplomatic service started somewhat later, in late 1954 and 1955, with the political denouement of Malenkov and the political ascendancy of Khrushchev. In some cases regional Party secretaries were shifted to diplomacy because they were aligned with Malenkov, but in some instances, reassignment was largely a lateral movement probably initiated to make room in the apparatus for deserving cronies and reliable supporters of Khrushchev and his allies. Aside from those who were demoted or moved laterally, still others actually registered advancement in Party standing after their assignment to diplomacy, in accordance with shifting factional lines.

Of the sixteen individuals in this group, eight suffered a demotion in Party rank after their entry into the diplomatic service (L. F. Ilyichev, M. V. Zimyanin, I. T. Grishin, G. A. Denisov, I. K. Zhegalin, Ye. A. Gromov, I. K. Zamchevsky, and S. A. Tovmasyan). Of these, Ilyichev and Zimyanin managed to recover and even improve their Party standings subsequently as factional lines shifted back and forth. Ilyichev first entered the diplomatic service in 1952, when he was a candidate member of the Central Committee. He was demoted to membership in the Central Auditing Commission in 1956, left the diplomatic service in 1958, was jumped to full membership in the Central Committee in 1961 and then advanced to the Party Secretariat. With the ouster of Khrushchev, Ilyichev was returned to the central apparatus of the Foreign Ministry and dropped from membership in all the central organs of the Party. Zimyanin's career has also been rather chequered and in some

TABLE 3
CAREER PATTERNS OF PARTY OFFICIALS IN THE DIPLOMATIC SERVICE

Career Category	Shiykov, T.F. (1907-1964) 1948*	Ilyichev, L.F. (1906-) 1952	Zimyanin, M.V. (1914-) 1953	Fryubin, N.P. (1908-) 1954	Grishin, I.T. (1911-) 1955	Yepishev, A.A. (1908-) 1955	Abrasimov, P.A. (1912-) 1956	Gromov, Ye. A. (1909-) 1957	Zamchevsky, I.K. (1909-) 1957	Chervonenko, S.V. (1915-) 1959	Denisov, G.A. (1906-) 1960	Zhegalin, I.K. (1906-) 1960	Tormasyan, S.A. (1910-) 1961	(Basov, A.V. (1912-) 1965	Titov, F. Ye. (1910-) 1966	Tolstikov, V.S. (1917-) 1970
Party rank																
Presidium-Politburo Mbr.																
CC Member	56-61	61-66	52-56 66-		52-61	64-	61-			61-	52-66	52-66	56-61	61-	52-71	61-
Cand. Member	39-52	52-56	56-66	56-66		52-64		56-61	56-61							
CAC Member		56-61														
Western countries																
Afro-Asian													65-			
Communist countries																
Yugoslavia				55-57		61-62			57-60							
China					55-60					59-65						70-
Poland				54-55			57-61									
Czechoslovakia			60-65							65-						
Rumania						55-61						60-65		65-		
Hungary	59-61							57-59			63-65					
Bulgaria											60-63				65-	
East Germany							62-									

654

	North Vietnam	North Korea
	48-54	61-64
Foreign Ministry		
Foreign Minister		
First Dep. or Dep. FM.	65-	57-
Dept. Head or Dep. D.H.	52-58, 57-60	59-, 56-57
Other	53-56	60-
Non-diplomatic work		
Government Bureaucracy	61-64	60-, 65-
Party Apparatus	54-59, 58-64, 65-	62-, 61-62
Unknown		66-

*The first date refers to life span; second date refers to year of entrance into diplomatic service.

respects was the mirror image of Ilyichev's and correlates strongly with the rise of Andropov. At the time of his entry into the diplomatic service, he was a full member of the Central Committee; he was demoted to membership in the CAC in 1956, but after Khrushchev's ouster, he was appointed chief editor of *Pravda* in 1965 and jumped to full membership of the Central Committee in 1966, the job Ilyichev held in 1952 before his shift to the diplomatic service.

Of the remaining six in this group, three (Grishin, Gromov, and Zamchevsky) entered the service in 1955–57, and all suffered a demotion in Party rank in 1961, and thus appear somehow to be associated with losing factions in the power struggle during this period. The other three (Denisov, Zhegalin, and Tovmasyan) entered the service in 1960–61. All three were full members of the Central Committee at the time of their entry. Tovmasyan was dropped from membership in 1961 and the other two failed to be re-elected in 1966.

In at least three cases, reassignment to the diplomatic service was a lateral move. P. A. Abrasimov entered the diplomatic service in 1956 as a full member of the Central Committee and has so remained continuously. In 1970, V. S. Tolstikov, a full member of the Central Committee since 1961, was appointed ambassador to China, but it is still too early to make a definitive judgment as to its significance for his political career. The youngest member of this group (born in 1917), his appointment to Peking may be a step to higher things in the Party or simply political stagnation. Yepishev, the third member of this trio, entered the diplomatic service in 1955 as a candidate member of the Central Committee, and left diplomacy in 1962 to become Chief of the Main Political Administration of the Armed Forces, without any change in Party rank. He was elevated to full membership in November 1964, immediately after Khrushchev's fall, thus suggesting retrospectively the factional character of his diplomatic sojourn.

Two individuals in the Party functionary class, aside from the ups and downs of Ilyichev and Zimyanin, were promoted in Party ranking *after* their entry into diplomacy. N. P. Firyubin entered the service in 1954 and was elected a candidate member of the Central Committee in 1956, only to be dropped in 1966 after Khrushchev's eclipse. Firyubin, the husband of Ekaterina Furtseva, after brief tours as ambassador to Czechoslovakia and Yugoslavia, has functioned as a Deputy Foreign Minister since 1957. Chervonenko entered the diplomatic service as ambassador to Peking in 1959, and was elected a full member of the Central Committee in 1961. An obscure secretary in the Ukrainian Party apparatus, Chervonenko's appointment to Peking in place of Yudin was a sign of Moscow's displeasure with the state of Sino-Soviet relations, but a definite promotion for Chervonenko. Recalled from Peking in 1965, he was reassigned as ambassador to Prague, retaining his Party rank, and supervised the Soviet quashing of the Dubcek regime in 1968.[72]

[72] Chervonenko was replaced in 1965 with S. G. Lapin, a professional journalist, who has served at various intervals in the diplomatic service since

Khrushchev's ouster apparently created gratuitous diplomatic opportunities for F. Ye. Titov and A. V. Basov, both of whom were shifted out of the Party Apparatus into diplomatic work in 1965. Although both retained their full membership in the Central Committee at the 23rd Party Congress, they have clearly suffered a diminution of power and their Party rankings may be in jeopardy.[73]

The final individual in this group of diplomats, T. F. Shtykov, entered the diplomatic service in 1948 as ambassador to North Korea, from where he was reassigned to the Party Apparatus in 1954. Elected a candidate member of the Central Committee in 1939, he was elevated to full membership in 1956, and after a brief tour as ambassador to Hungary (1959–61), he was dropped in 1961 upon his reassignment to bureaucratic obscurity. Shtykov's career was similar in many respects to that of the Stalinist career diplomats of the Laverentiev and Pushkin type, although his Party ranking was consistently higher. Shtykov died in 1964.

Of the sixteen Party functionary diplomats in Table 3 ten were still in the diplomatic service in 1970, and of these, five were full members of the Central Committee.

The assignment pattern of the Party functionary diplomats varies significantly from that of the two previous groups of diplomats, but shares features with both. The Party functionary diplomat is appointed almost exclusively to Communist capitals and to this extent his function overlaps that of the political diplomat. On the other hand, the Party functionary diplomat serves frequently in the central apparatus of the Foreign Ministry as a Deputy Foreign Minister, Department Head, or Member of the Collegium, but usually in charge of Eastern European or Communist countries' affairs. Again, as the political diplomat, the Party functionary diplomat frequently re-enters the Party or government bureaucracy from the foreign service. Of the sixteen Party functionary diplomats in Table 3, eleven have served only as ambassadors to various Communist countries, as four have served both as ambassadors and in the Central Foreign Ministry bureaucracy. One (Ilyichev) has served only in the Central office when in the Foreign Service, as Head of the Press Department before he started to reclimb the slippery rungs of the Party ladder in 1958, and as a Deputy Foreign Minister since his fall from grace after his patron Khrushchev was dethroned.

1954. Appointed Director-General of TASS in 1967, Lapin represents a new breed of Soviet diplomat, who enters laterally into the service at various times and returns to his main professional career — journalism, education, culture, science, etc. Lapin was recalled in 1967 and Tolstikov was appointed in 1970.

[73] A major shake-up in ambassadorial appointments to Eastern European capitals was set in motion on the eve of the Twenty-fourth Party Congress, meeting on March 31, 1971. Both Basov and Tito were withdrawn from their posts in Bucharest and Budapest, respectively, as was Aristov from his long tenure in Warsaw. At the time of this writing, it appears that Chervonenko is also being replaced in Prague. All four are full members of the Central Committee, and given the circumstances of their entry and exit into the diplomatic service, they are likely to be demoted in party rank.

4. *Soviet Diplomacy and Party-State Relations*

The relationship between State and Party functions in Soviet diplomacy since the death of Stalin betrays a reversion to earlier practice in some degree. During the first years of the Soviet regime, the inexperienced Soviet leaders perceived Soviet ambassadors and ministers as both formal representatives of the Soviet State accredited to bourgeois governments and also as the informal representatives of the Soviet Party to the proletariat and Communist parties of the countries to which they were sent. He thus served in the dual capacity of diplomat and revolutionary agent simultaneously, a condition that soon proved untenable and hence counterproductive. When Soviet diplomatic representatives abroad were formally shorn of their revolutionary garb in 1924 by a decree that directed them to refrain from interfering in the internal affairs of the countries to which they were accredited, the function of revolutionary agitation and propaganda was redirected principally through the Party apparatus to the Comintern and foreign Communist parties, although Soviet diplomatic establishments continued to provide legal cover and covert support. With the advent of new Communist countries after World War II, the formal practice of separating State and Party functions in Soviet diplomatic relations was retained even in relations with Communist states. This became difficult to sustain as Soviet ambassadors to Communist countries increasingly were assigned functions that impelled them to interfere in their domestic affairs. Since Soviet intervention in the internal affairs of Communist countries would be a gross travesty of the norms of international law (sovereignty, nonintervention, etc.), and Stalin wished to preserve the formal sanctity of these norms because it served Soviet interests, Soviet ambassadors conducted their intervention at the Party level in accordance with the Stalinist conception of "socialist" or "proletarian internationalism." Consequently, Soviet ambassadors were invested *de facto* with the status of Soviet Party representatives to the Central committees of fraternal ruling parties. Although this recombination of diplomatic and revolutionary-ideological functions was never made publicly explicit, Soviet practice clearly suggested that Soviet ambassadors to Communist countries were dual representatives. Thus, Stalin, in rebutting Tito's complaint that the Soviet ambassador was exceeding his functions by interfering in the affairs of the Yugoslav Party, outlined in lucid terms his conception of the Soviet ambassador as a dual representative:

> Tito and Kardelj . . . identify the Soviet Ambassador, a responsible Communist . . . with an ordinary bourgeois ambassador, a simple official of a bourgeois state. . . . The Soviet Ambassador, a responsible Communist . . . not only has the right but is obliged, from time to time, to discuss with Communists in Yugoslavia all questions which interest them.[74]

[74] *The Soviet-Yugoslav Dispute* (London, Royal Institute of International Affairs, 1948), pp. 34–35. The Soviet ambassadors involved at the time were Sadchikov (1945–46) and Lavrentev (1946–1949).

As noted earlier, Soviet ambassadors to Communist countries during the Stalin period constituted a special quasi-political corps, who specialized in Eastern Europe and the Middle East: Pushkin, Lavrentev, Sadchikov, Lebedev, and Lavrishchev. There is some indication that they were also under the administrative control of the Ministry of State Security as well. Soon after Stalin's death, however, they were no longer assigned to foreign posts abroad and their positions were occupied by the incoming Political and Party Functionary diplomats.

What was largely an informal arrangement under Stalin has since become more expressly institutionalized. Since almost all Soviet ambassadors accredited to Communist capitals are full or candidate members of the Central Committee, their dual capacity is more or less explicit and the Soviet ambassador is frequently the official Soviet Party representative to Party Congresses held in the host country.

Since Stalin's death, and particularly since the de-Stalinization campaign was started in 1956, some Communist countries, particularly China, have sought to invest their ambassadors to Moscow with a similar dual capacity. This has rendered the role and functions of not only the Soviet ambassador to Communist countries, but of all diplomatic envoys between Communist countries, murky, ambiguous, ambivalent, and subject to misconstruction, as unilateral Soviet interference in the domestic affairs of Communist countries was used by the Chinese as justification for Peking's interference in Soviet Party affairs.

The issue of mutual interference was raised in June 1963, when Chinese embassy personnel distributed the Chinese letter of June 14, 1963 criticizing Soviet policy to members of the Soviet Central Committee and to other key State and Party officials. After Soviet protests failed to stop the distribution, several Chinese embassy officials were expelled for engaging in illegal activities, whereupon Peking complained as follows:

> Since Soviet establishments and personnel can do, and have always done this in China, why cannot the Chinese establishments and personnel do the same in the Soviet Union? What justification has the Soviet Government to lodge a protest with the Chinese Embassy in the Soviet Union in this connection? What justification has it to demand that the Chinese Government recall the said Chinese personnel?[75]

Moscow angrily retorted that the Chinese embassy officials "were conducting themselves in the Soviet Union as though they were still in one of the provinces of China," and then went on to erect the shield of state sovereignty and seek refuge behind the norms of international law:

> The attempts on the part of the Chinese to represent the matter as though such norms [i.e. international law] as respect by one socialist state for the laws and regulations of another socialist state and its sovereignty have no force in the relations between socialist states are contrary to Leninist principles.[76]

75 *The New York Times*, June 30, 1963.
76 *Pravda*, July 5, 1963. Soviet writers and jurists were frequently carried away in their imputation of motives to Peking, and sometimes they

The Soviet reply to the Chinese denied that Soviet personnel would disseminate Soviet literature in violation of Chinese laws, but the Chinese retorted that no such restrictions existed in China, that none would be invoked, and demanded reciprocity in the name of proletarian internationalism.

There was, of course, just a touch of sweet irony in the Chinese assertion of their right to behave in the Soviet Union as if it were a Chinese province on grounds that "proletarian internationalism" transcended the ordinary restrictions and artificialities of such bourgeois concepts as sovereignty. The Chinese were demanding nothing less than the exercise of extraterritorial rights on Soviet soil similar to those demanded by Stalin with respect to Yugoslavia in 1948, and essentially on the same grounds. It may be recalled that when Tito and Kardelj complained about the activities of Soviet personnel on Yugoslav soil in contacting individuals and organizations outside ordinary administrative and legal channels, Moscow retorted as follows:

> Soviet workers are politically mature people and not simple hired laborers, who have no right to be interested in what is happening in Yugoslavia. It is only natural for them to talk with Yugoslav citizens, to ask them questions and gain information, etc. One would have to be an incorrigible anti-Soviet to consider these talks as attempts to recruit people for the intelligence service. . . . It must be emphasized that Yugoslav comrades visiting Moscow frequently visit other cities in the USSR, meet our people and freely talk with them. In no case did the Soviet Government place any restrictions on them. . . . According to the Yugoslav scheme, information about the Party and State can only be obtained from the leading organs of the CC of the CPY or from the

---

unwittingly caricatured Soviet attitudes toward other Communist states. Thus, on August 21, 1963, *Pravda* charged that Peking was arrogating to itself the right to represent the true interests of the Soviet people: "The CPR leaders attempt to present matters as though their statements, which are aimed at undisguised interference in the internal affairs of other socialist countries, specifically the Soviet Union, are dictated allegedly by a sense of 'proletarian international duty. . . .' It must be said that no imperialist state has yet gone so far as to assert that it and not the Soviet Government represents the Soviet Union in international affairs or to speak in the name of the Soviet people. . . . If any government . . . began to assume that it, and not the government of another state, expressed the will of the people of the latter state, chaos and confusion would reign in international affairs. . . . In the statement of the representative of the CPR Government, the claim to determine for the Soviet people what furthers their interests and what does not, what ensures their security and what does not, grows to simply fantastic proportions." A few days later, the Soviet jurist, G. Tunkin, asserted that the Chinese leadership was even claiming a right to represent the U.S.S.R. in international affairs: "The leaders of the CPR have gone even farther in their policy of flouting the norms of international relations than imperialist governments permit themselves to go. The Chinese leaders have gone so far as to assert insolently that they, not the Soviet Government, represent the Soviet Union in international affairs." F. Kozhevnikov, "On That Which is Obligatory For All — Position of the Chinese Leadership From Standpoint of International Law," *Izvestia*, August 24, 1963. Cf. also, G. Tunkin, "State Borders and Peaceful Coexistence," *Izvestia*, August 27, 1963.

Government. . . . It may be asked now: Why should Soviet Communists in Yugoslavia have fewer rights than Yugoslavs in the USSR?[77]

Although the Soviet-Yugoslav and Soviet-Chinese situations are logically comparable, they are by no means symmetrical in their effects. What is interesting in both situations is the shameless manner in which Moscow manipulated the principles of "sovereignty" and "reciprocity" to its advantage even when the Soviet Union reversed its position. Thus, in 1948, the Soviet Union condemned the Yugoslavs for invoking "sovereignty" and demanded "reciprocity" on Soviet terms, whereas in 1963, the Soviets were invoking "sovereignty" and denied that "reciprocity" had any applicability in the situation. In 1948, Moscow wanted the right to freely conduct its activities on Yugoslav territory, whereas such a "right" was of no advantage to Yugoslavia; in 1963, Moscow wanted to exclude Peking's personnel from conducting its activities on Soviet soil and saw no advantage in gaining or preserving a similar "right" on Chinese territory.

In 1967, at the height of the Great Proletarian Cultural Revolution in China, the impasse on this issue was resolved by the mutual withdrawal of ambassadors by Moscow and Peking. Representation at both the Party and State levels was thus ruptured until the restoration of ambassadorial exchanges in 1970. It appears clear, however, that neither the Soviet nor Chinese ambassadors will attempt to assert rights and prerogatives of Party representatives.

The enunciation of the "Brezhnev Doctrine" (or Socialist Commonwealth Doctrine) of limited sovereignty creates new horizons of possible Soviet abuse of diplomatic relations in the Communist world. The Brezhnev Doctrine, in effect, attempts to unilaterally impose certain self-contained parameters around a constellation of ideologically related sovereign states belonging to a universal interstate system, in which the principles of "socialist internationalism" would intersect with the norms of international law to produce a distinctive ideo-legal interstate subsystem. Two types of sovereignty result from this fusion: ideological and legal-juridical, in which the former enjoys primacy and must be preserved even to the extent of infringing upon the second.

The progressive intertwining of international juridical norms with ideological norms was reflected in Foreign Minister Andrei Gromyko's address to the United Nations General Assembly on October 3, 1968, when he declared the "socialist commonwealth" to be a distinctive juridico-ideological community, with an overall sovereignty of its own, and thus immune from the normal rules governing sovereignty and nonintervention. Socialist states, individually, and the Socialist Commonwealth, collectively, have invisible ideological frontiers (called "socialism") and if these invisible frontiers are transgressed by hostile forces (who may also be invisible), then the Soviet Union is entitled to violate state sovereignty in order to defend ideological sovereignty:

The countries of the socialist commonwealth have their own vital interests, their own obligations, including those of safeguarding their mutual

77 *The Soviet-Yugoslav Dispute*, pp. 40–41.

security and their own socialist principles of mutual relations based on fraternal assistance, solidarity and internationalism. This commonwealth constitutes an inseparable entity cemented by unbreakable ties such as history has never known. . . . The Soviet Union and other socialist countries have on many occasions warned those who are tempted to try to roll back the socialist commonwealth, to snatch at least one link from it, that we will neither tolerate nor allow that to happen. . . . The Soviet Union deems it necessary to proclaim from this rostrum, too, that the socialist States cannot and will not allow a situation where the vital interests of socialism are infringed upon and encroachments are made on the inviolability of the boundaries of the socialist commonwealth and, therefore, on the foundations of international peace. It goes without saying that such an action as military aid to a fraternal country to cut short the threat to the socialist order is an extraordinary step, it can be sparked off only by direct actions of the enemies of socialism inside the country and beyond its boundaries, actions creating a threat to the common interests of the camp of socialism.

But it remained for Leonid Brezhnev to merge the sovereignty of socialism and state sovereignty into a definitive doctrine of "limited sovereignty," and so the doctrine justifiably bears his name:

The socialist states stand for strict respect for the sovereignty of all countries. We emphatically oppose interference into the affairs of any states, violations of their sovereignty. At the same time the establishment and defense of the sovereignty of states, which have embarked upon the road of building socialism, is of particular significance for us, communists. . . . The CPSU have always advocated that each socialist country determine the specific forms of its development along the road of socialism with consideration for its specific national conditions. However, it is known, comrades, that there also are common laws governing socialist construction, a deviation from which might lead to a deviation from socialism as such. And when the internal and external forces hostile to socialism seek to revert the development of any socialist country toward the restoration of the capitalist order, when a threat to the cause of socialism in that country, a threat to the security of the socialist community, as a whole, emerges, this is no longer only a problem of the people of that country but also a common problem, concern for all socialist states.[78]

In some respects, the "Brezhnev Doctrine" emerges as a logical extrapolation of the earlier Chinese interpretation of "proletarian internationalism," although Peking now recoils from the logical extension of her earlier position. The nexus of the "Brezhnev Doctrine" was postulated by *Pravda* as follows:

[78] *Pravda*, November 13, 1968. The fusion of the two sovereignties was explicitly stated by *Pravda* on April 7, 1969: "Socialism and sovereignty are indivisible. Marxist-Leninists believe that when a threat arises to the revolutionary achievements of a people in any country, and thereby its sovereignty as a socialist country, and a threat to a fraternal community, then the socialist states' international duty is to do everything to preserve this threat and to insure the progress of socialism and the strengthening of the sovereignty of all socialist countries."

There is no doubt that the peoples of the socialist countries and the Communist Parties have and must have freedom to determine their country's path of development. However, any decision of theirs must damage neither socialism in their own country nor the fundamental interests of the other socialist countries nor the worldwide workers' movement, which is waging a struggle for socialism. This means that every Communist Party is responsible not only to its own people but also to all the socialist countries and to the entire Communist movement. Whoever forgets this in placing sole emphasis on the autonomy and independence of Communist Parties lapses into onesidedness, shirking his internationalist obligations. . . . The sovereignty of individual socialist countries cannot be counterposed to the interests of world socialism and the world revolutionary movement.[79]

Tito, consistent with his earlier position, of course, denounced the doctrine as an attempt to ideologically justify Soviet interference in the domestic affairs of other Communist states:

In the name of the alleged higher interests of socialism, attempts are made to justify even the open violation of the sovereignty of a socialist country and the adoption of military forces as a means of preventing independent socialist development.

The Chinese also predictably condemned the doctrine, but did so at the expense of undermining an earlier Chinese assertion of the right to intervene in the domestic affairs of other Communist states, although, of course, Peking never maintained that the right of interference extended to the use of military force:

"Limited sovereignty" in essence means that Soviet revisionism can encroach upon the sovereignty of other countries and interfere in their domestic affairs at will, and even send its aggressor troops into the territory of these countries to suppress the people there, while the people invaded have no right to resist aggression and safeguard their own sovereignty and independence. This is an out-and-out fascist "theory" . . . The fascist theories of the Soviet revisionist renegade clique are of the same kind as the tsars' imperialist ones created to invade other countries.[80]

The increasing and consistent employment of higher Party officials as ambassadors to Communist countries symbolizes perfectly and precisely the Soviet fusion of the diplomatic realm with the ideological where Communist states are concerned. Soviet ambassadors, and in theory at least all Communist ambassadors to Communist countries, under the Brezhnev Doctrine, are simultaneously obliged to respect state sovereignty in accordance with international law, but to violate it in conformity with the principles of socialist internationalism, if the sanctity of state sovereignty endangers the preservation of socialist sovereignty. The Brezhnev Doctrine, although abstractly conceding to the Chinese and other Communist parties the right to function as the

[79] *Pravda*, September 25, 1968.
[80] *Jenmin Jihpao*, March 17, 1969.

joint or collective guardians of the socialist sovereignty of the U.S.S.R., attempts to re-invest Soviet ambassadors with viceregal functions particularly in Warsaw Pact countries, which they had largely forfeited after 1956.[81]

The movement of former Party leaders and Party bureaucrats into the Soviet diplomatic service since Stalin's death thus represents not only a transformation of the diplomatic service itself, but even more importantly a transformation of relations among Communist countries. Stalin's two-track system of relations could no longer be sustained after his death and was gradually replaced with a single-track system performing two functions. Before the invasion of Czechoslovakia in 1968, the fusion of Party-State functions in the person of the Soviet ambassador served to enhance the sovereignty and autonomy of the smaller Communist states, since, as diplomats, the Party officials serving as ambassadors were governed by diplomatic protocol and limited in their activities by the norms of international law. In other words, during this period, their official status as ambassadors restricted their behavior as Party representatives.

With the advent of the "Brezhnev Doctrine," however, and the unilateral Soviet incorporation of the principles of socialist internationalism into the corpus of international law, the sovereignty and autonomy of the smaller Communist states are seriously compromised since those states that accept the principles of the "Brezhnev Doctrine" (Poland, Hungary, Czechoslovakia, Bulgaria, East Germany, and Mongolia) have in effect legally surrendered their right under international law to be protected against the collective external intervention by Communist states, if they independently judge that the socialist character of the Communist state in question is in danger of ideological erosion, internal subversion, or external pressures. Under these circum-

---

[81] Party-State relations were further blurred by provisions of the new Soviet-Czech Treaty of Alliance concluded in 1970. One Soviet commentator expressly noted that the Treaty formally interlaces Party and State relations, thus endowing the documents and statements of the international Communist movement with a juridico-diplomatic status. The Treaty literally fuses international law and socialist internationalism within the Communist inter-state subsystem: "The main principle determining the relations between socialist countries is the principle of socialist internationalism. This is now not only a political principle, but also a principle of international law. Mutual assistance of the socialist countries in their struggle against imperialism, for the triumph of socialism and communism, and in defense of the gains of socialism is a fundamental principle of socialist internationalism. This is constantly emphasized in the documents adopted by the socialist countries and the documents of the international Communist movement, which has always regarded defense of socialism as the principal task of the fraternal parties in all countries. The incorporation in the Soviet-Czechoslovak treaty of the provisions on joint defense of the socialist gains of the peoples of the two countries, and on strengthening and defending the socialist community is a concretisation in this bilateral treaty of the principles of socialist internationalism as a legal obligation of the requirements flowing from the general principles determining relations between socialist countries." O. Khlestov, "New Soviet-Czechoslovak Treaty," International Affairs, July 1970, pp. 12–13.

stances, as official representatives of the most powerful Communist state, Soviet ambassadors are quasi-legally empowered — as ambassadors — to function as guardians of the ideological purity and physical safety of the socialist system in the Communist country to which they are formally credited. Before the "Brezhnev Doctrine," the norms of international law limited the behavior of Soviet diplomats; after the "Brezhnev Doctrine," international law "obligates" Soviet diplomats to intervene in the internal affairs of other Communist countries. This appears to be the major implication of the Brezhnev Doctrine for Soviet diplomacy.

19. THE UNION REPUBLICS AND SOVIET DIPLOMACY: CONCEPTS, INSTITUTIONS, AND PRACTICES

Vernon V. Aspaturian

Ever since the constitutional improvisations of February 1, 1944, one of the enigmatic and obscure aspects of Soviet diplomacy has been the precise role of the Union Republics in its execution, administration and procedures. Aside from the participation of the Ukraine and Byelorussia in the work of the United Nations and its affiliated bodies and conferences, little attention has been paid to the role or potential of the Union Republics in Soviet foreign policy. Their apparent diplomatic inertia, however, is misleading, for in marked contrast to their meager formal participation in external affairs is their increasing implication in the quasi-diplomatic maneuvers of the Soviet Government. Furthermore, the juridical capacity of the Republics to embark on diplomatic adventures meets the formal canons of internal and international law, and remains intact in spite of the past dormancy of their diplomatic organs. At opportune moments it may be transmuted into concrete diplomatic benefits.

Reprinted from *The American Political Science Review*, June, 1959, pp. 383–411. Reprinted by permission.
This article is part of a forthcoming book on Soviet Diplomacy, the research for which was made possible by a grant from the Rockefeller Foundation. The author wishes to express here his appreciation to the Foundation.

I. Introduction

A close inspection of the formal internal administrative and institutional implementation of the Amendment of 1944 reveals more than a dozen diplomatic embryos — at various stages of development — placidly incubating, patiently awaiting the warm rays from Moscow to burst forth fully hatched. The diplomatic inactivity of the Soviet Republics in the past has been due, not so much to the reluctance or refusal of other states to recognize their diplomatic status, as to Moscow's calculated refusal to stimulate their diplomatic reflexes.

Contrary to widespread impression, the participation of the Soviet Republics in Soviet foreign relations finds considerable support not only in Soviet history and constitutional law, but in the doctrine and practice of international law as well. The role of the Union Republics in Soviet diplomacy falls into four distinct phases, each marked by its own peculiarities corresponding to the changing internal and external requirements of the Soviet regime. The first phase — from 1918 to the *de facto* formation of the Union in mid-1923 — was characterized by the existence of the Republics as formally independent states with their separate diplomatic establishments.[1] The second period covered the approximate life of the 1924 Constitution and was marked by an institutional centralization of foreign affairs in Moscow, yet within a framework which gave the Republics limited but significant internal administrative responsibility and restricted representation abroad. This phase came to a violent and inscrutable demise about a year before the outbreak of World War II. The third phase covered the years from the purges to the adoption of the 1944 Amendments, a period during which the Republics were deprived of all participation — fictional or otherwise — in the administration of Soviet foreign relations.[2] The current phase, which began with the juridical renovation of the Soviet federation to empower the Republics to maintain separate but subordinate diplomatic establishments alongside the Union, has yet to achieve its definitive contours.

Juridically the present phase bears a remarkable resemblance to the first, but in actual practice the similarity is more formal than real. The genuine distinctions which demarcate the four phases are to be found neither in the legal nor the ideological shifts of the past four decades of Soviet rule, but rather almost exclusively in the changing security requirements of the Soviet center and its power to impose absolute and undeviating conformity over the periphery of the Soviet

---

[1] For accounts of the diplomacy of the Republics before the formation of the Union, *cf.* O. I. Chistyakov, *Vzaimootnosheniya Sovetskikh Respublik do Obrazovaniya SSSR* (Moscow, 1955), and *Desyat Let Sovetskoi Diplomatii* (Moscow, 1927).

[2] This phase of Soviet diplomacy, together with an extensive analysis of the complex motives behind the adoption of the amendments and the concrete postwar diplomatic missions of the Republics in Soviet diplomacy, are treated in detail elsewhere by the author in "The Union Republics as Instruments of Soviet Diplomacy."

multi-national federation, irrespective of juridical formalities. Each phase thus represents distinctions not only in the role of the Republics as actors in Soviet diplomacy, but also as pawns, and so corresponds not only to the internal metamorphosis of the Soviet power structure but also to the rapidly fluctuating balance of diplomatic opportunities in the international struggle for power. This was made abundantly clear by Molotov in 1944:

> During the early period when our State was not yet gathered into one Union State, but consisted of separate parts . . . Comrade Stalin said . . . that "at that time the Soviet Republics, although they acted together, marched separately, occupied primarily by the problem of their existence." That was inevitable at the initial stage. When the U.S.S.R. was founded . . . it was decided to unify foreign relations with foreign States in one center. Then was created the All-Union People's Commissariat of Foreign Affairs, in which were vested the powers of the People's Commissariats of Foreign Affairs of the separate Soviet Republics. . . . This was necessary at a certain stage of the development of our State and yielded its positive results by having strengthened the State and highly enhanced its part in international affairs. But even then, as far back as the Party Congress in 1923, Comrade Stalin said: "We shall still take up the national question more than once, since national and international conditions are subject to change and may still change. I do not preclude the possibility that subsequently we may have to separate certain commissariats which we are now merging in the Union of Republics."[3]

Whereas in 1922 the danger was that Republics which marched separately might fall out of step, by 1944 the central control was sufficient to ensure that the Republics would act and march in unison even if they possessed the formal capacity to set their own pace. Legal decentralization of foreign affairs for a weak Soviet state might conceivably encourage separatism and invite intervention, but for a powerful Russia it could considerably enhance its diplomatic flexibility and enable it to exploit manifold opportunities in international politics. As in any federal system, legal decentralization of foreign affairs can weaken or strengthen the Soviet position in international affairs, depending upon the cohesion and stability of political power in the center; thus Soviet leaders have always been cognizant of the ambivalent and double-edged character of institutional and juridical forms. Speaking of the Soviets, Stalin warned:

> The Soviets are only a *form* of organization — true enough, a socialist form, but only a *form* or organization for all that. Everything depends upon the *content* that is put into this form. We know of cases when Soviets . . . for a certain time supported the counter-revolution against the revolution. . . . Hence, it is not only a matter of Soviets as a form. . . . It is primarily a matter of the content of the work in the Soviets; it

[3] Molotov's Report to the Supreme Soviet on February 1, 1944. The text to which references are made in this article is that reprinted in *International Conciliation*, No. 398, March 1944, p. 239. Hereinafter cited as *Molotov Report*.

is a matter of the character of the work of the Soviets; it is a matter of *who* leads the Soviets. . . . We must assume that the anti-Soviet elements take all this into account . . . and use these as a screen for their underground organizations. . . . The Soviets, taken as a form of organization, are a weapon and a weapon only. Under certain conditions this weapon may be turned against the revolution. . . . It all depends upon who wields this weapon and against whom it is directed.[4]

In the concrete implementation of the 1944 Amendments, the Kremlin recognizes that, unless proper precautions are taken, the Amendments may unwittingly provide a legal cover for separatists in the Union Republics or furnish a gratuitous fissure into which hostile powers might insert their diplomatic wedges. These hazards would be increased in the event of a serious political crisis. The Soviet Government manifestly has no intention of frivolously or indiscriminately expanding the diplomatic activities of the Union Republics and so running the risk of permitting continuous contact between potential secessionists and the representatives of hostile states behind a screen of legality. As a general rule, the latitude allowed the republics in foreign affairs has been, and will continue to be, determined by a careful calculation of the constantly fluctuating balance between the requirements of internal security and cohesion on the one hand and the fleeting expediencies of foreign politics on the other.

II. THE CONSTITUTIONAL INNOVATIONS OF 1944: THEIR JURIDICAL SIGNIFICANCE

By empowering the Union Republics to establish separate foreign offices, diplomatic relations, defense establishments and national troop formations,[5] the Amendments of February 1, 1944 struck a new juridical equilibrium between the center and the circumference in the Soviet federal system and provided the basis for multiple recognition under international law. Constitutionally, the Amendments transformed the Union into a *de jure* confederation remarkably similar to the political

[4] J. V. Stalin, *Leninism* (International Publishers, 1942), pp. 278–279.
[5] Although not strictly a diplomatic emendation, the Amendment simultaneously adopted which authorized the Republics to establish separate defense departments and national troop formations is intimately connected with foreign affairs. Unlike the Amendment on foreign affairs, however, this Amendment has never been given implementation even in form. Although all the Republic Constitutions were altered to include a Defense Ministry in the list of Union-Republican Ministries, not a single Republic has ever established a Defense Ministry or even so much as appointed a Defense Minister. Molotov in his speech to the Supreme Soviet claimed that Latvian, Lithuanian, Estonian, Georgian, Armenian, Azerbaidzhanian and Kazakh (but not Ukrainian or Byelorussian) national armies were already in existence. Assorted deputies boasted in the Supreme Soviets about the number of divisions, generals and officers of their respective nationalities in the Red Army; but after the War the national formations were dissolved and have never been revived. The entire Amendment remains a dead letter. Cf. D. L. Zlatopolsky, *Obrazovaniye i Razvitiye SSSR kak Soyuznovo Gosudarstvo* (Moscow, 1954), pp. 203–205.

structure proposed by Rakovsky and Skrypnik at the 12th Congress of
the Party in 1923, and contemptuously denounced then, with both
juridical logic and eloquent realism, by the principal architect of the
1944 Amendments, J. V. Stalin:

> What becomes of the single union state if each republic retains its
> own People's Commissariat of Foreign Affairs and People's Commissariat
> of Foreign Trade? . . . It is obvious, however, that we are creating not a
> confederation, but a federation of republics, a single union state, uniting
> military, foreign, foreign trade and other affairs, a state which in no
> way diminishes the sovereignty of the individual republics. If the Union
> is to have a People's Commissariat of Foreign Affairs, a People's Com-
> missariat of Foreign Trade, and so forth, and the republics constituting
> the Union are also to have all these Commissariats, it is obvious that
> it will be impossible for the Union as a whole to come before the out-
> side world as a single state. One thing or the other: either we merge
> these apparatuses and face the external enemy as a single Union, or
> we do not merge them and create not a union state, but a conglomera-
> tion of republics, in which case every republic must have its own
> parallel apparatus.[6]

Although the 1944 Amendments did not disturb the central government's exclusive control over foreign trade, they did establish what
Stalin condemned as a confederation in 1923 and what Molotov hailed
as a "new forward stride" in the development of the Soviet federation in
1944, thus permitting the Soviet Union to masquerade as a confederation under international law and a federation under internal law.

(1) *The International Legal Status of the Union Republics.* From
the standpoint of Soviet legal doctrine, the Republics have from the very
beginning, and without interruption, been paraded as sovereign states.
Theoretically, according to Stalin and his juridical exegetes, the republics in joining the Union in 1923 did not surrender their sovereignty
irrevocably, but voluntarily entrusted certain powers of statehood to the
central government, which they were free to recover by virtue of their
right to secede from the Union:

> If the R.S.F.S.R., the Ukraine, Byelorussia and the Transcaucasian
> Republics are not each to have its own People's Commissariat of Foreign
> Affairs, it is clear that the abolition of these commissariats . . . will be
> accompanied by a certain restriction of the independence enjoyed by
> these republics. . . . Some people ask a purely scholastic question —
> whether after amalgamation the republics remain independent. This is a
> scholastic question. Their independence is restricted, for every amalga-
> mation involves a certain restriction of the rights of the amalgamating
> parties. But the elements of independence of each of these republics

[6] J. V. Stalin, *Works*, 13 vols. (Moscow, 1952–1955), V, pp. 341–344;
cf. also pp. 302–303. According to Vyshinsky, the "Ukrainian Confedera-
tionists" wished to retain separate Foreign Affairs Commissariats so that they
could "preserve the legal possibility of contact with their masters — the big
imperialist powers and Poland — so as to betray their people and the Union
in its entirety." A. Y. Vyshinsky, *The Law of the Soviet State* (Macmillan,
1948), p. 264.

undoubtedly remain, for each republic retains the right to leave the union at its own discretion. *There you have the elements of independence, the maximum of independence, which is potentially retained by each of the republics forming part of the Union and which each of them is always at liberty to exercise.*[7]

Within the context of Soviet juridical theory, the 1944 Amendments represent a partial recovery by the republics of powers which they entrusted to the Union in 1923 and again in 1936, and signify an expansion of their sovereign authority into the sphere of international relations. Thus, in a Declaration of the Ukrainian Republic, dated April 26, 1945, and circulated at the San Francisco Conference, the Ukraine rested its juridical right to membership in the United Nations on grounds that it had redeemed portions of its sovereignty which it had earlier surrendered voluntarily and temporarily to the Union:

> The Ukrainian Soviet Socialist Republic, on the basis of its Constitution of January 30, 1937, and the constitutional revisions and amendments adopted by the Supreme Soviet of the Ukrainian Soviet Socialist Republic on March 4, 1944, has recovered the right which it formerly had and which it voluntarily ceded to the Union of Soviet Socialist Republics in 1922, to establish direct relations with foreign states, to conclude agreements with them and to have independent representation at international conferences and bodies set up by the latter.[8]

A similar Declaration was circulated by the delegation of the Byelorussian Republic. In a press conference held by D. Z. Manuilsky in San Francisco on May 22, 1945, the Ukrainian Foreign Minister further elaborated by maintaining that all of the Union Republics had always possessed diplomatic rights but that they voluntarily chose not to exercise them until now. Since these rights could only be exercised on the basis of an Amendment to the Union Constitution, the question of juridical initiative involved in the partial redemption of sovereign rights by the Republics is a moot one. It would be more correct to say that these rights were not recovered by the Republics but that they were delegated to them by the Union. Nevertheless, Soviet jurists maintain that:

> The Soviet Union as a whole and every Union Republic in particular are autonomous subjects of international law with all the rights and obligations towards other states which derive from this status. . . . Union Republics, as well as the Soviet Union as a whole, are truly sovereign states.[9]

[7] J. V. Stalin, *Marxism and the National Question* (International Publishers, 1942), pp. 140–141 (my italics). Cf. also *Works*, V, pp. 247–248.

[8] *Vneshnyaya Politika Sovetskovo Soyuza v Period Otechestvennoi Voiny* (Moscow, 1947), III, p. 229. Also cited in F. I. Kozhevnikov, *Sovetskoye Gosudarstvo i Mezhdunarodnoye Pravo* (Moscow, 1948), p. 63.

[9] V. V. Yevgenyev, "Subjects of International Law, Sovereignty and Non-Interference in International Law," *Sovetskoye Gosudarstvo i Pravo*, March 1955 (No. 2), 76–77. Cf. also F. N. Kozhevnikov, *Mezhdunarodnoye Pravo* (Moscow, 1957), p. 89.

Furthermore, as members of the Soviet Union, the republics not only enjoy all legal rights under international law but also the extra-legal prerogatives of a Great Power in international politics:

> Membership in the USSR guarantees each Republic full protection of its rights and interests on the international level. If each Republic acted in international affairs as a separate state . . . it would have little participation and influence in the consideration of major international questions. It is only as part of the Union structure that each Republic, irrespective of its size, has equal opportunity with others to assume the position of a Great Power — the USSR — in international affairs.[10]

This is not the first time that a single political entity enjoys the capacity for multiple representation under international law.[11] In the recent past, one need only recall the Imperial German Federation, the Ottoman Empire, the British Commonwealth in its early development, the Weimar Republic and even the Bonn Federal Republic today to realize that the Soviet formula was not an invention of Stalin's devious genius.[12] It is not necessary that a Union be a confederation in law for

[10] V. Vadimov, *Verkhovny Sovet SSSR i Mezhdunarodnye Otnosheniya* (Moscow, 1958), p. 17. *Cf.* also p. 16.

[11] Soviet jurists, by drawing distinctions between "state" sovereignty and "national" sovereignty, even claim that the lesser national units in the Soviet Union are "sovereign." "The struggle of nationalities for the realization of their national sovereignty need not take the form of a struggle for an independent state, *i.e.*, state sovereignty . . . as a nationality may just as well express the wish to be included in a multi-national state as a member of a federation or as an autonomous unit." L. A. Modzhoryan, "The Notion of Sovereignty Under International Law," *Sovetskoye Gosudarstvo i Pravo*, February 1955 (No. 1), p. 70. But Yevgenyev maintains that "a nation, which has not yet created its own independent state or seceded into such a state, may not be recognized as a subject of international law, because the lack of any public authority deprives this nationality of the capacity for contracting international obligations and guaranteeing their fulfillment." Yevgenyev, "Subjects of International Law," p. 77. The most eloquent practical demonstration of the interchangeability of the Soviet conceptions of sovereignty was the liquidation of the Karelo-Finnish Union Republic and its transformation into a lesser unit as the Karelian Autonomous Republic by a mere stroke of the pen. Neither the population nor the Supreme Soviet of the Republic were consulted in a move which deprived the Republic of its cherished right to secede, its separate foreign affairs and defense establishments, fourteen deputies in the Council of Nationalities and its Vice-Chairman on the Presidium of the Supreme Soviet of the U.S.S.R. *Pravda*, July 17, 1956. *Cf.* also A. Y. Vyshinsky, *The Law of the Soviet State*, pp. 275–280; Kozhevnikov, *Mezhdunarodnoye Pravo*, pp. 86–107; and V. N. Durdenevsky and S. B. Krylov, *Mezhdunarodnoye Pravo* (Moscow, 1947), pp. 109–168.

[12] The most relevant precedent in recent times was Imperial Germany. The twenty-three monarchies and three city Republics of the Empire enjoyed the power of separate diplomatic relations and their representatives were often to be found alongside the Imperial Ambassadors and Ministers. Only Prussia was denied this privilege. *Cf.* Otto Esch, *Das Gesandtschaftrecht der Deutschen Einzelstaaten* (Bonn, 1911); Riess, *Auswärtige Hoheitsrechte der Deutschen Einzelstaaten* (1905); and Windisch, *Die Völkerrechtliche Stellung der Deutschen Einzelstaaten* (1913). Under the Weimar Constitution, while foreign relations were centralized in Berlin, the Länder were permitted limited authority to conclude treaties with foreign states, although Berlin

its component units to qualify as diplomatic entities, any more than it is necessary that a state be actually independent to enjoy recognition under international law or to engage in diplomatic relations. Should the United States, for example, aspire to gain separate diplomatic recognition for its constituent states, it need only make the requisite juridical alterations and await the individual decisions of other powers to grant or withhold recognition. Certain hazards are always inherent in any devolutionary process: one need only point to the attempts of France to preserve her Empire by permitting members of the French Union to enjoy autonomous diplomatic status. It is perhaps the serious risks involved, more than any other single factor, that have prompted the Kremlin to stifle what initially appeared to be a promising, if limited, diplomatic future for the Soviet Republics.

Although all the Soviet Republics have equal diplomatic powers, only the Ukraine and Byelorussia have any recognized status under international law, and this stems solely from their membership in the United Nations. In marked contrast to the Soviet Government's sedulous refusal to permit the republics to establish bilateral diplomatic contacts with other states, it has been persistent in efforts to gain their entry into international organizations and conferences. Aside from minor agreements signed by three of the republics with the Lublin Polish Provisional Government, virtually all the formal diplomatic activity of the two republics has been confined to the United Nations, its affiliated and associated organizations, and conferences and commissions based upon United Nations membership.[13] Failure to win further international legal recognition of this sort has only stimulated the Soviet Government to enhance the prominence of the republics, if not in its formal diplomacy, then on the fringes. Since 1950, their informal participation on the margins of diplomacy has been progressively expanded and accelerated. This reflects Moscow's resourcefulness in reaping the benefits of a confederation under international law and those of a federation under constitutional law, without risking the obligations and hazards of either, while it remains in fact a highly centralized state. In this way, the Soviet leaders hope to gain the best of three worlds.

(2) *The Constitutional Distribution of Diplomatic Powers.* The constitutional decentralization of foreign affairs in the Soviet system is ingeniously devised to preclude any legal or political conflict between formal devolution and actual centralization of control. Although the supremacy of the center might appear to be sufficiently guaranteed by the monolithic organization and monopolistic control of power by the

---

reserved the power of final approval and ratification. Bavaria was permitted to maintain relations with the Holy See and a French Minister-Plenipotentiary continued to be accredited to Munich. *Cf.* L. Oppenheim, *International Law,* ed. H. Lauterpacht, 2 vols., 6th ed. (Longmans, 1947), I, pp. 115–116; 161–192. In an era of petty personal monarchs in Europe, diplomatic recognition perhaps performed a social prestige function comparable to the issuance of free railroad passes to the executives of minor roads here until Congress put a stop to the practice.

[13] *Cf.* pp. 688–693, this text.

Communist Party, the constitutional provisions of both the All-Union and the several Republic documents nevertheless allow for the erection of parallel diplomatic apparatuses not coordinate with, but subordinate to, the central Ministry of Foreign Affairs. *Kompetenz-kompetenz* clearly resides in the Union. The Amendments assert the absolute supremacy of the central government over foreign affairs and establish essentially a permissive authority for the center to delegate limited diplomatic functions to the republics, at its own discretion.

When the author asked Foreign Ministry officials in Moscow and in the Republics why the latter had not established diplomatic contacts with foreign countries, he was quickly told that the Constitution does not make mandatory the exchange of diplomatic representatives, but merely provides the juridical authority. Although all Union Republics have the juridical capacity to enter into diplomatic relations, this equality is not thought to be infringed by an unequal implementation of their diplomatic powers. So their juridical status, while it remains uniform under internal laws, can develop unevenly under international law, as witness the special status of the Ukraine and Byelorussia.[14] Their diplomatic relations can be expanded selectively and with discrimination, in accordance with the requirements of policy and the opportunities of international power politics.

The general authority permitting the republics to engage in diplomatic relations is governed by Articles 14a and 18a.[15] The first gives the central government jurisdiction over "representation of the U.S.S.R. in international relations, conclusion, ratification and denunciation of treaties of the U.S.S.R. with other states," and "establishment of the general procedure governing relations of the Union Republics with foreign states," while Article 18a asserts that "each Union Republic has the right to enter into direct relations with foreign states and conclude agreements and exchange diplomatic and consular representatives with them."

Article 60e of the Constitution stipulates that the Supreme Soviet of the individual republic "decides questions of representation of the Union Republic in its international relations," while Article 67d states that the Union Council of Ministers "exercises general guidance in the sphere of relations with foreign states," and Article 68a stipulates that it "co-ordinates and directs the work of the All-Union and Union-Republican Ministries of the U.S.S.R." Article 76 defines the jurisdiction and administrative status of the Union-Republican Ministries, while Article 78 lists the Foreign Ministry in this category. Article 87 further elaborates by pointing out that "each Union-Republican Ministry directs the branch of state administration entrusted to it, and is subordinate both

[14] The same could be said of the various Imperial Acts, culminating in the Statute of Westminster in 1931, which governed the relations between Great Britain and her Dominions.

[15] Constitution of the U.S.S.R., as amended to January 1, 1957, in *Istoriya Sovetskoi Konstitutsii* (*v Dokumentakh*), *1917–1956* (Moscow, 1957), pp. 944–964.

to the Council of Ministers of the Union Republics and the corresponding Union-Republican Ministry of the U.S.S.R."

The constitutions of the fifteen individual republics have also been
appropriately altered to conform with the Amendments of 1944, and
they make six separate references to the powers of the republics in
foreign affairs. Using the Constitution of the Uzbek Republic as reference, Article 16a establishes that "the Uzbek Soviet Socialist Republic
has the right to enter into direct relations with foreign states and to
conclude agreements and exchange diplomatic and consular representatives with them," but neither the power to ratify and denounce treaties
nor to declare war and peace is mentioned.[16] Article 19aa gives to the
Supreme Soviet of the Republic and its Presidium power to authorize the
"establishment of the representation of the Uzbek S.S.R. in international
relations," while Articles 30h and 39i give to the Presidium the power to
appoint and recall diplomatic representatives of the Republic as well as
to receive the letters of credence and recall of foreign emissaries. Article
46g states that the Republic's Council of Ministers "exercises guidance
in the sphere of the relations of the Uzbek S.S.R. with foreign states, on
the basis of the general procedure established by the U.S.S.R. governing
the relations of the Union Republics with foreign states." Article 50
provides for a Ministry of Foreign Affairs as a Union-Republican
Ministry.

The constitutional provisions of both the All-Union and republican
documents are sufficiently elastic to permit a wide degree of initiative for
the republics in establishing diplomatic contacts and negotiating international agreements. In practice, they possess no initiative at all and act
only upon signal from Moscow. There is nothing, however, to prevent
foreign states from approaching either Moscow or one of the republican
Foreign Ministers at the United Nations with a bid to exchange diplomatic representatives with individual republics. In all probability, at this
stage, such a bid would be received with both suspicion and embarrassment.

III. Representation of the Union Republics in Federal Organs of Policy and Administration in Foreign Affairs

Although the republics obviously cannot act independently, scrupulous attention, almost to the point of extravagance, has been paid to the
formal and decorative aspects of republican participation in the internal
organs of foreign policy and administration at all levels of the central
government. As in any federation, the Union Republics might be expected
to have appropriate unit representation in the legislative organs of the
federal government, and formal decentralization in foreign affairs should
give them participation in the executive and administrative institutions
of the central state structure as well. From a purely constitutional

[16] *Constitution of the Uzbek S.S.R.* (Moscow, 1949). The numbering of
the corresponding articles may vary among the republican constitutions, but
the language is identical in all cases.

standpoint, the Soviet system meets both these expectations, although in varying degrees of implementation.

(1) *The Presidium of the Supreme Soviet.* The Presidium of the Supreme Soviet of the U.S.S.R. possesses a wide and impressive range of ceremonial and substantive (executive, legislative and judicial) powers in the sphere of foreign relations and functions as the collegial Chief of State of the Soviet Union. It is recognized by Soviet jurists as the highest institutional symbol of state representation under international law. Normally, however, the Chairman of this body performs all the symbolic and ceremonial acts in the name of the Presidium as a whole. As the highest personal symbol of state sovereignty, he is invested with its *jus repraesentationis omnimodae* in the traditional rituals of diplomacy:

> In accordance with the universally recognized doctrine of international law, the supreme representation of the modern State is vested in the chief of state, whether he be an actual person (monarch, president of the republic) or a collective body (Presidium of the Supreme Soviet of the U.S.S.R., Federal Council of Switzerland). . . . As a general rule, the competence of the chief of state includes the declaration of war and conclusion of peace, nomination and reception of diplomatic agents, granting powers for the conclusion of international treaties and agreements of special significance, and the ratification and denunciation of these treaties and accords.[17]

Not only does the Presidium of the Supreme Soviet perform the acts enumerated above, but it is also empowered to interpret all Soviet laws in operation, convene and dissolve the Supreme Soviet, annul decisions and orders of the Council of Ministers of the Union and of the republics, appoint and remove the higher commands of the armed forces, declare martial law and act as custodian of supreme state power during the intervals between sessions of the Supreme Soviet.[18]

In this organ of thirty-three members, there are fifteen Vice-Chairmen — one for each of the Union Republics. By custom only, and not by constitutional imperative, the Chairmen of the fifteen Presidia of the republics are elected as Vice-Chairmen of the All-Union Presidium;[19] this accounts for nearly one-half the total membership of that body. Frequently, selected Party leaders of high rank are also to be found

---

[17] V. P. Potemkin, editor, *Istoriya Diplomatii*, 3 vols. (Moscow, 1945), III, p. 765. The Presidium was not expressly authorized to *denounce* treaties until the Supreme Soviet revised Article 49 of the Constitution on February 25, 1947. *Istoriya Sovetskoi Konstitutsii*, p. 831.

[18] Articles 48 and 49.

[19] Cf. B. P. Kravtsov, *Verkhovny Soveta SSSR* (Moscow, 1954), pp. 69–70. The law on the composition of the Presidium, adopted on March 19, 1946, does not specifically state that each Republic is entitled to a Vice-Chairman — or even a representative — but the number of Vice-Chairmen has always corresponded to the number of Union Republics. *Sbornik Zakonov SSSR i Ukazov Prezidiuma Verkhovnovo Soveta SSSR 1938–1956* (Moscow, 1956), p. 77. Cf. *Pravda*, March 28, 1958, for the composition of the current Presidium. Among the ordinary members are high Party functionaries from the Uzbek, Ukrainian, Byelorussian and Kazakh Republics.

among the sixteen ordinary — in actuality, the working — members of the Presidium. Thus in the highest organ of diplomatic representation in the Soviet system, the Republics are generously represented. In two cases, the Byelorussian and Ukrainian Republics, the Chairman of the Republic's Presidium functions separately as representative of a collegial Chief of State in his own right under international law; the other Vice-Chairmen possess only the legal capacity to function similarly. While the Soviet system of multiple sovereignty combines in many ways the characteristic configurations of suzerainty and vassalage of old Oriental Empires (the Parthian, Persian and Ottoman), the feudal multiple monarchies of Europe (the Holy Roman Empire and Imperial Germany), and the progressively attenuated subordination which marked the British Commonwealth, the Soviet collegial formula of a Chief of State composed of subordinate Chiefs of State constitutes a unique departure in modern diplomatic practice.

(2) *The Supreme Soviet.* In the bi-cameral Soviet legislature — the formal repository of all state power and the source of basic legislation — each republic is entitled to 25 deputies in the Council of Nationalities and a complement of deputies in the Council of the Union proportionate to the size of its population. The one supposedly expresses the juridical equality of the Union Republics and the other their demographic inequality; but, unlike our Senate and the upper chambers in other federal states, the Council of Nationalities was devised to serve a further purpose. According to Stalin, it was organized in order that "the nationalities of the USSR have *their particular, specific* interests, connected with their specific national characteristics," represented.[20] It is an expression not only of the federal nature of the Soviet State but also of its multi-national character; of course, both elements are organically connected.

The fourteen non-Russian republics account for 350 deputies in the Council of Nationalities, or slightly more than one-half, while the remaining contingents represent lesser national units (mostly within the R.S.F.S.R.) which do not possess formal diplomatic powers. Thus some of the republics, because of lesser national units within their borders, actually possess far more than their basic contingent of 25 deputies in the Council of Nationalities. For instance, the Ukraine, with a population in excess of forty million, has only its basic complement of 25 deputies, while the Georgian Republic, with a population of four million, has 52, thus in effect shattering the principle of equality which ostensibly prevails in this chamber. Unlike upper chambers in some other federations, the Council of Nationalities enjoys no special prerogatives in the area of international relations. Although it is constitutionally coordinate with the Council of the Union, the latter actually carries more prestige and status in the Soviet scheme because it symbolizes direct and proportionate representation.

[20] Stalin, *Leninism*, p. 401. *Cf.* also Kravtsov, *Verkhovny Soveta SSSR*, p. 35 and Vadimov, *Verkhovny Sovet SSSR i Mezhdunarodnye Otnosheniya*, p. 15.

Until recently, the Supreme Soviet played only a passive role even in the formalities of legislating policy dealing with foreign affairs. Convoked only rarely and then for sessions of very short duration, it did little but hear and approve reports of the Government on foreign policy, give assent to the decrees of the Presidium, and adopt laws and resolutions initiated by the Council of Ministers. Since 1954, however, a calculated effort has been made to give the Soviet legislature a more conspicuous and active role in foreign affairs; as yet this has been more ornamental than real. Aside from being called into session more frequently to hear reports on foreign policy, its expanded participation has been characterized by three main developments: (1) the stimulation of the withered functions of its two Foreign Affairs Commissions and their recent reorganization; (2) the establishment of direct contacts with legislative bodies of other countries, either through the exchange of parliamentary delegations, participation in international legislative associations or conferences, and the use of Supreme Soviet officials in quasi-diplomatic capacities; and (3) the issuance of propaganda declarations, resolutions and appeals on international questions. Under the first two categories the more active role of the Supreme Soviet has automatically enhanced the formal role of the republics in the legislative aspects of Soviet foreign policy.

(a) The Foreign Affairs Commissions. Although the two Foreign Affairs Commissions (one for each chamber) are not mentioned in the Constitution, each chamber organized a Permanent Commission on Foreign Affairs at its first session in January 1938, in accordance with Article 51.[21] According to A. Y. Vyshinsky, the chief function of the Foreign Affairs Commissions is to make "a preliminary examination of all matters connected with foreign affairs to be considered by the Supreme Soviet (and its Presidium)."[22] The Commissions, which superficially resemble their counterparts in the American Congress and the parliaments of western Europe, are empowered to sit separately or jointly (the usual procedure) whether or not the Supreme Soviet is in session. Between sessions of the Supreme Soviet, the Commissions exercise the power of legislative control and surveillance over the execution and administration of Soviet foreign relations.[23]

The competence and authority of the Commissions are quite broad and embrace three general functions: (1) to examine and recommend action to the respective chambers on matters concerning foreign policy which come before the Supreme Soviet; (2) to examine and recommend action to the Supreme Soviet or its Presidium on motions or proposals concerned with the ratification, denunciation or nullification of treaties and agreements concluded by the Soviet Union; and (3) to prepare on its own initiative and introduce for the examination of the Supreme

[21] S. G. Novikov, *Postoyannye Komissii Verkhovnovo Soveta SSSR* (Moscow, 1958), p. 33.
[22] *The Law of the Soviet State, op. cit.*, p. 349.
[23] Vadimov, *Verkhovny Sovet SSSR i Mezhdunarodnye Otnosheniya*, p. 8.

Soviet or one of its chambers draft legislation and other acts touching on questions of foreign policy. In carrying out their functions, the Commissions are authorized to organize subcommissions, summon government officials and experts to give testimony, and demand that the government furnish documents and materials necessary for their work.[24]

Historically, the record shows only one occasion when the Commissions have criticized the work of the Foreign Ministry. At the initial meeting of the Supreme Soviet under the new Constitution, on January 17, 1938, Zhdanov in his capacity as Chairman of the Foreign Affairs Commission of the Council of the Union sharply questioned Molotov about the espionage activities of foreign consulates and asked why the Foreign Affairs Commissariat was tolerating such a condition. Molotov acknowledged the criticism and promised action.[25] Since Stalin's death a determined effort has been made to embellish the work of the Commissions. Whatever passes for debate or discussion in the Soviet legislature on foreign affairs is almost always conducted by members of the Commissions, who comment approvingly upon the proposals of the Government or are inspired to introduce motions and resolutions to be adopted by the Supreme Soviet, allegedly upon their own initiative.[26]

The spokesman for the Commission is its chairman, who is also its most powerful and influential member. Normally, the chairmen of the two Commissions are full or alternate members of the Party Presidium (Politburo) and have no formal executive or administrative posts in the government. When the Commissions act jointly, the Chairman of the Commission of the Council of the Union, who is usually a full member of the party's highest body and of the Party Secretariat, as well as the party's most authoritative professional theoretician and its specialist on relations with foreign communist parties, acts as presiding officer and spokesman. This post is usually reserved for an ethnic Russian. The first chairman of this Commission was Andrei Zhdanov; its current presiding

[24] Novikov, *Postoyannye Komissii Verkhovnovo Soveta SSSR*, pp. 33–39. For details on the organization and procedures of the two Commissions, cf. Vadimov, *Verkhovny Sovet SSSR i Mezhdunarodnye Otnosheniya*, p. 9; D. A. Kerimov, *Zakonodatelnaya Deyatelnost Sovetskovo Gosudarstva* (Moscow, 1955), pp. 54–57. Full texts of the Statutes on the organization and procedure of the Commissions are reprinted in *Istoriya Sovetkoi Konstitutsii*, pp. 837–840.

[25] Cf. *Pervaya Sessia Verkhovnovo Soveta SSSR, 12–19 Yanvaria, 1938* (Moscow, 1938), pp. 135, 151. Cf. also Kravtsov, *Verkhovny Soveta SSSR*, p. 66.

[26] For a concrete illustration of the way in which the Commissions present their reports, cf. *Materialy Pyatoi Sessi Verkhovnovo Soveta SSSR po Voprosam Razoruzheniya i Zapreshcheniya Atomnovo i Vodorodnovo Oruzhiya* (Moscow, 1956). Cf. also Novikov, *Postoyannye Komissii Verkhovnovo Sovet SSSR*, pp. 34–39 and Vadimov, *Verkhovny Sovet SSSR i Mezhdunarodnye Otnosheniya*, p. 8, for a list of treaties which have been submitted in the last few years to the Commissions for examination and approval prior to their ratification by the Presidium. The procedure is evidently perfunctory, cursory and ceremonial, since in almost all cases examination, approval and ratification have been completed within one or two days.

officer is Mikhail Suslov. The chairman of the Commission in the Council of Nationalities is usually a party figure of less imposing rank; its first chairman was Nikolai Bulganin and the current incumbent is N. A. Mukhitdinov, First Secretary of the Uzbek Party and a member of the Presidium and Secretariat of the CPSU.[27]

The membership of the two Commissions reflects the careful selection of a balanced slate. It includes representatives from republican governments and party organizations, the Komsomol, trade unions, the armed forces, the cultural elite and Party specialists on relations with foreign communist parties (Comintern and Cominform overseers before 1957). As a general rule, members of the All-Union Presidium, and Council of Ministers and officials of the Foreign Ministry are excluded from the Commissions, presumably to maintain the fiction that the Commissions are independent agencies of review and investigation. Because of this incompatibility, members of the Commissions who subsequently are appointed to executive or administrative positions in the government, related to foreign affairs, cease to be active and are eventually dropped from the Commissions. This happened in 1958 to some Commission members elected in 1954. The fact that this rule does not apply to republican executive and administrative officials (including Premiers and Foreign Ministers) unwittingly betrays the insignificant part they have in the execution and administration of foreign affairs. On the other hand, the active Premiers and Foreign Ministers of the Ukrainian and Byelorussian Republics (because of their more direct participation in diplomacy) apparently are excluded from membership in the two Commissions.

In March 1958, the size of the two Commissions was more than doubled — from eleven each to twenty-three each.[28] They were completely reorganized and the equilibrium among the various republics and organizations was radically altered. Formal and informal representation of the republics in the two Commissions is numerically impressive, particularly in the Council of Nationalities, and reflects careful planning and discrimination in selection. In the reorganized Commissions, however, the balance between formal representation (republican government officials) and informal representation (republican party officials) has been significantly altered — perhaps indicating a contemplated expansion of the responsibilities of the republics in formal diplomacy.

Before March 1958, the composition of the Commission in the Council of Nationalities included two republican Premiers (Azerbaidzhan and the Turkmen Republic), two Foreign Ministers (Kirgiz Republic and Georgia), three Central Committee members of republican party

[27] Mukhitdinov's predecessor was Dmitri Shepilov, who resigned after his appointment as Foreign Minister in July 1956. Only the two Commissions on Foreign Affairs have had such a succession of powerful personalities as Chairmen, although members of the Politburo and Presidium appear in other Commissions as ordinary members.

[28] *Pravda*, March 28, 1958. When first organized, the Commission elected by the Council of Nationalities had only ten members.

organizations (Ukrainian, Latvian and Kazakh), and the First Secretary
of the Uzbek Party.[29] The composition of its counterpart in the Council
of the Union before its reorganization embraced no republican government officials, but included the First Secretaries of four republican party
organizations (Byelorussia, Tadzhik, Estonia and Lithuania) and a
former Premier of the Uzbek Republic.[30] In the two Commissions
elected in 1954, all the republics except the Armenian and Moldavian
were represented in one or the other of the two Commissions by either a
republican governmental official or a high party functionary.

In the newly expanded and reorganized Commissions, elected on
March 27, 1958, the number of high republican government officials has
been drastically reduced in favor of a generous influx of regional party
officials and members of the cultural elite. In the newly elected Foreign
Affairs Commission in the Council of Nationalities, the R.S.F.S.R. has
six members (including one each from the Daghestan Chumash and
Buryat-Mongol Autonomous Republics), while the Ukraine has three.
Georgia, Azerbaidzhan, the Uzbek and Tadzhik Republicans are represented by two members each, while the Byelorussian, Lithuanian,
Latvian, Moldavian, Armenian and Kazakh Republics have one representative each. In the corresponding Commission in the Council of the
Union, the R.S.F.S.R. has no less than eleven members (including one
each from the Karelian and Tatar Autonomous Republics), against three
for the Ukraine. The Lithuanian, Byelorussian, Latvian, Estonian,
Georgian, Azerbaidzhanian, Uzbek and Kazakh Republics each have one
representative in this Commission. The composition of the two Commissions indicates a calculated attempt to allot representatives to the Republics in accordance with their size, importance and ethnic complexity.[31]

High republican government officials have been reduced to only
two, both in the Council of Nationalities: the Foreign Minister of the
Georgian Republic (who is also a First Deputy Premier) and a Deputy
Premier of the Armenian Republic. In the Commission elected by the
Council of the Union, the membership includes the First Secretaries of
the Estonian and Lithuanian Parties, while the Chairman of the Commission in the other Chamber is the First Secretary of the Uzbek Party.
The balance of the membership in both Commissions is made up of
regional party officials from the republics, Komsomol and trade union
functionaries, writers, educators and propagandists — most of whom

[29] *Izvestia*, April 21, 1954, and July 14, 1956.

[30] *Izvestia*, April 21, 1954.

[31] Of the 46 members in both Foreign Affairs Commissions, 17 are from
the R.S.F.S.R. (including deputies from 5 Autonomous Republics), 6 are from
the Ukraine, 3 each are from the Uzbek, Georgian and Azerbaidzhan Republics (including 1 representative each from an Autonomous Republic within
the Union Republic), 2 each are from the Byelorussian, Lithuanian, Latvian,
and Tadzhik Republics, while the Armenian and Estonian Republics have one
each. The remaining member is Marshal Grechko, representing the armed
forces. The ethnic distribution does not necessarily follow the distribution by
Republics, since representatives from some of the Republics are often ethnic
Russians.

also belong to a *mélange* of mass propaganda organizations which have been spawned by the World Peace Council and its affiliated associations.[32]

Although the Commissions have been more than doubled in size, two republics, the Turkmen and Kirgiz, are currently unrepresented in either Commission. Since international treaties altering the boundaries of the republics must have the approval of the republic concerned, under Article 18, it would appear logical to give every republic at least one representative in the Commissions.[33] The practice appears to be in that direction, but at present there is no formal rule which either governs the ethnic composition of the two Commissions or makes representation from every Union Republic mandatory.

(b) Republican Participation in Soviet Parliamentary Groups. Before 1955, the Supreme Soviet as such engaged in little para-diplomatic activity nor did it exhibit any great passion for establishing contacts with parliaments in other countries. On February 9, 1955, in synchronization with Malenkov's demise as Premier, the Supreme Soviet issued a number of declarations on foreign policy matters, one of which was an appeal to the other parliaments of the world to exchange visits of parliamentary delegations with the Soviet Union.[34] Since then, the Soviet legislature has exhibited an extraordinary enthusiasm for quasi-official parliamentary contacts and has engaged in a veritable flood of exchanging visiting delegations. Whereas in 1954 the Soviet Union received parliamentary delegations from only two countries and dispatched only one of its own, between 1955 and 1957 it entertained delegations from 26 countries and sent visitors to seventeen.[35] Parliamentary delegations and other dignitaries from Asia and Africa have also been received by the Supreme Soviets of the Uzbek and other Moslem republics, while Soviet Asian deputies have been given unusual prominence in Soviet delegations visiting the East.[36]

The quasi-diplomatic functions of the Supreme Soviet were further embellished on June 29, 1955 when it declared adherence to the Inter-Parliamentary Union and sent an energetic delegation to the 44th Annual Conference of the association held in Helsinki in August of the same year.[37] Since it was first organized, the Parliamentary Group of the U.S.S.R., which is by far the largest from any member country, has played a conspicuous role in the executive organs of the IPU and in its

[32] *Pravda*, March 28, 1958. The governmental, party and professional positions held by the members of the Commissions were identified by scrutinizing lists of government, party and other organizations appearing in local newspapers and various issues of central newspapers.

[33] *Cf.* pp. 691–692, this text.

[34] *Izvestia*, February 10, 1955. *Cf.* also Vadimov, *Verkhovny Sovet SSSR i Mezhdunarodnye Otnosheniya*, pp. 77–78. This declaration was supplemented by a resolution of December 28, 1955 by the Supreme Soviet on the exchange of parliamentary delegations with other countries.

[35] Vadimov, *Verkhovny Sovet SSSR i Mezhdunarodnye Otnosheniya*, p. 78.

[36] Z. A. Lebedeva, *Parliamentskaya Gruppa Sovetskovo Soyuza* (Moscow, 1958), pp. 51–53.

[37] *Ibid.*, pp. 9–10.

annual conferences.[38] Although the Ukrainian and Byelorussian Republics have also declared their adherence to the IPU, they have not yet been admitted as separate members. Both republics, however, have organized Temporary Bureaus in anticipation of their formal admission.[39] In the composition of the 21-member Executive Committee of the Soviet Parliamentary Group, each of the other Republics has been allotted at least one representative.[40]

(3) *Organs of Central Administration: The Council of Ministers and the Foreign Ministry.* In the highest state organ of diplomatic policy and administration in the central government, the Council of Ministers, the Union Republics play a minor formal role and exert an even lesser influence in its deliberations and decisions. Although the Premiers of the republics have been *ex-officio* non-voting members of the Council of Ministers since the formation of the Union and are authorized to maintain their plenipotentiaries in Moscow, they are excluded from the Presidium of the Council of Ministers, where major policy decisions are made, unless they are specifically invited for consultation.[41] The main administrative link between the organs of the center and those of the republics is the Union-Republican Ministry, to which corresponding Ministers are appointed at both levels, each theoretically responsible to his respective supreme organs of state authority. The Union-Republican Ministry in each republic, furthermore, is clearly subordinated to the administrative control of its counterpart in the central government, making an ingenious pattern of dual subordination. Since the Constitution empowers the All-Union Presidium to annul, and the federal Council of Ministers to suspend, decisions and orders of the Council of Ministers in any republic, the supremacy of the central government is assured, in the event of conflict.[42]

The Union-Republican Ministries, of which the Foreign Ministry is one, have proved useful devices for decentralizing the burdens of administration and responsibility without at the same time relinquishing control or direction of policy. This distributive purpose can be served, however, only if there are activities which can be decentralized for administrative convenience. Since the Foreign Ministry has limited internal responsibilities and these are not at present either functionally or territorially diffused throughout the Union, there is virtually nothing for the Union-Republican Foreign Minister to administer, aside from the minor diplomatic responsibilities of the Ukraine and Byelorussia.

The Ministry of Defense has also been a Union-Republican Ministry

[38] More than 96 per cent of the deputies of the Supreme Soviet belong to the Soviet Parliamentary Group. See Lebedeva, *Parliamentskaya Gruppa Sovetskovo Soyuza*, p. 10; *cf.* ibid., pp. 14–44, for a description of the activities of the Soviet delegations and individual deputies.

[39] *Pravda*, July 2, 1955. Each has also nominated two representatives to the Council of the IPU.

[40] Lebedeva, *Parliamentskaya Gruppa Sovetskovo Soyuza*, pp. 11–12.

[41] *Cf.* Vadimov, *Verkhovny Sovet SSSR i Mezhdunarodnye Otnosheniya*, p. 17. This practice was first adopted by decree of the Sovnarkom on August 7, 1923. *Sistematicheskoye Sobranie Deistvuyushchikh Zakonov S.S.S.R.* (Moscow, 1926), I, pp. 33–34.

[42] Articles 49f and 69.

since 1944, but has never been decentralized beyond the provisions of the Constitution. So the Foreign Ministry has been in a curious half-way stage, neither internally decentralized like the Ministries of Justice and Culture nor completely aborted like the Ministry of Defense. Before 1938, under the provisions of the Narkomindel Statute of November 12, 1923, many consular and administrative functions in the territories of the republics were entrusted to a special Narkomindel Representative attached to the Republican Council of People's Commissars.[43] Should the Soviet Government expand its consular exchanges to the degree which prevailed before 1938, one way of decentralizing the administrative machinery of the Foreign Ministry might be to assign the consular duties and responsibilities performed by the old Narkomindel Representative in the territories of the republics to the Republican Minister of Foreign Affairs.

[Since this article was published in June, 1959, important changes have taken place in the composition, size, legal status and powers of the Supreme Soviet, its Presidium and its Standing Commissions: (1) the size of the Presidium has increased to thirty-seven members, with the addition of four more ordinary members; (2) in 1966, the number of deputies allotted to each Union Republic in the Council of Nationalities was raised from twenty-five to thirty-two, for a total of 448 deputies from the non-Russian republics, thus giving them an absolute majority in this Chamber of 750 members; and (3) the size of the two Foreign Affairs Commissions was increased to thirty-two each, thus giving the Union Republics greater representation in the Commissions. More importantly, however, the legal status and powers of all Standing Commissions were strengthened in October, 1967, with the promulgation of a Supreme Soviet Statute (Zakon), "On Standing Commissions of the Council of Union and the Council of Nationalities." According to M. S. Solomentsev, Secretariat member and Chairman of the Legislative Proposals Commission of the Council of Union, the Commissions have been transformed from organs created by "only internal acts of the chambers" into organs "having the force of law." The jurisdiction of the Commissions has been somewhat expanded, but more significantly, under the new law their formal legal authority has been enhanced, since the Statute gives the Commissions "control over the activity of U.S.S.R. ministries and departments" and entrusts them with the promotion "in all their activities during U.S.S.R. Supreme Soviet sessions and the period between sessions, of uninterrupted and effective work by the Supreme Soviet as the highest representative body of state authority in the U.S.S.R." (For text of the Statute and Solomentsev's report, cf., Izvestia, October 13, 1967.) The new law furthermore explicitly stipulates that, among others, membership in the Presidium of the Supreme Soviet or the Council of Ministers is incompatible with membership in the Commissions. The continuing importance of the two Foreign Affairs

---

[43] Full text of the Narkomindel Statute, as amended to 1928, is reprinted in *Yezhegodnik Narodnovo Komissariata po Innostrannym Delam na 1929 god* (Moscow, 1929), pp. 65–74. Chapter V of the Statute describes the functions and authority of the Narkomindel Representative.

Commissions is highlighted by the fact that M. A. Suslov continues as Chairman of the Foreign Affairs Commission of the Council of Union, and Secretariat member Boris Ponomarev was appointed Chairman of the counterpart body in the Council of Nationalities in 1970. Other high-ranking party secretaries were appointed Vice-Chairmen in each Commission. (*Izvestia,* July 15, 1970.) The expanded membership of the Commissions ensures at least one representative from every Union Republic, in addition to representatives from some of the larger autonomous Republics.]

IV. Diplomatic Institutions and Procedures in the Union Republics

The juridical latitude allowed the Union Republics in foreign affairs is remarkably generous for a federation. The 1944 Amendments give the republics far greater legal autonomy in foreign relations than the provisions of the Narkomindel Statute under the Constitution of 1924, and their juridical status now approximates what it was before their amalgamation into a single Union. In actuality, however, their real participation falls far short of their status at that time in external affairs and in internal administration under the 1924 Constitution.

In accordance with their constitutional capacity to conduct separate diplomatic relations, modest institutional organs and procedures have been adopted by the republics, which appear capable of rapid expansion and activation should the signal ever be given by Moscow. The complexity of these arrangements, however, varies from republic to republic, reaching its maximum development in the Ukraine and Byelorussia.

(*1*) *Republican, Executive and Legislative Organs of Diplomacy.* Since the governmental structures of the republics are faithful microcosms of the central government, their Presidia, Supreme Soviets and Councils of Ministers are empowered to play analogous roles in republican diplomacy.[44] The Presidium of the republican Supreme Soviet functions as a collegial chief of state and is authorized to appoint and recall republican diplomatic representatives and to receive letters of credence and recall of foreign envoys accredited to the republics. It is not, however, specifically empowered to institute military titles or diplomatic ranks, appoint or remove members of the high command of the armed forces of the republics, ratify or denounce international treaties signed by the republics, declare war or peace, or to order general or partial mobilization of republican military formations. Presumably, in accordance with past Soviet constitutional doctrine and practice, the Presidium of a republic can be authorized by the center to exercise these powers.

Since the Chairman of the Presidium of the republic is almost always simultaneously a federal official by virtue of his *ex officio* status as a Deputy Chairman of the All-Union Presidium, he plays a dual role in international relations — as representative of the federal Chief of

[44] Kravtsov, *Verkhovny Soveta SSSR*, pp. 73–78.

State and as authorized spokesman of his republic's collegial Chief of State. In recent years, the Chairmen of the Presidia of some of the republics have played a larger personal role in Soviet diplomacy, serving as heads of Soviet delegations abroad, as Acting Chairman of the All-Union Presidium in the absence of the Chairman, and as ornamental adjuncts to junketing Soviet leaders. The Chairman of the Uzbek Presidium, Sharaf R. Rashidov, for example, has been assigned a pivotal role in Soviet relations with Asian and African countries. As the highest official of the most important Soviet Asian Republic, Rashidov accompanied Marshal Voroshilov, Khrushchev and Bulganin, and Mikoyan on their respective diplomatic tours through the countries of Southeast Asia and the Far East.[45] In December 1957, he served as the chief of the Soviet delegation to the Asian-African Conference held in Cairo.[46] In line with this trend, the Chairman of the Presidium of the Supreme Soviet of the Armenian Republic, Sh. M. Arushanyan, headed the Soviet delegation to the 47th Annual Conference of the International Parliamentary Union, held in Rio de Janeiro in July 1958.

Whereas the Presidium and/or the Supreme Soviet of the republic is authorized to establish the diplomatic representation of the republic, the republican Council of Ministers is invested with the functions of administering whatever diplomatic relations are established, but under the general procedure laid down by the central government. Using the powers of the federal Council of Ministers as a guide, the republican Council of Ministers, through the medium of its Chairman and Foreign Minister, can be authorized to: (1) grant, withhold or withdraw recognition of governments; (2) sever and restore diplomatic relations; (3) order acts of reprisal against other states (by virtue of the authority to establish separate Ministries of Defense and military formations); (4) appoint negotiators and supervise the negotiation of international treaties and agreements not requiring formal ratification by the Presidium; (5) declare the adherence of the republic to international conventions not requiring formal ratification; (6) conclude agreements with other heads of government not requiring ratification; (7) give preliminary examination to all treaties before submission to the Presidium for ratification; (8) confirm all treaties and agreements not requiring formal ratification; (9) oversee the "current work of the diplomatic organs, effectively direct that work and take the necessary measures in the field"; and (10) appoint, accredit and recall all diplomats below plenipotentiary rank.[47]

The Supreme Soviets of all the republics are unicameral chambers, but the ambit of their authority in international relations is once again

[45] Vadimov, *Verkhovny Sovet SSSR i Mezhdunarodnye Otnosheniya,* pp. 74–75.

[46] *New York Times,* December 29, 1957.

[47] *Cf.* Vadimov, *Verkhovny Sovet SSSR i Mezhdunarodnye Otnosheniya,* pp. 10–12; Kozhevnikov, *Mezhdunarodnoye Pravo,* pp. 111–117; Durdenevsky and Krylov, *Mezhdunarodnoye Pravo,* pp. 130–139; and O. E. Polents, *Ratifikatsiya Mezhdunarodnykh Dogovorov* (Moscow, 1950), pp. 32–36.

modelled on the parent body, though in severely diminished form. After the adoption of the 1944 Amendments, the Supreme Soviets of the republics were empowered to establish Foreign Affairs Commissions, patterned after the central legislature.[48] At least seven of them (Byelorussia, Ukraine, Georgia, Turkmenistan, Tadzhikistan, Uzbekistan and the R.S.F.S.R.) have done so.[49] What these Foreign Affairs Commissions do remains a mystery, but presumably they are primed to play a role similar to their prototypes. Like their models, the Chairmen of these shadowy bodies are party functionaries. The Chairman of the R.S.F.S.R. Commission, A. B. Aristov, for instance, is a full member of the Party Presidium and Secretariat and member of the Central Committee's Bureau for the R.S.F.S.R. (which is a surrogate for its Party organization).[50] The Chairman of the Ukrainian Commission is a Secretary of the Ukrainian Party, as was the last known Chairman of the Georgian Foreign Affairs Commission.[51] The other Chairmen are Central Committee members of their respective party organizations.[52]

(2) *The Republican Ministry of Foreign Affairs.* All the republics, including the Karelo-Finnish up to the time of its demotion in 1956, have established Ministries of Foreign Affairs and all have at some time or other actually appointed Foreign Ministers. In recent years, neither the R.S.F.S.R. nor the Moldavian Republic appears to have appointed a Foreign Minister, though for different reasons. The absence of a Moldavian Foreign Minister may reflect its sensitive relationship to neighboring Communist Rumania, of which it is in reality an unredeemed ethnic territory; while in the case of the R.S.F.S.R., it may be considered superfluous or potentially risky (just as there is no separate Russian Communist Party organization). Since the Soviet federation is erected upon the principle of the juridical equality of the Union Republics, the Constitutions of the R.S.F.S.R. and Moldavia continue to preserve their capacity to participate in international affairs.

Aside from the Foreign Ministers of the Ukraine and Byelorussia, the Foreign Ministers of the republics do little but carry empty diplomatic portfolios, greet foreign dignitaries, attend diplomatic receptions and banquets, serve on various Soviet diplomatic or quasi-diplomatic delegations to international organizations, conferences and meetings, and take part in the foreign policy "discussions" in the Supreme Soviet or its Foreign Affairs Commissions. Soviet Foreign Ministry officials in Moscow and republican authorities in Georgia and Armenia, when asked

[48] Kravtsov, *Verkhovny Soveta SSSR*, p. 75.

[49] As in the case of the Union Constitution, the Foreign Affairs Commissions are organized in accordance with the constitutional authority of the Supreme Soviets to establish "commissions of investigation and audit on any matter."

[50] *Pravda*, March 23, 1955.

[51] S. V. Chervonenko, *Pravda Ukrainy*, July 3, 1956; D. V. Mchedhishvili, *Zarya Vostoka*, September 2, 1956.

[52] Byelorussia, F. A. Novikova, *Sovetskaya Byelorussiya*, December 15, 1955; Turkmen Republic, A. M. Annanurov, *Turkmenskaya Iskra*, March 18, 1955; Tadzhik Republic, Ya. A. Rakhimov, *Kommunist Tadzhikstana*, March 29, 1955; Uzbek Republic, R. G. Gulanov, *Pravda Vostoka*, December 7, 1956.

during the Summer of 1958 what precise functions were performed by the Foreign Ministers of the republics, informed the author that a principal function was to be consulted in all diplomatic matters which specifically affected the interests of their republics. In Tbilisi and Yerevan, he was further told that the republican Foreign Ministries were responsible for arranging and administering cultural relations and exchanges between the republics and foreign states. One of the specific functions of the Armenian Foreign Ministry, the author was told, was the organization and administration of the repatriation of more than 100,000 Armenians from abroad to the Armenian Republic.

The post of republican Foreign Minister remains, however, essentially honorific and is clearly a part-time responsibility, since most of them have additional administrative duties. As of the beginning of 1958, in three republics (Armenia, Estonia and Tadzhikstan), the Chairman of the Council of Ministers also holds the post of Foreign Minister, while in another (Georgia), the Foreign Ministry is presided over by a First Deputy Premier.[53] In five others (Byelorussia, Kazakhstan, Kirgizia, Turkmenistan and Uzbekistan), a Deputy Chairman also serves as Foreign Minister, and in one instance (Latvia), the position is simultaneously held by the Minister of Culture.[54] Only in three Republics (the Ukraine, Azerbaidzhan and Lithuania) does the Foreign Minister have no other visible means of support.[55]

Information on the organization and structure of republican Foreign Ministries and the composition and size of their diplomatic establishments is obscure, since Soviet sources provide little systematic descriptive information. The diplomatic structure of the republics must be reconstructed from scattered and fragmentary references in the Soviet press and from lists of delegations furnished to international organizations and conferences in which the republics participate.

Only the Ukraine and Byelorussia maintain any semblance of a permanent diplomatic establishment. This is due to their membership in the United Nations and six of its specialized agencies, and their participation in international commissions and conferences based on U.N. membership. The two Slavic Republics must maintain a minimum roster of diplomatic functionaries and a staff to handle routine clerical and administrative work made necessary by their modest participation

[53] A Ye. Kochinyan, *Pravda*, December 9, 1956 and September 13, 1956; A. A. Myurisep, *Izvestia*, December 11, 1956; N. Dodkhudoyev, *Pravda*, February 10, 1957 and *Izvestia*, May 27, 1956; M. I. Kuchava, *Zarya Vostoka*, August 9, 1956.

[54] K. V. Kiselev has headed the Foreign Ministry of the Byelorussian Republic since its formation. T. T. Tazhibayev, *Pravda*, November 3, 1956; K. K. Konduchalova, *Izvestia*, February 16, 1957; B. Ch. Charyyev, *Pravda*, January 20, 1957 and *Izvestia*, October 3, 1956; G. S. Sultanov, *Izvestia*, January 26, 1957 and November 3, 1956; Ya. P. Ostrov, *Sovetskaya Latviya*, March 25, 1955 and *Izvestia*, December 2, 1956.

[55] L. F. Palamarchuk (the fourth Foreign Minister of the Ukraine since 1944), *Izvestia*, December 3, 1956; M. I. Aliev, *Bakinsky Rabochye*, October 23, 1956; I. I. Gashka, *Sovetskaya Litva*, October 10, 1956. Aliev, Azerbaidzhan's Foreign Minister since 1944, died on September 28, 1958.

in diplomatic affairs. The most fruitful single source of information on the diplomatic establishments of the Union Republics is the lists of delegations furnished the United Nations several times a year.[56] Since 1946, the compositions of the Ukrainian and Byelorussian delegations to the meetings of the General Assembly have revealed a gradual but rudimentary differentiation in administrative organization, broken down into Ambassadors, department heads, "expert-consultants" to the Foreign Ministry, interpreters, and clerical secretaries. With but few exceptions, the diplomatic functionaries of the republics are not "on loan" from the central Ministry of Foreign Affairs, as might be expected, but are primarily republican government officials or university professors with relatively minor rank in republican party organizations. The low party status of republican diplomats also corresponds with All-Union practice. Neither of the two republics maintains permanent delegations at United Nations headquarters and presumably a substantial part of their Foreign Ministry staffs moves to New York each Fall to assume their single most important diplomatic responsibility. The temporary headquarters of both delegations are separate from that of the U.S.S.R. and from each other — a calculated attempt to maintain the appearance of autonomy.

The composition and size of the delegations of the two Soviet Republics reveal minor variations. This is due in part to the uneven nature of their responsibilities at the U.N. at different times. As full-fledged members of the international organization, each is entitled to be elected as a non-permanent member of the Security Council (whereupon they automatically serve as members of the Atomic Energy Commission and the Commission for Conventional Armaments), the Economic and Social Council, and the Trusteeship Council; and their representatives may also serve as Chairmen and rapporteurs of various committees and commissions. Depending upon the extent and diversity of their responsibilities, the size and complexity of the two delegations are subject to corresponding fluctuations, since they must maintain sufficient personnel to occupy these various positions. The only major U.N. body from which they are technically excluded is the World Court.[57]

Although in most cases the republican Foreign Minister is coterminous with the Foreign Ministry itself, the Ukrainian Republic boasts a diplomatic establishment which includes a Deputy Foreign Minister, a Secretary-General, a Political Department (with a Director and Deputy Director), a Protocol and Consular Division (although it has no consular

[56] *Delegations to the United Nations,* issued for every regular and special session of the General Assembly and *Permanent Missions to the United Nations,* issued monthly or bimonthly, both published by the Protocol Section of the U.N.

[57] Article 3 of the Statute of the Court stipulates that no two members of the Court may be nationals of the same state and that for this purpose, any person who could be regarded as a national of more than one state "shall be deemed a national of the one in which he ordinarily exercises civil and political rights."

representation and precious little protocol), a Press Division and a Counselor on Economic Problems. Its diplomatic ranks correspond with those of the Union and include Ambassadors, Ministers, Counselors, and first and second secretaries. The Foreign Ministry also lists a number of Expert-Consultants.[58] The structure of the Byelorussian Foreign Ministry, for some reason, reveals more sophistication if not sophistry, for in addition to the officials, divisions and ranks reported by the Ukrainian Republic, it includes a Collegium of the Foreign Ministry (like its parent prototype in Moscow) with several otherwise untitled members and junior diplomats at the level of third secretary, thus hinting that it may be an organization not only of Chiefs but of Indians as well.[59] Members of the republican Supreme Soviet, university professors and sundry government officials have also appeared on the diplomatic delegations of the two republics. Presumably, the Political Departments are in charge of U.N. affairs, while the Secretary-Generals are in charge of administrative matters. The expert-consultants advise on legal and other technical questions, but the duties of the Chiefs of the Consular Departments in the two Foreign Ministries remain an enigma. Since the Byelorussian Republic joined UNESCO, it has appointed a Commission for UNESCO Affairs attached to its Council of Ministers, as has presumably the Ukrainian Republic as well.[60]

Various other republics have also listed Deputy Foreign Ministers, but none can claim so elaborate a diplomatic apparatus as these two. The size of the buildings which house the republican Foreign Ministries can also convey an impression of the complexity and diversity of their diplomatic functions. While the Ukrainian Foreign Ministry is housed in an office building of respectable proportions, the Georgian Foreign Ministry has its headquarters in a dilapidated structure in a dark corner of Tbilisi and consists only of a single reception chamber.

(3) *The Union Republics and International Treaties.* Soviet writers rarely fail to invoke the limited treaty relations of the Ukrainian and Byelorussian Republics as concrete proof of their diplomatic autonomy in international affairs. These relations, however, have been quite modest and carefully circumscribed, restricted almost exclusively to the Byelorussian and Ukrainian Republics.

Soviet constitutional law recognizes two general categories of international agreements: treaties requiring formal *ratification* by the su-

---

[58] *Delegations to the United Nations,* Eighth Session of the General Assembly, September 1953, p. 91; ibid., Ninth Session, September 1954, p. 91; ibid., Eleventh Session, November 1956, p. 126; ibid., Twelfth Session, September 1957, p. 133; ibid., Thirteenth Session, September 1958, pp. 131–2.

[59] *United Nations Handbook,* General Assembly Supplement (United Nations, 1946), p. 16; *Delegations to the United Nations,* Second Regular Session of the General Assembly, September 1947, p. 28; ibid., Twelfth Session, September 1957, pp. 24–25.

[60] *Izvestia,* October 13, 1956. Its Chairman is G. Ya. Kiselev, who was also designated as one of the Byelorussian representatives to the Council of the IPU.

preme organs of state power (the Supreme Soviet or its Presidium, usually the latter), and international agreements requiring only *confirmation* by the Council of Ministers. Whereas Article 14a gives to the Union the power of "conclusion, ratification and denunciation of treaties of the U.S.S.R.," Article 18a allows the republics only "to conclude agreements" with foreign states, and makes no mention of *treaties* or of the ratification and denunciation of international compacts. The Union Republics, like the Union, are governed by the provisions of the Law on the Procedure for the Ratification and Denunciation of International Treaties of the U.S.S.R., adopted by the Supreme Soviet on August 20, 1938, ostensibly upon the initiative of its Foreign Affairs Commissions. According to this law, "peace treaties, treaties of mutual defense from aggression and treaties of mutual non-aggression" are subject to ratification, as are treaties specifically requiring ratification,[61] whereas "economic and other treaties upon the conclusion of which no provision was made for subsequent ratification do not require such ratification and may be confirmed by . . . the Council of People's Commissars [Council of ministers] of the U.S.S.R. according to general procedure."[62]

International agreements contracted by the republics have fallen into both categories. No specific provisions in either the Union or republican constitutions empower the republics to ratify or denounce treaties, nor do they explicitly deny this authority either. In accordance with past and current Soviet constitutional practice, this means that the republics can ratify and denounce treaties upon direct authorization by the central government or in the absence of its disapproval. Since final jurisdiction resides in the federal government, all agreements signed by the republics with foreign states are subject to nullification, disavowal or denunciation by the Union government in the unlikely event of disagreement between the republics and the central government. The same holds true for any declaration of war and peace, for which there is neither authorization nor prohibition in the Soviet Constitution.

The first international agreements contracted by the republics were in 1944 and were bilateral in nature. On September 9, 1944, the Ukrainian and Byelorussian Republics, and on September 22, 1944, the Lithuanian Republic, concluded population accords with the Lublin Committee of Poland. The agreements were signed by the Premiers of the republics and were not subject to ratification by the republican Presidia.[63] Three years later, on May 6, 1947, these three republics signed a final protocol with Poland affirming that the agreements of 1944 had

[61] *Second Session of the Supreme Soviet of the U.S.S.R.*, August 10–21, 1938, verbatim report in English (International Publishers, 1938), p. 678 for full text.

[62] Ibid., p. 595, comment by Deputy O. J. Schmidt on behalf of the Foreign Affairs Commission of the Council of Nationalities. For details concerning ratification procedure in the U.S.S.R., cf. Polents, *Ratifikatsiya*, pp. 32–36.

[63] *Vneshnyaya Politika Sovetskovo Soyuza v Period Otechestvennoi Voiny*, 2 vols. (Moscow, 1946), II, pp. 202–204; 230–232. No texts of the agreements were published, only descriptive information bulletins.

been fulfilled.[64] These agreements were the first and so far the only bilateral compacts signed by any of the Soviet Republics.

The Charter of the United Nations was the first international instrument to be signed by the republics which required formal ratification, and since the two republics deposited instruments of ratification in 1945, the procedure permitting their Presidia to ratify international documents was established early in their diplomatic development.[65] The two republics also deposited separate instruments of ratification in connection with the Peace Treaties signed with Italy, Bulgaria, Hungary, Rumania and Finland. Furthermore, the Ukrainian Republic participated in the Belgrade Conference on the Danube Convention as one of the riparian powers and deposited a separate document of ratification.[66] The two republics have also adhered to the Conventions on Genocide and Human Rights, have joined six U.N. specialized agencies, and have adhered to other multilateral conventions, some of which required formal ratification.[67] The agreements signed separately by the two republics with UNRRA on December 18, 1945 required only the confirmation of their Councils of Ministers.[68]

The authority of the Union Republics to conclude international agreements under the Soviet Constitution does not make it mandatory that they negotiate with foreign powers on matters specifically affecting their interests nor does it require that they participate in negotiations and treaties signed by the U.S.S.R. even though they may be directly affected. The Soviet Union has signed treaties with Poland, Czechoslovakia, Rumania, Finland and Iran altering the territorial boundaries of various Union Republics without the participation of representatives from the interested republics in the negotiations or even in the ceremonies at the time of signature. The only restrictions upon the powers of the federal government in this connection are Articles 18 of the Union Constitution and 16 of the republican Constitutions which require the consent of the republics prior to the ratification of any treaty which alters the boundary of the republics concerned. No established procedure in law has been adopted for securing this consent and in the past this provision of the Constitution has not always been honored even in form. Under the broad latitude of the Constitution, the Soviet Government could, if it so desired, require formal preliminary approval by the Presidia of the affected republics before formal ratification, but the customary procedure is for a republican deputy to grant this consent

[64] *Vneshnyaya Politika Sovetskovo Soyuza na 1947 god*, 2 vols. (Moscow, 1952), II, pp. 383–384; *cf.* also Korovin, ed. *Mezhdunardonoye Pravo* (Moscow. 1951), p. 365.

[65] *Cf.* Polents, *Ratifikatsiya*, p. 36.

[66] *U. N. Treaty Series*, Vol. 33, No. 518, pp. 181–224; *Vneshnyaya Politika . . . na 1948 god*, II, p. 29.

[67] The two republics are members of the International Labor Organization, UNESCO, the World Health Organization, Universal Postal Union (although neither Republic has a separate postal system nor distinctive postal issues), the International Telecommunications Union, and the World Meteorological Organization; *cf.* Kozhevnikov, *Mezhdunarodnoye Pravo,* pp. 338–348.

[68] *New York Times,* December 18, 1945.

before a joint meeting of the two Foreign Affairs Commissions of the Supreme Soviet. This was the procedure employed in gaining the formal consent of the Azerbaidzhan and Turkmen Republics to the frontier rectifications made in the Soviet-Iranian Treaty of December 2, 1954.[69]

V. THE SCOPE AND FUTURE OF REPUBLICAN DIPLOMACY

At the time the constitutional Amendments were adopted in 1944, the Soviet Government undoubtedly envisaged that the diplomacy of the republics would develop more extensively than has proved to be the case. According to Molotov, the changes adumbrated a "great expansion of the activities of the Union Republics" in international relations. "It cannot be said," he reported to the Supreme Soviet on the day the Amendments were adopted, that a single Foreign Commissariat

> could fully cover not only the requirements of the whole Union but also the multifarious and growing requirements of the Union Republics in foreign affairs. Thus the Union Republics have quite a few specific economic and cultural requirements which cannot be covered in full measure by All-Union representation abroad and also by treaties and agreements of the Union with other States. These national requirements of the Republics can be better met by means of direct relations of the Republics with corresponding States.[70]

Three days later, on February 3, 1944, *Izvestia* and other Soviet newspapers predicted that the sixteen Republics would seek to establish diplomatic relations with all countries in diplomatic communion with the U.S.S.R.

Main attention was focused upon the largest of the non-Russian republics, the Ukraine, whose representative in the Supreme Soviet hailed Molotov's report and asserted that "a specifically national aim of the Ukraine is the need to establish a close, direct contact between a Slavic State — the Ukraine — and two of her Slavic neighbors — Poland and Czechoslovakia."[71] The resurgence of Ukrainian nationalism during the war and the key role of this republic in Soviet claims upon the territory of pre-war Poland tended to indicate that the Ukraine at least would be permitted to establish diplomatic contact with neighboring countries. The population agreements signed in September 1944 and Gromyko's electrifying proposal at Dumbarton Oaks in August 1944 that the sixteen republics be given separate membership in the projected international organization further demonstrated that the Kremlin was serious about its avowed intention to usher its republics into the diplomatic community. This expectation was given additional support on May 14, 1945 in San Francisco when the Ukrainian Foreign Minister, Dmitri Manuilsky, cavalierly announced to a massive press conference that the Ukraine was "ready at any time to exchange diplomatic and

---

[69] Novikov, *Postoyannye Komissii Verkhovnovo Soveta SSSR*, p. 34. The Azerbaidzhanian deputy was also the Foreign Minister.

[70] *Molotov Report*, p. 241.

[71] D. L. Zlatopolsky, *Obrazovaniye i Razvitiye SSSR kak Soyuznovo Gosudarstvo* (Moscow, 1954), pp. 202–203.

consular representatives with any country," and added that his government would "consider with gratitude any proposals by other states with regards to foreign relations."[72]

An important diplomatic role for the Ukraine was apparently expected by high Czech officials as well. President Benes predicted that the Ukraine would be a key member of the "Slav Bloc," and in August 1945, Zdenek Fierlinger, the Czech Ambassador to Moscow (and later Premier), ventured to envisage that:

> The Ukraine and Czechoslovakia, as neighbors, must make decisions on a whole series of important questions . . . through special treaties and agreements between Czechoslovakia and the Ukraine. . . . The development of these friendly relations of a political and economic character will be facilitated to a great extent by the amendments which were recently made by the Supreme Soviet of the U.S.S.R. . . . The changes permit the Union Republics not only to enter into direct diplomatic dealings with other countries, but also to conclude treaties and agreements. Considering the diversity of economic dealings between two neighboring industrial countries, this situation in practice will have an important result.[73]

In spite of these expectations, no bilateral diplomatic contacts between Czechoslovakia and the Ukraine — or any other Soviet Republic — ever materialized. Even the Soviet-Czech Treaty of June 29, 1945, transferring the Carpatho-Ukraine to "its ancient motherland — the Soviet Ukraine," was negotiated and signed without benefit of even sham participation by Ukrainian functionaries, although the Treaty was drawn up in the Ukrainian, Russian and Slovak (but not Czech) languages.[74] With the annexation of the Carpatho-Ukraine, the great Ukrainian passion for diplomatic relations with Czechoslovakia evaporated as abruptly as it had appeared.

The only pretense at bilateral diplomatic contacts by the republics were with the Soviet-sponsored Lublin Regime in Poland. Aside from the population accords of 1944 and a so-called "state and visit" paid by the "Ukrainian" Premier, none other than Nikita Khrushchev, to Warsaw in December 1945, and reciprocated the following October by a Polish visit to Kiev, nothing ever came of the "specifically national aim of the Ukraine" to establish diplomatic relations with the Poles.[75] Notwithstanding various reports and speculations to the contrary, the author confirmed in Moscow that not a single republic has ever exchanged diplomatic or consular representatives with a foreign power. Even the cultural contacts are arranged on an *ad hoc* basis, since none of the republics maintains cultural attachés with Soviet diplomatic missions abroad.

[72] *Soviet News*, May 25, 1945; cf. also *New York Times*, May 23, 1945.
[73] Z. Fierlinger, "Soviet-Czechoslovak Economic Relations — Past and Future," *American Review on the Soviet Union*, VI, August 1945, p. 30.
[74] *Sbornik Deistvuyushchikh Dogovorov, Soglashenii i Konventsii Zaklyuchennykh SSSR s Inostrannymi Gosudarstvami*, XI (Moscow, 1955), pp. 31–32.
[75] Cf. *New York Times*, October 12, 1946.

There is no question but that the Soviet government subsequently revised its estimate of the advantages to be gained by stimulating the diplomatic reflexes of the republics, for not a single instance exists where a Soviet Republic, or the Union on its behalf, has ever made a formal bid to another state to exchange diplomatic or consular representatives. On the contrary, when the British Ambassador, more in jest than in earnest, suggested to Molotov in 1947 that London was interested in exchanging representatives with the Ukrainian Republic, Molotov retorted with evident annoyance that Kiev was not interested in expanding its diplomatic contacts.

One complicating legal factor which prevented the republics from taking any initiative in making such contacts, down at least to the beginning of 1948, was the Decree of August 26, 1926 which made it a criminal offense for republican officials at home or abroad to deal directly with functionaries and institutions of foreign states without going through the channels of the Foreign Ministry in Moscow. According to this decree, which remained in force even after the adoption of the 1944 Amendments, should republican officials "receive from foreign governments offices or officials abroad, or from foreign diplomatic missions in the U.S.S.R., written communications of a political or economic nature, they must forward such communications to the People's Commissariat for Foreign Affairs without answering them." An identical procedure was established for verbal communications.[76]

On December 16, 1947, this decree was nullified and superseded by a new decree of the Presidium which removed its application to republican officials and authorized the republics, in conformity with the Union decree, to establish analogous procedures governing contact between republican institutions and officials with those of foreign powers.[77] Using the Decree of February 10, 1949, issued by the Presidium of the R.S.F.S.R., as a model, the republican decrees, which are closely patterned after the All-Union decree, authorize contact with foreign powers only through the channels of the republican Ministry of Foreign Affairs, unless expressly permitted otherwise by treaties signed by the U.S.S.R., agreements concluded by the republic, or else by special permission of the Foreign Ministry of the U.S.S.R. or the republic.[78]

Although the nullification of the 1926 Decree did not result in a surge of diplomatic contacts by the diplomatic officials of the republics, it did eliminate a legal incongruity in Soviet law, whereby republican officials acting under the provisions of the Constitution granting diplomatic powers to the republics could be prosecuted under the criminal provisions of the Decree. Furthermore, as long as this decree was in force, the formal pretense of diplomatic autonomy for the republics was hardly tenable even in Soviet law.

[76] *Sobranie Zakonov i Rasporiazhenii Rabochye-Krestianskovo Pravitelstva SSSR*, 1926, Part II, No. 60, Article 448.
[77] Full text in *Sbornik Zakonov SSSR . . . 1938–1956*, pp. 169–171.
[78] Full text in *Sbornik Zakonov R.S.F.S.R. i Ukazov Prezidiuma Verkhovnovo Soveta R.S.F.S.R. 1946–1954* (Moscow, 1955), pp. 107–108.

The role of the Union Republics as actors in Soviet diplomacy, aside from the activities of the two Slavic Republics in the U.N. and its affiliated bodies and conferences, remains essentially ceremonial and ornamental. Up to now, the Kremlin has shown serious interest only in gaining multilateral acceptance of its republics, and has sedulously prohibited them from engaging in purely bilateral diplomatic contacts. Its feeble, half-hearted and scattered attempts to win recognition for additional republics in the international community should not, however, be construed as exhausting the Kremlin's bag of diplomatic tricks. Since its initial success in gaining the admittance of the Ukraine and Byelorussia into the U.N., Moscow has failed to win acceptance of its other republics under international law. After it was rebuffed in its attempt to gain admission for the three Baltic republics to the Paris Peace Conference in 1946, the Soviet government resorted to a backdoor maneuver by attaching the Foreign Ministers of the three republics to the regular Soviet delegation. Subsequent attempts to get other Soviet Republics into international organizations like the International Telecommunications Union and the Universal Postal Union were equally unsuccessful.

Failure to make headway on the legal level has challenged the Soviet Union to contrive more ingenious diplomatic formulas. In recent years, the Soviet Republics have been given an increasingly prominent role on what might be called the fringes of international diplomacy. For example, beginning in September 1950, at the Fifth Session of the General Assembly, the Soviet Government initiated the practice of including the Foreign Ministers of selected Soviet Republics (principally Central Asian) as members of the Soviet delegation. In 1950, the Foreign Ministers of the Uzbek and Kazakh Republics were named alternate representatives;[79] in 1951, it was the turn of the Turkmen Foreign Minister,[80] and in 1952, it was once again the Uzbek Foreign Minister and the Deputy Foreign Minister of the Latvian Republic who were designated as alternate representatives.[81] After Stalin's death, the Uzbek Republic, in accordance with the policy of granting greater prominence to the most vigorous of Moscow's Central Asian Republics, was awarded virtually a permanent berth on the Soviet delegation and its Foreign Minister (or Minister of Culture) was elevated to the status of a full representative.[82] This practice not only permits Moscow to accustom

[79] *Delegations to the United Nations,* Fifth Session of the General Assembly, September 1951.

[80] Ibid., Sixth Session, September 1951.

[81] Ibid., Seventh Session, October 1952.

[82] Ibid., Eighth Session, p. 94, and Ninth Session, September 1954, p. 93. In the following year, the U.S.S.R. delegation included a member of the Presidium of the Lithuanian Republic, the Chairman of the Georgian Supreme Soviet and Rector of the State University, and a Deputy Chairman of the Kazakh Council of Ministers. In 1956, only the Kazakh functionary was retained on the Soviet delegation; but in 1957, it was the turn of a Latvian official and the Uzbek Foreign Minister once again. At the 1958 Session of the General Assembly, the Foreign Ministers of the Lithuanian and Armenian Republics appeared on the Soviet delegation. *Cf.* corresponding numbers of *Delegations to the United Nations,* cited above, note 58.

the outside world gently to the presence of republican officials at diplomatic gatherings, but also to convey the impression to the republics that they have a definite role in foreign affairs.

Perhaps not surprisingly, in relations among the states of the Soviet orbit, the republics have achieved no greater prestige as distinct diplomatic personalities, although if Moscow were to become seriously interested in enhancing their diplomatic respectability, it could easily arrange for their recognition by its client states in Europe and Asia. In November 1954, however, at the Moscow Conference on European Peace and Security, attended only by countries in the Soviet orbit, the official Soviet delegation included the Premiers of the R.S.F.S.R., the Ukraine, Byelorussia and the three Baltic Republics.[83] Six months later, at the Warsaw Pact Conference, the Premiers of the six Soviet Republics were once again in attendance as members of the Soviet delegation, but they did not sign or join the Pact as separate members.[84] Significantly, neither the Karelo-Finnish nor the Moldavian Republic was represented — a calculated omission which adumbrated the dissolution of the Karelo-Finnish Republic less than two years later and cast an ominous shadow over the juridical status of Moldavia.

Two republics, the Ukrainian and the Uzbek, appear on the verge of being invested with significant diplomatic responsibilities, the former in Soviet relations with Europe and the latter in Afro-Asian affairs. In August 1955, the Chairman of the Uzbek Presidium, Rashidov, boasted in the Supreme Soviet of the extensive "cultural ties between the Uzbek Republic and foreign countries," and reported that since the beginning of 1954, the Republic has been visited by delegations from 36 countries, of which 27 were from Asia and Africa.[85] Less than a year later, he asserted that the number of delegations had increased to more than 100, including numerous parliamentary groups.[86] Since 1955, the Uzbek Republic has played host to the leaders of virtually every neutralist power in the Middle East and Southeast Asia. With almost ritual regularity, visiting Asian dignitaries embark on a pilgrimage to the principal centers of the Uzbek Republic when touring the Soviet Union.

Although it is doubtful that the Ukraine can play as effective a role for Soviet diplomacy in European affairs as the Uzbek might in Asian and African, from the tenor of a recent speech by A. I. Kirichenko, it would seem that an enhanced diplomatic role for the Ukraine will be a consequence more of Ukrainian national egoism than of any anticipation of concrete diplomatic advantages for Soviet foreign policy:

> Look at the Soviet Ukraine! Today it is one of the major countries of Europe and the world. . . . Today the Soviet Ukraine, with its population of 42,000,000, is one of the biggest European powers. . . . Our Republic occupies a worthy place in the international arena. It is one of

[83] New Times (No. 49), December 4, 1954, special supplement, p. 64.
[84] New Times (No. 21), May 21, 1955, special supplement, p. 69.
[85] Materialy Pyatoi Sessii Verkhovnovo Soveta SSSR, pp. 40–41.
[86] New Times (No. 33), August 11, 1955, special supplement, p. 22.

the founders and a member of the United Nations and many other international organizations; it is strengthening its ties with socialist countries.[87]

An expanded role for the republics in Soviet diplomacy may assume three possible patterns, alone or in combination: (1) a steady expansion and acceleration of their role in quasi-diplomatic activity on the fringes of international relations; (2) transfer of internal consular, passport and visa functions to the republican Foreign Ministries; and (3) formal bids by the Republics, or the Soviet government on their behalf, to exchange diplomatic or consular representatives with foreign powers, not necessarily all at once, but selectively. At the minimum, the Soviet Republics could expect a warm reception from the countries in the Soviet orbit, but it is quite possible that non-Communist states, for their own reasons, may also wish to establish relations with individual republics. Diplomatic or consular exchanges between the Uzbek Republic and individual countries of the Middle East and Southeast Asia are a definite possibility and are likely to reap rich dividends for Soviet foreign policy.[88]

[87] *Pravda,* December 25, 1957.

[88] The increasing importance of the Uzbek Republic has been given legal confirmation in the Soviet Constitution. In the original version of the Constitution, the Uzbek Republic was listed eighth in the hierarchy of Republics enumerated under Article 13. On February 25, 1957, the Supreme Soviet revised Article 13 to list the Republics, not in the order of their admission to the Union, but in accordance with the size of their population. The Uzbek Republic was moved from eighth place to fourth, immediately after the R.S.F.S.R., the Ukraine and Byelorussia, although its population is less than that of the Kazakh Republic. Text of revision is in *Istoriya Sovetskoi Konstitutsiya,* p. 829, and the original at page 730.

VII EXTERNAL INPUTS AND INSTRUMENTS OF SOVIET FOREIGN POLICY

20. THE SOVIET UNION AND INTERNATIONAL COMMUNISM

Vernon V. Aspaturian

THE SOVIET UNION AND WORLD COMMUNISM
UNDER LENIN AND STALIN

As rulers of the first country in which a Marxist revolutionary party had been elevated to power, the Bolsheviks early had to define their relationship with kindred Marxist parties engaged in revolutionary activity in other countries.

Although the international communist movement has been institutionalized only in two organizations, the Comintern and the Cominform, Moscow's relations with foreign communist parties before 1956 falls into three distinct, but closely interrelated, periods: (1) the Leninist period (1919–1928); (2) the Stalinist period (1928–1953), and (3) the residual-Stalinist period (1953–1956). These distinctions are purely arbitrary, based neither on the programmatic nor the institutional metamorphosis of the world communist movement, but exclusively on the degree to which foreign communist parties participated in the formulation of decisions concerning revolutionary strategy or Soviet foreign policy.

The Leninist Phase: Partners in World Revolution

The Comintern, founded by Lenin in 1919, was invested with two basic and interdependent functions: (1) to coordinate the strategy and direction of the world revolutionary movement; and (2) to defend the

From Vernon V. Aspaturian, "The Soviet Union and International Communism," in Roy C. Macridis, editor, *Foreign Policy in World Politics*, © 1968. By permission of Prentice-Hall, Inc., Englewood Cliffs, New Jersey.

702 THE SOVIET UNION AND INTERNATIONAL COMMUNISM

Soviet state against counterrevolution and foreign intervention. These two purposes, in turn, rested upon two fundamental assumptions concerning the world revolutionary movement: (1) the Russian Revolution was merely the first phase of a general revolution, and had neither a justification nor a purpose independent of it; (2) the revolution in Western Europe, particularly in Germany, was imminent.

The entire history of the relationship between Moscow and foreign communist parties has been determined by the two essentially contradictory purposes — world revolution, and the defense of the Soviet Union. The proper defense of the Soviet Union, in turn, has rested on the shifting assumptions concerning the fortune and direction of the revolutionary movement outside Russia.

When Lenin convened the first Congress of the Comintern, in 1919, neither the concept of a world communist movement nor of foreign communist parties existed. Under Bolshevik sponsorship, radical or left-wing factions of the social-democratic parties splintered off to form separate communist parties which affiliated with the new Third International. At the Second Congress, in 1920, statutes were drawn up defining: "The Communist International [as] . . . a universal Communist party of which the parties operating in each country [including Russia] form individual sections," whose aim was "the establishment of . . . the international Soviet Republic."[1] Although the Russian Party was the only Communist Party in power — except for the Hungarian during a brief period — and although a Russian, Grigori Zinoviev, was installed as president, the Party was not invested with a privileged and dominant status in the organization, but, like all the others, was subordinate to the decisions of the World Congress and its executive committee. However, since the Soviet Union was the only soviet state in the world, and since the headquarters of the Comintern could be established only in Moscow, it was inevitable that, as the prospects of the revolution faded, the position of the Party would, correspondingly, be enhanced.

Disagreements between Bolshevik leaders and foreign communist parties, particularly the German, were frequent. Revolutionary doctrine and strategy, and the role of Soviet diplomacy, were discussed in the World Congress and in the meetings of its executive committee. The participation of foreign communist parties was by no means a mere formality, and the Soviet state, which was conceived primarily as an instrument of the world revolution, frequently had to adjust its foreign policy to the views of these other parties, over which it did not exercise full control. The failure of revolution to take hold in Hungary and Germany, plus the ability of the Bolshevik regime to survive, forced a corresponding modification of the assumptions upon which the Comintern rested.

The struggle for power unleashed by Lenin's death, in 1924, also found its reflection in the Comintern and within communist parties abroad. A reexamination of the previous estimates of the revolution in

[1] W. H. Chamberlin, ed., *Blueprint for World Conquest* (Chicago, Human Events, Inc., 1946), p. 36.

Germany, and the victory of Stalin's policy of "socialism in one country," in opposition to Trotsky's idea of "permanent revolution," forced leaders in the Comintern and in foreign communist parties to choose sides. As Stalin squeezed out his rivals at home, his supporters in the Comintern and in foreign communist parties carried out corresponding purges in their organizations. By 1930, Stalin had established his mastery over the party apparatus at home, and this was immediately followed by a corresponding subjugation of the Comintern.

The Stalinist Phase: The Primacy of Soviet Interests

The Soviet state soon assumed an identity and existence of its own, separate, yet related, to that of the Comintern. The entire history of Soviet relationships, first with foreign communist parties, then with other communist states, and then with rivals for leadership (i.e., China), has been determined by the Soviet Union's two essentially contradictory purposes — to serve the interests of foreign constituencies (world revolution, other communist states, China), and to reflect its internal interests (survival as a state, national interests, Soviet elites). This contradiction was resolved by adjusting the interests and behavior of the Comintern and foreign communist parties to those of the Soviet Union. From 1928 to 1953 foreign communist parties, even after they assumed power in their own countries, played little part in the formulation of Soviet foreign policy and were, on the contrary, completely subservient to it as pliable and expendable instruments.

The world communist movement during the Stalinist period rested upon assumptions radically divergent from those upon which the Comintern was originally founded. These were: (1) the Soviet Union is the center and bulwark (not simply the advanced guard) of the world revolution; (2) revolution independent of Moscow's support is impossible; and (3) the preservation of the Soviet Union as the indispensable base of the world revolution is the most important objective of all communists, who must owe undeviating loyalty to Russia as the "proletarian fatherland." These new assumptions were incorporated into the 1928 *Program of the Comintern,* and the extension of world revolution became identified with the expansion of Soviet power:

> The U.S.S.R. inevitably becomes the base of the world revolutionary movement. . . . In the U.S.S.R., the world proletariat for the first time acquires a country that is really its own. . . . In the event of the imperialist declaring war upon and attacking the U.S.S.R., the international proletariat must retaliate by organizing bold and determined mass action and struggle for the overthrow of the imperialist governments.[2]

The basic philosophy justifying this submission to Moscow's control was euphemistically defined by Stalin himself as "proletarian internationalism":

> A *revolutionary* is he who without evasions, unconditionally openly and honestly . . . is ready to uphold and defend the U.S.S.R. . . . An

[2] Ibid., pp. 220–223.

704 THE SOVIET UNION AND INTERNATIONAL COMMUNISM

internationalist is he who unconditionally, without hesitation and without provisos, is ready to defend the U.S.S.R. because the U.S.S.R. is the base of the world revolutionary movement, and to defend and advance this movement is impossible without defending the U.S.S.R.[3]

Communist parties abroad were subordinated as expendable instruments manipulated in the interests of the Soviet state. Orders transmitted through the Comintern were followed with unquestioning obedience, even if they invited self-destruction (China, Germany) or conflicted with the fundamental interests of their own people (France). As Moscow changed its policies, foreign communists followed suit, even if the new policies were diametrically opposed to the current line. The Kremlin functioned as a GHQ of the world communist movement, sacrificing a division or corps here and there in the interest of the movement as a whole.

The dissolution of the Comintern in 1943 did not materially alter the relationship between Moscow and foreign parties, except, as noted by Andrei Zhdanov at the founding of the Cominform in 1947, that "some comrades understood the dissolution of the Comintern to imply the elimination of all ties, of all contact, between the fraternal Communist Parties [which] . . . is wrong, harmful and . . . unnatural."[4]

After World War II, when communist parties were installed in power in the countries of Eastern Europe and the Soviet Union was deprived of its unique position as the only communist state in the world, the theory of "proletarian internationalism" was transformed from a system justifying Moscow's control of parties into a system justifying her control of entire countries and subordinating their interests to those of Russia. Some satellite communist leaders considered the Soviet theory of "proletarian internationalism" applicable only to parties in capitalist countries, otherwise it became a philosophical justification for Soviet colonialism.

As satellite leaders betrayed signs of uneasiness and independence in their new role as government leaders with the interests of their own countries and peoples to consider, Stalin organized the Cominform, ostensibly as an organ of mutual consultation based on the equality and independence of its members, but in reality to solidify his control over the satellites and to root out all tendencies toward independence. Unlike the Comintern, the new organization was carefully restricted to only the seven communist states of Eastern Europe (Albania was denied membership) and to the two largest parties in the West, the Italian and the French. The refusal of Tito and other ∟tellite leaders to place the interests of Russia above those of their own communist countries and to act as Moscow's subservient agents of plunder and exploitation of their own people led to the expulsion of Yugoslavia from the Cominform and the wholesale slaughter of satellite leaders who showed signs of independence. "Loyalty to the Soviet Union," ran the Moscow line, "is the touchstone and criterion of proletarian internationalism."[5]

[3] J. V. Stalin, *Sochineniya* (Moscow, 1949), Vol. X, p. 61.
[4] *Strategy and Tactics of World Communism*, p. 229.
[5] *For a Lasting Peace, For a People's Democracy*, June 30, 1950.

This was echoed by satellite communists and by communist leaders in capitalist countries, who agreed with Dimitrov that "proletarian internationalism . . . means complete coordination of the activities of Communist Parties and of the leading role of the Bolshevik [i.e., Soviet] Party."[6]

In rebuttal, Yugoslav leaders complained:

> The leaders of the U.S.S.R. consider that Yugoslavia as a state should be subordinated . . . and its entire development in a general way should be made dependent upon the U.S.S.R. At the same time, they have forced other socialist states to act in a similar manner. . . . The political relations . . . are also based upon . . . the need to maintain in the various socialist countries the kind of regimes that will always be prepared to agree . . . to accept such unequal status and exploitation of their country. Thus — subservient and vassal governments and vassal states are actually being formed.[7]

Stalin's insistence that the communist parties in Eastern Europe and in the Far East continue their subservience to Russia's interests introduced serious strains in the communist orbit, of which Tito's defection was merely the most obvious manifestation. Moscow continued to interfere crudely in the internal development of the satellite states, while disclaiming interference; it plundered their economies and called it disinterested aid; and it rigidly dictated their progress toward socialism, while paying lip-service to national peculiarities. On all these matters, satellite leaders were not consulted before decisions were taken in the Kremlin, but were simply commanded to carry them out as efficiently as possible.

Whereas the small communist states of Eastern Europe were at the mercy of Soviet power, the attempt to dictate to Peking provoked considerable resistance. Satellite leaders elsewhere were slaughtered by the score, but no Stalinist purges took place in the Chinese Party. One measure of Stalin's patent contempt for Chinese interests or national sensitivities was his refusal to relinquish the Soviet stranglehold on Manchuria, dissolve joint stock companies, or surrender the special extraterritorial interests in Port Arthur and Darien, although this refusal was clearly resented by the Chinese. According to Walter Ulbricht, Stalin's brazen attempts to treat China like an ordinary satellite almost forced Mao to desert the Soviet camp.

The Residual Stalinist Phase: The Primacy of Soviet Interests Defied

When Stalin died, in March, 1953, the dominance of the Soviet Union in the communist system appeared fixed and permanent, and the primacy of its interests established and assured. His death, however,

[6] G. Dimitrov, *Report to the 5th Congress of the Bulgarian Communist Party* (Sofia, 1948), p. 55.
[7] Milovan Djilas, *Lenin on Relations between Socialist States* (New York, 1949), pp. 16, 31.

unleashed rivalries among his successors, and this created opportunities for other communist states to stir and come back to life. Since Stalinist sycophants were installed in all the satellite countries, and their constituency was in Moscow rather than at home, they had no vested interest in loosening the Soviet grip. With their patron dead, however, they faced an uncertain future. As they anxiously sought to identify their new patron in Moscow, "collective leadership" was proclaimed. Malenkov was invested only with the formal trappings of state authority, and he clearly was forced to share power with Beria and Molotov. Factional groupings assumed shape in the satellite capitals, corresponding to those in the Kremlin, and Beria's arrest, in June, sent a ripple of fear through Eastern Europe. Soon, collective leadership became the new orthodoxy, as Party and state posts in Eastern Europe were separated and redistributed.

Stalin's successors were thus almost immediately confronted with the vexing problem of trying to perpetuate his system of vassalage, or of modifying it. This reexamination unleashed a "great debate" within the Kremlin, one which divided the leadership into one faction which insisted that the old system be retained with minor adjustments and another which advocated a liberalization that bordered on revolutionizing the entire relationship between Moscow and her allies. While Malenkov was Premier, no radical departures from Stalin's policies toward Eastern Europe could be detected, but it now appears that the faction headed by Khrushchev and Bulganin was pressing for a complete rupture with the past. Its program included: (1) elimination of the developing schism with Peking; (2) rapprochement with Marshal Tito; (3) halting the economic exploitation of the satellites; and (4) permitting the gradual evolution of partial political autonomy. These proposals presupposed not only a break with the past, but also an actual repudiation of Stalin's policies, and consequently they were strongly resisted by Molotov and others, as dangerous to the unity of the communist movement.

As the internal controversy became more acute, uncertain, and incapable of resolution on the basis of the internal political balance, the factions in the Kremlin reached out into their empire for incremental support. Communist leaders were once again about to become power constituencies, starting with the most powerful and the most independent, China and Yugoslavia. China had been humiliated by Stalin, who had tried to make her subservient and this was clearly resented by the Chinese, not only as unconsonant with its national pride and dignity, but as contrary to proper relations between communist states.

Obviously, Chinese resentment promised possible political support to some in the Kremlin. We can date the beginnings of the Soviet Union's loss of primacy in the communist world from Khrushchev's opportunistic use of China and Yugoslavia against his rivals. Presumably, both Mao and Tito would reciprocate by supporting Khrushchev. And for the next three years, both China and Yugoslavia played significant roles in shoring up Khrushchev's position at home and vis-à-vis the Eastern European communist countries.

The defeat of the Malenkov-Molotov policy was clearly apparent by July, 1954. Neither Premier Malenkov nor Foreign Minister Molotov accompanied the Khrushchev-Bulganin mission to Peking, in the autumn of 1954, where it was their purpose to assuage Peking's resentments and inaugurate a new era in the relations between the two countries. The Soviet grip on Manchuria was relinquished, the joint stock companies liquidated, and full Chinese sovereignty restored over Darien and Port Arthur.

The Chinese apparently submitted an additional list of grievances and demands. Mao apparently interpreted the Soviet action as a sign of fear and weakness, and demanded further adjustments: the return of Mongolia; a rectification of Sino-Soviet frontiers in China's favor; and perhaps a demand that the Soviet Union cancel Chinese debts incurred as a result of the Korean War, which, after all, was fought in the interests of the socialist camp as a whole. All these were presumably rejected. The Mongolian issue and the general territorial question became a matter of public record only in August 1964, when Mao Tse-tung raised them in an interview with a visiting delegation of Japanese socialists:

> In keeping with the Yalta Agreement the Soviet Union, under the pretext of insuring Mongolia's independence, actually placed this country under its domination. . . . In 1954 when Khrushchev and Bulganin were in China we took up this question but they refused to talk to us. . . . Some people have declared that the Sinkiang area and the territories north of the Amur must be included in the Soviet Union.[8]

The Soviet version of the 1954 events placed them in a broader context, as revealed in a rebuttal by *Pravda:*

> Maps showing various parts of the Soviet Union . . . as Chinese territory continued to be published in the CPR. Chinese representatives recently began mentioning with increasing frequency hundreds of thousands of square kilometers of Soviet territory which allegedly belong "by right" to China. . . . In his talk, Mao Tse-tung bemoaned the fate of Mongolia which, as he said, was put by the Soviet Union "under its rule. . . ." The existence of an independent Mongolian state, which maintains friendly relations with the U.S.S.R. . . . does not suit the Chinese leaders. They would like to deprive Mongolia of its independence and make it a Chinese province. The CPR leaders offered "to reach agreement" on this with N. S. Khrushchev and other Soviet comrades during their visit to Peking in 1954. N. S. Khrushchev naturally refused to discuss this question.[9]

Thus, by 1954, China felt assertive enough to demand territorial restitution in the name of Chinese national interests. Mao was also apparently informed of the impending resignation of Malenkov, an unprecedented gesture on the part of Soviet leaders, in that it was an implicit request for clearance from a foreign communist leader.

[8] *Pravda,* September 2, 1964.
[9] Ibid.

The decision to seek a reconciliation with Tito proceeded more cautiously, but it, too, was a Khrushchev-Bulganin gesture in search of new external constituencies. And since the effort to return Yugoslavia to the communist fraternity was bound to have repercussions in Eastern Europe, Khrushchev saw a need to ameliorate conditions in other communist states as well. Comecon (Council of Mutual Economic Aid) was converted from a vehicle of exploitation into an institutionalized conference, and regular meetings were devoted to mutual economic problems. In November, 1954, a conference in Moscow laid the foundations for the Warsaw Pact, which was signed on May 14, 1955, binding all the European communist states in a military alliance. While the Pact did little more than legalize the presence of Soviet troops on the territories of the Eastern European states, it was significant psychologically. Unilateralism was replaced with formal multilateralism, and Stalin's divisive, bilateral arrangements were disowned.

The rapprochement with the Yugoslavs was preceded by a bitter controversy in the Kremlin, and Molotov, who was strenuously opposed to the whole idea, was overruled. At Tito's insistence, the following measures were taken: (1) Stalin's satellite policies were openly condemned and repudiated; (2) Stalin's victims in Eastern Europe, like Rajk in Hungary and Kostov in Bulgaria, were posthumously rehabilitated, their trials pronounced a fraud, and Tito absolved of all implications of subversion and deviation; (3) "national deviationists" or "Titoists" still alive, like Gomulka in Poland and Kadar in Hungary, were released from prison and restored to high rank in the Party; (4) "Stalinists" in Eastern Europe were dethroned and replaced with personalities more acceptable to Tito; (5) the Cominform was liquidated; (6) Molotov was ousted as Foreign Minister because he was *persona non grata* to Tito; and (7) Moscow accepted the Yugoslav theory "that the roads and conditions of socialist development are different in different countries . . . that any tendency of imposing one's views in determining the roads and forms of socialist development is alien."[10] Never before had a foreign communist leader — and a former outcast, at that — demanded and received such an influential role in the policies of the Kremlin.

THE SOVIET UNION AND INTERNATIONAL COMMUNISM: THE EROSION OF SOVIET PRIMACY

The Twentieth Party Congress represented a new level in the evolution of Soviet relations with the rest of the communist world. Locally responsive communists, like Gomulka and Nagy, were catapulted into power in Poland and Hungary by powerful internal pressures which were set into motion by the revelations of the Twentieth Party Congress. The demolition of Stalinism at home could only have resulted in the progressive disintegration of Stalinist structures in Eastern Europe. The repercussions in China, Yugoslavia, and Albania were smallest, since

[10] The *New York Times*, June 21, 1956.

they were governed largely by indigenous Stalinist regimes, particularly China and Albania.

The Polish and Hungarian "Octobers" were the immediate and most serious consequences of de-Stalinization, and the demands these two events placed upon the communist system, as then organized, threatened to reduce it to ruins. Nationalism of the Soviet variety could no longer be obscured and nationalism of the smaller states could no longer be denied. The year 1956, thus, inaugurated the gradual dissolution of proletarian internationalism into its constituent proletarian or communist nationalisms. This process unfolded gradually and pragmatically in response to situations and events.

Before Stalin's death, the flow of demands in the communist system had been in one direction only, from the center to the periphery. After Stalin's death, and especially after 1956, the flow was substantially and progressively altered. First Peking, in 1954, then Yugoslavia, in 1955, then Poland, in 1956, made demands upon the Soviet Union which were met and which have since been repeated by other communist states. By 1958, the Soviet Union was bombarded with demands, trivial and serious, from all directions. Moscow's demands on other communist states became more limited and less coercive. During the years 1957–1961, demands flowing in from the periphery gradually exceeded those flowing outward from the center.

The Council of Mutual Economic Aid (Comecon), for example, which was originally operated to the economic advantage of the Soviet Union, was reorganized to control and arrest Soviet exploitation. No sooner had this happened, than it was converted into a vehicle for channeling economic aid from the Soviet Union to the other communist states, as demands came in for restitution, reparations, economic assistance, and commercial autonomy. The joint stock companies were dissolved, and deliveries of raw materials and finished goods were made in accordance with world market prices. Eastern European states asserted the right to receive economic assistance from, and engage in profitable commercial transactions with, capitalist countries.

Economic demands upon the Soviet Union spilled over into the political and ideological realms, as individual states demanded and received greater autonomy. Institutions modeled after those in the Soviet Union were, in many cases, dissolved or modified, while Soviet-type ideological controls over the arts, sciences, professions, education, and media of information were renounced in accordance with the local demands of each state. No overt attempt was made to organize joint or concerted action on Moscow until 1961, however, when China and Albania forged an anti-Soviet factional alliance.

The role of the Soviet Union underwent modification with each successive stage in the continuing evolution of the system and movement. Four distinct phases are discernible in the Soviet Union's relationship to the communist universe of states and parties during the period from 1956 to 1967.

The first phase was a short one, covering the period from the

Twentieth Party Congress to the World Conference of Communist Parties in November, 1957. During this period, the Soviet Union was clearly a crippled leader, mauled and bruised as a consequence of its de-Stalinization program. Split and divided at home, with its prestige tarnished and its power tattered and ragged, using both Belgrade and Peking as crutches, it hobbled its way from one capital to another seeking to preserve its authority.

The World Conference of November, 1957, marks the end of the first phase and the beginning of the second, which lasted until the Twenty-second Party Congress of the Communist Party of the Soviet Union (CPSU), in October, 1961. Unable to assert its former primacy, the Soviet Union was soon challenged by China, which attempted to introduce Chinese interests as a prime factor in proletarian internationalism, by making successive demands on the Soviet Union, on the system, and then on the movement itself. Khrushchev's excommunication of China's echo, Albania, at the Twenty-second Party Congress, signaled a successful Soviet quashing of the Chinese bid for primacy and an attempt to reassert positive Soviet leadership in Eastern Europe and over Western communist parties.

The third phase, which covers the period from the Twenty-second Party Congress to the limited Test Ban Treaty of July, 1963, was marked by the progressive transformation of a polycentric communist universe into a movement grouped around two opposite poles, Moscow and Peking. This meant that not only was Marxism-Leninism incapable of guaranteeing an ideological consensus, but that the international communist movement was no longer even capable of containing the conflict.

The fourth phase, beginning with the limited Test Ban Treaty and still continuing, was marked by open mutual denunciation and abuse, the possible transformation of a polarized communist universe into two hostile camps, and the dissolution of the communist world as a military bloc. Peking accused Moscow of conspiring with the United States against her, while Moscow charged Peking with seeking to maneuver the Soviet Union into a thermonuclear war of mutual annihilation with the United States so that it might pick up the pieces and dominate the ruins. The ouster of Khrushchev, in October, 1964, postponed the climax of this phase, but China's refusal to send a delegation to the Twenty-third Congress of the CPSU in April, 1966, may have inaugurated a new phase in the evolution of the world communist movement, the phase of two hostile communist camps and movements, and the evolution of a Soviet-American *détente*.

Crippled Leader: The Primacy of
Soviet Interests Subdued

Theoretically, of course, proletarian internationalism demands that national interests be subordinated to an international interest. In the case of the Soviet Union, the subordination of its interests to proletarian internationalism could only mean to reverse roles and allow the national interests of other communist states to prevail over its own. This, Moscow was not prepared to do. From 1956 to 1958, therefore, an attempt was made to find a way to coordinate several national interests. The effort proved futile, however, as it became apparent that the Chinese were demanding a disproportionately large role for their national interests in the calculation of proletarian internationalism. Soviet recognition of the primacy of proletarian internationalism, under these conditions, would have been tantamount to the subordination of its national interests to those of the Chinese.

The cracking of the monolith in Eastern Europe approached its climax in October, 1956, with an independent-minded Gomulka in Warsaw and a secessionist-minded Nagy in Budapest. Moscow fluctuated between adventurism and paralysis. The Poznan uprising and its aftermath elicited a Soviet threat to intervene militarily but, according to Chinese accounts, Chinese pressures exerted a moderating influence and Poland was saved from Soviet military occupation. The Hungarian national uprising, which threatened to sweep communism out entirely, was met with hesitation and vacillation in Moscow; according to the Chinese version, it was only the wisdom and firmness of Mao Tse-tung which induced Khrushchev to save Hungary for the socialist camp.

Events in Eastern Europe soon outpaced both Soviet thought and action. The "palace revolution" in Warsaw introduced an autonomous and significant center of heretical pressure within the bloc. Gomulka successfully defied Soviet threats, purged Stalinists from key positions, and demanded and received a veto on the movement of Soviet troops in Poland. The Polish revolution was praised in Peking and Belgrade, but generally condemned by the Stalinist-oriented leaders in other satellite capitals.

Soviet intervention in Hungary also evoked divergent reactions in various capitals. Peking pressured for military intervention, the other satellites applauded it, Warsaw deplored it, and Belgrade condemned it. This brought Tito into direct conflict with Peking. Tito openly condemned the Soviet explanation of the revolution and deplored the use of troops. In his famous Pula speech, Tito revealed the existence of "Stalinist" and "anti-Stalinist" factions in the Soviet hierarchy and in the communist movement as a whole, and Yugoslavia was once again removed to the periphery of respectable communism. The situation over Hungary was so serious that Moscow asked Peking for support. A statement was issued condoning the Hungarian repression and repudiating the Yugoslav criticisms. Belgrade temporarily lost influence, but Peking and Belgrade were to emerge as the two poles of the communist axis.

On October 30, 1956, the Soviet leaders, in consultation with Peking, issued a statement entitled "The Foundations of the Development and Further Consolidation of Friendship and Cooperation between the Soviet Union and other Socialist States," in which Moscow conceded grave errors in its relationships with other communist states, promised amends (and eventually reparations), and called for the transformation of the communist system into a commonwealth of socialist nations:

> In the process of constructing a new system and effecting profound revolutionary changes in social relationships, there have arisen many difficulties, unsolved problems and outright errors. The latter have in-

cluded infringements of the mutual relationships between socialist countries and mistakes which have weakened the principle of the equality of rights in the mutual association of the socialist countries.[11]

Moscow also pledged that "the Soviet Government is ready to discuss, together with the governments of other socialist states, measures . . . to remove the possibilities of violating the principle of national sovereignty and . . . equality."

The dissolution of the Cominform — the only multilateral party organization in the entire movement — made it a matter of urgency to devise new processes and institutions of mutual consultation as quickly as possible. Since the Cominform was viewed as a discredited symbol of Soviet primacy and Stalinist domination, Moscow's stated preference for a new, permanent, multilateral organization was rejected by Peking, Warsaw, and Belgrade as too suggestive of the Cominform and Comintern. It was opposed by the Italian Party. In all cases, the opponents of a revival of institutionalized multilateral forms betrayed a fear that this might relegitimize Soviet primacy, in view of Moscow's command of the loyalty of a majority of both communist states and parties. Moscow, accordingly, resigned itself to a position of flexibility, but called for immediate action:

> The establishment of businesslike contact between Communist, Socialist, and Workers' Parties in order to eliminate the split in the international labor movement has become one of the most urgent problems of our times.[12]

With Tito discredited, Peking boldly moved in and unilaterally assumed the role of an honest broker between Moscow and its rebellious Eastern European client states. On December 29, 1956, the Chinese issued a long statement, in which they condemned the extremes of both Stalinism and Titoism, and, at the same time, attempted to suggest a new orthodoxy for the entire system. The legitimacy of national interests in determining common action was explicitly recognized:

> Marxism-Leninism has always strongly advocated that proletarian internationalism be combined with patriotism. . . . The Communist Parties of all countries must . . . become the spokesmen of the legitimate national interests and sentiments of their people [and] . . . effectively educate the masses in the spirit of internationalism and harmonize the national sentiments and interests of these countries.[13]

Chou En-lai was dispatched by Peking on a fence-mending tour designed to find a new common ground between Moscow and its recalcitrant satellites in Eastern Europe. The Chinese action was welcomed by Gomulka, who saw, in Peking's intervention, a useful counterpoise to Soviet pressure. Tito, however, viewed it with resentment and anxiety, since Peking was seeking to strike a compromise between Polish and Soviet positions, rather than between Yugoslav and Soviet. Chou En-lai

[11] *Pravda*, October 31, 1956.
[12] Mikoyan's speech to the Eighth Congress of the Chinese Communist Party, *Pravda*, September 18, 1956.
[13] *Pravda*, December 31, 1956.

carefully steered a course which simultaneously renounced "great power chauvinism" and preserved the "leading role" of the Soviet Union. Peking's intervention apparently also helped to improve Khrushchev's position in the Soviet hierarchy. As a consequence, the balance of factions in the Kremlin was altered, and the February, 1957, Plenum of the Central Committee reversed some of the key decisions of the December, 1956, Plenum, which seemed directed at Khrushchev.

The forging of a new international interest or communist consensus was, during most of 1957, restricted mainly to bilateral discussions between communist parties and leaders and consultations at various Party Congresses, but this soon proved inadequate and ineffective. Warsaw continued its refusal to accept even the formalities of Soviet primacy, while Peking became an increasingly assertive spokesman for the camp as a whole. During the "anti-Party group" crisis, in June, 1957, Khrushchev again apparently sought and received support from Mao, which further contributed to the image of China as virtually a codirector of the socialist camp. In return for Chinese support, Khrushchev apparently agreed to contribute to China's nuclear development, and an agreement on nuclear technology was signed in October, 1957.

Not only did the communist countries fail to agree upon new forms of supranational organizations of consultation, but they failed to find any operational consensus at all. In 1957, the Soviet Union was unable to convince the other communist countries of the necessity for a new multilateral communist organization similar to the Cominform in structural outlines. And by 1964, Moscow was unable even to persuade the communist states to convene a general conference of communist parties. None has been convened since November, 1960. An alternative pattern of multilateral consultation, reportedly suggested by Moscow, was the exchange of permanent Party representatives. Both suggestions were frowned upon by Peking, Warsaw, and the Italian Communist Party, and Belgrade was not consulted.

The principal resistance to a new Cominform came from Yugoslavia, although both Poland and China also opposed a revival of the organization in any form, which they still feared might once again be employed by Moscow as an instrument of centralization and domination. The Yugoslav-Polish view was that consultation be primarily a bipartisan affair:

> Both parties recognized that the bilateral interparty relations in the present conditions constitute the most appropriate form of consultation between Communist and Workers' Parties. This does not exclude, however, a broader cooperation of Communist and Workers' Parties and progressive movements in connection with individual questions of common interest.[14]

Pending the formation of definitive institutions and methods of consultation, bilateralism and *ad hoc* multilateralism have been the

[14] The *New York Times*, January 1, 1957.

general rule. This has followed three patterns: (1) mutual exchanges of Party delegations to Party conferences and congresses; (2) bilateral discussions throughout the communist world, followed by the issuance of joint communiqués, which have deviated interestingly from the crude uniformity of the past; (3) multiparty conferences, in the form of periodic gatherings of delegates from all communist parties, and selective conferences restricted to parties which exercise power in their respective states. The first of these post-Cominform conferences was a rump meeting held in Budapest in January, 1957, which was attended only by delegates from Moscow, Budapest, Sofia, Prague, and Bucharest.

November, 1957, saw the first attempt to establish a multilateral process for arriving at a communist consensus. Since two distinct consensuses were involved, one among communist states and another among all parties, two separate conferences were organized. The first, held from November 14 to 16, included only representatives from the communist states; the second, which met from November 16 to 19, included representatives from sixty-four communist parties. This was in line with the evolving formula that the communist camp as a whole should offer direction to the movement It is now known that serious controversies between Moscow and Peking developed at the November Conference. The expulsion of the "anti-Party group" and the successful disposition of Zhukov had improved Khrushchev's position to the point where Peking's support was no longer required or desired. A number of Mao's proposals were successfully resisted, but the Chinese leader was successful in altering a Soviet draft declaration which proved unacceptable to Yugoslavia. On the issue of Soviet primacy, Peking was even more emphatic than Moscow in having the declaration incorporate the formulation, "the socialist camp headed by the Soviet Union."

The Yugoslav representatives refused to accept the declaration issued by the ruling communist parties, which embodied a common core of ideological principles and policy positions which had been hammered out after long and arduous negotiation. The purpose of the declaration was to restore the unity among the various ruling parties, but it became impossible to reconcile the extreme positions of China and Yugoslavia, in spite of the wide latitude which the November Declaration afforded for individual variation within a common program.

The concessions made by Moscow, however, did earn the public support of Peking for the ideological innovations introduced at the Twentieth Party Congress, as well as the denunciation of at least some aspects of Stalinism, but the Chinese could not accept positions which would be acceptable to Belgrade. Now that China supported the Russian position, Warsaw had no alternative but to alter its heretical position and support the declaration. The main points at issue, which the Yugoslavs could not accept, were the questions of the leading role of the Soviet Union in the communist world, the dogmatic insistence that all international tensions were generated by Western imperialism, that peace was possible only after the liquidation of capitalism but that peaceful coexistence would govern relations with the capitalist world pending its final liquidation and, finally, that revisionism (i.e., Titoism) constituted the chief threat to the unity of the communist orbit. Dogmatism (i.e., Stalinism) was condemned as a lesser deviationist evil and threat to communist unity.

The net result was the elimination of Yugoslavia as a factor in making decisions for the communist orbit, and the elevation of Peking to a position of rivalry with Moscow for power and influence in the communist world. The November, 1957, meeting signaled China's political and ideological independence from Moscow and underlined the voluntary character of her recognition of Soviet Russian primacy, with the implication that she could withdraw this recognition at will. The auspicious inauguration of the People's Communes in China in 1958, and the bitter attacks leveled against them by Soviet leaders betrayed a bold attempt on the part of China to claim primacy for the Chinese state as the most advanced society in the world.

The 1957 declaration also called for a new authoritative international journal of the communist movement, presumably to replace the defunct paper issued by the Cominform, and a third multiparty conference, held in Prague in March, 1958, without benefit of the Yugoslavs, could only agree to issue a theoretical and informational monthly, the *World Marxist Review*. This journal has, however, been repudiated by Peking and its followers in the international communist movement.

Outwardly, the 1957 conference seemed to reflect harmony and concord, and its declaration outlined new procedures for determining the content and direction of proletarian internationalism:

> Following their exchange of views, the participants in the discussion have come to the conclusion that in the present circumstances it would be expedient, in addition to the meetings of leading officials and in addition to an exchange of information on a bilateral basis, to arrange more far-reaching conferences of the communist and workers' parties in order to discuss topical international problems, to exchange experiences, to get to know one another's views and attitudes and to coordinate the common struggle for common aims, for peace, democracy, and socialism.[15]

Challenged Leader: The Chinese Bid for Primacy

The full implications of the resurgence of nationalism were not immediately apparent in 1956–1957. The enthronement of the nation-state as the definitive form of the communist state meant that the idea of a world communist state had been jettisoned in favor of a communist inter-state system for the indefinite future. Party conflicts would inevitably be transformed into state conflicts, and state conflicts would inexorably reflect national conflicts, as the nation-state once again preempted the highest loyalty of its citizens. Highest loyalty to the proletariat, yes, but to the *national* proletariat and its nation-state.

The Chinese were caught in a peculiar dilemma. They insisted that the movement required a center or leader, but more than any other

[15] *Pravda,* November 22, 1957.

communist state, they demanded autonomy. What Peking wanted, of course, was to assume direction herself, but since there was little immediate prospect of displacing Moscow directly, the Chinese sought to use Moscow as an unsuspecting instrument in their drive for power and influence.

The Chinese insisted that Moscow be recognized as the leader of the camp and movement because a leader was required, although the Soviet leaders had demonstrated their unworthiness since the Twentieth Party Congress. Peking refrained from criticizing the Soviet leadership openly and expected, in return for preserving the unity of the movement, that Moscow would cater to Chinese superior wisdom and advice. The Soviet Union would thus lead a world communist movement whose policies would reflect Chinese interests. Perhaps at the appropriate time, China would then displace Moscow as the *de jure* leader of the movement.

This strategy is only thinly concealed by subsequent Chinese explanations of why they followed an unworthy leader for so long a period of time. Thus, in February, 1964, in response to a Soviet charge that Peking wished to "seize the leadership," the Chinese rhetorically asked:

> From whom? . . . Who now holds the leadership? In the international communist movement, is there such a thing as leadership which lords it over all the fraternal parties? And is this leadership in your hands?

And then, somewhat inconsistently, Peking refers to the events of 1957:

> At the 1957 Moscow meeting of fraternal parties, our delegation emphasized that the socialist camp should have the Soviet Union at its head. The reason was that, although they had committed some mistakes, the leaders of the C.P.S.U. did finally accept the Moscow declaration. . . . Our proposal that the Socialist camp should have the Soviet Union at its head was written into the declaration.[16]

An earlier statement by the Chinese, issued in September, 1963, reveals that Peking's motivation, in pressing for the recognition of Soviet leadership, was a compound of cynicism, fear, and timing, while their behavior was arrogant, self-righteous, and patronizing:

> Ever since the 20th congress of the C.P.S.U. we have watched with concern as the C.P.S.U. leadership has taken the road of revisionism. Confronted with this grave situation our party has scores of times and for a long period considered: What should we do? . . . Should we keep silent about the errors of the C.P.S.U. leadership? We believed that the errors of the C.P.S.U. leadership were not just accidental errors . . . but rather a whole series of errors of principle which endanger the interests of the entire socialist camp and the international Communist movement. . . . We foresaw that if we criticized the errors of the leaders of the C.P.S.U. they would certainly strike at us vindictively and

[16] *Jen Min Jih Pao*, February 4, 1964. Citation is from the version published in the *New York Times*, February 7, 1964.

thus inevitably cause serious damage to China's socialist construction. . . . We took into consideration the fact that the C.P.S.U. . . . is the party of the first Socialist state, and that it enjoyed high prestige in the international Communist movement and among the people of the whole world. Therefore, over a considerable period of time we were particularly careful and patient in criticizing the leaders of the C.P.S.U., trying our best to confine such criticism to interparty talks between the leaders of the Chinese and Soviet parties. . . . But all the comradely criticism and advice given to the leaders of the C.P.S.U. by responsible comrades of the C.C.P. Central Committee in scores of inter-party talks did not succeed in enabling them to return to the correct path.[17]

Peking's description of Mao Tse-tung's behavior at the 1957 Moscow conference could scarcely conceal the manner in which he apparently lectured Khrushchev and other Soviet leaders:

> The delegation of the C.C.P., which was headed by Comrade Mao Tse-tung, did a great deal of work during the meeting. On the one hand, it had full consultations with the leaders of the C.P.S.U., and where necessary and appropriate waged struggle against them, in order to help them correct their errors; on the other hand, it held repeated exchanges in views with the leaders of other fraternal parties in order that a common document acceptable to all might be worked out. . . . In their original draft of the declaration, the leadership of the C.P.S.U. insisted on the inclusion of the erroneous views of the 20th Congress on peaceful transition. . . . The Chinese Communist party resolutely opposed the wrong views contained in the draft declaration submitted by the leadership of the C.P.S.U. We expressed our views on the two successive drafts put forward by the Central Committee of the C.P.S.U. and made a considerable number of major changes of principles which we presented as our own revised draft. Repeated discussions were then held between the delegations of the Chinese and Soviet parties on the basis of our revised draft before the "joint draft declaration by the C.P.S.U. and the C.C.P." was submitted to the delegations of the other fraternal parties for their opinions.[18]

Under Khrushchev's direction, Soviet policies were gradually oriented toward the avoidance of thermonuclear war and a relaxation of international tensions, based on a limited accommodation with the United States. By achieving an agreement with the United States when Soviet prestige was high, the diplomatic consequences might be correspondingly advantageous. This strategy, however, conflicted with Chinese aspirations. Mao made dramatically clear, at the 1957 Moscow meeting, that he calculated the Soviet Union to be militarily superior to the United States and that instead of settling for an accommodation, his superior wisdom dictated that the Soviet Union should use its military superiority to oust American power from marginal areas, particularly in the Far East.

These divergent national interests were bound to collide, although Peking apparently thought that its leverage was still sufficient to force

[17] *Peking Review*, No. 37, September 13, 1963, pp. 6–23.
[18] Ibid.

Moscow's acceptance of its demands. The Chinese decided to press the issue and confront Khrushchev with an agonizing choice between supporting a major ally or seeking an accommodation with the major enemy and thus risking a rupture with Peking. The Chinese leaders apparently thought that Khrushchev would hardly dare to alienate Peking in return for an uncertain and fragile accommodation with the United States. Mao probably calculated — on the basis of past experience — that Khrushchev would not dare oppose him for fear that his rivals might use his opposition as a pretext to successfully discredit his leadership.

From Peking's standpoint, China possessed all the necessary credentials for primacy in the communist world except nuclear power and stage of development. In 1958, China had the world's largest population, which was three times that of the Soviet Union and about twice the size of the combined populations of all party states. It was blessed with the longest and most continuous civilization and culture in the world; it was truly universal in an historical sense as the direct successor of the Celestial Empire, whose civilization and culture had extended to the Middle East and Eastern Europe by Genghis Khan and his successors, who destroyed 40 states, large and small, in order to erect a more beautiful civilization. Furthermore, China had the largest communist party in the world, nearly one-half the total of all communist party members on the globe. Its party and state were graced with the most politically adept, verbally eloquent, and ideologically elegant leader in the communist world, Mao Tse-tung, the true inheritor of the tradition of Marx, Lenin, and Stalin. Although the Soviet Union remained a powerful military and industrial state, this was only a temporary phase, since its prestige and that of its leaders, was soiled by inept and fumbling behavior. The Soviet Union was an unworthy leader whose primacy had crumbled as a consequence of its own political opportunism and ideological sophistry. This was the perception which the Soviet leaders thought Mao held, and it probably was not too inaccurate. Thus, a Soviet leader was to complain in 1964:

> It is known that beginning in ancient times the ideologists of China created a concept of their country as the "Middle Kingdom," the oldest civilization, the custodian of world order and spiritual harmony, as a "universal land" with power over everything under the sun. The imperial ideology concerning China's special role in the history of mankind to some degree affects the consciousness of China's present-day leaders.[19]

Sometime in late 1957 or early 1958, the Chinese leaders decided to overcome the two deficiencies in their credentials for an assertion of primacy: (1) the lack of nuclear weapons; and (2) a retarded stage of economic development. Apparently, Mao perceived an opportunity, in the summer of 1958, to force the issue of nuclear weapons with the Soviet Union and, at the same time, to disrupt Khrushchev's attempts to bring about a new summit meeting in order to establish some sort of accommodation with the United States.

[19] L. Ilyichev, "Revolutionary Science and the Present Day," *Kommunist*, No. 11, July, 1964, pp. 12–35.

Peking's fears and suspicions were apparently reinforced by Moscow's mild response to the landing of American Marines in Lebanon and Khrushchev's assent to Eisenhower's suggestion that a summit conference be held within the framework of the United Nations Security Council, to discuss the Middle Eastern crisis. Such a conference would not only exclude Peking, but possibly include India and even Chiang Kaishek, since Nationalist China continued to occupy China's seat on the Security Council.

Peking's reaction was sufficiently violent to impel Khrushchev not only to withdraw his acceptance, but also to make a hurried and unannounced trip to Peking to offer explanations. On August 4, Khrushchev withdrew his suggestion for a summit meeting altogether.

The Chinese had apparently prevailed again. It appears, however, that they may have used the opportunity to make an additional demand, that Moscow supply China with sample atom bombs, but Moscow refused. The Chinese may also have demanded that Khrushchev be prepared to issue a public statement of nuclear support for a forthcoming Chinese initiative in the Taiwan Strait to test American determination and perhaps, also, to force Moscow to choose between communist unity and an agreement with the United States.

The unsatisfactory nature of the Soviet response during the Taiwan Straits crisis of 1958 was confirmed in 1963, when the entire episode was raked over in acrimonious public debate after the Test Ban Treaty was signed. In reply to a Soviet claim that China was spared nuclear destruction during the Taiwan Straits crisis because of the Soviet Union's readiness to retaliate with nuclear weapons if China were attacked, the Chinese delivered their own version of the episode:

> It is especially ridiculous that the Soviet statement also gives all the credit to Soviet nuclear weapons for the Chinese people's victory in smashing the armed provocations of U.S. imperialism in the Taiwan Straits in 1958. What are the facts? In August and September, 1958, the situation in the Taiwan Straits was indeed very tense. . . . The Soviet leaders expressed their support for China on 7 and 19 September respectively. Although at that time the situation in the Taiwan Straits was tense, there was no possibility that a nuclear war would break out and no need for the Soviet Union to support China with its nuclear weapons. It was only when they were clear that this was the situation that the Soviet leaders expressed their support for China.[20]

The issues of a Soviet nuclear capability for China and unspecified Soviet military demands upon China were revived in connection with the events of 1958.

Speaking for the Soviet Union, Suslov reported to the Central Committee in February, 1964:

> It is known that the CPR leaders have stubbornly sought to get the Soviet Union to hand over atomic bombs to them. They took extreme offense that our country did not offer them samples of atomic weapons.[21]

[20] *Peking Review*, No. 37, September 13, 1963, pp. 6–23.
[21] *Pravda*, April 3, 1964.

It seems clear that the Soviet Union began to resist Chinese demands after Khrushchev's return from Peking in 1958, when he decided, instead, to pursue his policy of seeking an agreement with the United States. This was confirmed by the Chinese in September, 1963:

> The leaders of the C.P.S.U., eager to curry favor with U.S. imperialism, engaged in unbridled activities against China. . . . They thought they had solved their internal problems and had "stabilized" their own position and could therefore step up their policy of "being friendly to enemies and tough with friends."[22]

The Chinese later complained bitterly that the Soviet refusal to supply them with nuclear assistance and bombs was a betrayal of "proletarian internationalism." Moscow retorted that, since the Chinese could always rely for their security upon Soviet nuclear power, Peking's desire for a separate nuclear capability had little to do with proletarian internationalism and probably was motivated by a desire to engage in adventures which would be subversive and detrimental to Soviet interests:

> If the leaders of China are actually following the principles of proletarian internationalism, why are they striving so hard to obtain their own atom bomb? People who stop at nothing in their desire to provide themselves with new types of destructive weapons must have some motive. What is behind this desire? From our point of view, the very idea of the need to provide themselves with nuclear weapons could occur to the leaders of a country whose security is guaranteed by the entire might of the socialist camp only if they have developed some kind of special aims or interests that the socialist camp cannot support with its military force. But such aims and interests can manifest themselves only among those who reject proletarian internationalism, who depart from socialist positions on questions of foreign policy. . . . After all, it is impossible to combine with the peaceloving foreign policy course of the countries of the socialist system plans for nuclear weapons of one's own order, for example, to increase one's influence in the countries of Asia, Africa and Latin America or to create for oneself a "position of strength" in disputed international questions or, finally, to exacerbate international tension.[23]

Further insight into China's motivations during this period, was provided when Chen Yi, the Chinese Foreign Minister, conceded, in 1963:

> Atomic bombs, missiles and supersonic aircraft are reflections of the technical level of a nation's industry. China will have to resolve this issue within the next several years; otherwise, it will degenerate into a second-class or third-class nation.[24]

The Chinese demands, in 1958, for a nuclear arsenal of some sort were paralleled by a series of bold moves designed to secure an ideological foundation for a future Chinese claim to primacy. According to a

[22] *Peking Review*, No. 37, September 13, 1963, pp. 6–23.
[23] *Pravda*, September 21, 1963.
[24] As reported by *Kyodo* (Tokyo), October 28, 1963.

subsequent account, Moscow interpreted Chinese behavior at that time as follows:

> In the spring of 1958 the Chinese leadership began to change its line sharply. Instead of the approximately 15 years that had been envisioned for setting up the base for socialism in China, in 1958 a period of only three years was proclaimed to be adequate even for the transition to communism. The so-called "great leap" was announced — a political-economic adventure unprecedented in both design and scale. This was a policy . . . built on the desire to solve grandiose tasks faster and to "teach" others the newly invented methods of building socialism and communism. It was then that the slogan was proclaimed of the "people's communes," which formed the basis of the attempt to leap over natural stages of socialist construction in the . . . effort to get "ahead of progress" here.[25]

Khrushchev, a resourceful politician, quickly perceived the challenge, and while he did not overtly condemn the communes or criticize the Chinese Great Leap at the time, he ignored it publicly and ridiculed it privately. The Soviet press was conspicuously silent about the entire affair, but the Yugoslavs openly denounced the communes and other Eastern European leaders privately expressed disgust and apprehension over Mao's abrupt leftward turn. In April, 1964, Khrushchev revealed what he had obviously discerned, six years earlier, to be the motivation behind China's behavior:

> But in that same year, 1958, the Chinese leaders unexpectedly proclaimed the so-called course of the "great leap" and the "people's communes." The idea behind this course consisted in skipping over the stages of socialist development into the phase of communist construction. At the time, Chinese propaganda asserted that China would show everyone an example of entry into communism ahead of schedule.[26]

Who was ahead of whom was no idle question, since both Moscow and Peking were aware that spearheading the dialectic of history was a necessary ideological prerequisite for a serious and legitimate claim to primacy, although it could not by itself be sufficient. Nuclear power was also necessary. Consequently, Khrushchev took immediate and effective steps to deny both nuclear weapons and economic success to the Chinese. Moscow curtailed its economic and technical assistance to China on the pretext that the Great Leap forward was disrupting and distorting Chinese economic development, and aid, hence, constituted a waste of Soviet resources. Although Peking later confessed that the Great Leap had failed, the episode remained a sobering experience for the Soviet Union's leaders.

The Chinese then sought new ways to press their demands upon Moscow and enhance their power and influence in the communist movement. They shifted to the strategy of denying the ideological significance of the Soviet Union's material and social achievements, and maintained that both the Soviet Union and China were in a transitional

---

[25] L. Ilyichev, "Revolutionary Science," pp. 12–35.
[26] *Pravda*, April 16, 1964.

stage of development and more or less equidistant from communism. This shift in design was fully appreciated in Moscow.

> The mania of hegemonism drove them onto the path of adventurist leaps in the economy. . . . The first successes in economic development and in the cooperation of the peasants turned the heads of the Chinese leaders, gave them the idea that the transitional period was already past and that through communes China would be able to reach communism fast — before the socialist countries of Europe, the Soviet Union included. . . . Then the Chinese leadership, to conceal its miscalculations, launched a noisy propaganda campaign designed to present matters as though not only in China but in the U.S.S.R. and all socialist countries the tasks of the transitional period have not been carried out, that the U.S.S.R. is a country somewhat richer than China, but, in the sense of social gains, as far from communism as China is.[27]

Since Soviet interests required a rapprochement with the United States, and Chinese interests dictated an aggravation of Soviet-American relations, the interests of the two countries were to drift further and further apart. On this point, compromise was impossible. Each was convinced that its vital interest — the avoidance of thermonuclear war, from the Soviet point of view, and the expulsion of the Americans from the Far East, from the Chinese — dictated the proper course to pursue. If Moscow, China's chief ally, were to become reconciled to the United States, her major enemy, then of what value was the Sino-Soviet alliance to the Chinese? On the other hand, if solidarity with China required that the Soviet Union risk nuclear annihilation in a confrontation with the United States, her alliance with China was tantamount to a suicide pact. These divergent interests made it imperative that each chart its own policy toward the United States in accordance with its individual goals.

Khrushchev, in a series of ripostes to the Chinese bid for primacy, continued to apply various forms of political, military, and economic pressure. The Chinese were later to complain about this period rather bitterly:

> In 1958 the leadership of the C.P.S.U. put forward unreasonable demands designed to bring China under Soviet military control. These unreasonable demands were rightly and firmly rejected by the Chinese Government. Not long afterward, in June, 1959, the Soviet Government unilaterally tore up the agreement on new technology for national defense concluded between China and the Soviet Union in October, 1957, and refused to provide China with a sample of an atomic bomb and technical data concerning its manufacture.[28]

Two months after the nuclear agreement with China was nullified by Moscow, on August 3, 1959, it was announced in Moscow that Khrushchev would meet with Eisenhower in the United States. Almost simultaneously, Marshal Peng Teh-huai was dismissed by Peking. The

---

[27] *Pravda*, April 21, 1964.
[28] *Peking Review*, No. 37, September 13, 1963.

Chinese military leader, who had been Peking's observer to the Warsaw Pact Organization, apparently shared Khrushchev's misgivings about Mao and, furthermore, was professionally concerned over the imminent suspension and withdrawal of Soviet military support. The Chinese have hinted that Khrushchev tried to bring about the ouster of Mao by intriguing with his rivals.

> On more than one occasion, Khrushchev has gone so far as to tell leading comrades of the Central Committee of the C.P.C. that certain anti-party elements in the Chinese communist party were his "good friends." He has praised Chinese anti-party elements for attacking the Chinese party's general line for socialist construction, the big leap forward and the people's communes, describing their action as a "manly act."[29]

On August 7, while the Chinese Central Committee Plenum which dismissed Marshal Peng was still in session, the Sino-Indian border conflict flared up, leading to an invasion of Indian territory by the Chinese which continued into September. The Sino-Indian dispute, which Moscow interpreted as a device to frustrate the Eisenhower-Khrushchev meeting, unleashed acrimonious discussion between the two communist giants, culminating in a Soviet statement deploring the conflict and virtually disassociating Moscow from Chinese actions. Three years later, Peking complained:

> On the eve of the Camp David talks in September, 1959 — on September 9, 1959, to be exact . . . a socialist country, turning a deaf ear to China's repeated explanations of the true situation and to China's advice, hastily issued a statement on a Sino-Indian border incident through its official news agency. Here is the first instance in history in which a socialist country, instead of condemning the armed provocations of the reactionaries of a capitalist country, condemned another fraternal socialist country when it was confronted with such armed provocation.[30]

All these anti-Chinese moves by Moscow, according to Peking, were sacrificial offerings at the altar of a *détente* with the United States:

> The tearing up of the agreement on new technology for national defense by the leadership of the C.P.S.U. and its issuance of the statement on the Sino-Indian border clash on the eve of Khrushchev's visit to the United States were presentation gifts to Eisenhower so as to curry favor with the U.S. imperialists and create the so-called "spirit of Camp David."[31]

Peking charged that Khrushchev further sacrificed Chinese interests by informing Eisenhower that the Soviet Union would not give nuclear weapons to China and that Moscow would accept a "two Chinas" solution to the Taiwan problem. After the Camp David talks, which

[29] *Jen Min Jih Pao*, February 4, 1964.
[30] *Whence the Differences? A Reply to Comrade Thorez and Other Comrades* (Peking, 1963), pp. 11–12.
[31] *Peking Review*, No. 23, September 13, 1963.

Khrushchev considered a signal success, the Soviet leader's stature and prestige visibly increased. In his next confrontation with Mao in Peking, almost immediately afterward, his self-assertion did not go unnoticed:

> Back from the Camp David talks, he went so far as to try to sell China the U.S. plot of "two Chinas" and, at the state banquet celebrating the 10th anniversary of the founding of the C.P.R. he read China a lecture against "testing by force the stability of the capitalist system."[32]

Serious conflicts of national purpose and interests were only obliquely revealed in the Sino-Soviet dialogue but, as the conflict continued and intensified, they gradually broke through the ideological shells in which they were encrusted. Although ideology and national interests are so intimately intertwined in communist politics that they cannot be distilled out completely, yet they were separating out as visible quantities in the equation of conflict. Soviet interests veered more and more in the direction of an acceptance of the *status quo*, whereas Chinese interests demanded that the United States be expelled from the Far East.

What the Chinese failed to do, Gary Francis Powers and the flight of an American U-2 over Soviet territory succeeded in doing, on May Day, 1960. The Chinese felt themselves justified and congratulated themselves on their superior wisdom. Three years later, they were still exulting: "The 'spirit of Camp David' completely vanished. Thus, events entirely confirmed our views." Khrushchev, however, berated both Eisenhower and Mao, the former for cupidity or stupidity, and the latter for belligerent dogmatism. Relations with China deteriorated even faster than those with the United States, however. In June, Moscow suggested that the forthcoming Rumanian Party Congress be turned into an *ad hoc* meeting of ruling parties to discuss the implications of the abortive summit meeting with the West, and Peking accepted only grudgingly, because it was opposed to Moscow's purpose in calling the meeting. Moscow's interest in seeking a *détente* with the United States seemed to coincide with the interests of the Eastern European states, and the Chinese were unenthusiastic about placing themselves in the minority, so they had the meeting broadened into a general conference of communist parties. Peking's relations with the Kremlin were not visibly improved by the shooting down of the U-2, but it appears that Khrushchev's rivals at home were strengthened and Soviet attitudes towards the United States hardened.

The Chinese initiated their new strategy of reaching outward from the fraternity of communist countries into the larger movement for support by engaging in factional activity against Soviet positions at a WFTU meeting held in Peking on June 5–9, 1960. This was the first instance of one communist state, other than the Soviet Union, organizing opposition against another. This factional activity was to accelerate and become the main organizational weapon against Moscow's seemingly permanent majority in the fraternity.

[32] Ibid.

Anticipating China's factional strategy, Khrushchev laid an ambush for the Chinese at Bucharest:

> At Bucharest, to our amazement, the leaders of the C.P.S.U. . . . unleashed a surprise assault on the Chinese Communist Party. . . . In the meeting, Khrushchev took the lead in organizing a great converging onslaught against the Chinese Communist Party as "madmen," "wanting to unleash war" . . . "being pure nationalist" on Sino-Indian boundary question and employing "Trotskyite ways" against the C.P.S.U.[33]

Khrushchev's crude, but probably warranted, retaliation against the Chinese failed to halt them. Instead, the Chinese escalated the level of their demands, expecting that Moscow would back down eventually. Moscow had no alternative but to retaliate again. In the words of the Chinese:

> Apparently the leaders of the C.P.S.U. imagined that once they waved their baton, gathered a group of hatchetmen to make a converging assault, and applied immense political and economic pressures, they could force the Chinese Communist Party to abandon its Marxist-Leninist and proletarian internationalist stand and submit to their revisionist and great power chauvinist behests. But the tempered and long-tested Chinese Communist Party and the Chinese people could neither be vanquished nor subdued. Those who tried to subjugate us by engineering a converging assault and applying pressures miscalculated.[34]

Nationalism continued to spill over from the communist system into the larger movement. Non-ruling parties were drawn more and more into the struggle, as the twelve communist ruling parties failed to find an area of common agreement for the movement as a whole. A separate conference of parties has not been convened since 1957, and is not likely to occur in the future, although the European group has met, as the Warsaw Pact Organization and as Comecon.

The second conference of all the communist parties was convened in November, 1960. Both the Chinese and Soviet leaders lobbied vigorously before, during, and after the conference. The Chinese found themselves in the minority. They made virtually no headway among the European and Western parties, and their behavior completely bewildered and confused the others, most of whom did not want to be placed in the uncomfortable position of being forced to choose, although they were not averse to exploiting the dispute to their own ends. Stung by Chinese charges of great power chauvinism, the Soviet leaders emphasized that theirs was the majority position and correctly claimed that, of the eighty-one parties represented at the conference:

> The overwhelming majority of the fraternal parties rejected the incorrect views and concepts of the C.C.P. [Chinese Communist Party] leadership. The Chinese delegation at this meeting stubbornly upheld its own particular views and signed the Statement only when the danger arose of its complete isolation. Today it has become absolutely obvious

[33] Ibid.
[34] Ibid.

that the C.C.P. leaders were only maneuvering when they affixed their signatures to the 1960 Statement.[35]

The Chinese ruefully conceded a Soviet majority at the conference, which reaffirmed the primacy of the Soviet Union as the senior partner in an association of equal members:

> The communist and workers' parties unanimously declare that the Communist Party of the Soviet Union has been, and remains, the universally recognized vanguard of the world communist movement, being the most experienced and steeled contingent of the international communist movement.[36]

The Soviet Party was thus unambiguously enthroned as an ambiguous leader. Khrushchev, in a widely publicized speech on January 6, 1961, virtually renounced the dubious distinction of being the leader of a movement which was fractured beyond repair. It was also, simultaneously, a signal that Moscow could no longer be held responsible for, or be associated with, Peking's actions:

> The C.P.S.U. in reality does not exercise leadership over other parties. All communist parties are equal and independent. . . . The role of the Soviet Union does not lie in the fact that it leads other socialist countries but in the fact that it was the first to blaze the trail to socialism, has the greatest positive experience in the struggle for the building of socialism, and was the first to enter the period of comprehensive construction of communism. . . . It is stressed in the Statement that the universally acknowledged vanguard of the world communist movement has been and still remains the C.P.S.U. . . . At the moment, when there exists a large group of socialist countries, each of which is faced with its own tasks, when there are eighty-seven communist and workers' parties functioning, each of which, moreover, is faced with its own tasks, it is not possible for leadership over socialist countries and communist parties to be exercised from any center at all.[37]

Rump Leader: Polarization of the
International Communist Movement

The course of the controversy between the Soviet Union and China since the conference in November, 1960, and the nature of the demands each has placed upon the other has resulted in the release of more information, greater employment of abuse and invective, less sophistication and discretion in argumentation, and greater visibility of underlying motives and intentions — all, more or less, variations on themes which are now familiar.

The deterioration of the ideological quality of the conflict revealed the naked national interests which were in conflict. This did not signify that ideology was rendered insignificant, but it did mean that it was becoming progressively national and internationalized. Furthermore, issues of national interest are more likely to mobilize popular support

---

[35] *Pravda*, July 14, 1963.
[36] Cited from full text in the *New York Times*, December 7, 1960.
[37] *Kommunist*, No. 1, January, 1961, p. 34.

than are abstract ideological imperatives. The emergence of Communist China as well as of national communist states in Eastern Europe required the dozen communist states involved to reconcile their divergent interests into a common ideology which could command universal respect. The result appears to be little more than a demand that the non-ruling communist parties subordinate their interests to those of the twelve communist states. The debilitating struggle between Moscow and Peking has further revealed the degeneration of a once universalistic ideology into a vehicle of national power.

The polarization of the communist system and movement has largely followed lines of geography, stage of economic development, and even race, rather than ideology, although each pole continues to justify its position ideologically. More and more, the Soviet Union is being forced to surrender its pretensions to universalism as it emerges as essentially the leader of a coalition of European communist nations and a group of Western communist parties.

By the time of the Twenty-second Party Congress in October, 1961, the crystallization of national conflicts was already yielding to a new polarization. Soviet primacy had been dethroned, and the Chinese bid for leadership rebuffed. Each communist state was chartering its own road to socialism, and Soviet classifications of each country's stage of development seemed to be essentially a barometer of its relationship to Moscow. The Soviet position in the communist world was largely defined by its military power and economic strength, rather than by its ideological wisdom. Moscow adjusted to the new distribution of power in the system with grudging grace, although residual aspects of its former aspiration to centralized control continued to assert themselves. More out of habit than conviction, Soviet leaders continued to pose as the source of ideological innovation. Khrushchev announced a grandiose plan for the construction of communism, promulgated new statutes for the Party, which introduced the principle of rotation, and proclaimed a new Party Program, after discussion of a draft which had been widely circulated. Innovations like "all-people's state" and "all-people's party" were evidences more of the ideological exhaustion of the Soviet regime than its creativity. Although these enunciations were offered as guides to other states and parties, it was evident that each communist country and party would examine the new ideological wares and carefully select and reject in accordance with its own needs.

After halfhearted attempts to oust the Albanian leader, Enver Hoxha, had failed, Khrushchev publicly excommunicated the Albanian Party. As the most outspoken defender of the Chinese position, Tirana was a thorn in Khrushchev's side and had to be removed from the communist bloc. Albania also served as a useful surrogate target for Peking, since China's darts were hitting closer and closer to Moscow, although they were ostensibly aimed at Belgrade. The Chinese reacted by defending Albania, and by ordering Chou En-lai to leave the Congress in a huff. Khrushchev and other Soviet leaders appeared indifferent.

Albania was China's first recruit in her anti-Soviet campaign within the system. She was soon joined by North Korea (which has since assumed a neutral position), and then by an ambivalent, but practical, North Vietnam. The Chinese were also ultimately able to entice the numerically powerful Indonesian Party (which has since been all but destroyed) to their side, but they succeeded in generating factionalism and splinter groups in other countries more often than they won over their parties. Some communist states and parties, in Europe and elsewhere, offered and tried to mediate, since most of the parties had a vested interest in preventing an open and formal break, though few were really interested in healing the split. As long as the two most powerful communist states were locked in controversy, it allowed the widest latitude of autonomy for the others. The advantages for the non-ruling parties, however, were not as clear.

As early as December, 1961, the Italian communist leader, Luigi Longo, openly admitted the pattern of polarization which was assuming shape in the communist world:

> The quarrel between the Soviet and the Chinese Communist Parties refers to a much more important question than that of peaceful coexistence, possibilities of avoiding atomic war or the dispute over the cult of Stalin's personality. The real issue is a difference between their views on the true way to socialism and communism. The Chinese believe that the development of communism in the various countries of the socialist bloc should be indivisible. The countries that are more advanced economically should therefore take more interest in the troubles and sufferings of the more backward socialist countries and place all their material resources at their disposal. Those who hold this view cannot accept the competition between the Soviet Union and the United States and the capitalist countries. Nor can they accept peaceful coexistence or Soviet aid to underdeveloped countries. This help should be given to the economically backward countries in the socialist camp. The Chinese comrades do not hide their misgivings but we Italian communists believe that the Soviet policy of competition with the United States is more useful for the development of world communism than a concern for the equal economic development of all the countries in the socialist camp. The effect of Soviet policy is to accelerate the development of conflicts within the capitalist camp and to draw the colonial peoples in the socialist camp.[38]

The Cuban missile crisis, resulting at least in part from a Soviet attempt to demonstrate its ability to protect all socialist countries, accelerated the fragmentation and polarization and brought into question the credibility of what Moscow was seeking to demonstrate. Accusing Khrushchev of engaging in both "adventurism" and "capitulationism," and of risking thermonuclear war without prior consultation of other communist states (by dispatching missiles and then withdrawing them over Cuban objections), the Chinese sought to cast doubt on Moscow's willingness to defend other communist states against American imperialism. The Chinese gesture backfired, as the European parties rallied to the support of the Soviet Union, although Castro was obviously

[38] L'Unita, December 23, 1961.

humiliated and peeved by the quick Soviet retreat. Moscow sought to salve his wounds by dispatching Mikoyan on a fence-mending mission and by promising additional economic assistance. Peking's charge of a Caribbean "Munich" struck most of the other parties as unnecessarily inflexible and a verification of China's belligerence.

The episode served to isolate China even more. Moscow organized its counterstroke against the Chinese, as Peking was subjected to an unprecedented crossfire of invective and abuse at a series of European Party Congresses, held from November, 1962, to January, 1963 (Bulgarian, Hungarian, Italian, Czechoslovak, and East German). Moscow concentrated its fire on Albania, while the European parties converged upon the Chinese directly. Some parties, including the Cuban, attempted to preserve a posture of neutrality, but as the conflict escalated, polarization accelerated. Peking struck back in a series of unusually long, documented, and systematically organized attacks on Western parties, still adhering to the phrase "certain comrades" when referring to the Soviet leaders, but naming Italian and French leaders in their indictments. The conflict flared into the open in March, 1963, when Khrushchev's position seemed precarious at home. But the Test Ban Treaty was soon signed, and the first phase of the long sought-after *détente* with the United States was a reality.

Compromised Leader: The Soviet-American Détente and World Communism

The Soviet Union's relations with both the United States and Yugoslavia improved rapidly, and Moscow's image of American intentions underwent a radical change. From the Chinese point of view, something resembling a *reversement des alliances* had taken place, and they saw the Soviet Union and the United States as conspiring to deny China nuclear weapons and plotting to jointly dominate the world.

> The leaders of the C.P.S.U. have completely reversed enemies and comrades. . . . The leaders of the C.P.S.U. are bent on seeking Soviet–United States cooperation for the domination of the world. They regard United States imperialism, the most ferocious enemy of the people in the world as their most reliable friend and they treat the fraternal parties and countries adhering to Marxism-Leninism as their enemy. They collude with United States imperialism, the reactionaries of various countries, the renegade Tito clique and the right-wing Social Democrats in a partnership against the socialist fraternal countries. When they snatch at a straw from Eisenhower or Kennedy or others like them, or think that things are going smoothly for them, the leaders of the C.P.S.U. are beside themselves with joy, hit out wildly at the fraternal parties and countries adhering to Marxism-Leninism, and endeavor to sacrifice fraternal parties and countries on the altar of their political dealings with United States imperialism.[39]

The Chinese, having failed in their bid for primacy, and Moscow, having failed equally to bring the Chinese to heel, are now both looking

[39] The *New York Times,* February 7, 1964.

for an appropriate occasion to fasten responsibility for an organizational split upon the other. Recognizing that few Eastern European or Western communist parties can identify their interests with those of the Chinese, Peking has virtually abandoned Eastern Europe states and Western parties as possible instruments with which to organize a new revolutionary movement which would embrace both communists and non-communist revolutionaries. Since Moscow has succeeded in virtually isolating Peking from the European communist states, the Chinese have retaliated by trying to freeze the Soviet Union out of Asia, Africa, and Latin America. Resorting to bonds of race and under-development, Peking appears to be seeking to mobilize the nonwhite under-developed world against the white developed world, whether communist or non-communist. Chinese representatives vigorously propagate the view that racial bonds are stronger than class bonds in Soviet calculations, and that Moscow will inevitably associate itself with whites against non-whites. According to a Soviet indictment, the Chinese reason that, since nonwhites outnumber whites, the most effective road to Chinese hegemony is to organize them under Chinese direction, in preparation for the day when they will displace the white race as the dominant element on the globe. This, according to Moscow, is the real meaning of the Chinese slogan, The East Wind prevails over the West Wind:

> The Chinese leaders represent matters as though the interests of the peoples of Asia, Africa, and Latin America were especially close and understandable to them, as though they were concerned most of all for the further development of the national liberation struggle in order to turn them into a tool for the realization of the hegemonic plans. . . . The Chinese . . . suggested to the representatives of the African and Asian Countries that inasmuch as the Russians, Czechs, and Poles are white, "you can't rely on them," that they will allegedly "always be in collusion with the Americans — with whites," that the peoples of Asia and Africa have their special interests. . . . The Chinese leaders are trying to fan these feelings, in the hopes of setting the peoples of the former colonies against the socialist countries, against the working people of the developed capitalist countries. . . . China, they reason, is the largest country of the East and embodies its interests; here are born the "winds of history" that are to prevail over the "winds of the West." Thus this slogan is nothing but an ideological and political expression of the hegemonic aspirations of the Chinese leadership.[40]

The Chinese strategy now seems as follows: (1) to undermine the traditional Soviet claims to a special position in the communist world, by charging its leaders with "modern revisionism" and "the restoration of capitalism"; (2) to undermine the credibility of Soviet promises to defend and look after the military security of its smaller allies; (3) to isolate the Soviet Union from the under-developed countries and from the revolutionary movement in Latin America, Africa, and Asia. They are, in effect, energetically preparing the groundwork for a separate and rival revolutionary movement, in these continents.

[40] *Pravda,* April 3, 1964.

One of the consequences of the Sino-Soviet split is that it leaves the Soviet Union as a badly wounded leader of a rump, essentially Western communist movement. And within this orbit, it is now defied even by its formerly most servile minions, the leaders of the Rumanian Communist Party, who, in an unexpected and unusual gesture of defiance, refused to accept the agricultural role assigned to Rumania under the new Comecon plan for the international socialist division of labor. Rumania has not only offered itself as a mediator in the Sino-Soviet dispute, but also deals with both Peking and Moscow, while it seeks expanded and more profitable commercial relations with the West. This is likely to be the pattern pursued by other communist states remaining in the Soviet sphere, as they exercise their right to adopt and pursue policies tailored to their national interests, just as does the Soviet Union.

The sudden and unexpected ouster of Khrushchev from his posts of authority in October, 1964, diminished Soviet prestige further. The humiliating manner of Khrushchev's removal conveyed the impression that Chinese pressure and demands on the Soviet Union had somehow prevailed again. And the sense of outrage expressed by Eastern European leaders and by Western parties, most of whom had associated their interests with Khrushchev's policies, indicated that they were using the removal of their champion as an occasion to assert their increasing independence and autonomy. Some parties, like the Polish, Hungarian, Yugoslav, Italian, and French, were critical of Khrushchev mainly because he did not pursue the ultimate logic of de-Stalinization with sufficient vigor. Disturbed in particular by the nature of Khrushchev's ouster, they demanded and received an explanation. Togliatti's testament, issued in September, 1964, explicitly called for a greater public disclosure of factional and policy differences among Soviet leaders:

> It is not correct to refer to the socialist countries (including the Soviet Union) as if everything were always going well in them. . . . Some situations appear hard to understand. In many cases one has the impression there are differences of opinion among the leading groups, but one does not understand if this is really so and what the differences are. Perhaps it could be useful in some cases for the socialist countries also to conduct open debates on current problems, the leaders also taking part. Certainly, this would contribute to a growth in the authority and prestige of the socialist regime itself.[41]

This represented a further development in the reverse flow of demands from the periphery to the center in the communist world. Up to now, only Moscow exercised the right to interfere and intervene in the factional squabbles in other communist states, while changes in Moscow were immune from outside scrutiny and intervention. The chorus of demands and criticisms which descended on Khrushchev's detractors and successors resulted, first, in arresting any further design to downgrade and degrade Khrushchev and, second, in accepting the demands for a detailed explanation of the sudden change in Soviet leadership. Further, the concern expressed by Eastern European and Western party

[41] Quoted in the *New York Times*, September 5, 1964.

leaders is a reflection of their determination to complete the transition from pawns to actors in the world communist system and movement. Either they participate in decisions pertaining to communism as a whole, and their interests are taken into account in arriving at these decisions, or they will assert their right to chart their own course.

Although the escalation of the Vietnamese war in 1965, and the systematic bombing of North Vietnam by the United States, has caused a deterioration of Soviet-American relations and has arrested the *détente*, it has poisoned Sino-Soviet relations even more. In March, 1966, just prior to the opening of the Twenty-third Communist Party Congress, which the Chinese refused to attend, Moscow and Peking once again exchanged denunciations. These summarized their complaints against one another, revealed new information about their past relations, and disclosed additional sources of continuing conflict and rivalry. In a secret letter circulated to communist parties, Moscow leveled a series of charges against the Chinese leaders which seemed almost deliberately designed to provoke the Chinese into absenting themselves from the Congress. In this letter, the Soviet leaders made the following charges: (1) China has interfered with Soviet attempts to send material and military assistance to North Vietnam; (2) Chinese leaders have rebuffed all Soviet overtures for a meeting in order to settle their differences; (3) the Chinese have organized anti-Soviet demonstrations and have tried to incite the Soviet population against its leadership; (4) "the C.P.R. [Chinese People's Republic] leadership propagates ever more obstinately the thesis of potential military clashes between China and the Soviet Union"; (5) the Chinese have been "provoking border conflicts . . . [which] have increased again in recent months . . . [and] allegations are being spread to the effect that the Soviet Union unlawfully holds Chinese territory in the Far East"; (6) and, finally:

> There is every reason to assert that it is one of the goals of the policy of the Chinese leadership in the Vietnam question to cause a military conflict between the U.S.S.R. and the United States. They want a clash of the U.S.S.R. with the United States so that they may, as they say themselves, "sit on the mountain and watch the fight of the tigers."[42]

In conclusion, the Soviet letter reiterated the charge that Peking was manipulating the international communist movement and the national liberation movement for its own hegemonic purposes.

The Chinese leaders retorted, in a public statement, that the circulation of "an anti-Chinese letter to other parties, instigating them to join you in opposing China," was eloquent proof of insincerity in inviting the Chinese to attend the Twenty-third Congress of the C.P.S.U. Peking accused Moscow of spreading false rumors that China was obstructing Soviet assistance to Vietnam, and "encroaching on Soviet territory." The Soviet leaders were charged with stating that China was no longer to be viewed as a socialist country and of viewing the Chinese Communist

---

[42] Quoted in the *New York Times*, March 24, 1966.

Party as an "enemy." The Chinese statement made a brief but spirited defense of Stalin, and accused Khrushchev's successors of intensifying his "revisionism" and "splittism," but the main burden of its attack was that Moscow, far from wanting to aid North Vietnam, was encouraging the North Vietnamese to negotiate with the United States in order to clear the way for the Soviet Union and the United States to accelerate their joint conspiracy against China:

> Despite the tricks you have been playing to deceive people, you are pursuing United States–Soviet collaboration for the domination of the world with your whole heart. . . . You have all along been acting in coordination with the United States in its plot for peace talks, vainly attempting to sell out the struggle of the Vietnamese people against United States aggression and . . . to drag the Vietnam question into the orbit of Soviet–United States collaboration. You have worked hand in glove with the United States in a whole series of dirty deals inside and outside the United Nations. In close coordination with the counter-revolutionary "global strategy" of United States imperialism, you are now trying to build a ring of encirclement around socialist China. . . . You have even aligned yourselves with United States imperialism . . . and established a holy alliance against China, against the movement and against the Marxist-Leninists.[43]

Thus, beginning in late 1958 and continuing into the Sixties, was the gradual emergence of Peking and Moscow as the two poles of ideology and power in the communist camp. A new Soviet policy was to seek to solidify Soviet control and influence over the Eastern European communist states, as a separate and distinct process from maintaining the unity of the communist world as a whole. This has led to the existence of a European communist bloc, led by the Soviet Union. Only Albania, whose special fear is Yugoslavia — the main focus of attack by Peking — remains outside the Soviet bloc, playing a strange game of pitting Peking against Moscow. China has not yet organized a comparable regional communist bloc, but indications are that Peking would like to organize such a regional grouping, made up of the four Asian communist states — China, North Korea, Mongolia, and North Vietnam, but her geographical position vis-à-vis the smaller Asian countries, is not as decisive as the Soviet position with respect to Eastern Europe since three of the four Asian communist countries border on the U.S.S.R. itself. Mongolia, which fears Chinese power, has solidly associated itself with Moscow, while North Korea has issued a plague on both houses, and North Vietnam straddles the fence, using the Soviet Union as a counter-poise against Chinese domination, and relying upon Chinese threats to deter the U.S. from carrying the war to the north.

The Soviet Union and China appear to be significantly divided on questions of ideology and policy sufficient to prevent the development of a common outlook and the forging of a common policy toward the noncommunist world. These divisions reflect a basic conflict of national interests between a maturing social and industrial order — the Soviet

[43] Ibid.

Union and the European satellites — which has a greater stake in avoiding nuclear war, and a pre-industrial revolutionary society which feels that its political and economic goals can be achieved only by destroying the vestiges of the old social and economic order.

Irrespective of the detailed nature, causes, and motivations of Sino-Soviet controversies — and these range from traditional, historical, and territorial questions to fundamental differences between the basically European character and culture of Moscow and the orientalism of China and transcend ideological matters — the significant point is that the world communist movement has been divested of its single directing center and threatens to fragment into several centers. Regardless of what institutional forms of cooperation are adopted, the Kremlin has abdicated its monopoly on making decisions for the entire communist world and to some extent must coordinate its foreign policy with that of its allies, rather than the other way around.

21. RUSSIA AND CHINA VIEW THE UNITED STATES

Alexander Dallin

In a lengthy statement, ostensibly addressed to their Italian comrades, the Chinese Communists in March 1963 acknowledged:

> . . . It is obvious that differences of principle exist in the international Communist movement today as to how to appraise and how to deal with U.S. imperialism, the arch-enemy of the peoples of the world.[1]

Even a cursory perusal of recent statements does indeed reveal significant differences between the Soviet and Chinese images of the United States, its goals, and its capabilities and between their prescriptions for coping with it.

Making some allowance for Peking's proclivity to give an "unfair" account of the Soviet position, one finds confirmation for the divergence in remarks such as these:

> Those [in Moscow] who slanderously attack the Chinese Communist Party allege that our unremitting exposure of imperialism and especially of the policies of aggression and war of U.S. imperialism, show our disbelief in the possibility of averting a world war; actually what these people oppose is the exposure of imperialism. . . . They prettify U.S. imperialism in one hundred and one ways and spread among the masses

Reprinted from *The Annals of the American Academy of Political and Social Science*, September, 1963, pp. 154–162. Reprinted by permission of the author and publisher.
[1] "More on the Differences Between Comrade Togliatti and Us," *Hung-ch'i*, No. 3/4, 1963; English translation in *Peking Review*, No. 10/11, March 15, 1963.

of the people illusions about imperialism, and especially about U.S. imperialism.[2]

ANTECEDENTS

Some predisposing factors antedate the current Sino-Soviet rift. It has been correctly argued that the Communists' victory in itself constituted a major defeat for half a century of American policy in Asia: The reciprocal relation of American failures and Communist successes in China set the stage for what ensued. In an interview with Anna Louise Strong, held in August 1946 and repeatedly quoted by the current leadership since 1960, Mao Tse-tung made a number of comments which remain valid in his eyes. On the one hand, he argued, the United States is out to maximize its conquests. On the other hand, it does not threaten the Socialist camp directly, if only because it must first dispose of the rest of the non-Communist world, which was labeled a vast "intermediate zone."[3]

Mao was thus able to tell the Soviet Union that a more vigorous stand would not invite war with the United States — a point Peking has not failed to reiterate.[4]

Victory did not significantly alter the Communists' attitude toward the United States. On the contrary, it instilled in the Peking leadership a sense of pride in its isolation, reinforced by American and United Nations nonrecognition of the mainland regime, and it found therein further cause for suspicion of the outside world. The Korean war was fought, by the Chinese, as a "resist America" campaign.

At least three major sources of Sino-American enmity are commonly recognized to have been apparent in China prior to the fundamental shift in policy in 1957–1958: the quest for national "unification," especially the claim to Taiwan and the offshore islands; a drive for prestige and recognition as a great power; a commitment to further the cause of communism at home and abroad. Traditional and "ideological" facets thus combined, on the Chinese side, to prepare the ground for the growth of intense anti-Americanism.

On the Soviet side, at least the first two of these three compulsions

---

[2] "The Differences Between Comrade Togliatti and Us," *Jen-min jih-pao* (Peking), December 31, 1962; English translation in *Peking Review*, No. 1, January 4, 1963.

[3] Mao Tse-tung, *Selected Works* (in English) (Peking, 1961), Vol. 4, pp. 99–100. This concept helps "explain" the alleged American tendency toward aggrandizement, which includes an encirclement of China (from Japan, South Korea, Taiwan, South Vietnam, Thailand), but puts the showdown into the indefinite future. True, "as everybody knows, what the U.S. ruling clique calls the 'national purpose' is to achieve world domination." Yet (in harmony with the Chinese view of local wars) Peking insists that "seizure of the 'intermediate zone' plays an increasingly important role in U.S. global strategy." *Jen-min jih-pao*, January 21, 1963.

[4] *Selections from China Mainland Magazines* (Hong Kong), No. 233, October 31, 1960, cited in Donald S. Zagoria, *The Sino-Soviet Conflict, 1956–1961* (Princeton, 1962), p. 404.

were lacking. If anything, the ubiquitous hostility toward imperialism had on several occasions been moderated by the fact that Russia and America appeared to share, if not interests, then enemies, in Europe and in the Far East. As one of the Big Three in 1941–1946, the Soviet Union gained that aura and legitimation which the Chinese Communists lacked. Yet, in the following years, Moscow, much as the Chinese comrades, properly identified Washington as its first and most dangerous foe. There was nothing "inevitable" about the parting of their ways.

In the post-Stalin decade, the picture became significantly more blurred. First, the inherent tensions in the traditional Bolshevik love-hate for the "citadel of capitalism" became more apparent as the search for new answers and new policies began after Stalin's death. Second, Moscow soon began to modify some of its stereotypes — either explicitly (for instance, on violence) or by omission (for instance, on the prospects of economic crises) — securing, on the whole, a more realistic assessment of the world environment. And, third, the changes, in the Soviet Union and in the Communist movement at large, created and then sanctioned a measure of diversity in Communist attitudes unprecedented in the past generation.

Conflict or Coexistence?

After a variety of crises, the search for new solutions was still on when events in the fall of 1957 spurred a profound reassessment by both Moscow and Peking. Having consolidated his own position, Khrushchev viewed the latest accomplishments — notably, the intercontinental ballistic missiles and space satellites — as indicators of Russia's new might and as a wise investment that would automatically pay rich dividends. To the Chinese leaders, by contrast, these developments seemed to produce new opportunities for action. While Moscow agreed that it had at last achieved near-parity in effective nuclear and deterrent power and thus undermined the United States "position of strength," the wind of rosy optimism which swept the Soviet capital led to the assertion that "a new stage of coexistence" had begun. The Chinese Communist line, on the contrary, saw "the east wind prevailing over the west wind" in a perspective of greater revolutionary potentials and enthusiasm. Essentially, Peking pressed for a "forward" policy, while Moscow sought a *détente;* one prepared to rely on men and will, the other on history and power-in-being; one responded to "left" and the other to "right" impulses and formulas in the Communist world.

There was some truth in the Chinese charges of Soviet inconsistency. Moscow no longer had simple or single answers. In Soviet analysis, too, the United States was *the* major antagonist. Yet it was also (as Moscow put it at times) the major partner — the other superpower, the other major industrial state, the only one behind which the Soviet Union lagged. Unlike the Chinese, Moscow sensed some identification — precisely thanks to the rivalry the two were engaged in. At times, Soviet leaders no doubt recognized the fact that the two superpowers — unlike the Chinese — were both "modern" — and perhaps also "Western" and "white." In 1959–1960 and intermittently since then, Soviet media have developed the notion that the United States was not ruled by "madmen" and "maniacs" but that there were powerful "men of reason" in Washington.

Now the Chinese asked of Moscow what it believed or planned: "With regard to the U.S. imperialists, one day you will call them pirates and the next you say they are concerned for peace. . . ." After agreeing to the so-called Moscow Statement, which in December 1960 recognized that "U.S. imperialism is the chief bulwark of world reaction and . . . an enemy of the people of the whole world," the Soviet leaders, Peking charged, maintained "that the destiny of mankind depended on 'cooperation,' 'confidence' and 'agreement' between the heads of the two powers, the United States and the Soviet Union."[5]

The difference was more profound, perhaps, than either protagonist knew. As one American expert wrote, "much of recent Soviet foreign policy toward the United States appears to be based on the calculation that forces at work within American society are bent on achieving a *modus vivendi* with the USSR and are willing to pay a relatively high price for it."[6] Especially during and after the Khrushchev visit to the United States, in 1959–1960, Soviet statements abounded in references to the "peaceful" American people, with whom the Soviet people wish to live in "friendship." Even later, in April 1962, Khrushchev told an American editor that, except for the difference in the two systems:

> We really have no cause for serious quarrels. Nowhere do our interests directly clash, either on territorial or on economic questions. The Soviet Union and the United States are both countries that are excellently provided with natural resources and possess large populations and well-developed industry and science. . . .[7]

To Peking, such views were bound to sound like treason. The "modern revisionists" in Moscow were, in Chinese eyes, guilty of many things, of which their view of the United States was but one. Here was only one, but one important instance of broad differences in world view — differences which also encompassed the East-West dilemma, the inevitability of war, alternative ways of economic development, and the nature of the colonial world.

DOCTRINE AND REAPPRAISAL

The Chinese position, since 1958, combines some elements of the earlier Maoist argument with echoes of the rigid Stalinist view. A unique aspect of the Soviet scene, under Khrushchev, by contrast, is a timid

[5] "More on the Differences."
[6] Zbigniew Brzezinski, *Ideology and Power in Soviet Politics* (New York, 1962), p. 105.
[7] Khrushchev interview with Gardner Cowles, *Pravda*, April 27, 1962.

diversity and at times uncertainty of comments emanating from within the Soviet Union. One may find in Soviet speeches and publications reiteration of certain concepts which are held by Peking; more significantly, one also finds instances in which the present Soviet leadership repudiates or ignores these views. By the logic of the two positions, the Chinese argument is more systematic, more consistent, and more extreme; the Soviet argument, torn between doctrinal assumptions and realistic reappraisals.

The common point of departure is the assessment of "imperialism." Peking adheres to the orthodox view that "imperialism is by nature predatory. . . . When its policy of plunder meets with obstacles which cannot be surmounted by 'peaceful' means, it resorts to war."[8] While Moscow does not dispute this proposition "in principle," Peking in turn does not use it to dispute explicitly the Khrushchevian tenet that wars are no longer to be considered "inevitable" even while "imperialism" survives. But Peking did insist that the warlike nature of imperialism was immutable, hinting, in 1962–1963, that "some persons" had dangerous illusions about it.

Despite the verbal concessions to the Chinese in the "compromise" Moscow Statement of December 1960, Moscow rarely went so far as to argue — as Peking did — that American imperialism is "the most vicious enemy of peace . . . the most ferocious and most cunning enemy of the peace-loving peoples of the world." In Chinese eyes, the Russians were guilty of not exposing and assailing the United States and, instead, of talking seriously — "strategically," and not merely "tactically" — of hazardous matters like disarmament. "These [Soviet] friends, when discussing disarmament, talk very little or not at all of the facts of U.S. expansion of armaments and preparation for war. . . ."[9] At the center of the debate was, then, the Chinese contention that nothing had led, indeed nothing could lead, to a change in the essence of American objectives — or of imperialism in general — and the Soviet reply that a qualitative change had occurred in the international situation, for a variety of reasons, such as the greater might of the "socialist camp" and the destructiveness of thermonuclear weapons. To any reasonable person this made global wars "unthinkable."[10]

[8] Yu Chao-li, "On Imperialism as the Source of War in Modern Times," *Hung-ch'i*, No. 7, April 1, 1960.

[9] Liao Cheng-shih, speech at World Peace Council meeting in Stockholm, December 16, 1961. The theme is further developed in "The Differences Between Comrade Togliatti and Us."

[10] When Khrushchev visited the United States, in September 1959, Peking commented that "in view of the U.S. cold war record and its aggressions of all kinds in the past," its intentions should be judged "not by its words but by its deeds." *Jen-min jih-pao*, September 29, 1959. The following spring, Peking devoted lengthy articles to the question, "Is There Any Change in U.S. Foreign Policy?" — only to conclude that, while there was "a certain change of methods," the "substance" of American objectives remained the same. The argument pointed to American efforts to break out of its "isolation" and to "gain time, restore military predominance, and tighten up control over its 'allies.'" Tsui Ch'i and T'an Wen-jui, "Comment on the Present Foreign Policy of the United States," *Shih-chieh Chih-shih*, No. 6, March 20, 1960.

Time and again, Peking warned Moscow that the United States still wanted and expected war: the professions of the Eisenhower administration were not to be trusted; the Kennedy administration was bound to be as bad as its predecessor — in fact, worse.[11] As for Khrushchev's and his followers' illusions, Peking retorted with venom:

> It will be recalled that three years ago, following the "Camp David talks," some persons in the international Communist movement talked a good deal about Eisenhower's sincere desire for peace, saying that this ringleader of U.S. imperialism was just as concerned about peace as we were. . . . Now we again hear people saying that Kennedy is even more concerned about world peace than Eisenhower was and that Kennedy showed his concern for the maintenance of peace during the Caribbean crisis.
>
> One would like to ask: Is this way of embellishing U.S. imperialism the correct policy for defending world peace? The intrusion into the Soviet Union of spy planes sent by the Eisenhower administration, the hundred-and-one acts of aggression around the world by U.S. imperialism, and its threats to world peace — have these not repeatedly confirmed the truth that the ringleaders of U.S. imperialism are no angels of peace but monsters of war? And are not these people who try time and again to prettify imperialism deliberately deceiving the people of the world?[12]

How could Mao and his followers reconcile the image of a United States madly arming and preparing for war with their insistence that a tougher policy did not amount to "brinkmanship"? The answer was Mao's "paper tiger" formula. As the Chinese told their American comrades on December 10, 1959, "On the surface, this enemy [the United States] seems strong, but actually it is hollow and feeble. . . . The situation in the United States, in which the new forces are still inferior

[11] For an exposition of Chinese views of the Kennedy administration, see Mei Yi, "Kennedy and his Clique," *Shih-chieh Chih-shih*, No. 3, February 3, 1961, which described the Kennedy election as "a victory for the Rockefeller financial group in the struggle among the various financial groups for the control of the [U.S.] government" and Lyndon Johnson's place on the ticket as a victory of certain financial, oil, and arms interests. In fact, it made every member of the cabinet and White House inner circle a puppet of some monopoly interests. See also Huang Kang, "A Few Things About Kennedy," *Hung-ch'i*, No. 13, July 1, 1961; Chen Yü, "Kennedy's 'Brain Trust,'" *Shih-chieh Chih-shih*, No. 14, July 25, 1961, which finds: "The fact that Kennedy employs these so-called college professors, experts, and scholars shows that his tactics are more sinister and vicious" than those of his predecessor.

[12] "The Differences Between Comrade Togliatti and Us." See also Zagoria, *The Sino-Soviet Conflict*, pp. 240 ff, and *Jen-min jih-pao*, June 13, 1960. On the Kennedy administration, see also *Jen-min jih-pao*, December 1, 1961; English translation in *Peking Review*, No. 49 (December 8, 1961), which concluded that the United States had "sustained a series of disastrous defeats," and, because of the uneven development of capitalism and the struggle among the imperialist countries, the entire imperialist world was "slithering further down the slope of disintegration." The Kennedy administration was accused of "preparing for both all-out nuclear war and limited wars of various types." See also Alexander Dallin and others (eds.), *Diversity in International Communism* (New York, 1963), pp. 213–214, 222–226, 234–236.

and the decaying forces have the upper hand, is definitely a temporary phenomenon, which must change to the opposite."

Here was a morale-building lesson which the Chinese Communists had brought with them to power from civil-war days. As Mao reiterated in November 1957, "Over a long period we formulated the concept that strategically we should despise all our enemies, but that tactically we should take them seriously." This applied to the United States, to imperialism in general, and to the atom bomb.

When Peking sought to invoke this thesis during the Cuban crisis of October 1962 — presumably to demonstrate that Moscow was guilty of unnecessary cowardice, having retreated in the face of United States threats — Khrushchev felt compelled to take open issue with the "paper tiger" theme. Accusing unnamed would-be Marxist-Leninists of trying to provoke a thermo-nuclear clash between the Soviet Union and the United States, in which these *provocateurs* would "sit it out," he went on to argue that "imperialism is now no longer what it used to be. . . . If it is a 'paper tiger' now, those who say this know that this 'paper' tiger has atomic teeth."[13]

But the Chinese Communists indignantly reaffirmed their formula, insisting that it was "of great importance for the question of whether the revolutionary people will dare to wage a struggle, dare to make a revolution, dare to seize victory"; it was important also to "destroy the arrogance of the enemy" and to instill "revolutionary determination and confidence, revolutionary vision and staunchness" in the masses.[14] The two capitals were speaking different tongues.

In the same speech defending his Cuban policy, Khrushchev had referred to the "reasonable" men in Washington. Here was another area of Sino-Soviet disagreement. While Soviet publications and, at times, leading figures continue to resort to the primitive stereotypes of monopoly rule, politicians as tools of economic interests, and crude exploitation, the total image of the United States as conveyed by a Khrushchev or Adzhubei reflects some sense of meaningful diversity in American life, in which individual actors, such as the President, are their own masters; in which depressions no longer figure as inevitable phenomena; in which, Moscow argues, even disarmament could be absorbed by the existing system without serious dislocations; and in which a tug-of-war is being fought between "lunatics" and "wild men," who are prepared to "go down with music," to start a thermonuclear war, and the "men of reason," who put survival ahead of the achievement of American objectives.

The Soviet image, as it has evolved, suffers from considerable ambiguities and contradictions.[15] But the gap between it and the Chinese picture of America is so striking that Peking inquired whether

[13] Nikita Khrushchev, report to the Supreme Soviet of the Soviet Union, December 12, 1962, in *Pravda*, December 13, 1962.
[14] "The Differences Between Comrade Togliatti and Us."
[15] For an astute attempt to analyze the Soviet view, see Nathan Leites, "The Kremlin Horizon," RAND Memorandum RM-3506-ISA, March 1963.

Moscow still believed in the Leninist theory of the state, which posits that the entire state apparatus is "the tool of monopoly capital for class rule."

> And if so, how can there be a president independent of monopoly capital; how can there be a Pentagon independent of the White House; and how can there be two opposing centers [one, moderate; the other, "ultra"] in Washington?

Those who portray President Kennedy as "sensible," Peking added, are presumably "serving as willing apologists for U.S. imperialism and helping it to deceive the people of the world."[16]

IMPLICATIONS

References, since 1962, to the "willing" or "deliberate" assistance which Khrushchev was lending the imperialists hinted at a new and perhaps fundamental element in the Sino-Soviet debate. Paradoxically, the Chinese argument that American-Soviet contradictions are *not* paramount[17] in the present stage of world affairs makes more credible to its proponents the idea that the United States and the Soviet Union may be working toward an accommodation detrimental to the cause of communism and, more particularly, to the cause of China. The old suspicion of the "outsider" was rekindled when, in mid-1958, precisely when Peking was executing its shift toward a "leftist" policy, Khrushchev proposed to solve the Middle Eastern crisis by a summit meeting which would have included Nehru and Hammarskjold but not Mao Tse-tung.[18]

The Chinese Communists readily applied their sweeping skepticism about negotiations with the leading imperialists to the specific context of impromptu summitry. Peking would henceforth remind unnamed comrades that the problems dividing the two worlds were so basic that it was both naive and treasonous to believe in the ability of a handful of men to overcome or resolve them.

Chinese suspicions of Moscow's outlook are likely to have been reinforced by Soviet pronouncements regarding the decisive nature of Soviet-American agreements. Gromyko, speaking in December 1962, was but one of several to point out, after the Cuban crisis:

> . . . how closely associated the destinies of the world are today with Soviet-American relations. It is an historically established fact that without understanding between the USSR and the USA not a single serious international conflict can be settled, no agreement can be reached on any important international problem. . . . If the USSR and

---

16 "More on the Differences."

17 While Moscow has insisted that "the chief contradiction of our epoch is the contradiction between socialism and capitalism" (Boris Ponomarev, "With the Name of Lenin . . . ," *Pravda*, April 23, 1963), Peking has "pointed out that the real and direct contradictions of the world [after the Second World War] were the growing internal contradictions of the capitalist world itself" (Yu Chao-li, *op. cit.*). See also Mao's *Imperialism and All Reactionary Cliques Are Paper Tigers* (Peking, 1958).

18 See Zagoria, *The Sino-Soviet Conflict*, pp. 199–206.

the USA pool their efforts to iron out the conflicts and complications which arise in these regions, the emerging flames of war die down and the tension subsides.[19]

Peking's answer was plain: The view that "every matter under the sun can be settled if the two 'great men' sit together" smacked of "great-power chauvinism" and of "power politics," and was alien to Marxism-Leninism.[20] Evidently with the Cuban crisis in mind, a prominent spokesman for the Chinese regime told an Afro-Asian conference in Moshi, Tanganyika:

> The attempt to decide major problems of the world and to manipulate the destinies of mankind by one or two countries will certainly end in utter failure and be condemned by history. The countries of Asia and Africa as well as all peoples are firmly opposed to the big powers bullying, oppressing, and giving orders to small countries.[21]

For years China has maintained that it would not let the Soviet Union negotiate binding agreements for it — for instance, on nuclear testing. The very real fear of a closed Soviet-American "nuclear club," from which Communist China was barred, added fuel to the suspicions which alienated Peking from Moscow. Thus, the "hot line" agreement in the spring of 1963 was apt to be viewed by the Chinese as further evidence of Soviet subservience to the West and by Moscow as incidentally strengthening the Soviet hand by demonstrating to Peking that Moscow had options regarding its foreign policy, while presumably Peking had none.[22]

Out of these fears and suspicions, then, there also emerged an ideological element: the identification by Peking of the Soviet line as an exemplar of "modern revisionism," which "objectively" helps the imperialist camp. With good Bolshevik logic, it found the chain linking Khrushchev with Tito and Tito in turn with Washington. The communiqué released following the tenth plenum of the Central Committee of the Chinese Communist party (September 28, 1962) did indeed speak of modern revisionists who "betray the cause of communism ever more shamelessly and give aid and comfort to the plans of imperialism." *Pravda* omitted this passage from its version of the communiqué.

"UNITY OF THEORY AND PRACTICE"

Richard Lowenthal has suggested that the potential rivalry of the two powers could become actual only when concrete policy disagreements arose which took the debates out of the realm of abstractions. As it happens, it has been precisely around relations with the United States

[19] Andrei Gromyko, speech before the Supreme Soviet of the Soviet Union, *Pravda*, December 14, 1962.
[20] "More on the Differences."
[21] Liu Ning-yi, "Unite to Fight Against Imperialism," February 4, 1963; English translation in *Peking Review*, No. 7, February 15, 1963.
[22] Peking interpreted Kennedy's American University speech precisely in this fashion, as part of "a most cunning and vicious move in his 'peace strategy.'" *Jen-min jih-pao*, June 22, 1963.

that the divergences have crystallized since 1958. On a succession of issues, from Taiwan, over Soviet-American summitry, to the Congo and Cuba, the problem has been how the Communists must handle the United States. Each of the two positions here assumes a good deal of coherence and consistency. The Chinese aversion to serious negotiations with the enemy and to efforts to achieve a *détente* with the United States is entirely in keeping with the general world view and the view of modern war, in particular, as held in Peking. Similarly, the Soviet effort to avoid a showdown, the orientation toward a build-up of economic and military might over time, and a willingness to arrive — at least for the time being — at a *modus vivendi* with the West is in harmony with broader assumptions made in Moscow about the drift of world affairs.

Here the attitude toward war becomes significant again. True to itself, Peking argues that nuclear weapons — any more than other changes in military technology — cannot change basic and durable historical laws. It denies the Soviet thesis that, in the nuclear age, war is no longer the continuation of politics and reasserts the classic distinction between just and unjust wars. Moreover, Peking was prepared to argue, even after nuclear war life would go on, with communism inevitably victorious.[23]

Moscow's firm rejection of this and other instances of "dangerous ultra-revolutionary pyrotechnics" in turn implied a search "for sensible agreements with all who demonstrate that they take a realistic approach to the present alignment of forces and who understand what the consequences of a thermo-nuclear war would be."[24] Here the arguments had a direct bearing on actual conduct. Since 1958, if not earlier, Peking has variously sought to apply pressure on Moscow to help it secure its objectives abroad. But it must have realized, with a good deal of frustration, that it had no effective leverage to compel the Soviet Union to do what China wished — least of all, to commit Soviet armed forces to assist in the seizure of Taiwan.

Peking needed Soviet assistance to attain its goals. Yet, by seeking to compel Moscow to back Peking's political strategy, it contributed to the rift between them without thereby advancing its own ends. While Peking was no doubt outraged by Soviet "cowardice" — be it in Laos or in Cuba — it was futile for the Chinese to argue that a policy of greater risks was certain not to provoke war with the United States and that local wars need not escalate into general, nuclear conflicts. Moscow was sure it knew better.

CONSTANTS AND VARIABLES

There are few obvious limits to Sino-Soviet divergences regarding the United States. The only thing, perhaps, that could make the Sino-Soviet military alliance operative would be a United States attempt to replace the Communist regime in China with a pro-American govern-

---

[23] E.g., "The Differences Between Comrade Togliatti and Us."
[24] B. N. Ponomarev, "With the Name of Lenin."

ment: if the alternative to the present system is an extension of United States power along the perimeter of the Soviet Union, Moscow would be prepared to intervene in force.

Beyond this most unlikely contingency, the prospects are uncertain. The political fundamentalism in Peking is by no means immutable, and its eventual moderation could contribute to a *détente* in the Far East. But, it is important to note, even short of such a radical change, the Chinese leadership has not been "fanatical" or "irrational" in its policy. It has repeatedly recognized superior force when confronted with it, and, as in Korea, it has been prepared to "compromise" when necessary. More recently, it has sought to involve the Soviet Union in various operations but has carefully observed its own rules of conflict management to keep out of involvements in India, Laos, or Vietnam, which might provoke United States intervention in force.

One may point to three major components to describe the divergence of outlook discussed above. (1) China has certain national goals — such as the quest for territorial "unification" and for international acceptance — for which Russia has no equivalent needs. (2) China sees the world — and appeals — from the vantage point of an underdeveloped country. Thus it naturally strives to identify with other "have-nots"; its anti-imperialist animus logically turns its point against the United States. In many respects — the rational, but not the racial — this is a valid Leninist approach. Yet, the Soviet Union, which pursued a somewhat similar policy in earlier days, increasingly seems to have outgrown such an outlook, even though it professes to champion the cause of the new states. (3) Finally, the Sino-Soviet alignment today happens to coincide with the division of international communism into "left" and "right" movements, each advocating strategies scarcely susceptible of reconciliation with the other's. While none of these three elements need remain static, there appears to be little prospect for an early or substantial change of heart.

Either of the two great Communist powers can, but neither needs to, present a grave challenge to the United States. Either may, under different circumstances, become the more dangerous or the more difficult to cope with. Yet the future remains "open-ended": All permutations remain possible, and, at some future stage, any two of the three — Russia, China, United States — may find parallel interests in restraining or isolating the third on this or that cause.

Recent events have helped to dispose of a widespread American myth which invites political indolence, namely, the assumption that the Sino-Soviet dispute has no direct bearing on the United States because it is "a family quarrel."[25] Quite the contrary, the attitudes and policies of

[25] This article was written before the eruption of Sino-Soviet differences in July 1963. In its "open letter" of July 14, 1963, the Central Committee of the Communist party of the Soviet Union charged that the Chinese leaders "consider it to their advantage to preserve and intensify international tension, especially in the relations between the USSR and the USA." The Chinese People's Republic refused to adhere to the partial nuclear test ban treaty,

the two powers toward the United States are a central issue in their rift, and, within limits, the United States, by its own response and behavior, can perhaps affect the course or balance of the dispute, whose outcome must not be a matter of indifference to this country.

---

charging officially (in its Statement of July 31) that Soviet sponsorship of the treaty amounted to "capitulation to U.S. imperialism" and "allying with the United States to oppose China." The Soviet reply (*Pravda*, August 4, 1963) in turn accused Peking of lining up with the "madmen" in Washington, Bonn, and Paris in abetting thermonuclear war.

22. THE WARSAW PACT: ITS ROLE IN SOVIET BLOC AFFAIRS

United States Senate Committee on Government Operations

Summary

The Warsaw Pact was created in May 1955 by the USSR as a political response to West Germany's rearmament and admission to NATO.

The establishment of the pact was in part an outgrowth of the desire of Russia's post-Stalin leadership to replace the methods of Stalin, which were no longer practicable, with a new mechanism for maintaining its position as the supreme arbiter of Soviet bloc affairs. The Warsaw Pact provided a new basis for the presence of Soviet troops on the territory of some of the Eastern European countries.

The Russians probably thought — although they were later proven to be wrong — that the pact was also a form of insurance against effective political initiatives by the leaders of the East European Communist parties. The Political Consultative Committee of the Warsaw Pact was designed as a convenient sounding board for Soviet foreign policy views, particularly about West Germany and its admission on May 9, 1955, to NATO.

At the outset, the Eastern European members gained some limited military benefits from their membership in the Warsaw Pact, but they had no opportunity to function as other than the military and political

From *The Warsaw Pact, Its Role in Soviet Bloc Affairs*, A Study submitted . . . to The Committee On Government Operations, U.S. Senate, 89th Congress, 2nd Session (U.S. Government Printing Office, 1966).

vassals of Moscow. This is no longer the case, however, because of political evolution within the Soviet bloc and of changes in the relations of the Soviet bloc states to each other. The effect has been to give the Warsaw Pact a political role in Soviet bloc affairs at least as important as its function of bringing about military integration.

Today, it is no exaggeration to say that the Warsaw Pact is one of the few remaining effective devices available to Moscow for holding the Soviet bloc together at a time when the forces of national self-interest are increasingly coming into play in Eastern Europe. The Eastern European states, for their part, probably regard the pact as surety that the USSR will continue to underwrite their regimes and to safeguard their boundaries.

The USSR, in response to this view and to protect its own interests, has had to tolerate the gradual achievement of some measure of equality among pact members. Meaningful military coordination among the armies of the signatories has advanced, so that the Eastern European armed forces are a more useful adjunct to Soviet military power.

HISTORY OF THE ORGANIZATION

Why It Was Established

The Warsaw Treaty Organization (WTO), established formally on May 14, 1955, is composed of eight European Communist states — the USSR, Albania,[1] Bulgaria, Czechoslovakia, East Germany, Hungary, Poland and Rumania. In the past Communist China, North Korea, North Vietnam and Mongolia, all of which remain outside the formal structure of the treaty, have attended pact meetings as observers. Thus the WTO, which has both a military and a political character, is primarily a European organization. . . . Its specific purpose was to serve as a counter to NATO, and internally as the formal device for the perpetuation of close ties between the Soviet Union and the Eastern European regimes.

Developments in East-West Relations

The act of forming the Warsaw Pact climaxed a series of unsuccessful attempts by the USSR to prevent the inclusion of the Federal Republic of Germany in the Western alliance, NATO. At the Berlin Conference of Foreign Ministers in February 1954, Soviet Foreign Minister, V. M. Molotov renewed earlier Soviet suggestions for the neutralization of Germany and proposed an all-European treaty of collective security. By the terms of the Soviet proposal, cooperation

---

[1] Although still nominally a member of the Warsaw Pact, Albania apparently no longer takes part in pact activities. It rejected a pact invitation to send Albanian representatives to the last Political Consultative Committee meeting known to have been held, that of January 1965. Moreover, because of its diplomatic break with Moscow in 1961, it is unlikely that Albania has had any formal type of military relationship with the Soviet bloc for at least the last five years.

among treaty signatories would be confined to the military field, and agreements on mutual aid among participants would be determined by special procedures to be worked out later. Like the North Atlantic Treaty, the proposal specified that armed aggression against one treaty partner was to be considered an attack on all. Initially the United States and the Chinese People's Republic were to be accorded only observer status in the treaty organs, but the following month the USSR indicated its willingness to accept the U.S. in the all-European security pact and at the same time suggested its own entrance into NATO.

Although the Soviet proposals were unacceptable to the Western powers, the USSR renewed its efforts to undermine the European Defense Community and in July 1954 suggested the holding of an all-European collective security conference. The invitation was rejected by the Western powers. Some months later, in December 1954, the USSR convened a meeting in Moscow of its Eastern European allies. The Chinese People's Republic was invited to send an observer, and did so. After the Moscow gathering it was announced that the bloc would "take common measures for the organization of armed forces and their commands" in the event that the Western powers ratified the agreement signed in Paris on October 23, 1954, permitting the rearming of West Germany and its subsequent admission to NATO and the Western European Union.

When the Paris Agreements went into effect on May 5, 1955, the USSR carried out its threat and annulled its treaties of alliance with Great Britain (1942) and France (1944). The entry of the Federal Republic of Germany into NATO occurred on May 9, 1955. Two days later the "Conference of European Countries for the Protection of Peace and the Security of Europe" began in Warsaw. On May 14 the Treaty for Friendship, Mutual Assistance and Cooperation was signed, and the eight countries party to the treaty issued a "Resolution on the Formation of a Unified Command of Armed Forces."

The establishment of the Warsaw Treaty Organization thus coincided in time with the accession of the Federal Republic of Germany to membership in the Western alliance. Pact signatories explained its creation primarily as an answer to the expansion of NATO and the creation of the Western European Union. Conversely, observers in the West initially tended to view the provisions of the Warsaw Pact primarily as an effort to hasten the military integration of the Soviet Union and its Eastern European neighbors and to justify the maintenance of Soviet troops in those countries.

The Situation in the Soviet Bloc

The death of Stalin and the resultant political uncertainty that beset the Communist leaderships in Eastern Europe were also among the key factors which made a formal arrangement governing military and political matters within the Soviet bloc desirable in the eyes of the new Soviet leadership. Already there had been manifestations of popular discontent in Berlin and in Pilsen, Czechoslovakia, in addition to economic problems and the appearance of factional dissent within some local Communist parties.

The two years from Stalin's death in 1953 to the creation of the Warsaw Pact in 1955 were marked by the attempts of Georgi A. Malenkov, Molotov and Nikita S. Khrushchev to consolidate their individual power bases. Soviet political and economic problems demanded immediate answers, and these problems became the issues over which the internecine struggle was waged within the "collective leadership."

Malenkov, whose "new course" proposed to cure Soviet economic ills without disrupting the Stalinist political structure, tended to ignore the effect of such a program on the stability of the Eastern European regimes, then floundering under the legacy of Stalin's economic structures. Moreover, the Eastern Europeans at this point erroneously interpreted Malenkov's denigration of Stalinist economics as meaning that there would be a concomitant loosening of Stalinist political controls. Malenkov also overlooked the fact that a softer foreign policy line might undermine stable intra-bloc relations.

Molotov, the die-hard Stalinist, doggedly persisted in his espousal of the hard line in both the economic sector, where he was unwilling to abandon Stalin's emphasis on heavy industry, and the international arena, where he opposed rapprochement with Yugoslavia and a soft-pedaling of East-West antagonisms.

Khrushchev alone attempted a fusion of past with present on both the domestic and intra-party front, pursuing a course that sought improvement of the agricultural situation, revitalization of the economy and betterment of the standard of living without abandoning past Soviet commitments to the prior development of heavy industry.

Under Stalin's rule, the Eastern European party hierarchies had become accustomed to receiving instructions from their Soviet advisors, and they followed uncritically the line developed by Moscow. They reacted with considerable disorientation to the absence of clearly defined economic and political formulas. The Eastern European regimes were also uneasy because of popular pressures to take initiatives for economic and political reform on the home front. Popular resentment of terrorism, economic stagnation and party incompetence were becoming increasingly widespread in Eastern Europe.

In East Germany, the Party had already been shaken by the workers' riots and general strike of June 1953, which had been quelled only by Soviet troops. Although the Socialist Unity Party (SED) rejected general criticism of the Party line at its 15th Central Committee Plenum that July, it did admit that an accelerated effort "to construct the socialist foundation had erred in ignoring practical internal and external considerations." Economic concessions were made, including a reduction in wage taxes and prices, and a partial amnesty was granted for those convicted of minor offenses.

A similar state of affairs existed in Czechoslovakia, where citizens rioted in Pilsen in the summer of 1953 to protest a regime-inspired currency reform. Subsequent party appeasement gestures included a reduction in delivery quotas and a slowdown in the rate of industrial production, as well as a limited and short-lived "de-collectivization" program.

In Poland, widespread poverty, economic instability and a restive populace added to the problems facing the Polish United Workers Party (PZPR). The PZPR was hampered in attempting a relatively calm transition to reform programs by the presence of the imprisoned but not forgotten former Party boss, Wladyslaw Gomulka, whose rehabilitation many party members thought should logically follow regime espousal of economic change and limited liberalization. In fact, his release in April 1955, after incarceration since 1949 for "revisionist tendencies" and "Titoism," and a reorganization within the Ministry of Public Security preceded the Polish Communist leadership's endorsement of a less rigid domestic policy.

In Hungary, the cumulative effect of the violent purge trials, the executions of non-Communist leaders and an extremely intensive industrialization drive necessitated the elevation of the "liberal" Imre Nagy to the Premiership. A subsequent government call for a "consolidation of legality" attempted to head off popular reaction to economic and personal repression.

In Rumania, rejection of the SOVROM — joint stock companies that facilitated Soviet exploitation of the country's resources — as well as the 1952 ouster of pro-Moscow Rumanian party leaders like hardline Vice Premier Anna Pauker, were further indications that a lack of firm leadership on the part of the USSR was leading to a corresponding lack of political cohesion in the bloc.

In an effort to buttress the individual regimes and to reverse the trend toward bloc disunity, Khrushchev began to emphasize the position of the Eastern European countries as equal partners with the Soviet Union. He hoped thereby to set the stage to bind them in a political and military alliance that would create a commonwealth of socialist states and ensure continued Soviet hegemony in Eastern Europe.

Instrument of Soviet Control over Eastern Europe

As an instrument of Soviet control, the Warsaw Pact had value as a device for monitoring political and military developments in the member states. In the political field, it reminded the signatories of their common ideologies and purpose, underscored the importance of formal inter-state ties and created a mechanism providing a common political forum, over which the Soviet Union at first exercised complete control. In its military aspect, it would eventually lead to the solution of such problems as the status of Soviet troops in the bloc countries, and the consolidation of the Eastern European armies as an effective front line of defense for the Soviet Union.

Instrument of Political Propaganda

Soviet Marshal G. P. Zhukov, in an article entitled "The Warsaw Pact and Questions of International Security," published in Moscow in 1961, observed,

> The Warsaw Pact appeared and exists as a defense pact of govern-
> ments that are threatened by a common danger. This is confirmed, if
> only by the fact that the Warsaw treaty was born six years after the
> North Atlantic bloc in answer to their forming of a military threat.

This theme has been used frequently by the USSR to underscore the
allegedly defensive character of the bloc alliance, and to establish the
alleged intransigence of the Western powers. Related propaganda has
also directed considerable attention to the provision for dissolution of
the Warsaw Pact the minute that NATO ceases to exist.

According to Zhukov,

> the Paris Agreements formed a wide possibility for the rebirth of mili-
> tarism in West Germany. The coming into force of the Paris Agreements
> compelled them (the Warsaw Pact states) to take appropriate measures.

By harping on the presence of West Germany in the Western military
alliance, the USSR was able to capitalize on the all too recent memories
of World War II harbored by the Eastern European populations and was
able, with apparent logic, to suggest that the military organization of the
European Communist states was the only rational means of coping with
the alleged revival of West German revanchism. The inclusion of Bonn
in NATO was similarly helpful to local regimes in these states by providing them with a justification for their formal military and political
subservience to the Soviet Union; i.e., they were making a conscientious
effort to protect their citizenry from ravages by a newly militant
Germany, a subject around which some support for the party could be
rallied.

Thus, as a propaganda tool the pact served to illustrate "the defensive and peaceful character" of Soviet military relationships, to cast
the USSR in the role of protector of Eastern Europe and to gain some
popular backing for the local Communist parties.

Cooperative Military Alliance

Despite Soviet efforts to make the Warsaw Pact assume the character of a viable military alliance, the USSR until recently avoided
meaningful military integration of the member states. Prior to 1961,
military cooperation was limited largely to establishing and operating an
integrated Soviet-controlled bloc air defense, to providing the Eastern
Europeans with technical information necessary for the production of
Soviet-type weapons, and to a general standardization of weapons used
by the armed forces of the member states. Military leaders and delegations exchanged visits, and broad strategic tasks were given a general
definition, but there was neither real military integration nor frequent
and regular combined maneuvers of the various Communist forces.

Relationship to Series of Existing Bilateral
Agreements of Mutual Assistance

On May 15, 1955, one day after the signing of the Warsaw Treaty,
the Austrian State Treaty was signed in the Belvedere Palace in Vienna.
As a result, the original justification for the presence of Soviet troops in

Hungary and Rumania — protection of the USSR supply lines to Austria — no longer existed. The Soviet Union, moreover, was obligated to withdraw its forces from the two countries within 40 days after the new treaty took effect.

Thus, some new basis to permit the continued presence of Soviet troops in these two countries was necessary; the Warsaw Pact provided this. It also established terms under which the Soviet Union could claim legitimacy for its armed presence in other Eastern European countries, if necessary.

By 1950 the USSR had concluded bilateral mutual aid treaties with all of the members of the Soviet bloc which were to become signatories of the Warsaw Pact (except East Germany, with which it did not conclude such a treaty until 1964, and Albania, which has a mutual aid treaty only with Bulgaria). None of these treaties of friendship and mutual assistance, however, provided a firm juridical basis for the stationing of Soviet troops on the territory of a treaty partner. Although the terms of the Warsaw Pact agreement regarding this were general and referred vaguely to "agreed measures," they did provide for the formation of a Unified Armed Force and took the first step toward regularization of the status of Soviet troops in Eastern Europe.

After the widespread political turmoil that weakened Soviet hegemony in Eastern Europe in 1956, the stationing of Soviet troops in that area was further regularized by a series of "status of forces" agreements, which in effect used the Warsaw Treaty as their point of departure without any formal reference to it. Since the USSR certainly wielded the power necessary to conclude these agreements independently of the Warsaw Pact framework, its use as a point of departure for the agreements signified Soviet awareness of the pact's value as a means of coping with the threat of political diversity in Eastern Europe. (See Table 1.)

How It Is Organized and Operates

At the Warsaw conference of May 1955 establishing the Warsaw Treaty Organization, two major bodies were created to carry out the functions of the pact: the Political Consultative Committee, and the Unified Command of Pact Armed Forces, both headquartered in Moscow.

According to the terms of the treaty the Political Consultative Committee — on which each state is represented by a specially appointed official — is charged with coordinating all activities of the pact organization, with the exception of purely military matters. However, "general questions pertaining to the strengthening of the defense capacity and to the organization of the joint armed forces of the states that are parties to the treaty will be examined by the PCC, which will take appropriate decisions." Additional committee responsibilities involve consideration of important foreign policy decisions, and the use of the PCC by member states to consult "on their common interests" and to

TABLE 1
BILATERAL TREATIES OF FRIENDSHIP, COOPERATION AND MUTUAL ASSISTANCE SIGNED BY WARSAW PACT MEMBERS

	USSR	Poland	Czech	Hung	Rum	Bul	E.G.
USSR	—	FMA 4–45 r. 4–65	FMA 12–43 r. 12–63	FMA 2–48	FMA 2–48	FMA 3–48	FMA 6–64
Poland	FMA 4–45 r. 4–65	—	FMA 3–47	FMA 6–48	FMA 1–49	FMA 5–48	F 7–50
Czechoslovakia	FMA 12–43 r.12–63	FMA 3–47	—	FMA 4–49	FMA 7–48	FMA 4–48	F 6–50
Hungary	FMA 2–48	FMA 6–48	FMA 4–49	—	FMA 1–48	FMA 7–48	F 6–50
Rumania	FMA 2–48	FMA 1–49	FMA 7–48	FMA 1–48	—	FMA 1–48	F 8–50
Bulgaria	FMA 3–48	FMA 5–48	FMA 4–48	FMA 7–48	FMA 1–48	—	F 8–50
East Germany	FMA 6–64	F 7–50	F 6–50	F 6–50	F 8–50	F 8–50	—

FMA — Friendship and Mutual Assistance Treaty.
F — Friendship Treaty.
r. — Renewed.
The treaties are valid for a period of twenty years and commit the co-signatories to mutual defense against aggression, particularly aggression by a rearmed German state. In this regard the treaties concluded with East Germany were called only Friendship treaties. It was not until June 1964 that the GDR-Soviet Union agreement was upgraded to the level of a treaty of Friendship, Cooperation and Mutual Assistance. To date none of the other Pact countries have followed the Soviet lead with a similar upgrading. In two cases treaties have been renewed, between the USSR and Czechoslovakia and the USSR and Poland. Albania has not been included since it has signed a Treaty of Friendship, Cooperation and Mutual Assistance only with Bulgaria, an agreement the two states concluded in December 1947.

develop the "economic and cultural cooperation of the partners." Only the first of these functions seemed to be of importance until the early 1960's.

The PCC in May 1955 was further empowered to form auxiliary organs for which "a need may arise" in executing its responsibilities. Accordingly a Permanent Commission, located in Moscow, and a Joint Secretariat, also situated in the Soviet capital, were created at the second meeting of the Committee in Prague in January 1956. At this same meeting it was also decided that the Political Consultative Committee would convene at least twice a year but could meet more frequently if its members desired.

The Permanent Commission, the most significant of the two auxiliary organs, has competence for the development of recommendations on foreign policy questions of importance to pact members, while the Joint Secretariat is responsible for administering "those technical fields serving the realization of treaty goals." Both bodies are dominated by the

Soviets, and the Soviet head of the Joint Secretariat is also the Chief of Staff of the Unified Command of Pact Armed Forces.

The Unified Command of Pact Armed Forces has paramount authority over the troops assigned to it by the member states of the pact. According to the terms of the treaty, the Unified Command is enjoined to "strengthen the defensive capability of the Warsaw Pact, to prepare military plans in case of war and to decide on the deployment of troops" assigned to the pact forces, which consist of contingents of national units designated for assignment to the Unified Command.

At the initial convocation of the Warsaw Treaty Organization, it was agreed that the Supreme Commander of the Armed Forces would be a representative of the Soviet Union. He is supported by a General Staff, which includes permanent representatives of the general staffs of the member states, and is assisted by eight deputies, traditionally the ministers of defense of the countries party to the treaty, although the deputies theoretically may be drawn from a lower military echelon. Even though these deputies are appointed and recalled by the governments of their respective states independently of the Unified Command, the integrated staffs of the Command function supra-nationally.

On paper, the organization of the Warsaw Pact bespeaks impressive coordination among its members on political and military matters, but the actual operation is a different matter. The Political Consultative Committee meetings have served principally as a forum for the articulation of a common stand on important international issues as proposed by the USSR. The Joint Command of Pact Armed Forces has also been under complete Soviet domination, with both the posts of Commander-in-Chief and Chief of the General Staff held by Russian officers. (See Figure 1.)

The Warsaw Pact Today and Its Value to the USSR

Military Value

Since 1961, the Soviet Union has been carrying out a program to upgrade the military significance of the Warsaw Pact, particularly in terms of its use as an instrument of common defense of the Communist camp. This policy has resulted in the holding of combined pact training exercises and in considerable modernization of the equipment of the pact forces commensurate with their apparently enlarged responsibilities.

Coordination of Military Planning, Equipment and Strategy

The late 1950's were marked by the first steps to elevate the importance of the military contribution of the Eastern European countries in over-all Soviet military planning, with a concurrent increase in emphasis on a more active joint role for pact forces in defensive and offensive theater operations. Soviet attention to the cooperative aspects of the alliance was heightened during the Berlin crisis of 1961.

FIGURE 1
WARSAW PACT STRUCTURE

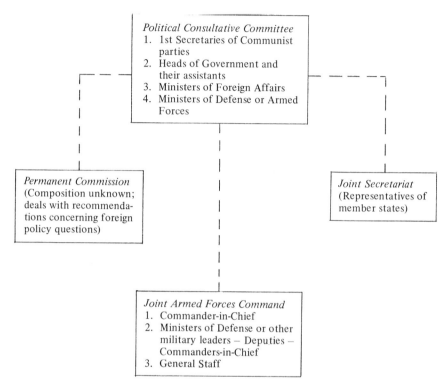

In September of that year, the defense ministers of the countries involved gathered in Warsaw for the first publicly announced meeting devoted wholly to military matters. In October, Soviet, East German, Polish and Czechoslovak forces participated in a major field exercise, the first of a series of such annual combined training exercises. According to Marshal Grechko, Commander-in-Chief of the Warsaw Pact forces, these exercises are of great importance because of their "contributions to further growth of the combat might of our joint armed forces, to higher standards of training, to better coordination of forces and staffs, and to the elaboration of common views on methods of nuclear and conventional warfare."

In addition to undertaking combined exercises, the Soviets introduced a program of re-equipment and modernization of the Eastern European armed forces. On the whole, the modernization program and the training given the Eastern European armies prepared them principally for conducting theater warfare under nuclear conditions. Except for Albania all of the Soviet bloc countries, however, have been furnished with potential nuclear delivery systems in the form of tactical missiles or aircraft. Even though the nuclear warheads for these weapons presumably are kept in Soviet hands, possession of missiles and attack aircraft by Eastern European armed forces increases the possibility of nuclear sharing within the pact at some future time.

Stationing of Soviet Troops in Eastern Europe

As noted earlier, the Warsaw Pact's initial military significance lay in the fact that it provided justification for the stationing of Soviet troops in Eastern Europe. This Soviet presence facilitated the adoption of Soviet organizational forms and field doctrine by the local armies, as well as the standardization of weapons and local arms production along Soviet lines. Finally, the deploying of Soviet troops in Eastern Europe (in East Germany, Poland and Hungary) serves as a guarantee of sorts for the existence of a political atmosphere which best serves Soviet interests.

Since the late 1950's, however, when the Soviet Union first showed a greater appreciation of the benefits to be derived from closer military integration within the pact, the role of the Soviet troops in Eastern Europe has undergone a significant change. The USSR was prompted to conclude status-of-force agreements after the events of 1956, and great pains were taken to stress the legal restrictions and juridical safeguards governing the actions of the Soviet military in the other pact countries. Emphasis now is placed on the equality between the armed forces of the host country and the Soviet troops, with considerable propaganda effort devoted to demonstrating "the development of comradely bonds" resulting from the combined exercises of pact troops.

Although military collaboration between the Soviet Union and the other pact members may not have proceeded as far as some official accounts seek to convey, the fact remains that the Soviet Union has found it useful to stress the close military bonds among the Warsaw Pact members. One important Soviet motive can be traced to the fact that Soviet forces in Eastern Europe, in addition to their deployment opposite NATO, have long had a kind of garrison function to insure that regimes sympathetic to Soviet policy remain in power. As the countries of Eastern Europe have gradually acquired a measure of autonomy in their economic, cultural and political affairs, the garrison aspect of Russia's military presence became increasingly awkward for Moscow. The Warsaw Pact, however, confers collective sanction on the Soviet presence in the name of defense against the NATO threat.

Forward Defense Area

Closer military integration of the Eastern European armies into Soviet operational plans has been noteworthy for the particular attention given to East Germany, Poland and Czechoslovakia, the so-called "northern tier" countries, referred to in public statements by bloc officials as "the first strategic echelon" of the Warsaw Pact. The regional differentiation between the states of the northern group and those constituting the southern sector of the alliance stems from their relative importance as a forward defense area. Since the territory of these northern countries would be the main axis for a central European campaign in time of war, the Soviets have shown greater interest in them. Another contributing factor is the role this area has traditionally played as a defensive buffer zone against a possible land invasion from the West, a concept that has remained alive in Soviet military thought despite the fact that such a traditional military invasion of the Soviet Union in the nuclear age is a remote contingency.

The difficulty of deploying substantial reinforcements from the USSR in the event of nuclear war makes an effective Warsaw Pact force, already in place close to the arena of European conflict, a highly attractive project.

Use to Plan Actions Elsewhere than Europe

There has been no evidence to suggest that the Soviet Union has contemplated use of the armed forces of the pact, committed by the terms of the treaty only to a European defense system, to initiate or support military actions elsewhere. For example, during the Suez crisis of 1956 there was no mobilization of pact forces. During the Cuban missile crisis of 1962, the Soviets attempted to maintain a non-provocative stance in terms of the treaty organization, and again there was no build-up or mobilization of pact forces.

The most significant concentration of Soviet forces and the most effective troop contingents assigned to the pact are in the previously mentioned "northern tier" countries, which have geographic and strategic political importance only in terms of a European conflict. Inasmuch as the pact armed forces have never been assigned a role outside of the context of the European theater, it is unlikely that they would be used in any other way — such as sending units to Vietnam — in the future, particularly since some of the Eastern European countries have been taking an increasingly independent stand toward pact command arrangements. The USSR, in fact, probably is finding that it can no longer singlehandedly decide in all cases the disposition of pact troops.

Political Value

On the surface, it seems inconsistent that the USSR has adopted a policy of strengthening its Eastern European allies at the very time they are becoming politically less tractable. The political benefits derived by the Soviet Union from the Warsaw Pact, however, are probably at least as great as the military benefits.

Thus Political Consultative Committee communiqués and resolutions have been so phrased as to indicate unanimity and to underline strongly the status of the USSR as the spokesman for the Communist movement. Even in 1961, when intra-bloc relations were exacerbated by the growing tensions of the Sino-Soviet dispute, the Russians were able to use the Warsaw Pact to maintain a show of unity by issuing strongly worded complaints against the West, particularly in regard to the German question and disarmament.

According to the articles of the Warsaw Treaty the Political Consultative Committee is obligated to meet at least twice a year and may convene as frequently as its members deem necessary. However, as the sporadic pattern of meetings indicates, the committee has never met biannually. The above table represents only those Pact meetings which have been held openly. It is probable that treaty members have met at unpublicized gatherings.

The USSR also used the periodic and irregular gatherings of the Political Consultative Committee (see Table 2) to pressure a reluctant member to accept the "majority view" or, if this was impossible, to persuade the other government in the alliance to join with them in isolating the dissident.[2] This method was employed to bring about and to justify the ouster of Hungarian Premier Imre Nagy. At the end of the 1956 revolution, Nagy was charged with violating the unity of the bloc by his unilateral decision to withdraw Hungary from the Warsaw Pact. Similar pressure was brought to bear against the Albanians in June 1962, when they were excluded from participation in a meeting in Moscow of the Pact's Political Consultative Committee.

The Soviets also found the Warsaw Pact a useful device for rebutting Chinese charges that Moscow was a disintegrating influence in the Communist camp. The communiqué issued after the March 1961 meeting of the Political Consultative Committee pointedly stated that the PCC was "guided by the theoretical and political conclusions of the November 1960 Conference of representatives of Communist and Workers Parties" and by the "historic documents" of that conference. Such an announcement was devised to put the Soviet Union firmly on the side of the angels, and to emphasize that it was the Chinese and Albanians (neither the Albanian party nor government chiefs attended the meeting) who were disrupting the unity of the bloc and rejecting the good offices of the USSR and its supporters.

With the growth of economic pragmatism and the appearance of more nationalistically oriented policy stands by the Eastern European regimes, a new situation in Soviet bloc relations gradually came into being in the early 1960's. Moscow's apparent hopes to use the Political Consultative Committee genuinely "for the purpose of consultations" among the parties to the treaty foundered on the rocks of national differences. Today the USSR has little capability to override dissenting elements within the pact by political pressure; even those countries willing to follow the Soviet line are reluctant to join in isolating more independent members in case they too should one day wish to pursue a path of their own choosing. The failure of the Warsaw Pact's Political Consultative Committee to meet since January 1965 is probably a reflec-

[2] This type of pressure tactic is one of the main reasons accounting for Rumania's oft-voiced view in recent years that bloc decisions are binding only with unanimous — rather than mere majority — support. Communist China has constantly reiterated this point also during the years of its dispute with Moscow and the Soviet bloc. The USSR has never been willing formally to accept this view because it would give any one of the Eastern European countries veto power. As a practical matter, however, it has on a number of occasions found it necessary to accede implicitly to the unanimity rule.

TABLE 2
WARSAW PACT MEETINGS SINCE MAY 1955

Date	Place	Type	Members Represented	Level of Participation
27–28 Jan. 56	Prague	PCC	All	Chief or Deputy Chief of Government. Defense Ministers.
24 May 58	Moscow	PCC	All	Chiefs of Party and Government. Defense Ministers. Foreign Ministers.
27–28 Apr. 59	Warsaw	Foreign Ministers	All + CPR	Foreign Ministers, CPR. Deputy Foreign Minister.
4 Feb. 60	Moscow	PCC	All	Chiefs of Party and Government. Defense Ministers. Foreign Ministers.
28–29 Mar. 61	Moscow	PCC	Albania did not send Party or Government Chief.	Chiefs of Party and Government. Defense Minister. Foreign Minister. Chief or Deputy Chief for Economic Planning.
3–5 Aug. 61	Moscow	First Secretaries	Albanian First Secretary did not attend. Representatives of Asian socialist countries attended.	Chiefs of Party.
Sept. 61	Moscow	Defense Ministers	Albania probably absent.	Defense Ministers, Chiefs of General Staff.
30 Jan.–1 Feb. 62	Prague	Defense Ministers	Albania probably absent.	Defense Ministers.
7 June 62	Moscow	PCC	All except Albania.	Chiefs of Party and Government.
27–28 Feb. 63	Warsaw	Defense Ministers	All except Albania.	Defense Ministers, Chiefs of Staffs.
July 63	Moscow	Heads of Party and Government	All except Albania.	Chiefs of Party and Government.
26 July 63	Moscow	PCC	All except Albania.	Chiefs of Party and Government. Defense Minister. Foreign Minister or Deputy.
19–20 Jan. 65	Warsaw	PCC	All except Albania.	Chiefs of Party and Government. Defense Minister. Foreign Minister.

tion of the growing weakness of this body as an instrument for achieving a political consensus, much less interparty unity.

Economic Cost to USSR of a Military Withdrawal from Eastern Europe

Although the military base system of the Soviet armed forces in Hungary, Poland and especially East Germany is rather extensive, a relinquishment of those facilities to the present Eastern European governments should pose no economically significant obstacle to a withdrawal of Soviet forces from Europe.

The question of the exact value of the Soviet military investment in fixed facilities in Eastern Europe is complicated, as is perhaps best illustrated by examining the case of East Germany. The bulk of the Soviet military forces outside the USSR are stationed in East Germany; and the extent of Soviet control and exploitation of the Eastern European countries has, in the long run, probably been greatest in East Germany.

The Soviet forces in East Germany (GSFG) are mobile field forces and hence can be withdrawn to the Soviet Union on short notice. Although available information does not permit any highly accurate computations of the economic value of the GSFG's fixed facilities, it is believed that a significant portion, if not all, were built at the expense of the Germans both before and after 1945. In any event, the East German economy suffers from a shortage of storage and housing facilities and could well use any facilities vacated by Soviet troops. There is little reason to suspect that the East Germans would not make it economically worthwhile for the Soviets to leave.

The purpose of the Soviet presence in East Germany is no longer the exploitation of the East German economy, but the maintenance of Soviet strategic interests. The only remaining aspects which may still have economic importance for the USSR are the relatively minor economic advantages of garrisoning troops in East Germany instead of the USSR, and the more significant operation of the uranium mines.

The Soviet Union has already given up most of the economic advantages derived from the 1945 occupation of the Soviet Zone of Germany and the Soviet sector of Berlin. At the end of 1953, the USSR cancelled the balance owed by East Germany on the reparations account, and arranged to turn back to East Germany the last of the enterprises seized after the war — except for the uranium mines, which the USSR will probably retain until the ore is exhausted.

By 1956, the East Germans finished paying for the enterprises which had reverted to their control. Occupation cost payments were progressively reduced in 1954, 1956, and 1958, and finally discontinued in 1959.

Soviet withdrawal, then, apparently would neither jeopardize significant economic interests, nor pose economic costs of a size that would be difficult to negotiate. (See Table 3.)

TABLE 3
ESTIMATED PERSONNEL STRENGTH OF THE
EASTERN EUROPEAN ARMED FORCES

	Poland	Czecho-slovakia	East Germany	Hungary	Rumania	Bulgaria	Albania[1]	Total[2]
Ground Forces	215,000	200,000	80,000	100,000	175,000	125,000	30,000	895,000
Naval Forces	17,000	—	17,000	—	8,000	7,000	3,000	49,000
Air Forces	45,000	35,000	15,000	9,000	15,000	20,000	5,000	139,000
TOTAL ARMED FORCES	277,000	235,000	112,000	109,000	198,000	152,000	38,000	1,083,000
Militarized Security Forces	45,000	35,000	70,000	35,000	60,000	15,000	12,500	260,000

[1] Although Albania no longer participates in Warsaw Pact affairs, it remains a nominal member and is included in this chart for comparative purposes.
[2] Not including Albania.

BENEFITS DERIVED BY EASTERN EUROPE FROM THE PACT

Assurance of Protection Against Germany

Whether the belief is justified or not, the Federal German Republic remains a real threat in the minds of many Eastern Europeans and thus has served the governments of the Warsaw Pact states as a valuable propaganda justification for their close relations with the Soviet Union. Typical of the attitude of Eastern European Communist regimes toward West Germany is the statement made on March 26, 1966 by Jan Karol Wende, Vice Marshal of the Parliament of the Polish People's Republic:

> . . . the Federal German Republic is the only state in Europe whose government wants to thwart the results of World War II, officially puts forward territorial claims to Poland, Czechoslovakia and the Soviet Union, and is striving, under the slogan of "reunification" for annexation of the GDR. . . . any attempts at undermining the political and territorial status quo in Europe threaten an armed conflict, which in this part of the world would inevitably turn into a world conflagration. . . .

As a consequence of this fear of a possible revival of German militarism, the Eastern Europeans view a military alliance with the USSR as the most practical means, and perhaps the only feasibility, to protect themselves from the traditional German threat to the area. Certainly the collective security arrangements of the pact give them a greater measure of defense than they could ever obtain with their own resources.

Both the regimes and the people of these countries are also highly sensitive to situations which, in their eyes, constitute potential nuclear war hazards. They regard the presence of NATO nuclear weapons in West Germany as a principal deterrent to conclusion of the German peace treaty and stress that their reliance on the nuclear capability of the Soviet Union is necessary in order to avert the possible aggressive aims of a reactionary West German Government.

For some of the countries — specifically Poland and Czechoslovakia — membership in the Warsaw Pact under the aegis of the USSR gives them some measure of assurance that they will be able to retain the territories they acquired from Germany at the end of the war — acquisitions which more than 20 years later still lack the legality of a peace treaty.

Modern Armaments

As a result of the extensive supply program begun by the Soviets almost 15 years ago, and the local manufacture of military equipment in Eastern Europe, a high degree of standardization of materiel has been achieved among the armed forces of the pact member states (see Table 4, p. 768, for Eastern European military budgets). This process has not only facilitated simpler wartime weapons coordination but has also made peacetime production and supply of modern weapons easier. No

Eastern European country has been permitted to establish either an autonomous manufacturing capability for a complete range of military equipment and supplies, or a fully adequate war reserve.

Despite some time lag between the appearance of particular weapons and supplies as standard in the Soviet army and the supply of the same items to the Eastern European armies, Moscow has generally made up-to-date military materiel available to them. The bulk of equipment used by these forces today is concurrently standard in the Soviet military forces.

Although nuclear weapons currently deployed in Eastern Europe are under the control of the Soviet forces stationed there, tactical missiles and new generation aircraft have been directly assigned to the armed forces of Poland, Rumania, East Germany, Hungary, Czechoslovakia and apparently Bulgaria. Possession of these weapons undoubtedly increases the stature of the bloc armed forces, and there is no doubt that their ability to conduct modern warfare has become far greater as a result of Soviet tutelage.

Support for Regimes in Power

Although the Warsaw Pact plays a role as the guarantor of power for local Communist regimes in Eastern Europe, this should not be given undue emphasis. Dissolution of the pact as a formal organization, and even the subsequent withdrawal of Soviet troops from the territory of the Eastern European countries, would not spell the end to Communist domination in those countries. In fact, particularly in view of the growing strength of "national Communism," and its acceptability to most Soviet bloc leaders, such a turn of events would probably make the several Communist governments more palatable to the populations of those areas. The majority of the citizens of Eastern Europe tend to regard some form of socialist government as the only practical method for establishing and maintaining sound economies in their respective countries.

However, it would also be unwise to underestimate the psychological advantage the Eastern European governments derive from emphasizing their membership in the Warsaw Pact. Reiteration by the Eastern European leaders of the closeness of cooperation between the local army and Soviet troops, as well as pointed references to Soviet military might, are subtle but effective reminders. They deter any considerations of political independence among the satellite populations as forcefully as the more flagrant methods of coercion, terrorism and blatant Soviet domination experienced under Stalin. The "psychological shadow," as it has been termed by George Kennan, cast by the presence of the Soviet troops in Eastern Europe certainly falls across the consciousness of those who are citizens of the states belonging to the Warsaw Pact, and can only serve to remind them that in all probability their destinies are bound with that of the Soviet Union for some time to come.

PROBLEMS WITHIN THE PACT

Eastern European Countries Becoming Less Tractable

The CPSU is against any hegemony in the Communist movement, for genuinely internationalist relations of equality among all the parties. . . . The strengthening of unity requires observance of the standards of relations among the parties worked out collectively by them; complete equality and independence, non-interference in each other's internal affairs, mutual support and international solidarity.

These remarks, made by Leonid Brezhnev, Secretary General of the Communist Party of the Soviet Union, at the 23rd Party Congress in March 1966, are not hollow words. They reflect Soviet recognition and acceptance of the growing diversity within the Communist world, and particularly of the centrifugal forces at work within the Warsaw Pact. The USSR, by deciding to accept what it cannot prevent without an undue and counterproductive show of force, has given its stamp of approval to an increased independence on the part of its pact partners. In so doing, Moscow obviously hopes to preserve the unity, as well as the military and political effectiveness, of the Warsaw Treaty Organization.

In admitting the necessity of working out problems collectively, the USSR is apparently responding to pressures from the Eastern European regimes for a greater voice in the conduct of pact affairs. Indeed, by accepting that "business-like contacts and political consultations between leaders of the fraternal parties of the socialist countries have become a system," the Soviet Union again has given necessity the mark of virtue. Even so, the USSR has not been able to convene a meeting of pact states at the first secretary or ministerial level since the last convocation of the Political Consultative Committee in January, 1965. Under the terms of the pact, it is supposed to meet twice a year.

Even in those instances where an Eastern European regime has deliberately rejected the lead of the Soviet Union, the others have been reluctant to condemn the dissenting member. For instance Rumania's unilateral reduction of the term of service in its armed forces from 24 to 16 months has drawn no censure, at least in public, from the other members of the alliance. They have also been willing to tolerate Bucharest's insistence on full independence in economic policy and foreign policy — Rumanian determination to straddle the fence in the Sino-Soviet dispute — as well as the Rumanian overtures to the West. The reasons for this are clear. By refusing to criticize Rumania's right to pursue an independent course, the other members of the alliance are establishing a precedent that will serve them well should their own national interests diverge from those of the pact as a whole.

There is also evidence that the Eastern European members of the pact, including those who consider maintenance of the alliance at least a military if not a political necessity, disagree over the current organization and chain of command under which the pact now operates.

Marshal Grechko has referred to the need to reorganize the structure, and Vaclav David, Minister of Foreign Affairs of Czechoslovakia, in his March 15, 1966 speech to the National Assembly, spoke of the need for "further strengthening the Warsaw Pact organization." Disagreements on the future structure and organization of the Warsaw Pact reportedly became evident at the last PCC meeting in January 1965. They apparently remain unresolved.

Another factor which obviously has considerable bearing on the smoothness with which the Warsaw alliance operates is the differing relationships that its various member governments have with the Soviet Union. The greatest degree of friction exists, of course, between the USSR and Albania, which for all practical purposes has read itself out of the pact; the friction stems from Albania's rigidly pro-Chinese stand. Rumania has maintained correct relations with the USSR, but has pointedly refused to take sides in the Sino-Soviet dispute. Within the pact, Rumania has refused to attend meetings whenever it appeared possible that the gathering might prove to be a forum for anti-Chinese propaganda. Poland and Czechoslovakia support the USSR in the Sino-Soviet dispute, although Poland has taken a more moderate stand on the problem. Both of these countries tend to regard close support of the Soviet lead as a guarantee of protection against Germany. East Germany has had no choice but to be a faithful and willing ally of Soviet foreign policy. The relationship of the Hungarian regime to the USSR tends to be passive, largely because of Hungary's economic dependence on the Soviet Union. As party First Secretary Kadar said at the 23rd CPSU Congress, "We support enhancing the effectiveness of international organizations of such great importance for socialism and peace as the Warsaw Pact and CEMA."

Reliability of Eastern European Forces

The inclusion of the armed forces of the Eastern European countries in the pact has greatly increased the quantity of manpower available to the USSR, but the question of their reliability, if called upon to fight with the Soviet Union, remains a major factor for consideration. If the bloc forces were called upon to support the USSR in a defensive campaign in hostilities initiated by West Germany, it is likely that the pact's Eastern European armies would fight with their Soviet comrades. It is also possible that the countries individually might fight an effective offensive campaign, provided that it was directed against one of their traditional national enemies; for example Poles and Czechs would wage an offensive campaign against the Germans, or the Bulgarians against the Greeks and Turks. History indicates, however, that the national armies of the bloc countries are hardly entirely reliable allies. Units of the Hungarian Army actively fought the Russians in the 1956 revolution. A decisive portion of the Polish Army was prepared to resist any use of military force by the Russians to prevent the appointment of Gomulka in October 1956.

The current Soviet Party leaders have had difficulty in persuading the various pact members to pull their proper weight within the alliance, as has been noted in Rumania's reluctance to accept the burdens entailed by larger pact commitments. Nationalism has also created problems elsewhere, even among stalwart Soviet supporters. In April 1965, for instance, a nationalist faction of the Bulgarian army attempted a coup apparently aimed at directing Bulgarian policy along more independent lines. The Soviets have sought to explain away such soft spots in the pact by claiming publicly that "imperialist" attempts to split the bloc would prove futile. This type of comment reflects, of course, a certain helplessness in dealing with the problem of obtaining cooperation at a time when the national interests of the Eastern European countries are permitted greater play in their policy making.

Eastern European Members Fear Nuclear War

Another reason for the determination of Eastern European members to assume a greater voice in Warsaw Pact decisions is their reluctance to become involved in a nuclear war. Leaders of the non-Soviet member governments are apparently interested in achieving a policy-making role for themselves commensurate with the vulnerability of their positions as sites for Soviet nuclear weapons. The possibility of their involuntary involvement in a nuclear war became clear to them during the Cuban missile crisis of 1962. As members of the Warsaw Pact and therefore allies of the USSR, they were implicitly involved and would have been subject to the same consequences as Moscow if the Soviet missile build-up in Cuba had led to war.

Effect on Decision-Making Process

The divisive factors which have been at work within the Warsaw alliance are having repercussions within the policy-making mechanisms of the pact as the Eastern European members of the alliance have begun to press for a more influential voice in matters affecting their own interests, such as choice of strategy, sharing of military and economic burdens and resolution of foreign policy issues bearing on the question of war or peace. It seems fairly certain that efforts to alleviate these pressures will take the form of some sort of reorganization of the pact structure. In mid-September 1965 Brezhnev, in commenting on the need to strengthen bloc unity, remarked that "the current situation places on the agenda the further perfection of the Warsaw Pact organization. We are all prepared to work diligently in order to find the best solution." The Soviet party leader revealed shortly thereafter that a series of talks with Eastern European leaders had dealt with the need for establishing within the Warsaw Pact organization "a permanent and operating mechanism for considering urgent problems."

However, the role and nature of the Warsaw Pact appear to be conditioned in large part by two closely related factors: the degree to which the Soviets place reliance upon the other pact forces, and the extent of actual Soviet dependence upon them. The USSR will doubtless be prepared to accept some diminution of its authority within the

Warsaw alliance to the extent that it feels dependent on the other pact forces. Although the advent of the missile age seems, on the surface at least, to have somewhat reduced Soviet military dependence on the Warsaw allies, other considerations, both military and political, suggest that on balance Soviet dependence on the Warsaw allies probably is becoming greater.

Trends along the above lines, with greater emphasis on military integration and interdependence and assertion of separate national interests, will probably result in a new balance of decision-making power among the pact's members. From the Soviet viewpoint, the alliance continues to perform an important political function. It has proven more effective than any other multilateral institution in holding the bloc together and still provides the basic treaty obligation binding the Eastern European states to the Soviet Union.

Although it would be unrealistic to suppose that the USSR will cease to play a predominant role in pact affairs, the trends at work within the treaty organization suggest that the pact may be evolving toward an alliance of a more customary kind, subject to a greater degree than previously to the interplay of coalition politics, and that the Eastern European partners may derive greater political, cultural and economic autonomy in the course of such an evolution.

TABLE 4
MILITARY EXPENDITURES IN THE EASTERN EUROPEAN COMMUNIST COUNTRIES 1958–59 AND 1963–66

	1958	1959	1963[1]	1964[1]	1965[1]	1966[1]
	Announced military expenditures in current prices					
Bulgaria (million leva)	173	163	297	260	231	240
Czechoslovakia (million crowns)[2]	8,933[1]	8,790[1]	11,332	10,948	10,220	10,800
East Germany (million DME)	([3])	([3])	2,700	2,800	2,900	3,300[4]
Hungary (million forints)	2,080	2,410	6,610	6,150	5,567[5]	5,219
Poland (million zlotys)	11,220	14,259	20,694[6]	21,881	23,500	25,300
Rumania (million lei)	3,600	3,446	4,143[6]	4,346[6]	4,700[6]	4,800

[1] Planned expenditures, unless otherwise indicated.
[2] Including expenditures for public security.
[3] East Germany began publishing realistic defense figures in 1962 following a reclassification of military expenditures among categories of the state budget which made the military budget more inclusive.
[4] The figure shown is the upper limit indicated in the plan.
[5] Actual expenditures in Hungary reportedly were 190 million forints less than the plan of 5,757 million forints.
[6] Actual expenditures.

VIII RECENT SOVIET FOREIGN POLICY

23. SOVIET FOREIGN POLICY PERSPECTIVES IN THE SIXTIES

Vernon V. Aspaturian

INTRODUCTION

The most conspicuous over-all characteristics of Soviet foreign policy since Khrushchev are: the progressive disengagement of foreign policy goals from ideological norms; the diffusion of policy-making; the globalization of Soviet power and influence; the personalization of Soviet diplomacy; and finally, the vigorous pursuit of both confrontation and collaboration with the United States.

All of these trends were set into motion under Khrushchev. Brezhnev and Kosygin have attempted to arrest or attenuate most or all of these trends but without much success. Ideology as a motivational force in Soviet foreign policy continues to wane. Moscow has retrenched somewhat from the global overcommitment of its power and resources made under Khrushchev, but it cannot abjure its global role without serious injury to Soviet prestige and influence. While Soviet foreign policy is no longer symbolized by a single personality, it has not been completely depersonalized either; Kosygin, Brezhnev, and Podgorny now appear on the world stage almost as equals, whereas before there was only one. The division of diplomatic labor symbolizes the collectivity of the current Soviet leadership, but it also reflects the fragmentation of power and authority.

From Vernon V. Aspaturian, "Foreign Policy Perspectives in the Sixties," from *Soviet Politics since Khrushchev*, Alexander Dallin and Thomas B. Larson, eds., © 1968. By permission of Prentice-Hall, Inc., Englewood Cliffs, New Jersey.

The ouster of Khrushchev may have been prompted at least in part by the conviction that he had become too closely identified with the policy of alienating Peking in order to woo Washington, which was viewed with concern by some of the other leaders, who may have favored a different equilibrium between Soviet commitments to China and Soviet cooperation with the United States. As matters turned out, both Peking and Washington have been further alienated.

The de-ideologizing of Soviet foreign policy, set into motion at the XX Party Congress, and the repudiation of some sacrosanct ideological principles within which it operated, served to free it from Stalinist fetters, but it also shattered the myths of Soviet ideological infallibility and political omniscience. This, in turn, released disintegrative forces. Factional politics became the rule throughout the Communist world and have become increasingly institutionalized, making it virtually impossible to coordinate policy or resolve conflicts among Communist regimes and Parties.

De-Ideologizing Soviet Foreign Policy

Viewed in historical perspective, ideology has not been a constant in shaping Soviet behavior but a relative factor whose relationship to others relevant to Soviet behavior has fluctuated widely. This protean and variable characteristic has been a prime source of controversy in assessing the significance of ideology for Soviet policy.

Soviet foreign policy has always been the product of ideology in combination with other variables: capabilities, perceived opportunities, personalities, internal group and factional interests, and extra-volitional institutional and functional restraints. The long Stalinist era served to distort and dull the perception and analysis of Soviet behavior from abroad. Soviet policy was judged to be the product of two variables: ideological goals, as interpreted by Stalin, and Soviet capabilities. Ideology determined long-range goals, while short-range goals were limited by Soviet capabilities. An extremely complicated process of interaction and metamorphic development was thus reduced to an oversimplified two-factor analysis and prediction of Soviet policy. Stalinist behavior was mistakenly assumed to be the immutable behavior of the Soviet state. The leader's personality and the internal political order were accepted as constants, while ideology was viewed as an instrumental extension of Stalin's personality. Stalin's long-range ideological goals were no secret; it was his short-run intentions which were inscrutable. On the assumption that Stalin would take what he could get, the most common method for predicting short-run Soviet behavior was the measurement of Soviet capabilities. While such an approach had its utility during the Stalin era, it unfortunately spilled over into the post-Stalin period when it served to obscure the influence of other important variables which had been largely muted or latent until then.

Since the ideological goals of the Bolshevik movement were enunciated long before there was even a problem of Soviet security or interests to defend, ideology in its pristine form cannot be defined as an expedient defensive response to the behavior of a hostile environment.

After the Revolution and the Soviet state merged, this dual entity made itself the self-appointed custodian of the interests of the world proletariat. A national revolutionary movement was metamorphosed into a world revolutionary movement; and the interests of the Soviet state were merged with those of the movement.

The relative influence of ideology as a motivating force in Soviet foreign policy cannot be properly separated from the utility of the world Communist movement as an instrument of Soviet policy: the disutility of the latter was bound to subvert the animating force of the former. "In the change from Lenin to Stalin," observes George F. Kennan, "the foreign policy of a movement became the foreign policy of a single man,"[1] and one might add that in the changeover from Stalin to his successors, the foreign policy of an autocrat became the foreign policy of an oligarchy.

Under Stalin, the interests of the world movement fused with that of the Soviet state, and the interests of the state were largely merged with the personal and political interests of Stalin. World revolution, i.e., the extension of Communist power, became indistinguishable from Soviet expansion, and while this was largely a hypothetical relationship until 1939, after the outbreak of World War II it became a practical matter which ultimately resulted not only in the territorial expansion of the USSR but in the establishment of a system of vassal states, which was first successfully challenged by Yugoslavia in 1948 and has been in a state of progressive dissolution since 1956.

While Stalin's death set the stage for the disintegration of the world Communist movement into its constituent states and national Parties, the underlying cause for the divorce of Soviet interests from those of other Communist Parties was the rapid growth in Soviet capabilities. As Soviet power grew, so did the risks and costs of implementing a forward policy. The general tendency was for Soviet ideological goals to recede or to erode into ritualistic rhetoric, while the growth in Soviet power created greater opportunities for the pursuit of traditional great-power goals.

In the years since Stalin's death, the Soviet Union has been forced to adjust to changing configurations of interests and power at home, in the Communist inter-state community, in the world Communist movement, and in the international community at large — changes which have resulted in a fundamental restructuring of priorities among the various interests and purposes which motivate Soviet foreign policy.

The progressive de-ideologization of Soviet foreign policy goals under Khrushchev took place more by inadvertence, as a consequence of his opportunism, than by design. Once domestic pressures — for instance, in favor of raising the standard of living — were given equal legitimacy with ideological pressures, it was axiomatic that they would become a factor in internal politics and in turn impel Khrushchev to cater to them, while spurning the simultaneous demands of foreign Communist states and Parties. To assign higher priority to China and

---

[1] George F. Kennan, *Russia and the West Under Lenin and Stalin* (Boston, Little, Brown and Company, 1961), p. 223.

the world Communist movement might have been necessary to preserve Soviet pre-eminence in the world of communism. But it was bound to be of little value in preserving Khrushchev's authority at home, which increasingly depended upon his ability to meet the demands of powerful domestic constituencies.

Thus the traditional operational norms and assumptions of inter-state behavior — national interest, security, survival, economic and material well-being, national pride and prestige — have been increasingly supplanting the abstract goals of "world revolution" and "world communism" in Soviet foreign-policy behavior. In the words of Peking:

> The Soviet leaders seek only to preserve themselves and would let other people sink or swim. They have repeatedly said that so long as they themselves survive and develop, the people of the world will be saved. The fact is they are selling out the fundamental interests of the people of the world in order to seek their own momentary ease.[2]

. . . In the process of gradually disentangling ideological norms from policy goals, however, Soviet ideology has assumed a new function, whose effects are not altogether an unmixed blessing. It now functions to legitimize Moscow's behavior as a *global power*, i.e., a power which asserts a right to intervene in any dispute or conflict in any part of the globe. While the Soviet leaders have abjured ideology as a norm-defining mechanism, they have by no means abdicated their self-appointed role as the guardian and spokesman of the oppressed masses of the world against international imperialism. Otherwise Soviet global intervention-ism could be justified only in terms of raw power and naked self-interest, an impression which Moscow avidly desires to avoid. . . .

The Globalization of Soviet Foreign Policy

If it was Stalin who transformed the Soviet Union into a great power, it was under Khrushchev that Soviet Russia was transformed into a global power, challenging the United States for paramountcy and asserting the right to influence developments in any part of the world. Khrushchev broke out of the doctrinal shell confining Soviet diplomacy and embarked upon a bold global strategy of reaching out in search not only of possible recruits to the Communist bloc but of diplomatic client states.

Khrushchev's global strategy, pursued against the background of Soviet space spectaculars which he tried to metamorphose into military power, was designed to breach the non-Communist world at its most vulnerable points — in the Middle East, Southeast Asia, Africa, and even Latin America — irrespective of the strength of local Communist Parties. The maximization of possible diplomatic gains in the non-Communist world invited a minimization and dilution of the ideological content of Soviet foreign policy. This was to prove self-defeating (although advantageous momentarily) since it dictated the abandonment

---

[2] "Statement by the Spokesman of the Chinese Government . . . August 15, 1963," *Peking Review*, VI, No. 33, August 16, 1963, p. 7.

of foreign-policy strategies associated with Moscow for decades. Thus it meant, in some instances, sacrificing the future of local Communist Parties in return for diplomatic gains in the third world; it meant the diversion of scarce resources from internal development and from allied Communist countries to seduce the newly-independent countries of Asia and Africa with economic aid; it meant the assumption of new burdens in areas vulnerable to United States sea and air power, far from the centers of Communist power. For a time Khrushchev capitalized on the alleged "missile gap" to unfurl a protective nuclear-missile umbrella over Asia, Africa, and Latin America in the mistaken conviction that the United States could be thereby deterred from interfering with Soviet policy or from intervening to arrest local revolutions.

While Khrushchev successfully transformed the Soviet Union into a global power, he did so at the expense of weakening Soviet control in its own sphere; alienating Moscow's strongest ally, China; over-committing Soviet power; and maximizing the risks of thermonuclear war by his persistent probing of weak spots in the Western world hoping to force the United States into the settlement of outstanding issues on Soviet terms. These were the orientations and relations which the Soviet leaders inherited when they retired Nikita Khrushchev.

KHRUSHCHEV AND SOVIET DÉTENTE STRATEGY

One serious consequence of these trends in Khrushchev's foreign policy was the abandonment of a structurally-assured leadership of the Communist bloc in return for a tacit bid to be a co-ruler of the world with the United States. This simultaneously alienated the Chinese, who saw in Moscow's desired partner their chief enemy, and created a spiritual and power vacuum in the international Communist movement which Peking tried to fill. The consequence was a fracturing of the Communist bloc and the establishment of a new fluid and uncertain equilibrium in Sino-Soviet-America relations.

Soviet and Chinese Perceptions of the United States

Since the United States has become a major factor in the evolving relationship between the Soviet Union and China, its perceptions and behavior become important variables of the situation. It is difficult to ascertain whether Sino-Soviet differences are a consequence of divergent perception of American intentions and behavior or a root cause of these differences. By the November, 1957, conference of ruling Communist Parties in Moscow, it had become rather clear that the United States, its intentions, and the threat it posed were being perceived differently in Moscow and Peking, and this gap was straining the Sino-Soviet alliance. Khrushchev emphasized more and more the horrors of nuclear war and made its avoidance the first objective of Soviet foreign policy. Since the avoidance of thermonuclear war depended also upon the United States, such a policy presupposed a revised image of the United States, which would allow for an equal commitment on the part of the American "ruling class" to the avoidance of such a holocaust.

Khrushchev's policy was facilitated by the fact that, with the exception of the German question, both the United States and the Soviet Union were prepared to accept the political and territorial status quo in Europe. Neither the Soviet Union nor the United States had any direct demands upon the other which could encumber an accommodation. The principal obstacles originated in ideological differences and the inherent tendency of the two hegemonial powers to view one another with suspicion and fear as natural rivals.

China's relationship with the United States was fundamentally different. From China's standpoint, the United States was not only its major ideological opponent, but its major national enemy as well. Not only had China been involved in a proxy war with the United States in Korea, but the United States persisted in its refusal to recognize the Peking regime, remained the decisive force in keeping Peking out of the United Nations, and sustained a rival regime on Taiwan which it recognized as the legitimate government of all China. The United States policy toward China's two major Far Eastern allies, North Korea and North Vietnam, was substantially identical, and since both bordered on China, this created the appearance of hostile encirclement by the United States, which appeared as the major obstacle to the national unification and juridical recognition of China and its two acolytes and directly or indirectly seemed to threaten the interests and very existence of the Far Eastern Communist regimes. Not only did the United States continue to deprive them of territories which they claim as part of their state, but in all three instances it actively supported rival regimes.

No comparable perceptions of American deprivations existed on the Soviet side. The Soviet elite still views the United States as the leader of a hostile ideological-military coalition and as a global power rival in international affairs; but these are matters subject to compromise and accommodation. These differeng perceptions of American intentions and expected behavior have shaped corresponding attitudes across a spectrum of issues which, while couched in ideological terms, are actually distorted by the national interests of each side and organized into different orders of priority.

The areas of tangible agreement between the two have shrunk considerably, since Moscow and Peking have divergent perceptions of the nature of the American threat and divergent assessments of the risks and costs necessary to deal with it. Because of these divergent perceptions, the further expansion of communism is no longer viewed by both Moscow and Peking as automatically beneficial; it all depends on, What kind of communism is being proliferated? Whose power is being expanded? Whose interests are being served?

The Realignment of Forces

In the decade between 1956 and 1967, Soviet and Chinese images of one another and the international scene have undergone fundamental alteration. These perceptions, in turn, are a function of changing Soviet perceptions and unchanging Chinese perceptions of American behavior and reflect the essentially conflicting national and state interests of two states unable to manipulate a common ideology in such a way as not to jeopardize the interests of one while advancing those of the other. What the Chinese leaders perceive as necessary for their own security and well-being, the Soviet leaders perceive as inimical to their requirements. These differences arise partly because of divergent internal demands and pressures as well as different security requirements. The limited test-ban treaty of 1963 constitutes the major watershed in the evolution of Sino-Soviet-American relations, with both Peking and Moscow conceding that an important realignment of world political actors has taken place.

In the eyes of both Peking and Moscow, the Soviet Union and the United States had been transformed from total enemies into limited partners-and-adversaries. Cooperation-and-conflict were to characterize their relations, with the center of gravity shifting from conflict toward cooperation. Even American bombardment of a common ally in Southeast Asia was insufficient to restore Sino-Soviet cooperation and friendship, and while the escalation of the Vietnam war impeded the Soviet-American détente, it failed to provoke a direct confrontation. The Soviet reaction has been one of dismay, disappointment, and embarrassment. There is little question but that Moscow expected the nuclear test-ban treaty to be followed up by a series of further agreements, most notably an East-West non-aggression pact, a nuclear non-proliferation treaty, and possibly a German settlement.

On the other hand, the Soviet Union and China were transformed from full allies into partial adversaries and potential enemies. Conflict-and-cooperation were to characterize their relationship as well, with the center of gravity shifting from cooperation toward conflict. The escalation of the Vietnam war, instead of increasing cooperation between them, actually reduced it even further.

From the Chinese point of view, the test-ban treaty and its implications brought about a virtual reversal of alliances. This observation, a typical Peking exaggeration, appears valid as a statement of Chinese expectations, if not fact:

> The leaders of the CPSU have completely reversed enemies and comrades. . . . The leaders of the CPSU are bent on seeking Soviet-United States cooperation for the domination of the world. They regard United States imperialism, the most ferocious enemy of the people in the world, as their most reliable friend, and they treat the fraternal parties and countries adhering to Marxism-Leninism as their enemy. They collude with United States imperialism, the reactionaries of various countries, the renegade Tito clique and the right-wing Social Democrats in a partnership against the socialist fraternal countries. When they snatch at a straw from Eisenhower or Kennedy or others like them, or think that things are going smoothly for them, the leaders of the CPSU are beside themselves with joy, hit out wildly at the fraternal parties and countries adhering to Marxism-Leninism, and endeavor to sacrifice fraternal parties and countries on the altar of their political dealings with United States imperialism.[3]

[3] *Hung Chi*, editorial, February 6, 1964; translated in *The New York Times*, February 7, 1964.

Strangely enough, the new Soviet and Chinese images of world realignments held much in common. Essentially extra-Marxist, these revised images of world realignments in effect abandoned the canons of class analysis. Instead of a world divided into peace-loving Communist states and warlike imperialist countries with a broad belt of non-aligned states in between, Moscow now perceived the world as being divided into peace-loving states and social forces, on the one hand, and warlike states and social forces, on the other. Some sectors of the imperialist "ruling classes" were numbered among the peace battalions, while some Communist states and Parties were consigned to the warlike forces. The peace-loving forces were united in singling out the avoidance of thermonuclear war as their overriding objective; they enthusiastically embraced the test-ban treaty and were opposed to the dissemination of nuclear weapons and the proliferation of nuclear powers. Acceptance of the test-ban treaty, in the Soviet view, became the litmus test of peace-loving tendencies.

Peking divided the world into nuclear and non-nuclear powers, irrespective of ideology or social systems. It saw the struggle as one between those who wanted to preserve their monopoly over nuclear weapons and those who wanted to break it. Whereas Moscow argued that proliferation was against the best interests of the "socialist camp" and would increase the possibility of war, the Chinese retorted that the capitalists already had a clear numerical advantage in nuclear weapons and that non-proliferation would freeze the West's advantage.

Concealed in all the verbiage was the implicit Chinese charge that a freeze of the thermonuclear status quo would give the white and developed countries a monopoly on nuclear weapons, which would continue to ensure their domination over the non-white, underdeveloped nations of Asia, Africa, and Latin America, who would be denied nuclear weapons. That the Soviet Union was a Communist country was less significant in this connection than the fact that it was European, "white," and developed. It could not be assumed that Soviet interests and those of the underdeveloped countries, including China, were congruent. The Soviet claim that China and other countries could rely upon Soviet nuclear might in defense and promotion of their interests was viewed by Peking as amounting to an intolerable dependence upon the Soviet Union, which meant that in return for Soviet nuclear protection other countries would have to tailor their interests to coincide with those of the Soviet Union and thus become its dependent appendages.

When one slices through all of the invective, esoteric jargon, and self-serving rhetoric of the Sino-Soviet dispute, what emerges are two variants of the classic image of a world divided into revisionist[4] and status quo forces, with the Chinese enrolled among the revisionist forces and Moscow associated with those of the status quo. A principal objective of the test-ban treaty for the Soviet Union was to deny the forces of

[4] The reference to "revisionism" here and hereinafter does *not* imply use of this label in its specific Marxist-Leninist connotation, i.e., "rightist" deviation.

revisionism access to nuclear weapons. From Moscow's perspective, the threat came from those who wanted to alter the international status quo through resort to war, if necessary. These included both revolutionary and reactionary opponents of the status quo. Moscow considered both equally dangerous to Soviet interests. They included West German "revanchists," "madmen" in the United States, the Chinese Communist leadership, and the Parties that followed the Chinese lead.[5]

The Soviet leaders correctly perceived that the Soviet Union was the main target of all these forces, East and West, Communist and non-Communist. And although the Soviet Union had only recently been the most revolutionary center in the world, its leaders were realistic enough to understand that revolutionary revisionism was likely to provoke counterrevolutionary revisionism and that, on balance, this would be detrimental to Soviet interests.

The Cuban missile debacle apparently convinced Khrushchev that Soviet interests could best be served by pursuing an essentially status quo foreign policy with residual traces of political and ideological revisionism. Soviet national and territorial objectives were largely satisfied, and Moscow found the existing distribution of power at least tolerable if not enthusiastically acceptable. This was particularly true with respect to the division of Europe, where the juridical status of East Germany and West Berlin constituted the only areas of concern and anxiety. Moscow's European allies were similarly inclined toward the status quo.

The nuclear test-ban treaty highlighted the transition of the Soviet Union from revolutionary global power to a mature state whose national goals have been largely satisfied and whose ideological goals have been largely eroded. The erosion of the Soviet commitment to violence and world revolution reflects the growing maturity of the Soviet Union and further signifies that the manipulation of a world revolutionary movement is no longer either indispensable or perhaps even desirable as an instrument of Soviet policy or purpose.

Khrushchev's repeated call for an international treaty outlawing the use of force in the settlement of territorial questions was a reflection of Moscow's relative satisfaction with the territorial status quo, while the Soviet signature on the test-ban treaty reflects Moscow's relative satisfaction with its status as the second of two global nuclear powers. Content with her state frontiers, equipped with a powerful arsenal of nuclear weapons, and surrounded with a retinue of client states in Eastern Europe, the Soviet Union remains revisionist only in the ideological sense. Ideology has become increasingly ritualistic as Moscow's passion to preserve national gains exceeds its passion to achieve ideological objectives.

Verbally, of course, the Soviet leaders deny that they have become partisans of the status quo, as Khrushchev did in December, 1963:

> No Marxist-Leninist ever interpreted peaceful coexistence of countries with different social systems as preservation of the *status quo*, as a sort

[5] *Pravda*, August 5, 1963.

of truce with imperialism, as a "safe conduct" against revolutionary processes of national and social liberation. No one applies this principle to the relations between imperialism and oppressed peoples, since the principle of coexistence by no means places a "veto" on the struggle of these peoples.[6]

But, contrary to Soviet expressions of intent, Soviet behavior and the objective consequences of Soviet policy unmistakably stamp the status quo character of her foreign policy, as the Chinese have correctly assessed.

What remains of Soviet ideological revisionism continues to be blunted for the following reasons: (1) It tends to stimulate ideological counter-revisionism in the United States, which manifests itself among the "madmen" who demand a foreign policy of "roll-back," "liberation," "export of counterrevolution," and "atomic blackmail." (2) It has a tendency to revive and reinforce all other proponents of violent change, especially in West Germany and Japan. Both countries have national claims against the Soviet Union and its client states. As the country most vulnerable to territorial revisionism, Moscow has a conspicuous interest in stifling territorial revisionism in general. (3) Soviet revisionism sustains and reinforces Chinese national and ideological revisionism, which is aimed in large part against the Soviet Union itself.

The Condominium Approach

Khrushchev's détente strategy assumed the faint but definite contours of a Soviet-American condominium, or dyarchy, in the international community, whereby the two super-powers would demarcate their respective areas of vital interest, define their area of common interest, delineate the status quo to be preserved, and establish the guidelines which would govern their competition in areas peripheral to their vital interests. Khrushchev came to believe that no problem of international relations could resist the imposition of a joint Soviet-American solution. Such a condominium would, in effect, ensure American non-intervention in areas of Soviet vital interests and Soviet non-intervention in areas of American vital interests. Thus Khrushchev had on various occasions stressed that "history has imposed upon our two peoples a great responsibility for the destiny of the world," and that as regards the two countries, "our interests do not clash directly anywhere, either territorially or economically."[7]

This approach was most pungently described by Peking with its customary self-serving rhetoric of exaggeration, but it was also discernible in the speeches of Soviet statesmen and in Soviet writings. It finds reflection in two Soviet books published in 1965, *The Motive Forces of U.S. Foreign Policy* and *The U.S.S.R. and the U.S.A. — Their Political and Economic Relations.* Accordingly, the two books were pounced upon by Chinese critics as ample confirmation that the policy

[6] *Pravda,* December 22, 1963.
[7] *Pravda,* December 31, 1961.

of the Brezhnev-Ko.ygin regime was indistinguishable from that of its predecessor. According to an official Chinese review, the first book

> . . . proclaims that "Soviet-American relations, the relations between the two greatest powers in the world, constitute the axis of world politics, the main foundation of international peace." Using the words of U.S. Secretary of State Rusk, it preaches that "the two great powers — the USSR and the U.S.A. — bear special responsibility for the destiny of the world and of mankind." It says that the Soviet Union "strives for peace and cooperation with the United States, realizing that Soviet-American relations are the primary thing in contemporary world politics and in the question of war or peace. . . ." The book stresses that an "extremely important feature in Soviet-American relations" is the so-called "community of national interests of the two countries." It says, "Except for the black spot — the U.S. participation in the military intervention against Soviet Russia from 1918 to 1920 — Russian-American and Soviet-American relations have not been clouded by any military conflicts or wars." "At the present time, too, no territorial or economic disputes or conflicts exist between the two countries, and their national interests do not clash either on a world scale or on any regional scale."[8]

Hence, *Hung Chi* correctly noted, Moscow and Washington can shift the competitive aspects of their relations to the periphery of their vital interests:

> The book asserts that provided there is "peaceful coexistence" between the Soviet Union and the United States, "the competition between the two socio-economic systems and the ideological struggle between the two main antagonists on the international arena will proceed within the confines of broad economic, diplomatic, scientific, and cultural competition and cooperation, without sanguinary collisions and wars."[9]

Khrushchev's détente strategy was thus based upon two assumptions:

1. The Kennedy Administration represented the "sober" forces in the American "ruling class," who perceived a détente with Moscow to be in their self-interest and thus could be "trusted."
2. The United States could speak for the entire West, and thus the détente would assume the configuration of an international condominium between the two major world powers.

As a consequence of the "condominium" Moscow appeared to harbor several expectations:

1. The Soviet Union and the United States together would retain overwhelming nuclear superiority and thus be able jointly to enforce the peace.

---

[8] "Confessions Concerning the Line of Soviet-U.S. Collaboration Pursued by the New Leaders of the CPSU [*Hung Chi*, editorial, February 11, 1966]" (Peking, Foreign Language Press, 1966), pp. 3–4.

[9] Ibid., p. 3.

2. Japan and Germany would be prohibited from acquiring nuclear weapons and their revisionist ambitions blocked by joint Soviet-American action.
3. The nuclear development of France and China would be considerably inhibited and retarded.
4. China's expansionist aspirations would be contained and blocked by the United States with the tacit support of the Soviet Union.
5. The "madmen" in the United States would be isolated and kept out of power.
6. A general relaxation of international tensions would ensue, which would undercut the attractiveness of the appeals for more aggressive action. Without a Soviet "threat," Khrushchev reasoned, internal social revolution in various parts of the world would no longer be perceived as a threat by the United States.
7. A rapid growth in Soviet economic development would take place with a corresponding rise in the standard of living.

Deficiencies in Khrushchev's Policy

The entire structure of Khrushchev's détente strategy rested upon the assumption that the Kennedy Administration represented the "sober" forces in the United States and that they would continue to determine American policy. This strategy implicitly posed a serious threat to the social position, role, and interests of powerful socio-institutional groups in the Soviet Union, like the Party apparatus, heavy-industrial managers, and the traditional military. Instead of executing his détente policy so that their interests might be painlessly accommodated, Khrushchev brusquely attempted an "end run" by appealing to other constituencies whose interests would be enhanced by his policy. Khrushchev's strategy and behavior also exposed the Soviet Union to new diplomatic and security vulnerabilities. This, too, contributed to a tactical agreement between Khrushchev's associates and his opposition. His opportunistic behavior in going outside the normal arena of Soviet politics, together with his capricious judgments, frightened his own partisans. Khrushchev's policies threatened the interests of his factional opposition; his behavior alienated his own faction. These currents merged to topple him in October, 1964.

It remains a matter of speculation to what extent the background of his ouster included the concern of the Soviet elite that Khrushchev's détente policy threatened to expose the Soviet Union to new vulnerabilities. To some of Khrushchev's colleagues it may have appeared that the Soviet Union was being cleverly encircled by shrewd American diplomacy, aided by an inept and over-zealous Khrushchev, who had not adequately covered either his eastern or his western flank. The cutting edge of Peking's revisionist aspirations was now being turned against the Soviet Union in revenge, without any assurance of a restraining influence by the United States at a time when West Germany's revisionist edge had not yet been blunted. In August, 1964, for example,

Mao Tse-tung virtually invited Japan, East Germany, Poland, Rumania, and Finland to join Peking in dismembering the Soviet Union:

> There are too many places occupied by the Soviet Union. In correspondence with the Yalta agreement, the Soviet Union, under the pretext of guaranteeing the independence of Mongolia, actually put that country under its rule. . . . In 1954, when Khrushchev and Bulganin arrived in China, we raised this question, but they refused to talk with us. They have appropriated part of Rumania. Detaching part of East Germany, they drove out the local inhabitants to the Western area. Detaching part of Poland, they included it in Russia and as compensation gave Poland part of East Germany. The same thing happened to Finland. They detached everything that could be detached. Some people have said that Sinkiang Province and the territory to the north of the Amur River must be included in the Soviet Union. The USSR is concentrating troops on its borders.[10]

Khrushchev, in effect, was relying for Soviet security upon the uncertain good will of the Kennedy Administration and upon the even more dubious trust of his successor, who was an unknown quantity.

Anxieties and Uncertainties

Against this background of Soviet anxiety and uncertainty concerning Khrushchev's possible misperceptions of the Kennedy Administration's intentions and his possible miscalculation of the magnitude of the common interest between Moscow and Washington, the assassination of President Kennedy could only intensify these apprehensions. Now the Soviet leaders were seriously in danger of being victimized by their own fantasies about "ultras," "extremists," and "madmen."

Deciphering Kennedy's motives and intentions was difficult and treacherous enough, but their initial doubts about Kennedy had been dispelled in the minds of the Khrushchev faction after 1,000 days of dealing with him. Besides, Khrushchev and Kennedy had experienced a number of harrowing crises together, and a certain mutual respect had developed between the two men, so that an element of "trust" in their relations was conceivable. In short, Kennedy was a known quantity to Khrushchev, whose strategy rested upon the conviction that this known quantity would continue in power through 1972. Actually, Khrushchev's policies were based upon a virtually pre-determined assumption that the "sober" group would continue to prevail through any administration.

During the first six months of the Johnson Administration, the Soviet leadership remained non-committal about the character of the Johnson presidency. It was obvious that the Soviet leadership was concerned lest the delicate balance of forces which it detected in the American leadership be upset in favor of the "ultras," whose activities and views were given increasing prominence in the Soviet press.

These doubts and uncertainties continued into the months of the United States election campaign of 1964. If Lyndon B. Johnson was re-

[10] *Pravda*, September 2, 1964.

elected, Soviet observers seem to have reasoned, the uncertainty would continue; if Barry Goldwater were to become president, all of Khrushchev's assumptions and expectations would be shattered beyond repair.

The tendency of Khrushchev to accept Johnson as a spokesman for the "sober" group in America probably not only alarmed his conservative detractors, who had never accepted his perception of an American "ruling class" divided into "sober" and "mad" groups, and the traditional military (such as Marshal Rodion Malinovsky), who shared an image of the United States with the conservatives, but also frightened his own factional associates as well, who viewed his clumsy and capricious style with apprehension.

Khrushchev's ouster thus came hard on the heels of a number of events which pointed toward crises in Sino-Soviet and Soviet-American relations. What their relevance was can only be surmised. At any rate, the displacement of Khrushchev did not resolve Soviet doubts or end Soviet backstage debate about the entire détente policy.

SOVIET DIPLOMATIC STRATEGY AFTER KHRUSHCHEV

Unlike Khrushchev, the new Brezhnev-Kosygin team was probably prepared for any contingency which might develop as a result of the American election, ready to plug the gaps in Khrushchev's détente strategy if the détente policy continued, and also amenable to try a new approach to Peking.

The Soviet Image of the Johnson Administration[11]

For more than three years the Brezhnev-Kosygin team has been taking its measure of the Johnson Administration, and while the latter has not been consigned to the "mad" category (this would have generated irreversible and highly unpalatable implications for Soviet policy and behavior), neither has it been classified as "sober." The doubts and uncertainties about the Johnson Administration persist in Moscow and probably find expression in different ways among various Soviet leaders. Although voices uttering different views are periodically heard in the Soviet press, the dominant view in official Moscow is evidently that the Administration is subject to pressures from both "doves" and "hawks," and this accounts for the vacillation in its policies and behavior. It is noteworthy, however, that Anastas Mikoyan, once the most outspoken advocate of the view that Washington is dominated by "sober" men, was dropped from the new team, perhaps as being too committed to the Khrushchev line.

The image of the Johnson Administration held by the Brezhnev-Kosygin regime is not identical with Khrushchev's image under Kennedy. Whereas Kennedy was perceived as a representative of the "sober" forces in the American "ruling class," Johnson has not been viewed as a member of this group. Voices are still to be heard which seem to assign

[11] See also Alexander Dallin and Thomas B. Larson, eds., *Soviet Politics since Khrushchev* (Englewood Cliffs, N.J., Prentice-Hall, 1968), Chapter 7.

Johnson to the "sober" camp, while others consign him to a more "bellicose" or "aggressive" wing; still others emphasize that he tries to satisfy both groups and thus vacillates in his own posture.

In May, 1965, after the Administration had involved itself more deeply in the Vietnam war, Brezhnev charged that Johnson had betrayed the American public (and, in effect, double-crossed the Soviet leaders) by contravening his campaign promises. President Johnson, he charged, had campaigned "under the slogan of allegiance to peace and fidelity to the traditions of Franklin Roosevelt," and the American voters,

> aware of the catastrophe a world war would mean for the United States in today's conditions, put their trust in the politician [Johnson] who in campaign speeches had spoken out for peace and a realistic approach to international problems.[12]

The following month, Premier Kosygin bluntly charged:

> The government of the United States is in essence pursuing the foreign-policy line proposed by Goldwater at the time of the elections but rejected by the American people. It is carrying out an aggressive policy directed against the countries of socialism, against the states that have liberated themselves from colonial domination, against the revolutionary movement of the peoples.[13]

Moscow's perceptions of the Johnson Administration are also shaped by its view of Chinese intent and behavior, and while it may still have doubts about Johnson, it seems to have none with respect to Mao Tse-tung. Indeed, it has blamed the Chinese leader for discouraging a Vietnamese settlement in the hope that a prolongation of the conflict would inevitably force a confrontation between Moscow and Washington, which the existing regime fervently seeks to avoid. Thus, in a letter circulated among friendly Communist Parties, dated February 23, 1966, the Soviet leaders alleged:

> . . . the Chinese leaders need a lengthy Vietnam war to maintain international tensions, to represent China as a "besieged fortress." There is every reason to assert that it is one of the goals of the policy of the Chinese leadership in the Vietnam question to promote a military conflict between the USSR and the United States. They want a clash of the USSR with the United States so that they may, as they say themselves, "sit on the mountain and watch the fight of the tigers." New facts constantly prove the readiness of the Chinese leaders to sacrifice the interests of the national liberation movement to their chauvinist big-power plans.[14]

For their part, the Chinese retorted that the new leaders were plotting with the United States to encircle China:

> You have worked hand in glove with the United States in a whole series of dirty deals inside and outside the United Nations. In close

[12] *Pravda*, May 9, 1965.
[13] *Pravda*, June 19, 1965.
[14] *The New York Times*, March 24, 1966.

coordination with the counterrevolutionary "global strategy" of United States imperialism, you are now actively trying to build a ring of encirclement around socialist China. Not only have you excluded yourselves from the international united front of all the peoples against United States imperialism and its lackeys, you have even aligned yourselves with United States imperialism, the main enemy of the peoples of the world, and established a holy alliance against China, against the movement, and against the Marxist-Leninists.[15]

In spite of all, the dominant view in Moscow has been that the "sober" groups would ultimately prevail, particularly if the Vietnamese war is settled, since this is presumed to be the main inspiration of the more aggressive forces in American society.

The contrast between the cautious, prudent, and restrained style and tempo of the Brezhnev-Kosygin foreign policy and the ebullient, highly idiosyncratic style of the Khrushchev era, with its exercises in adventurism, bluffing, and vulgarity, should not obscure some essential continuities between the two foreign-policy lines. The two sets of policies share a common point of departure in pursuit of a common goal but differ in methods and strategies.

One conspicuous departure from the Khrushchev policy was a determined attempt to heal the rift with China, which was made promptly after Khrushchev's ouster and permitted to linger for over a year. Another was to reassert the Soviet presence in Vietnam, and a third but less obvious departure was a new approach to the West designed to provide greater security against Germany. None of these departures signified a shift away from the top priority item in Soviet foreign policy — the avoidance of thermonuclear war with the United States — but rather suggested that the leadership thought the new approaches need not be incompatible with a Soviet-American rapprochement.

The Brezhnev-Kosygin Strategy: Double Encirclement

The retirement of Khrushchev did not solve Moscow's problems of West Germany and China, which the new regime inherited from its predecessor, but it did set the stage for a fresh review and re-examination of policy. The new leaders were certainly aware that West Germany and China were problems which transcended personalities, systems, and ideologies. Moreover, the two countries pose different problems for Moscow. China has already reasserted itself and has successfully rebuffed Soviet hegemonial ambitions in the Far East and established an effective barrier to any further expansion of Russian power southward. Germany, on the other hand, remains divided and thus constitutes as yet only a potential threat to the eroding hegemonial position of Moscow in East Central Europe, either because West Germany might become an instrument of American policy against the Soviet Union or because, under certain circumstances, West Germany might be able to involve

---

[15] Chinese reply to the Soviet invitation to send a delegation to the XXIII Congress of the CPSU, in *The New York Times*, March 24, 1966.

the United States in a war with Moscow in pursuit of her own aspirations.

Moscow perceives of the German threat as real but *potential* or *latent*, and Soviet policy is designed to prevent its development, whereas the Chinese threat is viewed as much more immediate and ominous.

In the Far East, the Soviet Union has envisaged the United States as a partner in the encirclement and containment of China and thus, with some reservations, desires a United States presence in that area. On the other hand, in Europe the United States is viewed as the chief bulwark of West Germany and the main source of her power and influence.

While the détente with the United States established an over-all strategic balance between the Communist and non-Communist worlds and minimized the threat of direct confrontation and possible annihilation, it also diminished the need for bloc unity and afforded individual member-states the luxury of allowing their submerged and latent local and national grievances against one another (inside and outside blocs) to surface. This serves to create instability on the periphery of both power-blocs and disturbs the equilibrium, which was artificially frozen by the bi-polarization of power after World War II.

It is the threat to local balances on the eastern and western marches of the Soviet Union that has agitated the new regime in Moscow. Moscow has sought to maintain the status quo in the West by restructuring a new configuration in the local balance of power, while in the East it has sought to preserve the status quo by maintaining the existing balance of forces.

Isolation and Containment of China

Whereas the United States may have embarrassed, alarmed, and humiliated the Soviet leadership by its conduct in Vietnam, it poses no threat to the Soviet Union; nor does it aim to upset the status quo in the Communist world. The Chinese leaders, on the other hand, seek to overturn the present leadership of the Soviet Union and have hinted that they might even resort to force to redeem China's "lost" lands now "occupied" by the Soviet Union. Thus, on February 23, 1966, the CPSU informed other Communist Parties that Peking was even contemplating war:

> The idea is obstinately being suggested to the Chinese people that it is necessary to prepare for a military conflict with the USSR. The CPSU Central Committee has already informed the fraternal parties that the Chinese side is provoking border conflicts. Such conflics have again increased in recent months. . . . At the same time, allegations are being spread to the effect that the Soviet Union unlawfully holds Chinese territory in the Far East. The official Chinese representative in the bilateral consultations on border questions threatened directly that the CPR authorities would consider "other ways" of settling the territorial question and stated: "It is not out of the question that we will try to restore historical rights." But the CPR has no "historical rights." The

territories of which the CCP leadership now talks have never belonged to China.[16]

The recrudescence of Chinese expansionist ambitions has left the Soviet Union little choice but to pursue a policy of isolating, encircling, and containing China. The efforts, immediately after the ouster of Khrushchev, to heal the rift with Peking were to no avail.

> Since the Plenum of October, 1964, the CPSU Central Committee has done everything possible to normalize relations with the CCP and to insure unity of action in the struggle against the common imperialist enemy despite existing differences of view. In this connection we considered the fact that the interests of the Socialist camp and of the entire Communist movement will suffer from the continued differences of view.[17]

Moscow views the United States as its main partner in the encirclement and containment of China, with India and Indonesia playing subsidiary roles.

The United States has always subscribed to an "Open Door" policy in the Orient. The policy implies a door open to all outsiders, not only the United States, since several outside powers are necessary to ensure their presence and are thus mutually reinforcing. The presence of peripheral powers serves to displace a hegemonial equilibrium with a balance of power involving several actors. As a corollary to the "Open Door" policy, the United States, since 1905, has encouraged Russian presence in the area as a counterpoise to Japanese ambitions, and after the Bolshevik Revolution, when a power vacuum developed in the Russian Far East, it was the presence of United States troops and American insistence on the territorial integrity of Russia which deterred the Japanese from detaching the Russian Far East in one form or another, thus allowing the bogus Far Eastern Republic to be reabsorbed into the Soviet state. Moscow is also not unmindful of the fact that Japan's attack upon Manchuria and her further ambitions in the area were instrumental in the recognition of the Soviet Union by the Roosevelt Administration.

Historically, the presence of both the United States and Russia in the Far East has been mutually reinforcing. Russian and American interests have come into direct conflict in the Far East only when the indigenous powers have been weakened by internal strife or defeat in war. This was the case after World War II when the defeat of Japan created a power vacuum which could not be filled by a weakened and divided China and thus led to a direct confrontation between Moscow and Washington, and the two indigenous powers of the region, China and Japan, temporarily became instruments of Soviet and American policy respectively.

The reassertion of China's bid for hegemony in the Far East thus once again endangers the interests of both the United States and the Soviet Union, as they interpret them, just as Japan's challenge did in

[16] *The New York Times*, March 24, 1966.
[17] Ibid.

1931. Since Peking has publicly repudiated Moscow's claim to being an Asian power and has declared the Soviet Union to be a European power "in Asia," the Soviet leaders are under no illusions concerning Peking's conception of the role Moscow is to assume in Asian affairs. Furthermore, the Chinese have claimed virtually the entire Soviet Far East including the Maritime Province (with Vladivostok). Similarly, Peking is determined to drive American power and influence out of the Far East and thus slam the door against both Moscow and Washington, the two remaining foreign "imperialist" powers in East Asia.

Khrushchev's downfall provided an occasion for Moscow to review its relations with China and its Far Eastern policy in general. Essentially, this led to two departures from Khrushchev's policy. The first was a decision to attempt once again to arrest the deterioration in Sino-Soviet relations. The second was to reassert Soviet interest in Southeast Asia and restore Soviet influence and involvement in Vietnam. Khrushchev had virtually dissociated Moscow from Southeast Asia, fatalistically abandoning the area during the Sino-Soviet conflict, assuming that both race and geography favored the Chinese. The escalation of the war and American bombardment of North Vietnam, however, confronted Moscow with serious problems involving the prestige and credibility of the Soviet Union's obligation to defend all socialist states from attack — a commitment which was first made in 1960 (and repeated thereafter):

> Today the whole world has had an opportunity to receive assurance that anyone who dares to encroach upon the inviolability of the Soviet Union's borders, as well as those of other socialist countries, will receive a crushing rebuff. The Warsaw Treaty Organization is based on the principle of "all for one and one for all." The Soviet government has frequently stated that the borders of all its true friends — the socialist countries — will be defended by the Soviet Union exactly as if they were its own borders. This is how we understand proletarian internationalism and this is how all the peoples of the socialist countries understand it.[18]

Apparently Khrushchev had been unwilling to make even a gesture which would have satisfied the formalities of Moscow's existing obligations toward North Vietnam. The Soviet Union was in danger of becoming an object of ridicule, some Soviet officials held, and the credibility of its commitments was subject to serious erosion.

The reassertion of Soviet influence in Southeast Asia was designed to serve four objectives:

1. To reassert the credibility of the Soviet promise and ability to protect its allies against American power;
2. To find a common ground for a rapprochement with China, whose joint support of North Vietnam would maximize chances for a settlement;
3. To re-establish a measure of control over a situation which might conceivably involve the Soviet Union in another confrontation with the United States, which Moscow avidly sought to avoid; and

[18] *Pravda,* May 14, 1960.

4. To be in a position to influence a settlement of the Vietnamese conflict which would not subvert the détente with the United States.

The second and fourth objectives were and are incompatible, but apparently the Brezhnev-Kosygin regime thought that a reconciliation with China and a détente with the United States were possible simultaneously, provided Moscow approached the whole problem in a different way — or at least acted as if no choice between these orientations needed to be made.

An Olive Branch to China Rebuffed

The Soviet approach to Peking was apparently based upon the conviction that the Sino-Soviet dispute had been exacerbated by the personality conflict between Mao and Khrushchev and hence was irreconcilable while both remained in authority. The Brezhnev-Kosygin regime may have felt obliged to explore whether Peking was prepared to find a face-saving formula to heal the split. But, according to Moscow's later review of its efforts to heal the breach, Peking rebuffed every Soviet overture:

> We submitted an extensive program for normalizing Chinese-Soviet relations at both the Party and the state level. This program included proposals on implementing bilateral meetings of delegations of the CPSU and the CCP on the highest level, on the mutual discontinuation of polemics, concrete proposals on extending Chinese-Soviet trade and scientific, technical and cultural cooperation, and on coordinating the foreign policy activities of the CPR and USSR.[19]

The Chinese, for their part, revealed that they had obstinately attempted to impose their views upon the new Soviet leaders and extract a confession of "repentance" which they must have known was unacceptable:

> Since Khrushchev's downfall, we have advised the new leaders of the CPSU on a number of occasions to make a fresh start. We have done everything we could but you have not shown the slightest repentance. Since coming to power, the new leaders of the CPSU have gone farther and farther down the road of revisionism, splittism and great-power chauvinism. The moment you came to power, you declared that you would resolutely carry out the Khrushchev revisionist general line of the XX and XXII Congresses. You told us to our faces that there was not a shade of difference between Khrushchev and yourself on the question of the international Communist movement or of relations with China.[20]

In Search of a Vietnamese Settlement

Khrushchev had disassociated Moscow from the Vietnam war except in the most perfunctory way. In his speech of January 6, 1961, he conspicuously failed to classify the Vietcong uprising as a "just" war,

[19] *The New York Times,* March 24, 1966.
[20] Ibid.

although the Vietminh war against the French was so categorized and described as successful and terminal. Khrushchev's lack of interest in the Vietnam war probably stemmed from a desire to avoid a possible confrontation with the United States in Southeast Asia and perhaps also from a belief that Hanoi would ultimately cast its lot with Peking.

Moscow may have perceived in the American escalation of the war in Vietnam an opportunity to facilitate simultaneously a reconciliation with Peking and also a détente with the United States. But Peking was not interested in settling the war, even on Hanoi's terms, since from the Chinese perspective a Vietnamese settlement would clear the way for a full resumption of the Soviet-American détente. As a consequence North Vietnam was caught in the Sino-Soviet crossfire while being pounded by the United States.

The Vietnam war impaled the Soviet leaders on the horns of a painful dilemma. By restoring the Soviet presence in Hanoi, Khrushchev's successors hoped to regain a measure of control and influence over a matter vitally affecting their interests elsewhere, but they simultaneously incurred the risk that failure to achieve a settlement could only worsen relations with Hanoi, Peking, and Washington.

Soviet exploration of a reconciliation with China thus did not necessarily signify an intention to repudiate its détente policy, but rather a drive to minimize sources of friction in its foreign relations. Unlike previous Soviet regimes, which frequently perceived opportunities to muddy international waters and were interested in sustaining a degree of tension on the international scene, the Brezhnev-Kosygin team has shown a passion for tension reduction and interest in international stability. The Tashkent settlement between India and Pakistan, engineered by Kosygin, is indicative of this reorientation in Soviet policy.

In retrospect, Khrushchev's judgment that Soviet and Chinese interests and objectives were incompatible appears to have been valid, especially after Mao's startling and gratuitous claim to some 500,000 squares miles of Soviet territory in the summer of 1964. While Khrushchev had apparently judged the Chinese situation well if not wisely, the abortive attempt of his successors to heel the rupture was not without its compensations. The basic miscalculation of the Brezhnev-Kosygin team was the obverse of the fundamental correctness of Khrushchev's judgment. As long as avoidance of thermonuclear war remained the top priority item in Soviet foreign policy, Soviet and Chinese interests were bound to collide. China's price for a reconciliation was a complete repudiation and reversal of Soviet policy, including a repudiation of the resolutions of the XX, XXI and XXII Party Congresses. This Moscow was not willing to do. Thus, before the end of 1965, Sino-Soviet polemics were resumed in more aggravated form and were further exacerbated the following year by the sharp factional conflict which broke out in Peking.

What the new team in Moscow managed to convey in the process of dealing with Peking was a novel posture of sensitivity, moderation, and rationality, in contrast to Peking's obstinacy, dogmatism, and rigidity. This served further to isolate China in the Communist world. But Moscow's sobering experience with the Chinese could not but impel it to reintensify the uneasy search for a détente with the United States, made both more urgent and more difficult by the continuing conflict in Vietnam.

Soviet Policy in the West

If it is a major Soviet objective to contain China in the East, a major goal of its diplomacy in the West is to forge a preventive containment of West Germany. But whereas the American presence is necessary in the Far East to encircle China, Moscow views the American presence in Europe as an obstacle to its policy with respect to the German Federal Republic.

Hence, current Soviet policy in the West is designed to eject the United States from Europe, not so much to weaken the United States or to make West Germany more vulnerable (although these are subsidiary objectives) as to remove the protective umbrella of American power under which West Germany might develop into a major military power in her own right. Soviet leaders have viewed with increasing concern the steady rise in West Germany's power and influence. Especially since France's virtual defection, they have claimed to perceive an evolving Washington-Bonn axis within NATO, which might develop a momentum of its own. They see three possible dangers which might develop: (1) the United States might choose to permit the full revival of German military power as a bulwark against the East; (2) West Germany might, in pursuit of her own revisionist ambitions, set into motion a chain of events which would involve the United States and the Soviet Union in war; (3) West German power might evolve to the point where, if it decides to assert an independent policy and chart its own course, its containment by the United States would require measures which Washington might choose not to invoke.

It is the third possibility which has probably disturbed the Soviet leaders most. Just as China managed to develop its power under the umbrella of Soviet protection and then declared its independence of Soviet policy, Moscow sees the real possibility of a similar performance by West Germany. The sudden outburst in West Germany of vehement opposition to a nuclear non-proliferation treaty during Kosygin's visit to Britain in 1967 surprised many in the West and could only reinforce the Soviet conviction that influential forces in West Germany secretly harbor a lust for nuclear weapons.

Moscow seeks to ease the United States out of Europe so as to deprive West Germany of its protective umbrella, which would clear the way for Moscow to devise new arrangements to ensure the maintenance of the status quo in Europe. It would, of course, also create other opportunities for Soviet diplomacy, giving Moscow greater flexibility in pursuing whatever objectives it might choose in Western Europe.

While the Soviet approach to China proved abortive, the new approach to the West has been bearing fruit. Khrushchev may have

perceived that the Soviet Union could hardly expect American cooperation in an encirclement and containment of Germany, and during his
last few months in power rumors were rampant that he was planning a
deal with West Germany at East Germany's expense. If this was so, the
new regime reversed this strategy almost immediately, and all talk
about a special deal with West Germany in exchange for generous lines
of credit and other concessions suddenly ceased. Just as Washington's
approach to Eastern Europe aims to isolate East Germany, the Brezhnev-
Kosygin approach to Western Europe is designed to isolate and encircle
West Germany. Instead of relying on the condominium approach, the
new strategy is to deal with Great Britain and France individually, on
the assumption that their interests *vis-à-vis* West Germany are different
from those of the United States.

Khrushchev's successors perceived that Moscow's willingness to
pursue a détente with the United States enabled London and Paris to
resume an autonomous foreign policy. Once the Soviet threat was lifted,
London and Paris could pursue policies independent of the United
States. Since the American presence in Europe not only shielded Western Europe from Soviet power but also implicitly served to protect
Britain and France from a possible German revival, a withdrawal of the
United States from Europe on the basis of a détente with Moscow would
remove the main restraining influence on German power.

With respect to Germany, the Brezhnev-Kosygin regime thus perceives a common interest between Moscow, on the one hand, and
London and Paris, on the other, which is not shared by the United
States. Moscow's approach signifies a subtle bid to establish an informal
containment of Germany as a part of the crypto-entente arrangement
with those two countries. Such an encirclement would be reliable
because it would rest upon the self-interest of the three countries. It
cannot be said that London and Paris were totally unresponsive to these
subtle overtures.

The multi-pronged Soviet approach is thus designed not so much to
divide Western Europe and open it to Soviet penetration, but rather to
protect Moscow's western flank at a time when the main danger appears
on the eastern horizon. While it cannot rely upon the self-interest of the
United States to contain and limit German power, it can rely upon
British and French self-interest to resist the revival of German power.

It should be noted that, while it may not be the intention of the
regime in Moscow to weaken the West by this strategy in order to make
it vulnerable to Soviet attack or penetration, objectively it does expose
the three countries to potential hazards, should the intentions of the
regime change, or should a new militant faction come to power in
Moscow, or should the present strategic balance change radically in
favor of the Soviet Union.

As long as the threat from Moscow was more immediate and real
than the threat from Germany, the United States, according to the
Soviet view, could impose an ideologically-inspired policy upon the West
as a whole, subsume the long-range German threat, and actually spon-

sor a partial revival of German military power. Once the Soviet threat was lifted, however, the Soviet leaders perceived that West Germany's growing power in NATO and America's increasing reliance upon Bonn as its chief ally in Europe posed a more immediate threat to London and Paris than did Moscow. This view has been outlined by a Polish international affairs expert in a leading Soviet journal:

> Up to the early 1960's, the United States as a rule managed to impose its own political ideas as regards Germany on the West European countries, although these, far from being enthusiastic, even objected to them. It was not until the balance of forces turned against the U.S.A. that the West European countries were able to pursue a more independent policy on the German question among others.[21]

With the United States out of Europe, West Germany's ambitions would be kept in check by the European status quo powers acting in concert. This is the main thrust of the periodic Soviet call for a conference on European security. Thus, in response to a question concerning the possible American participation in such a European security conference, Kosygin replied at his Paris press conference:

> In our opinion the countries of Europe would gather to discuss the situation on the European continent with the aim of easing tension and ensuring security in Europe. As to U.S. participation in this conference, it seems to me that this is a question that should be decided by the European countries themselves. When they do decide the question, you will receive an answer to it.[22]

At the same press conference, Kosygin lucidly described the status quo which Moscow seeks to preserve in Europe:

> I think the major contribution that the Federal Republic of Germany can make to the solution of the problem of European security is that it must have a clear and accurate conception of the situation in Europe, where two German states exist — the GDR [German Democratic Republic] and the FRG — and no forces from outside can change this situation. Any other judgments on this score are unrealistic. This is the first circumstance. The second is that the boundaries in Europe that were formed after World War II are inviolable. Moreover, West Germany must renounce forever any claims on nuclear weapons. If the FRG recognizes these circumstances, it will make a great contribution to the cause of easing tension in Europe and to the cause of ensuring European security.[23]

Khrushchev's successors do not perceive in de Gaulle's ambitions and anxieties the policies of a front man for nameless French extremists (which apparently was the view of Khrushchev). Rather they view de Gaulle's attitude toward the United States as reflecting a profound conflict over the future of Germany's role in Europe.

[21] L. Pastusiak, "Dangerous Bonn-Washington Deal," *International Affairs*, No. 7, July, 1966, p. 45.
[22] *Pravda*, December 5, 1966.
[23] Ibid.

De Gaulle's emphasis on the "grandeur" of France is perceived as symbolic of his intention to establish and preserve a clear and permanent position of military superiority *vis-à-vis* Germany, which de Gaulle views as France's eternal and natural rival for paramountcy in Western Europe.

> France's withdrawal from the NATO military structure has enabled her to regain freedom of action, which naturally strengthens her positions in the world arena. This step has also removed the danger of France being automatically involved in a world conflict against her free will which, in the nuclear age, would jeopardize the future of the entire country. . . .
>
> The Soviet Union has always emphasized France's rights as a world power particularly responsible for European security. Naturally, this attitude of the USSR makes it easier for France to defend her rights and interests in the world arena and, in particular, to rebuff the attempts of the United States and West Germany to dictate their will. It is no accident that de Gaulle wrote in his memoirs that the solidarity of the two countries "is in keeping with the natural state of affairs as regards both the German menace and the Anglo-Saxon desire for hegemony."[24]

The Franco-Soviet rapprochement is described in almost rhapsodic terms as not stemming from "temporary expediency," but as "a long-standing tradition to maintain mutual contacts and act jointly in politics,"[25] which is frankly put forward as nothing less than a policy of encircling Germany:

> . . . In these circumstances, the interests of the Soviet Union and France dictate the imperative need to join their efforts so as to prevent a dangerous source of tension in the center of Europe.
>
> Many commentators point out that the interests of the two countries coincide on such important problems of European security as preventing West Germany from gaining access to nuclear weapons and the inviolability of the existing frontiers.[26]

Britain's interest in isolating and encircling Germany is not viewed in Moscow as being as natural and durable as is the French interest. At times Britain has not been averse to a revival of German military power as a counterpoise to either Russia or France, or both. Furthermore, the Anglo-American relationship is viewed as more intimate and durable than the Franco-American relationship and hence less susceptible to subversion. Whereas French and American national interests may actually come into direct conflict over Germany, it is likely that Anglo-American problems will reflect themselves as differences over policy rather than as a conflict of national interests. Thus, while it is plausible for Moscow to believe that the American presence might be excluded

[24] Y. Nikolaev, "Soviet-French Relations — An Important Factor of World Politics," *International Affairs*, No. 12, December, 1966, p. 12.

[25] N. Yuriev, "Soviet-French Cooperation and European Security," *International Affairs*, No. 6, June, 1966, p. 7.

[26] Nikolaev, "Soviet-French Relations," p. 13.

from the continent, it is not likely that it can be expelled from the British Islands.

Nevertheless, the present Soviet leadership views the Wilson Government as at least partly amenable to its encirclement strategy, provided that it is muted and played in low key, recognizing that British policy with respect to Germany is based on fleeting expediency rather than a durable vital national interest as in the case of France.

The present Soviet leaders thus aim for a relationship with Great Britain and the strategic détente with the United States.

IMPLICATIONS OF CURRENT SOVIET DIPLOMACY

Khrushchev's détente policy and its implications for the world Communist movement emerge, in retrospect, not as simply reflections of his personal idiosyncrasies but as a realistic course corresponding to the vital interests of the Soviet Union as a global power. This policy could be executed within a different priority of internal interests (heavy industry over light, armaments over butter, etc.), carried out with greater or lesser flexibility, prosecuted with greater or lesser enthusiasm, implemented with more or less finesse, and compressed within the shell of a "harder" or "softer" line, but any Soviet group which placed survival at the top of its priority list would have to seek some form of rapprochement with the United States to maximize its chances for survival. Khrushchev in his own bungling way had intuitively grasped the essentials of a realistic foreign policy. The challenge of Communist China made it impossible for Moscow to continue its half-century of oscillation between being a state and the center of a world revolutionary movement. Moscow had to choose between survival and doctrinal virtue. It had chosen the former, leaving the latter to Peking, which need not yet decide between the two.

Moscow's decision to seek a rapprochement with the United States and the American response plunged both alliance systems into disarray. Priorities in the policies of more than a score of states are in the process of being restructured, and various realignments are likely to take shape. This process will be accelerated if an over-all strategic détente between the United States and the Soviet Union becomes a durable reality, since it will provide a protective umbrella for other states to resurrect demands upon one another.

Just as the Soviet decision to give higher priority to a détente with the United States than to China's national hegemonial interests alienated China from Russia, the United States may have to choose whether to place a higher priority on a détente with the Soviet Union than on its support for West Germany's territorial and other national claims. Moscow's strategy is to isolate West Germany, just as China has been isolated. One of the nightmares of Western statesmen has been a replay of the Rapallo scenario, but this is hardly a likely prospect at this time.

Today the Soviet Union is a global power, while Germany is a dismembered state still slightly tainted by its Nazi past; today, the

Soviet Union holds East Germany in thrall and supports Polish positions on the boundary question and thus holds many prizes which Bonn would like to retrieve; but what can Bonn give in return? The relationship is totally asymmetrical. Furthermore, there is reason to believe that Moscow is implacably committed to a divided Germany, and there is hardly a conceivable circumstance under which the Soviet Union might find a reunited Germany in its interest. Even the hypothetical vision of a united Communist Germany can hardly be a cause for jubilation in the Kremlin after the Chinese experience. The Rapallo nightmare of Western statesmen is matched or exceeded by the Soviet nightmare of being caught between two Communist great powers with territorial and other national grievances against Russia.

The erosion of NATO, which has been a consistent goal of Soviet foreign policy, contributes in turn to the dissolution of the Warsaw Pact, which Rumania already considers obsolete and superfluous. This, of course, is an unintended consequence of Soviet policy. The absence of a Western coalition not only contributes to the erosion of the Eastern bloc but further encourages the smaller Communist countries to make their own arrangements with individual countries of Western Europe and thus creates the possibilities of new realignments. The greater the number of ties established with Western countries and the greater the number of Western countries involved, the greater will be the areas of autonomy for the smaller Communist states; and in the absence of a Western threat, these ties cannot be viewed by Moscow as seriously detrimental to its security and vital interests.

Soviet Foreign Policy at the Crossroads

After 50 years of the Soviet state, the successors to Lenin, Stalin, and Khrushchev face painful problems in foreign policy which demand resolution. The Soviet leaders must decide finally whether they are directing a state or a movement; in the face of the Chinese challenge and American pressures, the current transitional attempt to behave like a state while hanging on to the rhetoric of revolution cannot be sustained indefinitely. And if they choose to play out their role as a global power, the Soviet leaders must decide whether to challenge the United States once again for paramountcy or settle for second place, whether to continue to postpone the maximum utilization of scarce resources for internal development in order to maximize foreign-policy options and the achievement of diplomatic goals. Moscow must also decide whether to seek spheres of influence on four continents or retrench to the Eurasian land mass. No matter what the decisions, they will be cause for renewed factional conflict.

There is substantial evidence to suggest that the Soviet leadership is divided over the direction of its next major moves in foreign policy. As a consequence, most decisions have postponed rather than resolved existing differences of opinion. It would be an over-simplification to divide the Soviet ruling group into "hawks" and "doves"; but it is true that the sharpest point of internal factional conflict is over the allocation of resources, which frequently divides the Soviet leadership into two broad groupings: those advocating a greater relaxation of international tensions, a retreat from overcommitments in foreign policy, and a demand that peripheral international disputes be resolved through compromise and mutual concessions; and those advocating a build-up in Soviet strategic capabilities, perhaps even to the point of challenging the United States for strategic pre-eminence, greater assistance to allies under attack to whom the Soviet Union is committed in one form or another, and the deferral of maximizing internal development in the interests of national security.

It would be grossly incorrect to characterize the second group as being made up entirely of expansionist-minded or ideologically-oriented leaders, although both types are undoubtedly included. Rather, it is, on the whole, a grouping which is skeptical of United States intentions and has little confidence in lasting international stabilization. Instead it envisions a continuous period of challenge and response between the two global powers. It does not rule out the possibility that China may become an object of attention from both sides. Hence, this group may be more amenable to an ultimate reconciliation with China than is the first grouping, even if it retards or reverses the détente with the United States.

The Arab-Israel war, in June, 1967, served to bring these contradictory currents of Soviet attitudes into sharp relief. Soviet policy seemed to veer from one extreme to another during the crisis, as if some leaders were demanding a more vigorous Soviet response while others were counseling prudence. Although there appears to be some evidence to show that at least some sectors of the Soviet leadership encouraged the Arabs in their provocations against Israel, there is also evidence to indicate that part of the Soviet leadership was alarmed at Nasser's excesses as well as those of the Syrians. Once the war broke out, the Soviet government strenuously supported the Arab states diplomatically and politically on every point except the destruction of Israel.

One may surmise that some Soviet leaders called for more vigorous and direct action on the premise that an Israeli victory of the magnitude which it assumed would undercut the credibility of Soviet military and diplomatic support and simultaneously enhance that of the United States as Israel's patron.

The refusal of Moscow to go beyond the strong diplomatic support given to the Arabs suggests that the counsels of moderation won out, and Premier Kosygin's appearance at the United Nations General Assembly was designed as much to emphasize Soviet support for the Arabs as it was to arrange a personal meeting with President Johnson.

Confronted with a wide range of rapidly changing problems, the Soviet leadership will probably continue to "muddle through," allowing itself to be dominated by events rather than domesticating them. Until the Vietnam war is settled, there will always be serious apprehensions and suspicions in the Soviet leadership concerning ultimate American intentions. As a consequence, the Soviet leadership is likely to continue to make compromise decisions, postpone the resolution of problems, and remain vulnerable to the demands of those whose counsels would lead to a new and more dangerous spiral in the arms race. It is a question as to how much longer Moscow can evade some hard decisions on the direction of its foreign affairs.

24. RECENT SOVIET FOREIGN POLICY: SOME PATTERNS IN RETROSPECT

Marshall D. Shulman

The law of life is change, but rarely it seems, has the life of inter-national politics changed in so many of its dimensions and with such accelerating speed as in the present. Continents seethe with change and conflict; nations form, unite, and disunite; the guerrilla and the missile transform the art of war. In the words of Leonid Brezhnev: "Foreign political tasks have become more complex."

Indeed, the impression is inescapable that the leadership of the Soviet Union has been groping for the most effective way to deal with some complex and unanticipated problems, and that it may now be poised at a fork in the road. It is evident that the Vietnam issue, only recently a small cloud on the horizon, now darkens the skies over every continent; but the question it poses is whether this issue will prove to be but a transient interruption in the long-term evolutionary trends in Soviet policy, or whether this conflict, and the complications flowing from it, will mark a significant turn in the direction of Soviet policy.

Over the postwar period as a whole, and especially after the death of Stalin, it has appeared that the long-term trends in Soviet policy were moving in the direction of traditional power-bloc politics based on nation-state interests, with increasing reliance upon the indirect strat-egy of "peaceful coexistence." Within this formulation, significant fluc-tuations have been marked, particularly in response to changing perceptions of the power balance. What is in question now is whether the efforts to deal with the events of the last few years, and in particular those growing out of the Vietnam conflict, are to be regarded as fluctuations within this evolutionary pattern, or whether some new departures may be in the making.

It is not the Vietnam issue alone which creates this necessity for choice, but the many underlying factors in international politics which are sharply highlighted by this conflict: the potentialities for revolutionary upheavals elsewhere in the underdeveloped areas; the continued militancy of the Chinese Communist regime; the diplomatic isolation of the United States on the Vietnam issue; the widening of divisive trends in the non-Communist world, including Europe; the rise in United States military capabilities; and the smarting inferiority of Soviet strategic and local military power, pressing against other claims on Soviet resources. It has been the interplay of such considerations as these that has posed the alternatives confronting the Soviet leaders in thier recent deliberations on foreign policy.

A brief review of certain main trends in Soviet foreign policy between the Twenty-Second Congress of the Communist Party of the Soviet Union (October 17–31, 1961) and the Twenty-Third Congress (March 29–April 8, 1966) offers an illuminating impression of the mounting claim these issues have made upon the attention of the Soviet leadership, and of the evolution of Soviet responses to them.

I.

In the fall of 1961 when the Twenty-Second Congress assembled, Soviet policy was suffering from a hang-over as an aftermath of Khrushchev's inflated claims to a "shift in the balance of power" during the post-Sputnik euphoria. From 1958 until mid-1960, the main thrust of Soviet policy had been an effort to translate into political advantage the general impression that the achievements of Soviet science and technology in orbiting the first artificial space satellite and in testing the first intercontinental ballistic missile in late 1957 signified at least a potential gain for Soviet power. This effort proceeded along three main lines: (1) pressure for political concessions from the West (in particular, on Berlin in 1958); (2) a damping-down of international tension to restrain Western over-reaction to Soviet achievements (the Khrushchev visit to America in 1959, from which emerged the "spirit of Camp David"); and (3) an intensified cultivation of Soviet influence among the new nations of Africa and Asia. By the time of the U-2 episode in May of 1960 and the subsequent disintegration of the Summit Conference, it had already become apparent that the symbolic effect of Soviet space and missile demonstrations had not produced Western concessions on Berlin or on Eastern Germany. Moreover, the atmosphere of detente had not headed off an intensified United States effort to close the presumed "missile gap" — as evidenced by the testing of the first Atlas intercontinental missile and the launching of the first Polaris submarine. In fact, it became evident that Khrushchev's effort to squeeze maximum advantage out of the Soviet test demonstrations had so galvanized the American missile production effort that the strategic balance in the coming missile period favored the United States even more than it had in the preceding period of the strategic bomber, and the Soviet Union became the "Avis" of international politics. As a result of information from over-flights and other intelligence sources, it became clear that Khrushchev had not backed up his claims by going into large-scale production of intercontinental missiles (as the Soviet Union had done in missiles of shorter range). The net effect of this effort to capitalize on purely symbolic demonstrations was therefore massively adverse to the Soviet power position.

Nevertheless, Khrushchev's impulse was to respond to the puncturing of the "missile gap" by going over to the attack. Influenced perhaps by his reading of President Kennedy's susceptibilities, and by the weakening of the American position as a result of the "Bay of Pigs" disaster, Khrushchev reopened the Berlin crisis in the spring of 1961. Thus the international climate in the background as the Twenty-Second Party Congress opened that fall was one of tension. There had been a confrontation of Soviet and American tanks in Berlin; the exodus from East Germany had reached such flood proportions that a Berlin Wall was required to staunch it; and the three-year moratorium on nuclear testing was ended as first the Soviet Union and then the United States began a new round in the development of more advanced missiles and nuclear warheads. Khrushchev did his best to wring maximum political advantage out of the test exposition of a weapon in the 55 to 60-megaton range, and spoke of the possibility of a 100-megaton weapon.

What is interesting about this brief recapitulation of the events prior to the Twenty-Second Congress is the way they illustrate several persistent elements in the Soviet experience:

1. A major determinant of the policy emphasis in this period appears to have been an essentially political calculation of the effect of present and future power upon political behavior.

2. Related to this was a (perhaps distinctively Khrushchevian) tendency to give great weight to the anticipated political effect of demonstrations of token military capability, rather than to actual military capability.

3. The dampening of the atmosphere of tension to restrain Western policy and military preparations was carried forward at the same time as pressure was applied to gain advantages and resources were concentrated on building the Soviet power base, notwithstanding the contradictory effect of those policies.

4. In this period, as has so often been the case in the Soviet experience, the effort to apply pressure to gain political advantages tended to have counterproductive results, stimulating the cohesion and mobilization of the Western powers.

II.

The central strategic conception of the Soviet leadership, as it emerged from the proceedings of the Twenty-Second Congress, appeared to have been that the urgent immediate task was the strengthening of the Soviet economic base as the source of future power in its multiple aspects, meanwhile relying upon an easement of international tension to prevent further disadvantageous trends in the Soviet power position. The main business of the Congress was intended to center around a twenty-year economic plan, but foreign policy questions would not remain in the background, particularly because of the Albanian-Chinese attack upon the fundamental direction of Soviet policy. Against this attack, Khrushchev elaborated and defended "peaceful coexistence" as a strategy which was both prudent and effective, emphasizing the following three considerations:

1. The development of thermonuclear weapons is a qualitative change in the international situation which requires the avoidance of a general nuclear war.

2. The advanced industrial countries, while showing no signs of imminent revolutionary potentialities, are vulnerable to internal and external pressures that can weaken their international power position, and are susceptible to a policy of division and detente.

3. The newly independent nations, following a more-or-less "neutral" course, have become a favorable factor in international politics, which can be brought by a "peaceful coexistence" policy to augment the influence of the Soviet bloc.

While it was clear that the absorption of the significance of thermonuclear destructiveness into Soviet thought was resulting in an increasing conservatism in regard to general war, this did not remove the military plane of conflict from a significant place in the struggle, even under the strategy of "peaceful coexistence." This is reflected in continuing efforts to find ways to make effective political use of military capabilities, thereby achieving gains without general war. This may be observed in the intimidatory pressure of Soviet military capabilities upon Western public opinion to produce a spirit of accommodation. Examples are Khrushchev's reminder to the countries of Western Europe that they are "hostages" to Soviet medium-range rockets, and Gromyko's enjoinder to the Western powers to be "realistic" in the spirit of Franklin Roosevelt and accommodate themselves peacefully to the changes which the growing power of the Soviet Union necessitates. This effort may be seen also in the Khrushchev speech of January, 1961, and in the declarations at the Congress regarding the necessity of Soviet military aid for those local conflicts described as "wars of national liberation." The declarations were nevertheless tempered by some ambiguous recognition of the danger that limited conflicts might enlarge into general war.

What was not expressed at the Congress, but what, in the light of subsequent actions must have been in the forefront of the consciousness of the Soviet leaders and an active issue in behind-the-scenes debates, was the conviction that the strategic military superiority of the United States must be overcome as soon as possible. This lesson had been dramatized during the Berlin crisis of 1961, when the confrontation of tanks at "Checkpoint Charlie" made it clear that however great might have been the advantage of the Soviet Union in local forces, the risk of escalation would have carried the encounter to a strategic plane at which the comparative advantage of the United States would have been decisive. The anticipatory awareness of this advantage necessarily narrowed the limits beyond which Soviet diplomacy could press the issue. But the question was how, given the limitations of Soviet resources, the American lead could best be overcome? With a gross national product roughly half that of the United States, with serious problems in the administration of the Soviet economy reflected in a slow-down of the rate of growth, and with political considerations limiting the capacity of the leadership to deflect resources into the military sector at the enormous levels required, the choices were obviously difficult.

It is now apparent, in the light of Soviet behavior in the course of the following year, that three lines of action were followed to try to narrow the gap of Soviet strategic inferiority:

1. Efforts were made to slow down the American strategic advance (still accelerating in response to the crisis of the previous year) by recreating a climate of reduced tension. The Berlin issue was cooled by a private message from Khrushchev to Kennedy in September, 1961, and more specifically in March, 1962, at a meeting of the Foreign Ministers of the Soviet Union, the United States, and the United Kingdom. Significantly, that meeting took place at the re-opening of disarmament negotiations, which had been broken off by a Soviet walk-out from the ten-nation disarmament conference two years earlier. A conference on Laos successfully reached agreement on the neutral status of that trouble-spot. Agreements were reached with the United States on the extension of cultural exchanges and for technical cooperation in the peaceful uses of outer space. An exchange of private correspondence with Kennedy was opened by Khrushchev in this period. It was evident that Khrushchev had hoped his improvement of relations with Kennedy would head off the resumption of atmospheric testing by the U.S. in response to the Soviet tests in the fall of 1961, and he was angered when the American tests were announced in March, 1962.

2. Some additional resources were transferred to the military sector. It was explained that the rise in the retail price of butter and meat by 25 and 30 percent, and the postponement of the scheduled reduction in income tax, were made necessary by increased defense expenditures. Some of these expenditures were clearly absorbed by the development of nuclear weapons tested in a series beginning in September, 1961, and in a new series of tests which lasted from August until November of 1962; some by the large number of space experiments, including a number

identified as "cosmic satellites," and one referred to by Khrushchev as a "global rocket"; and some, to judge by the lead-times involved, must have gone toward the increase in the Soviet stockpile of intercontinental missiles which began to make its appearance in the following years.

3. The most daring effort to find a short-cut toward strategic parity was of course the abortive emplacement of medium and intermediate-range missiles (of which the Soviet Union had an abundance) in Cuba. The targetting of the United States from Cuba would have enabled the Soviets to perform a strategic function, substituting for their deficiency in intercontinental missiles.

The failure of this third action produced such a spectacular crisis that all parties concerned and most spectator nations seem to have experienced something of a catharsis. Largely because of this experience, but also because of several coincidental factors to which we will turn in a moment, Soviet foreign policy reflected a marked shift of emphasis during the two years which followed, from the end of 1962 until the last months of 1964.

The most striking feature of this period is that it marked the lowest level of tension between the Soviet Union and the United States of the entire postwar period. For a brief period at least, while the memory of the Cuban missile crisis was fresh in mind, the function of detente measures qualitatively deepened. In the previous periods, intermittent efforts to damp down the atmosphere of tension seemed specifically intended to reduce the United States military effort and the cohesion of the Western alliance. Now, although these purposes were also served, the measures involved had a somewhat more substantive character, and appeared intended to defuse the conflict relationship with the United States to some degree in order to reduce the risk of general war and bring down the level of military expenditures required.

III.

In the post-crisis atmosphere, the Soviet Union moved with relative speed toward a number of arms control measures. In December, 1962, Khrushchev indicated to Kennedy his willingness to accept two or three on-site inspections, plus three "black boxes," in verification of a ban on underground testing; since the United States position at that time was that a minimum of eight inspections were required, no agreement resulted. The following July, Khrushchev accepted an earlier American proposal for a test ban in the three environments in which no on-site inspection was required: outer space, the atmosphere, and under-water — with an ambiguous suggestion that this agreement be tied to a non-aggression treaty between the Warsaw Pact and NATO powers. Although the latter proposal was not realized, the Partial Test-Ban Treaty was quickly negotiated within a month. The fact that the United States and the Soviet Union had both completed a series of atmospheric tests the previous summer and fall was doubtless a contributory circumstance. Among other measures taken in this period was an agreement for a "hot line" of immediate communications between the Soviet and American leaderships, acceptance by both powers of a resolution in the General Assembly of the United Nations prohibiting the orbiting of nuclear weapons, and a reciprocal exchange of unilateral pledges by the Soviet Union and the United States to reduce the production of fissionable materials for weapons purposes. The Soviet Union also announced a reduction in its military budget, although the impression prevailed in the West that Soviet production of intercontinental missiles in this period was intensified following the Cuban crisis. Foreign Minister Gromyko also announced that the Soviet Union was now prepared to accept the Western proposal for a "nuclear umbrella" — a certain residual number of missiles to remain in the hands of the Soviet Union and the United States in the earlier stages of the disarmament process, but the proposal remained tied to the Soviet plan for "general and complete disarmament," and came to naught.

A number of actions by the Soviet Union in other fields during this period strengthened the impression that it was seeking to improve relations, such as the cessation of jamming the Voice of America and the British Broadcasting Corporation programs, and the agreement on the designation of U Thant as Secretary-General of the United Nations without any further pressure that the U.N. Secretariat be reorganized along "troika" lines. The period was not without incidents that might under other circumstances have given rise to considerable tension: some interference with American and British convoys on the road to Berlin, the arrest of Professor Frederick C. Barghoorn, and a dispute over the financing of U.N. peacekeeping operations, but these were handled by the Soviet Union with an evident desire to minimize the disturbance to the over-all relationship of diminished tension.

Although the Cuban missile crisis was the most dramatic cause of the turn toward low-tension policies in this period, there were a number of other factors present which operated in the same direction, and may have played important contributory roles. Among these factors was Khrushchev's impression of current American politics and policies. Once Kennedy's firmness in the Berlin and Cuba crises had dispelled Khrushchev's earlier impressions of Kennedy's vulnerability to pressure, there developed an obvious interest in the Kremlin in cultivating a private relationship of confidence with the American President. Kennedy's appeal for an end to the Cold War in his commencement address at American University on June 10, 1963, had a powerful public impact in the Soviet Union (many Russians carried the clipping of the speech in their wallets) and made an obvious impression on Khrushchev. The sale of wheat to the Soviet Union and the tone of confidence and candor in the private communications between the two leaders strengthened the Soviet impression that some collaboration was possible between adversaries. After the death of the President, and particularly during the election campaign between Johnson and Goldwater in the autumn of 1964, the Soviet leadership exercised great care that no action on its part should strengthen any potential "hard line" tendencies in American politics.

In other parts of the world, political trends also argued for the advantage of a low-tension policy. In Western Europe, although the Bonn-Paris Treaty evoked some harsh and anxious reactions from the Soviet Union, the famous press conference of General de Gaulle in January, 1963 was regarded in Moscow for the most part as a positive development. Prospects for the continued momentum of the European Common Market, which had been a source of mounting concern in the Soviet Union and in Eastern Europe, now appeared diminished. Moreover, the influence of the United States and the effectiveness of NATO were both diminished by the French line of sovereign independence, and Soviet diplomacy, despite some sensitivity about the General's conception of "Europe from the Atlantic to the Urals," accepted his thrust toward national independence as an "objectively progressive" development. During the last months of the Khrushchev regime, Soviet diplomacy also began to explore the possibility of influencing the orientation of the Federal Republic in a more favorable direction, notwithstanding the continuous drumfire of Soviet propaganda on the themes of German "militarism and revanchism." These divisive trends clearly depended upon a Western European perception of a diminished Soviet threat, and therefore added further weight to the argument for a low-tension policy.

Meanwhile, acute problems within the Communist bloc became a major preoccupation. The Sino-Soviet dispute had by now burst into an open exchange of polemics; Chinese incursions into Africa and Chinese encouragement of an independent line on the part of the Eastern European states, Rumania in particular, occupied the attention and energies of the Soviet leadership. At home, the declining growth rate of the Soviet economy was dealt with by a succession of administrative and political reorganizations, piling one improvisation upon another, the effect of which was to strengthen Soviet requirements for trade and credits from the West, create stringent claims upon Soviet resources, and dissatisfactions within the Party that were to lead to the ouster of Khrushchev in October, 1964.

One other important contributory factor in the background during this period was the effect of changing military technology. A significant revolution had been taking place in the qualitative character of the strategic weapons system on both sides during the four or five years preceding, and it was to have important political consequences. Both the Soviet Union and the United States had been moving away from reliance upon vulnerable "first-strike" weapons systems. The advent of "hardened" intercontinental missile systems and missile-bearing nuclear submarines encouraged the evolution of "second-strike" retaliatory strategic doctrines and diminished the fear of surprise attack. The prevailing conception of a balance of mutual deterrence, insensitive to substantial inequalities in the number of weapons in any particular category available to either side, encouraged a certain sense of stability in the strategic military confrontation. Although military strategists on both sides continued to be concerned about the requirements for a war-fighting capability in the event that deterrence should break down, the political climate during this period encouraged a relatively low expectation of general war.

IV.

As of the fall of 1964, therefore, it appeared that a combination of circumstances tended to push the Cold War into the background. Domestic preoccupations, fragmenting alliances, and a certain strategic stabilization all added encouragement to a relationship of low tension and even tacit restraint between the Soviet Union and the United States. It is of course difficult to document the presence and the growth of this tacit restraint; perhaps the most that can be recorded now is the impression that the political and military decision-makers on both sides had begun to take into account the interacting processes in the defense field, and that certain decisions regarding procurement, deployment, the staging of maneuvers, etc., were affected by the desire to avoid stimulating undesired reactions from the other side.

The transition to a new inflection of policy during the year and a half which followed, from the fall of Khrushchev to the Twenty-Third Party Congress in March–April of 1966, mainly resulted from the interaction of three factors: the intensification of the Vietnam conflict, a further heightening of Chinese power and militancy, and changes in the substance and the style of decision-making under the new Soviet leadership.

Toward the latter part of 1964, the tide of battle and politics in Vietnam appeared to be moving toward an early Communist victory. One clear departure in policy by the new Soviet leadership, in contrast to the contraction of Soviet commitments to Southeast Asia in the latter Khrushchev period, was to reassert Soviet interests in the area. A major motivation for this decision may have been the desire to limit the extension of Chinese Communist influence, advanced by the apparent validation of militant Chinese support for the Viet Cong and the North Vietnamese regime. The reassertion of Soviet interests was dramatized by the visit of Premier Kosygin to Hanoi and North Korea in February, 1965. Stopping in Peking en route, Kosygin continued the effort of the new leadership to effect a *modus vivendi* with the Chinese. From later exchanges of recriminations, it appeared that Kosygin may have been urging Hanoi and Peking to encourage a graceful withdrawal of the United States from the area by allowing negotiations to begin. The Chinese Communist regime, however, was adamant. Fortified by the recent explosion of the first Chinese nuclear device and by the favorable course of events in Vietnam, the Peking leadership refused to support any moves toward negotiation, and offered no terms of reconciliation short of Soviet surrender. Moreover, during the ensuing period the Chinese intensified their attack, accusing the new Soviet leadership of continuing the policy of Khrushchev "revisionism," of sacrificing the interests of the world revolutionary movement to Soviet national interests, and — worst of all — of entering into a collaboration with the American imperialists.

Meanwhile, the United States opted for a heightened commitment in Vietnam to try to stem the deterioration of the position of the Saigon government. American forces were not frankly committed to a combat role, and American military power began to flow into the area in greatly increased volume. The attack by United States planes upon North Vietnam territory, coincident with the visit of Kosygin to Hanoi, dramatically engaged Soviet prestige in the conflict. By the late spring of 1965, Soviet planes and surface-to-air missiles were engaged in unacknowledged combat with American airpower and the Soviet leaders were beginning to talk of the possibility of sending Soviet "volunteers" to support the allied government of North Vietnam. After a declining interest in accepting the hazards of meditation following the spring of 1965, Soviet diplomacy appears to have been temporarily active in encouraging a reliance upon negotiations during the United States bombing lull and "peace offensive" of December, 1965–January, 1966, but without success. In the period following, particularly after the bombing of oil installations in the vicinity of Hanoi and Haiphong, the Soviet Union turned determinedly away from any role as mediator.

By the time of the Twenty-Third Party Congress, Soviet pronouncements and actions made it clear that there was now little expectation of a return to the kind of detente that had prevailed two years earlier; instead, the conviction seems to have taken root that a qualitative change was beginning to alter the international picture. Among the elements associated with the Vietnam conflict which are cited or implied in the Soviet analysis as signifying a change in the international situation are the following:

1. The increase in military expenditures by the United States, not only for Vietnam, but to raise its military capabilities generally. The United States, said Kosygin at the Congress, "has used the war in Vietnam to begin a new stage in the arms race." He went on to cite the supplementary defense appropriations requested by the Administration, and the increased military budget for the next fiscal year. The possibility that the war may continue to expand leads to an expansion of military effort in all categories, and in research and development of new weapons systems; moreover, as it appears to Moscow, the United States is building up mobile forces and acquiring valuable training experience in local and guerrilla combat as a result of the conflict in Vietnam, thereby adding to its military capabilities.

2. American policy appears to have taken a turn toward greater militancy. From the Soviet point of view, this seems indicated by the United States effort to use force to reverse the course of a local revolutionary trend. The impression is strengthened by the action of the United States in the Dominican crisis, in the Congo airlift, and by the bombing of North Vietnam. (Purely as a conjecture, it may be added that the frontal challenge to Soviet prestige and influence in Hanoi presented by the bombing of the North, particularly of the Hanoi and Haiphong areas, may have appeared to Moscow as violative of the tacit restraints assumed to exist between the United States and the Soviet

Union during the 1963–1964 period.) Gromyko's references at the Congress to American "preachings of diktat and arbitrariness," "glorifying the policy of strength in international relations," and the frequent references to American "violations of international law" and of "norms of international conduct," obviously have a propaganda function but also reflect a Soviet assessment of a change in American policy.

3. The possibility of general war appears greater now than it did two years ago. While the balance of mutual deterrence may still be operative as a restraint against deliberate attack, the risk of escalation out of the Vietnam conflict, even though unintended, now appears to be given increasing weight in the Soviet outlook. At least, policy no longer proceeds on the assumption that a larger war is out of the question in the foreseeable future.

4. There may be other Vietnams. That is to say, this war may be a forerunner of a whole category of conflicts, arising out of the political turbulence to be seen in Asia, Africa, and Latin America. Some of these conflicts may be in situations which the Soviet Union identifies as "struggles for national liberation," and are more likely now to result in violence than was formerly thought because of the general heightening of the propensity for violence in the underdeveloped world in recent years, and because of the assumed disposition of the United States to interfere in these transitions with force, as the "gendarme of the world."

5. The United States is growing more isolated in the world, and there is a tempting opportunity to derive advantage from furthering this isolation by unifying opposition to the United States under the theme of "anti-imperialism." The slogan of "anti-imperialism" is evidently regarded in the Soviet analysis as an increasingly successful rallying-cry in Europe as well as in the underdeveloped areas.

6. The exploitation of this theme against the United States has also been regarded as advantageous in the context of the Sino-Soviet competition. The Chinese are thereby deprived of an opportunity to capitalize on potent "anti-imperialist" attitudes around the world, and they are also given less grounds for a plausible charge of Soviet-American collusion.

These elements of the international situation growing out of the Vietnam war as seen from Moscow deeply influenced the whole range of foreign policy projected at the Twenty-Third Congress, although the impression suggested is one of tentativeness, of uncertainty, of changes in degree. The feeling that seems most marked in the discussion is that events have taken over, that the initiative is in the hands of external forces whose shape is not yet clear, and that the main business at hand is not in foreign policy but at home, in the repair of the economy. Also implicit, particularly in the "consensus" tone of Brezhnev's report on behalf of the Central Committee, is the suggestion that events have released many voices from among contending interests in the Soviet bureaucracy, and that many decisions remain to be made, particularly in regard to the allocations of resources and the administration of the economy.

V.

One area in which fundamental policy alternatives have been opened up for discussion is that of military doctrine and the nature of military forces to be built. Since early 1965, as a consequence of the change in leadership in the Soviet Union and the intensification of the fighting in Vietnam, arguments have been more widely aired concerning the need for the diversion of additional resources to military purposes in the light of the perceived "dangerous trends" in American policy, although, as might be expected, there have been sharp differences about which services should be the beneficiaries. On the whole, the Soviet leadership appears to have followed a middle course in meeting these pressures. The military budget for 1966 reflected a five percent increase in acknowledged military expenditures, and the new Five Year Plan allows for some substantial military increases — just how much, it is difficult to say.

Notably, the ground forces, economized upon in favor of the rocket forces since the decline of Zhukov in October, 1957, have tended to come back into their own, along with other theatre forces required to strengthen the Soviet capacity to deal with local wars, including non-nuclear wars, and if need be, in distant places. This has meant increases in merchant shipping, amphibious and air-lift capacity, naval infantry, and conventional weapons.

Soviet strategic capabilities, however, are not neglected. From about mid-summer, 1965, claims of Soviet advances in this area began to be assorted and demonstrated. At the Congress, the Soviet Defense Minister spoke of new Soviet capabilities in mobile rocket launchers and of a missile-equipped nuclear submarine which had just completed a trip around the world under-water. Implicit in the military discussion is the question whether enlarged research and development expenditures can lead to a technological break-through that might make it possible for the Soviet Union to overcome its situation of strategic inferiority. The question appears to be posed with more urgency than in recent years, and the amounts budgeted for scientific research have risen substantially, but no signs of such a potential break-through are in sight. Neither an anti-missile deployment nor an orbital missile system holds the promise of a drastic shift in the strategic balance. The deployment of an anti-missile system risks precipitating another upward spiral in the arms race, that would greatly increase military expenditures on both sides without any substantial increase in security. On an *a priori* basis, one would surmise that the Soviet leadership is carefully weighing the stimulation of a higher arms race against such disadvantageous economic odds, but the question of anti-missile deployment is complicated on both sides by the existence of smaller nuclear powers, China in particular.

In sum, the partial stabilization in the strategic military field is reduced; the previously accepted assumption that the likelihood of general war was extremely remote is weakened; and the trend toward tacit restraints in the U.S.-Soviet inter-adversary relationship, although still apparent in the Vietnam conflict, commands less confidence than in the recent past.

The tone of the discussion at the Twenty-Third Congress regarding military preparations is conveyed in the following minatory paragraph from Brezhenev's report:

> We must never forget about the possibility of future trials which can again fall on the shoulders of the Soviet people. In the complex and tense international situation of today, our duty is to display unremitting vigilance. The Party considers it necessary to insure the further develop-ment of the defense industry, the perfection of rocket-nuclear weapons, and all other types of equipment. Such are the demands of our home-land's security.

Brezhnev also called for the perfection of civil defense prepara-tions, for the further extension of the current Soviet practice of equip-ping the Warsaw Pact forces with "the most modern weapons," and for joint training maneuvers with those forces "in the face of the intensified aggressive actions of the imperialist forces headed by the United States of America."

VI.

On the political side of Soviet foreign policy, the broad strategy of "peaceful coexistence" is reaffirmed, although in somewhat harder terms and with some new differentiations in political strategy toward the advanced industrial countries and the underdeveloped areas.

Brezhnev's formulation of "peaceful coexistence" at the Congress illustrates the difficulty of reconciling its various aspects:

> At the same time that we expose the aggressive policy of imperialism, we consistently and unswervingly pursue a policy of peaceful coexis-tence of states with different social systems. This means that while regarding the coexistence of states with different social systems as a form of the class struggle between socialism and capitalism, the Soviet Union at the same time consistently advocates normal, peaceful relations with capitalist countries and a settlement of controversial issues between states by negotiation and not by war. . . . Naturally, there can be no peaceful coexistence when it comes to internal processes of the class and national-liberation struggle in the capitalist countries between oppressors and the oppressed, between colonialists and the victims of colonial oppression.

Although the various elements involved in this formulation have all been expressed before, this combination of them has an unmistakable unsmiling emphasis upon the "struggle" side of the "peaceful coexis-tence" strategy. What this means in operational terms becomes clearer from an examination of the policies projected for the industrialized and the underdeveloped areas of the world.

One of the active fronts in recent Soviet diplomacy has been Western Europe and the cultivation of the Pan-European idea. In contrast to the freeze on Soviet relations with the United States and efforts to isolate the United States by an intensive "anti-imperialism" campaign, the Soviet detente policy has flowered in relation to Western Europe.

The notion of an "All-European Conference" to discuss European security problems "without outside interference" has been advanced by the Soviet Union and the Warsaw Pact powers without actually pushing for an early convocation of such a meeting. For the time being, the Soviet Union seems content to have the idea in circulation, and perhaps, it has suggested, the convocation might better come, when the time seems ripe, from the neutral nations of Europe, or possibly from Rome, where Foreign Minister Gromyko publicly restated the proposal.

The fullest expression of the idea has come from a statement issued at Bucharest on July 5, 1966, by the Warsaw Treaty members. This makes it clear that the Pan-European proposal has a broader political sweep than the Rapacki or Gomulka proposals, which it may be intended to supplant. Among other things, the measures proposed would liquidate NATO and the Warsaw Pact organization, eliminate United States troops and bases from Europe, bring about recognition of the German Democratic Republic, commit the Federal Republic of Germany not to have access to nuclear weapons in any way, and substitute an all-European trade arrangement for the European Common Market.

The Soviet Union clearly sees the reduction of United States influence in Western Europe as a favorable development, and it has cultivated General de Gaulle with this thought in mind. However it is not yet clear whether the Soviet leadership has decided how far it would like to see this political strategy pushed. A central theme in current Soviet propaganda is the liquidation of all foreign military bases and the withdrawal of all foreign troops. At the Party Congress, Gromyko quoted Roosevelt as saying at Yalta that American troops would be out of Europe two years after the war. "Ten times two years has passed," he went on, "but the American Army is still in Europe and by every indication claims a permanent status here. But the peoples of Europe are saying and will yet say their word on this score." In his discussion of the German problem, however, Gromyko evokes the principle of the Potsdam agreement that would imply a continued American presence in Germany.

This is perhaps the heart of the dilemma for the Soviet Union. Under present circumstances, the most obvious immediate effect of the reduction or elimination of American influence from Europe is to strengthen the possibility of the Federal Republic of Germany becoming the dominant power on the continent, economically, militarily, and politically. This prospect may account for the increasing intensity of the Soviet concentration on the themes of German "militarism and revanchism." Soviet commentators on international affairs have made clear their awareness that the de Gaulle withdrawal from NATO is a mixed blessing. In their opinion, it is leading into a situation in which the Federal Republic now becomes the principal partner of the United

States and later, with the decline of American influence, may stand in decisive control of Western Europe and whatever may remain of the Western Alliance.

The Soviet diplomatic response to this problem is by no means fully resolved, but it has begun to move along the following lines, not altogether consistent with each other:

1. A continued campaign to isolate the Federal Republic by hammering away at the themes of "militarism and revanchism."

2. A strong effort to inhibit the military strengthening of the Federal Republic by advancing the nuclear-free zone proposal for Central Europe, and by making the renunciation of access to nuclear weapons by the FRG a condition for West German participation in Pan-European discussions. The Soviet insistence on the exclusion of West German participation in a Multilateral Force, an Atlantic Nuclear Force or a European Nuclear Force, as a prior condition for a treaty on nonproliferation, is a further effort in this direction; so also is its pressure for the withdrawal of American tactical nuclear weapons under the present "two-key" arrangement from West German territory.

3. An effort to encourage other West European countries — particularly France, Italy, Britain, and the Scandinavian countries — to take the lead in European affairs.

4. The cultivation of political elements within the Federal Republic that seem disposed to improve relations with Eastern Europe and the German Democratic Republic. This, it is believed, is best achieved by dangling the possibility of German unification. Gromyko, at the Party Congress, declared: "We stand for the normalization and improvement of relations with the Federal German Republic on the basis of its turning to the policy of peaceful cooperation and realism." The Bucharest communique was even more specific:

> As for the unification of the two German states, the road to this goal lies through a relaxation of tension, a gradual rapprochement of the two sovereign German states and agreement between them, through agreements on disarmament in Germany and Europe, and on the basis of the principle that once the unification of Germany is achieved, the united German state will be genuinely peace-loving and democratic. . . .

5. At the same time, the Soviet Union continues to consolidate its position in Eastern Germany, and effectively deepens its commitment to the continued division of Germany. A major theme of Soviet diplomacy and a fundamental Soviet condition for the improvement of relations between Eastern and Western Europe is the recognition of the sovereignty of the German Democratic Republic and the acceptance by the Federal Republic of existing borders.

While the German issue is far and away the central pillar of Soviet policy toward the advanced industrial countries, there are a number of other continuing lines of action in this area which require at least brief mention. The central theme of this part of Soviet policy draws its sanction from Lenin's injunction to play upon differences within the capitalist camp. Gromyko sounds the note in these terms: "Weighing the facts of modern international life, analyzing the differences and shades in the foreign political platforms of bourgeois parties, tendencies, and groupings, one should say that the conclusions drawn by the founder of the Soviet state in the first years of Soviet power are as topical today as then." In practice, this means an increasing effort to differentiate policy in order to take advantage of conflicting interests between and within the Western countries, and to cooperate "with those forces in the bourgeois camp that understand the need to improve international relations."

While accepting the high level of economic growth in Western Europe and the progress of the European Economic Community as a fact of life, Western Communists are enjoined to work within the framework of the Common Market to "democratize" it by using the "anti-monopoly" theme. The French Communist Party is encouraged to increase its political effectiveness by working with "the working class and all the leftwing forces of France." The Italian Party is given encouragement to proceed with its efforts to form a "broad progressive front," and Gromyko's visit to the Vatican was a sign that religious differences should be no ideological barrier to this effort. Kosygin emphasizes that a further expansion of trade with the capitalist countries would be welcomed, and visits by Soviet officials to Canada and Japan have translated this desire into specific terms.

Meanwhile, the Soviet Union has not allowed the Vietnam issue to be compartmentalized in its relations with the U.S., and has thereby sought to exercise some direct pressure by generalizing the tensions of that issue into the fields of cultural exchanges, arms control discussions, and many other forms of overt contact. But the level of tension has been carefully modulated by the continuation of negotiations toward a treaty regarding celestial bodies, negotiations at the Eighteen-Nation Disarmament Committee in Geneva, and by the preservation of a certain decorum in the everyday business of international life. As noted earlier, Soviet diplomacy seeks to exert indirect pressure upon the United States and a weakening of its international influence by a broad political coalition organized around the twin themes of opposition to imperialism and to war.

VII.

While the industrialized areas have always occupied the forefront of Soviet attention because of their capacity to influence the balance of power even by small shifts in orientation, the underdeveloped world has been claiming an increasing share of Soviet attention in recent years for two principal reasons:

1. The dynamism of political life in Asia, Africa, and Latin America, seized by the travails of nation-building, susceptible to sudden and violent changes, constantly presents new problems, dangers, and opportunities to which the Soviet leadership finds itself obliged to respond.

2. This area is an important locus of the Sino-Soviet competition, with the consequence that Soviet policy finds itself operating in a triangular configuration, against the West on one side and the Chinese on the other, requiring innovative responses to particular situations according to the strength of interests engaged on each side of the triangle.

As a consequence, both Soviet theory and policy have a particularly tentative character in this sector. In broad terms, Soviet doctrine as reflected in the Brezhnev report to the Twenty-Third Congress tends to distinguish between four categories within the underdeveloped world:

1. "neo-colonialist" states, which may have achieved political independence, but are dominated by pro-Western regimes;
2. states which are following the "road of progressive social development," or, to use a particular term of art, are moving along the path of "non-capitalist development";
3. countries which are "building socialism";
4. states or political forces which are "fighting for national liberation."

Tactics vary accordingly. Principal attention is focused on the second and fourth categories. In the case of the "neo-colonialist" countries (Saudi Arabia and the Portuguese colonies are mentioned) relations are minimal and the struggles are not in an active phase. As regards the third category, no countries are mentioned by name, reflecting some disappointments in the recent past. At the time of the Twenty-Second Congress, a corresponding category of present or potential "national democracies" included, in addition to Cuba, the names of Indonesia, Ghana, Guinea, and Mali. The whole discussion of how states might evolve from "national democracy" to "socialism" (in the Soviet sense) received minimal attention at the 1966 Congress.

Instead, the second category has been enlarged, to embrace countries that are not pro-Western in orientation, and that are engaged in processes of social change which are accepted as "progressive," even though they may not correspond with the Soviet conception of socialism. A great deal of sad experience in the recent past has moved the Soviet Union to take a much less doctrinaire view of indigenous forms of socialism. In his report, Brezhnev indicates an attitude of broad tolerance toward the states that are following the "non-capitalist path of development":

> Major social reforms have been carried out in such countries as the United Arab Republic, Algeria, Mali, Guinea, Congo Brazzaville, and Burma. . . . It goes without saying that the form and scale of these processes vary in different countries. The revolutionary creative work of the people who have proclaimed the construction of socialism as their objective introduces distinctive features into the forms of movement along the road of social progress.

Brezhnev indicates a willingness to continue collaboration with nationalist leaders in these areas, but he goes on to say that the closer these countries come to socialism, the better their relations are likely to be with the Soviet Union.

The developments in Algeria, Ghana, and Indonesia posed especially painful problems for the Soviet Union. For awhile, Soviet analysts toyed with the conception of "proletarian democratic dictatorships" to deal with the phenomenon of military dictatorships potentially anti-Western in outlook, but this formulation did not make its appearance at the Congress. Breshnev confined himself to a modest hope for an improvement of relations with Indonesia, and a plea for an end to the mass slaughter of Communists in that country.

Category four, however, is where the action is. Here are the liveliest questions about future decisions to be made in Soviet foreign policy. In those conflict situations defined as "struggles for national liberation," Soviet leaders have already made it plain that the strategy of "peaceful coexistence" does not apply. However the questions remain how active Soviet intervention should be, whether it should operate directly or only through intermediaries, how great a risk of general war this might entail, and what enlargement of Soviet capabilities would be required to intervene effectively in a number of such local conflict situations. The last question particularly depends upon the Soviet assessment of whether United States policy in Vietnam and in the Dominican Republic reflects a general American intention to intervene actively and with force wherever pro-Communist movements are successful.

The other side of Soviet policy is illustrated by its response to the fighting between India and Pakistan over Kashmir, a conflict which was not regarded as a "struggle for national liberation." The success of Soviet mediation at Tashkent was hailed as a victory for "socialist diplomacy . . . something completely new in the practice of international relations," and Gromyko spoke proudly at the Congress of the widespread recognition and respect gained for the Soviet Union as a result of this act of statesmanship.

These two experiences, Tashkent and Vietnam, open up and define a spectrum of possible responses to local conflict situations. In each case, Soviet policy was directed toward containing the expansion of Chinese influence, and in the former case, the Soviet and Western interests were not in sharp opposition.

Several other aspects of Soviet policy toward the underdeveloped areas require at least passing mention. Relatively little attention is given to Latin America in current Soviet discussions; the prospects there are clearly for the future rather than for the immediate present, and little encouragement is given to Cuban efforts to stimulate an active revolutionary front on that continent. Soviet representatives at the Tri-Continental Conference in Havana during January, 1966, did sound like revolutionary enthusiasts, but Moscow took pains afterwards through diplomatic channels to disassociate itself from these sentiments. At the

Twenty-Third Party Congress, the Cuban spokesman was alone in trying to drum up enthusiasm for a policy of revolutionary militancy.

Soviet economic aid programs have shown some modest increases, after declining in recent years. Most of these programs take the form of long-term, low-interest credits, and are concentrated in relatively few countries. The largest recipients by far are India and Egypt, and recently Soviet and Eastern European economic aid programs have been extended into Africa.

Finally in this connection it should be noted that Brezhnev implied a possibly greater interest in the United Nations, anticipating that the great increase in the number of new nations admitted to that organization might operate, if not in the Soviet favor, at least against the interests of the United States. The context of his remarks, however, emphasized the potentialities of the organization "as an arena of active political struggle," rather than as an instrument of conciliation and collaboration.

CONCLUSIONS

It is manifest, even in so brief a review of the principal trends in recent Soviet foreign policy, that the area of choice is severely constricted in comparison to the complexity of the environment in which this policy must operate. The possibility of further violence in the underdeveloped areas; the rise of nationalism in the world, with its prospects of further fragmentation and disorder; possibilities for upsetting technological developments in weapons; uncertainties regarding the future unfolding of Chinese behavior in the world — those are but a few of the determinants to which the Soviet leaders will find themselves obliged to respond in the period ahead.

And yet the area of choice, though limited, remains decisive.

The Soviet leadership can decide whether the most effective response to the Chinese challenge is by proving its revolutionary militancy, or by championing the issue of peace.

The Soviet leadership can decide whether to try for short-term advantages in a political campaign against the United States, or to make the effort to restore some measure of restraint in their competitive relationship — provided, of course, the United States makes a reciprocal effort in this direction.

The Soviet leadership can decide whether to ride the crest of a wave of revolutionary violence in the former colonial territories, or to make an effort toward collaboration in international procedures to contain and pacify these conflicts.

Most important of all, it will be for the Soviet leadership to decide whether a competition for military advantage under conditions of an uncontrolled arms race better serves Soviet long-term interests than the compromises that would be required (and not from the Soviet Union alone) to allow for some safeguards against the increasing risk of war.

25. THE SOVIET UNION AND EASTERN EUROPE

Vernon V. Aspaturian

I.

The brutal Soviet occupation of Communist Czechoslovakia in August 1968 on the thirtieth anniversary of Munich and the twentieth anniversary of the internal Communist Party coup of 1948 signals an ominous turn in Soviet·relationships with Eastern Europe, whose full implications for internal Soviet developments, Sino-Soviet relations, the World Communist movement, East-West relations and particularly for Soviet-American relations are as yet not fully predictable. There is little question but that all of these relationships will undergo multiplex re-examination and change.

Not only has the Soviet occupation of Czechoslovakia reversed a welcome tendency on the part of the Soviet leaders in exercising self-restraint in their dealings with Moscow's former vassal states, but it also calls into question the internal political stability, judgment and even basic honesty of the Soviet regime in its dealings with other countries. The circumstances of the Soviet occupation, coming as it did hard on the heels of the Cierna and Bratislava meetings between the Soviet and Czech hierarchies, is bound to raise once again the entire question of the role of duplicity as a conscious and calculated instrument of Soviet diplomacy.[1]

The 1968 subjugation of Czechoslovakia signifies therefore a new phase in the evolving relationship between Moscow and its allied states

---

[1] Cf. V. V. Aspaturian, "Dialectics and Duplicity in Soviet Diplomacy," *Journal of International Affairs*, No. 1, 1963, pp. 42–58, and "Diplomacy in the Mirror of Soviet Scholarship," in J. Keep, editor, *Contemporary History in the Soviet Mirror* (New York, Frederick C. Praeger, Inc., 1965), pp. 243–274.

of Eastern Europe — a phase in which the naked security and national interests of the Soviet Union have been unambiguously given a higher priority in Soviet calculations than ideological considerations. Whatever the ideological rationalizations that were used by Moscow to justify its intervention in Czech affairs they were only routinely and cursorily invoked and failed to persuade most of the Communist parties of the world. The Soviet action provoked condemnation by China, Rumania, Yugoslavia and Albania among Communist countries and elicited denunciation by the leadership of the French and Italian Communist Parties. The flimsiness of Moscow's ideological pretext was further exposed by the frank Polish admission that Warsaw cooperated in the venture on grounds of *raison d'etat* — surely as distant from the cherished Marxist-Leninist principle of "proletarian internationalism" as one can visualize.

In subordinating ideological interests, norms and goals to Soviet State interests, needs and requirements, the Soviet Union not only has tended to confirm Peking's charge that Moscow's behavior is solely determined by the interests of the Soviet "revisionist clique," but by its outrageous violation of the principle of "proletarian internationalism," the Soviet Union has also subverted whatever remained of the underlying theoretical basis of the World Communist movement and system. In addition, the Soviet action has seriously risked, *inter alia,* the following hazards and dangers as well to its position in world affairs:

1. The further disorientation and division of the World Communist movement.

2. The weakening of Communist parties in non-Communist countries and the erosion of their electoral support, particularly in France, Italy and India.

3. The further disorganization and fracturing of the Communist Bloc into factional and hostile groupings, particularly in Eastern Europe.

4. The tarnishing of its carefully cultivated image as a mature and responsible Global Power that exercised its enormous power with consummate self-restraint and prudence.

5. Exposed itself as a blatant violator of the elemental norms of international law (non-intervention, non-interference, independence and sovereignty) which Moscow has repeatedly proclaimed before various forums as sacrosanct.

6. Demonstrated once again that it had precious little concern for "world public opinion" after a decade of praising its virtues.

7. Endangered the Soviet-American détente, by jeopardizing senate ratification of the non-proliferation treaty; provided Bonn with a credible justification for refusing to accede to it, aroused and encouraged the "hard-liners" in the United States, risked the revitalization of NATO and probably assured that there would be little or no U.S. troop withdrawal from Europe.

8. Provided a possible precedent and/or justification for the intervention of the United States and other great powers in the affairs of smaller states.

There is little reason to doubt that the Soviet leaders were not oblivious of these grave risks and one must assume that the action was conscious and deliberate although it may have been taken after acrimonious and bitter controversy and probably against the better judgment of a substantial segment of the Soviet leadership. Why? The indications are that once again the interests of the Soviet Union as the leader of a revolutionary movement and the interests of the Soviet Union as a state had come into direct and flagrant contradiction and that one set of interests had to be subordinated to the other.[2] This has frequently happened in the past and the resolution has nearly always been in favor of Soviet State interests, but what makes this particular action unique and transcendentally significant is that the Soviet leaders were unable to credibly correlate and identify their state interests with a transcendental ideological interest in a way to persuade perhaps the overwhelming majority of Communists throughout the world.[3]

Even Fidel Castro was moved to concede that the Soviet action was illegal, immoral and contrary to basic Communist precepts, but he nevertheless supported it on grounds of Cuban self-interest. Significantly, support for the Soviet action, tacit or open, came only from those states (Communist and non-Communist) and Communist parties that perceived their self-interest to be more in tune with Soviet self-interest than in conflict.

When the Soviet Union established its sphere of influence in Eastern Europe after World War II, Soviet State interests and ideological interests were conveniently and logically largely in tandem. The establishment of a Soviet bloc simultaneously satisfied the historic and strategic necessity of a security belt and the convenience of a springboard for the further communization of Europe in accordance with the self-imposed mission assumed by Moscow.

Increasingly, however, these two purposes of the Soviet presence in Eastern Europe have been rendered incompatible and as the Soviet role and position in the international Communist movement has been challenged from within and eroded by the obstacles and hazards from without, Moscow has been forced to reexamine the basic premises of its presence in Eastern Europe. By resorting to the military occupation of Czechoslovakia, the Soviet leaders have signified their determination to maintain a sphere of influence in the traditional great power sense and have thereby simultaneously signified an implied admission that the Eastern European countries, for all practical purposes, can no longer serve as a springboard for the further communization of Europe.

[2] The specific causes of the Czech intervention are discussed below, pp. 835 ff.

[3] For a fuller treatment of the author's view of this point, cf. the following: "Soviet Foreign Policy," in R. C. Macridis, *Foreign Policy in World Politics* (Englewood Cliffs, Prentice-Hall, Inc., third edition, 1967); "Moscow's Foreign Policy," *Survey*, October, 1967, pp. 35–60; "Internal Politics and Foreign Policy in the Soviet System," R. B. Farrell, editor, *Approaches to Comparative and International Politics* (Evanston, Ill., Northwestern University Press, 1966), pp. 212–287.

The Soviet occupation thus does not imply that Communism is once again "monolithic"; rather it proves the opposite. Neither does it signify a militant resurgence of "World Communism" as a motive force in Soviet behavior, but rather signifies the full flowering of the Soviet State as a traditional imperialistic state, whose influence and role in the world is determined not by the attractiveness of its ideology but by the enormity of its power and its determination to employ it in its self-interest.

The occupation of Czechoslovakia by the military forces of the Soviet Union and four of its Warsaw Pact allies thus inaugurates the latest phase in the evolution of a relationship between Moscow and Eastern Europe that has gone through several distinct phases of development during the past half-century, many of whose influences antedate and transcend the Bolshevik Revolution.[4]

II.

The relationship between the Soviet Union and Eastern Europe which emerged after World War II was shaped by a complex of factors which almost defy comprehensive analysis. History, geography, culture, language, religion, psychological attachments, national character and ideology have all played a role in shaping both the direction and configuration of the relationship. The impact of these factors has varied considerably in uneven and changing proportions in Soviet relations with the individual countries of Eastern Europe and this fact has contributed enormously to the differentiation evident in the developing relations between Moscow and the different countries of Eastern Europe. Some of these factors have served to bind the countries of Eastern Europe to Moscow, while others have served to alienate them. And it is not always a simple matter to sort out and disentangle the contradictory and converging forces which operate to influence and shape the attitudes of individual countries to the Soviet Union.

Soviet interest in Eastern Europe, of course, has its origins in the pre-Bolshevik period. History and geography alone would be sufficient to guarantee a special role for Moscow in this region. Historically, the area has been a buffer zone between Russia and other major powers of Central Europe for many centuries and for the past two hundred years, Russia has sought to assert a dominant influence in the region. Indeed, there are some observers who suggest that history and geography alone are sufficient to explain the subjugation of Eastern Europe by Moscow

[4] For the standard work on the evolution of Soviet relations with Eastern Europe, cf. Zbigniew Brzezinski, The Soviet Bloc (Cambridge, Mass., Harvard University Press, revised and enlarged edition, 1967). For the author's interpretation of the Soviet role, cf. V. V. Aspaturian, The Soviet Union in the World Communist Movement (Stanford, Calif., The Hoover Institution, 1966), and the author's "The Soviet Union and International Communism," in R. C. Macridis, Foreign Policy in World Politics, pp. 216–246.

after World War II. Yet the specific character and form of the subordination suggest that other factors have been equally influential.

The response and reaction of the various countries of Eastern Europe to the Russian interest in the area have varied widely over time from one country to another, and this has enormously influenced the widely varying perceptions and images of Russia generated in the region. Many of these attitudes and perceptions were shaped by the events and circumstances of nineteenth century European diplomacy. Less than two hundred years ago, all of the nationalities of Eastern Europe (except the Serbs of Montenegro) were languishing under Ottoman or Hapsburg domination. The circumstances of their liberation and independence were to shape national attitudes toward Russia for many decades.

Since all of the subject nationalities of the Ottoman and Hapsburg Empires in the region were either Slavic and/or Orthodox (with the exception of the Magyars who became a co-ruling nationality in 1848), the fact that Russia was the largest and most powerful Slavic and Orthodox state was destined to assume a signal importance in Russia's diplomatic calculations and the national perceptions and images of the nationalities struggling for liberation. Russia was instrumental in liberating the Rumanians, Bulgars and Serbs and was eager to pose as the champion and potential deliverer of the Croats, Slovenes, Czechs and Slovaks (all Catholic but Slavic) from Hapsburg domination. Thus was forged a symbiotic relationship between Russia and the Slavic/Orthodox nationalities of Eastern Europe, which was manifested before World War I in the Pan-Slavic movement and has in many ways survived the vicissitudes of revolutionary upheaval, social convulsions, elite hostilities, military occupation, territorial dismemberment, political subjugation, ideological conflict and two World Wars. The Rumanians, being Orthodox but non-Slavic, have conflicting perceptions, because while historically Russia was instrumental in freeing them from Ottoman rule, Moscow has insisted upon retaining territories considered to be part of Rumania *irredenta* (Bessarabia). Hungary and Poland, on the other hand, have traditionally viewed Russia both as a rival for power and influence in the region and as an oppressor. This is particularly true of Poland, a Catholic Slavic nation, with its own proud historical credentials as a great power in the area, the bulk of whose population languished under Russian rule and oppression for over a century.

The complex and intersecting ethnic, religious, political, geographic and historical variables which have contributed to the shaping of Eastern European attitudes toward the Soviet Union can perhaps be best summarized, if not with complete adequacy, by Table 1.

III.

While both history and geography ineluctably impelled the Soviet Union to assert its dominance and influence in Eastern Europe, the precise nature and configuration of the relationship that emerged owes

TABLE 1
VARIABLES AND FACTORS SHAPING EASTERN EUROPEAN IMAGES AND ATTITUDES TOWARD THE U.S.S.R.

Country	Positive							Negative									Ideological				
	Slavic	Orthodox	Russia viewed as liberator	Friendly dynasty before World War I	Allied State, World War I	Allied State, World War II	Amicable official relations before World War II	Non-Slavic	Non-Orthodox	Russia viewed as enemy or oppressor	Hostile dynasty before World War I	Enemy State, World War I	Hostile official relations before World War II	Enemy State, World War II	Territorial conflict with Russia/U.S.S.R.	Soviet Military Occupation	Strong Communist Party before World War II	Strong Guerrilla Movement	Warsaw Pact	CEMA	Support Moscow over Peking
Albania		1				X		X	1		X		X					X	2	2	
Bulgaria	X	X	X								X	X	X	X		X			X	X	X
Czechoslovakia	X		X			X	X		X						X				X	X	X
East Germany								X	X	X	X	X	X	X	X	X	X		X	X	X
Hungary								X	X	X	X	X	X	X	3	X			X	X	X
Poland	X					X			X	X	X		X		X	X			X	X	X
Rumania		X	5	6				X		1		4	X	X	X	X			X	X	
Yugoslavia	X	1	X		6	X			1									X			X

its character neither to history, language and culture nor to the strategic and security imperatives of geographical propinquity, but rather is to be found in the history of the relationship between the Communist party of the Soviet Union and the World Communist movement, of which the pre-War Eastern European Communist parties were an integral part.

The entire history of the Soviet relationships, first with foreign Communist parties, then with Communist states, and then with rivals for leadership (China), has been determined by two essentially contradictory purposes: either serving the interests of foreign constituencies (world revolution, party-states, China), or reflecting the interests of internal constituencies (survival as a state, national interests, Soviet elites). The first purpose is inherently self-abnegative, since it demands that the interests of the Soviet Union's internal constituencies be subordinated to the interests of external constituencies, while the second is subversive of internationalism, since it gives higher priority to internal needs than to external obligations.

Tension between these two conflicting sets of demands was inevitable and not capable of easy resolution. One purpose was bound to subordinate the other. Either the Soviet State was to become an expendable instrument of the international proletariat or the Communist movement would be reduced to a creature supinely responsive to the demands of the Soviet State. This contradiction was resolved by adjusting the interests and behavior of the movement and foreign communist parties to those of the Soviet State, and from 1928 to 1953, foreign Communist parties, even after they assumed power in their own countries, remained instruments rather than partners of the Soviet Union.

With the installation of Communist regimes in the countries of Eastern Europe, the Soviet Union was automatically deprived of its unique position as the only Communist state in the world, whose ruling proletariat preempted the articulaton of the class interests of the entire world proletariat languishing in oppression and exploitation in capitalist countries. As long as the Soviet Union was the only Communist state, it could be rationalized that good Communists everywhere should display first loyalty to the only fatherland of the proletariat. Loyalty, however, was not founded on the inherent moral superiority or priority of interests of the Soviet proletariat over all others, but on the basis that as the only country ruled by a proletariat, class interests dictated highest loyalty to the base and center of the world revolutionary movement. This is the principle known as "proletarian internationalism." The international proletariat gave its loyalty to the Soviet Union on the premise that the Soviet Union was the only authentic representative of the class interests of proletarians in all countries. That it was the Russian proletariat which ruled the first Communist state was simply a function of historical fortuity and legitimatized neither its moral nor political superiority.

Proletarian internationalism became, in effect, a device for converting party subservience into state vassalage. Entire countries were subjugated and their interests subordinated to that of the russianized

Soviet State. Some satellite leaders, however, demurred and interpreted the Stalinist theory of "proletarian internationalism" as applicable only to parties in capitalist countries; otherwise it became a philosophical justification for Soviet imperialism and colonialism.

The refusal of Tito and other satellite leaders to place the interests of the Soviet State above those of their own Communist states and to act as Moscow's subservient agents of plunder and exploitation in the name of "proletarian internationalism," resulted in Tito's expulsion and the wholesale liquidation of satellite leaders who betrayed signs of wavering loyalty.

When Stalin died in March 1953, the dominance of the Soviet Union in the Communist system appeared fixed and permanent and the primacy of its interests established and assured. Stalin's death, however, unleashed internal divisions among his successors and this created opportunities for other Communist states to stir and come back to life. Amorphous factional groupings assumed shape in satellite capitals corresponding to those in the Kremlin. The more inconclusive the struggle in Moscow, the greater the apprehension in Eastern Europe. Stalin was dead and Stalinism was dying. The Communist world entered into a period of turmoil and confusion. Direction from Moscow became contradictory, inconsistent, wavering and hesitant. Surviving anti-Stalinists in satellite countries were emboldened to move and challenge their own Stalinist leaders left in the wake of Soviet confusion. Satellite leaders were soon drawn into the vortex of the Kremlin intrigues as pawns, not as pawns of Moscow, but as pawns of factional groupings in the struggle for power.

As the internal controversy became more acute, uncertain and incapable of resolution on the basis of the internal factional balance, Kremlin factions reached out into their empire for incremental support. Communist leaders were once again about to become power constituencies, starting first with China and then Yugoslavia, the most powerful and the most independent.

Yugoslavia's defection in 1948 had thus prophetically adumbrated the eruption of national Communism in the Communist system and the progressive erosion of Soviet primacy. The divisive and corrosive factional squabbles in the Kremlin after Stalin's death, the kowtowing to Peking in 1954 and the apologies in Belgrade the following year, all combined to undermine Soviet prestige and authority in the Communist universe. Uncertainty and hesitation in Moscow encouraged arrogance in Peking, insolence in Belgrade and dissidence in Eastern Europe.

The flow of demands and the resolution of conflicts in the Communist system and movement underwent systematic and fundamental alteration, as the primacy of Soviet interests was defied, subdued and challenged. Up to Stalin's death, the flow of demands in the Communist system was in one direction only, from the center to the periphery. Since Stalin's death, and with accelerated momentum after 1956, the equilibrium of demands has been substantially and progressively altered. First

Peking in 1954, then Yugoslavia in 1955, and Poland in 1956, made demands upon the Soviet Union which were met and have since been repeated by other Communist states. The demands of the Nagy regime in Hungary were such that they could be met only at the risk of permitting the system to disintegrate and so they were forcibly denied. By 1958, the Soviet Union was bombarded with demands, trivial and serious, from all directions. While Moscow continued to make its own demands upon other Communist states, they were more limited and less coercively executed. The balance in the flow of demands, however, was radically upset during the years 1957–1961, as demands flowing in from the periphery gradually exceeded those flowing outward from the center.

As the Eastern European states continued to assert the priority of their own national interests in one area after another in their dealings with the USSR, it was virtually axiomatic that, as they succeeded in resisting or trimming the demands made upon them by Moscow, they would reverse the flow of demands. The Council of Mutual Economic Aid (CMEA), for example, which was originally conceived to facilitate the economic plundering of Eastern Europe by Moscow, was reorganized to control and arrest Soviet exploitation. No sooner had this happened, than it was converted into a vehicle for draining economic resources from the Soviet Union to the Eastern European countries, as demands were made in Moscow for restitution, reparations, economic assistance and commercial autonomy, and Eastern European states asserted the right to receive economic assistance from and engage in profitable commercial transactions with capitalist countries.

Economic demands upon the Soviet Union spilled over into the political and ideological realms, as individual states demanded and received greater internal autonomy. Soviet-modeled institutions were, in many cases, dissolved or modified, while Soviet-type ideological controls over the arts, sciences, professions, education and information media were renounced in accordance with the local demands of each state, and the Cominform itself was abolished in response to these demands. The extent to which these demands were successfully asserted, depended in large measure upon the power and leverage exercised in individual cases. No overt attempt was made to organize joint or concerned action in making demands upon Moscow until 1961, when China and Albania forged an anti-Soviet factional alliance. Up to that time, only the Soviet Union enjoyed the luxury of mobilizing other parties and states against another member of the Communist confraternity.

The 20th Party Congress constitutes a major watershed in the evolution of Soviet relations with the rest of the Communist world. Locally responsive Communists like Gomulka and Nagy were catapulted into power in Poland and Hungary by powerful internal pressures which were set into motion by the revelations of the 20th Party Congress. The demolition of Stalinism at home could only result in the progressive disintegration of Stalinist structures in Eastern Europe, which had been erected in response to the dictates of Moscow. The internal effects in China, Yugoslavia and Albania were minimal since they were governed largely by indigenous Stalinist regimes, particularly China and Albania.

The Polish and Hungarian "Octobers" were the immediate and most serious consequences of destalinization, and the demands both events placed upon the Communist system as then organized threatened to reduce it to ruins. Nationalism of the Soviet variety could no longer be obscured and nationalism of the smaller states could no longer be denied by the smokescreen of proletarian internationalism. The year 1956 thus inaugurated the gradual dissolution of proletarian internationalism into its constituent proletarian or Communist nationalisms, a process that unfolded gradually and pragmatically in response to situations, events and opportunities.

Thus, little more than a decade ago, Eastern Europe, in the eyes of most Americans had been reduced to little more than an amorphous grey blob destined to languish as a permanent appendage to the Soviet Union. It seemed as if 60 million people divided among more than half-a-dozen nationalities had been suddenly and irrevocably stripped of their proud histories, deprived of their national identities and shorn of their cultural individualities. They became part of an expanding Soviet or Communist Empire. With almost indecent unanimity, the outside world forgot their national identities and for more than a decade they were almost universally consigned to anonymous oblivion as Soviet "satellites," "captive states," "slave states" or vassal states. But this apparently successful synthetic homogenization of Eastern Europe was purely superficial and illusory.

While it was Tito's defection in 1948 that pointed the way and Stalin's death in 1953 that created the opportunity, it was the denunciation of Stalin by Khrushchev in 1956 at the Twentieth Party Congress that gave initial impetus to pluralistic Communism, and it was the Sino-Soviet split, the détente with the United States (as a consequence of the partial nuclear test ban treaty signed in July, 1963) and Khrushchev's sudden and unceremonious ouster in October 1964, that created new opportunities and successively accelerated the fragmentation of the Communist Bloc and the liberalization of internal regimes. The Sino-Soviet conflict enabled the smaller states of Eastern Europe to play off the two Communist giants against one another and thus afforded them the opportunity to develop greater autonomy *within* the Communist movement as both Peking and Moscow bid for their favor and support against one another in their rivalry for leadership within the Communist movement. First Albania succeeded in using China to separate herself from Soviet paternalism and then Rumania offered herself as a "neutral" mediator between Russia and China while simultaneously enlarging her own freedom of action.

If the Sino-Soviet conflict created the opportunity for the smaller Communist countries to expand their latitude of freedom from Soviet influence within the Communist world, the Test Ban Treaty of July, 1963 and the Soviet-American détente provided the further opportunity to expand their freedom of action outside the Communist world. The Soviet-American détente served to diminish both the U.S. threat to Moscow and the Soviet threat to the West and thus contributed to the progressive erosion of both NATO and the Warsaw Pact Organization. The expansion of internal autonomy spilled over in the realm of foreign policy when Rumania, in April, 1964 announced what amounted to a virtual declaration of independence when her leaders refused to subordinate their economic development of the central coordination and planning of the Bloc's Council of Mutual Economic Assistance (Comecon) and supinely accept its dictate that Rumania concentrate on agricultural development and spurn industrialization.[5]

Khrushchev's ouster in October of 1964 accelerated the erosion of Soviet influence, and Rumania in the following year refused to accept a Soviet demand through the Warsaw Pact Organization that all of the pact countries adopt uniform rules on military conscription and instead reduced the military obligation of its conscriptees to below the suggested level. In 1966, Rumania issued her first independent call for the dissolution of all military blocs and in the same year demanded that Moscow not employ nuclear weapons without consulting the other members of the Warsaw Treaty Organization. At the same time, Bucharest questioned the right of Moscow to select the Commander of the Warsaw Treaty forces and suggested that it be rotated among the other members.[6] The same year saw Rumania concluding a number of important commercial arrangements with Western countries which reduced her trade with the Soviet Union to about 30 percent of the total by 1968, thus further reducing Moscow's capability to take punitive action. Beginning in 1964 and continuing to the present, the Rumanian leaders refused to condemn Red China and side with Moscow in the Sino-Soviet split and adopted a policy of pursuing friendly relations with *all* countries, including the United States. In apparent pursuance of this policy, Rumania has served as a diplomatic conduit between Washington and Hanoi, has established normal diplomatic relations with West Germany, refused to condemn Israel as the aggressor in the June 1967 Arab-Israeli war and continued to maintain diplomatic relations with Israel while the other Communist countries, including Yugoslavia, severed theirs, and also voted independently of the Soviet bloc on a number of issues in the U.N.

During the first half of 1968, Rumania's defiance of the Soviet Union accelerated and was no doubt encouraged by developments in Prague. As the Czechs expanded their area of internal freedom, Bucharest expanded hers in foreign policy and the two processes appeared to

[5] *Cf.* D. Floyd, *Rumania, Russia's Dissident Ally* (New York, Frederick A. Praeger, Inc., 1965), and Ghita Ionescu, *The Break-up of the Soviet Empire in Eastern Europe* (Baltimore, Penguin Books, 1965).

[6] *Cf.* Excerpts from Ceausescu's speech in *The New York Times*, March 14, 1966. The Rumanian leader, in this speech also condemned past Soviet interference in the affairs of the Rumanian Communist Party and Rumanian internal affairs, and expressed resentment at the manner in which Bessarabia was annexed by Moscow.

feed back and forth upon one another. Thus, in rapid fire order, Rumania withdrew from the Budapest Consultative Conference of Communist Parties (March 1, 1968) and a week later at the Sofia meeting of the Warsaw Pact powers, she refused to sign the "unanimous" declaration endorsing the draft treaty against the spread of nuclear weapons sponsored by Moscow and Washington. Rumania's objection to the draft treaty was similar to those raised by West Germany and other NATO powers, but she also demurred on grounds that it represented another infringement on the sovereignty of the smaller non-nuclear powers by Russia and America. This declaration marked the first time that a document of this character was issued without the signature of all the members of the Warsaw Pact, although the meeting was sufficiently important to attract all the Party Heads, Premiers, Foreign Ministers and Defense Ministers of the seven allied powers.[7]

This was followed by Bucharest's refusal to participate in the Dresden Conference of Warsaw Powers and its crude threat to intervene in Czechoslovakia (March 23–24, 1968). She similarly refused to participate in the Warsaw Meeting of the Alliance (Prague also refused to attend) on July 14–15, 1968, which issued an even more threatening ultimatum to the Dubcek regime, while Warsaw Pact forces were deliberately delaying their departure from Czech territory although their summer military exercises (which Rumania refused to join) had been completed. During this period, Rumanian leaders publicly encouraged the Czech reformers and at the height of the Crisis, President Ceausescu offered to lend his personal presence in Prague in a joint gesture of defiance. Dubcek prudently declined the offer, but after the Cierna and Bratislava meetings with the Soviet leadership, Ceausescu followed Tito to Prague in a display of solidarity. To Moscow, it would seem that the pre-War Little Entente was being resurrected as a hostile grouping of Communist states in its erstwhile placid garden of client and vassal states. After the Soviet intervention, Rumania continued its gestures of defiance: She condemned the invasion, demanded that all Communist states be masters of their own affairs, vowed never to allow Warsaw Pact forces on Soviet territory, placed the entire country on the alert and threatened to actively resist any possible Soviet encroachment on its sovereignty.

IV.

Before the Czech invasion, the countries of Eastern Europe could be grouped into four distinct general categories in reference to their relationship to the Soviet Union: (1) Yugoslavia, an independent, virtually "neutralist" and "non-aligned" Communist state that exercised complete sovereignty in its domestic and foreign policy. (2) Albania, an independent, anti-Soviet (anti-Revisionist) Communist state, ideologically allied to but not under the control of China or any other Communist state. (3) The Warsaw Pact countries of Poland, Czechoslovakia, Bulgaria, East Germany and Hungary, which were residual satellite states, or more properly client states of Moscow.[8] (4) Rumania, a dissident and non-cooperative member of the Warsaw Pact and CEMA, a "neutral" in the Sino-Soviet conflict, and quasi-independent in its foreign policy. After the Czech invasion, both Yugoslavia and Rumania were further alienated from Moscow and the Bloc, Czechoslovakia was returned to vassalage, while Poland was forced into greater dependence on the Soviet Union and, like East Germany, was threatened with *de facto* diplomatic isolation.

The current diversity in Eastern Europe is the consequence of two distinct but closely interrelated and often confused processes: destalinization and desatellitization.[9] Destalinization refers primarily to the dismantling of Stalinist institutions and practices in domestic life and originally closely followed the destalinization taking place in Russia itself. Desatellitization refers to the process whereby the individual countries of Eastern Europe gradually reasserted their autonomy and independence from Soviet control, a process that is still continuing. Desatellitization has been a universal phenomenon, but destalinization has not involved all countries. At a certain stage of development the two processes came into conflict, since some countries asserted their independence in order to retain certain Stalinist institutions and norms or to resist their complete dismantling. In Albania, for example, desatellitization has resulted in the intensification of Stalinist norms rather than greater internal liberalization. Destalinization was also resisted in varying degrees in Rumania, Bulgaria and Czechoslovakia as well, although it had recently been almost completely repudiated in Czechoslovakia. Destalinization is, in effect, a process of internal liberalization, a process that has progressed at varying tempos in Eastern Europe, sometimes faster and sometimes slower than in the Soviet Union itself. The two most independent countries of Eastern Europe reflect opposite tendencies with reference to Stalinism, with Yugoslavia the most distant in its departure from Stalinism and Albania the least.

Yugoslavia thus represents one pole in the spectrum of Communisms in Eastern Europe, while neighboring Albania constitutes the opposite pole. Although the two regimes represent opposite deviationary patterns of development, curiously enough the two countries share a

[8] East Germany, the only divided national state in Eastern Europe, was actually under full Soviet military occupation, while Poland and Hungary were under partial Soviet occupation and Bulgaria was and remains supinely servile. East Germany's status was improved by the Czech occupation while the autonomy of Poland and Hungary was seriously compromised.

[9] For an accounting of the diversity in institutions, policies and tendencies developing in Eastern Europe, cf. the following: Ghita Ionescu, *The Politics of the European Communist States* (New York, Frederick A. Praeger, Inc., 1967), and H. Gordon Skilling, *The Governments of Communist East Europe* (New York, Crowell, 1966); Kurt London, *Eastern Europe in Transition* (Baltimore, The Johns Hopkins Press, 1966); and J. Triska, *The World Communist System* (Stanford, Stanford Studies of the Communist System, 1964).

number of distinctive features which set them apart from the other Eastern European states. Both countries do not share a territorial frontier with the Soviet Union; both regimes are largely indigenous and guerrilla in origin; neither experienced a Soviet military occupation, although Soviet troops did pass through Yugoslavia; each has been governed by a single dominant personality since the inception of their Communist regimes and "personality cults" flourish in both countries. In both instances, this phenomenon can be characterized as a modified institutional residue of the Stalinist era. The "cult of personality" survived in Yugoslavia because Yugoslavia departed from the Soviet model at a time when this was the universal mode in the Communist orbit. It fell victim to the destalinization policies ushered in by Khrushchev, when Yugolslavia was no longer a part of the Bloc. In the meantime, the "Titoist" variant of the "cult of personality" developed its own inner dynamic and momentum. The "cult of personality" survived in Albania because Enver Hoxha was sufficiently isolated geographically from the Soviet Union to defy destalinization, and as a consequence "defected" from the Soviet orbit, or rather claimed that Moscow has abandoned orthodox or true Communism in favor of "revisionism." Instead of remaining politically and ideologically isolated, however, Albania had the option of associating itself with a powerful China, which also disassociated itself with Moscow's destalinization policies.[10] It should be noted that when Yugoslavia defected from the Soviet orbit, China was not yet a Communist country and Belgrade did not have the option of aligning itself with another major Communist power.

Albania and Yugoslavia represent not only the two extreme poles of Communism in Eastern Europe, but are also the most independent. This curious situation is not only a function of their relations with Moscow, but more pertinently results from their relations with each other. Albania has traditionally feared Yugoslav imperialism and initially Albania was more a satellite of Yugoslavia than of Moscow. Hoxha modeled himself more on Tito than on Stalin and given the distribution of power and interest in the area, Stalin was probably content to allow a reliable Belgrade to deal with Albania as it saw fit. Under the circumstances a Communist Albanian regime had little choice but to accept Yugoslav tutelage. With the defection of Tito in 1943, however, new options emerged for Tirana and Hoxha allied himself with Moscow and used Russia as a counterpoise against Yugoslavia in order to assert its independence from Belgrade. Since Russia was geographically removed from Albania, Hoxha could be a voluntary rather than coerced satellite of Moscow.

Among the Warsaw Pact states of Eastern Europe, Rumania and Bulgaria remain tightly run oligarchical states, while Hungary, Poland and Czechoslovakia betray varying degrees of liberalization. Poland initially was the boldest in its liberalization, but it soon relinquished its lead to Hungary, whose liberalization continues in spite of the presence

[10] Cf. William Griffith, *Albania and the Sino-Soviet Rift* (Cambridge, The M.I.T. Press, 1963).

of Soviet troops. With the displacement of Antonin Novotny as Secretary-General of the Czech Communist Party by Alexander Dubcek in January 1968, the stage was set for perhaps the most thorough-going liberalization in all Eastern Europe. Czechoslovakia is the only country in the region with a genuine democratic heritage and it was quite possible that Prague may have actually developed into an authentic Communist democratic state had not Moscow intervened. Bulgaria, the most pro-Russian and pro-Soviet country (regime and population) in Eastern Europe closely patterns itself on the Soviet Union, while Rumania chooses its own pace irrespective of changes in Russia itself.[11]

The terms "destalinization" and "desatellitization" are no longer either accurate or appropriate in describing the manifold transformations taking place in Eastern Europe. Both processes, it is now clear in retrospect, were but transitional episodes in the drive for greater autonomy internally and independence in foreign policy. In the case of destalinization, the process had moved into the phase of de-sovietization in some countries and could eventuate even in decommunization, whereas desatellitization might logically result not only in withdrawal from the Soviet alliance and neutralization, but eventually culminate in a reversal of alliances. Either development would affect the balance of power between East and West and both taken together could alter the balance irreversibly. All of these fears and hazards, which were repeated and candidly expressed by Moscow, Warsaw and East Germany, congealed to trigger the Soviet occupation of Czechoslovakia.

It is not always easy to determine which of the two processes — internal autonomy or independence in foreign policy — is perceived by the Soviet leadership as posing the greatest danger to its interests. Undoubtedly the Soviet leaders are sharply divided on this point, as they are on many others, and it is also quite possible that the relative danger of the threat of each process varies over time and from one country to another. The Soviet leadership might thus tolerate varying degrees of autonomy and independence, which would in turn depend upon their perception of the strategic importance of the country concerned or the reliability and prudence of its leadership, which further involves an intuitive calculation of the historical images of Russia prevailing in each country. The two processes pose distinct, if not entirely unrelated, sets of dangers and risks for Moscow, which seem to coincide not only with the two main purposes of the Soviet presence in Eastern Europe but also with the two major factional cleavages in the Soviet leadership. Thus growing internal autonomy directly challenges the ideological values and norms of the Soviet system and indirectly the security of the Soviet State, while independence in foreign policy erodes directly Soviet power in world affairs and indirectly constitutes a challenge to Soviet ideological goals and values. Concomitantly, some Soviet leaders, especially those that are ideologically conservative, are more likely to be disturbed

[11] For an analysis of the sources of diversity, cf. R. V. Burks, *The Dynamics of Communism in Eastern Europe* (Princeton, Princeton University Press, 1961).

by deviations and departures from the Soviet system, while others might be agitated more by the degree of independence asserted in foreign policy, and still others might find both processes equally unpalatable and any combination of the two downright intolerable. Aside from factors such as inertia, factional paralysis, and the impact of cumulative developments, these conflicting perceptions of the "main" danger may account for the extraordinary self-restraint exercised by Moscow toward Rumania's growing independence in foreign policy and her intolerance of developments in Czechoslovakia.

Leaving Albania and Yugoslavia aside, which are special cases, it is evident that Rumania and Czechoslovakia constitute contrasting case studies in Soviet behavior. But before we address ourselves specifically to the question of why Moscow behaved differently in each case, it might be useful to distinguish and segregate the dangers and risks perceived by the Soviet leadership in the two processes taking place in Eastern Europe, keeping in mind that the degree of danger or risk perceived varies from faction to faction and from individual to individual in the Soviet hierarchy. It should also be borne in mind that both processes and variations of the basic human drive for freedom and thus either process can begin first and ignite the other or develop in isolation.

While the Soviet leaders have accommodated and adjusted to the impulse of the Eastern European states to manage their own affairs, as long as they remain "socialist," the absence of any common or universal criteria of what constitutes "socialism" since Khrushchev's denunciation of Stalin in 1956, creates a wide area of ambiguity which causes anxiety in Moscow and inspires boldness and innovation in Eastern European capitals. What started out as "destalinization" was soon legitimatized in the doctrine of "separate roads to socialism," but it quickly became evident that the "separate roads" doctrine created both logical possibilities and practical opportunities for subverting and displacing the social orders inspired and established by the Soviet Union. Thus was born the Soviet equivalent of the "falling dominoes" theory: Destalinization leads to "separate roads," which proliferate into various "national deviations," which may in turn inspire "modern revisionism," which is but a prelude to "social democracy" that quickly degenerates into "bourgeois democracy" and the "restoration of capitalism."[12]

[12] Cf. "Is the Situation Normal?" a denunciation of "creeping counter-revolution" in *Izvestia*, July 31, 1968 and A. Butenko, "Under the False Flag of 'Building Bridges,'" *Izvestia*, May 16, 1968, where it is alleged, "first 'bridges' and then a 'revision of the status quo,' *i.e.*, a revision of the existing boundaries in Europe." Cf. also M. Volgin, "Bridges on Rotten Foundations," *Izvestia*, July 11, 1968; "The Strategy of Imperialism and the Czechoslovak Socialist Republic," *Pravda*, July 15, 1968; I. Aleksandrov's article in *Pravda* (July 11, 1958), "Attack on the Socialist Foundations of Czechoslovakia," in which he ominously compares the "counter-revolutionary" situation in Czechoslovakia with that of Hungary in 1956; V. Bakinsky's "Whom Doctor Henzl is Defending," *Izvestia* (July 13, 1968), which stresses the ultimate consequences of allowing "anti-socialist" elements and "counter-revolutionaries" free rein in Czechoslovakia, and finally the *Pravda* editorial of August 22, 1968, justifying the intervention, "Defender of Socialism is the Highest International Duty."

V.

At what point in this process are the Soviet leaders apt to intervene? Does the Czechoslovak intervention provide clear-cut criteria for judging what might be called the Soviet "threshold of intolerance"? On the surface, it might appear that the threshold of intolerance in the Czechoslovak case was reached at a point somewhere between "modern revisionism" and "social democracy," and that a precedent for future interventions has thus been established. In concrete terms, the Czechoslovak intervention suggests that the Soviet Union will intervene when the following developments take place:

1. The removal of all censorship, restraints and sanctions on freedom of expression in the press, arts and sciences and the restoration of the freedom of expression and assembly generally.[13]

2. Pressures develop for the restoration of a mutiparty system that would jeopardize the political monopoly and control of the Communist party.[14]

3. Economic innovations are planned that would seriously dilute the "socialist" character of the economic order returning some sectors of the economy to private hands and allowing a greater latitude for the further expansion of the private sector.

4. The restoration of Parliamentary government, whose power, responsibility and accountability would be to the electorate rather than the Communist party.

Internal changes in Czechoslovakia alone, however, were not sufficient in themselves to provoke Soviet intervention, given the grave risks and costs that such intervention would entail. If these developments could be *contained* and *restricted* only to Czechoslovakia, then intervention might have been averted. It appears that it was precisely this as-

[13] For the ventilation of Soviet fears concerning press freedom in Czechoslovakia, cf. Yuri Zhukov, "Strange Undertaking of *Obrana Lidu,*" *Pravda,* July 27, 1968, and "Double Game," *Pravda,* July 28, 1968. For Soviet attacks on Czeck "revisions" of recent history, cf. A. Nedorov, "Contrary to the Facts," *Izvestia,* June 29, 1968, and "What Does 'The Student' Teach? — The Prague Weekly 'for Young Intelligentsia' and Its Concept of Democracy," *Komsomolskaya Pravda,* June 21, 1968. Moscow was particularly incensed at the renewed interest in the Masaryks and attempts to rewrite the recent history of Czech-German relations, which it interpreted to be an intellectual preparation for a rapprochement with Bonn. Cf. also A. Kamshalov, "Socialism and Young People," *Komsomolskaya Pravda,* July 20, 1968 and the attacks upon Jan Prochazka in *Literaturnaya Gazeta,* May 19 and June 26, 1968.

[14] This was reflected in the vicious Soviet attacks upon the political manifesto, "2000 Words," which called upon the Dubcek regime to purge the party of Novotny followers, and contained a savage criticism of the party as the source of Prague's ills for the past 20 years. Cf. abridged text in *Washington Post,* July 21, 1968 and for Soviet attacks, cf. *Pravda,* July 11, 1968, the attack upon Frantisek Kriegel in *Liternatunaya Gazeta,* July 10, 1968, the attack upon Josef Boruvka, a member of the Czech Presidium, for approving the notion of a non-Communist opposition in *Pravda,* March 9, 1968, and N. Vladimirov's attacks on the new "political clubs" in Czechoslovakia, "The 'Political Instincts' of Vaclav Havel," *Literaturnaya Gazeta,* May 15, 1968.

surance that Dubcek and his reformist colleagues gave to Moscow, which the Soviet leaders initially accepted. Upon further reflection, however, it was judged that Dubcek was either unwilling or incapable of controlling the situation at home and certainly unable to prevent the contagion of liberalization from spreading across Czech frontiers.[15]

Thus, if the infection could not be isolated, then one might conclude that it was the danger of contagion rather than the infection alone that was considered the graver risk. Once Czech liberalization was legitimatized by accepting it as a *bona fide* variant of Marxism-Leninism, then it would be legitimate for Communists and others to demand the same measures in other Communist countries, particularly in Poland, East Germany and in the Soviet Union itself. Internal dominoes falling in Czechoslovakia alone was bad enough but might be tolerated, but apparently the nightmare of dominoes falling all over in Eastern Europe and in the Soviet Union was too much. Too many vested interests and cherished goals and values were involved.

The Soviet fear of the consequences of both processes operating simultaneously in Czechoslovakia was first formally registered in the Dresden Conference warning to Debcek[16] that events inside Czechoslovakia were threatening the stability and endangering the security of other Communist states and then formalized more specifically as an explicit threat to intervene in the Warsaw Powers statement of July 15, 1968:

> We cannot agree to have hostile forces push your country from the road of Socialism and create a threat of severing Czechoslovakia from the Socialist community, that is something more than your cause. . . . This is the common cause of our countries, which have joined in the Warsaw Treaty to ensure the independence, the peace and security in Europe. . . . We shall never agree to have imperialism, using ways peaceful and non-peaceful, making a gap from the inside or from the outside in the Socialist system and changing in imperialism's favor the correlation of forces in Europe.[17]

VI.

A third major risk in allowing the unimpeded expansion of internal autonomy is that it might create the conditions that would allow the generation of pressures for greater independence from Moscow in foreign policy. This brings us logically to a discussion of the risks and dangers perceived by the Soviet leaders as its former satellites demand greater freedom in dealing with the outside world.

[15] This was the crux of the warnings in the Dresden and Warsaw statements and a major reason given for the necessity of intervention in *Pravda,* August 22, 1968.

[16] Cf. *Pravda,* March 25, 1968, for text of communique and for Soviet commentary, *cf.* I. Aleksandrov, "Slanderer's Fabrications are Doomed to Failure," *Pravda,* March 28, 1968.

[17] Full text in *Pravda,* July 18, 1968.

These risks and hazards, of course, vary from one country to another, depending largely upon its strategic importance to Soviet security, economic significance, natural resources and its impact and influence upon the other Communist countries as a possible model to emulate. While the Soviet leaders might tolerate varying degrees of independence in foreign policy just as they might allow differentials in internal autonomy, the latitude of freedom is less than that permissible in internal affairs because it strikes more directly at the Soviet power position in world affairs and more vitally affects its security. While in the case of Czechoslovakia, the traditionally favorable image of Russia combined with the Czech fear of German "revanchism" might have been sufficient to allay Soviet qualms that an independent foreign policy would erode Prague's commitments to the Soviet Union and the Warsaw Pact, it was nevertheless true that some developments in the direction of an independent foreign policy raised apprehensions in Moscow, frightened Gomulka and appeared downright ominous to Ulbricht. This included not only a possible political and diplomatic rapprochement with West Germany (encouraged by Bonn's repudiation of the Munich agreement of 1938) originating within the Dubcek regime itself, but also the prospect of a large hard-currency loan from West Germany that might set the stage for a radical reorientation of Czechoslovakia's trade from the Soviet Union and Eastern Europe to Western countries.[18] The fact that such a rearrangement of trade relations eminently coincided with Czech economic interests and was indispensable for economic recovery served to reinforce the fear that a change in trade relations would soon be followed by significant alterations in Prague's political and ideological alignments.

Furthermore, when Brezhnev's mission to save Novotny failed in December 1967 and particularly after Novotny's suspension from the party and the discrediting of the Secret Police by the Dubcek regime, opinion on foreign policy became bolder and, from the Soviet point of view, outrageous. The Jan Mesaryic affair was reopened and Moscow's complicity through Mikoyan was alleged, past Soviet interference in

[18] Moscow feared that not only Prague but other Eastern European states might be attracted by the blandishments of West Germany's "new Eastern Policy," which became a focus of Soviet attack. Cf. Gromyko's speech to the Supreme Soviet, Pravda, June 28, 1968; "What They Hope for in Bonn," Izvestia, May 15, 1968; "Secret Arms Caches at the Border with the F.R.G.," Pravda, July 19, 1968; "F.R.G. Interference in Czechoslovak Affairs," Pravda, July 20, 1968; V. Mikhailov, "In the Revanchists Sights," Pravda, July 22, 1968; L. Kamyin, "Revanchists' Orgy," Izvestia, July 26, 1968; V. Zhigulenko, "To the Beat of Drums," Izvestia, July 27, 1968; and Ye. Grigoryev, "A Hoof Wrapped in Rags," Pravda, July 28, 1968. Professor Zbigniew Brzezinski, a former member of the State Department's Policy Planning Staff came in for considerable condemnation as the ideologist of the "building bridges" policy and the architect of the plan to "isolate" East Germany. Cf. Brzezinski's Alternative to Partition (New York, McGraw-Hill, 1965); Willy Brandt, "German Policy Toward the East," Foreign Affairs, April, 1968, Adam Bromke and P. E. Uren, The Communist States and The West (New York, Frederick A. Praeger, 1967), and The Atlantic Community and Eastern Europe (The Atlantic Institute, 1967).

Czech affairs was roundly condemned, and demands for a new and more thorough investigation made their appearance in the press. A prominent Czech general challenged Soviet domination of the Warsaw Pact command structure,[19] others called for a reexamination of Prague's role in the Warsaw Pact Organization, while still others demanded that future Czech foreign policy be based on Czech national interests and not on the interests of Moscow, other Communist states or the World Communist movement.[20] Some even called for a frankly "neutralist" foreign policy.

It is still conceivable that the Soviet leaders might have adjusted to a wide degree of Czech autonomy in domestic and foreign affairs if they were convinced that it would be restricted only to Czechoslovakia and would not spill over and generate similar pressures in more sensitive and less reliable Communist allies. The national and renowned Czech penchant for prudence and caution reinforced by the traditional Czech fear of Germany might have been sufficient to inspire a continuing loyalty to the Soviet Union and also sufficient to inspire Moscow's confidence in Prague's reliability. The decisive factor in a sharply divided Soviet leadership may well have been the real fear that Ulbricht would not be able to resist the pressures for liberalization in East Germany that would inevitably be generated if Dubcek was successful in resisting Soviet pressures. Greater internal autonomy in East Germany would inevitably result in further popular pressures for an independent reexamination of East Germany's role as a separate state bound in permanent vassalage to Russia. Under these conditions Moscow would be confronted with a crisis of incalculable magnitude. The situation might spin out of control and result in a reunited Germany that would fundamentally alter the entire balance of power in Europe and conjure up the nightmare of another German march to the East. At best, an autonomous East Germany would sap Soviet energies and constitute a permanent drain on Soviet power, resources and nerves.

One might even make out a case that the desperate and hasty disavowal of the Bratislava agreement was actually triggered not so much by Dubcek's refusal or inability to satisfy some reputed secret commitment to arrest liberalization but rather by Ulbricht's unexpected gesture of reconciliation with West Germany made soon after his

---

[19] Lt. General Vaclav Prchlik, Head of the Military Department of the Central Committee of the Czech Communist Party. *Cf. The New York Times,* July 16 and 19, 1968. For the Soviet reaction, cf. the *Krasnaya Zvezda* editorial, "Whose Favor is General V. Prchlik Currying?" July 23, 1968, which prompted Prague to reassign the General, which failed to satisfy Moscow.

[20] In particular, the views of Jan Prochazka, who advocated a restricted role in international affairs for Czechoslovakia, based upon her own needs and interests: "We are a small country. . . . We should have a modest foreign policy, one conforming to our possibilities. I do not understand why we have to intervene in the affairs of Madagasgar, Guatemala or Nigeria." *Cf.* "The Train Jan Prochazka Missed," *Literaturnaya Gazeta,* May 19, 1968, and N. Vladimirov, "On Which Roof is Jan Prochazka Sitting?" *Literaturnaya Gazeta,* June 26, 1968; *cf.* also Moscow's attack on "The Student," *Komsomolskaya Pravda,* June 21, 1968.

disagreeable meeting with Dubcek and just a few days before the forces of the Warsaw alliance moved across Czech frontiers.[21] To Moscow this may have been an evil omen of impending catastrophe unless she intervened to stop the falling Czech domino.

VII.

The Soviet intervention in Czechoslovakia has been widely compared to the Soviet crackdown in Hungary twelve years earlier and contrasted to Soviet restraint in the face of Rumanian defiance. What accounts for the differences and similarities in Soviet behavior in the three cases? First of all, it should be pointed out that the Soviet Union shares a common frontier with all three countries, the absence of which was an important factor in the successful defiance of both Yugoslavia and Albania. Aside from the factor of time, which is important in itself, the Soviet intervention in Hungary was inspired by fears that were both genuine and credible and triggered by provocations that transcended any indulged in by Prague and Bucharest. A national anti-Soviet uprising swept Hungary, during which the Imre Nagy regime virtually disestablished the Communist system: the Secret Police was dismantled and many of its members executed in summary fashion by outraged vigilante groups and the military; the multi-party system was restored as the Communist party disintegrated; political prisoners were released, including Cardinal Mindszenty; Nagy announced Hungary's unilateral withdrawal from the Warsaw Pact and enunciated a "neutralist" foreign policy. It should also be remembered that the Hungarian uprising took place against the background of the Eisenhower-Dulles policy of "liberation," which was avowedly dedicated — in words at least — to the emancipation of the satellites from Soviet domination. It might be added that the appeals and encouragement of Radio Free Europe appeared to the Kremlin as a further indication of U.S. malevolence and mischief.

Neither Czechoslovakia nor Rumania have threatened to *withdraw* from the Warsaw Pact, although both have criticized its current organization and Rumania has refused to cooperate with it in recent years. Neither have threatened to disestablish the Communist social order although the Czechs planned to "humanize" it, and neither have threatened to pursue a "neutralist" foreign policy, although some Czechs discussed the possibility while Bucharest has proclaimed its "neutrality" in the Sino-Soviet conflict. And the Communist party has never been threatened with disintegration in either country, although the Czechs were dreaming of the prospect of opposition parties if not a full-fledged multi-party system. And most importantly, developments in Czechoslovakia were proceeding in an atmosphere of détente and the total absence of any U.S. provocations, verbal or otherwise.[22]

[21] Cf. *The New York Times*, August 18, 1968.
[22] This did not prevent Moscow from indulging in fantasies and fabrications concerning the role of the U.S. Cf. V. Ragulin and I. Chushkov,

The causes of Soviet intervention in Hungary are relatively un-complicated when contrasted to the combination of Soviet restraint with respect to Rumania and Soviet intervention in Czechoslovakia. Perhaps an analysis of differences and similarities in Soviet behavior toward developments in the two countries will aid us in developing criteria by which to determine the Soviet "threshold of intolerance." First of all, it should be realized that the Soviet *threat* to intervene has always been omnipresent in relations with both countries and for that matter is a perennial hazard faced by all of the Eastern European countries as they have advanced from vassalage to clientage. A second general observa-tion is that the factional divisions in the Soviet leadership, resulting in periods of inertia and paralysis in the face of difficult decisions, is an uncertain and incalculable variable since the balance of factions within the Soviet hierarchy is in a state of continuous flux and the decision to intervene or exercise restraint (whether calculated or resulting from factional paralysis) may be a product of fortuity and chance. A third general point is that the developments in Czechoslovakia took place after Rumania's defiance and the sheer cumulative impact of the Ru-manian situation was a crucial incremental factor in the Soviet percep-tions of threat and danger in the Czech case.

Both Czechoslovakia and Rumania share frontiers with Russia, as already noted above. Both have ceded territory to the Soviet Union, but unlike the Czechs who have no irredentist claims to the Carpatho-Ukraine, the Rumanians have not resigned themselves to the loss of Bessarabia, which is considered to be part of the Rumanian national patrimony. The Czechs and Slovaks are Slavs but not orthodox; the Rumanians are orthodox but not Slavs. The Czechs have traditionally viewed Russia as a potential liberator and protector, whereas in recent decades, the Rumanian image of Russia has been rather negative. The Czechs were allied to the Soviet Union during World War II, whereas Rumania joined the Axis, participated actively in the war against the Soviet Union, re-annexing Bessarabia and adding "Transdniestria" to their territories for good measure. The Czechs fear Germany which has been the traditional and historic national enemy and oppressor of the Czechs (the Slovaks, however, do not share this perception), whereas Germany has never constituted a direct threat to Rumania, whose dynasty was a branch of the Hohenzollern family. Thus, while it would be natural for the Czechs to rely upon the Russians as their protector against Germany, the Rumanians have no need of Russian protection, but on the contrary, are apt to view Russia as a national enemy not above threatening to support Hungarian territorial claims against Bu-charest, if the need and opportunity arises. Whereas the Czechs perceive

---

"Adventurist Plans of the Pentagon and the C.I.A." *Pravda*, July 19, 1968; B. Strelnikov, "Trojan Horse of American Propaganda," *Pravda*, July 29, 1968; Yuri Zhukov, "Instigators," *Pravda*, August 16, 1968; and N. Matveyev, "Poisoned Pens," *Izvestia*, August 17, 1968. Rusk's tepid protest at this gratui-tous involvement was routinely shrugged off by Ambassador Dobrynin and the Soviet Foreign Ministry.

Germany as the greatest threat to their security and independence, the Rumanians tend to see the Soviet Union in this light. And finally, the Czech Communist party was a broadly based national party in contrast to the Rumanian Communist party which had virtually no national base and whose leaders were largely non-ethnic Rumanian *emigres* sojourning in Moscow as Soviet lackeys.[23]

While Rumania's isolated geographical location rendered her vulnerable to Soviet pressure, it simultaneously made her defiance of the Soviet Union a minimal threat to Soviet power and security interests. Furthermore, Rumania's independent policy posed little danger to the vital interests of any other Eastern European state and thus most of her Warsaw Pact allies viewed Rumania's gestures of independence from Moscow with not a little sympathy. Only Hungary has long standing grievances against Rumania, but Bucharest's disaffection from Moscow could only benefit Hungary, not injure her. In short, Rumania's defection did not pose a real threat to Russia or any other Eastern European country since she was surrounded entirely by Communist states (if one includes Yugoslavia).

On the other hand, Czechoslovakia's geographical location was of signal strategic and security importance not only to Russia but to Poland and East Germany as well. Whereas Rumania's independent behavior in foreign policy would be largely of symbolic significance, an independent Czech foreign policy could seriously interfere with coordinated Bloc military or diplomatic action, particularly where West Germany is concerned. Geographically, Czechoslovakia slices Eastern Europe into a "northern tier" (East Germany and Poland) and a "southern tier" (Hungary, Rumania, Bulgaria, Albania and Yugoslavia). Significantly, the countries to the north of Prague supported and indeed encouraged Moscow to apply pressures and threaten sanctions of the liberalization program was not arrested and indeed reversed, while the southern tier, with the exception of Moscow's perennially loyal satrapy of Bulgaria, *i.e.*, Hungary, Rumania and Yugoslavia, supported the Dubcek regime's right to recover its full sovereignty. Even Albania supported the right of Prague to declare its independence of Muscovite control, although the substance of Czech liberalization was anathema to both Enver Hoxha and his distant patron in Peking. Although Janos Kadar gave Dubcek muted moral support, Hungary reluctantly participated in the Warsaw military occupation because as a country still under Soviet military occupation it had little choice.[24] In contrast, East Germany and Poland participated in the occupation with considerable enthusiasm, while

[23] Ceausescu charged in May, 1966 that Moscow deliberately staffed the Rumanian Communist party with non-ethnic Rumanians and emigrés to keep it in a permanent condition of servility. *The New York Times,* May 14, 1966.
[24] One prominent Hungarian, the chief editor of *Nepszabadzag,* for example, rejected in a speech before the Hungarian Parliament, the Moscow charge that the situation in Czechoslovakia was similar to that of Hungary in 1956. *The New York Times,* July 14, 1968.

Bulgaria faithfully followed the Soviet lead, hoping perhaps to pick up Soviet support for its latent claims to Yogoslav Macedonia.

These cleavages in the Communist Bloc are likely to survive no matter how the Czech crisis is finally resolved and while they may be submerged temporarily, they are likely to be resurrected with greater force later on.

Not only does Czechoslovakia cut the Eastern European countries into two parts geographically, but it is the only Eastern European country that simultaneously borders on West Germany and Russia and indeed is the only Warsaw Pact state that shares a border with two non-Communist states. Thus it is the most exposed to the West geographically just as it is more related to the West in political traditions, historical associations and general way of life than the other countries of Eastern Europe (East Germany excepted). When one looks at the map of Eastern Europe, Czechoslovakia conjures up the image of an "invasion funnel" leading from West Germany to Russia, or one might even visualize Czechoslovakia as a knife aimed by West Germany at the heart of the Ukraine. Decisions, unfortunately, are often influenced by such banal metaphors, as they are by clichés like Bismarck's, "The master of Bohemia is the master of Europe."

In short, one might say that while the risk of a Czech defection from the Soviet Bloc in foreign policy was lower than that of Rumania, the danger to Russia and other countries of Eastern Europe would be infinitely greater than a Rumanian defection. Even gestures of Rumanian-type noncooperation posed a threat to Russia and the two countries to the north. The Czech armed forces could be relied upon to resist a German invasion but it would be unlikely that they could be depended upon to act in order to make diplomatic gains for the Soviet Union, the Bloc as a whole or "World Communism." As a consequence of the occupation, it is doubtful now that the Czech army can be relied upon to cooperate efficiently in any venture with the other members of the Soviet Bloc.

One final factor that distinguishes the Czech case from the Rumanian. As noted earlier, there might be a cause-and-effect relationship between internal autonomy and independence in foreign policy, moving in either direction. In domestic matters, the Rumanians did not challenge the legitimacy of Marxism-Leninism, did not seek to "humanize," "revise" or "liberalize" Communism, and hence posed little direct threat to the legitimacy and stability of Soviet-type social orders. Czech liberalization, on the other hand, directly challenged some of the basic principles of Marxist-Leninist ideology. Even the validity of the Soviet doctrine that Leninism was an integral and inseverable extension of Marxism as a universal truth was questioned when a prominent Czech leader had the audacity to suggest that Leninism was a purely Russian variant of Marxism and hence not necessarily applicable to other socialist countries.[25]

[25] C. Cisar, a Secretary of the Czech Central Committee, in *Rude Pravo*, May 7, 1968, Cisar later attempted to soften his position, but he was never-

This type of challenge should be distinguished from the successful repudiation of the Soviet leaders as the ultimate fount of ideological infallibility and orthodox truth. The Soviet leaders have long ago adjusted themselves to the loss of their monopoly on doctrinal omniscience and indeed are busily engaged denying it to the Chinese. To relinquish the claim of doctrinal infallibility merely means to give up the right to dictate future ideological interpretations for the Communist world, but to accept Leninism as relative and restricted truth rather than absolute and universal writ, would be to accept the legitimacy of dismantling existing Communist systems and putting Lenin on the same footing as the descredited Stalin. Such an acceptance would threaten the existing systems not only in Eastern Europe but in the Soviet Union itself, where a small but growing body of disenchanted Soviet intellectuals welcomed developments in Czechoslovakia with quiet enthusiasm.[26]

There is some reason to believe that the conservatively oriented members of the Soviet leadership were just as frightened — if not more so — by the prospect of a successful humanized Communist system in Czechoslovakia that would endeavor to join democratic freedoms and procedures with a socialist economic order as they were by the specter of a "restoration of capitalism." A humanized, democratized Communist state in the heart of Europe might not only discredit the Soviet model itself, exposing it as a transitional regional product of Marxism grafted on to the Russian autocratic heritage, but might serve as an attractive model to be emulated by other Eastern European countries. Even the Russians might be attracted to such an option in preference to their own primitive and outmoded political and economic institutions, which appear to many members of the Soviet scientific, intellectual and technological elite to be monumental symbols of embarrassment and disgrace in the second most powerful and scientifically advanced country in the world as it moves into the 21st Century.[27]

In analyzing Soviet behavior in Eastern Europe, one cannot exclude the conditioning character of the international environment outside the Communist world itself. At this point, one can only ask questions without answering them. To what extent was the Soviet move against Czechoslovakia a reflection of the relative growth of missile and nuclear power *vis à vis* the United States? Does this mean that as the Soviet Union approaches parity with the United States that it will manifest less self-restraint in its behavior? To what extent was the

---

theless severely attacked by the prominent Soviet ideologist, F. Konstantinov, in *Pravda* on June 14, 1968, "Marxism-Leninism is a Unified International Doctrine," and on July 24, 1968, "Leninism is the Marxism of the Present Era." *Cf.* also I. Pomelov, "Common Principles and National Characteristics in the Development of Socialism," *Pravda*, August 14, 1968, which concentrated its fire on national variations of "socialism" and "communism."

[26] *Cf.*, for example, the remarkable document on "convergence" by the Soviet scientist, Andrei D. Sakharov, who called upon the Soviet leaders to support and praise Czech liberalization. Full text in *The New York Times*, July 22, 1968.

[27] *Cf.* The Sakharov statement, cited above.

Soviet decision to occupy Czechoslovakia conditioned by the prior knowledge that the United States was unwilling or unable to take either preventive or retaliatory measures? Was the U.S. warning to Moscow not to occupy Rumania a factor in a deterring Soviet sanction against Bucharest in retaliation for its past recalcitrance and its shrill condemnation of the Soviet occupation of Czechoslovakia? To what extent is there a tacitly acknowledged, never admitted but indeed denied, Soviet-American "spheres of influence" arrangement which recognizes that each Global Power has untrammelled power to act with relative impunity in its own domain, subject only to the constraints of its own sense of moral propriety, the restraints imposed by its internal factional conflicts and institutional procedures, the deterrence inspired by its sensitivity to the inevitable cries of moral outrage, the reluctance engendered by the prospect of tarnishing its carefully cultivated image of a mature and responsible power, and the fears aroused by the prospect of further fracturing its own alliance system and alienating the diplomatic affections of countries in the Third World? To what extent was the action conditioned by the eroding credibility of the Soviet Union to act promptly and decisively to protect its interests brought about by American intervention in Southeast Asia and the Caribbean, the challenge of Communist China, the dissolution of Soviet control over the World Communist Movement, the apparent disintegration of its empire in Eastern Europe, and the disenchantment of its Arab client states with Moscow's inability to prevent an Israeli victory in the 1967 war or to force Israel out of the Sinai and the West Bank? The fall of Nkrumah in Ghana, Ben Bella in Algeria and Sukarno in Indonesia may have also reinforced the image of an impotent Soviet behemoth, paralyzed by the fear of thermonuclear war and mesmerized by the subtle and seductive blandishments of a cunning and disarming American détente diplomacy.

And finally one must ask whether the Soviet move was further conditioned by a debilitating fear of the uncertain intentions of a faction-ridden Chinese leadership, armed with a growing arsenal of thermonuclear weapons and a developing missile capability, thus prompting the Soviet leaders to shore up their disintegrating European flank in order to minimize the possibilities of a two-front diplomatic or military maneuver against Moscow, no matter how remote, calculated or fortuitous it may be.

VIII.

What of the future?

It is now apparent in retrospect that the Czech crisis confronted the Soviet leaders with its moment of truth in Eastern Europe: to intervene or not to intervene? Either course would have produced unpalatable and distasteful consequences. Down to virtually the moment of occupation, it appeared that the Soviet Presidium, after its meetings with the Czech leadership at Cierna and Bratislava, had decided, perhaps by a slim margin, that the consequences of non-intervention would be less disagreeable than those of intervention. Unless we succumb to the view that the Soviet leaders engaged in an act of calculated perfidy, it must be assumed that a prior decision was precipitously reversed. This seems to be confirmed by the gross ineptness of the political side of the occupation as contrasted with the quick and smooth efficiency of the military operation. The Soviet action is thus simultaneously a frightening tribute to the immensity of Soviet military power and a dismal monument to its diplomatic ineptitude, political incompetence, grotesque morality and the utter and complete bankruptcy of Communist ideology. The enormity of the Soviet debacle was permanently enshrined by the pathetic inability of 650,000 Warsaw Pact troops to find the elusive and nameless Czech political leaders who invited them to expel the "Western imperialists," subdue the "counterrevolutionaries" and crush the treacherous "Dubcek clique."[28] Unable to pressure an aged, but unyielding President Svoboda to legalize their intervention and unable to persuade even a handful of Czech and Slovak Communists to betray their country by signing the prefabricated Soviet document of invitation and to form a Quisling government, Moscow was forced to deal with the very government which its military forces had arrested. Svoboda was whisked off to Moscow and given a shameless red carpet welcome, while Dubcek, Premier Oldrich Cernik and National Assembly President Josef Smirkovsky were transported to the Soviet capital in chains to "negotiate" a compromise settlement.

It is an eloquent tribute to Czech courage and perhaps Dubcek's Slovak obstinacy that the Soviet intervention has not been endowed with even a shred of legality and that the faceless sponsors who "invited" the Warsaw Powers to occupy their country have not come forward to identify themselves, if indeed they do exist at all.

Clearly the Soviet Union has reached an important crossroads in its relationship with Eastern Europe. Before the Czech intervention in Czechoslovakia, the Soviet position in Eastern Europe had been clearly slipping in response partly to the apparent erosion of NATO and the diminution of the U.S. threat to the Communist system. Either the Soviet empire was on the verge of dissolution as Rumania virtually

---

[28] The "invitation" was necessary to provide the bare minimum basis of legality for the intervention, since the Warsaw Treaty does not give the member states the blanket authority, collectively or individually, to unilaterally declare the existence of "counter-revolutionaries" and/or external "imperialist forces" and intervene on their own initiative. The juridical scenario employed by Moscow was virtually a carbon copy of the U.S. and OAS's intervention in the Dominican Republic. The so-called invitation, published by *Pravda* and *Izvestia* on August 21, 1968, justified the intervention on both internal and external grounds:

Tass is authorized to state that party and state leaders of the Czechoslovak Socialist Republic have requested the Soviet Union and other allied states to give the fraternal Czechoslovak people immediate assistance, including assistance with armed forces. The reason for this appeal is the threat posed to the socialist system existing in Czechoslovakia and to the constitutionally established state system by counter-revolutionary forces that have entered into collusion with external forces hostile to socialism.

seceded from the Warsaw alliance and Czech liberalization appeared to be irresistible and threatened to infect all of Eastern Europe, or it was on the brink of a fundamental transformation.

The transformation of relationships could have assumed one of three forms:

1. The conversion of the Warsaw Pact and CEMA into an authentic socialist "commonwealth of nations," in which the individual members would be allowed a wide latitude of internal deviation from the Soviet norms of socialism, exercise greater freedom in trade and cultural relations with the West, while remaining tightly bound to the Soviet Union in a purely defensive alliance. Such a transformation would presuppose a continuation and expansion of the détente, a tacit disavowal of ideological aggressiveness in foreign policy, and give greater form and shape to the new commonwealth as a purely regional association, in which the interests of the smaller members would no longer be sacrificed to those of the Soviet Union in the name of the bogus principle of "proletarian internationalism" or subordinated to purely Soviet great power diplomacy in its dealings with the United States or Communist China. The chief objections to such a transformation before August 1968 were that it threatened to isolate East Germany, render Poland even more dependent upon Russia *vis à vis* West Germany, and deprive the Soviet Union of some useful levers and pressures in dealing with the German problem, the United States and Communist China.

2. The natural *devolution* of the Warsaw Pact, CEMA and other multilateral organizations and their replacement with a series of bilateral and tri-lateral agreements. The Soviet Union could make periodic *ad hoc* adjustments to the situation, allowing the natural interests of each state to more or less shape its individual relationship with the Soviet Union. Moscow would rely upon a common ideology, intersecting interests, the prudence and good sense of the smaller countries and the reservoir of goodwill toward Moscow that would flow from such a policy to become the foundations of a new relationship. Under these conditions, the relationship of the individual member states with Russia could vary considerably as would their relations with one another. The artificiality of imposed "fraternal" relations would be replaced by something more uncertain but perhaps more durable and natural.

3. The reconstitution of the Soviet Empire as a "sphere of influence" or domination, similar to the U.S. position in the Caribbean. Wherever and whenever necessary, naked force and fear would replace reliance on the shibboleths of ideology, pliable local leaders and a common social system, in order to preserve Soviet control.

Apparently Moscow has chosen the third option which effectively forecloses the other two. It would seem that the Soviet Union by its action in Czechoslovakia has not only expended whatever reservoir of goodwill that remained of the historical, cultural and ideological associations of the past, but has reduced its options to only two: Preserving its position by force, threat and periodic intervention, or allowing its control of Eastern Europe to completely disintegrate. For the moment, the Soviet Union has enhanced the credibility of its determination to use its immense power to control its immediate environment, but simultaneously has restored its reputation for diplomatic perfidy, impetuous brutality and psychological insecurity. Not only the Communist world, but the Communist states of Eastern Europe are now irrevocably split. Although there is no discernible military threat in sight from any quarter in Europe, the Soviet Union is now in military occupation of no less than four Eastern European countries (Poland, East Germany, Hungary and Czechoslovakia). Albania has unilaterally withdrawn from the Warsaw Pact as a result of the Czech crisis, while Rumania refuses to allow Warsaw Pact forces to maneuver on its territory and refuses to participate in their exercises elsewhere. Yugoslavia has never belonged to the Warsaw Pact and at the height of the Czech crisis announced its determination, together with Rumania, to resist by armed force any attempt on the part of Russia to occupy her territories.

The liberalization in Czechoslovakia has been arrested and is being reversed. Soviet leaders have announced not only their intention to heap Soviet troops on the Czech-West German frontier indefinitely, but are also imposing their dictates on purely internal Czech affairs, and have refused to allow Prague to expand its trade relations outside the Soviet bloc. Like Hungary, Czechoslovakia has been retroverted from clientage to vassalage. While the initial reaction in the other countries of Eastern Europe was fear and apprehension combined with outrage and shame, they are now on notice that Moscow will not hesitate to reduce its fraternal allies to vassalage if the Soviet Union disapproves of either their internal or external policies. Nevertheless, as the initial shock wears off and the Czechs continue their passive resistance and active non-cooperation, the people of Eastern Europe are likely to become more restive than quiescent. Disturbances might even spread among disaffected and alienated Soviet intellectuals, scientists and students. The moral position of Gomulka has been probably irretrievably damaged, now that Gomulka stabbed his defenseless neighbor in the back with neither justification nor provocation. Poland, as a consequence, has been more tightly riveted to dependence upon the Soviet Union and is now completely surrounded by countries under Soviet military occupation and its people even more thoroughly alienated from Moscow. It may be that Gomulka sold his country's honor mainly to gain a tactical advantage over his internal rival, General Moczar, and in return for a mess of potage established a precedent for a future Soviet military occupation of Poland in the guise of "multilateral" action.

The Soviet military occupation of Czechoslovakia ushers Soviet relations with Eastern Europe into a new phase — a phase of Soviet military control. This new phase should not be confused with the earlier Stalinist period. During the Stalin era, Moscow relied not only upon the Soviet military presence, but upon a common ideology and more importantly upon the reliability and servility of the local Communist party.

This is no longer even residually the case in Rumania, Yugoslavia, Albania and Czechoslovakia (in spite of the occupation). Communist parties in Eastern European countries will continue to pay greater and greater attention to national needs rather than Soviet dictates and interests, although the danger of a desperate Soviet intervention has increased. But interventionism itself is a wasting asset and cannot be sustained indefinitely, and thus the Soviet military occupation of Czechoslovakia simultaneously signifies a Soviet determination to reintensify its control, but at the same time risks contracting its range of control.

In spite of the Soviet action, as time goes on the ideological bond of Communism will continue to erode and Eastern European countries will become more European and less "Communist." Today everywhere in Eastern Europe, in stark contrast to the Soviet Union, Communism appears as a thin, almost transparent, veneer, ready to be shed the moment the climate is felicitous. Fundamental and far-reaching transformations are still imminent in Eastern Europe, and perhaps for at least another decade, these changes will take place in the name of Communism while simultaneously subverting it. While similar changes will also take place in Russia, the necessity or desire to disavow Communism as an ideology may not be nearly as intense. After all, Soviet society and Marxism-Leninism are Russian creations and thus are not as incompatible with Russian nationalism as they are with the nationalisms of non-Soviet countries. It must be remembered that whereas the Communist system is an indigenous Russian phenomenon, in Eastern Europe, it is an alien, imported system imposed from the outside by force. Thus while Communism and nationalism may be fused into a "Soviet patriotism" in the Soviet Union, this is by no means an assured amalgam in Eastern Europe.

Communism is now irrevocably associated with Russian and/or Soviet imperialism, domination and control, and while this may have a minimal vitiating effect in countries traditionally pro-Russian, it may simultaneously be a barrier to its complete acceptance, assimilation and adaptation in the traditionally anti-Russian countries of Eastern Europe. At least another decade will be required before permanent trends are conclusively discernible, when a new generation of leaders and citizens make their appearance in both Russia and Eastern Europe.

IX THE SOVIET UNION AS A
GLOBAL POWER

26. THE SOVIET UNION AS A GLOBAL POWER

Vernon V. Aspaturian

As a Russianized socialist multinational state, the Soviet Union operates in two distinct but overlapping interstate environments whose relationship to one another is subject to constant change. These are, first, the general interstate system and, second, the Communist party-state subsystem. The dynamic relationship between the Communist subsystem and the general system, as an optimistic Khrushchev viewed it in 1960, was perceived as follows:

> The world is made up of socialist and capitalist countries. They can now be regarded as two communicating vessels. At present the capitalist vessel is, in terms of number of states, the larger. But this is a temporary situation. History is developing in such a way that the level in the capitalist vessel will be dropping while the socialist vessel will be filling up.[1]

This optimism has since been clouded by the Sino-Soviet split, which has subverted two basic Communist tenets. First, the fact of the Sino-Soviet conflict itself has undermined the original assumption that common bonds of ideological purpose and a common social order of

Reprinted from Vernon V. Aspaturian, *The Soviet Union in the World Communist System,* with the permission of The Hoover Institution on War, Revolution and Peace, Stanford University. © 1966 by the Board of Trustees of the Leland Stanford Junior University.

[1] *Pravda,* June 4, 1960. See also George Modelski, *The Communist International System* (Princeton, Center of International Studies, 1960); Z. Brzezinski, *The Soviet Bloc* (Cambridge, Mass., Harvard U. Press, 1960), esp. pp. 104–137, 445–479, for perceptive analytical discussions of the Communist interstate system.

Marxist-Leninist inspiration would be sufficient to submerge potential conflicts of interest, generated by the national impulses of individual Communist states. Second, the Chinese theory of "intermediate zones" controverts the original belief in the impossibility of socialist and capitalist states' uniting against other socialist states. In the Chinese theory, the Soviet Union and the United States are in partnership to establish a sort of dyarchy over a world divided into respective spheres of influence. According to *Pravda,* the Chinese image of international realignments emerges as follows:

> The theory came into being as early as 1946. In its original form it boiled down to the following: The Chinese leaders divided the entire world into three parts or zones. The first — American imperialism, the U.S.A. The second — the Soviet Union and other socialist countries. The third zone, as if lying between them — hence, intermediate — mainly the countries of Asia, Africa, and Latin America. Now Mao Tse-tung is introducing a correction into this "theory." Slanderously declaring that the U.S.S.R. "entered into a compact with the United States to struggle for world domination," he actually combines the two main zones into one. This scheme leaves him with two zones: "Soviet-American" and the so-called intermediate which actually includes China as well. The division of the world into two opposing social systems, recognized by all Marxists, thus disappears. According to the Chinese theoreticians, the intermediate zone represents revolution and progress. As regards the Soviet Union and the United States, they, according to this theory, "entered into a conspiracy" to struggle for world domination. Hence the conclusion is drawn on the necessity of the struggle of the peoples of the intermediate zone against American imperialism and, at the same time, against the Soviet Union.[2]

The Chinese have since divided the intermediate zone into two intermediate subzones, one including the Western developed nations, and the other embracing the socialist and underdeveloped countries, minus the Soviet Union. According to the Chinese view, since the Soviet Union has violated the basic principles of "proletarian internationalism" by colluding with the United States and India against China, it is permissible and perhaps imperative for China to seek alignments with countries in both intermediate zones against the Soviet Union and the United States. The Soviet leaders consider the Chinese position to be mere hypocrisy:

> One of the directions of the Chinese leaders' struggle for hegemony is flirting with the imperialist powers, under the cover of talks about an "intermediate zone." The political reason for this strategic "innovation" is to substantiate China's separate political collaboration with imperialist states — West Germany, England, France, Japan — while at the same time it loudly accuses others of "collusion with imperialism."[3]

[2] *Pravda,* September 2, 1964.
[3] L. Ilyichev, "Revolutionary Science and the Present Day," *Kommunist,* July 1964 (No. 11), pp. 12–35.

To their interstate relations, both the Soviet Union and China bring their national interests and the interests of their various internal constituencies. These interests intersect in the two interstate environments in which China and the Soviet Union operate. However, the Chinese and Soviet roles are qualitatively different in both environments. The Soviet Union operates as a fully recognized Great Power in both systems, whereas the Chinese aspire to Great Power status in each. The U.S.S.R. is the most powerful state in the Communist subsystem and the second most powerful in the general system, while the Chinese are a poor second in the Communist subsystem and are not even fully recognized as a Great Power in the general interstate system.

The Soviet Union responds to different responsibilities in both systems, and consequently its two roles may conflict, harmonize, or overlap. These roles have been subject to alteration in both environments, and they are still in the process of assuming a definitive configuration in each case.

In the Communist subsystem, the Soviet Union has functioned as the leader and director of an ideological community of states, a European alliance system within it (the Warsaw Treaty Organization), and a multilateral European (plus Mongolia) economic organization (Council of Mutual Economic Aid). It is the only state in the Communist system armed with intercontinental ballistic missiles and an operational stockpile of nuclear weapons, and it is the only Communist state militarily allied by treaty with both European and Asian party-states. The Soviet Union has multilateral or bilateral military ties with all party-states except North Korea, North Vietnam, and Cuba. There are no formal military ties between the Asian and European party-states, although China, North Korea, and North Vietnam have sent "observers" to Warsaw Treaty Organization meetings.

The Soviet Union, until recently, was charged with the responsibility of representing and defending the interests of all Communist states in their confrontation with the non-Communist world, although this responsibility has suffered considerable attenuation since 1956. Over and above its formal contractual obligations, Moscow has unilaterally assumed responsibility for the external military protection and of the entire socialist camp and for the preservation of their internal social orders against subversion and upheaval. Thus, on May 14, 1960, *Pravda* issued the following blanket statement of military protection:

> Today the whole world has had an opportunity to receive assurance that anyone who dares to encroach upon the inviolability of the Soviet Union's borders, as well as those of other socialist countries, will receive a crushing rebuff. The Warsaw Treaty Organization is based on the principle of all for one and one for all. The Soviet government has frequently stated that the borders of all its true friends — the socialist countries — will be defended by the Soviet Union exactly as if they were its own borders. This is how we understand proletarian internationalism and this is how all the peoples of the socialist countries understand it.

In spite of the wide array of bilateral military agreements, in spite of the Warsaw Pact and the U.S.S.R.'s unilateral assumption of military obligations for the entire camp, the precise nature of Soviet military commitments remains unsettled. While the statement of blanket protection cited above was issued after the Paris summit meeting proved abortive and at a time when Soviet military capabilities in relation to the United States were believed to be at their zenith, this unilaterally asserted commitment has been repeated many times. The Soviet leaders remain, however, the final judges of when their obligations are to be discharged, and on several occasions disputes have arisen between Moscow and its allies, particularly China, as to whether Soviet obligations have been properly met. Since the Cuban missile crisis, the credibility of the Soviet Union's willingness to protect its allies under certain conditions has been considerably undermined. The level of risk which Moscow will assume depends on a number of internal and external variables, but it is absolutely clear that the Soviet Union is not likely to discharge military obligations on behalf of another ally if the consequences are tantamount to a suicide pact. Furthermore, Soviet willingness to discharge military obligations to allied states must be subordinate to Soviet state interests and responsibilities in the general interstate system.

The Chinese, as part of their design to discredit the Soviet Union and undermine its authority in the Communist system, have denounced Soviet promises of protection as worthless, since according to Peking, the Soviet Union refuses to place the security interests of its allies over its own purely domestic and diplomatic interests, to say nothing of its security interests:

> The conclusion of the tripartite treaty [i.e., the Test-Ban Treaty] once again shows that the Soviet leaders seek only to preserve themselves and would leave other people to sink or swim. They have repeatedly said that so long as they themselves survive and develop, the people of the world will be saved. The fact is they are selling out the fundamental interests of the people of the world in order to seek their own momentary ease.[4]

While it is natural that the Soviet Union, like the United States, is not disposed to allow its allies to involve it in military adventures that might result in a direct confrontation with another nuclear power, there is considerable substance in the Chinese view that Moscow now appears to give higher priority to the purely internal interests of its domestic constituencies than to the national interests of its allies, and that its passion for a settlement with the United States seems to override its military obligations to support its allies in pursuit of their national goals. According to Peking:

> The revisionism and split-ism of the leaders of the Communist Party of the Soviet Union are the product of both the lush growth of the bourgeois elements inside the Soviet Union and of imperialist policy and

[4] "Chinese Statement of August 15, 1963," *Peking Review*, August 16, 1963.

particularly of the United States' imperialist policies of nuclear blackmail and "peaceful" evolution. In turn, these revisionist and divisive theories and policies cater not only to the widespread capitalist forces at home but also to imperialism, and serve to paralyze the revolutionary will and to obstruct the revolutionary struggle of the people of the world.[5]

The Chinese indictment of Soviet military promises as unreliable, while self-serving, is warranted in some degree. To be sure, in almost all concrete instances of alleged Soviet delinquent behavior, the Chinese have accused Moscow of defaulting on their commitments to China. The single exception is the hardly sustainable charge that Moscow, by withdrawing its missiles from Cuba without prior approval of Castro, had treacherously defaulted on a unilaterally assumed military commitment to Cuba:

> The fact is that when the leaders of the CPSU brandish their nuclear weapons it is not really to support the people's anti-imperialist struggles. Sometimes, in order to gain cheap prestige, they just publish empty statements which they never intend to honor. At other times, during the Caribbean crisis for instance, they engage in speculative, opportunistic, and irresponsible nuclear gambling for ulterior motives. As soon as their nuclear blackmail is seen through and is countered in kind, they retreat one step after another, switching from adventurism to capitulationism and lose all by their nuclear gambling.[6]

One might also place in the same category the Chinese charge that Khrushchev is preparing to sacrifice the independent existence of the German Democratic Republic in return for expansion of the *détente* with the United States. This is an accusation of a political rather than a military sellout, although East Germany is now a full member of the Warsaw Pact.

The other Chinese charges of Soviet military unreliability and even treachery refer to Soviet reluctance to offer firm military support publicly to China during the Taiwan Strait crisis of 1958, to Soviet military assistance to India in 1962, and to alleged Soviet collusion with the United States in order to prevent China from becoming a nuclear power:

> As far back as 1959, the Soviet leaders made a gift to the United States of their refusal to provide China with technical data required for the manufacture of nuclear weapons, but, for the sake of larger interests, we never mentioned this before, not even between fraternal parties. If the Soviet leaders had not colluded with the U.S. imperialists in an effort to force China to undertake not to manufacture nuclear weapons, we would not have wanted to talk about this. . . . Not only have you perfidiously and unilaterally scrapped the agreement on providing China with nuclear technical data, but you have blatantly given more and more military aid to the Indian reactionaries, who are hostile to China and have made incessant armed provocations against it. . . .

[5] "Chinese Statement of February 4, 1964," *Jen Min Jih Pao*, February 4, 1964. *Cf.* also *New York Times*, February 7, 1964.

[6] "Two Different Lines on the Question of War and Peace," *Peking Review*, No. 47, November 27, 1963, pp. 6–16.

The real point is that the Soviet leaders hold that China should not, and must not, manufacture nuclear weapons, and that only the few nuclear powers, and particularly U.S. imperialism . . . are entitled to the continued production of nuclear weapons.[7]

Chinese charges of Soviet unreliability have forced Moscow to respond by threatening to exclude China from its umbrella of nuclear protection. In August 1963 an article in *Krasnaya zvezda* warned:

> China today is indebted to the power of Soviet nuclear weapons for the fact that it can calmly engage in solving its internal tasks of economic and state construction. The leaders of the Chinese People's Republic ought to recognize that they can permit themselves such luxuries . . . as their gross attacks on the Soviet Union and the CPSU only because the external security of China is guarded by the might of the Soviet Union and of the whole socialist commonwealth. . . . The great Chinese people have an ancient proverb: "When you drink water, remember who dug the well." It seems the Chinese leaders, judging by their statements, assume this wisdom can be disregarded.[8]

Almost a year later, *Izvestia* hinted that perhaps Peking may have taken itself out of the socialist camp:

> Casting doubts on the efficacy of the Soviet-Chinese treaty of friendship, alliance, and mutual aid, C.P.R. Minister of Foreign Affairs Chen Yi alleged in December 1963 that Soviet assurances are of no value. "Such promises are easy to make," he said cynically, "but they aren't worth anything. Soviet protection is worth nothing to us." Trying to justify the C.P.R. government's flirting with reactionary regimes, Marshal Chen Yi today declares that China is a "nonaligned" country. In political language, this means in fact that Chen Yi does not consider China a part of the world socialist camp. . . . True, the Chinese leaders assert occasionally that in a "complex situation" the U.S.S.R. and the C.P.R. would line up together against imperialism. A legitimate question arises: When are the Chinese leaders to be believed?[9]

Although the Soviet Union demonstrated in October 1962 that it was willing to assume a high level of risk in order more effectively to discharge whatever military obligations it had assumed, it is also true that by meeting its military obligations to Cuba, Khrushchev anticipated possible diplomatic and political advantages elsewhere. In this instance, the interests of its Cuban ally and its own interests coincided and the risks involved were considered worth taking. On the other hand, the precipitous withdrawal of Soviet missiles as well as the other concessions made to President Kennedy tended to confirm the Chinese view that the U.S.S.R. will quickly abandon any ally to the mercies of its

---

[7] "Chinese Government Statement of September 1, 1963," *Peking Review*, September 6, 1963.

[8] Colonel A. Leontyev, "Dogmatists at the Well," *Krasnaya zvezda*, August 25, 1963. See also *Pravda*, August 21 and September 21, 1963.

[9] "Combine National and International Interests," June 4, 1964. Foreign Minister Chen Yi added: "no outsiders can give us protection, in fact, because they always attach conditions and want to control us." (Reported in the Washington *Post*, December 8, 1963.)

enemies if Soviet security interests dictate such a course. Moscow's rebuttal that it had exacted a promise from Washington not to attack Cuba and that its missiles on Soviet territory stood ready to retaliate in the event of an American assault against its Caribbean ally was hardly taken seriously in Peking, Washington, Havana, or elsewhere.[10] The continued presence of Soviet troops in Cuba many months after the crisis indicated, however, that Moscow was willing to assume lower-level risks on behalf of its ally's security interests.

On the other hand, Moscow's tepid response to the systematic aerial bombardment of its military and ideological ally, the Democratic Republic of Vietnam, which it has repeatedly vowed to defend, would seem to verify Peking's accusations that not only Moscow's unilateral commitments but its legal obligations to its socialist allies as well are subordinate to its passion for avoiding another thermonuclear confrontation with the United States. Peking stridently predicted in one of its statements issued after the signature of the Test-Ban Treaty that Khrushchev's abject surrender during the Cuban missile crisis exposed the entire socialist camp to U.S. nuclear blackmail, and Moscow's behavior during the Vietnamese war, in Peking's eyes, is eloquent confirmation of its prophecy. The Brezhnev-Kosygin regime's inaction in the face of the aerial destruction visited upon its North Vietnamese ally for more than a year would suggest that Khrushchev's abandonment of Cuba in October 1962 on the strength of a vague U.S. promise not to invade Cuba was neither an isolated response generated by unique geographical circumstances nor the impulsive reaction of a particular Soviet leader, but represented a more fundamental and durable structuring of Soviet

[10] Thus Peking taunts Moscow: "We should like to ask the Soviet leaders, since the transport of rockets to Cuba was a matter of such great importance, did you ever consult the Soviet people, or the other socialist countries, or the working class in capitalist countries about it? Without consulting anybody you willfully embarked on a reckless course and irresponsibly played with the lives of millions upon millions of people. . . . There is no need whatsoever to transport rockets to Cuba in order to protect the Cuban Revolution. That was what the Soviet leaders said in the past, and it is also what they are saying now. . . . For instance, the Open Letter of July 14 of the Central Committee of the CPSU said that 'in case of aggression by American imperialists we shall come to the assistance of the Cuban people from Soviet territory. True, in this case the rockets would take slightly longer in the flight, but their accuracy would not be impaired by this.' That being so, why did you have to ship rockets to Cuba . . . ? And inasmuch as the rockets were withdrawn afterwards, why had they to be introduced before . . . ? The withdrawal of rockets is said to have gained in exchange a guarantee from the United States that it would refrain from invading Cuba. The Americans have said there was no such guarantee. You have said there was. But where is the guarantee? Do you really believe that the United States will not invade Cuba again? Unfortunately, you do not seem to have much confidence in that." ("Chinese Statement of September 1, 1963.") For Soviet explanations of the Cuban adventure see "The Open Letter" of July 14, 1963 and the Soviet Government Statement of September 21, 1963, which states that "the Soviet Union, acting in the spirit of proletarian internationalism, supplied without hesitation its nuclear missile weapons for the defense of Cuba's revolutionary gains." *Pravda,* September 22, 1963.

priorities and interests as between its commitments and responsibilities in the Communist interstate subsystem and the general interstate system.

Increasingly, Soviet responsibilities in the Communist system are colliding with its responsibilities and interests as a global power in the general interstate system, with Moscow frequently assigning higher priority to the latter. This follows from the Soviet realization that its security and well-being depend more upon its relationship to the United States than upon its role and position in the Communist system. Since the United States has the capability independently to annihilate the Soviet Union, regardless of the latter's degree of solidarity with its allies in the Communist world, Soviet security interests demand some sort of accommodation with the United States. No amount of solidarity between Peking and Moscow can deprive the United States of this objective and independent capability. Thus, if the price of solidarity with China is a more militant or aggressive policy toward the United States, Soviet security interests must come into conflict with system interests: the Soviet Union has a vital area of common interest with the United States, and the intensification or expansion of this interest in view of the current Chinese position almost automatically insures the shrinkage of its area of common interest with the C.P.R. The security interests of the East European party-states also seem to dictate an accommodation with the West. Their interests being thus in harmony with those of the Soviet Union, they are deaf to Peking's charges of Soviet military unreliability.

Moscow's dilemma is both politically and ideologically enervating. Revolutionary ideological imperatives dictate solidarity with China, while Soviet defensive instincts demand a *détente* with the United States. Since these two impulses conflict, Khrushchev sought an alternative that proved non-existent: he hoped to transform a *détente* into a disarmed world which would deprive the United States of its capability to "export counterrevolution" when revolutions spontaneously erupted around the world. Peking considered this an incredible expectation and viewed Soviet justifications as puerile at best and perfidious at worst.

In the general interstate system, the Soviet Union, as the second most powerful economic and military state in the world, functions as a global power with self-proclaimed rights and responsibilities in all parts of the world. At many points its role in the Communist system intersects harmoniously with its role in the general interstate system, particularly in supporting revolutionary movements and regimes in the underdeveloped areas; but they also often collide, as noted above. This dual role imposed upon the U.S.S.R. calls for both conflict and cooperation with the United States; conflict, as the leader of the Communist camp, and cooperation as a partner-rival in the general international scene. This cooperative imperative has been intensified by Soviet awareness that its very physical existence depends upon the exercise of mutual nuclear self-restraint on the part of Washington and Moscow. It means assigning a premium to the relaxation of international tensions, since this not only tends to maximize Soviet physical security but enhances the possibility of more intensified internal development. On the other hand, such a course involves the sacrifice of the interests of some of its allies and the postponement or abandonment of certain of its diplomatic and ideological objectives in foreign policy.

To minimize these conflicts, Soviet leaders have endeavored to find surrogates for the obligations they have deferred or renounced in the Communist subsystem. They are providing greater material assistance to party-states; and in underdeveloped countries they are supporting local nationalist revolutionary regimes and movements rather than focusing exclusively on Communist revolutionary movements. Soviet flirtation with such leaders as Nasser, Ben Bella, Nkrumah, Sukarno, and Nehru, is designed to move their countries gradually into the Soviet diplomatic orbit and then, as in the case of Cuba, to orient their "ethnic" socialisms in a Soviet direction.

This pattern of Soviet behavior virtually abandons local Communist movements to their own devices and tends to frustrate the development of Communist parties where they are weak or nonexistent. This has created a gap that the Chinese have begun to exploit. Communist parties in underdeveloped countries tend to have a greater interest in becoming constituencies of China than of the Soviet Union, since China shows a preference for working through them, while Moscow upholds regimes which they may temporarily support but which they ultimately seek to subvert and replace. Thus, Soviet policy increasingly resembles the behavior of a Great Power seeking client states, rather than the leader of a revolutionary movement cultivating spiritual adherents.

Soviet policies have naturally been supplied with ideological rationalizations. The necessity of Soviet cooperation with the United States is covered by the rubric of "peaceful coexistence," its flirtation with nationalist regimes is justified by the notion of "peaceful transition," and its zeal for domestic material development is ideologically explained as "building communism." These policies in turn, according to the Soviet leaders, fully meet Moscow's obligations to the "world revolution":

> In creating the material and technical base of socialism and communism, the socialist countries are delivering imperialism blow after blow in the decisive sphere of social activity — the sphere of material production . . . All this revolutionizes the masses, helps accustom them to the active struggle against the capitalist system and for social and national liberation. . . . It is the internationalist duty of the Communists of the socialist countries to build the new society well and successfully, to develop the economy, to strengthen defense capability, to consolidate the socialist camp, and to strive to insure that through practical implementation the ideas of socialism become increasingly attractive to all working people.[11]

11 Suslov report, *Pravda*, April 3, 1964.

The Chinese, however, perceive these policies in a different light:

> In putting up the signboard of "building communism" . . . Khrushchev has ulterior motives. . . . He is using it to fool the Soviet people and cover up his effort to restore capitalism. He is using it to deceive the international proletariat and revolutionary people the world over and betray proletarian internationalism. Under this signboard, the Khrushchev clique has abandoned proletarian internationalism and is seeking a partnership with U.S. imperialism for the partition of the world; moreover, it wants the fraternal socialist countries to serve its own private interests and not to oppose imperialism or to support the revolutions of oppressed peoples and nations, and it wants them to accept its political, economic, and military control and be its virtual dependencies and colonies.[12]

The erosion of the Soviet commitment to violence and world revolution represents the growing maturity and responsibility of the Soviet Union in world affairs. The control and manipulation of a world revolutionary movement is no longer either indispensable or desirable as an instrument of Soviet policy and purpose. In some ways it has actually become counterproductive and dysfunctional. In retrospect, one might say that the Soviet Union used its control of a world revolutionary movement as a *de facto* (not necessarily an intentional) surrogate for other attributes of Great Power status and behavior. As the Soviet Union developed economic and military power, the world revolutionary movement correspondingly lost its former utility: it was no longer necessary, for the Soviets had the acquired conventional instruments of Great Power status.[13]

On the other hand, China finds herself in a condition of impotence comparable to that of the Soviet Union before the Second World War. China is an aspiring world power, and she still perceives a world revolutionary movement and support of Communist parties as significant

[12] "On Khrushchev's Phony Communism and Its Historical Lessons for the World," *Jenmin Jih Pao*, July 14, 1964. In another statement, Peking charged: "The leadership of the CPSU has become increasingly anxious to strike political bargains with U.S. imperialism and has been bent on forming a reactionary alliance with Kennedy, even at the expense of the interests of the socialist camp and the international Communist movement." ("The Origin and Development of Our Differences," *Peking Review*, September 13, 1963).

[13] According to Peking, Moscow is seriously misjudging the necessity of outside Communist support: "It should be understood that the relationship between the Soviet people and the other peoples of the world is one of mutual reliance, like that between lips and teeth. The existence and development of the Soviet Union are a support to the revolutionary struggles of other peoples. While in turn these people's revolutionary struggles and victories support the Soviet Union. There is no reason whatsoever to think that the Soviet Union no longer needs others' support. In fact this is not the case. If the lips are gone, the teeth are exposed. If U.S. imperialism should be given a free hand to put down the revolutionary struggles of other peoples, and if the Soviet leaders should ally themselves with U.S. imperialism against the fraternal countries, eventually it will not be possible for the Soviet Union itself to be preserved." "Chinese Statement of August 15, 1963."

and useful power-substitutes during the current transition period. As in the case of the Soviet Union, China's success in organizing and manipulating a world revolutionary movement will depend upon her ability to find foreign constituencies who believe they can best serve their interests by becoming instruments of China's Great Power aspirations.

As a global power in the general interstate system, the Soviet Union demands and is accorded all of the legal rights and privileges of such status: permanent membership on the U.N. Security Council and the right to be consulted on all major problems of international relations. It also asserts its informal prerogatives as a global power by unilaterally intervening in any dispute or problem in any part of the world to the degree which its power permits. It organizes alliances and coalitions, seeks client states, and buys the support of smaller powers. The Soviet Union has interjected its presence in Latin America, Africa, and Southeast Asia, and it maintains an extensive program of military and economic assistance. As a global power, the world, not merely the Communist system, is its sphere of activity.

The Chinese were quick to perceive the growing incompatibilities between these world-wide interests of the Soviet Union and its narrower obligations to its Communist allies. These incompatibilities were implicit in Khrushchev's doctrinal emendations at the Twentieth Party Congress, to which the Chinese at first subscribed, and then reneged when they became aware of their full implications. From Peking's standpoint, Soviet behavior since 1956 exhibits a desire to strike a global accommodation with the United States — an accommodation involving a sphere of influence for the U.S. and the U.S.S.R., their joint monopoly of nuclear weapons, and an informal agreement to maintain the existing equilibrium. Soviet adherence to the Test-Ban Treaty and Moscow's call for a general convention outlawing the use of violence in boundary disputes are intended to give legal recognition to precisely such an accommodation. "The real aim of the Soviet leaders," according to Peking,

> is to compromise with the United States in order to seek momentary ease and to maintain a monopoly of nuclear weapons and lord it over the socialist camp.[14]

The emergence of the Soviet Union as a thermonuclear power with global interests and responsibilities, the resurgence of nationalism in the Communist system, the emergence of China as a rival to the Soviet Union, and the unmitigated fear of thermonuclear annihilation — all these have all combined to give the Soviet Union a greater interest in maintaining the *status quo* than in attempting, through high-risk policies, to alter it in its favor. Moreover, the increasing cleavage between the interests of developed and underdeveloped nations, the fading prospects for revolution in the former, and the growing prospects for revolution in the latter might serve to enhance Chinese, not Soviet, power. The proliferation of Communist regimes under these conditions would alter

[14] Ibid.

the balance between developed and underdeveloped, European and non-European Communist states — a situation which Moscow increasingly perceives as both dysfunctional and counterproductive to its interests.

As a consequence, the Soviet Union has been impelled to restructure the order of priorities among its obligations and interests in the Communist party-state subsystem and the general interstate system. This means, as the Chinese have charged, that the Soviet Union will protect its interests in the general interstate system, even if doing so adversely affects the interests of its Communist allies in the subsystem. Stripped of its ideological jargon, the following Chinese perception of Soviet intentions and behavior in foreign policy would be difficult to quarrel with:

> According to the leaders of the CPSU, with the emergence of nuclear weapons the contradiction between socialist and imperialist camps, the contradiction between the proletariat and the bourgeoisie in the capitalist countries, and the contradiction between the oppressed nations and imperialism have all disappeared. The world no longer has any class contradictions. They regard the contradictions in the contemporary world as boiling down to a single contradiction; that is, their fictitious contradiction between the so-called common survival of imperialism and the oppressed classes and nations on the one hand and their total destruction on the other. . . . Guided by this theory . . . the leaders of the CPSU maintain that the way to defend world peace is . . . for the two nuclear powers, the United States and the Soviet Union, to cooperate in settling world problems. Khrushchev has said: "We (the United States and the U.S.S.R.) are the two strongest countries in the world and if we unite for peace there can be no war. Then if any madman wanted war, we would but have to shake our fingers to warn him off." It is thus apparent to everybody how far the leaders of the CPSU have gone in regarding the enemy as their friend.[15]

Chinese criticism and denunciation of Soviet cowardice during the Cuban missile crisis and Soviet behavior in the face of the U.S. escalation of the war in Vietnam, however, has been considerably undermined by China's own refusal to discharge similar obligations to its North Vietnamese ally. More than a year after Peking blustered and threatened that it would not "stand idly by" while the U.S. attacked a neighboring ally, the Chinese have been doing precisely that, all the while condemning the Soviet leaders for not doing what they prudently dare not do. The Communist interstate system thus reveals itself as a failure not only as a conflict-containing system but as a mutual-protection association as well.

[15] "Two Different Lines on the Question of War and Peace," *Peking Review*, No. 47, November 27, 1963, pp. 6–16. For an incisive analysis of the divergent and conflicting order of national priorities which China and the Soviet Union employ in formulating their foreign policies see Herbert S. Dinerstein, "Rivalry in Underdeveloped Areas," *Problems of Communism*, March-April 1964, pp. 64–72.

27. PEACE AND POWER:
LOOKING TOWARD THE 1970s

Zbigniew Brzezinski

Power tempts — not only serves — policy. In the coming decade, the power of the two super-states will begin to overlap globally and, because of this, the competition between the United States and the Soviet Union could become more intense and less stable, especially as conditions in some areas come to offer inviting targets for big-power involvement. Both powers may then be drawn into hostile confrontations, even though they may not actually desire them. The termination of the Viet Nam war, far from ushering in a new era of *détente* between Washington and Moscow, might be followed by a more complicated phase in international politics, unless thought is now given how to construct a new framework for peace in the 1970s.

The nature and implications of the new phase are more readily perceived if approached from a historical perspective. The last few years have seen a striking change in the respective attitudes of the two powers toward each other. The United States has come to stress the theme of "peaceful engagement" and, by and large, the Soviet Union is no longer portrayed as the principal threat or enemy. The Soviet Union, on the other hand (particularly since the fall of Khrushchev), appears to be adopting toward the United States a stance reminiscent of John Foster Dulles' toward Moscow: moral condemnation is combined with emphasis on "containment" of Washington's allegedly unbridled ambitions.

The change in official American attitudes was initiated in the last days of the Eisenhower Administration by both J. F. Dulles and Chris-

Reprinted from *Encounter*, November 1968, pp. 3–13. Reprinted by permission of the author and publisher.

tian Herter. To the established notion of containment, the theme of collaboration was added. This additional element was given high priority by the Kennedy Administration, especially after the Cuban confrontation of 1962. The American University speech, with its stress on the need for "a new start," was clearly designed to communicate to Moscow the new American interpretation of the relationship. President Johnson continued along the same path and on October 7, 1966, despite the growing acrimony between Washington and Moscow over Viet Nam, appealed for broad East-West reconciliation. In so doing, he revised substantially some key U.S. concepts: he stressed that Europe's reunification would have to precede that of Germany and he called for closer relations with both the Soviet Union and Eastern Europe, implicitly moving away from the tactic of separating the East Europeans from Moscow.

Underlying the emerging American posture was not only a simplistic yearning for U.S.-Soviet accommodation. It reflected increasing concern that Moscow must be "educated" into sharing a sense of nuclear responsibility in a world possessing increasingly numerous and devastating nuclear weapons. Thus the United States continued to seek to expand its tenuous links with Moscow, even as the war in Viet Nam intensified; it continued to exercise restraint in language, even in the face of increasingly violent anti-American abuse from Moscow, much of it personally directed at the President, abuse without parallel since the early '50s; it continued to exonerate the Soviet Union of any desire to prolong the Vietnamese war, even though Soviet arms shipments were increasingly designed to assist the waging of the war in the South and not merely to defend the North; it avoided exploiting the Soviet invasion of Czechoslovakia to fan anti-Soviet sentiments; it continued its policy of cautiously calibrating its defence programmes, lest they precipitate excessive Soviet concern.

Perhaps, more generally, the break-up of the Stalinist monolith and the Sino-Soviet dispute encouraged American hopes of a major evolution in the Soviet outlook, and the U.S. posture was clearly designed to encourage such evolution. Previous fears, tempered by a sense of nuclear security, thus gave way to hopes, only occasionally clouded by Soviet rocket-rattling.

If the change of American attitude can be traced — in a relatively steady line — over a period extending close to a decade, Soviet posture toward the United States has zigzagged more pragmatically. In some ways, the removal of Khrushchev in the fall of 1964 can be considered the most significant recent turning point. Though in the preceding years Khrushchev's policy had been far from consistent, it appeared to put a priority emphasis on the American-Soviet relationship. Having learned at some risk during the Cuban missile crisis that there was no short cut in the long road to replacing the U.S.A. as the preponderant world power, Khrushchev was apparently willing to settle down to a longer period of U.S.-Soviet quiescence or even accommodation, at least until Soviet arms development had erased the imbalance revealed in 1962.

In the pursuit of the Soviet-American priority he was even willing to sacrifice his relations with the more militant Communist states. On the eve of his fall Khrushchev was obviously preparing the ground for a final split with China, and a few months earlier he almost literally disowned the North Vietnamese, after they had had their first taste of U.S. aerial bombardment.

The new Soviet leaders — as revealed by their speeches and actions — came to power with a rather different set of priorities. Though concerned with keeping American-Soviet relations on an even keel (and they made a major effort to communicate that intent to Washington), they were more preoccupied with repairing international Communist unity and with shoring up the domestic authority of the ruling Communist bureaucracy. Themselves middleaged bureaucrats of Stalinist vintage (most of them obtained their first major promotions during the painful days of the "Great Purge"), they were inclined to cultivate the more radical parties of North Viet Nam and North Korea; they were disinclined to push the Chinese into a final split; and they saw in the restoration of some ideological unity direct implications for political stability at home.

These priorities interacted with actual developments, and in the course of the next two years the new Soviet attitude toward Washington crystallised. First of all, it continued to rest on an intelligent recognition of the Soviet stake in maintaining a working relationship with Washington. It is noteworthy that, despite the Vietnamese war, more U.S.-Soviet agreements were successfully negotiated during this time than during the preceding decade. It should be noted, however, that these were primarily treaties designed to enhance specific bilateral interests, or common negative ones (such as the Non-Proliferation Treaty), without any broad accommodation on the more conflicting issues — the arms race, Berlin, etc. At the same time the new Soviet leaders, convinced that the United States was about to move out of Viet Nam, energetically strove to establish Soviet presence in Hanoi. Evidently they hoped to help shape a settlement that would formalise the American setback, and thus permit Moscow to obtain some "revolutionary credit," without jeopardising its relationship with Washington. In a way, Moscow hoped to "have its cake and eat it too," much as Washington hoped to continue "improving relations with Moscow" while bombing a Communist state.

There also matured in the Kremlin a strong conviction that the United States, particularly under President Johnson's stewardship, was pursuing an increasingly assertive policy, based on its recently acquired long range air- and sea-lift capabilities. The new Soviet leaders were accordingly inclined to dismiss initiatives such as President Johnson's speech of October 7, 1966, as deceptive "window dressing" for a more belligerently anti-Communist policy. That was the official interpretation shared by Moscow with its East European allies, some of whom had been tempted to respond more positively to the American plea for East-West reconciliation.

It would appear that by 1967 the Soviet leaders reached the conclusion (which they then shared with many foreign Communist leaders) that the Communist forces were faced with a new imperialist offensive, led by the United States. The Soviet leaders argued — as Brezhnev did during the fiftieth anniversary celebration, or Suslov to the international Communist meeting in Budapest in March 1968 that events such as the killing of Lumumba, the fall of Goulart, the denigration of Sukarno, the Dominican intervention, the Greek coup, and even the Israeli surprise attack on Egypt, were all part of a very deliberate U.S.A.-engineered political offensive. Symptomatically, these views were repeated by Tito after talks with Moscow. They were also systematically developed in the theoretical organ of the Italian Communist party (*Rinascita*, August 4, 1967), which asserted:

> For the policy of the *status quo* and the attempts to divide the world into zones of influence between the two super-powers, U.S. imperialism is gradually substituting a revised and corrected re-edition of the old policy of *roll back*, giving birth, within the framework of nuclear co-existence with the U.S.S.R. (caused by reasons of *force majeure*), to a series of local interventions (economical, political, military) designed to modify the world equilibrium by means of setting up reactionary régimes, or by support given to them, and liquidation of the progressive forces and movements in individual countries.

The Soviet concern was exacerbated by the realisation that effective "containment" of the U.S.A. was not possible through reliance purely on the apocalyptic power of the Soviet military establishment. The Soviet leaders recognised that the United States, having developed its long-range conventional capabilities, had ceased to be an apocalyptic nuclear power and was in effect a global power. The Khrushchevian reliance on rocket threats (much like Dulles' "massive retaliation") was too awesome to be credible in situations requiring moderate but effective military pressure. Hostility, frustration, and concern were thus important ingredients of the new analysis, and they reinforced ideological biases that shaped the over-all Soviet perspective on world affairs.

These considerations provided the general framework within which the Soviet leaders reacted to specific dilemmas. Thus, in respect to China, the new Soviet leaders showed a special concern over the possibility of American-Chinese collusion. Russian concern over such a "new encirclement" is historically understandable, but the new Soviet leaders, precisely because they were less inclined to split with China and less concerned with improving U.S.-Soviet relations, were more prone than Khrushchev to fear U.S.-Chinese collaboration. During the last three years, Soviet diplomats in the United States have made repeated probes to establish if any serious thought was being given in official circles to such collaboration. By the same token, they must have been reassured by several very high-level U.S. statements which appeared to go out of their way to present China as "the number-one threat to peace." These statements also had the effect of encouraging the Soviet leaders to be patient in their relations with Peking — in the hope that they might be repaired after Mao's death.

With the passage of time, the war in Viet Nam became increasingly the central issue in Soviet-American relations. At first the Soviet concern was that the United States should not escalate the war too rapidly, thereby posing for Moscow some difficult dilemmas. The U.S. did not do so, and the Kremlin was doubtless reassured by the highly measured pattern of U.S. escalation (which also inured the North Vietnamese to its consequences). So reassured, and at the same time concerned with improving its relations with the more radical parties, the Soviet Union gradually increased its own involvement, becoming in time the key factor in supplying the actual war effort in the South.

Soviet commitment grew parallel to the Soviet reassessment of the war's international implications. The Kremlin's initial concern — perhaps it was even an ambivalence — gradually gave way to a growing appreciation of the relative political benefits of the war to the Soviet Union and of its political cost to the U.S. By 1967, the Soviet leaders must have concluded that the war was straining bonds of amity between the United States and Western Europe; that it was paralysing any progress in the policy of "peaceful engagement" on the East-West front and making it easier for the Soviet Union to maintain its position in Eastern Europe; that it was intensifying domestic and financial strains in the United States; that it was consuming roughly the equivalent of the annual U.S. GNP growth advantage over the Soviet Union; and that it was diverting Chinese hostility away from the Soviet Union.

To be sure, the Soviet leaders were doubtless aware that the war involved some liabilities for them as well. It was embarrassing to see a Communist state bombed day after day, without an effective Soviet response. U.S. military were obtaining the needed experience and testing. The war did cost the Soviet Union economically, and it certainly reduced the chances of increased East-West trade. But on balance, unless a direct U.S. defeat could be attained, a continuation of the war seemed preferable to an American victory. It may be safe to assume that the Soviet leaders, as realists, knew that a true compromise solution was about as feasible as in the Spain of 1938, and that at the present time it could only be a thinly transparent mask for one side's victory and the other's defeat.

Soviet strategy was hence primarily concerned with limiting the risks of the war while politically exploiting its continuation — a point which so far among statesmen only U Thant came close to making in his February 1968 declaration and Lord Avon in his March 1968 Cornell speech. Naturally, the Kremlin could not stop Hanoi from deciding on peace and it would certainly be willing to serve as the diplomatic midwife for a settlement favourable to Hanoi. But short of that, the major thrust of Soviet diplomacy in the last two years has been to contain the risks of the war while exploiting it politically against the United States. (It is noteworthy that the occasional and short-lived bursts of Soviet interest in promoting negotiation have generally corresponded to times of heightened expectations of U.S. escalation.) These considerations should temper any excessive optimism concerning the likely Soviet role in the peace negotiations initiated in late March 1968 by President Johnson.

The official U.S. posture made it easier for the Soviet Union to maintain this attitude. On the one hand, some American spokesmen talked of Viet Nam as a "global crucible" — hence involving Soviet interests as well — while simultaneously exonerating the Soviet Union for the war's continuation and reassuring it about the risks involved. The result was that the Soviets gradually became more deeply involved without having to pause and weigh the consequences of transforming a purely regional problem into a direct U.S.-Soviet confrontation.

Elsewhere in the world, one discerns in the Soviet behaviour (rather in contrast to Khrushchev's) the absence of a grand pattern, though a quick willingness to exploit specific opportunities. Soviet policy in Europe thus seems in abeyance. The Soviet leaders apparently have not decided whether to reverse their standing hostility toward Bonn and to seek to capitalise on growing West-German frustrations. A policy of accommodation could contain some grave risks for the Soviet position in Eastern Europe. It appears that a majority in the Soviet leadership counselled a conservative posture, pointing to "growing German influence" in Rumania and Czechoslovakia, and warning that an about-face on Bonn could have grave repercussions in Warsaw and East Berlin. The Soviet ambivalence and conservatism have been classically shown in the Czechoslovak case. Fearful of democratisation, the Soviets acted — but their military operation was not matched by a clearcut political conception.

In Latin America, current Soviet policy bears a striking resemblance to American policy in Eastern Europe: a region where one must tread lightly, speak softly, carrying not a "big stick" but only gifts. Hungary in 1956 and the Dominican Republic in 1965 both reasserted for each major power the principle of "geographic fatalism" — excessive change in an area immediately contiguous to the respective major power provokes an overwhelming response. Hence one must rely on courting the established élites, count on gradual change and avoid encouraging revolutions, while developing closer economic and cultural links with the ruling circles. Pursuit of this policy chilled Soviet relations with Fidel Castro in a manner very much like the frost which Kennedy's Eastern policy caused in his relations with Konrad Adenauer.

Although events in the Middle East in June 1967 initially represented a major setback for the Soviet Union, the Soviet leaders exploited both American and Israeli ambiguity concerning the specific conditions of an eventual settlement and managed to maintain their links with the ruling governments. This has permitted Moscow to advance both the traditional Russian interest in establishing a direct presence in the Mediterranean and its Communist stake in radicalising the Arab élites and masses. It may be calculated that the basic Soviet tactic is to prevent a new war, which could only lead to another Arab defeat, and a real settlement, which doubtless would require active U.S. diplomatic participation.

The rest of Africa, and also Asia, with the important exception of India, seems to interest the present Soviet leaders less than it did Khrushchev. His policy of undifferentiated political-economic offensive has given way to a much more selective approach, concentrating Soviet resources on only a few targets. Apparently the conclusion has been reached that a longish process of evolution will be first required before most of the new states become "ideologically ripe for socialism." The abortive revolutionary spasm of Indonesian Communism must have been thoroughly examined in Moscow. Though Soviet military assistance programmes are still extended, and they do enable the Soviet Union to exploit such conflicts as that in Nigeria, one gets a sense on the whole of lesser expectations and lowered interest in Third World problems.

The only exception is India. The Soviet stake in Indian stability is, in all likelihood, a function of Sino-Soviet relations. Soviet assistance has accordingly grown, and India represents perhaps the only major region in the world where tacit U.S.-Soviet cooperation to enhance both political stability and economic development is actually taking place.

Finally, to conclude this quick overview of the Soviet posture in the context of Soviet assessment of U.S.-Soviet relations, the Soviet leaders have made the first major effort in years to forge anew some Communist unity on an "anti-imperialist" basis. The last such effort was made in 1957. The subsequent 1960 international Communist conference was more ambivalent and dominated by the Sino-Soviet dispute. The Budapest meeting in early 1958 was keynoted by anti-U.S. themes, and though the new "anti-imperialist" front is still more verbal than real, it would be an error to dismiss it as involving mere semantics. Seen in a larger framework, it represents yet another symptom of the current Soviet mood.

The political change is accompanied by a gradual shift in the American-Soviet strategic balance. A mere six years ago (*i.e.*, during the Cuban missile crisis of 1962) the Soviet Union already had the second-strike capacity to inflict on the U.S.A. the loss of several tens of millions of lives — but at the cost of its national existence. Today, though the U.S. still possesses the capacity to inflict on the Soviet Union the ultimate penalty of national extinction, the Soviet Union can destroy a hundred million Americans. Thus, in effect, parity in non-survivability almost exists and, as Soviet missile strength reaches U.S. levels, it will shortly be attained.

This is a major shift. It is misleading to argue that the potential loss half-a-dozen years ago of twenty or thirty million American lives was already then unacceptable to the United States. Naturally so from the American point of view, and from a moral standpoint certainly so. But, looking at the American-Soviet confrontation from Moscow, the then existing asymmetry did have a crucial political import: it lent some credence to U.S. threats and it imposed restraints on Soviet bluffing. The Soviet leaders knew that the cost of miscalculation was still qualitatively different for the Soviet Union than for the United States. The United States would certainly feel most concerned if the situation was reversed.

The deployment of Soviet ICBMs to a level matching that of the United States, the introduction of the *FOBS* (Fractional Orbit Bombardment System), the possibility that some recent Soviet space experiments are designed to develop a *MOBS* (Multiple Orbit Bombardment System), the Soviet interest in ABMs and civil defence — and the expected rapid development by the United States of *MIRVs* (Multiple-Individually-Targeted-Re-entry Vehicles), the implacement of some ABMs, perhaps the development of the spectrum bomb, will all contribute to an increasingly complex posture, defiant of clear-cut calculations and inimical to psychological self-assurance. Whether this condition will lead to greater mutual restraint or, on the contrary, prompt more maneuver and bluffing cannot be answered with certainty, but there may be some reason for entertaining some pessimism.

The emerging American-Soviet relationship involves potentially a fateful incompatibility between the emerging balance of forces and the structure of the international system. During the last twenty years, there was a harmony of sorts. Two rather homogeneous blocs were led respectively by a relatively status-quo-oriented superior nuclear power and by an anti-status-quo-oriented inferior nuclear power, with the rest of the world by and large quiescent. We are now moving into a setting in which the two blocs are beginning to dissolve, in which during the next decade the inferior and essentially apocalyptic nuclear power will also become militarily (though not yet in other respects) a global power, and in which the Third World threatens to dissolve into sporadic violence and international anarchy.

Until now peace was safeguarded through asymmetrical deterrence. U.S. self-restraint and one-sided deterrence ("we can do fundamentally more damage to you than anything you can do to us") interacted with the Soviet instinct of self-preservation and Moscow's deliberately fostered ambiguity and even exaggeration of its own power. That system worked for twenty years. It is being replaced by a novel state of symmetrical deterrence, in which U.S. instinct of self-preservation and rationality ("we can do to you what you can do to us") interacts with the Soviet instinct of self-preservation and rationality. Perhaps that, too, will suffice to promote restraint, but the fact is that until now deterrence was unbalanced, and the United States never had to face a crisis with the Soviet Union in the setting of parity.

In the past, there had been many warnings against becoming obsessed with the allegedly evil character of Soviet intentions, and admonitions to concentrate primarily on Soviet capabilities. Today the tendency is to rely more on the allegedly peaceful character of Soviet intentions and to downgrade the importance of increased Soviet capabilities. Yet the scope of capabilities does make a difference, irrespective of motives. One does not know how the Soviet leaders retroactively interpret the Cuban missile crisis, but might they not now speculate that the U.S. leadership would have acted differently if symmetrical deterrence existed? On reading the record, one might well wonder. And could not one speculate that the Soviets might have responded differently to the U.S. nuclear threat? During the Cuban missile crisis, the U.S. asserted its interests not only in Cuba but in Berlin where they were tactically inferior but which they protected by their nuclear superiority. In the setting of parity, a counterblockade of Berlin might well have been the Soviet response.

Not having faced a crisis in the setting of nuclear parity, we have not had to think seriously in post-deterrence terms. Subconsciously, we have assumed that deterrence will work because it has to. But this restraining imperative imposed itself more strongly on the weaker party in the nuclear equation. Hence deterrence may just not work as well in the future. To say that is not to predict a comprehensive nuclear war, but it is to note that, added to Third World instability, symmetrical deterrence could have lower effectiveness in avoiding war.

It can be argued that the new situation will have the positive effect of creating in Washington and Moscow a sense of shared destiny. It could reduce the fears of the weaker and the self-assertiveness of the stronger. To some extent, that is true already. But the argument would be more reassuring if in all other respects — attitude, ambition, interests — the two powers were truly similar, and if the international context and the arms race were both relatively stable.

There is still another imponderable to be considered. The 1970s will see for the first time in history the presence of two overlapping global military powers. U.S. and Soviet intercontinental weapons, perhaps space weapons, as well as marines and air-borne intervention forces, will crisscross, float side by side, and rub shoulders. One does not need to assign aggressive designs to the Soviets and purely pacific intentions to the United States in order to ask whether global peace can be preserved with two overlapping global military powers pursuing conflicting global policies in a dynamic setting of Third World instability. In the past, imperial systems were territorially confined; overlapping fluid (or mobile) imperial power is new. The present international system appears ill-equipped for containing it.

To be sure, for the next few years considerable disparity will continue to exist in relative long-range air- and sea-lift capabilities. But here, too, the Soviet Union appears determined to offset its current weakness. The Antonov-22 troop airships, the three helicopter carriers under construction, and the current expansion of the Soviet marine infantry strength, all provide self-evident clues to the thrust of Soviet military programming and to the kind of role that the Soviet Union envisages itself playing in the world.

It is unlikely that changes in international climate will alter the picture. It can be said with some confidence that the expansion of Soviet military power has a momentum of its own, subject obviously to technological and fiscal restraints but not to oscillations in international atmospherics. The occasional periods of *détente* did not slow down Soviet military development and some decisions which could perhaps be labelled as involving "aggressive" or "destabilising" consequences (for example, the Soviet ABM programme), appear in fact to have been made during periods of *détente*. Moreover, given the traditional impetus of international relations, the Soviet leaders are naturally determined to match and perhaps, or even probably, surpass what the United States can develop and deploy.

Greater capacity to become involved in the world's trouble spots will, in all probability, stimulate greater temptations to become so involved. The Soviet Union was generally excused for not becoming directly engaged in the Vietnamese conflict because even militant Communists knew that it could not. It would have been much more difficult for the Soviet Union to avoid becoming the prisoner of its power if it demonstrably possessed the means for long-range intervention. There is thus no *a priori* reason to exclude the possibility that in ten years from now Soviet marines could be landing in Nigeria or Ceylon. Accordingly, as Soviet long-range air- and sea-lift capabilities grow, the probabilities of a new type of confrontation — a direct one between U.S. and Soviet intervention forces — will similarly grow. Indeed, apprehension over this possibility could increase the inclination of each of the major powers to move in first, in the hope that by "staking out" a claim it will discourage the other from moving. But the implicit premium on preemption would mean a spiral of intervention.

The foregoing discussion takes for granted Soviet staying power in the international rivalry involving the two super-states. It also assumes staying power for the United States. A domestic crisis in America, and especially a panicky disengagement from world affairs because of frustrations spread by the Vietnamese war, would have a catastrophic effect on world stability. It would probably result in a wave of upheavals that could not but stimulate a dangerously erratic sense of optimism in Moscow, conceivably precipitating the Soviet Union into courses of action that so far Moscow has been careful to eschew. A belated, extreme right-wing reaction in the United States would then have the effect of polarising a world which had become even more unstable and chaotic.

Soviet staying power could also be sapped by growing contradictions between the Soviet political system and Soviet society. Today that society has the wherewithal for further social development, and it rebels against many of the dogmatic restraints imposed by the ruling élite. Those concerned with rapid economic development call for major economic reforms; others desire more intellectual freedom; still others reach out for greater autonomy for the non-Russian 50 per cent of the Soviet population. It is obvious from recent East European experience that socio-economic reforms cannot be long compartmentalised, and giving in to the economic reforms opens the doors dangerously to reforms in other spheres.

Yet not to open the doors at all also has its dangers. Stagnation in the Soviet economy would impinge ominously on the Soviet relationship with the United States. By 1985, assuming a U.S. growth rate of about 3 to 5 per cent, the U.S. GNP will be circa 1.5 trillion dollars; even with 5 per cent growth, the Soviet will be only about 800 billion, and thus the gap in absolute figures will have widened. If the Soviet rate of growth should decline, the contrast would be even more startling, with grave implications for the Soviet position in the relative power balance.

The need for reforms does not mean, however, that reforms will follow. Given the political realities in the Soviet Union, one cannot altogether ignore the possibility that instead of evolving toward a more moderate posture the Soviet political system could pass into the hands of a more dogmatic chauvinist leadership, resting on an alliance linking the *Agitprop*, some party *apparatchiki*, and the military. This, too, would have a polarising effect on the world scene.

An additional factor of uncertainty concerning the future Soviet orientation is injected by China. A complete break in Sino-Soviet relations, not to speak of open hostilities, could compel the Soviet leaders to seek greater accommodation with the West. Similarly, a moderate China, responding to cooperative overtures from Washington, could make the Soviet Union more aware of its stake in better East-West relations. But short of these extremes, China tends to induce a more rigid posture in the Kremlin. Mao's verbally militant China creates pressures on Moscow to prove its own orthodoxy by creating the new "anti-imperialist front" and giving support to North Viet Nam and North Korea. A post-Mao, somewhat more moderate China could increase the Soviet temptation to seek accommodation with Peking, which again would involve further stiffening in the Soviet posture toward the West. Finally, a China disintegrating domestically could prompt both Soviet and American efforts to promote the interests of favoured contenders, thereby creating another new focus of competition.

To be sure, in some areas there may be growing cooperation. India, as already noted, may be the one example. The space race, after the moon has been reached, may become another. The two countries will, in all probability, continue to expand those ties that result in direct benefits for each. It is also possible that Europe, reacting against the two "hegemonies" (a feeling exacerbated by U.S. passivity in the face of the Czech invasion), could opt out of the Cold War and become *de facto* a neutral zone.

All this is a far cry, however, from real and positive international cooperation. It is unlikely that the Soviet Union will soon become a partner of the United States in creating international stability. The Soviet mediation in Tashkent between India and Pakistan had a very specific purpose in mind, given Soviet concerns with China's position; before such cases are generalised to reveal some fundamentally new Soviet attitude toward Third World stability, recent Soviet behaviour in the Middle East ought to be taken into account.

For the time being, the Soviet attitude remains essentially guided by tactical principles that can be labelled "risk reduction and opportunity exploitation." It was applied to the Middle East, to Viet Nam and even to the *Pueblo* incident. In each instance the Soviet Union attempted to extract the maximum political advantage at U.S. expense, while striving to contain the possible risks. The Soviet concern with reducing risks is in itself a welcome and positive element; but the first factor in the tactic should be assessed before the second is construed as revealing a widespread identity of interests with the United States.

Open conflict in the American-Soviet relationship may become more frequent if some Third World countries degenerate into anarchy because of social fragmentation, bred by failures in economic development and continued inefficiency of political leadership. That dismal prospect appears likely to be the case for at least several of the developing states. Sporadic violence, in the context of a premium on preemption, may have a suction effect on U.S. and Soviet intervention forces, resulting by the '70s in some unprecedented confrontations. At the minimum, at least one "Fashoda"[1] is to be expected. The question is, of course, whether in the context of the new nuclear equation an American-Soviet "Fashoda" will work out as peacefully as the Anglo-French one did in the late 19th century.

The issue is made more urgent because the nuclear equation is likely to remain a highly dynamic one. It is improbable that a system of U.S.-Soviet arms control, or weapons freeze, can be arranged in the foreseeable future. It is sometimes suggested that parity may make it more feasible. The problem, however, is how to define parity, given different felt needs, different commitments, different industrial-population distributions and different historical perspectives. Indeed, it could be argued that an artificially contrived parity arrangement could encourage a false sense of calculable certainty, and thus stimulate rash risk-taking.

Both powers are also likely to continue feeling that there is utility from the standpoint of peace in maintaining the present advantage over other nuclear aspirants, such as China, and this they can only do by matching advances in their own weapons systems. Furthermore, since formally contrived parity appears unlikely, it is to be expected that the Soviet Union will seek to undo what remains of U.S. strategic superiority and, in the process, whatever the Kremlin's actual calculations, will inevitably appear to be seeking superiority. This will exact its price in ideological and psychological terms, making peaceful adjustments of conflicting interests more difficult.

How to construct an international system geared to reducing these new hazards? This will be the central question of the coming decade. Definition of the new goal will require creative vision, capable of mobilising the minds and spirits of peoples who sense drift but who are unable to define the needed response. Past conflicts and present suspicions will make this task even more complicated than it already is. Nor is it clear what the specific objective ought to be and who can take the

[1] The 1898 Anglo-French colonial expeditionary confrontation, with the French eventually backing down.

lead in seeking it. Europe is in a mood of withdrawal, in spite of the reactions produced by the Soviet occupation of Czechoslovakia. The Soviet Union, more hostile to the U.S.A. and preoccupied with its crumbling position in Eastern Europe, may seek solace in its increasing military power. The U.S.A., frustrated in Asia, absorbed by domestic problems, and increasingly unable to say anything attractive to the Europeans, may — out of sheer inertia simply opt for more of the same in foreign affairs. Yet it should be clear by now that *more of the same simply will no longer do.*

The needed response should involve an effort to forge a community of the developed nations, embracing the Atlantic states, the more advanced European Communist states (including the Soviet Union), and Japan. This need not be — and for a very long time could not be — a homogeneous community, like the EEC or the once-hoped-for "Atlantic community." But deliberately seeking to define certain common objectives in the fields of development, technological assistance and East-West security arrangements could help to stimulate a sense of common involvement and the growth of some rudimentary institutional framework (for example, through formal links in the economic sphere between OECD and CEMA; in the security sphere between NATO and the Warsaw Pact; or the creation of an informal political consultative body).

Progress in that direction would have the important effect of helping to terminate the civil war among the developed nations that has dominated international politics for the last hundred and fifty years. The nationalist and ideological disputes among these nations have less and less relevance to the real problems of mankind, yet their persistence has precluded a constructive response to the human dilemmas that both democratic and Communist states increasingly recognise as being the key issues of our times. The absence of a unifying process of involvement has kept alive old disputes and has clouded the purposes of statesmanship.

To postulate the need for such a community — and to define its creation as the task for the coming decade — is not Utopianism. Mankind is moving steadily toward larger-scale cooperation, under the given economic, scientific, and technological pressures. All of human history, despite periodic reverses, clearly indicates progress in that direction. The question is whether a spontaneous movement will suffice to counterbalance the dangers already noted. And since the answer is probably no, it follows that efforts to accelerate the process of international cooperation among the advanced nations are needed and represent a realistic response to the present challenge.

Movement toward the larger community of the developed nations will necessarily have to be piecemeal, and it will not preclude more homogeneous relationships within the larger entity. The Soviet Union and Eastern Europe, or the OECD countries, not to speak of EEC, for a long period will continue to enjoy more intimate relationships among themselves. The Soviet Union is in a conservative mood and is not likely to be initially responsive. The point, however, is to develop a broader structure, linking the foregoing in various regional or functional forms of cooperation. Such a structure would not undo the basic reality of U.S.-Soviet nuclear confrontation, which would remain the axis of world power. But in the broader cooperative setting, the conflicts between the United States and the Soviet Union could become reminiscent of late 19th-century Anglo-French colonial competition; "Fashoda" did not vitiate the emerging European *entente*.

The Soviet Union would be more likely to become involved in such a larger framework because of the inherent attraction of the West for the East Europeans, whom the Soviet Union would have to follow lest it lose them altogether, and because of the Soviet Union's own felt need to collaborate more in the technological and scientific revolution. That the Eastern Europeans will be moving closer to West Europe is certain. Recent events in Czechoslovakia are merely an augury of what will follow; Soviet power can only slow down — but not stop —the process. It is only a matter of time before individual Communist states come knocking at the doors of EEC or OECD, and hence even for Moscow wider East-West arrangements may become a way of maintaining some effective links with the East European capitals. Last but not least, the threat from China could also have the desirable effect of inducing in the Soviet leaders a less doctrinaire outlook.

Very important, too, is the consideration that a broad community of the developed nations, involving a variety of links among the various powers and sub-communities (such as EEC or CEMA), avoid a semblance of a bilateral U.S.-Soviet deal. Such a deal would be resented by most Europeans, both West and East, and they would work against it. Furthermore, it is unlikely that the Soviet Union could be seduced into a direct U.S.-Soviet arrangement as long as it feels itself weaker and poorer than the United States. A Soviet Union that is becoming stronger against the United States would be less tempted by such an arrangement, and the United States' attitude could also become more ambivalent.

The definition of the broader goal would also have other beneficial effects. For one thing, it is likely that initially the Soviet Union would be hesitant or even hostile. An approach based on the bilateral concept, favoured by many critics of U.S. policy, could thus quickly prove to be abortive, and the consequence presumably would be increased tension. Efforts to create a larger cooperative community have the advantage that they need not be halted by an initial Soviet reticence nor can they be easily exploited by Moscow to perpetuate a cold war. On the contrary, Soviet reticence would only result in more costly Soviet isolation. By 1985, the combined GNP of the United States, Western Europe, and Japan will be roughly somewhere around 3 trillion dollars or four times that of the Soviet Union (assuming a favourable rate of growth for the Soviets). With some Eastern European states gradually shifting toward greater cooperation with the EEC and the OECD, the Soviet Union could abstain only at great cost to its own development and world position.

Much of the initiative and impetus for an undertaking of so grand a scale will have to come from the United States. Given the old divisions in the advanced world and the weaknesses and parochialism of the developing nations, the absence of a constructive American initiative would mean, at the very best, the perpetuation of the present drift in world affairs. The drift would certainly not be halted if the United States were to follow the paths which nowadays it is so fashionable to advocate, mainly that of disengagement. Even if America could do so — despite the weight and momentum of its power — there is something quaintly old-fashioned in the eloquent denunciations of U.S. global involvement, especially when coming from Europeans, whose record for successful maintenance of world peace is not exactly admirable. Moreover, even the most brilliantly contrived, though one-sided, indictments of U.S. policy, for example Stanley Hoffman's *Gulliver's Troubles* (1968), cannot erase the fact that the United States, despite its allegedly long records of errors and misconceptions, has somehow become the only power that thinks in global terms and actively seeks constructive world-wide arrangements. It is revealing in this connection to note that initatives such as the Test Ban Treaty or the Non-Proliferation Treaty were opposed by governments that some critics of global involvement usually praise. The fact that the U.S. commitment to international affairs is now on a global scale has been decided by history. It cannot be undone, and the only relevant question that remains is what will be its form and goals.

One of the important functions of the United States in the process of shaping the new structure will be to help convince the Soviet Union of the futility of its strategy of conflict in international politics. The Soviet leaders must learn that concentration on either rebuilding "an anti-imperialist communist community" (which in any case present East European trends defy) or heavy reliance on military development will not serve the long-term interests of the Soviet Union itself. This means that in the process of striving to create a broader framework from which the Soviet Union could only abstain at a disadvantage to itself, and until such time as workable arms control arrangements are mutually agreed upon, it will remain necessary for the United States to seek to maintain what might be called asymmetrical ambiguity in the nuclear relationship, *i.e.*, a qualitative advantage in deliverable weapons (though no longer a clearly calculable superiority in survivability), and to develop new weapons systems, so that Soviet leaders may not become tempted to take calculated gambles based on the new equilibrium.

In general, the effort to induce cooperation and to limit hostility will require an intricately nuanced balance between courtship and reciprocity. The latter, it must be said bluntly, is a necessary component, lest a premium be put on uncooperative behaviour, thereby strengthening the case of the more dogmatic elements in the Soviet leadership who argue that a unilateral policy involves few, if any, costs. That reciprocity, to be educational yet not escalatory, must be calibrated very precisely. The most educational form it can take is to duplicate as exactly as possible the action to which it is a response, be it a matter of an arbitrary and one-sided cancellation of previously contracted exchanges or abuse of diplomatic privileges. Even then, such necessary steps should not be taken in the spirit of cold war conflict but as regrettable reactions to unilateral actions.

Finally, persistent efforts will be necessary to "de-demonise" the U.S.-Soviet relationship. Much progress has been made on both sides since the 1950s but strong suspicions linger. A useful device — both symbolically and practically — would be to initiate the practice of holding annually an informal two-day working-discussion meeting between American and Soviet heads of governments, in addition to regular meetings with friendly or allied governments. The meeting need not always have a formal agenda, and it should not involve official state visits. Indeed, it would be best to hold it in places that minimise public exposure and avoid fanfare: one year in Alaska, another in the Soviet Far East, etc. Its purpose would be to provide the heads of the neighbouring two leading nuclear powers with a regular opportunity for personal exchange of views and for the maintenance of personal contact. If held regularly even at times when the two powers may be disagreeing over some major issue — it would avoid generating false expectations and wrong impressions (such as conveyed by the appearance of excessive eagerness on President Johnson's part in August 1968), while perhaps stimulating gradually a sense of mutual involvement in world affairs and a new, more mature pattern in the relationship between the world's two principal powers.

We live in a time of an emerging global consciousness. This consciousness, still timid and uncertain, inevitably clashes with perspectives shaped by the last hundred and fifty years of national and ideological conflicts. The national policy of the first global power must be in keeping with this trend toward a universal awareness. It must reflect the decisive need of mankind to terminate conflicts whose historical roots and objectives belong to another era. Thus, irrespective of initial Soviet responses, it behoves the United States to move beyond doctrines shaped by the recent confrontation and to seek broader solutions and more ambitious goals than those that have dominated American foreign policy during the last twenty years. In the short run, it would also be good tactics. Most Europeans (and the Japanese) would welcome a broadly gauged effort to create a new structure and this, in itself, would be a step toward shaping a new core for international policies. For the longer run, it represents the imperative strategy of peace in the age of overlapping total power.

28. THE TRANSFORMATION OF ALLIANCE SYSTEMS

Herbert S. Dinerstein

The pattern of international relations has always been in flux. The further we are removed from a period, the easier it is to discern its most salient features. So the fifteenth century now emerges as the time of the birth of the nation-state which was to become the key factor in international relations. Yet the supra-national church was not successfully challenged until the next century. Today it is clear that the French Revolution completed the conversion of dynastic states into national states. In retrospect the 18th and particularly the 19th centuries are seen as the high point of the world expansion of Europe and the extension of its system of international relations. Now we realize that the Japanese victory over Russia in 1904–1905 marked the beginning of the counter-offensive against Europe. But what emerges sharply now was obscured then by a welter of incident.

Is the twentieth century the century of the ideological polarization of politics, or will it be the century of the end of ideology? At the end of the twentieth century will its first half seem to have been the period of world wars and its second half the period of peace? Fifty years from now it will be much easier to discern which features of the present international scene were transient, which permanent; now it is only possible to peer at the mass of events and try to make out some of the pattern. The hypothesis of this paper is that, first, the increased destruc-

Reprinted from *The American Political Science Review*, September, 1965, pp. 589–601. Reprinted by permission.

Any views expressed in this paper are those of the author. They should not be interpreted as reflecting the views of the RAND Corporation or the official opinion or policy of any of its governmental or private research sponsors.

tiveness of world war and the very small likelihood of its occurrence and, second, the establishment and expansion of a Communist state system have transformed the nature of international relations.

I. War as an Instrument of Policy

The investigation will begin with an examination of the change in the conception of war as an instrument of policy, treating separately the periods before the First and Second World Wars and the period since the Second World War.

A. Pre-World War I

Before World War I statesmen believed, on the whole, that war could be profitable. Political leaders initiated wars, expecting gains commensurate with costs. The classic case comprised Bismarck's three wars against Denmark, Austria, and France, which achieved the unification of Germany at a cost probably no greater than expected.

The corollary to this assumption that some wars were worth the price was that some were not. Price was calculated not only in terms of prospective gain but also in terms of avoiding losses. Thus Great Britain reluctantly entered World War I pursuant to the guiding principle that no single nation — Germany in this case — should be permitted to dominate the European continent. Had any of the major powers before World War I foreseen its consequences, each would probably have been willing to accept greater shifts in the balance of power before engaging in war. The low tolerance for political loss in the European capitals of 1914 was a function of their underestimate of the cost of a general war.

B. Pre-World War II

For the victorious powers, the terrible, unexpected destructiveness of World War I produced a conception of war midway between that of 1914 and that of the present. Clausewitz's remark, made in a different context,[1] that "a conqueror is always a lover of peace," also applied to the Entente powers, since after 1918 a new war could bring them no great benefits. A profound anti-war spirit permeated all levels of British and French society. Consequently, in contrast with their position before World War I, Great Britain and France were willing to tolerate great and unfavorable changes in the balance of power before judging war to be necessary.

The defeated powers, on the other hand, in particular Germany after 1933, were too absorbed in the consequences of defeat to worry much about the possible hollowness of victory in a new war. The harsh, punitive nature of the Treaty of Versailles had outraged practically all Germans who felt, at the very least, that guilt for the war was not exclusively theirs. (Increasingly this judgment on war guilt was shared outside the country, especially in Great Britain and the United States.)

[1] Karl von Clausewitz, *On War* (New York, Modern Library, 1943), p. 332.

The more moderate elements in German society expected an eventual voluntary modification of the terms of defeat. The German right wing, however, scorned concessions from the victors and proposed to get, by an aggressive policy, and quickly, what they believed to be their due. The great depression that hit Europe in 1931 greatly enlarged the dissatisfaction and frustration in German society and two years later helped bring Hitler to power. Hitler promised radical solutions for Germany's external and internal problems. The Nazis were convinced and acted upon the conviction, that the Versailles Treaty should be revised only by force, or the threat of its employment. Hitler continued and hastened the rearmament of Germany begun, in part secretly, during the Weimar Republic. Finding himself unopposed by the West, he became more bold in throwing off the hampering restrictions of Versailles. Since Britain and France felt that war could only produce further national decline, while Germany felt that only the threat of war, and perhaps war itself, could restore the nation, retreat followed upon retreat until London and Paris were driven to choose reluctantly between the two extremes: to acquiesce in Hitler's aims — which was tantamount to complete defeat in war, though without fighting — or to face up to him, with ostensibly inferior armaments, at the grave risk of highly destructive general war. Either course seemed to promise only disaster, but war was finally accepted as the lesser evil.

In the 1930s Germany viewed war as an instrument of policy, as "have-not" nations have traditionally done. Hitler's strong desire for German expansion was coupled with a belief that his enemies could be beaten one by one. Had he foreseen how many, how powerful, and how united his enemies would be, he might have been slower to provoke war. Between the two world wars Great Britain and France followed the traditional policy of victors: they upheld the status quo established by the last war, eschewed aggression for themselves and deplored its practice by others. Their attitude toward war as an instrument to prevent losses had become more cautious since 1914, for they feared that air bombing would make the next war a cataclysm of destruction.[2] Consequently, they tolerated great defeats in Europe before resorting to war and exposed themselves to further defeats in the early years of the armed conflict.

C. Post-World War II

Today, neither the Soviet Union nor the United States has any goals commensurate with the expected cost of a nuclear war. Hence, given the present balance of military power, the initiation of total war is unacceptable. With the development of nuclear weapons, *both* major powers have now all but ruled out large-scale nuclear war as an instrument of policy.

In the past the initiator of a war seldom thought it would be a total

[2] Chamberlain, particularly, and even Churchill, expected that aerial bombing would produce far more casualties than it actually did. However, 50,000 British civilians died in German air raids, a figure that would have seemed horrible enough to the statesmen of 1938.

war; he always hoped to control the arena and intensity of war so as to maximize his chances of victory. Today it is commonly believed that a possible consequence of a direct military confrontation between the two super-powers would be a rapid transition to total war accompanied by unprecedented destruction. Both sides now say they will, and presumably intend to, retaliate with nuclear weapons if attacked with them on a large scale; but it is quite uncertain what lesser assaults, if any, would move them to nuclear war. Obviously both sides want to avoid such difficult decisions, and this is the basis of whatever mutual understanding exists. What differentiates the present situation from that preceding the outbreak of World War II is that *both* sides rather than *one* have rejected total war as an instrument of policy. Furthermore — in contrast to the situations preceding both world wars — the Soviet Union and the United States now have a very low tolerance for *any* changes in the balance of power in Europe. Since 1948 no changes comparable to those that took place in the periods 1904–1914 and 1933–1939 have occurred. The comparative rigidity of the present arrangements in Europe is to be explained, first, by the mutual awareness of the consequences of a nuclear war and, second, by the fear on both sides that any shift in the balance of power would cause the losing side to suffer further losses in rapid succession. Dominoes falling, has been the favored image. As early as December 1953, when the United States still enjoyed what was practically a monopoly in nuclear weapons, President Eisenhower stated the conviction that has dominated American attitudes ever since. By asserting that a nuclear war would mean the end of civilization, he implied that only the gravest threat to American interests could justify a decision to launch nuclear war. By maintaining American superiority in weapons, he reduced the likelihood that such threats would emanate from the Communist world.

In the Soviet Union, as early as 1954, Malenkov said that a nuclear war would mean the destruction of world civilization. Khrushchev, who was soon to replace him as the head of the Soviet government, rejected that view. As long as the Soviets had no significant nuclear capabilities of their own, the victorious Khrushchev faction insisted that a nuclear war, undesirable as it might be, would mean the destruction of the capitalist part of the world, not of the whole of civilization; and that Communism would rise like a phoenix from the ashes. The Soviets probably feared that if they accepted a cataclysmic view of nuclear war, while only their opponents had the means to wage it, they would be inviting pressure from the West to yield political positions under the threat of such a war. However, after the Soviet Union itself gained acceptance for its claim to possess substantial nuclear capabilities, Khrushchev moved to Malenkov's position that a nuclear war would be a common disaster for all mankind. In fact some Soviet writers, referring to nuclear war, now deny the validity of Clausewitz's doctrine, adapted by Lenin, that war is the continuation of politics. In simple terms, they mean that nuclear war does not pay.

At present, the public Chinese Communist position is similar to that taken by the Soviet Union down to about 1958 or 1959, although somewhat more stridently expressed. The Chinese apparently are reluctant to admit that nuclear war would mean the end of the world while their enemies are the only ones in a position to wage such a war. The Soviet Union, they charge, has become a status quo power that sees more advantage in freezing present arrangements by agreement with its opponents than in a forward policy that entails some risk of conflict with them. Since the Chinese are willing to risk conflicts between the Communist world and its enemies — as an essential condition for altering the status quo — they cannot say that a total nuclear war would mean the end of mankind. The Chinese argue that the opponent is a "paper tiger"; that an aggressive joint Communist policy would produce concessions, not war, but that if capitalism initiated a war, it would be the tomb of that system. Communism, however, would survive. But the Soviet Union, with fewer unfulfilled aspirations than the Chinese, has put forward a much more apocalyptic view of nuclear war than the Chinese and has been less willing to take risks, especially to promote the objectives of Chinese foreign policy. The Chinese have recommended that the whole Communist camp combine in pursuit of their objectives, but they have failed to impose their view on the others. In their consequent isolation, the Chinese have scrupulously avoided actions that might have provoked the United States to employ its nuclear weapons against them. Whether Communist China's policy will become bolder as it develops nuclear weapons, only time can tell.

Meanwhile, the two super-powers have rejected war as an instrument of policy because of their fear of its consequences. How this has influenced international affairs we shall shortly see.

II. Is War Likely?

Before World War I, wars were more frequent than today. More than a dozen regular wars were fought between 1870 and 1914, almost all bilateral, and many of them could have expanded into larger wars.[3]

[3] The following is a partial list:
  a. Franco-Prussian War, 1870.
  b. Serbo-Montenegrin War against Turkey, 1876.
  c. Russo-Turkish War, 1877–1888.
  d. British-Afghan War, 1878.
  e. The Zulu War, 1879.
  f. War of the Pacific, 1879–1883.
  g. British-Egyptian hostilities, 1882.
  h. Serbo-Bulgarian War, 1885.
  i. Sino-Japanese War, 1894–1895.
  j. Italo-Ethiopian War, 1896.
  k. Greco-Turkish War, 1897.
  l. Spanish-American War, 1898.
  m. The Boer War, 1899–1902.
  n. The Russo-Japanese War, 1904–1905.
  o. Tripolitan War between Italy and Turkey, 1911–1912.
  p. The First Balkan War, Bulgaria, Serbia, and Greece against Turkey, 1912–1913.
  q. Second Balkan War, Bulgaria against Serbia, Greece, Rumania, and Turkey, 1913.

In addition, many international crises, almost all multilateral, threatened war. Since some of the wars of this period, including the two largest, the Franco-Prussian War and the Russo-Japanese War,[4] yielded benefits to the victor that were apparently commensurate with the sacrifices, the recurrence of similar wars was not "unthinkable."

At present the chances of a large-scale war with the most modern weapons seem small, certainly very much smaller than in say, 1913 or 1938. But the awful realization that the human race could be in jeopardy often dominates the imagination, obscures the reduced likelihood of war, and produces the emotionally based conviction in times of crisis, that war is likely, or inevitable in the long run unless radical changes are made in the international system. The truth, however, is that statesmen in the competing camps share a catastrophic view of the consequences of nuclear war, and this has made warfare *less* likely.

Not only general war, but apparently also wars on a smaller scale, with or without the employment of nuclear weapons, have become less likely. Only a few years ago it was generally expected that limited wars would become more likely when the Soviet Union had acquired nuclear parity. With both sides in possession of nuclear weaponry, the reasoning went, either side, trading on the common fear of a general nuclear war, might conduct war on a lower scale with relative impunity.

The validity of this prediction has not undergone a genuine test, since the United States has maintained nuclear preponderance. Although the Soviet Union has disposed of a substantial nuclear capability for some years now, the United States has enjoyed a mutually recognized superiority. In this situation both sides have been concerned about the escalation of local conflicts and have sought to avoid them. Whether local wars would be more likely *if and when* the Soviet Union achieved rough nuclear parity, or when China achieves a real nuclear capability, can only be a matter for speculation.

III. The Nature of the Alliance Systems

A. Pre-World War I

The great powers before World War I were organized in a balance of power system first systematically described by Machiavelli. A power shifted from one alliance to another, either to "balance" another power or a coalition which had become too strong, or to place itself in a position to gain territory at the expense of a former ally. In the nineteenth and early twentieth centuries, nations sought territorial alterations within Europe, competed for empire in Asia and Africa, jockeyed for positions of advantage in the expected demise of the Ottoman Empire. Some, but not all, of their goals were interchangeable. Thus

---

[4] It is not generally appreciated that the Japanese, despite their naval victories, were staggered by the extent of their losses and probably would have soon taken the initiative in suing for peace, had not Russia done so because of the revolutionary situation in the latter country. I am indebted to Paul Langer for this realization.

Italy, by alliance with the Central Powers, increased its chances of getting the territories it claimed on the French Riviera, but thereby relinquished claims to *irredenta* in the Austro-Hungarian Empire. And Bismarck tried, but failed, to compensate France for the loss of Alsace-Lorraine by holding out opportunities in Africa. But it was not only the prospect of gains that caused nations to shift from one alliance to another. Fear of loss could be equally, or more impelling. Thus, the German naval program of the turn of the century played a major role in persuading France and Great Britain that they had more to fear from Germany than from each other.

In contrast to the present, ideology was not an inhibition to diplomatic realignments (*renversements des alliances*). The ideological differences between Imperial Russia and Republican France and Liberal England were residual; for neither the Russians on the one hand, nor the French on the other, were intent on a political revolution within the other country (unlike the period from 1791–1815). These nations formed an *entente* which survived the crisis preceding the war, three years of war, and the democratic revolution of February 1917, only to collapse after the victory of the Communists in October 1917.

Great powers shifted their alignments rapidly and radically. For example, in 1898 in the Fashoda crisis, Great Britain and France were on the brink of war over competing ambitions in Africa. The crisis that erupted brought the two countries closer to war than they had been for many years. The French, for a combination of domestic and foreign policy reasons, yielded and war was avoided. The name applied to this easement was *détente*. Several years later, largely because of a changed perception of the danger from Germany, the two powers formed an *entente* — practically an alliance — first settling territorial disputes between themselves on a basis of give and take. Thus, they proceeded from the brink of war immediately to a *détente* and eventually to an *entente*. A *détente* sometimes developed into an *entente;* enemies sometimes became friends. How much, or how little, this has changed we shall examine shortly.

Remaining outside the alliance system was only possible for countries without territorial ambitions and against whom others did not have territorial claims. Even so, in time of war or imminent war, another power might invade for strategic reasons. Of course, distant and powerful nations separated by oceans, like the United States, could remain outside the system of alliances.

B. Pre-World War II

By World War II the character of the system had begun to change in that the status quo and the revisionist groups were more firmly fixed in their positions. France, Great Britain, and the new states of Eastern Europe, created in part at the expense of Germany and of Russia, supported the status quo. Germany, especially after Hitler's rise to power, was revisionist, and the Soviet Union shunted between the two positions, although it was basically revisionist.[5] Neither the Soviet Union nor any other major power was able to remain neutral. Small powers like Austria, the Baltic States, and Finland, outside the major alliance systems, or secured only by bilateral nonaggression pacts, lost their independence to the revisionist powers. Even within the status quo alliance system, weaker powers did not enjoy genuine security. Although the great powers never formally renounced their obligations to Czechoslovakia, in essence they abandoned her to Germany. Before the First World War neutrality would not necessarily survive the outbreak of war; before the second, even membership in an alliance did not protect weaker powers from absorption before the inception of general war. How different the position of the weak and unaligned has become!

In the interwar period, the threat of internal revolution inhibited the formation of alliances. For example, the Franco-Russian treaty of mutual assistance signed in 1935 was never implemented by joint military arrangements as in the case of the Franco-Russian alliance whose negotiation was completed in 1894. Although the alliance proved abortive for more reasons than the ideological tension between Republican France and the Communist Soviet Union, ideology did play a major role.

C. The Present

1. GENERAL CHARACTER

Alliances now differ in three large respects: (1) political goals have superseded military; (2) the relative power and the number of participant states have altered significantly; and (3) ideology has become a major factor.

a. The Primacy of Political Goals. The determination of the major powers to avoid war, noted above, has caused a qualitative change in international relations. The expectation that war can be avoided makes the primary purpose of alliances deterrence of war rather than preparation for its conduct. Although success in the former purpose is dependent on the latter, the primacy of deterrence is of great consequence. The great questions of war and peace are the almost exclusive concern of the Soviet Union and the United States; the secondary powers in both alliances benefit, or suffer, from the military balance produced by the rivalry of the two greatest powers. But the influence of secondary powers on the balance of power in comparison with their influence in earlier alliances is modest. The relations between the two greatest

---

[5] The Soviet Union was revisionist when Germany was weak, a defender of the status quo after Hitler came to power, and revisionist again in 1939 when it seized the opportunity to gain territory and remain neutral in a war between its foes. The status quo position of the Soviet Union at various times must be distinguished from that of Great Britain and France, for unlike them it had great expectations of radical favorable chances in the future. The Soviet Union favored the status quo when its relative weakness permitted no other course, but was prepared to shift when opportunities for aggrandizement offered themselves. Professor Vernon V. Aspaturian suggested this and other formulations.

powers are increasingly conducted on the assumption that outstanding issues will be resolved only by political means. The secondary members of both alliance systems pursue their particular goals in the confidence that there will be no world war. Thus conflicts with the hegemonic power within each alliance involve only political and economic costs. The question of isolation and abandonment in a world war need hardly be considered. The Chinese Communists would hardly have permitted relations with the Soviet Union to deteriorate to the point of withdrawal of Soviet military aid if they had expected war with the United States; de Gaulle would not have presumed to challenge the American position in Western Europe if he expected a world war. Hence secondary powers, while less influential in alliance military arrangements, enjoy more freedom of action within the alliance. The consequences of this increased freedom of action are quite different for each system. They will be examined at the point where intra-alliance arrangements are discussed.

b. *The Increase in the Number of Participants in the International System and the Change in their Relative Power.* Since the Second World War the distribution of power within the international system has changed significantly. Earlier there were greater powers (more than two); secondary participants in alliances who, at the lower end of the power spectrum, merged with client states protected by a major power and without a genuinely independent foreign policy; and finally a great fraction of the world's population, largely non-European, lived in colonies or semi-independent political entities.

At present there are two super-powers, the Soviet Union and the United States. In time, probably, Communist China and, possibly, a united Western Europe will join the ranks of the super-powers. But now the gulf in power between the largest power in each alliance and the next largest is greater than ever before. Consequently, the very magnitude of the power of the two greatest states creates, despite their rivalry, some common concerns and common interests not shared by their allies.

By now almost all the former colonies and semi-independent states have become independent and have largely remained unaligned. The reduced likelihood of world war makes it possible for them to contemplate continued existence without becoming minor members of a diplomatic system. They no longer worry that their independence would constitute the victor's spoils in a new world war. From being the objects of international politics they have become active participants, adjusting and readjusting their relationships with each other and with the major powers. And client states, especially in Eastern Europe, as we shall see, are increasingly asserting some control over their own foreign policy.

c. *Ideology.* Soon after the conclusion of the Second World War it became a truism that ideology was the major determinant in international relations. But like many truisms it turned out to be a half-truth. As early as 1948 Yugoslavia, after ejection from the Communist camp, was able to survive as an "unaligned" nation. The Soviet Union failed to gobble up weak nations on its periphery and communize them on the model of the Eastern European nations largely because, both before and after it acquired nuclear weapons, the Soviet Union feared a large war that might result from aggression against a small country protected within the American alliance system. The American system of guarantees and alliances of the 1950s has been much criticized of late on the ground that the Soviet Union was really unaggressive and that the system extended American commitments beyond American strength and willingness to play a world role. But the success of the policy and the containment of Soviet expansion by superior military strength does not prove that containment was unnecessary. It was just because some countries joined in the effort to contain the Soviet Union that other countries could afford non-alignment and enjoy the freedom of a position between the two main antagonists. But whatever the origin of the present security of the smaller powers, the present reality is that both diplomatic and ideological non-alignment are realistic policies for the weaker nations in the international system.

After 1947 it was widely believed, on both sides, that the passage of a particular country from one camp to the other, regardless of its size, would precipitate a series of such changes. In the West this fear rested on the over-facile assumption that Western European nations, which had not been occupied by Soviet troops, were as much in danger of communization as the Eastern European countries had been. In the Soviet Union, on the other hand, it was feared that the successful departure of Yugoslavia from the Soviet satellite system would be emulated. This fear lay at the basis of the brutal imposition of strict police controls in all the satellite states after 1948. Since then in Europe both sides have felt that any alteration of the status quo would produce a chain reaction.

But the very stability, caused in part by the mutually shared apprehension of the consequences of change, has produced a measure of relaxation. The conversion of some of the satellite states of Eastern Europe into client states with incipient independent foreign policies has been an embarrassment, and may presage serious losses; but it has not been a disaster for the Soviet Union. Castro's personal conversion to Communism, which (given his position) meant the communization of Cuba, caused great agitation in the United States. But it is now tolerated largely because of Castro's failure to spread the revolution, the relatively minor importance of Cuba, and the frustration of the Soviet attempt to make a major strategic change on the basis of a political victory in a small country.

In the overall balance of power, new Communist states, ideologically much diluted and little controlled by the largest Communist state or states, may become important. If, again, modernizing dictators adopt Communism and impose the new faith on their people like the pagan princes converted to Christianity, will it be an extension of the international power of Communism or a dilution of its strength? It all depends on what happens to such states. If some stumble and founder, then the pattern maintained since 1920 when Hungary ceased being a

Communist state will have been broken — communization will no longer be irreversible, and each case can be separately assessed on its own terms. If, on the other hand, each new regime consolidates itself (and no established regimes abandon Communism), then forceful measures to prevent what will seem to be permanent losses can be expected. Thus, ideology will play a greater role in internaional relations or a reduced role; the present situation seems to be transitional.

Very likely the importance of ideology in foreign policy calculations will persist longest in areas vital to the interests of the greatest powers. For example, it is difficult for the near and proximate future to imagine political changes in Europe in which ideology would not figure largely. Reckoning on the basis of power politics alone, the Soviet Union would have much to gain from the abandonment of the Communist regime in Eastern Germany. A serious proposal to Western Germany for reunification on the basis of demilitarized neutrality would have good chances of acceptance and at the very least would precipitate a major political crisis in Western Germany. Such a settlement, presumably including the settlement of the Polish (and Czech) western borders, would constitute a political settlement in Europe which would probably bring in its train major modifications of NATO and the Warsaw Pact. The enormous saving in money would greatly ease the dilemma of resource allocation within the Soviet Union. This projection of future events seems unrealistic only because the ideological value of Eastern Germany cannot be exchanged for other values. But the reconversion of Castro, or the collapse of his regime would probably not be viewed as fraught with disaster by the Soviet Union.

2. INTER-ALLIANCE RELATIONS

a. As between the United States and the Soviet Union. Earlier the familiar point was made that the Soviet Union and the United States have a common interest in avoiding nuclear war. But beyond that common interest, rivalry is the keynote of the relationship. In that rivalry, relative military strength is crucial. At present both sides accept United States superiority in nuclear weapons, but Soviet acceptance followed upon efforts to create a balance more favorable to the Soviet Union. The Soviet Union failed to convert its priority in ballistic missiles into a superiority in intercontinental forces, largely, probably, because of its industrial and economic inferiority. It also failed in its effort to alter the military balance by the expedient of putting medium and intermediate-range missiles into Cuba in the fall of 1962. For the Soviet Union, a test-ban treaty promised to, and has tended to, stabilize the weapons balance at roughly the present level, namely an inferior Soviet position in intercontinental nuclear weaponry. The Soviet Union probably accepted such a state of affairs for the interim, at least, because the alternatives might be worse. A continuation of the arms race at a faster pace might well produce no relative advantage. The economic cost, which the Soviet Union can ill afford, might well be paid without military and political improvements relative to the United States, perhaps even with a decline in the Soviet Union's relative position. The United States, on the other hand, enjoying a military superiority which it believes has contributed to the frustration of Soviet aims in Cuba, West Berlin, and elsewhere, is willing to continue the present situation. It is uncertain, of course, whether opportunities, especially in the technological sphere, to alter the weapons balance will emerge and be exploited by the Soviet Union. But at present the United States and the Soviet Union seem to accept roughly the present balance because the former finds it satisfactory and the latter can see no way to alter it significantly for the better.

An unusual feature of the treaty, and significant for the altered nature of international relations, was that both the Soviet Union and the United States knew that a major ally of each would refuse to sign it. The leading powers of the rival alliances thus agreed on a major issue concerning which, one differed with France and the other with Communist China — both disagreements being between allies. Furthermore, the conclusion of the treaty legally bound the signatories to resist their allies' demands for assistance in developing nuclear weapons. Whatever political costs were involved in opposing the wishes of their alliance partners the United States and the Soviet Union were ready to bear. Both major powers opposed the further proliferation of nuclear weapons, and the treaty represented a common resolve not to assist in such proliferation. It was generally recognized, however, that even without help France and Communist China could acquire nuclear weapons by their own efforts.

The corollary of the Soviet and American determination to reduce the danger of war by controlling nuclear weapons as much and as long as possible by themselves is the determination to avoid small-scale conflicts which could grow into larger ones, eventually threatening war. Most often this has meant the frustration of a secondary ally's desire to use force to his own advantage. The two super-powers, in a sense, have a tacit pact to keep the peace even if it frustrates an ally's ambitions. Thus, the United States vetoed the Anglo-French-Israeli adventure in Suez, with the Soviet Union adding menace from the sidelines. Whatever the extent of Chinese desires in India in the fall of 1962, the joint — though not concerted — United States and Soviet support of India set limits on Chinese objectives. In both cases it was a non-aligned nation that was protected against an ally. As a consequence, the United States and Soviet partnership in keeping the peace reduces the policy alternatives traditionally enjoyed by secondary members of an alliance. Thus, not only the nuclear powers, but their weaker allies, also must pursue their foreign policy objectives with much less reliance on military force as an instrument to attain desired goals.

The recognition of an area of common Soviet-American interest, symbolized by the test-ban treaty, has been referred to as a *détente*. But unlike the traditional *détente*, the present arrangements cannot be converted into an *entente*, *i.e.*, the alliances cannot be reshuffled because several essential features are lacking.

First, the present situation is essentially bipolar, since as has already been remarked, the difference between the power of the strongest member of each alliance and the next strongest is unprecedentedly great. Traditionally, great powers shifted from one alliance to another because another power of the same size was perceived as threatening. Thus, the British *entente cordiale* with France in 1904 required the existence of a Germany. At present the Soviet Union and the United States have no peers in power.

Second, in most reversals of alliances at least one partner was revisionist, that is, considered territory held by another power as rightfully belonging to itself. Thus, the Anglo-French *entente cordiale* of 1904 eventually brought Alsace-Lorraine back to France; the Italian shift from the Triple Alliance to the Triple Entente brought them Fiume, etc. Now *both* the Soviet Union and the United States, having been victorious in the last war, are essentially status quo powers. This generalization requires serious modification only when the present arrangements for Germany are challenged, but hardly at any other time.

Concerted action to keep the peace between two powers is not equivalent to common action to ward off a common threat from a third power, or to gain something at the expense of third powers. Unless and until the Soviet Union and the United States perceive a threat from a third power of equal rank, or both develop aggrandizing goals which can be achieved only at the expense of third powers of equal rank, the necessary basis for the conversion of *détente* to *entente*, for the reversal of alliances, does not exist.

Thus, even if the ideological tension between the Soviet Union and the United States diminishes rather than intensifies, they can only become more friendly; they cannot become friends.

But from the point of view of secondary allies, this partial accommodation between the two super-powers has some of the features of a reversal of alliances, especially if the accommodation is in an area of vital interest to the secondary power. Thus, in the Chinese view, the Soviet accommodation with the United States on the peace issue has deprived the Chinese of practically every advantage which the alliance had afforded. But unlike the classic reversal of alliances, the Chinese do not find themselves in another diplomatic constellation. The improvement in the relations between the two super-powers does not lead to the reshuffling of alliances but to alterations within each alliance which will be considered subsequently.

b. As between a Super-Power and a Secondary Power in a Rival Alliance. On several occasions the United States and the Soviet Union have given limited support to a secondary power in the rival system in order to increase the leverage of that power in relation to the hegemonic power, with the object of reducing the cohesion of the rival system. American aid to Yugoslavia was an example of such a tactic — after the fact to be sure, but relevant nonetheless. After the increase in Poland's independence in 1956, United States aid to Poland was offered in the hope of consolidating that independence rather than out of any farther reaching community of Polish and American foreign policy interests. Recently, Rumania has taken first steps toward similar arrangements. Other East European Communist states may well follow suit. Thus far these measures have not caused departures from the Warsaw Pact, but have rather contributed to the process of desatellitization in Eastern Europe.

Similarly in Cuba, the Soviet Union offered Castro, then not yet a Communist, limited political and economic assistance with the purpose of reducing the cohesion of the American diplomatic system in the Caribbean. Castro, a modernizing *caudillo*, deemed it necessary to provoke sharp conflict with the United States in order to demonstrate that he was not merely another dictator, who after eloquent promises of reform would relapse into corruption. In order to guarantee continued Soviet support and also to control his own Communist Party, Castro declared himself and Cuba to be Communist. If Paris was worth a mass to Henry IV, Cuba was worth a party card to Castro. In contrast to the Russian and Chinese revolutions, which derived largely from internal impulses with subsequent effects on foreign policy alignments, the basic impulses in Cuba were in the realm of foreign policy with subsequent effects on domestic policy.

Attempts by both the United States and the Soviet Union to weaken the rival coalition by approaches to some of its members seem to be a permanent rather than a transitory phenomenon.

c. *As between Secondary Members of Rival Alliance Systems*. The main purpose of cross-alliance relationships between secondary alliance members is to gain leverage as against the alliance hegemon, often on issues which are of secondary importance to the hegemonic power but of primary importance to the weaker power. For the United States, relations with Pakistan are important, but no more important than relations with a dozen other powers. For Pakistan nothing is more important than the Indian problem. Hence Pakistan's arrangements with China have as their main motive the improvement of her position *vis-à-vis* India.

The Franco-Chinese exchange of courtesies (*rapprochement* would describe more than has occurred), was motivated by consideration of lesser urgency than the Pakistani-Chinese gestures of friendship. The French desire a larger voice in allied policy in general, and in Southeast Asian policy in particular, but their national interest in that area can only be residual and sentimental. It is more a case of, "I will be heard." For the Chinese it represents a symbolic escape from the diplomatic isolation caused by the Sino-Soviet breach.

Recently, both the French and the Germans have sought to improve their relations with some of the Eastern European countries. In part the motive resembles that of the United States in seeking to stimulate the growth of the independence of these states from the Soviet Union, but in part it expresses the rivalry of France and Germany for dominance in Europe.

In these cases, to greater or lesser extent, the approaches of second-rank members of one alliance to second-rank members of another alliance have been un-ideological and represent an effort to satisfy desires thwarted by the hegemonic power. Thus Pakistan wants a settlement of the Kashmir dispute which the United States will not support; France wants to be the first power in Western Europe; the countries of Eastern Europe want to improve their bargaining power with the Soviet Union by establishing better relations with France and especially West Germany.

Since only the hegemonic power can satisfy the demands represented by these cross-alliance overtures between secondary powers, these overtures do not lead to switching alliances. After all, it is the United States, not China, to whom Pakistan must look for effective pressure for its solution of the Kashmir question. France wants American acceptance of its claim to primacy in Europe; Soviet or Chinese assent is meaningless. Poland and Rumania require Soviet acceptance of their desire for greater freedom in foreign policy. West Germany or France cannot satisfy that wish, they can only serve as instruments for its accomplishment. Therefore, these approaches to members of the rival alliance are really methods of improving negotiatory power against the hegemonic power. The basis impulse is from within the alliance, not from without.

d. *As between Non-Aligned Powers and Alliance Members.* (1) *Competition between Members of Rival Alliances for Influence with the Non-Aligned.* In the immediate postwar period, only the Western alliance system drew non-aligned states to itself. These states fell into several categories: first, states against whom the Soviet Union or China had territorial claims or was presumed to have territorial ambitions (Turkey and Iran in the Near East). In the Far East, South Korea and South Vietnam were under threat when not under attack.

A second category of states entering the American mid-eastern and far-eastern alliance systems comprised those who wanted American economic or political aid but were under no immediate threat from either the Soviet Union or China. Iraq, Pakistan, and the Philippines are the obvious cases. Most new states, however, perceiving no threat from the main Communist states, and hoping for economic support from both systems, have remained unaligned.

When it was realized that the Soviet Union had abandoned the policy of the absorption of contiguous states out of fear of the consequences, states in the tier beyond those immediately bordering on the Soviet Union and China dropped whatever ideas they had had of joining a Western defense system, thus putting a term to the Western process of alliance building.

Furthermore, beginning in 1955, the Soviet Union began to furnish military, and sometimes economic, support, especially to former colonies who were at odds with their former imperial masters. Indonesia and Egypt are the two most important in this category.

For the great majority of the non-aligned countries, national interest is best served by joining neither alliance system and being wooed by both. Above it was argued that the international tension produced by the communization of new states (the unaligned or undeveloped, or both, being the most likely candidates) would not remain at its present level. It would either increase or decrease. If concern increases, efforts to draw unaligned countries into alliance systems would resume, with the leaders of the unaligned countries seeking to exploit the advantages of the middle position. In a period of intense rivalry for their allegiance, the leaders of non-aligned countries could combine appeals to magnanimity with the threat or promise to move from one camp into another. But this is a threat of limited utility, because all concerned know that the first choice for the unaligned is the medial position.

If fears for the definitive passage of presently unaligned (or loosely aligned) powers to one of the systems decline, the bargaining power of the unaligned will be sharply reduced. They will be reduced to a position commensurate with their power. They can appeal to the magnanimity of the great powers, but they cannot negotiate effectively because they have little to give or withhold.

The super-powers in their rivalry and mutual fear of war have permitted the birth of a host of new nations and have protected their independence. These now act on the international stage, but the political importance of any single one of these nations becomes a multiple of its true power only when it becomes an object of rivalry between the two super-powers.

(2) *Competition between Members of the Same Alliance System for Influence among Uncommitted States.* The first area of Sino-Soviet rivalry for influence in underdeveloped countries has been Southeast Asia. By the time of the Bandung Conference at the latest, it was clear that Sino-Soviet rivalry for the adherence of the unaligned was at least as important as Communist-capitalist rivalry.

Since the Soviet signature of the test-ban treaty, the Chinese have challenged Soviet influence wherever they could: in Africa, in the Near East, in Latin America, and even in Europe. This competition is really a function of intra-alliance dissension, to the examination of which we shall now proceed.

Competition within the non-Communist alliance for influence among the unaligned, by contrast, is of slight significance, because no conflict comparable to the Sino-Soviet conflict exists. Greek-Turkish rivalry in Cyprus, however sharp, is consequently localized; and French oil interests in North Africa, as against other European powers are not the occasion of NATO's troubles.

a. The Non-Communist Alliance System. The purpose of the non-Communist alliance system or, more correctly, systems, is the containment of the Communist states. This is a familiar goal in international diplomacy, namely, not allowing an opponent to grow too strong. Two novelties characterize this effort: its geographical scope and its duration. The French Revolution, in its time, also presented a threat to the established political order, but it was essentially confined to Europe, and conclusively contained in 1815, only a quarter century after its beginning. The Communist Revolution is almost half a century old and still presents challenges in many parts of the world.

The ideological character of the Communist system has impelled a search in the non-Communist alliance for a suitable ideological label for its system, but none has been found, for the internal regimes of the member nations are based on different principles. Outside of Western Europe, only in countries populated by settlers from Northwestern Europe, and in Japan, are societies based on a broad consensus. In most of Latin America, the Near and Middle and Far East, ruling strata are too narrow and middle classes too small to make representative democracy a genuine possibility at present. Although frequently deplored, this political diversity in the non-Communist alliance is a source of strength rather than weakness, as we shall presently see.

The non-Communist alliance system truly deserves the appellation of polycentric because it is a congeries of alliances with different purposes suited to the different threats posed by Communism in various parts of the world. In each of these alliances the hegemonic power, the United States, plays a different role.

In the NATO alliance, after setting into motion the economic and political restoration of Western Europe, the United States by the maintenance of nuclear military superiority has limited the options open to Communist expansion. Since 1948 when Czechoslovakia became a Communist country, the Communist state system has made no progress in Europe. Hence the anti-Communist purpose of the NATO alliance has receded into the background, and NATO's main task is to maintain a credible deterrent against the Soviet Union. Since this task has been successfully accomplished, its importance tends to be forgotten, except when the Soviet Union offers a challenge such as the Berlin crisis, or even more dramatic, the Cuban missile crisis.

With security against both internal and external threats seemingly assured, the nations of Western Europe can and do devote much of their energies to jockeying for favored positions, as against each other, and as against the hegemonic power of the United States. France has put herself forward as the claimant for leadership in Europe. Western Germany cannot compete for this position despite her greater economic resources, because the unresolved problem of unification makes her politically dependent on the United States. The issues on which the NATO allies differ are well publicized: the sharing of nuclear control in NATO, the terms of economic integration, support for Western Germany's position on the Berlin issue and what lies behind it — the political future of all Germany. Yet despite these very genuine differences, the system is not disintegrating, but is rather rearranging the relationship of its parts. After all, the economic integration of part of Western Europe goes forward; economically Western Europe and the United States are growing closer rather than apart. The basic stability of the NATO alliance can be explained on two grounds. First, no claimant for second place presents a genuine challenge to United States power. China may someday be a greater power than the Soviet Union, but neither France nor Germany can challenge the preeminence of the United States. Thus, de Gaulle is claiming the position of the first among the secondary powers in the alliance, rather than the position of first in the alliance. Since goals are limited, the conflict does not pass beyond a certain point. Second, the modesty of NATO's goals makes of it an alliance which can withstand a great deal of turbulence. Since its main purpose is to prevent the spread of Communism and Soviet power in Europe, differences which do not threaten the accomplishment of that objective are not really subversive. If the purpose of NATO encompassed a common political direction of all Western Europe, or a common economic policy directed from the center, then NATO would be even more disrupted than the Soviet system in Eastern Europe. It is because the true purpose of NATO is *merely* anti-Communist that the alliance is capable of accommodating so much change.

A striking feature of the NATO alliance system is the limited power of the hegemonic partner. The Cyprus issue illustrates the increased independence of the weaker power within the alliance. In a traditional alliance system, both Greece and Turkey would have had to consider the consequences of defying the wishes of the hegemonic partner for peace in Cyprus. The Turks would have had to calculate that bad relations with the United States might encourage the Soviet Union to press its claims once again for *irredenta* in Eastern Anatolia. The Greeks, for their part, would have had to worry that bad relations with the United States would encourage Yugoslavia or Bulgaria, or both, to renew claims for Greek Macedonia. But neither Greece nor Turkey need concern themselves overmuch about such contingencies, because in a common desire to avoid territorial conflicts which might cause even greater conflicts, the Soviet Union and the United States have consistently avoided territorial conflicts in Europe in which both alliances were involved. The consequence has been to make territorial conflict within alliances easier.

The problems of the hegemonic power in the CENTO and SEATO alliances are very different from those in NATO. In the band of territory stretching from the Bosporus to the China Sea, the economic base for political institutions of the Western European type does not exist. Unresolved internal, political, and economic problems of varying intensity characterize every member of the CENTO and SEATO alliances. And in Vietnam, a situation exists which the Communists expected would be common to the majority of the former colonies.

The speed and relative ease of decolonization since World War II has come as a surprise to all. Communist theorists expected that the imperial powers and the colonies would have been involved in long armed conflict, during which the national liberationist movement would have been captured by Communist parties. However, only in Indo-China is the Communist Party engaged in active combat to become the successor to a colonial regime.

In Vietnam, therefore, the United States is trying in the midst of a civil war to create the political conditions in which democracy might be able to grow, and it is not an easy task. Had the British been as reluctant to face the necessity of liquidating empire as the French, Burma today might be in the position of Vietnam, rather than an independent and unified country.

In the CENTO and SEATO alliances the hegemonic power has two tasks: first to create the conditions for economic growth, which it is hoped will permit the establishment of broadly based governments of the West European type in which the internal threat is practically nonexistent; and second, as in Vietnam, to aid a regime actually engaged in a civil war with Communists.

The role of the United States as the hegemonic power in Latin America is again very different. Opposition to the extension of the Communist state system is a very different task in Latin America than in Europe or Asia. The geographical proximity of part of Latin America enables it to play a role in the military relationship between the two super-powers. The United States' successful opposition to the emplacement of missiles in Cuba was in pursuit of the goal of maintaining strategic superiority over the Soviet Union. As pointed out earlier, Soviet acceptance of this relationship is the condition of the existing *détente* between the super-powers.

A second United States purpose in Latin America is to prevent the establishment of Communist regimes in these countries. The hegemonic position of the United States in this alliance is complicated, first, by the circumstance that the danger from Communism is internal rather than external. The United States and Latin America are in a very uneasy relationship because of their different assumptions about the nature of their relationship. Although Latin American countries display a very wide variety of stages of development, they share the belief that the United States plays a dominant role in the affairs of each country. For each country of Latin America the United States is the most important foreign power; for the United States, each Latin American country is only one of many. The natural consequence is resentment at neglect.

Second, the belief is almost universal in Latin America that United States policy toward Latin America is largely determined by American private investors in Latin America.

Third, any United States involvement in the internal affairs of Latin American countries awakens the suspicion that North American imperialism is again active.

Yet the very formulation of the problem necessitated active North American involvement in Latin American internal affairs. The operative theory in the United States is that the unresolved developmental problems of Latin America may create good opportunities for Communism, and that therefore it is in the interests of the United States to help Latin American countries develop their economies.

In Latin America, however, the danger of Communism from within is not perceived as so great, and the dominant feeling is that the United States *owes* Latin America assistance because of the profits that American business has made in the last century. Moreover, the United States, it is believed, owes such a debt even if the businesses of its citizens are confiscated.

The situation is further complicated by vacillations in the United States judgment as to the danger of Communism in Latin America. The Cuban conversion to Communism, at first seen as a pattern for the future, is now increasingly perceived both by the Soviet Union and the United States as unique. As the danger of Communism is perceived to diminish, quite naturally United States interest in Latin America declines.

The Rio Pact is not, then, a traditional alliance against a foreign threat but an agreement about United States economic and military assistance against internal threats, variously perceived by the signatories of the pacts. Is this a transitional or a permanent feature of the international scene? The answer seems to depend very much on the future prospects of Communism discussed above. If Communism loses as well as gains, then new variants of syncretic Communism in Latin America, if they emerge, will probably be viewed as reversible phenomena which might do world Communism more harm than good in the long run. If on the other hand, Communism continues to gain, the pressure for intervention before and after the fact of conversion will be high.[6]

b. The Communist Alliance System. The members of the Communist alliance system share with the members of the non-Communist alliance system the security from war which results from the common interests of the two super-powers in keeping the likelihood of war low. But beyond this the resemblance ceases. The major distinguishing features of the Communist alliance are the following: (1) It is a fragmented system meant to be universal. (2) It is divided into revisionist and status quo powers. (3) Its members have territorial and economic claims against each other.

The greatest difficulty in the Communist alliance system is to establish a common agreement on its goals. As we have seen in the non-Communist alliance system where the purpose is essentially to contain Communism, the alliance system is divided into different parts in accordance with the nature of the task, with the United States being the hegemonial power in each of the sub-alliances. No such satisfactory solution is possible in the Communist alliance because its goals go far beyond containing the opponent; they encompass, eventually, overwhelming him. It has not been possible to reach agreement on how to do so safely in a world full of nuclear weapons.

For a long time the Communist camp could preserve the fiction of the existence of a correct political and military strategy to be discovered by divination from the entrails of Marxism. While the *pontifex maximus* was established in Moscow, the question of variant interpretations never arose. But just as the United States and the Soviet Union finally succeeded in establishing the security of their respective allies from attack, the primacy of Moscow was challenged from within the Communist alliance system by China, and the leadership of the United States within the Atlantic Alliance was sharply disputed by de Gaulle. The protected secondary powers challenged the hegemon, but the consequences were much more serious for the Communist system.

---

[6] These lines, like the rest of the paper, were written in March 1965. No changes have been made in the text to accommodate subsequent events like the Dominican crisis.

For one, the main challenger, Communist China, was potentially a greater power than the Soviet Union, which lent a special bitterness to the conflict. Second, the problem of mutual economic aid is much more severe in the Communist camp than in the other. In the non-Communist system, in each of the sub-alliances, economic demands have been made only on the hegemon, that is, the United States. In Western Europe economic assistance is no longer necessary; in other areas the extent of economic assistance is under continuous assessment. But in the Communist camp the direction of demands has been reversed. The Soviet Union at one time exploited Eastern Europe, but since 1956 it has responded to demands upon itself from Eastern Europe. The Soviet Union also exploited China by reasserting Tsarist rights in the Treaty Ports and on the Manchurian railroad. Moreover, as has been revealed since, the Chinese Communists had to pay for Soviet military aid during the Korean War. After Stalin's death the flow of demands was reversed until 1960, when the Soviet program of military and economic assistance came to an end.

These reversals in the flow of economic wealth are profoundly disturbing to the Communist camp because a critical goal for all its members, including the hegemonic power, is the attainment of the standard of living of the advanced Western capitalist countries. Since the United States has already attained this goal, offering assistance to its allies does not mean postponing the achievement of the aim of an adequately fed and clothed population.

A further cause for division in the Communist alliance is the existence of status quo and revisionist powers. These claims are not only against members of the non-Communist alliance, but against each other.

The Soviet Union, being a victor in the last war, is essentially a satisfied power territorially. Communist China is not, having active claims to Taiwan and inactive but not abandoned claims in Southeast Asia. A common policy of pressing these claims would produce gains for China, not the Soviet Union, and what is more, the costs to the Soviet Union are higher. Soviet support of Chinese territorial claims could cause conflict with the United States, but even if that were avoided it would most probably produce a new phase of the arms race with the attendant economic embarrassment of the Soviet Union. Since China is too far behind the United States in weapons to be in competition, this cost does not enter into her calculations.

Thus in the Communist alliance, agreement cannot be reached on a common policy of promoting the expansion of Communism, nor on some scheme for sharing economic resources to build Communism in each country. The frustration produced by these differences is so high that Communist China has raised her territorial claims against the Soviet Union and Outer Mongolia and has encouraged Rumania to raise the question of Bessarabia obliquely. Poland, Czechoslovakia, and East Germany have not claimed the territory they lost to the Soviet Union, but these demands are just beneath the surface.

Originally, in the Communist system the tendency was for each country's internal institutions to be pressed into conformity with those of the Soviet Union; but since Stalin's death diversification rather than *Gleichschaltung* has been the trend. This aggravates internal political problems in the Soviet Union. For example, the freedom of action of Soviet leaders in domestic agricultural policy is limited by the existence of a Poland without collective farms.

Within the Western system the necessity to maintain uniformity in the political regimes of all its members has never been felt, and centrifugal tendencies do not create pressures for domestic reforms. As the originally looser system becomes more so, there is little feedback in internal politics. As the rigid system loosens, however, the feedback is significant and, what must be deeply disturbing, of dimensions difficult to foresee and assess.

Thus it is hard to imagine Eastern Europe as anything but much altered ten years from now and Western Europe as remaining essentially the same. Paradoxically, it seems that the cohesion of the Communist alliance system, once pressed into a rigid mold, will suffer much greater disintegration than the always loose non-Communist system. And the multiplication of ideological variants of Communism probably will eventually attenuate the ideological force of Communism.

Perhaps the second half of the twentieth century will indeed be the time of the end of ideology and a time of peace.

29. UNITED STATES–SOVIET CO-OPERATION: INCENTIVES AND OBSTACLES

Robert C. Tucker

ABSTRACT: Since Stalin's death the Soviet and American governments have moved into a new post-cold-war relationship in which continuing political rivalry is combined with some political co-operation to keep this "competitive coexistence" peaceful. Incentives for co-operation are strong, centering in common interest in reducing the danger of thermonuclear war. But obstacles, too, are strong: resistance by some Third World states, resistance by some elements of both of the co-operating governments, and the continuing intense competition for influence in the Third World, which creates imbalances and crises. Despite all the obstacles, the incentives to United States–Soviet co-operation may prevail. But if a co-operative relationship is to endure, it will have to become more extensive and evolve into an *entente*. The precondition of this is some curtailment of power rivalry, which would not, however, mean a global bargain. Furthermore, some element of trust would have to be built into the Soviet-American relationship. The Soviet-American co-operative arrangement could take two different forms: either a "condominium" based on a division of spheres of influence or an alliance on behalf of the growth of international order. The latter would be more in accord with the needs of the situation and the genius of the two peoples.

One of the most significant realignments of the recent past, East and West, is a *rapprochement* between the United States and Soviet Russia, an uncertain move by the two military superpowers and erst-

Reprinted from *The Annals of the American Academy of Political and Social Science*, July 1967, pp. 1–13. Reprinted by permission of the author and publisher.

while cold-war adversaries into limited collaborative relations for purposes of maintaining international peace and security.

This realignment was made possible, on the Soviet side, by the
death of Stalin and ensuing reorientation of Soviet policy in both internal and external affairs. It emerged slowly in the course of a post-Stalin
dialogue between leaders of the two countries. The Geneva summit
meeting of 1955 and the Camp David talks in 1959 between President
Eisenhower and Premier Khrushchev were landmarks in the growth of
this dialogue. The late 1950's and early 1960's witnessed a series of
concrete steps that gave substance to the new trend in the relations
between the two countries.

These steps included the limited nuclear-test-ban agreement of
1963, the previous year's agreement on neutralization of Laos, the
creation of the permanent direct communication channel between Moscow and Washington called the "hot line," the agreement on peaceful
uses of the Antarctic, the agreement not to place bombs in orbit, the
recently concluded multilateral treaty on principles for the use by all
states of outer space, the growth of cultural and scientific exchange, the
regularizing of contacts and discussion between the political leaders and
diplomatic officials of the two countries, the continuing negotiations on
arms control and disarmament, the talks on measures to prevent proliferation of nuclear weapons, the United States–Soviet agreement on
direct air connections, and the conclusion of the consular convention. At
the same time, there have also been a number of setbacks to the new
trend in United States–Soviet relations. The U-2 episode of 1960 and the
Cuban missiles crisis of 1962 are both noteworthy examples. In the
middle 1960's, moreover, the growth of Soviet-American political cooperation has been seriously retarded and complicated by war in Vietnam, and especially by the United States policy, initiated in early 1965,
of bombing raids on North Vietnam, a Soviet ally. At this time of writing
(May, 1967), the future of Soviet-American co-operation is deeply
clouded.

Even without these serious setbacks, the *rapprochement* between
the two great powers would by no means have been describable as a
"condominium," not to mention the Conspiratorial "collusion" for joint
Soviet-American world rule which has been conjured up in various
statements emanating from Peking. On the other hand, we should not
minimize the potential importance of the emergence in the post-Stalin
era of a new Soviet-American relationship, the replacement of the old
cold-war antagonism with a more complex and constructive interaction
in which competition and co-operation are conjoined. What I wish to do
in what follows is to explore the possible meaning of this realignment,
and to consider some requisites of stable co-operative relations between
the two countries.

The Historical Background

Although ideologically at opposite poles, the United States and
Soviet Russia were not wholly unprepared in a psychological sense for

the new trend in their relations which developed after Stalin. There was no tradition of enmity between their peoples. America has always enjoyed great popularity in the minds of many Russians, and even the Soviet Communist regime, speaking through Stalin, once defined the Bolshevik "style" in work as a combination of "Russian revolutionary sweep" with "American efficiency."[1] Americans, for their part, were perhaps less inclined to positive feelings toward Russia. But during the Second World War, they generally admired the Russian war effort, and ordinary Russians were more aware than their government ever acknowledged of the contribution of American Lend-Lease assistance to that effort. A large fund of mutual good will resulted.

Not surprisingly, the idea and, to some extent, the fact of Soviet-American political collaboration have a history going back to that period. For in 1941 the two countries suddenly became involved in a "cooperative relationship" of the most elementary kind — a coalition war for survival against a common enemy. It was only natural under those conditions that some should conceive of a continuing co-operative relationship in the postwar period. Such a concept entered into the architecture of the United Nations as an organization, the Security Council in particular. Optimistic expectations were not borne out, however, and the wartime alliance gave way to the cold-war hostilities of 1946–1953. Not until after Stalin's death did a change in the Soviet leadership and political outlook begin to make possible the more hopeful and constructive pattern of United States–Soviet relations that some had envisaged during World War II. The prerequisites for this development had been present in the Soviet internal situation ever since the end of the war. But Stalin, the most absolute of twentieth-century dictators, was for psychological reasons unable to recognize and accept them, and continued to the end of his days to press the cold war against the manifold "enemies" with which his paranoid personality and hostile actions peopled the world.[2]

The men who came to power in the Soviet system after Stalin's death represented a generation of somewhat younger leaders who, unlike Stalin himself, had never been revolutionaries. Rather, they had come up in political life as executives and managers. They were typified by Malenkov and Khrushchev and, more recently, by Brezhnev and Kosygin. Communist in ideology, the post-Stalin leaders give little evidence of being radical in their outlook; they are an essentially *post-revolutionary* leadership presiding over a relatively deradicalized Soviet Marxist movement, one that has gone very far toward accommodating itself to the world that it remains ideologically committed to transform.

The deradicalization of Soviet Communism has certain obviously important foreign-policy implications. They could be summed up by

---

[1] J. Stalin, *Works* (Moscow, 1953), p. 194. The statement was made in Stalin's lectures of 1924 on "The Foundations of Leninism."

[2] This thesis has been elaborated with supporting evidence in this writer's *The Soviet Political Mind* (New York, Frederick A. Praeger, 1963), chaps. 2 and 8.

saying that fifty years after the Bolshevik Revolution, the Soviet Union can no longer accurately be described as a "revolutionary power." Its leadership remains ideologically committed to the goal of a world-wide Communist revolution, but the pattern of Soviet conduct in world affairs has increasingly become that of a status-quo power rather than a revolutionary one.[3] Of course, "status-quo power" is itself a concept with a range of possible meanings. In the Soviet case, we do not have a power so rigidly wedded to the international status quo that it would actively resist revolutionary change in the non-Communist part of the world. As its response to the Cuban revolution makes clear, for example, Soviet Russia, even in this era of deradicalization, is still willing to welcome and give assistance to a regime moving on its own into the Communist orbit. The thesis here being advanced is simply that the commitment to world Communist revolution, while still intact ideologically, has become very weak as a political motivation and has ceased to be a mainspring of Soviet initiative in world affairs. Soviet ideological behavior has registered the trend in question through emphatic pronouncements against "export of revolution" and through affirmation of the idea that Communist revolution should occur, if at all, as an indigenous development in the country concerned and, if possible, as a nonviolent one.

If the contemporary Soviet Union is no longer to any significant extent a revolution-making power but rather one which finds the international status quo not hard to live with, the explanation is to be sought not solely in the change of leadership and outlook attendant upon the death of Stalin and the passing from the political scene of the remnants of the Bolshevik old guard (such as Molotov) who had survived in power with Stalin. Among other factors reinforcing the status-quo tendency is the growing polycentrism of the Communist world in our time. The fourteen Communist-ruled states and the eighty or so Communist parties elsewhere in the world are no longer under Soviet control as in Stalin's time. Moreover, Soviet political and ideological ascendancy in the polycentric world of Communist states and parties has been powerfully challenged by Communist China under Mao. Further enlargement of the sphere of Communist political power could, in these conditions, complicate the Soviet effort to retain an ascendant position. Indeed, Moscow's position as capital of world Communism could be further undermined rather than bolstered by Communist revolutions that brought to power parties looking to China for leadership. The otherwise curious spectacle of Soviet support for a non-Communist India in its latter-day hostilities with Communist China finds part of its explanation here.

Still another force behind the evolution of the Soviet state from the role of a revolutionary power to that of a status-quo power is the need for international stability as a setting for internal Soviet development

[3] This refers, of course, to the pattern of action in the non-Communist part of the world. Soviet policy toward the *Communist* part has long been protective of the status quo, as was best shown by the Soviet intervention in Hungary in 1956 to keep communism intact in a country where its fortunes were uncertain owing to popular revolution.

and reform. The post-Stalin leadership inherited from Stalin a country in internal crisis caused by the long regime of terror, bureaucratic stultification, gross mismanagement, neglect of crying welfare needs of the people, and resulting catastrophically low morale. In Stalin's final years, all these problems had gone largely unrecognized in an atmosphere of relentless pursuit of the Cold War abroad. Indeed, it may have been in part Stalin's unwillingness to face the necessity for change and reform inside the Soviet Union which spurred him to keep the nation's attention constantly fixed upon the machinations of foreign "enemies." With his death, there was an underlying change in the relationship of internal and external politics of the Soviet regime.

Instead of predicating the internal policy upon the needs of the Cold War abroad, the post-Stalin leadership, under Malenkov and Beria at first and subsequently under Khrushchev and others, tended to give the position of priority to internal needs and problems and to seek a cold-war *détente*. Not only would such a *détente* relieve external dangers to Soviet security (for example, by ending the Korean war); it might also make it possible to reallocate scarce Soviet funds to internal developmental needs, and especially to the long neglected consumer-goods industries. Thus, the commitment to internal development and reform was a factor favoring international stabilization.

Nor is this, as might be supposed, a strictly short-term proposition. A Soviet regime attempting, as part of its reform policy, to rule Russia without the terror that was the hallmark of Stalinism must necessarily seek substantial and continuing improvement in the living standards of the Soviet population, and the pressure to do this rises as public opinion emerges as a force in the no-longer-totalitarian single-party system. But with a gross national product far lower than America's, Soviet Russia can divert large resources to welfare needs only if it can substantially reduce or control defense expenditures. These considerations point to *détente* and international stabilization as a long-range Soviet interest, to arms control and negotiated disarmament measures as a way of enabling Russia to control arms outlays without falling behind in relative military power vis-à-vis the United States, and to a new political relationship with the United States as a precondition of achieving such ends.

COMPETITIVE COEXISTENCE

The new foreign orientation of the post-Stalin Soviet leadership reflected these underlying realities. Ideologically, it expressed itself in the doctrine of "competitive coexistence," which was advanced in the time of Khrushchev and incorporated into the Program of the Soviet Communist party in 1961. That doctrine portrays the United States and the Soviet Union as, respectively, the leaders of two ideologically opposed "systems" competing by peaceful means — economic, political, cultural — for dominant world influence, the chief stake in the contest being the future development of the underdeveloped countries of the

Third World either toward Soviet Communism or American capitalism. Internal economic development is a principal arena of this external competition, for it is a question of which developmental model, the Soviet or the American, will prove more compellingly attractive in the long run.

But competitive coexistence was presented in the post-Stalin Soviet doctrine as involving a measure of co-operation between the competitors. Rather in the manner in which our economists have described "oligopolistic competition," in which two or more dominant firms co-operate to prevent price wars and maintain general market stability while competing (for example, through advertising) to improve their relative shares of the market, Soviet theorists of competitive coexistence have envisaged the Soviet Union and the United States as engaging in political cooperation to prevent war and maintain over-all international stability while they carry on long-range nonmilitary competition (for example, through propaganda and ideology) to enhance their relative influence in the world. Being Marxist, they have presented this notion of a dual competitive-cum-co-operative relationship with America as a "dialectical" approach to coexistence. The basis of the co-operation, according to the Soviet view, as formulated by both political leaders and theoretical specialists, is the shared vital interest of the two great powers in reducing the chances of war. Co-operation for this purpose would involve the development of close and regular contact on all problems of mutual concern, the attempt to negotiate solutions of issues concealing threats to peace, the defusing of trouble spots in various parts of the world (Laos, for example), and the stopping of local conflicts before they grow into great conflagrations threatening to involve the major powers. In effect, the new Soviet doctrine has seen in United States–Soviet political co-operation a way of keeping competitive coexistence peaceful, of maintaining a relatively stable international environment within which the nonmilitary competition for influence can proceed.

The United States government has, since President Eisenhower's time, tended to respond favorably to the concept of a changed relationship involving some co-operation as well as continued political rivalry with Soviet Russia. It, too, has shown awareness that such co-operation could prove a requisite for cosurvival in the nuclear age. It, too, has an interest in curbing the astronomical costs of modern military technology, the spiral of the arms race. Without some success along that line, it can no more get to what is now called the "Great Society" than Soviet Russia can get to what it calls "Full Communism" (two visions of the social goal which have, by the way, more than a little in common). So, the new Soviet foreign orientation of the post-Stalin period found a receptive audience in Washington. President Kennedy's speech at American University, "Toward a Strategy of Peace," was one of the significant markers of this trend in United States official thinking. President Johnson, too, has strongly endorsed the concept of a co-operative relationship with Russia. "We've got to get into the habit of peaceful co-operation," he said, for example, in a public pronouncement of September 1966 to the Soviet people, emphasizing the common interest of the two countries in the avoidance of war, the historical record of friendliness between the two peoples, and the desirability of extending co-operative relations beyond what had so far been accomplished.[4]

Obstacles to Co-operation

Taking stock of the outcome so far, it must be admitted that the experiment in Soviet-American collaboration has not yet borne great fruit in deeds or brought about a stable *entente* between the two governments. Although by no means insignificant in their cumulative entirety, the co-operative acts and agreements noted earlier are little more than a series of tentative and cautious beginnings. Let us consider, for example, some of what has *not* yet been done. So far, progress on arms control and disarmament has been small. The treaty on nonproliferation of nuclear weapons would, it is true, be a very great step forward in this field. But at present it still remains under negotiation, and the outcome is uncertain. Part of the responsibility for that rests with the failure of the United States and Soviet Union to match the renunciation being asked of others with some renouncing on their own parts — such as the renouncing of the right of *first use* of nuclear weapons — and to give guarantees to the nonnuclear states against nuclear blackmail or nuclear attack by governments which might try to violate the system.

What is more, the United States and Soviet Union may be on the threshold of another fateful round of the arms race, involving the deployment of anti-ballistic missiles systems and resulting further development of offensive weapons by both sides, all of which may represent a serious setback for the cause of arms control (for example, by necessitating a resumption of nuclear tests above ground). They have not so far been willing to transform the costly competitive race to the moon into a co-operative venture. They have done next to nothing to place economic assistance to underdeveloped countries on a co-operative and multilateral basis, although the emerging crisis of economic growth and overpopulation makes the need for a co-operative approach to the problem painfully obvious.

There is no single or simple explanation for the tentativeness of United States–Soviet co-operation and for the modest character of the positive results so far. One of the explanations, however, lies in the strength of the resistances and obstacles on both sides to a working accord between the United States and Soviet governments on important international problems. Realism not only compels us to acknowledge the existence of these obstacles, but also to admit that they make themselves felt on both sides. Thus, both great powers encounter resistances within their respective alliance systems to a Soviet-American *entente*. They emanate in particular from certain governments whose leaders fear that United States–Soviet co-operation could be injurious to their

[4] *The New York Times,* September 28, 1966, p. 14.

own national interests. The importance that both the United States and Soviet Union attach to the preservation of their alliance structures forces them to take account of these counter-pressures. Soviet policy-makers have had to contend in particular with Communist Chinese objections to the relationship with the United States; and the United States government has had especially to contend with concern in West Germany over the possible impact of Soviet-American co-operation upon German reunification and other interests.

A further obstacle to collaborative relations between the two great powers is the persistence on both sides of old habits of mind born in the era of the Cold War, habits of ingrained hostility and distrust, habits of seeing the struggle against the other side as the supreme proper concern of national policy, and co-operation between Russia and America as unnecessary for security purposes or undesirable, or both. To make matters still more complicated, these habits of mind are unevenly distributed on both sides. Some American and Soviet political leaders are more flexible and conciliation-minded, more able and willing to conceive of collaborating with adversaries and to experiment along those lines, whereas others are more rigid and doctrinaire, more inclined to rely on military might in relations with the other side, more convinced that the only effective way to talk to them is in the language of cold power. In the jargon of recent times, we have the "softliners" and the "hardliners," the "doves" and the "hawks." These terms are obvious oversimplifications, but the divisions to which they point are real and enormously important facts of political life in *both* of the capitals. The recent United States Senate debate over ratification of the consular convention with the Soviet Union made the division on the American side more dramatically apparent than before. Because of the single-party system and official control of the press on the other side, the division is less apparent in the Soviet leadership. Yet those of us who regularly study the Soviet press have found abundant evidence that it exists.

And so, on both sides, there are influential elements who *oppose* a Soviet-American working relationship and who resist efforts in that direction to the extent that they can. In a curious way, moreover, they reinforce each other. For insofar as the Soviet hardliners gain the ascendancy inside the Soviet Union's regime, the policy orientation that they pursue tends to support the arguments of their opposite numbers in Washington about the difficulty of working co-operatively with the Russians. The same process also works in reverse: ascendancy of those who favor a hardline policy in Washington plays into the hands of the Moscow opponents of Soviet-American co-operation, for it leads to actions by the United States government which make the latters' arguments in the internal policy debate on the Soviet side more plausible. Thus, the tough policy that the United States government has pursued in Vietnam during the last two years has resulted, among other things, in a growth of influence of hardline elements inside the Soviet government and a worsening of the position of the proponents of better relations with Washington.

Still a further serious obstacle to a stable and self-sustained United States–Soviet working relationship is the continuance of political rivalry between them at the level of intensity that has marked it during the past decade. Both great powers have vigorously engaged in a political influence contest, particularly in the Third World, employing diplomacy, economic assistance, arms exports, technical aid, propaganda, and so on. Experience makes it quite clear that this influence contest can create situations that, in turn, impose great strain upon the fabric of Soviet-American relations. Thus, for example, Moscow, pursuing political influence, has in recent months created an arms imbalance in North Africa by shipping much military equipment to Algeria, which has led to a plea from Morocco to the United States for matching arms assistance. The dynamics of situations of this kind contain within themselves the potentiality of armed conflicts which, in turn, create more international tension and threaten to involve the superpowers. The earlier history of present events in Indochina bears witness in its way to the relevance of this proposition.

So, the whole concept of a "nonmilitary" Soviet-American competition for influence in the uncommitted countries has a certain unreality. For competitive coexistence tends to remain peaceful only so long as neither side is conspicuously or irretrievably *losing*. The game shows a dangerous tendency to cease being peaceful when: (1) a change of regime seriously adverse to one or the other side occurs or threatens to occur within a given country that has been an object of competition, and (2) circumstances permit the application of force to prevent or reverse this adverse outcome. An intense competitive struggle to draw uncommitted countries into one orbit of influence or another is, therefore, a serious bar to the development of stable co-operative relations between the United States and Soviet Union.

All of these obstacles to Soviet-American co-operation have made themselves felt in recent years and help to explain why more has not been achieved. In this connection, special mention must be made of the war in Vietnam. On the surface, this war has not completely put a stop to United States–Soviet political collaboration. Yet, in a deeper way, the war, and especially the bombing of North Vietnam which began in early 1965, has had a very depressing effect upon the whole post-Stalin growth of working relations between Moscow and Washington. Changes that slowly were taking place in the official Soviet image of the American political leadership have been set back or reversed, and an image of the American leadership that resembles the old cold-war stereotypes has re-emerged in the Soviet official press. A relapse into old suspicions, old animosities, and old anti-American Soviet reflexes may be reflected in this. In part, it may reflect increased influence of the hardline element in the Soviet leadership under the impact of Vietnam, and in part it may express a general tendency of the Soviet political mind to reconsider its earlier more hopeful view of American leaders. Furthermore, in the general atmosphere of West European apathy or opposition to America's Vietnam action, the Soviet leadership has been presented with fresh opportunities to cultivate political relationships in Europe that might not otherwise have existed or have been so beckoning, and consequently we have seen in the past two years a tendency for Moscow to exploit centrifugal forces in the Western alliance structure, to give the emphasis not to closer relations with Washington but rather to closer relations with West European capitals, Paris included. Finally, the dialogue between Soviet and American leaders, a dialogue which lies at the core of the co-operative relationship, has suffered and greatly been diminished as a result of Vietnam. On the whole, the injury done to the emergent *entente* with the Soviet Union may be far from the least of the tragedies of the Vietnam war from the American point of view.

Yet I do not believe that the new Soviet-American relationship is or need be permanently impaired. Given in the near future a negotiated peace in Vietnam, the underlying forces in the world situation which impel the two superpowers to collaborative action should reassert themselves. Fundamental security interests of both powers, and indeed of all peoples, are involved. Hence it seems premature to assume a permanent shift of Soviet diplomatic emphasis to the western European scene or to treat the whole venture of co-operative relations between the United States and the Soviet Union as a matter of historical interest only. What may be useful, then, is to reflect on the experience of the past decade in this field, and try to draw some lessons from it.

REQUISITES OF SOVIET-AMERICAN CO-OPERATION

(1) It appears that, notwithstanding all the obstacles explored above, the incentives to co-operative action by the two superpowers are quite strong, sufficiently so to provide a basis for greater success in this field than has been achieved so far. The fundamental incentive is the common interest in reducing the danger of a thermonuclear holocaust. This primary common interest, reinforced by a further common interest in curtailing the cost of military preparations and establishments, dictates United States–Soviet co-operation in all feasible measures of arms control and disarmament. Further, the primary common interest in preventing a general war gives rise to a set of secondary common interests in stabilizing or settling crisis-situations in which the threat of armed violence is latently present.

Beyond these shared interests in avoiding war, in bringing the arms race under control, and in the defusing of world trouble-spots, the United States and the Soviet Union have an underlying, although as yet imperfectly cognized, common interest in working together to meet certain other problems and dangers. The population explosion, the growing disparity between the wealthy nations and the poor nations and the associated problem of economic development, and the problem of air and water pollution are high on the list or situations that contain a mounting threat of disorder on a world scale, situations of unprecedented urgency and seriousness. Only through international co-operation can these dangers be contained, much less allayed, and without cooperation between the two most powerful and wealthy of industrialized nations, no efforts by the United Nations or regional associations of states can bear great fruit. In effect, international co-operation is becoming a vital necessity in the face of the rise of a plethora of problems that, by their very nature, cannot be satisfactorily resolved within the confines of the nation-state. In the continuing absence of an effective system of world order, the United States and Soviet Russia can alone provide by their co-operative action an interim response to the need for a co-operative international approach to these problems. It is not only, then, the danger of war which provides the underlying motivation for their co-operation, but also the political, demographic, economic, and technological challenges to prolonged meaningful human living on this planet.

(2) A co-operative arrangement between the United States and the Soviet Union cannot easily be enduring and stable unless it becomes more close and extensive than political leaders on either side have apparently envisaged, and unless it takes precedence over such important competing concerns as the integrity of their regional alliance structures. Up to now, the tendency on both sides has been to think in terms of a modicum of co-operation combined with a high level of continued political rivalry throughout the world. The experience of the past decade suggests, however, that unless the co-operative working relationship transcends this, unless it goes beyond a *détente* and becomes an *entente,* it may not be viable at all.

This view is admittedly at variance with the thinking of some respected American specialists in foreign-policy problems. They take a continued intense process of Soviet-American competition for influence as a constant and feel, in part because of pressures from within the Western alliance system, that co-operative relations with Moscow neither need be nor ought to be extended beyond a minimum of mutually advantageous action, chiefly in the sphere of arms control, to reduce the hazards of nuclear war.[5] However, such a scenario for American-Soviet relations may be more of a utopia than the just-mentioned *entente.* For it overlooks the essential indivisibility of these relations, the virtual impossibility of maintaining stable co-operative arrangements in one field — the delicate and difficult area of arms control — while pursuing as vigorously as ever a world-wide political competition for influence which keeps the competitors mutually estranged and periodically generates high tension between them. The co-operative links between Washington and Moscow cannot be expected to prosper if frequently subjected to extreme political turbulence in a world of intense Soviet-American political rivalry.

This is not to argue that some sort of global bargain between the two powers is the precondition of their successful co-operation in world affairs. An antecedent general settlement of outstanding international issues, however desirable in the abstract, does not appear realistically

[5] See, for example, the argument of Marshall D. Shulman in " 'Europe' versus 'Détente'?," *Foreign Affairs,* April 1967.

attainable in the near future. Undoubtedly, there are various issues — and German reunification is almost certainly one of them — which will have to be lived with until the slow passage of time and efforts of diplomacy can bring possibilities of resolution that do not now exist. The point being made here is simply that the competitive process, although it clearly cannot altogether be stopped, need not on the other hand be taken as a simple given, an unalterable fact of international life, something over which the two governments have no control. Rather, it has an interactive dynamic of its own which can be curbed and brought under control, given the settled will on both sides to do so. It is something to which limits can be set. And difficult as this might be to achieve, it would probably be less difficult than to achieve progress on the terribly complex technical problems of arms control and disarmament *without* curtailment of the power rivalry between the two principals. On the other hand, progress on arms-control measures should become increasingly feasible in a setting of lessened political competition between the chief governments concerned.

The theory of competitive coexistence, as elaborated on the Soviet side and more or less accepted with much ideological rationalization on the American side, envisages an indefinitely prolonged process of political competition tempered by co-operative steps to keep this competition peaceful. But that is a formula for an inherently unstable and deeply troubled United States–Soviet relationship. To stabilize it, the co-operative aspect will have to be given primacy over the competitive aspect. The two governments will have to show a settled disposition to reach settlements where possible. They will have to neutralize or otherwise defuse various danger points in world politics, such as Southeast Asia; to forestall the eruption of crisis-situations that place great strain upon their relations; to avoid getting into conflicts which give rise to domestic pressures against co-operative relations; and, in general, to adopt a conflict-resolving posture in their interrelations and their approach to world problems. Clearly, this would imply certain significant modifications in the habitual modes of thought and conduct of both main powers on the international scene. Above all, instead of regarding the promotion of a particular form of society as their highest mission in history, the leaders would have to conceive it as their supreme goal to serve the cause of order in human affairs, pending the slow creation in time of order-maintaining institutions on a world scale.

(3) This raises the whole question of the form that a United States–Soviet *entente* might take. Manifestly, close relationships between great powers can take a multitude of forms, depending upon the purposes that animate them and other factors. A United States–Soviet working relationship could conceivably fall into the pattern of imperialistic great-power alliances of the past, with a division of Soviet and American spheres of influence in the world. In effect, the interests of the two powers, narrowly conceived, would become the touchstone of their co-operative action. Although the United States and Russia have the combined physical power to enforce such a condominium, an at-

tempt to co-operate along those lines would not, for a great many reasons, be likely to succeed for long. Not only would it be beset by manifold resistances from smaller states whose interests were being overridden by the great powers; it would conflict with the aspirations of the two peoples themselves, and would encounter resistances, both internal and external.

An alternative form of *entente*, although historically unprecedented, would be more in accord with the needs of the situation and the spirit of the two peoples. Instead of co-operating politically in their own national interests, narrowly conceived, the governments of the United States and Soviet Union would seek to exert their influence separately and jointly on behalf of the growth of order, which is in the interest not simply of these two major nations but of all. They would work not only in their bilateral relations but in the United Nations and its working bodies, in their regional alliances, and in every aspect of foreign policy, to promote constructive change and peaceful solutions of world problems. In effect, the United States–Soviet co-operative relationship would become a kind of trusteeship under which the two governments would jointly act as sponsors of international order pending the creation of a workable formal system of world order in the future. They would form, as it were, an informal interim system of order, a holding operation to help man survive long enough to move into the new form of international life that is needed but does not yet exist.

Such an undertaking would tap the deeper sources of idealism present in both the American and Russian peoples. Among contemporary nations, these two are notable for the stubborn streak of idealistic aspiration that marks them both in very different ways. Both have a universalism and a commitment to world order. They conceive it differently, it is true. Americans tend to think in terms of a world order under law, whereas Russians, insofar as they are Communists, tend rather to think in terms of a world order under ideology. No easy reconciliation of these disparate approaches to world order will be possible. But the younger generations, those who come to positions of power and influence in ten or fifteen years' time, may find it easier than their elders did to make the necessary mutual adjustment. What their elders can do is to give them a chance to try.

(4) Finally, it is, in my opinion, an essential requisite for stable co-operation between the United States and Soviet Union that an element of mutual trust be built over time into their mutual relations. The foundation of this trust might be the recognition by leading persons on both sides that the two countries have acquired, by virtue of modern military technology, not only certain common security interests but a *mutual* security interest. That is to say, given the unheard-of possibilities of destruction inherent in total thermonuclear war in our time, each of the two superpowers has, whether it recognizes this or not, acquired a certain interest in the *other's* security, or (what amounts to the same thing) its sense of security. For nervousness, tension, insecurity on either side have become dangerous to both. It is in this context

that the growth of mutual trust becomes a factor of great potential importance.

Considering the heritage of mutual mistrust and suspicion born of the Cold War and the whole past history of our relations, the idea of building trust into Soviet-American relations may seem wildly unrealistic. Moreover, there is a certain tendency to suppose that the sole proper basis for Soviet-American relations, including co-operative action in arms control, is the rationally calculated self-interest of both parties, their common desire to survive. This may be so, but it is not self-evidently so. For it may be that in certain situations now emerging on the horizon of Soviet-American relations, the dictates of calculated self-interest will depend on what image of the other side goes into the calculation: the picture of a malevolent force operating only on the basis of calculated self-interest, or, alternatively, that of a force moved by certain human feelings and not foreign to benevolence. If this is so, then the growth of trust — the kind of trust that may have been emerging, for example, in the relations between Kennedy and Khrushchev — could prove of decisive significance.

To build mutual trust into United States–Soviet relations will at best be a long slow process, and probably never complete, at least in the present generation. But without it, there can be no genuine *entente,* and many problems will be far harder to resolve. In particular, the arms race will probably not be brought under control.

30. SOVIET FOREIGN POLICY AT THE CROSSROADS: CONFLICT AND/OR COLLABORATION?

Vernon V. Aspaturian

I. INTRODUCTION

The decision of the Union of Soviet Socialist Republics to occupy Czechoslovakia in August 1968, while it represents a fundamental turning point in Soviet foreign policy, most of whose implications are ambiguous yet ominous, should not be permitted to obscure the fact that the Soviet regime remains confronted with a wide array of postponed internal and external problems that demand action and yet defy resolution. The decision to arrest forcibly the processes of liberalization in Czechoslovakia stands out as an uncharacteristic act of will on the part of a regime whose four years in power have been marked by drift, indecisiveness, vacillation, paralysis, and "muddling through." For five years the government of Leonid Brezhnev and Alexei Kosygin has postponed action on painful problems, has permitted events and situations to accumulate dangerously, and in general has allowed itself to be dominated by events rather than domesticating them. During its first two years in office the regime's inaction was perhaps inaccurately ascribed to prudence, caution, and calculated restraint. It now appears in retrospect that paralysis was confused with prudence, inertia was mistaken for caution, and factional indecisiveness was accepted as self-restraint.

The inaction of the Brezhnev-Kosygin government was viewed as a welcome respite from the erratic, contradictory, and irrational pattern of

Reprinted in edited form from *International Organization*, Summer, 1969, pp. 589–620. Reprinted by permission.

behavior during the decade of Nikita Khrushchev's rule[1] which contrasted unfavorably with what appeared to be the calm, controlled, and rational demeanor of his two principal successors whose bland, bureaucratic, and pragmatic personalities seemed eminently to correlate with their behavior. It soon became apparent that the Brezhnev-Kosygin team represented not so much a new unified collective rationality as it did a latently explosive marriage of factional convenience in which the partisans of Khrushchev's policies joined forces with his detractors to topple the Soviet leader for divergent reasons.

Khrushchev's successors inherited not only his policies but also the problems his policies had created, and for at least a year it appeared that Moscow's policies indeed corresponded to what Peking labeled as "Khrushchevism without Khrushchev." The continuity in policy between the Brezhnev-Kosygin regime and its predecessor is indeed greater than the differences. It may be that this continuity represents more the automatic consequences of indecisiveness and drift than of conscious deliberation. The personalities and groups that supported Khrushchev's détente policies remain powerful forces within the Soviet hierarchy, but they may not possess sufficient power and leverage to exercise anything exceeding a veto over fundamental departures.

After more than five decades of revolution, civil war, social convulsion, and unprecedented destruction which witnessed the growth of the Soviet state from a near cipher in world affairs to a mighty modernized and industrialized global power second only to the United States in the magnitude of its influence and the scope of its interests the Soviet leaders are now faced with a series of fundamental questions which cannot be postponed indefinitely and whose resolution may be impossible without provoking a leadership crisis.

The Soviet leaders must first make a decision regarding the root problem of all their problems, the question of purpose. It is the loss of purpose and the search for a surrogate that has divided the Soviet leadership and undermined the Soviet will to act in the face of both new dangers and new opportunities. This is the fundamental cause for the malaise and indecision that grip this aggregation of mediocrities whose mandate is as obviously transitional as its passions are inferior to those of its predecessors. The Soviet leaders must decide whether they are directing a state or a movement; in the face of the Communist Chinese challenge and pressures from the United States the current transitional attempt to behave like a state while clinging to the rhetoric of revolution cannot be sustained indefinitely. If they choose to play out their role as a global power, the Soviet leaders must once again decide to challenge the United States for paramountcy, demand parity, or settle for second place as did Khrushchev when his bluff was called in the 1962 Cuban missile crisis. Furthermore, they must decide whether to postpone maximum utilization of scarce resources for internal growth in order to widen

[1] Khrushchev held both the post of First Secretary of the Communist Party and that of Chairman of the Council of Ministers. Brezhnev succeeded to the former post and Kosygin to the latter.

foreign policy options and achieve diplomatic goals. Moscow must also decide whether it will seek spheres of influence on four continents or retrench to the Eurasian land mass. No matter what the decisions, they will affect the delicate internal social equilibrium and cause renewed factional conflict.

There is substantial evidence to suggest that the Soviet leadership is seriously divided over the direction of its next major moves in foreign policy, just as it was probably divided over the occupation of Czechoslovakia and continues to be wrenched by factional controversy on how to deal with passive resistance. As a consequence most decisions are still being postponed rather than resolved. It would be a gross oversimplification to divide the Soviet ruling group into "hawks" and "doves" although the issues and options represented by these avian symbols are the focal points of controversy. The Soviet leadership appears to be gravely agitated over the allocation of resources and to be divided into two broad groupings: those advocating a greater relaxation of international tensions, a retreat from overcommitments in foreign policy, and a demand that marginal international disputes be resolved through compromise and mutual concessions; and those advocating a buildup in Soviet strategic capabilities, perhaps even to the point of challenging the United States for global primacy, greater assistance to allies under attack to which the Soviet Union is committed in one form or another, and the postponement of internal growth in the interests of national security and the exploitation of international opportunities.

It would be an overstatement to characterize the second group as being made up entirely of expansionist-minded or ideologically oriented leaders although both types are undoubtedly included. Rather, it is on the whole a grouping that feels that Khrushchev surrendered the initiative to the United States, overestimated its capabilities and staying power, overlooked its domestic contradictions, and allowed many opportunities to slip by. This group is skeptical of American intentions and is inclined to the view that the Administration of Lyndon Johnson used the détente to the detriment of Soviet interests and that international stability works to the advantage of the West not only because it preserves the Western status quo but also because it undermines the Soviet position in Eastern Europe and in the international Communist movement. Instead of a détente it envisions a continuous period of challenge and response between the two global powers with periodic respites in the form of *ad hoc* arrangements and *de facto* stalemates. It does not rule out the possibility of China becoming an object of attention from both sides, and hence this group would probably make more concessions to achieve an ultimate reconciliation with China in order to preclude the unpalatable prospect that Moscow might become the chief victim of a Sino-American understanding. Hence it might be willing to risk mending relations with China even if that should retard or reverse the détente with the United States.

The Arab-Israeli war in June 1967 and the occupation of Czechoslovakia a year later served to bring these contradictory currents in the

Soviet leadership into sharp relief. Soviet policy in both instances seemed to veer from one extreme to another, as if some leaders were demanding a more vigorous response while others were counseling prudence.

Since most of the tendencies as well as the problems of Soviet foreign policy were inherited from the Khrushchev era, it might be useful to examine the conditioning factors which have shaped and continue to shape Soviet attitudes and behavior in international affairs. Three conditioning factors are of crucial significance. These are: 1) the erosion of ideology and the consequent loss of the sense of purpose and direction which has always been a strong point in Soviet decision-making; 2) the fragmentation of the decisionmaking process which has contributed to the erosion of ideology and which in turn has been accelerated by it; and 3) the globalization of Soviet foreign policy which has extended the range and scope of Soviet commitments in world affairs at a time when that country has suffered both a loss of purpose and a weakening of will.

The contemporary crises in Soviet foreign policy can thus be defined in terms of a divided leadership confronted with expanding obligations while being shorn of its purpose. This serves to create instability at the top, unpredictability in behavior, and diminished capability for the rational control and containment of dangerous situations.

II. The Erosion of Ideology: The Loss of Mission

One of the most conspicuous characteristics of Soviet foreign policy during the Khrushchev era was the increasingly agnostic character of its operative norms, to say nothing of its actual policy behavior. This feature has continued to distinguish the foreign policy of his successors. In fact, the erosion or waning of ideology as a motivating force in foreign policy has not only accelerated but has also assumed a variety of dimensions. The traditional ideological goals of "world revolution," "world Communism," and "proletarian internationalism" have lost much of their relevance for Soviet foreign policy although they continue to be intoned systematically for rhetorical effect and residual pragmatic value. This is not to say that the erosion of ideological commitment has progressed evenly in all sectors of the Soviet population, the Soviet elites, and the Soviet leadership. For some, of course, the waning of ideology is viewed as a catastrophe whereas for others it may appear as an unmitigated blessing.[2] Although the spectrum of views in the leader-

[2] Cf., for example, the remarkable document, "Thoughts on Progress, Coexistence and Intellectual Freedom," by the celebrated Soviet scientist, Andrei D. Sakharov, which represents a virtual repudiation of ideology as a factor in Soviet foreign policy calculations. Although this document has restricted circulation inside the Soviet Union, it apparently represents the views of a significant number of Soviet scientists, artists, and other intellectuals. For the text see The New York Times, July 22, 1968.

ship is probably much narrower, it is this very difference of outlook which contributes to the erosion.

The concept that ideology is eroding in the Soviet Union has provoked considerable controversy and is subject to varying constructions. The erosion of ideology can mean the lessening of its intensity or value as a variable in foreign policy; it can mean the lessening or waning of both commitment and conviction on the part of the leadership, individually or collectively; it can mean a contraction in its scope or range of application; and finally it can mean its subversion by resort to purely pragmatic and opportunistic behavior which debases its character, undercuts its functionality in shaping policies or decisions, exhausts its potential as a source of innovation, and subverts its appeal and effectiveness for internal and external audiences.

The erosion of ideology in the Soviet Union has been characterized in varying degrees by all of these processes. With specific reference to foreign policy it would perhaps be more appropriate to refer to *de-ideologization* rather than the erosion of ideology to define the process whereby foreign policy goals have been progressively disengaged from ideological norms. The de-ideologization of Soviet foreign policy set in motion at the Twentieth Party Congress in 1956 and the repudiation of some sacrosanct ideological principles served to free foreign policy from Stalinist fetters, but it also shattered the myths of Soviet ideological infallibility and political omniscience. This in turn released disintegrative forces. Factional politics, having spread throughout the Communist world, has become increasingly institutionalized, making it virtually impossible to coordinate policy or resolve conflicts between Communist regimes and parties.

The progressive de-ideologization of Soviet foreign policy goals under Khrushchev took place more by inadvertence and as a consequence of his opportunism than by deliberate design. Once domestic pressures — for instance, in favor of raising the standard of living — were given equal legitimacy with ideological pressures, it was axiomatic that they would become a factor in internal politics and in turn impel Khrushchev to cater to them while spurning the simultaneous demands of foreign Communist states and parties. To assign higher priority to Communist China and the world Communist movement might have been necessary to preserve Soviet preeminence in the world of Communism, but it was bound to be of little value in preserving Khrushchev's authority at home which increasingly depended upon his ability to meet the demands of powerful domestic constituencies.

The loss of purpose, i.e., the loss of the sense of historic mission which has characterized Soviet foreign policy since the establishment of the Soviet state and which animated the Bolshevik Party long before it gained control of the state, created a vacuum which has been spontaneously filled by the traditional operational norms and assumptions of great-power behavior — national interest, security, survival, economic and material well-being, national pride, prestige, and power — which are increasingly displacing rather than supplementing the abstract goals of "world revolution" and "world Communism" in Soviet foreign policy behavior.

While the Soviet subjugation of Czechoslovakia in 1968 is not the first time the naked security and national interests of the Soviet Union have been given a higher priority in Soviet calculations than ideological considerations, the ideological rationalizations employed by Moscow to justify its intervention in Czechoslovakia were so patently transparent that they earned the scorn, ridicule, and condemnation of virtually every important Communist leader in the world. The flimsiness of Moscow's pretext was further exposed by the candid Polish admission that Warsaw cooperated in the venture on grounds of pure raison d'état. What makes this particular Soviet subordination of ideological norms to state interests unique and transcendentally significant is that the Soviet leaders were unable credibly to correlate and identify their state interests with ideological norms in a manner that persuaded the overwhelming majority of Communist leaders throughout the world. Even Fidel Castro felt called upon to recognize the action as contrary to basic Communist precepts although he embraced it on grounds of Cuban self-interest.

In spite of the brazen enunciation of the so-called "Brezhnev" or "Socialist commonwealth" doctrine attempting to justify Soviet intervention in any "Socialist" country on grounds of higher ideological interests, the military occupation of Czechoslovakia signifies a Soviet determination to maintain a sphere of influence in the traditional great-power sense. Contrary to an impression in some quarters, the Soviet decision to intervene does not imply that Communism is once again "monolithic" but the exact opposite. Neither does it signfy a militant resurgence of "world Communism" as a motive force in Soviet behavior. On the contrary, the Soviet occupation signifies the full flowering of the Soviet state as a traditional imperial power whose influence and role in the world are determined not by the attractiveness of its ideology or its social system but by the enormity of its power and the determination to employ it in its self-interest.

While the Soviet Union appears to have exhausted ideology as a motivating force in its foreign policy because it has become increasingly dysfunctional, ideology has not exhausted its utility in other dimensions. It continues to serve the Brezhnev-Kosygin regime as a valuable instrument of epistemological, political, and social analysis, i.e., as a theory of reality, as a repository of moral truths and standards of ethical conduct, as a medium of communication, as an effective and necessary vehicle for the rationalization and explanation of the Soviet social order, and as the indispensable foundation of legitimacy upon which the entire Soviet structure reposes. While ideology wanes as a motivating force, it may simultaneously wax in its other functions, much as religions have undergone similar functional metamorphoses.

In the process of gradually disentangling ideological norms from policy goals Soviet ideology has assumed a new function whose effects are not altogether an unmixed blessing. It now functions to legitimize

Moscow's behavior as a *global power,* i.e., a power which asserts a right to intervene in any dispute or conflict in any part of the globe. While the Soviet leaders have abjured ideology as a norm-defining mechanism, they have by no means abdicated their self-appointed role as the guardian and spokesman of the oppressed masses of the world against international imperialism.

Correspondingly, however, and with considerable irony the residuary Soviet commitment to the transcendental normative goals of ideology serves simultaneously to legitimize the global behavior of the United States. For if the Soviet Union is the self-appointed defender of the weak and the oppressed from imperialist aggression and the "export of counterrevolution," the United States is the self-proclaimed defender of the weak, vulnerable, gullible, and unstable nations which are the natural prey of "international Communism" operating through the manipulation of "national liberation movements" and "popular uprisings" which are viewed as mere euphemisms for "export of revolution" and "subversion." Without the omnipresent threat of "international Communism" (now presumably to read "Asian Communism") the United States would find it difficult to explain and justify its behavior in terms other than might and self-interest which it too wishes to avoid. This is not to imply that without the presence of "international Communism" as a legitimizing instrument Moscow and Washington would halt or even limit their penchant for global interventionism but rather that they would have to contrive new legitimizing instruments for behavior that is essentially a natural function of their power and status in the international community and which is animated more by self-interest than by messianic fervor or purpose.

III. The Fragmentation of the Decisionmaking Process: The Paralysis of Will

Under Stalin policy formulation and decisionmaking were tightly centralized in Stalin's person: Thought and action were coordinated by a single personality. Under his successors, however, the inconclusive struggle for power resulted in the fragmentation of the decisionmaking structure, distributing power among various individuals and factions, each in command of parallel institutional power structures. Ideology was divorced from policy formulation which in turn was frequently out of phase with the administration and execution of policy as rival factions assumed control over policymaking bodies. The fragmentation of the decisionmaking structure was artlessly concealed by the figleaf of "collective leadership" as factional politics replaced one-man decisions in the Soviet leadership. Personalities, factions, and eventually sociofunctional and socioinstitutional groupings assumed a more variable role in the shaping of Soviet behavior, and a new fluid relationship was established among Soviet capabilities, ideology, personalities, and institutions in the decisionmaking process. While this made it even more difficult to judge Soviet intentions and predict Soviet behavior, it was compensated for by the corresponding inability of the Soviet Union to pursue the single-minded and precisely calibrated type of foreign policy which was characteristic of the Stalin era since Soviet leaders are apparently as uncertain as Western Kremlinologists in charting the course and outcome of internal factional conflict.

Factional conflict in the Soviet hierarchy has thus introduced a new and fortuitous element in Soviet behavior since it is by no means predictable that a given Soviet personality or faction will continue, repudiate, or modify the policies of its predecessors. Even more significantly, Soviet policy may fluctuate not only in accordance with obvious institutional and personality changes but with the changing equilibrium of factions within the hierarchy on a more or less continuing basis. As Soviet capabilities expand, these factional conflicts register changing and conflicting perceptions of risks involved in relation to possible returns; they represent shifting configurations of interest, both domestic and external; and finally they represent conflicting and changing sets of priorities as new choices and options proliferate out of expanded capabilities. In the absence of a stable consensus in the policymaking Politburo the tendency in post-Stalinist Russia has been for various factions to implement their own views and policies through Party or state institutions and organs under their direct administrative control, thus conveying the impression of contradictory, inconsistent, and ambivalent behavior in Soviet policy. While this is the net effect for the Soviet system as a whole, it is not necessarily true of individual groups, factions, or personalities whose own views may be consistent and firm but are simply unable to prevail over equally consistent and obdurate views held by other groups and individuals. The possibility of factional vacillation and ambivalence is, of course, not ruled out.

Whereas the United States has always been accustomed to self-restraint in the exercise of its power, the self-restraint introduced into Soviet behavior because of factional politics confronts Soviet leaders with a new and bewildering experience to which they have not completely adjusted. Accustomed to being guided in their behavior by the principle of "pushing to the limit," the Soviet leaders have in the past assumed that the American "ruling class" was guided by the identical principle and have behaved accordingly. It should be emphasized that Soviet behavior in this connection was encrusted in a conceptualized doctrine concerning the behavior of capitalist ruling classes which existed long before the advent of the Cold War and thus could not be explained as a spontaneous response to American behavior, except in concrete cases. Correspondingly, American decisionmakers have always assumed, on the basis of both Soviet doctrine and past behavior, that the Soviet leaders do not exercise self-restraint and will always "push to the limit," not recognizing that self-restraint is not entirely a subjective phenomenon but can be imposed upon decisionmakers objectively as well. Hence, American decisionmakers have yet to adjust completely to this new departure in Soviet behavior. This element of self-restraint is not necessarily deliberate or calculated in all instances but has also resulted from institutionalized factors such as internal power rivalries, conflicts of judgment, perception, and interests, and sheer bureaucratic inertia, i.e., the fragmentation of the decisionmaking process.

The fragmentation of the decisionmaking process combined with the erosion of Soviet ideology has produced a new element of both instability and uncertainty in Soviet behavior, an institutionalized irrationality, particularly in crisis situations.

Collective leadership, therefore, may not necessarily contribute to more rational or controlled action but may, under certain conditions, be even more dangerous and difficult to contend with than one-man rule. Under some circumstances collective leadership may turn out to be collective irresponsibility as decisions are made and unmade by shifting conditions or autonomous action is taken by powerful socioinstitutional bodies in the face of factional paralysis or bureaucratic inertia. The deliberations of a divided oligarchy are not only secret but anonymous as well and can yield many surprises. In the words of Professor Leo Mates of Yugoslavia in referring to Czechoslovakia:

> If it is possible for unprovoked military intervention to follow negotiations and agreement, then the danger to peace is transferred to the domain of the unpredictable, which can but leave deep traces on the general behavior of states in international relations.[3]

This suggests that if the Soviet Union could unleash massive military forces *after* tensions had been presumably dissipated, the Soviet leadership is capable of virtually any kind of rash and irresponsible behavior. The Soviet occupation of Czechoslovakia thus is bound once again to raise the entire question of the role of duplicity as a conscious and calculated instrument of Soviet diplomacy and conjure up the specter of a Soviet "Pearl Harbor" in the minds of the American public.[4] More than ever Soviet decisions in foreign policy may reflect the anxieties, fears, insecurities, and ambitions of individual factions and personalities involved in secret and faceless intrigue and maneuver. This cannot but tarnish the image of rationality, sobriety, and predictability which had emerged during the first years of the Brezhnev-Kosygin regime. We may, of course, be witnessing the disintegration of a hitherto stable equilibrium or consensus sustained by the lowest common denominator of factional interest, i.e., sheer inertia. Whether the assumption of mutual rationality which has formed the foundations of Soviet-American relations has been seriously undermined remains to be seen.

In the absence of crisis situations, whether acute or chronic, the

[3] Cited by Anatole Shub, "Lessons of Czechoslovakia," *Foreign Affairs*, January 1969 (Vol. 47, No. 2), p. 267. *Cf.* also Vernon V. Aspaturian, "The Aftermath of the Czech Invasion," *Current History*, November 1968 (Vol. 55, No. 327), p. 263.

[4] *Cf.* Vernon V. Aspaturian, "Dialectics and Duplicity in Soviet Diplomacy," *Journal of International Affairs*, 1963 (Vol. 17, No. 1), pp. 42–60, and "Diplomacy in the Mirror of Soviet Scholarship" in John Keep and Liliana Brisby (ed.), *Contemporary History in the Soviet Mirror* (New York, Frederick A. Praeger, 1964), pp. 243–274. (Selection 13.)

assumption of Soviet rationality will continue to be valid. As personalities and as individual factions the Soviet leaders appear to be a sober and calculatingly rational group and in their separate capacities are determined, forceful, and animated by purpose. But in the absence of a stable majority or durable consensus and with the fluidity of the decisionmaking process characterized by rapidly dissolving and reconstituted majorities on various issues the behavior of the Soviet leadership as a collectivity is likely to be fluctuating and inconsistent. The multiplication of divergent rational inputs can thus produce a collective irrational output. It is in this restricted sense that the real possibility of institutionalized irrationality may come to characterize Soviet behavior.

IV. THE GLOBALIZATION OF SOVIET FOREIGN POLICY: THE EXPANSION OF COMMITMENT

It was during the Khrushchev decade that the role of ideology underwent its most significant transformation although the process of erosion had already started during Stalin's last years as the risks of a militant ideological foreign policy escalated at a faster pace than the growth of Soviet power. Under Khrushchev ideological erosion was accelerated by the inadvertent de-ideologization of Soviet foreign policy in order to exploit new diplomatic opportunities. In the process Khrushchev abdicated Moscow's assured status as leader of the world Communist movement in return for the dubious status of acting on the world stage as a global power whose oyster was not only the world of Communism but the great glove itself.

There is a sharp distinction between a Great Power or even superpower and a global power, of which there are only two, the Soviet Union and the United States. Under Stalin the Soviet Union was transformed from a sprawling, rickety, and weak giant into an authentic Great Power — a superpower. Stalin not only created the technical-industrial base for the transformation, but he also presided over the conversion of the Soviet Union into a nuclear power and through skillful diplomacy and military conquest created a new territorial and hegemonial base for the further intensification and expansion of Soviet power and influence under his successors.

If it was Stalin who transformed the Soviet Union into a Great Power, it was under Khrushchev that Soviet Russia was transformed into a global power directly challenging the United States for paramountcy and unilaterally commanding the right to intervene in any part of the world to assert an interest and to influence developments. Stalin pursued essentially a cautious continental policy oriented toward the communization, first of the Soviet periphery and then of the new geographical periphery of the expanded Communist bloc, relying on direct physical contiguity and the concentrically radiating expansion of Communism from the Soviet base. He was loath to overcommit the Soviet Union militarily, politically, or ideologically and was reluctant to burden himself with ideological obligations which he could not or preferred not to fulfill.

While Khrushchev successfully transformed the Soviet Union into a global power, he did so at the expense of weakening Soviet control in its own sphere, alienating Moscow's strongest ally, China, overcommitting the power and resources of the Soviet Union, and maximizing the risks of thermonuclear war by persistently prodding and probing weak spots in the Western world and by forcing the United States into a series of confrontations in the hope that these confrontations would result in the settlement of outstanding issues on Soviet terms and would force the United States to withdraw from exposed positions. The Suez crisis of 1956, the spasmodic Berlin crisis of 1958–1961, and finally the Cuban missile crisis of 1962 were all grim consequences of Soviet risk-taking in foreign policy in pursuit of substantial diplomatic gains.

V. SOVIET OPTIONS IN FOREIGN POLICY:
CONDOMINIUM, DÉTENTE, PRIMACY, OR ENTENTE

Each of these conditioning processes will have an important impact on future trends in Soviet foreign policy, individually as well as in dynamic interaction with one another. To the degree that Marxist-Leninist ideology relies on the epistemological imperative of viewing conflict and contradiction as the mainsprings of progress, then to that degree will the progressive de-ideologization of Soviet foreign policy reduce the compulsion to turn to conflict and violence as inevitably fruitful sources of political and diplomatic gain. While this may sweep away certain dogmatic preconceptions that have interfered with Soviet perceptions of international stability as a desirable goal, at the same time it may incite the Soviet state to behave more in the fashion of a traditional imperialist power whose behavior will be shaped by the logic of its role in world affairs and the momentum of its capabilities. Ideologically calculated employment of violence to promote world Communism may thus be supplanted by opportunistic and expedient resort to force to promote Soviet power and prestige, irrespective of its relevance to world Communism.

Similarly, the fragmentation of the Soviet leadership into factional groupings will tend to institutionalize self-restraint in Soviet behavior. While this is a factor favoring international stability, at the same time it creates the possibility of instability in the leadership and an element of fortuity and unpredictability in its behavior which will tend to create further barriers to collaboration and international stability. Dealing with a divided oligarchy whose deliberations remain concealed and whose fluctuating dominant coalition remains essentially anonymous can induce irrational anxieties and provoke impulsive responses and over-reactions in the behavior of other powers. Greater rather than less emphasis might be placed on external countervailing power as a restraining mechanism, and the result might be a spiral of rivalry and intense competition rather than collaboration.

On the whole, however, the globalization of Soviet foreign policy is a factor working in favor of international stability since global pretensions require that the Soviet leaders transcend their parochial responsibilities to the interests of Communist states and parties in order to cultivate an image of concern for the interests of a wide spectrum of states with variegated regimes and social systems. This would tend to encourage the Soviet leadership to develop a vested interest in the virtues of prestige, self-image, sensitivity to world opinion, and appreciation for outlooks and attitudes different from its own. At the same time, however, it weakens Moscow's role as the leader of an ideological coalition, sacrifices the interests of Communist parties, and creates openings for an ambitious ally like China to compete for the favor of neglected Communist states and parties. Global concerns will also run the risk of overextension and overcommitment that might divert scarce resources away from pressing domestic problems and thus contribute to internal unrest and discontent.

Furthermore, as a global power the Soviet Union will inevitably find itself in worldwide competition with the other global power, the United States, in areas remote from its vital interests in distant parts of the globe. This will increase the possibilities and risks of confrontation and will force the Soviet Union to assume positions for the sake of prestige and its standing as a global power. Since much of this rivalry will take place in an increasingly unstable third world, the danger of being sucked into the center of rapidly developing vacuums will be enhanced with the distinct possibility of the Soviet Union being maneuvered unwittingly and inadvertently into assuming explicit and implicit obligations forcing it to commit its power and prestige over relatively trivial issues. Soviet commitments to the Arab states illustrate what might happen in other parts of the world although the Soviet leaders have so far shown great prudence and caution in this regard by spurning a major effort in sub-Saharan Africa and in Latin America.

Only in the Indian subcontinent have the Soviet leaders undertaken commitments comparable to those to the Arab states and in this case the solicitude is motivated more by their preoccupation with the Chinese danger than anything else. Moscow is both displacing and supplementing American military assistance to both India and Pakistan in the interests of local stability which works in favor of Soviet interests. Hans Morgenthau's observation that the American policy of arming both India and Pakistan was an illogical exercise in that the United States was conducting an arms race with itself seems not to have persuaded the Soviet leaders of its perversity since Moscow is now similarly engaged in a race with itself in this vital region. Both Moscow and Washington apparently feel that it is the better part of wisdom, if not strict logic, to conduct an arms race with oneself in preference to one with the other global power since it can be more precisely calibrated and controlled.

It appears that the Soviet Union is irrevocably committed to function on the world stage as a global power irrespective of its problems of purpose and divided leadership, but the precise contours of that role have by no means been delineated. It is likely that the Soviet leaders will avoid pressing confrontations with the United States in peripheral areas and instead will utilize the United Nations as both a forum and an arena to either postpone decisions, induce stalemates, settle for provisional and *de facto* settlements, or work out mutually agreeable compromises. Neither the problem of purpose nor of divided leadership, however, can be settled by outside agencies or powers, for both must be resolved at home. Similarly, it is not likely that either Soviet-American relations or Sino-Soviet relations can be fruitfully ventilated in international bodies, and the Soviet Union will continue sedulously and relentlessly to treat its relations with Eastern European countries as internal rather than international problems in accordance with the "Socialist commonwealth" doctrine.

The decisive factor in international stability, of course, remains the state of relations between the United States and the Soviet Union. This will, in turn, depend in large measure upon the Soviet leadership's perceptions of Washington's intentions and capabilities as measured against its own purposes and power. The Soviet leadship appears sorely divided over the precise character that Soviet-American relations should assume. Some, apparently, like Kosygin, seem to favor a continuation and expansion of the détente ushered in by the 1963 Treaty Banning Nuclear Weapons Tests in Atmosphere, in Outer Space, and Under Water; others may wish to challenge the United States overtly for primacy in an increasingly hierarchically structured international system; still others, perhaps including Brezhnev, may perceive a limited or arrested détente as the best formula to assure the sanctity of the status quo where Moscow would like to preserve it while freeing the Soviet Union to alter it elsewhere. A fourth possibility, entente, may have attractiveness for sectors of the Soviet intelligentsia, for people like Andrei Sakharov, but it is not likely that the Soviet leaders conceive of it as a viable possibility at the present time. Therefore, the debate probably revolves around the three other alternatives enumerated above.

VI. THE KHRUSHCHEV OPTION: CONDOMINIUM

Khrushchev had opted for a policy of accommodation and détente with the United States in July 1963 but only after his vigorous attempt to overcome American strategic superiority had failed and the world was twice brought to the brink of thermonuclear war — once over Berlin and again over Cuba. The Soviet Union found itself politically overcommitted, financially overextended, militarily vulnerable, ideologically challenged by Peking, and economically on the verge of bankruptcy. In return for the respite gained by signing the test ban treaty, which was a tacit recognition and acceptance of American strategic superiority, Khrushchev elevated American-Soviet relations to the top-priority item in Soviet foreign policy since only an understanding between the two global powers could guarantee the avoidance of thermonuclear war. In addition, Khrushchev expected a long period of international stability and Soviet-American cooperation which he thought would strengthen his position at home and further Soviet interests abroad.

Khrushchev's détente policy assumed the faint but definite contours of a Soviet-American condominium or dyarchy in the international community whereby the two superpowers would demarcate their respective areas of vital interest, define their area of common interest, delineate the status quo which was to be preserved, and establish the guidelines which would govern their competition in areas marginal or peripheral to their vital interests. . . .[5]

VII. THE FAILURE OF CONDOMINIUM

Undoubtedly the condominium conception of a détente still holds some attraction for individual members of the current Politburo, and it remained, by default, the basis of the Brezhnev-Kosygin foreign policy for the first two years or so although with significant modifications.

The entire structure of Khrushchev's détente policy, however, rested upon the assumption that the Kennedy Administration represented the "sober" forces in the United States and that these forces would continue to determine United States policy. Furthermore, it presupposed that Moscow and Washington shared an interest in containing German, Japanese, and Chinese revisionism. Khrushchev's policy posed a serious threat to the social position, status role, and general interests of powerful, but numerically small, sociofunctional and socioinstitutional groups like the Party apparatus, heavy industry managers, and the traditional military. Instead of conceiving and executing his détente policy so that the interests and needs of these groups might be painlessly accommodated, Khrushchev brusquely attempted an "end run" by appealing to those broad social constituencies whose interests would be enhanced by his détente policy in a bold effort to envelop and isolate his detractors in a sea of "democracy."

Aside from the serious internal dislocations among social priorities implied by his policies Khrushchev's strategy and behavior were also exposing the Soviet Union to new diplomatic and security vulnerabilities, and this too contributed to the tactical area of agreement between Khrushchev's faction and his opposition. Khrushchev's policies threatened the interests of his factional opposition while his behavior alienated his own faction and his détente strategy made the Soviet Union diplomatically and militarily vulnerable.

Both Kosygin and Brezhnev were closely associated with Khrushchev's détente policy; they subscribed to the Khrushchevite division of the American "ruling class" into "sober" and "mad" elements. Although they too were predisposed to recognize President Johnson as a representative of the former, they probably showed more concern about a possible shift in the American political equilibrium to the right. Khrushchev's ouster in October 1964 thus came hard on the heels of a number

[5] For details, see Vernon V. Aspaturian, "Foreign Policy Perspectives in the Sixties," in Alexander Dallin and Thomas B. Larson (ed.), *Soviet Politics Since Khrushchev* (Englewood Cliffs, N.J., Prentice-Hall, 1968), pp. 141–144. (Selection 23.)

of events which ominously pointed toward the crystallization of simultaneous crises in Sino-Soviet and Soviet-American relations. The nomination of Senator Barry Goldwater as a Presidential candidate in 1964, President Johnson's Tonkin Bay retaliatory strikes, Mao Tse-tung's open bid for some 500,000 square miles of Soviet territory, and China's imminent explosion of an atomic bomb all likely played a catalytic role in Khrushchev's ouster since they all took place in the months just prior to Khrushchev's denouement.

A new flexibility, combined with a more soundly conceived, better integrated, and more systematic strategy and bolstered by a revitalized consensus, was needed in order for Soviet leaders to be better prepared for whatever unforeseen contingencies might evolve out of the new and confused American political situation as well as out of the ominous uncertainties of China's new capabilities.

The displacement of Khrushchev probably did not dispel the doubts of the factional groupings that were unenthusiastic about the entire détente policy although the new Brezhnev-Kosygin regime was probably more likely to assuage the wounds and grievances of the factional opposition, particularly the traditional military, and to show greater sensitivity to their interests and hence may have been initially armed with a new consensual mandate charged with reviewing and revising existing policy if necessary. Thus, unlike Khrushchev, the new team was poised and prepared for any contingency which might develop out of the American election, ready to plug the gaps in Khrushchev's détente strategy if the détente policy continued, and also amenable to trying a new approach to Peking.

After five years of the Johnson Administration the Soviet leadership, on balance, probably feels that international stability works to the advantage of the United States in particular and the status quo in general. Since international stability is inherently antirevolutionary, it surrenders the political and diplomatic initiative to the United States as the paramount power in the world and as the chief guardian of the status quo. The Soviet position in world affairs, instead of being enhanced, was diminished to that of a tired, worn-out revolutionary power content with permanent status as "Number 2" while the United States was left free to flex its diplomatic and military muscles all over the world and subtly to undermine the Soviet position in Eastern Europe with seductive policies of "bridge building" and "peaceful engagement." While the Johnson Administration faithfully refrained from aggressive and overtly hostile moves against the Soviet position in Eastern Europe, its selective enticement of individual Communist states proved to be a device against which the unimaginative Soviet leaders had no defense except military intervention to arrest the growing forces of autonomy. Furthermore, China had been progressively transformed from an alienated ally into a hostile and threatening neighbor while the world Communist movement was fractured and demoralized and the national liberation movement was deprived of its protective umbrella.

Confident of its superior power and relying on the Soviet Union to

refrain from any action that might endanger Soviet-American collaboration, the United States massively escalated the war in Vietnam, systematically bombed Moscow's ally, and landed Marines in the
Dominican Republic to prevent the establishment of a revolutionary-
oriented regime. Furthermore, not only in Moscow but also in Belgrade,
Cairo, and elsewhere, particularly after the Arab-Israeli war of 1967, the
impression that the Johnson Administration had been using the détente
not to preserve international stability but to devise a cleverly conceived
political offensive against Soviet and radical nationalist positions all
over the world achieved widespread acceptance. The Dominican affair,
the ouster of President Sukarno in Indonesia and of João Goulart in
Brazil, the fall of Kwame Nkrumah in Ghana, the overthrow of Mo-
hammed Ben Bella in Algeria, the Greek military takeover, and finally
the Israeli attack upon Egypt appeared to many in Moscow as part of an
overall United States design. Abdul Nasser openly complained in Cairo
that the chief danger to peace and progress was the absence of any force
that could deter or contain the United States while the Italian Communist paper, *Rinascita*, flatly claimed that the Johnson Administration
was pursuing a cleverly concealed "roll-back" policy:

> For the policy of the *status quo* and the attempts to divide the world
> into zones of influence between the two super-powers, U.S. imperialism
> is gradually substituting a revised and corrected re-edition of the old
> policy of *roll back*, giving birth, within the framework of nuclear coexis-
> tence with the U.S.S.R. (caused by reasons of *force majeure*), to a series
> of local interventions (economical, political, military) designed to
> modify the world equilibrium by means of setting up reactionary
> régimes or by support given to them, and liquidation of the progressive
> forces and movements in individual countries.[6]

VIII. THE TEMPTATIONS OF STRATEGIC SUPERIORITY

One of the constants of the world situation during the past six
years has been the American superiority in missile and thermonuclear
capability. Instead of contributing to international stability it has been
accompanied by instability, but an instability which the Soviet leaders
may have perceived as favoring American interests. This has raised in
the Soviet mind the entire question of whether the United States is
deceptively palming off disequilibrium working in its favor as international stability. The degree to which the Soviet leaders perceive this
asymmetric relationship in strategic power as contributing to the Johnson Administration's audacity and boldness in assuming the role of
"international gendarme" is crucial to any realistic assessment of meaningful arms control agreements with the Soviet Union.

Since the Brezhnev-Kosygin regime soon after taking office embarked upon an accelerated program of narrowing or eliminating the
American lead in strategic striking power not only by stepping up the

---

[6] *Rinascita*, August 4, 1967, as cited in Zbigniew Brzezinski, "Peace and
Power," *Encounter*, November 1968 (Vol. 31, No. 5), p. 5.

production of intercontinental ballistic missiles (ICBM's), improving and refining existing weapons, hardening its launching sites, and expanding its nuclear naval capability but also by deploying a modest antiballistic missile (ABM) system around Moscow, it is obvious that the Soviet leaders are convinced that the narrowing or elimination of the strategic gap is a necessary prerequisite to an effective policy of deterring the United States from acting out its role as "world policeman." On the other hand, it has been the dominant view of the Johnson Administration since about 1965 that the United States possesses an invulnerable and "assured" capability whose effectiveness will not be eroded by the achievement of Soviet strategic and nuclear parity. While this view is not without its detractors, there is an equally forceful view that the achievement of parity will contribute to a more stable mutual deterrence and improve the chances for arms control and other agreements because it will eliminate the essentially psychological and symbolic sense of inferiority in Moscow without at the same time affecting the actual power equilibrium.

This view, of course, assumes that psychological and symbolic inferiority exerts only a peripheral influence on the behavior of nuclear powers. But we really do not know to what extent the strategic superiority of the United States was the decisive incremental factor impelling it to behave with relative impunity in peripheral areas of the world while simultaneously deterring vigorous Soviet action against its own recalcitrant client states in Eastern Europe, to say nothing of deterring more aggressive Soviet activity in other areas, i.e., deterring a possible Soviet intervention in the Arab-Israeli war to prevent the ignominious defeat of its Arab client states. To what extent, for example, were the Soviet move against Czechoslovakia and its threatening gestures against Rumania and Yugoslavia the reflection of a greater confidence inspired by the relative growth of its missile and nuclear power? Does this mean that as the Soviet Union approaches parity with the United States it will manifest less self-restraint in its behavior?

The assumption that the Soviet leaders seek parity as a terminal goal in order to establish symbolic equality with the United States and as a necessary prerequisite to negotiations on other issues on equal terms bears careful scrutiny. Undoubtedly, some Soviet leaders subscribe to this view, but others probably do not. The crucial unknown is the degree to which a significant element in the Soviet leadership believes that Soviet strategic superiority is a feasible goal and that its achievement will transfer the initiative to Moscow and bring about a reversal of roles between the two global powers. It is an unpalatable but ineluctable fact that once the Soviet Union achieves parity, it will be in a better position to strive for superiority.

Although the Soviet proponents of parity might warn the advocates of superiority that given the resources and capabilities of the United States, the Soviet Union cannot hope to win a renewed arms race without straining its economy, provoking internal discontent as a consequence, and forever forfeiting an opportunity to reach substantial agreements on the basis of equality, the advocates of superiority might well rebut as follows: The United States is now psychologically, militarily, and politically on the defensive, bruised and humiliated by the Vietnamese war, alienated from its allies in Western Europe as a consequence, wracked by internal racial disorders, youthful rebellion, and conflict between rich and poor, and afflicted by political malaise and war weariness. No administration could confidently hope to mobilize the necessary social support and political unity to engage in another arms race without aggravating even more these "internal contradictions." Furthermore, the argument might run, the United States position in the third world has been discredited by its counterrevolutionary interventionism, and a strategically superior Soviet Union could not but revive the morale of revolutionary forces, regimes, and movements in underdeveloped countries, frighten America's NATO allies into opting for neutrality, isolate West Germany, solidify the Soviet position in Eastern Europe, reunify the world Communist movement, force Israel into a dictated settlement with the Arab states, and place China on notice that Moscow is not to be trifled with. While such a policy might run the risk of encouraging a mutually defensive Sino-American rapprochement — which they might argue is even more likely otherwise — this view might hold that it is even more likely that China, confronted with a powerful Russia, might alter its attitude toward the Soviet Union, particularly if Mao Tse-tung passes from the scene in the meantime.

Will the Soviet leaders opt for such a policy? Probably not, but it cannot be excluded as a tempting possibility. If it has any viability as an alternative, considerable responsibility must be placed upon the Johnson Administration for demonstrating that strategic superiority does make a difference in spite of the fact that the Soviet Union possessed an "invulnerable" second strike with "assured" destructive capabilities. But the "assured" destructive capability of a strategically inferior Russia was of a limited character as compared with the nearly *absolute* level of "assured" destructive capability possessed by the United States, and it was this condition of asymmetry that made the difference.

The diplomatic utility of strategic superiority defined in terms of a unilateral first-strike capability should not be obscured by the miasma of controversy generated over the rationality or irrationality of nuclear war. As an instrument of diplomatic blackmail strategic superiority apparently retains its effectiveness, for such a capability can be a powerful factor in the deterrence and paralysis of responses to military and diplomatic initiatives in areas marginal to the interests of the global powers. The Soviet leaders may opt for a first-strike capability not for the purpose of initiating and winning a nuclear war with the United States but in order to escalate the risks of American counteraction to Soviet initiatives. Strategic superiority thus could provide a kind of protective umbrella for Soviet diplomatic maneuvers and would enable Moscow to maximize its options in foreign policy. Whereas parity enables a power to opt for stalemate or various levels of de-escalation in its diplomacy, strategic superiority allows not only stalemate or de-escalation but also a limited range of escalation in foreign policy behavior.

If it is a main current objective of the Soviet Union to contain and deter American power rather than to erode or roll it back, then the achievement of strategic parity might be sufficient to achieve this goal. Since it appears that the Administration of Richard Nixon is seriously contemplating a reduction in American international obligations — surely neither withdrawal nor isolationism, neo or otherwise — agreements on arms control which would stabilize the existing distribution of power might well offer a welcome respite to both parties. Unfortunately, however, parity as a concept and as a reality virtually defies the precise, calibrated measurement which is demanded to make it a mutually acceptable formula, whereas superiority is much easier to measure and define, particularly when the margin of superiority is substantial. The inability to arrive at a mutually satisfactory definition of "parity" may constitute an insuperable roadblock to agreement in spite of the willingness of both parties to accept it in principle, and the temptation for either Washington or Moscow — or both — to strive for a measurable degree of superiority as a consequence may be unavoidable.

Even if the Soviet leaders opt for parity and if an acceptable formula is devised, it is not likely that the Soviet Union will abandon its role as a global power. This means that although Moscow may accept a freeze on missile or atomic capability and even a limited cutback in strategic force levels, the Soviet leaders will continue to develop conventional military capabilities sufficient to enable them to compete with the United States on a global scale. This means that the Soviet leaders will perceive a need for expanded naval capabilities — aircraft carriers, helicopter carriers, naval infantry (marines) — and long-range air troop carriers to enable them to provide sufficient forces either to deter the United States from intervening or to permit their own intervention. This also suggests that the Soviet Union will seek to acquire the use of foreign ports and bases in friendly countries in the Mediterranean, the Indian Ocean, and Southeast Asia. Latin America, except for Cuba, will probably remain off limits for the time being, but this does not exclude a little Soviet reverse "bridge building" and "peaceful engagement" with Latin American regimes of various hues, the current flirtation with Peru being a good example of future Soviet behavior. While such a policy might infuriate Castro and Latin American revolutionaries, it will nevertheless be a useful device to weaken the United States position in Latin America in the interests of Moscow as a global power if not a revolutionary one.

On the other hand, the Soviet Union will probably erect new barriers and obstacles to "peaceful engagement," "bridge building," and "Ostpolitik" in Eastern Europe. Moscow is determined to preserve its empire in Eastern Europe — the "Socialist commonwealth" doctrine is sufficient indication of this — and it may even take additional measures to domesticate Rumania and intimidate Yugoslavia, but its fear of an increasingly bellicose China may be the decisive factor exercising a restraining influence on Soviet behavior in Europe. Moscow's quick and prudent withdrawal of its Berlin threat in March 1969 was probably encouraged by the armed incursion of the Communist Chinese in the Ussuri Valley region of the Soviet Far East.

IX. THE CHINESE PUZZLE: THE TRIANGULATION OF GLOBAL POWER

Any realistic assessment of the prospects for international stability will increasingly depend to a large extent upon the growing capability of China and the intensity and scope of its ambitions as a world power. For the moment Chinese aspirations and behavior pose a greater threat to the Soviet position than to the American, and Peking may actually be in a position to cripple the Soviet ambition to be an effective global competitor with the United States just as it has effectively crippled the Soviet leadership of the world Communist movement. Soviet-American relations are thus an integral part of a complex and intricate triangular relationship between Moscow, Peking, and Washington in which cause and effect have become inextricably merged and incapable of being disentangled. The behavior and conduct of each actor in this curious *ménage à trois* have a multiplier impact upon the reactions and responses of the other parties in the triangle which in turn set in motion feedback effects upon the actors themselves and then radiate out to affect their relations with other states in the international community. This strange triangular relationship was apparently set in motion back during the days of the "spirit of Geneva" in 1955, although the United States was unaware of its intimate involvement as a third party in a fragile Sino-Soviet partnership until after the Cuban missile crisis when it became unambiguously clear that the single greatest factor affecting Sino-Soviet relations was United States conduct, behavior, and intentions. Unwittingly, American responses and reactions were registering their impact upon Sino-Soviet relations in an active and fundamental way which in turn reshaped Chinese and Soviet attitudes toward the United States although it has been recognized since the Camp David era that the United States was always at least a peripheral and passive influence on Sino-Soviet relations.

While it cannot be documented with absolute certainty, the root cause of Sino-Soviet differences appears to be the United States and the divergent images of its intentions and behavior which are perceived in Moscow and Peking. If it is the root cause, Khrushchev's détente policy and its implications for the world Communist movement emerge, in retrospect, not as simply the reflections of his personal idiosyncrasies (which certainly dominated his style and mood) but as a realistic policy corresponding to the vital interests of the Soviet Union as a global power and hence virtually unavoidable in its essentials if survival is accorded top priority in Soviet foreign policy calculations. The policy could accord different priorities to internal interests (heavy industry over light, armaments over butter, etc.), could be carried out with greater or lesser flexibility, enthusiasm, finesse or style, cynicism, and wisdom, and could be compressed within the shell of a "harder" or "softer" line, but any Soviet group which placed survival at the top of its priority list would have to seek some form of rapprochement with the United States to maximize its chances for survival rather than depend indefinitely upon the vagaries of spontaneous deterrence, chance, accident, miscalculation, or error. Khrushchev in his own clumsy and bungling way had intuitively grasped the vital essentials of a realistic foreign policy. The challenge of Communist China made it impossible for Moscow to maintain its half-century oscillation between being a state and the center of a world revolutionary movement, and Soviet leaders were finally confronted with the moment of elemental contradictory truth: Pursuing world revolution could only maximize the prospects of total physical annihilation as both a state and the center of a messianic movement, and Moscow had to choose between survival and doctrinal virtue.

Ironically enough, continued Sino-Soviet hostility would encourage Soviet tractability elsewhere. Because of its geographical position the Soviet Union is peculiarly vulnerable to an encirclement strategy. As long as China sustains its hostility, Moscow cannot afford to antagonize its neighbors in the West for fear of some nightmarish Sino-German coordination of pressure, if not actual collaboration, against the Soviet Union. The inopportune Chinese military incursion in the Soviet Far East just as Moscow was reapplying pressure on West Berlin may have been an esoteric Chinese bid to Bonn for informal cooperation. Moscow, a capital not unversed in the nuances and subtleties of esoteric communication, lost no time in sounding out both Kurt Georg Kiesinger and Willy Brandt about the state of Sino-German relations, noting in particular that West Germany is China's most active trading partner in the West. The quick relaxation of Soviet pressure on Berlin, however, was certainly not unnoticed by Bonn, whose leaders soothingly assured Ambassador Semyon Tsarapkin that West Germany would not seek to exploit Soviet difficulties with the Chinese — which of course can be interpreted as a threat as well as a promise.

The Chinese danger thus serves to encourage the Soviet leaders to seek some sort of accommodation with the United States, but at the same time they probably realize that their open paranoia concerning China exposes them to some serious vulnerabilities. For example, the United States may thus find a vested interest in sustaining and aggravating Sino-Soviet relations in order to dampen Soviet appetites for adventures elsewhere.

As long as China is hostile to the Soviet Union, Moscow retains a vested stake in the perpetuation of Sino-American hostility, for a rapprochement between Peking and Washington would enable the Chinese to concentrate their full fury against the Russians. A Chinese-American reconciliation is by no means considered an impossibility by Moscow. Significantly, the Soviet press has charged on more than one occasion that the Chinese leaders are plotting a rapprochement with the

United States and Soviet writers condemn with unusual vigor any intimation by Western writers or spokesmen that a Sino-American rapprochement might be a distinct possibility. On February 21, 1967, *Krasnaya Zvezda*, for example, charged that both Washington and Peking were maneuvering toward a possible reconciliation. The Russian Army newspaper complained that the "Taiwan lobby" was curiously inactive and had been replaced with a "Red China lobby." It condemned the alleged secret understanding between China and the United States about the Vietnam war designed to prevent a Sino-American confrontation and accused the "ruling circles" of Washington of favoring Mao Tse-tung's retention of power because of his anti-Soviet policies:

> About the middle of 1964, something strange began to happen with the Taiwan Lobby. The press which earlier carried a hard line against Peking and had stood like a mountain behind Chiang Kai-shek, began to soften its tone. The same metamorphosis occurred with leading businessmen, senators and government leaders. . . . In Washington, there is open talk that the ruling circles of the United States are interested in the retention of power by Mao Tse-tung.[7]

One of the genuine fears of some Soviet leaders is that a Sino-American rapprochement might enable China to devote greater attention to its unredeemed territories in the north.

The peculiar fluidity of Sino-Soviet-American relations has seriously complicated the impact of the Vietnamese war on future international stability. Khrushchev had virtually abandoned Vietnam; his successors reasserted Moscow's presence for a complex of reasons, some of them contradictory: It was expected to give Moscow a measure of control over the situation and an opportunity to claim credit in the event of its successful resolution and was designed to be part of a plan to reduce or eliminate the sources and causes of Sino-Soviet friction. While Khrushchev's successors wanted to heal the breach with China, they also wanted to pursue the détente with the United States, although in different form. Since the Chinese felt that a Soviet-American détente was incompatible with a Sino-Soviet reconciliation, they spurned the Soviet olive branch. In the meantime the war in Vietnam escalated, Moscow became the chief supplier of arms to the North Vietnamese, and Soviet-American détente was thus made more difficult.

On the whole, the Soviet leaders have exerted their influence in favor of a negotiated resolution of the war, which the proponents of

---

[7] *Krasnaya Zvezda*, February 21, 1967. *Cf.* also *The New York Times*, July 21, 1966. On the other hand, Taipei has expressed concern that the turmoil on the Chinese mainland might precipitate a joint Soviet-American intervention resulting in "another Yalta, a Russo-American deal at China's expense." (*The New York Times*, February 19, 1967.) And in March 1969 Peking made the strange charge that the visit of Soviet journalist Victor Louis to Taiwan was part of a scheme to collude with Chiang Kai-shek against Peking. The Soviet fear of a Sino-German and a Sino-American rapprochement directed against Moscow has become a recurrent theme in the Soviet press since March 1969.

expanded Soviet-American détente viewed as an obstacle to improved relations. As the war was intensified and prolonged, the balance of sentiment in the Politburo shifted as suspicions of the Johnson Administration's intent increased. Relations with both Peking and Washington seemed to have deteriorated and the Soviet perspective on Vietnam became ambiguous and ambivalent. To some Soviet leaders the war remained an insuperable barrier to expanded cooperation while to others the inconclusive character of an intensified conflict which strained American economic and military capabilities, aroused domestic agitation, and diverted the United States' attention away from other areas appeared to pay off greater dividends than would a settlement itself. Thus, while Moscow continued to work on behalf of a settlement, it simultaneously exploited the war by exacting informal and implicit concessions from the United States concerning Eastern Europe in return for Soviet efforts on behalf of ending the war.

Since the advent of the Paris negotiations the Vietnamese war has become essentially a peripheral factor in Soviet-American relations although the Nixon Administration is still relying on Moscow to influence Hanoi toward an acceptable conclusion of the conflict.

X. THE SOVIET UNION AND THE UNITED NATIONS

How will all this affect Soviet behavior in the United Nations? Probably not very much. It is not necessary to recapitulate at this point the Soviet view of the UN as essentially an expedient instrument of policy. Increasingly, the Soviet leaders resort to UN bodies when it is clearly in the Soviet interest to utilize its facilities and forums to block whatever action it may take that adversely affects Soviet interests. Moscow stepped up its interest in the UN after Stalin's death, particularly after 1955, not because its basic image of the UN had been altered but rather because Khrushchev reasoned that Stalin was too dogmatic and rigid to exploit fully the possibilities offered by the UN and had too quickly dismissed it as no more than an instrumentality of United States foreign policy.

Generally speaking, Soviet behavior in the United Nations is usually an extension or reflection of Soviet behavior elsewhere. Soviet interest shifts from one organ to another depending upon their relative usefulness, always primed, however, to insist upon the right of a Soviet veto, whether formal or informal. Thus, when the Soviet Union was making its principal thrust in the third world, Soviet utilization of the General Assembly as a vehicle for its policies was at its zenith. Since Moscow was wooing the excolonial states of Africa and Asia, Soviet policy was essentially supportive of Afro-Asian positions. Soviet disenchantment with the General Assembly took form when Moscow realized that Soviet support of anticolonial positions could not be converted into effective Afro-Asian support for Soviet causes and coincided with the disappointing results of Khrushchev's efforts to gain influence in the third world in return for an expensive outlay of resources invested in an ambitious economic assistance program. Moscow retrenched from its overextended position to a few key countries ruled by radical nationalist regimes and moved toward an accommodation and détente with Washington. As a consequence Moscow betrayed a renewed interest in the Security Council where the two global powers could arrive at mutually acceptable positions with minimum intrusion by the smaller powers.

One might conclude that as a general rule if the Soviet Union resorts to the General Assembly as its chief UN vehicle, then Moscow is in a state of intense rivalry with the United States, while if it employs the Security Council as the principal forum in the UN, Soviet policy is oriented toward accommodation and détente with the United States. One might even go further and suggest that a certain functional division of labor has been devised for the Security Council and the General Assembly. On matters of shared interest and concern with the United States the Soviet Union will turn to the Council; on matters reserved for competition and rivalry Moscow will employ the General Assembly. The Security Council thus becomes a forum of accommodation and the General Assembly an arena of conflict. Issues which the Soviet leaders prefer to handle outside the UN represent residual areas of condominium, i.e., the duo-monopolistic preserve of the two global powers.

The area of possible Soviet-American agreement remains fairly large, but perhaps it has contracted somewhat from earlier possibilities and is under constant scrutiny by more skeptical members of the Politburo. Even during the grimmest period of American escalation in Vietnam the Soviet leadership entered into a number of agreements with the United States, the most important of which was the 1968 Treaty on the Nonproliferation of Nuclear Weapons. Various bilateral cultural exchange programs, treaties on outer space, the consular agreement of 1964, the Moscow–New York air agreement of 1968, and the important agreement adopted as Security Council Resolution 255 (1968) of June 19, 1968, whereby the United States and the Soviet Union jointly agreed to come to the assistance of nonnuclear powers threatened or attacked with nuclear weapons,[8] were all signed during this period.

Both the United States and Russia will probably reaffirm the sanctity of their respective spheres of influence, the latest manifestation of this tacit agreement being the mild American reaction to the events in Czechoslovakia. The questions of "bridge building" and "peaceful engagement" remain moot at the moment while Yugoslavia's relationship to the "Socialist community" remains an undefined area. Although the European status quo has been somewhat disturbed, both parties seem to have a greater interest in preserving it than upsetting it.

In the Middle East Russia and the United States appear to be moving in the direction of an imposed settlement whose outlines remain obscure. Moscow will continue to expand its involvement in the Arab

[8] This resolution was adopted in connection with the 1968 Nonproliferation Treaty.

world, seek naval bases on Arab territories, and provide more credible and effective guarantees against another Israeli attack. What the Soviet leaders will do if the Arab states take the initiative or if a conflict inadvertently breaks out remains an enigma. Apparently this is one of the most controversial issues in the Politburo, with some members apparently encouraging the Arabs and others counseling caution.

In the Far East Moscow still appears to have more of an interest in ending the Vietnamese war than in seeing it continue despite its obvious usefulness in maintaining a large American military force on the Asia mainland to the south of China. Moscow's relative indifference to the destruction of the Indonesian Communist Party and its support to Pakistan and India are reaffirmations of its Chinese encirclement policy. The key to Soviet success here largely depends upon the United States, and Sino-American relations may turn out to be the most important conditioner of Soviet behavior elsewhere.

Since the Soviet Union is too powerful not to challenge the United States, we can expect a continuing rivalry between the two global powers during the next decade, but increasingly it will assume traditional patterns. Not only will the leadership crisis in the Soviet Union be temporarily resolved, but given the advanced average age of the Soviet gerontocracy,[9] the world can expect a sudden and massive generational shift in Soviet leadership during the next decade. This new leadership, unlike the existing one, will be largely a product of the post-Stalinist era. It will not be psychologically crippled or morally corrupted by the cruel Stalinist legacy; it will be neither ideologically committed to the residuary rotting corpus of Stalinist mythology nor obligated by self-interest to preserve and perpetuate residual Stalinist institutions and processes. This new leadership, furthermore, will not be conditioned by the fears and anxieties of the Stalinist years which have been such a crucial factor in shaping the outlook of the current leadership. How this next generation of Soviet leadership will repudiate or reaffirm the Soviet past remains an enigma, but it is extremely likely that all of our assumptions concerning Soviet behavior and purpose will once again be subject to critical reexamination and reassessment.

[9] The average age of the Politburo is 59. The youngest member is 51, the oldest is 70.